BUSINESS IN GREAT WATERS

BUSINESS IN GREAT WATERS

The U-Boat Wars, 1916–1945

John Terraine

They that go down to the sea in ships,
that do business in great waters;
These see the works of the Lord,
and his wonders in the deep.
Psalm cvii, 23, 24

WORDSWORTH EDITIONS

First published in the United Kingdom in 1989
by Leo Cooper Ltd.
Leo Cooper is an independent imprint of the Octopus Publishing Group
Michelin House, 81 Fulham Road, London SW3 6RB

This edition published 1999
by Wordsworth Editions Limited
Cumberland House, Crib Street, Ware,
Hertfordshire SG12 9ET

ISBN 1 84022 201 8

Printed and bound in Great Britain
by Mackays of Chatham plc, Chatham, Kent.

Contents

Page

INTRODUCTION xiii
Abbreviations xix

PART I: THE FIRST ROUND

1	Free From All Scruples	3
2	The Most Formidable Thing	17
3	Engage The Enemy More Closely	40
4	Convoy Acted Like A Spell	57
5	Slack Water	85
6	Foiled Rather Than Defeated	105
7	Small Advantages	130
8	The Battle Done	141

PART II: INTERVAL

The Insidious Submarine	153

PART III: THE SECOND ROUND

1	Dearth Of U-boats	213
2	Nothing Of Major Importance	242
3/i	The Steep Atlantick	255
3/ii	The Very Nadir Of British Fortunes	275
3/iii	As Though The Defence Had Won	311
4	By The Narrowest Of Margins	353
5	A Roll Of Drums	403
6	The Heartbeat Of The War	444
7	We Had Lost The Battle	513
8	Unconditional Surrender	614

NOTES 674

APPENDICES

A	British, American and German Naval Ranks	761
B	The German U-boats of World War I	762

C	Gross Tonnage of Merchant Shipping Lost Through Enemy Action, to 11 November, 1918	766
D	Shipping and U-boat Losses 1939–45, yearly and monthly	767
E	U-boat Deployment in the Biscay Bases (July, 1943)	770
F	Shipping Losses in British Home Waters, 1939–45	771
G	Analysis of U-boat Losses 1914–45	772
	SELECT BIBLIOGRAPHY	774
	General Index	783
	Index of Aircraft	826
	Index of Convoys	829
	Index of Merchant Vessels	831
	Index of U-boats	833
	Index of Warships	837

Illustrations

1 *Flotillenadmiral* Hermann Bauer (*Bundesarchiv*)
2 *Kapitänleutnant* Walter Forstmann (*Bundesarchiv*)
3 Engine room of a submarine (*Imperial War Museum*)
4 Vice-Admiral Roger Keyes (*Robert Hunt Library*)
5 *Korvettenkäpitan* Max Valentiner (*Bundesarchiv*)
6 *Korvettenkäpitan* von Arnauld de la Perière (*Bundesarchiv*)
7 Bruges – base of the Flanders flotillas (*Imperial War Museum*)
8 British drifters at sea (*Imperial War Museum*)
9 Hydrophone drill aboard a drifter (*Imperial War Museum*)
10 3.5 inch stick bomb thrower (*Imperial War Museum*)
11 Felixstowe F2A flying boat (*Imperial War Museum*)
12 Curtiss H12 Large America flying boat (*Atlantic Fleet Audio Visual Command*)
13 Short Type 184 seaplane (*Imperial War Museum/MARS*)
14 Admiral William S. Sims (*Naval Photographic Center, Washington, DC*)
15 *Leutnant* Karl Dönitz, 1917
16 U-boats at Kiel, 2 October, 1918 (*Robert Hunt Library*)
17 U-boats surrendering at Harwich, 1 December, 1918 (*Imperial War Museum*)
18 Hitler with *Admiral* Erich Raeder (*Personality Pictures*)
19 Type VIIC U-boat, La Pallice, 1942.
20 Type IXC 'U-cruiser' leaving Kiel (*F. Urbahns, Schleswig-Holstein/ MARS*)
21 *Fregattenkapitän* Otto Kretschmer (*Robert Hunt Library*)
22 Dönitz with *Kapitänleutnant* Gunther Prien

23 *Kapitänleutnant* Joachim Schepke (*Bilderdienst Suddeutscher Verlag*)
24 *Kapitänleutnant* Julius Lemp (*Robert Hunt Library*)
25 Admiral Sir Percy Noble (*Imperial War Museum/JMPPL*)
26 HMS *Columbine* (*Crown Copyright (Admiralty)/MARS*)
27 'The steep Atlantick stream' (*Imperial War Museum*)
28 Hoisting a depth-charge into ready position (*Imperial War Museum*)
29 St John's, Newfoundland.
30 Convoy Conference, Liverpool (*Imperial War Museum*)
31 HMS *Icarus* off Iceland (*Imperial War Museum*)
32 HMS *Broadway* (*Imperial War Museum*)
33 HMCS *Restigouche*
34 HMS *Spey* (*Imperial War Museum*)
35 HMS *Audacity* (*Imperial War Museum/MARS*)
36 Consolidated PBY-5 (Catalina) flying boat (*Imperial War Museum/J. G. Moore*)
37 Short Sunderland flying boat (*Short Bros Ltd, Belfast/MARS*)
38 B-24 (Liberator) bomber (*Smithsonian Institute/Robert Hunt Library*)
39 Air Marshal Sir Philip Joubert de la Ferté (*Imperial War Museum/MARS*)
40 The Enigma cypher machine (*Imperial War Museum*)
41 Alan Turing (*Bassano & Vandyk Studios*)
42 Professor P. M. S. Blackett (*MARS*)
43 Bletchley Park (*ET Archive*)
44 U-boat pews at Bordeaux
45 Night sky over Brest during an RAF attack
46 Commander D. F. F. W. MacIntyre (*Imperial War Museum*)
47 Lieutenant-Commander P. W. Gretton (*Imperial War Museum*)
48 Lieutenant-Commander G. J. Luther
49 Captain F. J. Walker (*Imperial War Museum/Personality Pictures*)
50 Fleet Admiral E. J. King USN (*US Navy Official Photograph/Personality Pictures*)
51 Henry J. Kaiser (*Personality Pictures*)
52 'Hedgehog' with 24 anti-submarine missiles (*Imperial War Museum*)
53 USS *Bogue* (*Naval Photographic Center, Washington, DC*)

54 Operations Room, Derby House, Liverpool, April 1945
   (*Imperial War Museum*)
55 Admiral Sir Max Horton
56 Admiral Horton aboard *U523*, Londonderry, May, 1945
   (*Imperial War Museum*)
57 Type XXI U-boat (*W3 – Bilddienst, Wilhelmshaven*)
58 Type XXIIII U-boat (*W3 – Bilddienst, Wilhelmshaven*)

Maps
Drawn by Chester Read

1 Area of U-Boat operations 1914–1918   18
2 Five months of Restricted Submarine Warfare September, 1916–January, 1917   39
3 1st Quarter of Unrestricted Submarine Warfare February–April, 1917   39
4 Western Approaches   43
5 The Spider Web patrol pattern   75
6 2nd Quarter of Unrestricted Submarine Warfare May–July, 1917   89
7 3rd Quarter of Unrestricted Submarine Warfare August–October, 1917   89
8 The U-Boat Ambush, October, 1917   94
9 4th Quarter of Unrestricted Submarine Warfare, November, 1917–January, 1918   103
10 5th Quarter of Unrestricted Submarine Warfare, February–April, 1918   103
11 The Northern Barrage   114
12 6th Quarter of Unrestricted Submarine Warfare, May–July, 1918   129
13 7th Quarter of Unrestricted Submarine Warfare, August–October, 1918   129
14 The Battle of the Atlantic, 1940–1943   208–9
15 Typical Convoys & Anti-Submarine Escorts, 1940–1941   291
16 Convoy SC 42   374
17 British & American Naval Commands, 1942   415
18 Situation in North Atlantic, 5–7 March, 1943   548
19 Situation in North Atlantic, 17–19 March, 1943   559

Introduction

TEN BOOKS ON the First World War published between 1960–82; a substantial statement on the Royal Air Force in the Second World War published in 1985; now U-boats, conducting Unrestricted Submarine Warfare between 1916–45: is there any connection between the subjects that have kept three decades of my life very fully occupied – or does this diversity indicate mere dilettantism? I believe that a connection does exist and that it is an important one – but I will readily confess that this perception is hindsight, and does not imply any deliberate intention at the time of writing, least of all when it all began some thirty years ago.

I belong to a generation to which the two World Wars were present realities marking the most impressionable part of a lifetime. In 1921, when I was born, my father worked in Brussels, where the signs of German occupation between 1914–18 were still visible even to a very small boy, where its weight still lay heavily on the people and continued to do so for the next eighteen years; I grew up with the Great War never far from people's minds and very often in their conversation. And it was usually very difficult indeed to make head or tail of what they were saying. It was a mystery – not surprisingly, because I should say that no event in history has ever been so steeped in mythology since the time of the Old Testament.

World War II, which I lived through in what I now consider to have been a state of incomprehension at least equal to my confusion about its predecessor, added new layers of mythology, fresh fantasies to addle the minds of young and old alike. However, these did not stand up for long to the harsh audit of peace (if I may borrow a phrase from Correlli Barnett). Birds which had been well on their way to the roost in the 1930s flocked home in the 1950s. 1956, I suppose, was the year when they arrived, and one could begin to measure the enormous change that the wars had brought, to Britain, to the British Empire, and to the world.

It was during that decade that I began thinking to some recognizable purpose about the wars, especially 1914 to 1918, to try to unravel some of the mysteries. My first book taught me my first lesson: *Mons: The Retreat to Victory* was commissioned for Batsford's 'British Battles' series, and Mons has, indeed, occupied a significant pedestal in British legend, even including Angels! I learned that the truth was otherwise; General Smith-Dorrien's half-day skirmish at Mons on 23 August, 1914 took on a different look when I contemplated the long battle-line of the French armies, grappling with their massive, well-trained, well-equipped and courageous German enemy. This struggle cost the French over 210,000 officers and men – which is considerably more than the full strength of the British Expeditionary Force – in the month of August alone: a sobering thought. It dawned on me that exclusive inspection of the British contribution would not supply adequate explanation of the First World War's mysteries – and soon I also recognized that the same was true of World War II. If the 'British Battle' at Mons in 1914 shrinks perceptibly in the perspective of the main action on the main front, so, I fear, does the 'British Battle' of El Alamein in 1942.

More and more, as one book followed another, I became concerned with this matter of the main front and the main action – the *decisive* point, or what the Germans would call the *Schwerpunkt*. I did not, for a very long time, express it, even to myself, with such precision, but it steadily became my preoccupation: the *Schwerpunkt*, the centre of gravity of each of the two wars. And that is the connection: the Western Front in World War I, where first the French and then the British Armies bore the burden of the main action against the main enemy; the RAF, taking its position on 'the Right of the Line' in World War II; and the defeat of the U-boats, which in 1943 provided the only means by which the Western Allies could deploy their full forces against the main enemy once again. I was well aware that this amazing enterprise was *not*, in fact, the *Schwerpunkt* of World War II itself, which from June 1941 was always on the Eastern Front, where the German Army was ground down in even costlier Verduns, Sommes and Passchendaeles with Russian names. Yet as far as Britain and America were concerned, Operation OVERLORD was the main action of the German war, and that was no light matter.

My aim in this book has been to try, as far as a single volume permits, to identify and observe the ingredients of submarine and anti-submarine war. They belong very firmly to the new warfare of the Industrial Revolution whose nature was first glimpsed in America between 1861–65,* and which bared its teeth in World War I. It was a warfare which owed almost everything to Technology and which demanded the ever-increasing participation of Science. It called into existence a new anti-submarine armament – ship- and air-borne depth charges, bombs and projectors, acoustic and magnetic mines and torpedoes, U-boat detectors (Hydrophones, ASDIC and magnetic), special vessels and aircraft loaded with instruments and devices of wonderful sophistication. It made heavy demands on discoveries like Radar, on Wireless Telegraphy and the intercepts thereof, on Direction-Finding, on Radio-Telephony – and always, unceasingly, on the courage, endurance, ingenuity and skill of the men in the U-boats, the men who fought them at sea and in the air, and the helpless merchant seamen who were their quarry or their wards.

As always in such studies, I was struck by the great advances made (on both sides) between 1914–18; if I were to rewrite this book, I would give even greater emphasis to this. Equally striking was the astonishing readiness in Britain and America between the wars to forget so much that had been learned so painfully. The unity of the whole 'unrestricted submarine warfare' period, from its effective beginnings in 1916 right up to the last actions in 1945, speaks, I think, for itself. It is the unity of a finite story, an unique phase in technological development. Nothing quite like it will be seen again – for the simple reason that the nature of the beast has changed. The U-boat wars were not really submarine warfare at all; they were fought by submersibles – torpedo boats with the power to dive. It certainly surprised me to see how tightly the U-boats were locked to the surface, and this, in most cases, was what caused their downfall. When, at the very end, the Allies made a brief encounter with vessels approximating to true submarines, their techniques were rendered obsolete. So the story ended with a bleak view of what I have called 'the unappealing landscape of

* The first sinking of a warship by a submarine was that of USS *Housatonic* by CSS *H. L. Hunley* in Charleston harbour on February 17 1864.

Square One', as true submarine warfare powered by nuclear energy comes upon the scene.†

It remains for me now to acknowledge the help I have received in writing this book. First I must thank two associates at the Royal United Services Institute, retired naval officers: Rear-Admiral E. F. Gueritz and Captain A. B. Sainsbury, who saw this craft down the slipway, for which I am most grateful. I am indebted also to David Brown and his helpful colleagues at the Naval Historical Branch (Ministry of Defence), to Air Commodore Henry Probert at the Air Historical Branch, to Dr W. A. B. Douglas, Director of History at the National Defence Headquarters, Ottawa, and Marc Milner whom I met in the Directorate and whose work has proved invaluable on matters concerning the Royal Canadian Navy. An acknowledgement which is also full of regret is to the late Patrick Beesly, who gave me much valuable assistance with Intelligence problems, and whose untimely death came as a great blow. I must also mention here Dr Jürgen Rohwer, the outstanding German historian of the U-boats, on whom I have leaned heavily, Captain Stephen Roskill, the British Official Naval Historian, a prolific chronicler of the Royal Navy and its affairs in this century without whom no book like this could exist, and Peter Padfield, whose biography of Admiral Dönitz has also been a foundation-stone, together with the Memoirs and War Diary of that singular and redoubtable enemy. Finally, I must sincerely thank my publisher, Leo Cooper, who saved the craft from foundering and has been unfailingly supportive and patient, often under trying circumstances; my editor, Tom Hartman, for his calm, his industry, and his experienced professionalism; and Mrs Beryl Hill, at her place on the bridge exercising her extraordinary ability to make rough seas smooth.

John Terraine
March 1989

---

† A true submarine is an artificial fish, capable of indefinite submerged existence, identical performances on and below the surface and is powered by one set of machinery for all purposes.

Acknowledgements

The author and publishers are grateful to the following for permission to quote copyright material in this book; B. T. Batsford Ltd, *Battle of the Atlantic* by D. MacIntyre; Victor Gollancz Ltd, *Dönitz; The Last Führer* by Peter Padfield; William Collins Sons & Co. Ltd, *Hankey, Man of Secrets* by Captain S. W. Roskill; Penguin Books Ltd, *Convoy* by Martin Middlebrook; Cassell Publishers Ltd, *The Crisis of the Naval War* by Admiral of the Fleet Lord Jellicoe; *Three Corvettes* by Nicholas Monsarrat; *The Far Distant Ships* by Joseph Schull; Longman Group Ltd, *Naval Operations*, by Sir Henry Newbolt; George Weidenfeld & Nicolson Ltd, *Iron Coffins* by Herbert A. Werner.

Abbreviations

AA: anti-aircraft
ACM: Air Chief Marshal
ACNS: Assistant Chief of Naval Staff
Adml: Admiral
  R/Adml: Rear-Admiral
  V/Adml: Vice-Admiral
  A–F: Admiral of the Fleet
AHB: Air Historical Branch, Ministry of
  Defence
AI: Air Interception (radar)
A/M: Air Marshal
  AV/M: Air Vice-Marshal
AMC: Armed Merchant Cruiser
AOC (-in-C): Air Officer Commanding
ASDIC: Allied Submarine Detection
  Investigation Committee sonar
ASV (I, II, III): Air-to-Surface-Vessel
  radar
ASW: Anti-Submarine Warfare
BdU: Befehlshaber der U-boote
BEF: British Expeditionary Force
BP: Bletchley Park
BT: Bathythermography
CAM: Catapult Aircraft Merchant (ships)
CBO: Combined Bomber Offensive
CCM: Combined Cipher Machine
CCNF: Commodore Commanding
  Newfoundland Force
Cdr.: Commander
Cdre.: Commodore
CHOP: Change of Operational Control
C-in-C, Commander-in-Chief
CINCWA: C-in-C, Western Approaches
CNS: Chief of Naval Staff
CO: Commanding Officer

COAC: Commanding Officer, Atlantic
  Coast (RCN)
COMINCH: C-in-C, United States Fleet
COS: Chiefs of Staff
CPO: Chief Petty Officer
CSA: Confederate States of America
CTF: Commander, Task Force
Cttee.: Committee
CVE: Aircraft Carrier, Escort (USN)
DCNS: Deputy Chief of Naval Staff
D/F: Direction Finding
DNI: Director of Naval Intelligence (RN)
EG: Escort Group
FAA: Fleet Air Arm
FAT: Federapparattorpedo (or
  Flächenabsuchender torpedo)
FdU: Führer der U-boote
FFI: Forces Françaises de l'Intérieur
FFN: Free French Navy
F-M: Field-Marshal
F/O: Flying Officer
GAF: German Air Force
GC & CS: Government Code & Cipher
  School
G-H: RAF navigation aid
GNAT: German Naval Acoustic Torpedo
GR: General Reconnaissance (aircraft)
HF/DF: High Frequency Direction
  Finding
HSF: High Sea Fleet
H2S: RAF radar navigation aid
KG: Kampfgeschwader (Bomber Group)
LCT: Landing Craft, Tank
L/R: long range
LST: Landing Ship, Tank

MAC: Merchant Aircraft Carrier
MAD: Magnetic Airborne Detector
MF/DF: Medium Frequency Direction
    Finding
MN: Merchant Navy
MOEF: Mid-Ocean Escort Force
MOMP: Mid-Ocean Meeting Point
M/RAF: Marshal of the Royal Air Force
M/V: Merchant Vessel
NCS: Naval Control Service
NCSO: Naval Control Service Officer
NEF: Newfoundland Escort Force
NID: Naval Intelligence Division
OBOE: RAF blind bombing system
OIC: Operational Intelligence Centre
OKH: Oberkommando des Heeres
OKW: Oberkommando der Wehrmacht
P/O: Pilot Officer
PR: Photographic Reconnaissance
RA: Royal Artillery
RAF: Royal Air Force
RAN: Royal Australian Navy
RCAF: Royal Canadian Air Force
RCN: Royal Canadian Navy
RCNR: Royal Canadian Naval Reserve
recce.: reconnaissance
RFC: Royal Flying Corps
RN: Royal Navy
RNAS: Royal Naval Air Service
RNR: Royal Naval Reserve
RNVR: Royal Naval Volunteer Reserve
RNorN: Royal Norwegian Navy
R/T: Radio-Telephony
SAC: Supreme Allied Commander

SBT: Submarine Bubble Target
    (*Pillenwerfer*)
SEAC: South East Asia Command
sitrep: situation report
S/L: Squadron Leader
S/M: submarine
SO: Senior Officer
SOCC: Senior Officer, Canadian Corvettes
SOE: Senior Officer of Escort
sqdn: squadron
SS: Schutz Staffeln (Protection Echelons)
TBS: Talk Between Ships (R/T)
TEK: Torpedo Erprobungs Kommando
TVA: Torpedo Versuchs Anstalt
U/B: U-boat
UK: United Kingdom (of Great Britain)
USA: United States of America; US
    Army
USAAF: United States Army Air Force
USCG: United States Coast Guard
USN: United States Navy
USS: United States Ship (USN)
VHF: Very High Frequency
VLR: Very Long Range
VMT: Very Many Thanks
WA: Western Approaches
WACIS: Western Approaches Convoy
    Instructions
W/C: Wing Commander
WLEF: Western Local Escort Force
WOMP: Western Ocean Meeting Point
WRNS: Women's Royal Naval Service
WSF: Western Support Force
W/T: Wireless Telegraphy

PART I

THE FIRST ROUND
1916–1918

'. . . the essence of war is violence, and moderation in war is imbecility . . .'
Admiral of the Fleet Lord Fisher, 1913

1

Free From All Scruples

'The gravity of the situation demands that we should free ourselves from all scruples.'

Admiral von Ingenohl, November, 1914

On 13 November, 1916, in the half-light of a dripping fog, the British 51st (Highland) Division captured the wrecked remains of the hamlet of Beaumont Hamel on the River Ancre. Beaumont Hamel had been an objective of the first day of the Battle of the Somme, 1 July, and on that day it had been a conspicuous scene of the terrible disaster which then befell the British Army – the worst day in its history, with 57,470 casualties, of whom 19,240 were killed. During the four months that followed the Germans fortified Beaumont Hamel with great skill, turning it into one of their most important strong-points on the Somme front. Its capture in November symbolized their defeat in the great battle, which ended five days later. A month after that (15 December), at Verdun, the French launched a four-day attack which took 11,000 prisoners and 115 guns; on the 18th that battle also came to an end. Thus closed the fighting on the Western Front in 1916, a dreadful year for Germany, the turning-point of World War I.

German losses in 1916, according to their Official History,[1] amounted to 'a round figure of 1,400,000' – a total which we know to be incomplete. Fighting at Verdun had gone on for ten months; on the Somme for four and a half months – and simultaneously, General Alexei Brusilov, in Russia's last great offensive of the war, inflicted crippling losses on the Austro-Hungarian Empire, forcing the Germans to enter that battle also. Thanks largely to their efforts, the Russian attack was halted after four months – but at a cost. The subsequent swift overthrow of Romania by the Central Powers was their only gleam of light in the dark story of the land warfare of the year. By the time it ended, in the words of General Erich Ludendorff, 'The Army had been fought to a standstill and was utterly worn out.' [2]

On 29 August, while these dire events were still unfolding, Field-Marshal Paul von Hindenburg was promoted from supreme command on the Eastern Front to Chief of Staff of the German Army, the highest post that it offered,[3] with Ludendorff as his 'First Quartermaster-General' (effectively his own Chief of Staff). The very next day, at the Imperial headquarters at Pless in Silesia, the two new Army chiefs were plunged into a top-level conference on a subject far removed from operations on the battle-fronts, but no less important for Germany. With the Imperial Chancellor, Theobald von Bethmann Hollweg, in the chair, the conference *personae* assembled: Karl Helfferich, State Secretary for the Interior, Gottlieb von Jagow, State Secretary for Foreign Affairs, the War Minister, General Wild von Hohenborn, with Hindenburg and Ludendorff, *Admiral* Eduard von Capelle, Secretary for the Navy, and *Admiral* Henning von Holtzendorff, Chief of the Naval Staff. All were conscious of the increasing pressures of the Allied blockade of the Central Powers, the privations of the civilian population and the effect of these upon its will and capacity to continue the war, as well as the shortages of raw materials which were already affecting munitions production. The subject before the conference was how best to combat this hazard, and at the same time strike at the continuing flow of overseas supplies into the European Allied countries: in other words, the submarine blockade of Britain.

The German admirals were discontented; they had the sense of holding a war-winning weapon in their hands, but not being allowed to use it properly. Yet the word itself required careful interpretation; the actual weapon was double-edged. On the one hand, the submarine enjoyed the priceless asset of invisibility, making it more difficult to counter than any naval craft previously built. On the other hand, there were certain things it could not do, or could not do in the traditional manner of naval warfare. One – most significant – was pointed out by Admiral of the Fleet Lord Fisher, in retirement, to Winston Churchill, First Lord of the Admiralty, in June, 1913; the submarine, he wrote:

cannot capture the merchant ship; she has no spare hands to put a prize crew on board . . . she cannot convoy her into harbour. . . . There is nothing else the submarine can do except sink her capture . . . (this) is freely acknowledged to be an altogether barbarous method of warfare . . . (but) the essence of war is violence, and moderation in war is imbecility.[4]

Neither Churchill nor his advisers were prepared to accept this; Fisher's successor as First Sea Lord, Admiral Prince Louis of Battenberg, said that the suggestion of such barbarity 'marred' an otherwise brilliant paper. A strong body of naval opinion was prepared to assert that the submarine accordingly had no value for a war against trade, and the Imperial German Navy, before the war, had made no preparations to use it in such a manner. It did not take long for the Imperial Navy to change its mind.

Much was heard, from 1914 onwards, about 'international law', the 'Law of the Sea', and so forth; the truth is that there was no such thing. Blockade, of course, was a familiar practice to all maritime nations from distant times, and an attempt at codifying such operations was made in the Declaration of Paris in 1856. Nothing more was done about the subject until the series of Hague Conferences on the humanizing of war and progress towards disarmament which began in 1899 and culminated in the Peace Conference of 1907. No sooner was its business concluded than the British Government convened a group of international jurists to examine sea warfare, especially the questions of blockade and contraband (obviously intimately linked); their deliberations resulted in the Declaration of London of 1909, an instrument whose force was substantially diminished by the fact that none of the future belligerents ratified it (although the Liberal majority in the House of Commons proclaimed the intention of adhering to the terms of the Declaration). That, for what it was worth, was the state of 'international law' on the subject of maritime war against trade in 1914.

By 1909, of course, the advent of the 20th century and the advance of the Industrial Revolution had transformed the whole subject of blockade. In the past it had reposed upon two fundamentals: that it should be visible and that it should be effective. It meant a squadron (or a fleet) sitting outside an enemy port, preventing entrance and exit; and it meant a squadron or fleet strong enough to overawe or fend off all attempts either to break out of or to relieve the blockaded port. The first element – *close* blockade – was ruled out by modern weapons: mines, torpedoes – and submarines. The alternative was distant blockade, and this was adopted by the Royal Navy immediately on the outbreak of war: the British Grand Fleet exercised its naval supremacy from a base some 500 miles distant from the nearest German port – sometimes from even further away. It was evident that even such a large navy as Britain's could not be in strength simultaneously at every point; this was not considered a limiting factor – indeed, 'effective' blockade had taken on a new meaning as far back as 1861, when the United States Government declared a blockade of some 3,500 miles of Confederate coastline when it had no more than about twenty ships available for the purpose of enforcing it. This proclamation was indeed 'little more than an act of faith' [5] – a faith soon justified by the astonishing expansion of the United States Navy. The British blockade of Germany in 1914 must at times have seemed as tenuously maintained; yet it proved immediately to be as effective as the United States blockade of the Confederacy ultimately became. In a matter of weeks – some authorities would say days – the first stage was victoriously concluded:

> the enemy's . . . merchant navy had been swept away, and he had no ships on the high seas except one or two armed merchantmen, which, one by one, went to their doom. [6]

What this meant was that, except in the Baltic, the only vessels serving German ports were neutrals, and one thing at least the Declaration of London had done: it had clarified, though it had not simplified, the procedures by which a blockading power dealt with neutral shipping. It is important to note what these were. Cargoes were divided into three categories: first there was 'absolute contraband', a very short list of material and articles used exclusively for war, and whose destination was in enemy territory; these could be seized outright. Secondly, there was 'conditional contraband', which comprised goods which might or might not be used for war (food, fodder and fuel, for example) and which could only be seized if they were clearly destined for the enemy; even so, the seizure depended on the carrying vessel being bound for an enemy-held port – such cargoes could not be taken if they were heading for a neutral port, even though they might then be

6

re-consigned to the enemy. We have to recall that Sweden, Norway, Denmark and Holland were all neutral, and that ports like Rotterdam, Amsterdam and Copenhagen were all important centres of German supply. Clearly, 'conditional contraband' was a problem area; no less so was the third category, 'free goods', which were not to be considered as contraband at all, though they included such materials as metallic ores, textile substances, rubber, and a variety of machinery and manufactured articles:

> This latter list was most disastrous to the exercise of belligerent rights, for it would enable Germany to import in neutral bottoms, to any extent that she could arrange, such vitally important materials for the manufacture of munitions and armaments as cotton, copper, iron ore, etc., as well as the principal raw materials of German industry.[7]

Not only was the whole question of contraband thus made hideously complicated and absurd, but the Declaration also insisted that blockade itself should only apply to enemy coasts – thus striking at the very principle of distant blockade which was to guide the Royal Navy in two world wars. It is difficult indeed to surmise what it was that induced the naval members of the British delegation to the conference even to listen to, let alone to accept, these lethal stipulations.

One thing was perfectly clear: whatever one might think of the categories of contraband specified, the only way of discovering which one a cargo belonged to was by going aboard the ship and examining the manifest – even, perhaps, the cargo in the hold. If the decision was then taken to seize it, a prize crew would be put aboard the ship, which would be taken to a British port. The normal procedure after that would be compulsory purchase of the cargo and the return of the ship to its home port with its own crew. It was, from the neutral point of view, all very inconvenient and irritating, but except in circumstances so rare that they are hard to imagine, no question whatever arose of loss of life, or injury or sinking. This, of course, was where the submarine parted company; as Fisher had pointed out, boarding, prize crews and capture were precisely what the submarine could *not* do. What it could do, and most frequently did, especially in the early days, was to surface, threaten the ship with gunfire, order the crew to take to their boats and then sink her. The riposte to that was to arm the merchantmen – it was only in the 20th century that large merchantmen ceased to be armed in the normal course of events. A refinement in 1915 was to introduce heavily armed merchantmen with Royal Navy crews on the trade routes, to decoy submarines to the surface and then sink them – these were known as 'Q-ships'. The response of the submarine commanders to both these measures was increasingly to remain submerged and sink their quarries without warning by torpedoes. It was at that stage that the brutal, shocking quality of the new style of warfare became apparent, and the revelation came very quickly indeed. The first sinking of a merchant ship by a German submarine was on 20 October, 1914; the first sinking without warning was 26 October.

The risk of sinking without warning – what very soon became known as 'unrestricted submarine warfare' – was the outrage to world opinion, especially in the maritime neutral countries. The question was whether neutral outrage or neutral terror would prevail – and German naval planning in both world wars was marked by

> a fatal belief in simple, preferably 'ruthless' plans on which the enemy would allow himself to be impaled.[8]

Angered by the effectiveness of the British blockade and frustrated by his inability to damage the Grand Fleet, *Admiral* von Ingenohl, the Commander-in-Chief of Germany's High Sea Fleet, stated:

> We can wound England most seriously by injuring her trade. . . . The whole British coast, or anyway a part of it, must be declared to be blockaded, and at the same time the aforesaid warning (to neutrals) must be published. . . . The gravity of the situation demands that we should free ourselves from all scruples which certainly no longer have justification.[9]

On 7 November, 1914, the Chief of the Naval Staff in 1914, *Admiral* von Pohl, made the formal proposal to the Chancellor of a submarine blockade of Britain; it was not well received. Bethmann Hollweg was no fool and, despite the assurances of the Naval Staff, he was able to perceive without difficulty that sinking without warning and without surfacing would inevitably put neutral shipping in such danger as to alienate those countries – including, of course, America. This was a fear that never left him. In the discussions of November and December

8

he had useful support – from the Emperor Wilhelm II, who disliked using his beloved Navy for such a purpose, and from the submarine officers themselves. A pre-war study by a commanding officer, *Korvettenkapitän* Blum, had prophetically concluded that to be effective a force of 222 submarines would be needed to blockade the British Isles. In December, 1914, Germany had precisely twenty-eight, of which twenty-one were in the North Sea, and as their *Führer*, *Fregattenkapitän* Hermann Bauer, pointed out, of these only three or four could be maintained on patrol. Nevertheless the admirals persisted; the Kaiser was won over, the Chancellor unwillingly persuaded, and on 4 February, 1915, the announcement was published:

1. The waters around Great Britain and Ireland, including the whole of the English Channel, are herewith declared to be in the War Zone. From February 18 onward, every merchant-ship met with in this War Zone will be destroyed, nor will it always be possible to obviate the danger with which passengers and crew are thereby threatened.
2. Neutral ships, too, will run a risk in the War Zone, for in view of the misuse of neutral flags by the British Government on January 31,[10] and owing to the hazards of naval warfare, it may not always be possible to prevent the attacks meant for hostile ships from being directed against neutral ships.

Between the lines of a certain amount of sanctimony, the meaning of this proclamation was clear enough. Clearer still were parts of the instructions issued to submarine commanders, above all this fundamental principle of both wars:

The first consideration is the safety of the submarine.[11]

No risks were to be taken in order to make sure recognition of targets; and although in the instructions issued on 18 February it was clearly stated (paragraph 3) that 'Neutral ships are to be spared', the difficulties of recognizing them were emphasized, and Paragraph 7 added:

If in spite of the exercise of the greatest care mistakes should be made, the commander will not be made responsible.

On these principles the first submarine campaign was launched; the

9

commanding officers waged it according to dictates of circumstance and their own natures. It says something for the survival powers of nineteenth century liberal humanitarianism that in 1915 no more than 21% of sinkings were performed without warning.[12] Among them, however, was one that Germany would have cause to regret – an endorsement of all Bethmann Hollweg's misgivings: the sinking of the 32,500-ton Cunard liner *Lusitania* on 7 May with a loss of 1,198 lives out of 1,957 on board (passengers, 1,257; crew, 700). Of the 785 passengers drowned, 124 were American. Also aboard the *Lusitania* were 1,250 boxes of field artillery ammunition and 18 boxes of percussion fuses containing fulminate of mercury, a highly explosive substance. The latest research indicates very strongly that it was the explosion of these munitions, following the impact of a single torpedo, which produced the damage that caused the great ship to go down in under 18 minutes.[13] From the point of view of the German Navy, the munitions cargo justified the destruction of the liner; from the point of view of the Chancellor and the Foreign Office, these boxes of shells and fuses were dearly bought. The loss of the *Lusitania* 'had sown the seed, slow-germinating as it might be, which would eventually grow into America's entry into the war.'[14] Until the sinking, American discontent with Britain's conduct of the blockade had threatened a serious rupture of relations between the two countries; after the *Lusitania*, it was Germany, not Britain, that chiefly occupied the hot seat of American disapproval.

The sinking of the Cunarder, much as it might alarm the German Foreign Office, did not lead to abandonment or even deliberate diminution of the 1915 submarine campaign. It was sheer shortage of vessels that brought about a tapering-off of effort at the end of the year: in October the North Sea and Flanders flotillas combined could only maintain four boats at sea; in November only three; and in December four again, but all small boats belonging to the Flanders flotillas. The total loss of world shipping by submarine attack during the year amounted to 1,307,996 gross tons; of this the British quota was 855,721[15] – both high figures, and startling to a generation facing this menace for the first time. Yet the British loss amounted to only just over 4% of the available amount of British merchant shipping, so Churchill was not wrong in saying:

No substantial or even noticeable injury was wrought upon British commerce by the first German submarine campaign.[16]

And as this petered out in the last quarter there was every reason to suppose that it had accepted defeat. This was by no means the case. It required another political gaffe to force the suspension of the submarine war against trade. That came in March, 1916, when the Germans were able to put seven North Sea and Flanders boats to sea, and on the 24th of the month one of them torpedoed the Channel packet *Sussex* with a loss of fifty lives in the explosion, a number of them once more being American. In a speech on 13 April President Woodrow Wilson said that this act

> must stand forth, as the sinking of the *Lusitania* did, so singularly tragical and unjustifiable as to constitute a truly terrible example of the inhumanity of submarine warfare as the commanders of German vessels for the past twelve months have been conducting it.

Six days later the United States Government presented an ultimatum to Germany:

> Unless the Imperial German Government shall now immediately declare and carry into effect its abandonment of the present method of warfare against passenger and freight carrying vessels, the Government have no choice but to sever diplomatic relations with the German Government altogether.

And this was, at last, enough; the Imperial Government at once ordered that all German submarines should revert to standard blockade practice (boarding and searching); rather than expose them to the dangers of this procedure, the Naval High Command recalled all the North Sea boats. The submarine war in British waters was reduced to the activities (chiefly minelaying) of the Flanders flotillas. For the next four months the world total of shipping sunk averaged just under 130,000 gross tons, and the British monthly average was just under 57,000 — both figures entirely containable.

This, then, was the position that faced the Pless conference on 30 August; this was why *Admiral* von Holtzendorff and *Admiral* von Capelle came to the deliberations with impatience and discontent. It was von Holtzendorff who opened the proceedings by reading a carefully prepared paper, arguing for the earliest resumption of 'unrestricted' warfare, and dismissing the likely effect of it on the neutrals. Even if the United States declared war on Germany, said the Naval Chief of Staff, there was scarcely anything that she could do about it; Holland and Denmark would not abandon neutrality unless they were invaded; the South American states, needing foreign shipping to carry away their grain harvests, would be helpless against submarines. Meanwhile, the Admiral pointed out, the condition of Germany's allies was deteriorating fast. Could they bear another winter of war? He concluded:

> I do not see a *finis Germaniae* in the use of a weapon which cripples Great Britain's capacity to support her allies; but rather in the neglect to employ it.[17]

Holtzendorff's paper brought the absolute division of opinion between the Navy and the political leaders into the open. The Foreign Minister, von Jagow, found the prospect of war with America appalling; its effect, especially on other neutrals, would be incalculable, he said:

> Germany will be treated like a mad dog against which everybody combines.

Helfferich supported von Jagow, and went even further; he had the temerity to challenge the statistics on which the Naval proposals were based. Although his own estimate of the available British shipping tonnage was far too low, he cogently argued that there was enough of it for Britain to supply herself and maintain a general trade, whatever the submarines might do. He also strongly challenged the assertion that Germany had nothing to fear from war with America:

> If she declares war, America, with all her reserves, will be at the disposal of the Allies, for their cause will be hers. . . . I can see in the employment of the (submarine) weapon nothing but catastrophe.

To this *Admiral* von Capelle could only reply that in his opinion unrestricted submarine warfare would lead to peace; what sort of peace he did not say.

It was now Bethmann Hollweg's turn; he saw unrestricted warfare as 'an act of desperation' and bluntly opposed the naval view with a warning that the continued neutrality of countries like Denmark could not be counted upon if it was adopted. Holtzendorff retorted with the conviction 'that a fortnight's unrestricted war will have this effect, that the neutrals will keep aloof from England'. Through all this, the new Army leaders followed only one thread: they had no moral scruples about submarine warfare, nor did they rate too highly the long-term effects, even of an American declaration of war.[18] They were, however, concerned about the new enemy already in the field: Romania. Conscious of the strain that the year had already imposed on the existing fronts, and with another now demanding further resources, they could not risk any additional burden:

> The intervention of Holland and Denmark on the side of the Allies would, it was thought, be the last straw to break the back of the vastly over-stretched German Army.[19]

This notion, in the brilliant light of hindsight, seems grotesque – yet on reflection it is not so surprising that the new leadership, in the very moment of taking up the reins, should hesitate over accepting further risks. They needed some clarification of the military situation; they needed a little time. And since this fitted well with Bethmann Hollweg's own desire to seek once more for a diplomatic approach to peace, he suggested that he should shortly inform the Reichstag that

> the decision (with regard to submarine warfare) had been postponed; and that Field-Marshal von Hindenburg had stated that he must wait for the issue of the Romanian campaign before he could form a definite opinion.[20]

This was agreed.

It was a postponement in name rather than in fact; within a fortnight of the Pless decision, Ludendorff was assuring the Naval Staff that 'he was in favour of beginning unrestricted submarine warfare as soon as the military position on the continent was secure.'[21] *Kapitän zur See* von Bulow, the emissary of the Naval Staff who visited Ludendorff at Great Headquarters on 10 September noted:

> General Ludendorff believes in a successful issue to submarine war . . . he has no faith in being able to force a favourable decision by means of war on land alone.

This was not surprising; Ludendorff and Hindenburg had just returned from their first visit to the Western Front; neither had ever experienced anything resembling what they now learned. At a conference at Cambrai on 7 September the Army Group and Army commanders had painted a frightening picture of warfare in the west; of the crushing Allied material superiority in what the Germans came to call '*die Materialschlacht*' (the battle of matériel), and the 'fearful wastage' of the German forces on the Somme and at Verdun. What the new High Command heard, it quickly translated into a fundamental change of strategy:

> Within days of assuming Supreme Command, [Hindenburg and Ludendorff] came to the conclusion that the armies must move on to the defensive in the West. Such a situation had already been forced upon the German forces; now Ludendorff believed it must be formally recognized and steps taken accordingly regardless of possible consequences to morale – indeed, he maintained that morale would sag even further, both on the fighting front in the West and at home, if the slaughter was allowed to continue. As early as September, therefore, orders were given for construction to start on the powerful defensive positions later to be famous as the Hindenburg Line. . . . Ludendorff fully realized the shortcomings of such defensive lines. 'They were sufficient to postpone the decision . . . but they could never lead to victory.' The strategy could therefore be used in three ways: as a means of forming a basis for an eventual land offensive, as a strong foundation from which discussions for peace could begin, or as a background to the adoption of unrestricted submarine warfare.[22]

Steadily, through the remainder of the year, the pressure on Bethmann Hollweg grew. Romania proved to be a thing of straw: the Central Powers' offensive against her began in September; by the beginning of November the Romanians were cut off from the Black Sea; on 6 December Bucharest fell – the 'threat' in the East had evaporated. Heavy Italian attacks on the Isonzo front against Austria were held. By tremendous efforts the Anglo-French offensive on the Somme was also halted, though fighting continued at high intensity. The German High Command could feel that affairs were being gripped; it could throw off some earlier constraints. And the Naval Staff never ceased to press the submarine solution. Worst of all, it became apparent that President Wilson would not undertake any peace moves until after the presidential election, which was not due until November. And during these autumn months the submarines themselves had been writing a new chapter of sea history: a sudden leap from the already increasing figure of 162,744 tons of shipping sunk in August to 230,460 tons in September – the largest monthly total so far – rising again to the really alarming figure of 353,660 tons in October. It would be a year before the monthly rate fell below 300,000 again; 'in effect the second Submarine Campaign had started.' [23] And what was equally ominous, in 1916 sinking without warning rose to 29%. The issue between the Chancellor and the Service chiefs had become scarcely more than the recognition and formal endorsement of a *fait accompli*.

It required one more powerful broadside from von Holtzendorff to clinch the matter. This came in the form of a strong memorandum on 22 December, in which he deployed the full battery of statistics to prove that a monthly rate of sinking of 600,000 tons would bring Britain to her knees, and this, he asserted, was well within the powers of the German submarine fleet:

> I arrive at the conclusion that an unrestricted war, started at the proper time, will bring about peace before the harvesting period of the 1917 summer, that is, before 1 August; the break with America must be accepted; we have no choice but to do so. In spite of the danger of a breach with America, unrestricted submarine war, started soon, is the proper, and indeed the only way to end the war with victory. [24]

A brisk exchange of Peace Notes, via the re-elected President Wilson, concluded with the rejection of German proposals on 30 December; this cut the last ground from under the Chancellor's feet. By now the Emperor had changed sides, and Bethmann Hollweg, 'a mere civilian, could not face army, navy and Kaiser acting in concert.' [25] The final decision was taken at another conference at Pless on 9 January, 1917: it was agreed that unrestricted submarine warfare would be declared on 1 February.

This was a moment for history to take note of; from the very foundation of the Empire, the Army had provided the power base of German policy; from 1 August, 1914, it had been the 'motor' of the war. Now Germany's thrust was transferred from her great and revered Army to the young and relatively untried Navy – a revolutionary change indeed, and a measure of the defeats that she had sustained, chiefly on the

15

Western Front. The consequences were not slow to appear: in the short term they began to reveal themselves immediately, when the United States Government severed diplomatic relations with Germany on 3 February. In the somewhat longer term, a further consequence of very great import indeed, would follow on 6 April, 1917, with the United States declaration of war. In the longer term still, a succeeding generation would have cause to rue the style of war which became established by the February declaration, and the weapons with which it was conducted.

2

The Most Formidable Thing

The submarine is the most formidable thing the war has produced – by
far – and it gives the German the only earthly chance he has to win.
U.S. Ambassador Walter Page to his son, 1917

IN FEBRUARY, 1917, the German submarine fleet numbered 111 'U-
(*Untersee*)boats' – precisely half the number that *Korvettenkapitän*
Blum had said would be needed for an effective blockade of Britain.
Of these, forty-nine belonged to the North Sea flotillas under the command of the High Sea Fleet,[1] and thirty-three to the Flanders flotillas,
which came directly under the Naval Staff. The differences between
the two groups were not merely organizational, they were also functional. 'U'-boats proper were the larger, more heavily armed, longer-
ranged craft – 'overseas' submarines; these formed the High Sea Fleet
flotillas, and until May, 1915, they constituted the whole of Germany's
submarine force. The early occupation of the Belgian coast (Ostend
was entered by German troops on 15 October, 1914) suggested further
possibilities: small coastal boats, easy and quick to build, which could
operate in the Channel and the narrower parts of the North Sea out of
Ostend and Zeebrugge. These were the 'UB'-boats, ordered and designed in November, 1914; deliveries began early in 1915, and the first
flotilla was formed in March. The UB-boats were prefabricated in
Germany, brought across to Bruges in sections and put together in
assembly yards that had been prepared there. By May there were seven
in process of assembly, and in June two put to sea. Bruges was the

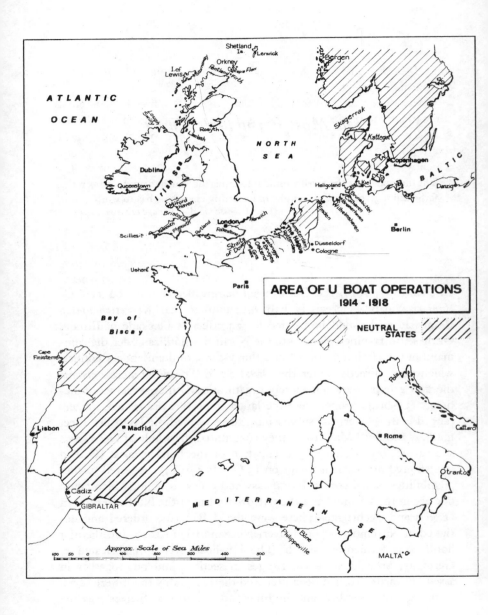

ATLANTIC
OCEAN

Shetland Is.
Lerwick

I. of Lewis
Orkney Is.
Pentland Firth
Cape Flex

NORTH SEA

Bergen

Skagerrak
Kattegat
Copenhagen
Kiel
BALTIC
Danzig

Roeyth
Lamlash

IRISH SEA

Dublin
Queenstown

Milford Haven
Bristol
Plymouth
Scillies

London
Harwich
Portland
Folkestone
Straits of Dover
Heligoland
Emden
Wilhelmshaven
Cuxhaven
Bremen
Berlin

Dusseldorf
Cologne

Paris

AREA OF U BOAT OPERATIONS
1914 - 1918

NEUTRAL STATES

Ushant

Bay of Biscay

Cape Finisterre

Pola

Lisbon
Madrid
Rome
Cattaro

Cadiz
GIBRALTAR

MEDITERRANEAN SEA

Otranto

Bone
Philippeville

MALTA

Approx. Scale of Sea Miles
100 50 0   100   200   300   400   500

true base of the Flanders flotillas, which made their way by canal to the exit ports, Zeebrugge and Ostend. By 1917 the Bruges base offered the U-boats the protection (against air attack) of massive concrete shelters with six-foot-thick roofs, prototypes of the even more solid 'pens' in the French Atlantic ports in World War II. 'UC' minelayers joined the UB-boats in late 1915, and soon became a valued adjunct to the submarine campaign.

When we reflect that $U1$, the German Navy's first experimental submarine, only underwent her trials in 1907, and its first diesel-driven boats (which were also the first real ocean-going types) only made their appearance in 1913, we have to admire the ingenuity and vigour which were displayed in all directions during the first decade of the U-fleet. Development, be it noted, did not proceed with even progress; the decade was a period of continuous experiment, balancing the elements of armament, endurance and speed, sometimes successfully, sometimes less so, but always with a trend towards larger, further-ranging, faster and more powerfully armed boats. A highly successful type was the 'Thirties' class, $U31–41$; ordered in 1912 and launched in 1915, five of these boats became in 1916 the scourge of the Mediterranean. They had a displacement of 680/870 tons (surface and submerged); their armament consisted of four torpedo tubes (two bow, two stern), six 50-cm torpedoes and a 105-mm gun; their surface endurance was 4,440 miles at 8 knots (80 miles at 5 knots submerged) – a high figure; they could manage $16\frac{1}{2}$ knots on the surface and $9\frac{1}{2}$ submerged – these also were very good performances. They carried a crew of four officers and thirty-five ratings, which was already the standard complement. Early though their design was, they were not in all respects the best performers to have appeared: the four boats of the $U23$ type, ordered in 1911, had speeds of 16.8/10.3 knots, while the four $U27$s, ordered four months before the $U31$s, were not only faster but also boasted an endurance of 5,520 miles.

Too much experiment, too much striving for improvement is always the enemy of production (as the British would shortly discover with their tanks); numbers were by now a matter of some importance and the ten $U31$s had that important advantage, as Allied shipping in the Mediterranean learned to its cost. The most famous of them was $U35$, commanded by *Korvettenkapitän* von Arnauld de la Perière, who has been called 'the ace of aces of the U-boat commanders in World War I'; in one 24-day cruise in 1916 he sank no fewer than fifty-four ships, totalling 90,150 tons – 'an all-time record, never even approached in either war.' He is credited with sinkings amounting to 400,000 tons. Another notable boat of this type, also operating in the Mediterranean, was *Kapitänleutnant* Walter Forstmann's *U 39*. Forstmann was another 'ace', scarcely less famous than von Arnauld; his total of sinkings, chiefly in the Mediterranean, was 380,000 tons.[2]

1916 was an important year in U-boat history; it saw the commissioning of more boats than any other year of the war – 108, with a peak of fifteen in December. These were the craft which were to be the mainstay of the unrestricted campaign in 1917. The eight boats of the *U 43* type[3] were slow in production: they began to appear in April, 1915, but were still trickling through until the following July. Although designed considerably later, they were no particular improvement on the 'Thirties' boats; displacing 720/940 tons, they carried the same armament as the *U 31*s (two extra torpedo tubes in the bow, but no extra torpedoes); their diesels generated 2,000 hp (compared with 1,850) but they were still underpowered, with an endurance of only 400 miles more than their predecessors, and slower speeds (15.2/9.3 knots). A real advance was made with two types both ordered in June, 1915: six boats of the *U 81* type, completed between August and December, 1916, of 810/950 tons displacement, 2,400 hp (thereafter the norm), speeds of 16.8/9.1 knots, carrying ten torpedoes, and with an endurance of no less than 7,630 miles. Two further 1915 orders came to fruition in 1917: *U 93*s (850/1,000 tons) with sixteen torpedoes and speeds of 16.8/8.6 knots, but endurance of only 3,800 miles, and *U 99*s (750/950 tons) carrying twelve torpedoes, with speeds of 16.5/8.2 knots and endurance of 4,080 miles.[4] Such was the long-range equipment with which the German Navy entered upon its 1917 campaign.

The UB- and UC-boats had meanwhile undergone a considerable transformation. The early types had been feeble instruments of war: *UB 1–17*, delivered in 1915, displaced only 127/142 tons; their 60 hp diesel and 120 hp electric motors gave them endurance of 1,650 miles at 5 knots on the surface and 45 miles at 4 knots underwater and speeds of 6.7 and 6 knots respectively. Their armament was almost laughable: two 45-cm torpedoes and a machine-gun; they carried one officer and thirteen ratings. *UB 18–47* appeared in 1916, far higher-powered with 280 hp from each set of engines; these gave them endurance of 5,700 miles at 6 knots on the surface, but still no more than 45 miles at 4 knots submerged, and speeds of 9.2/5.8 knots. They were armed with four 50-cm torpedoes and either a 50- or an 88-mm gun; their crew was increased to two officers and twenty-one ratings. It will be appreciated that none of these types, nor the 168/183-ton UC mine-layers of 1915, were war-winners. The real improvements were still largely on the drawing boards in 1916, and made their appearance in the flotillas throughout the next year: a total of eighty-four UBs, belonging to three types, *UB 48, 72* and *88*, and sixty-nine UCs of four types, *UC 16, 34, 49* and *80* (only six completed). The three UB types were much of a muchness: 510–520/640–650 tons displacement; all had the same engine-power, 1,100/760 hp, giving endurance of 3,500–4,200 miles at 6 knots and 50–55 miles at 4 knots, with speeds of 13.4–13.5/7.5–7.8 knots. Their armament was ten 50-cm torpedoes (a big stride) and an 88- or 105-mm gun; their crews numbered three officers and thirty-one ratings.

The new UCs were also much larger than the early types: 410–480/490–560 tons, with 500–600/460–620 hp engines. These gave very good surface endurance: 6,910–8,200 miles at 7 knots, or 40–55 at 4–4.5 knots submerged, with speeds of 11.5–12/6.6–7.2 knots. The *UC 16*s, *34*s and *49*s carried eighteen mines, seven 50-cm torpedoes and an 88-mm gun, with crews of three officers and twenty-three ratings; the *UC 80*s carried fourteen mines, seven torpedoes and a 105-mm gun, with crews of three officers and twenty-nine ratings. More than half the German submarine losses in 1917 would be UC-boats, which is an indicator of the increasing use of submarine-laid mines, and of the vulnerability of these still small and comparatively under-powered craft.

There is a story of Field-Marshal Sir William Robertson, when he was Chief of the Imperial General Staff in 1917, going aboard a small British submarine and when he had completed his inspection asking the young commander whether he liked the life:

> The commander said he did, whereupon R. gave a grunt and a glance, and said, 'Umph, well you're d——d easily pleased.'[5]

It is not only landsmen who are prone to take that view of the submariner's existence, for obvious reasons. The danger element requires no emphasis – the risks involved in trusting one's life to a complicated piece of machinery with virtually no possibility of any help should anything go wrong – especially in those early days when so much remained unknown, so many hazards were waiting to be met – are clear enough. Enemy action seems superfluous, but in 1917 enemy action became a serious factor to reckon with, as we shall see. At all times, however, the crews of Germany's submarines had to endure the conditions dictated by the complications of their diminutive craft:

> There was little privacy and little comfort in a U-boat. There was no bath and only one lavatory for the use of all officers and men aboard. Few shaved, no one changed their clothes from the beginning to the end of a voyage. The officers used eau de cologne to mask body odour and the indescribable damp, oil-laden, stale smells of the sweating interior of the boat. But because of this closeness and the shared hardship and danger, and because there was no room for men who could not be relied on, a U-boat's complement was a uniquely tight brotherhood. '"One for all and all for one," as it was expressed, we were like a great family isolated on the wastes of the oceans . . . I cannot conceive of a finer or more loyal community of life and labour than that of a U-boat.' Thus one typical description.[6]

To catch the full savour of the conditions described above, we have to remember that the ocean-going U-boats of the High Sea Fleet flotillas, by February, 1917, were normally spending three to four weeks at sea, and with the advent of unrestricted warfare their rest-time in harbour was sharply curtailed. *Flotillenadmiral* Bauer, their *Führer*, told the commanders in January that the objective now was:

> to force England to make peace and thereby to decide the whole war. *Energetic* action is required, but above all *rapidity* of action . . . the sole aim is that each boat should fire her entire outfit of ammunition as often as possible. . . . Short cruises, short visits to the dockyard, considerable curtailment of (routine) practices. . . . During periods of overhaul only what is absolutely necessary to be done.[7]

So the great campaign arrived at its formal opening, but, as we have seen, this was hardly more than formality; for the commanders and crews, 1 February signified no more than a hotting-up of a process already well launched; for the world at large it was only 'a public notice of what had virtually been happening for some time'.[8] For Britain and her allies, the sense of crisis was already present: a total of 355,139 gross tons of shipping (British: 182,292) was lost in December,

1916, rising to 368,521 in January (a new record; British: 153,666). In that month the mordant diarist, Colonel Repington, recorded a conversation in which he had expressed the view that

> it was at present a question whether our armies could win the war before our navies lost it.[9]

An unnamed officer in Naval Intelligence told him on the same day that 'frankly he knew no way of combating the submarine menace'. Unrestricted warfare was still eight days off.

Because the effects of the German declaration would soon display some dramatic and amazing features, and the remainder of 1917 would be spent in unremitting effort and unremitting strain, it is important to understand the reasons for the timing. First and foremost, there was the dread of further heavy fighting on the Western Front; as Hindenburg said,

> the German General Staff is bound to adopt unrestricted U-boat warfare as one of its measures, because among other things it will relieve the situation on the Somme front.[10]

It was an open secret that the Allies, under the direction of the new French Commander-in-Chief, General Robert Nivelle, were intending to launch a great joint offensive at the earliest possible moment; if this was to be anticipated and possibly averted, 1 February was none too soon. Secondly, the overthrow of Romania meant that there would now be troops to spare to meet any threat from Holland or Denmark. And finally, as significant as anything, there was the encouraging rise in the numbers of the U-boats themselves:

> It was this rise in the number of U-boats operating at sea that caused the rapid increase in sinkings and not the 'unrestricted' nature of U-boat warfare.[11]

In both world wars in this century, numbers proved to be profoundly important in all spheres: numbers of men, of guns, of aircraft,[12] of ships, of escort vessels – and of submarines. When the U-boat fleet rose to over 100 craft in January, 1917, it reached a milestone of development; these were the tools, and without them the work could not have begun. Optimistically, the Naval High Command hoped there would be enough to bring it to the desired fruition.

* * * * *

The U-boats' great enemy was the Royal Navy, and 1917 found it not in the best of spirits. The Grand Fleet, the nation's pride, with its imposing squadrons of battleships and battle cruisers, supported and protected by armoured and light cruisers and over 100 destroyers, lay fretfully at anchor in its Orkneys base at Scapa Flow, reflecting upon the disappointments of 1916: the failure to achieve a decision in its sole encounter with the High Sea Fleet at Jutland in May, and the failure even to make contact when the Germans came out again in August. The Grand Fleet's new Commander-in-Chief, Admiral Sir David Beatty, was well aware of certain grave deficiencies in British matériel, above all the big-gun ammunition, and despite his dashing and aggressive nature, he was not sorry that matters were not to be put to the test of battle again until some of his worst wants had been remedied. Meanwhile, the unpleasing spectacle unfolded, as it would again in the next war, of a large and powerful element of the Royal Navy sitting mostly idle in its bases, while another (comparatively feeble) portion worked itself to the limits in the attempt to overcome the most serious naval threat that Britain had faced since the Dutch Wars of the 17th century.

It was fortunate indeed that the Germans had displayed their hands in the 1915 campaign; at least, as a result, some necessary steps were taken to provide means of countering a threat which had no precedent, and for which no preparations whatever had been made.[13] Despite the unwarranted general euphoria when the first campaign died down, a lot of thinking had been done, some material progress had been made, and although the Admiralty mood was not rosy by any means, it was at least being professional. Admiral Sir John Jellicoe, who had commanded the Grand Fleet since the beginning of the war, became First Sea Lord on 29 November; just over a week later, Mr David Lloyd George became Prime Minister, and in his new government Sir Edward Carson became First Lord of the Admiralty, and a new ministry was created: Shipping, under the shipbuilding magnate, Sir Joseph Maclay. The first practical fruits of so much change were seen on 18 December, with the setting up of the Admiralty Anti-Submarine Division under Rear-Admiral A. L. Duff. Anti-submarine warfare would now be conducted on staff principles by staff methods; these do not, of course, include magic spells.

24

Submarine warfare was all new in 1914, and anti-submarine warfare was, by definition, even newer. The Germans at least had the weapon; what they still had to discover was its proper purpose, and the right way to use it, and by 1917 they had made substantial progress in both respects. The Royal Navy, for its anti-submarine rôle, did not have a weapon, which was a serious drawback when it came to considering methods: it is difficult to think of a manual without a car to go with it, and, lacking a weapon, the Navy's 'manual' for anti-submarine warfare could only be the thinking and the attitudes that it had evolved for use of the weapons it did have – all designed for quite different purposes. Certain things, however, became immediately apparent: battleships, battle cruisers and large armoured cruisers, on which naval construction had concentrated during the ironclad period, were useless against the new enemy – indeed, a liability, requiring their own lavish protection against underwater attack. Fast modern light cruisers might do, but they were a very expensive kind of hammer to use against the nut; and there were destroyers. It is to be noted that, apart from its own submarines, the Navy in 1914 had almost no smaller craft than destroyers: just fifteen over-gunned but underpowered sloops and gunboats built between 1882 and 1900.[14] When war came, and the need for smaller craft became apparent, it was met by the 'conscription' of various types of basically non-military craft: trawlers and drifters above all, a handful of 'whalers' (ordered by Admiral Fisher in 1915), motor launches and motor boats, yachts and ancient paddle vessels. By November, 1918, this 'Auxiliary Patrol' numbered over 3,000 vessels, a total which, as Lord Jellicoe said, was in itself an indication of the difficulty of dealing with submarines.[15]

That left the destroyers: 320 of them in January, 1917, all but thirty-seven in home waters. Their proper name was 'torpedo boat destroyers', recalling the function for which they had originally been designed before the advent of the submarine: to repel torpedo attacks by very fast surface craft on the great ships of the fleet. Introduced in 1893, speed was the first consideration in their design, and the coming of turbines in the following year brought amazing development. HMS *Viper*, in 1899, could manage over 37 knots, and could hold 34 knots for as long as three hours[16] – astonishing performances indeed. The quest for speed now took hold of naval thinking and construction for all categories; it had no advocate more vigorous than Sir John Fisher, who told Churchill in 1912:

The most damnable person for you to have any dealings with is a Naval Expert! Sea fighting is pure common sense. The first of all its necessities is SPEED, so as to be able to fight —

> *When* you like
> *Where* you like
> and *How* you like.[17]

Churchill needed little persuading; on becoming First Lord in 1911 he had inherited, among other things, the 'Tribal Class' destroyers, twelve boats launched between 1907–9, whose engines generated 14,250–15,500 hp, producing a speed of 34 knots. But by the standards of the day these were expensive craft, and the Board of Admiralty recoiled from their cost; the next three classes (*'Beagles'*, *'Acorns'* and *'Acherons'*) were all smaller and slower (27–28 knots). The *'Acastas'* of 1912–13 were larger, their engines generating 24,500 hp for a speed of 30 knots. The 'L' class, which followed, was larger still, but lost on speed (29 knots). Not until 1914, when the excellent 'M' class began to appear, was the 'Tribal' performance matched; all told, there were 108 'M's, mostly averaging over 1,000 tons displacement, generating up to 27,500 hp, with speeds between 34–36 knots, and a basic armament of three 4-inch guns, a 2-pounder and four 21-inch torpedo tubes.[18] They supplied the core of the Grand Fleet's flotillas, and set the standard of British destroyer performance throughout the war. But they were not designed to deal with submarines.

The feature of all destroyers in both wars was the massive engine-power required to yield their high performance; by 1918 the Royal Navy's vessels were generating 30,000, even 40,000 hp. The slim hulls were sheaths for the great turbine engines (and their fuel) with which they sliced through all but the most hostile seas. The contrast between these racers – frequently called the 'greyhounds' of the sea – and the U-boats with their 15–17 knot surface speeds is at once apparent. Speed enabled the destroyers to race towards a U-boat, if it could be located; but once in proximity, the tight turning-circle of the submerged U-boat taking evasive action put the fast destroyer at a disadvantage. And there was another contrast, too, which required no expert to perceive it: that which existed between the dashing destroyer and the 6–10 knot merchantman whom it might have to protect or assist. Destroyers were maids-of-all-work, because they were there, and very little else was; but for some of the work they had to do they were costly servants and not easy to come by; on average, it took eighteen months to build one. Fortunately, in 1917, there was other help at hand.

Before we consider this, it will be as well to look at the armament of the destroyers themselves. Like all other surface craft, designed for surface action, their chief reliance was on their guns, and with these they could certainly blast a U-boat out of existence – if they could get it into their sights. However, the first recourse of the U-boat against enemy naval craft was to invisibility; it vanished as rapidly as possible beneath the waves – and even by 1917 'as rapidly as possible' meant rapidly indeed: a diving time of 40–45 seconds, reduced to 30 seconds in 1918. Thereupon the destroyer's guns were useless, unless the U-boat could be forced back to the surface, and the same, of course, applied to the torpedo tubes.[19] It is here that we make acquaintance with the weapon that would shortly dominate anti-submarine warfare, and become primary in World War II: the depth charge. As is so often the case, its antecedents go back further than one might suppose – it was in 1911 that the idea of a 'dropping mine' was first put forward, and Jellicoe's predecessor as Commander-in-Chief, Sir George Callaghan, made a request for some in July, 1914. It was not until two years later (June, 1916), however, that an effective depth charge was produced: the Type D, with a bursting charge of 300 lbs of TNT. It is indicative of the rudimentary state of the weapon that for the benefit of slower vessels, to preserve them from damage by their own device, a Type D*, with a bursting charge of only 120 lbs of TNT, had to be brought in shortly afterwards. In 1917 the introduction of a new pistol capable of firing the charge at depths of 100, 150 or 200 feet made the Type D* unnecessary. A thousand Type Ds were ordered in August, 1916, but so slow was production that in early 1917 the normal equipment of any vessel was precisely two Ds and two D*s.[20] By July, production was still only 140 per week, rising to 500 in October and over 800 in December. It was not until early 1918 that anti-submarine craft received the complement of thirty-fifty depth charges which thereafter became normal in both wars. But it was in 1917 that it rapidly became apparent that 'the weapon with the greatest future was evidently the depth charge'.[21]

As numbers of depth charges increased, the problem of delivery increased also; it became standard practice to drop the charges in patterns worked out to counter the U-boat's evasive manoeuvres, with pistols set to fire at varying depths. Dropping was normally done from rails over the stern of the ship, but it did not take long to perceive that there was a lot to be said for projecting the charges to some distance in order to widen the pattern. Accordingly, in July, 1917, first (very slow) deliveries of depth charge throwers began, one to be fitted on each rear quarter to throw the charges to a distance of 40 yards while others went out over the stern. Another piece of standard anti-submarine equipment had arrived. And with it one more, which was to make an effective return to the scene in 1942: in 1917 it was called by its simple proper name – a howitzer – which could throw its projectile to ranges of 1,200–2,600 yards. Its limitation was its small bursting charge, requiring a direct hit to be effective; orders for 2,056 of these weapons were placed by the end of May, 1917, but by the end of July only thirty-five had been issued, and only 377 by the end of the year.[22] The improved 1942 version was called a 'hedgehog', and came to be much admired.

What began to amaze beholders straight away, and continued to amaze them right up to 1945, was the strength of a submarine's hull. Not only was it discovered that U-boats could dive to unsuspected depths, enduring the anticipated pressures of the deeps with impunity, but they also proved capable of standing up to ferocious pounding by their enemies. Even with the 300-lb burster of the Type D depth charge, says Jellicoe,

> it was necessary to explode it within fourteen feet of a submarine to ensure destruction; at distances up to about twenty-eight feet from the hull the depth charge might be expected to disable a submarine to the extent of forcing her to the surface, when she could be sunk by gunfire or rammed, and at distances up to sixty feet the moral effect on the crew would be considerable and *might* force the submarine to the surface.
>
> A consideration of these figures will show that it was necessary for a vessel attacking a submarine with depth charges to drop them in very close proximity, and the first obvious difficulty was to ascertain the position of a submarine that had dived and was out of sight.[23]

This was, indeed, the $64,000 question of both wars: 'Where has he gone?'; 'Where is he now?' It was in 1917 and 1918 that the first steps towards answering it were taken.

It required no great stroke of imagination to appreciate that if one could devise a method of listening to a submarine's engines under water, one would at least be aware of that proximity which, as Jellicoe observes, was so essential for a successful attack. The answer that technology provided (in 1915) was the hydrophone, which could pick up the sound of a submerged U-boat in movement at a range of some two miles, but, as Jellicoe says,

> all the devices for use afloat suffered from the disadvantage that it was not possible to use them whilst the ship carrying them was moving, since the noise of the vessel's own machinery and of the water passing along the side prevented the noise made by other vessels being located. What was required was a listening instrument that could be used by a ship moving at least at slow speed, otherwise the ship carrying the instrument was herself, when stopped, an easy target for the submarine's torpedo. It was also essential, before an attack could be delivered, to be able to locate the *direction* of the enemy submarine, and prior to 1917 all that these instruments showed was the presence of a submarine somewhere in the vicinity.[24]

Necessity produced, as it so frequently did between 1914–18, a burst of inventive originality; no fewer than eleven types of Non-Directional (2) and Directional (9) hydrophones were perfected and produced by the end of the war. This was largely thanks to the work of the Anti-Submarine Division set up at the end of 1916, and in particular the Hawkcraig Experimental Station under Captain C. P. Ryan R.N. Two types of directional hydrophones were produced in 1917, one devised by Ryan, the other by the Board of Invention and Research; they began to be distributed to bases for training purposes in April, 1917, and shortly afterwards there were gramophones with recordings of various types of engine- and propeller-noises as they sounded under water. Systematic hydrophone training for officers and ratings was instituted in March under a qualified Hydrophone Officer at each base. By 31 December, 3,680 General Service (non-directional) hydrophones had been supplied to naval vessels, and 1,950 Mark I and Mark II Directionals. A civilian inventor named Nash had meanwhile perfected a further improvement: the 'fish' hydrophone (of shark-like appearance) operated outboard while a ship was in motion; production of these began in October and thirty-seven were received by the end of 1917, rising to 199 at the end of the war.

The advances in hydrophone technology during World War I were impressive and this would remain a most useful equipment both for anti-submarine forces and for U-boats themselves throughout World

War II. Thanks to further progress, by then the U-boat hydrophone equipment was capable of detecting convoys of merchant ships at distances of up to 50 miles; in the final, inshore campaigns of 1944–45 the anti-submarine escort vessels once more came to rely upon it heavily. But it was, in fact, in June, 1917, that it began to be displaced as a prime submarine detector. It was in that month that the *Allied Submarine Detection Investigation Committee* decided to explore the possibilities of an entirely different technology. This consisted of a sound transmitter sending a fan-shaped beam through the water ahead of a patrol ship; if the beam encountered an obstacle it would be reflected back as an echo. Known at the time as the 'Electrical Detector', it was familiar in both world wars by the name derived from the initial letters of its sponsor: ASDIC (now known as sonar). Even the early versions could give a fair indication of the direction of the target, but accurate depth-finding was always a problem. ASDIC had the advantage that it could be operated from a ship moving at speeds up to 15 knots, but it also had drawbacks: echoes might be obtained from many other types of obstruction than submarines, calling for considerable skill and experience in the operator; it was valueless for detecting submarines on the surface: and at less than 100 yards it lost contact, as the submarine target came below the fan of the beam. It was, however, without doubt the instrument of the future; in November, 1918, seven ships were fitted with it, and 'promising results'[25] were obtained, but it was never operational. So in World War I it was hydrophones or nothing, and the Allied navies were very glad of them. How far they had advanced, with the necessary skills, is indicated by the duration of some of the hunts that they made possible – in one case as long as thirty hours of continuous contact, closely matching some of the longest ASDIC hunts of World War II (see p. 621, Note 13).

Hydrophones for short-range detection; for longer-range information, effective in a longer term, the Navy relied upon yet another of those 'first-time-ever-used' inventions which were the distinguishing feature of the 1914–18 war. As well as being the first effective war of the underwater weapons, it was the first war of Wireless Telegraphy (W/T) with all that implied. Obviously, one thing it implied was a degree of distant control never before enjoyed, making the Admiralty itself in effect a commander-in-chief. It also implied an opportunity of penetrating enemy dispositions which was a complete novelty. In addition it offered a potential of disruption by jamming (extensively practised by the Mediterranean Fleet as early as its 1902 manoeuvres) and a detective potential by Direction Finding (D/F). Thanks to the foresight of Admiral Sir Henry Jackson, Jellicoe's predecessor as First Sea Lord, and Admiral (later Admiral of the Fleet) Sir Henry Oliver, the Chief of the War Staff, an organization already existed in August, 1914, for intercepting German radio messages, and this was quickly built up into what in World War II was called the 'Y' Service. To sift and decode the mass of intercepted material which then poured into the Office of the Director of Naval Intelligence, another organization was required; this came into formal existence in November, 1914 – the now famous Room 40, predecessor of Bletchley Park in September, 1939. By May, 1915, a further organization was in existence whose purpose was to locate German warships of all types by taking bearings on their radio signals – this was Direction Finding. It was in that month that the course of a U-boat was tracked by this method right across the North Sea, a procedure which had become commonplace by 1917. By 1941 D/F was tracking U-boats across the Atlantic and far further afield, and by 1943 it had become a prime agent of their swift destruction.

Fortune, in war, is apt to deal out its high and low cards with an even hand. Virtually from the beginning of the war, the Royal Navy enjoyed one impressive advantage over its enemies: by the end of 1914, all three of the German Navy's codes were in the possession of Room 40, with the result that

> virtually any wireless signal made by the German Navy which could be intercepted, was to become equally available to Winston Churchill, Admiral 'Jacky' Fisher (now 1st Sea Lord) and their immediate subordinates. No one, on either side, had anticipated such a swift and overwhelming intelligence defeat for the Germans; it was one from which the Imperial German Navy was never to recover.[26]

The full extent of the defeat only emerged when the 'Y' Service had time to grow and Rear-Admiral Sir W. R. Hall, Director of Naval Intelligence, found that

> it was able to intercept and record almost every naval wireless message, and diplomatic, consular and commercial messages as well, which were transmitted by the German authorities.[27]

It must be added that the German Navy had its own equivalent of Room 40, the Decrypting Service (*Entzifferungsdienst*: '*E-Dienst*') at Neumünster. Unlike its formidable successor in World War II, the *B-Dienst*, of which we shall hear much more, this Service never matched the achievements of Room 40. It was badly based, for a long time wrongly recruited, and treated with unusual indifference and lack of understanding by the Naval High Command. The British admirals have been accused of being slow to grasp the advantages that science and technology were putting in their hands; in some respects their use of radio intelligence was lamentably ill-organized and unappreciative, yet their lead over the Germans was clear and strategically of profound importance.

It was also ironically the case that the German advantage in one particular field worked to their disadvantage. They surprised themselves (as well as their enemies) by the high quality of their radio transmitters; their main naval station at Nauen, near Berlin, transmitting on 800 metres, could be received in the Mediterranean and the Adriatic, but also as far afield as America, South-West Africa and even China. In late 1917 the Zeppelin L 59, over Khartoum, was able to receive direct operational orders from the Nauen station. Even the earliest U-boats carried excellent transmitters (400 metres) and receivers which enabled them to communicate with their bases at distances of hundreds of miles (in May, 1916, *U 20* set up a record with an exchange of radio signals across 770 miles).[28] This unexpected attribute proved, however, to contain a built-in hazard: the Germans made 'excessive and quite unnecessary use of wireless'; the High Sea Fleet flotillas, in particular, became 'unduly garrulous'. By 1917,

> The increase in the number of U-boats at sea, the improvements in their already efficient wireless sets, and the need of the U-boat command to direct its boats to the most profitable areas caused a rise in the volume of wireless traffic. This was of much assistance to Room 40's experts in breaking the changes in key, by now much more frequent, in solving the disguised grid squares in which positions were given, and in identifying changes in call signs. . . . The U-boat's themselves were becoming more talkative. Although there was nothing like the stream of signals necessitated by the Wolfpack tactics employed in World War II, the more distant operations being undertaken by the beginning of 1917 did require more frequent reports from U-boats at sea and instructions from their shore command.[29]

Thus, with the aid of the efficient French listening and D/F organizations, Naval Intelligence had a far clearer picture of U-boat movements and broad location than ever before; the twin problems remained – of narrowing detection down to a precise position, and making an effective attack.

For the Royal Navy, 'attack' was the key word; all naval tradition, and the training based upon it, was founded upon the principle of carrying the war (or the battle) immediately to the enemy. Inspired by the examples of Drake, of the great seamen of the 18th century, and above all of Nelson (whose final signal at Trafalgar, No. 16 – 'Engage the enemy more closely' – was as well-known to naval officers as 'England expects . . .' to the public at large), the Royal Navy chafed at the lack of offensive opportunities which characterized World War I and the restrictions imposed by the underwater weapons. All its instincts were to go out and seek the enemy, and to destroy him; all anti-submarine warfare was conceived in terms of hunting the submarine to destruction; every weapon or system was judged by its value in this regard. It may be imagined what intense chagrin and bitter disappointment was endured when no technological advance, no improvement in production figures, seemed to bring this object nearer. In the whole war up to the end of March, 1917, according to Sir Henry Newbolt,

> there had been one hundred and forty-two actions between German submarines and British destroyers, and the destroyers had only sunk their opponent in six of them. When therefore a German submarine commander fell in with a British destroyer, though he would certainly have to submerge and perhaps to change his ground, still his chances of escaping destruction were about 23 to 1.[30]

As 1917 opened, in some two and a half years of war no more than forty-six U-boats had been lost from all causes, which included the explosions of their own mines, in one case the torpedo of another U-boat, and the variety of accidents to which so youthful a weapon was certain to be prone. It was not an auspicious situation or prospect for the Royal Navy. How to make its attack effective was its new $64,000 question', and the irony is to observe how, with the answer already in its hands, the Navy clung to every solution but the right one for so long.

An obvious form of offensive against U-boats, which the Navy was eager enough to adopt, was the mining of the approaches to their bases – the Heligoland Bight and the Belgian coast. Unfortunately, even as late as January, 1917, in Jellicoe's sorrowful words,

> we did not possess a mine that was satisfactory against submarines.[31]

How serious this matter was is depressingly revealed in his revelation that in a trial which he ordered to be carried out by bumping British mines against a British submarine (with reduced charges, be it understood!) only 33% of them actually detonated. By April, the Navy had a stock of 20,000 mines, but only 1,500 of them were fit for laying; not only did they often fail to explode, but sometimes they did not take their intended depths, and sometimes they even exploded themselves by floating to the surface:

> Energetic measures were adopted to overcome this latter defect, but it took time and but few mines were available for laying in the early months of 1917.[32]

A much superior mine, the 'H' Type, had been designed in 1916, and orders for 100,000 were placed; deliveries, however, did not begin until the summer of 1917, and only 1,500 were ready for use by September. Thereafter the position improved, and over 10,000 were laid in the last quarter of the year; but as unrestricted U-boat warfare began, all that was in the distant future.

This dismal story of the quality of British mines was regrettably matched in the case of torpedoes. British torpedoes had a habit of not running straight, of passing right under even large ships, and failing to explode when they did make a hit. For submarine officers who had taken high risks to bring their enemies into their sights, this was, to put it mildly, infuriating. It says much for the morale of the Submarine Service that it was able to rise above such a failure. In the event a total of seventeen U-boats were destroyed by British submarines; it might have been a lot more – but even so, the submarine itself could never be a major submarine-killer. What this further fault displayed – taken in conjunction also with the Grand Fleet's ammunition defects referred to above – was what Correlli Barnett has harshly but accurately defined as 'the decline in the creativeness and quality of British technology' which had already been taking place through several decades.[33]

In a struggle whose very essence was technology, this was serious indeed.

It was, then, with its existing equipment, good and bad, and ideas born in earlier wars and different conditions, that the Royal Navy now braced itself against its enemy once more. There were, however, two significant additions, both in substantial measure due to Germany's premature disclosure of her hand in 1915. This had the effect of focusing attention on the Navy's grave lack of small craft suitable for anti-submarine work, in consequence of which the once familiar category of sloop was revived: the 'Flower' class, 112 vessels built between 1915–18. All had displacements of 1,200–1,300 tons, speeds of $16\frac{1}{2}$–$17\frac{1}{2}$ knots (well above those of the UB- and UC-boats, but outclassed by some of the later U-boats) and an armament of two to four guns, 12-pounders, 4-inch or 4.7-inch (3-pounder anti-aircraft guns were a notable novelty, in response to North Sea contingencies). The sloops must have seemed strange items to many naval officers; although officially divided into five types,[34] there were numerous variations of design (within the specified dimensions) according to the fancies of the contractor. To speed production, all were built on merchant ship lines, with armament hidden in order to tempt U-boats to their doom – an unlikely event by 1917. To the naval eye, used to the sleek, trim lines of the man-o'-war, they did not look like naval vessels at all – yet they were the Royal Navy's first specifically anti-submarine craft. Originally intended for patrolling and minesweeping (hence their shallow draught), in 1917 they proved their general versatility. Often seen in company with them by that year were the P- (Patrol) Boats, 612 tons displacement, 20-knot speed and armed with two 14-inch torpedo tubes as well as two guns. A feature of these was their ram bows made of hardened steel.

It was with these instruments – destroyers (the older types proving highly useful), P-boats, sloops and flocks of trawlers – warned by radio intercepts and D/F bearings, hopeful of precise detections by the improving hydrophones and impatient for more depth charges, that the Navy applied itself to the unremitting task of what it called 'offensive patrolling'. Periodic sweeps, some in great strength, were carried out along the main shipping routes, and in waters where U-boats were known to be passing or operating. Special 'hunting patrols' were formed for the purpose as more vessels became available. And with 1917 the Navy began to receive increasingly valuable aid from another of the war's great innovations: air power.

The Royal Naval Air Service was constituted on 1 July, 1914, and once war was declared it lost no time in making its mark. On 22 September four aircraft set out from Antwerp to attack the Zeppelin sheds at Düsseldorf and Cologne (two to each city); in thick mist, only one found its target; Flight Lieutenant Collett succeeded in bombing the Düsseldorf shed from a height of 400 feet, thus inaugurating a style of warfare which Germany would come to rue. In September, 1914, it was somewhat less than devastating:

> One of [Collett's] bombs fell short; the others probably hit the shed, but failed to explode. Germans ran in all directions.[35]

A second attempt on 8 October by two Sopwith Tabloids was more successful; the machine piloted by Flight Lieutenant Marix bombed the shed at Düsseldorf from 600 feet, scoring a direct hit and causing a spectacular gush of flame which announced that an inflated Zeppelin had been inside the shed. This was good going, but there was better still to come: the attack on the birth-place of Zeppelins, Friedrichshafen, far away on Lake Constance, by four Avro 504s which took off from Belfort in eastern France on 21 November. One was forced to return before reaching the target; the other three pressed on, making their final approach at about 10 feet above the level of the lake, then climbing to 1,200 feet and diving to 700 to make their attack. Each dropped its load of four 20-lb bombs and this time it was a gas-works which exploded in gigantic flames while a Zeppelin was badly damaged. One aircraft was shot down and the pilot taken prisoner (he was treated with great care and courtesy). As the Official Air History remarked,

> There have since been many longer and greater raids, but this flight of 250 miles, into gun-fire, across enemy country, in the frail little Avro with its humble horse-power, can compare as an achievement with the best of them.[36]

Finally, to round off these curtain-raisers by the naval air service in 1914, came the seaplane attack on Cuxhaven on Christmas Day. The feature of this was the use of three carriers (converted Channel packets), each with three seaplanes aboard. Two failed to take off, but the remaining seven continued with the operation; they were all supplied by the prolific firm of Short Brothers – three Admiralty Type 74, two Admiralty Type 135 and two 'Folders' (one of the earliest aircraft to have folding wings). As a raid, the operation was not a success: the seaplanes failed to find the Zeppelin sheds they were looking for, but as a reconnaissance and an alarm raiser it was certainly effective – and it was another milestone passed in a rapidly growing collection. By the end of 1914 there was no doubt that the RNAS was definitely 'on the map'.

One savours these exploits all the more when one adds the consideration that in a matter of just over half a year all the aircraft that had taken part in them were already museum pieces. For the RNAS as well as for large parts of the rest of the British war-making machine, 1915 and much of 1916 was a time of trial and error, of ceaseless development, ceaseless search for effective weapons. 1917 was when, for the Air arm perhaps above all, this began to be rewarded. For the RNAS, a conspicuous newcomer in 1915 was the Short Type 184 seaplane; this 'was to the First World War what the Swordfish became in the Second World War; both types made history as torpedo–carrying aircraft.'[37] In the case of the Type 184, this was on 12 August, 1915, when, piloted by Flight Commander C. H. K. Edmonds, it became the first aircraft in the world to sink a ship at sea by torpedo attack. All told, Shorts built 650 Type 184s for the RNAS, and in 1916 they became a mainstay of anti-submarine patrol; starting with one 225 hp engine, their power plant increased to 275 hp by 1918, with speeds of $88\frac{1}{2}$ mph at 2,000 feet, or 85 mph at 6,500, and endurance of $2\frac{3}{4}$ hours. A 1917 addition was the Curtiss H 12 Large America flying-boat, developed from an earlier type by Wing Commander J. C. Porte of the RNAS who was also 'a designer and innovator of genius'.[38] The particular feature of the H 12s was their greater sea-worthiness, thanks to Porte's hull designs, and their endurance of six hours. Seventy-one H 12s were delivered to the RNAS, but in late 1917 they began to be superseded by the even better Felixstowe F 2a, which also owed much to Porte's pioneering. Just under 100 of these were built before the war ended; their power plant was two 345 hp Rolls-Royce Eagle VIII engines, giving a maximum speed of $95\frac{1}{2}$ mph (at 2,000 feet) and a normal endurance of six hours; they were also formidable combat machines, carrying from four to seven Lewis guns and two 230-lb bombs.

Finally, in the air armoury, there were airships; this was a field in which Germany had enjoyed a commanding lead, with her rigid Zeppelins. In 1913 all British airships came under naval control, and the

British preference was for non-rigid types; effective production of naval airships began with the SS (Sea Scout) type of 1915, followed by an improved SSZ (Sea Scout Zero) design in 1916. Their range and endurance were limited and they were regarded mainly as coastal patrol craft, especially useful in narrow waters such as the Strait of Dover or the Severn estuary. In 1917 the last of the British non-rigid types began to appear: the NS (North Sea) class. NS 1 was delivered in February, and in June it performed a flight of 1,500 miles and $49\frac{1}{2}$ hours' duration. This, of course, was the outstanding airship characteristic – range and endurance, whose virtues became more and more apparent as 1917 wore on. It had some other important advantages over heavier-than-air machines: an ability to hover, which greatly assisted the task of observation; a greater weight-lifting capacity; and, probably most important of all, room to carry the cumbersome wireless apparatus of the period, enabling it to transmit and receive messages with relative ease. Its faults were its slow speed, making it virtually useless for attack, its instability in any degree of wind which made accurate aiming of guns or bombs impossible, and its liability to devastating fire if its hydrogen bags ignited. Despite these drawbacks, as 1917 opened the British airships stood on the threshhold of their most valuable service, in a manner that might have been foreseen, but was not.

No aircraft, when 'unrestricted submarine warfare' was declared, had sunk a submarine, or even, so far as could be proved, inflicted significant damage on one, though numerous claims were made on both counts. The truth was – and hard it proved to swallow – that *no* measures so far adopted by the Royal Navy were sinking U-boats in any quantity that might influence events. The record, by 1 January, was dismal enough, and it showed no sign of improvement in the new year: only two sunk in January, and in February, the first month of unrestricted war, only five, one by its own mine. These figures were not, of course, known with precision at the time; the British disposition is normally to take an optimistic – often an over-optimistic – view of difficult situations, yet, as we have seen, taking into account the obviously increased numbers of U-boats at sea, the damage they were doing, and the condition of the anti-submarine armament, senior naval officers who knew the position were in a state of lively apprehension about what might be in store. So even before 'unrestricted warfare' got into its stride, there were good grounds for calling the German U-boat, as Ambassador Page would shortly do, 'the most formidable thing the war has produced'.

1ST QUARTER OF UNRESTRICTED S/M
WARFARE: FEBRUARY-APRIL,1917
WESTERN APPROACHES, CHANNEL
& EAST COAST

No Ocean Convoys: No Coastal Convoys:
French Coal Trade Convoys
Running (Night Sailings).

● ....Ship sunk by U-Boat.

North Sea
sinkings
omitted

FIVE MONTHS
OF RESTRICTED
S/M WARFARE
SEPT.,1916-JAN.,1917

Scale of Sea Miles

WESTERN APPROACHES & CHANNEL

● ....Ship sunk by U-Boat.

3

'Engage the Enemy More Closely!'

(*Royal Navy Signal No. 16; Commodore Sir Home Popham's Telegraphic Code, 1803*)

UNRESTRICTED U-BOAT warfare, from the German point of view, began most promisingly: there was a swift and lasting rise in the amount of shipping sunk – 540,006 gross tons in February, 593,841 tons in March.[1] This was the beginning of the great shipping massacre: over 500 ships went to the bottom in the first two months of the campaign, and it was noted with alarm that a high proportion of this loss consisted of the ocean-going vessels on which Britain's supplies depended. Equally ominous was the statistic that showed the effect on the neutrals whose shipping constituted an important factor in British trade: neutral entrances and clearances of British ports during the two months were 'little more than 25 per cent of the previous year's total'.[2] In informed circles anxiety grew; each week's account lent more point to Colonel Repington's question whether the Navy was losing the war and on 11 February Lord Derby, Secretary of State for War, reported it to Field-Marshal Sir Douglas Haig, commanding the British Expeditionary Force; Derby added:

> Rather cruel on the Navy because they are really at their wits' end as to how to deal with these submarines.[3]

Repington recorded in his diary further proof of this condition. On 21 February he was talking to another naval officer working at the Admiralty:

He is not at all sanguine about overcoming the menace, and thought we should tunnel the Channel and improve our air transport service. What a prospect for the Navy! He thought that it had become a disadvantage to be an island.[4]

At the end of March, with the picture darkening all the time, Lord Hankey recorded the fear that oppressed him: 'we may yet be beaten at sea.'[5] Already there seemed to be every possibility that *Admiral* von Holtzendorff's confident prediction of 'victory before the harvest' would be borne out; and the worst was yet to come.

At the root of Britain's problem, accentuating her weaknesses in anti-submarine weaponry and system which have been described above, and lending point to the anonymous naval officer's opinion that being an island was now a liability, lay the grim facts of geography. No ruses, no stratagems could alter the inescapable truth that all shipping seeking to enter British ports must ultimately follow certain obvious and unchangeable routes. These formed what one authority aptly called the 'three great cones of approach';[6] Lord Jellicoe adds a fourth, but there is no disagreement on what the cones signified. It is important to understand a profound difference between the anti-submarine campaigns of 1916–18 and 1940–45. Although the World War I U-boats could cross the Atlantic, and operated (to the rage of Americans) off the coast of the United States and as far south as Madeira, their real battle was fought relatively close to the European mainland. When the *Alnwick Castle* was sunk in the Atlantic on 19 March, and the survivors came ashore after a severe ordeal in their boats, it was startling news that the sinking had occurred 320 miles from the nearest land; this was the furthest distance yet recorded, only fourteen ships having been sunk over 100 miles off shore, and of these only three over 200 miles. The reason was very simple; the authorized sailing system for merchant vessels coming from distant parts was wide dispersal in mid-ocean, closing as they entered the 'cones', and drawing into conspicuous flocks as the 'cones' narrowed. The three 'cones' pointing towards the ports of Liverpool, Bristol and Southampton constituted the Western Approaches, which rapidly became the decisive point of the action. Reading from south to north, they were:

A: from the Mediterranean and South Atlantic, making for Bristol and the Channel ports, converging on the Scilly Isles;

B: from the Caribbean and southern American ports, making for Bristol and Liverpool, converging at Fastnet Rock;

C: from the northern American ports and Canada, making for Liverpool and the Clyde, converging on Tory Island.

Jellicoe adds a fourth approach ('D'), northabout to the East Coast, converging on the Orkneys. Where these routes converged, they entered a zone of 'protected concentration', where all available light craft prowled incessantly, guarding against U-boats. Since the danger area in each 'cone' covered some 10–15,000 square miles, it is scarcely surprising that most of this prowling was completely ineffective:

> In these circumstances the areas of concentration were, in the long run, little better than death-traps.[7]

The U-boats simply stationed themselves on the flanks of these unmistakable concentrations, waited for the patrols to pass, and fell upon the flocks.

What the nation's peril meant in terms of private misery is exemplified by the *Alnwick Castle* survivors. On the day before she was torpedoed, she had rescued the crew of another British ship, so her six boats had to accommodate two crews and two lots of passengers. One boat, which ultimately reached the Spanish coast, contained twenty-nine people; by the time it had made its landfall, eight of them had died, and the survivors were all suffering from frostbite. The chief officer of the *Alnwick Castle*, Mr A. H. Blackman, was in another boat, containing thirty-one people; in his report to the Company, Mr Blackman told of the deaths, among others, of 'the storekeeper, who the night before went raving mad and had to be lashed down for the safety of all concerned', of a cattle-man who 'jumped overboard after three frustrated attempts, and was drowned, the wind and the sea, and the enfeebled state of us all making it impossible to save him', and the deck-boy, who died one evening, having 'been quietly dying all day'. Mr Blackman continued:

> Although we had occasional showers of rain everything was so saturated with salt that the little we did catch was undrinkable. We even tried by licking the woodwork (oars, tillers, seats, etc.) to gather up the rain spots, and so moisten our mouths, but the continual spray coming over

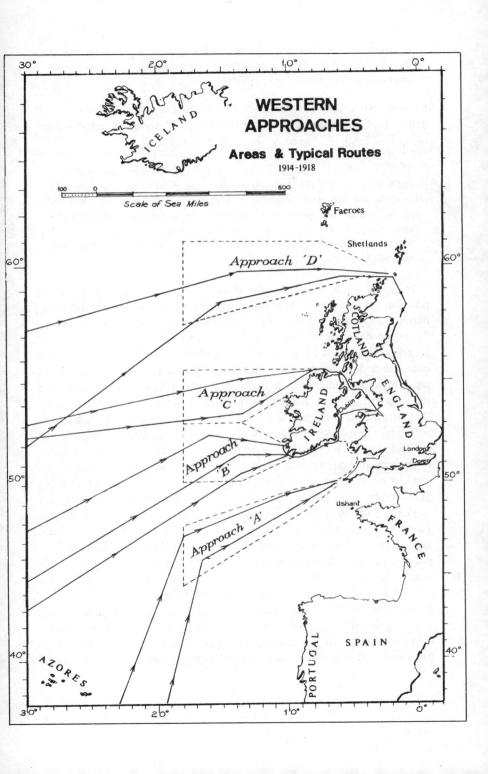

rendered this of little use. In fact, we actually broke up the water 'breaker' in order to lick the inside of the staves, which we found quite saturated with moisture, and to us delicious.[8]

Even so, when they reached port, two of the crew were demented, and had to be forcibly dragged out of the boat, and another died as he was being lifted out. As one naval writer and editor said,

> The case of the *Alnwick Castle* was typical of hundreds; with the sudden explosion, the disappearance of the great ship, the miserable struggle for life in open boats on a stormy sea by men who had no comforts and no warmth, and who were exposed to the waves and the bitter cold, with every prospect of perishing of starvation and thirst. Many boats were never heard of again; many ships vanished leaving no trace.[9]

It is not at all to be wondered at, if a generation brought up to take for granted the shelter and immunity from harsh reality that the Royal Navy had provided for a hundred years reacted to the scenes described by such survivors as the *Alnwick Castle*'s with shock and outrage. Already in 1915, the common reaction to U-boat warfare had been fierce denunciations of 'piracy' and German 'atrocity'; this was a well-worn theme dating from certain events during the German advance through Belgium in August, 1914.[10] It had then earned the name 'Frightfulness', from the German *'Schrecklichkeit'*, which is perhaps better translated as 'terribleness'; it was, in fact, a deliberate policy of intimidating a civilian population by iron-handed behaviour in order to prevent any interference with military movements. It is obvious that even in its least brutal manifestations there is bound to be an element of *Schrecklichkeit* in submarine warfare; as the proportion of vessels sunk by torpedo without warning increased in 1917 (from 37.5% in January to over 60% in April) the sense of atrocity deepened. Quite apart from the more frequent resort to torpedoes (the U-boats appearing in 1917 carried ten, twelve or even sixteen, as compared with the normal six of earlier types), some U-boat commanders displayed a relish for cruelty. *Korvettenkapitän* Max Valentiner, whose *U 38* was a noted terror of the Mediterranean in 1916, was one to whom 'killing was a pastime'.[11] Another was *Korvettenkapitän* Wilhelm Werner (*U 55*) who in 1917 'behaved with particular savagery, killing and drowning 100 seamen in the course of a single patrol'.[12] Yet it should be noted that out of eighteen U-boat commanders listed as war criminals by Britain in 1918, only four names also appear among the 'top twenty' U-boat 'aces' (credited with over 100,000 tons of shipping sunk). Even with unrestricted warfare, it is apparent that, in the words of a once-popular song, 'It ain't what you do, it's the way that you do it'.

Public rage at the style of war that the U-boats were conducting, and fear of its consequences, spilled over into mounting discontent with the Royal Navy, a frame of mind which expressed itself more vehemently as one mounted the ladder of responsibility. On 9 February Colonel Repington (still Military Correspondent of *The Times*) was lunching at the House of Commons with the Prime Minister, Mr Lloyd George:

> We began on the Navy. L. G. said that the Admiralty had been awful, and the present submarine menace was the result. . . . He thought that the apathy and incompetence of the naval authorities were terrible. I asked him why he did not hang somebody. He said that, at the time of the French Revolution, the heads of the incompetents would certainly have fallen.[13]

History was never Lloyd George's strongest suit; with better qualification Lord Esher, special envoy in Paris, was telling Sir Douglas Haig three months later:

> It is time that something was done at the Admiralty. There has been no critical or creative movement within its antique walls since the War began. That celebrated phrase of Mahan's about Nelson's ghostly, unseen, storm-tossed fleet, has been the Navy's undoing.[14]

Lord Esher was referring to one of the great naval text-books: the American Admiral Alfred T. Mahan's famous work, *The Influence of Sea Power upon the French Revolution and Empire* (1892). Mahan was referring to the Royal Navy's blockade of the French Channel ports (Nelson was in the Mediterranean at that time) and his actual words were:

> those far-distant, storm-beaten ships upon which the Grand Army never looked, stood between it and the dominion of the world.

But if Lord Esher was incorrect in these details, he was on the right scent all the same; modern naval thinking is much inclined to agree with him that Mahan's influence was sometimes baleful to a serious degree.[15] If he was also unfair, as well as incorrect, about 'creative movements', it is more understandable. He was not to know about Room 40, or about the various secret devices already in process of development, or about the new designs approved and orders placed for new ships which were only just beginning to bear fruit. Nevertheless, it was fair to say 'It is time something was done'; the U-boat campaign had reached its terrible peak, and though we know now that it had passed that point, no one could know that on 6 May.

'April is the cruellest month,' says T. S. Eliot; April, 1917, was a cruel month indeed for a world at war. It was in that month that Vladimir Ilyich Lenin returned to Russia, to give the revolution which had broken out in March a different character which would soon affect the war itself and the world thereafter. On 9 April (Easter Monday) the British offensive at Arras opened with a brilliant feat of arms by the Canadians at Vimy, and successes elsewhere. The British Army had come a long way since its 1915 misfortunes and the early days of the Somme in 1916; it could now expect to break *into* even very strong enemy positions almost at will, but it had a long way still to go before it learned how to break *through*. The Battle of Arras quickly deteriorated into another grim slogging match – the costliest of the British offensives.[16] Worse still, this battle was launched as a diversion to assist General Nivelle's main offensive in Champagne; the French attack was launched on 16 April and almost immediately turned into a disaster from which the French Army scarcely recovered during the remainder of the war. In the air, April was also the cruellest month; the Royal Flying Corps was passing through a tragic phase, with the Germans enjoying technical superiority until a flow of the new generation of British machines could be established. The RFC lost 316 aircraft in April, a ghastly time for the boy pilots sent out with less than twenty hours' solo flying to face better-equipped and experienced enemies. The only gleam of light on this dark horizon was the declaration of war by the United States on Germany on 6 April, but so dense did the darkness grow that many wondered whether all might not be lost before America's aid could begin to become effective. It was the submarine war above all that gave April, 1917, the quality of terror: 395 ships sunk, a total of 881,027 gross tons of shipping, of which 545,282 tons were British, 96% of this result being due to U-boats.[17]

The 'crunch' of the war at sea came on the day after Nivelle's offensive began to falter in Champagne. Until 16 April shipping losses, though severe, were no worse than they had been in February and March – (but on the 17th the storm broke with terrible violence.'[18] There is a certain confusion at this point on precise dates and figures; according to Fayle, the 17th saw the catastrophe move immediately to its peak:

> On that day alone the submarines destroyed nearly 34,000 tons of British shipping, and on the 19th the losses were over 32,000 tons.[19]

Sir Henry Newbolt, on the other hand, selects 21 April as the worst moment:

> On a single day, April 20, 27,704 tons of British shipping were reported sunk, and 29,705 on the following day.[20]

It scarcely matters which set of figures or which dates are exact: both groups spell a perfectly appalling state of affairs – only matched on three dreadful occasions in 1942. Either way, this sudden steep increase in sinkings which prevailed between 17–27 April gave the month a daily average of just over thirteen ships sunk; this compared with a daily average throughout 1916 of three, and in ten months of 1918 (January–October inclusive) 3.6. In Churchill's words:

> The great approach route to the south-west of Ireland was becoming a veritable cemetery of British shipping, in which large vessels were sunk regularly day by day about 200 miles from land. During this month it was calculated that one in four merchant ships leaving the United Kingdom never returned. The U-boat was rapidly undermining not only the life of the British islands, but the foundations of the Allies' strength; and the danger of their collapse in 1918 began to loom black and imminent.[21]

All these dire matters were implicit in the terse statement of Lord Derby to Field-Marshal Haig on 18 April:

> The state of affairs now existing is really very bad indeed, and we have lost command of the sea.[22]

This also would have its loud, clear echoes in 1942.

The general public, it need hardly be said, was almost totally oblivious of the peril that now threatened it; the Government had ceased to publish figures for tonnages sunk, nor were Allied and neutral losses mentioned in the Press. And very soon (beginning on 25 May) a very different matter occupied public attention: the damaging attacks by the Gotha bombers on British targets, chiefly London, which could not be disguised. Perhaps it was as well that these became the great preoccupation; the civilian population between 1914–18 was considerably less stoical than it was between 1939–45, and had it had an inkling, for example, that by the end of April only six weeks' corn supplies remained in the country, it is likely that some very hysterical manifestations would have taken place. Rear Admiral W. S. Sims, shortly to command American naval forces in European waters, was let into the secret of shipping losses at the hands of U-boats by Admiral Jellicoe on 9 April – over a week before the real holocaust began. Sims recorded:

> I was fairly astounded; for I had never imagined anything so terrible. I expressed my consternation to Admiral Jellicoe. 'Yes,' he said, as quietly as though he was discussing the weather and not the future of the British Empire, 'it is impossible for us to go on with the war, if losses like this continue.'
>
> 'What are you doing about it?' I asked.
>
> 'Everything that we can. We are increasing our anti-submarine forces in every possible way. . . . But the situation is very serious, and we shall need all the assistance we can get.'
>
> 'It looks as though the Germans were winning the war,' I remarked.
>
> 'They will win, unless we can stop these losses – and stop them soon,' the Admiral replied.
>
> 'Is there no solution for the problem?' I asked.
>
> 'Absolutely none that we can see now,' Jellicoe announced.[23]

'Increasing our anti-submarine forces in every possible way': on 23 April, as the U-boats enjoyed the pinnacle of their power, Jellicoe addressed a memorandum to the Government, outlining the situation and such remedies as he could propose. 'Immediate action' was required, he said, but what? He demanded more destroyers; he urged that the United States should send a large force to British waters; he wanted more merchant shipping to be laid down and suggested building very large 'unsinkable' ships; he planned intensive mining of the

German harbour approaches, conceding nevertheless that until new, improved mines were delivered in large numbers there was no likelihood of this being very effective; finally, he recommended laying in large reserves of foodstuffs while the shipping still existed to do it with. It was not a cheerful prognosis, and the most discouraging thing about it, as Newbolt says, is that it showed clearly that the First Sea Lord 'hoped to master the German submarines or to hold them in check by multiplying the weapons used in our existing methods of attack.' [24] There was nothing new. The 'existing methods', as we have seen, were not doing much good. Newbolt adds:

> Possibly the First Sea Lord was right in thinking that fast light craft were the best answer to the submarines that we possessed; but it was becoming apparent that they were not being used in such a way as to achieve the desired result. [25]

What emerged from all this, as Newbolt goes on to say, was the need to take a fundamental decision on which naval opinion was still (and to a considerable extent remained) sharply divided:

> Either our whole forces must be thrown into the attack upon the German submarines, or else the defence of our merchantment must be made the first consideration and the anti-submarine offensive the second. [26]

On 23 April Jellicoe and his Director of the Anti-Submarine Division, Admiral Duff, still believed in the anti-submarine offensive, for want of anything better in view; among others, Admiral Sir David Beatty, commanding the Grand Fleet, argued that, on the contrary, the whole force employed against U-boats should concentrate on escorting merchant ships. There was an impasse; and as Jellicoe had said to Sims a fortnight earlier, this meant that 'no solution' was in sight. But not for long; the sands had now run out.

There is a statistic which is not commonly quoted in connection with the U-boat war of 1915–18, but which is of the deepest significance, and justifies my statement on page 33 that the Navy had the answer to its problems in its hands. It is this: between August, 1914, and November, 1918, 5,399,573 officers and men of the forces of the British Empire served on the Western Front. That vast array was carried to France (the overseas contingents making journeys of thousands of miles) under the noses of the High Sea Fleet and the Flanders flotillas, without ever losing a man, horse or gun at sea. This was an unquestionable achievement of the Royal Navy, one of its major contributions to the war; how was it done? The question is no sooner put than answered; every particle of that gigantic army was watched over and protected during every minute of its final crossing by the destroyers and light craft of the Navy – it was, in other words, escorted in convoy.

There was nothing new about this; convoy was a system hallowed by history and tradition. It was, as Captain Donald Macintyre has said, firmly based upon the principles of concentration and economy of force:

> During the centuries of almost incessant warfare which came to an end with the defeat of Napoleon, the application of these principles to the defence of merchant shipping had resulted in the unquestioned adoption in time of war of the convoy system. The gathering together of the season's shipping engaged in any particular trade and sailing it in an organized fleet with a naval escort enabled the maximum protection to be afforded. At the same time it enabled the available naval force to be concentrated where the enemy was bound to come if he wished to do you hurt. So obvious was this to the seamen of Nelson's day that any other system would have been unthinkable to them.[27]

Indeed, so firmly established was this system by the end of the 18th century, and so well accepted, that Marine Insurance underwriters demanded 30–40% higher premiums for ships sailing independently of convoy, and in 1798 an Act was passed which gave the Admiralty the power to enforce the convoy system for all ocean-going ships. Nevertheless there were always some ships, even in the worst days of 1917, 1942 or 1943, which preferred to sail alone for one reason or another (they were called 'runners' in Nelson's day). Macintyre says:

> The fate of many of these ships foreshadowed in a remarkable way that of merchant vessels of the steam age in the First World War prior to the introduction of convoys. They fell easy prey to fast privateers and small warships who were always able to evade patrolling or blockading warships, just as submarines were to prove themselves able to do.[28]

Why, we may wonder, with this experience so firmly bedded in the national and naval consciousness, and with the example of the immediate resort to convoy for military transports in 1914 present before its eyes, did the Admiralty hesitate for so long before extending the same protection to the nation's vital trade?

The answer that will always spring readily to the minds of some, and give them full satisfaction, is stupidity; others, taking into account the characters and qualities of the men concerned – they would not be human if these did not include some degree of prejudice and error – will be less pleased with that answer. As may be supposed, it is too simple; the arguments against convoy also had some history behind them, and presented considerable force.

At every stage of the Industrial Revolution we meet the same regrettable characteristics: the over-confident assertion of the absolute superiority of modern methods and techniques over all past practices, and the absolute right to pursue 'progress' and riches by the shortest possible route, with a minimum of obstruction. Steam-power, the 19th century firmly believed, had 'changed everything'. Shipping companies, revelling in the new freedom of action, the greater assurance of regular departures and arrivals that steam conferred, were impatient of anything that suggested restriction upon their commercial profit-making. A long period of peace, with no visible serious naval threat,[29] reinforced these attitudes; in 1872 the Compulsory Convoy Act was repealed, and without being too clearly aware of the fact, the Navy underwent a major change in its war strategy. Macintyre comments:

A new jargon grew up in which to describe the Navy's task. It was to 'secure the sea communications', 'protect the ocean highways', 'preserve the sea-routes' – all phrases which screened the fact that merchant ships would no longer receive direct protection. That the 'patrols' which were to achieve these objects would each be, in the illimitable spaces of the ocean, like a single rifleman trying to protect a caravan in the Sahara by strolling at random to and fro along the route, was ignored by those who knew the sea and left unexplained to those who did not.[30]

Meanwhile, the amount of shipping that might need protection was steadily growing beyond all previous expectation. In Nelson's day the critical phases of the naval year were the arrivals of the great convoys from the East and West Indies with all the wealth that they contained – a matter of some hundreds of relatively small wooden ships. By June,

1914, the total tonnage of the world's sea-faring nations was 43,144,000 gross, carried in much larger vessels whose number could not be measured. The British Empire's tonnage alone amounted to 20,524,000 gross, of which the United Kingdom supplied 18,892,000.[31] Britain's nearest competitor, Germany, possessed 5,135,000. By 1917, even with the hazards of war, the weekly figure for entrances into British ports was 2,500 vessels, with as many clearances. With this background, it is not entirely to be wondered at if the Admiralty balked at the sheer size of the task if it attempted constant trade protection on the lines of the old convoy system. It was difficult to see how this could be done without suspending all other activities of the Royal Navy with all that that implied. Jellicoe and his colleagues would have had no difficulty in understanding Nelson's words over a hundred years before:

I am pulled to pieces by the demands of merchants for convoys.[32]

But as Mahan remarks, these were demands that he never refused, no matter what the cost to his fleet and his peace of mind.

There were, furthermore, other strong arguments against convoy in 1917. Naval officers gravely doubted the ability of merchant ships (especially neutrals because of the language problem) to keep station in convoy, above all at night; this proved to be a reasonable doubt in both world wars, shared also by Nelson ('They behaved, as all convoys that ever I saw did, shamefully ill; parting company every day'[33]) – and shared also by many merchant skippers. It was pointed out that the speed of a convoy is always the speed of its slowest ship, which was likely both to delay the arrival of essential supplies and to make the convoy itself very vulnerable to attack. And on the same tack, the doubters stressed the difficulty of large numbers of ships arriving simultaneously at the ports and requiring dock facilities and transport to move their cargoes. This was not a dream-problem; it became very real.

The final and overwhelming argument against convoys, however, was that collecting large numbers of ships together into groups would be to provide the U-boats gratuitously with perfect targets. The Operations Division of the Admiralty expressed itself officially on this subject in January, 1917:

The system of several ships sailing in company, as a convoy, is not recommended in any area where submarine attack is a possibility. It is evident that the larger the number of ships forming the convoy, the greater is the chance of a submarine being enabled to attack successfully, and the greater the difficulty of the escort in preventing such an attack.

In the case of defensively armed merchant vessels, it is preferable that they should sail singly rather than that they should be formed into a convoy with several other vessels. A submarine could remain at a distance and fire her torpedo into the middle of a convoy – with every chance of success. A defensively armed merchant vessel of good speed should rarely, if ever, be captured. If the submarine comes to the surface to overtake and attack with her gun, the merchant vessel's gun will always make the submarine dive, in which case the preponderance of speed will allow of the merchant ship escaping.[34]

There is an apparent logic in this; alas, it is only apparent, it is not real. What these two deadly paragraphs display is the acute lack, in January 1917, of real analysis of anti-submarine warfare. The second paragraph, in particular, is detached from reality; it cannot have had the benefit of advice either from a British submarine officer, or from naval or Merchant Marine officers with actual experience of U-boat attack. We have to recall that the Naval Staff itself had only been in existence for five years, and the Anti-Submarine Division for less than a month. Staffs, military or naval, cannot be improvised; Churchill had more to do with the creation of the Naval War Staff in January 1912, than anyone, and he wrote:

It takes a generation to form a General Staff. . . . At least fifteen years of consistent policy were required to give the Royal Navy that widely extended outlook upon war problems and of war situations without which seamanship, gunnery, instrumentalism of every kind, devotion of the highest order, could not achieve their due reward.
Fifteen years! And we were to have only thirty months![35]

In the case of the Anti-Submarine Division, it was more like thirty days; the system of statistical analyses (the foundation of sound staff work) which could already have revealed the increasing tendency of U-boats to sink at sight and have monitored that tendency in the future did not exist. But by April matters were improving; there was an inkling that most torpedoed crews never even saw the U-boat that had sunk them. Better still, someone had had the acumen to examine the statistic of the entrances and clearances of ports. Did the Navy really have to think of escorting some 5,000 vessels a week? Might it not be that the task was rather simpler than that?

Key figures in answering this all-important question were Mr (later Sir) Norman Leslie of the new Ministry of Shipping, and a junior naval officer, Commander R. G. H. Henderson.[36] It was Henderson who subjected the entrances and clearances to a close examination which revealed that the figure which had so frightened the Admiralty was a gross total which included small coasters making several calls, cross-Channel steamers, everything, in fact, above 300 tons. This was not what submarine warfare was about; it was about ocean-going vessels, the ships that were vital for the nation's survival – and of these the true number was between 120 and 140 a week. It seems certain that Commander Henderson made this conclusion known to Sir Maurice Hankey, the influential Secretary to the War Cabinet, who was already a supporter of convoy by February. By April Hankey was confirmed in his view; his lively mind was much occupied with the U-boat crisis, and on 30 March he noted in his diary:

> I have many ideas on the matter, but cannot get at Ll. George in regard to it, as he is so full of politics.[37]

As April wore on, however, Lloyd George was forced to take his mind off politics and concentrate it on the matter of survival; and the Admiralty at last came to grips with some of the facts that stared it in the face.

The most important of these was that the convoy system was already in use and working well. At the stage of the industrial revolution then reached, coal was the primary source of power, and Britain's inexhaustible supplies gave her great advantages. Coal was a major export, not least to Britain's chief ally, France; the extent of the French trade may be measured by the fact that in one month alone (November, 1916) 800 colliers plied across the Channel, 580 of them coming from South Wales, the rest from the North-East coast. Losses to these vessels (small craft for the most part) had been mounting, and the French asked that they should be protected. The Admiralty responded with what it called 'controlled sailings' – there was a reluctance to use even the word 'convoy' – giving groups of colliers the escort of a few armed trawlers for which the name 'warship' was scarcely more than a courtesy title. But rough and ready though this system was, it worked amazingly well – Jellicoe, writing after the war, still cannot conceal his surprise. The first 'controlled sailing' was from Mount's Bay to Brest on 10 February; by the end of August the number of ships in the French coal trade effectively convoyed in this fashion was 8,871, of which no more than sixteen had been sunk – 0.18%. The man directly in charge of the coal trade convoys was none other than Commander Henderson; it was, in fact, this experience that set him thinking, and not least about the light it threw on the question of vulnerability.

Nothing was harder to shift than the belief that convoys presented magnificent targets, and would lead to even greater losses. This conviction ruled not only in the Admiralty, but in the French and American Navies also, and was much in the minds of merchant ship Masters, expressed at a conference in February. What, then, asks Churchill, was overlooked 'in this high, keen and earnest consensus'? His answer goes to the very roots of the subject, as exposed in two world wars:

> The size of the sea is so vast that the difference between the size of a convoy and the size of a single ship shrinks in comparison almost to insignificance. There was in fact very nearly as good a chance of a convoy of forty ships in close order slipping unperceived between the patrolling U-boats as there was for a single ship; and each time this happened, forty ships escaped instead of one. Here then was the key to the success of the convoy system against U-boats. The concentration of ships greatly reduced the number of targets in a given area and thus made it more difficult for the submarines to locate their prey. Moreover, the convoys were easily controlled and could be quickly deflected by wireless from areas known to be dangerous at any given moment. Finally the destroyers, instead of being dissipated on patrol over wide areas, were concentrated at the point of the hostile attack, and opportunities of offensive action frequently arose.[38]

So accurately does this passage summarize the experience of 1940–45 that we have to remind ourselves that the book in which it appeared, *The World Crisis*, came out in 1923. If Churchill profited by hindsight, it was only to a very limited degree; rather more so, and with characteristic inexactitude and exaggeration, Lloyd George in the '30s picked up his final point – offensive action:

the convoy also served the purpose of bringing the submarine to the destroyer instead of the destroyer having to range the Atlantic looking for a periscope.[39]

In other words – and this was perhaps hardest of all to grasp until the thing was tried – convoy offered the Navy its chance, its *only* chance, of being able to do what it most desired to do: to 'engage the enemy more closely'.

4

Convoy Acted Like a Spell

'If losses went on rising as they rose in April – and what was to stop them? – the Central Powers would win the war. . . . We see now that the introduction of convoy acted like a spell.'

Captain Cyril Falls

IT HAS BEEN a widespread belief, persisting for a very long time, that the British High Commands in World War I, military and naval, were afflicted from beginning to end by a universal outbreak of peculiar imbecility. It is a view which received powerful expression from the Prime Minister (1916–18), Mr Lloyd George, in his memoirs which appeared in the 1930s, and was cordially endorsed by the writings of supporters both inside and outside the Services. A phrase was coined as a label for the disease: the 'Military Mind'. It meant a mind totally trapped in routines and routine thinking, incapable of accepting or appreciating any kind of novelty, and closed to rational argument. This belief drew strength from the undoubted fact that military institutions are certainly conservative; they draw heavily upon tradition, and they are, of course, hierarchical. And the men at the top, except in most unusual circumstances, are generally well into middle age. What this meant, in 1914–18 terms, was that they would have been brought up in a Victorian world which, when they were boys, knew nothing of cars or aeroplanes, telephones or radio, high explosive or automatic weapons. And upon that generation of senior officers fell a fate that was unique. As I have said elsewhere:

never before or since has so much innovation been packed into such a short space of time. The imagination of that generation (in every country) had no option but to work overtime; those who were short of imagination had to develop it rather fast. The truth is that those ruddy-cheeked, bristling-moustached, heavy-jawed, frequently inarticulate generals rose to challenge after challenge, absorbed weapon after weapon into their battle systems, adapted themselves to constant change with astonishing address.[1]

The same was, by and large, true of the admirals, whose Service was, if possible, even more dominated by technology, and the pace of technological change, than the Army. In the case of submarine and anti-submarine warfare, it is a simple fact that, until 1915, everything about it was new; there was no previous experience for guidance, and everything was changing all the time. If Jellicoe and other members of the Board of Admiralty seem at this distance in time, with all the benefits of hindsight that it brings, to have moved slowly on the question of convoys, that was not (as we have seen) without reason. And in any case, as Sir Maurice Dean has said, referring to the British Government's prolonged hesitation in regard to aviation after the Wright brothers' great stride towards the future in 1903,

It is seldom wrong for governments to adopt a cautious approach, especially in military or commercial matters.[2]

However, by 27 April 1917, the admirals (Jellicoe and Duff) were convinced – sufficiently convinced for Jellicoe to approve on that day a detailed minute in favour of the adoption of convoy which Duff had submitted to him the day before, and to order a full-dress experimental convoy to be run on the homeward route from Gibraltar. This was duly done on 10 May. Even before that, at the end of April, a convoy system was instituted between Lerwick and the Norwegian ports, under the protection of a flotilla leader and six destroyers of the Grand Fleet, which also gave protection to certain other vessels in northern waters.[3]

The timing of these actions knocks a famous yarn on the head; it is a version of events admired by Lloyd George and well honed by Lord Beaverbrook (then Sir Max Aitken) who always tended to see contemporary history in terms of yarns of that sort that the less sophisticated newspaper readers enjoyed. It relates to the visit which Lloyd

George (Hankey in attendance) paid to the Admiralty on 30 April. On that day, wrote Beaverbrook,

> with the submarine peril at its height, the Prime Minister descended upon the Admiralty and seated himself in the First Lord's chair. This was possibly an unprecedented action. It was well within the powers and competence of the Prime Minister; yet there may be no parallels in our history. For one afternoon the Prime Minister took over the full reins of Government from the head of a major department of state. . . . The meeting was a minor triumph for the Prime Minister. . . . Lloyd George had staged a deliberate encounter with the Naval High Command, and had emerged triumphant.[4]

It is good stuff for the port and brandy or the gossip columns, but for nothing else. The decisions were already taken three days before Lloyd George's 'descent', which gives the ring of conflict a somewhat hollow sound – and, indeed, there was no conflict. Hankey was a deeply interested party to the whole argument about convoys; his diary for 29 April explicitly states that the Admiralty was undertaking convoy 'on their own initiative', and on the 30th he tells us:

> This morning Lloyd George and I went to the Admiralty and spent the whole day there very pleasantly, lunching with Jellicoe and his wife and four little girls – Lloyd George having a great flirtation with a little girl of three.[5]

Those who believe that the Admiralty should have acted earlier are unlikely to change their minds. Hankey, a warm advocate of convoy since February, was one of them, and his biographer may be given the last word on this subject:

> In sum, although one can reasonably criticize the Admiralty for their slowness and reluctance to introduce the traditional strategy, it is also reasonable to ask why Lloyd George should escape all the blame for the delay in starting convoy and be accorded so much of the merit for the change, when Hankey's original memorandum on the subject had been in his hands since 1st February. If the Admiralty was slow to adopt convoy, the Prime Minister and his colleagues in the War Cabinet showed no very marked alacrity in picking up the ball which Hankey had placed at their feet.[6]

Having reached their decision, the admirals lost no time; on 28 April the Senior Naval Officer at Gibraltar was informed that convoys would begin from there in about ten days. The Convoy Commodore, Captain H. C. Lockyer, arrived on 7 May; by 10 May a convoy of sixteen merchant ships had been collected, and on that morning the masters and chief engineers were briefed; the convoy sailed that evening. It was escorted by two 'special service' ships (converted merchantmen) supplemented by three armed yachts in the most dangerous area; on 18 May, after a passage without incident and without loss, the convoy was met by six destroyers from Devonport and a flying-boat from the Scillies, who took it safely to its sundry destinations. Naval officers, keeping sharp watch with critical eyes, were pleased (if also surprised) to observe that the merchantmen had, on the whole, kept station satisfactorily, and had paid due attention to signals. The only problem had been the inability of the lower-powered vessels to keep up their nominal speeds. Newbolt comments:

> The success of this initial experiment was extremely encouraging, and went far to allay misgivings as to station-keeping. Further, the opinion of the masters, as expressed to the Convoy Committee, was that sailing in convoy greatly relieved the strain in the danger zone, by freeing them from the risk of capture, if not of sinking, and from all anxiety as to courses and the procedure to be adopted in view of war warnings.[7]

Such was the first of the ocean trade convoys; it would have been foolish then, and would be foolish now, to generalize too much from this single experience, but three points deserve notice. The first, by a long lead, is the fact that the convoy never met a U-boat (or if it did, the U-boat would seem to have been more concerned with remaining invisible than with carrying out an attack). There could be several reasons for this (we shall refer to a likely one in another context shortly), but the vanishing capability of a convoy in the ocean wastes is an obvious candidate, with a hopeful message for the future. Secondly, and less hopeful (contributing also, perhaps, to the first) is the size of the escorting force: eleven warships of one kind or another to guard sixteen merchantmen was a number likely to daunt any U-boat captain, certainly, but also daunting to even the most robust supporter of the convoy system, and which reflected a serious error in the whole organization in the early days. Thirdly, there is the matter of station-keeping and convoy discipline; merchant skippers, in both wars, tended to be highly idiosyncratic, tough, practical men with independent minds, who did not by any means accord automatic respect to the Royal Navy. Barring only the captains of great liners or other show-piece vessels, they had no time for spit and polish, for rank and protocol; their lives were harder, their work (in peacetime) more continuous than that of men-o'-war. A World War II convoy Commodore wrote:

> The men sailing under the Red Duster felt that they were the only real sailors and the sailors who manned our warships were a bunch of softies ... the blunt fact was that they preferred to have as little contact with us as possible.[8]

It was satisfactory indeed to find that these hard-bitten specimens could and would accept a degree of discipline, and that their own misgivings about keeping station were after all exaggerated.

The introduction of convoy has been written about as though it acted like the wave of a magic wand. Even so normally cool and balanced a historian as Captain Cyril Falls has said:

> We see now that the introduction of convoy acted like a spell.[9]

If we really look carefully, we see nothing of the kind. There was indeed a very sharp drop in the amount of tonnage sunk in May, by nearly 300,000 tons (British, nearly 200,000) to 596,629 gross. But this is not in any way attributable to convoy – indeed, only a small percentage of ships actually were convoyed during that month, pending the full organization of the system. The main cause of the decline was, quite simply, that the U-boats were not able to sustain the tremendous effort they had made in April. It was estimated that whereas, in that awful month, there had been fifty boats at work, totalling a cruise time of 660 days, in May the number of boats dropped to forty, and their time at sea to 535 days. It was in particular the larger boats, the U-boats proper, which operated in the Western Approaches, whose numbers most significantly declined, with a natural decrease in sinkings in that area, from 191 vessels in April to 156. But when all the statistics are given careful consideration, it will be agreed that the 'magic wand' or 'spell' was taking time to produce its effect: 596,629 tons is a very great deal, and justified no complacency. As the American Ambassador in London, Mr Walter Page, told President Wilson on 4 May,

At the present rate of destruction more than four million tons will be sunk before the summer is gone. Such is this dire submarine danger. The English thought that they controlled the sea; the Germans, that they were invincible on land. Each side is losing where it thought itself strongest.'[10]

War's ironies abound; this was a shrewd perception of one of them.

Before the Gibraltar convoy had even reached home waters, the Admiralty had set up the Convoy Committee referred to above. It convened on 17 May, and when it presented its report some three weeks later, having taken into account the examples of the Gibraltar convoy, the Scandinavian and Dutch convoys, and the colliers, this document proved to be the foundation of convoy organization and procedure, a blueprint at last, to which World War II would only add refinements and numbers. The committee[11] proposed a programme of eight homeward and eight outward convoys in every eight-day period. Four assembly ports were designated for the homeward-bound convoys: New York, where vessels from the northern American ports would collect, and then be joined at a sea rendezvous by those from Canada; Hampton Roads, collecting point for the southern American ports, the Gulf of Mexico, the Caribbean and Panama; Dakar, for the South Atlantic, and the Australian and Far East trade via the Cape of Good Hope; Gibraltar, for the Mediterranean. Each of these four collection ports would provide a convoy for Britain twice in every eight days, one serving the West Coast, the next serving the East Coast and the Channel (including northern France). The three trans-Atlantic convoys would be brought across under protection of an old battleship or a cruiser (either regular RN, or an auxiliary) to a point outside the U-boat danger zone, where they would meet a destroyer escort; this would bring them to their dispersal point, and their final passage to their destinations would then be protected by coastal escorts. For the outward-bound convoys, the assembly-points were Lamlash, Queenstown and Plymouth for the Atlantic ports, Milford Haven and Falmouth for Gibraltar and Dakar. The outward-bound convoys suffered the particular hazard in winter or bad weather of being in ballast (that is to say, carrying no cargo) which made them at times almost unmanageable in company, and station-keeping virtually impossible. The homeward convoys were already in operation and developed at once on the lines indicated; outward-bound convoys had to wait until August.

In both wars, speed was a constant curse of convoys, and the 1917 committee's attempt at a solution of the problem was not a great success. It set a limit of 12 knots maximum and 8¼ minimum, which was not altogether realistic, and left the vulnerable slow-sailers unprotected. The Gibraltar convoys, which normally contained a number of somewhat ancient ships plying the coal and ore trades, were permitted a minimum of 7 knots. The thinking on this was that it would be fatal to allow slow-sailers to delay the rest. In World War II the practice was adopted of running 'fast' and 'slow' convoys from the same ports, which was sensible; but in both wars there remained the problem of ships which could not attain (or at any rate, could not hold) their nominal speeds, or whose machinery broke down when pushed too hard for too long. As Admiral Creighton says:

> A freighter might waddle across the ocean in peacetime for years without any undue demands being made on the engines; normally, the engine-room telegraphs would be pushed to the 'Full Ahead' position after clearing port and dropping the pilot and often remain there for thousands of miles. In convoy, a ship had to make frequent alterations of speed to keep station.[12]

In 1917 it was discovered that many such ships did not even have voice pipes connecting the bridge and the engine-room, and the Admiralty had to take measures to supply these, as well as the necessary signal apparatus; in 1940 the same deficiencies were encountered.

The most serious mistake made by the 1917 Convoy Committee was in the matter of escorts. The Committee contemplated an average convoy size of about twenty ships, and it considered that six vessels would be required to provide the destroyer escort of each convoy. This meant fourteen flotillas of that size in all, three each at Lough Swilly, Queenstown, Portland and Plymouth, and two at Gibraltar: eighty-four vessels in all. No fewer than fifty-two cruisers (or similar) were needed to supply the ocean escorts. The Admiralty's hesitations were not entirely without reason. It must be stated at once that 'destroyer escort' was interpreted as including sloops and P-boats as well as destroyers, though the latter were always the most numerous. In July, 1917, there were available: sixty-four destroyers, eleven sloops and sixteen P-boats – a total of ninety-one craft;[13] this figure would rise to a peak of 195 (115 destroyers) in April, 1918. Meanwhile the Admiralty had laid down certain rules:

The normal number of ships in any convoy to be 20 (26 maximum; any increase requiring special Admiralty permission).[14]

Escort for a convoy of over 22 ships:	8 destroyers;
Escort for a convoy of between 16–22 ships:	7 destroyers;
Escort for a convoy of under 16 ships:	6 destroyers.[15]

It was a feature of the whole 1917–18 anti-submarine campaign that, as Admiral Jameson says, the Admiralty insisted on 'unnecessarily small convoys with over-abundant escorts'.[16]

The Committee's report was studied carefully, and formally approved on 14 June. There is, of course, a substantial gap between formal approval and full implementation; nevertheless, it was found possible to run four convoys from Hampton Roads (with emphasis on oil tankers) before the end of the month, and the extension of the system awaited only the availability of the requisite forces. The safe arrival of all four of these convoys (as well as the one from Gibraltar), says Newbolt,

> supplied a fairly conclusive answer to all who had doubted the success of the system on tactical grounds. The experience gained showed that *a convoy had intrinsically great powers of evasion*, in that it was almost impossible for a submarine commander to place himself right upon its track, at the right time of day, and in a good position for attacking it, *when its course and time of arrival were completely unknown to him*.[17]

Previously, a submarine had only to position itself somewhere in the Western Approaches, keep a sharp look-out for patrols, and wait – and victims were there for the taking. The whole of that immense stretch of water had been, in the U-boat sense, 'productive'; now it was no longer so; for both sides – Royal Navy and Merchant Marine as well as the U-boat commanders,

> the most surprising result of convoy was to make the waters suddenly very empty. Instead of a stream of ships at more or less regular intervals there were days when U-boat lookouts saw nothing at all.[18]

Hitherto it had been the submarines that had enjoyed the attribute of invisibility; now, in their fashion, the convoys also enjoyed it. Newbolt comments:

The passage of these convoys through the danger area showed that, if the system could be developed and extended, it would alter the whole aspect of submarine warfare.[19]

Meanwhile, the aspect of submarine warfare was not a pretty one; convoys or no convoys, the U-boats had found a second wind. Shipping losses in June totalled 687,507 gross tons (British, 417,925), the second highest monthly figure for the whole war. And during the month only two U-boats were sunk, though this precise figure was not then available. However, even the most optimistic naval officer must have found little cause for satisfaction, watching the weekly statistics and striking off the names of the lost, or seeing the limping survivors struggling into port. And what they would not know, perhaps fortunately, was that eight new U-boats had been commissioned in June, more than ample replacements for such losses. The U-boat fleet at this stage, according to *Flotillenadmiral* Andreas Michelsen, who took over from Bauer in June, numbered 132 boats, of which sixty-one were at sea, forty of them in British home waters.[20]

It is obvious that no magic wand or spell was visible in June.

Everything hopeful was still in the future. Important changes had taken place in the Admiralty in May, but, like everything else connected with the anti-submarine war, they required time to take effect. The struggle to drag that august institution right into the twentieth century was long and hard; Admiral Fisher had made an excellent beginning on the material side and with Service conditions during his period as First Sea Lord from 1905–10, but the thinking side was his blind spot. He had bitterly opposed the creation of a Naval Staff, whose lack, as we have seen, had already had serious effects. When Churchill did at last introduce such a body, for various reasons it failed to produce its full potential effect. He himself considered the time factor to be the most significant, and few will dispute that; in more concrete terms, it meant that a generation of senior officers occupied key positions who knew little about the proper use of a General Staff, and if anything cared less; these men would have to pass away into retirement before a true staff machine could be forged. As a shrewd observer remarked, with special reference to the U-boats, at about this time,

whether we get the better of them or not depends, in my opinion, on whether the Admiralty succeeds in scaling off its semi-opaque upper layer of senior respectabilities who behave with perfect propriety, but have neither knowledge of modern conditions, nor initiative, nor imagination. The beating of the submarines – indeed, naval work as a whole of every description – is a young man's job. In spite of all its virtues I think there is more obstruction and 'old chappery' in the Navy than in any other branch of administration.[21]

This may be somewhat cruel – naval officers at that time were mostly tight-lipped men, not much given to smooth talk, and therefore readily liable to misunderstanding – but it was an opinion widely held in informed circles. The Shipping Controller Sir Joseph Maclay even went so far as to tell the War Policy Committee of the Cabinet that 'he considered the Admiralty was not a good office!'[22] What critics tended to lose sight of was the Admiralty's unique rôle, to which Jellicoe draws attention:

> The Admiralty Staff organization necessarily differed somewhat from that the War Office, because during the war the Admiralty in a sense combined, so far as Naval operations were concerned, the functions both of the War Office and of General Headquarters in France. This was due primarily to the fact that intelligence was necessarily centred at the Admiralty, and, secondly, because the Admiralty acted in a sense as Commander-in-Chief of all the forces working in the vicinity of the British Isles.[23]

Yet the criticism holds that the organization did not serve this double function well, and Jellicoe himself provides an explanation for this fault, tracing it to unclear thinking about the duties of the Chief of Staff, which had always been defined as being advisory:

> He possessed no executive powers. Consequently all orders affecting the movements of ships required the approval of the First Sea Lord before issue, and the consequence of this over-centralization was that additional work was thrown on the First Sea Lord. The resultant inconvenience was not of much account during peace, but became of importance in war, and as the war progressed the Chief of Staff gradually exercised executive functions. . . . The fault in the organization appeared to me to lie in non-recognition of the fact that the First Sea Lord was in reality the Chief of the Naval Staff, since he was charged with the responsibility for the preparation and readiness of the Fleet for war and for all movements.[24]

66

Stated thus, the whole thing appears as a blinding glimpse of the obvious; the lesson of history is that nothing is obvious until the moment comes that makes it so.

For the Admiralty, that moment came in May, 1917. On the 14th of that month, the offices of First Sea Lord and Chief of the Naval Staff were merged; Jellicoe took both titles and functions. Vice-Admiral Sir Henry Oliver, who had been 'Chief of the War Staff' since November, 1914, now became Deputy Chief of the Naval Staff, responsible for the surface operations of the Navy, while Rear-Admiral Duff became Assistant Chief of the Naval Staff, responsible for anti-submarine warfare. It was an important step towards decentralization, marred only by the characters of Jellicoe and Oliver, both men who tended to regard delegation of duty as dereliction, both accustomed to accept enormous, unremitting work-loads. It was said of Oliver that 'he never left the War Room, night or day'; his custom was to draft every signal to the Fleet with his own hand – with the inevitable result that, as Fisher told Churchill as early as March, 1915, he 'so overburdens himself he is 24 hours behind with his basket of papers'.[25] Yet, as Churchill said of Oliver:

> His accuracy in detail and power of continuous and tenacious mental toil were extraordinary. He combined with capacious knowledge an unusual precision of mind and clarity of statement. His credentials as a sea officer were unimpeachable.[26]

He was now 52 years old; the difficulty of getting rid of such men, of replacing such compendious knowledge and capacity for work, will be appreciated.

The kernel of truth within the wilder accounts of Lloyd George's 'confrontation' with Jellicoe on 30 April was a set of useful agreements cordially arrived at between the two men. Lloyd George urged decentralization, and Jellicoe entirely agreed; the difficulty was his temperamental inability to carry it out. One thing, however, could be done, and Jellicoe accepted it with misgivings, but as a necessity: the First Sea Lord/Chief of Staff could be freed from the burden of supply. For this purpose Sir Eric Geddes was brought in as Controller, with the task of supervising all shipbuilding, not merely for the Royal Navy but also for the Merchant Marine – an enormous undertaking, but of a kind that Geddes revelled in. His true field was railways – he had been manager of the North-Eastern Railway, and Lloyd George had been quick to bring him into the Ministry of Munitions when it was created in 1915. In 1916 he went to Haig's General Headquarters in France to reorganize the BEF's railway system, and after the chaos of the fearful winter of 1916–17 he became Director-General of Transport. While he was serving with the army in the field, it seemed appropriate to give him the rank and badges of Major-General, which meant that he could issue direct orders. Haig, in his Despatch of 31 May, 1917, acknowledged a particular debt to Geddes, 'to whose great ability, organizing power and energy the results achieved are primarily due'.[27] When he came to the Admiralty, it once again seemed appropriate that he should hold rank and wear uniform – a 'promotion' to Vice-Admiral, placing him on a par with Sir Henry Oliver, who was no more than an acting Vice-Admiral after a lifetime in the Navy. It did not go down too well with older officers. Lord Esher thought there was a Gilbert-and-Sullivan element in all this. Oliver had the last laugh; he was ten years older than Geddes, but survived him by twenty-eight years, to die as an Admiral of the Fleet at the age of 100.

Other suggestions which Lloyd George put forward or supported were a weekly Admiralty appreciation of the course of the war, on the lines of one already emanating from the War Office, close liaison with the Ministry of Shipping (really only a matter of degree), diversion of shipping from the east to the west coast, an appeal for Japanese destroyers in the Mediterranean (they were already on their way) and various other matters of detail. More importantly, he urged that there should be a portion of the Naval Staff freed from day-to-day considerations, which could look ahead to study policy and plans. A planning section was accordingly created, which later in the year developed into the Plans Division, a clear step forward. The sardonic Repington, when he heard of all these transactions, was inclined to attribute them to the First Lord, Sir Edward Carson, with whom he lunched on 15 June. Carson, he noted,

is stopping minute-writing, and is asking heads of departments to see each other more and settle things by word of mouth. He has started a thinking branch to make plans, and there will be a similar branch in the Grand Fleet. It is surely a sound thing to begin to think after fighting for three years.[28]

Churchill's comment on all this change was more benign:

> Younger officers were called to the Admiralty and more responsibility was given to them. Without this reorganization of the Staff, the measures that defeated the U-boat, even if conceived, could not have been executed.[29]

Churchill was correct, but this fruition was still far distant and not very probable in June. Convoy was still in its infancy, sinkings mounted, and what Newbolt calls 'the widest and most elaborate operation that had as yet been undertaken against the German submarines'[30] proved totally ineffective. It covered a broad stretch of sea at the north of Scotland, from Stornoway on the Isle of Lewis to the Pentland Firth, where U-boats were known to make their passage to and from the Atlantic. The operation lasted for nine days (June 15–23) during which there were sixty-one sightings of U-boats and twelve attacks on them; there was no indication of any loss or damage being caused to them, or of any effect on their own operations in the Western Approaches. This may serve as a final condemnation of 'offensive action' pure and simple, by which the Admiralty set so much store.

And while the Navy was thus occupied another matter was exercising the nation's leaders. 1917 was the year of the great Flanders offensive, the Third Battle of Ypres, generally known as 'Passchendaele'. The connection between the Flanders offensive and the U-boats was intimate; it dated from the first U-boat campaign and the formation of the Flanders Flotilla. When the second campaign began in the latter half of 1916, and the strain on the Royal Navy became very great, naval and ministerial minds turned once more to the sallyports at Ostend and Zeebrugge. What was then called the War Committee of the Cabinet met on 20 November, and when the meeting was over the Prime Minister, Mr Asquith, laid a note before the Chief of the Imperial General Staff, General Sir William Robertson. Asquith knew that Robertson, with Haig, was to meet the First Sea Lord (Sir Henry Jackson) in three days' time, so he did not sign this note; its provenance, however, was evident, and its import unmistakable. In it Asquith said:

> There is no operation of war to which the War Committee would attach greater importance than the successful occupation, or at least the deprivation to the enemy, of Ostend, and especially Zeebrugge.

I desire therefore that the General Staff and the Higher Command in France, in consultation with the Admiralty as necessary, shall give the matter their closest attention and that you will report to me personally at an early date what action you consider feasible.

As I have said elsewhere.

Although this note never received the final authority of signature, there can be no doubt that it constitutes the true point of origin of the Flanders offensive of 1917. Ultimate responsibility is thus seen to lie where it ought to lie – with the country's political leaders.[31]

There were, of course, other considerations governing the decision for or against the offensive. Much had happened since November, 1916, including a change of government (and of top Admiralty personnel), America's entry into the war, the first Russian revolution, the failure of the French offensive from which so much was hoped, the long-drawn-out Battle of Arras – and the unrestricted U-boat campaign. Throughout it all, British General Headquarters had clung to the idea that there would, at some stage, be an offensive in Flanders, with the clearing of the Belgian coast as a main objective; preparations for it were well advanced, and the stage had been reached when it was imperative to have an official yea or nay from the Government. For the purpose of arriving at this, a succession of meetings of the newly created War Policy Committee took place between 19–26 June; their proceedings vividly reveal the problems and conduct of a democracy at war, which do not concern us here (I have examined them in some depth in *The Road to Passchendaele*, pp. 144–76). What does concern us, with the light it throws on our present subject, is the intervention of Jellicoe on 20 June. The First Sea Lord had already circulated two papers to the Committee, and he was now asked to develop the ideas expressed in them. He said

that two points were in his mind, the first was that immense difficulties would be caused if by the winter the Germans were not excluded from the Belgian coast.

What was weighing on Jellicoe's mind was the strong possibility that the Germans would reinforce their destroyer force at Zeebrugge and make a concentrated sortie which would then 'sweep up' the Navy's relatively weak anti-submarine patrols in the Channel and attack cross-Channel traffic and French warships for good measure. His second point was

> that if we did not clear the Germans out of Zeebrugge before this winter we should have great difficulty in ever getting them out of it. The reason he gave for this was that he felt it to be improbable that we could go on with the war next year for lack of shipping.[32]

Haig noted in his diary:

> A most serious and startling situation was disclosed today. At today's Conference, Admiral Jellicoe, as First Sea Lord, stated that owing to the great shortage of shipping due to German submarines, it would be impossible for Great Britain to continue the war in 1918. This was a bombshell for the Cabinet and all present. A full enquiry is to be made as to the real facts on which this opinion of the Naval Authorities is based. No one present shared Jellicoe's view, and all seemed satisfied that the food reserves in Great Britain are adequate. Jellicoe's words were, 'There is no good discussing plans for next Spring – We cannot go on.'[33]

'Bombshell' is clearly no overstatement; the effect of this pronouncement coming from such a quarter, may be imagined. From this moment Jellicoe's days as First Sea Lord were numbered. He had borne the burden of responsibility for the Grand Fleet from the very beginning of the war until the end of 1916 – as Churchill said, in that capacity he was 'the only man who could lose the war in an afternoon'. He moved straight from that exacting task to the anti-submarine war, which was no less of a burden. He had adopted the convoy system because he was forced to by the national emergency, but he knew that if it was going to work it would not do so immediately and might, indeed, be too late; all the Navy's other methods and weapons seemed to break in his hands. It is small wonder if this highly realistic professional, well used to looking grim facts in the face, was now over-tired and despondent. And in that condition, despite all his great qualities, it has to be said that Admiral Sir John Jellicoe was no longer an asset to the main campaign of the Royal Navy, the struggle against the seemingly invincible U-boats. Yet it would take until the end of the

71

year to remove him; the immediate victim of the Government's understandable dismay was Carson.

Lloyd George, in his confusing (when not actually mendacious) *War Memoirs*, informs us that, strangely enough, it was a conversation with Haig that decided him upon further changes. He dates this to 'early summer', which could mean anything; Haig's diary, however, records that he and Geddes breakfasted with Lloyd George on 26 June, and discussed Admiralty matters. Geddes spoke critically of the Admiralty system (he had already told Haig that Carson was 'very tired', that Jellicoe was 'feeble to a degree and vacillating' and that there was no 'fixed policy', nor any digested information on which to base one). Lloyd George says (if this was the conversation to which he was referring) that while Haig expressed great admiration for Jellicoe's knowledge as a technical sailor,

> he thought him much too rigid, narrow and conservative in his ideas. As to Sir Edward Carson, I am afraid Sir Douglas Haig had no opinion of his qualities as an administrator. He thought he was distinctly out of place at the Admiralty. He strongly urged upon me the appointment of Sir Eric Geddes to that post.[34]

There is no knowing with Lloyd George; he has a trick of making others say what he himself was thinking, particularly if this can in any way discredit them while leaving him personally blameless. At any rate, the indefatigable recorder Hankey informs us that two days later Lloyd George was expressing the determination to move Carson from the Admiralty, but was still wondering how to replace him. For a brief moment Hankey himself was considered as a possible First Lord – a very striking promotion for a substantive Lieutenant-Colonel of the Royal Marines. However, it was not to be, and on 6 July he recorded:

> It has been decided that Eric Geddes is to be First Lord. Ll. George has offered it to him and he told me on the telephone he had accepted.[35]

Geddes became First Lord on 20 July, Carson becoming a member of the War Cabinet by way of a palliative. Lloyd George informs us:

> Sir Eric Geddes, in his acceptance of the position of First Lord, stipu-

lated that Jellicoe should not be immediately removed. Geddes knew that Jellicoe had the confidence of the senior officers in the Navy, and that it would therefore be a distinct advantage to secure his co-operation if that were at all possible.[36]

That is a way of putting it. Admiral Schofield, the naval historian, expresses the situation somewhat differently:

> [Geddes] took a long time to settle down. His instructions were to pick up the ropes where Churchill had left off, in developing and expanding the Naval Staff. It was not an easy task and it was rendered more difficult by an overbearing manner which antagonised the naval members of the Board with whom he had to work. Further, his relations with the First Sea Lord, who should have been his closest colleague, were soured by the knowledge that he was to be used as the instrument for his dismissal.[37]

The overdue and necessary reforms of the Admiralty did not all happen at once – here, as elsewhere, there was no question of 'magic wands' – and they occurred under mixed auspices. What Geddes *was* able to do, and fairly quickly, was to expand the Plans section into a Division, under Rear-Admiral R. J. B. Keyes with Captain A. D. P. Pound as his Assistant (names that would be heard again). He was also able to form a Statistics Division, under an Army officer, Lieutenant-Colonel J. G. Beharrell, with a predominantly civilian staff qualified to analyse and draw conclusions from the mass of information about shipping and losses which poured in. This was long overdue, but drew the wrath of Admiral Oliver; this revealed, according to Professor Marder, 'Oliver's inability to see that foresight must be based on sound knowledge of the past' – which could be one explanation of the Admiralty's long hesitation over convoys. Clearly, as long as Oliver (and Jellicoe) remained there would be stumbling-blocks in establishing true modern staff methods. It was a not particularly well-designed step towards that end to bring in, against Jellicoe's protests, Vice-Admiral Sir Rosslyn Wemyss as Deputy First Sea Lord. As Jellicoe pointed out, it was difficult to fit an officer with that title into an organization which already had a Deputy and an Assistant Chief of the Naval Staff. He remarks:

This appointment was frankly made more as a matter of expediency than because any real need had been shown for the creation of such an office[38]

– the expediency being, of course, the need to groom a successor to himself.

While these very important organizational measures were being set in motion, on the material side there were steady advances, mostly initiated by Jellicoe, Duff and the exceptionally able Director of Naval Intelligence, Rear-Admiral (later Sir Reginald) Hall. The flow of depth-charges and hydrophones, already ordered, was now beginning to be effective. A similar flow of new anti-submarine vessels was coming from the shipyards, promising some alleviation of the strain of finding convoy escorts. At the same time, a most useful accretion of strength appeared with the arrival of three divisions (eighteen vessels) of American destroyers at Queenstown to reinforce the Western Approaches forces there under Vice-Admiral Sir Lewis Bayly.

A further accretion of strength, of a totally different kind, was the increasing effectiveness of the RNAS. It was in April that the advent of the Large America flying boats (H 12s) initiated what was known as the 'Spider Web' patrol system in the North Sea. Operating first from Felixstowe (and then also from Great Yarmouth, 1 May), the H 12s kept ceaseless watch on the surface movement of U-boats in the North Sea. The 'web' was centred on the North Hinder Light Vessel (see diagram); it formed an octagon 60 miles in diameter, with eight radiating arms, each 30 miles long, and three joining arms at 10-mile intervals. This allowed for the search of some 4,000 square miles of sea; at cruising speed on the surface (to save batteries), the U-boats took about ten hours to pass through this area. In normal conditions, a flying boat could search two sectors (a quarter of the whole web) in five hours or less; its mere presence would force a U-boat to dive, slowing its progress markedly, and probably ensuring that it reached its operating station with flat batteries requiring immediate recharge. D/F plots guided the flying boats to the most profitable sectors of the web. Obviously the keen desire of every crew was to destroy a U-boat; in the first eighteen days, with only five flying boats available, twenty-seven patrols were completed, resulting in eight sightings of U-boats and three attacks. The first of these was on 20 May:

On the evening of this day, Flight Sub-Lieutenants C. R. Morrish and

74

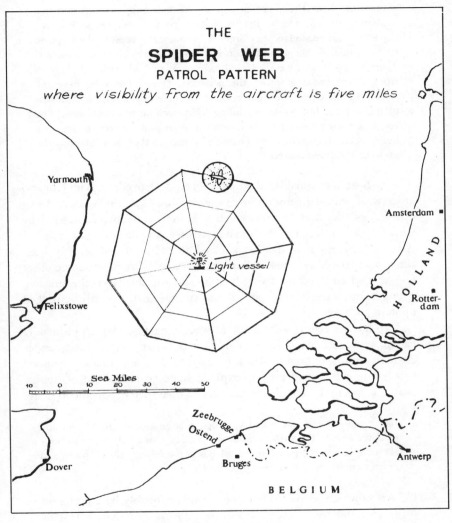

THE
SPIDER WEB
PATROL PATTERN
where visibility from the aircraft is five miles

North Hinder Light Vessel
The *Spider Web* patrol pattern. The circle round the aircraft represents the area
covered if the visibility is five miles.
Source: Alfred Price: *Aircraft Versus Submarines* p. 22; Kimber 1973

H. G. Boswell, with 1st Air Mechanic W. P. Caston, engineer, and Leading Mechanic A. E. Shorter, wireless operator, were on patrol, when, about ten miles east of the North Hinder, they sighted an enemy submarine about five miles distant at full buoyancy. Course was immediately altered, and as the flying boat passed over the submarine, three recognition signals were fired. As no answer was given the seaplane (*sic*) was turned sharply and again met her adversary end on, as she was diving. Two bombs were released, which hit the submarine directly in front of the conning tower, the periscope being then still above the water. A large patch of oil was noticed for some time after the explosion of the bombs, but owing to failing light nothing else was seen. The seaplane then returned to Felixstowe at 9.30 p.m., where, owing to a heavy swell, the machine crashed on alighting on the water. Happily the personnel were uninjured.[39]

The U-boat was considered to have been destroyed, and in January, 1919, was identified from German sources as *UC 36*, the occasion being claimed as 'the first . . . on which a British seaplane, unassisted by surface craft, effected the destruction of a hostile undersea boat.'[40] Alas, subsequent investigation showed that *UC 36* had already been sunk, on 17/18 May, cause unknown.[41] On 20 May it was some other U-boat that endured the flying boat attack, and displayed the amazing strength and survival capacity of the species so frequently remarked upon in both wars.

Two further claims were made for the flying-boats which ultimately had to be set aside. A flight of five boats, led by Wing Commander Porte in person, sighted a U-boat on 24 July. The first attacker dropped two bombs which appeared to explode some 50 feet ahead of the U-boat as it was in the act of diving, a second boat then dropped two more,

and as soon as the water had subsided a large amount of air, oil and wreckage rose to the surface. Later in the day a small circular red buoy was observed by the patrolling seaplanes at the edge of the oil patch and served to mark the last resting place of *UC 1*.[42]

UC 1 is now considered to have been sunk, probably by a mine, on 19 July. No U-boat is recorded as lost on 24 July. The same is true of 29 July, when two flying boats attacked a submarine which they claimed to have sunk, and which was later thought to have been *UB 20*. But *UB 20* is now listed by Grant as lost the previous day off Ostend (a long way from where the flying boats had their action) and is considered to have been a certain victim of an undetected British minefield laid on 25 July. The only U-boat kill now definitely attributed to aircraft in the 1914–18 war was *UB 32*, attacked by an H 12 piloted by Flight Sub-Lieutenant N. Magor on 22 September inside the 'Spider Web'. As with all other aircraft, the value of the flying boats against U-boats was as a deterrent rather than a killer, and of this there was no doubt; their reconnaissance capabilities have already been indicated.

Some doubt still surrounds the fate of *UB 32*; according to Newbolt, she was sunk on 18 August by Seaplane No 9860; according to Grant (who confirms the sinking on 22 September) her killer was 'a seaplane from Dunkirk'. All inherent probability suggests that the flying-boat was the aircraft really responsible, but it must not be forgotten that it was on the seaplane squadrons that the main anti-submarine work fell. This was especially true in the Channel, which by the early summer of 1917 was fringed on both sides by allied seaplane bases, British and French. Their work was recognized as increasingly important, and on 11 May, at the suggestion of Commander Laborde, head of the French Naval Aviation Service, a conference assembled at the Admiralty to work out the details of co-ordination between the two Air Services; its result was clearly useful:

> The limits of the British and French patrol zones were settled, and a common code of visual and wireless signals was drawn up, in order that submarines when located in one zone should not be lost sight of, but should be followed up by the aerial and surface forces of any zone which they might subsequently enter.[43]

Life was becoming more difficult for the U-boats; but it was difficult for the RNAS also. In the course of his electrifying statement to the Ware Policy Committee on 20 June Jellicoe also said

> that the German position on the Belgian coast was very bad from the point of view of our air position. For the moment we had lost the command of the air over the sea as the Germans had a better seaplane than we had. Only yesterday two of our seaplanes had been destroyed by the enemy and Rear-Admiral Commanding at Dover said he could not maintain an aerial seaplane patrol without better machines.[44]

The RNAS, in fact, was passing through a phase similar to that which had so seriously affected the RFC a month or two earlier, while awaiting the delivery of better types of aircraft. Very shortly the Naval Service would introduce high-performance non-amphibious fighters to escort its seaplanes on bombing or torpedo missions. Mostly from the redoubtable firm of Sopwith – '$1\frac{1}{2}$ Strutters', 'Pups', Triplanes and 'Camels' – these satisfactorily redressed the balance.

The introduction of convoy evidently encouraged the search for new methods of detecting U-boats – some, to our eyes, distinctly far-fetched. The slow speeds of even surfaced U-boats made possible, for example, a use of kite balloons which would be impossible in a fast-moving naval surface engagement. On 12 July, during another U-boat-hunting operation off the Shetlands, a balloon flown from the destroyer *Patriot* (Flight Lieutenant O. A. Butcher observing) sighted a U-boat at a distance of 28 miles. *Patriot* was able to close the enemy and make a depth charge attack which succeeded in destroying *U 69*. There was sharp debate about the value of this method with convoys:

A balloon flown from a vessel escorting a convoy might advertise the presence and course of the ships to a distant and invisible U-boat which would then be able to submerge and get into position for attack. For this reason balloons were not, at the outset, used by convoy escorts.[45]

In the Second World War the sight of ships flying balloons – merchantmen or escorts – was commonplace, but they were usually anti-aircraft barrage balloons, not observation balloons.

The obvious instruments for the work of convoy protection, possessing the attributes of height, wide visibility and motion, were, of course, airships, and it was now that they came into their own. Indeed, we learn that

the bulk of this class of air work during the remainder of the war fell to these ships . . . With regard to actual airship patrols, these were standardised, definite patrol areas being laid down for each station. In consequence, shipping routes were systematically swept, and adjoining stations co-ordinated their efforts so as to avoid overlapping or breaks. Patrols were also carried out in conjunction with destroyers and other patrol vessels.[46]

The weakness of airships, as stated above, was their uselessness in attack, owing to being so visible themselves and so slow to manoeuvre.

On the other hand, their very presence kept U-boats submerged, thus preventing their attacks. An interesting example of the air deterrent at work was seen on 9 August, when a convoy bringing American troops to Europe entered the Channel: first there appeared an H 12 from the Scillies which escorted the convoy until relieved by a seaplane from Newlyn, which was in turn relieved by two airships from Mullion which took station on the starboard and port bows of the convoy. In these positions, after about an hour and a half, both airships simultaneously sighted a U-boat on the surface about seven miles away, coming in at full speed on an intercepting course. The airships closed the enemy, who immediately submerged, when they dropped two 100-lb bombs in the U-boat's wake. Another seaplane then arrived and the three aircraft began a search, but without success. One airship returned towards the convoy and signalled 'Submarine submerged under us'; this brought two British and two American destroyers to the position, making depth charge attacks while the convoy continued on its course. The aircraft, reinforced by aeroplanes from Mullion, kept up their guard duties for several hours, but no more was seen of the U-boat. There is little doubt that it escaped unscathed – but what is more important, so did the convoy.

All these air elements in the anti-submarine war developed in numbers and efficiency by leaps and bounds in 1917: forty-seven airships and 160 heavier-than-air craft at the end of 1916 mounted to sixty-three airships and 314 flying boats, seaplanes and landplanes by the end of 1917 – and expansion was only beginning.

As important as all these improvements of matériel, and of great future promise, was the incorporation at last of Room 40 into Admiral Hall's Intelligence Division. This, too, was part of the May reforms; unbelievably, until that date, this invaluable Intelligence source had been kept separate from other branches of Intelligence work by Oliver, who treated it as 'his private cryptographic bureau'; as Patrick Beesly says:

> The fact that Room 40 was not a part of the Intelligence Division and was deprived of often useful information from ID's sections, and even more important, that those sections were totally cut off from the priceless information available in the decodes, was an error of such magnitude that it is now almost impossible to explain.[47]

In anti-submarine terms, what this obvious step forward meant was that the work on tracking and recording U-boats that Fleet Paymaster E. W. C. Thring had been doing for three years without benefit of radio decodes would now at last enjoy that increment. When to this was added a connection by pneumatic tube to the Convoy Section of the Mercantile Movements Division under Fleet Paymaster H. W. E. Manisty and the D/F Section under a civilian, Frank Tiarks, the makings of what in World War II would be called a Submarine Tracking Room were present.

It was a hard summer, the three months April–June marking the very peak of the U-boat effort: 2,165,163 gross tons of British, Allied and neutral shipping sunk, of which no less than 1,316,065 was British. The next two months saw an improvement, but nothing sensational: 557,988 tons sunk in July (British, 364,858), 511,730 tons in August (British, 329,810). With sinkings still running at over half a million tons a month, it is small wonder that there were long faces. What the British authorities could not know was that there were even longer faces in Germany.

'Unrestricted U-boat war,' *Admiral* von Holtzendorff had promised, 'will bring about peace before the harvesting period of the 1917 summer, that is, before 1 August.' It is always dangerous, often fatal, to make such predictions – especially to name dates. The harvesting period had arrived; 1 August came and went; there was no sign of peace. A number of people in the Central Powers had had reservations about the unrestricted campaign from the first; as the weeks and months went by, their scepticism increased. For Austria–Hungary, for example, peace was no mere pious aspiration, it was a clear necessity. As early as April, the new Austrian Emperor Karl had warned his German cousin that hunger was breeding social revolution – 'a new and more dangerous enemy than the Entente'. His Foreign Minister, Count Czernin, added a memorandum stating that it was essential for Austria–Hungary to have peace before the summer was out. He put a searching question:

All the information we receive about England combines to prove that a collapse of our most powerful and dangerous adversary is simply out of the question. Submarine war would damage but not ruin her; would it not, then, be better to abandon the idea that the campaign would be an instrument of final, decisive victory, and to make a serious effort to begin peace negotiations?[48]

As voices crying in the wilderness, the Austrians might have been ignored; but they were not 'in the wilderness'; there were voices in Germany growing louder to the same effect. The Army High Command itself, whose influence in favour of the campaign had been so significant, had now changed its opinion. *Oberst* Bauer, of the General Staff, who has been called 'Ludendorff's chief political agent',[49] approached the leading Centre Party member, Mathias Erzberger, in June. Erzberger (no left-wing revolutionary) had been making an independent study of the Naval Staff's tonnage claims, and had come to the conclusions that these were substantially spurious, that the campaign was in reality a total failure,[50] and that the only logical course for Germany was to seek a negotiated peace – echoing the Austrians. Bauer now told him that Ludendorff had also lost all confidence in the naval claims; this did not draw the First Quartermaster-General to the idea of peace negotiations, however; on the contrary, he was laying his plans for a winter campaign – clear evidence that in the minds of the High Command peace was a long way off. When he realized this, Erzberger was profoundly shaken. The main Commission of the *Reichstag* was due to meet on 3 July to begin its deliberations on war credits; in the debate that ensued, Erzberger threw in his lot with the Social Democrats, whose left wing had already broken off to form an Independent Socialist Party dedicated to an early peace. Their mood was well expressed by the deputy Gustav Hoch on 5 July:

The situation cannot become more serious than it is. . . . Submarine warfare was to have been the solution, but it has failed. The Government is continuously admonishing us to hold out. But can we do that? We have now exhausted our strength. We are in the midst of revolution. The thoughts of the working men are already revolutionary. Confidence in the Government had gone. Hope is gone, and it cannot be resurrected.[51]

To this Erzberger added two days later:

The government says: We must hold out! That is true. But we can and must hold out only if there is a prospect that the next year will bring a better peace than we can now secure. . . . I do not hesitate to say: *I do not believe that we can obtain a better peace at the end of another year.* I consider it my duty to express myself quite frankly.

The Left-Centre combination was decisive; Erzberger and his associates drafted a resolution which they placed before the Committee; its key section ran:

> The *Reichstag* is striving for a peace of understanding, for a durable pacification of peoples. Forced annexation of provinces, and political, economic and financial oppression are incompatible with a peace of the kind.

This was the stone in the pond, whose ripples would be more like tidal waves as one produced another. The first reaction of the High Command was total disgust and rejection of the resolution; the second was grave fear that Bethmann-Hollweg was not the man to block it. Hindenburg and Ludendorff telephoned to Berlin on 12 July, threatening to resign if the Chancellor was not removed. Since he had now lost all useful support in the *Reichstag*, he resigned the next day, and was replaced by a nonentity, a Prussian official named Georg Michaelis, who was, in fact, simply the nominee and mouthpiece of the High Command.

This was a black moment for Germany – and for the peace hopes of the world. By accepting Michaelis, the *Reichstag* abdicated its right to control the political decisions of the war. Worse still, by this act the deputies

> meekly allowed both their authority and that of the Emperor to be usurped by Ludendorff, who in his own name and that of Hindenburg exercised dictatorial power over the country for the next sixteen months.'[52]

Imperial Germany, in other words, now became what it had never been, an outright military dictatorship; Bismarckian Germany was dead. And with its passing, the Empire itself was fatally weakened. By his totally inept handling of this whole crisis, Wilhelm II forfeited all confidence in the *Reichstag*. It was, in Erzberger's words, 'the turning of the first sod for the grave of the old régime'.

The Peace Resolution was duly passed (despite the fierce opposition of the High Command) on 19 July. But Michaelis served his masters well; in accepting the principles enunciated in it, he added the words, 'as I understand them'. As he wrote to the Crown Prince a few days later,

I have deprived it of its greatest danger by my interpretation. One can, in fact, make any peace one likes, and still be in accord with the Resolution.[53]

It meant, in other words, precisely nothing.

19 July also held other significance; it was on that day that about half of the crew of the battleship *Prinzregent Luitpold*, moored at Wilhelmshaven, refused all duty. The next day 140 men marched off the light cruiser *Pillau*. On 1 August fifty men from *Prinzregent Luitpold* also went over the side, and by 4 August two other battleships of the same division, *Kaiserin* and *Friedrich der Grosse*, were also seriously affected. Some days later the crews of two more battleships, *Westfalen* and *Rheinland*, also displayed grave symptoms of discontent. With the exception of *Pillau*, the disorders were confined to the battle fleet, which had been virtually locked in its harbours for nearly a year. Since the outbreaks occurred on the very day that the *Reichstag* Resolution was passed, it is obviously nonsense to say that they were caused by the Resolution. There were, nevertheless, links between the Peace Party in the *Reichstag* and the ratings in the fleet, and evidence came to light of a regular organization for distributing Independent Socialist literature demanding 'peace without annexations' – the central matter of the Resolution itself. But over and above this, says Newbolt,

> it is quite impossible to dissociate this breakdown in the most rigorously disciplined fleet in the world from the promises which the admirals had so freely scattered before the German nation some months before. Beneath the shouting of the seamen who broke ashore, the jeering and whistling of the men who refused to receive their rations, the wild talk of the stokers who held free speech meetings in the *Friedrich der Grosse*, there is evident a deeper and more estranging resentment, the bitter anger of brave men, who had at last realized the true nature of the policy for which they and their people were now called upon to endure starvation.[54]

This is both sententious and inaccurate – Germany's worst food privations (the ghastly 'turnip winter' of 1916–17) were over, and the Russian collapse promised further alleviation. However, there is this core of truth in Newbolt's words: the German seamen, like the French soldiers earlier in the year when Nivelle's offensive failed to redeem its promise, felt bitterly deceived. It is a bad feeling, pregnant with evil consequence. The disaffection in the High Sea Fleet was not stilled until the end of August; the future would show that it was never eradictated. This was a harvest of which *Admiral* von Holtzendorff had never dreamed.

5

Slack Water

'The flood-tide of German success seemed for the first time to be slowing down towards a period of slack water.'

Sir Henry Newbolt

IT IS OFTEN possible, with the great decisive battles of past periods, to put a finger on an almost exact moment when the issue was determined. Thus Lady Longford identifies a period of crisis in the Battle of Waterloo: 7–9 p.m. on 18 June, 1815 (Richard Aldington says it was from 'about 7.30 until dark'[1]). At Trafalgar we can identify a period of the battle when the combined French and Spanish fleet lost ship after ship, and the dying Nelson knew that he had won the day: it begins at about two o'clock in the afternoon of 21 October, 1805, and by half past three the thing is settled. The crises of great modern battles are less discernible; the greatest surface naval action of the First World War – Jutland – produced no crisis at all. And the underwater battle, spread over about two years, moved into its critical phase almost imperceptibly, and was resolved without anyone being really aware of the fact. Sir Henry Newbolt expresses himself on it with due and significant caution:

the month of September was, in some respects, the month in which the flood-tide of German success seemed for the first time to be slowing down towards a period of slack water, possibly even towards an ebb.[2]

85

Fayle permits himself more precision:

The summer months witnessed the turn of the tide.[3]

'Witnessed' – by the deity, perhaps; for mortals the vision was less clear.

The two sets of statistics which are most commonly used to illustrate the progress of anti-submarine war are the figures for shipping losses due to submarines, and the corresponding losses of the submarines themselves. September, 1917, showed dramatic improvements for the Allies in each case. The world tonnage of shipping sunk dropped by 160,000 tons to 351,748, the lowest monthly figure of the year to date (British, 196,212). The reasons for this are not clear; redeployment of the U-boats is a likely one, and also a measure of the same sort of temporary exhaustion that had affected them in May (see p. 61). The main fact is that October's figures showed another steep rise, to 458,558 gross tons (British, 276,132). Surface attack, as we shall see, accounted for some part of this, and Mediterranean losses were high. There was another satisfactory fall in November: to 289,212 gross tons (British, 173,560) – only to be followed by another depressing rise in December, to 399,111 gross tons (British 253,087). The permanent drop in world tonnage sunk to below 300,000 tons a month does not occur until the second quarter of 1918. It is therefore not surprising that Fayle, having specified a turn of the tide, goes on to say:

The turn, however, had come only just in time: indeed, it was impossible as yet to assert with certainty that it had not come too late.[4]

He points out that the first six months of unrestricted U-boat warfare had reduced the world's total tonnage by 3,850,000 tons which, however correct Erzberger's calculations may have been, was a daunting figure for the maritime powers. And to that total of absolute loss there has to be added a mounting quantity of temporary loss by damage, blocking the shipyards with essential repairs, which in August reached 537,000 tons. Shipbuilding, both in Britain and even more so in America, was entirely failing to keep pace with such a rate of loss.

The doubtful portents of the shipping statistics were matched by those of U-boats disposed of. In the month of September an unprecedented ten (possibly eleven[5]) U-boats were lost.[6] This compares with a February–August average of just over four, which makes September

86

look highly encouraging, but it also compares with a commissioning rate of seven per month in the same period, which leaves a solid margin of advantage with the U-boat fleet. And it also has to be compared with the average monthly rate of loss during the next three months, which exactly matched the average commissioning rate: seven boats in each case. Clearly, there is nothing here to match the marked *and sustained* upturn in U-boat destruction which occurred in July, 1942, which we shall examine later. Indeed, only twice during the remainder of the war did the monthly total of U-boats sunk go into double figures. However, this is probably the appropriate place to point out a truth which naval officers, with their attack tradition, found it difficult – indeed, virtually impossible – to take in:

> The defeat of the unrestricted U-boat campaign did not depend on the number of U-boats sunk.[7]

Or, as Professor Marder summarized the essence of the anti-U-boat war,

> Sinking submarines is a bonus, not a necessity . . . what matters is that the ships deliver cargoes regularly and adequately. . . . Indeed, one can safely go a step further: it really did not matter how many U-boats the Germans had, if they were forced to keep out of the way and the British and their Allies got their ships with their literally vital cargoes through and without being delayed by fear of attack.[8]

This was an easier perception after the event than during it; and, as Newbolt says, the true sign of the 'slack water', the first hint that the U-boat might be heading towards defeat, was at the time so subtle that anyone might be forgiven for not detecting it. It was a matter of contrast: not a very emphatic contrast, but real nevertheless. Up to September, he says, whatever successes the Allied counter-measures may have achieved (in particular the reduction of shipping losses),

> they cannot be said so far to have caused the German submarine commanders to alter their tactics or procedure in any important particular.[9]

During all that time, one finds

> week after week, month after month, nearly the same number of U-,

UB- and UC-boats working in nearly the same areas. The almost monotonous regularity of their proceedings during these critical months is perhaps the strongest existing proof that our counter-measures were as yet practically ineffective.

In truth, he adds, up to this point anti-submarine operations had in no way persuaded the enemy to revise or change his plans; in other words, they had failed.[10] And then,

> In September this state of things comes to an end; for it was in September that the U-boat commanders changed their tactics for the first time since the campaign began.

It was not a very big change, merely some shifts, of position by the U-boats, dictated by the 'empty waters' referred to above. To the U-boat commanders, it must have seemed as if the Admiralty had performed some massive shipping diversions, in effect 'evacuating' the normal approaches, and the obvious thing to do was to find out where the shipping had gone. So they explored new ground, in the Bay of Biscay and the eastern Channel, and up into the North Sea. They did not yet understand that

> so far from being emptied, the zones to the west and south-west of the Scillies and to the south-west of the Fastnet were more crowded with traffic than they had been in the days when [the U-boats'] devastations were most easily executed, when their daily records were filled up with entries of ships sunk, seamen drowned and boats destroyed. What was to tell them that through the very zone which they were abandoning as no longer fruitful, the indispensable British merchant fleet with all its vital cargoes was passing unobserved and in increasing numbers?

It was a straw in the wind; but this was a wind that would prevail. It signified the first diminution of U-boat initiative, the first imposition of the Allied will upon them – and it was due entirely to the adoption of convoy. It was thus the first manifestation of the *offensive* quality of the convoy system which, to so many naval officers, had the look of pure defensive. And it was, certainly, the defensive aspect which was at this stage most obvious. In August outward-bound convoys (to dispersal points well out into the Atlantic) had been adopted, and the system was extended from the North to the South Atlantic. There

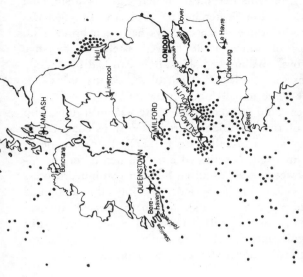

3RD QUARTER OF UNRESTRICTED
S/M WARFARE: AUG.-OCT., 1917
W. APPROACHES, CHANNEL & E. COAST

Aug. 17: Homeward S. Atlantic & Gibraltar Convoys started.
Mid. Aug: Outward Convoys (dispersing in 12°-15° W) started.
Sept. '17: Convoys organised on a Speed & Destination Basis.
Mid. Oct: Outward Gibraltar Convoys kept together until
arrival at Gibraltar.
Oct. '17: Through-Mediterranean Convoys started.

● ....Ship sunk by U-Boat.

✦ .... Ocean Convoy Assembly Port

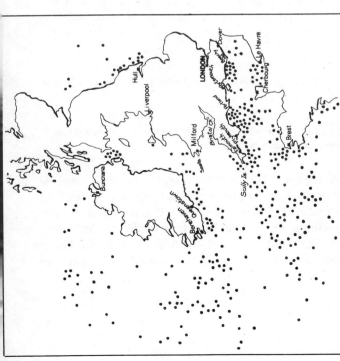

2ND QUARTER OF UNRESTRICTED
S/M WARFARE: MAY-JULY, 1917
W. APPROACHES, CHANNEL & E. COAST

April: 1st Scandinavian Convoys run.
May: 1st two experimental Ocean Convoys run.
June: Four N. Atlantic (Homeward) Convoys run.
July: Regular Homeward N. Atlantic Convoys begin.

● ....Ship sunk by U-Boat.

were further important additions to be made – coastal traffic in home waters, and, above all, the Mediterranean, which was now a shipping graveyard – but by the end of September the protective function was firmly established. Eighty-three ocean convoys had been brought in, totalling 1,306 ships, of which 1,288 arrived safely; in fifty-five outward-bound convoys, totalling 789 ships, only two had been sunk. Even more significant was the fact that out of the twenty ships lost, only twelve were sunk while actually under escort.[11]

Once these statistics could be established, there was no arguing with them; for the whole of 1917, the figures are: 5,090 ships convoyed of which sixty-three were lost, a casualty rate of 1.23%. It scarcely needs to be said that this, in itself, constituted a severe defeat for the U-boats. Its severity, however, was disguised by their continued success against independent sailers; in the period May–July, this amounted to 356 ships (93% of all independents), and in the period August–October, 221 ships (83% of the total).[12] Comment is superfluous. But perhaps the most significant fact of all to emerge was the quite unexpected security of convoys under attack. By September,

> Although nearly twenty convoys had been attacked, in no instance, even when the attack was successful, had such wholesale havoc been wrought as the opponents of convoy had anticipated; *generally only one ship was sunk; in no instance had a formed convoy lost more than two vessels.* On several occasions the escort, on sighting a submarine, had been able to take the offensive, and to hunt it so continuously that no attack was made.[13]

To this already sufficiently remarkable statement we need only add one more fact: that

> down to the end of 1917 there was only one instance of a ship being lost from a convoy receiving air escort.[14]

In the first week of September an Allied Naval Conference gathered in London to review the state of the anti-submarine war. It was unfortunate that this gathering was not, say, a month later, when some of the better news of the month might have been available. As it was, prospects were still bleak, with a new threat to consider in the North Atlantic, where the Germans had introduced 'U-cruisers', capable of carrying the attack out to great distances,[15] and of holding their stations for as long as three months, thanks to their large fuel supplies and improved living accommodation. With this and other disturbing considerations in mind,[16] Jellicoe addressed the conference in serious vein – indeed, in tones of desperation. His first proposal was 'a stupendous blocking operation against all the German harbours in the North Sea and the Baltic'.[17] 'Stupendous' is indeed the word for such a plan; Jellicoe himself, writing immediately after the war, seems to distance himself from it. The idea of completely sealing the exits from the German ports was, he says,

> most attractive in theory and appealed strongly to those who looked at the question superficially. . . . It was not a matter of surprise to me that the idea of sealing the exits from submarine bases was urged by so many people on both sides of the Atlantic. It was, of course, the obvious counter to the submarine campaign, and it appealed with force to that considerable section which feels vaguely, and rightly, that *offensive* action is needed, without being quite clear as to the means by which it is to be carried out.[18]

It was possibly with some relief that Jellicoe discovered that the grandiose project held out little appeal to the practical naval officers attending the Allied conference – among them Admiral Funakoshi from Japan, with discouraging memories of the Japanese Navy's attempts to block Port Arthur in 1904. The alternative was mining; minelaying in the Heligoland Bight and off the Flanders coast had so far proved to be a disappointing exercise, partly due to the very serious defects of British mines mentioned above, and partly also to the skill and perseverance of the German minesweepers. Thanks to their unremitting efforts, though U-boat commanders had to be exceedingly cautious in navigating the swept channels, very few U-boats had been lost. What was now proposed was a huge minefield to block the northern exit from the North Sea between Norway and the Shetlands, where minesweepers could not reach. It was believed that this passage was a main U-boat thoroughfare, the 'barrage' in the Straits of Dover being still regarded as a virtually total deterrent to U-boats making for the Atlantic. The proposed new minefield, which would be known as the 'Northern barrage',[19] was also a project on the grand scale: Jellicoe estimated that it would require 100,000 mines – and, evidently, an immense force of minelayers and escorts to sow the field. Such a number was clearly quite beyond the capacity of British industry, so large-scale American help would be needed, and this was soon promised. The conference endorsed the 'Northern barrage' policy, which now became a major Admiralty and Allied commitment.

It was from America – or rather, an American – that the conference obtained its clearest beam of light on the realities of anti-submarine warfare. At an early stage Admiral Sims made a significant reference to the convoy system; it was, he said, a genuinely offensive measure, inasmuch as it forced the U-boats to fight at a disadvantage. He returned to this theme later, and put the telling question,

> Was not the future of every form of anti-submarine warfare bound up with the extension and development of the convoy system; in fact, was not this system the one and only method of placing the U-boats on the chess-board of submarine warfare in a position of strategical and tactical checkmate?[20]

As Newbolt says, it is not difficult, from a post-1918 standpoint, to recognize in the convoy system 'a decisive counter-attack against the German warfare upon merchant traffic'. (Writing in 1930, and no doubt fully preoccupied with his own particular historical period, he seemed not to be aware of the resurgence of official resistance to this interpretation between the wars.) At the time, however, in the midst of 'a mass of daily incidents which . . . seemed no more than a disorderly succession of disasters', what Sims was saying had a distinct ring of novelty, if not heresy:

> The leading naval authorities were by no means inclined to give the convoy system this pre-eminent position amongst the many other measures of anti-submarine warfare which they were trying. To them, the convoy system was an item on a list, a measure amongst many others; and Admiral Sims must be given the credit of being the first naval expert in high position who had the insight to realize that the remedy for which the Allies were still seeking had actually been found.

The percipience of Admiral Sims went even further; if he startled the delegates with his analysis of the potential effect of convoy, he gave them distinct cause for alarm with his prognostication of what the result might be. What, he questioned, would the Germans do if they reached the conclusion that convoys were wrecking the U-boat campaign? Clearly, they would attempt to riposte:

> It was not likely that the enemy would entrust his counter-attack solely to submarine cruisers armed with six-inch guns; he might, on the contrary, be expected to make a determined attempt to break up the whole convoy system by attacking it with heavy, powerful ships. 'To counteract that,' concluded Admiral Sims, 'you have got to do one of two things: either you have got to convoy with Dreadnought battleships, or else you have got to make the best terms of peace you can.'

Such foresight was both remarkable and timely; as it turned out, the use of capital surface ships to destroy convoys was reserved for World War II, but the attack by powerful surface elements was introduced within a matter of weeks of Sims's speech. Its effect on the Grand Fleet was immediate, as we shall shortly see; the percipience of Sims lies, not so much in the precise course of the 1917 riposte, as in a dawning awareness that the great dreadnought battleships, on which both sides prided themselves, might find their true value not in Trafalgar-style encounters, but in their threat to trade and the need to meet that threat. To put it another way, anti-submarine warfare, which had seemed to be a subject quite separate from 'real' naval warfare, was showing itself to be part and parcel of the general theme, inextricable from it. And this, too, was a lesson that would take a very long time to sink in.

October was a bad month, with the fresh upcurve of shipping losses; it began badly for the Royal Navy, though the extent of the setback was not realized at the time. Intercepts indicated a considerable number of U-boats about to return to Germany by the northabout route and down the North Sea; the Admiralty planned an extensive ambush for them. Between the latitudes of 50° and 54°N (a distance of some 300 miles) it deployed a force of twenty-four trawlers, forty-two drifters, twenty-one destroyers, a flotilla leader and four submarines down the long, narrowing funnel of the U-boat passage, with ten miles of mined nets in the narrowest portion. The operation began on 1 October and continued until the 10th; the weather was so bad that the destroyers in the central section were driven back to harbour three times, and at others had to abandon their patrol and turn their heads into the

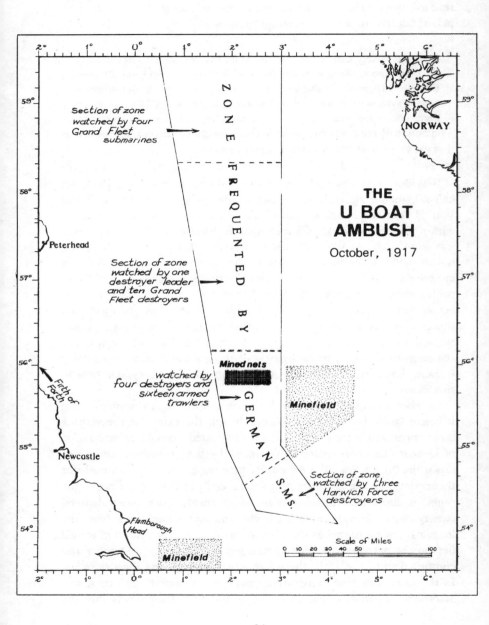

Section of zone
watched by four
Grand Fleet
submarines

ZONE FREQUENTED BY GERMAN S.M.S.

NORWAY

THE
U BOAT
AMBUSH

October, 1917

Peterhead

Section of zone
watched by one
destroyer leader
and ten Grand
Fleet destroyers

Firth of
Forth

Mined nets
watched by
four destroyers and
sixteen armed
trawlers

Minefield

Newcastle

Section of zone
watched by three
Harwich Force
destroyers

Flamborough
Head

Minefield

Scale of Miles
0 10 20 30 40 50   100

mountainous seas. The fishing boats of the Auxiliary Patrol were better able to ride out these gales. Sir Henry Newbolt, calling his other style of writing to his aid, paints a picture of the drifters holding their stations on the nets, while

> the trawler skippers, lashed and buffeted by sea, rain and wind, listened through their hydrophones for any sounds that might come up from the motionless depths below the turmoil of waves and spray.[21]

The noises of the deep, however, served only to confuse; a phenomenon that was becoming familiar in anti-submarine warfare haunted this operation from the first. Unidentified underwater explosions were reported by numerous vessels, on one occasion accompanied by inexplicable green lights like rockets. On 3 October,

> At half-past ten in the morning the watch-keepers on the hydrophone in the trawler *William Tennant*, which was stationed at the western end of the net line, heard sounds of a submarine moving through the water beneath her. The sounds were followed by a loud explosion, which again was followed by complete silence; the trawlers *Oyama* and *Chieftain* were near, and their hydrophone listeners heard the same succession of sounds and noticed the same following silence. Later in the afternoon the trawler *Swallow*, which was also near the western end of the nets, heard the sound of a submarine's electric motors so distinctly that the listeners thought the U-boat was directly underneath them. The captain dropped a depth charge; it exploded and again there was complete silence.

What were these underwater detonations? What was the meaning of these silences? They might be faulty mines exploding; they might be some ruse by wily U-boat captains and well-disciplined crews; they might be simply a product of fatigue and strain in the hearers – but the number of witnesses seemed to rule that out. An attack on the destroyer *Tancred* on 9 October, and the sighting of a U-boat by the trawlers *Sir John French* and *Swallow* somewhat later, confirmed that U-boats were present. The combined evidence seemed conclusive, and the Admiralty claimed three U-boats destroyed 'in the vicinity' of the ambush. German sources afterwards seemed to identify these as *U 50*, *U 66* and *U 106*. It has subsequently transpired that *U 50* (Berger) had been sunk by a mine, probably as far back as 31 August, and her commander's body had been washed ashore on 23 September; *U 66* was also sunk by a mine, on 3 September. Of the three named, only *U 106* (Hufnagel) was sunk during the period of the ambush operation, but there is very strong evidence that she, too, fell victim to a mine, probably one of the newly-arrived Mark H2, laid by the submarine *E 51* on 7 October off the Dutch coast – very close to the last position reported by *U 106* on that day. The only other possibility is *UB 41* (Ploen), sunk on 5 October; her position, near Flamborough Head, was well away from the ambush site, but she may have strayed into it on the way and suffered damage. All the firm evidence, however, points to a complete failure of an 'offensive' operation once again.

Worse was to follow. The Scandinavian convoys had now been plying the Lerwick-Bergen passage for over five months without any major untoward incident, though losses had been high due to an incorrigible tendency to straggle. There can be little doubt that a sense of false security existed both in the merchant ships and in the Grand Fleet destroyers escorting them. It is extraordinary that no instruction relating to action in the event of attack by surface vessels had been issued to destroyer captains, nor, apparently, had there been any discussion of such action among themselves. The consequences fell out as may be imagined.

Once more, on 15 October, the Listening Service had given warning of imminent movement by German warships; substantial counter-moves were at once set in train by both the Grand Fleet and the Harwich Force. It seems scarcely possible, yet it is a fact, that the following day, with over eighty British vessels out on patrol in the North Sea, two fast (34-knot) German minelaying cruisers, *Brummer* and *Bremse*, each armed with four 150-mm guns, should be able to carry out a 500-mile dash to a position north of Bergen, close to the convoy route. There, on the 17th, they encountered the destroyers *Strongbow* (Lt-Commander C. L. Fox) and *Mary Rose* (Lt-Commander E. Brooke) with two armed trawlers, escorting a loose convoy of twelve merchant ships (two British, one Belgian, the rest Scandinavian). The two British destroyers were widely separated, and for some reason out of radio touch when the German ships were sighted. Both behaved in the Royal Navy's loftiest tradition of self-sacrificing endeavour; both were quickly sunk without any perceptible damage to the enemy,[22] and the convoy was wiped out with the exception of the British and Belgian ships. Having paid due tribute to the heroism of the destroyer companies, there is not much to add to Newbolt's comment:

Little can be done if two destroyers and a number of unarmed merchant-men are attacked by two powerful cruisers; and still less is likely to be done if the contingency has never been considered or discussed.

The incident proved, moreover, that, if the Germans decided to raid the Scandinavian route with surface ships, it would be very difficult to stop them.[23]

Brummer and *Bremse*, to fill the bitter cup, eluded the Royal Navy's patrols on the way back as they had done on their northward dash; the Admiralty and Admiral Beatty were left to count the cost.

The immediate damage – the loss of two destroyers and nine merch-antmen – was bad enough; far worse was the new sense of vulnerability where things had seemed to be reasonably secure, and the new strain on already stretched resources. For Beatty it was worst, because it spelt a further weakening of his fleet in relation to its main designated task – combat with the High Sea Fleet. Obviously he would now have to provide extra cover for the Scandinavian convoys from his already depleted light forces, and once more the cry went up for destroyer reinforcements. Something could also be done in the way of reducing the number of convoys while at the same time increasing their size. Better still was the proposal to adopt a shorter route – from Methil in the Firth of Forth instead of Lerwick. And at last the destroyer escorts were given clear instructions in regard to attack by greatly superior force. The situation, they were reminded, would be quite different from that of attack by U-boats, when it would be their clear duty to counter-attack immediately. Against a strong surface force, all they could do would be to report as soon as possible,[24] disperse the convoy, and try to distract and harass the attackers while this was happening, making fullest use of their speed. They were *not* to engage superior forces; they were not to be risked uselessly. All these steps were in hand or in consideration, but before any fully effective solution to the problem had been reached, the Germans struck again.

In sharp contrast with October's events, when the next attack on the Scandinavian convoys was delivered on 11–12 December Room 40 was able to offer no help at all;[25] the Germans were learning the value of wireless silence. This time the instrument was a full flotilla (eight ships) of the newest and fastest German destroyers. One half-flotilla made for the English coast to harry vessels gathering for the Scan-dinavian convoy, the other headed north towards Bergen. It was at 11 a.m. on 12 December, just as the east-bound convoy was turning up towards that destination, with a stiff north-westerly bringing squalls of rain and a heavy swell which hid all but the masts and funnel-tops of the destroyers, that the German force fell upon its prey. This time the escort consisted of the two destroyers *Pellew* (Lt-Commander J. R. C. Cavendish) and *Partridge* (Lt-Commander R. H. Ransome), with four armed trawlers and six merchant ships in company. Some distance to the west – too far for participation in what followed – were two power-ful Grand Fleet cruisers with four more destroyers, acting as a covering force for both this convoy and its west-bound counterpart. Long before this reinforcement could appear, the doom of the east-bound convoy was sealed. German gunnery was, as usual, excellent, and in a matter of minutes HMS *Partridge*, unable to move or resist, was reduced to, in effect, a practice target. Torpedoed three times, she sank after about half an hour, having during that time contributed one more minor epic of indomitable courage to the history of the Royal Navy.[26] The *Pellew*, with her port engine-room full of water, fell out of the fight and disap-peared behind a blinding rain squall; by a miracle she was able to reach Norway, and later Scapa Flow – the sole survivor of convoy and escort. Once again the German ships made a safe escape; their sister half-flotilla had already returned intact, having succeeded only in sinking two small stragglers off the Northumberland coast. The sum total of events on 11–12 December, however, could only be regarded as very disturbing. It says much for the fortitude of the naval authorities that they persevered with the decision to adopt the Methil–Bergen route; though the full journey was much shorter, the North Sea passage was longer, and closer to the German bases. When the new route came into operation in the new year, Admiral Beatty regularly attached a Grand Fleet battle squadron to the covering forces. Newbolt tersely remarks:

This allocation of a battle squadron to the defence of trade was a great departure from the principle of rigid concentration which had dominated the organization and employment of the Grand Fleet since the war began: it was illustrative of the extent to which the war against commerce had engaged our strength and resources.[27]

It is not often that prophets are proved so quickly and comprehensively correct as Admiral Sims.

Meanwhile, what of the U-boats? In the Mediterranean, in October, they enjoyed a triumphant feast: 142,519 gross tons of shipping sunk and damaged.[28] This total dropped sharply in November, but rose in December to a most alarming 176,767 tons. In that month *UC 38* (Wendlandt) was sunk in the eastern Mediterranean, being only the fifth German U-boat to have been lost in that sea since the beginning of the war.[29] Convoy was not introduced in the Mediterranean until November; even then, escorts were pitifully weak, and remained so, not so much on account of a lack of suitable vessels as of protracted devotion to 'offensive' methods which scarcely troubled the U-boats at all. Add to that the problems of divided command – France and Italy were Mediterranean naval powers with an indisputable say in the conduct of affairs; in addition, there was an important Japanese destroyer flotilla, and a growing American commitment – and the special circumstances which made the inland sea a U-boat paradise will be appreciated.

In British home waters and in the Atlantic there was disappointment for the Admiralty at the failure to destroy U-boats. September's high score was halved in October, all five being victims of mines,[30] one of them *UB 41* possibly blown up by a German mine. November was more promising, with eight kills, four of them positively attributable to British action: two torpedoed by British submarines, one sunk by depth charges and one rammed. In December there were eight once more, two by ramming and one by depth charge attack. Even allowing for some false optimism it was not a very impressive performance. What made it particularly depressing was the failure of the remarkable hydrophone development during the year to produce the expected results. Much had been hoped from hydrophone-equipped hunting flotillas such as those that we have seen operating in the North Sea in October. A substantial degree of decentralization had taken place, permitting local commanders to dispose of these flotillas without reference to the Admiralty. This succeeded in cutting the time-lag between alert and action from forty-eight hours or more to six to eight hours. It was still too much, and the weapon proved ineffective. The local commanders reflected sorrowfully upon this, and at least one of them, Vice-Admiral C. H. Dare at Milford, reached the conclusion that the only answer was to convoy everything – including ships sailing to join or being dispersed from ocean convoys and all coastal traffic. This, clearly, would mean breaking up the hunting patrols, but Admiral Dare argued:

This method would have at least one great advantage, in that a submarine would be compelled to attack within reach of a vessel capable of active retaliation. With the present system of patrols this is not the case: the enemy can, with the greatest ease, evade them, and only attack a merchant ship when they are absent. The hydrophone flotillas might still be retained at work on their present patrols, but I am of opinion that, with the present instruments, and the incessant bad weather ... these vessels are a waste of useful ships.[31]

Acting on his own precepts, Admiral Dare instituted the first local convoy on 1 December – and the results were exactly what one might suppose. During the month his forces escorted twelve convoys, a total of seventy-four ships, within their area – and not one was lost. Yet another six months would have to pass before this system became universal around the British Isles. As Admiral Jameson says, despite the extremely useful work done by Jellicoe and the Anti-Submarine Division which he had set up a year earlier,

it is difficult to resist the conclusion that Jellicoe and other senior officers at the Admiralty were at heart still opposed to convoy and were rather too ready to consider almost any alternative.[32]

Paradoxically, the rising curve of losses in coastal traffic during the last quarter of 1917 represented, in reality, a U-boat defeat rather than a victory. For it was in this period that they made their most significant acknowledgment of the effect of the convoy system to date. Unable to find the quarries which had abounded in the open stretches of the Western Approaches, they now changed their tactics altogether: they came inshore. Fayle informs us:

During the first three months of unrestricted submarine warfare only 20.4 per cent of the losses in European waters (excluding the Mediterranean) were due to attacks made within ten miles of land; exactly half the casualties occurred outside the fifty-mile limit. Now, for the three months November to January inclusive, only 1.7 per cent of the successful attacks took place more than fifty miles from land, and 62.8 per cent of the losses were incurred within ten miles from shore.[33]

This was the second tactical innovation imposed upon the U-boats by Allied methods, and it reflected a marked falling-off of their performance in the main Approaches and consequently against the big ocean-going ships which were Britain's mainstay.

The new threat was, nevertheless, dangerous, and had its effect on the convoy system; the fast outward-bound convoy from Queenstown had to be abandoned, and its vessels merged with the slow convoy from Milford:

> The loss of speed was regrettable, but it was more than compensated by the advantage of escort from so early a period of the voyage.[34]

A third innovation forced upon the U-boats by their lack of success was an omen of a very different kind. As the year drew to an end, it was perceived with dismay that an ever-increasing number of attacks on shipping were taking place by night. An average of 22.5% of attacks in darkness between February and October suddenly mounted to 54.2% between November and January (January, 60%).[35] This tendency continued into 1918, with results that we shall see.

Reviewing the 'state of play' at this stage of the 'period of slack water,' with its mixture of discouragement and hope, Newbolt remarks:

> If all the outstanding facts of the year's campaign were reviewed they supported no positive conclusion and justified no hard and definite forecast.[36]

This is a perfectly correct assessment of the uncertainty of the time; it is possible, however, equally to approve Lloyd George's contention with hindsight, that

> The great Allied triumph of 1917 was the gradual beating-off of the submarine attack. This was the real decision of the War.[37]

That fact, however, was insufficiently apparent in December, 1917, to save Jellicoe. Relations between him and Geddes had been deteriorating; the sharp upward jolts which punctuated the curve of shipping losses, and the evident failure to sink any considerable number of U-boats, kept discontent with the Admiralty alive. On Christmas Eve, Jellicoe discovered this letter on his desk:

My dear Sir John Jellicoe,

    After very careful consideration I have come to the conclusion that a change is desirable in the post of First Sea Lord. I have not, I can assure you, arrived at this view hastily or without great personal regret and reluctance. I have consulted the Prime Minister and with his concurrence I am asking to see The King to make this recommendation to him . . .

Yrs Sincerely E. C. Geddes[38]

Jellicoe replied the same day. He permitted himself only to remark,

    You do not assign a reason for your action, but I assume that it is due to a want of confidence in me.

    Under these conditions you will realise that it is difficult for me to continue my work . . . I shall therefore be glad to be relieved as soon as possible.

So departed one of Britain's most devoted and unsparing public servants; his great services were rewarded by a peerage whose title was engraved on his heart: Viscount Jellicoe of Scapa. In 1919 he also became an Admiral of the Fleet. Admiral Oliver did not long survive him at the Admiralty; in January, 1918, he went to the Grand Fleet to command a Battle Squadron.

    Jellicoe's successor was – predictably – Sir Rosslyn Wemyss, a man of very different stamp. Compared with the dedicated, almost monkish professional Jellicoe, Wemyss was a man of the world, accustomed to moving in influential society. Indeed, as a very old friend of George V, he was regarded by some as a 'Court sailor'. Immediately on his appointment he confided to the King, 'I am fully aware of my limitations'; but the ex-sailor George V wrote back in his own hand:

My dear Rosy,

    . . . during this war wherever you have served and whatever you had to do, you have done *right well*. You have many excellent qualities, but you are too modest to mention them, anyhow I consider that you have three which will enable you to fill the very important and responsible post of 1st Sea Ld. namely common sense, great tact and you are an absolute gentleman. For these reasons I at once gave my consent to your appointment. I feel sure you will have the support and confidence of the whole Service . . .

Believe me
Yr. sincere friend

G. R. I.

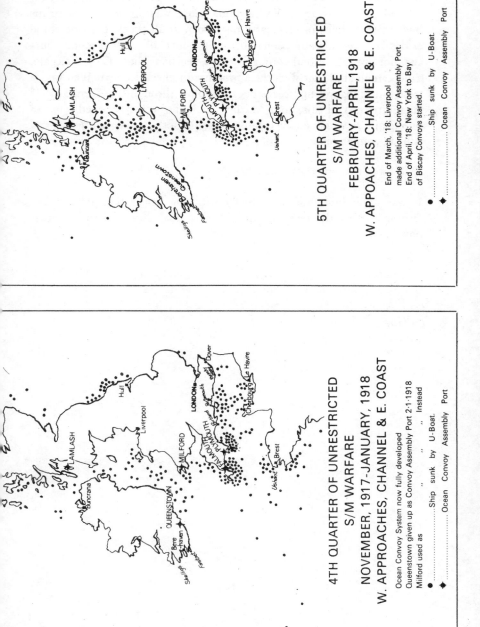

5TH QUARTER OF UNRESTRICTED
S/M WARFARE
FEBRUARY-APRIL, 1918
W. APPOACHES, CHANNEL & E. COAST

End of March, '18: Liverpool
made additional Convoy Assembly Port.
End of April, '18: New York to Bay
of Biscay Convoys started.

● .... Ship sunk by U-Boat.
◆ .... Ocean Convoy Assembly Port

4TH QUARTER OF UNRESTRICTED
S/M WARFARE
NOVEMBER, 1917-JANUARY, 1918
W. APPROACHES, CHANNEL & E. COAST

Ocean Convoy System now fully developed
Queenstown given up as Convoy Assembly Port 2·1·1918
Milford used as   "   "   "   "   " Instead

● .... Ship sunk by U-Boat.
◆ .... Ocean Convoy Assembly Port

It was asking a lot that the *whole* Navy should suddenly become supporters of an officer whose previous career had little of high distinction
and showed scant signs of exceptional ability. He was, nevertheless,
says Marder, 'one of the most popular senior officers in the Navy',[39]
his judgment was good, his common sense was obvious, as were his
buoyancy in times of crisis and his charm at all times; even potential
critics admired his approachability. But above all, he had moral courage, not only the moral courage to take decisions, but also to delegate.
So it came about that with the appointment of Sir Rosslyn Wemyss, 'a
fresh and invigorating breeze began to blow through the Admiralty'.[40]
In addition to all this, adds Marder, he had a well developed sense of
public affairs which enabled him to handle both British politicians and
Allied commanders:

'He was, in short, a naval statesman.'

It was upon him, building chiefly with the bricks that Jellicoe had
fashioned, that the task of administering final defeat to the U-boats
now fell.

6

Foiled Rather Than Defeated

'The German submarines . . . had been foiled rather than defeated.'
Admiral Jameson

THE YEAR 1917 was one of the worst in history; its tale of calamities
still casts long shadows. For the Allies it was full of disappointments
and missed chances. There was, first, the failure to exploit the hard-
won, grievously costly victory on the Somme the year before, capped
by the unhindered German withdrawal to the 'Hindenburg Line' which
bore clear witness to that victory.[1] Shortly after this came the news of
the Russian revolution in March, which some expected to act as a re-
juvenating force, but which for the time being could only mean that
Russia, previously a mainstay, was now an uncertain quantity. Then
came the disaster of General Nivelle's Champagne offensive in April,
and the widespread mutinies in the French Army on the Western
Front which followed it. The British Flanders offensive, haunted by
bad weather,[2] did not produce the results anticipated – the amphibious
operations originally planned on the Belgian coast near Ostend were
abandoned on 22 August, and thereafter the axis of the British offensive
shifted eastwards in the direction of Roulers, a railway junction, rather
than towards the U-boat exits.[3] In October the misfortunes of the
Western Front were repeated with interest on the Italian Front, with
the Caporetto catastrophe. The same month witnessed the second Russian revolution, which brought the Bolsheviks to power and shortly

took Russia out of the war. The entry of America, from which so much had (somewhat unrealistically) been hoped, showed no sign yet of compensating for this serious weakening of the coalition; by December, 1917, only one American divison was actually in line on the Western Front, on a quiet sector in eastern France. And throughout all these depressions, all through the year the U-boats maintained their ominous refrain, with another upcurve on the graph of shipping losses in December. Only the future – and that not immediate – could show that this was a misleading signpost: that the real turning-point of the U-boat campaign was at hand.

A turning point was definitely due: by the end of January, 1918, with the unrestricted U-boat campaign a year old, the reduction of world shipping by war losses alone during that period amounted to nearly 6,200,000 tons gross (British, 3,750,000). In addition, a further 1,175,000 gross tons (British, 925,000) had been damaged, mostly to the extent of putting the ships concerned out of action for four to six months. It did not require, on top of those figures, an increase in normal marine hazards; yet such there was, sufficient to raise the amount of British shipping under repair to 1,500,000 tons. This has to be compared with an output of merchant shipping from British yards of only 1,163,000 tons – 30% below the average for the last three years of peace. It was, as Fayle says, a 'profoundly unsatisfactory' situation,[4] and a poor prospect.

By the end of 1917 the inshore movement of the U-boats had become very clear and the Flanders flotillas[5] were, erroneously, again regarded as the villains of the piece. Strenuous efforts had been made during the year to close the exits from Zeebrugge and Ostend with minefields; during the first six months these had produced no results at all. This was undoubtedly chiefly due to the poor quality of British mines on which we have already several times remarked. Just how bad this was is illustrated by the case of *U 70*. Generally speaking, a mine was lethal to a submarine, a single explosion being quite sufficient to tear a great hole in the hull. On 27 September at 0058 *U 70* struck a mine while submerged off the Goodwin Sands; she was nevertheless able to surface and report to headquarters in Bruges. She made further signals at 0330 and 0530; the intercepts brought British aircraft and ships to the scene at 0745, and *U 70* herself picked up a signal saying 'Submarine directly beneath us', clearly from a British aeroplane. She dived, not without difficulty, and remained on the bottom for several hours. At 1430 she signalled to Bruges again, asking for escort to take her home, and reporting damage to her rudder and engines, at the same time giving her position, course and speed. This brought British patrol boats to her at 1515, sending her quickly to the bottom again, to endure eleven depth charges. At 2240 she surfaced, and there was another exchange of signals with Bruges, thanks to which, when she arrived at what she expected to be a rendezvous with German torpedo boats, it was only to find that these had encountered a British flotilla leader with five destroyers in that vicinity at 0120 (28 September) and had understandably beaten a hasty retreat. *U 70* sighted the British ships at 0325, reported her position and course to Bruges, and dived again. She came up at 0440, but only to sight more ships in the distance; they may well have been her intended escort, but there was no point in waiting to see, so down she went again. At 0848 she was back on the surface and receiving orders to come straight into Zeebrugge; at 0930 she was sighted by a German aircraft which told her that it was going to find the torpedo boats, and twenty minutes later these appeared. However, six British destroyers arrived first, accompanied by an aircraft which machine-gunned *U 70* and dropped three bombs which exploded close to her. This sent her down again until midday, but when she came up it was only to be attacked by another aircraft which drove her down again. At 1600 she told Bruges that she would stay down until 1900, giving another position which Bruges then checked, and when she came up for the last time she finally met the torpedo boats, and was towed into Zeebrugge at 2330.[6] The point of the story is that none of this should have happened; it tells us much – about the robust construction of the U-boat, about the sophistication of radio interception at that stage of the war, but chiefly about the mine.

In the second half of 1917 new minefields and better mines, laid closer to the shore in the Zeebrugge approaches, improved the British performance; Grant (a cautious recorder) attributes the loss of six U-boats to this cause in the period July – December.[7] Shipping losses, however, continued to be severe, and the density of U-boats in the Channel area showed no sign of diminishing. It was at this stage that Room 40 and the listening Service took a significant part in reshaping anti-submarine strategy.

One does not have to pore for long over an atlas in order to perceive the naval significance of the Straits of Dover. Narrowing to a span of just over 20 miles between Folkestone and Cap Gris Nez, it forms a highway between the North Sea and the English Channel both for merchant shipping[8] and for warships – including submarines. For the U-boats, whether coming from the Flanders base or from the High Sea Fleet, the quickest way to their hunting-grounds in the Western Approaches was through the Straits.[9] It was a priority consideration for the Admiralty to block this passage; its narrow width and the relative shallowness of its waters seemed to lend themselves to such a project. Even before war broke out, a study of anti-submarine defence had produced the recommendation of a net barrage (first tried in the 1904 Spithead manoeuvres) suspended from a steel hawser held up by floats and constantly patrolled; if a submarine struck the net the agitation of the floats would bring the patrol craft to the spot to attack with depth charges. Indicator buoys to mark an entangled submarine, which would light up at night, were a further refinement. Some 750 miles of nets were on order by 1915, each 100 yards long and 60 feet deep; it was another obvious refinement to lay mines beneath the nets – the Channel floor being in some places 120 feet below the surface. Yet another, sanctioned by the Admiralty but never actually carried out, was a boom right across the Strait. Aircraft patrols supplied a fourth, and there were more to come: magnetic and acoustic mines, 'indicator loops' to lie on the sea floor and give notice of submarines passing over them, and hydrophones in the same position for the same purpose. The whole of World War I was marked by a constant progress of technology; its two chief novelties, air warfare and submarine warfare, displayed this at its most impressive. But the three main elements of a barrage remained the same throughout: the net, the mine and the patrolling craft.

It is sad to relate that so much ingenuity was in vain. Grant's compendious and most authoritative list of U-boats sunk (with locations and dates) shows only two U-boats (*U 8*, 4 March; probably *U 37* in April) sunk in the Strait during 1915, one only in 1916 (*UB 29*, 13 December), one possible (*UC 36*, 17/18 May) and one certain (*UB 56*, 19 December) in 1917. This was a poor reward for great efforts, great expenditure of time, labour and materials. But by the last boat named, *UB 56*, there hangs a tale.

In April, 1915, the Dover Command was conferred upon Vice-Admiral Sir Reginald Bacon, an officer of great intelligence and an inventive turn of mind. He had supplied Churchill, in September, 1914, with designs for a 'landship' (tank) which carried its own bridge for crossing trenches and means of raising the bridge behind it. He had designed and constructed[10] in a very short time a 15-inch howitzer. In September, 1916, he had been highly receptive to Haig's idea of 'special flat-bottomed boats for running ashore and landing a line of Tanks on the beach',[11] and in July, 1917, he took pleasure in showing Haig a portable ramp equipment for climbing a steeply inclined sea wall with an overhanging lip (as at Ostend), and Haig remarked:

> I saw the tanks ascend the wall twice – wonderful performance to look at and done without any effort![12]

The problems of the Dover Barrage were meat and drink to a man like Bacon, and he threw himself into their solution with enthusiasm. As Churchill says,

> In everything that concerned machinery, invention, organization, precision, he had few professional superiors.[13]

Unfortunately, like others with similar talents, Admiral Bacon found it difficult to believe that he could be mistaken; he was quite certain that his devices were destroying U-boats to the extent of deterring them from attempting the passage of the Straits, and the temporary relaxation of the U-boat campaign in 1916 (see p. 11) powerfully reinforced this belief. He was consequently unmoved and, indeed, scornful when a stream of decrypts from Room 40 revealed that, in Newbolt's words,

> the German submarines were passing through the Straits of Dover in an unbroken procession.[14]

Or, in Churchill's caustic verdict that

> During 1917 the failure of the 1916 Barrage across the Dover Straits had been total.[15]

By the autumn of 1917 Room 40's voice had acquired considerable authority, and the evidence of failure at Dover gave the Admiralty sufficient anxiety for Rear-Admiral Keyes, who had only recently been made Director of the new Plans Division, to be appointed chairman of a 'Channel Barrage Committee'. That was on 17 November, and only twelve days later the Committee presented its report. Fortified by on-the-spot investigations, it was severely critical of the existing barrage, even going so far as to suggest that the Germans would regret the removal of the obstacle in view of the false complacency that it en-gendered. When it came to making positive proposals, the Committee was less forthcoming, but one which it strongly urged drew an equally strong response from Admiral Bacon. The Committee insisted that the nets and minefields should be illuminated at night by searchlights and flares, as the only sure way of forcing U-boats to dive into minefields. Admiral Bacon was very much against these illuminations; recalling a damaging raid by German destroyers in October, 1916,[16] and other forays in 1917, he protested against turning his small craft into obvious targets. The picture which he formed (and which shortly became a reality) is well described by Churchill:

> About a hundred little vessels of no military quality – trawlers burning flares, drifters, motor-launches, paddle mine-sweepers, old coal-burning destroyers, P-boats, with a monitor in their midst – all lay in the glare of the searchlights. The area was as bright as Piccadilly in peacetime; and its occupants scarcely better armed. Some miles to the eastward five patrolling divisions of destroyers offered their only possible protection. But if these were evaded by a raiding enemy, a massacre seemed inevitable.[17]

Not only did Admiral Bacon protest against lighting up the barrage area, he also challenged the Admiralty order to concentrate his patrol craft on the eastern end of it and strengthen them by withdrawing vessels from the more distant barrages which he had to maintain on the Belgian coast. Again, he saw in these orders the probability of a massacre (and he was not wrong); a conference on 18 December served only to show how fundamentally opposed were Bacon's ideas and those which were now prevailing at the Admiralty. When Bacon returned to Dover, he had given an undertaking at least to try out the illumination, and this he did on the night of 19 December. It was precisely on that night that *UB 56* (Hans Valentiner) was driven down into the deep mines and there destroyed. Bacon's arguments were torn to ribbons, his tenure of command was clearly at its end. On 1 January, 1918, he was replaced by Keyes, promoted to Vice-Admiral.

Keyes was a friend of Churchill, who never stinted praise of his friends; the results of the change of command, he said, 'were amazing'; Keyes 'revolutionized the situation'.[18] Professor Marder's judgment is also friendly, but probably more exact:

one of the most attractive of men, warm-hearted and full of boyish enthusiasm – a born leader with few brains.[19]

Keyes himself was diffident about his intellectual prowess, but claimed 'the knack of getting the right people about me and making good use of them'.[20] His first concern was to concentrate along the minefield, keeping it well lit at night; he accepted the risk to the covering forces, giving orders that the approach of enemy destroyers should be signalled by green Very lights, whereupon the drifters and trawlers were to disperse rapidly, making for the British or French coasts according to position. The immediate results were good: four U-boats were sunk in the Straits (three by mines) between 8 January and 8 February, which made a striking contrast with the record for the whole war to date. Keyes, always an optimist, believed that the figure was larger, and was well pleased. The German destroyer foray on 14 February, referred to above (Note 17), in which seven drifters and a trawler were sunk, with five more drifters, a trawler and a paddle minesweeper severely damaged (eighty-nine officers and men killed or missing) while the Germans escaped unharmed, wiped away his pleasure:

The fishermen were deeply angered. They thought the Royal Navy had failed to give them the protection which it had guaranteed, and which they deserved. They saw themselves exposed on any night to merciless attacks. For a while they lost confidence in the new Dover Command, and, indeed, in the Royal Navy. . . . Keyes's reputation hung on a thread.[21]

Keyes, in fact, was hardly to blame. The events of 14 February were distinguished by a series of unforeseeable accidents and mischances which, added to the ordinary difficulties of action on an extremely dark and hazy night, merely underlined the inevitable vulnerability of defences entrusted almost entirely to small Auxiliary vessels close to an enemy base. Fortunately for him, Keyes was soon able to restore his reputation by planning and executing a real failure in the best British manner: the famous Zeebrugge Raid on St George's day (23 April).

Intended to block that U-boat and destroyer exit once and for all, the operation was marked by great dash and gallantry on the part of all concerned, but failed completely in its purpose at a cost of 635 casualties. However, it was trumpeted as a great success (at a time when success was in short supply) and Keyes was saved.

Meanwhile the activities which had drawn criticism upon him were proceeding well. By the time of the Zeebrugge Raid, the Dover Barrage had (genuinely) claimed four more U-boats; the Germans – for reasons that are not at all clear, though the Raid may have had something to do with them – never repeated their February foray, and the Barrage became, within its limits, a success story. 'Within its limits'; it never achieved what Keyes and his loyal supporters believed that it achieved. He was convinced that as many as twenty-six U-boats perished in the Barrage during 1918; Grant demurs:

> The true figure, in our opinion, was fourteen.[22]

The lower figure was nevertheless sufficient; increasing evidence of U-boats using the northabout route showed that the Dover Barrage in its new form was having a definite deterrent effect. This is not to be wondered at; the fate of a U-boat caught in the minefield could be horrible. Among the (chiefly Flanders) U-boats which continued to attempt the passage was *UB 55* on 22 April; whether her crew had worse expereinces than others we cannot know, but since some survived we do know with precision how horrible theirs were:

> Near the Varne Buoy the commander had ordered a dive to 12 metres. As the boat took this depth a net or mine scraped along the hull, exploding violently at the stern. Water poured in and the stern went down. The crew were ordered forward to restore trim, but the motor room was soon full of water. The ballast tanks aft could not be blown, although the engineer officer was able to set the boat level on the bottom at 25.3 metres. Water leaked into the control room, however, and the batteries were emitting chlorine gas. As the air pressure increased, several men committed suicide by stuffing their mouths and nostrils with wadding and putting their heads under water. Others tried to shoot themselves, but the damp cartridges would not fire. Finally two men got out through the conning tower hatch and twenty more through the bow torpedo hatch. The change of air pressure killed most of them, but after an hour and a half in the water a patrol drifter, searching for wreckage, picked up the commander and seven others.[23]

Even the real successes of the Dover Barrage had to be paid for; on the debit side we have to reckon an over-heated enthusiasm in the Admiralty for barrages in general as an anti-submarine device. If, by May, it could be said that 'the eastern entrance to the Channel was virtually sealed',[24] the same could not be said of the northern project which had been agreed at the conference in September, 1917. As finally planned, this vast enterprise would comprise a complex of deep minefields right across from the northern Orkneys in the west to somewhat south of Bergen in the east – an area of over 30,000 square miles of sea. This was a very different scale of things altogether. And there was a further, highly significant difference also to take into account: unlike Dover, the Allies did not possess a firm base at each end of the complex. There was no question of infringing Norwegian neutrality or of coercion.

The whole Northern Barrage project depended on the American supply of mines; the Navy Department ordered 100,000 in September, 1917, and much was hoped of a new type with long antennae (originally designed to extend 100 feet, they were soon shortened to 70). Work on the barrage began on 3 March, with a large patrolling force of flotilla leaders, destroyers, sloops, P-boats and trawlers in attendance. From the beginning there were problems, which came to a head on 22 March, when the sloop *Gaillardia* blew up while buoying one of the new minefields. The mines in this field were of the new American type, adjusted to a depth of 65 feet below the surface; *Gaillardia* drew only 10 feet, and at the time of the explosion was some distance away from the line of buoys. Work was accordingly suspended, pending enquiries, and not resumed until 20 April. The American mines were concentrated in the central section of the barrage, which began to be filled in early June. It was soon clear that all was still not well: a single trawler reported hearing twenty-eight distinct and about thirty distant explosions between 8–15 June. The Americans pointed out that this number of explosions accounted for no more than about 4.5% of the total of mines laid, and that even this proportion would shortly be reduced by a new mechanical device that was in process of delivery. This, however, did not live up to expectations and premature and unexplained explosions in the American minefields continued to be reported. Then, on 8 July, the Listening Service picked up a signal from *U 86*, reporting that she had struck a mine. Another signal, from *U 60*, provided some details of *U 86*'s mishap: she had been at a con-

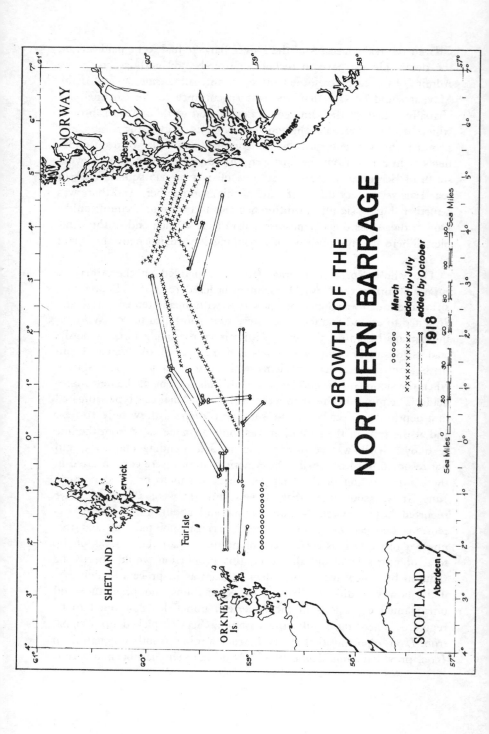

GROWTH OF THE
NORTHERN BARRAGE

March   ooooooo
added by July   xxxxxxxxxxx
added by October   ⊶⊶⊶⊶
1918

siderable distance from a floating glass ball (indicating a deep mine-field) when the explosion happened. Since, on Admiralty admission, a mine would only destroy a surfaced U-boat if it exploded 15 feet or less from the hull, this was obviously another premature and, not surprisingly, *U86* was able to reach home despite her damage – and despite British submarines, warned by the decrypts, lying in ambush in the Skagerrak and the Kattegat. However, the two navies, British and American, persevered with their task; in the event, the Americans laid no fewer than 56,571 mines, and the British 13,546.[25] U-boats continued to move out through the northern North Sea exit, as well as exploring the supposedly impenetrable Pentland Firth. The last mine-laying exercise took place on 26 October, 1918. Grant tells us the final count:

> Six submarines certainly or almost certainly perished in the Northern Barrage, and one more may have done so.[26]

Admiral Beatty, irritated at the constriction of the Grand Fleet's freedom of manoeuvre by the barrage, was only one who thought the whole thing had been a fearful waste of time and resources.

At least the Northern Barrage was not positively harmful to the anti-submarine war; the same could not be said of the Otranto Barrage at the southern end of the Adriatic. Here the width of the straits is almost 50 miles – a more manageable distance than the Orkneys–Bergen passage, but still a great deal more than Folkestone–Calais. We have noted the late introduction of convoy in the Mediterranean and the serious weakness of the escorts; the reason was, quite simply, grotesquely misplaced faith in the Otranto Barrage. Its object was to prevent all egress from the two Adriatic U-boat bases, Pola (Austrian) and Cattaro (German). The Barrage (mines and nets) was supported by a Mobile Force, backed by an Allied Submarine Patrol and air forces. In April, 1918, a great 'hunting' operation was mounted in conjunction with the Otranto Barrage; convoy escorts were stripped to the bone to build up the formidable force required –

> 35 destroyers, 4 torpedo boats, 6 sloops, 52 trawlers, 74 drifters, 31 motor launches, 36 USA submarine chasers, 8 submarines, excluding French and Italian, 3 squadrons of bombers, 2 of fighters and various seaplanes. In addition, there were some 200 large and small craft in the

British Adriatic force. These sustained efforts were rewarded in August by the destruction of one U-boat – the sole kill. At the same time the losses amongst independently sailed vessels, which had been at the rate of ten for every one lost in convoy, continued to the end to be heavy. The barrage had quite failed in its purpose.[27]

It only remains to add that, during these final months of the war, the attenuated Mediterranean convoy escorts succeeded in sinking six U-boats, prompting the reflection that 'had the rôle of convoy been appreciated, namely that of *protector of ships and killer of U-boats*, and the barrage force used to augment the escorts, kills would have been more numerous, not, as was evidently believed, fewer.'[28] The extraordinary thing is the persistence of such a false belief, right to the end of the war, despite all the evidence. It is perhaps fortunate that the military geography of World War II ruled out these barrages; far-stretched navies might other wise have once more seen their insufficient strength dissipated in the same unrewarding activities.

Meanwhile, the long-awaited turning-point of the campaign remained obstinately out of sight. In the first quarter, monthly shipping losses never fell below 300,000 gross tons, and were actually increasing.[29] However, they were (just) containable, by comparison with the dreadful peaks of 1917; the more serious impact of unrestricted U-boat warfare is to be observed in a different quarter – in Whitehall, where a naval conference was convened on 2 January in the course of which

recognition of the exceedingly narrow limits to which command of the sea had now shrunk was forced upon our naval command for the remainder of the war.[30]

The crux of the matter was the North Sea, and what had to be recognized there was nothing less than, in Newbolt's words, 'the dispersion of our principal naval forces' leading to 'extraordinary changes . . . in our higher strategy'.[31]

It was not a matter of numbers: the Grand Fleet still held its bases at Scapa Flow and Rosyth in great strength (augmented in December, 1917, by the arrival of a squadron of six powerful modern American dreadnoughts); the Harwich Force remained constantly active on its multifarious duties; but these considerations were deceptive. The truth was that anti-submarine warfare had now become a continuous activity of Britain's first-line forces – something never foreseen, and constituting a real victory for the U-boats. As Newbolt says,

> Just as we had found, in the early stages of the campaign, that a submarine, operating in a given area, would immobilize great numbers of watching and hunting forces, so, in its later phases, when the whole submarine fleet of the Central Powers was striving to obtain a decision at sea, we found ourselves obliged to take counter-measures, which, in their total consequences, were equivalent to a strategical division of the fleet.
>
> As a result the Commander-in-Chief informed the conference that it was, in his opinion, no longer desirable to provoke a fleet action, even if the opportunity should occur. Such large contingents of our naval forces were now absorbed in the regular duties of the anti-submarine campaign, that he could no longer be certain of meeting the German fleet even on terms of equality.[32]

Proceeding logically from this, Beatty's conclusion was that what had been fundamental Grand Fleet strategy throughout the war – namely, to try to bring the German battle fleet to action at any cost – was no longer applicable; his function now would be simply to contain the enemy until some new factor restored the Royal Navy's traditional advantage. And to this the Admiralty agreed. It was a moment in history: a moment of farewell to the supremacy of British sea-power that had been taken for granted since Trafalgar.

When the war began, the Germans, like other belligerents, had very little idea of how to use their submarines. Their instinct, in accordance with their general military policy, was to find an offensive use for the new weapon, and it was a normal part of their strategy to support the sorties of the High Sea Fleet with U-boats whose purpose was to weaken the Grand Fleet by picking off its capital ships on their way to battle. Using submarines to sink battleships was good war trading – if it could be done; the stark fact is that in the whole course of the war, though some older battleships were duly sunk,

> Not a single dreadnought was sunk by a submarine and the strength of the main combatant fleets was never seriously affected.[33]

Thus Admiral Jameson. In the sense that dreadnought numbers were never diminished by U-boat attack, he is correct; in the sense of the

Grand Fleet being truly 'unaffected' by submarines, he is quite wrong. The final sortie of the High Sea Fleet (22–25 April, 1918) is proof of the matter; the German foray was based squarely on the information (largely from U-boats) that battleships and cruisers from the Grand Fleet, with their full destroyer escorts, were covering both the North Sea mine-laying operations and the Scandinavian convoys – thus presenting a perfect opportunity for what Beatty feared most: defeat in detail. Fortunately, the sortie failed in its purpose, but it caused a great fright. This division of the opposing main force was not what the unrestricted U-boat campaign had been launched for; it was not the way of weakening the Grand Fleet that the Germans had envisaged, but it was highly effective nevertheless.

The number of U-boats in commission in January, 1918, was 132;[34] it is not a very meaningful figure, because, for one reason or another, only thirty-three (25%) were at sea when the count was taken. From January onwards the totals dropped steadily to a lowest for the year of 112 in June, rising again to 128 in September. However, in February a total of 129 saw fifty at sea (38.7%) and 125 in April saw fifty-five at sea (44%). The percentages began to matter less, as the totals decreased, and other factors reduced the effectiveness of the U-boat fleet. Building programmes were deeply in arrears, reflecting the crisis of the German economy. The programmes themselves reflected an optimism which is hard to explain at this distance in time: ninety-five boats ordered in June, 1917, of which only about five ever materialized – in time for the surrender. In addition there were eighteen 1,200-ton cruisers (see pp. 133–4 Note 7) ordered between June and December; 102 boats of various types ordered in December; 148 in 1918 (plus seventy-two of a new, 360-ton single-hull type for coastal defence known as UF-boats); none of these were ever completed. U-boat losses, meanwhile, were significantly increasing; a mere eleven sunk in the first four months of 1917 grew to twenty-four in the equivalent period of 1918. Nine of these were from the Flanders flotillas, and Colonel Repington recorded on 28 April:

A Boche officer blown up and saved said that it was now a point of honour to go to the Flanders flotilla owing to the severity of its recent losses.[35]

This was April, and the turning-point was at hand at last.

It was in April that the losses of merchant shipping fell, permanently, below the 300,000-ton mark. But, far more important, it was also in April that the construction of merchant ships exceeded losses for the first time since the unrestricted campaign had begun. The second quarter of 1918 showed a remarkable – and once more, permanent – change:

	Losses (War & Marine) (1,000 gross tons)	Output (1,000 gross tons)
1915 (total)	1,724	1,202
1916 (total)	2,797	1,688
1917 (total)	6,623	2,938
1918 (first quarter)	1,143	870
(second quarter)	962	1,243
(third quarter)	916	1,384
October	178	511

April, 1918, the month in which the British Expeditionary Force fought with its 'backs to the wall',[36] and few gleams of light shone upon the Allied cause, was nevertheless the month in which the first of Germany's final desperate throws for outright victory came to a fruitless end, and also the month when failure finally stamped the submarine campaign.

It scarcely needs to be said that these satisfactory signs were not at once apparent; in the following month, on land and at sea, the Germans showed themselves capable of what proved to be dying kicks, but at the time had the appearance of dangerous threats. Frustrated in March and April on the British sector, the German Army summoned up its strength for a mighty blow against the French in Champagne on 27 May which produced the deepest one-day advance on the Western Front since trench warfare had begun. This heralded the opening of another series of offensives which carried the Germans back to within sight of the Eiffel Tower – as close to Paris as they had been in 1914. World attention naturally focused on this great drama, missing the significance of what was happening in the U-boat war; yet the connection between the two aspects of warfare was very close. The heavy losses and great discouragement of the Allied armies in the spring of 1918 gave American reinforcement a new urgency; by the end of May, that is to say after 13 months of belligerency, there were 650,000 Americans in France. It was a disappointing figure, after such a long time, but worse still was the fact that this was a largely paper army; only one division was in the line on 1 May and only three in June. But in that month, by a concentrated Allied shipping effort, 250,000 Americans poured into France, with the same number again in July. The U-boats proved wholly unable to interfere with this programme, a fact which must in itself rank as another major defeat for them.

A further failure, with overtones of defeat, casting ominous shadows towards the distant future, also took place in May. The form that it assumed was described by Newbolt (and followers) as an attempted 'concentration' of U-boats against the convoys themselves. As such, it takes its place in history as the first essay in the group, or 'pack', tactics which became the outstanding feature of U-boat warfare in 1941. Even in May, 1918, the idea was not new:

> In 1917 when the initial experience with British convoys showed that a single U-boat had only slender chances against the strong defence, the Officer Commanding U-boats in the High Sea Fleet, Commodore Bauer, suggested that several U-boats should operate jointly. For this purpose he wanted to put a flotilla commander on one of the submarine cruisers of the *U 151* class, converted as a command U-boat, and to allow him as tactical commander to co-ordinate by radio an attack by several U-boats on a convoy.[37]

The key elements of 1941 were thus present in Bauer's proposal: a tight command system operated by radio communication. Bauer himself, however, was relieved of his command in June, 1917, before the idea could be put into practice, and in May, 1918, when his successor, *Flotillenadmiral* Michelsen, revived it, he did so in a cruder form, without the essential ingredient of intelligence-fed control.

Newbolt's account of what happened in that month has not been basically challenged; Grant only adds two or three to the numbers of U-boats participating, though he fills in the important aspect of counter-U-boat intelligence. Since the resulting operation, feeble though it looks in the hindsight of World War II, underlines a fundamental difference between the two U-boat wars, it is worth inspection. The fundamental difference, of course, is that, whereas in World War I the U-boats proved incapable of mounting an effective campaign against convoys, in the next war it was the grim and costly convoy battles that held the centre of the stage. What is surprising, as Newbolt says, is that it took almost a year of steadily increasing success of the convoy system before the Germans mounted a real attack on it (other than the two surface-vessel raids on the Scandinavian convoys described above), 'that is, when the mischief done to the German plan of commerce destruction was beyond remedy'.³⁸

The operation began on 10 May and lasted in a desultory fashion until 25 May, involving about a dozen U-boats; the location was, as may be supposed, the Western Approaches. Not all the U-boats engaged during that period were identified by Room 40, but a reasonable track of what was taking place was made possible by the garrulity of some of the captains: eight calls from *U 70* were identified and located between 9 May and 21 May; *U 43* proclaimed herself with five calls between 15–22 May, and *U 94* also offered up five calls between 16–24 May; *U 55* and *U 46* each made four calls between 16–22 May. On the day the 'concentration' began, nine convoys were in the danger area, homeward or outward-bound, and four U-boats 'by knowledge or luck' lay more or less in their path. 'Throughout the whole twenty-four hours, however, there were no sinkings, nor was any one of the convoys attacked.' Even with 1918 equipment, this was a poor performance, but it was characteristic. The next day *U 86* succeeded in sinking the steamer *San Andres* on her way into Bristol; this was the solitary success of the day, during which 'the procession of convoys filed past the watching submarines'.

During the night five U-boats, *U 43*, *U 70*, *U 92*, *U 103* and *UB 72*, regrouped themselves around the entrance to St George's Channel; this proved to be an unfortunate manoeuvre. Just before 4 a.m. on 12 May the troopship *Olympic*, laden with American soldiers, sighted a surfaced U-boat on her starboard bow; this was *U 103*, and it was her end, rammed by the *Olympic* before she had time to submerge. Within the hour *UB 72* had followed her to the bottom, torpedoed by the British submarine *D 4*. The fate of the two boats was not immediately known, but it must have been clear to the U-boat commanders concerned that the combined attack was not going well, for reasons that are not hard to discover: 'their movements bear no trace whatever of a combined plan for discovering the exact places in which convoys could be met'. The only possibility of a success on 12 May was mid-morning, when *U 70* fell in with the thirty-five ships of convoy HS 38 from Sydney, Nova Scotia, escorted by eight destroyers and three sloops:

> It would have been imagined that the submarine commander had an exceptional opportunity: it was a fine summer morning, the sea was smooth, and what wind there was blew from the west. The convoy covered a wide front, and should have been a good target: yet all the German could do was to fire two torpedoes, which both missed, at the rear ship of the starboard wing column, and then get out of the way.

Once more, a disappointing performance; and this pattern continued until 17 May:

> The initial situations at daybreak on each successive day seem often enough to promise exceptional opportunities to the U-boat captains; but the opportunities slip mysteriously away as the day goes by, and – more important – the steady uninterrupted flow of convoys slips past the U-boats at the same time.

Evidently Bauer had been, in the broad sense, correct: 'pack' attacks required control. But what they did not require, as World War II displays, was the local tactical commander that he envisaged. Radio communication had not yet come of age; when it did, it would supply the answer to this conundrum.

May 17 and 18 saw the only worthwhile successes of the concentration. It was on the 17th that *U 55* (Werner) sank the steamer *Scholar*, belonging to the homeward Gibraltar convoy HG 75, and shortly afterwards followed this by sinking the *Denbigh Hall* from a combined convoy of six ships from HL 33 and HJL 2. These were skilful performances, but not exactly famous victories: *Scholar's* displacement was no more than 1,635 tons, and *Denbigh Hall's* was 4,943. On the 18th, however, *U 94* found another convoy (to which *U 55* had directed her) and sank the 10,644-ton *Hurunui*, which was more to the point. And that was the sum total of sinkings from convoys in what Newbolt calls 'the most methodical and elaborate attempt that the German Staff had as yet made to interfere with the convoy system'. The operation can be said to have ended by 25 May; all its successes were contained in the first eight days, and they amounted to this:

> The U-boats had sunk and damaged only five vessels in what, a year

before, had been their most productive zone: three [actually four] of these ships had been in convoy, it is true, but during the same time 183 convoyed vessels had reached harbour safely, and 110 had been escorted outwards through the danger zone.

So the convoy system handsomely survived the first serious attack upon it; the U-boats, like so much else at that period, would require further advances of technology to overcome this adversary. Meanwhile, as Jameson says, 'a golden opportunity had been missed'.[39]

Two illuminations of the U-boat warfare of this period are worth mention. We have already had occasion to notice the sturdy construction of the U-boats, even of this early vintage; *UB 72*, *D 4*'s victim on 12 May, is a case in point. Her tribulations did not begin when she encountered *D 4* in Lyme Bay; she had been in serious trouble before the 'pack' even assembled:

> On May 7 and 8 a total of 51 depth charges were dropped on *UB 72*. The first three were from a dirigible, and apparently caused no damage. Next, she was pursued for two hours by a destroyer which dropped 23 depth charges, opening a leak in an oil tank and causing her to leave a track of oil in her wake. Next day the submarine was again trailed by a destroyer, which dropped 20 depth charges, shaking up the boat considerably and extinguishing five lights. Later in the day, a patrol boat dropped 5 more charges on her.[40]

This daunting experience before the main action had even begun has been understandably cited as an example of 'the amount of punishment a submarine can stand from depth charges'. It is also an indicator of the high degree of courage and resolution of the captain (Träger) and his crew who nevertheless continued the attempt to carry out their attack as ordered. It is satisfactory to record that some, at least, of these brave men survived *UB 72*'s sinking as prisoners of war.[41]

There is also a coincidence to be noted and accorded its due measure of importance. May, 1918, saw the largest number of U-boat losses of the whole war – fourteen boats. This at once puts one in mind of May, 1943, which was also distinguished by the loss of many U-boats – no fewer than forty-one. But when one has said that, one has said it all. May, 1943, signalled an enduring trend in a war that still had almost two years to run; May, 1918, was a high-water mark of U-boat losses, soon followed by the end of the war. The U-boat defeat was reflected in a marked diminution of U-boat effectiveness, not in the tally of loss; in June this dropped to a mere three, rising to six in July and seven in August, but never again reaching double figures. Newbolt, indeed, somewhat disparages the May total, attributing it to 'extraordinary misfortune', and commenting that the Allies 'could not possibly count upon keeping the monthly destruction at such a figure'.[42] However, Newbolt was under the impression that the figure itself was seventeen; Grant's revised total of fourteen contains one (*UB 70*, Mediterranean) whose cause is unknown; all the rest are due to normal anti-submarine practices – three rammed, three destroyed by depth charges, two by mines, one by gunfire, and four torpedoed by British submarines. The only special misfortune in such a list is that of meeting as many hostile submarines in one month as one might normally expect in almost a year; all that one can really infer from it is a general improvement of skills and weapons in the anti-submarine forces, and the declining losses of the U-boats in the following months indicate only their declining activity.

In one area in particular of weaponry and skill great strides were made in 1918: the air rôle. It was chiefly in the last six months that this became most apparent, but progress was continuous throughout the year. On 1 April all air activity, whether conducted by the Royal Flying Corps or the Royal Naval Air Service, was concentrated in the hands of the new-born Royal Air Force. This measure proved to be of mainly administrative and organizational significance:

> To the end of the war ... maritime air policy and dispositions were virtually directed by the Admiralty and the control of actual operations continued to be exercised by the naval area commanders.[43]

The pattern here created remained valid throughout the next war; anti-submarine air organization also anticipated the future arrangements of Coastal Command:

> For work in the coastal areas an operational air group was to be formed for each strategic zone. The Headquarters was to be in touch with the Senior Naval Officer and with the Local Base Intelligence Officer and linked by telephone with all air stations and wireless stations in the group.[44]

A new conscious professionalism, right through the whole anti-submarine effort, was clearly visible on the air side: a school for observers in anti-U-boat squadrons and flights was opened at Aldeburgh; books and pamphlets on U-boat tactics were issued to all stations and expert lecturers arrived to disseminate their knowledge.

As ever, in both wars, the aircraft themselves constituted the chief problem – either in the matter of performance, or of numbers, or of both. By January, 1918, when 60% of shipping losses were occurring within ten miles of the shore, this opened up a new area of air activity: the constant watch on coastal waters and (somewhat later) escort of coastal convoys. The question was, what with? 1918 would see a substantial increase in the numbers of anti-submarine aircraft against a background of general permanent shortage, and this proved to be salvation from the scrap-heap for one of the aviation industry's lamentable failures. The de Havilland 6 had been born in crisis for quick production as a trainer for the rapidly expanding RFC in 1916; already by 1917 it was being supplanted, and there seemed to be no possibility of alternative use for it, which was a pity, because no fewer than 2,200 had been actually built. Then, early in 1918, the Admiralty asked for aircraft patrols in the Tyne-Tees area, where U-boats had become dangerously aggressive. Two flights of DH 6s were accordingly formed in March, and in June thirty-two more flights (five operated by the US Navy), a total of 192 aircraft, were formed along the coast. It is salutary to reflect upon the military capabilities of this machine, which makes even the Avro Anson of 1939 look powerful and warlike. Its maximum speed was 75 mph; its armament consisted of 100 lb. of bombs – but in order to lift even this small amount the observer had to be dispensed with; those aircraft powered by the Curtiss OX-5 engine turned out to be highly unreliable, and made frequent descents into the sea. The good news was that DH 6s floated for a long time, so there was a reasonable chance of rescue and casualties were few in relation to the number of engine failures. In April, 1918, a promising replacement for this paragon appeared – the Blackburn Kangaroo, powered by two 250 hp Rolls-Royce Falcon engines giving it a maximum speed of 98 mph; its outstanding features were its excellent view ahead and its loaded weight of 8,017 lb. The Kangaroo remained in RAF service, in fact, until 1929 – but in 1918 only one squadron (fourteen aircraft) saw service.

By mid-1918 the Navy and RAF alike had a much clearer idea of aircraft capabilities, and working systems or air/sea cooperation were standardized and operated as a matter of course. Radio contact, either direct between aircraft or via their base, was a fundamental of all operations; this was the year in which airmen were 'given the power of speaking and listening to speech in flight'[45] – an acquisition which would one day augment the potential of air power out of all recognition. It was still a crude and chancy gift in 1918, with quavering signals often blotted out by static, but it was a beginning, from which operations could only benefit. Functions for these were now well defined. Landplanes (DH 6s and others) maintained intensive patrols – one aircraft every twenty minutes – over an inshore zone some 15–20 miles wide and ultimately stretching from St Abb's Head in Scotland, down through the Channel and round to the Irish Sea. For work further out, convoy escort, patrols or in conjunction with hunting flotillas, there were the seaplanes and flying-boats. For deep sea work, there were still only the kite balloons (not to be despised), but auxiliary cruisers were being fitted to carry seaplanes, and consideration was even given to towing airships from surface craft. The principal use of the airships (of which there were about 100) was for convoy escort, especially searching ahead and out on the flanks; they had the advantage over heavier-than-air machines of being able more easily and economically to keep station with a convoy. They were also used for diverting ships for mine-searches, and to help the hunting groups. In the barrage areas, endurance and weather permitting, the aircraft maintained patrols whose purpose was to force the U-boats to dive in amongst the mines. And finally, there was air power's favourite resource: bombing. Air attacks on the Flanders base and its exits were always much in favour; like most 1914–18 bombing (and later also) this proved to be an over-rated activity. It was widely practised in the Adriatic as well as the North Sea, but in neither area did it produce worthwhile results:

> These attacks did not influence U-boat operations and did not result in the destruction of, or significant damage to, any U-boats.[46]

It will be noted from the above that the Admiralty's deep-seated faith in submarine-hunting operations (a dogmatism seen at its most obdurate in the Mediterranean) was still as alive and vigorous in 1918 as in previous years. A latter-day complication was to fit, at first seaplanes, then flying-boats and finally (it was intended) also airships with hydrophones. Success still eluded the hunters, but no amount of failure seemed able to diminish the enthusiasm for these laborious and demanding efforts:

> Even with the experience gained in 1917, there were in 1918 far more air sorties on area patrols[47] than on escort to convoys but the proportion devoted to convoys rose from one in eight to one in five sorties and only three ships were sunk from convoys receiving air escort.[48]

One cannot help wondering what the result might have been if those proportions had been reversed. And what is worse, all this had to be relearned between 1941–43.

So April, 1918, had seen the turning-point of the U-boat campaign, and May saw the ebb in unmistakable progress. Churchill, indeed, has stated that

> By the middle of 1918 the submarine campaign had been definitely defeated.[49]

He was writing in 1923; Admiral Jameson, in 1965, was more circumspect. He even cast doubt on the drooping morale of U-boat crews which was confidently proclaimed by Allied propaganda:

> Prisoners captured from sunken U-boats showed that the men had not lost confidence in their officers, but many of the ratings were young and clearly inexperienced. What had suffered was efficiency.[50]

As he says, efficiency, in a submarine, is unusually dependent on the personality of its commander, but every member of the small crew is important; each man must possess definite skills and the initiative to use them. (This was probably more true in the early days of the weapon than at any time thereafter, because there was then less 'automation', fewer mechanical aids for the essential tasks.) One thing was certain: every crew needed time and experience together in order to arrive at the mutual reliance that makes a team. And time was fast running out:

> By the end of June 150 boats had been lost, usually with all their crews. The German submarine service, never a very large body of officers and men, had had heavy casualties ... After every war patrol proved men had to be drafted away to form an experienced nucleus in new boats

commissioning, and their replacements, straight from the submarine school, did not always measure up to what had become a nerve-racking life. Not all the officers now being given command possessed the combination of guts and instinctive good judgment for the lone and difficult task of attacking well-protected, moving targets glimpsed through a periscope or dimly seen when on the surface at night. There had always been a great difference between the results obtained by the best and run-of-the-mill commanding officers. The aces, though liable to be let down by inefficient crews, still did quite well, but their less gifted and less aggressive colleagues had too much to compete with.

This seems a fair analysis, and it draws Jameson to this conclusion about the condition of the U-boats as 1918 moved into its second half:

They had been foiled rather than defeated.

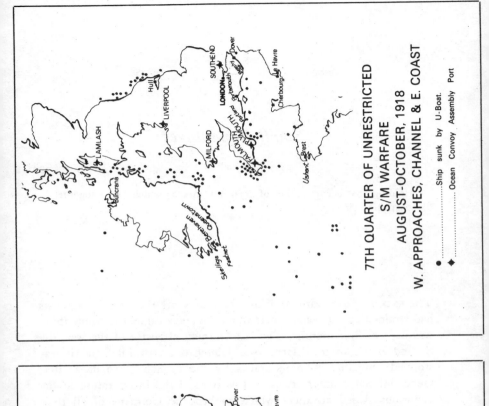

6TH QUARTER OF UNRESTRICTED
S/M WARFARE: MAY–JULY, 1918
W. APPROACHES, CHANNEL & E. COAST

By May, '18: Dover Strait Barrage fully effective. Passage
abandoned by U-Boats.

● ....Ship sunk by U-Boat.
◆ .... Ocean Convoy Assembly Port

7TH QUARTER OF UNRESTRICTED
S/M WARFARE
AUGUST–OCTOBER, 1918
W. APPROACHES, CHANNEL & E. COAST

● ....Ship sunk by U-Boat.
◆ .... Ocean Convoy Assembly Port

7

Small Advantages

'Holding that accumulation of small advantages which taken together constituted victory.'

Sir Henry Newbolt

THE END, IN 1918, came quickly; for four years the giant antagonists had strained against each other; when the crack came, the whole thing was over in four months. The last German offensive of the war, the Second Battle of the Marne, was launched on 16 July, and it was stopped immediately in its tracks by the French. Two days later, General Foch counter-attacked; this marked the inauguration of the victorious Allied advances which robbed the Germans of all their earlier gains and continued until they sued for peace in November. At sea the signs and portents of defeat were already visible, before the guns of the Marne began to speak.

It was the wrecking of the German Army – the 'motor' of the war (see p. 15) – in the violent Western Front battles of 1918 that brought about the crumbling of Germany's allies on the secondary fronts, and finally of Germany herself on the main front. The pattern of the war at sea was different: it was not battle, but inaction, that wrecked the High Sea Fleet; and, as regards the submarines, the crumbling was simultaneous in the North Sea and the Mediterranean. Six of the fourteen U-boats sunk in May belonged to the Flanders flotillas; this loss followed upon nine in the previous four months – a considerable total for a force which never numbered more than thirty boats.[1] By June the strength of the flotillas had dropped to twenty-three, with eleven at sea, but losses continued to mount up: out of three U-boats lost in that month, two were Flanders boats; out of six in July, four were from Flanders; out of seven in August, six. By now, says Churchill, a Flanders boat 'could hope for only six voyages before meeting its dark doom'.[2] Small wonder that, as Grant says,

> From the beginning of June . . . the effectiveness of the Flanders flotillas steadily declined.[3]

The main burden of the submarine war in the north was thus thrown upon the High Sea Fleet flotillas, which manfully did their best. On 10 June they numbered forty-nine boats, of which fifteen were at sea, plus nine cruisers of which one was at sea; these figures improved to a total of fifty-six in July, with twenty-two at sea, and four out of the nine cruisers, and fifty-eight in August, with nineteen at sea, but with twelve cruisers of which five were at sea. During these months the totals of shipping losses were:

	World	*British*
June	255,587 gross tons	162,990 gross tons
July	260,967 gross tons	165,449 gross tons
August	283,815 gross tons	145,721 gross tons

But these totals conceal a more serious matter: that whereas in March, 1917, the High Sea Fleet U-boats had been destroying an average of more than one ship every two days (0.55 ships per U-boat per day), by June, 1918, this had dropped to an average of one ship every *fourteen* days – 0.07 ships per U-boat per day. The picture in the North Sea and the Atlantic was bleak for the Germans and the prospects even more so.

The U-boat war in the Mediterranean was always significantly different from that in Home Waters. That sea had always been a 'happy hunting ground' for the U-boats, while their losses, as we have seen, were few and far between; by June, 1918, the tally for the whole war was only ten. As a result, the dilution which so seriously affected the efficiency of the North Sea boats left the Cattaro Flotilla practically untouched. Nevertheless, its effectiveness showed as dramatic a decline as in the Flanders flotillas: while sinkings in the Mediterranean had remained at a monthly rate of well over 100,000 gross tons for the first five months of 1918, suddenly, in June, there came a drop to 78,322 tons, and an average for the next three months of 73,767.

> This was due to no relaxation on the part of the enemy. They had not been able to maintain quite as many submarines at sea as during the previous month; but the total number of days spent by the submarines on cruise – the figure which gave the truest measure of the enemy's exertion – was not below the average. They had expended the same amount of oil, machinery, courage, cruelty, ingenuity and labour in destroying seventy-eight thousand tons of shipping as they had in sinking one hundred and seventy-six thousand tons a few months previously. The setback was final: the enemy never restored the position by a counter-attack or a special exertion. It can therefore be said that during June the naval campaign in the Mediterranean ended in an Allied victory second in importance only to the victory in Home waters.[4]

No roll of drums or peal of bells greeted these victories; they were of the nature of things that are real enough, but imperceptible. Certainly the German Naval Command did not perceive them. *Admiral* Scheer, now Chief of the Naval Staff, continued to believe that the U-boats were Germany's only hope of obtaining an acceptable end to the war:

> We could achieve it by this means alone. . . . We must and will succeed.[5]

It was, in fact, in June that the bulk of the 1918 U-boat building programme referred to above was ordered: forty U-boats proper, forty-four of the new Mark III UBs and forty Mark III UCs. Since these orders could not possibly bear fruit for at least a year, it is evident that the Naval Staff did not consider that defeat was staring it in the face. And since it was also able to procure the transfer of some 50,000 workers from Army contracts to U-boat construction, it is also evident that the German Government had not lost faith in the underwater weapon either.

In July two of what we can now describe with easy assurance as the dying kicks of the U-boat arm were seen, both of much greater future than present significance. On the 19th the outward-bound convoy OLX 39 was off Skerryvore Rock; it consisted of seven ships, including the 32,234-ton White Star liner *Justicia*, escorted by no fewer than seven destroyers. A small U-boat 'pack' (one source says four boats) was in the vicinity, and *UB 64*, with great temerity, braved the powerful escort and torpedoed the *Justicia*, bringing her to a standstill. The destroyers at once closed in with depth charges, but *UB 64* escaped while the listing liner was taken in tow. After two hours the submarine came to periscope depth and fired another torpedo; it missed, and once again the depth charges descended. Undaunted, the U-boat came up again three hours later, and fired yet again, without success; this time the answering depth charges caused such damage that *UB 64* was compelled to break off the action, and was glad to creep away. The next day, however, another U-boat, *UB 124* (Wutsdorff), on her first war cruise, had arrived on the scene and saw the *Justicia* being towed back to port under protection of a massive concentration of escort craft – no fewer than twelve destroyers, two sloops, two armed yachts and eight trawlers. In spite of them all, the U-boat was able to hit her with two more torpedoes which spelt her doom. However, there was a price to pay:

> *UB 124*'s crew was brave but inexperienced. She lost her trim, broke surface, got under again as the destroyers rushed in and plunged to the bottom in a veritable rain of depth charges. Damaged and shaken she lay on the bottom all day and was trying to come up and escape on her diesel engines at 7.0 p.m. when she got into serious difficulties, lost her trim, broke surface and was abandoned as she finally sank.[6]

Naval Intelligence consoled itself for this episode with valuable information gathered from the *UB 124* survivors – but that could not bring back the *Justicia*. Yet the whole thing was very much a flash in the pan – two further attempts at 'pack' operations in August came to nothing. But now we can see that the performances of *UB 64* and *UB 124* were heralds of what might be done, and in due course was, even against convoys with powerful defence.

Later in the month there was another portent. Over the protests of Admiral Scheer, the decision was taken to attempt a 'blockade' of the American coast; the word has to appear with quotation marks because only three U-boats (*U 117*, *U 140* and *U 156*) took part in this vast enterprise, making it as impudent as the Union blockade of the Confederacy in 1861 (see p. 6). The three boats were not ineffective: their mines sank the US crusier *San Diego* and damaged the battleship *Minnesota*; in addition,

> Twenty-eight steamers displacing more than 1,000 tons were sunk by bombs or gunfire and fourteen torpedoed; over fifty small, unarmed

craft, including sailing vessels, tugs, barges and motor boats were destroyed, mostly by bombs. For the submarines it was a return to the older, happier days with ships sailing independently and unprotected, in a large area where patrols were easily dodged.[7]

Newbolt's count of vessels sunk off the American coast is substantially less, but he agrees that the total was 'considerable'. He adds:

> But during this same period convoys had passed through the new U-boat zone without loss. These convoys were the real quarry, and they had escaped entirely. On the American coast, as indeed in every other theatre, U-boat operations had ceased to be operations for a large strategical purpose and had become no more than sporadic attacks upon trade.[8]

What may now astound us is that when the later U-boats sounded their own 'roll of drums' on the American coast in early 1942, it took the United States Government and the US Navy utterly by surprise, as though this very precise warning of what might happen had never taken place – only twenty-four years earlier.

The quiet victory pursued its course. Newbolt describes it with perception:

> To all outward appearance the war at sea was still a quite indecisive succession of attacks, ripostes, counter-attacks and counter-ripostes, yet it was during these monotonous days that the naval campaign was definitely won. The exact date of the Allied naval victory is difficult to determine, for it was not announced in the despatches of a naval commander, or in the log books of vessels engaged in a great action, but in a few columns of statistics kept in an office in the centre of London.

He refers, of course, to those decisive, crushing statistics of shipping losses and output which we have noted; they reflected, as he says,

> success in its most comprehensive sense; and from midsummer, 1918, British operations at sea may be regarded as measures for holding that accumulation of small advantages which taken together constituted victory.[9]

It is not at all to be wondered at that the victory was unnoticed; an 'accumulation of small advantages' is thin gruel compared with what was happening on the battle-front. The British armies under Haig had entered the general Allied offensive on 8 August – the Battle of Amiens, in Ludendorff's words 'the black day of the German Army in the history of the war', causing the Kaiser to say on 11 August,

> I see that we must strike a balance. We have nearly reached the limit of our powers of resistance. The war must be ended.[10]

In this battle the British Fourth Army took 22,000 prisoners and more than 400 guns – visible and tangible proofs of success. On 21 August the Third Army joined in the fray – the Battle of Bapaume, which produced 34,000 prisoners and 270 guns. When the First Army also came in on 26 August, the British Expeditionary Force established itself as the very spearhead of the whole Allied advance. In September it performed what must surely be the most tremendous feat of arms in British history: the storming of the 'Hindenburg Line' on 29 September. The next day the Second Army, forming part of the Army Group commanded by the King of the Belgians, took its place in a new offensive in the north towards Ostend and Bruges. The Germans did not wait for the Allied soldiers to reach these places; on 1 October the Bruges radio station instructed such Flanders U-boats as were at sea to return to German ports. Ten others also departed for Germany and five were blown up in their base; it was the end of the Flanders Flotillas, scarcely noticed amid the cheers of the triumphal entries into liberated cities.

This was, in effect, the last month of the war, and though the U-boats did their best to maintain some activity, all attention that could be spared from the steady advance of the armies was drawn more and more towards the High Sea Fleet. By now, indeed, the still large U-boat fleet was reduced by the lowered quality of crews to virtual impotence; yet there were still some resolute commanders capable of doing damage, as witness the cruises of *UB 87* (33,000 tons sunk), *UB 57* (32,000 tons) and *U 82* (26,000 tons). The mettle of the best of the U-boat commanders and their crews is displayed in the story of the last cruise of the legendary von Arnauld de la Perière, now commanding *U 139*. On 1 October he sighted a ten-ship convoy with strong escort near Finisterre:

After missing a torpedo shot he allowed the convoy to pass overhead, surfaced and pursued it, attacking with gunfire as soon as he could close the range. Von Arnauld sank one ship which had straggled behind, disabled another and, when put down by the escort, remained in the vicinity to finish her off. Dusk was now falling; patrols were all around, but he closed the crippled ship and fired a torpedo. Judging that the safest place was close to his victim, he went deep to pass beneath her. Suddenly there was a crashing noise overhead, the lights went out, water poured through the conning tower hatch and *U 139* took on a heavy list and started to plunge towards the bottom, 500 fathoms down. Von Arnauld had collided with the sinking ship and was pinned under her bottom! By blowing main ballast he managed to get clear, only to break surface amongst the patrols. Very skilfully handled, *U 139* got under again, escaped further damage from a deluge of depth charges and got clear away. All three periscopes were damaged beyond repair, but von Arnauld remained at sea. *U 139* was still able to dive, though quite blind when submerged. She could use her torpedo tubes on the surface and she had her guns, as she demonstrated a few days later by sinking a Portuguese gunboat after a sharp engagement. Von Arnauld remained on patrol until recalled to Germany.[11]

It is impossible to withhold admiration from such an officer as von Arnauld; such high degrees of resolution and seamanship are rare. Other U-boat activities, however, rebounded at this stage of the war to Germany's considerable disadvantage. Outright defeat in the field was a daily more imminent prospect, only staved off by devoted rearguard actions. But, as the Allies advanced, the spectacle of destruction, some of it deliberate, left behind by the retreating enemy, and the plight of the civilian population, hardened their hearts. Negotiations for peace had just begun (3 October) between the German Government under a new Chancellor, Prince Max of Baden, and President Wilson of the United States.[12] It was no favour to the German side when news came on the 4th of the torpedoing of the passenger vessel *Hiramo Maru* off the Irish coast with a loss of 292 lives out of 320 on board. Six days later the Irish Mail Boat *Leinster* was torpedoed without warning, and torpedoed again while she was sinking, with a further loss of 527 lives. President Wilson, in a formal Note on 14 October, pronounced that neither the United States Government nor its allies

will consent to consider an armistice so long as the armed forces of

Germany continue the illegal and inhuman practices which they still persist in. At the very time that the German Government approaches the Government of the United States with proposals of peace, its submarines are engaged in sinking passenger ships at sea – and not the ships alone but the very boats in which their passengers and crews seek to make their way to safety.[13]

Among the Allies there was, as Lloyd George says, 'a howl of indignation',[14] neatly expressed by Britain's Foreign Secretary, Mr Arthur Balfour, whose comment was:

Brutes they were, and brutes they remain.[15]

The chances of any merciful compromise in the peace negotiations were always slender – such as they may have been, they were torpedoed in the Irish Sea as surely as the luckless ships.

The Germans replied to President Wilson on 20 October; their tone was circumspect, as befitted the continuous deterioration of their military condition. However, they denied 'illegal and inhuman practices', and denied specifically that the U-boats had destroyed lifeboats and their occupants. Since neither the *Hiramo Maru* nor the *Leinster* was mentioned in the British list of incidents later considered to have been war crimes, this denial would seem to have been justified. But at the same time the German reply also contained the promise that U-boats would cease torpedoing passenger ships and orders to that effect went out that day. General Ludendorff wrote:

This concession to Wilson was the heaviest blow to the Army and especially to the Navy. The injury to the *moral* of the fleet must have been immeasurable. The Cabinet had thrown up the sponge.[16]

Reading the signs aright, Admiral Scheer on the next day recalled all the U-boats still at sea. The unrestricted submarine campaign against commerce was over; it had lasted just under twenty-one months; Scheer's order acknowledged that it had failed, as had all Germany's other expedients.

The U-boats had failed; the Army was approaching a condition described as 'capable neither of accepting nor refusing battle';[17] there remained only the High Sea Fleet. For this great, expensive and mainly idle instrument of war a final desperate operation was planned: a last attempt to inflict crippling damage on the Grand Fleet by action in the North Sea. It was not quite the entirely suicidal venture that is often suggested; it was wrapped in at least a light cloak of plausibility by proposed manoeuvres against British forces and shipping along the Flanders coast and in the Thames Estuary, in order to draw detachments of the Grand Fleet southward and fulfil the old German dream of defeating it in detail. U-boat cooperation was an essential part of the plan, in the form of attacks on the British forces coming down from Rosyth and Scapa Flow. Thus the last designated task of the U-boats was what had first been intended for them: offensive action against the Royal Navy itself. Those that were available accordingly began to gather in the North Sea in the region of the Firth of Forth – under the ever-watchful 'eye' of the Listening Service and Room 40. One boat, *UB 116* (Emsmann), was even ordered to Scapa Flow itself – in anticipation of a famous deed almost exactly twenty-one years later.[18]

Admiral von Hipper, commanding the High Sea Fleet, issued his orders on 24 October; the Admiralty noted

> an unusually large number of messages in a most secret cipher on the night of 23–24 October, but purport unknown.[19]

Room 40's work was made more difficult by a major change in the German call-signs in September, but even if vessels could not be readily identified the volume of signals was always indicative. On the 28th the Listening Service overheard orders to the German 3rd Battle Squadron to coal at Wilhelmshaven, orders to five U-boats to take up North Sea positions, and also orders to the Cattaro Flotilla to leave the Mediterranean if possible, if not, to seek internment in a Spanish port. By now seven or eight U-boats had been located, and it was clear that some major enterprise was brewing. Beesly rightly draws attention to the change in the manner in which this information was now handled under the Wemyss/Fremantle (DCNS)/Hall régime:

> Beatty was being taken fully into the Admiralty's confidence, and was being given the Admiralty's best guess and the reason behind it. The Chief and Deputy Chief of Naval Staff were at last consulting Hall and his experts before coming to conclusions. The Operations and Intelligence Divisions were working in concert instead of in separate watertight compartments. It was very much overdue.[20]

It is a fair comment; it is also fair to call this a long stride towards the ULTRA system of World War II.

28 October was a bad day for the U-boats: *U 78* was sunk by the British submarine *G 2* south-west of Norway, and that night *UB 116*, trying to enter Scapa Flow, was blown up on shore-controlled mines – the last U-boat casualty of the war. 29 October was even worse for the High Sea Fleet; the great sortie was due to begin the next day, and orders were given to raise steam. They were the signal for mutiny, which spread rapidly through the battle squadrons and the rest of the fleet. At 0833 the Admiralty learned that the German Fleet was to remain at anchor, and at 1312 that movement was postponed until the next day. On the 31st there were no indications of German activity – for very good reasons; it was on that day that *U 135*, commanded by a distinguished officer, *Kapitänleutnant* Johannes Spiess, found herself, by command of von Hipper himself, pointing her torpedo tubes and manning her 150-mm gun, not against British vessels on the open sea, but against the German battleship *Helgoland*, at anchor in the fleet base at Wilhelmshaven. It had come to that.

In the German bases (Kiel was the hotbed) revolution was already at work. The sailors began to organize on the lines of the 'Workers' and Soldiers' Councils' (imitating the Russian Soviets) springing up elsewhere. Red flags were being flown. On 1 November Room 40 knew that the U-boats in the North Sea were under orders to return home, and that disorders were rife in the Fleet. By the 5th it was clear that these were extremely serious, and at 0226 on 6 November a signal from *Flotillenadmiral* Michelsen to U-boats in the Baltic was picked up, ordering them to

> fire without warning on ships with the red flag. The whole of Kiel is hostile. Occupy exit from Kiel harbour.... Use all means to break down resistance.[21]

By now the U-boats were the only element of the Imperial Navy that could still be relied on to obey orders; but all the loyalty and determination in the world will not keep a modern warship operational without a due supply of food and fuel. Michelsen had to have a base of his own, and on that same day he set out in *U 135* for Heligoland, accompanied by about a score of other U-boats and a collection of destroyers and small craft which were still performing their duties. They were too late; the mutiny had already reached there. Still looking for a loyal harbour, Michelsen took his variegated flotilla to Sylt, only to find that a 'Soldiers' Council' was in process of taking over the island:

> With no reserves of fuel and other supplies and abandoned by their fellow countrymen [Michelsen's ships] could do nothing. On 9 November Michelsen sadly ordered his ships to return to their home ports. In the words of Spiess it was 'Goodbye to the Imperial Navy. Goodbye to the German North Sea'.[22]

It was not quite 'goodbye' to the U-boats; their final – and characteristic – gesture was made at 0715 that morning off, of all places, Cape Trafalgar. Here there was a great gathering of Allied warships, watching for U-boats trying to come out of the Mediterranean through the Straits of Gibraltar. Among these was *UB 50* (Kukat), and among the warships was the old battleship HMS *Britannia* with an escort of two destroyers. Kukat nevertheless fired two torpedoes which narrowly missed *Britannia*, and then a third which duly hit her and exploded a quantity of cordite; she went down after a three-hour struggle to save her, and *UB 50* got clean away. Newbolt remarks:

> The *Britannia* was the last British warship sunk by the enemy. She was destroyed by a German submarine within one of those zones which had been specially defended, and which, of all places in the high seas, should have been more dangerous to German U-boats than to Allied warships. Her destruction within two days of the final armistice was a stern reminder that the German submarine commanders were still undefeated and defiant, though their campaign against the commercial highways of the sea had been ruined and brought to nothing.[23]

The Armistice took effect at 1100 hours on 11 November. The First World War was over:

> The weapon purchased so dearly by the German war leaders had first been blunted and then broken in their hands. It remained for them only to pay the price, and meet the fury of the world in arms. But from this they did not shrink.[24]

8

The Battle Done

The strife is o'er, the battle done;
Now is the Victor's triumph won;
O let the song of praise be sung. Alleluia!
Francis Pott, hymn, translated from Latin,
Finita Iam Sunt Praelia

BY THE TERMS of the Armistice with Germany signed on 11 November, 176 U-boats were handed over to the victorious Allies – the whole existing fleet except those interned in neutral ports or broken up in Germany. The majority crossed the North Sea in batches during the month to surrender to the Royal Navy, and by 1 December 122 had arrived at Harwich; eight 'sank' on the way, but, as Jameson says, 'without any particular inconvenience to their crews'.[1] Others were dispersed among the Allied naval powers sooner or later to find their way to the breakers' yards. The 'most formidable thing' the war had seen declined into a memory, almost into oblivion.

Through accident, through enemy action or unknown causes, Grant lists 178 U-boats lost during the war.[2] In addition, there were the five destroyed when the Flanders base was abandoned and eleven similarly disposed of in Cattaro when that flotilla was ordered home.[3] Losses thus amounted to just under 50% of the 390 boats built between 1914–18.[4] Casualties in the U-boat service numbered 515 officers and 4,894 ratings killed – a trifling figure by comparison with what had been normal from the first in land warfare, but a high proportion (certainly not less than 30%) of a service which was always numerically small. Accidents claimed nineteen boats, and nineteen more were lost by unknown causes. The chief U-boat killer in the First World War was undoubtedly the mine, which claimed at least forty-eight certain victims (according to Grant); but as he says, 'Its usefulness was chiefly due to the geographical situation'. He refers here to the barrages, especially at Dover, and the type of fixed defences that sank *UB 116* at Scapa Flow, and clearly he is quite right. But he goes on:

> The weapon with the greatest future was evidently the depth charge, independent of geography and usable wherever and whenever U-boats made attacks upon shipping.[5]

Depth charges were definitely responsible for the sinking of thirty U-boats, all but eight of them in 1918. The next best total was due to ramming: nineteen U-boats, of which five were the work of merchant ships or transports. British submarines, as we have seen (p. 34), accounted for seventeen U-boats, a very creditable score.

Certain important and permanent truths about submarines had emerged between 1914–18. The first, dating from the very beginning of the war and restated constantly throughout it, was what Gibson and Prendergast call 'the unsuspected sea-keeping endurance displayed by submarines generally'.[6] Since sustained cruises are of the very essence of submarine warfare, it is difficult to overstate the importance of this discovery. Linked to it was the further discovery that U-boats were capable of operating for substantial periods at great distances – right across the Atlantic, in fact, on America's doorstep, nearly 4,000 miles away. As early as April, 1917, the ingenious *Flotillenadmiral* Bauer had foreseen not merely a 'headquarters ship' rôle for the long-range boats, but also what would later be known as a 'milch cow' (supply ship) rôle; haphazard attempts at this were made the next year. Finally, both sides discovered that these slim, delicate-looking, complicated craft were capable both of resisting the pressures of surprising depths and surviving apparently annihilating attacks.

On the other side of the ledger, we see the U-boats operating under some real disadvantages. German Naval Intelligence was never able to supply them with the flow of accurate information about Allied shipping that their successors enjoyed between 1940–3. Nor did they ever receive the strong, authoritative direction of World War II; this was, obviously, in part a penalty of being newcomers to the naval scene (overshadowed by the High Sea Fleet) but also, of course, in part a result of the lack of Intelligence. Thirdly, though radio was in constant and increasing use, it was still an unreliable means of communication; this is not surprising – when unrestricted U-boat warfare began, only twenty years had passed since Signor Marconi had amazed the world by transmitting a radio signal across the English Channel. By 1918 it was daily routine to transmit orders, information and reports across the Atlantic – though sometimes they did not come through very clearly. And there was the further problem – the fact that what I have elsewhere called 'the indiscreet clatter of distant invisible voices'[7] was now already a major Intelligence source, a weapon not merely for the U-boats but also for their enemies. However, it was clear by November, 1918, that with firm leadership based on sound Intelligence and exercised through improved transmitters and receivers, 'the most formidable thing' stood a distinct chance of becoming a true war-winner.

Nevertheless, as long as words continue to possess their accepted meanings one thing is clear: the U-boats of 1914–18 had been defeated. How had it been done? Grant, whose account of how both British and French naval Intelligence kept track of U-boat movements is impressive, claims that 'the work of interception and decryption was all-important, especially when it was coordinated and acted upon'. He adds:

For the anti-submarine war of 1914-18 it was perhaps the most significant contributor to British and Allied victory.[8]

This is a large claim indeed. Patrick Beesly fully accepts the central rôle of Intelligence in what was still considered to be the main theatre of naval war – the confrontation of the two great surface fleets:

It was Room 40, despite its imperfections and despite the Admiralty's repeated failures to make the best use of its information, which enabled the Grand Fleet to meet every German move and which confirmed the German High Command in its essentially defensive, unenterprising use of the *Hochseeflotte*. Room 40 robbed the Germans of the advantages of surprise.

It is less easy to be so precise about Room 40's contribution to the defeat of the U-boats.[9]

143

Recalling how, after 1943, thanks to ULTRA, Naval Intelligence was able to keep as close a guard upon Dönitz's U-boats as Room 40 had upon Scheer's High Sea Fleet from 1914–18, Beesly soberly concludes:

> Neither in World War I nor in World War II did British Intelligence win the U-boat war, but in both cases it certainly shortened it.

The simple truth is, as Ronald Lewin pointed out when he came to write the story of ULTRA, that knowing what the enemy is doing or intending is not enough:

> even the best of secret intelligence diminishes in value if the enemy is overwhelmingly superior.[10]

For victory, force is required as well as knowledge; and force, in such a context as this, means the right weapons and the right system. The system, clearly, was convoy. Jameson, posing the question, 'what defeated the U-boat?', firmly replies:

> Convoy is, of course, the short answer, for it was convoy which had foiled them of their prey. Convoy was by far the most important factor in robbing the U-boats of victory.

He goes on:

> the fact that submarines were destroyed in large numbers was highly relevant, and most of them met their fate not whilst attacking convoys, but elsewhere. Without these casualties quality would not have fallen away, as it did from late 1917 onwards, and convoys would have been subjected to heavier and more skilful attacks.[11]

There is an obvious conflict here with Marder's dictum that 'sinking submarines is a bonus, not a necessity' (see p. 87). And since both arguments contain a clear measure of reason, we need to consider them further. Marder's main proposition, that a submarine which is not sinking enemy shipping is a failure, is incontrovertible. It is equally hard to dispute that heavy casualties lead to loss of efficiency. Two facts nevertheless tell against Jameson; the first is that loss of efficiency is not *solely* caused by casualties; as the Royal Air Force discovered

144

between 1936–43, and the U-boats themselves discovered again between 1940–43, the dilution which is inseparable from rapid expansion has to bear a proportion of the blame. Secondly – and this is surely decisive – *at no time* during the First World War were U-boats effective against convoys. As we have shown above, this failure was an established fact long before U-boat losses reached significant numbers. The important truth within Jameson's contention would seem to be this: as both wars showed, victory over the U-boats was a 'two-tier' business. Preventing the loss of shipping was stage one; stage two was holding the victory. And in this connection, casualties were obviously extremely significant, hastening a decline of morale in already diluted crews.

The infliction of casualites was a direct product of the development of weapons. It was not, in 1916–18, to any extent worth dwelling upon, a product of convoy; as Jameson says, the great majority of U-boats lost met their fate elsewhere. Grant, indeed, attributes only sixteen U-boat sinkings to the work of escorts.[12] It is, however, in the increasing number of sinkings and even more, the increasing fear of sinking, that we find the striking improvement in anti-submarine warfare; as *Admiral* Tirpitz expressed it: 'a mere work of destruction (wolves amongst a flock of sheep) had become an operation of war involving great danger and loss.'[13]

When we consider the unrestricted U-boat campaign of 1916–18 it is as well to begin with the mortal dread that they had inspired in those who knew the truth – with, in other words, the meaning of that pregnant phrase of Lord Derby's to Haig in April, 1917:

we have lost command of the sea.

A prophecy had been fulfilled. In 1805 the inventor, Robert Fulton,[14] who had already built a practical submarine for France, demonstrated the devastating effect of an underwater charge to the First Lord of the Admiralty, Lord St Vincent. Fulton already had the support of the Prime Minister, William Pitt, for his advanced ideas. St Vincent, however, shocked by the explosion, viewed them with an admiral's eye, and he remarked:

Pitt was the greatest fool that ever existed to encourage a mode of war which those who commanded the seas did not want, and which, if successful, would deprive them of it.[15]

As we have seen, the deprivation, in 1917, did not last very long; yet it had sufficed to create a very real risk of losing the war. One would have supposed that that fact would be unforgettable, but it was not.

Secondly, since we speak of prophecies, it is right to recall Fisher's warning in 1913, that submarines could take no prizes, and that by their very nature they would be forced to sink their prey, whatever might become of its crew. This had been amply borne out despite initial disbelief in Fisher's prediction; the submarine commander's first responsibility could only be the safety of his ship. It was not an easy course to steer, between sinking as many ships as possible (building up the tonnage 'score' which marked the 'ace'), ensuring the safety of the boat, and some measure of outright brutality. '*Schrecklichkeit*' came quickly to sea warfare as well as land; the submarine was a natural vehicle for it. Looking back with the calm perspective of hindsight, it is possible to see now that it was not so much 'unrestricted submarine warfare' (which would be met again) as 'unrestricted industrial technology' that was to blame for the hideous scenes which accompanied the U-boat campaign. In particular, it was the torpedo that was the guilty party.

The enemies against whom convoy was first instituted (see note 32, p. 679) were known as 'corsairs' or privateers, and were very much feared. The original Arab corsairs of the Barbary Coast had a fearful reputation for cruelty, and boldly carried their depredations right up to the Channel and beyond. Their European followers were no less a force to reckon with: the 'corsairs' of St Malo, for example, between the years 1672–97, captured 1,300–1,400 enemy ships (mostly, of course, British) in addition to those they sank – and this was just one French port. To this day, the names of Duguay-Trouin (1673–1736) and Robert Surcouf (1773–1827) are treated with pride and reverence as distinguished sons of the town; British records would, of course, speak of them somewhat differently. But Duguay-Trouin, Surcouf and their comrades did not carry torpedoes; their attacks were visible and 'natural' – and they took prizes and prisoners. In World War I the contemplation of great vessels suddenly smitten, perhaps in the dead of night, by shattering explosions caused by unseen foes, and rapidly disappearing under the waves with passengers and crews drowned, blown up, or left exposed to lingering death in open boats, came as a deeply shocking novelty. It must be noted, however, that this was very much a civilian reaction; the Royal Navy did not love its dangerous enemies, but it did not treat them as pirates (whatever the Press might say). U-boat crews in both wars, struggling in the water as their boats foundered after an unsuccessful fight, were picked up and looked after by the craft that had hunted them; they were not hung in chains. In the Navy's own submarine service, the attitude was chiefly one of mutual respect.

In the minds of an outraged public, moral indignation against the U-boats was much on a par in both wars. In terms of the practicalities of U-boat warfare, the similarities are also striking, the differences being almost entirely matters of degree or finesse. In both wars the U-boat fleet had to undertake rapid expansion, made more difficult in World War I by the claims of the very large High Sea Fleet. In both wars the lesson of numbers was rammed home; numbers permitted the formation of packs (and larger numbers allowed larger packs); the air threat which produced the World War II-style 'pens' at Bruges in 1917 also compelled the addition by 1918 of an 'altiscope', an extra, angled periscope to search the sky for the U-boat's new enemy. The tactic of night attack on the surface (i.e. using the U-boat's best speed under cover of the darkness), always hard to counter, had become normal: during the last nine months of the war, 37% of attacks in the Atlantic and Home Waters were conducted in that manner; in the Mediterranean the proportion was as high as 67%. All this, taken in conjunction with the range, endurance and communication system already mentioned, shows that the lineaments of 20th century submarine warfare were now well defined, not merely in outline, but in some important respects fleshed in as well, in this seminal period between February, 1917, and November, 1918.

The same is, of course, true of anti-submarine warfare. We have followed the development of the all-important weapons: the increasing effect of mines (including the acoustic and magnetic varieties), the emergence of the depth charge – even to the point of early use by aircraft, the anti-submarine howitzers and bomb-throwers (p. 28), the growing sophistication of hydrophones leading to the invention – just too late – of ASDIC, the new vessels (sloops) introduced purely for anti-submarine action. All in all, the material effort was massive (and without benefit of any blue-prints); indeed, it has been said that the most significant effect of the U-boat compaign, at least during the last year of the war, was the tying down of Allied Forces.[16] Bearing in mind the inventive and productive effort involved, as well as the numbers (some 300 Allied destroyers and nearly 4,000 auxiliaries), this seems a fair judgement, valid again between 1940 and 1945.

It is, however, in a quite different field that we see the most striking material advance; it is closely linked with the growth of the convoy system, whose central importance has been sufficiently stressed. So valuable had aircraft shown themselves in naval warfare (but above all in anti-submarine operations) by 1918 that a truly amazing expansion programme was agreed for completion by December: no fewer than 353 flying-boats and seaplanes, and 920 landplanes – a total of 1,273 machines. This was clearly too much, more than was needed, and more than industry could supply or trained manpower could support. In the event, the figures achieved were 305 and 382 respectively. This was, nevertheless, an impressive performance:

> Although the immense expansion in the maritime air forces planned to be attained by the end of the war did not materialise, the strength of the purely maritime side of the RAF in Home Waters on 11 November 1918 was 43 squadrons and seven flights numbering about 685 planes and 103 airships. No less than 37 of these squadrons (285 flying-boats and seaplanes, and 272 landplanes) were engaged on anti-U-boat duties, together with all the airships.
>
> It can therefore be seen that the outstanding task was anti-U-boat and under cover of this heading it was agreed that the provision of air escort and cover to convoys, both ocean and inshore, was a most essential task.[17]

The Air Historical Branch tells us that by the Armistice 'much confused reasoning had been clarified' – as one might expect; anti-submarine air warfare had to a large extent, in fact, been systematized. Among the many important details that had emerged with clarity was the appreciation (by the end of 1917) that, pending the development of satisfactory airborne depth charges (which would require over twenty more years),

> the optimum weapon of air attack against submarines was a bomb containing at least 300 lb of explosive. This had been standardized in a light casing giving a total weight of 520 lb and fitted with an impact fuse in the case of a direct hit and a delay fuse which detonated at about 40 feet after entering the water.[18]

This should have been valuable progress indeed, and in the light of such accurate prescription it is sad indeed to record (as we shall in due course have to do) that the RAF entered its second maritime war without a lethal weapon, and that this state of affairs persisted until the middle of 1942. On the other hand, it has to be agreed that in World War I it was not by killing U-boats that the Air arm made its mark. Its most useful rôle was seen to be convoy protection, and on this subject experience and reflection had hardened out into a clear doctrine which, alas, was also lost to view in the years that followed:

> The conclusion of the Naval Staff in 1918 on the correct usage of air escort was that 'a single escorting machine should keep close to the convoy as, for fear of being betrayed by the track of their torpedoes, the U-boat commanders refrain from attack on convoys with aerial escort. The ideal is that a convoy should be escorted by at least two aircraft, one keeping close and one cruising wide to prevent a submarine on the surface from getting into a position to attack. The rear of the convoy should not be omitted, for a submarine may be following on the chance of getting in an attack after dark.'[19]

All this has the clear ring of prophecy, as does the addendum:

> the mounting of searchlights in aircraft was advocated.

That pointer to effective anti-submarine warfare at night would also have to wait for over two decades for fulfilment.

It was thus with a remarkable multiplication of its material strength and with a well-esteemed new partner that the Royal Navy concluded its first great battle against the submarine. But its most significant advance, as we look towards the future, was an organizational matter: the linking of the new kind of Intelligence deriving from radio (monitoring, decryption and judicious dissemination, together with the scarcely less important D/F) to existing sources to begin an approach towards a real Submarine Tracking Room, and the application of all the information thus gained by an Operational Intelligence Centre. These would prove to be new dimensions indeed.

When we survey this war against the U-boats in 1916–18, and seek to estimate its contribution to the 1914–19 war as a whole, once more we catch a strong hint of what the future would hold. The issue was not merely a matter of the 3,329 British and Allied ships sunk by U-boats between February, 1917, and November, 1918,[20] or the 14,879

Merchant Navy dead in the whole war.[21] The German intention had been to bring Britain rapidly to impotence and surrender by severing her vital supply lines. This strategy failed, as was plain to see. And there was another failure, of almost matching importance, but not explicit and so less easily recognizable; it is indicated in the striking statistic quoted on p. 50. During the whole war, the critical theatre was always the Western Front in France and Flanders – this was the main front, where the main body of the main enemy stood, and had to be fought. That is why the British Empire sent 5,399,563 officers and men across the Channel between 1914–18. In 1917 American forces began to follow in their footsteps; in the crisis of the summer of 1918 the steady flow of Americans across the Atlantic became a flood. At the Armistice the American Expeditionary Force, with a ration strength of 1,876,000, was actually larger than the BEF. For both Britain and America, this huge concentration of military strength constituted the main effort of the nation in the war. And the U-boats proved powerless to prevent it, or even diminish it; the great hosts crossed the oceans of the world and the Narrow Seas without losing a man, a horse or a gun. This, too, was a preview of things to come, when a second generation of U-boats would in turn prove unable to prevent – though they might hinder – the main Anglo-American effort of the Second World War.

All in all, there was much for the Admiralty (and the new Air Ministry) to brood upon, if they felt so inclined, when the great conflict at last came to an end, and peace (of a sort) returned with the signature of the Treaty of Versailles on 28 June, 1919.

PART II

INTERVAL

THE INSIDIOUS SUBMARINE

'. . . to protect convoys against the insidious submarine and aircraft'.
Admiral Sir Ernle Chatfield to Churchill, May 28 1936

No BRITISH NAVAL officer could doubt the message of the war that had been won:

> The Royal Navy emerged from the conflict stronger than at any time in its history.[1]

Correlli Barnett, in the first volume of his lament for the passing of British power, spells out the meaning of that in greater detail:

> The total destruction of German seapower marked for Britain the supreme gain of the Great War, since the British Empire was a maritime empire and Britain herself, owing to some seventy years of Free Trade, depended on sea-borne supplies for her very existence. The year 1919 therefore appeared to witness the apogee of English supremacy at sea. Sixty-one battleships flew the White Ensign: more than the French and United States fleets together; more than twice as many as the Japanese and Italian fleets together. There were 120 cruisers and light cruisers and 466 destroyers to escort the battlefleet and protect the tens of thousands of miles of sea-routes that converged on the British Isles from all over the world. This was nearly twice as many cruisers and destroyers as the French and United States navies combined; nearly three times as

many destroyers as the Japanese and Italian navies together. England and the empire rested secure again behind the overwhelming gun-power of the Royal Navy.[2]

The nub of the matter was 'the total destruction of German sea-power'; without that central fact firmly in mind it is not possible to make sense of much of what followed during the next twenty years. We have always to remember that by the terms of the Treaty of Versailles the German Navy was reduced to no more than six 'battleships' of no more than 10,000 tons, six cruisers, twelve destroyers and twelve torpedo-boats. There were to be no German submarines. When the knowledge of the naval terms that were about to be agreed at Versailles filtered through, the High Sea Fleet, surrendered and anchored at Scapa Flow, was scuttled by its crews in protest. By the time the Treaty was signed, the whole fleet lay on the bottom of the North Sea, scene of the failures of its disastrous lifetime. The U-boats were passing through the breakers' yards. The U-boat menace had died with German sea-power.

It is in the light of this fact that the frequent stricture, prompted by hindsight of World War II, that the Admiralty's neglect of anti-submarine warfare between the wars was a product merely of blindness and folly, has to be reconsidered. For most of the inter-war period, there was no submarine threat, no specific anti-submarine war to prepare for. What there was, however, was a continuing diminution of naval strength dictated by a Treasury in a permanent condition of dire dismay, and a major reorientation of naval strategy itself.

Retrenchment after war is a British tradition. The profligacy of war, the pouring out of resources only for destruction, has always outraged the country's 'solid citizens', the professional and trading classes. And this was never more true than in the aftermath of the First World War, which had witnessed destruction on a scale and in manners never previously experienced, but calling to mind such past horrors as the Thirty Years' War or the devastations of the Mongols and the Huns. When the Treasury and the new Chancellor of the Exchequer (Mr Austen Chamberlain)[3] came to count the cost of it all in 1919, they discovered a National Debt which had mounted from £650,000,000 in 1914 to £7,435,000,000 in 1918, and foreign debts amounting to £1,340,000,000.[4] These seemed to be very terrible figures – indeed, they were; and to Government, Industry and the City alike the necessity of making the earliest possible return to the international and domestic economic practices of 1913 seemed unquestionable and paramount. Above all, government expenditure, which had been practically limitless during the war, had to be cut – and in a world panting and exhausted by its greatest war, expenditure on arms was a very obvious target.

Of all military expenditures, the Royal Navy's was the most intransigent; the only cheap item in the Navy's locker was an Able Seaman. All major warships are very expensive indeed; in the 1920s it cost £1 million merely to modernize the battleship HMS *Queen Elizabeth* (her sister ship, *Warspite*, cost £2 million), while an entirely new battleship (HMS *Nelson*, 1925) cost £7,500,000. Out of a budget whose annual total sank to £51 million by 1930, these were large sums; and every class of vessel down to minesweepers, already expensive by the standards of other Services,[5] was tending to cost more and more right through the inter-war decades as equipment became more complicated and expensive, and sophistications multiplied. It is not surprising if two points of view, both devoutly and sincerely held, came quickly into head-on conflict. On the one hand there was the ingrained belief of the Admiralty and all navalists in an 'irreducible "minimum"' of British naval strength,[6] somewhat breathtakingly propounded in a Naval Staff memorandum in May, 1919. This proposed a post-war fleet of thirty-three battleships, eight battle-cruisers, sixty light cruisers and 352 destroyers, which, as Captain Roskill says,

> judged by any standard, was a generous provision for naval defence during the long period of peace towards which the whole world was then looking forward.[7]

It may be imagined how this programme was received by a Government which only three months later enunciated the policy which was effectively to hamstring all three Services for about a decade and a half. This was the other side of the argument: the notorious 'Ten Year Rule', laid down by the Cabinet in August, 1919:

> It should be assumed, for framing revised Estimates, that the British Empire will not be engaged in any great war during the next ten years.

It was the particular contribution of Winston Churchill, as Chancellor of the Exchequer in 1928, to make this Rule self-perpetuating, and thus completely crippling. In 1919 it had the effect of reducing an original Navy Estimate of £171 million to £90 million, which had already dropped to £58 million by 1923. Between 1920–1938 (inclusive) the average of annual Naval expenditure was £64.3 million; this is the grim fundamental fact against which all policies have to be judged. It is, however, important to hold it in perspective: the average of Army Estimates during the same period was £54.4 million, and of Air Estimates, £24 million.

For three centuries naval supremacy – or at the very least, naval invincibility – had been the cornerstone of British policy. In 1919 that ceased to be the case; built into the structure of the Treaty of Versailles was a League of Nations dedicated, among other things, to Disarmament, and meanwhile advocating that its members should no longer seek security through national armaments and alliances, but collectively, through the League. Britain was an enthusiastic member of the League of Nations, and 'collective security' – whatever that might mean – became Government policy at about the same time as the Ten Year Rule. And it was at this juncture also that two other disturbing factors swam into view: on 19 November, 1919, the United States Senate refused to ratify the Peace Treaty, thereby rejecting 'collective security'. And simultaneously, for the Royal Navy, a new potential enemy hove in sight. In the words of Stephen King-Hall:

> When the German battle fleet surrendered for internment to Sir David Beatty and the British-American battle fleet at Rosyth, the stage upon which the struggle for sea-power had been enacted revolved. The admiralties saw, not the shallow and narrow waters of the North Sea in which, since 1906, Germany and Great Britain had contended, nor did they see the blue waters of the Mediterranean where British and French had struggled in the time of Nelson and Napoleon. Instead of these restricted and historic waters the vast expanse of the Pacific Ocean came into view.[8]

It was Jellicoe himself, visiting India, Australia and New Zealand in late 1919, who first officially drew attention[9] to the probability of future war with Japan – and promptly received a sharp rap on the knuckles from the Board of Admiralty for daring to discuss such a matter. Yet before the year was out the Naval Staff was talking in

156

identical terms, and pointing out that in such an event a fleet base at Singapore would be needed. By May, 1921, the Naval Staff was assuming that there would be war with Japan in 1930. This was a startling development, and a poor accompaniment to Disarmament and 'collective security' – especially in the light of Jellicoe's warning that it would be 'unwise to depend upon United States naval co-operation'.[10] How had it come about?

Britain and Japan had been allies since 1902; the treaty of alliance was subject to review every five years, and so was due for renewal (or otherwise) in 1922. It had been of considerable value to Britain and her other allies between 1914–18, enabling the Royal Navy and its associates to concentrate in the main theatres of war. Japanese warships had helped to overcome the threat of German surface raiders by convoying the Australian and New Zealand forces to the Middle East; a Japanese destroyer flotilla did useful work in the Mediterranean, helping to escort troop convoys threatened by U-boats. For their part, the Japanese profited by the capture of the German base at Tsing-Tao and the extension of their influence in the province of Shantung. However, they were not satisfied with this and in 1915 they alarmed all and sundry (none more than the Americans) with their notorious 'Twenty-one Demands' to China – a warning that they had moved into an expansionist phase which was inadequately masked by their membership of the new League of Nations in 1919. When Jellicoe spoke of 'trouble with Japan', this was what he had in mind. And it was this sharp deterioration in relations between the two great 'Anglo-Saxon' naval powers and the rising force in the Far East that makes some sense of otherwise bewildering proceedings at the Washington Conferences of 1921–2.

From the naval point of view, it would be hard to overstate the importance of the Washington Treaties. They constituted, according to Correlli Barnett:

one of the major catastrophes of English history.[11]

Two in particular call for mention: the Five-Power naval treaty, which laid down ratios of naval strength, and the Four-Power treaty which was the device adopted by Britain to camouflage her non-renewal of the direct alliance with Japan. This it conspicuously failed to do; after 1922 the Japanese were increasingly isolated from the great Western Powers, and they knew it. And in the Admiralty,

It was clearly assumed by the makers of war plans that the Trafalgars and Jutlands of the future would be fought east of Singapore.[12]

The key words here are 'Trafalgars and Jutlands'. It is already evidence of some confusion of mind that the two battles could be bracketed at all: the only valid connection between them is the fact that both were fought almost entirely by the surface capital ships of their respective periods – the battle fleets. When one looks at their outcomes, it is contrast, not similarity, that seizes the attention. Nelson's victory was absolute, and supplied the warrant of British naval supremacy for a hundred and nine years. Jutland was a British victory, inasmuch as the High Sea Fleet, though it inflicted greater damage, failed to weaken the Grand Fleet to anything like the extent intended, and then fled the field, never to return to it.[13] But already, as we have seen, the decisive naval struggle had moved away from the surface fleets, and was being fought out by the Navy's anti-submarine forces against the enemy under the water. The battles 'east of Singapore', however, were not envisaged as contests with the Japanese submarine fleet; the spine-chillers for naval experts were such items as the already-commissioned battleships *Mutsu* and *Nagato* (33,800 tons, eight 16-inch guns) and two planned successors, *Kaga* and *Tosa* (39,000 tons, ten 16-inch guns). And to these traditional power-symbols would be added, as the brief inter-war decades slid by, a new dimension, a new distraction.

The outstanding feature of the story of aviation is the speed of its development. The maritime rôle of aircraft tells the same tale: only six years elapsed between the Wright brothers' breakthrough at Kitty Hawk in 1903 and Blériot's Channel crossing in 1909 which first made light of the sea. Thereafter, the air assault on the water barrier, which throughout human history had been the chief constraint upon the movement of man, progressed by rapid strides. The year after Blériot's flight saw the first step taken towards a sea-carrier for aircraft, when Eugene Ely took off from the deck of an American cruiser; the next year (1911) he capped that by landing on USS *Pennsylvania* and then taking off again. In May, 1912, Lieutenant R. Gregory RN made the first British flight from a ship under way. 1913 was the year when the term 'seaplane' came into general use, and as we have seen this type of aircraft swiftly became a mainstay of maritime air operations; but the challenge to it was not long delayed. The basic fault of the seaplane was that it was a fair-weather craft: taking off or attempting to come down on rough water could easily be fatal. The problem was how to make landplanes operationally effective at sea — in other words, to carry the feats of Ely and Gregory the necessary further stage forward so that aircraft could not merely take off from but also return to a ship under way. What was needed was an aircraft carrier [14] with a proper flight-deck, and by 1916 such a vessel was about to appear — a conversion of the 'fast battle-cruiser' HMS *Furious*. In August, 1917, Squadron Commander E. H. Dunning, RNAS, made air history by landing on *Furious* while she was under way. In July, 1918, the same ship made more history by flying off the first carrier-based landplane strike, when seven Sopwith Camels attacked the Zeppelin sheds at Tondern in Schleswig, destroying the airships *L54* and *L60*. Just under a year later, John Alcock and Arthur Whitten Brown made their non-stop crossing of the Atlantic in a Vickers Vimy bomber, conveying a strong hint that the very term 'landplane' might soon prove to be no more than a figure of speech.

So the aircraft carrier arrived, offering vast, if still imprecise new opportunities to the air arm. Three rôles for it were instantly perceived: reconnaissance, which seaplanes had failed to perform at Jutland, defence of the Fleet against enemy aircraft, and a strike capacity using torpedo-carrying aircraft. An excellent machine for that purpose was produced by Sopwith's in 1917, the Cuckoo; at the end of the year Admiral Beatty asked for 200 of these for use with the Fleet, and a squadron was actually embarked on the carrier HMS *Argus* (a converted foreign merchantman) in October, 1918. It was too early to envisage the aircraft-carrier as the capital ship of the future, but it was already impossible to contemplate a properly-balanced fleet without them. The misfortune was that, by the terms of the creation of the Royal Air Force on 1 April, 1918, the manning of aircraft, even on carriers, was an RAF function, while the ships themselves belonged to the Navy. This dual control was a running sore throughout the inter-war years, not resolved until 1937 when the Fleet Air Arm returned in its entirety to the Royal Navy.

Admiral Beatty, who became First Sea Lord in 1919, was at all times a stout defender of the battleship as the Navy's capital ship for the foreseeable future, but he was also a great supporter of the aircraft carrier. In July, 1920, he urged that, in addition to a fairly modest programme of new capital ship construction (modest, that is to say, in relation to existing United States and Japanese programmes and the advancing obsolescence of many of the Grand Fleet's battleships), it was essential to complete the conversion and construction of three aircraft carriers: *Furious*, *Eagle* and *Hermes*.[15] The total cost of this work was estimated at £84 million spread over five years. By later standards this is a trifling sum, but in the 1920s, with economic crisis mounting, and economy the Treasury's overriding aim, it seemed to be a great deal of money. Even the Admiralty could only contemplate it if construction of cruisers, destroyers and submarines was suspended for a year. However, the Washington agreements shortly wiped out even such modest progress as this (much, one may suppose, to the relief of the Treasury and the Disarmament lobby alike). In the event, only four new battleships were launched between 1918–39, and five carriers, of which only two were originally designed as such.

It has been thought necessary to discuss all these matters so that what might, as I have said earlier, otherwise be incomprehensible may assume at least some degree of rationality. To recapitulate, the esssence of the matter is that, first and above all, no submarine threat was visible in Home waters or their approaches; secondly, as regards the new potential naval enemy, it was Japanese battleships, not submarines, that were chiefly feared, and the building of the Singapore base that took financial priority; thirdly, as regards the advance of technology, the future danger was believed to be in the air, rather than under the waves. And so we find that the reduction of the large-ship building programme was not accompanied by any increase in the number of small craft which might be suited to anti-submarine warefare – indeed, rather the contrary. The 466 destroyers and flotilla leaders of November, 1918, (on which the burden of convoy escort and U-boat hunting had overwhelmingly fallen) were reduced to 201 destroyers and sloops in September 1939, of which 100 were Fleet destroyers which were neither available nor suited to escort work.[16] Perhaps worst of all was the fact that anti-submarine warfare, as a naval specialization, came to be regarded as a definite backwater holding out little prospect of promotion.

* * * * *

On 14 November, 1918, *Korvettenkapitän* von Arnauld de la Perière brought his boat, *U 139*, back into Kiel for the last time. He took in the scene that awaited him. Red flags were flying from all the warships in the base; Sailors' and Workers' Councils were in control of the port. When he had secured his boat, von Arnauld went below, put on his civilian clothes and quietly walked ashore to disappear from view. It was, as Admiral Jameson says, 'a queer finale for the most successful submariner in history'.[17]

For another U-boat captain, the commander of *UB 68*, taken prisoner on 4 October, the homecoming was delayed until July, 1919, by which time Kiel was barely recognizable as a naval base. The fleet had gone; most of it was already on the sea-floor at Scapa Flow. A few U-boats, excluded from the surrender, were being broken up under the supervision of an allied Control Commission.

> The naval station itself presented a dismal spectacle, the sentries offhand if not actively insolent, careless in dress and manner, smoking on duty, allowing their rifles to rust. These were some of the visible effects of mutiny and defeat; the inner scars left on the officers were probably not so apparent, but certainly more permananent.[18]

On 28-year-old *Oberleutnant zur See* Karl Dönitz, who came back to Kiel in July, 1919, the scars cannot have been easy to conceal. He had not taken easily to being a prisoner of war; he felt deeply the loss of four members of his crew when *UB 68* was scuttled. The British, military and civilian, regarded U-boat crews with considerable loathing in 1918, and made that clear. And all the news that Dönitz was able to glean from Germany was bad. He put on a convincing act of madness which resulted first in his being sent to Manchester Lunatic Asylum, but later, more satisfactorily, in his being among the earliest prisoners to be repatriated. The Germany to which he returned could only deepen, not heal, these scars.

Karl Dönitz entered the Imperial Navy as a cadet in 1910; in 1912 he was appointed to a ship which had a *rendez-vous* with destiny: the cruiser *Breslau* in the Adriatic. A Prussian Army custom adopted by the junior Service was the election of cadets to officer status by the officers of their unit – regiment or ship; election had to be unanimous and there was no appeal; the custom 'was designed as the final bar to any dilution of the social and spiritual homogeneity of the officer corps.'[19] Karl Dönitz passed the test and was gazetted *Leutnant zur See* (Sub-Lieutenant) on 27 September, 1913. He quickly won the high opinion of his captain and became the *Breslau*'s signals officer. August 4, 1914, found *Breslau*, in company with the new battlecruiser *Goeben*, off the Algerian coast, bombarding the French bases at

Philippeville and Bone. At 10 o'clock that morning the German ships had the enlivening experience of finding themselves in company with two British battlecruisers which stationed themselves on each quarter of *Goeben*, awaiting news of the expiry of Britain's ultimatum to Germany. *Breslau*, a light cruiser with no part to play in a contest of giants, was sent off to Messina to arrange coaling facilities; *Goeben*, forcing the last knot out of her engines, succeeded in drawing away from the British ships before their authority to open fire came through. So began the historic race eastwards to the Dardanelles Straits and through to Constantinople which tipped the balance of Turkey's entry into the war on Germany's side – there can be few parallels for such a large result ensuing from the action of such a small force. For Dönitz it marked the beginning of almost two years of distinctly active service in the Black Sea during which he made his mark in his profession; in his personal report in August, 1915, his captain wrote:

> Dönitz is a charming, dashing and plucky officer with first-rate character qualities and above-average gifts.[20]

These did not pass unnoticed in the quarters where it mattered; in the autumn of 1916 (now an *Oberleutnant*) he was ordered home to train for the submarine arm on which, as we have seen, Germany was by then pinning her hopes. So he bade farewell to *Breslau*, in which his most formative professional years had been spent, taking with him another glowing report:

> above-average talent, especially good professional ability, great professional interest and a strength of judgment exceeding that to be expected from his age and experience.[21]

The career of Dönitz as a submariner began on 1 October, 1916, not voluntarily, but in fulfilment of his duty as an officer of the Imperial German Navy, obeying orders. It was on that day that he reported to the U-boat School in Flensburg-Mürwik, and the next day his course of instruction began. He passed out on 3 January, 1917, with another excellent report which ended with significant words:

> Among his comrades he is very well liked.

And with this recommendation he went off to Pola to join his first U-boat, *U 39*, commanded by the already famous *Kapitänleutnant* Walter Forstmann (see p. 20). He could scarcely have found a better tutor in practical U-boat warfare. The declaration of 'unrestricted' warfare had just been made, to the great satisfaction of the U-boat arm, Forstmann not least. *U 39* sailed from Pola on 12 February, passing through the Otranto Barrage in the night of the 13th, and the next day Forstmann found his first quarry, an Italian steamer, which he promptly sank. This was the beginning of ten months of vigorous activity for Dönitz, under a prime submariner and leader who came to think as highly of him as had his previous commanders. Forstmann's report at the end of the year said:

> Sailed and navigated the boat calmly and confidently, is reliable as watch-keeping officer and understands the management of his subordinates . . . Lively, energetic officer, who enters into each duty with diligence and enthusiasm . . . Popular comrade, tactful messmate.[22]

The portrait of the true submariner comes out clearly from these words: diligent, enthusiastic (but also calm), tactful – the essential qualities. Efficiency and comradeship were the watchwords; Dönitz revelled in both.

Recognition was not long delayed; in December, 1917, Dönitz was ordered to a commanding officers' gunnery course in Kiel, and then came that memorable moment in a naval officer's life when he receives his first command – in Dönitz's case the 417-ton minelayer *UC 25*, also at Pola. In her he made two cruises, distinguishing himself in the first to the extent of being awarded the Knight's Cross of the Hohenzollern Order. When *UC 25* was paid off, he received a better command, *UB 68*, in which he made the one cruise which ended in disaster and captivity. According to his own account, this particular group of UB-boats suffered from a structural fault which had already required several modifications; this, he says, was his undoing. He had made one successful attack on an Allied convoy 150 miles east of Malta on the night of 3/4 September, 1918, and in the early morning gave orders to dive for another attack at periscope depth, but instead

> we suddenly found ourselves submerged and standing on our heads. The batteries spilled over, the lights went out, and in darkness we plunged into the depths.[23]

In theory, a depth of 180–200 feet was the maximum permitted by the UB-boat's pressure hull, but *UB 68* continued her frightening dive until the indicator quivered between 270 and 300 feet. Then, at last, her compressed air succeeded in blowing the tanks, giving her extreme buoyancy; *U 68* now shot upwards stern first, one-third of her length rising into the air with screws racing as she crashed to the surface:

> I tore open the conning tower hatch and glanced hastily all round. It was now broad daylight. I found that we were right in the middle of the convoy. All the ships, destroyers and merchantmen alike, were flying signal flags, sirens were howling all round us. The merchant ships turned away and opened fire with the guns they had mounted on their sterns, and the destroyers, firing furiously, came tearing down upon me. A fine situation! What I should have liked to do would have been to crash dive as quickly as I could. That, however, was impossible. My supply of compressed air was exhausted, the boat had been hit and she was making water. I realized that this was the end and I gave the order 'All hands, abandon ship'.

He omits to say that *Leutnant* Jeschen, the Chief Engineer, had the task of opening the seacocks; *UB 68* went down, according to survivors, in only eight seconds, and Jeschen was not able to get out in time. All in all, it was a bitter moment.

This, then, was the officer who stood on the quayside at Kiel in July, 1919, wondering how to pick up the threads of a shattered career. He was, to his fingertips, an officer of the Imperial Navy; it is important to be clear what that means. In that still young and predominantly middle-class Navy,[24] which has been called 'the one truly national institution in the German Empire',[25] the neuroses of the *parvenu* were visible. Socially it was overshadowed by the Army, itself under the shadow of the Prussian nobility; professionally it dwelt in the shade cast by the Royal Navy's three centuries of supremacy at sea:

> The compulsions of its officers were to be in attitude and conduct more noble than the nobility of the sword, in professional matters more professional than the officers of the Royal Navy, originally its professional model.[26]

Naturally, in middle-class officers born in the 19th century, there were likely to be some strong residues of the Liberalism and romanticism of that time. The powerful streak of chivalry in the make-up of, say, *Korvettenkapitän* Karl Müller of the famous cruiser *Emden* – whose boast was that in all his successful career as a commerce-raider, not one civilian life had been lost, nor even any civilian injured – was acknowledged by his enemies. Hans Langsdorff, of the *Graf Spee* in 1939, kept alive this tradition of 'gentlemanly' war – and no doubt there were others of the same cast of mind but less fame. But the Imperial Navy was not officered by Arthurian knights – middle-class or not, its traditions were rather those of the Teutonic Order.

It has been remarked that in 1900, when the Imperial Navy was well embarked upon its most ambitious and fateful expansion,

> The European world – was obsessed with the ideas of imperialism and world policy and the idea of sea power was an integral part of the larger imperial idea. Even sane people were victims of the obsession.[27]

It had been the mission of the Teutonic Knights to spread German religion and *kultur* eastwards by force of arms against the savage pagan tribes of Prussia and what were later known as the Baltic States. In the early 20th century, German expansion could only be overseas expansion, and this was the avowed aim of *Weltpolitik*; but wherever the Germans looked across the world, they saw the Union Jack, proclaiming that they had come too late. The whole purpose of the Imperial Navy was, by war if necessary, to reverse this state of affairs. It was no accident that 'the one truly national institution' should also be

> the very same institution at the heart of the struggle with Britain. . . . The fact that the Navy was middle class, liberal, nationalist and commercial, helps us to see why its fundamental strategy was aggressive and anti-British.[28]

In Dönitz the anti-British motivation of the Imperial Navy was always strong, intensified by the experience of captivity, and never faltering thereafter. He believed, as did his contemporaries, in the

Navy's historic destiny for Germany; at the backs of their minds, even amidst the worst humiliations of defeat, lingered the anticipation of *Der Tag*, however long delayed. Absolute loyalty to the Service and to the German State pervaded them all. They were accustomed to, respected and desired an iron discipline. The U-boat man, in particular, had no sense of having been beaten in battle, and viewed the miserable end of the U-fleet as a false, unjustified outcome which must be corrected. They were, in other words, highly combustible material.

Meanwhile, in the depressing condition of post-Versailles Germany, what was Dönitz to do? The Treaty permitted the Navy only 1,500 officers, which meant that it could choose carefully, selecting those most likely to prepare well for the day when it could once more point the way to German greatness. Significantly, Dönitz was among those who were asked if they would like to remain in the Service; his reply was equally significant:

> I answered with a counter-question addressed to the Director of Personnel. 'Do you think that we shall soon have U-boats again?' . . . 'I'm sure we shall,' he answered. 'Things won't always be like this. Within a couple of years or so, I hope we shall once again have U-boats.'
> This answer was all that I needed to persuade me to serve on in the navy.[29]

He was now heart and soul a submariner, and his explanation of this attachment helps us to understand the sympathetic authority which he would later display as the leader of the re-born Service:

> During the war . . . I had been fascinated by that unique characteristic of the submarine service, which requires a submariner to stand on his own feet and sets him a task in the great spaces of the oceans, the fulfilment of which demands a stout heart and ready skill; I was fascinated by that unique spirit of comradeship engendered by destiny and hardship shared in the community of a U-boat's crew, where every man's well-being was in the hands of all and where every single man was an indispensable part of the whole. Every submariner, I am sure, has experienced in his heart the glow of the open sea and the task entrusted to him, has felt himself to be as rich as a king and would change places with no man.

It is positively lyrical; it seems to belong to a different world from the shattering explosions, the fine ships torn apart or blazing from end to end, the last heart-rending plunges, the emaciated corpses of merchant seamen in open boats or rafts. However, the submariner's is a desperate trade, and it is understandable that they would fortify their spirits with a certain strumming of the lyre.

So Dönitz remained a naval officer, taking up an appointment as assistant to the Personnel Director (who was, in fact, his old flotilla commander, *Korvettenkapitän* Otto Schultze) on 14 August. It would, however, be a good deal longer than Schultze's 'couple of years' before he would actually handle U-boats again. In the meantime, surviving a third mutiny in the German Navy,[30] like a number of other submariners he went to torpedo boats, commanding *T 157*, one of the twelve permitted to Germany by the Treaty of Versailles. Circumventing the disarmament provisions of this treaty was now a prime object of the German Forces, quietly condoned by the Weimar Republic. Actual submarines would have been impossible to hide, but naval warfare studies could be continued, and in the winter of 1921 three such were concerned with U-boat topics, with emphasis on the night surface attacks which had become standard in 1918. As Dönitz's latest biographer remarks, 'a surfaced submarine *is* a torpedo boat',[31] so exercises in the torpedo boat flotilla could be directly related to the work that was nearest to Dönitz's heart. He spent nearly three years with these boats, rising in rank to *Kapitänleutnant*, and once more winning the golden opinions of his superiors: 'exemplary service outlook and fullest devotion to duty'; he handled his volatile and uncertain crew 'very sharply and militarily; despite this he is respected and popular with them'. Under a stiff exterior, it appears that he was also a good comrade on his small craft, 'full of hearty merriment at appropriate times'.

Dönitz's period as an active torpedo boat commander was interrupted by two shore appointments which could only further his main career. In 1923 he went to Kiel as an adviser (*Referent*) to the Torpedo, Mine and Intelligence Inspectorate, where once more his 'cheerful joy of life', which made him 'a very popular comrade', was remarked upon. Then, in the autumn of 1924, he was summoned to the very centre of naval affairs, the *Marineleitung* (High Command) in Berlin. Before taking up his post there, he attended a staff course presided over by *Konteradmiral* Erich Raeder, who would later loom large in his life. Raeder's first impression was a good one:

Clever, industrious, ambitious officer. Of excellent general professional knowledge and clear judgement in questions of naval war leadership. Good military as well as technical gifts.

With some perspicacity, Raeder recommended that 'he be employed not in one-sided technical positions but given opportunity for general military-seamanlike further training'. In the small post-Versailles Navy, this sequence of golden opinions, added to all that is implied in the phrase 'popular comrade', was already marking Dönitz out as a man with a future.

The *Marineleitung* at this time has been called 'a powerhouse of clandestine rearmament'.[32] The determination to thwart the drastic provisions of Versailles ran powerfully through the whole German Officer Corps – Army, airmen, surface Navy and submariners. In his new post (concerned with organizational and other internal matters) Dönitz did not have a direct hand in the subterfuges and ruses that were being adopted, but there is no doubt that he totally approved of them, and indeed, though his political position had not yet hardened out, it was the disgust that he and others felt at being compelled to serve a government which they regarded as having betrayed the Services, that would soon shape his thoughts. This sentiment was only partly eased by the accession of Field-Marshal von Hindenburg as President of the Republic in 1925. Hindenburg was a national hero – but Versailles remained.

Under its heavy shadow the Navy was nevertheless making small progress towards a revived U-boat arm. In 1922, under the direction of a former Chief Constructor at the *Germaniawerft* of Kiel, assisted by naval officers, a highly secret submarine construction office was set up in The Hague, camouflaged by the name of a Dutch firm: *Ingenieurskantoor voor Scheepsbouw* (IvS). The purpose of this was to ensure that a design staff should be maintained and built up. Another secret company (*Mentor Bilanz*) was formed in Berlin to become a clandestine building section, linked to IvS; technical staff from the naval construction office were provided for this in 1927. Carrying this story to the end of the Weimar Republic (since it marked the first provision of the tools of Dönitz's future trade and for a decisive battle in world history), we may note that already (July, 1926) trade missions had been sent to the Soviet Union to look for U-boat contracts; little came of these, but the subject was clearly becoming more pressing because, in the winter of 1926–7, eight out of ten naval studies were concerned with U-boats. 1928 was the year when *Admiral* Raeder became Commander-in-Chief, and in that year also *Mentor Bilanz* was replaced by a new company, *Ingenieursburo für Wirtschaft und Technik* (*Igewit*), whose purpose was to prepare for rapid rebuilding of a U-boat arm. At the same time an agreement was reached with Spain for the building of a 750-ton U-boat at Cadiz; after thorough trials by German officers and technicians, this boat was sold to Turkey in 1931. Meanwhile agreements had also been reached with Finland, which resulted in 1930 in the building of a small coastal (250-ton) U-boat designed by IvS which became the prototype of Germany's own renewed construction:

> Finally in November, 1932, two months before the National Socialists achieved power, General von Schleicher, probably the most devious character of the period, who had recently been appointed Minister of Defence and was to become the last Chancellor of pre-Hitler Germany in the following month, approved the plans to rebuild the German Navy, including 16 U-boats. Such plans had in fact been gestating in the utmost secrecy for at least five years.[33]

Dönitz, by now, was back at sea, as navigator of the cruiser *Nymphe*, the flagship of the Commander-in-Chief, Baltic. In November, 1928, he was promoted to *Korvettenkapitän*, and returned to torpedo boats to command the 4th Half-flotilla, which he called

> a magnificent command. . . . I was independent. Some 20 officers and 600 men were under me, a large number for a young officer such as I was.[34]

He was 37 years old. And in a sense, he now took up again where he had left off in 1923; it can scarcely have been accidental that once more the torpedo boats were understudies for submarines – the 1929 manoeuvres consisted of an attack on an 'enemy convoy' which the 4th Half-flotilla was fortunate enough to find and 'destroy' in a night attack. This command suited him perfectly, and his 1929 report reflects a leader in full control, right on top of his work; it concludes glowingly:

All in all – a splendid officer of worthy personality, equally esteemed as officer and man, an always tactful subordinate and excellent comrade.

The next year's report endorsed all that had been said before, and added this statement:

the welfare of his men claims his very energetic attention.

This is an attribute which the rank-and-file, at sea or on land, are always quick to perceive, and in their appreciation it reaps rich rewards.

It is at this stage that we encounter the first hint of a discordant note. The period 1930–34 is a somewhat shadowy passage in Dönitz's life; illumination falls only upon its less important moments. In October, 1930, he received a posting which he later described as 'first Admiralty staff officer and leader of the Admiralty staff office of the High Command of the North Sea station in Wilhelmshaven'.[35] It is not very clear what his duties were, and his own terse description serves more to conceal than to inform:

My tasks included measures of protection against inner (service) unrest. Often these questions were discussed in the Defence Ministry in Berlin with the competent representatives of all service commands.[36]

His only other comment was that this was 'truly a time filled with work' – overwork, perhaps, because his next report, while acknowledging his professional competence and calling him 'an excellent officer', also said this:

Very ambitious and consequently asserts himself to obtain prestige, finding it difficult to subordinate himself and confine himself to his own work-sphere . . . His strong temperament and inner verve frequently affected him with restlessness and, for his age, imbalance. Must therefore be brought to take things more calmly and not to set exaggerated demands, above all on himself . . . character is not yet fully formed and [he] is in need of strong and benevolent leadership.[37]

The officer who wrote this was Wilhelm Canaris, the enigmatic ex-submariner admiral who later became head of the *Abwehr* (Military

Intelligence) and was executed in 1944 for complicity in the July Plot. Canaris was devious, subtle, a man with private thoughts, not carried away by passions for the causes which he served; as Peter Padfield says, his comments

> are extraordinarily interesting because, for the first time ... we are receiving an impression as it were from outside the charmed circle of like-minded and dedicated career officers.[38]

Canaris was not the only one to detect, behind the cool, correct mask of the disciplined naval officer, a suggestion of abnormality, an apartness from the ordinary processes of the mind. This was not a rare characteristic in the early 1930s.

'Inner unrest' – inside or outside the Services – can very easily be a political matter, and political matters were very much to the fore in Germany as the Weimar Republic entered its last days. Adolf Hitler was the rising star – the touchstone; Germany divided on him, for and against. For traditional Army officers, the leader of the National Socialist German Workers' Party was still a corporal, an Austrian upstart and rabble-rouser. But for many naval officers, his message held an altogether different scale of importance. Padfield argues, with authority, that the notion of a set of dispassionate, politically neutral professionals is a myth:

> Hitler's racial and world views were nothing more than the propaganda of Imperial Germany rendered more brutally simple in his crude mind, and therefore keyed in with the naval officers' basic prejudices ... most naval officers who met Hitler personally were impressed. He had the Kaiser's extraordinary memory for technical detail and interest in ship design and weaponry; he appeared to have the future of the Navy at heart; above all he spoke of the future of Germany in terms they approved.[39]

The misreading of the frame of mind of men brought up in the Imperial Navy is really only an extension of a still widespread misreading of Wilhelmine Germany itself, based on sentimentality and a nostalgia for a German version of the '*Grande Époque*' which is largely a figment of imagination; as a German writer has said, it is only a part-truth that Hitler was the destroyer of Germany:

we must learn to understand that the destruction started with Bismarck's work and that the Wilhelminian epoch externally so glamorous contained the seed of death.[40]

And another, as early as 1920, recalled memories

of the byzantine emptiness and falsity of the spectacle and of the theatricality of the parades. . . . The brooding atmosphere of this empire of money-grubbers, in which, from time to time, there sounded the rattling of sabres or the music of waltzes.[41]

Through it all ran the undercurrent of premeditated aggression of which the Navy itself was the symbol, so that now, in the 1930s,

There was a deeper understanding between the frustrated officers of the *Reichsmarine* and the Nazis than a hatred of Communism and the Versailles Treaty; it was nothing less than a revival of the national goals of 1914.[42]

It was against this background, fully sharing these sentiments, that Dönitz formed his political stance; during this period he became a Nazi – not a 'half-Nazi', reluctantly forced into a position which he secretly disliked, but a real Nazi, a believer, the man who would one day succeed Hitler because he was by then the one man that Hitler could trust. His first meeting with Hitler was on 2 November, 1934, but there is no record of it; we do not know what subjects were discussed; we do not know what impression the new German Führer made upon him – all he ever said about it (on record) was that he had thought Hitler '*brav und würdig*' (both words can be translated as 'worthy') which is cryptic to say the least. It scarcely matters; he was already Hitler's man. Like every German serving officer he had taken the oath of 'unconditional obedience to Adolf Hitler' on 2 August, when the latter took supreme power on the death of Hindenburg. The point about the oath-taking, for Dönitz, was that he undoubtedly meant it. And very shortly he would be able to offer his most valuable service in fulfilment of it.

Dönitz missed the alarms and excursions which marked Hitler's march to power; he was travelling in the Far East on a Service grant while the Reichstag burned, the March election of 1933 swept Hitler into office, Germany became a dictatorship and the opposition was suppressed in a reign of terror. A year back in Wilhelmshaven followed. Padfield remarks:

> He must have found his internal security duties very much easier since active Communists had been rounded up and thrown into concentration camps.[43]

In October he was promoted to *Fregattenkapitän* and his annual report spoke of his 'magnificent intellectual and character gifts . . . outstanding leadership qualities'. These had their reward in June, 1934, when he was given command of the light cruiser *Emden*, built in 1925 and at that time undergoing a major refit. He took her to sea immediately after his interview with Hitler, on a prestige cruise which brought him once more to the Far East. He returned from this in July, 1935, by which time the naval scene had undergone a significant change: by the end of 1934 there were already parts of twelve U-boats awaiting assembly in Kiel.[44] On 1 February, 1935, Hitler gave orders for U-boat building to be openly resumed, and Dönitz, who was expecting to take *Emden* on a second Far East cruise, was told that instead he would be taking on the task of raising a new U-boat arm. His reaction was not quite what one would expect, but perhaps a measure of the ambitions which had been awakened within him:

> I cannot say that I was altogether pleased. The idea of a cruise to the Far East had been very alluring, while in the formation of the new, balanced fleet which we were planning, the U-boat would represent only a small and comparatively unimportant part. I saw myself being pushed into a backwater. Subsequent events proved that my opinion at the time was quite wrong.[45]

* * * * *

1935, a turning-point for Karl Dönitz, was a bad year for the world, for Europe, and not least, for the Royal Navy. In the Far East, the Japanese seemed poised for new aggression;[46] their last act of 1934, at the very end of the year, had been to repudiate the Washington naval treaty. No progress had been made with the Singapore naval base to offset the patent threat implied in this. In the Middle East, Italy (still in theory an ally) was making menacing gestures towards Abyssinia.

On 3 January the Emperor of Abyssinia appealed to the League of Nations for protection against this intimidation by a fellow League-member. This posed for Britain a hard choice between championing the League of which she had been an enthusiastic founder, or preserving the main line of communication of the Empire by turning a blind eye to Italy's wrongdoing. It was on the Fleet that the defence of the Mediterranean artery chiefly depended and the likelihood of Italian hostility was bad news indeed for the Royal Navy at a time when it had to contemplate implementing the 'main fleet to Singapore' policy and reckon with a revived threat in the North Sea as well. For on 16 March Hitler denounced the military clauses of the Treaty of Versailles, serving notice of the intention to raise a German mass army once again, with an appropriate air force to back it, and a new navy.

It was this background of mounting difficulties in all directions – the Japanese posture above all – that guided the Admiralty, and through it the Government, towards the 'abject surrender'[47] of the notorious Anglo-German Naval Agreement of June, 1935. It is a good measure of the general demoralization of politicians and Services alike in the mid-Thirties that a nation conscious of depending above all on its sea-power could voluntarily accept the German demand for a fleet amounting to 35% of British naval strength. What looks like wilful blindness is the further acceptance of a claim to build submarines up to 45% of British tonnage; yet the Naval Staff expressed the view that, by doing so, Britain had in some unexplained fashion 'mastered the submarine danger'.[48] One cannot be too harsh on the Admiralty and its advisers who defended the Agreement when one finds no less a figure than Admiral Beatty telling the House of Lords that 'now there was at least one country in the world with which Britain need not fear an armaments race'.[49] Padfield comments that in June, 1935,

> Both sides to the Agreement showed an amateurish gullibility about the real interests of the other; of the two the greater mistake was made by the Germans. . . . In the event they deceived themselves more dangerously than the enemy.[50]

That has the look of hindsight from a long way on.

So the U-boats signalled their return to the naval scene, greeted with a strange mixture of dismay and euphoria in British naval circles.

There were those who would echo what Sir Maurice Hankey[51] had confided to his diary already in 1932:

> it would be worth a lot to get rid of submarines and aircraft,[52]

but as no practical means of achieving this desirable end suggested themselves, the sentiment did not translate easily into policy. Admiral Chatfield, an energetic First Sea Lord who spoke with the authority of having been Beatty's Flag Captain at Jutland and a close associate of the Navy's hero, seemed to entertain two attitudes. On the one hand he could write in a Hankey vein of 'the insidious submarine and aircraft',[53] but in almost the same breath he would be asserting that the Navy's anti-submarine techniques would be found 80% successful, and even saying:

> our methods are now so efficient that we will need fewer destroyers in the North Sea and the Mediterranean.[54]

On 9 July, less than a month after the signature of the Anglo-German Agreement, the Germans revealed their own interpretation: the new building programme was announced, comprising two battleships (*real* battleships, not the pocket variety), two heavy cruisers, sixteen large destroyers, and no fewer than twenty-eight submarines, including two ocean-going (or 'Atlantic') boats of the kind that would later go down in history as Type VII. Those who had permitted themselves to suppose that the Agreement had been no more than a matter of principle received a rude shock; it was clearly a matter of considerable practicality as well. And those who had eyes to see derived little comfort later in the month when Britannia paraded her might at Spithead; 160 vessels lined up for royal inspection, among them two aircraft carriers. But experts could see without too much difficulty that, after one and a half decades of retrenchment, and talk of disarmament, 'the shop window was mainly filled with obsolete goods'.[55] Meanwhile, as the new German threat unfolded, this seriously weakened Service was faced with mounting crisis in the Mediterranean, culminating in Italy's declaration of war on Abyssinia on 3 October. Britain's support for League sanctions against Italy as the aggressor nation made it more than likely that hostilities would ensue; attention accordingly focused on the Mediterranean Fleet, whose deficiencies and weaknesses had previously been masked by more serious matters elsewhere. Worst of all was the evident fact that the fleet base at Malta was clearly untenable in the face of Italian land-based air power; in 1933 the Commander-in-Chief, Mediterranean, had estimated the cost of putting Malta's air defences in order at £150,000. It was more than the Navy could afford. So now, in the autumn of 1935, the fleet abandoned Malta – a sign of things to come. It has been said that British rearmament dates from 1934; as regards the Navy, in the sense that some progress was made from the rock-bottom expenditure of £50.5 million in 1932, the statement may be technically justified, but the bitter struggle with the Chancellor (Mr Neville Chamberlain) to raise the 1935 Estimates to just over £60 million, despite all the evident signs of the times, is indicative of how limited the progress was. And these were *estimates*; reality was a long way behind. It did not include very much in the way of effective preparation against submarines, of whatever nationality.[56]

The Admiralty's view of anti-submarine warfare now calls for further consideration. We have seen the formidable array of distractions which diverted attention from the subject between the wars; what we have not examined is what was probably the most formidable factor of all – the Admiralty's own frame of mind. At the centre of this, for reasons which still remain elusive despite Captain Roskill's exhaustive researches, is the curious but persisting belief that the main threat to trade in the event of war would be from enemy surface vessels, not submarines.[57] So firmly held was this belief that in March, 1935, the Parliamentary Secretary to the Admiralty, Lord Stanley, stated in the House of Commons:

> I can assure the House that the convoy system would not be introduced at once on the outbreak of war.[58]

He meant, of course, the *mercantile* convoys evolved with such success between 1917–18. As before (see pp. 49–50) there was no doubt or hesitation in the matter of *military* convoys. The Combined Exercises of the Home and Mediterranean Fleets in 1934, for instance, featured an attack by the Mediterranean Fleet on a convoy from the West Indies to Spanish waters, which the C-in-C, Home Fleet, escorted *with his battle fleet*. As late as 1938, in an exercise designed to demonstrate the protection of a large convoy against surface, *submarine* and air attack, we discover an escort consisting of two battleships, two battlecruisers, a carrier, a cruiser squadron and three destroyer flotillas! As Captain Roskill, who took part in some of these exercises, remarks, such a scale of protection (to say nothing of the 10-knot speed of the convoy) 'would of course be absurd for a mercantile convoy'.[59] And the same source brings us the amazing information that.

> not one exercise in the protection of a slow mercantile convoy against submarine or air attack took place between 1919 and 1939.[60]

Why? The answer seems to be as devastatingly simple as it is extraordinary. As we have seen (p. 30) ASDIC (sonar) had actually been brought into use in 1918, but too late to be effective in that war. In the post-war years very considerable progress was made with the development of this obviously important weapon. The Admiralty would appear to have been somewhat hypnotized by this. After a period of experiment, destroyers began to receive ASDIC in 1923, and after 1932 all destroyers were (as money permitted) fitted with it. By 1937 the Naval Staff felt able to pronounce that:

> the submarine should never again be able to present us with the problem we were faced with in 1917.[61]

What makes this statement the more remarkable is the fact that, in August of that very year, the destroyer *Havock*, passing through the western Mediterranean, through waters where Spanish Government, Nationalist, Italian and German warships were intermittently in combat, was narrowly missed by a torpedo. She obtained an ASDIC contact, but lost it, and though joined by other destroyers in an anti-submarine attack, no result was obtained. The submarine was, as it turned out, the Italian *Iride*, and though she was shaken by the attack, she survived. It was not a very encouraging performance, yet:

> This comparative failure of the Asdic does not appear to have shaken British confidence in its effectiveness.[62]

On the contrary, as late as March, 1939, Churchill asserted in a memorandum to Chamberlain: 'The submarine has been mastered.' It was an extraordinary delusion; one fact alone should have choked it at birth –

ASDIC, a valuable detector of a submarine submerged, was demonstrably useless against a submarine on the surface. Since, as we have seen, surface attacks at night were already a favourite tactic in 1918, this defect of ASDIC was clearly likely to become a serious matter. It certainly lends a strange colour to the Admiralty's confident prediction in 1937; we seem once again to be in the presence of that absurd but prevalent belief in all three Services between the wars that there was nothing to be learned from 1914–18 experience except how not to do things.

It was in keeping with all else in that depressing period – and yet another pernicious result of the perpetual shortage of money – that Naval Intelligence, like anti-submarine warfare, had become a backwater. The admirable organization built up by Rear-Admiral Hall, with its invaluable Room 40, was allowed to wither away; by the mid-Thirties there was little left of it. However, the *men* remained; it was fortunate indeed that one of them, Admiral Sir William James, who had been head of Room 40 in 1917–18, had risen to the position of Deputy Chief of Naval Staff in 1936, and at once took steps to correct what he perceived as a potentially fatal state of affairs. What was lacking and urgently needed was Operational Intelligence – the comprehensive scan of information from many sources to give a filled-in picture of enemy intentions, locations and capabilities. The activities of the Italian fleet, and especially its submarines, in the Spanish Civil War acted as a vigorous spur, and James, working through the Director of Naval Intelligence, Rear-Admiral J. A. G. Troup, won his point in 1937. In June of that year the task of co-ordinating Naval Intelligence was entrusted to Paymaster Lieutenant-Commander Norman Denning,[63] 'a born intelligence officer', who thus became the 'Father' of the Operational Intelligence Centre (OIC) of which we shall hear a great deal more. A vital subsection of this was created by Troup's successor, Rear-Admiral John Godfrey, early in 1939: the Submarine Tracking Room under Fleet Paymaster E. W. C. Thring who, like James, was an old Room 40 hand. Thring was now over 60 years old, but

he possessed a highly sceptical and analytical mind and a stubborn integrity which was not to succumb to browbeating from superiors in the Admiralry or the optimistic blandishments of juniors afloat.[64]

It was late in the day to be picking the brains of the men of 1918, but better late than never.

It was also in 1937 – a year which displays the Admiralty in a condition of marked perplexity and contradiction – that Lord Stanley's astonishing 1935 dictum received its quietus. A Shipping Defence Advisory Committee was formed, not a moment too soon, in February; at its second meeting it was once more Admiral James who brought light into a dark place. He stated:

> 'that the convoy system is considered by the Admiralty to be the most effective form of protection against surface, submarine or air attack', that plans had been prepared to introduce it in 'possible war areas', and that steps had been taken 'to ensure that there will be available for convoy work sufficient escorts' in whatever areas convoy 'may be deemed necessary'.[65]

At last a 1917 lesson had sunk in – but not universally, and not without difficulty, whatever history might say: shipowners and merchant masters were not all best pleased. As stated earlier, the Red Duster and the White Ensign did not readily seek each other's company.

Admiral James's third point, that 'steps had been taken "to ensure that there will be . . . sufficient escorts"', was, it has to be regretfully concluded, moonshine. True, in 1933 the Estimates had included a specially designed 'Convoy Sloop' – just one. And in 1935 the designation reappeared – one more. In December, 1936, the Admiralty had gone so far as to approve a 'legend' for convoy sloops,[66] but it can be a long haul from legend to launching. The battles of the Estimates, bitterly contested between the Treasury and the three Services, continued into 1938 and even into 1939, but it was in 1938 that the real national awakening came. The Czechoslovak crisis and the Munich agreement, which was greeted by many with heartfelt relief, but described by Winston Churchill as 'a total and unmitigated defeat', were in fact a turning-point; from then onwards the economists were in retreat – slow, reluctant, but nevertheless retreat. As late as February, 1939, the Treasury believed it had won some sort of victory by paring the naval Estimates down to £149.5 million; this was nearly twice the amount for 1937, and every penny of the increase had to be fought for.[67] But it was in this total that, as Roskill says,

for the first time heavy emphasis was placed on convoy escorts by including two score escort destroyers ('Hunt' class) and 56 of the new, easily built 'Whalecatcher type' corvettes ('Flower' class).[68]

We shall meet these ships again; meanwhile enthusiasm is somewhat tempered by the Admiralty's intrinsic contradiction. The need for escorts was recognized, but with it there remained an inexplicable addiction to the 'hunting groups' which 1917–18 had shown to be a complete waste of time and important resources. In a sharply critical vein, and with all the authority of Official Historian status, Roskill comments:

> If at the end of 1936 signs were not lacking that the navy was going to be very short of first class men at or near the top of the promotion ladder, the next two years were to make matters far worse.[69]

He was, in saying this, drawing attention to an unusual incidence of illness and death in the higher ranks at this time; illness would certainly help to explain what too often has the appearance of sheer lack of grip. One has to take into consideration also the exhaustion due to having to fight for pennies at every turn while the fleet visibly deteriorated and vital matters were ignored. Chatfield's very obvious pre-eminence only highlights the inadequacies of the men around him, and Chatfield ceased to be First Sea Lord in September, 1938.

Progress (or otherwise) with anti-submarine measures has, clearly, to be looked at always against the background of naval progress generally; in the last year of peace, if the anti-submarine element has a disappointing look, it merely reflects the condition of the Royal Navy itself – and the condition of the nation. Rearmament was at last in 'full swing'; which is to say that, by the standard of true requirement, some hesitating steps were now being taken (alongside a substantial expansion of the Royal Air Force and belated re-equipment of the Army) which seemed massive at the time but were still far short of the pressing necessities of war. The whole programme was, furthermore,

> blunted by inadequate home steel production from the very beginnings of pre-war rearmament in 1936. As early as December, 1936, the Admiralty was reporting to the Cabinet Defence Policy and Requirements Committee that new warship construction was being held up by delays in delivery of structural steel.[70]

Already, between 1914–18, the British steel industry had shown ominous signs of backwardness and inadequacy for modern war needs; by the late 1930s the situation was far worse. Correlli Barnett sums up the defects of this vital defence industry:

> plant already mostly obsolescent or even obsolete in date and design, organisation of production and marketing fragmented, leadership outmoded in outlook and often technically ignorant, research and development neglected and underfunded, workforce wedded to traditional methods and demarcations.[71]

It was a discouraging foundation for all rearmament (inevitably now undertaken against the clock). As may be supposed, such a situation produced some bizarre results, like, for example, in desperation ordering 15,000 tons of armour plate from Czechoslovakia's Skoda works for delivery by October, 1938.

There were other serious defects in a fleet whose modernization was long overdue: defects of design (some going back a long way, as in the battlecruiser HMS *Hood*, sunk in May, 1941, in a manner all too reminiscent of her three predecessors at Jutland in May, 1916). There were failings in gunnery, well attested by senior officers, and due in large part to production shortfalls of fire-control equipment. There was an even more serious weakness in the anti-aircraft department, which British industry was unable to remedy; once again the Navy (and the Army and Air Force) had to shop abroad, for Swiss 20-mm Oerlikon guns, the Swedish 40-mm Bofors and the American Browning machine gun. The contract permitting manufacture of the Oerlikon in Britain was not signed until 3 October, 1939. This AA shortcoming would account for the loss of many fine ships. Security was gravely compromised by the Admiralty's steadfast refusal to adopt the Typex signal ciphering machine (based on the German Enigma), despite having taken the original initiative in this direction in 1928. Lord Mountbatten, a vigorous advocate of the advantages of Typex, attributed this stubbornness to 'sabotage' by ultra-conservative members of the Board.[72] There was a general inability to see or foresee the effect that developments of air power would have on sea warfare, not least trade protection. The Navy, having won its battle for the return of the Fleet Air Arm in 1937, seemed to take the view that that was all that mattered; the Air Force, having lost the battle, lost interest in maritime uses of air power also. The result was that the RAF's Coastal Command became a 'Cinderella', with pitifully small numbers of antiquated aircraft, and no visible rôle in 1939 except North Sea reconnaissance.[73] In a sense epitomizing the general backwardness of naval thinking, matching the backwardness of *matériel*, there was a continuing attachment to, and religious belief in, the 'capital ship', which was seen as the battleship, and correspondingly grave apprehension about Britain's weakness in this category. The Empire's total of battleships and battlecruisers in September, 1939, was twelve, which was few indeed in the light of the 'worst possible case' – simultaneous war against Germany, Italy and Japan. As it turned out, battleships were *not* the capital ships of 1939–45, merely very costly items; but it must be acknowledged that this mistake was one shared by the Naval Staffs of *all* the major maritime nations, Germany as much as any.

Against this catalogue of woes, there were some longer-term gleams of hope in the scientific and technological pipeline. 1914–18 was, of course, the period of sensational technological take-off, with the *début* of military aviation, submarine warfare, radio communication and the wide application of the internal combustion engine amidst much else. There were not many things that were absolutely new in World War II, but those that there were had profound significance, while in many other fields the progress made was practically tantamount to innovation.

One such case was aviation. The 1930s saw great strides forward in all aspects of aeronautics, and as British rearmament, limping though it was, gained momentum, a striking transformation took place:

> The Royal Air Force in 1934 was a force of wooden bi-planes. By 1939, with a few exceptions at home and rather more overseas, it was a force of metal monoplanes.[74]

The metal monoplanes were capable of performances far beyond those of their predecessors; the advent of the high-performance 8-gun fighter was dictated by the anticipation of unprecedented combat speeds, and speed was what took the public eye during those years. When war came, the greatly increased range of the modern aircraft was to have even greater significance; it meant the ability to carry effective bomb-loads to Berlin and beyond; it meant land-based aircraft truly reducing the Atlantic to a 'pond'; it meant a rôle hardly foreseeable in 1939 for Coastal Command. And to enable the RAF's Commands to fulfil their rôles round the clock in all weathers, the aircraft borrowed from civil aviation a range of well-developed flying aids controlled by instrument panels (just beginning to appear in RAF machines in 1937)[75] incorporating ever-increasingly sophisticated navigational and identification systems. It was not easy at first to connect such matters with U-boats and underwater menaces, but it did not take very long for the connection to become apparent, and once more some attention paid to past lessons would have paid good dividends.

As we have seen, another innovation of 1914–18 was radio. It is difficult now to grasp and interpret a scene in which radio had become a familiar weapon of war of growing value and efficiency, but entirely lacked a commercial production base. It was not until the advent of the British Broadcasting Company in 1921 that manufacturers could look forward to a mass civilian market for radio sets and components. Unfortunately, this never produced the highly-skilled labour force and advanced methods of the great American corporations of which the British companies became, by 1939, in effect only out-stations. This was a serious matter in what proved to be, even before it had begun, a 'wireless war'. World War I has been aptly called 'the only war ever fought without voice control',[76] and the frequent criticisms of generalship in that war need to be carefully reconsidered in that light. In contrast,

> The Second World War was the first in which radio played a dominant part in tactical control.[77]

The Operations Rooms and sector Controllers of Fighter Command, the intercommunication between aircraft in flight or in combat, the Army's universal 'walkie-talkies', all illustrate the point. But nothing does so more vividly than the system of distant tactical control by radio employed by Dönitz for his U-boats, of which we shall have much more to to say. And to all of these voices in the air the indefatigable Listening Services paid unceasing attention, while D/F stations waited to pounce upon a 'fix'. It was, indeed, in the late Thirties that the British Services found themselves quietly 'entering the era of sophisticated electronic eavesdropping'[78] which would add a new dimension to war, and in the process test severely the scientific and technological capabilities of the nation.

Radar was something new. It was not, as British folklore long insisted, a breathtaking British secret, born at Weedon in February, 1935.[79] German research and development had begun in 1934 and, without realizing it, the RAF's Bomber Command would encounter the results operationally at the very beginning of the war. In 1939, indeed, German radar technology was more advanced than Britain's, but for once, and largely due to the thrust and coordination imparted by the Tizard Committee for the Scientific Survey of Air Defence, it was Britain that took the operational lead. British radar was undoubtedly cruder,

> but it worked and was proved operationally. These, in electronics, are the only two things that matter. Very advanced ideas are only useful if they are available off the production line when they are wanted.[80]

So it came about that in September, 1939, though the Germans could make good use of a few experimental '*Freya*' sets at particular points, Britain's 'Chain Home' screen could mount an effective 24-hour-a-day radar watch around a substantial length of the south and east coasts. There was a price to pay – there usually is: Sir Henry Tizard's prime concern was Air Defence, and it was towards this end that development was almost entirely directed. It is difficult to complain about that, but the fact often hides from view simultaneous movement in other directions. While Watson-Watt's team in the Radio Department of the National Physical Laboratory pushed vigorously ahead with Chain Home, Dr Edward Bowen and another group at Bawdsey Research Station were investigating airborne radar with an eye to two uses whose importance would soon be acknowledged: AI (Air Interception, for night-fighters) and ASV (Air-to-Surface Vessel, to locate ships at sea). In 1937 Bowen achieved important results in the latter direction, obtaining echoes from large warships at ranges up to five miles. He reported:

> these results encourage the hope that it will ultimately be possible to discover and locate ships at sea at distances up to about ten miles from an aircraft.[81]

The implications for anti-submarine warfare, as the essential complement to ASDIC, require no emphasis. In 1937, however, it was not German submarines, but German aircraft that preyed on men's minds. Bowen's work was a benefit for the future, but in the future it would remain for a long time yet.

Obviously, for the well-informed observer, these potentials in the late Thirties – long-range aircraft, radio control and penetration, D/F and radar – held out much hope in the long term, if one was permitted. For those requiring more immediate encouragement, hope could best be found in the condition of the enemy.

* * * * *

Dönitz's misgivings on taking up his new appointment in 1935 were not without reason. It is a simple, if extraordinary, fact that, as Padfield says, 'big-ship, big-gun men ruled at the *Marineleitung* in Berlin as they did at the British Admirality'.[82] The Kaiser's large surface fleet of 1914–18 had, one would have thought unmistakably, been Germany's outstanding failure of World War I. Yet in 1935 the German admirals (Raeder himself conspicuously) seemed unable to drag their minds away from big ships and big guns. Well before Hitler's advent, in May, 1931, in derision of the Versailles clause limiting German battleships to 10,000 tons displacement, the first of the 'pocket battleships', *Deutschland*, had been launched:

> At the sound of the *Deutschland's* name a shudder of apprehension vibrated down the keel of every 10,000 ton cruiser and of many a battleship of the world. And she was to be the first of six![83]

Well might the world tremble; the pocket battleships, actually displacing 12,000 tons, carried six 11-inch guns and had a maximum speed of 26 knots despite heavy armour. By 1935 there were two more, *Admiral Graf Spee* and *Admiral Scheer*. The classic development of a naval arms race at once ensued: the French riposted with the battlecruiser *Dunquerque* and her sister ship, *Strasbourg*, 26,500 tons, mounting eight 13-inch (330-mm) guns and capable of about 30 knots. This brought forth a German retort in 1934, the laying down of two fast battleships (the Royal Navy would call them battlecruisers), *Scharnhorst* and *Gneisenau*, 31,800 tons, mounting nine 11-inch guns,[84] and capable of 31 knots at deep load. Convinced that the threat to commerce was from fast surface raiders, the Admiralty was much alarmed at what it knew about these designs (if it had known the full truth it would have been far more so); but now it was at last able to begin upon the construction of a modern line of battleships at the maximum limit of the Washington Treaty (35,000 tons). This was the *King George V* class, originally planned to carry twelve 14-inch guns (later reduced to ten) with a

185

speed of 29 knots. The Germans immediately responded: it was in 1936 that they laid down the *Bismarck* (with *Tirpitz* to follow), ostensibly also conforming to the 35,000 ton limit, but actually displacing about 42,500 tons, mounting eight 15-inch (380-mm) guns and with a speed equal to that of the *King George V*s. Germany was thus on the way to possessing seven fast modern battleships, with another planned; *Admiral* Raeder even contemplated a ninth at one point. In addition there was to be a squadron of five heavy cruisers of the *Admiral Hipper* class, capable of 32 knots and mounting eight 8-inch (203-mm) guns. Inasmuch as the German Navy contemplated a trade war, it was to these fast, powerful surface units that it looked, rather than towards the few small U-boats which actually appeared in 1935. Even Dönitz himself is on record in that year saying that the U-boat was 'little suited' to the trade war 'in consequence of its low speed'.[85] How are these phenomena to be explained?

Hindsight is a trap; we have here to dismiss from our minds the coming Battle of the Atlantic; we have to forget the Nazi-Soviet Pact of 1939; we even have to forget Munich and the power-equation of 1938. In 1935 Nazi Germany was still an infant, unsteady on its feet. Its ideological message – for external as well as internal consumption – was a fierce anti-Communism which would find its expression the following year in the Rome-Berlin Axis and the Anti-Comintern Pact. The Soviet Union was a visible potential enemy; so was France. On 13 January, 1935, the Saar, administered by the League of Nations to make its coal available to France as reparation for war damage, cast its vote in a plebiscite controlled by an international force to decide its future. 80.8% of voters in a 97.9% poll voted for return to Germany – a triumph for Hitler and National-Socialist propaganda. Hitler thereupon pronounced:

> With the return of the Saar there are no more territorial claims by Germany against France, and I declare that no more such claims will be raised by us. We are now certain that the time has come for appeasement and reconciliation.[86]

On 1 March the Saar formally reverted to German sovereignty, and within a week Hitler's declaration lost much of any savour that it might have had for France with the revelation that a German Air Force once again existed, followed a week after that by the denunciation of the military terms of the Treaty of Versailles and the statement of intention to raise a conscript army of thirty-six divisions. For all the German military, Army or Navy, the implications of these factors were quite clear: in any immediate term, Germany's enemies were likely to be the USSR and France, soon linked in a treaty of mutual assistance.[87] And after June, as Dönitz tells us, with the signature of the Naval Agreement the rôle of the Navy became very much easier to define:

> Britain, in the circumstances, could not possibly be included in the number of potential enemies.[88]

This was only a half-truth; as we have seen a day of reckoning with the Royal Navy was built into the make-up of ex-Imperial Navy officers and the new Nazi intake alike. But that day was thought of as being at some distance in the future – somewhere in the mid-40s.[89] Meanwhile, strategy would be directed against Russia and France, and it is easy to see the immediate attraction of the battleship programme: once completed, it would ensure complete domination of Germany's 'private' sea, the Baltic. As for the U-boats, they might well find a rôle (as in World War I) interrupting communications in the Mediterranean – not British communications, but French communications with North Africa and the French possessions in the Levant. It all has a far-fetched sound about it; but there were some very far-fetched people at large in 1935.

Such was the confused but lively picture of policy and strategy when Dönitz returned to his beloved U-boat arm in June of that year; it was an exciting, but challenging moment, despite his reservations – as he says,

> Body and soul, I was once more a submariner.[90]

The main problem was that there were so few submarines; the full strength of the arm that summer was twenty-six boats, completed or under construction, made up as shown in the table on p. 188.

The pressing need was clearly to build more U-boats, and while this was being done Dönitz had a short interval between appointment and actual command during which he could clarify his ideas and evolve a system for their implementation. Always prominent in his mind was the faith which had come to him in 1917 and never faltered:

I believed in the fighting powers of the U-boat. I regarded it, as I had always regarded it, as a first class weapon of offence in naval warfare and as the best possible torpedo carrier.

In view of the part played by submarines in the two wars, it is easy, but incorrect, to think of them as Germany's natural arm of sea war. This was not the case; as we have seen, there was a powerful big-ship faction to contend with, and this was considerably fortified by scepticism about the real value of U-boats prompted by the British Admiralty's evident confidence that it had found the answer to them. Dönitz flatly rejected these thoughts:

> I did not consider that the efficient working of Asdic had been proved, and in any case I had no intention of allowing myself to be intimidated by British disclosures. The war was to show that I was right.

Type	Number	Displacement on surface/ submerged	Speed on surface/ submerged	Range on surface/ submerged	Armament	Crew
IA	2	862 tons 983 tons	17.8 knots 8.3 knots	6,700 miles at 12 knots; 78 miles at 4 knots	4 bow, 2 stern torpedo tubes; 1 105-mm gun	43

[This apparently powerful type was based on the boat built in Cadiz and sold to Turkey in 1931. Dönitz comments: 'Not a very satisfactory type: when diving rapidly it was inclined to become dangerously down by the bows and demanded very expert handling.' No further Type Is were built.]

| IIA | 12 (6 completed) | 254 tons 303 tons | 13.0 knots 6.9 knots | 1,050 miles at 12 knots; 35 miles at 4 knots | 3 bow TT | 25 |

[Dönitz comments: 'A very simple and successful vessel, but very small.' It was based on the design of the Finnish *Vesikko*.]

| VIIA | 4 (2 completed) | 626 tons 745 tons | 17 knots 8 knots | 6,200 miles at 10 knots; 94 miles at 4 knots | 4 bow, 1 stern TT; 1 88-mm gun | 44 |

[This type was also based on a Finnish model, the *Vetehinen*; Dönitz called it, very briefly, 'an excellent type'.][91]

He is entitled to that little piece of self-congratulation; in 1935, however, he did not have the benefit of the hindsight on which it is founded, yet he had to convert his officers and men to his way of thinking:

> I wanted to imbue my crews with enthusiasm and a complete faith in their arm and to instil in them a spirit of selfless readiness to serve in it. Only those possessed of such a spirit could hope to succeed in the grim realities of submarine warfare. . . . One of the first things I had to do was to rid my crews of the ever-recurring complex that the U-boat, thanks to recent developments in British anti-submarine defence, was a weapon that had been mastered.

This was the chief mission with which he took command of Germany's first new U-boat flotilla on 28 September. It was called the 'Weddigen Flotilla', after *Leutnant* Otto Weddigen, the famous commander of *U9* and *U29* in 1914 and 1915.[92] Despite its prestigious name, it was not a vastly impressive formation to outward appearances – just three Mark II U-boats. But this was the incubator of a prodigious brood, and Dönitz brought all his formidable powers of leadership and inspiration to his task. How well he succeeded with his main purpose is related by one of his original commanders:

> The salient feature of this training year, 1935–36, was the fact that it eradicated from the minds of all the commanders and their crews the inferiority complex which had undoubtedly been prevalent among them, and the idea that the U-boat had been mastered and rendered impotent as an instrument of war by recent highly developed anti-submarine devices.[93]

In those words we may read the rebirth of the high morale which had sustained the U-boat crews of the Imperial Navy to the very end and would be remarked upon equally in their successors.

Morale was the first fundamental; the second, as with all naval matters, was the nature of the sea itself. No true mariner takes liberties with the sea; no true mariner pretends to know all that is to be known about it. Dönitz (now *Kapitan zur See*) and his Chief Engineer, *Fregattenkapitän* Thedsen, were the only officers in the whole of the new U-boat arm with war experience, knowledge of what tricks the sea might play in operational conditions and what their effects might be:

The U-boat had to be equally at home on the surface and beneath it, for long periods at a time in the widest possible expanses of the open seas and in all weathers. Our aim, then, had to be to ensure complete acclimatization of the crews to life aboard ship, *complete familiarity with the sea under all conditions and absolute precision in navigation*, and particularly astronomical navigation.[94]

Dönitz kept the flotilla constantly at sea; always, as he says, 'an advocate of personal contact in leadership', he and Thedsen joined the boats in turn, supervising every aspect of a carefully thought out, detailed programme. The results were gratifying:

Very quickly the crews of the Weddigen Flotilla acquired a happy enthusiasm for their jobs and for their branch of the service. The systematic and thorough manner in which the training programme was carried out, the fact that we were always at sea, the feeling among the crews themselves that the training made sense, that they were improving and that their efficiency was increasing – all these combined very swiftly to give great impetus to the flotilla's endeavours.

It is hard to resist the conclusion that, in both wars, the German Army and the Navy took training more seriously than their British counterparts. (Whether the same is true of the 1935–45 *Luftwaffe* vis-à-vis the RAF is a moot point.) The German Navy insisted on a minimum of six months' training for all its crews, and succeeded in keeping to this even in the critical later stages of the war. Dönitz, in 1938, even put forward a scheme for a three-year training period which, if it does nothing else, shows how far he then was from recognizing the imminence of war. In 1935 he tried to put the Weddigen Flotilla through every possible circumstance or combination of circumstances that war might bring. His curriculum throws light on what it means to be starting at the very beginning, and what he meant by 'thorough'; it covered:

conduct of the ship when in enemy waters; the problem of remaining unseen – the commander being required to try and develop a kind of sixth sense with regard to whether he had or had not been observed when on the surface; the study of the question when to submerge in the face of a sighted aircraft or surface vessel and when it was permissible to remain on the surface; the invisible attack at periscope depth and with minimum use of periscope – by night taking advantage of background light, wind and sea to offer the smallest possible silhouette; the basic tactical principles, e.g. unobserved maintenance of contact and the reaching of a position ahead of the target, the changeover from day routine to night routine and vice versa; action in face of enemy defensive action, e.g. withdrawal on surface or submerged, when to remain at periscope depth and retain the power to observe, and when to dive and become blind, when to withdraw submerged at speed on a zig-zag course and when to slip away noiselessly at low speed; the technical control of the U-boat and the technique of diving, at all depths, at all times, and under conditions as close to those of war as possible; defensive surface and AA gunfire prior to an emergency dive.[95]

Every U-boat in the flotilla had to carry out sixty-six attacks on the surface and another sixty-six submerged before it even fired a torpedo. And when it did so, instead of firing at the officially prescribed range of 3,000 yards (to avoid ASDIC), Dönitz proclaimed his entire confidence in his arm by cutting the range to 600 yards.

In 1939 the U-boats seemed to spring fully-fledged, highly competent and lethal into the fray. It is an extraordinary reflection that they had had only four years to bring themselves to that state – and a tribute to Dönitz and his small (but growing) band of competent assistants. No other great power submarine service had to start from so far back; they all had a continuum of experience to draw upon, commanders and crews long past the 'A, B, C' stage of their profession. The Germans in 1935 started from scratch; for Dönitz this meant some very fundamental thinking, and since his conclusions left an unmistakable mark on the coming war, they deserve to be inspected. He divided his problems into three categories; the first proved to be the one in which he made his own most visible personal mark – the matter of control. He formulated this succinctly while in prison in Nuremberg in 1946:

The exercise of control. How far is it possible to exercise command over a number of U-boats? Is it possible during the actual attack or only as far as to ensure co-ordinated action before the attack? What is the ideal balance between the exercise of overall command and giving the U-boat its independence of action? Must command be exercised by a person actually at sea? In a U-boat? Or in a surface vessel? Is it, anyway, possible to exercise command from a U-boat? Can command be exercised wholly or partially from the land? Would it then be necessary to have some sort of subordinate, intermediate command post at sea? If so, where would the division of responsibilities between the two lie?[96]

All these were very basic questions. Other navies might have taken the answers to them for granted (perhaps unwisely); Dönitz could not. As commander of the Weddigen Flotilla he had to find his own answers; and when, on 1 October, 1936, he was appointed *'Führer der U-boote'* (*FdU*, U-boat Leader) the need for answers became even more pressing, for they would shape the whole arm. We shall shortly see how swiftly his ideas moved on this vital matter. Meanwhile, he had perceived another, arising from it:

> *Communications.* How can a U-boat be contacted when it is surfaced, when it is at periscope depth, when it is completely submerged, from another U-boat, from a surface ship and from a land station? What means of communication will be required? What wave-lengths, short, long, very long, should be used? What would be their range – by day, by night, in varying conditions of sea and weather? What about transmitting conditions aboard a U-boat? What facilities for transmitting and receiving must a U-boat have, if it is to exercise command? The whole question of transmitting, receiving and reporting beacon signals. Evolving of practical codes and phrases to be used in the passing of orders and reports.

Here we enter, through another door, that new world of radio communication which had been revealed in World War I and now offered such amazing possibilities. It was no bad thing to have to survey it now entirely afresh. From personal experience, Dönitz was very aware that, contrary to every other fighting system, the World War I U-boats had 'operated and fought alone'.[97] The introduction of the convoy system, he believed, had shown up the grave disadvantage of solitary operations:

> I was therefore clear in my own mind that this problem of the employment of U-boats operating together had to be solved.

'U-boats operating together', 'group tactics', 'wolf packs' – whatever the form of words, it would all depend absolutely on communications. Only with that problem solved could the next be approached:

Tactical. How should U-boats, operating together, act? While approaching their zone of operations should they proceed together and if so, how? Or should they be split up and, if so, in what sort of formation? What are the best formations and movements for conducting a reconnaissance, for giving support to other reconnoitring groups or for the U-boats to take over reconnaissance effectively from such other groups? What formation should U-boat groups detailed to deliver the attack use – close formation or extended, and if the latter, should they be extended abeam or ahead and what should be the distance between groups and between individual boats? Or should they be completely split up and, if so, how – in line, in echelon or what? How many U-boats are required to ensure maintenance of contact, should they and can they be detailed for this duty? How is relief to be effected, when will a U-boat maintaining contact be at liberty to attack? And many more questions.

It is as one ponders this list of searching queries that the deeply disturbing implications of the fact that in the Royal Navy at this time 'anti-submarine warfare . . . came to be regarded as a definite backwater' become apparent.

In 1937, after considerable trial and error, Dönitz reached one conclusion of the greatest significance; it was in the matter of control. He had been seriously considering whether it might be necessary to construct a 'special command U-boat, equipped with the necessary means of communication and with adequate quarters for the staff'. Clearly, it would be no easy matter – was it really necessary? In the autumn manoeuvres of 1937, he tells us,

> I was aboard a submarine depot ship in Kiel, from which by wireless I directed the operations being conducted by U-boats in the Baltic.

The next question was whether the same thing could be done for operations in the vast spaces of the Atlantic. It was not finally resolved until 1939, when further experiments indicated that 'control of operations could and should be exercised exclusively from a shore base'. This conclusion was to shape the coming U-boat war.

In the mood of euphoria following the Anglo-German Agreement, with a World War I style all-out attack on British trade ruled out, it was hard to reach realistic decisions about the tactics of U-boat groups. This meant, in turn, that it was hard to reach realistic decisions about the type or types of U-boats that Germany should build. Wrestling with these problems, Dönitz was able to arrive at some fundamental conclusions about the nature of the submarine as a weapon which would at the very least save him from serious errors and could lead him towards a wise choice of vessel. He was clear about one thing: a submarine, with its always restricted vision, is a very poor instrument of reconnaissance. This drew him to the appreciation that 'it must act in co-operation with a branch of the armed forces more suited to reconnaissance duties. And for these the best instrument is the aeroplane'. This awareness constituted the opening paragraph of what would become an unhappy chapter in the U-boat story. Meanwhile, by the same token, restricted vision made the submarine also 'a very poor gun platform'; nor was it suited to combined action with other types of naval craft. On the other hand, it was a 'first class torpedo-carrier', and also very suitable for mine-laying. In other words, its prime weapons would be what they had been between 1914–18, and the best U-boat would be one which could use those weapons with consistently good effect.

All this was considerably ahead of the thinking of the Naval Staff. It did *not* look favourably upon group tactics for U-boats, and the reasoning behind this is interesting in the light of what we now know but what Dönitz did not know when he wrote his memoirs in 1958. The Naval Staff, he tells us, rejected group tactics because:

> their use in action would involve too much breaking of wireless silence, which in its turn would enable the enemy to locate the U-boats and pin-point their position. I, on the other hand, held the view that the maintenance or breaking of wireless silence should be regarded purely as a matter of expediency and a means to an end and that the disadvantages inherent in the breaking of wireless silence should be accepted.[98]

What he naturally does not mention is the *Enigma* cipher machine which was in universal use by the German Services, and which proved in the Navy's hands to be a formidable opponent even for the best cryptological brains in Britain. But what we can now see is that in the matter of radio vulnerability, Dönitz was wrong and the Naval Staff was right.

In other respects, it was a different matter. For reasons now difficult to understand, the 'big-ship men' of the Naval Staff extended their dogmas into the U-boat arm; they believed, says Dönitz, that it was particularly necessary to build really big U-boats, U-cruisers of some 2,000 tons with a wide radius of action, spacious storage room for torpedoes and, above all, a vessel well found to fight a gun-battle on the surface. These cruisers, asserted the High Command, should stand first on the construction priority list.

The 'U-cruisers' were, as we know, another 1917–18 revival; we have observed their début in May, 1918, and their unimpressive perform-ance on the American eastern seaboard. There was nothing in that to warrant a fresh attachment to them, but the Naval Staff was quite determined, and Dönitz blames this for the very slow rate of construc-tion and delivery which followed:

1935	14 U-boats
1936	21 U-boats
1937	1 U-boat
1938	9 U-boats
1939	18 U-boats [99]

1937 was clearly a very disappointing year. Dönitz says that his differences with the High Command had by now become 'increasingly acute', which is understandable since it was at this time that Raeder was contemplating a ninth battleship – despite a serious steel produc-tion shortfall which Hitler appeared to believe that he could dispose of by a flourish of the pen, and Göring supposed that nationalization could instantly cure. Meanwhile the Spanish Civil War was polarizing Europe, and peace looked more precarious with every passing week. Dönitz says:

I became more and more inclined to the opinion that Hitler's policy and the resultant steady growth of German power must, notwithstanding the Naval Agreement, inevitably provoke an attitude of hostility in Bri-tain. . . . I believed . . . that war with Britain would soon be upon us and I pressed with increasing vehemence for an acceleration of the German submarine building programme.

The question remained, what kind of U-boats to build? Dönitz had no doubts, and the breakdown of construction figures between 1936–9 shows that he was able to prevail to a large extent, though not able to prevent the delays which he so much regretted. Out of the forty-six boats laid down in those years, twelve were Type IIs, thirteen were of the large type favoured by the High Command (Type IX), and twenty-one were Type VIIs. Dönitz had been doing some more fundamental thinking; he was persuaded that the torpedo, not the gun, was the true U-boat weapon. He also perceived that:

> The submarine is the sole class of warship which is called upon only on the rarest and exceptional occasions to fight one of its own kind ... The type of submarine can therefore be chosen without regard to the size of the submarines possessed by any other navy.[100]

Thus freed from the necessity for any kind of 'race' with any potential opponent in the manner of the surface craft, whose various types showed a universal tendency to grow bigger and bigger, Dönitz could assess the qualities of a boat purely in terms of its targets and its tactics. He definitely rejected size as a criterion; to build big submarines, he was sure, was simply wrong policy; it is worth considering what he has to say on this with some care:

> The fighting power of a submarine does not increase, as it does in the case of other warships, in proportion to an increase in its size. On the contrary, many of those characteristics from which the submarine derives its own particular value as a fighting unit tend to decrease in value once a certain size is overstepped.

He proceeds to enumerate the disadvantages of the large submarine; it is a formidable list, and one wonders, in view of his reputation and experience, what impelled the Staff to argue with him for so long. With a large boat, he says:

> The time which it requires to dive from the surface to a safe depth is increased. Submerging becomes a more difficult operation, too sharp a downward inclination enhances the hazards, because the greater length of a large vessel much increases the tendency to become down by the bows. The same applies when the submarine is submerged; the whole technique of submerging and surfacing becomes more complicated and, for the Chief Engineer, the technical officer responsible, more filled with imponderables. A large submarine is more difficult to con at peri-

scope depth than a smaller one. . . . This applies particularly to a submarine proceeding at periscope depth in rough weather or a swell. . . . Moreover the larger the vessel, the less handy and the less easy to manoeuvre it becomes; both on the surface and submerged it has a greater turning circle and therefore requires more time to turn through any given angle. Then again it is slower and more clumsy than a small craft in following the swiftly changing phases of an engagement – a particularly serious disadvantage where night operations are concerned. Finally, the larger vessel offers a larger silhouette and is therefore more liable to be discovered.

By contrast with this damning catalogue, the advantages of the Type VII were clear and decisive:

it was a reliable boat, easy and safe to handle. For its size it had the greatest possible fighting power. . . . Its diving time was 20 seconds; it behaved very well under water; and it was relatively fast – 16 knots – and handy on the surface.

The only important fault of the VIIA was that its fuel capacity gave it too small a radius of action – 6,200 miles. The ingenious Thedsen, however, soon came up with an idea for making better use of the existing space, and with only a slight increase of displacement he was able to increase that figure to 8,700 miles in the VIIB. It is interesting to compare the VIIB with a 1918 type – *U 105–114*, ordered in May, 1916, and completed by June, 1918:

	1918 U 105–114	*1939 Type VIIB*
Displacement: surface	800 tons	753 tons
submerged	1,000 tons	857 tons
Oil capacity	122 tons	108 tons
Maximum speed: surface	16.4 knots	17.2 knots
submerged	8.5 knots	8.0 knots
Maximum range: surface	3,900 miles at 8 knots	8,700 miles at 10 knots
		6,500 miles at 12 knots
submerged	50 miles at 5 knots	80 miles at 4 knots
Minimum diving time	approx. 60 seconds	20 seconds
Maximum safe depth	160 feet	650 feet
Torpedo tubes	4 bow, 2 stern (16 torpedoes)	4 bow, 1 stern (14 torpedoes)
Torpedo calibre	500-mm (395 lb warhead)	533-mm (770 lb warhead)
Torpedo range	1,100 yards at 40 knots	2,700 yards at 50 knots
Guns	1 105-mm or 88-mm	1 88-mm [101]

It will be noted that the Type VII was actually smaller and carried less fuel than the *U 105* class, and had one fewer torpedo tubes; the significant improvements were in diving time and permissible depth (stated figures for the latter, both in 1918 and in 1939, were often exceeded), and in the performance of weapons (when working properly). The most important improvement of all, however, does not appear in the table: radio equipment.

With small modifications, the Type VIIB became, in January, 1939, the Type VIIC – 'the main operational submarine used by the Germans during the war'.[102] Out of 691 Type VII boats built and commissioned, 650 were VIICs.[103] They were 220 feet long, with a 20.3-foot beam; in normal circumstances they could remain at sea for seven to eight weeks without refuelling. For their day, they were 'miraculous masterpieces of shipbuilding and weapons technology'; as regards comfort, little had changed since 1917 (see p. 22):

> There are no compartments aboard a submarine, such as you find on surface vessels. Even the customary divisions between the engine room, the hold, and the crew's quarters are absent. The inside of a submarine is rather like an express train carriage with an aisle down the middle and open areas leading off on either side. Even the 'wardroom' has traffic going through all the time. All those coming off or going on guard duty have to squeeze by the officers' mess table, which protrudes sideways into the aisle. The padded bench which seats the captain, an officer of the watch, and the engineer officer at mealtimes is actually the latter's bunk, serving double duty during the day. All paperwork is done atop the selfsame mess table, and that includes coding and decoding radio signals. The 'captain's cabin' is no more than a narrow recess separated by a green curtain from the centre passage.

Actually, there were functional divisions along this 'aisle', which comprised four sections. The aftermost contained all the machinery and electrical equipment, the air compressor and the stern torpedo tube. Here resided the two diesel engines, capable of generating 2,800 hp, and the two electric motors. Half the 50-ton storage batteries for these were under the adjacent deck plates, with a tiny galley, a washroom and the petty officers' quarters above. Midships was 'the heart and brain of the boat, the control room';[104] it contained a gyro and a magnetic compass, pumps, a fresh-water producer, the lower periscope, a chart closet with table and electrical gear to control the rudder and the hydroplanes. Forward of this was a radio room, a listening room, the four bow torpedo tubes, the other half of the storage batteries under the deck, a minuscule washroom, the captain's 'cabin', officers' and warrant officers' wardrooms and the crew's quarters. Finally, there was the conning tower, containing the attack periscope, the torpedo computer and the helm. Not an inch of space inside the pressure hull was wasted; along its whole length ran pipes, ducts and cables, interspersed with handwheels and instruments, with sausages and joints of smoked meat and oilskins among them; every locker concealed some link or junction behind its thin wooden door:

> In fact, the whole thing is nothing but a steel cigar crammed with machinery and weapons. Anything not of iron or steel looks totally out of place.[105]

Within this mechanical cloister, for weeks on end, forty-eight enforced celibates cohabited in close confinement; forty-eight was the regular complement, not counting passengers or trainees. Some of them, no doubt, had volunteered at the beginning, but the majority were conscripts drafted to the U-boat arm and then subjected to a rigorous selection process to make sure that they had the stuff of real submariners; in a submarine there could be no odd-men-out, no lone wolves in these packs. Conscripts they may have been, but conscripts with the right frame of mind; any misfits left after the stern training would be swiftly weeded out by the captain of the boat, who would almost certainly have started the same way. He was generally an *Oberleutnant* or *Kapitänleutnant*, whose word was always law, but who maintained his authority in a continuous proximity beyond anything known in all but the smallest surface craft. The Executive Officer and First Watch Officer was usually also an *Oberleutnant*, and was held responsible for the torpedoes. The Second Watch Officer was a *Leutnant*; his special duties were the radio and, in surfaced action, the gun. And there was the Chief Engineer ('the Chief'), usually a *Leutnant* too:

> The Chief Engineer is the commander's right hand. He is the absolute ruler of the engine rooms and responsible for precise depth control. He has to have something more than mere technical ability; as the man in charge of underwater steering he has to have a special sense which will enable him to anticipate the boat's every tendency to sink or rise, because by the time these show up on the instruments, it is usually too late.

These four constituted the normal complement of commissioned officers, with one or more midshipmen temporarily attached for training, and the occasional specialist aboard to observe or advise.

The Third Watch Officer and Navigator was a warrant officer (*Obersteuermann*); there were two more of these, and fourteen petty officers. Finally, there were the twenty-seven ratings with their various special skills. To accommodate all these men – often fifty or more – there were two lavatories, but one of these was frequently used as a storeroom holding extra provisions to keep the boat longer at sea. That meant one lavatory only, and even that could not be operated at depths below 80 feet. To use it above that depth involved manipulating various valves in proper sequence – 'a circus act to cope with the intricate machinery'. In prolonged rough weather, even on the surface, conditions inside the boat were purgatory:

> The stench of 51 sweating seamen, diesel oil, rotting food, and mouldy bread mingled with the noisome odours that emanated from the galley and the two tiny washrooms. The overbearing smells and the never-ending rocking made the men in the narrow drum dizzy and numb. Only the daily trim dive brought partial relief from the perpetual swaying. . . . Down in the quiet depth we finished the work we otherwise could not perform, had a meal without losing it on the deck plates or in the bilges. And for an hour or two we recuperated while waiting for the next assault of water and wind. These routine dives were never long enough, and surfacing always came too soon.[106]

Working beneath the sea is, like aviation, an unnatural occupation. Man is not a bird; he is not meant to fly. For that reason, as both civil aviation and the Royal Air Force well knew,

> Fear of flying was a factor to be reckoned with. Fear of *operational* flying was something that very few escaped.[107]

A very distinguished and highly decorated night fighter gunner and radar operator, Squadron Leader 'Jimmy' Rawnsley, bears witness to the constant struggle

> against an enemy that was much deadlier than the Luftwaffe. Human frailty and inexperience, and inadequate and unreliable equipment joined forces with the relentless and ever-present law of gravity, and a

foe so implacable just had to be given a name. We called him Sir Isaac Newton.[108]

Another name for him, of course, is Stress. For the submariner, one may substitute for 'fear of flying' 'fear of the depths', and the name of his Stress could be Davy Jones, whose famous locker too often came all too close. These basic stresses were things to be overcome as best one might – those who couldn't did not last the course. For each Service concerned, there were devices to help men to do this – the Royal Air Force's 'tours of duty', and for the U-boat men, whose living conditions were almost unbearably squalid without the addition of Stress as a shipmate, these were made bearable by a simple fact – that

> nobody lives on board when the sub is in harbour. This, too, distinguishes the submarine from other vessels. It does not provide the crew with a home.[109]

So the misery was finite, as the RAF airman's was, terminated by the end of a cruise and dry land once more – or Davy Jones's Locker after all.

Such, then, were the Type VIIs on which Dönitz increasingly relied; what depressed him was how few they continued to be – by the end of 1937 a mere nineteen. He was still a long way from persuading the Naval Staff to give them anything approaching the priority that he urged, and meanwhile Hitler's policies were bringing war palpably closer. This was the period of the 'Greater Germany' agitations, the demand for 'self-determination' for all Germans living outside the Reich. In the territory of the 'Free City' of Danzig, administered by the League of Nations, the Nazis obtained a two-thirds majority in the Diet in May, 1937, making conflict with Poland virtually certain. Meanwhile the scene shifted to Austria and Czechoslovakia to the familiar accompaniment of Nazi agitation, outcries about oppression and demands for 'self-determination', with the threat of direct German intervention barely concealed, if at all. Austria was specifically prohibited from political union with Germany by the terms of her peace treaty (the Treaty of St Germain, signed on 10 September, 1919). But Hitler was in no mood to be trapped by treaties; on 11 March, 1938, German troops crossed the frontier, and union (*Anschluss*) was proclaimed. Once more the League and the democracies proved powerless, encouraging Hitler to step up pressure on Czechoslovakia, with its three-million-strong German minority in the Sudetenland. The Nazis (who had gained over $1\frac{1}{4}$ million votes in the 1935 elections) demanded complete autonomy, and proceeded to stage 'incidents' to justify secession. This was the first Czechoslovak Crisis, which blew up in May, with partial mobilizations and troop movements on both sides of the frontier. May 21–23 were the critical days, but this time the world was granted a little breathing space. The immediate crisis died down, but it was on 28 May that Hitler told his Service chiefs of his 'unalterable decision to smash Czechoslovakia' and warned *Admiral* Raeder that Britain must henceforth be reckoned as an enemy – as Dönitz had concluded some time back.

Hitler's warning was accompanied by proposals for accelerated building of U-boats – and battleships. This should have been at least in part good news for Dönitz, but it turned out not to be, because the German Navy now gave an exhibition of muddled thinking and indecision beyond anything seen in Whitehall. Raeder appointed a committee, under the chairmanship of the Deputy Chief of Staff, *Vizeadmiral* Günther Guse, to make firm proposals for 'an agreed strategic basis on which the Navy can be built'. At the same time, as an aid to the committee, he ordered his chief staff officer, *Kapitän zur See* Hellmuth Heye, to draw up a plan of action against Britain. Heye's plan came before the committee for consideration on 23 September; the first presentation came as a shock to the 'big-ship' men present. Guse told them:

> Gentlemen, the plan of action that you have before you argues that we cannot successfully try conclusions with Britain by means of battleships.[110]

This was a promising beginning, but no more than that. When Heye's proposition met the response that may be imagined, the committee immediately went into defensive positions to protect the battleship programme. Heye argued that:

> Britain's vulnerability lies in her maritime communications. This postulates that all resources should be applied to mercantile warfare.

This was interpreted once more as the attack on trade routes by large surface vessels, leaving only the argument whether heavy or light ships would be better for the purpose. Heye was a believer in speed, and wanted light forces, but *Admiral* Carl Witzell, head of the Ordnance Department, argued:

> Only the heaviest ships could get the Atlantic striking force through.

And this opinion won the day.

What is amazing, in the light of 1915–18 experience, is first that there is no indication that the committee at any time felt any necessity to consult the *Führer der U-boote* about the rôle of his arm, even in the mercantile warfare for which it might be regarded as the natural instrument. And secondly, having expended much time and breath on the pros and cons of battleships, the committee appears to have uncritically accepted the view of U-boat potential put forward by Heye:

> There are grounds for assuming that the English counter-measures against U-boats, in particular (sound) detection, have reached an especially high standard. U-boats' attacks on English forces will therefore not be too successful. So long as no unrestricted U-boat war can be allowed, 'cruiser war' against merchant ships – if it is *only* conducted by U-boats – will have a limited effect. It comes down to the fact that the single U-boat by its nature does not come into question for 'cruiser war' on the high seas, but must be employed in a more or less stationary rôle.[111]

Evidently the German Navy, like much else in the Third Reich, was operating in closed compartments. Only *Admiral* Hermann Böhm, the Fleet Commander designate, disputed this extraordinary statement – extraordinary because it was so totally at variance with Dönitz's teachings within the U-boat arm itself. At the seventh meeting of Guse's committee on 17 October, Böhm stated:

> In a war with Britain I place the strategic possibilities in the following order: firstly the use of U-boats and mines; secondly, a series of raids against the vessels of the British strategic blockade . . . thirdly, the type of mercantile warfare which rightly figures so prominently in the plan before us.[112]

Even coming from such a quarter the wind of sanity did not prevail.

It will be convenient to take this story to its termination, which was not long withheld. Seizing on every word that favoured the big ships, and either omitting or diluting every contrary opinion, the committee made the report which found its expression in the barely credible 'Z Plan'[113] for future naval expansion, launched on 29 January, 1939. As originally envisaged, it was a long-term project, due for completion in 1948. By that date it called for:

Type H battleships (56,000 tons +)	6
Bismarck type battleships (42,500 tons)	2
Gneisenau type battleships (31,800 tons)	2
Pocket battleships (12,000 tons)	3
Battle cruisers (30,000 tons)	12
Aircraft carriers	8
Heavy cruisers	5
Light cruisers	24
Scout cruisers	36
Destroyers	70
Torpedo boats	78
U-boats (Atlantic types)	162
(Coastal)	60
(Special Purpose)	27

U-boats total: $162 + 60 + 27 = 249$

In German naval parlance, this was a 'balanced fleet'; in the sense of containing a bit of everything, the phrase may stand; in the sense of any practical utility, the whole thing was rubbish. Indeed, it was worse than rubbish; it was fantasy of a kind that men in positions of power entertain at their peril. Padfield questions both Raeder's intelligence and his moral courage at this juncture; rightly, for the Commander-in-Chief knew, if no one else did, how far existing construction programmes were lagging. He knew about the perennial shortage of steel, he knew the gigantic labour force this Plan would call for, and he could envisage the technical problems that it was bound to throw up. Yet he endorsed it, and put it to Hitler, who seized upon it, giving it 'priority over all other rearmament plans and even over exports'[114] – but demanded at the same time that the Plan should be completed not in ten years but in six. Even at that, Raeder did not protest. Hitler told him:

For my political aims I shall not need the Fleet before 1946.[115]

And Raeder believed him.

Dönitz's mind, during this time, was working on entirely different lines – as Raeder also knew. During that winter, 1938–9, the *FdU* conducted a war game 'to examine, with special reference to operations in the open Atlantic, the whole question of group tactics – command and organization, location of enemy convoys and the massing of further U-boats for the final attack'.[116] From the progress and result of this game he drew certain highly important conclusions:

> If, as I presumed, the enemy organized his merchantmen in escorted convoys, we should require at least three hundred operational U-boats in order successfully to wage war against his shipping.

Padfield questions how he arrived at this number, remarking that 'for all the explanation in [Dönitz's report] the figure might have been drawn out of a hat'. But Dönitz tells us:

> In arriving at this figure I assumed that at any given moment one hundred U-boats would be in port for overhaul and to give the crews a period of rest, a further hundred would be on their way to or from the theatre of operations, and the remaining hundred would be activiely engaged in operations against the enemy. Given this total, however, I believed that I could achieve a decisive success.

By the time Dönitz submitted his official report (13 April, 1939) the Z Plan was in full swing. The discrepancy between his own demand for 300 'operational' boats for the Atlantic, the 162 projected for that area in the Plan *by 1948*, and the actual number in commission (only thirty-eight Type VIIs and Type IXs completed by 1 September) was glaring, and its meaning obvious:

> With the number of U-boats already available and with the additions which, according to prevailing construction priorities and speed of building, we would hope to receive, we should not, for the next few years, be in a position to inflict anything more than 'a few pinpricks' in a war against merchant shipping.

It was a depressing prospect, and this recognition of it marks the beginning of a long, uphill struggle to set it right. But the immediate future held only more shocks and even more alarming expectations.

Europe's tolling bell was already strident and persistent; German troops entered Czechoslovakia on 15 March, and a week later the (mainly German) 'autonomous region' of Memel was seized from Lithuania. On 3 April Hitler ordered his Service chiefs to draw up plans for 'Case White' – an attack on Poland to be timed for 1 September or thereabouts. On the 28th of that month he repudiated the 1934 Non-Aggression Pact with Poland and the 1935 Naval Agreement with Britain. The latter, remarked Dönitz, 'was an exceptionally strong political measure',[117] which is no more and no less than the truth. Scarcely had its implications had time to sink in, when with much trumpeting Hitler and his Italian understudy, Benito Mussolini, signed their 'Pact of Steel' (22 May). The next day Hitler explained to the Service chiefs what his reasons were for attacking Poland; he warned them that this could mean war with France and Britain and even mentioned the need to occupy the Low Countries as a base for operations against the British. The Army leaders took the opportunity to produce their plan for the overthrow of Poland in three months' time. In the teeth of all these signals, the admirals and the *FdU* clung to their hopes that there might still be time to carry out at least a fair part of the Z Plan, and get more U-boats built. As late as 22 July Raeder, addressing the officers of the U-boat flotillas at Swinemünde, gave them a personal assurance from Hitler:

He would ensure that in no circumstances would war with Britain come about. For that would mean *Finis Germaniae*. The officers of the U-boat arm had no cause to worry.[118]

With a mind as devious and deluded as Hitler's, it is impossible to tell whether he really supposed that deceiving the men whose loyalty was vital to him was some clever move, or whether he actually believed his own utterances. For Raeder and Dönitz, this promise was the last ray of hope for the fulfilment of their own plans, but within a month it would be extinguished in the diving swirls of the U-boats moving to their war stations, and the demise of the stillborn Z Plan fleet.

All through August the political tension grew; by the middle of the month the imminence of war could not be disguised. On 19 August fourteen Type VII and Type IX U-boats left Kiel and Wilhelmshaven, bound for the Atlantic; two more very shortly followed. The pocket battleship *Admiral Graf Spee* left Wilhelmshaven on the 21st, followed by her sister ship *Deutschland* on the 24th; favoured by dense fog, both entered the Atlantic undetected. On 25 August fourteen Type IIs took up positions in the North Sea. Thus thirty U-boats and two major surface units were already at large and ready to strike by the last week of August. And, what was worse, the Royal Navy (and the RAF) was entirely oblivious of the fact; as one naval officer, holding what would soon become a key position, remarked:

Our Intelligence was not so much inefficient as totally inadequate.[119]

Certainly the contrast with World War I is very painful, and it has been distinctly misleading. The apparent high state of German preparedness is a mirage; as Cajus Bekker says:

Despite all the tactical precautions it set in train, the High Command of the German Navy did *not* believe that there was to be war with Britain. Not then, at least, in 1939 – and not because of Poland.[120]

Dönitz, nearly twenty years later, wrote with undiminished bitterness:

Everything had gone contrary to my expectations. . . . The navy was like a torso without limbs. . . . We were now paying dearly for the holiday years, so far as U-boat construction was concerned, of 1936–7 and for the very inadequate use we had made in 1938 and 1939 of the tonnage allotted to us under the Anglo-German Naval Agreement. And in consequence we now found ourselves at war with a meagre grand total of fifty-six boats in commission [actually fifty-seven]. . . . And to crown all, we were haunted by the knowledge that even this state of affairs did not represent the lowest ebb in our U-boat strength, which would only be reached later. In fact, we did not come to it until February, 1941, when the grand total of our operational boats fell to twenty-two. Seldom indeed has any branch of the armed forces of a country gone to war so poorly equipped. . . . If only in view of the very weak state of our naval power, then, war in 1939 should have been avoided at all costs. . . . But our leaders failed to appreciate the real situation . . . and there then arose one of the most tragic situations in naval history.[121]

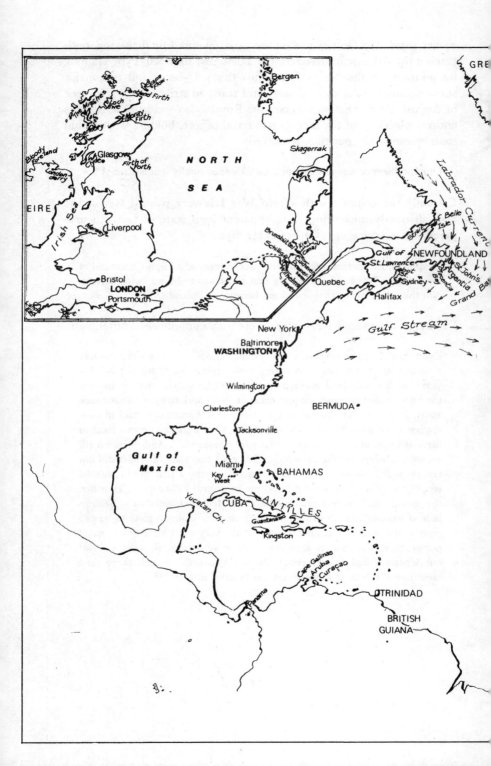

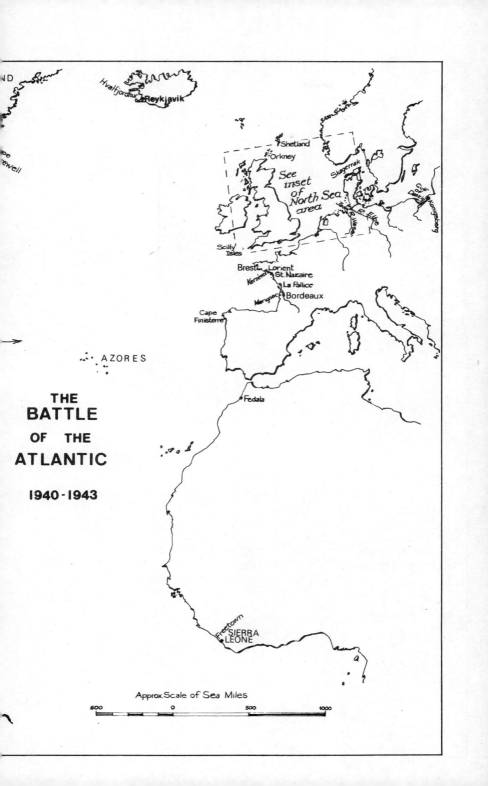

THE
BATTLE
OF THE
ATLANTIC

1940-1943

Approx. Scale of Sea Miles

PART III

THE SECOND ROUND
1939–1945

'In all the long history of sea warfare there has been no parallel to this battle, whose field was thousands of square miles of ocean, and to which no limits of time or space could be set.'
Captain S. W. Roskill, DSC, RN: The War at Sea ii p. 335; HMSO 1956

1

Dearth of U-boats

'The salient feature of our present position is the dearth of U-boats at our disposal.'

Admiral Dönitz, 1 October, 1939

ON THE DAY that war with Poland began (but still believing there would be no war with Britain) Dönitz moved to the timber barracks on the edge of Wilhelmshaven which housed the headquarters of U-boat Command West. The ocean-going U-boats were at his personal disposition, for which he answered directly to the Naval Staff; for the time being, however, he came under the authority of Naval Group West in matters regarding the operations of the Type IIs in the North Sea. His Chief of Staff was *Fregattenkapitän* (later *Konteradmiral*) Eberhardt Godt, whom he described as 'a man of unshakeable imperturbability, who was of immense assistance in arriving at a factual appreciation of any given situation'.[1] Godt would remain with him to the end, and Padfield remarks that

The two made an excellent combination, Dönitz providing the fire and drive and inspiration, Godt the calm efficiency of the ideal staff officer.

But he adds:

All that was missing from the team was a strong critical, analytical brain.[2]

Also present for a while at Wilhelmshaven was *Fregattenkapitän* Hans von Friedeburg, described by Dönitz as 'a particularly gifted organizer and a man endowed with an exceptional capacity for work'.[3] Just over a fortnight later, he sent von Friedeburg back to Kiel to become Chief of the Organization Section, U-boat Command. As such, his most important duty was to provide the crews of newly-commissioned U-boats with that thorough and well-thought-out training which sustained the arm through all its adversities and contributed so greatly to its triumphs.[4]

Wilhelmshaven, once the unlovely [5] home of the High Sea Fleet and scene of its mutiny and humiliation, stood in a roomy bay about ten miles across at its widest point at the mouth of the River Jade. Outside the bay, and offering an outlet both from the Jade and the River Weser, on which stood the great port of Bremen, were the Schillig Roads and then Cuxhaven at the mouth of the Elbe, leading to Hamburg. Twenty miles across the estuary from Cuxhaven stood Brunsbüttel, the western exit of the Kiel Canal. The whole of this complex has been called, in naval terms, Germany's 'back-yard'. So it was; her 'front door' was the Baltic coast, some 450 miles of it as the crow flies from Flensburg in the west to Königsberg in the east. But the Baltic is a poor starting point for the world's great oceans, its sole exit being through the Belts and Sounds of the Danish islands and then the Skagerrak with all the North Sea beyond. In World War I, the High Sea Fleet had been more or less confined to the 'back yard', a circumstance whose disadvantages, as Dönitz remarked, 'had become very obvious'; now, from his own viewpoint as *FdU*, disadvantages were again apparent:

> Britain's vital arteries, which had to be attacked, lay to the west of the British Isles on the high seas of the Atlantic. . . . Germany's position for the deployment of her naval forces in the Atlantic is just about as unfavourable as it could possibly be. We live, in relation to the British sea lanes, in a sort of blind alley.[6]

All this became very material on Sunday, 3 September, when all doubt and hope were swept away; the British ultimatum was received at 9 a.m., with a two-hour time limit. No answer having been received, at 11.15 the Admiralty sent out the signal 'Total Germany' to all its fleets and stations. This was naturally picked up immediately by the

German listening service (*Horchdienst*) and disseminated through the *xB-Dienst*, the cryptanalysis section of Naval Intelligence (*B-Dienst*). At Wilhelmshaven, the Signals staff officer, *Leutnant* von Stockhausen, interrupted Dönitz's daily conference to show him the teleprinter message. Evidently disconcerted, he crumpled up the paper, tossed it down in front of Godt and began to pace up and down. Staff officers heard him murmur to himself and repeat:

> *Mein Gott! Also wieder Krieg gegen England!*
> (My God! So it's war with England again!)

Then he abruptly left the room and was gone for about half an hour. When he came back he was a changed man: 'Dönitz had come to terms with himself.'[7] He brought to the assembled officers a message whose ingredients would become familiar:

> We know our enemy. We have today the weapon and a leadership that can face up to this enemy. The war will last a long time; but if each does his duty we will win.[8]

Absolute loyalty to the Nazi leadership, deep faith in the U-boat arm itself, and a realistic appreciation that this was going to be a hard war to win: that was Dönitz's stance and he did not depart from it.

The U-boat war lost no time in declaring its nature and indicating where its decisive theatre would be. Among the boats positioned around the British Isles in preparation for war was *Leutnant* Lemp's *U 30* (Type VIIA), out in the Atlantic some 250 miles north-west of Ireland. That very evening Lemp sighted a large vessel, with a high superstructure, outward-bound and zigzagging on a course which seemed to him to be well off the normal shipping routes. He concluded, it was later said, that it must be a British armed merchant cruiser, and at 2100 hours he fired two torpedoes, both of which hit the target. This proved to be the 13,851-ton Donaldson liner *Athenia*, carrying over 1,100 passengers, of whom more than 300 were Americans, from Liverpool to Montreal. One hundred and twelve lives were lost, of whom twenty-eight were American:

> From the sinking, without warning, of a passenger ship, both Allies and neutrals concluded that Germany had consigned the laws of naval war-

fare to the scrap-heap and from the outset released her submarines from all restrictions.[9]

The echoes of the *Lusitania* were loud and clear; the memories of 'unrestricted' submarine warfare flooded back. This time, it seemed, the Germans had been even quicker off the mark than in 1914; 1917 had returned in one swift bound.

The contrary was true. Still reeling from the shock of the British ultimatum, it was no part of Hitler's policy to risk offending neutral – above all, American – opinion. Accordingly, acting on instruction from above, Dönitz's orders to his Command on the afternoon of the 3rd had been quite definite:

> U-boats to make war on merchant shipping in accordance with operations order.[10]

That meant, he says:

> The U-boats had to wage war in accordance with the conditions laid down in the Prize Ordinance. These were the same as those contained in the London Submarine Agreement of 1936. That is to say, *the U-boat was required to act in the same manner as a surface vessel*; whether the merchant ship were armed or not, the U-boat had first to surface before it could halt and examine it. If, under the conditions of the Prize Ordinance with regard to nationality and/or cargo, the U-boat was entitled to sink the vessel, it was first required to ensure the safety of the crew; on the high seas the lifeboats carried by the merchant vessel were not deemed to be adequate for the purpose.[11]

The only exceptions to this rule were merchant ships which could reasonably be said to be performing as instruments of war – vessels under armed escort, vessels taking part in an operation or resisting inspection, vessels acting as military transports. In all other cases, the Prize Ordinance held good.

Dönitz had never much cared for this inhibition, which he regarded as seriously reducing the operational value of the submarine, but he had faithfully passed on the directive issued to him. And now Lemp had put the fat in the fire. What was almost as bad was that he made no report, so that the only information available in Germany was what London chose to say about the sinking. Undeterred, the German Propaganda Ministry roundly asserted that no German warship had been anywhere near the *Athenia*, that what had sunk her must have been either a British mine or a British torpedo and that it was most probable that the deed had been instigated by Churchill as First Lord of the Admiralty in order to inflame American opinion. Since Dönitz and his staff knew quite well what *U 30*'s location was, they were, says Padfield, 'whether they liked it or not, accomplices to this deliberate campaign of lies'.[12]

Lies and deceptions are, of course, stock features of the weaponry of every nation, and it is difficult to see what other procedure the U-boat Command could have adopted towards the propaganda outpourings. Operationally, what it did on 4 September was to issue at 1655 a reminder to all U-boat commanders that:

Existing orders for mercantile warfare remain in force,

and to follow this up at 2353 with:

By order of the Führer passenger ships until further notice will not be attacked even if in convoy.[13]

When Lemp came home from his cruise at the end of the month, he did not return to a hero's welcome. On Raeder's instructions, he and his entire crew were sworn to secrecy, the log was 'doctored' to omit all mention of the *Athenia* sinking, and the Headquarters record similarly corrupted to credit *U 30* with the sinking of only two small vessels totalling 9,699 tons. All this, says Padfield, made the U-boat Command not merely accomplices, but 'active accomplices' of the propagandists.[14] He is on safer moral ground when he looks a little further ahead, to 24 September, when Dönitz signalled to his boats:

Armed force should be used against all merchant ships using their wireless when ordered to stop. They are subject to seizure or sinking without exception.

There had obviously been a change of mind at U-boat Headquarters since 4 September; this was, as Padfield says, 'the first turn of the screw'.[15] The second was not long delayed: permission to sink without warning any vessel sailing without lights was given on 2 October. Once more, logs were to record such occurrences 'as due to possible confusion with a warship or auxiliary cruiser'. None of this need occasion any surprise; it merely bore out what Sir John Fisher had prophesied in 1913, and pointed up his dictum that 'the essence of war is violence, and moderation in war is imbecility' (see p. 5). Moreover, the momentum of such thinking, once accepted, appears impossible to check; by the end of November Dönitz's ideas had moved on again, as we discover from his Standing Order No. 154:

> Rescue no one and take no one aboard. Do not concern yourselves with the ships' boats. Weather conditions and the proximity of land are of no account. Care only for your own boat and strive to achieve the next success as soon as possible! We must be hard in this war.[16]

Once again, the echo is precise – February, 1915: 'The first consideration is the safety of the U-boat' (see p. 9). So much for the Prize Ordinance; clearly, whatever name it might now be given, Unrestricted Submarine Warfare was once more coming on apace.

It was easier to dispose of the inhibitions of 'International Law' than to overcome the inhibition of the dearth of U-boats. The thirty boats at sea when war broke out were a freak circumstance; when, one by one, they came in from their cruises there was very little to replace them on the distant patrol stations. The actual total available for operations rose slightly in October, but according to the U-boat War Diary it was unusual for more than six to eight boats (about a third of the 'Atlantic' Types VII and IX) to be on station at any given moment.[17] And thereafter the totals themselves began to fall:

December 1939	38
March 1940	31
June 1940	26
November 1940	25
February 1941	22 (the all-time low)

These were the figures that haunted Dönitz and his Operations staff for the first two years of war as debts haunt a bankrupt. Indeed, so conscious was Dönitz of the centrality of this issue that, at the very outbreak of war, he came to an astonishing decision which he inscribed in the War Diary:

I have made up my mind. The obviously right thing is for me to take over control of the U-boat expansion programme as Director General, or something of the kind at Naval High Command ... if we do not swiftly succeed in building up a numerically powerful and efficient U-boat arm, the fighting efficiency of the arm as it now stands might well deteriorate to such an extent that even the presence of its commanding officer would be of no avail. For this reason the task of supervising the expansion of the U-boat arm as a whole must be regarded as by far the most important task which Naval Command can be called upon to under-take.[18]

Not surprisingly, Raeder disagreed. He refused to sanction Dönitz's application for transfer to Berlin on the simple grounds that he was 'indispensable where he was with his combatant forces'.

The campaign in Poland in September, 1939, was a triumph for the German Army and Air Force. Warsaw fell on 27 September and all organized Polish resistance ended a few days later.[19] Flushed with a victory whose speed surprised even him, Hitler nevertheless found time to spare a thought for the Navy, engaged in its very different war against its very much more powerful enemy. On 28 September he visited the U-boats and their Command Headquarters in Wilhelms-haven. Dönitz seized the opportunity to urge once more the matter that was closest to his heart. He told Hitler:

After a careful examination of the whole question of U-boat warfare, I am convinced that in the U-boat we have, and always have had, a weapon capable of dealing Britain a mortal blow at her most vulnerable spot.

The U-boat war, however, can only be successfully waged if we have sufficient numbers available. The minimum requisite total is 300 U-boats. . . . Given this number of boats, I am convinced that the U-boat arm could achieve decisive success.[20]

Hitler, says Dönitz, 'made no comment at the time'. The truth would seem to be that, in this moment of wonderful success, the *Führer* was actually in dire strategic confusion. To the last moment he had clung to the hope that there would not be war with Britain; even now he continued to hope that this war could be limited and short. He had just partitioned Poland with his Non-Aggression partner, Stalin, and apparent cordiality reigned between them. But his anti-Soviet sentiments were only in temporary hiding awaiting an opportunity for a fulfilment which the brilliant performance of the Army and Air Force now made credible. He knew enough history, however, to recall that in 1914 *Generaloberst* von Schlieffen's famous war plan had called for no more than holding operations on the Eastern Front, pending the overthrow of France, which was intended to take place in only forty days. The failure to defeat France in the time given had led to the long war which ended with Germany's defeat. This time, Hitler determined, there should be no such mistake – and what the Army and Air Force had done in Poland promised to bear him out; this time France would definitely be smashed first. So U-boats, though he saw the point of them well enough, and admired their enthusiastic and highly professional *FdU*, came some distance down the production priority list.

When the coming of war swept away the Z Plan, all that survived of it intact was the U-boat building programme, calling for production of twenty-nine boats a month. This looks impressive, but even at its face value, Dönitz remarks, the prospect was far from brilliant:

> The time between the placing of the order and the delivery date was estimated at between two-and-a-half years and one year and seven months. This, in my opinion, was far too long; and before the U-boat became fit for operations it would require a further three or four months for trials and training. It seemed therefore that I could not count on any increase in the number of boats available for operations before the second half of 1941, practically two years after the outbreak of war.

No, indeed; not a brilliant prospect; and any attempt to improve it ran at once into the block of Hermann Göring in his capacity as economic overlord of Germany. Raeder, on 10 October, asked Hitler for full powers to regulate U-boat priorities in industry, raw materials and manpower. He was told:

> As Field-Marshal Goering already possesses the widest possible powers, the Fuehrer and Supreme Commander of the Armed Forces has refrained from granting any subsidiary emergency powers to cover the period of the U-boat building programme.

As a consequence, in March, 1940, Raeder was compelled to drop the monthly target from twenty-nine boats to twenty-five. As Göring proved immovable in the matter,[21] the figure of twenty-five, accepted as an expedient, became a permanent programme; but even that was illusory:

> In actual fact the monthly delivery of submarines in the first half of 1940 averaged two boats; in the second half of the year this rose to six boats per month. In the first six months of 1941 the monthly delivery rate was only thirteen . . . and it was only in the second half of the year that this rate started to rise, and then it only reached twenty boats a month.

These numbers form the bedrock fact about the first stages of the second U-boat war.

Considering their implications, the U-boats themselves did well. According to his naval adjutant, *Fregattenkapitän* von Puttkamer, Hitler, at the end of his visit to the U-boats,

> carried back to Berlin an excellent impression of the leadership of the U-boat arm as well as of the liveliness and spirit of the crews.[22]

Well he might; they had had a good month. For a submarine, the way to avoid trouble was to remain well below periscope depth – at the price of blindness and passivity. Dönitz called this 'surrendering oneself to the deeps', and his Standing Order No 151 warned against such a course.[23] He need not have worried; these resolute, peace-trained commanders and crew did not need to be exhorted. In September fifty-three Allied and neutral ships were sunk, a total of 194,845 tons; U-boats accounted directly for no fewer than forty-one ships (153,879 tons), while mines, whether laid by U-boats, destroyers or aircraft, were responsible for another eight sinkings (29,537 tons). This was a substantial achievement, at a cost of only two boats (to which we shall return); it contained a disappointment, but that was offset by a particularly brilliant success.

The disappointment was on 15 September, when *U 31* (*Leutnant* Habekost) sighted and reported an outward-bound convoy in the Bristol Channel. Dönitz ordered three more boats to the area (commenting 'if only there were more boats at sea now!'), but the concentration came to nothing and no attack developed. The success came two days later; on 17 September the fortunes of war smiled upon *Leutnant*

Schuhart's *U 29*. She was almost at the end of her patrol, and looking for a convoy in the Western Approaches from which she might add to the three ships she had already sunk, when with some amazement Schuhart saw a large aircraft carrier in his periscope. It was the 22,500-ton *Courageous*, on anti-U-boat duty not normally part of a carrier's curriculum, in fact taking a risk which according to Churchill 'it was right to run',[24] but which the Official Historian calls 'surprising'. It was only by chance that *U 29* sighted her; it was by chance also that her escort consisted of only two destroyers (the other two had gone to help a merchantman), and it was by chance that her turn in order to fly on her aircraft brought the U-boat into an ideal position for attack. Schuhart made no mistake, firing three torpedoes at less than 3,000 yards of which two hit the target, which was enough. *Courageous* sank in fifteen minutes, taking with her 518 of her complement of 1,260. It was 'the first major U-boat success of the Second World War',[25] and it is scarcely surprising that Dönitz, in the War Diary, called it 'a glorious success'. It was the very thing to lift morale sky-high – as Hitler found it on 28 September.

Scarcely had this feat entered the annals of submarine warfare than another, even more spectacular, followed. This was an exploit very close to Dönitz's heart – indeed, one stemming particularly from him. He tells us:

> From the very outset I had always had in mind the idea of an operation against Scapa Flow.[26]

The famous home of the Grand Fleet in World War I, and of the Home Fleet in World War II, was one of the most formidable, or forbidding, targets that the U-boats could have attempted. Not merely was it defended by every device that the Royal Navy could muster at its vitals, but through the sounds and channels of this miniature Orkney archipelago within an archipelago run some of the most alarming currents and perplexing tides in the world. In the Pentland Firth, dividing the Orkneys from the mainland of Scotland, are whirlpools capable of turning a dreadnought round and a race running at 10–14 knots[27] – which can create difficulties for a submarine with a maximum underwater speed of 7 knots. Dönitz brooded upon these matters until 26 September, when an excellent, informative set of aerial photographs supplied by the *Luftwaffe* revealed a difficult but just possible means of entry into the broad, calm waters of the Scapa Flow anchorage. He decided to make the attempt, and entrusted it to *Kapitänleutnant* Günther Prien of *U 47*:

> He, in my opinion, possessed all the personal qualities and the professional ability required.[28]

Dönitz was right, and what followed on 14 October is now familiar naval history. Prien's log does it full justice:

> 14.10.39 . . . We are in Scapa Flow.
> It is disgustingly light. The whole bay is lit up . . .
> We proceed north by the coast. Two battleships are lying there at anchor, and further inshore, destroyers. Cruisers not visible, therefore attack on the big fellows. Distance apart, three thousand metres. Estimated depth, seven and a half metres. Impact firing. One torpedo fired on northern ship, two on southern. After a good three and a half minutes, a torpedo detonates on the northern ship; of the other two nothing is to be seen.
> About! Torpedo fired from stern; in the bow two tubes are loaded; three torpedoes from the bow. After three tense minutes comes the detonation on the nearer ship. There is a loud explosion, roar, and rumbling. Then come columns of water, followed by columns of fire, and splinters fly through the air. The harbour springs to life. Destroyers are lit up, signalling starts on every side, and on land, two hundred metres away from me, cars roar along the roads. A battleship had been sunk, a second damaged, and the three other torpedoes have gone to blazes. I decide to withdraw . . .
> at 02.15 we are once more outside. A pity that only one was destroyed.
> . . . The crew behaved splendidly throughout the operation.[29]

It is difficult to think of any U-boat exploit during the war to equal this; the battleship sunk was the *Royal Oak* (launched in 1914) destroyed by Prien's second salvo; she went down in thirteen minutes, with twenty-four officers and 309 men. With her went all sense of security in the Scapa anchorage, and the Home Fleet, which since early September had been 'commuting' between the Firth of Forth, Scapa and Loch Ewe on the west coast of Scotland, gave up once more the idea of returning to its main base. It was 1914 all over again, but with the destruction of two of the fleet's major units now to contemplate.

It is small wonder, then, that of all the U-boat commanders, Prien was Dönitz's favourite. He was, said Dönitz,

> all that a man should be, a great personality, full of zest and energy and the joy of life, wholly dedicated to his service and an example to all who served under him. Typical of the man and his outlook is a remark he made before the war, when he said: 'I get more fun out of a really good convoy exercise than out of any leave!' In war, notwithstanding his sudden leap to fame and popularity after the Scapa Flow exploit, he remained a simple, frank and courageous fighting man, intent only on doing his job and adding to his exploits.[30]

A somewhat different impression of Prien is recorded by William Shirer, the American foreign correspondent, who encountered him in Berlin only four days after the sinking of the *Royal Oak*:

> October 18
> Captain Prien, commander of the submarine, came tripping into our press conference at the Propaganda Ministry this afternoon, followed by his crew – boys of eighteen, nineteen and twenty. Prien is thirty, clean-cut, cocky, a fanatical Nazi, and obviously capable. Introduced by Hitler's Press chief, Dr Dietrich, who kept cursing the English and calling Churchill a liar, Prien told us little of how he did it. He said he had no trouble getting past the boom protecting the bay. I got the impression, though he said nothing to justify it, that he must have followed a British craft, perhaps a minesweeper, into the base. British negligence must have been something terrific.[31]

Prien was evidently giving nothing away, and telling his tale with some cunning. Shirer's deduction that he had followed a British vessel into Scapa Flow was clever but very wide of the mark. *U 47*'s route had been chosen by Dönitz, using charts and the air photographs,[32] and endorsed by Prien, who had visited the Orkneys as a 'holiday-maker' before the war and had carefully studied the entrances to the Flow.[33] This route did not go near any boom. However, Shirer's last remark seems to be not without substance: if the Germans, on the strength of such information, could see a way into Scapa Flow, it should surely not have been impossible for the Home Fleet's staff to do likewise and take special precautions until the danger point could be permanently sealed.

Dönitz, meanwhile, had been coming to certain conclusions about the trade war, irrespective of operations against the Royal Navy. On 1 October he had been promoted to *Konteradmiral*, and on the same day he decided to switch his main effort down to the vicinity of Gibraltar, which he considered 'a focal point for the concentration of shipping'. His reasons for this were, first, the strength of British defences, sea and air, operating from numerous home bases; secondly, the deteriorating weather of northern latitudes; and thirdly, as ever, the difficulty of finding convoys with so few U-boats. It is interesting to note that he still thought in terms of local tactical control of U-boat operations, exercised from one of the boats themselves:

Commander (*Fregattenkapitän*) Hartmann will proceed to sea in *U-37* in command of this Atlantic group and will direct operations against convoys as opportunity occurs.[34]

On the day after Prien's success, Dönitz was appointed *Befehlshaber-* (Flag Officer) *der-U-boote* (*BdU*), a sign of Hitler's satisfaction with the U-boat arm. He now took control of all U-boats, no matter where they were operating. And for a little longer, until his main force was compelled to return to refuel and rearm (and rest), his business continued to thrive excellently. Out of forty-six Allied ships sunk in October (196,355 tons), the U-boats accounted for twenty-seven (134,807 tons; mines, often laid by U-boats, took another eleven ships, 29,490 tons). So the 'brisk initial skirmish'[35] of the submarine war drew to an end, with the creditable score of sixty-eight ships (288,685 tons) to the U-boats' account in two months. The price was seven U-boats: three IXAs, one VIIA, one VIIB, two IIBs; between 300–350 officers and men. Dönitz was alarmed at these losses (three of them by mines) and noted in the War Diary on 23 October that they

must lead to paralysis of U-boat warfare if no means can be devised of keeping them down.

The five Type VIIs and Type IXs represented almost 25% of the total available, which was indeed a serious matter, to say nothing of the loss of trained crews. But the U-boat arm had made its mark in unmistakable fashion.

Pride goeth before destruction, and an haughty spirit before a fall (Proverbs xvi, 18).

The next two months saw a steep fall in sinkings by U-boats[36] – to 51,589 tons (twenty-one ships) in November and 80,881 tons (twenty-five ships) in December. In January, 1940, there was an improvement: 111,263 tons (forty ships), and in February the best total so far: 169,566 tons (forty-five ships). But this was a flash in the pan; the average tonnage sunk during the next three months was no more than 50,275. Undoubtedly the main reason for this was the everlasting 'dearth'; Jürgen Rohwer tells us:

> The few new U-boats coming into service were only enough to make good losses, and to keep the number of U-boats capable of operating in the Atlantic more or less stable at twenty or so. But ... there were rarely more than six or eight U-boats in the area of operations at the same time; usually there were between three and five, and sometimes fewer.[37]

The situation was exacerbated by the length of time that was being taken over dockyard repairs, due, says Rohwer, mainly 'to insufficient shipyard workers having been allotted to U-boat repair work'. Dönitz fulminated in the War Diary:

> I will not tolerate the lack of organization which causes the boats to remain days longer in the yards.

The situation would improve, but in December, 1939, it only reflected the chaos of much of Göring's economic 'empire' brought about by the premature declaration of war. The overlord of the Four Year Plan had dimly apprehended some such outcome as far back as 1938, when he told an assembly of manufacturers:

> It is a bad thing if a man has to confess, once the battle has started – 'damn it, I should have done this before'.[38]

Well, the battle had started, and Dönitz was not the only one who would feel its pinches.

Even in this darker period, there were some consolations; the attack on trade might be faltering, but the U-boats continued to take a toll of the Royal Navy – using their secondary weapon, the mine. Well served by the *B-Dienst*,[39] Dönitz had ordered mining operations in the Firth of Forth, the Firth of Clyde and Loch Ewe; they paid good dividends. On 21 November the modern cruiser *Belfast*, 'commuting' in the Firth of Forth, was struck by a mine and her back broken by the explosion. She was saved with difficulty, but out of action for a long time. This was the work of *U21*, commanded by *Korvettenkapitän* Frauenheim. Even better was the work of *U31* (Habekost) on 4 December; a mine laid by her some time earlier in Loch Ewe struck the Home Fleet flagship, HMS *Nelson*, and caused damage so serious that she was out of action for the best part of a year.

As 1939 drew to an end, the morale of the U-boat crews was high. Only nine boats had been lost all told, seven by the end of October, *U35* in November to British escort destroyers, and *U36* in December to the submarine *Salmon*; both these U-boats were Type VIIAs. Dönitz's crews may have been few in number, but they had a sense of being on top of their job and had a good deal to congratulate themselves on. William Shirer spent Christmas Day in Kiel, and broadcast interviews for the Columbia Broadcasting Service with the crew of a U-boat which had just come in, then spending the evening with them aboard the submarine tender in which they celebrated the festival:

Surprising with what ingenuity these tough little sailors had fixed up their dark hole – for that it was – for Christmas. In one corner a large Christmas tree shone with electric candles, and along one side of the room the sailors had rigged up a number of fantastic Christmas exhibits. One was a miniature ice-skating rink in the midst of a snowy mountain resort on which couples did fancy figure-skating. A magnetic contraption set the fancy skaters in motion. Another showed the coastline of England and another electrical contraption set a very realistic naval battle in action. After the broadcast we sat around a long table, officers and men intermingled . . . [rum and tea and 'case after case of Munich beer' were then served; a sing-song followed]. Towards midnight everyone became a bit sentimental. . . . Impressive, though, the splendid morale of these submarine crews, and more impressive still the absolute lack of Prussian caste discipline. Around our table the officers and men seemed to be on an equal footing and to like it.[40]

In one respect, at any rate, the lessons of 1918 had been well learned.

It was during this period, too, that another lesson became apparent. With so few boats, 'group' or 'pack' tactics were not possible, and Dönitz was forced to order his captains in the Atlantic to think chiefly in terms of individual operations. But all the experience gained pointed in one direction,

> namely, that the tactical direction of an attack on a convoy could not always and with certainty be exercised by a commander at sea in a U-boat, and that it was in any case not necessary.[41]

This realization marked the inception of a revolutionary system of command made possible only by the great strides in radio communication referred to above. Their full fruition would not be seen until real 'packs' arrived; in 1939/40 Dönitz was adapting his system by stages. The first was the recognition of the drawbacks of local control – and, since this went against all previous military teaching in all dimensions, it was revolutionary indeed. It was axiomatic, in 1939, that an admiral should go to sea with his fleet, and that each section of that fleet should have its own commander present aboard his flagship. The armies had learned, in World War I, that the front line was not the right place for anyone except the junior officers to exercise command, but it was still firmly believed that generals should be as near the front as possible,[42] and that control should be exercised downward through a hierarchy which would be located progressively nearer to the battle. Effective mass tank warfare, for example, only became possible when radio permitted tight local control. But World War II was about to provide two remarkable exceptions to what had always seemed a most obvious and unarguable rule: they were the night bomber[43] and the submarine.

The drawback of local U-boat control in attacking convoys was, as Dönitz now perceived, insurmountable. The local commander would have to remain out of sight of any escorting aircraft, if his command (and his boat) were to have any duration of life at all. But that would mean that he would be out of sight of the operation, and therefore robbed of all the advantages associated with the 'man-on-the-spot'. This was unanswerable, and furthermore, since the 'command boat' would be of such dubious value, it would merely represent the unwarrantable diminution of an already too-small force. Finally, all this being so, the qualities that a local commander would require could more profitably be employed on the training of new crews. It was difficult to counter these arguments.

The only possible strong argument against them would have been the lack of any alternative to local control, and this was something that only mounting war experience could elucidate. By the turn of the year the basic decision was made:

> we were able, by experiment, to reach the positive conclusion that I could myself quite easily direct the *whole* tactical operation against a convoy from my headquarters ashore.[44]

It was all a matter of communication: the boats must communicate their sightings and observations promptly and accurately to U-boat HQ. U-boat HQ had then to correlate this information, add to it any further information from other sources – aircraft, cryptanalysis and observation by surface craft (if any) would be the main ones – and instruct the U-boats as quickly as possible:

> My control, therefore, extended *up to the moment of launching an attack*, but *not* to the actual attack itself. In this latter each commander acted independently, and on the efficiency, initiative and determination of each one of them depended the success of the operations to which I had severally led them.

It is difficult to translate this sytem into the language of any other Service. It implies direct tactical communication between, in Army terms, the General Officer Commanding-in-Chief and company commanders, or in Royal Air Force terms, the Air Officer Commanding-in-Chief of Bomber Command and the flight commanders, omitting all intermediaries. The Royal Navy, however, does offer examples of this kind of distant direct command; one such was Admiral Pound's disastrous intervention in the action of Convoy PQ 17 in 1942 – not a happy parallel. More cheering (if less exact) was the British campaign in the Falkland Islands in 1982.

What it meant in 1939 was, in words that still convey a hint of wonderment though written some twenty years later, that:

> My 'on-the-spot knowledge' and my ability to 'get the feel' of how things were out there in the Atlantic proved to be greater than we had hoped.

After each operation I called upon each individual captain to report to me personally and in detail. These reports, together with the additional information on any special points passed on by the commanders to members of my headquarters staff and the entries in the war diaries of the U-boats, gave me a good overall picture of the situation at sea throughout the war.

It was, above all, to the commanders' personal reports that Dönitz attached the greatest importance, and it was these reports that established the undoubted *rapport* between leader and led; as Rohwer says,

the discussions which followed them were always conducted with great frankness on both sides. It was certainly these uninhibited discussions with his commanders that saved Dönitz from losing contact with the grim realities of front-line action, and helped to forge a bond of union between him and his staff on the one hand, and the commanders and crews of the U-boats on the other.[45]

This 'bond of union' was perhaps the most important reality of the U-boat war; it is, indeed, hard to see how it could have been conducted at the pitch to which it attained without such a thing. The personal contact was absolutely essential, and the returning crews did not miss the significance of the slim, upright figure of the *Befehlshaber* standing on the dockside to greet them at the end of their exacting missions:

It was, I must confess, when I saw them thus, emaciated, strained, their pale faces crowned with beards of many a week at sea and in their leather jackets smeared with oil and flecked with the salt of the ocean, that they seemed nearest to my heart. There was a tangible bond between us.[46]

Dönitz neglected nothing that would make this bond firmer. It was a regular feature of return to base that at once, probably the very next day, there would be a distribution of decorations earned by officers and men. As an ex-submariner, Dönitz did not like to contemplate the thought of a man who had done well and won recognition going to sea again without being rewarded, perhaps never to return; he would have felt guilty and ashamed:

Where decorations were concerned, there was no correspondence and no red tape in U-boat Command. . . . I regard this practice of immediate awards to those engaged upon operations as psychologically important.

As 1940 dawned the U-boat crews were going to need some psychological sustenance.

From the very start of their campaign the U-boat captains had been aware (it was only a suspicion at first) that all was not well with their chief weapon. They could not know that their first losses were, in fact, due to precisely this. On 14 September, three days before *U 29*'s triumphant sinking of the *Courageous*, *U 39* (*Kapitänleutnant* Glattes) nearly stole her laurels. Operating off the Orkneys, by what he no doubt considered to be a stroke of unbelievable luck, he came up with *Ark Royal*, Britain's most modern aircraft carrier – indeed, her *only* truly modern one. Glattes succeeded in reaching a good firing position at a range of only 800 metres and despatched two torpedoes. Both exploded some 80 metres short of the target, whereupon the carrier's escort immediately pounced upon *U 39* – so fast that the captain of the destroyer *Foxhound* could actually see the U-boat in the water below him as he let go his depth charges. *U 39* was blown to the surface and her crew captured before the boat foundered to become Germany's first U-boat loss of the war. But of course, none of these details were known at U-boat Headquarters.

Nor was the fate of the next casualty known at first; this was *U 27* (*Kapitänleutnant* Franz), lost on 20 September. Attacks and sinkings of fishing trawlers revealed her presence, off the Butt of Lewis, and the Commander-in-Chief, Home Fleet, having had two aircraft carriers attacked – one sunk – in the space of a week, reacted very strongly, as may be supposed. He at once sent off ten destroyers and some naval aircraft to deal with the menace, which they faithfully did. *U 27* was sunk by the destroyers *Fortune* and *Forester*, and her crew, also, was captured. From his prisoner-of-war camp *Kapitänleutnant* Franz succeeded in smuggling out a message telling Dönitz what had happened:

Three torpedoes fired – three premature detonations – then enemy depth charges.[47]

By the time this information reached U-boat HQ it only corroborated what was becoming an ever-thickening file.

Reports of such incidents were now coming in at depressingly regular intervals. On 25 October *Kapitänleutnant* Schultze returned to Kiel with *U 48*, to report that five of his torpedoes had misfired. On the 31st came a signal from *Kapitänleutnant* Schütze in *U 25*, complaining that, in a salvo of four torpedoes, every one had been a failure. *U 46* came in on 7 November with her commander, *Kapitänleutnant* Sohler, in a state of fury; in four weeks he had succeeded in sinking only one ship, despite a wonderful opportunity of doing serious damage to a convoy; he told Dönitz:

> Three times we got into the convoy. Once I fired seven torpedoes against a mighty wall of overlapping ships without getting a single strike! Then, with a great cruiser laying stationary and broadside-on right in front of our bows, my two torpedoes detonated before reaching it. Naturally the cruiser was alerted, and got clear.

Then on 10 November came the worst report of all, when the Type IIC *U 56* returned to Wilhelmshaven with her commander, *Kapitän-leutnant* Zahn, in a state of very great depression, as well he might be. On 30 October his small boat had found itself in amongst the Home Fleet and at 1000 hours the flagship *Nelson* presented an admirable broadside target; Zahn at once fired off a salvo of three torpedoes,

> lined up well and truly to strike the flagship forward, amidships and aft. As the *U 56* dived deeper, Zahn squeezed into the narrow radio room. The petty officer in charge held the stopwatch in his hand, counting the seconds. Zahn himself donned the earphones of the listening apparatus, which buzzed and droned with the thrashing of the mighty battleship's propellers.
>
> Suddenly, above this constant noise, they both heard the metallic clang of iron against iron. Many others heard it too, even without the aid of listening apparatus. But after the clang – the strike – nothing followed: no thunderous crash, no explosion.
>
> Then came a second, fainter clang. And that was all.

Zahn said in his report:

> The torpedoes' failure to explode undermined the morale of the whole crew. . . . One torpedo finally detonated when it stopped running at the end of its fuel. I watched through the periscope as two destroyers dashed at top speed to the spot.

Zahn's own morale was so affected by this awful failure – though it was none of his fault – that Dönitz felt obliged to take him off operations for a while and send him to von Friedeburg as a training instructor.

Clearly a situation of the utmost seriousness was coming to light. On 31 October, when he received Schütze's signal, Dönitz recorded in the War Diary:

> *At least* 30 per cent of torpedoes are duds. They do not detonate or they detonate in the wrong place . . . Commanders must be losing confidence in their torpedoes. In the end their fighting spirit must suffer.

This now became another preoccupation. Sailors – but submariners in particular – like airmen are peculiarly at the mercy of their technical apparatus. One recalls Beatty's famous comment at Jutland in 1916, when two of his six ships had vanished in gigantic funeral pyres of smoke and steam, and his own ship was on fire:

> There seems to be something wrong with our bloody ships today.[48]

It was not a pretty thought. Nor was it a pretty thought, in 'Bloody April', 1917, for the boy pilots of the Royal Flying Corps to take off in the knowledge that the Germans had the better aircraft, and that their own life-spans would probably be measured in days. Soon Dönitz was recording in the War Diary:

> It is my belief that never before in military history has a force been sent into battle with such a useless weapon.[49]

His military history was at fault; as we have seen (p. 34) the British Submarine Service had been through exactly the same miseries; but his feelings are understandable.

What was now breaking was the greatest scandal of the German Navy in the Second World War:

> a story of vanity and presumption, of departmental competition and jealousy, of thinking too little and demanding too much; all the ingredients of a man-made *débâcle*.

To understand what was happening we need, as usual, to go back some distance in time. As far back as 1915 – yet another example of the technological strides in World War I – Dr Adolf Bestelmeyer had developed for the Imperial Navy's torpedoes a 'distant pistol' which would be activated by the magnetic field of the target's hull. Between the wars this idea was further explored in Germany, with the hope of devising a torpedo capable of breaking the back of a battleship with a single warhead. The new pistol was known as MZ, a well-guarded secret and a favourite child of the designers. Two delivery systems were produced: the G7a torpedo, reliable, but still using the old compressed-air motor which displayed a bubble track, and G7e, specially for U-boats, electrically driven, making no track, but at 30 knots maximum speed slower than a destroyer and therefore considered only suitable for operations against merchantmen. For both types there were available both MZ (magnetic) pistols or percussion pistols (AZ) similar to those used in World War I, but a good deal more complex (and more liable to go wrong).[50]

On 14 November Professor Cornelius of the Berlin Technical High School, who had been working on torpedoes throughout the interwar period (an interesting insight into the realities of German disarmament in the Versailles/Weimar period) came to U-boat HQ and Dönitz left him in no doubt about his feelings. But Cornelius was unable to throw any light on the current problem or offer any remedy. Just over a month later there was a more hopeful portent, when *Konteradmiral* Kummetz was appointed Inspector of the Torpedo Department. Dönitz says:

> He approached the problem of the torpedo failures with a completely unprejudiced mind. The torpedo was not his child. With great energy he set about the task of tracking down the possible causes for the torpedo failures. And first and foremost it is thanks to him that many of these potential causes were traced and one by one eradicated.[51]

It took Kummetz some time to make any progress – he was hampered by the freezing over of the Baltic in the severe winter of 1939–40 which made it impossible to use the practice ranges. Before he could come to any useful conclusion, justifying any change in U-boat procedures, Hitler had begun his western campaign with the attack on Norway, and it was now that the full extent of the torpedo débâcle became apparent.

234

The Norwegian campaign was the first real test of the reborn German Navy, and it was clear that the U-boats would be required to participate with everything they could throw in. The German invasion took place on 9 April, anticipating Allied landings which were already in preparation and actually began on 15 April. Once these started, geography dictated that the North Sea, criss-crossed by troop transports and their escorts and covering naval forces, would be full of targets for U-boats. Their tasks, says Dönitz, were three-fold: first, to protect the German seaborne landings, secondly, to strike at the Allied landings, and thirdly, to prevent the Royal Navy from cutting German sea communications. For this purpose thirty-one boats in all were available, including six from the Training School; all but one are displayed on a map in his Memoirs, and they comprise:

Type IA	1 (*U 25*)
IIA	6 (*U 1–6*, from the Training School)
IIB	6 (*U 7, 9, 10, 13, 14, 19*)
IIC	6 (*U 56–60, 62*)
VIIA	8 (*U 30, 34, 46–49, 51, 52*)
IXA	2 (*U 38, 43*)
IXB	1 (*U 64*; *U 65* followed)

Their operations were, according to Jürgen Rohwer, 'a complete failure',[52] and the reason is not difficult to see. Already worried by the lack of results, on 11 April Dönitz called for reports to be signalled, and when these began to come in they proved, he says, 'to be 'calamitous':

U 25. 10 April evening, two destroyers torpedoed. Effect of explosion not observed.
U 48. [10 April] 1230. *Cumberland* type cruiser salvo of three. Missed, one failed to explode until the end of its run. 2115, salvo of three, cruiser *York*. Salvo exploded prematurely . . .
U 51. 10 April, 2210. Two misses. One exploded at end of safety run, the other after 30 seconds, 300 feet ahead of large destroyer.
U 48. 14.4, Westfjord, torpedo failures against *Warspite* and two destroyers.
U 65. Two shots at a transport. No success.[53]

On 16 April Dönitz's star performer, Prien of *U 47*, reported an attack on transports at anchor disembarking troops in the Bygdenfjord, protected by two cruisers:

> 2242, fired four torpedoes. Shortest range 750 yards, longest range 1,500 yards. Depth setting for torpedoes 12 and 15 feet. Ships stretched in a solid wall before me. Result nil. Enemy not alerted. Re-loaded. Delivered second attack, on surface, after midnight. Fire control data precise. Thorough inspection of all adjustments by Captain and First Lieutenant. Four torpedoes. Depth setting as for first attack. No success. One torpedo off course exploded against the cliff. While turning away ran aground. Refloated under extremely difficult conditions and very close to passing patrol vessels. N.B. Pursued with depth charges. Compelled to withdraw owing to damaged engines.

Prien believed in living dangerously; not satisfied with this hair-raising adventure in very narrow waters, only three days later he reported again:

> Sighted *Warspite* and two destroyers and attacked the battleship with two torpedoes at a range of 900 yards. No success. As the result of the explosion of one of them at the end of its run I was placed in a most awkward predicament and was pursued by destroyers coming from all directions.

And so it went on; four attacks on a battleship (*Warspite*), fourteen on cruisers, ten on destroyers and ten on transports, 'and the net result had merely been the sinking of one transport'. But the causes of the failures seemed to be narrowing down:

> In the twelve torpedoes with magnetic pistols discharged by *U 25*, *U 48* and *U 51* on 11 April ... there were six to eight cases of premature explosion – anything, that is, between 50 per cent and 66 per cent certain failures. The torpedoes with impact pistols fired at the anchored transports on 15 April by *U 47* were all failures.

The last fact contained the full measure of the disaster; if the fault could have been identified entirely with the magnetic pistols, matters would have been bad but not fatal. The answer – and this was indeed what Dönitz ordered – would simply be to rely on the contact pistol; but Prien's report shattered that hope of salvation:

> And so we found ourselves equipped with a torpedo which refused to
> function in northern waters either with contact or with magnetic pistols.
> ... To all intents and purposes, then, the U-boats were without a
> weapon.

It was a crushing realization – crushing for Dönitz, but if anything
worse for the U-boat captains and crews. Faith in their torpedoes was
now completely lost; Prien, in fact, told Dönitz that he 'could hardly
be expected to fight with a dummy rifle'. There was nothing for it; on
17 April Dönitz ordered the U-boats to withdraw from the Norway campaign.

It need hardly be said that the torpedo investigation now proceeded as
a matter of extreme urgency, and fortunately for the U-boats the prime
fault of the contact pistol was quickly discovered. It was a defective
action of the striker when hits were made at certain angles of incidence.
This, at least, could be quickly remedied. The running fault, which
caused German torpedoes to go deeper than intended and often run
right under their targets, was not properly identified until January,
1942. It was found to be a matter of excess pressure in the balance
chambers containing the hydrostatic valve controlling the horizontal
rudders. It turned out that a great many of these chambers were not
airtight. This meant that they were vulnerable to changes of air pressure
inside the submarine, and such changes were naturally inevitable when
the boat dived. Releases of compressed air caused a considerable build-
up of internal pressure; penetrating the torpedo balance chambers where
the pressure had to be atmospheric in order to regulate the depth of the
torpedo's run, this had the inevitable effect of forcing the torpedo
downward. It was a fault that could occur anywhere (as the early
examples in 1939 displayed), but in the Norwegian campaign it was
normal for the U-boats to remain submerged for very long periods –
perhaps as many as twenty hours in a day – thus building up exceptionally
high pressures; this is the most likely reason for there being so many
failures in April, 1940. Once known, the fault could be corrected.[54]

The magnetic pistols suffered from another drawback, which was
not overcome until December, 1942, with the introduction of the Pi2.
Until then, says Dönitz,

> the effectiveness of our torpedoes was no greater than it had been in the
> First World War.[55]

In this case the 'guilty party' was nothing less than the earth's magnetic field, which varies in different areas. In northern latitudes (northern Norway, for example) it is very strong – quite capable of detonating a magnetic torpedo automatically, and so producing the 'prematures'. The designers tried to counter this by adjustments to the pistol according to zones, numbering sixteen between the North Cape and the Bay of Biscay. North and south of those areas, magnetic pistols were not to be used – a somewhat cramping rule. But even with zonal adjustments, there were further hazards, such as 'interference areas' where the normal magnetic field was greatly strengthened. Volcanic rock could produce such interference – off the Scottish islands, for example; another activator of interference was iron ore, large deposits of which are found in northern Scandinavia – e.g. the Narvik area. And finally, there was the unusual hazard of 'magnetic storms', caused by sun-spots (particularly prevalent during the winter of 1939–40) which caused great difficulties with radio transmissions and reception, and made magnetic torpedoes behave very strangely indeed.

The remedies for all these matters were in the future; in the immediate present, in April, 1940, the simple fact was that the U-boats had suffered the equivalent of a heavy defeat. Careful examination of the available details of the thirty-six attacks carried out by the U-boats in the course of the campaign showed that with properly functioning torpedoes at least one out of four attacks on a battleship would have produced a hit, out of twelve attacks on cruisers seven would have scored hits, out of ten attacks on destroyers seven, and in five attacks on transports all five. As Dönitz says:

> The very important effect that successes on that scale would have had on the course of operations is obvious.[56]

The crews were naturally not aware of the whole story, but there was no doubt that their morale was very badly affected, and it took all of Dönitz's undoubted leadership charisma to hold it together.

The whole fiasco has the air of coming with shock effect in April, and there can be no doubt that the special conditions of the operations off Norway did play their part. But, as we have seen, Dönitz was already seriously worried by October, 1939; the wonder is that he had not been just as alarmed long before. It was not as though there had been no warnings. And it is here that we meet the scandal, the 'man-made *débâcle*', the bureaucratic complacency leading to what Dönitz would later call 'an error that cannot be condoned'.[57] To grasp it we need to look briefly at the Torpedo organization of the German Navy. At the head of this stood the Inspector of Torpedoes, the ultimate authority, and his staff. Beneath him was a department concerned with designing torpedoes (the Torpedo Experimental Institute at Eckenförde, near Kiel). In parallel with this was the Torpedo Test Institute (*Torpedo Versuchs Anstalt, TVA*) responsible for developing, testing and finishing. According to Bekker, the Experimental Institute was aware as early as December, 1936, 'or at latest June 1937', that G7a and G7e torpoedoes were not running true; an experimental test against nets showed that the fault might be as much as 3.70 metres. The immediate remedy suggested was the incorporation of a 'depth spring' which certainly gave good results in the trials to which it was subjected, but Dönitz tells us that there were only two trials, despite the misgivings of the Naval Chief Engineer. Nevertheless, *Kapitän zur See* Wehr, the head of the Institute, persuaded the Inspectorate that the spring should be adopted and introduced at once; industrial bottlenecks – the labour pains of the Four Year Plan once more – meant that none were ready before January, 1939.

It was, in fact, in 1937 that the warning bells rang most insistently. Max Valentiner, the redoubtable captain of *U 38* in World War I, arrived at the High Command headquarters to warn that even in 1917–18 there had been disturbing failures of torpedoes with magnetic pistols, including depth fluctuations of up to 30 metres. Valentiner made some practical suggestions, including depth recorders for practice torpedoes. Coming from such a source, one would have thought the warning might be heard, but the Ordnance Office told Valentiner that things had changed since 1918, the new pistol was the fruit of systematic research, and

There existed no grounds at all to doubt its absolute reliability.[58]

This was palpably untrue; it was at this time that reports from Spain brought 'the alarming news that the German torpedoes were no good'. The faults described were precisely those that came to light again in 1939–40, and were sufficiently disturbing to cause a new body, the Torpedo Trials Command (*Torpedo Erprobungs Kommando, TEK*) to be set up with orders to conduct further trials 'under the most rigorous conditions'. A fourteen-day test by a torpedo-boat was carried out:

> Result: the torpedoes were declared thoroughly unreliable both mech-anically and from the point of view of maintaining the required depth.

This entire proceeding was viewed with dislike and disdain by *TVA* and by Wehr, now a *Konteradmiral*, and jealous of any intrusion into an area which he clearly regarded as his own preserve. No progress had been made by October, 1938, when *TVA* itself carried out more trials, this time from a destroyer; her captain reported:

> Most torpedoes ran erratically as to depth . . . variations up to four metres . . . enough to shake one's faith in the weapon.

It did not, apparently, shake the faith of *Konteradmiral* Wehr; nor was the Torpedo Inspectorate alerted to the very serious state of affairs which existed at the outbreak of war.

When these matters came to light in the searching enquiries that were held in 1940, Raeder was appalled; he was particularly concerned at the effect that such revelations might have on younger officers and their faith in the Navy. In a memorandum of 11 June he said that as Commander-in-Chief he felt more strongly than anybody about the failures that had been revealed:

> I regard them as a grave misfortune not only for the Navy, but for the whole conduct of the war and thus for the German people. . . . By means of commissions of enquiry I have sought to establish whether there have been avoidable faults on the part of officers, officials or employees, and the Officer Corps may rest assured that if this is shown to be the case I shall bring the guilty persons to account with merciless severity.

He was as good as his word; Wehr and *Vizeadmiral* Götting (Kum-metz's predecessor) were dismissed, Wehr and leading officials were court-martialled and in December, 1941, the admiral and two officials were found guilty. Bekker questions whether they may have been, to some extent, scapegoats, whose punishment masked higher re-sponsibility, and he roundly asserts:

For the failure of the magnetic torpedoes the Naval High Command was itself highly culpable.

He says nothing about Dönitz. Yet it is surely a mystery how the *FdU*, with his intimate knowledge of the arm, and his passion for detail, could have missed such a thing as the failure of his main weapon. Did Valentiner say nothing to him? Did no one pass on Valentiner's warnings? Did he not see the reports from Spain? Did he know nothing about the trials and the reports of the torpoedo-boat and destroyer captains? His memoirs are silent on all these points; memoirs often are. The omissions are grave; they take some understanding.

So, on a low and depressing note, ended the first phase of the second round of U-boat warfare. Its cost, to 31 May, was twenty-four U-boats – one by cause unknown, one accidentally rammed by a German warship, one sunk by an aircraft of RAF Bomber Command, one by the Fleet Air Arm, three (possibly four) by mines; all but two of the rest were put down by the surface craft of the Royal Navy. The disastrous campaign off Norway exacted a price of three, perhaps four, U-boats (*U 1*, sunk by the British submarine *Porpoise*, *U 64* and *U 49*, and possibly *U 22*). But it was not the loss of the boats that mattered; it was the loss of the weapon. On the other side of the ledger, despite the torpedo failures and despite their paucity in numbers, the U-boats, so far in the war, had accounted for 241 British, Allied and neutral ships, a total of 852,813 tons. It was less than the single month's total for April 1917, but it was a beginning.

2

Nothing of Major Importance

'Nothing of major importance occurred in the first year of the U-boat warfare.'

Winston Churchill The Gathering Storm p. 371

THE COMING OF war is normally a 'moment of truth'; in 1939 the truth was particularly hard for Britain to bear, following upon what I have elsewhere called 'the 1920–40 madness', years of 'blindness, hysteria, dogma, credulity and at times sheer folly', of which the most conspicuous example was 'the folly of "never-againism" (never again a Continental commitment)' [1] – which also meant 'never again a Western Front', 'never again a British Expeditionary Force'. In that last fast, hectic span of time when everybody's mind was called upon to concentrate wonderfully, and reality reasserted itself, it was recognized that there *would* be a Continental commitment after all, there *would* be a BEF, fighting on a Western Front, in France, and that it would be a 'primary responsibility' of the Royal Navy to see that it got there. And, as in 1914, this was done; 161,000 men and 24,000 vehicles were transported to France by 7 October. Back-up stores and reinforcements followed in an unending stream, until by June, 1940, the total would mount to about half a million men and 89,000 vehicles – and as throughout the First World War, this was done entirely without loss. Once again, the U-boats proved powerless to hinder or damage the deployment of Britain's military forces in the chosen theatre, and once again the reason was plain to see: convoy.

This time, however, there was no delay over the convoying of merchant ships. We have already referred to the Shipping Defence Advisory Committee set up in 1936, and its pronouncement in favour of the convoy system. In a world and time infested by committees, many of which have the look of being more or less deliberate substitutes for action, the SDAC, according to Roskill, 'was a remarkably successful example of the co-ordination of many departments and interests'.[2] In its three-year span of life, it concerned itself with the training of Merchant Navy officers for defence and the preparation of a handbook for shipowners on *The Defence of Merchant Shipping*, strengthening ships in preparation to mount guns (low-angle for use against submarines, and also anti-aircraft), and signalling instructions. Considerable progress had been made by 1938, and in that year Paymaster Rear-Admiral Sir Eldon Manisty, whom we have already encountered as a member of the Admiralty's Convoy Committee in May, 1917 (see p. 62, Note 11) toured the convoy assembly ports to bring his experience to the creation of the organization known as the Naval Control Service. In January, 1939, the important subject of War Risks Insurance was tackled, and here also 'the committee drew heavily on the experiences of 1914–18'.

What no committee could remedy was the general shortage of the necessary means of making war. It was one thing to anticipate the arming of merchantmen by training their crews and preparing the ships. It was a different matter to supply the guns. A special section of the Trade Division was formed in June, 1939, to organize the arming of the whole Merchant Navy – a total of some 5,500 ships requiring armament, of which 3,000 were ocean-going. A fair number of low-angle guns could be supplied from Admiralty stores taken from scrapped ships; they might be old, but they were better than nothing. The difficulty was to procure anti-aircraft guns, and we have seen that British industry was very little help in this matter. There was an understandable (if unacceptable) reluctance to buy foreign weapons, but with the Fleet itself at risk this had to be thrust aside. A report in January, 1939, dwelt alarmingly on the vulnerability of aircraft carriers and cruisers, while destroyers were 'virtually defenceless against air attack' and 'the problem of the protection of merchant shipping . . . is at present unsolved'.[3] In March it was decided to order 500 Oerlikons from Switzerland and to buy the manufacturing rights; that transaction, however, was not concluded until 3 October. The British weakness in close-range AA weapons was a continuing feature of the war.

On 26 August, with war eight days off, the Admiralty assumed control of all British merchant shipping, whether sailing in convoy or not. This control was exercised through the Trade Division, headed by an Assistant Chief of Naval Staff who was, at the outbreak of War, Rear-Admiral H. M. Burrough. His authority over merchant ships began shortly before they sailed and continued until their safe return; the organization and conduct of convoys, the allocation of escorts, routing and briefing of masters all lay within the province of the Trade Division whose most valuable members were the Naval Control Service Officers at the ports. The first convoy (Gibraltar to Cape Town) actually sailed before the declaration of war – on 2 September. The 'cycle' of home-based convoys began four days later, on the east coast, and on the next day the first of the outward-bound ocean convoys set sail. At that stage of the war these had two originating points: the Thames, via the Channel (OA), and Liverpool (OB), with close escort only as far as $12\frac{1}{2}°$ West – which is not very far. The escort vessels remained at this point to bring in the next home-bound convoy. These started on 14 September, from Freetown (SL); the first Halifax convoy, with the famous designation HX, was on 16 September, and the first fast convoy from that port (HXF 1) on 19 September. Ships sailing at over 15 knots or less than 9 knots were not convoyed, and once more it was among these that the U-boats found the overwhelming majority of their targets. What we now know is that, thanks to the 'dearth of U-boats', the complex but practical convoy system built up on the foundation of past experience was not really tested for nearly a year – a valuable period of grace. Nevertheless, its message was clear: by the end of 1939, out of 5,756 ships which had sailed in convoy, the U-boats had only succeeded in sinking four.

It was as well that the U-boats were so few; even so, the Royal Navy's anti-submarine forces were at full stretch. For the task of continuously protecting some 3,000 ocean-going ships, the 101 destroyers and sloops that were available were a very small number. But worse, if anything, than the sheer lack of vessels was what Roskill has called 'an extraordinary ambivalence'[5] in the proposed manner of using them. It is indeed hard to reconcile the alacrity with which the convoy system was restored on the soundest First World War principles, and 'the persistence of the belief that to send out flotilla vessels and aircraft to hunt for U-boats was to take the offensive against them, whereas to use them to escort the convoys was to act wholly defensively'.[6] The intention, formulated by the Tactical Division in June, 1938, was to create nineteen hunting groups, each consisting of about five ships with reconnaissance aircraft, for use in 'a so-called "offensive rôle"'[7] at scattered points around the coast. Elementary arithmetic reveals that this would have left precisely six ships for escort duty, so it is not surprising that when war came the proposal was quickly forgotten. Yet, as Roskill says, 'the fallacy of the hunting group was to prove enduring – and costly'.[8] The whole idea was, in fact, a reversion to the pre-convoy doctrines of 1916, founded on the Navy's hallowed tradition of seeking out the enemy and destroying him in battle (see p. 33), fortified by the exaggerated belief in ASDIC that we have also noted. 'Ambivalence' is indeed the word; a committee headed by Vice-Admiral T. H. Binney, reviewing aspects of the maritime war in September, reported its view that 'the best position for anti-submarine vessels is in company with a convoy', and recommended

> that, for the present, every anti-submarine vessel with sufficiently good sea-keeping qualities should be employed with convoys rather than dispersed in hunting units.[9]

This eminently sensible conclusion was endorsed by the Deputy Chief of Naval Staff, Rear-Admiral T. S. V. Phillips, but unfortunately it ran counter to the thinking of the First Sea Lord, Admiral of the Fleet Sir Dudley Pound, as well as that of the First Lord himself, Winston Churchill, who expressed the offensive mystique in his own inimitable style:

> Nothing can be more important in the anti-submarine war than to try to obtain an independent flotilla which could work like a cavalry division on the approaches, without worrying about the traffic or U-boat sinkings, but could systematically search large areas over a wide front. In this way these areas would become untenable to U-boats, and many other advantages would flow from the manoeuvre.[10]

It would take some years of war to show that the offensive, so unexceptionably desired, could only prosper in the apparently 'defensive' company of the convoy. And this, at least, was not one of the unlearned lessons of World War I. The 1914–18 lesson had been that individual U-boats were generally reluctant to attack convoys, and unsuccessful when they did so; conversely, by the same token, escorts did not kill many U-boats in that war. It is necessary to hold this in mind if we wish to understand what can easily have the look of wilful blindness.

Far less encouraging was the condition of the Royal Navy's first ally – the RAF's Coastal Command. I have said that this was the 'Cinderella' of the RAF Commands, and the name is explained by a glance at its order of battle on the eve of war (as of 27 August, 1939):

Avro Anson (reconnaissance, first flight 1935)	10 squadrons
Saro London (flying-boat, 1934)	1 squadron
Supermarine Stranraer (flying-boat, 1935)	1 squadron
Vickers Vildebeest (torpedo-bomber, 1928)	2 squadrons
Short Sunderland (flying-boat, 1937)	2 squadrons
Lockheed Hudson (reconnaissance, 1938)	1 squadron [11]

The only modern aircraft in the whole collection were the Sunderlands, with their heavy armament of ten machine guns which caused the Germans to call them the 'Flying Porcupines',[12] their range of 2,980 miles and their endurance of $13\frac{1}{2}$ hours, and the Hudsons. These were a phenomenon; ordered in 1938, they were the first American aircraft to serve in the RAF (in the teeth of strenuous opposition); they had a maximum speed (Mark I) of 246 mph, a range of 2,160 miles and an endurance of six hours. A Hudson of No 24 Squadron gained the RAF's first air victory of the war, shooting down a Dornier flying-boat on 8 October, 1939, and on 27 August, 1941, it was a Hudson of No. 269 Squadron that became the first aircraft actually to capture a submarine (see pp. 364–5). At the other end of the scale of combat worthiness, the Ansons ('Faithful Annie') were only military aircraft by courtesy (or default); their armament consisted only of one fixed forward-firing .303 machine gun and one more in a turret behind, with four 100-lb bombs; reconnaissance in the North Sea was their only possible use, but restricted by the fact that at extreme range there still remained a 50-mile gap between the Anson's flight limit and the Norwegian coast. In fact the general state of Coastal Command, as Sir Maurice Dean says, only illustrated another distressing circumstance:

> The Admiralty and Air Ministry gravely underestimated the importance of aircraft for the protection of shipping, especially of convoys against U-boat attack. This was surprising because the importance of aircraft in this rôle had been fully demonstrated in the First World War.[13]

246

In January, 1938, triangular discussions between the Admiralty, the Air Ministry and Coastal Command Headquarters examined the anticipated functions of the Command and established certain priorities. These faithfully reflected the Admiralty's preoccupations at that time. A Fleet action – given the state of the German Navy in 1939 – was not to be expected or feared; as to U-boats, the belief was that 'the submarine has been mastered', and consequently nothing very serious was apprehended from that quarter. Surface raiders, on the other hand, especially the fast, powerful pocket battleships, were considered to be a very real threat, and this pointed immediately to Coastal Command's first task: a vigilant watch on the North Sea for their movements. So this function took first priority, and it is one of the war's emphatic ironies that the movement of the pocket battleships into the Atlantic in August, 1939, took place while a joint Navy/Air exercise was being held to practice the prevention of that very thing.[14] Next in Coastal's priority came cooperation with the Navy's Northern Patrol, a force of cruisers whose prime purpose was to enforce the British blockade of Germany; the aircraft were to cover gaps between the ships and divert suspected merchantmen for boarding or inspection in a port. Finally, in third place, came cooperation in defence of trade, in the form of the hunting groups referred to above. It was not very exhilarating, nor very impressive; it was not even very practical, with the numbers and equipment available. It is, indeed, small wonder that by December the AOC-in-C, Air Marshal Sir Frederick Bowhill,[15] was dwelling on the difficulty of carrying out his instructions.

Bowhill was 59 at the outbreak of war; he had joined the Royal Navy in 1904, entered the Naval Wing of the Royal Flying Corps in 1913 and continued in the Royal Naval Air Service in 1914; in 1919 he transferred into the Royal Air Force with the rank of Wing Commander. He was, in the words of Sir Maurice Dean,

> an ideal Commander-in-Chief for the early days of the war . . . he had seawater in his veins. He had an appreciation of naval needs based on a lifetime's experience.[16]

With Bowhill at Coastal Command HQ (Northwood) was another naval man of some distinction, Commander (later Captain) D. V. Peyton-Ward RN, an ex-submariner, now the Naval Liaison Officer, who would soon take a significant part in the development of anti-submarine warfare. After the war it was he who wrote the RAF's Coastal Narrative, *The Royal Air Force in the Maritime War*. Anyone who reads it will quickly see that here was a 'dark blue' officer with a definitely 'light blue' mind. It is Peyton-Ward who sums up the bleak prospect facing Bowhill and his whole Command in these early days:

> Apart from reconnaissance, the striking power of Coastal Command against enemy surface units was almost non-existent and action against U-boats had hardly been considered, other than reporting their presence to naval anti-submarine craft.[17]

Apart from the small number of his aircraft and the obsolescence of too many of them, Bowhill also faced a weapon problem somewhat akin to that which Dönitz was having to recognize at the same time. From 1925 onwards an anti-submarine bomb had been developed – in a leisurely fashion – and this came into service in 1931, with a new design (Mark III) in 1934. Without testing, it was decided to build up reserves of the Mark III in three sizes: 100 lb, 250 lb and 500 lb. It turned out to be 'quite useless' with repeated and apparently ineradicable fuze failures and 'unpredictable under-water travel'. Furthermore, there was no proper bombsight, which meant that crews had to attempt accurate placing by eye from low altitudes – at which the bomb, 'skipping' and exploding in the air, was more dangerous to the aircraft than to the target. The bombs were, in any case, far from lethal: the 100 lb anti-submarine bomb carried by Ansons proved to be practically harmless even with a direct hit,[18] while the 250 lb version used by the flying-boats had to explode within six feet of the pressure hull if they were to do any serious damage and even the 500 lb bomb had to be no more than eight feet away. It was all very depressing for the hard-driven pilots and crews of Coastal Command. As Peyton-Ward says,

> The result was that attacks on U-boats developing out of intelligent design of anti-U-boat patrols and sweeps came to nought as regards inflicting any serious damage.[19] All we could do was to harass and frighten.

The real answer to all this, of course, as Bowhill soon perceived, was to give up the bombs altogether, and adopt what had already been perceived as 'the weapon of the future' in 1918 – the depth charge (with suitable modifications for dropping from aircraft). And, as 1940 came in, this was what Bowhill was urging, but when it came to abandoning the bombs, a situation arose all too resminiscent of that in the German Torpedo Development department:

> Although circles in direct contact with this problem were convinced of the uselessness of the existing anti-submarine bombs there was an influential body of fixed opinion which refused to admit this.[20]

Not until the summer of 1940 was any real progress made in this matter.

In the meantime, however, a significant reorientation of Coastal Command thinking had taken place. Even before the end of 1939, the normal patrols in the North Sea had made frequent sightings of U-boats taking the northern passage into the Atlantic.[21] From these it was possible to build a picture of U-boat movements – arrival times in particular areas and returns – so as to intercept them by special patrols for that single purpose. There was not much these patrols could do when they made their sightings beyond alarming the U-boat and slowing it by making it dive. However, says Roskill,

> This led, before the end of the year, to a full realization of the great contribution which aircraft could make to the defence of merchant shipping against submarine attack – once an effective anti-submarine weapon had been provided.[22]

As Peyton-Ward puts it, Coastal Command 'had become 60% U-boat minded'.

As 1939 drew towards its conclusion, the Royal Navy was in a state of mild euphoria; the four months of war had been no picnic, and though losses were light in their total number, seven ships all told, they included two major units, *Royal Oak* and *Courageous*, whose loss was painful, as well as the 16,600-ton armed merchant cruiser *Rawalpindi*. On the other hand, the destruction of the pocket battleship *Admiral Graf Spee* in the River Plate in December brought great encouragement to the Navy and nation alike, while the general aspect of the U-boat war looked hopeful. The Admiralty did not, of course, have the corroborated information that we now possess about U-boat losses. It would also have found our present knowledge of U-boat numbers hard to believe. But, schooled by Admiral Hall and hard experience, the Intelligence Division from the first displayed a conservatism amounting at times to downright scepticism in its estimates of U-boats accounted for. This was good, and in marked contrast with other areas of the war, where claims and counter-claims sometimes reached towards fantasy.[23] Indeed, it was also in contrast with the U-boats themselves, whose tonnage claims have now been criticized as 10–40% too high (due in large part to the difficulty of assessing accurately a ship's tonnage by often hasty glances through a periscope). Of the nine U-boats lost by the turn of the year, the Royal Navy had accounted for six; deducting *U 36*, sunk by HM Submarine *Salmon*, five of these were the work of anti-submarine forces. So by the end of 1939 any doubts on a highly significant subject that may have existed appeared to have been laid to rest: 'that properly organized and promptly executed asdic search could sink enemy U-boats had been demonstrated'.[24] Time would shortly show that this was a deception.

For both U-boats and anti-submarine forces, in these early days, numbers were the prevailing preoccupation. It is not easy to throw a modern economy into war gear, and least of all a run-down economy, such as Britain's in 1939:

> Britain entered the Second World War in 1939 with a shipbuilding industry that was a rusting, partially dismantled and partly unmanned hulk of essentially Victorian technology; and, on the whole, no less rusting were its management and workforce and their operational methods.[25]

One of the worst effects of the blighting of British shipbuilding by the combined action of the great slump and the fixation with disarmament, over and above the technological retreat, was the evaporation of the potential workforce, especially the skilled labour on which all else depended. At the very beginning of rearmament, in July, 1936, the Ministry of Labour reported

> that a large and sudden demand for naval construction would be certain to overtax the labour capacity of the industry, and could only be achieved at the risk of serious delay or the disorganization of the labour force ordinarily engaged in the construction of merchant vessels. The results of the enquiry emphasize the importance of any naval programme

being envisaged from the point of view of enabling the industry to *recreate and train a skilled personnel* by the engagement of apprentices in adequate numbers (my italics).

By the end of 1937 unemployment in the shipyards still stood at 21%, and it was the lack of men with vital skills that made improvement difficult and slow. In 1939 the official expectation was an annual output of about 1,200,000 gross tons of merchant shipping and 370,000 tons for the Navy. This was not a very large amount for a run-down fleet, and once war losses and damage began to mount it would be still less impressive – *Courageous* and *Royal Oak* alone represented 51,650 tons which would have to be replaced.

It is against this background that we have to assess the growth of the anti-submarine force. In 1939 and early 1940 its 'star feature' was the 'Hunt' Class of escort destroyers mentioned on p. 180; three of these were launched in 1939, all in December (but of course not commissioned until 1940); eleven more launchings followed between January and May. Two *Black Swan* class sloops were launched in 1939 and four more in the following year. There were a few wartime conversions (the Admiralty yacht *Enchantress* into a useful sloop was a case in point) and some acquisitions of ships building for foreign countries; conspicuously and profitably among these were six excellent modern destroyers ordered by Brazil and acquired by the Royal Navy in 1939. And for a long time that was about the limit of progress – but there was a portent, also.

On 24 January, 1940, there was a launching at Smith's Dock, Middlesbrough; the craft concerned was not an impressive man-of-war – a displacement of 925 tons, 205 feet overall, a one-shaft reciprocating engine (2,750 hp) giving a speed of no more than 16 knots, a 4-inch gun and assorted AA, designed to hold a crew of eighty-five officers and men – but she was nevertheless the portent, the first of the 'whalers' included in the same 1939 Estimates as the 'Hunt' Class destroyers. In those Estimates, presented before the final pre-war crisis, the destroyers were masked from unfriendly Treasury inspection by the appellation 'fast escort vessels'; of the 'whalers' not much was said, except that they would not be fast, but they *would* be easy and quick to build, and the pattern chosen was that of the whale-catchers built chiefly for Norway at Smith's Dock. The First Lord did not much care for their name, and on 25 February, the day after the third

launching of one of these vessels, he addressed a memorandum to the
Controller of the Navy, Rear-Admiral B. A. Fraser: [26]

> I do not like the word 'whaler', which is an entire misnomer, as they are
> not going to catch whales, and I should like to have some suggestions
> about this. What is in fact the distinction between an 'escorter', a 'pa-
> troller', and a 'whaler' as now specified? It seems most important to
> arrive at simple conclusions quickly on this subject. . . . Let me see a list
> of the vessels built and building which fall in the various categories. [27]

Thus the 'fast escort vessels' took on their proper guise, and the
'whalers' became corvettes. It was not a name that appealed to everyone; Lenton and Colledge tartly remark:

> As the link between old sailing and modern steam counterparts is one of
> function and not of size a closer approximation to corvette was the
> modern light cruiser. [28]

They consider that this nomenclature set a 'groundless precedent' for
the further incorrect naming of the later 'frigates', which have also
been referred to as 'super-corvettes'. There seems to be a good deal in
this criticism; it will not have escaped notice that the genesis of these
vessels was distinctly similar to that of the 1915–18 sloops (see p. 35)
and the naming of the ships themselves certainly followed that precedent. The little ships that came down the slipways in 1940 and after
were also a 'Flower' Class, and the very first one of all, on 24 January,
was *Gladiolus*. She would see her first action on 30 May, and her last
on 16 October, 1941, when she was sunk by *U 558* in the North Atlantic. In the meantime, she and her sisters had been writing history.
Vice-Admiral Sir Peter Gretton has called the 'Flower' Class corvette
'the workhorse of the convoy escort force'. [29] Roskill says:

> it is hard to see how Britain could have survived without them, [30]

and others have uttered even higher praise. There was no disguising
the drawbacks of the corvettes – their slow speed, their cramped quarters almost rivalling the U-boats themselves for sheer discomfort, their
extraordinary liveliness in the water (it was even said that 'a corvette
would roll on wet grass' [31]). But Joseph Schull insists:

With all their limitations, they performed under the knowledgeable hand of a seaman with something of the spirit of a thoroughbred. They felt seaworthy; and they were to prove so.[32]

Another Canadian – since Canadians would come to know them so well – may have the last word:

The corvette navy was more a way of life than anything else.[33]

In all, 259 corvettes would be built in Britain and Canada, and thirty-three of them would be lost, mainly by the torpedoes of their special enemies.

It would be a wild exaggeration to suggest that the advent of a handful of these pygmies in the first half of 1940 brought great encouragement to the Admiralty, but it is a fact that even in May 'the state of the sea war, and in particular the war against U-boats, was not considered unsatisfactory'.[34] Some of the wilder flights of pre-war optimism were now seen to be mistaken, but comfort was taken from the toll of tonnage being lost to U-boats, running at 'a comparatively moderate average of 87,000 tons per month'. With an increasing flow of new escorts (of which the corvettes might be taken as a symbol) and longer range aircraft with better weapons for Coastal Command, it was confidently hoped that this figure would be substantially bettered. True, the Norwegian campaign had taken a toll,[35] including the aircraft carrier *Glorious*, reducing Britain's strength in that department to four out of the original six, but it was plain that the Germans had suffered heavily too. In Cajus Bekker's words:

The Norwegian campaign . . . ended with the bulk of the ships of the Germany Navy on the bed of the ocean, or else in the dockyards undergoing repair after being severely damaged.[36]

And the U-boats, for reasons which we know, but which cheerful observers at the time were disposed to attribute to defeat by the Royal Navy's anti-submarine forces and tactics, were blessedly – if strangely – quiet. It was all a delusion, a dream from which there would now be a nightmare awakening.

The great German offensive in the West opened on 10 May; by just over a fortnight later, the only option for the BEF was surrender on the battlefield, or a scramble back across the Channel to safety. By 4 June the latter manoeuvre was completed at Dunkirk – but the Army had lost virtually all its equipment, and the Navy had lost six more destroyers with nineteen others damaged. On 10 June Italy entered the war on Germany's side, creating a new area of maximum strain for the Royal Navy, and an impossible position for France. On 22 June the French signed an armistice with Germany, and on the 24th with Italy. France was effectively out of the war, and Britain stood alone. But Churchill was now Prime Minister, and, as Liddell Hart says,

> the British people took little account of the hard facts of their situation. They were instinctively stubborn and strategically ignorant. Churchill's inspiring speeches helped to correct the depression of Dunkirk, and supplied the tonic the islanders wanted. They were exhilarated by his challenging note, and did not pause to ask whether it was strategically warranted.[37]

Alas, the truth, in its stark simplicity, was that

> The course of no compromise was equivalent to slow suicide.

Churchill's statement that 'nothing of major importance occurred in the first year of the U-boat war' is one of his least perceptive; the opposite was true. The sea war had been utterly transformed. The real battle was only now about to begin.

3

i: The Steep Atlantick

'The Star that bids the Shepherd fold
Now the top of Heav'n doth hold,
And the gilded Car of Day
His glowing Axle doth allay
In the steep Atlantick stream.'

John Milton: Comus: a Masque

FROM BREST TO Bordeaux the shores of France look out towards
Milton's 'steep Atlantick' – but before you reach it you must first
traverse what Lord Byron later called 'Biscay's sleepless bay'. Un-
poetically but enthusiastically, Admiral Dönitz, when the German occupying forces arrived on the Biscay coast in June, 1940, perceived the
event as an 'outstanding improvement in our strategic position in the
war at sea'. Possession of this coast, he said,

/was of the greatest possible significance in the U-boat campaign.[1]

He did not exaggerate.

From the very beginning of what would be known as the Battle of
France, Dönitz and his staff had watched the progress of the German
Army with keen attention. Whatever the objectives of the Army may
have been, for the *BdU* the ports along the Biscay coast were the prize
that glittered, and in the mood of understandable German euphoria
after the victories in Poland and Norway, as the *Panzers* performed
their triumphant march in May and June, distances melted and what

had seemed far off suddenly came within easy grasp. Dönitz was not taken by surprise:

> While the conquest of northern France was in progress ... U-boat Command had had a train standing by, which, laden with torpedoes and carrying all the personnel and material necessary for the main-tenance of U-boats, was dispatched to the Biscay ports on the day after the signing of the armistice.[2]

Thus, in a very short time, the German Navy found itself in possession of the whole European continental coast from the North Cape to the Spanish frontier. The implications were clear:

> Never before in her history had Great Britain found herself faced by enemy forces on all sides except the West, a loophole which the German navy attempted to close and thus isolate this country from the rest of the world.[3]

As Dönitz succinctly expressed it:

> The first phase of the Battle of the Atlantic now began.[4]

With all the advantages of geography now on his side, Dönitz still faced the endemic difficulties of the U-boat arm at this stage of the war, the dearth of actual boats continuing to be the chief of these. It was at the very time that the Army was obtaining such important strategic advantages that the number of operational U-boats began to drop to its lowest totals: from thirty-one in April to only twenty-three in May, twenty-six in June and twenty-nine in July. On 7 July the first boat – *U 30* – to enter Lorient from the Atlantic arrived to refuel and rearm, advance-guard of a great array. The U-boat Command was impressed with Lorient; its repair facilities, says Dönitz, 'proved to be superior to those of the overburdened dockyards of Germany'.[5] It seemed to him also to be the right place for his command post, and work was immediately put in hand to convert a château at Kernével, at the mouth of the River Blavet, for this purpose.[6] Operating from Lorient offered several important advantages: the improved dockyard facilities made possible a 22% increase in the proportion of U-boats at sea; no longer did they have to make a 450-mile journey northabout to enter the Atlantic – which meant a saving of about a week on each patrol. These considerations also meant that the number of boats actively engaged actually increased, despite the drop in the operational total. Yet the number itself, in relation to the risk in hand, remained small – only eight or nine boats at sea at any one time. But it is wonderful what a handful of determined men in the right place can do.

The second endemic difficulty, source of endless complaints by Dönitz for at least another year, was what he called the 'lack of "eyes"' – a desperate shortage of intelligence about Allied shipping movements, above all the location of the convoys which he recognized as the truly profitable targets of his boats, and had desired from the very beginning of the war to smite with heavy blows.[7] Once again the lesson was being digested of the invisibility of convoys in the immensity of the sea (see p. 55), and this was something that the Biscay ports could not alter. Dönitz did, however, have another resource, which he was eager enough to make use of, and which in theory should have solved his problem to a large extent. The *xB-Dienst* had begun its penetration of British naval ciphers as far back as 1935–6, monitoring signals and observing corresponding movements in the Mediterranean during the period of the Abyssinian war crisis. Under its able director, *Fregattenkapitän* Heinz Bonatz, the *B-Dienst* developed this important advantage to the point where, during the Norwegian campaign, it was able to read between 30 and 50% of British naval signals without any undue delay.

Against merchant vessels it had possessed from the first, if anything, an even greater degree of penetration, checked briefly in January, 1940, when a new Merchant Navy Code was introduced, but this disadvantage was already largely overcome by March. Then in May the *B-Dienst* enjoyed a bonus: copies of the new Code were captured in Bergen in May, after which 'it was able to read the bulk of the traffic with very little delay'.[8] This was the theoretical solution to Dönitz's problem; the practical difficulty was that there was not much traffic. The dense volume of radio signals from Admiralty to convoys and from U-boat HQ to boats at sea was yet to come; sailing orders were received by convoy commodores in sealed envelopes and wireless silence was preserved at sea at all times except the most dire emergency. There was very little for the efficient *xB-Dienst* to feed on – and what there was decreased drastically when the Royal Navy replaced its Naval

Cypher No 1 by No 2 on 20 August. This change, with certain other timely security measures, limited the *B-Dienst*'s success very considerably until September, 1941. So, despite attempts to operate the U-boats on the prompting of decrypts even as early as June, 1940, and again in August, but always unsuccessfully, for the first year of the Battle of the Atlantic, in the words of Jürgen Rohwer,

Radio-intelligence played only an insignificant rôle during this time.[9]

Dönitz, as we have seen, had never been under any illusions about the reconnaissance capabilities of submarines themselves. Observation could never be more than the height of the conning tower permitted – and German submarine designers naturally aimed at low, clean profiles. It is surprising how much could, on occasions, be seen from a platform only a few feet above the sea: on a calm, clear day the collective smoke of a big convoy might be observed at a distance of fifty miles. But that would be exceptional; at most times that very quality which caused its enemies so much concern was also a severe handicap to the U-boat:

A submarine's conning tower, at night in a mid-Atlantic swell, is to all intents and purposes invisible.[10]

But by the same token, in a mid-Atlantic swell not only by night but also on a thick day, most of the world is invisible to the submariner. So, as Dönitz had foreseen, the U-boats would require help to overcome this problem – the help of aircraft, which lay firmly within the wide domain of Hermann Göring, now promoted to *Reichsmarschall*. For Dönitz the implication was clear enough: he faced 'war on two fronts'.

What Dönitz wanted, understandably enough (there were high-ranking officers of the Royal Navy who would have entirely agreed with him), was an equivalent of Coastal Command, under his own direction and serving the interests of the U-boat fleet exclusively. Göring, it need hardly be said, was bitterly opposed to this or any other diminution of his own authority, though not in principle hostile to the idea of trade warfare by aircraft. The Navy had been pressing for air-naval cooperation since 1938; 1940 was late in the day to try to improvise such a thing. Once again, Göring was betrayed by his lack of strategic vision before the war:

Too little effort was devoted to working out the advantages of air-sea warfare or to giving any sense of urgency to the material preparations it required.[11]

As with most air matters, 'material preparations' (i.e. production of suitable aircraft in sufficient numbers) were crucial. What Germany needed was a powerful, sturdy, combat-worthy, long-range bomber/-reconnaissance aircraft, or, at the very least, a prototype sufficiently advanced to be rushed into production. The only product in any way answering to that description at the outbreak of war was a large twin-engined machine which had begun life as *Projekt 1041* at the Heinkel *Flugzeugwerke* in June, 1937. Its first flight, under the designation He 177 V1, was in November, 1939, and terminated abruptly after only twelve mintues when the engine began to show signs of catching fire. This was just the beginning of a career which William Green describes as 'destined to provide the most dismal chapter in the wartime record of the German aircraft industry'.[12] When two later examples arrived for operational evaluation in a maritime rôle in August, 1940, they became the bane of all concerned 'and, subjected to interminable modifications to both airframes and engines, were declared totally unsuited for operational use'. The *Luftwaffe*, in its hour of need, persevered with the He 177, but it was not at all what either Dönitz or Göring was looking for in the summer of that year.

That left only a conversion, the Focke-Wulf FW 200 'Condor' airliner, which emerged as the FW 200C–1 for anti-shipping purposes in the spring of 1940. The unit nominated to operate the FW 200s was No 1 *Staffel* of No 1 *Gruppe* of *Kampfgeschwader* 40,[13] then stationed in Denmark. From there it began to attack British shipping, but at once encountered what was to become an outstanding characteristic of the aircraft throughout its war career, its 'chronic unserviceability'.[14] Out of six machines available at the outset of operations in April, only two were still serviceable by 11 May. The 200C–0 version was then withdrawn and replaced by the 200C–1, and with these No 1 *Staffel* recommenced operations from the airfield at Bordeaux-Mérignac at the end of June. Mérignac would henceforth be the prime 'Condor' base for the Battle of the Atlantic, but *KG 40* was not, to begin with, concerned with a battle that might never happen. Göring had promised Hitler that the *Luftwaffe* would be able to defeat the RAF and make possible an invasion of Britain, even taking into account the debilitated condition of the German Navy. Overconfident he may have been, but it is clear that with this task before him he was not likely to part with any aircraft that could serve him in a useful rôle. Dönitz's bald account of this phase of U-boat/*Luftwaffe* relations is disingenuous to the point of omitting all mention of the invasion (Operation SEELÖWE). Yet this is not entirely surprising. It was only one more difference between his character and Göring's that, while the ebullient but unintellectual Göring firmly believed in the possibility of successful invasion of Britain in July, 1940, the more practical Dönitz was convinced that a long war lay ahead. For both, however, the harsh fundamental remained: the sheer paucity of FW 200Cs.

The few there were did sterling work. The C–3 version, which appeared in the summer of 1941, had a maximum speed of 224 mph and an economical cruising speed of 158 mph, at which its range was 2,210 miles. Its armament comprised a 20 mm cannon in a forward ventral position, three 13 mm and two 7.9 mm machine guns and a bomb load amounting to 4,626 lb (a typical composition being two 500 kg + two 250 kg + twelve 50 kg). It had a crew of seven (five in the C–1). *KG 40*'s normal procedure was to fly out across the Bay of Biscay and then swing up round the western side of Ireland to Stavanger, where a detachment would refuel and rearm the aircraft, and shuttle back the next day to Bordeaux. Opinions of the Condor were mixed: Churchill called it 'the scourge of the Atlantic' and constantly urged the necessity of eliminating it from the scene. Captain Eric Brown, RN, who, as the Navy's Chief Test Pilot at the Royal Aircraft Establishment, Farnborough, had the opportunity of flying a number of German aircraft, called the FW 200 'this aesthetically most appealing of large aeroplanes' and summed its flight performance up as 'thoroughly competent'.[15] He agrees with Green, however, that its Achilles Heel was a structural weakness due chiefly to the speed with which it had been converted; it did not stand up well to the strain of continual operational flying at low altitudes and tended to break up if subjected to violent manoeuvres.[16] Alfred Price said:

> lacking armour and self-sealing fuel tanks this rather fragile aircraft could not absorb much punishment.[17]

The Condors may not have been combat-worthy, but with the Battle of Britain at its height there was not very much available to offer them combat. They began to add an increasing quota to the *Luftwaffe*'s anti-shipping campaign and Göring had every reason to be pleased with the results of this. In May, despite the claims of the Battle of France, his aircraft had sunk forty-eight ships, totalling 158,348 tons – a tonnage nearly three times that of the U-boats, still in the grip of their torpedo crisis (thirteen ships, 55,580 tons). June saw a startling transformation. With three evacuations (from Dunkirk, from northern Norway and then from Normandy and Brittany) to handle, and invasion threatening, the Royal Navy was hard pressed indeed; the heavy decision was taken to build up the strength of the light craft flotillas in the Channel area even at the cost of sacrificing escort for the Atlantic convoys. The result was a large number of vessels in the western approaches either unescorted or with exiguous escorts incapable of preventing determined attack – from the U-boat and *Luftwaffe* points of view in other words, a profusion of promising targets. Both took full advantage; the U-boats sank fifty-eight ships in June (284,113 tons) and the *Luftwaffe* sank twenty-two (195,193 tons). It was far and away the worst month of the war to date; losses from all causes[18] amounted to 140 ships, 585,496 tons, a total all too reminiscent of 1917. Jürgen Rohwer comments:

> morale in the U-boat service rose buoyantly so that when it entered the second phase of the Battle of the Atlantic ... spirits were high.[19]

Dönitz was still not receiving the reconnaissance support from the air that he required, but for the time being it did not greatly matter. This was the heyday of the individual U-boat 'aces', the 'grey wolves', as the propaganda machines of both sides would call them. Günther Prien (*U 47*), the hero of Scapa Flow, was ready-made for the rôle; two others reached pre-eminence during the next few months – Otto Kretschmer (*U 99*), known as the 'tonnage king', whose 'exploits stood alone',[20] and Joachim Schepke (*U 100*), full of confidence and aggression. These were the most famous names, all three sailing in Type VIIBs, but there were others in the list: Jenisch (*U 32*), Oehrn (*U 37*), Endrass (*U 46*), Schultze and later Rösing (*U 48*), Frauenheim (*U 101*) and more besides. They had two things in common:

> They had all received thorough training in peacetime and had all given proof of their merit during the first months of the war. And now they

261

threw themselves with daring, skill and ripe judgment into this on-slaught on the British lines of communication.[21]

The 'grey wolves' descended upon the flocks of practically defenceless ships approaching or leaving the western ports of Britain and devoured them, as their fathers had done in the pre-convoy days of 1916–17 (see p. 42). In the three months, July–September, they sank 153 ships, a monthly average tonnage of 252,926. During that time they lost only five boats; this was their first 'happy time'.[22]

By August, Brest and La Pallice as well as Lorient were operational U-boat bases (see Appendix E), these starting-points enabling the boats to cruise out as far as 25°W. Surface escort at this stage was only as far as 17°, and Coastal Command (barring only the Sunderlands) was hardly effective beyond 15°W. On 17 August Hitler gave a name to a present fact by declaring a total blockade of the British Isles, warning that neutral shipping would be sunk at sight; to the men going down to the sea in ships this was hardly news. The numbers of U-boats available did not significantly increase – they hovered between twenty-eight and thirty-one through the third quarter, which meant about nine or ten operational. It was with these few that the 'grey wolves' took their daunting toll of independent sailers and stragglers, and Dönitz was sufficiently encouraged to consider once more the chances of forming the 'wolves' into packs.

The first effective pack action against a convoy – an important date in the history of the Battle of the Atlantic – began on 6 September and continued until 10 September. It contained ingredients which were to become lethally familiar. The first was contributed by the *B-Dienst*, which was able for once to pick up and decipher a signal in good time for operational use.[23] It was an Admiralty signal instructing the slow convoy SC 2 from Sydney (Nova Scotia) where and when to meet its escort. Dönitz promptly detailed four U-boats to find the convoy, which *U 65* duly did in longitude 19° 15′W. The escorts succeeded in driving off *U 65* (von Stockhausen), but she made her contribution nevertheless by trailing the convoy and reporting its position, bringing the other three boats quickly towards it. The Atlantic itself supplied the next grim ingredient – even so early in September, it produced a violent storm with a Force 8 gale; it is difficult to measure the exact degree of disadvantage such conditions created for attackers and at-tacked respectively. They would, however, become a running refrain of the wartime winters. Prien in *U 47* made the next contribution, coming up before dawn on 7 September and attacking at once on the surface; in the darkness of the wild night he managed to sink three ships. Then came the dawn – and the aircraft: Sunderlands, whose presence compelled the U-boats to dive and lose contact with the convoy. This air intervention, too, would be a running (and ultimately decisive) refrain. But on the night of 8/9 September *U 99* (Kretschmer) and *U 28* (Kuhnke) came up and resumed the attack. This was not Kretschmer's day; two more ships were sunk, one by Kuhnke, the other by Prien again, whose boat was thus reduced to only one remaining torpedo. So the pack attack had sunk five merchant ships (four of them to a single U-boat) and five out of the fifty-three comprised in SC 2 is not all that many, but as Cajus Bekker says,

> the U-boat Arm would have been pleased indeed had it been able to inflict ten per cent loss on every convoy. But most convoys were reaching their destination unscathed, and the main problem was to find them at all.[24]

September was putting down markers. As SC 2 reached safe waters, Dönitz ordered *U 47* to take on the rôle of weather-boat, reporting on weather conditions twice a day from a point west of 23° (mainly for the benefit of the *Luftwaffe* in its attacks on Britain). While Prien was doing this, HX 72 ran right across him – but, as we have seen, he had only one torpedo, which must have made him a very frustrated man. However, the convoy was shortly set upon by other U-boats and lost six ships before the month was much further advanced. The 'new' tactics were clearly succeeding (inverted commas because, as we know [p. 147], in the last nine months of 1918 37% of U-boat attacks in these waters had been conducted in the same manner). The defence, as Captain Peyton-Ward says, was caught at its weakest point by the night attacks:

> the inadequate surface escort dependent on visual lookout could neither prevent the attacks nor detach forces to take vengeance on the attackers. The air escort, such as could be afforded, was of a rigid out-of-date pattern close to the convoy, though this was considered essential for the morale of the merchant crews. There were not sufficient aircraft to give additional cover at a distance from the convoy.[25]

What took the Royal Navy most by surprise, however, and caused most dismay, because the 1918 lesson had been completely ignored, was the degree to which the U-boats were using the surface. They were exploiting their surface speed to catch the convoys, and the darkness of night to get right into them, only diving to escape when the attack was over. This tactic, as Donald McLachlan says, meant that

> U-boats ceased to be submarines properly speaking and became submersibles.[26]

The truth is that the U-boats did not 'become' submersibles in 1940; they had never been anything else. True submarines still lay in a distant future. But their practice of staying on the surface as much as possible certainly took the Royal Navy by surprise in 1940, and nullified the ASDIC on which it had come to rely so absolutely. As this realization sank in, all those who perceived its implications would share the sentiments which Churchill later expressed:

> The only thing that ever really frightened me during the war was the U-boat peril.[27]

September was not one-sided, however, in distributing favours. Germany had stolen a march with the *xB-Dienst*'s successes in decrypting British naval signals in the mid-1930s, and British cryptography (see pp. 321 ff) faced the additional discouraging obstacle of the German *Enigma* machine. After a year of war, however, some progress had been made against this, and it was the decrypt of a German signal authorizing the dismantling of air-loading equipment at certain Dutch airfields catering for supply and troop-carrying aircraft on 17 September that offered the first suggestion of a postponement of Operation SEELÖWE the threatened invasion. It was only one message, to one unit, but the unit in question was intimately associated with the invasion preparations and the message was an order to stand down. British Intelligence and the Chiefs of Staff were wisely cautious, but they knew (and the Germans knew even better) that the *Luftwaffe* had suffered a heavy defeat on 15 September at the hands of Fighter Command, and by 20 September there was further evidence from photo-reconnaissance that naval units and barges collected for SEELÖWE were being dispersed.[28] The threat had not vanished – indeed, the decrypts[29] continued to indicate preparations well into November, but the urgency was fading and that, at least, was something to be thankful for. In Professor Hinsley's words,

> Despite the conflict of evidence and the absence of what alone could have resolved it – an unambiguous indication from a Sigint source that the invasion had been abandoned – a sense of relaxation gained ground slowly in Whitehall from the beginning of October.[30]

This frame of mind would be encouraged by the recognition of the ending of the daylight Battle of Britain (the last large daylight attack was on 30 September). It might have been encouraged even more had the knowledge been available of a definite shift in German strategic emphasis. With *SEELÖWE* under *Luftwaffe* cover an evaporating prospect, Hitler now applied himself to his intended attack on the Soviet Union; for Britain, he was satisfied to settle for night attacks on cities and industry, and the cutting-off of essential imports by U-boats which had always attracted him, even before the war.[31] Dönitz gained in importance as the promise of quick victory in the west died; it was a timely symbol of this that now he could move from Paris to his completed new headquarters at Kernével.

He was, as it turned out, able to emphasize the new consequence of the U-boat Arm with an early demonstration. October produced the U-boats' most remarkable performance so far, prompting Captain Donald Macintyre, who was trying to contend with them, to the later assertion:

> The convoy battles of October, 1940, could be fairly classed as catastrophic.[32]

It was Dönitz's ambition that 'not one day should pass without the sinking somewhere or other of a ship by one of the boats at sea'.[33] In October they excelled themselves: just over two ships a day, a total of sixty-three; the 'grey wolves' were at their zenith. The brunt of this onslaught fell upon a group of home-bound convoys in the second half of the month. The first to set out on this fateful journey was SC 7, on 5 October; such was the Royal Navy's escort shortage at this juncture that all the convoy's thirty-five ships had for protection for the first eleven days was the sloop *Scarborough*, launched in 1930, converted to a surveying vessel and reconverted for escort duties in 1939; she was only lightly armed and her maximum speed was 14 knots – well below the capability of a VIIB or VIIC U-boat. On the fourth day out a southerly gale sprang up, and four ships in the convoy, Great Lakes steamers quite unsuited to Atlantic storms, fell out; three were in due course sunk by U-boats, ever eager to pounce on stragglers. The convoy itself lost formation in the gale, and its speed was reduced to 6 knots. However, for another week it was spared, and when on 16 October the escort was reinforced by another sloop of the same class as *Scarborough*, *Fowey* and the corvette *Bluebell*, hopes must have risen. Yet this was still, by any standard, a very feeble escort for a convoy with a wide front.

> These three ships, none of which had worked together before, and amongst which there was *no common tactical doctrine or prepared plan of action* in case of an attack, took station round the convoy, *Scarborough* on the port bow, *Fowey* to starboard and *Bluebell* astern. Visual communication between them was impossible by night. The radio link was tenuous and unreliable. The distance between them, some six miles, was more than enough for a surfaced U-boat to slink through undetected, even though a full moon was shining down from a clear sky on a smooth silver sea.[34]

The U-boats would soon be there; that night *Korvettenkapitän* Rösing in *U 48* observed the convoy silhouetted against the moonlight; he at once reported its location, course and estimated speed to U-boat HQ, which directed six more boats towards him. Meanwhile, *U 48* attacked and scored hits on two ships; SC 7's Commodore, Vice-Admiral L. D. Mackinnon, at once ordered a 45° emergency turn to starboard, while the two sloops hunted the U-boat and the corvette stood by to pick up survivors. *U 48* escaped the sloops without much difficulty, but daylight brought an early-rising Sunderland which forced her to dive and she lost the convoy. She was not the only one: *Scarborough*'s captain, who was also senior officer of the escort, Commander N. V. Dickinson, full of hope and determination, spent 24 hours searching for *U 48*; he never saw the U-boat – or the convoy – again. It was one of the classic early errors of anti-U-boat warfare, excusable only by inexperience; it meant that the escort was reduced to two ships by the afternoon of 17 October. Fortunately, more help was on the way: a third sloop, *Leith*, and another corvette, *Heartsease*. But the U-boats were closing in; the first to arrive was not a member of the pack that Dönitz had ordered up; it was *U 38* (Liebe), out on patrol. Liebe made two attacks, but only scored one hit which failed to sink the freighter. However, his reports to U-boat HQ helped to place the pack across the route of SC 7 by the evening of 19 October, and the attacks began at 2015 that night. In this pack were familiar names: Kretschmer (*U 99*), Schepke (*U 100*), Frauenheim (*U 101*), with *U 28* (Kuhnke), *U 46* (Endrass) and *U 123* (Möhle) in company. The high degree of confidence of the U-boat commanders is reflected in Kretschmer's log:

October 18. 2124 . . . Convoy again in sight . . . From outside I attack the right flank of the first formation.

2202. Weather: visibility moderate, bright moonlight. Fire bow tube by director. Miss.

2206. Fire stern tube by director. At 700 metres, hit forward of amid-ships. Vessel of some 6,500 tons sinks within 20 seconds. I now proceed head-on into the convoy.

2230. Fire bow tube by director. Miss because of error in calculation of gyro-angle. I therefore decide to fire rest of torpedoes without director, especially as the installation has still not been accepted and adjusted by the Torpedo Testing Department . . . [*U 99* is attacked by an escort vessel]

2330. Fire bow torpedo at a large freighter. As the ship turns towards us, the torpedo passes ahead of her and hits an even larger ship after a run of 1,740 metres. This ship of 7,000 tons is hit abreast the foremast and the bow quickly sinks below the surface . . .

2355. Fire a bow torpedo at a large freighter of 6,000 tons at a range of 750 metres. Hit abreast foremast. Immediately after the torpedo ex-plosion there is another explosion, with a high column of flame from bow to bridge. Smoke rises 200 metres. Bow apparently shattered. Ship continues to burn with green flame.

October 19. 0015. Three destroyers [35] approach the ship and search area in line abreast. I make off at full speed to the south-west and again make contact with the convoy. Torpedoes from other boats are con-stantly heard exploding. The destroyers do not know how to help and occupy themselves by constantly firing starshells which are of little effect in the bright moonlight. I now start attacking the convoy from astern.

The picture of a dreadful night comes through all too clearly: dire confusion in the ghostly moonlight, ubiquitous explosions, the cries of abandoned sailors in the water, the helplessness of the weak and distracted escort. Kretschmer went on to sink three more ships and fired his last torpedo just before 0400. By the time SC 7, or what was left of it in scattered groups, found safe waters, seventeen ships had gone down; the sea was littered with sinking, burning and crippled merchantmen and seamen in bobbing boats or clinging to rafts and wreckage. For the escorts, as Macintyre says, 'it had been a night of shame and frustration'. And there was worse to come.

U 99, *U 101* and *U 123*, their torpedoes expended, returned to base and heroes' welcomes. That left *U 46*, *U 48* and *U 100*, with *U 38* fairly close and *U 28* somewhat further off, in the operational area within 250 miles of the north-west corner of Ireland; this now became known as 'Bloody Foreland', matching the 'cemetery of shipping' in the south-west in 1917 (see p. 47). Here, off the Foreland, on the very next night, the U-boats were presented with another splendid quarry: the fast convoy (see p. 287) HX 79 of forty-nine ships which had left Halifax some days after SC 7 left Sydney, and was now only two days behind. Unlike SC7, it had what appeared on paper to be a powerful escort: two destroyers, four corvettes, three trawlers and a minesweeper. But, says Macintyre,

> the ships of which it was composed had been got together at random; the Flower-class corvettes were newly commissioned and mostly straight from the shipyards. . . . Their crews lacked training and experience. None of the commanding officers of the ships of the escort had had any opportunity of meeting to discuss and determine a common plan in the event of an attack.[36]

Homed in by reports from Prien, the U-boats opened their attack at 2120 on the night of 19 October with hits on two ships. Once more there was a bright moon with visibility up to five miles, but the escorts never sighted a U-boat, though this night, like the last, was punctuated by explosions. At the end of it, fourteen more ships had gone down, and this was still not the end of the count. The U-boats had the good fortune to meet HX 79A on the same night, and seven more ships were sunk. This loss of no fewer than thirty-eighty merchant vessels in three days (but almost all in two consecutive nights) marked, says Macintyre,

October, 1940, 'one of the black months of the war at sea', still had more to say.

It has been said that for Britain 'the severe mauling of a convoy was the equivalent of a lost battle on land';[38] there was, however, a faint consolation, even for such a triple disaster as had just befallen. At least these miseries could be to a large extent wrapped in a veil of secrecy; the next blow was one that could not be hidden. The Canadian Pacific liner, *Empress of Britain* (42,348 tons) was built at Clydebank by John Brown's and launched in 1927. She was a luxury vessel, designed for maximum prestige as well as for commercial gain, and in her thirteen years of active life, which included a hundred round trips between Southampton and Quebec and eight world cruises, she had become 'a proud symbol of the British Mercantile Marine'.[39] Like other large, fast liners she sailed alone (except when trooping), relying on her speed (25.5 knots at her trials) to escape U-boats. On 26 October she was returning to Liverpool from the Middle East via Cape Town and the north-western approaches with 223 passengers (mostly Servicemen and their families coming home) and her crew of 419. Some 70 miles north-west of Donegal Bay she was attacked by a Focke-Wulf 200 which flew along her length and hit her with the first bomb, starting a fierce fire; a second run caused no damage, but on the third the Condor made another hit which started an even worse fire, causing ammunition to explode. Very soon the *Empress of Britain* was ablaze from end to end; the Condor captain had no doubt that she was doomed and the huge column of smoke pouring out of her seemed to be her pall. However, by a miracle the ship did not go down and an attempt was made to salvage the burning hulk. But for once Dönitz had the 'eyes' whose lack he constantly bemoaned; the Condor's report was passed to him, and, fortified by information from *B-Dienst* that the *Empress* was still afloat, it resulted in *U 32* (Jenisch) being sent to finish her off. Sunderlands kept *U 32* submerged for most of 27 October, but her hydrophones picked up the sound of the *Empress* under tow and the two destroyers which were escorting her. At about midnight Jenisch actually sighted his target, and some two hours later (28 October) he hit her with two torpedoes, causing a boiler explosion. After ten minutes the *Empress of Britain* capsized and disappeared beneath the waves. It was a telling blow for a seafaring nation. The German Press exulted, with headlines like 'Plutocrats' Liner Sails No More!' etc.; the Condor captain received the Knight's Cross of the Iron Cross Order; *Oberleut-nant* Jenisch received nothing, being taken prisoner when *U 32* was herself sunk two days after his success. But Dönitz could now point to what might be achieved with proper air-sea cooperation, and returned to his pressure on that front with all the *réclame* of his October victories to back him.

He had reason to be well pleased. It was his custom to take careful note of what he called the 'effective U-boat quotient' of his Command –

by which I mean the average sinking per U-boat per day for all the U-boats at sea.[40]

A high 'effective quotient' was the hall-mark of success, and the four months, June to September, 1940, certainly supplied that:

June	541 tons
July	593 tons
August	664 tons
September	758 tons

October, with the battle of the three convoys as its centrepiece, excelled all: the 'effective quotient' was no less than 920 tons (and would have seemed at the time to be even greater, because of the persistent habit of exaggeration by the U-boat commanders). The total tonnage lost during the month was 352,407; it is small wonder if Churchill was 'really frightened', and Dönitz correspondingly pleased – but at the same time conscious of how much more could be done if only means permitted.

After October there was a marked falling-off of U-boat performance; the Atlantic, in early November, was in Dönitz's words, 'empty of U-boats'. This pause was partly a consequence of the high intensity of the three-convoy battle, after which most boats would be back at base together, rearming, refuelling and making running repairs. Partly also, it was due to assigning a number of the boats to training duties in preparation for the anticipated increase of construction in the spring. And partly, as always, it was due to the everlasting 'lack of "eyes"' – the hard information without which the concentrations were pointless.

Above all, however, it was the 'dearth' that was responsible – at times during the next three months, according to Dönitz, no more than three boats were what he calls 'in direct contact with the enemy':

> For the time being, then, the war against Britain, the mighty sea-power and our principal adversary, was being waged by 120 to 240 men of the German U-boat arm.[41]

Some of the boats were given high designation numbers – 551, 556, 651 etc.; these were 'solely . . . an attempt to conceal our real weakness from the enemy'. There is no indication that this simple ruse was in any degree effective.

Strength and weakness have a way of taking on a different aspect according to which side they are viewed from. Dönitz offers another reason also for the decline of U-boat activity and successes from November onwards:

> The British in the Western Approaches had become appreciably stronger, and their anti-submarine measures included patrolling by aircraft which greatly affected our conduct of operations.[42]

Admiral Sir Martin Dunbar-Nasmith V.C., C-in-C Western Approaches and an ex-submariner of great distinction, and Air Chief Marshal Sir Frederick Bowhill at Coastal Command would have been surprised to learn this; from their point of view

> we were in desperate need of more and better weapons: more aircraft, more destroyers, more ASV, more depth-charges, more R/T sets for communication between air and surface escorts – but aircraft of longer range, ASV of higher performance, depth-charges specially designed for dropping from the air. Means of illumination by aircraft, such as search-lights and slow-dropping flares, were also urgently required.[43]

However, the fact remains that it was at this stage that, whereas until then what Dönitz called 'the focal point of U-boat operations' had been between 10° and 15°W, it now moved out west of 15°. No doubt this shift was in considerable part due to the work of the Sunderlands which we have encountered in this narrative more than once. It also owed itself to certain other factors which we shall examine later, and became a theme of the Atlantic battle through the next two years.

There was no notable convoy battle in November, 1940. This is the sort of situation in which it is easy for history to project a false image of war. It has often been said that 90% of war is boredom – but how does history convey that? The unboring parts – the battles, the terrors, the hardships, the joys of leave and so on – are not too difficult to describe; it is the day-by-day continuing experience, whose main feature is probably sheer fatigue, that presents the difficulty. Certainly this is true of the U-boat wars: the actions, and above all the spectacular convoy battles, have had many chroniclers and the tale is always worth telling. But it is important to remember that, as Cajus Bekker wisely observes,

> for every two convoys that were attacked, there were twenty that passed through the danger zone unmolested.[44]

The next few months were witnesses to that, but they have the look of non-events. Admittedly, the irrepressible Kretschmer won Oakleaves for his Knight's Cross by sinking two armed merchant cruisers, *Laurentic* and *Patroclus*, on 3 November. And on the night of 1 December he was back in action in a pack of four U-boats which sank ten merchant ships and the armed merchant cruiser *Forfar* in an attack on convoy HX 90. But November saw only thirty-two ships sunk by U-boats, the lowest figure since May, and totalling only 146,613 tons, while the next three months produced an average of just over thirty-two ships and of 178,718 tons. After the earlier triumphs, this was disappointing indeed, but against that Dönitz could set the cheering fact that between 21 August, 1940, and 7 March, 1941, only three U-boats were lost. U-boat morale was understandably high, as the British interrogator of the crew of *U 32* could confirm. He wrote in his report:

> The prisoners were all fanatical Nazis and hated the British intensely. . . . German successes during 1940 appear to have established Hitler in their minds not merely as a God but as their only God. Maintaining that Germany is at present only 'marking time' until after the consolidation of a series of political victories and corrective 'adjustments' in the Balkans and elsewhere, they think at any moment deemed suitable a German attack on Great Britain would be overwhelmingly successful and profess to be amazed at the British failure to see the inevitability of our utter defeat at any moment convenient to Hitler.[45]

These hard, well-trained young veterans were the best of a special breed, speaking at the very apogee of German power. The proof of his crews' quality was contained within another disappointment that Dönitz had to face at this period. Back in July, when their own forces seemed overwhelmingly strong in the Mediterranean and it looked as though Britain would in any case shortly be crushed by invasion, the Italians had offered direct help to Dönitz by a detachment of their own submarines operating from Biscay bases. Dönitz was delighted to accept – at the very least, he thought, he would now reap the benefit of more 'eyes'. A flotilla of twenty-seven Italian submarines duly arrived one by one at Bordeaux, and when Dönitz visited them the officers and crews made a good impression. Naturally, they needed Atlantic experience, and this it was hoped they would obtain by a training spell of some two months in the Azores area. They joined the U-boats in the north-western approaches in October, and Dönitz stationed them where they had a good chance of performing effective reconnaissance. That month and the next brought his disappointment:

Not on one single occasion did the Italians succeed in bringing their German allies into contact with the enemy. Their reports were invariably either inaccurate or they came too late; they failed to deliver any attacks of their own or to maintain contact with the enemy.[46]

Between 10 October and 30 November the Italian submarines aggregated 243 sea-days; during that time they sank one ship, of 4,866 tons – an effective quotient of 20 tons. The German aggregate of sea-days during the same period was 378, during which the U-boats sank eighty ships and worked up a quotient of 1,115 tons.

What Dönitz said about this at the time we do not know, but it may be imagined. When he came to write his memoirs nearly twenty years later, he was markedly restrained and sought for reasons which would excuse the bad Italian performance. He singled out lack of training over a period of years in the kind of mobile warfare which he had taught to his U-boats. He noted design faults in the submarines themselves: conning towers that were unnecessarily high, making the boats conspicuous, lack of an air supply mast for the diesels, which meant that the conning tower hatch had to be open when running on the surface – in the Atlantic that could mean green water pouring in and probably playing havoc with the electrical equipment. One thing was clear – it was no use trying to conduct joint operations with these allies; the Italians were allocated zones of their own, where they did somewhat better in their own way. The reason for this, he concluded, lay

> in their natural character and their martial characteristics. They are perfectly capable of delivering an assault with great gallantry and devotion, and, under the stimulating impetus of an offensive, will often display greater dash and daring than the Germans, who are less prone to be carried away by the thrill of battle.

This contrast drew him to an illuminating analysis of the style of war which he had invented and which his boats were practising:

> A convoy battle, however, demands not only gallantry and the offensive spirit, but also the toughness and endurance required to carry out the exacting task of remaining for hours and days on end in close and dangerous proximity to the enemy, compelled at the same time to abstain from any action until all the other boats have reached the spot and the time for the general attack comes. It is these qualities of toughness and endurance that we possess – or so I believe – to a greater degree than do the Italians; and it is for these reasons that they were of no great assistance to us in the North Atlantic.[47]

The ocean itself, having already given some ominous warnings, now declared its hand:

> That year exceptionally heavy and continuous storms swept across the Atlantic. Visibility was very restricted. With the U-boat twisting, rolling and plunging any attack was often quite out of the question. In storms like these, the sea broke clean over the conning tower. The bridge watch, consisting of an officer and three petty officers or ratings as lookouts, had to lash themselves fast to the bridge to prevent the foaming, boiling breakers from tearing them from their posts and hurling them overboard. During those winter operations the German submariner learned only too well the grandeur and might of the raging Atlantic.[48]

U-boats and escorts alike, this was their apprenticeship to the ways of the steep Atlantick stream.

3

ii: The Very Nadir of British Fortunes

'The very nadir of British fortunes in the Battle of the Atlantic.'
Captain Donald MacIntyre

WITH NO ALLIES, virtually no army, threatened by invasion, Britain depended more than she ever knew upon her one sure shield down the centuries, the Royal Navy. Exhilarated, understandably, by Fighter Command's evident successes in the Battle of Britain, the British public never knew how dangerous the real position was, or how weak the Navy was in relation to its swelling task, still less how severe was the cost of its concentration for the defence of the south-east coast. The Battle of the Atlantic crept up slowly upon the public consciousness; in the late summer of 1940 there was a lot else to think about.

From the Admiralty's point of view two features predominated: the dearth of escort vessels which fully matched Dönitz's dearth of U-boats, and the impossibility of establishing any firm escort organization as long as the invasion threat lasted. The main burden of convoy protection fell upon Western Approaches Command under Admiral Nasmith at Plymouth; [1] the very location of this Command came into question after the Fall of France. Lacking the bases in southern Ireland which it had possessed in the previous war, and now faced with a direct U-boat menace from the Bay of Biscay, the Admiralty abandoned the South-Western Approaches in early July. The Anti-Submarine School at Portland was already proving inadequate for the expanding task, and was in quite the wrong place; it was moved to Dunoon in Argyll, and a second establishment soon followed at Campbeltown. A further development in Scotland, which was to achieve a lasting semi-affectionate, semi-shuddering fame was the sea-training centre at Tobermory on the Island of Mull known as HMS *Western Isles*, and commanded by Commodore G. O. Stephenson (later Vice-Admiral Sir Gilbert, always 'Monkey' to his friends and contemporaries, in unkind reference to a certain homeliness of feature) who made this an invaluable part of the anti-submarine warfare apparatus. In August Churchill raised the question whether this northward trend should not be completed by setting up a new Command in the Clyde; it was a fertile suggestion, but it took a little while to bear fruit.

The decision to bring in all shipping for western ports through the North Channel [2] naturally created an unavoidable bottleneck, and this was undoubtedly to a large degree responsible for the high rate of sinkings during the U-boats' 'happy time'. Another large reason was the break-up of what convoy escort did exist in order to meet the needs of the Channel Commands – the Nore Command alone, for example, absorbed thirty-two destroyers and five of the new corvettes. But the problem was not just one of numbers; it was very much to do with the situation described above by Captain Macintyre – ships brought together and flung straight into action scarcely knowing each other and with 'no common doctrine or prepared plan'. In this phase of the battle the scratch escort collections, made up of whatever type of vessel came to hand, had an inevitably amateurish look by comparison with the hard-bitten, peace-trained U-boat packs. However, this was something that could be overcome, and the lesson was emerging that 'tactical coherence was more important than homogeneity'. [3]

It was all hard going, a time full of discouragement for the Royal Navy and for the nation's leaders. Fighter Command might make the Germans think twice about invasion, but Fighter Command could not defeat Germany. The only weapon that held out the slightest hope of doing that was the RAF's Bomber Command, and as we look back on it now Bomber Command in 1940 seems a very feeble instrument for changing the whole course of the war. Its long-range bomber force consisted of Wellingtons, Hampdens and Whitleys, and only rarely could it put more than 200 of these in the air at once. And when they did reach Germany, it transpired that in the current state of development of navigational and bombing aids only one third of the aircraft which claimed to have reached their target areas actually did so; another way of saying it is that only one in three of the aircraft recorded as attacking a target actually got within five miles of it. It is just as well that this was not known at the time, because this was, feeble or otherwise, the *only* weapon in Britain that could hit Germany at all. But from outside Britain there came a steadily brightening gleam of light.

In September, 1939, the United States of America was neutral – not merely neutral by disposition, but neutral by law. Between 1935–7 a series of bills bound America to strictly defined neutrality in the event of a European war:

> There were to be no loans or credits to belligerents, no arms shipments, no travel by Americans on the ships of belligerents, no weapons on American merchant vessels. If the United States – the theory went – put itself in an isolation ward, it would effectively seal out the disease of war.[4]

The bills took final shape in the Neutrality Act of 1937, but the theory which it embodied became an early casualty of the realities of war. On 4 November, 1939, the arms embargo clauses of the Act were repealed in favour of 'cash and carry': those belligerents who could afford to buy arms from America, and who could take away their purchases, would be permitted to do so. The bias in favour of the maritime nations requires no comment. In the crisis of 1940 this profound modification of the Neutrality Act enabled Britain to obtain half a million rifles, 80,000 machine guns, 130 million rounds of small arms ammunition, 900 field guns and 100 million shells. All this was covered without difficulty by President Roosevelt's policy of 'all aid short of war'. But Churchill already had his eyes on a different prize, to fulfil a need which his experience as First Lord of the Admiralty had brought home to him.

On 15 May, 1940, only five days after becoming Prime Minister, he opened that intimate correspondence with the President in which he signed himself 'Former Naval Person'. It was a long letter, covering several subjects of great moment, and it included the following:

> Immediate needs are, first of all, the loan of forty or fifty of your older destroyers to bridge the gap between what we have now and the large new construction we put in hand at the beginning of the war. This time

next year we shall have plenty. But if in the interval Italy comes in against us with another hundred submarines we may be strained to breaking-point.[5]

Just under a month later the full dimensions of the catastrophe which he had inherited were becoming apparent; Italy had entered the war, throwing 105 submarines into the balance, against just over eighty British and French destroyers and light craft in the Mediterranean – the French already showing every sign of being a disappearing asset. Churchill wrote to Roosevelt on 11 June:

> The Italian outrage makes it necessary for us to cope with a much larger number of submarines, which may come out into the Atlantic and perhaps be based on Spanish ports. To this the only counter is destroyers. Nothing is so important as for us to have the thirty or forty old destroyers you have already had reconditioned. We can fit them very rapidly with our Asdics, and they will bridge the gap of six months before our wartime new construction comes into play.[6]

On 31 July Churchill repeated this request (now raised to 'fifty or sixty of your oldest destroyers', to be used in the Western Approaches, freeing more modern vessels for anti-invasion duties); he said to Roosevelt:

> Mr President, with great respect I must tell you that in the long history of the world this is a thing to do *now*. Large construction is coming to me in 1941, but the crisis will be reached long before 1941. I know you will do all in your power, but I feel entitled and bound to put the gravity and urgency of the position before you.[7]

It was not easy for Roosevelt. A transaction in May to sell twenty fast motor torpedo boats to Britain had caused a *furore* in the Senate Naval Affairs Committee, whose chairman was an isolationist. He raised a cry of betrayal of 'our American youth who may be called upon to fight for the defense of our country'; the Attorney-General pronounced the transaction 'totally illegal' – and the whole deal had to be cancelled at the end of June. In that same month, too, the Chief of Naval Operations, Admiral H. R. Stark, had gone to Congress to request an appropriation of $4 billion in order to construct a two-ocean navy. It was not an auspicious moment to be asking for the loan of a substantial number of warships, old though they might be. However, the 'grey wolves' in the Atlantic proved to be strong persuaders; Roosevelt was a politician who could be shrewd to the point of being devious in order to get his way, and, with his careful manipulation, the famous Lend-Lease Agreement was arrived at and ratified on 2 September. Bases in Newfoundland and Bermuda were leased freely to the United States, with further bases in British Guiana and the West Indies in exchange for fifty American destroyers of 1917 and 1918 vintage.[8] The first deliveries took place on 6 September, when eight ships were handed over to British crews at Halifax. Informing the House of Commons of this highly unusual arrangement, and remarking on the ready availability of the British crews, Churchill said:

You might call it the long arm of coincidence.[9]

He was highly satisfied with the whole transaction.

The crews themselves, and those (British and Canadian) who followed them aboard the American destroyers, were less pleased. They were named by the Royal Navy the 'Town' Class, drawing on American, British and Canadian place-names. Frequently they were called the 'Four-stackers', referring to the four distinctive funnels (the furthest forward taller than the rest) which, with their flush decks, gave them an unmistakable profile. It is an open question whether they or the corvettes more fully fitted Kipling's generic description of 'that packet of assorted miseries which we call a Ship'.[10] The United States Navy, with characteristic generosity, handed them over well stored, to the pleasure of the British crews:

Every square inch of storage space was crammed with a variety of provisions which were now only a memory in England. Accommodations and fittings were also of a nature unknown. . . . There were bunks in the mess decks instead of hammocks; there were typewriters, radios, coffee-making machines.[11]

Despite their age, the 'Town' class destroyers were capable of high speeds (up to 35 knots) which could at times be a very useful asset. On the other hand,

Their crews hated them. They were narrow ships which rolled viciously;

their propeller shafts stuck out several feet beyond the stern and they were difficult to handle. They had a huge turning-circle which was not of much help when attacking a U-boat. They were certainly unsuited to Atlantic weather.[12]

On this there is general agreement; one description of their rough-weather performance says:

> their progress through heavy seas was a bitterly bad-tempered fight which wracked their own frames and the frames of their ships' companies.[13]

'Wracked' is the word; two of them had their low, glass-windowed bridges smashed, in one of them the captain and others being killed, while other crew members were crushed in the 'steep Atlantick's' avalanche of water.

What Churchill had not taken into account in his enthusiasm for obtaining them was the amount of modification and modernization that would be needed before they were ready for action. When built, they were heavily armed, with as many as four 4-inch guns and six 21-inch torpedo-tubes. For anti-submarine work most of these were useless and had to be replaced by depth charge projectors, anti-aircraft guns and new weapons coming into use. New ASDIC sets had to be installed, and before long new radar equipment. All this had to be done in dockyards that were already groaning under the burden of repair. Progress was slow, and Churchill (who could be strangely obtuse about such matters) found that difficult to understand; why, he asked the First Lord and the First Sea Lord in November, were there only sixty destroyers available for the Western Approaches, and of these only thirty-three operational? Why had the effective strength only risen by nine destroyers in the last month?

> meanwhile you have had the American destroyers streaming into service, and I was assured that there was a steady output from our own yards. I cannot understand why . . . such an immense proportion of destroyers are laid up from one cause or another. . . . What has happened to the American destroyers?[14]

He still, at the end of the month, laboured under the impression of the

American destroyers coming into service by dozens, but disillusionment was at hand; on 14 December he minuted the First Lord of the Admiralty:

Let me have a full account of the condition of the American destroyers, showing their many defects and the little use we have been able to make of them so far. I should like to have the paper by me for consideration in the near future.[15]

So the 'Town' Class limped, rather than rushed, into commission (six of them in the Royal Canadian Navy); for all their crews,

they were to remain to the end of their not inglorious careers seagoing purgatories of which those who sailed in them still speak with mingled horror and affection.[16]

Captain Donald Macintyre writes with seamanlike bluntness:

That most of them performed splendid service in filling a critical gap in our convoy defences will not be denied. At the same time it has to be recorded that to their new British owners they seemed vile little ships.[17]

The unkindest cut of all came from one of their RN captains, referring to the demise of a sister ship, HMS *Campbeltown* (ex-*Buchanan*), filled with high explosive and blown up in the Commando raid on St Nazaire docks in 1942:

the best thing that could have happened to the Town Class destroyers.[18]

Yet they were, as Joseph Schull says, 'with all their faults, a saving transfusion of strength'.

It was the October convoy catastrophe that brought the full extent of the U-boat menace home; a special meeting of the Defence Committee[19] was called to consider it on 21 October, and this was preceded by a meeting at the Admiralty the day before under the chairmanship of the Vice-Chief of the Naval Staff, Rear-Admiral T. S. V. Phillips. The conclusions arrived at in this meeting were:

1. that the attempt to avoid the U-boats by diverting shipping to the North Channel had not succeeded, and it was agreed that a World War I expedient which had been seen to be a failure in 1917 should be tried again – permanently patrolled shipping lanes (known as 'tram-lines') along which all shipping would be required to travel. The revival of this desperate prescription is an indication of the extent to which the Admiralty was unnerved by the U-boat attack.
2. that the matter of air and naval bases in Eire should be re-examined; this, also, bears a ring of desperation;
3. that escort vessels, other than destroyers, were too slow, and new escorts must be capable of at least 20 knots;
4. that a form of radar similar to ASV must be specially designed for the use of escorts as quickly as possible;
5. that every available light naval craft must be concentrated in the area of the north-western approaches, and that deployment against invasion should now take second priority.

The Defence Committee, with Churchill in the chair, approved these conclusions the next day. The 'tram-lines' proposal fortunately came to nothing; the steady movement westward of the U-boat 'focal area', making the lanes to be patrolled longer and longer, made that project impracticable. The third and fourth conclusions were indisputable; it was a good thing to establish them as matters for urgent attention, but they could clearly bring no quick relief. It was the fifth conclusion that really mattered, spelling out the new *schwerpunkt* of the war; Western Approaches Command had become, in Churchill's words, 'almost our most important station'.[20] 'Almost'? It is hard to think of any station that would be more important during the next four years. But Churchill, one feels, always thought of the war against the U-boats as a 'defensive operation', and tended to downgrade it, while admitting that it was of crucial importance.

The Defence Committee gave considerable thought to the question raised in the second conclusion, the need for bases in southern Ireland. Churchill, in his memoirs, confesses to mounting indignation at the losses caused by Eire's strict adherence to neutrality, and this was shared by many in Britain. At its next meeting, on 31 October, the Defence Committee considered the subject again:

Regarding bases in Eire, it felt that negotiations with De Valera[21] would be difficult; that the seizure and maintenance of naval and air bases against the will of the government and people of Eire would involve a grave military commitment, but that it might have to be done if the threat on our Western Approaches became mortal.[22]

And there the matter remained.

The same meeting approved the reinforcement of Coastal Command by a third long-range squadron fitted with ASV radar. Apart from the invaluable Sunderlands, 'long-range' in Coastal Command meant Bomber Command's discards and left-overs: a Whitley squadron on loan and then grudgingly transferred, even a squadron of the Fairey Battles which had been so dreadfully mauled in the Battle of France. But beggars cannot be choosers: the full strength of the Command in September, 1940, was no more than twenty-eight squadrons. This represented an 'initial establishment' of 461 aircraft, but of these only 226 were available with fully trained crews; another 100 aircraft were serviceable, but their crews were incomplete. The Command now possessed an effective anti-submarine armament – the airborne depth charge; it had shared in two U-boat kills, but it had made none of its own. Its outstanding operational problem was finding the U-boats; this was not easy in daytime, but their night tactics made it impossible. In this essential matter, however, within its present gloom, 1940 held out much future promise. Trials of Dr Edward Bowen's first ASV production sets (see p. 184) took place in November, 1939; in January, 1940, twelve Coastal Command Hudsons were duly fitted, but it need hardly be said that for a device as new as this and in such a specialized field the production problems remained considerable. In any case, for finding U-boats, ASV I was not an impressive performer. But Bowen was already at work on a much improved version, with a hopeful difference:

> Most important of all . . . was the fact that the new set had been engineered for mass production from the start; for this reason it was far more robust and reliable than its predecessor.[23]

Pye Radio and E. K. Cole received orders as early as the spring for 4,000 ASV II sets, first deliveries to be in August. By October, however, only forty-five had been received – and Coastal Command now had to face severe competition for these. The night 'blitz' on British cities focused attention on night fighters, and the need to fit them with every kind of electronic aid for their otherwise baffling task. Air Chief Marshal Sir Hugh Dowding (one of radar's earliest backers) had said from the first that the only solution to the problem faced by night fighters was to use radar as a gun-sight, and the aircrews increasingly agreed. Pye and Cole were told to concentrate on AI (Airborne Interception) at the expense of ASV – a clash of priorities of a kind that Coastal Command would have to learn to live with.

ASV II, when production could be resumed, coupled with a system of aerials devised by Mr R. Hanbury-Brown to give perception at right angles to an aircraft's line of flight,[24] was an encouraging future promise. But even before 1940 was out, there was something still better to look forward to. Professor J. T. Randall and Dr H. Boot had been making progress throughout the year on a new leap in radar technique: centimetric radar powered by the magnetron oscillator, which promised a revolution in range and clarity. Towards the end of 1940 scientists at the Telecommunications Research Establishment at Swanage were observing a submarine moving on the surface at a range of seven miles, and were preparing to install the equipment in aircraft. The advantages of a similar set for the surface escorts were obvious (as the Admiralty had already pointed out). It was a problem still hidden in the future that the new ASV III would have a further and compelling attraction in the form of a bombing aid – H2S – and so bring a competition with Bomber Command even more formidable than Fighter Command's claim to AI in place of ASV II.

Far worse, however, than these rivalries was the business of actual production, an area where the war revealed what Correlli Barnett calls:

> a disharmony between scientific genius and industrial backwardness. For while Britain could devise all these technological wonders, she could not make them quickly enough or in large enough quantities. . . . Thus on the eve of the Second World War the British radio and electrical industry, though prosperous, was in no sense a world leader, as the German industry had been before 1913, or the Japanese industry was to become after 1970. Rather, it was a follower, technically and commercially – and, even in terms of productivity, for output per man-hour in radio production in 1935 was less than a quarter of the American figure.[25]

A crisis was building up in this essential part of the war economy which could only be solved by even greater dependence on American production carried at high risk across the Atlantic; such cross-fertilization of sorrows is a familiar attribute of penury. But, says Barnett:

> the major *wartime* cause of the ... crisis was that from 1939 onwards this newest technology had suffered from a galloping attack of the classic British industrial disease – fragmentation of resources and effort, overlaps in product designs, batch production virtually by hand, utter want of standardisation of parts and components.

For all the participants in this nadir of British fortunes, it was clear that the rule was a familiar one:

> Jam tomorrow and jam yesterday – but never jam today.

For none was this more apparent than for the sailors and airmen fighting the Battle of the Atlantic.

It was in this period that the convoys first felt the weight of the U-boat attack – nothing yet comparable to what would happen when Dönitz overcame his 'dearth', but as we have already seen, destructive and frightening enough. It is time to take a closer look at the problem and the remedy. First, the ships that made up the convoys; the Official History always scrupulously lists them as 'British, Allied and Neutral', and a convoy was generally likely to contain ships of all three categories. But the British predominance in merchant shipping at that time was overwhelming, both in number of ocean–going ships and in gross registered tonnage, and was reflected in the usual composition of convoys (shown in the table on p. 286). These were the world's chief maritime powers; after them there is a steep drop – the next in order was Greece, with a total of 389 ships, 1,663,000 gross registered tons. In addition to the 2,695 ocean–going vessels on the British Register, there were some 1,000 coasters; these were only rarely targets for U-boats, but were under constant threat (which the Royal Navy was expected to contain) from German light naval craft, especially their very effective E-boats,[26] from the *Luftwaffe*, and from mines. On any given day, the average number of British vessels at sea was likely to be in the region of 2,500. That is the measure of the task faced by the Navy in its long–established duty of protecting British trade.

WORLD SHIPPING, 1939 (vessels of 1,600 GRT and over)

	Dry Cargo		Tankers		Total	
	Ships	GRT (000s)	Ships	GRT (000s)	Ships	GRT (000s)
British Empire	2,250	14,352	445	2,977	2,695	17,429
USA	1,020	5,670	389	2,836	1,409	8,506
Japan	1,007	4,600	47	430	1,054	5,030
Norway	548	2,100	268	2,109	816	4,209
Germany	676	3,506	37	256	713	3,762
France	454	2,313	48	326	502	2,639
Holland	370	2,111	107	540	477	2,651 [27]

The convoy remedy, as we have seen, was adopted before the actual outbreak of war, and this was just as well. It is only one more illustration of the value of the system that, by the end of 1939, out of 131 ships that had been sunk or damaged, 111 were due to maritime accident and only twenty to enemy activity. It is a further indicative fact that

> during the entire war, in the Atlantic, British home waters, the Caribbean and the Arctic, only twenty-five ships (one per cent of our total losses) were sunk by U-boats when both air and surface escorts were present. [28]

So another lesson of World War I was amply confirmed. But it is Cajus Bekker's assertion already quoted, that for every two convoys attacked, twenty passed unscathed, that is most illuminating, since it was this fact, above all, that constituted Dönitz's defeat. It also means that the characteristic convoy experience of the war, while plentifully endowed with the hazards and discomforts of the seaman's lot, and always under threat from the U-boat enemy, was far less often actually endangered by him:

> Atlantic convoys were drab, monotonous and unending. Some commodores and a good many merchant seamen trundled backwards and forwards for over five years without seeing a ship sunk or hearing a shot fired in anger. [29]

For the remainder, there was more than enough excitement, and for all there was the strain of expecting danger, which would increase proportionately to the length of time during which one had escaped it. Twenty-one convoy commodores and 35,000 merchant seamen lost their lives during World War II (compared with the Royal Navy's 51,578 killed and missing). Some proportion of the Merchant Navy's loss must be attributed to the slow appreciation of yet another World War I lesson – the need to include at least one specific rescue ship in each convoy; this was only met in 1942 (see pp. 439).

Convoys were designated 'fast' and 'slow'; by 1941 fast convoys were those containing ships capable of not less than 9 knots and (with luck) as many as 14.8; slow convoys were those which, it was hoped, might manage 8.9 knots and not less than 7.5, but often made much less. The eastbound HX convoys from Halifax were fast; the slow SC convoys sailed from Sydney; their westbound counterparts from Liverpool in 1940 were designated OB, (ONS from July 1941) with a brief OL fast group between September and October. After July, 1941, the fast westbound convoys were re-designated ON. But whatever the designation, these outward-bound convoys would generally be sailing in ballast, and

against prevailing westerlies this condition usually made the distinction between fast and slow convoys academic.[30]

Later in the war it would emerge that ships sailing in slow convoys spent nearly 30% more time at sea, and stood a 30% greater chance of being torpedoed; this was very far from being academic. Winter passages, it need hardly be said, were usually slower than those in summer – and Atlantic winters could be very long.

In the second half of 1940 the Director of the Admiralty's Trade Division (Assistant Chief of Naval Staff [Trade]) was Rear-Admiral H. R. Moore.[31] It was the Trade Division which was responsible for convoys, and for this work the key figures were the members of the Naval Control Service. On the outbreak of war, NCS staffs, each headed by a Naval Control Service Officer (NCSO), were sent out to ports across the globe with the specific function of handling every aspect of convoy activity while in harbour. The NCS was responsible for the assembly of the merchant ships, their business in harbour, their instruction in convoy procedures, arrangement within the convoy, sailing orders, charts, code-books and briefings. For this work it was necessary to win the confidence of the merchant skippers, and we have seen (pp. 60–61) that this was never an easy matter in either war. The fact that complaints about this vital sector of convoy life and work are extremely rare is perhaps the highest tribute the NCSOs and their hard-driven staffs could have.

Once at sea, the man responsible for the convoy as a whole was the Senior Officer of the Escort (SOE), virtually always a regular RN officer, a Commander or occasionally a Captain, but often a Lieutenant-Commander. Upon these relatively junior ranks fell responsibilities usually associated with admirals. The Senior Officer's duty would soon (April, 1941) be defined in a famous Convoy Instruction issued by Western Approaches Command (WACIS):

> The safe and timely arrival of the convoy at its destination is the primary object, and nothing releases the Escort Commander of [sic] his responsibility in this respect.

It sounds simple, and obvious; often it was nothing of the kind. There was always the other little matter: the matter of killing U-boats. Few naval officers in either war could bring themselves to accept such a view as Professor Marder's dictum, referring to 1917–18 (p. 87):

> Sinking submarines is a bonus, not a necessity.

In October, 1940, the unambiguous clarity of the Instruction had not yet been arrived at, and as we have seen, it was the lack of such precision that drew the unfortunate Commander Dickinson into 'classic error' when the U-boats pounced on SC7. He was not the only one, certainly not the last, to succumb to the temptation of his aggressive instinct. Western Approaches Command did its best in the Instruction to help the men in action towards the right decisions:

> the escort shares with all other fighting units the duty of destroying enemy ships, *provided that* this duty can be undertaken without undue prejudice to the safety of the convoy.

Within the convoy itself, the control of the merchant ships was the responsibility of the Convoy Commodore. These were nearly all retired

Flag Officers who had left the Navy as real commodores, rear-admirals even admirals, stepping down in rank in order to serve again. Each one's new duty was

> to sail aboard one of the merchant ships and control the navigation, zig-zags and stationing of vessels in convoy. It was to him that the masters would signal their troubles, the commodore acting as their interpreter to the escort commanders, who would probably have little knowledge of the vagaries of merchant ships and the difficulties of trying to manoeuvre them in convoy. Within the convoy the commodore passed all the orders.[32]

A Control Service Officer left this impression of the breed of Convoy Commodores:

> My first recollection of them was when I saw three elderly men in naval uniform, slowly climbing the stairs to the Control Office. Weathered, grizzled, they had a look of command, of race, for all their weariness and veteran aspect. Each wore on his chest a blaze of ribbons; each on his sleeves carried the broad band of commodore.
>
> Half way up they paused, like ageing horses on a hill. 'The old pump,' said one, 'isn't quite as good as it was.' Three pairs of eyes, amazingly young in wrinkled faces, interchanged glances of agreement. Then three pairs of legs, grown slow and a bit unsteady, stumped on up to my office. These are the elders of the sea who command our convoys.[33]

The Convoy Commodore's normal position was at the head of one of the centre columns of merchantmen; he would usually be in a large ship, well equipped for communication with the rest of the convoy, with the escort and with shore bases. He had a staff of five, chiefly signallers; at this stage, communication by night between escorts, between escorts and commodore and commodore to convoy was by wireless telegraphy, each message having to be encoded and decoded – a lengthy business. One lesson of the October battles was the need for a better means of communication; another was that

> quick communication is almost always preferable to complete security.[34]

By day the Convoy Commodore would use visual signalling (weather

289

permitting). On the flanks of larger convoys there would be vice- and rear-commodores, also with small signal staffs. It all sounds neat and orderly; but in a Labrador fog or a Force 8 gale, with ancient, barely seaworthy freighters, wireless sets that were antique and uncertain, and U-boats closing in, the whole edifice of the convoy could fall apart, and then it would be the duty of an elderly, weary commodore to find a way of stitching at least some of it together again.

There was, in 1940, no fixed doctrine concerning the size of convoys; this was dictated by the availability and readiness to sail of the merchant ships. There was an inclination to try to keep convoys small, in keeping with the smallness of the escort groups – but the very paucity of the escorts tended to work the other way. Later in the war operational research would show that large convoys were more practical, but no one had heard of operational research in these early days. Yet a convoy at sea, even then, was a big affair, impressive but difficult to supervise, awkward to patrol. A convoy of forty-five ships, says Roskill, would cover 5 square miles of sea. A broad front was preferred; Roskill's diagram shows a 45-ship convoy disposed in nine columns each of five ships, and a 55-ship convoy in eleven columns of five. Macintyre, on the other hand, referring to the 35-ship SC 7, says:

a convoy of 35 ships would be formed up in five columns of four ships and three columns of five ships each, the longer columns being in the centre. The columns would be five cables (half a mile) apart, the ships in column three cables (600 yards) apart . . .

Such a formation was necessary for several reasons. Long columns invariably became strung out. Whereas a column of five ships would probably be one and a half miles long, 15 ships would rarely be less than six or seven. Thus the broad-fronted formation was more compact from the point of view of escorting, while signals from the Commodore, leading one of the centre columns, could be seen simultaneously from all the ships. Furthermore, it offered a smaller target to submarines which normally attacked from the flank.[35]

Slow convoys had a bad name. Scraping the barrel for shipping, as losses and damage mounted, the Ministry of Transport collected together a fair number of antiquated vessels which should never have had to face the steep Atlantick. Merchant skippers were always a race of individualists, in the main contemptuous of naval disciplines (though

TYPICAL CONVOYS & ANTI-SUBMARINE ESCORTS   –   1940-1941

A. *Large convoy (45 ships) with weak escort (1 Destroyer & 3 Corvettes).*

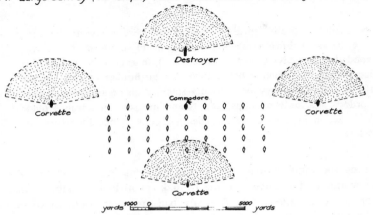

B. *Large convoy (55 ships) with strong escort (3 Destroyers & 7 Corvettes).*
Formation in fine weather with no indication of direction of U Boat attack.

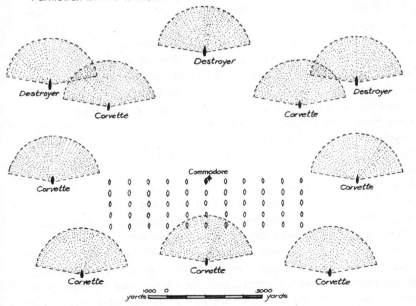

NOTE: *The shaded area ahead of each escort shows the area swept by its Asdic at 12 kts.*
and with 160° arc out to 2,500 yards.

Detection of a submerged submarine is, under average conditions, likely only with-
in 1200 - 1500 yards.

loud in demanding naval protection); some of the most stubbornly individualistic of them all were to be found in the slow convoys – perhaps because they had longer to nurse impatience and bad temper. Slow convoys, says Marc Milner,

> were characteristically unruly. Their ships were prone to belching smoke, breaking down, straggling (falling out of station in the convoy, beyond the protective screen of escorts . . .), or even romping ahead if stokers happened upon a better-than-average bunker of coal. In the early days slow convoys more often resembled an organized mob than an orderly assembly of ships, and their slow pace of advance made evasive action in the face of the enemy useless, if not altogether impossible.[36]

Making too much smoke was a heinous crime; on a clear day, the ordinary smoke of a convoy (trying to make as little as possible) could be seen from 50 miles away. A really bad emission could make this distance even greater.[37] Breakdowns were something that could not generally be helped; if they could not be put right quickly, the only thing to do was to send the ships concerned back to their port of origin or leave them behind (if past the mid-point of the voyage). Straggling was another matter; it implied, at best, a lack of due attention to sailing orders; at worst, it could signify a private intention to leave the convoy out of fear or sheer bloody-mindedness. For slow ships, the easiest way to do this was to fall behind, preferably at night; if caught by an escort, the captains of such stragglers developed a Nelsonian blindness to signals and sudden deafness to shouted orders, even through a loud-hailer from right alongside. If they were in that frame of mind there was nothing the naval officer could do about it. There was, however, a good deal the U-boat captain could do about it: in February, 1941, stragglers and their counterparts, the 'rompers' (ships with a few knots in hand which enabled them to push on ahead of the convoy),[38] accounted for half the sinkings performed by U-boats. Greek ships (still neutral during this winter) were notorious for both practices. Communication, in a polyglot assembly, presented more than usual difficulty; language was a problem, darkness was a problem. If a U-boat threat was perceived ahead, the commodore could order a zig-zag change of course, which meant turning the whole unwieldy mass 45° to port or starboard, all ships (in theory) turning simultaneously. The order for this could be conveyed by flags or coloured lights, and if the state of the sea was not too dreadful, and the commodore had drilled his convoy beforehand, the turn might be made without undue loss of formation – but that was not the end of the story:

> Probably the most dreaded thing of all to the commodore was the sudden clamping down of fog before he had a chance to hoist a signal telling the convoy to cease zig-zagging and resume the mean course.[39]

As regards the U-boats, all one could do, says Admiral Creighton, was to leave the escorts to deal with them and hope for the best:

> There was little of a practical nature one could do in a six-knot convoy.

A corvette officer puts it slightly differently. The main thing about a convoy, he says, is that

> it doesn't retreat, or re-form on a new line or execute strategic withdrawal to previously prepared positions. It sails on: having no choice and, in the last analysis, wishing none.[40]

It was not only U-boats and FW 200s that threatened the convoys as 1940 drew to an end. The 'big-ship, big-gun men' in the *Marineleitung* (see p. 185) still held their entrenched positions, even with a large part of Germany's surface fleet sunk or crippled. Under the interesting title, 'The Construction of a Post-War Fleet', a memorandum issued in early July stated:

> The Naval Staff holds that the salient lesson of the war to date should be the recognition that the remarkable development and performance of the Luftwaffe, and the achievements of the U-boat and mine-laying campaigns, have done nothing to undermine the importance of the capital ship.[41]

This document then proceeded to discuss very seriously 'The Rebirth of the Battleship', and propounded the somewhat amazing doctrine that

> The main protagonist in the war against the enemy's ocean communications is the battleship itself.

One of the most famous convoy posters of the war, with its bitterly ironical caption. It was drawn in 1941 by Captain Jack Broome who writes: 'It is worth emphasising how hopeless straggling was. Escorts couldn't cope. The only chap who enjoyed it was the U-boat fielding longstop.'

U-boats, it asserted, were needed only as a stop-gap until sufficient battleships were built to strike the decisive blow against Allied shipping; it envisaged a force of no more than 200 submarines (including training craft). The possession of the French Atlantic ports was seen as offering the perfect opportunity to put this belief to the test. Dönitz's private reactions to this expedition into the world of dreams may be imagined.

In any case, for the time being it faced a tiresome difficulty: in the summer of 1940 Germany had no operational battleships. *Bismarck* was still fitting out, and *Tirpitz*, the other very large exemplar envisaged in the 'Z' Plan, was not yet completed. *Scharnhorst* and *Gneisenau* were undergoing repairs after torpedo hits off Norway; *Lützow* had lost her stern in the same campaign and was also in dock. *Admiral Scheer*, one of the two surviving pocket-battleships, had been extensively reconstructed, and no sooner was this completed than she had to go back into dock with engine damage. The only available heavy unit was the cruiser *Admiral Hipper* and she, too, was in dock with engine trouble at the end of September. By the end of October, however, *Scheer* was seaworthy, and on the last day of that month she passed out into the Atlantic, the first German surface vessel to appear since the demise of *Admiral Graf Spee*. It now fell to her to carry out the injunction of *Vizeadmiral* Günther Lütjens, the Fleet Commander:

> Our job is to put as many (merchant ships) as possible under the waters.

There was, however, a rider to this: in view of Germany's weakness, the battleships were forbidden to engage a convoy if even only one British battleship was present. Cajus Bekker remarks:

> Consequently the British Admiralty did well to provide as many as
> / possible of their vital North Atlantic convoys with battleship escorts.

However, there was no battleship with the thirty-seven ships of convoy HX 84, sighted by *Scheer*'s reconnaissance aircraft on 5 November. Its escort consisted only of the 14,000-ton armed merchant cruiser *Jervis Bay*, with her eight elderly 6-inch guns. As the pocket-battleship closed the convoy and opened fire with her 280 mm (11 inch) battery, Captain E. S. F. Fegen of the *Jervis Bay* inscribed another page in the Royal Navy's long tradition of unhesitating self-sacrifice. This is not altogether to be wondered at – he was the representative of the fifth generation of his family to be naval officers. As he turned *Jervis Bay* towards her overwhelmingly more powerful opponent, he knew as well as anyone what the outcome was bound to be. He had ordered the convoy to disperse and his sole object now was to keep the raider busy while the merchantmen made their escape in the growing darkness of the late November afternoon. Captain Fegen was not permitted very much time even for this; in just over twenty minutes,[42] without having touched his enemy, his blazing ship went down taking her mortally wounded captain and some 200 of his crew with her. The merchant ships scattered in the failing light with the help of screens of smoke, and *Scheer* was only able to find five of them, totalling 38,720 tons – that, and a posthumous VC, were Captain Fegen's rewards for impeccable valour.

The reward of this action for the Germans was not to be measured by the tonnage sunk; it lay in the general consternation and disorganization resulting from the awareness of the new threat. For any kind of punitive or protective procedures against a pocket- (or any other type) battleship, the burden always fell upon the Home Fleet, itself none too strong (and not to be compared with the mighty array of heavy warships that Jellicoe and Beatty had disposed of). The British capital ships now moved individually to intercept the raider; all shipping was temporarily diverted; two more HX convoys, already at sea, were recalled to Canada, while a Bermuda-Halifax convoy also returned to port. These proceedings naturally caused serious congestion in the ports themselves, and delays in essential deliveries. The normal HX convoy cycle was not, in fact, resumed for twelve days, with HX 89.

Admiral Scheer's foray marked the beginning of a period which Cajus Bekker has identified as the 'zenith' of the German heavy ships and armed merchant cruisers. It will perhaps be convenient to summarize her own career. Having dealt with HX 84, she turned south, making first for the South Atlantic and then the Indian Ocean, thus cleanly evading the British ships searching for her. Her performance, says Roskill, 'demonstrated the excellent qualities of her class for commerce raiding.' Her outstanding quality was her range: 19,000 nautical miles without refuelling; this enabled her to make a voyage of 46,419 miles in five months without dropping anchor, during which she sank sixteen merchant ships over and above the *Jervis Bay*, totalling 99,059 tons. She returned to Kiel on 1 April.

In sharp contrast was the performance of the next heavy ship to enter the Atlantic, the cruiser *Admiral Hipper*, which made her appearance in early December. Her distinguishing characteristic was her high speed – 32 knots – as long as her sophisticated engines permitted. Otherwise, she was lightly armoured and therefore vulnerable; she carried eight 203 mm (8-in) guns, but her maximum endurance was no more than 6,800 nautical miles. To enable her to make her sortie, four tankers were also required. She was, in fact, 'suitable only for short-range operations'.[43] This first Atlantic venture by the *Hipper* was by no means brilliant; haunted by bad weather, engine trouble and fuel problems, she missed the Halifax convoys; turning south, she did find a convoy, but it was a troop convoy with a strong escort (WS 5A) making for the Middle East. *Hipper* turned away, having inflicted only slight damage, and entered Brest on 27 December – the first major German warship to use an Atlantic port. She did rather better in 1941, taking part in February in the only combined air, surface and U-boat operation that ever, according to Dönitz, took place in the Atlantic. At almost precisely the same time, the two most valuable units (as it proved) of the German surface fleet, the battleships *Gneisenau* and *Scharnhorst*, were at large there, beginning the most successful cruise by surface vessels of this whole period. But on 8 February they experienced the mortification of sighting a fine convoy target (HX 106), only to observe almost immediately the fighting top of a battleship amongst the merchantmen. It was HMS *Ramillies*, and, obedient to their categorical orders, the Germans turned away. However, their cruise was definitely successful: twenty-two ships (115,000 tons) in two months, sixteen of them in two days (15–16 March); on 22 March they entered Brest. The statistics of this period (table on p. 298) tell the story. The table is revealing. It is to be remembered that this was the absolute peak of the regular surface fleet's anti-shipping performance; yet its tonnage count was almost matched by that of six merchant raiders. And as will be seen, the heyday of the surface vessels coincided with the lowest level of U-boat strength; yet all of them together, naval and auxiliary, could only achieve a tonnage total of a little over half that of the U-boats. Dönitz was generous indeed in his acknowledgments to the big ships; their employment, he says,

> during the very months in which the U-boat arm was so weak in numbers proved to have been a sound decision and resulted in very successful support being given to the U-boats which until then had been operating alone in the fight against enemy shipping.[45]

| | Gross registered tonnage (number of ships) lost in sinkings by: | | |
	U-boats	Warship raiders	Merchant raiders
1940			
November	146,613 (32)	48,748 (11)	74,923 (9)
December	212,590 (37)	20,971 (3)	25,904 (5)
1941			
January	126,782 (21)	18,738 (3)	78,484 (20)
February	196,783 (39)	79,086 (17)	7,031 (1)
March	243,020 (41)	89,838 (17)	28,707 (4)
	925,788 (170)	257,381 (51)	215,049 (39)
		472,430 (90)	

Taking into account all the German Navy's activities at this time, Bekker says that it

> succeeded in keeping its powerful adversary busy in nearly all the oceans of the world. Unquestionably the naval initiative in early 1941 was held by Grand-Admiral Raeder in Berlin, whereas his opposite number, First Sea Lord and Admiral of the Fleet Sir Dudley Pound, was in a position of constantly having to react to the latest move of his German enemy, and guessing when and where he would strike next.[46]

However, looking at the tonnage sunk and the number of ships lost to the Allies, Bekker pertinently asks:

> was this figure any greater than the losses that the handful of German U-boats had been inflicting on the convoys month after month? Did the success won by the heavy surface ships justify the tremendous outlay that their use entailed?

For the time being Raeder and his staff clearly thought that the big ships had fully justified themselves, and they looked forward to repeating the exercise, eagerly awaiting the day when their two biggest units – *Bismarck* and *Tirpitz* – could come into action. Their awakening would not be long delayed.

* * * * *

It was of the essence of this nadir of British fortunes that everything seemed to be happening at once, blows falling from all directions on a nation almost totally unprepared. The background to the autumn convoy crises of 1940, whether from surface ships or FW 200s or from U-boats, was the Blitz, which from a maritime point of view took a very sinister turn on 7 September. On that day some 300 German bombers, escorted by virtually the whole available strength of the *Luftwaffe*'s fighters, made a deliberate attack on the London dock area, following it up that night and on the next two nights as well. In the course of this onslaught 21,000 gross tons of shipping were sunk and 48,000 damaged, and the decision was now taken to move all ocean-going ships out of the Port of London. One must beware of jumping to over-simple conclusions; the Official History says:

> Though . . . the bombing was the final reason for this decision, it was not the only one, nor the most cogent; the Port of London remained largely closed for several years after the bombing had ended; it was the E-boats and mines in the North Sea, and the air attack on ships sailing there, making the approaches to all the east coast ports extremely danger-ous for ocean-going ships, that brought on the port and transit system of this country its long-expected ordeal.[47]

So vastly have times changed that we need to be reminded that in the normal peacetime conditions of those days over 27% by weight of all Britain's imports came in through the Thames estuary, above all the Port of London, which was the entry point for more than half of the nation's meat supplies and the site of most of her cold storage. A similar proportion of butter and cheese came to London, for the same reason. In all, the east and south coast ports normally accounted for almost 60% of Britain's dry cargo imports; in the last quarter of 1940, this figure had dropped to 18%. It is obvious that a shift of traffic of these dimensions could only bring an immense burden to the ports in the west, and so it proved:

> By the end of 1940, conditions on Merseyside, Clydeside and in the Bristol Channel seemed to be fulfilling all the worst expectations about the confusion that diversion of ships from the east coast would cause. Complaints poured in about the multitude of difficulties – about shor-tages of transport, storage, labour and equipment, about consignees who could not be identified or who would not decide where they wished their goods to be sent. Suppose, on top of all this, there were heavy air raids on the west coast?[48]

The raids were not long withheld: Southampton on 23/24 November, Bristol on 24/25 November, Liverpool on 28/29 November. Southampton again on the last night of that month, and then Liverpool once more on three successive nights just before Christmas, 20/21, 21/22 and 22/23 December. The docks were at the centre of the bombing; Nicholas Monsarrat walked back to his corvette through streets blocked by the previous night's devastation:

> Across the street it was the same, and farther on the same, and all the way to the ship the same: what was not still burning lay in red-hot piles of brick and wood; what was not torn to pieces was blasted into a vile disorder. . . . We waited on board that same evening as the hands crawled round the clock towards another night, another testing-time, another ordeal. Hoses were rigged, sand-buckets filled and placed, wires run out to the opposite side of the dock in case the tall building alongside should take fire: the duty-watch were given their instructions and told to stand by: but all these precautions seemed to be off-set, rendered foolish even, by the opposing facts – the ship lay in the heart of the docks, and within a hundred yards two uncontrollable fires raged, unsubdued from the previous night, pointing beacons across the whole night sky. The day died, the fires showed stronger; at midnight the expected sirens went again.[49]

Even before the bombing of the west coast ports began, the disorganization caused by their sudden new burden entailed delays in handling estimated as equivalent to an annual rate of loss of imports of not less than $2\frac{1}{2}$ to 3 million tons a year (about 10% of the total). In addition, there was a mounting and seemingly intractable burden of repair of ships damaged by bombing, by U-boat or E-boat attack, by mines, or by the hazards of sea-faring through the 'frozen malice' of the Atlantic winters. By the end of the year the amount of dry-cargo shipping under or awaiting repair was some 2,000,000 gross tons, or 13% of the whole merchant fleet.[50] Losses at sea from all causes amounted to just under 4,000,000 tons (1,059 ships), of which the U-boats accounted for rather more than half the tonnage and just under half the ships. That was the size and shape of the crisis – only mitigated by the acquisition of some 3,000,000 deadweight tons of foreign shipping from countries overrun by the Germans earlier in the year. These gains, as the Official Historians say, were indeed a blessing – not because they made the shipping position easy but because without them it might, by the late spring of 1941, have become disastrous.

However,

The same blessing could not be bestowed twice.[51]

Furthermore, in the real condition of British shipbuilding referred to above it was clear that salvation would not come from her own yards; for the more distant future, that left only one hope – American shipbuilding. But in early 1941 neutral America's shipbuilding miracles were all in a future that could neither be assumed nor estimated.[52] It is not surprising, as one contemplates this complex of depressing circumstance, to find Churchill admitting that

it was to me almost a relief to turn from these deadly under-tides to the ill-starred but spirited enterprises in the military sphere. How willingly would I have exchanged a full-scale attempt at invasion for this shapeless, measureless peril expressed in charts, curves and statistics![53]

However, the peril was recognized and resolutely gripped by a deft mixture of democratic and undemocratic methods. It is a time-honoured recourse of democracy to appoint a committee – in this case a sub-committee of the existing Economic Policy Committee of the War Cabinet. On 19 December the Sub-Committee on Port Clearance was set up with instructions to find a solution to the chaos in the docks 'not later than 2 January, 1941', which may seem somewhat of a tall order, but in fact the sub-committee made its recommendation on 30 December. The decision was

to appoint 'dictators' to the chief west coast port areas. They were to be styled Regional Port Directors.[54]

Their function would be

to assume responsibility for the day-to-day operation of the ports in their areas and to co-ordinate all the activities involved in working them,

301

which was not merely highly undemocratic but another very tall order, too. That notwithstanding, the Minister of Labour, Ernest Bevin, now added substantially to it by insisting that the Port Directors must also be responsible for dock labour. He argued that the whole labour structure of the industry would have to be changed, and quickly, and the only people suitable for tackling that must be the Directors because 'there could not be two managers in the ports'. Mr Bevin was a strong character, a long-standing dockers' leader and founder of the Transport and General Workers Union; he gained his point. And that left only one more problem.

> To operate for the first time a scheme involving many thousands of men notorious for their intractability; to impose on them a degree of discipline to which they are unaccustomed and may be unwilling to submit; to make use of the services of some of the former employers on terms and, if necessary, to dispense with those of others – all this must require a very high degree of tact, judgment, skill and firmness, and could hardly be achieved by persons with no previous knowledge of the industry. But where was one to find a person of the right type, let alone several persons?

As the sub-committee debated this question, it quickly became apparent 'that it was no use looking for perfection, but necessary to do something and to do it immediately. The essential was to have a single over-riding authority in the ports.' Three appointments were made (for Bristol, the Mersey and the Clyde), of which two were to men with no previous knowledge of ports, shipping or industrial relations. The third was the Assistant General Manager of the Port of London, Mr (later Sir) Robert Letch, who now went to the Clyde. For all three, says Miss Behrens,

> The distinguishing feature of their position was that they were given virtually a free hand to override the various local authorities, and the various representatives of Government departments in the ports, including the representatives of the Service departments, who had for so long been a thorn in the flesh of the Port Emergency Committees. . . . Executive powers as unfettered as theirs were, apparently, granted to no other civilians in the country.

That fact alone displays the gravity of the crisis.

It is convenient to carry this story forward a short distance to the end of this act. Perhaps to the disappointment of incorrigible lovers of British amateurism, but not in any degree to the surprise of serious historians, it at once turned out that the man with the professional qualifications was the immediate outstanding success:

> The greatest achievements were in the Clyde, where diversion of shipping had caused the greatest difficulties. The Clyde had to deal not simply with different kinds of imports but with a larger total volume. Moreover, in the main port, Glasgow, there was a serious lack of shed and storage space, and the rail connections with the south and east were notoriously bad. Yet by the end of March the Regional Port Director could report that traffic congestion had been eliminated.[55]

If the success story on the Clyde was without question the most dramatic, Bristol and the Mersey also made significant progress, illustrated by turn-round figures which were already showing marked improvement in April. The test came at Liverpool in May. Starting on the night of 1/2 May, the Germans bombed Liverpool heavily on eight successive nights, the city's worst (but fortunately last) experience of this ordeal. Once again, the docks were at the centre; at one stage, out of 130 deep-sea berths normally available, only twelve were usable; the railways were largely paralysed by débris on the lines; the telephone system broke down; passenger transport in the city was in chaos; 3,966 people were killed and 3,812 seriously injured; 10,000 dwellings were destroyed and 184,000 damaged. Shipping losses, thanks to well-planned diversions, were negligible, but at the time there was no lack of Jeremiahs who proclaimed that one or two more nights of this treatment would have put the Port of Liverpool out of action altogether, and even that national defeat might have been in sight. The Official Historian, Miss Behrens, makes this riposte:

> There can never be any certain answer to assertions of this sort, but it must be confessed that the second of these seems to have no basis in fact. No one can say in advance what human ingenuity and endurance can achieve, or decide in retrospect where the limit must have come. All that can be said about the position in May is that the available evidence gives no support at all to the pessimists. On the contrary, not only had the average rate of turn-round throughout the country never been so good in any previous month as it was in May; even if one looks at the

figures of shipping in the Mersey in May and June, and compares them with the figures for the preceding and following months, *it is barely apparent that anything unusual had occurred.*[56]

This is a very remarkable statement; it is not only a deserved tribute to the personal qualities of the Regional Port Directors themselves, but it is the affirmation of a victory of immeasurable value in the trade war, a milestone in the progress of the Battle of the Atlantic without which it is hard to see how Britain would even have reached, let alone overcome, the terrible times that lay ahead.

* * * * *

This was, indeed, a time for milestones; while the harbour side of the battle was receiving this essential reorganization, the naval side was undergoing similar drastic change. It was at the beginning of February that the 'fertile suggestion' put forward by Churchill in August at last bore fruit. His proposal had been to set up a new Command for the Atlantic battle in the Clyde; this suggestion, he says, 'had encountered resistance, and it was not until February, 1941, that the increasing pressure of events produced Admiralty compliance.'[57] It is a familiar political line, to harp on, or hint at obstinacy and lack of imagination in the military hierarchies – here we have an audible echo of the Lloyd George–Jellicoe 'confrontation' in early 1917 (see pp. 58–9), with as little foundation. The Admiralty was never convinced that the Clyde was the right place for the headquarters of a new Command, which would necessarily (if it was to function properly) also have to accommodate an RAF headquarters. Its choice fell upon Liverpool, the central area fed by the Western Approaches, and Churchill agrees that this was the right decision.

The site chosen was Derby House, and work was quickly started to transform the interior of this building into a bomb-proof inter-Service headquarters of a new type – as though the famous Fighter Command Operations Room at Bentley Priory, Stanmore, had gained a second dimension. At Derby House the centrepiece was also an Operations Room, whose outstanding feature was the huge wall-chart and its subsidiaries known as 'the Plot'. Twice room height, and about twice as much as that in width, was the main Atlantic Plot which duplicated the Trade and U-boat Plot in the Operational Intelligence Centre at the Admiralty. By teleprinter link, these two nerve-centres fed information to each other, ensuring the most up-to-date indications on their respective charts. At Derby House the Plot showed at a glance

the position of every convoy, every escort group, every rescue tug, every
air patrol, every U-boat report, and every detatched unit of the Royal
Navy.[58]

Serviced 24 hours a day, the plot was changed every four hours to
indicate new positions by relays of the WRNS

who flitted up and down telescopic ladders with the agility of trapeze ar-
tists.[59]

Opposite, two up and two down, were four rooms looking out on the
Plot through glass fronts; the upper pair contained the Admiral Com-
manding in Chief, Western Approaches Command, and beside him,
with inter-communicating door, the AOC-in-C, No 15 Group of
Coastal Command. On 17 February these officers were, respectively,
Admiral Sir Percy Noble and Air Vice-Marshal J. M. Robb. The two
rooms below them contained the naval 'Duty Commanders' and the
RAF 'Duty Controllers' who presided over the Plot night and day.
There can rarely have been more intimate and continuous inter-Service
cooperation than that of the Operations Room in Derby House during
the next four years.

Sir Percy Noble has suffered in historiography through an attribute
which was not uncommon in naval officers of his generation: he did
not advertise. As a consequence, his is not one of the naval names that
spring immediately to the mind and lips. But it is significant that,
whenever he does obtain a mention, it is always approving; according
to a brother officer, writing in 1942, he was

A man of great personal charm, supremely fit both in mind and body,
immaculate in his dress and in his relations with others. An officer of
experience, with a brain always ready to grapple with new problems
from new angles, of great tolerance and with a passion for seeing points
of view other than his own.[60]

Every witness testifies to his charm; Admiral Creighton says:

He got his way not by the power of his position but by far more potent
weapons – charm and personality.[61]

305

Roskill goes beneath the surface with an analysis of what may, perhaps, have been a subconscious reason for this pleasing manner:

> He recognized from the earliest days that the Battle of the Atlantic would ultimately be won by the side whose morale was the higher; that to achieve a morale that would overcome all difficulties, and would rise above all tragedies and set-backs, demanded that the Captains of the escort vessels and aircraft should have complete confidence in his shore organization.[62]

Sir Percy Noble's recipe for this was twofold: to strive unremittingly for the maximum efficiency of all the shore departments, so that the men who had battled the U-boat enemy and the wild Atlantic should never have the sense of finding a new enemy waiting for them when they returned to port. His own part was characteristic:

> he constantly went to sea in the little ships and flew in the lonely aircraft of Coastal Command, sharing their dangers and their discomforts.

Admiral Noble, said the officer quoted above, in addition to this talent for a rare style of leadership, also possessed 'the qualities of a diplomat as well as of a sailor'.[63] This was a necessity, for giving leadership to the naval ships' companies and the airmen was only half the work of the C-in-C, Western Approaches; there were, in addition, the owners, masters and crews of the Merchant Navy, the ships that made up the convoys for whose routing and control he was also responsible. Here, too, his methods succeeded:

> The shipping interests had to be given faith in the organization for the protection of trade, and insight into the problems with which the naval authorities were faced. Sir Percy Noble accomplished these difficult tasks with conspicuous success. Frankness – a complete disarming frankness – as practised by Percy Noble, carried the day. Suspicion went by the board, and a fuller cooperation and mutual trust reigned in its stead.[64]

Derby House contained the brain cells that decided all the movements and policies of the Command, but, says Admiral Creighton, anyone wanting to flush a covey of commodores or a shoal of masters went not to Derby House but to the Liver Building, a miniature sky-scraper riddled with shipping offices, which dwarfed the humbler houses along the waterfront of the north of the Mersey.[65]

Here the reigning potentate was the Flag Officer in Charge, Liverpool, who was, in 1940, Rear-Admiral Ritchie. There were seven Flag Officers controlling the Western Approaches ports, and upon them fell the responsibility of ensuring that merchant ships were formed into convoys and ready to sail on their appointed dates; the Flag Officers, in other words, governed the convoy cycle. It was in the Liver Buildings that all the seemingly petty and often exceedingly tiresome details of a Liverpool convoy's existence were dealt with, and it was here, too, that

the individual battles of the Atlantic were refought. Here survivors came to tell their stories to avoid needless repetition of suffering and privation; here mistakes were analysed so they were not made again; here suggestions of masters, seamen, firemen and cooks were given equal consideration.

Once more it will be helpful to look ahead. Post mortems, held by all concerned, were the essential and continuing means by which, under Noble and his successor, Western Approaches Command strove for excellence, the only quality which could ensure the defeat of its resourceful enemies. And as with the U-boats themselves, training was the essence of the matter: training at Tobermory, under Admiral Stephenson, training at all odd hours of the day and night aboard the escort vessels themselves, to a degree which sometimes seemed to merit the adjective 'merciless', and later, under Noble's impulse in January, 1942, training in his new Western Approaches Tactical Unit. The Tactical Unit course was known as 'the Game'; it lasted a week, and some 5,000 Allied officers, 'from Admirals to Midshipmen', passed through it. And having done so, and returned to sea, they would endlessly discuss the problems which 'the Game' had thrown up, and by these discussions arm themselves against the surprises of real war:

In this way a common doctrine was established, enabling them to act as the Commander-in-Chief would wish them to act without signals.[66]

Only by these means could the distressing scenes of October, 1940, be avoided; what was also needed, of course, was a reasonable degree of permanence in the composition of the escort groups, and that would depend on the numbers available. Noble knew the need, and kept it before the eyes of those who had to provide for it.

The real war itself, in the steep Atlantick, after a lull in November and December, was once again 'rising in intensity'.[67] *Admiral Hipper*, *Scharnhorst* and *Gneisenau* were all at large, the FW 200s were active, and now joined by two groups of Heinkel 111s, one operating from Brest, the other from Norway; '90,000 tons of shipping was sunk by these aircraft.' In March the air offensive against the southern and western ports was stepped up: 238 German aircraft over Portsmouth on the night of 11 March, 316 over Merseyside the next night, and a follow-up attack on the one after that, on which same night (13/14 March) 236 aircraft attacked the Clyde, with 203 following on the 14th/15th; on the night of the 16th, Bristol, too, was attacked. The February shipping losses had mounted by over 80,000 tons to 403,493 (102 ships) and the First Sea Lord was already reporting heavy losses in March. Churchill wrote:

> this mortal danger to our life-lines gnawed my bowels.[68]

He decided that this was a peril which must be lifted 'to the highest plane, over everything else'. He accordingly 'proclaimed' the Battle of the Atlantic – though as we have seen, this had actually begun as far back as the previous July. His purpose, however, was not to produce accurate history, but something more immediate:

> This, like featuring 'the Battle of Britain' nine months earlier, was a signal intended to concentrate all minds and all departments concerned upon the U-boat war.

His next step was to form an Atlantic Committee consisting of the appropriate ministers, the Chiefs of the Naval and Air Staffs and their scientific advisers, with himself in the chair. Its first meeting was on 19 March, and the tempo of its further meetings matched that of the Battle itself in 1941: weekly until 8 May, then fortnightly, then less frequently until the final meeting on 21 October. At these meetings, says Churchill,

The whole field was gone over and everything thrashed out; nothing was held up for want of decision.

Even before the committee's meetings began, he had drawn up its Directive in unmistakable terms; this was entitled *The Battle of The Atlantic*, and dated 6 March, 1941; it is too long to quote in full, but substantial quotation is required because this document not merely outlines the practical approaches that would be made to the enormous problem, but also, by its tone, it reveals the stresses of the crisis:

1. We must take the offensive against the U-boat and the Focke-Wulf wherever we can and whenever we can. The U-boat at sea must be hunted, the U-boat in the building yard or in dock must be bombed. The Focke-Wulf and other bombers employed against our shipping must be attacked in the air and in their nests.

2. Extreme priority will be given to fitting out ships to catapult or otherwise launch fighter aircraft against bombers attacking our shipping. Proposals should be made within a week.

3. All the measures approved and now in train for the concentration of the main strength of the Coastal Command upon the North-Western Approaches, and their assistance on the East Coast by Fighter and Bomber Commands, will be pressed forward . . .

6. The Admiralty will have the first claim on all the short-range A.A. guns and other weapons that they can mount upon suitable merchant ships plying in the danger zone . . .

7. We must be ready to meet concentrated air attacks on the ports on which we specially rely (Mersey, Clyde and Bristol Channel). They must therefore be provided with a maximum defence. A report of what is being done should be made within a week.

8. A concerted attack by all departments involved must be made upon the immense mass of damaged shipping now accumulated in our ports. By the end of June this mass must be reduced by not less than 400,000 tons net . . .

9. Every form of simplification and acceleration of repairs and degaussing, even at some risk, must be applied in order to reduce the terrible slowness of the turn-round of ships in British ports. A saving of fifteen days in this process would in itself be equivalent to 5 million tons of imports, or a tonnage [equal to] $1\frac{1}{4}$ millions of the importing fleet saved . . .

10. The Minister of Labour has achieved agreement in his conference with employers and employed about the interchangeability of labour at

the ports. This should result in a substantially effective addition to the total labour force. In one way or another, at least another 40,000 men must be drawn into ship-repairing, ship-building and dock labour at the earliest moment . . .

11. The Ministry of Transport will ensure that there is no congestion at the quays, and that all goods landed are immediately removed . . . [The Minister] should also report weekly to the Import Executive upon the progress made . . .

12. A Standing Committee has been set up of representatives from the Admiralty Transport Department, the Ministry of Shipping, and the Ministry of Transport, which will meet daily and report all hitches or difficulties encountered . . .

13. In addition to what is being done at home, every effort must be made to ensure a rapid turn-round at ports abroad.[69]

It not infrequently occurs, in peace as well as in war, that there is many a slip 'twixt the Directive and the fulfilment. This was only the first crisis of the Battle of the Atlantic, and it would be deeds, not words, that resolved it. But Churchill had made a start; he was often wrong during the war, he could be infuriating to men doing their best under great strain, and absurdly exhausting in his manner of doing business, but it cannot be denied that he knew about running a war, and this Directive tells us that Britain's second battle for survival was being gripped.

3

iii: As Though the Defence Had Won

'The months of July and August saw the North Atlantic U-boat operations sink to their lowest level of effectiveness, and it looked almost as though the defence had won the race against the attack.'

Dr Jürgen Rohwer

ADMIRAL DÖNITZ, IN captivity, must often have reflected that 1941 had been a sickening year. Sixteen months into the war, it found the U-boat arm at its very lowest numbers; instead of the minimum of 300 boats which he had urged upon Hitler as an absolute necessity in September, 1939, Dönitz's front-line fleet could muster no more than twenty-one or twenty-two. The reasons for this appalling state of affairs, as listed by the Naval Ordnance Department, were numerous and irrefutable:

Delays caused by labour shortage, multiple conversions to auxiliary warships after the outbreak of war, delayed completion of dockyards, raw material shortages, economy in metals, overdue deliveries of steel castings and torpedo tubes. Transport difficulties, the black-out and air raid alarms, type alterations, crash programme for Operation SEALION.[1]

It is a catalogue which vividly exposes the conditions of the German economy at the zenith of Nazi power, and the incapacity of Hermann Göring who ruled over it. It goes a long way to explain why Germany lost the war. And for Dönitz it spelt that endless deferment of hope that 'maketh the heart sick'.

It is indicative of the farsightedness and strength of character of the *BdU* that, despite frequent urgings in these depressing phases of U-boat weakness, he would never obey the temptation to overcome the shortage of operational boats at the expense of training. It was during this period that *Fähnrich* Herbert Werner joined Type VIIC *U557* in Königsberg:

> The boat was weatherbeaten. The conning tower looked like a sur-realistic painting. The protective red undercoat showed in streaks through the splintered gray surface paint. Rust had formed everywhere, even around the barrel of the heavily greased 8.8 cm gun on the fore-deck. There was a light green shine of algae on the wooden deck that covered the steel hull.[2]

This run-down appearance was the consequence of a 'shakedown' cruise in the Baltic which had lasted no less than seven months. This kind of programme ensured that at the peak of its form, when the operational fleet received a reinforcement, the new boat would be fully operational. Dönitz clearly believed that, if the price for this was high, it was well worth paying. As we shall see, some of his opponents could not afford the luxury.

One development in January, 1941, seemed to hold out promise of needed help; haunted as ever by lack of 'eyes', Dönitz took up once more the fight for his own air arm (see p. 270), and on 7 January he won his point: *KG 40* was placed directly under his command by Hitler's order. This, he wrote in the War Diary,

> is a great step forward. It is, admittedly, only the first step in the right direction and, with the few machines available and the host of technical details that remain to be settled, its visible effects will not at first be very great. But in principle we are on the right lines, and I am confident that in time we shall reap the maximum rewards that are to be gained from such co-operation.[3]

His confidence was misplaced; *KG 40*'s Condors continued to take a toll of shipping, but the practical effects of air/sea cooperation were always disappointing. Göring, as may be supposed, was irate at this infringement of his prerogatives, and at a meeting between the two men (their first) he tried to persuade Dönitz to relinquish Hitler's 'gift'. Dönitz naturally refused:

> He then asked me to stay to dinner, but I declined the invitation, and we parted bad friends.

One more of the Third Reich's internal feuds was duly launched.

There was deceptive promise in the first joint actions under the new régime,[4] but there were warning signals also. Only two days after the meeting between Dönitz and Göring, on 9 February, *U 37* sighted the homeward-bound convoy HG 53 from Gibraltar some 160 miles south-west of Cape St Vincent. *Korvettenkapitän* Oerhn at once attacked and sank two ships. He then homed in six of *KG 40*'s Condors, which proceeded to sink another five. This was the reverse of the way it was intended to be done, but Dönitz did not complain. *U 37* then sank another ship from the convoy, and tried to bring the *Admiral Hipper* also to the scene. She arrived too late for the convoy, but found a straggler which she duly added to the bag. Dönitz remarks:

> This was the only combined air, surface ship and U-boat operation that ever took place in the Atlantic.[5]

Ten days later the procedure followed a more orthodox pattern. This time it was a Condor which called a U-boat to OB 288, which in turn called up others, and when the escort turned back at 20°W the pack fell to and sank nine ships. A week later, however, it was the other way round again. On this occasion Günther Prien found OB 290; he called up Kretschmer and six Condors, with the result that the U-boats sank three ships and the FW 200s nine with two more damaged – a very serious loss. These episodes fully explain Churchill's vehemence in his Directive on 6 March. In general, however, Dönitz was disappointed in the results achieved, and he admits:

> our main problem, how to locate convoys in the main North Atlantic theatre of operations, still remained unsolved in the summer of 1941.

Much harder to bear was the series of shocks that now followed. It was on the evening of 6 March that Prien's lookout in *U 47* sighted the smoke of the outward-bound OB 293. Prien's signals brought a number of U-boats to the scene, including Kretschmer in *U 99* and *Korvettenkapitän* Matz in *U 70*. When darkness fell the pack closed in, confident in its well-tried tactic of invisible surface attack. Kretschmer, as usual, soon scored hits; explosions and distress rockets gave promise of another convoy tragedy on familiar lines. But this time things worked out differently. This escort group reacted with an evident sense of purpose, showing no disposition to imitate earlier 'wet hen' procedures. *U 47* and the Turkish-ordered *UA* were forced to dive and driven off, the latter badly damaged; even Kretschmer had to break off his attack with half his torpedoes undischarged. Matz in *U 70* was unlucky; he was caught by the corvettes *Camellia* and *Arbutus*, forced back to the surface by depth-charge damage, and just had time to surrender with most of his crew before the boat foundered. The result of this brisk, effective action was that OB 293 escaped with the loss of two ships sunk and two damaged – a very light price in the face of such renowned enemies.

Prien was not the man to let a quarry escape as easily as this; for a short time he lost contact with OB 293, but reported on 7 March that he was resuming the pursuit, and by evening he had caught up again. He was closing in for a new attack when he was detected at 0023 on 8 March by Captain J. M. Rowland of the 1919 destroyer *Wolverine*, using one of the Royal Navy's earliest detection devices.[6] At that moment a sister ship, *Verity*, alerted Prien by firing starshell; he dived at once, and there followed a five-hour chase. At 0519 *U 47* was again sighted on the surface, and *Wolverine* attempted to ram. The U-boat crash-dived, and a pattern of depth charges instantly followed her down; a red glow lasting ten seconds was seen in the depths amid the explosions, and soon the débris of a shattered submarine came up to the surface:

In the days that followed the *U 47* was called by W/T again and again, but she never answered. Lieutenant-Commander Günther Prien and his crew had died in action.[7]

Five days later the U-boats suffered an even worse calamity; this time the intended victim was HX 112, fifty merchant vessels escorted by the five destroyers and two corvettes of Captain Donald Macintyre's 5th Escort Group, which already had the reputation of a hard-bitten set of fellows. HX 112 was first sighted south of Iceland by *U 110* (Lemp, who enjoyed the dubious fame of sinking the *Athenia* on the first day of war, and would soon make yet another mark on history). Lemp's report brought up Kretschmer and his friendly rival Schepke in *U 100* on the 15th; they attacked that night, but could only manage to sink one merchantman. The next night they did better; *U 100* was sighted on the horizon, which drew off three of the destroyers, thus enabling Kretschmer in *U 99* to get in amongst the convoy and pick off five more ships. But when *U 100* returned to join in this profitable action, making good speed on the surface and therefore undetectable by ASDIC, she fell foul of the latest device of anti-submarine warfare – one of the very first models of the new Type 271 seaborne radar mounted in the destroyer *Vanoc*. In pitch darkness the radar contact gave *Vanoc*'s captain a good idea of range and speed, and in thirty seconds he was on top of the unsuspecting *U 100*. Her rammed her on the conning tower. Schepke was crushed and went down with her; seven of his crew were saved.

And that was still not all. *Vanoc* now stopped to pick up *U 100*'s survivors, protected by Macintyre's own destroyer, *Walker*. *U 99*, circling the convoy with torpedoes all expended to make its way home, dived to avoid the destroyers and was at once picked up by *Walker*'s ASDIC. A prompt and accurate depth charge pattern, delivered 'by hand' because 'the beautiful instruments of precision provided for us all elected to break down at the crucial moment', wrecked her machinery and did other fatal damage. As *Walker* turned for another attack there

came the thrilling signal from *Vanoc* – 'U-boat surfaced astern of me'.

A searchlight beam stabbed into the night from *Vanoc*, illuminating the submarine *U 99* which lay stopped. The guns' crews in both ships sprang into action and the blinding flashes from the four-inch guns and tracers from the smaller weapons made a great display, though I fear their accuracy was not remarkable.... But fortunately we were able very soon to cease fire as a signal lamp flashing from the U-boat 'We are sunking' [sic] made it clear that the action was over. Keeping end on to the U-boat in case he still had some fight left, we prepared to lower a boat in case there was a chance of a capture, but even as we did so the crew of the U-boat abandoned ship and she plunged to the bottom.

I manoeuvred *Walker* to windward of the swimming Germans and as we drifted down on to them, they were hauled on board. Some of them were in the last stages of exhaustion from the cold of those icy northern waters when we got them on board....

The last to come over the side was obviously the captain, as he swam to *Walker* still wearing his brass-bound cap. We were soon to find out that we had made indeed a notable capture, for the captain was Otto Kretschmer, leading ace of the U-boat arm, holder of the Knight's Cross with oak leaves and top scorer in terms of tonnage sunk.[8]

Macintyre here omits to mention that he amiably relieved Kretschmer of the weight of an excellent pair of German naval glasses which served their new owner well for the rest of the war.

Matz, Prien, Schepke, Kretschmer – still the tally was not complete. On 23 March *Korvettenkapitän* Schrott's *U551* was sunk by the trawler *Visenda* south of Iceland, making the fifth in just over a fortnight. Coming after a period of three months during which there had been no losses at all, it is small wonder that this situation gave Dönitz very grave concern. Matz and Schrott were junior captains, but the other three were 'our most experienced and successful commanders', the aces, the stars of the cast, the best of the best. What did it mean? The tragedy, says Werner,

> stunned and baffled the country. Had the British introduced new wea-pons or techniques of anti-submarine warfare? So far, hunting had been relatively easy. U-boats were fast, manoeuvrable on and beneath the surface, and were also capable of diving below the British depth charges. Our losses were negligible compared with the casualties U-boats had inflicted upon our adversaries. We were without an explanation.[9]

U-boat HQ was obviously more anxious than all others to solve this puzzle, but with no survivors to question this was not an easy matter. Gradually, however, says Dönitz, it became apparent

> that the sudden increase of losses in March had not been due to any particular cause nor the result of the introduction of any new anti-submarine devices. The loss of three most experienced commanders at one and the same time had . . . been purely fortuitous.[10]

And soon something else also became apparent: with the removal of these three great submariners,

> The era of the grey wolves, and of lone 'aces', was over.[11]

* * * * *

An outstanding characteristic of Admiral Dönitz throughout the war was his resilience in adversity; even his resolute and optimistic spirit, however, would have been severely strained if he had been able to see the accessions of strength to the British Admiralty while his U-boats were passing through their dark hour. The accessions were of two kinds: mental (Intelligence) and material (ships). The outward (but deeply mysterious) symbol of the first was the near completion of that rust-coloured granite block at the north-west corner of the Horse Guards Paradeground which was sometimes disrespectfully known as 'Lenin's Tomb', but more properly as 'the Citadel'. Secret though its functions were, it had a convincingly bomb-proof look about it,[12] and this was, indeed, the key to its purpose – to protect the Admiralty's brain-cells. Into the bowels of this grim structure, in early 1941, moved the Operational Intelligence Centre, with both the Operations and Trade main plots, and the War Registry.[13] These were brain-cells of the highest power; so far neither side had been able to extract the full potential value of Intelligence in the war of the submarines, but that situation was about to change abruptly, and meanwhile Naval Intelligence in the Admiralty had been sharpening its tools and perfecting its system to the point where the OIC was soon to become 'in truth the nerve centre of the whole naval war'.[14]

Rear-Admiral John Godfrey, the World War II successor of the renowned 'Blinker' Hall as Director of Naval Intelligence, was 'a practical and successful seaman', but also

a somewhat unusual naval officer, a man of wide interests, great energy and determination, an innovator and original thinker and not one of those who considered that what was good enough for Nelson was necessarily good enough for the Royal Navy of 1939.[15]

It has also been said of him that he was

exacting, inquisitive, energetic and at times a ruthless and impatient master. Like the driver of a sports car in a traffic queue, he saw no danger or discourtesy in acceleration; with his own quick and penetrating mind he expected other minds to keep up.[16]

When Godfrey took up his post, he had two important advantages; one was that Hall 'was still about the place, advising and helping' (in 1941,

317

disliking the air-conditioned atmosphere of the Citadel, he moved into Hall's flat in Curzon Street), and in a number of essential matters such help could only be priceless.[17] And secondly, with war visibly imminent, the fetters of the Treasury would steadily relax. Godfrey could look forward to a time of expansion in a post which would again acquire great authority.

By the end of 1942 the Naval Intelligence Division was approaching its peak of some 2,000 people, a vast information-gathering and disseminating organism controlled by Godfrey.[18] For the day-to-day purposes of the naval war, the key section of it was the Operational Intelligence Centre to which we have several times referred but which now requires more careful notice. This was the organization 'fathered' by Lieutenant-Commander Denning (see p. 178) who defined Operational Intelligence in comprehensive terms:

> that part of naval intelligence organization which concerns itself solely with obtaining, deducing, coordinating and promulgating intelligence *which immediately affects* any naval operation being, or about to be, undertaken by British or Allied, or any part of the British or Allied, fleets.[19]

To understand what this entailed, what the texture of daily work in the OIC was like, it is perhaps most convenient to note the types of Intelligence material which it could expect to be handling on any given day:

> Material gleaned from enemy signals from Station X[20] . . . came by teleprinter to the teleprinter room, and delivered [sic] thence by hand into the various sections. All D/F bearings picked up in England were co-ordinated at one or two points and passed by teleprinter and tube to OIC. D/F signals from abroad came in by signal to War Registry and were sent by hand to OIC. Results of air reconnaissance came in from three Coastal Command headquarters at Plymouth, the Nore and Rosyth. Reports from local naval units and coast watchers were collated at area HQs and sent by teleprinter. Reports from agents were telephoned, if urgent; otherwise they came by teleprinter or handborne letter. Naval reporting organizations signalled by cable and telegram; and reports from Lloyd's and merchant ships came by special line. Where one man had operated with a trickle of fact there was now an organization as large as a great news agency.[21]

As early as 1940 more and more operational decisions were being taken where the operational Intelligence was most readily available – in the OIC. Foreseeing this, Godfrey had recognized the coming need for an officer of some seniority and weight to head this immeasurably important unit: he chose Captain (later Rear-Admiral) Jock Clayton, replacing Denning, who then concentrated on the part of the work concerning German surface ships. The U-boats, of course, came under the eye of the Submarine Tracking Room.

Officially known as NID 8(S), this part of the OIC was the very centre of the anti-submarine war, whose Director, Captain (later Admiral of the Fleet Sir) George Creasy, was a constant visitor. The Tracking Room itself was headed by an old Room 40 man, Paymaster-Commander E. W. C. Thring. Over 60 when he took on the job, by the end of 1940 Thring's health was giving way under intense strain, and his replacement was clearly due – but by whom? Thring himself supplied the answer to that question. Among the civilians who worked in this Holy of naval Holies was a barrister whose first ambition had been to serve in the Royal Navy, but who had been prevented from doing so by poliomyelitis which left him with a twisted back and a limp. His name was Rodger Winn. In 1939 he volunteered for any useful service to the Navy – what he had in mind was interrogating prisoners of war – and in August of that year he had been directed to the Submarine Tracking Room. Under Thring's training and with his advice and encouragement, Winn displayed such flair for this work as to make a very considerable impression on influential senior officers – in particular Captain Creasy and Captain Edwards (Director of the Operations Division [Home]).

A notable difference between Thring and Winn was that while the former was a first-class analyst of recorded events with very stringent views of what constituted evidence and what did not, he flatly refused to prognosticate. Winn, who became his deputy, was prepared to take a chance when this could be justified by strong supporting indicators. Donald McLachlan tells the story of how, at some point in 1940, Captain Edwards, staring at the great Atlantic plot in the Tracking Room, put a direct question to Winn:

'In this position are two very valuable tankers south-east of Newfoundland, unescorted, on a Great Circle course and bound for the North Channel. Tell me what you would do with them in the present state of U-boat dispositions?'

After studying his plot for a few minutes, Winn said: 'I have a definite view to offer here. At midnight last night, from a point 200 miles east and 100 miles south of the tankers' present position, there was a long U-boat signal, more than 300 groups of it. Either that boat is homeward bound at the end of her patrol and sending in her sinking claims to U-boat HQ, or she has suffered mechanical damage or faults which she is describing. I feel ninety per cent certain she will be bound north and the tankers should therefore be routed to the south.'

The Trade Division's Movements Section disagreed and expressed some umbrage at the idea of the Tracking Room telling it what to do. Edwards, however, decided on an experimental compromise: one tanker was ordered to take a north-east course, the other a south-east. The next morning he reappeared in the Tracking Room with a gloomy look and said:

'Well, that's the end of our precious experiment: one tanker sunk out of two.' Winn, not knowing what diversion had been ordered, asked 'But what course was she on, sir; presumably northward?' Unable to reply Edwards went next door to Trade Division, checked the Out signals and returned ten minutes later to apologize to Winn who, he admitted, had been right in his calculations. It was the northbound one.[22]

It is understandable that after such an experience (and there were others) Edwards should be a firm supporter of Winn. Creasy was another, and so was Godfrey. The Vice-Chief of the Naval Staff and the First Sea Lord were persuaded, and so the bold decision was taken to put a civilian in charge of NID 8(S) – preserving the decencies by giving him the rank of Temporary Commander RNVR (Special Branch).[23] Winn took up his new post in January, 1941; it was a significant moment in the anti-submarine war.

It will be noted that the OIC and the Trade Division occupied neighbouring rooms in the fastnesses of the Citadel. Next door to Winn was the Trade Plot, presided over by Commander Richard Hall RN, son of Sir Reginald. Between him and Winn sprang up 'one of the great and most cordial partnerships of the war'; their fierce but friendly arguments were constant and highly productive – later in 1941, as we shall see, their cooperation played a decisive rôle. Every day,

Hall gave Winn estimated positions for all merchant ships in the Atlantic from the Admiralty Plot; Winn gave Hall known and suspected U-boat positions. Their motto was 'Never the twain shall meet'. No ship – not even Churchill's – left Britain without a route from Hall in the lower war room which had been checked in Winn's.[24]

Normally there would be about twelve people at work in NID 8(S), the majority of them civilians. They comprised watchkeepers, who took in and sifted all messages and kept a signal log; they also plotted the convoys; there were the D/F plotters from Section 8X (Lieutenant-Commander Peter Kemp in charge,[25] otherwise civilians); there were civilian day workers whose task was basically research, studying prisoner-of-war interrogations, U-boat building etc, and keeping records and card indexes up to date. Presiding 24 hours a day over the whole scene were the Naval Officer watchkeepers, alert for signs of critical developments and carefully judging the moment when it would be necessary to inform Winn or his deputy, who would then decide when to bring in Creasy and Edwards. Captain Roskill pays this tribute to the work of NID 8(S):

> There is no doubt at all that the skill of this room's staff, and the vigilance which they never relaxed for over five years, contributed greatly to the defeat of the U-boats.[26]

Yet, as 1941 came in and Commander Winn shouldered the burden of his new responsibility, as his future deputy, Patrick Beesly, says:

> The Tracking Room was still feeling its way, and it cannot be said that it achieved any spectacular results If it was now fit and trained to go, the real race was still to be run.[27]

In other words, what was still grievously lacking was advance Operational Intelligence. U-boat W/T signals were virtually non-existent until they had actually sighted convoys and after their attacks, and such signals as there were were wrapped in the impenetrable veil of the naval *Enigma* cypher (*HYDRA*).[28] As a result,

> Apart from D/F fixes . . . the U-boat plotting room in the OIC had no information as to their whereabouts and movements other than the attacks they made and the occasional sightings of them by British ships and aircraft. . . . Against the U-boat danger, even more than against the

raids by surface ships, the lack of operational intelligence constituted a grave and mounting handicap.[29]

One thing was clear: if this default was to be remedied, the cure could come from only one quarter – 'Station X', the Government Code and Cypher School (GC & CS), now removed to Bletchley Park, a late Victorian mansion in Buckinghamshire. Here an astonishing assembly of brain-power, largely drawn from Cambridge, fruitfully mingling such diverse disciplines as mathematics, chess and the classics, conducted the attack on the *Enigma*. They were the cryptanalysts, one of the four prongs of Sigint, the new name for the whole area of Intelligence which, as we have seen (pp. 30–31) had come into existence with radio, which had developed rapidly in World War I, and would now become a central feature of World War II. Sigint is sometimes referred to as though it was just cryptanalysis; it was not. The four prongs of Sigint were:

interception: the 'Y' Service, allied to D/F;
traffic analysis: the study of enemy radio procedures, techniques, volume etc.;
cryptanalysis: breaking the cyphers;
interpretation: translation and appraisal of significance.

Together these formed the 'comprehensive study of communications systems'[30] which in due course became known as Signal Intelligence, hence Sigint, which was soon recognized as 'vastly superior to espionage'. A surprising amount of useful knowledge could be obtained just from D/F and traffic analysis, but clearly, for real value there was no substitute for cryptanalysis, which was also the *sine qua non* of that vital function, interpretation. Bletchley Park (BP) became central to the conduct of the war when it began to decrypt the enemy's signals effectively, thus not merely observing his movements but entering the mind that guided them.

The grounds of the BP mansion were trim with lawns and rose-beds in September, 1939. They did not long remain so. Where the roses had spread their fragrance, bleak huts sprang up to house the various activities of the GC & CS. Gordon Welchman, tutor at Sidney Sussex College and a specialist in algebraic geometry, presided over Hut 6 where the German Army and Airforce *Enigmas* were attacked; in Hut

8 the target was *HYDRA*, and the attack was directed by the distinguished King's College mathematician, Alan Turing.[31] Each of these centres had its satellite: Hut 3 where the Army and *Luftwaffe* decrypts were translated and interpreted, Hut 4 awaiting similar material from the naval side. It was a long wait, partly because in 1940 it was the activities of the German Army and Air Force that attracted the highest priority of attention for most of the year, but chiefly because of the special difficulty of the naval cypher and the careful manner in which it was used. The difficulty was that whereas the other *Enigmas* could vary the three rotors operating at any time from a store of five, the Navy drew on a store of eight. Obviously this immensely increased the number of possible permutations when the rotors revolved, to the point where it was quite simply impossible for the unaided human brain to fathom them in any space of time that would make the business operationally useful.

It was Alan Turing's great contribution that he played the leading part in seeing to it that the British human brain was not unaided. Thanks in considerable part to some brilliant work against *Enigma* in the decade before the war by the Polish mathematicians Rejewski, Rozycki and Zygalsky, with support also from the French, Turing was able to make an early start on the work of making a machine that would be able to defeat the machine. Rejewski's triumph was the construction of just such a device early in 1938, entitling him 'to be regarded as one of the greatest cryptanalysts of his day'.[32] In December of that year, however, the Germans added their fourth and fifth rotors, multiplying the task beyond the physical resources of the Poles to deal with it. In July, 1939, facing the certainty of war with Germany, and some at least of them also facing squarely the certainty of defeat, they took the heroic, warrior decision to present the full story of the progress they had made towards breaking the *Enigma* to their Western allies. By so doing they would ensure at least a chance that even in the midst of disaster Poland would be able to strike back at her foes; such vision is not common in history. The most important part of the Polish achievement was Rejewski's '*Bomba*', the machine by which he and his colleagues 'brought cryptanalysis into the twentieth century'.[33] This was a development well in line with the work that Turing had been concentrating on before the war, and the Polish invention could hardly have come to a more receptive user. Working forward from the '*Bomba*', and with important help from Gordon Welchman, Turing produced the prototype of his own 'Bombe' by May, 1940. Its function was direct assault:

'to test all the possible wheel or rotor orders of the Enigma, all the possible wheel settings and ... connections to discover which of the possible arrangements would match a prescribed combination of letters.' When the prescribed conditions had been matched the bombe stopped.[34]

One who was privileged to see this prototype says:

I was ushered with great solemnity into the shrine where stood a bronze-coloured column surmounted by a larger circular bronze-coloured face, like some Eastern Goddess who was destined to become the oracle of Bletchley, at least when she felt like it. She was an awesome piece of magic.[35]

Not many people knew of the existence of the Bombe; most of those who did would have confirmed the idea of it as an 'oracle'. Its 'voice' was 'a noise like that of a thousand knitting needles'[36] as it ran untiringly through its brutal programme of permutations. Its utterance was the teleprinter paper containing, when the Bombe stopped, a message which was at least in German, but might still be cryptic. The 'priestesses' attendant upon the oracle were members of the WRNS (in the end there were about a thousand of them at BP) constantly feeding it with new programme material and reporting instantly when it stopped. It was utterly repetitive, exacting and highly secret work, carried out for the most part in out-stations where the successive Bombes were lodged. By the end of June, 1941, there were six Bombes in operation; only six, and only one normally available for work on the naval *Enigma*. But by then the break-through had occurred.

Like many fine gifts, the Bombe brought with it a crop of problems. Turing's first model, in May, 1940, made possible the breaking of the operational and administrative communications of all Commands of the German Air Force:

From 22 May, 1940, until the end of the war GC & CS was to read its settings daily, with few interruptions, and to do so with little delay.[37]

324

Once this was done, the British Sigint system found itself overwhelmed by an embarrassment of riches. Machine-made and machine-broken,

the Enigma's cyphered messages were mechanically converted direct into plain language; so that it yielded up its end-product in cornucopian abundance once the daily setting had been solved ... its plain language end-product, while it opened up to British eyes for the first time an intimate view of a vast German organisation, presented British intelligence with immense problems in evaluation on account of the intricate procedures, the code-names, the pro-formas and the other conventions which it employed for the sake of brevity or in the interests of internal security − not to speak of the difficulties sometimes created by poor interception and other sources of textual corruption.

The priceless information so gathered extended far beyond the *Luftwaffe's* private affairs, and was stored away in BP's Index, 'that extraordinary memory-bank which grew into perhaps the most comprehensive storehouse of intelligence in the country'.[38] But still the naval *Enigma* remained obdurate, the U-boats remained invisible and secret; something more would have to be done to help the Bombes. One possibility was information from prisoners of war − there had been a fair crop of them in March, 1941, alone; but at this stage of the war the morale and discipline of the U-boat crews were intact, and there is no indication of anything relating to *Enigma* being obtained from this source. The only remaining recourse was to capture an *Enigma* machine with its current settings.

It was not easy. In all navies and in the Merchant Marine the destruction of code-books and signals material was an automatic drill whenever capture threatened. The protection of the *Enigma* was a prime consideration in every German ship. In February, 1940, three rotor wheels had been taken from survivors of *U 33* − but they were the wrong ones. In April of that year the patrol boat *VP 2623* was captured; her *Enigma* machine had gone overboard, but she had a store of papers which could have been very valuable if the boat had not been so thoroughly looted by the boarding party. Nothing more was collected for nearly a year. On 3 March, 1941, however, during the Commando raid on the Lofoten Islands, a spare set of rotors was found on the abandoned armed trawler *Krebs*. This was progress, at last; with these, BP was able to read the whole of the traffic for February, and some for dates in March. By

10 May the crytanalysts had also broken the whole April traffic and were reading May traffic with a delay of only three to seven days.

What also emerged in April was the fact that two German weather-ships, one in mid-Atlantic and the other north of Iceland, as well as the familiar weather cypher in which they made their reports, carried *Enigma* machines and *HYDRA* settings. On 7 May the Royal Navy succeeded in taking the weather-ship *München* and seizing her machine intact. Her settings would enable the June traffic to be read practically currently. Two days later came the dramatic episode of the capture of Julius Lemp's *U 110* by the destroyer *Bulldog* while attacking Convoy OB 318.[39] This produced a very useful haul indeed; the settings for the very high-grade 'officer-only' German naval signals, and the *Kurzsig-nale* ('Short Signals') code using standardized messages designed to defeat D/F fixes by their very speed. What was missing, however, was the *HYDRA* settings for May, which Lemp had managed to destroy. However, the capture of the second weather-ship, *Lauenburg*, on 28 June gave BP the ability to read the July '*Heimische Gewässer*' ('Home Waters')[40] traffic currently:

> By the beginning of August it had finally established its mastery over the Home Waters settings, a mastery which enabled it to read the whole of the traffic for the rest of the war except for occasional days in the second half of 1941 with little delay. The maximum delay was 72 hours and the normal delay was much less, often only a few hours.[41]

What all this means is that Operational Intelligence was at last becoming a factor to reckon with in the anti-submarine war. This, of course, was the very heart of the matter; but as well as the signals that could lead to immediate action, BP's attack now enabled the Submarine Tracking Room to build up an extraordinary and most valuable familiarity with the U-boat fleet, boat by boat – identification numbers, captain's names, types, speed, endurance, damage and other intimate details, all the way from their working-up cruises in the Baltic to the North Sea and the Biscay bases, out on their Atlantic patrols and back again, their leave and their refitting cycles. Dönitz would have been astounded – and appalled.

It was now, in early 1941, that Sigint began to fulfil its promise, and soon it would show its teeth. Its success was due to several things – some luck, obviously, because that can never be dismissed, the brilliance of some of the BP performers, a very remarkable assemblage of brain power, and the invaluable Bombes. But in addition there were two early decisions whose importance may be thought to have been in the last resort decisive; their conjunction illustrates

the importance of concentrating all cryptanalytical effort in one place. It emphasized, too, the wisdom of attacking all codes and cyphers, even the ostensibly insignificant.[42]

Among those successfully attacked at Bletchley in the spring of 1941 were:

a cypher briefly used between Berlin and overseas naval attachés for material concerning supply ships;
a new merchant navy code;
light-ship codes;
a naval-air code;
an air-sea rescue code;
a dockyards cypher, *Werft*, which proved invaluable because some of its signals were re-transmitted by *Enigma*;
the German meteorological cypher, which helped in the same way.

What was happening, in fact, was

the operation of the Bletchley establishment as a whole, attacking the German communication system as a whole.[43]

The result was a godsend to Rodger Winn and his assistants in NID 8(S). Ronald Lewin is somewhat astray in saying that 'Bletchley's command over Hydra cypher shifted the U-boat war into a new dimension'. It was not just *HYDRA*, enormously important though that was; it was the whole range of German radio signals now being brought 'from the realm of guess-work into that of increasing authority'.[44] It was the equivalent of a major victory at sea.

* * * * *

While this victory was being won, the sinews of others were being strengthened. The ships were beginning to arrive. The grim winter of 1940–1 was now easing its grip, and the anti-submarine forces benefited accordingly:

The last week of April brought the opening of the St Lawrence, and with the spring freshette came the expected deluge of new corvettes.[45]

'Deluge' is perhaps a strong word; the statistical rendering is that during the next seven months thirty-three warships were added to the Royal Canadian Navy List – a decided accession of strength, whatever word is used for it. Behind the bald statement lies a curious story of changing national attitudes and growth.

In the early years of the century, Defence was not a word to conjure with in Canada; it represented, chiefly, an expenditure which politicians of all parties tended to look upon as a millstone. Inasmuch as there was a military instinct and tradition, it was centred in the regiments which had defended the frontier against attacks from the United States during the American Wars of Independence and 1812. As regards naval defence, according to the longest and strongest tradition of all, this was the province of the Royal Navy. It was generally accepted that British sea power and supremacy constituted the 'bedrock principle of security' for the whole of the Empire:

> The call of the sea to the British race is a living reality, a constantly potent influence, directing the path and shaping the destiny of the Empire.[46]

As they advanced towards nationhood, the Dominions expressed their understanding and endorsement of this fact by making their own contributions to the Royal Navy, and the third Imperial Conference in 1902

> ended with all the self-governing Colonies, except Canada, contributing to the Navy in one form or another.

This was a continuing process, taking different forms; with Australia, for example, there was never any doubt that there would be a contribution, but there was no doubt either that this would be distinctively Australian.

> Alone among the self-governing Dominions, Canada, or rather the Canadian Government, seemed not to hear the call of the sea.

In consequence, although a Royal Canadian Navy was established in 1910, when war came in 1914 it was 'incapable of undertaking a sea-going rôle'.[47] Its total strength was only 350 regular officers and men, with 250 scarcely trained members of the Royal Canadian Naval Volunteer Reserve, and Canada's naval effort throughout World War I was insignificant. By contrast, there was massive recruiting for the Army – a total of 619,636 of all ranks, whose spearhead was the four-division Canadian Corps which already held the reputation of an élite formation in 1917. It was not, at that time, a practical possibility for Canada to field such a force as that and a large Navy also, and no one expected her to do so.

The performance of the Canadian Expeditionary Force was a source of intense pride to a large number of Canadians, but the cost of it was also a source of great sorrow: 56,639 men killed or died of wounds and many more wounded and disabled. Between the wars, the sentiment expressed in the treacherous phrase 'Never Again' was very strong in Canada: never again a commitment to European war, never again the mass army and the mass casualties. The Navy was caught in the mesh of misled policies – indeed, it was the worst sufferer:

> Anti-war sentiment, isolationism, and serious economic difficulties haunted the navy's inter-war years.[48]

The nadir was reached in 1933, when it was even proposed to scrap the Navy altogether, in order to preserve the other two Services in the face of economic depression. Thereafter matters improved; the return of the Liberals under Mr Mackenzie King in 1935, despite the new Premier's isolationist and anti-imperial attitudes, favoured the Navy. To Mackenzie King, a large army and 1914–18 scale of casualties were particular anathema, which drew him to favour 'less personnel-intensive services such as the air force and the navy'. He thought of the Navy as a means of insulating Canada from the obviously growing tensions of Europe; both he and important colleagues also saw enlargement of the Air Force and the Navy as valuable encouragements to the growth of Canadian industry. As a result, the RCN in 1939, while absurdly weak in relation to the tasks which devolved upon it, was a considerably healthier infant than that of 1914: it contained 3,684 of all ranks and a fleet of seven destroyers and five minesweepers divided between its two oceans.

It is easy to mock at such numbers; in truth they were less important – because, given time, this fault could be corrected – than the Navy's own misinterpretation of what its rôle would be. The key to this is in the word 'destroyers'. The seven destroyers of September, 1939,[49] formed the first expansion of the Royal Canadian Navy; a further expansion, planned in January, 1939, contemplated increasing their number to eighteen, with sixteen minesweepers and eight anti-submarine vessels, divided equally between the east and west coasts, with an extra flotilla of eight motor torpedo-boats in the east. The RCN, it will be observed, at this stage fully shared the Royal Navy's conviction that the submarine menace would be easily contained and that the main threat would be the German surface fleet (with a possibility of ship-launched air attack). The RCN planners wanted ships that could successfully engage German cruisers and even battleships, by high-speed massed torpedo action. What they had in mind – ultimately – was the Royal Navy's 'Tribal' Class Fleet destroyers, powerful ships whose 44,000 hp turbines could work up speeds of $36\frac{1}{2}$ knots, whose armament was eight 4.7-inch guns, four 21-inch torpedo tubes and a large AA battery. They had, in fact, reached that danger point perceived by Churchill in his capacity both as First Lord of the Admiralty and later as Prime Minister,

> where one is no longer building a destroyer but a small cruiser. The displacement approaches or even exceeds 2,000 tons, and a crew of more than 200 sail the seas in these unarmoured ships, themselves an easy prey to any regular cruiser.[50]

Their vulnerability is demonstrated by their losses: fourteen Tribals sunk out of twenty-six built by 1945. They had other problems too – notably a liability to structural damage (even bending of the keel) when their enormous power plant punched their thin shells through heavy seas. Worst of all was the time it took to build them – nearly three years. Yet in the RCN as in the Royal Navy these were the light craft that the professionals admired and preferred to serve in.

Corvettes, by comparison, looked feeble and clumsy, hardly deserving the name of 'warship'. And so, in Canada, while the regular RCN officers stood by, awaiting delivery of their 'big ships', a strange thing happened: in effect, two Navies developed side by side, one regular (RCN) and one reserve (RCNR and RCNVR), and the division between them was clear:

> few regular career Canadian naval officers ever kept watch aboard a

corvette, and only a handful of corvette crewmen were RCN ratings. . . . It was a situation worthy of Gilbert and Sullivan: trained seamen were put in offices ashore and trained office managers were sent to sea. As a result, Canada's professional naval officers were to play an ever-diminishing rôle in the Battle of the Atlantic.[51]

This was the strange (and sad) result of the surface-ship fixation which the Royal Navy itself was having difficulty in sloughing off; for the regular RCN officers the only present outlets were a handful of senior posts and staffs, the seven pre-war destroyers, the despised 'Town' Class – and offices ashore.

Meanwhile, the little jerry-built corvettes were filled up with reservists and packed off to do what they could in the squalid brawls with U-boats around the herds of merchantmen. . . . But a funny thing happened to the regular navy while it waited for the Big Ships that were to fight the Big Battle. For as the years wore on, it became clear that the little battle, the U-boat thing, was in fact the Big Battle after all, and the little ships that were fighting it were all that was going to matter.

Between 1939–45 over 400 vessels appeared on the Royal Canadian Navy List; over 120 of them were corvettes and Canada actually built more than 130 of that class. The RCN had, during the middle period of the war, when the Atlantic Battle was at its height, become a 'corvette navy'. In the kernel of these statements there lies a great achievement, attributable chiefly to determination, the quality once familiarly known as 'grit', ingenuity and seemingly limitless patience in adversity. Yet all these virtues functioned, and suffered by so doing, inside a framework of total unpreparedness for war and inevitably slow adjustment to it. It would be agreeable to write as though the advent of the Canadian corvettes down the St Lawrence in 1941 marked a turning-point, an access of immediately decisive operational strength. It did not. It marked a portent for the future and meanwhile a welcome lift out of the 'nadir of British fortunes'. Indeed the RCN contribution at this stage was not unlike that of the ex-American destroyers that it only grudgingly accepted for itself; like them, what it offered was not precisely what the Royal Navy would have asked Father Christmas for, but it was far, far better than nothing. There are good (or at least undeniable) reasons for this which were often ignored at the time, by British officers and others, and usually continue to be so by historians.

331

First of all, there was the sheer rawness of the corvette crews; the destroyers soon absorbed all the experience that was available, leaving the 'corvette navy' to find its own way by trial and error:

> A bewildered RCNR lieutenant, only a month or two away from his second mate's berth in some merchant ship, his two interwoven curly stripes of gold lace still bright on each cuff, was dumped off at a ship-building yard to take over his new corvette command, with three or four officers as green as himself and sixty or seventy young men fresh from the prairies or city pavements who had never seen the sea before. If the new captain was lucky, one of his officers might have some practical experience of pilotage or navigation, if not too seasick to care. If his chief engineer had worked in a locomotive round-house and knew a little about steam engines, the captain felt himself to be fortunate indeed.[52]

What the Royal Navy found hard to grasp was the sheer absence in Canada of the training establishments and facilities which, even in its darkest days, it took for granted. The tribulations of the Canadian anti-submarine forces display once more the extreme difficulties that small Services experience when they have to expand rapidly and search in vain for teachers. It was a self-perpetuating, insoluble conundrum; no sooner had a captain (learning his own job all the time) shaken his ship's company down into some sort of crew than, on returning to port, most of his best officers and men would be taken from him to leaven new crews for the latest launchings. In the Royal Navy's anti-submarine units, the complaint was the constant breaking-up of groups; in the Canadian force, it was the breaking-up of crews, which must have reduced many young captains to despair. It is easy now to see that the problem was simply a heightened form of one affecting all three of Canada's expanding Services: finding and distributing skilled men. The RCAF in particular was a competitor, forcing the Navy to drop its minimum age of entry from 21 to 19.[53] But even a superbly written volume explaining all this would not have eased the corvette skipper's lot.

Then there were the ships themselves. The Canadian corvettes were given the same class name as their British counterparts; they were 'Flowers' – which, says Marc Milner, was a serious mistake, because it merely concealed the very real differences between British- and

Canadian-built vessels. Late-comers to the escort scene, the Canadian versions lacked the modifications which the British had been steadily introducing to fit theirs for an ocean-going rôle.[54] An essential for this, quickly recognized by the Royal Navy, was the extension of the fo'c'sle; the first sixty Canadian corvettes did not incorporate this feature. Neither did they have a breakwater on the fo'c'sle, so that when the ship took in water (which it constantly did) this ran through to the open welldeck making the accommodation unnecessarily wet, thus adding to the strain on the crew. Also, there was no planking or other form of covering of the deck plates, making these extremely slippery and hazardous, especially for depth-charge crews. The Canadian ships, furthermore, lacked secondary armament, especially effective AA. However,

> The most telling shortcoming of Canadian corvettes, and the one that was to cause the most difficulty in the struggle for efficiency, was the lack of gyro-compasses. . . . The first Canadian-built corvettes (including those built to Admiralty accounts) were equipped with a single magnetic compass and the most basic of asdic, the type 123A. Even by 1939 standards the 123A was obsolete and in the RN was considered only suited to trawlers and lesser vessels.[55]

Royal Navy criticisms of Canadian performances in attacks upon U-boats might have been tempered by awareness of this very serious deficiency. Unfortunately, these and other too-frequent manifestations were

> indicative of the condescending and paternalistic attitude of the parent service towards what was often regarded as the 'kindergarten'.[56]

And now it was April, and the new corvettes were arriving at Halifax, the great east-coast port and base, for commissioning: three before the month was out, ten more in May, as well as another ten originally ordered by the Admiralty and now transferred. On 20 May the Admiralty requested that the RCN should undertake escort duties from St John's in Newfoundland, and this request was enthusiastically received. Three days later the first flotilla of corvettes left Halifax for St John's, marking a turning-point in the history of the RCN, if not of the Battle of the Atlantic. The Canadian seamen would now make the acquaintance of a place with a reputation already familiar to a great many British mariners.

Newfoundland, in 1939, was a Crown Colony, having forfeited Dominion Status by financial ineptitude in 1933. Its capital, St John's, had been a minor station of the Royal Navy for a very long time, and was known to English-speaking sailors as 'Newfyjohn', a word pronounced in tones that were only rarely affectionate:

> It was small and undeveloped, and it was remote from any industrial centre. Everything required for the construction of a large naval base would have to come from outside the island. Communications were inadequate; skilled labour was scarce; docking facilities, billeting facilities, fuel and fuel storage were all lacking. Everything would have to be brought, everything would have to be built, in the midst of battle to keep the convoys sailing.[57]

The one dry dock was in constant use, repairing damaged merchantmen; in any case, it was not equipped for naval work. Even the wharfs of what had always been primarily a fishing port would require to be rebuilt to meet the needs of warships. The fishing – the famous cod fisheries – was performed in large part on the Grand Banks, two hundred miles to the south-east of Newfoundland, where the warm waters of the Gulf Stream coming up from Mexico meet the ice-laden Labrador Current to produce dense fogs at all times of the year. Coming out of St John's harbour one looked east into the worst part of the Atlantic, where the nearest landfall would be the west coast of Ireland, some 1,500 miles away. For all the seamen, British, Canadian, Allied, naval or Merchant Marine, who had occasion to use St John's harbour, the exit round the short curve and out through the heads was a distinct and unforgettable experience:

> In Newfyjohn . . . you are either in the harbour or out of it; there is no long estuary leading to the sea. The transition is brief and dramatic; one moment you are trundling along in the comparative serenity of harbour, and the next you are in the open ocean, amid all the fury of the North Atlantic winter.[58]

Where winter – or winter conditions – could last for about seven months of the year, the weather demons waiting outside St John's made special purgatories:

The sea is getting up under the impetus of that shrieking wind; for the next few hours we shall be punching into the teeth of the freshening gale, and already a lot of us are having sudden doubts about our stomachs. There are retching sounds from behind us on the bridge, where one of the new signalmen is bringing up his innards as he greets his first Atlantic gale . . .

A green one crashes aboard; peering over the dodger we can see its dark shape engulf our foredeck, and we crouch for shelter as the ship plunges thunderously into it. A wall of water, tons of it, sweeps across our fo'c'sle to hurl itself against our bridge structure with a resounding thump. Water sweeps overhead; even in the shelter of the dodger we are drenched . . .

The messdecks of a corvette in bad weather are indescribable . . . There is absolutely no fresh air . . . Dim emergency lights, red or blue, provide the only illumination in the dark hours, and around the clock there is always at least one watch trying to catch a few hours of oblivion, while about them the life of the mess goes on: men coming and going from outside, or snatching a meal before going on watch. With the hammocks slung, there is hardly room anywhere to stand upright, and there is moisture everywhere – water swirling in over the coamings when the outside doors open, sweating from the chilled steel of the ship's side, oozing from the countless pipe joints and deck-welds and rivets and deck openings, and all the other manifold places where water forces an entrance from the gale outside. Plunging into a head sea, the noise and motion in the fo'c'sle must be experienced to be believed; a constant roar of turbulence, wind, and water, punctuated by a crashing thud as the bow bites into another great sea, while the whole little world is uplifted – up, up, up – only to come crashing down as the ship plunges her bows over and downward, to land with an impact which hurls anyone and anything not firmly secured down to the forward bulkhead.[59]

Let the last word go to the man who said 'a corvette would roll on wet grass' (see p. 252). Nicholas Monsarrat also says that this ceaseless rolling, in rough weather, became a special form of torture:

It never stops or misses a beat, it cannot be escaped anywhere. If you go through a doorway, it hits you hard; if you sit down, you fall over; you get hurt, knocked about continuously, and it makes for extreme and childish anger. When you drink, the liquid rises towards you and slops over: at meals, the food spills off your plate, the cutlery will not stay in place. Things roll about, and bang, and slide away crazily: and then come back and *hurt* you again. The wind doesn't howl, it *screams* at you, and tears at your clothes, and throws you against things and drives your breath down your throat again. And off watch, below, there is no peace: only noise, furniture adrift, clothes and boots sculling about on the deck, a wet and dirty chaos.[60]

Into such scenes as these, to this exacting lot, Canada's new contribution to the battle was born: the Newfoundland Escort Force, comprising in June, 1941, thirteen destroyers (seven RN, six RCN), four RN sloops, and twenty-one corvettes (seventeen RCN). It was commanded by a Canadian, Commodore (later Rear-Admiral) L. W. Murray, who was, says Marc Milner,

above all a competent and confident officer, an excellent ship handler (as his contemporaries attest), and an able administrator.[61]

All these qualities would be needed, with tact and diplomacy and an agreeable manner besides, to build up a working base at St John's and turn his new, untried corvette navy into an effective fighting force. It now had its particular function, its own sector of the war: protecting the convoys between the West Ocean Meeting Point (WOMP) east of Newfoundland, and the Mid-Ocean Meeting Point (MOMP) south of Iceland. This would be the NEF's parish, and a less salubrious one it would be hard to find.[62]

Newfoundland and Iceland, the terminal points of the NEF beat, now became international meeting-points. The Lend-Lease Bill, having received Congressional approval, was duly signed on 11 March, 1941; the American destroyers, as we have seen, were quickly delivered, and not much time was lost by America in picking up her side of the bargain – the bases. Argentia, halfway up Placentia Bay in Newfoundland, was selected as an advanced base for convoy escort work within the United States 'Security Zone', and work began on transforming a desolate stretch of shore into an operational naval station in December, 1940. The Americans were not usually disposed to loiter over much matters; sufficient progress had been made by February to warrant the raising of the flag, and on 15 July Argentia was commissioned as a United States Naval Operating Base and Naval Air Station.

Iceland's story, in the early 1940s, belongs to a different 'saga'. The

British presence in Iceland dated from 10 May, 1940, the day the Germans launched their great offensive in the West. Already their bold conduct of the Norwegian campaign, and perhaps above all their unexpected and skilful strategic use of air transportation,[63] had planted the idea that there was very little that they might not be capable of attempting and achieving. In fact, it would now appear that the Germans had no intention of making an attack on Iceland at that stage, but the Admiralty, with Churchill still at its head, preferred to take no chances and pressed for the setting-up of British bases in the island. It is easy now to be dismissive about these alarms; they had an air of ominous reality at the time:

> the Admiralty's action was the culmination of over seven years of observed German activity in Iceland which by 1939 seriously worried Foreign Office, Admiralty and Air Ministry officials, especially since so much of it seemed to be concerned with the possible military development of Iceland or fifth column activities.[64]

Mr Chamberlain's Government acted, for once, with decision and alacrity; pressures were put upon the Icelandic Government which it was in no position to resist, and the British forces landed unopposed. Relations between the occupying force and the Icelanders were correct but cool at both official and personal level. Some British Servicemen were able to find a magic in the empty, sweeping landscape, but not many; most of them could hardly wait to get away from

> bleak, unfriendly Reykjavik . . . where – on a rare and gala night – the lissom, blonde Icelandic girls danced with you, light as a feather, cold as an icicle, silent as the tomb, and left you without a word when the dance was ended.[65]

The transformation of the war by the Fall of France included the transformation of Iceland's importance. Now it was no longer just a matter of guarding against a suppositional German landing at some future date. The abandonment of the south-western Approach, shifting the whole burden of sea-borne supply to the north, now made it doubly important that there should be no German foothold in Iceland, and even more important to build up a naval base which would serve as a staging-point in the Atlantic crossing and an air base from which Coastal

Command could carry its anti-submarine activities far out into the ocean. The first RAF squadron to operate from Iceland arrived in August – No 98, still equipped with the Fairey Battle light bombers which had been such a disastrous failure in France. They were quite unsuited to maritime work, but in January, 1941, they were reinforced by one squadron of Hudsons and one of the invaluable Sunderlands. When the Battles were withdrawn in early summer, they were replaced by Northrop N3P-B seaplanes belonging to No 330 Norwegian Squadron. In due course they, too, would be exchanged for Sunderlands. These reinforcements ensured that

> by mid-summer Iceland was the base of a small but highly specialized and skilful maritime air force.[66]

For the Navy, refuelling was the matter at the very heart of all ocean convoy escort work, and the great promise of Iceland was a base for this purpose. It was not until April that this became operational, at Hvalfjordhur (close to Reykjavik), 'a dreary and unforgiving haven', says Marc Milner, 'by far the worst of those used by escort forces in the Battle of the Atlantic'.[67] This was the hated 'home' of the forces which came together at MOMP, the Canadians of NEF coming in from the west, and the British escort groups from the east, sharing the same sparse facilities:

> These consisted exclusively of auxiliary support ships capable of sustaining life, not embellishing it. Oil, basic stores, water, food, and the most elementary running repairs were available. The anchorage itself offered little respite to tired men and belaboured ships. When all-too-frequent gales swept down over the barren hills of Iceland, the layover period for escorts became even more demanding than life at sea. The poor holding ground of the fjord's bottom, the proximity of other ships, the rugged shoreline, swirling snow, and hurricane-force winds made a night on the open sea preferable to one at anchor in Hvalfjordhur.

To this enticing spot the Americans came in July, 1941, to set up a base of their own and (at Britain's urging) to relieve the British Army as the occupying force. They came, they said, to 'protect' the country, but, says their Official Historian,

338

the people did not accept the occupation with good grace. Intensely nationalistic and provincial in their outlook, they did not sense the need for protection.[68]

The American arrival signalled the penultimate stage of a remarkable process. This is not the place for an examination of President Franklin Roosevelt's motives, methods and morals as he wittingly drew America out of the neutrality so deeply prized by so many of her citizens by stages which one by one made war with Germany virtually inevitable.[69] We need only note that the process was at least as old as the war itself.

The American 'Security Zone' has been mentioned; this dated from 5 September, 1939, when the President ordered the formation of a 'Neutrality Patrol':

> The avowed object of this patrol was to report and track any belligerent air, surface or underwater naval forces approaching the coasts of the United States or the West Indies. The fundamental purpose was to emphasize the readiness of the United States Navy to defend the Western Hemisphere.[70]

It was a short step from the 'Neutrality Patrol' to a 'Neutrality Zone' – a United States proposal at the Inter-American Conference convened in Panama City on 23 September. By the 'Declaration of Panama' on 2 October the twenty-one American republics set up what was soon known as the 'Security Zone'. Starting in the North at Placentia Bay, the edge of the Zone ran down some 300–600 miles from the eastern American coastline to latitude 20°N, where it made a vigorous swing eastward into the South Atlantic to cover the great projecting salient of Brazil.[71] As must be the case with any such line on a map, the 'security' of the designated area was largely fictional, but it was a highly significant fiction. As Churchill said in one of his 'Former Naval Person' communications with Roosevelt,

> We do not mind how far south the prohibited zone goes, provided that it is effectively maintained. We should have great difficulty in accepting a zone which was policed by some weak neutral. But of course if the American navy takes care of it, that is all right.[72]

The 'Security Zone' was a marker in the movement of America

towards war; the 'Cash-and-Carry' arrangement and Lend-Lease marked further stages. In 1941 they came at a fast rate: first, an Anglo-American inter-Service conference in Washington at the end of January, to discuss the loaded question of 'methods by which the United States and Great Britain could defeat Germany and her allies "should the United States be compelled to resort to war".'[73] The agreements reached in these far-reaching considerations went considerably beyond the hypothesis on which they rested. 'The subject of immediate moment,' says the US Official Historian,

> one which did not depend on a declaration of war by the United States, was that of escort-of-convoy.[74]

Preparatory planning for this activity was already in hand, and the Director of the USN War Plans Division had reported that the Navy would be ready to escort convoys through to Scotland by 1 April (the Argentia base was clearly a prime factor). The requisite escort vessels had now to be gathered together; this was a two-stage process, the first being the transformation of the 'Patrol Force' into the Atlantic Fleet under Admiral Ernest J. King on 1 February, and the second, on 1 March, being the creation of a 'Support Force' for convoy work drawn from the destroyers of that Fleet. Intensive anti-submarine warfare training, much assisted by the Royal Navy's experience and weapons development, now began, and also construction of new terminal bases for the Support Force in Scotland and Northern Ireland.[75] The manner in which policies having broadly the same aim could nevertheless conflict may be seen in the fact that the creation of the Support Force coincided with the finalization of Land-Lease, which liberated ten of the admirable US Coastguard cutters for transfer to the Royal Navy – just when the US Navy was beginning to feel a shortage of escorts.[76]

April saw further acceleration of United States involvement in the war at sea. It was during this month that approval was given for the refitting of British warships in American yards:

> From this time onwards it was rare for any American Navy yard, and many private yards as well, not to have at least one British ship in its hands for refit or repair or action damage. The building of warships of many types and of merchant ships on British 'Lend-Lease' account also dates from this time.[77]

Direct US Navy involvement also came a step nearer on 10 April when the destroyer *Niblack*, collecting survivors from a torpedoed Dutch freighter, picked up the ASDIC echo of a submarine 'evidently approaching for attack'. The destroyer capatain at once went into a depth-charge attack, and the U-boat 'retired'. Dr Morison wrote:

> So far as can be ascertained, this bloodless battle of 10 April, 1941, was the first action of the war between United States and German armed forces. [78]

Later information prompted an amendment; having checked the logs of all U-boats in the vicinity on that day, he found no mention by any of them of any depth-charge attack; 'in all probability it was a false contact'.

It was a natural hazard of a trigger-happy time that the first 'action' of the US Navy should turn out to be a fiction. President Roosevelt's unswerving policies, however, made it certain that there would be some definitely non-fiction action before very long. On the day that *Niblack* was dropping her unfruitful depth charges, the President was discussing with his highly 'interventionist' Republican Secretary of War, Henry L. Stimson, how far he could push naval support for Britain. Stimson, and probably Roosevelt too, would have liked to start actual convoy by USN ships, but as practical politicians, they guessed that public opinion was not yet ready for that. The discussion, says Stimson, therefore centred round 'how far over in the direction of Great Britain we could get', and how that might be accomplished:

> We had the Atlas out and by drawing a line midway between the westernmost bulge of Africa and the easternmost bulge of Brazil, we found that the median line between the two continents was at about longitude line 25.... His plan is that we shall patrol the high seas west of this median line, all the way down as far as we can furnish the force to do it. ... Then by the use of patrol planes and patrol vessels we can patrol and follow the convoys and notify them of any German raiders or submarines that we may see and give them a chance to escape. [79]

Thus, on 11 April, the US Security Zone suddenly sprang eastward from approximately 60°W to 26°W. Churchill greeted this leap as a 'momentous message', and told Roosevelt:

341

Admiralty received the news with the greatest relief and satisfaction.[80]

Well it might; and naturally the reaction of Admiral Dönitz was equally predictable. The new demarcation line, he said,

> was more than 2,300 sea miles from the American coast at New York and only 740 sea miles from the coast of Europe at Lisbon; and it included the Azores, which are a European group of islands. In this way something like four-fifths of the Atlantic ocean was declared to be part of the western hemisphere, in which American naval forces would shadow German warships and at once report their position to the British. No justification of any sort will be found anywhere in international law for thus extending a security zone or for putting it to the uses to which it was thus arbitrarily put.[81]

All in all, April was a busy month for the US Navy; its base in Bermuda was commissioned on 7 April. Admiral King's Operation Plan No 3, for the extension of the Security Zone, followed on 18 April, and three days later a Task Force was created to enter northern Greenland waters, suppress German weather stations there and (in due course) set up weather, radio and radar stations and build airfields which would ultimately do great work for the Allies.

All this was against the background of a war otherwise going badly for Britain and her allies. On 30 March the *Afrika Korps* made its début under General Erwin Rommel, an offensive destined to carry it triumphantly across Cyrenaica. On 6 April the Germans attacked Yugoslavia and Greece; on the 13th they occupied Belgrade, and on the 17th the Yugoslav army capitulated. Greece fared no better; a British expeditionary force, sent immediately to her aid, had to be withdrawn, with a Dunkirk-style loss of equipment and injury to national pride, by 22 April. By the 27th the Germans were in Athens, all British forces flung out of Europe once again, and the Axis armies were back on the Egyptian frontier. On 20 May German airborne troops attacked Crete and ten days later there was another miserable British evacuation. During these operations Allied shipping losses mounted catastrophically; 687,901 gross tons (195 ships) lost in April, of which 292,518 tons (105 ships) were in the Mediterranean, and 323,454 tons (116 ships) due to air action. The May total of 511,042 tons (139 ships) was an improvement, but still a very serious matter. Even more alarming were the losses of the Royal Navy, chiefly in the operations around Crete: three cruisers, six destroyers and twenty-nine smaller craft sunk, a battleship, an aircraft carrier, three cruisers and a destroyer badly damaged, and another battleship, four cruisers and six destroyers needing extensive repairs. The already heavy strain on the Navy was thus multiplied, and once more it had been shown that

sea-power could not henceforth be exercised independently of air-power.[82]

America, in the persons of her President and his advisers, watched all these events unfolding with deep dismay. Closer to home there were other ominous happenings. On 21 May (though the facts did not become known until June) the freighter *Robin Moor*, on her way to South Africa with general cargo, was sunk by *U 69* – the first American casualty of the U-boat war. A week later, in the full glare of worldwide publicity and keen attention, the great German battleship *Bismarck* came to the end of her one dramatic foray into the Atlantic under the guns and torpedoes of the Home Fleet, shattering the hopes of the German Naval Command (see p. 298). The action took place well inside the newly defined US Security Zone, watched by those concerned with the sharp awareness that

neither the Atlantic Fleet nor the entire United States Navy at that time had a vessel capable of trading punches on anything like equal terms with the *Bismarck*.[83]

The spectacular disappearance of *Bismarck* under the waves was accordingly a matter of considerable satisfaction in the United States. Roosevelt told Churchill:

All of us are made very happy by the fine tracking down of the *Bismarck* and that she is literally gone for good.[84]

On that same day, 27 May, he broadcast a declaration of Unlimited National Emergency. 'The war,' he told the American people '. . . is coming very close to home . . . it would be suicide to wait until they are in our front yard.' This thought was gaining ever wider acceptance, and fortified by awareness of that the President moved towards the occupation of Iceland in July and the adoption of escort duties by the US Navy in September, pointers of a general eastward movement which would end at Londonderry in January 1942. Such are the helpful wonders that neutrality can perform when it is cunningly interpreted.

The U-boats lent their habitual emphasis to all these measures; in particular they underlined the unsatisfactory aspect of the system of partial convoy forced on the Royal Navy by the fuelling problem. Early in April a pack of seven U-boats found convoy SC 26 in longitude 28°W south-east of Greenland before the Western Approaches escort joined, and sank six ships (Dönitz says 10). Their total sinkings in that month were forty-three ships (249,375 tons), rising to fifty-eight ships (325,492 tons) in May. More than half of this loss was incurred on the Sierra Leone route, leading to further demands upon the Navy and Coastal Command for escorts. Freetown would now join St John's and Hvalfjordhur in the list of the Navy's least admired resorts – though its amenities were of a somewhat different kind:

'A bloody funny name for the place,' said one of the ratings who had apparently been there. 'The only things free are sweat and syph!' and he drew his hand across his neck, dripping with sweat.[85]

Freetown is nearly 3,000 miles from the U-boat Biscay bases, and in order to maintain his offensive in that area Dönitz had recourse to surface supply ships. These enabled his seven boats to double their patrol time, with excellent results. He was well pleased with their performance, singling out in particular *U 107* under *Korvettenkapitän* Günther Hessler, which he credited with fourteen ships (87,000 tons). Hessler, he said, was 'an excellent tactician and a master in the art of the use of the torpedo). He was anxious to reward this captain with a Knight's Cross, but there was a problem:

I found it a little difficult to recommend him, because he was my son-in-law. Eventually the Commander-in-Chief put an end to my hesitation by telling me that if I did not recommend Hessler at once, he would. My subsequent recommendation was approved forthwith.[86]

Dönitz also speaks well of *Korvettenkapitän* Metzler's *U 69*, which laid mines off Lagos and Takoradi, sinking some ships and forcing both ports to close temporarily; nine ships (23,194 tons) were sunk by mines in May, 1941.

The most significant U-boat action, however, was in the third week of May, when a pack of nine boats attacked HX 126, in longitude 40°W where, needless to say, there was no escort. Five ships were lost in the first night, and the Commodore in these unenviable circumstances ordered the rest to scatter. One needs a great deal of assurance to say whether he was right or wrong, but the unfortunate end result was the loss of another four ships. This was an unpleasant shock for the Admiralty; it clearly showed that there was no such thing as a 'safety zone' for convoys once out beyond the cover of the shore-based aircraft. However, there was a partial remedy: the completion of the Navy's Iceland base now made it possible to refuel there, which meant in turn that escort could be provided as far as 35°W, and the formation of the NEF further meant that this could be a handover point (MOMP). By the end of the month, says Churchill, 'continuous escort over the whole route was at last a reality.'[87] This was Canada's first big contribution to the sea war.

There remained, nevertheless, 'The Gap' – that sinister patch of ocean between Iceland and Newfoundland, south of Cape Farewell, some 600–700 miles wide, where air cover could not reach. With the help of Canada and soon America, there might be surface escorts enough at least to give the U-boats a hard fight, but it was now well proven that the thing that hampered them most, forcing them to dive, to break off their attacks and miss their chances, was the presence of aircraft overhead. This meant aircraft with greater range than any of those in action at this stage of the war, and the phrase that was going to be heard time and again was 'Very Long Range' (VLR). The battle with the U-boats would be unceasing, the struggle to replace the lost ships would never end, and the struggle to expand the escort forces and give them the equipment they needed was still just beginning; but to all these was added a further fight, against the urgent claims of the strategic bomber offensive, for the VLR aircraft which alone could close the Atlantic Gap.

* * * * *

The *Bismarck*'s disastrous foray in May, 1941, was the last Atlantic operation of Admiral Raeder's prized heavy units. When *Bismarck* went down, the whole burden of the Atlantic battle fell upon the U-boats, which was not a matter that would occasion any surprise to Dönitz. It would, in fact, turn out to be in one important sense a relief. As we have seen, the two battleships *Scharnhorst* and *Gneisenau* had entered

Brest on 22 March; on 1 June they were joined there by *Bismarck*'s surviving consort, the beautiful, sleek heavy cruiser *Prinz Eugen*. From that time onwards these three dangerous ships were the targets of repeated attacks by aircraft of Coastal and Bomber Commands. It was a daunting task; the aircraft came in through storms of *Flak* to bomb heavily camouflaged ships which were in any case unsinkable by virtue of lying in the shallow water of docks or dry dock.[88] Damage was exceedingly difficult to assess, and the Admiralty exceedingly difficult to convince, but damage was clearly being done, for there the three vessels remained until February, 1942. Air Chief Marshal Sir Arthur Harris, who later became AOC-in-C of Bomber Command, saw this situation as a victory for the German Navy:

> The presence of these warships in a base from which they could easily make forays into the Atlantic gave a new meaning to the phrase 'a fleet in being'; instead of containing a hostile fleet, they contained a large proportion of the bomber force which might have been used to attack Germany.[89]

The German Naval Command saw the thing differently; it was only too well aware of the damage that was being done, very conscious of the helpless condition of the three ships, and dreading hits that would be visible and finally fatal. It was also aware that all the supply ships on which the surface forays had depended had been sunk by the Royal Navy (what it did not know was that more than half these sinkings were the result of *Enigma* decrypts). And in November it was left in no doubt about the evil effect the presence of the big ships in Brest was having on the U-boats. A large element in the continuing dearth of boats was evidently the time required in dock for repair and maintenance; this was in large part due to the lack of dock labour, and it is not difficult to imagine Dönitz's feelings when he saw some 800 precious dockyard workers, previously employed on U-boats, now directed to the upkeep of the big ships. On 26 November, after months of frustration, he addressed a strong memorandum to Raeder:

> In view of the urgent need of maintenance personnel for the U-boat arm, U-boat Command is of the opinion that the whole question of the repair of battleships and cruisers and of the building and repair of destroyers should be re-examined. . . . In other words, are these types of vessels essential for the prosecution of the war?

346

We are in conflict with the two strongest maritime powers in the world, who dominate the Atlantic, the decisive theatre of the war at sea. The thrusts made by our surface vessels into this theatre were operations of the greatest boldness. But now, principally as a result of the help being given to Britain by the USA, the time for such exploits is over, and the results which might be achieved do not justify the risks involved . . .

Only the U-boat . . . is capable of remaining for any length of time and fighting in sea areas in which the enemy is predominant . . .

For these reasons U-boat Command is emphatically of the opinion that battleships and cruisers are *not* indispensable to the prosecution of the war in the Atlantic . . . the inevitable and only logical conclusion must be that they are no longer of major importance to the prosecution of the war as a whole. That being so, maintenance personnel, which is most urgently needed for the vital U-boat arm, should no longer be wasted on repairing battleships and cruisers.[90]

In this memorandum, Dönitz adds,

I had made very far-reaching demands on behalf of the U-boat arm. As Officer Commanding U-boats, I could not, I felt, have done otherwise. My memorandum, however, had no effect.

Yet, as we now know, relief was at hand; on 11 February, 1942, in fog and darkness, the three big ships with attendant destroyers, minesweepers and torpedo-boats, all under a *Luftwaffe* umbrella, made their celebrated dash up the Channel. There was much heart-searching in Britain over the failure to prevent what had all the appearances of a brilliantly triumphant performance. However, the truth is that *Scharnhorst* was seriously damaged as she reached German waters by airlaid mines on 13 February; *Prinz Eugen* was torpedoed by the submarine *Trident* on her way to Trondheim on 23 February, and *Gneisenau* suffered two direct hits in a Bomber Command attack on Kiel on 26/27 February. All three were out of action again for many months (indeed, *Gneisenau* never sailed again). Cajus Bekker sums up:

the tactical success of the (Channel dash) could not mask that this strategic withdrawal represented a serious reverse for the German surface fleet. The French Atlantic bases, in which the Berlin Admiralty had reposed such shining hopes when taken over less than eighteen months

347

before, had under the weight of British air attack proved untenable – at least for capital ships. Their 'unique strategic advantage' for the war at sea had proved a snare and a delusion.[91]

At the end of it all, neither the German nor the British Admiralties had much to congratulate themselves upon; the RAF had reduced what still indisputably remained an early failure; only Dönitz could view the outcome with complete satisfaction – now, at last, he had the full use of his Biscay bases and all their attributes (RAF permitting). But all this was in 1942; in June, 1941, there was only frustration.

It was made all the worse by the long-delayed and eagerly awaited improvement in U-boat production (see p. 221); in March and April the average number of operational U-boats had been thirty; in June this figure rose to forty-seven and in July and August it would reach sixty. This growth should have been reflected in increased activity, more successful convoy battles and a steep rise in sinkings. Instead, there was a perplexing lull in the Atlantic; in his memoirs Dönitz writes as though these occasions were explicable as 'natural breaks' in the intensity of the action – he describes this one as

> another long hiatus during which the U-boats swept the seas fruitlessly in a vain attempt to find the enemy.[92]

The idea of the 'natural break' is not far-fetched; most protracted operations of war have periods of rest, reinforcement or regrouping. The one that now took place, however, had special reasons. It will be recalled that June was the month when Bletchley Park began to read the HYDRA Enigma signals practically currently; the result was a degree of effective re-routing never before attained – hence the empty seas. And even on one rare occasion when the U-boats did sight a convoy, BP's decrypts played a new and notable part in spoiling the success.

After the HX 126 battle in May there was no major action against a convoy until 23 June, when ten U-boats converged on HX 133 south of Greenland. This occasion turned out to be a double 'first'. For the Canadians in the NEF, it was their first convoy battle, and their performance resembled all too closely some of those of the Royal Navy's earlier days which we have already described. HX 133 was sailing under the protection of the RCN destroyer *Ottawa* with one British and three Canadian corvettes in company. At the same time three more Canadian and two British corvettes were coming down from Iceland to meet the westbound convoy OB 336. HMCS *Wetaskiwin* was the senior officer's ship of this group.

Trouble began on the night of 23 June, when a merchantman in HX 133 was torpedoed. The main attack came the next night when five ships were hit one after another, producing as ever a flurry of fairly frantic activity in the escort. *Ottawa* succeeded in obtaining a quick ASDIC contact and at once dropped a pattern of depth charges, but as she prepared to let go another, ill chance and inexperience took a hand in the game:

> two corvettes turned in her wake and the wash of their propellers ruined her contact. After that piece of bad luck and bad management *Ottawa* rejoined the convoy, instructing the corvettes to continue the search for the U-boat. The signal was incompletely received and the corvettes broke off the hunt. *Ottawa* could send no orders to them by radio telephone because they did not carry the equipment. They were slow in reading her signals by lamp; and their own lamps were so low-powered as to be visible only at close range.[93]

It reads like a text-book example of the unwisdom of sending raw crews to sea in ill-equipped ships; as Joseph Schull remarks:

> Signalmen, youngsters who had attained a precarious efficiency in class-rooms or on barrack lawns a month or so before, were finding the task of reading Morse from rocking bridges in rain and fog across heaving miles of sleety sea beyond them. No one could expect it to be otherwise, and no one could hope that the war would wait while shortcomings were made good.

Already, however, the second 'first' was producing its effect. The U-boat signals reporting contact with the convoy on 23 June were promptly decrypted at Bletchley Park and relayed to Western Approaches Command. Admiral Noble ordered *Wetaskiwin*, still searching for OB 336, to detach two corvettes to support the hard-pressed escort of HX 133, which she promptly did – at the same time discovering that she did not have the cipher for many of the signals that were now reaching her, which suggests some very bad staff work somewhere along the line. When the full attack on HX 133 developed, Admiral

349

Noble ordered *Wetaskiwin* and her two remaining corvettes to stop their search for OB 336 and go at once to help the *Ottawa* group. Almost immediately, however, *Wetaskiwin*'s captain, Lieutenant-Commander Guy Windeyer RCN, received a signal which placed him squarely in the classic naval officer's 'hot seat'. It was from OB 336, reporting that she was now also being attacked, and Windeyer's professional reading of the two signals convinced him that Admiral Noble had been unaware of this fact when he had sent his last order. Windeyer reasoned out his problem thus:

> The convoy for which he was searching was under attack and had no escort at all. HX 133 had its own escort group; and the two corvettes he had sent to its assistance would soon be arriving.

Whether, as a professional, recalling the famous saying of the renowned Admiral 'Jackie' Fisher, that 'any fool can obey orders',[94] or merely displaying the initiative to which he had been trained, Windeyer decided to disobey the C-in-C, Western Approaches, and close OB 336. When he did so, at dawn the next day, he found that the convoy had already lost two ships, but no further attack developed. It is good to record that Lieutenant-Commander Windeyer's action was later endorsed both by Admiral Noble and by Commodore Murray, commanding the NEF.

So the action closed with a loss of seven merchant ships from the two convoys, but thanks in considerable part to the decrypts which had made it possible to reinforce an escort group at a moment of crisis, this was not a one-sided reckoning. In the operations between 24–25 June, *U 556* and *U 651* were sunk by groups of RN escorts. These losses brought Dönitz's total for the six months, January–June, 1941, to twelve, which was a figure that he could definitely live with, especially in the light of the improved deliveries referred to above. What was *not* easy to live with was the effect of the greatly increased American presence. On 20 June *U 203*, in a misguided moment, had attempted to attack the US battleship *Texas*; this act, thought not even noticed by the American ship, brought a sharp and immediate reproof from Hitler, and Dönitz was forced to signal to all boats the following day:

> Führer orders avoidance of any incident with USA during next few weeks. Order will be rigidly obeyed in all circumstances. In addition

attacks till further orders will be restricted to cruisers, battleships and aircraft carriers and then only when identified beyond doubt as hostile.[95]

What this meant in practical terms, says Dönitz, was

that the U-boats could no longer attack their most dangerous enemies, the destroyers, frigates and corvettes, whether British or of any other nationality. With this intermingling of British and American naval forces the U-boats found themselves in a situation which was unique in the history of war.

It was, as Jürgen Rohwer says, 'a grotesque situation',[96] which is not altogether surprising, since it was the product of a grotesque miscalculation.

The reason why Hitler became so agitated on 20 June about the possibility of an 'incident' involving the United States was that he was about to commit the greatest blunder of his life on 22 June: the attack on the Soviet Union, Operation BARBAROSSA. This was a date in history whose full significance is immeasurable. It was the second turning-point of the Second World War, creating an entirely new context for all that followed, an endless and mounting drain on Germany's resources which would ultimately consume them all, and with them the Third Reich and its Führer.

BARBAROSSA held no good news for Dönitz, now or at any time. It could not fail to spell a down-grading of the U-boats in the unending strife of priorities, as he was quick to perceive:

the war with Russia will be decided on land, and in it the U-boats can play only a very minor rôle.[97]

He was right in all respects; eight operational U-boats had to be detached to the Baltic in support of the great advance:

There they found practically no targets and accomplished nothing worth mentioning. They were accordingly returned to me at the end of September.

In July he was ordered to make another detachment of four to six boats to the Arctic; what these were intended to perform is not clear,

351

since there were as yet no Arctic convoys plying between Britain and the USSR with essential war materials to be harried. But the result of these diversions, on top of his other troubles, was that in July and August:

> In the whole vast sea area from Greenland to the Azores there were only eight to twelve U-boats, like minute dots, searching for shipping.[98]

And the consequences of that were what one might expect; whereas in June the U-boats had accounted for 310,143 tons of shipping (sixty-one ships), their third highest monthly total of the war to date, the July figures were 94,209 tons (twenty-two ships), and in August 80,310 tons (twenty-three ships). Dönitz, with marked restraint, calls this 'meagre success', but Jürgen Rohwer is more forthright:

> the months of July and August saw the North Atlantic U-boat operations sink to their lowest level of effectiveness, and it looked almost as though the defence had won the race against the attack.

In London there was a surge of optimism, and a disposition in certain quarters (particularly those connected with the bombing offensive) to regard the Battle of the Atlantic as won; a few weeks would show that this was only a false dawn.

4

By the Narrowest of Margins

'it was only by the narrowest of margins that . . . the U-boat campaign failed to be decisive in 1941.'

F. H. Hinsley, British Intelligence in the Second World War ii p. 169

BARBAROSSA ADVANCED WITH triumphant strides;[1] the U-boat war stagnated. With more boats than he had ever possessed before, Dönitz now endured the chagrin of steeply declining performance. In the first half of 1941 Axis submarines sank 363 ships (1,451,593 tons), a monthly average of some 242,000 tons; in the second half-year these numbers dropped to 169 ships (720,159 tons), a monthly average of just over 120,000 tons. The rate for the first half-year represented a loss of over five million tons of shipping as against the one million tons of new shipping which was the maximum that Commonwealth yards could produce. And what that would have meant was a deficit of seven million tons of supply imports, two million tons of food, and a further serious shrinkage of oil stocks which were already close to the danger mark.[2] It is against this potential that the falling-off of the U-boat performance has to be measured.

When we look for an explanation of the phenomenon (whose character began to be apparent in July), it is obvious that the break into the HYDRA cipher achieved by Bletchley Park in June was the dominant factor, making possible the forewarned re-routing which stultified the U-boat packs. In July, for example, they patrolled the trans-Atlantic routes for three weeks without sighting a convoy, and in August there was a similar period of ten days, causing Dönitz to bring them back eastward, only to be stultified again by Coastal Command's intensive patrolling. It is not in any degree a deflation of the Intelligence achievement to point out that other factors were also at work, and that it is, as usual, in a combination that we may find the key to the central striking fact about the summer of 1941: that after HX 133 in June,

No major attack on an Atlantic convoy took place until September.[3]

This is not to say that nothing positive was happening on the U-boat 'front'. As early as October, 1940, Hitler, who often displayed considerable technical prescience, was asking Dönitz what sort of protection the U-boats should have in their new Biscay bases, to which the *BdU* replied that whether afloat or in dry dock both the boats and the workshops that serviced them should be under concrete. Hitler said he would put the matter in hand, and he was as good as his word. An architect of the Todt Organization[4] was entrusted with what Dönitz rightly calls 'this truly gigantic task', and work quickly began at Lorient, La Pallice, Brest, St Nazaire and, somewhat later, at Bordeaux, to construct shelters very similar to those at Bruges in World War I (see pp. 17–19). Coastal Command photographic reconnaissance monitored its progress stage by stage; the foundation work was done behind caissons which kept the sea out, and while this was going on the whole project was highly vulnerable to blast bombing. In July, 1941, few of the bomb-proof roofs were completed, and there was still a good chance of delaying, if not preventing, the construction. Bomber Command, however, having reluctantly accepted the need to attack the German surface ships,[5] shied sharply away from this further task. Its heavy bombers had other things to do. The Air Ministry backed the Bomber Command view, its own position being revealingly displayed in a minute to the Chief of the Air Staff in September:

It considered that the AOC-in-C, Coastal Command, in common with the Admiralty, had overlooked the long term indirect contribution which the bomber offensive had made and was still making to our security at sea by attacks, not only on the main German ports, but on the German industrial effort as a whole. This industrial effort supported their naval just as much as their military or other war effort. The Air Ministry had accepted that the bomber force should support the naval strategy more

354

directly when the Battle of the Atlantic was in its earlier and critical stage but there seemed no justification whatever for a return to this defensive strategy now when conditions at sea had so much improved and we were beginning to develop fully the air offensive to which we must look for winning as opposed to not losing the war. [6]

Bomber Command at this period (which would continue for some time to come) was passing through a disagreeable phase when it bitterly opposed all 'diversions' from what it considered to be its 'proper' rôle – the strategic air offensive against German industrial centres and morale – despite the fact that that its fulfilment of this rôle was increasingly seen as far from brilliant. I have remarked elsewhere that

> Indeed, it is at times difficult, taking into account the ineffectiveness of Bomber Command's 'proper' activity, and its strong resistance to all 'improper' activity, to decide whether it is more correct to say that Bomber Command was irrelevant to the war, or that the war was irrelevant to Bomber Command. [7]

The result, in this case, was as one might suppose. The Germans roofed in their new U-boat pens with solid reinforced concrete sixteen feet thick; the U-boat campaign revived and became a mortal danger; then, and only then, did Bomber Command throw its weight against the Biscay bases, in particular Lorient and St Nazaire:

> From the cascade of fire and high explosive which descended on the two ports practically nothing emerged intact – except the U-boat pens [8]

Dönitz remarked with perceptible blandness:

> It was a great mistake on the part of the British not to have attacked these pens from the air while they were under construction. . . . But British Bomber Command preferred to raid towns in Germany. Once the U-boats were in their concrete pens it was too late. [9]

It was some consolation for the frustrated *BdU* to observe the completion of the pens as the year wore on; he had little else to console him. Anxiety at the persisting failure to find convoys naturally prompted some urgent questioning at U-boat Headquarters. Dönitz was always inclined to attribute this lack of success to his two everlasting banes – the dearth of boats and the lack of 'eyes' (*B-Dienst* had yet to offer a real remedy by breaking the Admiralty's Naval Cipher No. 2). He had, however, to accept that these circumstances might not contain the full truth:

> was it not possible that there might be other reasons to account for our meagre success in locating shipping? Was there any chance, for example, that the enemy had some means of locating U-boat dispositions and of routing his shipping clear of them?[10]

An obvious possibility was D/F, already an effective method of location in 1915 (see p. 31). The loss of the French D/F stations (which had been most helpful in the First World War) after June, 1940, had been a serious setback for the British system, but by 1941 the Admiralty was able to make up for this in the westward direction by a chain starting at Land's End, then circling via Northern Ireland and the west coast of Scotland through Iceland and (later) Greenland to Newfoundland and Nova Scotia, right round to the West Indies. For a reliable 'fix', it was considered that intersections from at least three stations were required; such a ring as this would cover the whole of the North Atlantic. Yet Dönitz and his staff tended to undervalue this information source; on the evidence of earlier days, they had concluded that D/F was only really effective at short range. Beyond 300 miles, they believed, D/F was liable to an average error of 60–80 miles, and Dönitz recorded an error of 320 miles at a distance of 600. Times had changed, but still under this impression, when they weighed the profit and loss account of their method of command by radio transmission, they concluded that, while radio signalling should clearly be reduced to a minimum, it still contained 'the information upon which was based the planning and control of those combined attacks which alone held promise of really great success'. Accordingly it was decided that U-boat Command would continue to do its best 'to pick its way along the narrow path between the pros and cons of radio transmission'.

There was, of course, another possibility: that as well as taking directional 'fixes' from the U-boat signals, the British might be reading them by cryptanalysis. This was discussed, but dismissed. To accept it would have been to accept the vulnerability of *Enigma*, and no responsible German was prepared to do that in 1941. As Ronald Lewin says,

The possibility that their ciphers were being broken vexed but never dominated the minds of Dönitz and the staff of U-boat Command.[11]

Dönitz himself admits:

> Whether and to what extent the enemy reacted to radio transmissions was something which, try as we might, we were never able to ascertain with any certainty.[12]

And there, for the time being, that matter rested, or rather it would be better to say that it was put on one side. Since the situation which prompted the question did not go away, neither did the question itself; it lingered, like a poltergeist, in the background of U-boat operations right through the year.

This is an illuminating story; it tells us a good deal about the U-boat Command. The lingering image of this phase of the U-boat war is of 'Germanic' military efficiency contrasted with British last-minute improvisations containing some brilliant strokes but eternally hampered by late starts and earlier unwarlike frames of mind. The picture is sometimes difficult to justify in either case. The elaborate machinery of anti-submarine warfare which had grown up in Britain by mid-1941 (virtually unchanged thereafter) had certainly had to wait for war to bring it into being. Yet vital components had been in existence for a long time, making the assembly of the whole a much less difficult matter than might otherwise have been the case. This was especially true in the Intelligence field and in the area of sophisticated technology. The personnel of Bletchley Park, for example, did not suddenly 'flock to the colours' like Kitchener's volunteers in 1914. Many, like Turing and Welchman, had been hand-picked years earlier and only awaited the summons. Key parts of the anti-submarine apparatus, like the OIC and the Submarine Tracking Room, in the hands of men like Denning and Thring, soon revived the promise of gaining the Intelligence advantage enjoyed in the previous war. The radar scientists, as we have seen (pp. 184–5), had begun work on airborne radar, an essential complement to ASDIC in anti-submarine operations, in the late 1930s. By now they were progressing with a second complement, seaborne radar, to defeat the night/surface tactics of the U-boats. As with ASV III, the secret of success lay in the 10-cm band, and a centimetric prototype had already been installed in a corvette in March; in July 25 vessels were fitted with the new model, known as 271M. These were still early days; performance was variable, and in daylight even in optimum conditions the radar field of vision was scarcely better than that of the human eye in a conning tower; but at night, except in bad weather, 271M gave well-defined pictures of U-boats approaching convoys at distances up to 8,000 yards. It would be a year or more before this valuable aid became fully effective, but the foundations of success were as firm as those of the U-boat pens.

Even more important, as it would later prove, was another advance in the closely allied field of radio: seaborne high-frequency D/F, able to trace even the shortest of the U-boat 'short signals', was here the aim, and once again July, 1941, was a milestone, with the introduction of an improved model, FH 2, itself shortly to be superseded by FH 3 in October. U-boat Command, already guilty of undervaluing the land-based D/F chain, would then have to reckon with mobile detectors close enough to their quarry to pounce lethally on every indiscreet signal. One can see now that time was of the very essence in 1941. Technology was performing miracles in the practice of anti-submarine warfare, but ultimately it always has its own pace which cannot be pushed beyond definite limits. The new blessings of mid-1941 were for effective performance in a still distant future. Now was the time for the U-boats to strike, and nothing would have pleased Dönitz better. Never lacking tactical flexibility, he was quick to notice that after their early success his boats in the Freetown area were now finding markedly fewer targets and meeting markedly more numerous enemies. By mid-July the Admiralty had increased the number of escorts on the Freetown and Gibraltar routes to the point where continuous protection could be given.[13] Dönitz responded by switching his main pack effort to the waters round Ireland and Iceland – but wherever he put them, *Enigma* advertised their presence, and these were areas where the defence was at its strongest. The U-boat performance remained abysmal, and time continued to slip away.

It was some mitigation of this late-summer disappointment that reduced action by the U-boats brought with it, as one might expect, reduced losses: only four boats in the two months, July and August. Yet even this satisfaction had to be offset by the weakening caused by the Baltic and Norway diversions and by an inevitable degree of dilution as the long-awaited new boats came into operational service. It was flexibility carried to a point close to desperation when, in August,

Dönitz gave orders that in future escorts rather than merchant ships should take priority as targets. Here dilution could be said to have worked on the side of his enemies, whose numbers were steadily growing. Roskill remarks:

> Though this change of policy caused the loss of a number of these hard-driven little ships and of their gallant crews, it did not materially affect the ebb and flow of the long-drawn battle, since others were now coming forward in increasing numbers to take their places. Probably it merely resulted in the safe arrival of a number of merchant ships which would otherwise have been sunk[14]

Intelligence and tactical failures on the U-boat side, though at times arresting, were in fact at this period less significant than certain strategic and organizational considerations. We have noted the immediate effects of BARBAROSSA – the useless diversion of U-boats to the Baltic and to north Norway. These paled to insignificance at the end of August, when Hitler embarked upon a policy which defies rational justification to this day: over the protests of both Dönitz and Raeder, he ordered naval forces including U-boats to be sent into the Mediterranean.[15] The prompting of this decision was the acute crisis in the German supply position in North Africa caused by attacks on Axis (mainly Italian) shipping by the surface forces and submarines of the Royal Navy and aircraft of the RAF and the Fleet Air Arm. In so far as these were conducted by surface ships, there was reason for a judicious reinforcement of the Italian submarine force. But in so far as RN submarines and RAF aircraft were the offenders, U-boats were not the answer, and never would be; nor would they find any large quantity of British and Allied shipping to attack – the heavily escorted Malta convoys were only spasmodic, the main supply route to the Middle East being the long haul round the Cape of Good Hope. In the Mediterranean, the U-boats' chief targets would be warships; attacking these dangerous enemies[16] meant a withdrawal of effort from the trade war which Dönitz always believed to be their real business. So the Mediterranean diversion amounted to a fundamental change of strategy, with most serious implications:

> A basic error of strategy was committed the moment submarines were deployed in support of the Mediterranean campaign instead of being

supported by it. Victory in the Atlantic would have guaranteed victory in all western and southern Europe; victory in the Mediterranean would have been limited to that very important but self-contained region.[17]

For Dönitz it meant that

> At the moment when a fresh chance to strike a crippling blow had come, the means with which to deal it was snatched from his hand.[18]

Since this condition was to continue, to the grave detriment of operations on the main convoy routes, for a long time, it will be convenient to follow it through at least until the end of Dönitz's sickening year. Hitler issued his ill-judged order on 26 August; the first six U-boats entered the Mediterranean at the end of September to be followed by four more in early November. They very quickly made their presence felt: on 13 November *U81* sank the *Ark Royal*, on 23 November *U331* sank the battleship *Barham*, and on 14 December *U557* sank the cruiser *Galatea*. Possibly over-excited by *U81*'s performance, on 22 November the Naval High Command, acting as Hitler's vehicle, told Dönitz

> that the Mediterranean was now to be regarded as the main theatre of operations and that the entire force of operational U-boats would now be transferred to the Mediterranean and the sea area west of Gibraltar.[19]

For some reason the German High Command had allowed itself to be persuaded that the British CRUSADER offensive, which had started in somewhat dubious fashion on 18 November, was linked to a 'British and Gaullist' landing in French North Africa. This combination, Dönitz was told,

> places Italy and our whole position in the Mediterranean in a situation of acute danger . . . the importance to our whole war effort of retaining our position in the Mediterranean necessitate(s) a complete reorientation of the focal areas of U-boat activities until the situation has been restored.

The *BdU* was peremptorily ordered to send another ten U-boats to the eastern Mediterranean, and to station a permanent force of fifteen astride the Straits of Gibraltar. What this really meant, as Dönitz at once perceived, was

> the commitment of the entire U-boat arm to the Mediterranean and the Gibraltar area and the cessation of U-boat activities in the main Atlantic theatre of operations.

In other words, the most severe defeat so far sustained by the U-boats in the Battle of the Atlantic was inflicted by their own High Command.

Dönitz objected to the manoeuvre at every level. He disagreed fundamentally with the strategy; he did not see a fruitful U-boat rôle in the Mediterranean; he did not believe in an Allied attack on French North Africa. Tactically, his own World War I experience taught him that Mediterranean operations would be fraught with difficulties, some of them irremediable. He disliked concentrating boats near Gibraltar, a British sea and air base from which constant patrols were operating. U-boats here would have to remain submerged almost all the time, which meant that they would be blind, useless and vulnerable. Worst of all, as he well knew, once inside the Mediterranean they would have great difficulty in ever getting out again. The currents in the Straits of Gibraltar are complicated: the predominant flow, through the centre of the passage, is a strong west-east current which makes entry easy enough; on either side, close inshore, the currents run in the opposite direction, east-west. To pass the Straits against the central current on the surface took longer than a single night, so that daylight would find the boats exposed to the Gibraltar patrols. Submerged, they would find progress practically impossible in the centre, while the inshore routes were full of navigational hazards. Thus, says Dönitz,

> Once they were in the Mediterranean, my U-boats found themselves as I described it in my War Diary, 'in a mouse-trap'. We had, therefore, to consider most carefully before committing any considerable forces to the Mediterranean for, once they were there, they would never again become available for operations in any other theatre.

To all these considerations the Naval Command remained deaf and blind, and no redirection came from *OKW* or the *Führer*.[20] This situation well illustrates what has been called 'the extraordinary amateurishness of the German war effort'.[21] 'Germanic efficiency' withered under the Nazi touch: Göring, as economic overlord or as head of the *Luftwaffe*, was a disruptive disaster. Hitler, as head of the Armed Forces, was the same; ignorant, dogmatic, suspicious, operating not by principles but by 'intuition', he in fact reduced military policy to gambler's throws, expedients and quackeries of which the diversion of the U-boats to the Mediterranean is a perfect example. His system had no parallel to the British Joint Chiefs of Staff, presenting weighty professional views supported by the findings of the Joint Intelligence Committee to a responsible War Cabinet. Thus a nonsensical story about Allied landings in French North Africa was never subjected to serious operational Intelligence analysis. Even a year later, with America firmly in the war and playing a major rôle in the operation, TORCH stretched Allied resources and capability to the limit available; yet in 1941 the mere rumour of such a venture (without American participation) was allowed to produce a violent swing of German strategy. So the Mediterranean suddenly became 'the main theatre of operations' – despite the fact that BARBAROSSA was at a critical stage,[22] and Britain herself still unbeaten, and above all, one must add, despite the normal prevailing view of the North African theatre at Hitler's headquarters. Hitler himself, with only 'intuition' to guide him, was an inconstant factor, but his general position was one of indifference to the idea of throwing the British out of Egypt, and of a desire to keep his military commitment in Africa down to minimal proportions.[23] *OKW*, inasmuch as it had a view at all (other than echoing Hitler's), looked upon General Rommel's dashing campaigns as a tiresome sideshow. *OKH* (the Army High Command) had very little say in anything by now, but if faced with a choice in, say, the matter of finding reinforcements, it knew very well that North Africa could never take priority over the Eastern Front. So for Raeder to call the Mediterranean 'the main theatre' was really rubbish. Quite soon he would realize that the key to the Axis problem in that sea was Malta, with its submarine, surface and air threat to Rommel's lines of communication, and that the answer lay with the *Luftwaffe*, in the form of devastating air bombardment or airborne assault.[24] But meanwhile, with characteristic German opportunism, he insisted on 'complete reorientation' of the U-boats, which meant throwing away with both hands the chance that increasing numbers offered of fulfilling the promise of the first half year.

All this was deeply disappointing for Dönitz; he argued copiously against what he could see was a grave mistake, but without success.

Yet it would be wrong to make too much of a contrast between his wisdom in this particular matter and the bad system reigning at the centre of Germany's military affairs. If he was right about the Mediterranean, it was largely because his own fixation was a somewhat healthier fault than Raeder's inconsistencies. His war-making apparatus at U-boat Command, on the other hand, reflected the weaknesses of *OKW* and Hitler's method. Once more the contrast with his enemies was striking: on the British side we find anti-submarine warfare presided over by a committee headed by the Prime Minister, backed by an Admiralty Division which contained the ramifications of the OIC, drawing upon the whole complex of Bletchley Park, and operationally conducted by Western Approaches and Coastal Command. Dönitz, on the other hand,

> was conducting a campaign of vital importance, which would help to determine – if not as in his own view actually *decide* – whether the overwhelming naval power of the British Empire was to strangle or be strangled by the *Reich* – literally the most important question facing Germany; yet he was attempting to do so with a staff of half a dozen young U-boat men! They had not been trained to think scientifically, indeed their education had in most cases been seriously undermined by the Nazi control of schools. But if they had been natural geniuses their routine tasks and their demanding schedule at U-boat headquarters would have precluded serious analysis of the problems of this hide-and-seek war; thrashing them out in forays across the Breton fields was no substitute for thorough scientific analysis and proper organization of intelligence.[25]

Looking back across the decades (though memory recalls that it did not look like this at the time) one can see that it was the often derided British, in both wars, who were pioneering the modern procedures, while the 'advanced' Germans were in some respects (like the Nazi ideological overlay) actually mediaeval. And this was just as well, because in the gap between promise and fulfilment of those procedures, if Dönitz and his Command had been able to redress the balance, even by brute force, things might have gone badly indeed. Just *how* badly would shortly be seen. And this was the meaning of the second half of 1941 in the war at sea: for Dönitz an opportunity missed that would never recur; for Britain a breathing-space, a chance to consolidate progress and complete researches before the next peals of thunder.

* * * * *

We return to August, 1941, to an extraordinary event which was also a portent. Among the boats which Dönitz ordered to take up station in Icelandic and Irish waters was *U570*; as it turned out, she was a good example of the dilution which was now beginning to affect the U-boat arm. On 27 August *U570* was on her maiden voyage in 62°15"N, 18°35"W (south of Iceland). Her captain, *Korvettenkapitän* Hans Rahmlow, was on his first operational trip, as were a number of his crew, some of them so new that they had been suffering painfully from seasickness. It was Rahmlow's bad luck, early that morning, to fall foul of the now dense and vigorous patrols by Coastal Command aircraft, in this case a Hudson of 269 Squadron, whose crew spotted *U570*'s diving swirl in spite of bad visibility. An hour later, however, the Hudson's pilot found the U-boat on the surface and at once attacked; the depth charges hung up, *U570* was able to dive again and escape for the second time. Meanwhile, however, alerted by the Hudson's radio, other aircraft were on their way to the area. Over four hours after the first sighting, a second 269 Squadron Hudson, piloted by Squadron Leader J. H. Thompson, had the very good fortune to catch the U-boat in the act of surfacing. As *Korvettenkapitän* Rahmlow came through the conning tower hatch he encountered the shocking sight of an enemy aircraft coming straight at him with bomb-doors open. *U570* crash-dived immediately, but not in time to avoid being straddled by a stick of four depth charges. This time all went exactly right for Coastal Command and very badly indeed for *U570*; the depth charge settings were correct, the four explosions gave the submarine a fearful shaking, smashing instruments, putting out lights and causing leaks through which sea water reached the batteries. This was the situation most dreaded by submariners in both wars (see p. 112) because it produced emission of chlorine gas, causing death by asphyxia with agonizing and horrible accompaniments.[26] When the spray from the explosions cleared, the crew of the Hudson were startled to see, stopped on the surface, *U570* with German sailors out on her deck. A burst of fire from the Hudson produced a white cloth which one sailor waved; it looked astonishingly like a dress-shirt – which indeed it was, one of Rahmlow's. The U-boat was surrendering.

Squadron Leader Thompson remained with his captive until a Catalina flying-boat of 209 Squadron appeared, and later a trawler from Iceland. The state of the sea made boarding impossible, but more aircraft and more ships arrived and the next afternoon *U570* was taken in tow. Interrogation of the crew elicited the facts that the chlorine had demoralized the young sailors; they had insisted on immediate surrender, and the situation had developed beyond Rahmlow's power to deal with it. He had, however, jettisoned his *Enigma* machine and code-books before the boarding party came aboard. In due course *U570* was repaired and commissioned in the Royal Navy as HM Submarine *Graph*, under which name she served until she was wrecked off the west coast of Scotland in March, 1944.

This episode gave a great fillip to Coastal Command. By now a new AOC-in-C was in charge, Sir Frederick Bowhill having departed in June to form a Ferry Command whose task was to bring much needed American aircraft across the Atlantic. His successor at Coastal was Air Marshal Sir Philip Joubert de la Ferté; it was his second tenure of this Command, his first having been in its early days, 1936–7; he found it a very different instrument of war from when he had last known it. Thanks to Bowhill's indefatigable efforts,

> From being concerned almost entirely with reconnaissance, the Command had developed into an offensive weapon capable of inflicting serious damage on enemy warships, merchant shipping, aircraft and shore targets. Its equipment had improved out of all recognition.[27]

The 'rag-bag' nineteen squadrons of 1939 had increased to forty, and while a few of the old types still lingered in service, the order of battle was beginning to contain some impressive names: Beaufighters instead of Blenheims as long-range fighters, Beauforts as torpedo-bombers, Wellingtons displaying their admirable strength and versatility, Hurricanes in Iceland, Spitfire IVs for photo-reconnaissance, and early deliveries of two highly important long-range aircraft from America, the Consolidated Catalina (which the Americans designated the PBY-5) and the same Corporation's Liberator (B-24).[28] More than half the Command's aircraft were now fitted with ASV II and work was in progress on an airborne searchlight which, in conjunction with ASV, might go some way towards winning the 'never-ending struggle to circumvent the law that we cannot see in the dark'.[29] As we have frequently observed, the U-boats had by now developed a very healthy regard for Coastal Command's aircraft; yet when all accounts were rendered, the fact remained that they had yet to kill a U-boat by their own unaided efforts. As Captain Peyton-Ward says:

Two major deficiencies still kept air power as only a potential, instead of being an actual, threat to the life of a U-boat – numbers of long-range aircraft and lethal weapons.[30]

Here lay the further significance of the capture of *U570*: Squadron Leader Thompson had attacked with *depth charges*, and they had been effective. It must be admitted that the effectiveness was more a matter of luck than judgment; there was a long way to go yet, before an optimum setting for depth charges was scientifically established, and a type of depth charge (Mark XI) devised which would truly obey this setting at the very shallow level of only 25 feet. Thompson's Hudson carried the Mark VIII 250-lb charge, and his success fully demonstrated the superiority of this weapon over the wretched anti-submarine bombs of early days. If Bowhill had done nothing else, his championship of the depth charge against the bomb would have been an invaluable contribution. What was now awaited was a new bomb-sight which would make possible an accurate attack at low altitudes without having to depend (as Thompson had done) on a sportsman's 'eye'.

The struggle for VLR aircraft would go on. Already Coastal Command had had the effect of pushing the U-boats further and further westward, beyond the range of help from the Focke-Wulf Condors, into the narrowing 'Gap'. Iceland, now the base of 120 Squadron's Sunderlands, played a big part in this process. Closer to home, Whitleys and Wellingtons could maintain a patrol for some two hours at a distance of about 500 miles from base, but it was really only the flying-boats that could significantly improve on this – two hours at 600 miles by the Sunderlands and the same at 800 miles by the Catalinas. By mid-August sixty-seven of these sturdy old warriors[31] had entered Coastal Command service, but nothing like so many were operational; supplies were uneven, with both the Canadian and the Dutch governments (to say nothing of the US Navy) in competition. The first Liberators had teething troubles which were not readily cured, and supplies of these were also exiguous, in competition with Bomber Command. All attempts to divert the new four-engined Handley Page Halifax to Coastal work were firmly resisted; the Air Ministry was determined that these should be for Bomber Command alone, fearing, as Air Marshal Harris (then Deputy Chief of the Air Staff) put it, that

twenty U-boats and a few Focke-Wulf in the Atlantic would have provided the efficient anti-aircraft defence of all Germany.[32]

Whether this thought would have given any consolation to Dönitz is a matter of speculation. The VLR position was certainly a disappointment to Bowhill; yet, as Denis Richards says, it was

> with the knowledge that many, though by no means all, of the basic problems and difficulties had been overcome that (he) handed over to his successor.[33]

Sir Philip Joubert has attracted a mixed 'press'. He was highly articulate, often contentious, sometimes dogmatic and outspoken to a degree that politicians disliked (that does not necessarily have to be a very high degree). Sir Maurice Dean, acknowledging Joubert's intelligence, imagination and understanding, adds tersely:

> But other qualities are needed in a Commander-in-Chief and Joubert was short on these.[34]

Sir Maurice does not specify these qualities. He merely says:

> Joubert was not an ideal Commander-in-Chief for Coastal Command.

Denis Richards, on the other hand, calls him 'an extremely keen-witted and versatile officer', and refers to his earlier term of office,

> when his ever-active intelligence had stimulated the development of airborne radar for locating ships at sea.[35]

It was, in fact, according to Richards, the ever-increasing importance of radar that caused Joubert to be brought back:

> His first task was accordingly clear: to develop the most effective operational technique for ASV aircraft, and in so doing to make the aeroplane at last a 'U-boat killer'.

These are well-chosen words; when Joubert took over, Coastal Command was in this highly significant respect no further forward than the RNAS in World War I. This was the 'Scarecrow Phase':

> Our aircraft could seek, find, report, strike and wound. They could not yet kill. It was the firm intention of Sir Philip Joubert to remedy this

defect. The new Coastal chief was determined not to rest until the aeroplane was thoroughly lethal to the submarine.[36]

Joubert's efforts ran along two main courses. There was, everlastingly, the battle for material – for more aircraft, for VLR aircraft, for the most advanced ASV radar, for the radio-telephones (R/T) which were now coming in (and which promised to do great things for the cooperation of surface escorts,[37] for cooperation between escorts and convoy, and between aircraft, escorts and convoy) – and much else. Enough has been said for the time being on this. His second battle was within the Command itself, for greater efficiency, for improvement of techniques to make the best possible use of the equipment that existed. In this Joubert enjoyed another legacy from his predecessor: three months before leaving Northwood, Bowhill had enlisted Professor Patrick Blackett as Scientific Adviser to Coastal Command. This, as Sir Maurice Dean says,

> was the beginning of the Command's long, imaginative and productive alliance with the world of science.[38]

Blackett's arrival marked the first step towards the formation of an Operational Research Unit which would now set about revolutionizing the procedures and the rôle of Coastal Command. Besides Blackett himself, four Fellows of the Royal Society were associated with this Unit (Sir John Kendrew, Professor E. J. Williams, Professor C. H. Waddington and Professor J. M. Robertson), justifying Sir Maurice Dean's remark that

> It cannot be said that the scientists attached to the work were lacking in prestige.

However, since not even the most brilliant scientists can operate without data, it is only right to link with this array of academic talent Coastal Command's Naval Liaison Officer, Captain Peyton-Ward (see p. 247). It was shortly after Joubert's arrival that, independently of his normal duties, Peyton-Ward

> commenced writing up each individual sighting and attack on U-boats as they took place, using every scrap of first-hand evidence obtainable and analysing the probable result from all the data available. Whenever

possible the attacking crews came to the Headquarters which enabled personal corroboration, discussion of detail and practical experience to be effected while the event was still fresh.[39]

For the remainder of the war, working in close collaboration with the Submarine Tracking Room, Peyton-Ward continued to carry out this invaluable task, becoming in the process a specialist in all aspects of air anti-submarine warfare.

By 25 July Joubert considered it possible and useful to issue a new Tactical Instruction (No. 15) which certainly illuminates the condition and problems of Coastal Command at that stage of the war. In summary:

(i) The attacking approach was to be made by the shortest path and at maximum speed.

(ii) The actual attack could be made from any direction relative to the U-boat. [Later modified; length-wise attack preferred.]

(iii) The depth setting of all depth charges was to be 50 feet, the spacing of depth charges in a stick was to be 60 feet and all depth charges carried were to be released in one stick.
[As we have seen, the depth setting would be reduced to 25 feet; a spacing of 36 feet was introduced for the larger aircraft, but both this and the 60-foot spacing were later abolished in favour of one of 100 feet. These were fruits of Operational Research, sometimes sharply opposed by the aircrews.]

(iv) *The ideal was to attack while the U-boat or some part of it was still visible.* Data was given, however, to enable pilots to estimate quickly how far ahead of the point of final disappearance their stick should be placed if the U-boat got under just before release was possible.

(v) *In cases where the U-boat had disappeared for more than 30 seconds it was pointed out that success was unlikely* owing to the progressive uncertainty of the U-boats's position either in plan or depth.

(vi) The height of release must not be greater than 100 feet until an aiming sight was provided but the restriction against aircraft carrying depth charges at night was modified.[40]

(vii) Great stress was laid on the need for training and constant exercises so as to attain a high standard of attack and aiming accuracy.[41]

This, obviously, was just a starting point; discussion and argument about technique would be unending, and changing with the introduction of each new piece of equipment. Success, however, the kind of success that Joubert was seeking, remained obstinately round the corner. Operational Research had no difficulty in establishing the great advantage of complete cloud cover (with the aid of ASV II) in attacking U-boats:

Even then it was discovered that, unless the cloud base was low, the U-boats could still get well under water after the aircraft had broken cloud and before the attack could be pressed home.[42] The new problem was to make the aircraft more difficult to see from the bridge of the U-boat. After various experiments in camouflage it was discovered that plain white on all sides and under-surfaces of the aircraft gave a remarkable degree of invisibility in the cloud and sky conditions generally prevalent in northern latitudes. This white camouflage, with certain refinements resulting from scientific investigation, remained the standard colour of anti-U-boat aircraft throughout the rest of the war. Thus started in the summer of 1941 the familiar 'White Crows' of Coastal Command.[43]

Even with the new styles and weaponry being introduced, by September the only certain results to show for all Coastal Command's long, weary hours of flying were the incalculable (but clearly substantial) 'Scarecrow' effects, *U 570* captured and three kills shared with surface vessels; in addition there were estimates of some ten or twelve U-boats seriously damaged in the course of no fewer than 245 attacks made during the whole preceding course of the war. It was discouraging – the more so now that depth charges were at last standard equipment; evidently there must still be a fundamental fault of method requiring the further attention of Operational Research. Accordingly, says Peyton-Ward,

an analysis was made of all attacks since August, 1940, when depth charges were first used. This yielded the information that in spite of depth charge settings having varied between 100 feet and 300 feet, only those attacks made on a still visible U-boat or within 15 seconds of disappearance resulted in damage or destruction being assessed. During this period 35% of the U-boats attacked had some portion visible at the time of release and 15% had disappeared for less than 15 seconds. No evidence of even slight damage followed attacks made at a longer interval than 30 seconds after disappearance. It was therefore suggested that all efforts should be concentrated on attacking the former which were classified as Class A targets and that far less attention should be paid to the remainder.[44]

370

This acknowledgment that some 50% of the offensive effort of the Command was a pure waste of time was the more galling in that Joubert had, on taking office, laid great stress on offensive operations. It was bad that nothing was being done about the concrete pens whose progress was visible in the reconnaissance photographs week by week, but at least something might be done about the U-boats in transit to and from the Biscay bases. Joubert could see that the Bay itself was what his successor would call, in a vivid phrase,

> the trunk of the Atlantic U-boat menace, the roots being in the Biscay ports and the branches spreading far and wide, to the North Atlantic convoys, to the Caribbean, to the eastern seaboard of North America and to the sea-lanes where the faster merchant ships sail without escort.[45]

Obviously, the argument ran, the thing to do was to fell the tree by cutting through the trunk – 'the little patch of water about three hundred by a hundred miles in the Bay of Biscay through which five out of six U-boats operating in the Atlantic had to pass within range of aircraft based in England and Gibraltar'. So Joubert started in June what became known as the 'First Bay Offensive'; he kept it up as best he could until the end of the year, but as Coastal Command's attacks were all made in daylight, the initial results were unimpressive. Nor did they greatly improve in the later part of the year. Between 1 September and 30 November, 3,600 effective flying hours produced thirty-one sightings and twenty-eight attacks of which only five were considered likely to have caused damage bad enough to make the U-boat return to base. In December a sudden fall in the number of sightings was noted – only four, of which three were at night. Peyton-Ward comments that this circumstance

> did bring out in sharp relief the necessity for an efficient method of night attack before a really effective offensive could be launched.[46]

More satisfactory as a consolation, and a big moment in the history of Coastal Command, was an encounter on 30 November. Bletchley Park detected a U-boat (*U 206*) outward-bound across the Bay; she was, in fact, making for the Mediterranean. The decrypt told where to look and a Whitley of 502 Squadron duly made for the area indicated.

By a fortunate combination of satisfactory performance on the part of two pieces of equipment whose general record was sadly variable, first the ASV operator in the aircraft was able to find *U 206* at a range of five miles, then guide the pilot into visual attacking distance – then the depth charges did the rest. This was the solitary U-boat kill of the Bay offensive, but for Coastal Command it was a turning point. One U-boat captured by its unaided efforts in freakish circumstances, and one 'properly' killed; twenty-six months of war was a long time to wait for such a meagre result. But everything has to have a beginning.

The contrast between Coastal Command's contribution to the growing elaboration and sophistication of anti-submarine warfare and Dönitz's primitive headquarters organization leaning on the efforts of no more than seven ex-U-boat commanders will once more be noted. Perhaps nowhere was the difference more vividly displayed than in what were known as Joubert's 'Sunday Soviets'. These meetings were held weekly at the Telecommunications Research Establishment at Swanage; those present might include Cabinet Ministers, and would normally number junior as well as senior officers and the scientists:

> There were the frankest exchanges between those who designed the equipment and those who used it in action; and on more than one occasion a senior officer had 'his ears pinned back' by an over-enthusiastic junior. The 'Soviets' fulfilled a most important function: they brought reality to the scientists, who were always in danger of becoming mesmerised by the sheer technical brilliance of what they produced; they gave the senior officers a clear idea of how, in fact, the devices were performing in action; and they provided the fighting men with much information on how to get the utmost out of their equipment.[47]

This, too, was a beginning, along a major road.

* * * * *

In September, 1941, Dönitz was at last able once more to mount an offensive in his 'decisive theatre', the North Atlantic. He had enough boats to be able to form two or four groups (according to operational availability) which he despatched into the waters around Greenland, where useful results were most likely to be obtained:

> Three factors combined to lead me to this conclusion. They were, first, the help which, without declaration of war, the Americans were already

giving to the British in 1941 ... second, the fact that these more northerly routes could be given air cover by aircraft based on Iceland and finally that we had failed to sight any convoys on the more southerly routes during July and August. The correctness of my deductions was quickly confirmed.[48]

Dönitz was helped, at this stage, by certain measures of disguise which his staff had adopted in its signals exchanges with the boats at sea, codifying references to the German naval grid before enciphering them. These expedients never fully checked the cryptanalysts at Bletchley Park, but they did cause delays in the passing of information vital for the successful re-routing of the convoys.[49] The combined result of Dönitz's reasoning and BP's difficulty was a sudden re-escalation of the Atlantic battle.

The narrowness of the gap between triumphant success and highly disturbing failure in convoy operations was now to be displayed. In August Dönitz formed the *Norden* Group of fifteen to seventeen U-boats, and deployed it in the new hunting-ground south-east of Cape Farewell. On the 30th of the month SC 42 sailed from Sydney, sixty-two ships formed in twelve columns, carrying half a million tons of supplies, under Commodore W. B. Mackenzie RNR. By 2 September the convoy had reached St John's, where it was joined by five more ships[50] and the escort for the first lap of its transatlantic journey: the all-Canadian 24th Escort Group under Commander J. C. Hibbard RCN, who was also captain of the destroyer *Skeena*, with the corvettes *Alberni*, *Kenogami* and *Orillia* in company. It was a weak escort indeed for a convoy covering some 25 square miles of sea, weakened further by the fact that *Kenogami* had only been in commission for three months and lacked certain essential items of equipment.

Escort Group 24 and *Norden* Group of U-boats were unevenly matched opponents, but destined now to fight 'the biggest convoy battle so far'.[51] Unfair it may have been (it is, after all, one of the arts of war to seize an unfair advantage) but for the RCN this was an occasion of particular significance; as Marc Milner comments:

The two nights during which NEF Group Twenty-four fought alone were the acid test of the expansion fleet, and the fleet failed.[52]

It was not a dishonourable failure, nor was it entirely unredeemed, but

373

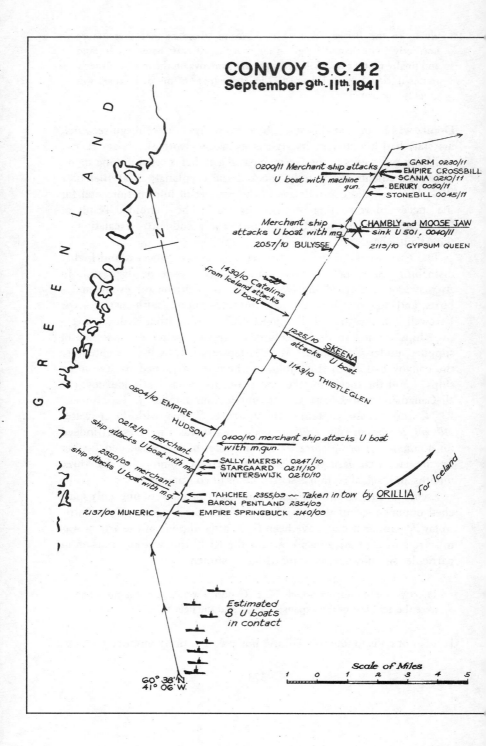

CONVOY S.C. 42
September 9th–11th, 1941

GREENLAND

N

0200/11 Merchant ship attacks U boat with machine gun.

GARM 0230/11
EMPIRE CROSSBILL
SCANIA 0210/11
BERURY 0050/11
STONEBILL 0045/11

Merchant ship attacks U boat with mg.

CHAMBLY and MOOSE JAW sink U 501, 0040/11

2057/10 BULYSSE

2115/10 GYPSUM QUEEN

1439/10 Catalina from Iceland attacks U boat.

1225/10 SKEENA attacks U boat

1143/10 THISTLEGLEN

0504/10 EMPIRE HUDSON

0212/10 merchant ship attacks U boat with mg.

0400/10 merchant ship attacks U boat with m.gun.

2350/09 merchant ship attacks U boat with m.g.

SALLY MAERSK 0247/10
STARGAARD 0211/10
WINTERSWIJK 0210/10

TAHCHEE 2355/09 ～ Taken in tow by ORILLIA for Iceland

BARON PENTLAND 2354/09

2137/09 MUNERIC

EMPIRE SPRINGBUCK 2140/09

for Iceland

Estimated
8 U boats
in contact

60° 38' N.
41° 06' W.

Scale of Miles

1 0 1 2 3 4 5

it was a costly one, pointing the most serious lesson to the autumn battles:

> the heavy losses sustained by such convoys as were attacked demonstrated that beyond the areas within the range of land-based air cover, which the U-boats now avoided, the continual improvement in the Allied defences was still not keeping pace with the continual increase in the number of U-boats.[53]

The first week of EG 24's escort was unremarkable, barring only the weather: easterly gales, producing a sea state of five (Very Rough) with a moderate swell to match,[54] reduced the slow convoy's speed drastically until, on 5 September, it was hove-to, barely keeping steerage way. This lasted for two days, when the gale fell off a little and SC 42 was able to work up to 5 knots. Commander Hibbard signalled that he would be 72 hours late at the Mid-Ocean Meeting Point where the fresh escort from Iceland was to take over. Meanwhile the Submarine Tracking Room had been fed decrypts which indicated a U-boat pack assembling close to the convoy's course; on 8 September SC 42 was re-routed due north, straight towards the rocky coast of Greenland whose precise location, in the prevailing bad visibility, was uncertain. *Skeena* went on ahead to reconnoitre, and this course was held for 25 hours, bringing the whole large assembly of ships to some five miles from the rocks, which was uncomfortably close for a convoy six miles wide. At that point SC 42 made a marked dog's-leg to the north-east, and it was hoped that it had rounded the U-boat patrol line. However, a periscope sighting in the moonlight by one of the merchantmen early on 9 September, and the (claimed) tracks of two torpedoes, warned that this might be a delusion. So it was; EG 24 succeeded in putting this U-boat down and keeping it there, but could not prevent it from making the report which would bring the pack to the quarry.

The first hits were made at about 2137 hours on 9 September; the first sinking was SS *Muneric* in the port column, loaded with iron ore which took her down like a stone. Thereafter, all was the familiar confusion of a night action, faithfully reflected by contradictions in the narratives. *Kenogami* quickly sighted the U-boat in question (*U 432*) and engaged her with the 4-inch gun, but as the ammunition was not charged with flashless powder the only effect of this was to make the crew temporarily night-blind. Hibbard ordered her to fire starshell –

but she had no starshell. Hibbard himself was about to join in this chase when rockets from the Commodore's ship called him to a U-boat sighting inside the convoy itself. By now some eight U-boats had gathered round SC 42, *U 432* had sunk a second merchantman (*Empire Springbuck*), U-boats were surfacing at intervals in different directions, and the Commodore was ordering emergency turns and resumptions of normal course in quick succession. Two hours can pass quickly in such a scene, and the next crisis did not develop until shortly before midnight (2348) when the last ship in the ninth column reported a U-boat on her starboard quarter. Mackenzie called Hibbard, and *Skeena* swung down between the seventh and eight columns to investigate; as she did so, Mackenzie ordered another emergency turn, with the destroyer in the middle of the convoy going at a fair speed:

Nightmare manoeuvres followed as the *Skeena* weaved her way through the great concourse of darkened ships, constant calls for full speed ahead or astern being necessary to avoid collision. In the midst of it all, a ship blew up as a torpedo struck home. Four minutes later two other explosions occurred, one in a ship right alongside the *Skeena*. Tracer bullets streaming out from several ships guided Hibbard to the U-boat. As *Skeena* passed closely across the bow of a ship in the seventh column, he saw her. A tight turn round the stern of another ship, his turbines screaming and his bridge structure rattling as every ounce of power wrenched the destroyer round, brought him in position to ram.

It was too late. The U-boat had dived.[55]

So 10 September came in with every promise of horrible events. It was as well that Hibbard was an experienced professional officer and a fine seaman; his responsibility, both as Senior Officer and as captain of the only really effective vessel of the escort, was daunting indeed. The two torpedoed ships were the *Baron Pentland* and the tanker *Tahchee*; *Orillia* doing her best to help the latter, soon fell far astern of the convoy. This was the last Hibbard would hear of corvette or merchantman for five days, when he learned (with presumably mixed emotions) that *Orillia* had taken the damaged tanker, towing her part of the way, into Reykjavik – a hazardous and skilful endeavour, but reducing SC 42's escort by 25%.[56]

Two more hours passed – hours of waiting, in anti-submarine operations perhaps the most testing ordeal of all:

we settled once more to a slow, minute-by-minute staring into the night and a continuous, nervous, over-the-shoulder consideration of the asdic dial. The strain was intense, chiselling minutely at patience and sanity through the long hours of the night. Attacks always came suddenly although always expected. The shock of that suddenness was made more emphatic by reason of our waiting.[57]

That was another corvette, another convoy – but the same hostile darkness, the same hideous eruptions of violent action, the same exhausting tension. And the battle of SC 42 had barely begun.

The next attacks came at 0210 from the port side of the convoy, and once more the attacker was *U 432*. Two ships, *Winterswijk* and *Stargaard*, were torpedoed within a minute of each other. Another merchantman, *Regin*, under a tough skipper, going to the help of *Stargaard*, sighted a surfaced U-boat and promptly opened fire with her machine gun. *Skeena* and *Kenogami* carried out searches, picked up contacts, genuine or false, dropped some depth charges, but achieved nothing. At 0247 a third ship in this phase, *Sally Maersk*, leading the starboard column, was sunk while the escorts were busy astern; this success was claimed by *U 81*. Almost immediately afterwards another U-boat was sighted and the convoy made yet another emergency turn. Once more *Skeena* and *Kenogami* searched, while *Alberni* occupied herself with picking up survivors. For a while the convoy had no close escort at all, then *Skeena* returned, leaving *Kenogami* to continue the rescue work. It is all too reminiscent of those bad October days of 1940 (see pp. 265–8) when the Royal Navy's own corvettes had been new to such scenes and far too few in number.

And now, once more, there was an interval for SC 42, about two hours of relative quiet, broken only by the steady ping of the escorts' ASDIC and another brief encounter between a merchantman using her machine gun and a surfaced U-boat. The last action of a dreadful night came at four minutes past 5 o'clock, when the newly converted CAM ship,[58] *Empire Hudson*, with a cargo of grain, fell victim to a particularly resolute commander, *Leutnant* Rollman in *U 82*. ASDIC searches once more produced no result, and a saddened, frustrated but by no means demoralized EG 24 sailed on into another ominous day. Seven ships were already lost, taking with them

thousands of tons of fuel oil, grain, phosphate, ammunition, stores and a fleet of trucks. Many plans afoot in Britain had been deranged that night; many small but much-needed cogs knocked out of the war machine.[59]

At this point the scene shifts – back to St John's, headquarters of the NEF, where an officer of some importance in RCN history was closely watching the progress of SC 42. He was Commander J. D. Prentice, a Canadian with 22 years' service in the Royal Navy, retired in 1934, and who happily returned to sea in 1939 in the RCN. He did not immediately feel again the sting of salt water in his eyes, for his first postings were to staff duties in Sydney and Halifax; there he met Murray, a man with whom he shared ideas and interests, and whose staff he joined with the title of Senior Officer, Canadian Corvettes (SOCC), a strange designation which indicates, if nothing else, the importance of those little ships in the RCN's development. Imaginative and vigorous, Prentice was also a training fanatic – 'he allowed his concern for efficiency to dominate his work'[60] – which, in view of the general rawness of the RCN expansion fleet, was no bad thing. In March, 1941, he was given command of a corvette of his own, *Chambly*, and strove continuously to make her the core of a permanent training group, but was continuously frustrated by the demands of actual operations. In August, 1941, he was preparing to make his first training cruise with five corvettes (including *Chambly*), but by 5 September operations had reduced the number to two – *Chambly* herself and *Moose Jaw*. Aware of the threat to SC 42 that was building up, Prentice shaped a course for his two ships that would bring him within supporting distance of the convoy, and by 10 September he was actually ahead of it, in a state of full alert.

This was not known to Hibbard, who now (10 September) faced sixteen more hours during which it would be EG 24 alone (except for one brief appearance by a Catalina from Iceland) that protected SC 42. The day was punctuated by periscope sightings, emergency turns by the convoy, ASDIC searches and depth charge attacks. The first casualty was the vice-commodore's ship *Thistleglen*; she was hit by *U 85* at 1145, and her cargo of steel and pig iron made sure that she would go to the bottom. EG 24 reacted with vigour, and about an hour later an attack by *Skeena* produced a huge air bubble and some oil coming to the surface. Hibbard was certain that he had made a kill, but the records did not confirm it. However, after the loss of *Thistleglen* there were no further misfortunes for some nine hours; then *U 82* returned to the fray; *Bulysse* went down at 2057, and *Gypsum Queen* at 2119. Once again, all that remained for EG 24 to do was to search vainly and cover the rescue of survivors.

This flurry of activity had not passed unnoticed, however; from the bridge of *Chambly*, now well west of SC 42, Prentice could see the rockets and starshell which marked the U-boat attacks, and he set course accordingly. Just after half past midnight his ASDIC operator, a member of his training team, Leading Seaman A. H. Johnson, called out, 'Contact-Red, Nine-O'. It was without doubt a submarine – and only 700 yards away. 'In view of the handiness and small turning circle of a corvette, it was decided to attack at once,' wrote Prentice in his report. Such short-range attack was against all current doctrine, but justified by the extraordinary event. Just two minutes after the first contact, *Chambly* laid a five-charge pattern, set for over 100 feet. Partly through malfunction and partly through human error, the first and second charges had exploded practically simultaneously which, it later transpired, had had the unintended effect of forcing the U-boat to surface by wrecking some of her instruments. As *Chambly* turned for a second attack, with *Moose Jaw* following, there was a swirl of white water ahead of the second corvette, and there, some 400 yards from *Moose Jaw's* port bow, was the submarine, running across. What followed was in keeping with the general confusion of the night. *Moose Jaw* had just time to fire one four-inch shell into the U-boat's conning tower, causing her captain to stop his engines, when the two vessels ran alongside each other. A single figure on the U-boat's bridge now made a wild leap and landed on the deck of the corvette, 'not even wetting his feet in the process'.[61] Not wishing to receive large numbers of such visitors, *Moose Jaw's* captain sheered off, whereupon the U-boat got under way again. Some of her crew were seen to make for the forward gun, but a couple of 4-inch rounds discouraged that manoeuvre, and a quick ram by *Moose Jaw* persuaded the Germans that it was now time to surrender. *Chambly* came up and sent over a boarding party, but the U-boat was clearly sinking. Lieutenant Simmons, the corvette's Number One, was nearly sucked down with her, and a stoker, William Brown, lost his life. Eleven Germans also died.

It turned out that the boat was *U 501*, on her first operational cruise. The leaper was her captain, *Korvettenkapitän* Hugo Forster, who explained that he had made his jump in order to insist that *Moose Jaw* should rescue his crew, 'but the explanation did not go down well either with friend or foe. When later he offered his hand to his chief quartermaster it was refused.' The sinking of *U501* might be called 'beginner's luck' – certainly, as was often the case, there was an element of luck in it, but, says Macintyre,

> Careful and conscientious training must also be credited to Prentice's success. *Kenogami*, for example, had three times had U-boats in sight at close range, but her inexperienced team had been unable to take advantage of it. In contrast stood out the instant, sure classification of contact by *Chambly's* asdic team, the prompt action by Prentice himself and the accurate attack which brought *U501* up in surrender.[62]

Galling it may have been for the over-worked and disappointed EG 24 to see newcomers take off the prize, but for the bruised feelings of the NEF generally this first kill was a consolation and a tonic.

It did not, however, bring an end to the sufferings of SC 42. Before *Chambly* and *Moose Jaw* had finished their business with *U501* the *Norden* Group closed in again. Now it was the turn of *U207* with two quick sinkings: *Stonepool*, at 0045, followed fourteen minutes later by *Berury*. Then there was a lull – if it can be called that – of an hour during which the seeds of further disaster were well planted when three corvettes, *Alberni*, *Kenogami* and *Moose Jaw*, which Hibbard believed to be at their escort stations, fell astern to collect survivors. The *Norden* Group struck again – and who was to know that this would be its last effort? – at ten minutes past two, when *Scania* and *Empire Crossbill* were both hit at the same time, bringing *U82's* score to five. Half an hour later came the last casualty of this doom-laden action – *Garm*, *U207*'s third victim, at 0239. When Hibbard counted the remains of the convoy in daylight, he found that twenty ships were missing, a shocking tally. Even reinforced, EG 24 still only numbered five ships, laden with survivors of lost merchantmen, and with deeply exhausted crews.

Fortunately, help was now at hand in two forms. First, a thick sea mist came up which Dönitz would have us believe was the sole reason for the suspension of the U-boat attacks. This mist, however, did not prevent the arrival of very substantial reinforcements: first, during the morning of 11 September, three more corvettes, *Gladiolus* (RN), *Mimosa* (Free French) and *Westaskiwin* (RCN), with the RN trawler

Buttermere, then in the early afternoon the 2nd Escort Group from Iceland under Commander W. E. Banks (who now became Senior Officer of the combined escort), comprising no fewer than five destroyers, *Douglas*, *Veteran*, *Saladin*, *Skate* and *Leamington*. And in addition to these ships there were aircraft from Iceland to give much-needed early warnings of U-boat presence. It was, in fact, one of these that shortly reported a U-boat on the surface 15 miles ahead of the convoy. With his now ample resources, Commander Banks had already had the foresight to detach *Veteran* and *Leamington* as long-range scouts and hunters, and they were nicely placed. Within half an hour *Veteran* sighted the U-boat and the two destroyers with their well-drilled and experienced anti-submarine teams instituted their established search proceedings; when they rejoined the convoy at dusk they brought the glad news of another definite U-boat sinking – *U 207* had reached the end of her luck.

This was not quite the last flicker of the SC 42 battle; on 16 September, as the convoy was approaching home waters and safety, a straggler was caught and duly sunk. This brought the total of ships lost to sixteen, nearly 24% of the combined total from Sydney and St John's. Such a percentage, if repeated on a considerable scale, spelt disaster, all the more startling by virtue of the preceding quiet spell. The most obvious and indisputable lesson of the battle was the need, even in the western Atlantic (hitherto regarded as a relatively 'safe' area) for more powerful escort groups. The RCN was asked to increase the strength of these from four to a minimum of six vessels, of which two would be destroyers. This would mean a minimum of forty-five corvettes at St John's, a figure which the RCN did not find unacceptable, in view of the state of corvette production. Ninety-nine of these admirable 'workhorses' were in commission (RN + Allies and RCN) by June, 1941, with another ninety-six building, forty-four of them in Britain, fifty-two in Canada. They were coming down the slipways at a rate of six-eight a month. Destroyers, however, were another matter. There were now six Escorts Groups in the NEF, which spelt a requirement of fifteen destroyers which the RCN just did not have available. This was a problem that Canada could only pass back to the Admiralty for solution, with results that we shall discuss. But in principle there was no dispute between the two Navies about the need for stronger escort.

The other needs, equally obvious, were for greater efficiency and better equipment. Efficiency is a function of training and experience;

and training, as we have seen, was what the RCN conspicuously lacked and found it eternally difficult to obtain. It lacked a proper training staff, it lacked training equipment, and it lacked also the training mystique which guided teachers and pupils in, say, Commodore Stephenson's establishment at Tobermory. It definitely lacked a Tobermory. A terse comment from a senior officer at St John's in September, 1941 leaves little on this subject to the imagination:

> At present most escorts are equipped with one weapon of approximate precision – the ram.[63]

We have observed (p. 287) the unfortunate lot of the slow convoys (a 30% higher chance of being torpedoed). It is clear, says Milner,

> that to some extent the high loss rate in slow convoys was due to the fact that they were largely escorted by the RCN.[64]

It is not necessary to say more. As for experience, one need only remark that the Royal Navy itself had only recently felt the same lack, that the Americans were about to do so, and that while it exists there is only one thing to be done – to 'sweat it out'.

In September the U-boats sank fifty-three ships (202,820 tons); it was a dramatic increase – more than double the totals for the previous month. Fifty-one ships were sunk in the North Atlantic (184,546 tons), and that, too, was more than double the August figures. Thirty-six of the fifty-three victims of the U-boats were accounted for by four convoys: SC 42, sixteen; SC 44, four; SL 87, seven; HG 73, nine. Dönitz's August instruction to make escorts a priority target produced no sensational effects,[65] but such as it did were now becoming apparent. In the SC 44 action, on 19 September, the Canadian corvette *Levis* was sunk by *U 74*, with the loss of half her ship's company, in addition to the sinking of four merchantmen. These Canadian disasters caused raised eyebrows and some tooth-sucking in Royal Navy circles, yet they were well matched by the RN's own experiences. HG 73 and SL 87 met their troubles just as SC 44 was emerging from its own; in each case the losses were very heavy, and made considerable mockery of 'continuous protection' on these routes.

SL 87 left Freetown on 14 September; it was a small convoy, with an escort to match – twelve merchant ships, guarded by an ex-American Coastguard cutter, an old sloop, a corvette and a small Free French vessel. Already weakened and still plagued by fuel shortages, the worst aspect of this group was that it was 'a mixed force, unused to working together'.[66] Four U-boats fell upon the convoy between 22–24 September and sank no fewer than seven of the merchantmen, over 58%, a rate of loss that would be surpassed but was nevertheless catastrophic. HG 73 was only marginally less so. Its twenty-five merchantmen sailed from Gibraltar on 17 September with Rear-Admiral Creighton as Commodore. His own ship, the 3,000-ton *Avoceta*, was carrying, in addition to her cargo, 128 refugees, mostly foreign women and children married to British citizens once living in France and now driven out by German occupation. They were not well disposed towards Britain, which they blamed for the war and their present plight; few could speak English and they were very frightened. Their presence did not make life easier for a commodore already only too well aware of the dangers of this journey, right under the eyes of the Condors at Bordeaux-Mérignac. Against these his best protection would be the Auxiliary Fighter Catapult ship *Springbank* which, in addition to a very powerful AA armament, carried a Fairey Fulmar fighter of No 804 Squadron, Fleet Air Arm.[67] This time the anti-submarine escort was a strong one – a sloop and eight corvettes.

For three days HG 73 was unmolested; the hazards and stresses of convoy operations even at quiet times are illustrated by a signals exchange on the third day out between the Commodore and a lagging ship (the fault turned out to be poor coal):

Either I had to reduce the speed of the whole convoy, slow as it was, or leave her an easy target for the U-boats. When it was clear she was dropping astern steadily I signalled:
　'Increase speed.'
No reply. Then again:
　'You will delay the convoy. Proceed at utmost speed.'
No reply. Finally:
　'What is the matter?'
This extracted an answer:
　'Nothing the matter. But there soon will be if any more bloody silly signals are made.'
The master was harassed enough trying to coax another knot out of his ship so I probably asked for that, but equally it might have been more sensible to have replied to my first signal.[68]

On the fourth day matters became much more serious; during the morning a FW 200 appeared, shadowing the convoy at a distance of under two miles. *Springbank* opened fire with her 4-inch AA guns and the Condor took herself further off; then the Fulmar was catapulted, and a chase began. It was in vain; half an hour later the Fulmar returned for the pilot to say that the FW had been too fast for him, and that he would now try to reach Gibraltar (which he did). Admiral Creighton comments:

> This was sad news for us, a bitter disappointment to the pilot and a poor reflection on what was supposed to be a fighter plane. . . . That was the end of our air protection.

A fuller report by the pilot, Petty Officer Shaw, showed that faulty ammunition had also jammed the Fulmar's guns; it was nevertheless true that the two-seater Fulmars were not by any means in the front rank of fighter aircraft, and in fact they were in course of being replaced by Sea-Hurricanes.

As well as losing his only aircraft to no avail, the Senior Officer of the Escort also heard from the Admiralty that U-boats were closing the convoy, and on the fifth day the Condors were back in position to home them in:

> Only two things could save us, a thick fog or a really bad gale. There was no sign of either.

Yet several more days were to pass before the U-boats were ready to make their attack – days of mounting terror among the refugees, who now spent most of their time huddled in the saloon, being too frightened to stay in their cabins alone. The Admiralty reported that U-boats were now only some 12 miles off, just over the horizon, stalking the convoy by its smoke and the Condor reports. There was nothing the escort could do about them; it had no fast ship to chase them and the radar sets chose this moment to develop faults. HG 73 was thus, in effect, blind when the U-boats came at it shortly before midnight on 25 September. The boats in question were *U 124*, claiming one victim, and *U 203*, claiming three – among them the *Avoceta*. Admiral Creighton survived, but out of a crew of forty and the 128 refugee passengers only twenty-eight were saved. On 26 September *U 124* sank three more

384

ships, and on the 27th *U 201* joined in, with two more including *Springbank*. Nine ships out of twenty-five is 36% – once more a disaster number.

One gleam of light, albeit faint, brightened a bad month. We have now noted the existence of the two types of catapult aircraft ships – the Royal Navy's auxiliaries and those that sailed under the Red Duster of the Merchant Marine. Both shared the same obvious fault – the great likelihood that, once projected, the aircraft would be lost even though the pilot was saved. It was, as Admiral Creighton remarked, 'a wasteful business', and furthermore there was the clear fact that these vessels offered only a 'one-off' advantage; without its aircraft, each one of them was just another ship. The only kind of ship that could carry a reserve was an aircraft carrier, and the truth was that the catapult ships were really only stop-gaps until escort-carriers came along. This they began to do in June, when the first of their line, HMS *Audacity*, was commissioned and began her trials. She was a dreadful-looking creature, converted from a captured German banana boat. Her dead-flat flight deck was 368 feet long and 60 feet wide (about half the length of the *Ark Royal*'s) and made her look, at a distance, like some large sinister raft or an upturned flat-iron. She carried six Grumman Martlet fighters, sturdy, reliable and highly manoeuvrable. In the land of their birth, America, these were known as Wildcats, a name later adopted also by the Fleet Air Arm; but in 1941, when 802 Squadron went aboard *Audacity*, the name was Martlet and it was a hall-mark of good service.[69] With a displacement of only 5,537 tons, *Audacity* had no space for a hangar; the aircraft were parked out on the flight deck in all weathers, and all maintenance had to be done there. It was evident that flying off and returning might be no joke, but the aircrew did enjoy one advantage: in peacetime the banana boats had carried a small number of passengers in very comfortable accommodation, and this would now be theirs.

On 13 September *Audacity* set out on her first voyage, with the outward-bound Gibraltar convoy OG 74, twenty-two merchantmen escorted also by a sloop and five corvettes. Her captain, Commander D. W. Mackendrick, adopted a routine of taking the carrier out of the convoy at night and rejoining in the morning, with two Martlets on patrol right through daylight hours. On the evening of 15 September they surprised a U-boat on the surface and forced it to dive – a useful result straight away. For three days OG 74's passage was uneventful, but on the 19th it suffered its first loss. This was not by enemy action, but by collison, and Macintyre remarks that it was

> one of the few occasions during the war when the natural hazards of steaming unhandy merchantmen in close formation led to such fatal results.[70]

The loss of the elderly collier *City of Waterford* thus offers an opportunity of paying a tribute to the seamanship which made such occurrences so rare during nearly six years of war.

For 802 Squadron in *Audacity* the real action was now about to begin. On 20 September a Martlet sighted a U-boat some 12 miles from the convoy; its report brought the sloop *Deptford* and a corvette to the scene to carry out an ASDIC search which led to a depth charge attack but no further result. The convoy, meanwhile, was zig-zagging in 40-degree turns which failed to throw off the U-boats; *U 124* made the first strike at about 2230, and another shortly afterwards. At this point OG 74 became somewhat broken up, with four ships separated from the main body. Among these was the rescue ship, *Walmer Castle*, with survivors of *City of Waterford* already aboard, and more being collected from *U 124*'s two victims. *Walmer Castle* was still alone when a FW 200 swept down upon her to make four attacks, the last of which was fatal, setting her on fire and causing many casualties. Somehow, though gutted, she remained afloat, and had to be sunk by gunfire some hours later. While she was still burning, *Audacity* took vengeance: two Martlets following a radar pointer found a Condor at 600 feet and attacked at once. The FW dived to sea level, but to no avail; a well-placed deflection shot broke off her weak tail unit and she dived into the sea – the first victory for an escort carrier against its prime designated enemy. At just over 27% OG 74's rate of loss was still a very serious matter, but the contrast with SL87 and HG73 is indicative of the deterrent effect of the carrier's aircraft, duly noted by U-boat Command. We shall hear more of the brief career of HMS *Audacity*.

* * * * *

The last quarter of 1941 marked a clear defeat for Admiral Dönitz. In those three months only seventy-one ships were sunk by submarines, a monthly average of 114,272 tons; in the North Atlantic the totals were fifty-two ships and 85,163 tons. This was not by any conceivable means what his mounting fleet was intended for.[71] And it was, as we have seen, a result not attributable to British action – certainly not to the first tentative performances of one escort carrier and a few catapult aircraft. It was largely a consequence of Hitler's absurd redeployment of the U-boats in a secondary and unsuitable theatre of war – the Mediterranean – with the consequence that in November their total sinkings were no more than 62,190 tons, while in that month and the next, in the great Atlantic shipping lanes only twenty-two ships went down. And now worse things still were befalling.

In August the world learned, with mixed emotions, of the historic meeting between Churchill and President Roosevelt at Placentia Bay, Newfoundland; the headlines were naturally captured by the formulation of the Atlantic Charter (which would later be the basis of the Charter of the United Nations). In particular, this identified 'the final destruction of the Nazi tyranny' as an aim of American policy. The Atlantic Charter painted political objectives with a broad brush – 'the right of all peoples to choose the form of government under which they will live' (quietly ignoring the fact that the German people had emphatically chosen 'the Nazi tyranny'), 'improved labour standards, economic advancement, and social security', 'freedom from fear and want', etc, etc. These would provide the talking points of the next fifty years and more. Of more immediate practical effect were certain precise agreements about the war against the U-boats in the Atlantic, which were not made public for obvious reasons. Churchill told the Cabinet when he returned:

clearly [the President] was skating on pretty thin ice in his relations with Congress, which, however, he did not regard as truly representative of the country. If he were to put the issue of peace or war to Congress, they would debate it for three months. The President had said that *he would wage war but not declare it*, and that he would become more and more provocative. If the Germans did not like it, they could attack American forces. . . . Everything was to be done to force 'an incident'.[72]

Events now succeeded each other somewhat swiftly. In his Labour Day broadcast on 1 September Roosevelt reaffirmed the American intention to 'do everything in our power to crush Hitler and his Nazi forces' and he warned again that if the Royal Navy and its allies should be defeated, the American Navy cannot now, or in the future, maintain the freedom of the seas against all the rest of the world.[73]

Roosevelt was preparing the ground for the implications of a naval agreement arrived at in the Placentia Bay meeting. The gist of this, fully in the spirit of the ABC-1 Agreement in January, was that the USN should now progressively relieve the Royal Navy of responsibility for the Western Atlantic, including convoy escort. Churchill told the Australian Prime Minister, Mr Robert Menzies:

> United States Navy is effectively taking over America-Iceland stretch of the Atlantic, thus giving us relief equal to over fifty destroyers and corvettes, soon to be available for home waters and Atlantic.[74]

This promise was, of course, potentially of very great value – all the more so in that at this very time Britian had undertaken the commitment of sending supplies to the Soviet Union by convoy on the Arctic route.[75] However, it must be said that Churchill's form of words suggests an immediacy which is misleading. It was, in fact, not until 25 August that the RCN itself assumed responsibility for the slow (SC) convoys; the USN's responsibility was to be for fast (HX) convoys only, and would not begin for some weeks to come. Yet

> In the interim, NEF passed from the operational control of C-in-C, Western Approaches, to that of Rear-Admiral A. L. Bristol, USN, Commander, Support Force, an officer whose nation was still neutral.[76]

Rear-Admiral Arthur LeR. Bristol Jr. was the senior officer at Argentia, with further far-flung duties entailing a heavy administrative workload. Fortunately, he possessed 'an immense capacity for work, a talent for administration, and a generous, genial disposition.[77] With this, it would appear, went a good deal of tact, which was just as well in a situation riddled with potential umbrage. The British and American leaders had taken this decision affecting the operational deployment of Canada's young Navy without any consultation with the Canadian Government or Naval Service Headquarters. This reflected an enduring American fault:

> Canada's fully independent status within a redefined empire was a

388

murky concept, poorly understood by Americans. Further, in appearance and practice the RCN was virtually indistinguishable from the RN. Not surprisingly, then, Canada and the RCN came under 'British Empire and Colonies' in the USN's filing manual. Americans preferred to deal with Commonwealth naval issues through the British Admiralty delegation in Washington. The presence of a Canadian naval attaché who professed to represent the views of an independent service only confused the situation.[78]

All this was no doubt true; a curious institution, full of anomalies, like the 'British Commonwealth' was hard to understand for people whose own national history dated from rebellion against the British Empire. (They may be forgiven; to have as neighbours an independent Canada and a colonial Newfoundland was a conundrum indeed.) Yet the main blame for misunderstanding can only lie with Britain. Self-satisfaction with the introduction of self-government for the Dominions (always for public and educational purposes contrasted with the satrapies of other imperial powers) was never matched by any worthwhile degree of sensitive interpretation of that same self-rule. Australians and New Zealanders had already experienced this in the Middle East; the RCAF, with its main weight actually in Britain, could add interesting footnotes, and the Canadian Army would soon be doing likewise. There was no party differentiation in this; flag-waving British Tories were as unperceptive of overseas attitudes and needs as anti-imperial Socialists. No doubt this helps to explain why the British in due course found it so easy to slough off their ties to those who, in two world wars, persisted in speaking of Britain as 'home' and acting accordingly.

In 1941 the Canadians did not make any difficult scene out of what could only be regarded as a slight, whether intentional or not, but as Marc Milner says,

the ill will generated by the failure to include Canada in decisions directly affecting her war effort could easily have been avoided.

As usual, it was the men on the spot who made an awkward situation work; Commodore Murray and Rear-Admiral Bristol were too sensible and businesslike to allow such a matter to spoil their cordial and efficient relations. In any case, the war itself had a way of brushing lesser matters aside. On 4 September the news came that a U-boat had attacked the American destroyer *Greer* south-west of Iceland and within the recently redefined US Security Zone. The U-boat (it was *U 652*) fired two torpedoes at the *Greer*, which succeeded in avoiding both of them. But Roosevelt now had the 'incident' he desired, and without 'forcing'. On 11 September he returned to the microphone – that ambivalent instrument of public persuasion of which he, Churchill and Hitler were all such masters – to denounce the attack on *Greer* as 'piracy legally and morally'. He now felt able to speak more frankly than ever before; the Nazis, he told the American people, were seeking to acquire 'absolute control and domination' of the seas; their aim was world mastery, and for this

> Hitler knows that he must get control of the seas. He must first destroy the bridge of ships which we are building across the Atlantic and over which we shall continue to roll the implements of war to help destroy him, to destroy all his works in the end. He must wipe out our patrol on sea and in the air if he is to do it. He must silence the British Navy.
>
> I think it must be explained over and over again to people who like to think of the United States Navy as an invincible protection that this can be true only if the British Navy survives. And that, my friends, is simple arithmetic.

A great practitioner of the homely metaphor, he tossed one in now with (apparently) no recognition that Dr Goebbels, if he had thought of it, could have used it with equal entitlement:

> when you see a rattlesnake poised to strike, you do not wait until he has struck before you crush him.[79]
>
> These Nazi submarines and raiders are the rattlesnakes of the Atlantic. They are a menace to the free pathways of the high seas. They are a challenge to our sovereignty . . .
>
> From now on, if German or Italian vessels of war enter the waters, the protection of which is necessary for American defense, they do so at their peril.

Some fifty years on, this utterance strikes false notes which are themselves revealing of that eternally fascinating subject, democracy at war. It is easy enough, in the security of time's arm-chair, to castigate the hypocrisies and deceptions which were the inevitable consequence of Roosevelt's privately admitted policy of waging war without declaring it. His main intention – to throw the full weight of the United States against aggressive Nazism – was entirely sound. Hitler and the Nazi system, down the years, have lost none of the evil aura already surrounding them in 1941, when the full extent of their iniquities was not yet known (some, indeed, not yet perpetrated, and the fullness of them never known to Roosevelt). But while he was consciously drawing America towards war in that year, he remained the prisoner of a public opinion which no American politician could defy without rueing the day. And American public opinion – like that of every western nation – was itself a prisoner of the pre-war falsehoods of peace through disarmament, isolation and neutrality. What we see, in other words, is the familiar sequence of one set of lies begetting another.

President Roosevelt was definitely waging war; as the American Official History says,

> From the date of the *Greer* incident, 4 September, 1941, the United States was engaged in a *de facto* naval war with Germany on the Atlantic ocean.[80]

To many people in Britain, including a number in positions of knowledge and responsibility, *de facto* war did not appear to amount to much, but the hard facts of the *Greer* episode show how far Roosevelt was prepared to go, in the full recognition that it was still 'the wish of 70% of Americans to keep out of war'.[81] These facts were actually made public on 1 October, following a Senate questionnaire to Admiral Stark, the Chief of Naval Operations:

> They showed that the *Greer* had been alerted by a British plane about a submarine that lay ten miles ahead. It went to general quarters and caught up with the submerged U-boat, making contact with it through its sound gear. For several hours the *Greer* and the British plane trailed the submarine. The British pilot finally broke off and, ascertaining that the *Greer* did not intend to attack, dumped his depth charges in the vicinity of the U-boat and returned to base. It was only after this that the U-boat turned and launched its first torpedo. The *Greer* then counter-attacked with depth charges to which the U-boat responded with a second torpedo. The *Greer* then lost contact and later resumed its course for Iceland.[82]

How American opinion might, in other circumstances, have adjusted itself to what soon emerged as 'The Case of the Reluctant Rattlesnake' we shall never know; by 1 October, in addition to the *Greer* incident, it had some other interesting matters to digest, and soon there would be more, of even greater import. As part of the acceptance of convoy escort duties, there was yet another eastward move of MOMP, to 22°W, which would now be the hand-over point for USN-escorted HX convoys to their Royal Navy home-run escort groups. The first convoy to have American escort was HX 150, fifty merchant ships which sailed out of Halifax with a local Canadian escort on 16 September, and was met the next day by four USN destroyers under Captain Morton L. Deyo. The convoy Commodore, Rear-Admiral E. Manners RN (Rtd.), greeted the Americans with the signal:

> I am very delighted to have all of you to guard this convoy for the next few days.

This courteous welcome was a sample of several exchanges in the course of the voyage, expressed, says the US history, 'in a courtly language which was exceedingly pleasant to read when decoded, but provoked somewhat uncourtly language among our inexperienced communications personnel'.[83] The passage of HX 150 was undisturbed by U-boats, but well stocked with marine hazards which were the standard fare of convoys throughout the war: breakdowns of ancient vessels, leading to straggling, a fire which caused one ship to be abandoned, a gale and heavy sea which made the rescue of her crew a test of seamanship (successfully passed) and a storm which delayed the British escort. By the end of the month, to those who observed events from the 'sharp end', American participation in the Battle of the Atlantic was a visible reality,

> and what that reality meant to the Admiralty, to the Flag Officers, to the captains and crews of the ships and aircraft who had for so long fought this vital and unending struggle alone, may not be easily realized by posterity.[84]

The 'price of admiralty', says Kipling,[85] is one that is paid in blood; this was a perception which the United States Navy would soon be in a position to endorse very fully. In the Atlantic the blood began to flow in mid-October. After days of battling with a gale which had caused no fewer than eleven ships to straggle (including the commodore's) and had dispersed about half of a strong Canadian escort in search of them, SC 48 had the ill fortune to encounter a U-boat pack which set upon it with enthusiasm. On 15 October they made two attacks which accounted for three merchantmen; the convoy's calls for help produced a powerful reinforcement – the RN destroyer *Broadwater* with the corvette *Lobelia* and in addition a division of five US destroyers which included USS *Kearney*. A confused night action on the 16th/17th gave the U-boats a harvest of six more merchant vessels, and it was against the glare of one of these, burning furiously, that *Kearney*, at about 0200, took a torpedo from *U 568* on her starboard side, causing many casualties including eleven killed. Her engines, however, continued to function, and she was able to reach Iceland under her own steam. SC 48 was another badly mauled convoy: 18% of her original merchant strength sunk, while the Royal Navy lost *Broadwater* and the corvette *Gladiolus* (the latter with all hands).[86] It would be wrong to suggest that the torpedoing of USS *Kearney* started or fundamentally changed developments in United States policy, but clearly this event was so very much in line with what President Roosevelt needed in order to push through his own policy that one questions whether, after all, it was not the battered convoy that won the victory.

Precisely a fortnight after the *Kearney* incident the inevitable occurred. As day was breaking on 31 October convoy HX 156, escorted by a group of five United States destroyers, had reached longitude 27°05′W. USS *Reuben James*, 2,000 yards out on the port beam of the convoy centre, moved to investigate a strong D/F bearing when a torpedo from *U 562* hit her on the port side. A nightmare scene ensued, probably due to an explosion in the forward magazine which blew off the whole fore portion of the ship, right back to the fourth funnel. The aft portion remained afloat for about five minutes, but as it went down some depth charges also exploded, killing a number of men in the water. Out of a ship's company of some 160, only forty-five survived, no officers among them. The blood price was being paid. It is small wonder that within a matter of days Congress had voted to revise the Neutrality Act on lines requested by Roosevelt – albeit by majorities that the President could only regard as disappointing. But ironically it was precisely now, when the U-boats were doing his work for him, that Roosevelt himself lost momentum – for a very good reason. On

16 October the relatively moderate Japanese government of Prince Konoye fell from power and was replaced by the aggressively military party. Here was a threat more real and immediate than any posed by the U-boats, and Roosevelt found himself in a situation which was already all too familiar to Churchill:

I simply have not got enough Navy to go round.[87]

While the MAGIC decrypts of the American counterpart to the GC & CS tracked the new departures of Japanese policy, there ensued what it is fair to call a breathless pause.

* * * * *

The battle of SC 48 was the last major action of 1941 on the main North Atlantic convoy routes; it was not quite the last action in that quarter. Despite the drain to the Mediterranean, Dönitz optimistically tried to maintain packs in the Newfoundland–Iceland area; in late October he had twenty boats there, formed in three groups, *Mordbrenner, Reisswolf* and *Schlagetod*. Thanks to Bletchley Park and the Submarine Tracking Room, they were able to achieve very little. On 28 October, after some harassment by Canadian and American aircraft off the north-east coast of Newfoundland, the *Mordbrenner* Group was ordered south. This movement threatened two convoys: the westbound American-escorted ON 26, on its way to Halifax, and SC 52, nearing Cape Race. On 31 October *U 374* sank a merchantman in the latitude of St John's, and on that same afternoon SC 52 was re-routed due north up the Newfoundland coast, passing inside the route of ON 26. The next day SC 52 was sighted by *U 374*, and Dönitz at once formed an *ad hoc* group (*Raubritter*) from *Mordbrenner* and *Reisswolf* to attack the slow convoy. The redeployment of the U-boats was considerably hampered at this stage by one of the periodic outbreaks of poor radio reception which were not uncommon in these waters. Weather conditions in general were deteriorating and neither convoy received any help from shore-based aircraft for some days, although well within range of RCAF and USN airfields. ON 26 was now out of the danger zone, but on 3 November *Raubritter* caught SC 52 as it approached the latitude of the Belle Isle Straits and three U-boats (*U 569, U 202* and *U 203*) sank four merchant ships. While this attack was in progress, the convoy received orders to return to Canada, and accordingly changed course for the mouth of the Straits. This move did not save it from its final losses at the hands of the U-boats and cost it two more ships which ran aground in dense fog. Thus, despite a strong escort of two destroyers and seven corvettes, SC 52 won the distinction of being 'the only transatlantic convoy driven back by U-boats alone during the entire war'.[88] But this was positively the last flicker of significant activity by the U-boats in northern waters in 1941. For the next two months the main enemy here would once again be the steep Atlantick, providing for all comers another 'macabre and desolate winter' marked by 'sleet, snow, rain, ice a foot thick on the forward superstructures: four hours on watch, two hours chipping ice, sleep and eat in between'.[89] The Canadian destroyer *Restigouche* received so much damage in a gale that she almost foundered; the corvette *Windflower* was rammed by a merchantman and sunk in a thick fog:

All corvette sailors remember their ships as a source of numbing fatigue and indescribable discomfort.

Such action as there was in the North Atlantic took place chiefly in its southern sector, in particular in and around the new U-boat concentration area west of Gibraltar. Two convoy battles claim special attention, with HMS *Audacity* featuring in both of them, and both were U-boat defeats. OG 76 left Liverpool on 31 October with twenty merchantmen and *Audacity* as part of its escort. No. 802 Squadron on this occasion had eight Martlets and ten pilots on the strength, but even on the Gibraltar run weather conditions had become so bad that flying was often impossible. Not only was visibility much reduced by low cloud and rain, but the state of the sea caused the flight deck at times to be pitching 65 feet and rolling 16 degrees, with spray sweeping over. The Fleet Air Arm was not easily deterred, and even in such conditions as these 802 Squadron flew off a patrol; one of the Martlets made a safe return, the other touched down just as the carrier's stern was rising and the aircraft went overboard, but floated just long enough for the pilot to be rescued.

On 8 November *KG 40*, whose reconnaissance was also affected by this weather, nevertheless sent up six Condors to try to find the Sierra Leone convoy SL 91, and guide U-boat Group *Stoerbrecker* to it. Just before midday two of these aircraft appeared on *Audacity*'s radar screen and a Martlet patrol was flown off. One Condor disappeared in cloud without contact, but Lieutenant-Commander Wintour and Sub-Lieutenant

Hutchinson found the second; Wintour attacked first and set the Condor on fire, but coming in too close he took a 7.9 mm shell just below the cockpit as he banked, and was killed instantly. Hutchinson then made five further attacks, expending 1,080 rounds of .5 ammunition before the Condor crashed into the sea. About three hours later Sub-Lieutenant Eric Brown, after a tense, remorseless hunt through the clouds, brought down a second Condor in a head-on attack. A fourth Condor was briefly sighted, but made good its escape. *KG 40*'s effort had failed completely; a loss of one-third of its operational aircraft produced no U-boat contact and no loss in either SL 91 or OG 76, which arrived safely at Gibraltar on the evening of 11 November. But *Audacity* was now a marked enemy of both *KG 40* and U-boat Command.

Her return journey began on 14 December, as part of the escort of HG 76, consisting of thirty-two merchant ships. Its Commodore was Vice-Admiral Sir R. Fitzmaurice, and the Senior Officer of the Escort, making his first voyage in that rôle, was Commander F. J. Walker – a name that would be heard again. His own ship was the sloop *Stork*,[90] a command which brought with it seniority in the 36th Escort Group comprising also a second sloop, *Deptford*, and seven corvettes. In addition, there were three destroyers on attachment, which made this escort unusually strong, but it was another destroyer, the Royal Australian Navy *Nestor*, which scored the first success in the saga of HG 76. A Gibraltar-based Sunderland had sighted a U-boat on the evening of the first day of sailing, and the next morning *Nestor* picked up an ASDIC contact which led to the destruction of *U 127* (Hansmann) at 1100 hours. She was part of a group which Dönitz had assembled to lie in wait for the convoy with orders to treat HMS *Audacity* as a prime target.

From 17 December HG 76 no longer enjoyed air cover from Coastal Command's newly established Gibraltar station,[91] and had to depend on *Audacity*'s patrols. It was soon after 0900 that one of these sighted another U-boat, surfaced some 20 miles from the convoy. The Martlet circled to give a good radar fix for the escort vessels, and a corvette made an ASDIC attack, but no result was perceived. At 1247, however, the destroyer *Stanley* made another sighting of a surfaced U-boat; Walker ordered a Martlet to attack immediately, while *Stork* and the destroyers made their best speed to the spot (in *Stork*'s case, not very great). The Martlet pilot, Sub-Lieutenant Graham Fletcher, gallantly

1. *above left* The first commander of U-boats in war, *Flotillenadmiral* Hermann Bauer.
2. *above right Kapitänleutnant* Walter Forstmann, Donitz's first commanding officer (*U39*).

3. 'There was little privacy and little comfort in a U-boat.'

4. *above left* 'A born leader with few brains': Vice-Admiral Roger Keyes, commanding the Dover Patrol, 1918. **5.** *above right Korvettenkapitän* Max Valentiner (*U38*), 'to whom "killing was a pastime"'.

6. *Korvettenkapitän* von Arnauld de la Perière (second from left) (*U35*), 'the ace of aces of the U-boat commanders in World War One'.

7. 'Bruges was the true base of the Flanders flotillas.' These submarine pens were prototypes of those built in the Bay of Biscay bases in World War II. Their concrete roofs were 6 feet thick, adequate against the aerial bombs at the time.

8. British drifters at sea; the fishing fleet supplied the greater part of the 'Auxiliary Patrol' which numbered over 3,000 vessels by November, 1918.

9. 'Advances in hydrophone technology during World War One were impressive'. Hydrophone drill aboard a drifter.

10. 'Stick Bomb Throwers "on the lines of trench mortar".' This 3.5 inch weapon threw a 200lb bomb to a range of 1,200 yards or a 350lb bomb to a range of 650 yards.

11. The Felixstowe F2A, which owed much to
Wing-Commander J. C. Porte RNAS, 'a designer and innovator of genius'.

12. The Curtiss H12 Large America flying boat as modified by
Wing-Commander J. V. Porte which came into operation in 1917.

13. The Short Type 184 seaplane which 'was to the First World War
what the Swordfish became in the Second'. (see p. 37)

(see p. 37)

14. *below left* Admiral William S. Sims, USN, whose 'foresight was both remarkable and timely'.
15. *below right* 'Body and soul, I was a submariner.' *Leutnant* Karl Dönitz,
watch officer in *U35*, 1917

16. U-boats in Kiel, October, 1918; 'revolution was already at work'. By 1 November the U-boats were in effect deprived of a base.

17. 'The "most formidable thing" the war had seen declined into a memory.' 122 U-boats arrived at Harwich to make their surrender by 1 December, 1918. The majority of their commanders 'were still undefeated and defiant'.

18. Hitler with *Admiral* Erich Raeder, German Naval C-in-C
and champion of a large German surface fleet.

19. 'Masterpieces of shipbuilding and weapons technology': a Type VIIC U-boat (*U258*),
the type chiefly used in World War II, approaching the bomb-proof pens at La Pallice in 1942.

20. 'Favoured by the High Command': a Type IXC 'U-cruiser' leaving Kiel.
With a surface displacement of 1,120 tons for increased bunkerage,
these were long-range boats (maximum endurance, 16,300 miles at 10 knots).
Admiral Dönitz considered them slow to dive and difficult to manoeuvre.

21. 'Grey Wolves': the 'tonnage king', *Fregattenkapitän* Otto Kretschmer, who was credited
with sinking 238,000 tons of shipping in eighteen months.
He wears the Knight's Cross with Oakleaves and Swords in this photograph which well
illustrates the relaxed off-duty relations between officers and men in the German Forces.

22. *above left* 'Grey Wolves': 'Of all the U-boat commanders, Prien was Dönitz's favourite.' The admiral with *Kapitänleutnant* Günther Prien, 'the Bull of Scapa Flow', wearing the Knight's Cross of the Iron Cross Order which he won for sinking HMS *Royal Oak* in October, 1939.

23. *above right* 'Grey Wolves': *Kapitänleutnant* Joachim Schepke, commander of *U100*, the third of the famous trio whose careers ended abruptly in March, 1941. Here he is appealing for volunteers from the Hitler Youth in the Berlin *Sportpalast*.

24. 'Memories of "unrestricted" submarine warfare flooded back': *Kapitänleutnant* Julius Lemp (left, in white cap), whose *U30* sank the liner *Athenia* in September, 1939. In 1941 Lemp is believed to have committed suicide on realising that the *Enigma* machine in his *U110* had been captured by a British boarding party.

25. 'A rare style of leadership': Admiral Sir Percy Noble (right), C-in-C Western
Approaches from February, 1941 to November, 1942. His
'potent weapons' of command were charm and personality.

26. 'More a way of life than anything else': HMS *Columbine*, one of the long line of
Flower Class corvettes which bore the brunt of escort duty in the
Royal Navy and Royal Canadian Navy. Inelegant and horribly uncomfortable,
they were also admirably seaworthy craft in the worst Atlantic weather.

27. 'The steep Atlantick stream': to hurricanes with Force 11 winds and Sea States 9, the Atlantic winter added frozen spray with ice forming on the decks and upper works, freezing up the depth-charge throwers and all working machinery, sometimes even capsizing the ship.

28. 'The primary armament of an escort was the depth charge': the charges could be rolled down chutes or projected to a distance by throwers. Depth-charge handling was always heavy work; on slithery, tilting decks in horizontal sleet, it was also highly dangerous.

29. 'In Newfyjohn . . . you are either in the harbour or out of it':
the harbour of St John's, Newfoundland, showing the heads where in winter
'the weather demons waiting outside made special purgatories'.

30. 'The Atlantic convoy was the heartbeat of the war': the conference,
organized by the Naval Control Service, was the first stage in establishing
convoy discipline for passages which were often uneventful, but if not . . .

31. 'A dreary and unforgiving haven': the destroyer *Icarus* (foreground) with naval and
merchant vessels (distance) in Hvalfjordhur anchorage, Iceland, where wind, snow and a
poor bottom could make conditions indescribable.

32. 'That packet of assorted miseries which we call a Ship': HMS *Broadway*, one of the 'Four-stackers', the ex-American Town Class destroyers acquired at the end of 1940, much hated but 'a saving transfusion of strength'.

33. 'Backbone of the RCN': HMCS *Restigouche*, a C Class destroyer purchased by Canada in 1938, part of the first expansion of the Royal Canadian Navy. The foremast carries a 286 radar antenna and the aftermast the HF/DF obtained by her captain 'by undefined means' while undergoing repair at the end of 1941.

34. 'It was rare to hear a bad word for frigates': the River Class frigates began to come into commission – slowly – in November, 1941. HMS *Spey* (December) was the second of the line; she is seen here escorting a well-spread convoy.

35. 'A dreadful looking creature': the first of the escort carriers, HMS *Audacity*, whose career lasted only from September to December, 1941, but in that time she amply demonstrated the value of such vessels.

dived on the U-boat which greeted him with all its AA armament. Just as Fletcher opened fire, a cannon shell hit the Martlet, bringing it down into the sea with its pilot's body. The surface escorts, however, had meanwhile opened fire at long range and very soon the U-boat's crew was seen to be abandoning ship. She sank at 1330 and survivors identified her as *U131* (Baumann); she was the shadowing boat for the pack, and was in fact the same boat that had been sighted at 0900. One member of her crew claimed that she had spent the whole of the previous night inside the convoy, homing in the rest of the pack.

December 18 brought yet another success. At 0906 *Stanley* again made a U-boat contact and a combined ASDIC attack ensued; fifty depth charges were dropped, and after half an hour of this treatment *U434* (Heyda) appeared on the surface just long enough for her crew to abandon her before she turned over and went down for the last time. Later that morning *Audacity*'s radar picked up two Condors; a Martlet patrol was immediately scrambled and intercepted the enemy aircraft, but by cruel luck the guns of both the Martlets jammed and the Condors escaped. The afternoon of the 18th was uneventful, but shortly after dusk a corvette reported another U-boat on the surface, indicating more attacks to come.

December 19 saw the U-boats striking back. Shortly after 0400 *Stanley* again sighted a U-boat, but just as her report ended she was hit by a torpedo and blew up in a huge explosion; there were only twenty-five survivors. *Stork*, close behind, swung round the stern of the blazing wreckage of *Stanley*, and at once obtained an ASDIC contact. She dropped a pattern of depth charges, ran on for half a mile, then turned for a second attack. Suddenly a U-boat surfaced two hundred yards ahead, and an eleven-minute chase took place, described in Walker's report:

As I went in to ram he ran away from me and turned to port. I followed and I was surprised to find later that I had turned three complete circles, the U-boat turning continuously to port just inside *Stork*'s turning-circle at only two or three knots slower than me. I kept her illuminated with snowflakes and fired at him with the four-inch guns until they could not be sufficiently depressed. After this the guns' crews were reduced to fist shaking and roaring curses at an enemy who several times seemed to be a matter of feet away rather than yards.

A burst of 0.5 machine gun fire was let off when these could bear, but the prettiest shooting was made by my First Lieutenant, Lieut. G. T. S. Gray, with a stripped Lewis gun from over the top of the bridge screen. He quickly reduced the conning tower to a mortuary. No men were seen to leave the U-boat although they must have jumped some time judging from the position in which we found the survivors later.

The U-boat was *U574* (Gentelbach); *Stork* rammed her at last just before the conning tower; the full length of the sloop scraped over her, and as the U-boat emerged at the other end she met a pattern of shallow-set depth charges which blew her to pieces. In this process *Stork*'s bows were crushed in and bent sideways, and her ASDIC dome so damaged that she was now powerless to attack submarines.

The U-boats were undeterred; an hour later *Audacity* was narrowly missed inside the convoy and a merchantman was hit. Then the Condors joined in the action, one of them very promptly shot down by Sub-Lieutenant Brown in another head-on attack, and its companion damaged. When more FWs returned in the afternoon, Sub-Lieutenant Sleigh pressed home a similar head-on attack with such determination that the Martlet actually hit the Condor, and came back with its wireless aerial wrapped round the tail wheel. That night was quiet, but 0730 saw another Condor back to shadow the convoy and a Martlet chased it for 45 miles before having to return because fuel was running low. In the afternoon another Martlet found two U-boats ahead of the convoy, which made an emergency turn; the U-boats dived and remained submerged while the Martlets were present. When they returned to *Audacity* it was so dark that they had to be signalled in with hand torches. The night of 20 December was also quiet.

December 21 came in with a succession of U-boat sightings. Walker reported:

> The net of U-boats round us seemed at this stage to be growing uncomfortably close in spite of *Audacity*'s heroic efforts to keep them at arm's length.

802 Squadron was by now becoming very tired, and it was only with difficulty that three Martlets could be kept serviceable. Take-offs and landings were made exceedingly dangerous by a heavy swell. When the last patrol was home, Commander McKendrick took *Audacity* out of

the convoy, as his custom was, but no escorts could be spared to go with her during the hours when she was defenceless. Walker was not happy to see *Audacity* pull away, but McKendrick was senior to him in the Navy List and this was his first Escort Group command.

Trouble began at 2033, when a merchantman at the rear of the convoy was torpedoed, causing immediate bursts of snowflake which lit up the whole area for friend and foe alike. They enabled *Oberleutnant* Bigalk, in *U751*, to observe the quite unmistakable silhouette of *Audacity* within convenient range. At 2037 the carrier took her first torpedo and immediately began to settle by the stern. While she lay helpless in the water, *U751* struck her twice more, this time causing a huge explosion (probably of aviation petrol) which blew off the whole of her fore portion. This reversed her sinking motion, and after a time she became almost vertical in the water with her propeller in the air and the sea around her full of heads. At 2210 she went down; among the many who died with her was Commander McKendrick, exhausted but almost saved when a big sea carried away his lifeline. Just over two and a half hours later, at 0040 on 22 December, EG 36 took vengeance; after a two-hour ASDIC pursuit, *Stork*'s sister sloop *Deptford* succeeded in destroying *U567*. This was a particularly grievous loss to Dönitz, because her captain, *Kapitänleutnant* Engelbert Endrass, was, as he says, 'one of the best and most experienced of our U-boat commanders'.[92] *U567* was also the fifth U-boat to be lost in this disastrous battle, of which Dönitz wrote in his War Diary on 23 December:

> The chances of losses are greater than the prospects of success. . . . Therefore the decision has been made to break off operations.[93]

This sequence of fiascos was a fitting end to a year marked by gross misdirection of the U-boat arm. The tailing-off of sinkings by U-boats in the last quarter of the year was watched by the Admiralty with, as may be supposed, great satisfaction, but at the same time with considerable puzzlement. The OIC report of 20 December remarked that 'the primary object seems, at least temporarily, to be no longer the destruction of merchant shipping'.[94] Dönitz would have echoed this interpretation – with the deepest disgust; and he would have cited as its reason the great command error of withdrawing the main body of the U-boat fleet from the North Atlantic. This was, of course, correct, as far as it went. There was, however, another reason which Dönitz was unaware of, but which we now know very well: the GC and CS penetration of *HYDRA*, enabling the Submarine Tracking Room to re-route the convoys so successfully from June onwards. Jürgen Rohwer has this to say:

> During the second half year of 1941, by a very cautious estimate the Submarine Tracking Room of the Admiralty, using 'Ultra' decrypts, rerouted the convoys so cleverly around the German 'Wolf-packs' that about 300 ships were saved by avoiding battles. They seem to me more decisive to the outcome of the Battle (of the Atlantic) than the U-boats sunk in the convoy battles of 1943 or in the Bay offensives.[95]

In other words, this was the true moment of decision in the Atlantic: not the early summer of 1943, when the U-boats met their 'Trafalgar' in spectacular fashion, but now, in this failure to sink ships in the second half of 1941. Rohwer's analysis echoes Marder's dictum on 1917 to which we have already referred more than once, that 'sinking submarines is a bonus, not a necessity', and what matters in submarine warfare is the safe arrival of cargoes. The same thought inspired Professor Hinsley when he wrote:

> it was only by the narrowest of margins that . . . the U-boat campaign failed to be decisive in 1941, and it is safe to assume that by the end of the year, before other developments had begun to increase the supply of shipping, the campaign would indeed have reached crippling proportions if its returns had gone on expanding at anything like the rate obtained during the first half of the year.

The command error comes back into the picture when we try to measure the extent to which the virtual doubling of the U-boat fleet might have offset the value of re-routing if all the boats had been available in the right place, the North Atlantic. Twice as many boats must surely have improved the chances of finding convoys, despite the decrypts – though it is exceedingly unlikely that they would have sunk an extra 300 ships, or anything like that number. So we have to conclude that, although Hitler's strategic blunder undoubtedly played its part, Professor Rohwer's final verdict stands:

There were many factors which influenced the outcome of the decisive

Battle of the Atlantic we experienced. I would put 'Ultra' at the top of this list of factors.[97]

Looking back upon it now, we can see that, when he lost his race with time in 1941, Dönitz really lost the battle. For whatever reasons one may cite, 1941 was the decisive year in the Atlantic – as it was in the war as a whole.

* * * * *

In the same paper that we have quoted above, Professor Rohwer makes the challenging statement:

Of course, there was never a doubt about the final outcome of the Battle of the Atlantic and the whole Second World War.

He seems here to be separating the actual Atlantic battle as it was fought between 1940–43 and a hypothetical 'final outcome' determined quite differently – determined, in fact, by the inevitable defeat of Germany. That outcome, it must be said, did not look at all inevitable as December, 1941, came in. Admittedly, close observers could see (with some astonishment) that Germany was suffering her second real defeat in the war. The first was the RAF's defensive victory in the Battle of Britain in 1940, leading to the cancellation of Operation SEELÖWE; now, in December of the next year, it was clear that she had failed again – failed to bring off the capture of Moscow which was intended to redeem the larger failure of BARBAROSSA itself. The Russians lost no time in seizing this failure as the cue for their own first successful counter-offensive which forced the Germans to make their first retreat. This event was greeted in the anti-Axis world with semi-incredulous delight, but only afterwards was its full significance seen, when it stood revealed as an omen underlining the great folly of the whole BARBAROSSA enterprise – Hitler's first step towards catastrophe. The misdirection of the U-boats, spoiling his most effective weapon, was a second; the third was not his doing – in fact he was as surprised as anyone by it.

On 7 December the Japanese fleet attacked the American base at Pearl Harbor. America was at war; and just to make sure that the full meaning of this was clear, on 11 December both Germany and Italy declared war on the United States, a gesture very promptly reciprocated by Congress. From this moment, indeed, as Professor Rohwer says, 'there was never a doubt about the final outcome of . . . the whole Second World War.' Not everyone could see into the future with that degree of clarity at the time, but when this immense news came through there were many in Britain who sensed with deep relief what Churchill could put into words:

> We had won the war. . . . Hitler's fate was sealed. Mussolini's fate was sealed. As for the Japanese, they would be ground to powder. All the rest was merely the proper application of overwhelming force.'[98]

How simple, how easy it sounds. But for the next three and a half years all the ingenuity, all the fortitude, all the courage of the free world would be exercised in the pursuit of this clear goal: 'the proper application of overwhelming force.'

5

A Roll of Drums

'On September 19th, 1941, Dönitz had suggested starting the war against the United States with a "*Paukenschlag*", or "a roll of drums".'
Jürgen Rohwer, Decisive Battles of World War II *p. 269*.

AMERICA'S SUDDEN ENTRY into the war called for an immediate conference to formulate war plans, an agreed grand strategy. No time was lost; the meeting was to be in Washington, and Churchill, thrusting aside urgent business in London, embarked in the battleship *Duke of York* with his staff and advisers[1] on 12 December. They arrived in Washington after dark on 22 December and plunged at once into the work of the conference with President Roosevelt; it was code-named ARCADIA and it would last just over three weeks. The fortnight which intervened between Pearl Harbor and the ARCADIA Conference was filled with frightening events, calculated to dash away all traces of long-term euphoria. Indeed, if matters went on in such a fashion, the very survival of the alliance was in doubt; and in fact, as things turned out, the year that was about to dawn would prove to be the hardest and worst of all the years of war.

Before the smoke had cleared over the wreck and ruin of Pearl Harbor the Japanese declared their hands across the North Pacific and South-East Asia. On 7 and 8 December their forces were landing in Thailand and Malaya; their bombers were active from Midway Island to Singapore; their attack on Hong Kong was begun. The next day they landed in the Philippines. On the 10th they sank the British battleship *Prince of Wales* and the battlecruiser *Repulse*; they captured the American advanced base at Guam Island and began their advance in Malaya. A week later they landed in Borneo. On Christmas Eve they took the American base at Wake Island and on Christmas Day Hong Kong surrendered. To such accompaniments the ARCADIA Conference continued: Manila taken on 1 January, a new attack developing against the Dutch East Indies on 10 January. But amidst it all, the most serious threat to Allied power was at sea.

Nineteen American warships were sunk or damaged in the Pearl Harbor attack; the hard core of the Pacific Fleet was virtually eliminated. Out of eight battleships present, two were irretrievably sunk, three damaged to an extent that would keep them out of action for one to two years, and the remaining three also damaged to varying extents.[2] To the loss of *Prince of Wales* and *Repulse* the Royal Navy had to add heavy losses in the Mediterranean. We have noted the sinking of HMS *Ark Royal* in the early part of November, followed by HMS *Barham* on the 23rd of that month. December added substantially to what Churchill called 'the series of major naval disasters': the flagship of the Mediterranean Fleet, HMS *Queen Elizabeth*, and her sister ship *Valiant*[3] were badly damaged in Alexandria harbour by what have been variously called 'human torpedoes' or 'chariots' – three Italian two-man craft carried to the locality by a submarine, the crews bringing limpet mines which they attached to the hulls of the battleships. These blew a hole some 40 feet square in the bottom of *Queen Elizabeth* and an even larger one in *Valiant*; both ships now rested on the floor of the harbour, their wounds concealed under the water, but both would be out of action for many months. All their attackers were captured and kept in close confinement for the sake of secrecy, but, as Admiral Cunningham says,

> One cannot but admire the cold-blooded bravery and enterprise of these Italians.[4]

And this was still not the full tally of December loss: it included also two cruisers sunk and another damaged, and a destroyer sunk. For the time being American naval power in the Pacific and British naval power in the Mediterranean had been, in Churchill's words, 'swept away'.[5]

It was against this bleak background that the ARCADIA Conference conducted its business. There is general agreement that its outstanding practical achievement was the creation of the body known as the Combined Chiefs of Staff – the American and British Joint Chiefs sitting together – the most effective instrument of democratic war direction ever yet seen. With it went the Supreme Commander principle, the appointment of a Supreme Allied Commander over all the forces, irrespective of nationality or Service, in each theatre of war. It is not difficult to write these words; overcoming national and inter-Service rivalries and differences of tradition, outlook and procedure was something else. In every theatre where it operated, the Supreme Commander principle, guided by the Combined Chiefs of Staff, worked so well that it is hard indeed to think of the Allies proceeding without it. We need to remind ourselves that one theatre never had a Supreme Commander: the Atlantic. There is no way of measuring a non-event, but, as we contemplate what the next eighteen months had in store, we may consider this a costly omission.

In the matter of grand strategy, ARCADIA settled one question whose fundamental significance it is difficult to exaggerate. Flung neck and crop into war by a surprise Japanese attack producing terrible disaster in mid-Pacific, how would America now frame her policy? At the secret Anglo-American staff talks in January (ABC–1) it had been agreed that 'should the United States be compelled to resort to war' the primary strategic objective of the two countries would be:

> The early defeat of Germany, the predominant member of the Axis, the principal military effort of the United States being exerted in the Atlantic and European area, the decisive theater. Operations in other theaters were to be conducted in such a manner as to facilitate the main effort.[6]

This was quite specific, but obviously weakened by the fact that the agreements arrived at in these exploratory and distinctly off-the-record discussions

> were never intended to be binding on the two nations, or to have any political or official character.

The immediate question now, in December, was how the ABC–1 accord would stand up to what Japan had done to outraged American feeling and thinking.

The question was no sooner asked than answered, in two simple but remarkable words: 'Germany first'. America would stifle her outrage; she would forego (for the time being) her natural desire to strike back as rapidly and as hard as possible at those who had struck her. Instead of instinct, the 'gut-reaction', this nation of over 130 million people of widely-differing origins, normally held together chiefly by emotional ties, would follow the course dictated not by emotion but by intellect, would adhere to the argument that

> the defeat of Germany meant the inevitable defeat of Japan, whereas the converse was not true.[7]

'Germany first' was indeed remarkable; down the centuries, however events may have been dressed up, it has not generally speaking been intellect that has ruled the human race.

To the vast relief of the British delegation, America reaffirmed the 'Germany first' strategy without demur, indeed, without discussion. And this was unquestionably fundamental to the whole future course of the war, on all fronts. The precise meaning of the strategy, interpreted into plans – plans relating to even tentative dates, areas and strengths – was not stated at ARCADIA. For this there were good reasons; the first was the stream of bad news pouring almost hourly out of the Pacific area on to the desks of the American Chiefs of Staff. The effect of these was inevitably some dilution of the pure doctrine of 'Germany first':

> It was politically impossible simply to write off the whole of this vast area without making some effort to hold it. ... It was clear to the Americans as to the British that some hard immediate decisions might have to take precedence at the Washington conference over long-term strategic plans.[8]

Secondly, there was the loss of sea power. In the paper which he laid before the conference, Churchill referred to 'the command of the sea, without which nothing is possible',[9] but Allied command of the sea at the turn of 1941/42 was seriously eroded. And thirdly, hand in hand with that sombre fact, was the shipping shortage created by the enormous demands of war and the performance of the U-boats. When any immediate project of any note was considered, the staffs came up against the same constant obstacle:

it appeared that shortage of shipping imposed an absolute ban.[10]

Nevertheless, in the minds of both British and Americans, for definite future reference, there was a clear intention which Churchill plainly expressed in the paper referred to above:

> We should . . . face now the problems not only of driving Japan back to her homelands and regaining undisputed mastery in the Pacific, but also of liberating conquered Europe by the landing during the summer of 1943 of United States and British armies on their [sic] shores.

Categorically he laid it down that

> The war can only be ended through the defeat in Europe of the German armies, or through internal convulsions in Germany produced by the unfavourable course of the war, economic privations, and the Allied bombing offensive.

Since this chimed exactly with American thinking, especially that of the Secretary of War, Mr Stimson, and the Army Chief of Staff, General George C. Marshall, there was no dispute. Perhaps that was a pity, because there was certainly disagreement— not with the intention, but on matters of significant detail of which the most potentially diversive was the date: 1943. Virtually the whole of the great Anglo-American debate of the next two years (whose echoes continue to roll) is to do with timing. At this early stage there were powerful voices in America (Marshall's for one) urging that the Allies should not wait for 1943, but make their onset in 1942; in the prevailing mood, it was fortunate that no one suggested a possibility of having to wait until 1944, for that might have led not merely to widespread apoplexy but also to a fatal revision of the fundamental agreement. That is another subject; what matters here is that, whatever the date of action might finally prove to be, the intention to attack the Germans in Europe, not 'planned' but accepted at ARCADIA, now became the lynch-pin of Anglo-American strategy. More than that, it was the foundation-stone of the Alliance itself. As I have said elsewhere:

> the whole thrust of the Anglo-American war effort from this time onwards would be towards a landing in north-west Europe, and a major

407

campaign by the joint armies, directed at the *Reich* as broadly agreed by the [ARCADIA] conference. Henceforth, whatever contributed to this end would promote the prime intention; whatever impeded it would be, to a greater or lesser extent, harmful.[11]

And I added:

Victory in the Battle of the Atlantic was an essential precondition of a major operation in North-west Europe.

* * * * *

The U-boats, in other words, were back in the centre of the stage.

When Dönitz made his proposal to greet America's entry into the war with 'a roll of drums', he had in mind the immediate despatch of twelve U-boats to the American east coast, of which six would be Type IXCs, capable of operating anywhere from the Gulf of St Lawrence to the Caribbean for two or three weeks at a time. Those waters, he noted, 'had hitherto remained untouched by war'; in them the U-boats could expect to find a great host of merchantmen, sailing independently towards the Canadian ports where they could join convoys heading for Britain. In accordance with what he always believed to be the unchanging principle of U-boat warfare, he pronounced the primary aim of his Service: 'to sink as much shipping as possible in the most economical manner'. In the 'virgin waters' of the American coast his captains could expect to enjoy another 'Happy Time' similar to their feast in British home waters in 1940–41. But, as he pointed out to the Naval High Command, speed was of the essence:

Sooner or later, of course, these favourable conditions would gradually disappear. . . . Ships would cease to sail independently, and the convoy system would be introduced. It was, therefore, of prime importance 'to take full advantage of the favourable situation as quickly as possible and with all available forces, before the anticipated changes occurred'.[12]

Hitler has sometimes been likened to Napoleon, and, indeed, some of their resemblances are profound: both came to grief in Russia; both entered a dream-world of mythical numbers, non-existent armies; both failed totally to grasp the matter of the sea and naval warfare. We have seen how Hitler disastrously gave his blessing to the diversion of U-boats into the Mediterranean; the glittering opportunities now presented in the western hemisphere did not cause him to change his mind – indeed, very shortly he would be afflicted with a new fixation, calling for a further diversion of U-boats: Norway.[13] To what extent Raeder really agreed with Hitler's 'intuitions' is unclear; that he absolutely failed to dislodge them is certain. Dönitz's request for release of twelve boats to drum down the American shipping lanes was refused. His request for Type IXCs was also turned down. That left him with only six boats available for Atlantic operations, of which only five were actually ready for sea. It was a pathetic situation.

It is extraordinary, and constitutes a perspective of the U-boat war that remains hard to grasp, that even now, after almost $2\frac{1}{2}$ years of war, Dönitz was suffering from his perennial malady – a 'dearth of U-boats'. On 1 January, 1942, he had more operational boats on his strength than ever before: ninety-one, with a further 158 undergoing training and trials. The figure ninety-one looks impressive, but breaks down immediately on inspection: twenty-three in the Mediterranean, with three more on their way there; six on the Gibraltar station; four already on the Norwegian coast, with four more shortly to follow. Already the ninety-one is reduced to fifty-one and of these

> 60 per cent were in dockyard hands undergoing repairs prolonged by shortage of labour.[14]

That left no more than twenty-two boats at sea, half of them on passage to or from their operational areas; and so it came about that after all this time

> there were never more than ten or twelve boats actively and simultaneously engaged in our most important task, the war on shipping, or something like a mere 12 per cent of our total U-boat strength.

Such was the result of 'intuition' linked to an amateurish system within an absolute dictatorship.

The U-boats had, of course, been to America before (see pp. 133–4), but even fewer of them, and of an earlier pattern which justifies the US Official Historian's observation that

> Admiral Tirpitz's coastal campaign of 1918 was a very faint taste of the foul dose that Admiral Doenitz administered in 1942.[15]

Nevertheless, the 1918 attack had been a shock, and the extent to which it had been forgotten and its lessons ignored is as surprising as it proved to be disastrous. The new U-boat campaign began on 12 January; by the end of the month twenty-three ships had been sunk off the American seaboard (142,320 tons). The second 'Happy Time' had begun and Dönitz records with satisfaction:

> The attack was a complete success. The U-boats found that conditions there were almost exactly those of normal peace-time. The coast was not blacked-out, and the towns were a blaze of bright lights. The lights, both in lighthouses and on buoys, shone forth, though perhaps a little less brightly than usual. Shipping followed the normal peace-time procedure and carried the normal lights.[16]

The US Official History comments:

> One of the most reprehensible failures on our part was the neglect of the local communities to dim their waterfront lights, *or of military authorities to require them to do so*, until three months after the submarine offensive started. When this obvious defense measure was first proposed, squawks went up all the way from Atlantic City to southern Florida that the 'tourist season would be ruined'. Miami and its luxurious suburbs threw up six miles of neon-light glow, against which the southbound shipping that hugged the reefs to avoid the Gulf Stream was silhouetted. Ships were sunk and seamen drowned in order that the citizenry might enjoy business and pleasure as usual.[17]

The unpreparedness for war of a democratic civilian population, three thousand miles from any warlike scene, reared on Isolationism and having enjoyed over three-quarters of a century of peace at home, is an understandable, if in such respects distasteful, phenomenon. The equal unpreparedness of those charged with the defence of the nation, with the recollection of 1918 and the vivid example of Britain since 1939 before their eyes, is something less understandable and less forgivable. For what now transpired was that the US Navy, for all the talk of 'Security Zones', and all the readiness to join in the Battle of the Atlantic, was simply not designed to protect America's own shipping. At the root of the matter lay a simple fact: the sheer lack of anti-submarine vessels and anti-submarine aircraft; and at the root of that lay the far less simple fact of a two-ocean war, with a second enemy of a totally different kind, who posed no submarine threat to trade but challenged American sea-power with capital ships, and against whom it was not American anti-submarine craft but American submarines that promised to be an effective weapon. Like the British Admiralty until 1939 (see p. 179), the Navy Department had neglected the small craft in large numbers which World War I had shown to be essential for dealing with submarine attack, believing that they could be improvised and quickly mass-produced in the smaller yards at short notice. How short is 'short'? Even with the start of the fifty-six 'whalers' in the 1939 Estimates, the Royal Navy still did not have enough escort vessels now, in 1942. Until this moment, in President Roosevelt's words, the US Navy 'couldn't see any vessel under a thousand tons'; the consequence was that, barring the invaluable Coastguard cutters, it entirely lacked an anti-submarine flotilla – and naturally it lacked also the equipment that goes with it. The US Official Historian comments in words and style unusual for official histories:

> This writer cannot avoid the conclusion that the United States Navy was woefully unprepared, materially and mentally, for the U-boat blitz on the Atlantic Coast that began in January, 1942. He further believes that, apart from the want of air power which was due to pre-war agreements with the Army, this unpreparedness was largely the Navy's own fault. . . . In the end the Navy met the challenge, applied its energy and intelligence, came through magnificently and won; but this does not alter the fact that it had no plans ready for a reasonable protection to shipping when the submarines struck, and was unable to improvise them for several months.[18]

The U-boats enjoyed themselves. Their technique was to lie submerged, sometimes at considerable depths, all day, and surface at night in the midst of a constant stream of ships which presented perfect targets against the coastal glare. While the original five boats were still present on the American coast, three Type IXs, at last released by the Naval High Command, came out to relieve them and so maintain a continuous presence. Shortly more Type VIIs would be on their way. All concerned were surprised and pleased at the performance of the VIICs:

> their radius of action was found in practice to be considerably greater than our theoretical calculations and previous experience had led us to assume.[19]

This was partly due to fuel-saving procedures adopted by their Chief Engineers on the outward passage, and partly to the fact that as they did not have to chase convoys they were able to avoid the heavy fuel consumption of high speeds. But there was another reason, which Dönitz describes, and which indicates the continuing high level of morale of the U-boat men:

> In their eagerness to operate in American waters the crews sought every means to help themselves. They filled some of the drinking- and washing-water tanks with fuel. Of their own free will they sacrificed many of the amenities of their living quarters in order to make room for the larger quantities of stores, spare parts and other expendable articles which an increase in the radius of action demanded. The German submarines even in normal circumstances were very much less comfortable to live in than the submarines of other nations because they had been built on the principle that every ton of their displacement must be used solely in fighting power, that is, for weapons, speed, radius of action. Now, however, the crews voluntarily gave up such 'comforts' as they had, and crammed their boats as full as it was possible to cram them. For weeks on end the bunks were stacked with cases of foodstuffs. Often there was hardly anywhere a man could sit, either in the forward or the after compartments; indeed, it was only possible to move about the boat along narrow gangways between the stacked cases.

It was, then, with a force mainly composed of Type VIICs and only a small admixture of Type IXs in their proper rôle[20] that Dönitz pressed his attack in what Jürgen Rohwer called 'the most successful period of the U-boat war against Allied supplies'.[21] The total sinkings in January (US seaboard and North Atlantic) were forty-eight ships (276,795 tons); in February thirty-one ships (199,695 tons) were sunk off the American coast, a further thirty-three (107,919 tons) in the Caribbean/Antilles area, and the full total for all the northern hemisphere areas was seventy-three ships (429,891 tons). Then came March, the first of the year's three dreadful months, when in all theatres 273 ships went down, totalling 834,164 tons, and taking with them all Allied hopes of speedy initiatives. Even the mobilization of American shipbuilding capacity planned at ARCADIA[22] would be hard put to it to offset such losses as these; the Atlantic areas accounted for ninety-five of the ships (534,064 tons), by far the worst experience yet, and of these forty-eight ships (274,295 tons) were lost in the coastal waters.

Well might Churchill speak of 'the terrible massacre of shipping along the American coast'.[23] The final emphasis of this bad time is contained in the losses of the U-boats themselves: eleven boats all told in three months, of which three were lost in the Mediterranean and two in Arctic waters, leaving only six accounted for in the Atlantic, none at all on the American seaboard.

As Dr Morison said, it is not possible to detach the US Navy from a large part of the blame for this state of affairs. What is in particular depressing is that as well as failing to make any effective preparation for anti-submarine warfare in its own manner, the US Navy displayed a rooted aversion to learning from the hard experience of the Royal Navy, or even from the wisdom of its own Admiral W. S. Sims in 1917 (see pp. 92–3). The senior American commanders, acknowledging the lack of small craft, instead of striving with might and main to remedy the evil in 1941, used it as an argument against convoy just as alarmists in the Admiralty had done twenty-five years earlier (see pp. 51–3). So the fatal doctrine was propounded that 'a convoy without adequate protection is worse than none',[24] and such vessels as were available, including destroyers from the Atlantic Fleet, were wasted in the vain hunts and 'tram-line' patrols that had exerted their fatal lure in the Royal Navy for too long.

When Admiral Harold Stark arrived in London to command the US Naval forces in the European theatre in March, the Admiralty prepared for him a paper summarizing its anti-submarine experience during the preceding thirty months. The four headings of this paper were:

1. The comparative failure of hunting forces.
2. The great value of aircraft in convoy protection.
3. The supreme importance of adequate training and practices.
4. The value of efficient radar.[25]

It must have been with some rueful reminiscent head-shaking that it addressed itself to the first heading, frankly admitting that

this is one of the hardest of all the lessons of the war to swallow. To go to sea to hunt down and destroy the enemy makes a strong appeal to every naval officer. It gives a sense . . . of the offensive that is lacking in the more humdrum business of convoy protection.[26] But in this U-boat war ... the limitations of hunting forces have made themselves very clear.

Captain Roskill expresses the hope that the last statement 'will prove the final epitaph of the U-boat hunting group'. The sad truth in 1942, however, was that the US Navy was prepared to try 'every conceivable measure – except convoy and escort'.

As far back as July, 1941, Admiral Stark had ordered a major reorganization of American coastal defences: the establishment of 'Sea Frontiers'. This was carried out on 6 February, 1942. A 'Sea Frontier' was not a linear concept; it expressed an area, a zone of particular responsibility, running out from a defined section of the coastline for a distance of roughly 200 miles. The northernmost, which contained the Argentia base, was known as the Canadian Coastal Zone; then came the Eastern Sea Frontier, extending from Nova Scotia to Jacksonville in Florida, and containing great ports like Boston, New York (the greatest in the world, with fifty clearances, inward and outward, every day), Chesapeke Bay, leading to the Navy's Norfolk base and to Washington and Baltimore, further south Wilmington, Charleston and Savannah – America's maritime citadel in the east; the Gulf Sea Frontier, whose headquarters were at Key West, took in the whole coast of Florida, most of the Bahamas, part of Cuba, the entire Gulf of Mexico and the Yucatan Channel; contiguous with this area as far as the Caymans, then running across to Cape Gallinas in Columbia, was the Caribbean Sea Frontier, containing the Antilles, Trinidad and the Dutch islands of Curaçao and Aruba with their oil refineries; the Gulf and Caribbean Frontiers, enclosed by oil-rich countries, were the homes of great tanker fleets in constant motion, vital supply areas of the Allied war; finally there was the Panama Sea Frontier, which straddled the Isthmus, facing both ways in America's two-ocean war. Admiral King estimated the total length of the sea lanes within these Frontiers at 7,000 miles,[27] which may be taken as the measure of the task facing the US Navy in the matter of establishing coastal convoys and finding escorts for them.

The day came, as it had to the Admiralty in 1917, when it was no longer possible to resist the pressures of necessity and historical example. The first step towards a comprehensive system of coastal convoys was taken by the US Navy on 1 April; it was unkindly known as the 'Bucket Brigades', and it consisted of a movement of ships from

BRITISH & AMERICAN NAVAL COMMANDS
ZONES OF STRATEGIC & OPERATIONAL CONTROL
ATLANTIC 1942

——————— Command & Frontier boundaries
– – – – – Boundary of British/American strategic zone
· · · · · · · Change of Operational Control (Chop) Lines

Miami H.Qs.

July 1942

Trondheim
Bergen
Scapa Flow

CANADIAN COASTAL ZONE

November 1942

St John's
Sydney

HOME STATION

Brest
St Nazaire
La Pallice

Halifax

New York   EASTERN SEA FRONTIER
Washington

Jacksonville   · BERMUDA

AZORES
Gibraltar   MEDITERRANEAN

NORTH ATLANTIC STATION

MADEIRA
Casablanca
Alexandria

GULF SEA FTR.
Miami
Bahamas

CANARY Is.

CARIBBEAN
San Juan
SEA FTR.

PANAMA
Colon   Aruba   TRINIDAD

SEA FRONTIER

November 1942

July 1942

C. VERDE Is.   Dakar

Freetown   Lagos
Aden

WEST AFRICA STATION

Pernambuco

ASCENSION   *March 1942*

Zanzibar

ST HELENA

Rio de Janeiro

TRINIDADE Is.

Lourenço Marques

Durban
Cape Town   EAST INDIES STN.

SOUTH ATLANTIC STATION

Montevideo

March 1942

FALKLAND Is.

80°   60°   40°   20°   0°   20°   40°

one Naval District to another up and down the long coastline under a series of local escorts. This, says Dr Morison,

> was the best defensive measure that could be put into effect given the paucity of escort ships and planes. Ships steamed during daylight hours as close to the shore as safety permitted, and at night took shelter in a protected anchorage. This system was practicable because the Atlantic Coast north of [Cape] Hatteras is divided into approximately 120-mile stretches between good harbors, which is about the maximum run that a slow merchant ship can make during daylight. South of Cape Henry, where there were no adequate harbors of refuge, the Eastern Sea Frontier established net-protected anchorages about every 120 miles[28]

Continuing losses rammed home the evident fact that 'Bucket Brigades' were no final answer to the U-boats, and even as they began to operate the US Navy was examining more effective measures. Whatever plan might be devised, the execution of it would depend on the availability of ships and aircraft. It is a matter of familiar history how the vast productive power of the United States grappled with both these matters.[29] This hard time in early 1942, before the great cornucopia spilled out its fruits, is not so well known; the Royal Navy's entry into the anti-submarine war was, by comparison, affluent. Of purpose-built vessels, the United States had only a dozen or so ancient PE-boats, built in 1918 by Ford's, of which the Official History says:

> Square-built, slow, weak, lively and wet, the PEs were almost completely useless.[30]

There were four or five wooden World War I Submarine Chasers, which were rather better, and five modern (post-1937) versions of the same type. Orders for sixty new Patrol Craft and Submarine Chasers had been placed, but were not due for completion until later in the year; the Royal Navy, on the other hand, had 300 escort vessels on order in United States yards – an irony which cannot have gone unremarked. As in Britain, from 1915–18, the first remedy was the mobilization of a very large auxiliary fleet – fishing boats, yachts, schooners, motorboats and any suitable craft that could be found around the coast. They were known as the Coastal Picket Patrol:

Civilian in its origin and always informal, the C.P.P. was affectionately known to its personnel as the 'Hooligan Navy'; the official Coast Guard title, 'Corsair Fleet', was little used.[31]

Laced with destroyers and Coast Guard cutters, this was the Escort Fleet. But America did not spend time in idle lamentation. In early April an escort-building programme of 'sixty vessels in sixty days' was proclaimed – and sixty-seven were actually built by 4 May, whereupon a second similar programme immediately followed. In the same period 201 minesweepers, which could be temporarily drafted to escort work, were also completed. Britain contributed a loan of ten corvettes and twenty-two anti-submarine trawlers – and a good deal of sound advice based on experience. Thus the 'Donald Duck Navy' came into existence, lacking only trained crews and officers. To cater for them the Subchaser Training School was set up at Miami in March and by 1944 10,396 officers and 37,574 enlisted men had been trained there for the US Navy alone. As the products of all these activities began to bear fruit, it was possible in May to strengthen the 'Bucket Brigades' with coastal convoys between New York and Key West, and ocean convoys between Guantanamo (Cuba) and Halifax. This marked an important step towards the 'Interlocking System' introduced at the end of August, which solved America's western hemisphere anti-submarine defence problem for the rest of the war (see p. 483).

Even worse, if possible, than the shortage of escort vessels was the shortage of aircraft. The United States had no organization comparable to Coastal Command, which was a lack severely felt. It meant, among other things, that when war came America was still the prisoner of the crude demarcation laid down in the Army Appropriations Act of 1920, by the terms of which the Navy controlled all sea-based aircraft (seaplanes, flying boats and carrier-borne) and all land-based aircraft were controlled by the Army. Thus, the two types so much coveted by the RAF, Consolidated's Catalinas and Liberators, both operated by Coastal Command, fell under different authorities when they were at home: Catalinas (PBY-5s) were USN, Liberators (B-24s) were USAAF. It is a sad fact that for most of the war against Germany and Japan there was also a running battle between the United States Navy and Army over many issues. In early 1942 it did not help to have inter-Service rivalry at work, but far more serious was the weakness of both air arms. When the U-boats arrived, and Pacific needs had been met,

417

the US Navy was left with precisely four PBY squadrons, a squadron of the more modern Martin Mariner (PBM) flying boats and a squadron of Lockheed Hudsons (PBO-1, designated A-29 by the Army) with assorted odds and ends of different vintages. The Army did its best to help in what was clearly recognized as a national emergency, and even placed all its units operating over the sea in the Eastern Sea Frontier under the operational command of Vice-Admiral Adolphus Andrews. However, by the end of March the total number of aircraft available in the Eastern Sea Frontier was no more than eighty-three USN aeroplanes and four airships, and eighty-four USAAF aircraft, divided between eighteen airfields distributed between Bangor in Maine and Jacksonville in Florida. By the end of July these numbers had grown to 178 aeroplanes and seven airships of the USN and 141 aircraft of the USAAF operating from twenty-six airfields. If the Royal Navy and the RAF grumbled – as they certainly did – at the difficulty of extracting VLR aircraft from the Americans, reflection upon these figures and their relationship to the 7,000 miles of sea lanes requiring patrol and protection goes a long way to explain the disappointment.

There were few consolations for an arduous existence, full of sudden alarms and long frustrations. Three months passed before the US Navy could claim a U-boat kill to set against the continuing toll of merchant shipping along the coast. It was, in fact, the Hudson squadron operating from Argentia, VP-82, which achieved this success, sinking *U656* on 1 March; fourteen days later another Hudson of the same squadron sank *U503*.[32] What with fog, ice, snow and the proximity of Canadian and USAAF airfields, as well as the US Navy's aircraft, Newfoundland waters were not well regarded by U-boats as hunting-grounds. Further south, on the American East Coast, the first U-boat kill, which was also the first kill by a US Navy surface craft, came after only another fourteen days: *U85* sunk by the old destroyer *Roper* (Lieut.-Commander H. W. Howe) after a determined chase some distance south of Norfolk. On 9 May the Coastguard cutter *Icarus* caught *U352* in shoal water near Cape Lookout; it was the U-boat's maiden and final cruise. Badly damaged by the cutter's depth charges, she surfaced to allow the crew to escape and then her captain scuttled her. Two more U-boats were despatched by US naval forces in June: *U157* off Cuba by the Coastguard cutter *Thetis* on 13 June, after a chase lasting three days and involving a very large number of aircraft and ships (leaving shipping unprotected during that time), and *U158* on 30 June some 130 miles southwest of Bermuda, following a high-frequency D/F fix by the Bermuda station, Hartland Point station in north Devon, Kingston in Jamaica and Georgetown, South Carolina. This enabled a patrolling Mariner of Squadron VP-74 in Bermuda to surprise the U-boat, some of whose crew were sunbathing on deck. Two well-placed depth charges, a near miss and one which actually hit the submarine and exploded alongside as it dived, finished the job.

There were two more kills in July, one in the Caribbean, one off the East Coast, making, says the US Official Historian,

> Eight kills in six and a half months – about as many new U-boats as were being produced every ten days. And in the meantime, in the areas where these submarines operated, over 360 merchant ships totaling about 2,250,000 gross tons had been sunk. An appalling rate of exchange for the Allies; one highly encouraging for the Axis.[33]

This is unarguable – yet one must note that the eight kills in the western Atlantic area (to say nothing of others in transit) have to be deducted from a force that, between February and the end of April, never numbered more than eight operational boats at any given time. Dönitz, however, had no doubt about the profitability of this zone of operations; the only question was where, within it, to achieve the maximum effect at minimum cost. In the Eastern Sea Frontier, hitherto the favourite U-boat target,[34] there was a perceptible change in April; the waterfront lights and neon sky signs of the resorts were put out on 18 April, at Admiral Andrews's orders, depriving the U-boats of their most helpless 'sitting ducks'. The 'Bucket Brigades', plus the slowly but steadily increasing numbers of the 'Donald Duck Navy' and its 'Hooligan' auxiliaries, produced the familiar effect of an 'empty ocean' between the movements of the groups of merchantmen, and gave them a little but appreciable extra protection when the U-boats did find them. Taking all these factors into account, says Dönitz:

> I therefore decided to use all U-boats becoming available for operations from the end of April onwards in a simultaneous attack on a number of other, and widely separated, focal points for shipping off the American coast. I would thus compel the enemy to split up and scatter his defensive forces, withdrawing considerable portions from the concentration he had just established off the east coast in order to protect other important areas which would now be equally threatened.[35]

He was enabled to look further afield by a long-awaited accession of strength: the advent of the Type XIV U-tanker. The first of the line entered service towards the end of April; she was *U 459* (*Korvettenkapitän* von Wilamowitz-Möllendorf),

> a clumsy great boat of nearly 1,700 tons. As she was not intended for offensive purposes, she carried no torpedo armament and mounted only AA guns for her own protection. She was immediately dubbed 'the milch-cow' by the submariners.

The Type XIVs carried 700 tons of fuel, which meant that one of them could keep twelve Type VIIs supplied for an extra four weeks, or five Type IXs for an extra eight weeks at sea. *U 459* carried out her first refuelling on 22 April, servicing *U 108* 500 miles north-east of Bermuda. Within a fortnight, according to Dönitz, she had refuelled twelve Type VIIs and two Type IXs before having to return with empty tanks. There was, he says, always a danger which 'filled me with misgivings' when a number of U-boats gathered at the same point to carry out an operation which was bound to keep them on the surface for a certain amount of time during which they would be vulnerable to roving aircraft. Nevertheless, the presence of the 'milch-cows'

> meant that in practice we had advanced our Biscay bases anything from 1,000 to 2,000 miles further westwards.[36]

With the help of *U 459* and her sister ship, *U 460*, as well as a large ocean-going minelayer converted to a supply ship, *U 116*, in May the U-boats renewed their offensive in the Caribbean and the Gulf of Mexico. Their first foray into the Caribbean Sea Frontier in February had been highly successful against defences so slender that when seen sideways they disappeared. On 16 February *U 156* came inshore and attempted to bombard the well-lit oil refineries at Aruba Island; if the gun-crew had managed to curb its enthusiasm sufficiently to give itself time to remove the tampion, it would not have had the distressing experience of exploding a shell in the barrel, in which case *U 156* might well have done extensive damage. When a second boat tried the same thing a little later it found the coastal lights extinguished and the target difficult to identify. But others provided full compensation: six tankers coming out of Lake Maracaibo on 16 February were sunk, and on 18 February *U161* (*Kapitänleutnant* Albrecht Achilles) entered the Gulf of Paria, sank two large ships at anchor off Port of Spain (Trinidad) and departed on the surface showing running lights. On 10 March Achilles went right into Castries Harbour, St Lucia, and torpedoed a passenger vessel and a cargo ship lying brilliantly lit beside the dock. Well might Dr Morison say:

U-boats showed the utmost insolence in the Caribbean, their happiest hunting-ground.[37]

In February the U-boats had sunk twenty-three ships (107,919 tons) in the Caribbean; it was merely a sketch of the damage they performed in May and June. It was now, across the full stretch of the Gulf and Caribbean Sea Frontiers, that the Type IXs came into their own, supported by a group of five Italian boats. In May, in the Gulf, the U-boats sank twenty-six ships (150,277 tons) and in the Caribbean forty-eight (203,265) while the Italians added three more (18,333 tons); a total of seventy-seven ships and 371,875 tons, constituting a major contribution to a bad month world-wide (151 ships, 705,050 tons). June was worse; world-wide it was the worst month of the whole war regarding shipping losses – 173 ships (834,196 tons), of which 144 ships (700,235 tons) were contributed by submarines. Nearly 60% of this vast total was attributable to their work in the Gulf and the Caribbean:

Gulf: eighteen ships, 83,444 tons; Caribbean: fifty-seven ships, 290,994 tons, Italians, six ships, 23,865 tons: total eighty-one ships, 398,303 tons.[38]

Within this invoice of catastrophe lay another set of statistics of special significance:

Between January and June 1942 (the Americans) lost seventy-three tankers in the Atlantic area, twenty-five of them off their own east coast. Eventually, in April, the Americans imposed a standstill on tanker movements along their eastern seaboard, pending the introduction of convoys. . . . Sixty-eight British-controlled tankers were sunk in the Atlantic area in the first six months of 1942, sixteen off the eastern seaboard and seventeen in and around the Caribbean.[39]

Taken in conjunction with the forty-nine tankers which the British Government had been compelled to send to the Indian Ocean in February, these figures spelt an oil crisis which appeared worse and worse the more you looked at it. By the beginning of May (with the U-boat offensive in the Gulf and Caribbean still to come) the British Oil Executive

calculated that their end-year stock level would be nearly two million tons below requirements unless they got tanker reinforcements.

These could only come from America, and the United States Government responded handsomely to the British appeal that was promptly made to it, despite its own mounting losses.

What all this was adding up to (with the Japanese advance still largely unchecked[40]) is clearly seen in an exchange of memoranda between General Marshall and Admiral King[41]. Marshall wrote on 19 June:

The losses by submarines off our Atlantic seaboard and in the Caribbean now threaten our entire war effort. . . . We are all aware of the limited number of escort craft available, but has every conceivable improvised means been brought to bear on this situation? I am fearful that another month or so of this will so cripple our means of transport that we will be unable to bring sufficient men and planes to bear against the enemy in critical theatres to exercise a determining influence on the war.[42]

King replied on 21 June:

I have long been aware, of course, of the implications of the submarine situation as pointed out in your memorandum of 19 June. . . . As you are aware, we had very little in the way of anti-submarine forces in the Atlantic at the outbreak of the war. . . . We had to improvise rapidly and on a large scale. We took over all pleasure craft that could be used and sent them out with makeshift armament and untrained crews. We employed for patrol purposes aircraft that could not carry bombs, and planes flown from school fields by student pilots. We armed our merchant ships as rapidly as possible. We employed fishing boats as volunteer lookouts. The Army helped in the campaign of extemporization by taking on the civil aviation patrol. These measures were worth something, but the heavy losses that occurred up to the middle of May on our east coast give abundant proof, if proof were needed, that they were not an answer to our problem ... the situation is not hopeless. We know that a reasonable degree of security can be obtained by suitable escort and air coverage. The submarines can be stopped only by wiping out the German building yards and bases – a matter which I have been pressing with the British, so far with only moderate success. But if all shipping can be brought under escort and air cover our losses will be reduced to an acceptable figure. I might say in this connection that escort is not just *one* way of handling the submarine menace; it is the *only* way that gives any promise of success. The so-called patrol and hunting operations have time and again proved futile.

As Captain Donald Macintyre remarks, this forceful language displays 'all the fervour of a convert'.[43] And thus, twenty-five years on and some $2\frac{1}{4}$ million tons of lost shipping into the bargain Admiral E. J. King came round to the opinion of Admiral W. S. Sims: convoy *was*, after all, 'the one and only method' of beating U-boats (p. 92). Admiral Dönitz[44] required little convincing:

Both the success achieved and the economy of effort required were very great in [the Caribbean] area. ... From the end of June, however, results in these areas, too, began to deteriorate. Here, too, as had happened off the east coast of the United States at the beginning of May, the convoy system was gradually introduced; and it became obvious that in the near future the main effort in the U-boat war would have to be switched back to wolf-pack attacks on convoys.[45]

Sinkings in the Caribbean did not immediately cease; they dropped markedly in July for organizational reasons (twenty-three ships, 90,229 tons), but mounted again in August (forty-one ships, 219,998 tons). In that month, however, the U-boats disappeared from the Eastern and Gulf Sea Frontiers; the *schwerpunkt* of the U-boat campaign shifted back towards the old hunting-ground, the main convoy routes across the North Atlantic. The American coastal campaign, however, had been an undoubted success for Dönitz and his men. In Churchill's words:

For six or seven months the U-boats ravaged American waters almost uncontrolled, and in fact almost brought us to the disaster of an indefinite prolongation of the war. Had we been forced to suspend, or even

423

seriously to restrict for a time, the movement of shipping in the Atlantic all our joint plans would have been arrested.[46]

* * * * *

By the end of June 989 ships (4,147,406 tons) had been sunk in 1942, 585 of them (3,080,934 tons) by Axis submarines. These appalling figures alone fully justify Churchill's verdict that the U-boat onslaught 'constituted a terrible event in a very bad time'.[47] According to where you sat, however, each separate section of 1942 seemed to provide its own 'terrible event': Singapore fell on 15 February, the worst defeat in British history; by 6 May the Japanese conquest of the Philippines was complete; by 20 May they had conquered Burma and arrived on the frontier of India; on 26 May General Rommel launched the offensive which took him to Tobruk and on into Egypt; in July Hitler began the advance that carried his once more triumphant forces to the Don, the Volga and deep into the Caucasus. Everywhere the Alliance was undergoing a degree of strain which at times seemed scarcely endurable. Only a small number of men were aware that within these dramas a crisis of a quite different kind had developed, containing a threat at least equal to any on the battlefield.

In late November, 1941, Dönitz and his staff, mystified by their continuing lack of success in locating convoys, had conducted another enquiry into security. Once more, taking into account the sundry alternative explanations that offered themselves – the absence of air reconnaissance when operations were pushed out beyond the reach of the Condors, for example, and close-order dispositions of the U-boats themselves which reduced their own reconnaissance capability – the Naval Staff concluded that the *Enigma* had not been broken, nor had there been any security leak from within the Service. Yet Dönitz and his senior officers remained dissatisfied, and on 1 February they took a very drastic step – drastic certainly for the GC & CS at Bletchley Park. They added a fourth rotor wheel to the *Enigma* machines serving the U-boats in the Atlantic.

When one considers the problem already posed by the three-wheel *Enigmas* it is difficult to resist using words like 'catastrophe' and 'disaster'. Patrick Beesly offers us a glimpse of the mathematical monstrosities which were being dealt with by the Turing 'Bombes' (see pp. 323-4):

Five spare rotors were carried, giving a total of eight, from which three could be chosen. This permitted 336 different combinations of rotor sequences. Each rotor had 26 positions giving 17,576 ring positions. In addition there were 1,547 possible plug connections and the operator could set each rotor to 26 different positions, giving 17,576 possibilities. The theoretical possible total of all these permutations was in the region of 160 trillion! [48]

Such were the spacious stratospheres where the Alan Turings operated. By the end of 1941 Bletchley Park had received sixteen '3-wheel Bombes' with which to conduct these operations, of which twelve were in action. Despite a heavy concentration of Bombe-time on German Army *Enigma*, they had, as we have seen, overcome the *HYDRA* cipher by their 'brutal' assault. But a four-wheel *Enigma* requires a 'four-wheel Bombe', and it did not exist (though the need had been foreseen). Thus darkness returned; as Andrew Hodges says:

> In 1941, Hut 8 had given sight to the blind, and if this experience had been traumatic, the taking of sight away was an even more cruel blow. [49]

Yet, as he adds, it was not quite the case that sight had been taken away:

> More precisely, the Admiralty again became, like Nelson, one-eyed.

There were several factors which reduced 'catastrophe' to the level of no more than (in Beesly's words) 'a major setback'. High among these was the fact that the new *Enigma* signals (designated TRITON by the Germans and SHARK by BP) were confined to the use of U-boats in the Atlantic. The *TETIS* cipher, used by U-boats in training in the Baltic, was unchanged, which meant that the activities and location of each new boat could be followed right up to the moment of commissioning and departure to an operational area. Also unchanged was the *HYDRA* cipher for Home Waters, enabling the Submarine Tracking Room to keep a check on U-boat movements in and out of Norwegian waters and the Bay of Biscay. By these means (and with the assistance of the now much more effective D/F chain and Photo-Reconnaissance), we continued to learn when a U-boat left for operations, and when and if it returned ... we knew the exact strength of the U-boat fleet and where each boat was based. We were able to make belated checks on the claims of kills from our own forces where there was no conclusive evidence from wreckage or survivors, although it might of course take some weeks before we could establish that a particular boat was overdue. Our estimates of the total number of boats at sea at any one time therefore remained remarkably accurate.[50]

What was missing was that invaluable, precise information about where a U-boat actually was, where it was going and what it intended to do, which had been the saving of so many convoys from the packs in 1941. Yet, as Jürgen Rohwer points out, in the first half of 1942, when shipping losses were mounting so alarmingly, this lack was not by any means as significant as it then seemed and often still looks:

> Up to the start of American convoy operations the German U-boats had no reason to operate in groups because they could find their targets easily enough by operating singly. Therefore the need to send operational or tactical radio-signals dropped off sharply and even with decrypting Bletchley Park could have done little to prevent the heavy shipping losses.[51]

In this 'very bad time', when troubles never came singly, it so befell that just as Bletchley Park lost its hold upon the U-boat signal traffic, the *xB-Dienst* took an important stride forward. In June, 1941, when American involvement in the Battle of the Atlantic was reaching a substantial level, the Admiralty had brought into use a reserve cipher for all American, Canadian and British forces engaged in convoy operations. It was known as Naval Cipher No 3, and as the year wore on it carried an ever-increasing traffic which attracted the attention of the watchful German cryptanalysts. Unfortunately, for reasons not altogether clear (unwise haste was probably at the head of them) the Admiralty did not protect this cipher with long subtractor tables, as it had successfully done with certain others. In January, 1942, sensing its vulnerability, *xB-Dienst* concentrated its resources against Naval Cipher No 3; by February the Germans had succeeded in reconstructing the book, and from then until December they were reading up to 80% of the traffic. In February, with the 'Happy Time' on the American coast in full swing, this success did not mean much, but some three months later, when Dönitz ordered a return to the main convoy routes, the advantage was palpable:

> 'B-Service' was able again and again to give U-boat Command timely and accurate information regarding the whereabouts of convoys.'[52]

The interlock of factors which governs the conduct of war is well displayed here. This interval, when U-boat Command was once more able to home in on convoys but for tactical reasons did not do so, was almost certainly an element of some importance in masking the fact that *Enigma* was not secure. If the U-boats had returned at once to the attack on convoys, and thanks to their new information had obtained dramatically better results, it seems hardly possible that someone at U-boat HQ would not have put two and two together and concluded that the previous lack of success had been due to the penetration of the *Enigma*. The results of such a realization, across the whole immensely valuable field of Sigint, hardly bear thinking about. Equally interesting is the reflection that, in turn, BP's inability to read the U-boat signals for the rest of 1942 meant that not until 1943 did any firm evidence appear that *B-Dienst* had penetrated the Admiralty's own ciphers. And so the truth of the parable was once more seen:

> For unto every one that hath shall be given, and he shall have abundance; but from him that hath not shall be taken away even that which he hath.[53]

The sense of being 'him that hath not' was very acute at both Western Approaches and Coastal Command HQs. Actual numbers are deceptive; Western Approaches, for example, in January, 1942, controlled twenty-five Escort Groups at its three bases, Liverpool, Greenock and Londonderry. These comprised some seventy destroyers, eighteen sloops, sixty-seven corvettes and ten ex-US Coastguard cutters. By 1941 standards this was a considerable force; measured against 1942 requirements, it was the reverse. For Britain as for America, 'Germany first' was a sound broad principle, but could never be an exact yardstick of practical policy. The Japanese were now at large in the Indian Ocean and the Bay of Bengal, threatening Calcutta, Madras and Colombo, and even, at this apogee of their power, the main supply lines to the Middle East up the east coast of Africa and the Red Sea.

On any given day there would be ninety-four ships at sea between Calcutta and Ceylon alone, open to attack by surface ships or Japanese submarines. In addition, there were the calls of the Arctic convoys carrying supplies to the Soviet Union whose value to the Soviet war effort can only be estimated by the force of the protests whenever there was any delay in delivery. And each week that passed underlined the necessity for the transfer of all available American escort craft to the East Coast convoys. An Anglo-American investigation in March produced this considered statement of the escort situation:

	Required	Available	Shortage
British	725	383	342
American	590	122	468 [54]

The conjunction of all these matters, added to the heavy naval losses sustained at the turn of the year and the unavoidable new Far East commitment, combined, says Roskill,

> to make the early months of 1942 among the most anxious of the whole war. As the First Lord said early in March, 'if we lose the war at sea we lose the war'. [55]

Sir Philip Joubert's position was on a par; between October, 1941, and January, 1942, he had been compelled to send 166 complete aircrews overseas, of whom only twenty-one came from the Training Units, all the rest being drawn from operational squadrons 'with a consequent heavy drop in availability of aircraft'. [56] As well as this drain, Joubert was called on to part with complete squadrons, especially of Catalinas, the long-range aircraft so badly needed in Coastal Command's ever-extending operations. It was, once more, the Far East, where the penury of aircraft of all types was most frightening, that caused these demands. The Admiralty assessed its requirements of aircraft in the Indian Ocean at 570 including the Fleet Air Arm. Including RAF, Royal Indian Air Force and South African Air Force, but excluding the Fleet Air Arm, the actual total available in March was forty-two. In place of the ninety flying boats considered to be needed, there were six.

36. 'Sturdy old warriors': A Consolidated PBY-5 (Catalina) flying boat of Coastal Command
over Gibraltar. The prototype first flew in 1935 but the Catalinas served both the
RAF and the United States Navy loyally throughout the Second World War.

37. 'The familiar "White Crows" of Coastal Command': a Short Sunderland flying boat
wearing the white camouflage paint prescribed by Operational Research. For three years
these and the Catalinas bore the brunt of long-range anti-submarine warfare.

38. 'VLR aircraft which alone could close the Atlantic Gap'; it was, in fact,
only the Consolidated B-24 (Liberator) bomber which rated as a true Very Long Range
aircraft so long desired by Coastal Command and so effective in 1943.

39. 'A familiar category of unfortunates': Air Marshal Sir Philip Joubert de la Ferté (*foreground, left*) was AOC-in-C, Coastal Command from June, 1941, to February, 1943. Like certain others, he saw the bad times, weathered the worst storms, but was not there for the victorious ending

40. 'A formidable opponent for the best cryptological brains':
the *Enigma* cipher machine which the Germans believed to be impenetrable.

41. *above left* 'An astonishing assembly of brain-power': Alan Turing, the Cambridge mathematician who headed Bletchley Park's attack on the naval *Enigma*. **42.** *above right* 'Long, imaginative and productive alliance with the world of science': Professor P. M. S. Blackett, who became Scientific Adviser to Coastal Command in 1941, where he launched the Operational Research Unit, and later to Western Approaches and the Admiralty itself.

43. 'Central to the conduct of the war': Bletchley Park (BP), also known as 'Station X', home of the Government Code and Cipher School, where the *Enigma* signals were decrypted.

44. 'Reinforced concrete sixteen feet thick'; for further protection of the
U-boat pens in the Biscay bases the Germans added a bomb-trap of
spaced concrete beams to detonate the RAF's bombs, with an 'explosion-chamber'
below to contain the blast. This example is at Bordeaux.

45. 'Aircraft came in through storms of *Flak*'; a night sky over Brest during an RAF attack.

46. 'A hard-bitten set of fellows': Commander (later Captain) D. F. F. W. MacIntyre,
whose 5th Escort Group ended the careers of Schepke and Kretschmer in 1941.
MacIntyre subsequently became a naval historian of distinction.

47. 'One of the First Division teams': that was MacIntyre's description of
Lieutenant-Commander (later Vice-Admiral Sir) P. W. Gretton's B7,
whose defence of HX 231 in April, 1943 marked 'the beginning of the end'.

48. 'Responsibilities usually associated with admirals': Lieutenant-Commander G. J. Luther, who was temporarily in command of Escort Group B4 in the ferocious HX 229/SC 122 battle of March, 1943.

49. 'The battle burnt him like a flame': Captain F. J. Walker, CB, DSO and three bars, DSC and two bars, the Royal Navy's outstanding U-boat killer. He is seen here on the bridge of his famous sloop, HMS *Starling*.

50. 'Reputation as . . . "a twenty-minute egg"': Fleet Admiral E. J. King, USN an officer
of great distinction who gave his British colleagues the impression of being obsessed
with the Pacific theatre, and 'disliked wars of mixed nationality'. **51.** *above right*
'A great production triumph': Mr Henry J. Kaiser, whose construction method resulted in
the launching of no fewer than 2,710 of the invaluable 'Liberty Ships'.

52. 'The never-ending battle of technology': this is the Hedgehog, with its 24 65lb bombs
designed to place a pattern 100 yards wide some 230 yards ahead of the ship. The Hedgehog had
long 'teething-troubles' but became an effective part of the anti-submarine armoury.

53. 'First . . . to see North Atlantic service': the escort carrier (CVE) USS *Bogue*.
She and her consorts became the scourge of the U-tankers in 1943.

54. 'At Derby House the centrepiece was . . . an Operations Room':
note the Coastal Command (No. 15 Group) officer at the indicator board and the
Leading Aircraftman (*left*). Western Approaches Command in Liverpool was an
inter-Service headquarters where cooperation was intimate and continuous.

55. 'New energy, a drive which was very soon felt': Admiral Sir Max Horton, who became
C-in-C, Western Approaches in November, 1942, with his Flag-Lieutenant.
A high proportion of the 1,000 officers and ratings at Derby House were members of the WRNS.

56. 'A token group of U-boats came to make their surrender': Admiral Horton and staff with
German officers aboard *U532* (Type IXC) in Londonderry in May, 1945.

57. 'An epoch-making U-boat': the Japanese Naval Attaché in Berlin inspected
a Type XXI U-boat at its moorings in August, 1944.
However, by the end of April 1945 only 12 Type XXIs had completed working-up,
and the first of them only became operational on April 30.

58. 'The unappealing landscape of Square One': the *Schnorchel* breathing-tube in conventional
types, and the advent of the Type XXIIIs in British Home waters in January, 1945,
nullified the techniques of anti-submarine warfare evolved during the preceding five years.
Fortunately the Second World War had only four more months go to.

The effect of these diversions (to use a loaded word that had become common currency), Joubert told the Under-Secretary for Air in February, was that

> the prospect of Coastal Command being able to work at reasonable efficiency appeared to be becoming more and more remote. The promise of centimetric ASV-fitted Liberators had come to nothing, the one Liberator squadron was being allowed to die out[57] and there had been a continuous change of policy in regard to his long-range aircraft.[58]

Proposals to 'compensate' him by loans of Whitleys from Bomber Command (now in process of receiving a new AOC-in-C in the formidable person of Air Chief Marshal Sir Arthur Harris) did not impress Joubert:

> Neither the Sunderland nor the Fortress, still less the Wellington or Whitley, were long-range aircraft by the Atlantic War standards. While fully aware of the importance of a sustained bomber offensive, it appeared to him that, if England was to survive this year, in which we were already losing shipping at a rate considerably in excess of American and British building output, some part of the bomber offensive would have to be sacrificed and a long range type such as the Lancaster diverted to the immediate threat to our Sea Communications.

Any proposal on these lines at any time tended to cause a rush of blood to the head in the Air Ministry and at Bomber Command, and to produce a response which would be more or less of a paraphrase of the minute quoted on pp. 354–5. The conflict of opinion between the Admiralty and the Air Staff at this juncture was acute. Sir Dudley Pound, as the file of disputatious memoranda thickened on his desk, referred to it as 'The Battle of the Air'. In essence, it may be reduced to the simple but basic divergence between the airmen, believing that the whole problem of the war, in whatever theatre, could be solved by bombing Germany into submission, and the sailors facing immediate crises which screamed for the application of air power, and who found it, as Captain Roskill mildly says,

> hard to believe that all these troubles could best be cured by bombing German towns.[59]

The 'man in the middle' of this sometimes definitely abrasive struggle

(Air Chief Marshal Harris was a man of very definite opinions who did not mince his words) was Joubert. As Peyton-Ward says:

> there is no doubt that on occasions during this depressing period in 1942 the AOC-in-C Coastal Command was, metaphorically, kicked by the Admiralty for not asking enough and blamed by the Air Ministry for demanding impossibilities.[60]

On 30 March, in a letter to the Air Ministry, he said outright that his position was becoming impossible. All the response he obtained was a bland homily from the Air Council to the effect

> that occasions on which an AOC-in-C's views were at variance with Air Staff opinion were not abnormal and should not give rise to embarrassment in the case of Coastal Command.

And with that he had to be content, relying on his hard-pressed crews to continue attempting the impossible and quite often achieving it.

As we have seen, Coastal Command's first attempt to carry the offensive to the U-boats – to sever the 'trunk' of their line of communication between bases and Atlantic operational areas – had not been a success in 1941. In the first five months of 1942 operations in the Bay of Biscay were much reduced; 5,041 flying hours failed to sink any U-boat and damaged only two, at a cost of six aircraft. During this time, says Dönitz, the U-boats

> experienced no difficulty in making the passage, either by night or by day when the weather was clear and visibility good.[61]

However, U-boat HQ did note a perplexing increase in the number of surprise daylight attacks. Dönitz found it

> difficult to believe that these had been due to slackness on the part of the lookout, who ought to have spotted the aircraft sooner; the suspicion therefore grew that the British aircraft, which always launched their attacks out of the sun or out of cloud, must have located the U-boat beforehand and have taken up position for the delivery of their attack while still out of sight from the target.

And then something highly disconcerting happened. In the early hours of 4 June for the first time U-boats in the Bay of Biscay were attacked from the air on a dark night. A searchlight had suddenly been flashed on at a range of 1,000 or 2,000 yards and had at once picked up the U-boat. The bombs followed immediately.

In detail this is incorrect; in substance perfectly true. The 'U-boat' was actually the Italian submarine *Luigi Torelli*, detected by the ASVII equipment of a Wellington of No 172 Squadron and illuminated by a 'Leigh Light'. This device was the product of a year of experiment and argument by its inventor, Squadron-Leader H. de V. Leigh, a World War I pilot at Command HQ.[62] The Wellington pilot in fact made two attacks on the *Luigi Torelli*; the first underlined the acute need for radio altimeters which we have already noted and which was now on the point of being met. Coming in at the specified 250 feet registered on his illuminated panel, the pilot (Squadron-Leader J. Greswell) found with disgust that his light beam, when switched on at the requisite 1-mile distance, had overshot the target substantially. The reason was obvious: the aircraft was too high – he had set his altimeter by a *forecast* pressure which placed him 100 feet higher than he should have been. Quickly correcting this fault, he prepared for another run. This time he had no trouble; the ASV worked admirably, the light was in exactly the right spot – but over and above all that, the submarine was shooting up red, green and white fireworks to mark its position. The Italians had concluded that an aircraft shining a bright beam of light in the Bay, but not making any attack with guns or depth charges, must be friendly. The question now arose whether a submarine sending up light signals might not perhaps be friendly to the aircraft – but Greswell remembered that British submarines did not signal with flares; they used candles in the water. The Wellington opened fire as it came in and then straddled the submarine with four 250-pound depth charges. The damage caused by these forced her to find a harbour (and begin a series of hair-raising adventures which she succeeded in surviving until 1946). But she was a fore-runner. Dönitz tells us:

In June three boats on their way to their operational areas were severely damaged in the Bay of Biscay in this manner, rendered incapable of submerging and compelled to return to base.

The implications of this event were not difficult to discern; they

431

were heavily underlined only a month later (5 July) when an American in 172 Squadron, Pilot Officer W. Howell, made the first ASV/Leigh Light kill – a text-book attack which ended the career of *U 502* (Rosentiel), returning from a 'happy time' in the Caribbean. A week later Howell illuminated *U 159* (Witte), also returning from the Caribbean. The U-boat crew attempted to shoot out his light, but failed; the depth-charge attack caused such damage to the U-boat that she was out of action until October. Never afraid to look unpalatable facts in the face, Dönitz perceived in this new style of air offensive a threat

> to our whole method of conducting submarine warfare, which was based on mobility and operations on the surface, and which reached its culmination in the wolf-pack tactics we had evolved. In areas where air cover was strong our most successful method of waging war would no longer be practicable.[63]

He did what he could, well aware of the inadequacy of his available counter-measures. He succeeded in obtaining twenty-four Junkers 88C6s for use as long-range fighters over the Bay. On 24 June he ordered the U-boats to cross the Bay submerged by day and by night (*U 502* and *U 159* had evidently not received this order, or were ignoring it for their own – fatal – reasons). This measure meant a loss of five days in the operational area, but it was better to accept that than to lose U-boats. And he began a policy of arming the boats with ever-heavier AA guns which threatened Coastal Command with increased losses to match its increased power. But he remained very acutely aware of the fact that

> the aircraft had suddenly become a very dangerous opponent.

It is one of the more unpleasing ironies of the war that at this very time Sir Arthur Harris was informing Churchill that Coastal Command was 'merely an obstacle to victory'.[64] The truth was precisely opposite, as the statistics reveal:

Between 1 January and 30 June 1942, only twenty-one U-boats were lost.
Of these, only $6\frac{1}{2}$ were attributable to air action.
Air action was therefore involved in 30.9% of U-boat losses.

British air action was involved in 16.6% of U-boat losses. Coastal Command claimed none.

This dismal picture changed abruptly in July: in that month eleven U-boats were lost (the highest monthly total to date), $5\frac{1}{2}$ being due to air action, two of these attributable to Coastal Command. These figures were not a flash in the pan: the U-boat losses during the remainder of 1942 were:

	Total	Due to aircraft [65]
August	10	5
September	10	$3\frac{1}{2}$
October	16	$9\frac{1}{2}$
November	13	7
December	5	1
	54	26

In the second half of 1942 the U-boats sustained sixty-five losses; thirty-one and a half were due to air action (48.4%). In other words, the air contribution rose steeply from 30.9% of a very small number to nearly 50% of a substantial number. Coastal Command's share of the air total was thirteen and a half U-boats (20.7%), which might not be brilliant in itself, but compares very brilliantly indeed with the zero return of January–June, and meant that now, at last, the Command was definitely 'in the game', where it firmly remained until the end of the Battle of the Atlantic. July, 1942, was thus an important milestone of the war.

As usual, it is not reasonable to look for any single cause to account for this transformation; rather we have to seek it in the fruition of a number of processes. Improving performance of ASV II, and increasing skill of its operators, were certainly among them; and meanwhile useful progress was being made towards the introduction of ASV III (see p. 284), with all that that promised for the future. The Leigh Light ('*das verdammte Licht*') was never a great killer of U-boats, but this is not the true measure of its effectiveness. A U-boat forced to return to base for repair, or arriving home in a condition that kept it in dock for several months, was a U-boat out of the war, and that was a result not to be despised. When Coastal Command did make an attack, it now had the satisfaction of using much improved depth charges –

the new Torpex explosive, 30% more powerful than the Amatol in previous use, began to be used as a filling in April at a rate of 150 charges a week, and began to reach the stations at the end of that month. Operational Research had carefully investigated the question of settings for the explosion of the charges, and opinion had now settled in favour of a very shallow setting of 25 feet. The introduction of a new pistol (Mark XIIIQ) for the improved Mark VIII charge ensured detonation at 34 feet, which was still too low but a step in the right direction.[66] Radio altimeters began to appear in June, very badly needed and gratefully received. The shortage of aircraft, especially VLR, and an accompanying shortage of aircrews trained and accustomed to maritime war requirements (exacerbated by the demands of other theatres) continued to exercise a drag on the advance to proficiency. Yet Coastal Command could look on the second half of 1942 almost as being born again, bidding definite farewell to the 'Scarecrow' phase, and resurrection as a killer.[67]

*   *   *   *   *

With the United States now in the war, as Churchill expressed it 'up to the neck and in to the death',[68] certain arrangements which had been acceptable as 'sweeteners' for the steady erosion of neutrality in 1941 now looked less attractive. Before Pearl Harbor American naval involvement in the Atlantic, and responsibility for Atlantic security, had seemed entirely desirable. After Pearl Harbor, with the US Navy plunged abruptly into the deep end of two-ocean war, the question of desirability became irrelevant; it was a matter simply of what was practicable and what was not. As the pinch of shortages tightened with every passing week, the withdrawal of the USN from the North Atlantic continued, until by mid-summer

> This left the Royal Navy to shoulder 50 per cent of the burden in that vital area and the Royal Canadian Navy 46 per cent. America's four per cent was represented by one or two coastguard cutters which led a mixed escort of American, British and Canadian ships, and a few destroyers based in Iceland.[69]

Yet it was the American admiral commanding Task Force 24 at Argentia[70] who continued to exercise control of convoy operations west of the CHOP (Change of Operational Control) line at 26°W which had been agreed at Placentia Bay in August, 1941. This was an anomaly which Western Approaches would work quietly to correct as the year wore on.

In the meantime other changes had been made with a view to replacing the dwindling American escort commitment in the Atlantic. The NEF 'beat' (Newfoundland to Iceland) was eliminated and a new escort force created in mid-February which would take the convoys all the way from Newfoundland to Londonderry. The name given to it was the Mid-Ocean Escort Force (MOEF), and its operation marked for the ships involved the beginning of the famous 'Newfy-Derry' run which lasted for the next three years,

> with the smile of the green Foyle rather than the scowling crags of Iceland greeting them at the end of each voyage.[71]

This arrangement made possible a useful economy of escorts, and was itself made possible by a return to the 'great circle route', the shortest distance between Newfoundland and the North-Western Approaches to the British ports. Diversionary re-routing in 1941 had tended to take the convoys further and further north, which made their passages longer and required reliefs of escorts – to say nothing of the sometimes horrific icing conditions encountered in those latitudes. While the U-boats were fully occupied along the American coast, there was no further point in wasting time and escort strength in that exhausting manner. On the other hand, the logic of the new manoeuvre would be easily apparent at U-boat HQ.

At the centre of all problems in Western Approaches Command was the matter of ships – *numbers* of ships. 'Numbers only can annihilate', said Nelson in 1805, and now Sir Percy Noble and his escort commanders knew too well that only numbers could keep a U-boat pack at bay, and only numbers could permit the long, implacable hunts that killed U-boats. But numbers were what they did not have. Destroyers were always too few – reminding us once more of Nelson and his eternal lack of frigates. The loss of thirty-two destroyers in the first six months of 1942 underlines a situation which was always anxious. By the middle of the year there were 200 corvettes in service, a reinforcement without which the anti-submarine war could not have been carried on. Ten of these invaluable craft were transferred to the US Navy; the remaining 190 were distributed as follows:

435

6 with the Arctic Convoys supplying the Soviet Union;

8 lent to the US Navy's Caribbean escort groups;

14 on the Gibraltar convoys;

47 between Gibraltar and the Indian Ocean, on the African coasts and the Pacific coast of America;

37 with United Kingdom-based escort groups;

78 with the groups based on Newfoundland and Canada.

The corvettes, as we have seen, were the 'workhorses' of the Atlantic escort groups, and remained so.

In April, 1942, they began to receive a reinforcement which would ultimately be their replacement: the 'super-corvettes' which another quirk of nomenclature caused to be named 'frigates'. Their resemblance to those that Nelson craved was negligible; not even their designated rôles were the same. They were larger than corvettes – 1,370 tons instead of 980, they were better armed, faster (20 knots compared with 16 – still not all that fast), and they carried a larger ship's company – 140 officers and ratings. Their endurance was greater than a corvette's, their living quarters were better, and they carried a doctor aboard instead of having to depend on the variable medical skills of the First Lieutenant. The doctor's presence also made it possible to relieve watch-keeping officers of the chore of cipher work when they came off watch. All in all, the frigates were a great improvement – but they had one serious disadvantage: they were slower to build. The first of the 'River' Class was HMS *Rother*, launched in November, 1941, and commissioned five months later. HMS *Spey* was launched in December, 1941, but the first six months of 1942 saw only seven more of these craft come down the slipways of Britain and Canada; a further twenty-eight followed in the second half-year, promising a substantial accession of strength in 1943. It is rare to hear a bad word for frigates (they remain, with modifications, an important naval type in the 1980s); the only common criticism of them in the late '40s was that there were never enough of them, and that was certainly true in 1942.

Frigates illustrate one aspect of the lack of escort numbers but, in truth, it was a universal disease. Convoys – even large convoys of more than fifty ships [72] – were still being escorted by only five or six warships which, as we have seen more than once, was a very small number to deal with a large pack of U-boats. It certainly did not permit the

436

sustained pursuit of a U-boat, once located, which was generally the only way to sink it. Commander Walker's very profitable defence of HG 76 in December, 1941, had shown what could be done if an escort was strong enough to form a 'strike force' while continuing to give the convoy close protection. But few indeed were the escort groups that could do that. On the other hand, the policy of keeping groups together, transforming a collection of ships into a true tactical unit, was beginning to show results; both group commanders and the captains of individual escorts were now developing a visibly higher level of expertise, an instinct for what they might expect from the U-boats and from their other eternal opponent, the 'steep Atlantick stream'.

Even though they lacked numbers, the escorts were beginning to enjoy certain other (belated) advantages. Together with Coastal Command, they were getting more effective depth charges, Torpex-filled, and capable of being set to a depth of 500 feet. The Navy's requirements in this respect were the exact opposite of Coastal Command's. For the airmen, who would only have the duration of their first sighting and the diving swirl of the U-boat in which to make their attack, success had to be immediate; once the U-boat was under the surface it was gone – hence the cry for a 'true 25-foot setting'. For the surface escort, the U-boat's dive was just the beginning of an ASDIC-chase which might last a great many hours (see p. 631, note 13) and which, it was now being realized, might take the U-boat down to very deep waters indeed. Despite the warnings of World War I, the Royal Navy in general, and Naval Intelligence in particular, had remained sceptical of the deep-diving capabilities of the U-boats of 1939–45. Even when prisoners-of-war spoke of dives to 600 feet, the disbelief continued right up to mid-1942. But at last they were persuaded.

The chances of locating a surfaced U-boat were, as we have seen, steadily improving. Type 271M radar was now standard equipment in escort vessels; Macintyre says that by mid-1942 'most of the escorts' had received this invaluable aid to convoy defence. Already other uses were discovered – the first step towards that almost total dependence on radar for navigation which came to exist after the war. In more or less fair weather, it was found possible to locate even such small objects as ships' boats and rafts by this means, enabling the rescue of survivors. Convoy control and station-keeping also shared the advantage; indeed, the Commanding Officer of HMS *Orchis*, the corvette in which Type 271M was tested, remarked that after being in a ship fitted with type 271, night navigation in one without will seem a perilous business.[73]

It was not infallible; bad weather could put Type 271M out of commission; there were disconcerting radar failures well into 1943 – but even taking into account the contribution of Bletchley Park at its best, there are some who speak of it as the most important element in the ultimate Atlantic victory.

In 1942 it received a valuable support. Parallel developments in Britain and America had now reached a point which, says Cajus Bekker, 'no German believed possible'.[74] In America this was the fruit of the very fortunate escape of the French research scientist, Professor Deloraine, with three of his colleagues in 1940. They carried to America the knowledge of a method of transforming a high-frequency directional fix, even of a very brief transmission, into a visual image on a screen. Already, by May, 1940, Deloraine and his colleague Busignies had produced four experimental models of such a device; when France fell, these were dismantled and the parts hidden. Deloraine arrived in America on 31 December, and the US Navy at once asked him to resume his work, which he did to such effect that a new experimental model was ready in April, 1941. Once more the briefest sound was made to appear as a spot of light – and more than that:

> A bright screen prepared with persistent fluorescent material ensured that, even after brief signals had ceased, the D/F direction was indicated with adequate accuracy.[75]

Expressed in simple words, this sounds a simple matter, and it is a process that is now quite familiar. But in 1940–41 it was a major breakthrough, and the further wonder is that the striking progress made by the French team had in fact been anticipated by British research much inspired by Sir Robert Watson-Watt. A prototype of a seaborne version of this HF/DF was tested in a destroyer in March, 1940, under the designation FH1. This proved unsatisfactory, and was replaced by FH2 in August, which in turn gave way to a prototype of an even better model, FH3, in October, and after some vicissitudes this began to be introduced in anti-submarine craft in 1942. We encounter it first towards the end of February, in one of the rare attacks on North Atlantic convoys in the early months of the year. Five U-boats attacked the convoy ON 67, thirty-five merchantmen escorted by four US destroyers and a Canadian corvette under Commander A. C. Murdaugh. From the US Navy's point of view, it was a depressing occasion: eight merchantmen sunk with no loss to the U-boats. It underlined, says the US Official History,

> the urgent need of a definite doctrine for depth charge attacks, and better training in following up underwater sound contacts. Commander Murdaugh's group was splendidly aggressive; but his officers were very deficient in attack technique.[76]

The real interest of ON 67, however, does not lie in the profit-and-loss account; it lies in two innovations which now saw the light. Both were lodged in the same ship, the SS *Toward* (Clyde Shipping Company) which revived yet another forgotten World War I procedure. She was the first of the specially designated rescue ships, carrying a surgeon and full medical staff, special rescue equipment, and space for several hundred survivors. Her function (and that of her successors as they came into general use) was to free the escorts from the distraction and burden of rescue work, which was a valuable step forward. The SS *Toward* also had another function; she carried FH3 HF/DF, and this enabled her to make the first U-boat detection of the ON 67 battle. It then became the normal practice, while this equipment was in short supply, to place it in the rescue ships; the U-boat captains had little compunction about sinking rescue ships – if they had known that these were carrying such important anti-submarine weaponry they would have felt completely justified.

In the field of weaponry further novelties were on the way. Echoing (but improving upon) the howitzers installed in World War I anti-submarine craft (see p. 28) was a device intended to overcome a major fault of ASDIC. In fact, this invaluable instrument of U-boat detection had two outstanding faults; the first was, in World War II, ineradicable:

> No method of accurately determining the depth of a submarine was ever found.

The second fault was what was known as the 'dead time', the period[77] when the attacking ship's conical ASDIC beam passed over the submarine (generally at a distance of 100–150 yards) and the sound contact

439

died. Then came the depth-charge attack, delivered from chutes and throwers, and causing such disturbance in the water that no further contact might be obtained for some minutes, or perhaps not at all. Obviously, if the submarine could be attacked without breaking ASDIC contact it would be a long step towards eradicating this serious weakness – in other words, what was needed was a forward-firing howitzer- or mortar-type weapon. This appeared in 1942, and was called the 'Hedgehog', but for security reasons when first installed under tarpaulin wraps it was often referred to as 'Anti-Dive-Bombing-Equipment'. Joseph Schull describes it:

> The square-set battery of twenty-four spigotted heads pointing forward and skyward at an acute angle might well have had some aerial intention. Actually it had not. The 65-pound bombs on the ends of the spigots were intended on firing to describe a brief arc through the air and enter the water some 230 yards ahead of the ship in an intricate circle pattern about a hundred feet in diameter. Around the circumference of the circle, and at points within its area, the bombs fell spaced some twelve feet apart. Each was loaded with thirty pounds of Torpex ... and any one of them, dropping straight down through the water, would explode on contact, with disastrous results for a U-boat.[78]

The Hedgehog was accurate, except in a heavy sea; its advantage over a normal depth-charge attack, says Captain Macintyre, 'was that the submarine commander had no warning of attack and so was unable to judge the moment to dodge'.[79] Less of an advantage was the fact that Hedgehog bombs only exploded if they hit their target:

> Thus, though an explosion signalled certain destruction of the submarine, a near miss did no damage at all, whereas under depth-charge attack damage sufficient to destroy or to force the submarine to the surface could accumulate from a succession of non-lethal near-misses.

As with so much else that concerned the war at sea and certainly the anti-submarine war, the Hedgehog had long-drawn-out teething troubles. It was in service (in limited numbers) in August, 1942, but it did not settle down into a dependable weapon until 1943, when it showed itself to be decidedly effective. An annoying and alarming fault of the early days was a tendency for some (occasionally *all*) of the bombs not to leave the spigots, thus ruining the pattern and threatening premature explosions in the ship. Later in the war (too late for the crisis in the Atlantic) the Royal Navy brought a heavier version of the Hedgehog into action, called the Squid (see p. 620). For the smaller types of anti-submarine craft even Hedgehog was too large, and the US Navy introduced 'Mousetrap' which fired a pattern of four or eight small rockets from a projector fastened to the deck, so that the ship had to be aimed in the direction (or supposed direction) of the U-boat.

It could be said that the whole story of anti-submarine warfare in the two World Wars was a matter of waiting for the right equipment to reach the right stage of efficiency. Yet this would be only partly true; there was something else as well which was at least equally important, as ON 67 had shown – what Dr Morison called 'attack technique'. An action on 14 April illustrated the same thing in the opposite fashion: the sinking of *U 252* in the course of defending convoy OG 82 by Commander Walker's sloop *Stork* and the corvette *Vetch*:

> During the action, the value of drills emerged as an essential to success. The depth-charge crews, the asdic team, the guns' crews and signalmen played split-second and vital rôles. A hitch anywhere and a determined, clever and slippery opponent might have escaped to sink more ships on another day.
>
> Throughout the attack the signalling of orders and reports between *Vetch* and *Stork* was kept down to a total of eight messages, embracing twenty-five words.[80]

This is proficiency indeed, at a level not to be obtained by any other recipe than constant and arduous training. We have already noted (p. 307) Admiral Noble's institution of the Western Approaches Tactical Unit ('The Game'), at which escort commanders and aircraft skippers were subjected to a week of simulated battle stress designed to prepare them for the sudden impact of successive crises which was the normal 'form' of a pack attack on a convoy. 'The Game', says Macintyre,

> had done much to instil a common doctrine of convoy defence, together with the team spirit and initiative which were the mark of a well-trained escort group.[81]

The Tactical Unit ranks high among the many contributions which entitle Sir Percy Noble to be called 'the architect' of the ultimate

Atlantic victory. Both the Royal Navy and the US Navy set great store by their training – though never to quite the extent of Dönitz's U-boats. With possibly a tinge of envy (reflecting on the pressures to which American escorts were being subjected) a USN officer sent to report in May on British anti-submarine training remarked that the Royal Navy always seemed to 'find time for this instruction somehow'.[82] The lack of this intensive training in the still expanding RCN continued to be noted.

New weapons and new systems, even if still imperfect, and increasing proficiency were gleams of light in a scene which at mid-summer was about as dark as it could be. The U-boats, in May and June, 1942, were at the very height of their powers in the Atlantic; they even penetrated into the Indian Ocean where surface raiders were also at work; the Japanese were still triumphant (no one could yet tell whether Midway was a true portent or a flash in the pan); and in the Mediterranean the Royal Navy's position continued to be precarious. Oppressed by all these ominous considerations, the Admiralty drew up on 23 June a paper addressed to the Chief of the Air Staff and the AOC-in-C, Coastal Command:

> A gloomy appreciation, therefore, formed the opening paragraphs of this survey in which it was stated that *we had lost a measure of control over the sea communications of the world* with all that this meant in the supply of raw materials and food for Great Britain and *the ability to take the offensive*. Succeeding paragraphs outlined the conception of maritime strategy which the Admiralty considered necessary to rectify the situation. . . . One major point, it was claimed, stood out clearly – *ships alone were unable to maintain command at sea*.[83]

Once again the 1917 echo is loud, and clear and appalling: 'we have lost command of the sea' (see p. 47).

This admission that the very nature of seapower had changed was a bitter moment for the Admiralty, following the long inter-war rearguard action against the apostles of unlimited air power. Right up to the moment when the Japanese, with trifling loss, sank the *Prince of Wales* and the *Repulse* by aircraft alone, the big-ship men could still maintain that the battleship was the core of the Fleet, and the Fleet was the core of seapower. Now their Lordships confessed that 'ships alone were unable to maintain command at sea' – a perception which Air Chief Marshal Sir Arthur

Tedder had considered to be proven after the lamentable losses incurred by the Royal Navy in the Crete operations of May, 1941 (see p. 343).

Now, a year later, the Admiralty was clamouring for

> A permanent and increased share in the control of sea communications . . . to be borne by air forces which must be mobile and must be trained and operated with naval forces in such a manner that they worked as a team.[84]

The Admiralty – and the Air Ministry did not greatly differ – estimated the deficiency of aircraft of all types for maritime use at about 800. The difference between the two Services was really only a matter of the urgency with which each approached a situation whose seriousness was perfectly visible to both. As the Admiralty said,

> We cannot await the fruition of a long-term programme when our hopes of even fulfilling that programme are being daily decreased by our lack of command of the sea.

It was against this background that the U-boat war now moved into its intense final phase.

6

The Heartbeat of the War

'The powerful ships of the great navies buttressed what remained of the world's old strategic framework and kept the tide of Axis triumphs from becoming a flood which would engulf the earth. Yet all their work . . . was secondary and contributory to the final objective, which was the defeat of Germany by an assault mounted from the British Isles. The conditions and necessities surrounding that long-envisioned and still far-distant objective had not changed. The Atlantic convoy was still the heartbeat of the war.'

Joseph Schull, The Far Distant Ships p. 124

THE DÖNITZ PHILOSOPHY of war was a simple one:

The enemy's shipping constitutes one single, great entity. It is therefore immaterial where a ship is sunk. Once it has been destroyed it has to be replaced by a new ship; and that's that.[1]

Much that to purer minds takes on the look of sheer opportunism – a fault to which German leadership was prone in both World Wars – can be explained by reference to this bald guideline. It supplies the adequate reason for his concentration against American coastal shipping from January to May, and his switch to the Caribbean and the Gulf in May and June:

the hub of both shipbuilding and the production of armaments lies in the United States. If, therefore, I go for the hub, and particularly the oil supplies, I am getting to the root of the evil.

444

The U-boat 'effective quotients' (see p. 270), from which his attention never wandered for long, though they never matched the high levels of the first *glückliche Zeit* ('happy time'), lent support to his convictions; in January the quotient was 209 tons sunk per boat per day at sea. Thereafter:

February	278 tons
March	327 tons
April	255 tons
May	311 tons
June	325 tons

These figures were very satisfactory, but Dönitz well knew that they were not the full story, that they had to be set against another reckoning which was far less encouraging. In mid-1942 the Naval High Command received a disturbing report to the effect that American shipbuilding alone was likely to produce a total of 15,300,000 tons in 1942 and 1943. Some experts in Germany doubted whether this was possible (in fact that figure was exceeded by some 2 million tons), but U-boat HQ, says Dönitz,

accepted in principle and as a matter of precaution the maximum figures given in the report.[2]

What these implied was that

to do no more than keep pace with the new tonnage being built – in other words, merely to prevent an increase in the enemy's total tonnage – we should in 1942 have to sink 700,000 tons of shipping per month. (Or, if the actual figures from British sources are taken as the basis in calculation, 590,000 tons per month.) Only sinkings over 700,000 tons (or 590,000 tons) per month would represent a lowering of the total tonnage available to the enemy.

The measure of the 1942 crisis at sea is that four times during the year the monthly total of shipping sunk exceeded the higher German figure, and only three times did it fall below the lower (British) figure. Dönitz, however, was working to the higher target, which meant hard labour for the U-boats – and as it turned out they were only able to reach it once in the second half of 1942.

June marked the high peak of the second 'happy time', but already there were ominous signs. The Americans knew now what they had to do, and were beginning to do it; with some reinforcement from the RN and RCN, escorts were collected and convoys began to appear in the Caribbean – with the usual results. The time had come for Dönitz to make another strategic shift in his accustomed manner – to return, as he had anticipated, to pack attacks on the North Atlantic convoys.[3] He had the satisfaction, in preparing his new strategy, of *B-Dienst's* penetration of the convoy ciphers, which promised much. And he had the further satisfaction, at last, of numbers which began to match his pre-war call for 300 boats (see p. 205). In January, 1942, he had begun his campaign with a total of 249 boats, of which ninety-one were operational. Both numbers improved significantly as the year wore on:

	Total	*Operational*
April	285	121
July	331	140
October	365	196 [4]

These were good auguries, but nothing could remove an uneasy nag of doubt which $2\frac{1}{2}$ years of war had planted in him:

My conviction grew that irretrievable time had been lost.[5]

The new offensive proper did not begin until July, but already there had been preludes and previews of what might be in store. By May *xB-Dienst* had firmly established that the North Atlantic convoys were using the great circle route between Halifax and Liverpool. With the U-boats fully occupied in American waters, it was in any case, says Dönitz,

logical to assume . . . that British homeward-bound convoys would now be using this, the shortest route without troubling to deviate from it.[6]

He had accordingly formed a group (*Hecht*) of eight boats 'for the purpose of attacking any convoy that might be sighted'. The group formed a patrol line abreast at maximum distance across the great circle route, and on 11 May *U 569* sighted a convoy which proved to be the outward-bound ONS 92. On the principle that a ship is a ship, whichever way it is going, and that all ships required to be sunk without

446

further ado, Dönitz launched the nearest five U-boats at ONS92. The escort was Group A3, consisting of the US destroyer *Gleaves*, with Commander J. B. Heffernan, USN, as Senior Officer. With him were the US Coastguard cutter *Spencer* and four RCN corvettes. It was thus a mixed group, a circumstance not favoured by any of the participating navies; worse still, it was, as Milner says, 'almost totally bereft of modern equipment'.[7] None of the escort vessels possessed HF/DF (though the rescue ship *Bury* did carry this), and only the corvette *Bittersweet* carried 271M radar worked by inexperienced operators. *Bury* plotted *U569*'s sighting signal on the morning of 11 May and reported it. The Admiralty also warned of the presence of U-boats near the convoy, but for unexplained reasons Commander Heffernan took no action on these warnings.

The action that followed was, as always, confused, but it would seem to have been made even more so by Heffernan's own procedures. In the afternoon of the 11th he took the two US ships on forward sweeps which produced a U-boat sighting some 17 miles ahead of the convoy. Heffernan then began a series of depth-charge attacks which he kept up until 0100 on the 12th, but without result. While he was so occupied, the U-boats struck; before *Gleaves* could rejoin the convoy, five ships were sunk, four of them by *U124* (*Fregattenkapitän* Mohr) and one by *U94*. During all this time, apart from *Gleaves*'s fruitless chase, A3 'had seen nothing except burning and sinking ships'. The daylight of the 12th was more productive of contacts, but not of U-boats sunk or damaged, and nightfall brought a fiasco whose penalty was duly exacted. Orders were given by the Commodore to make an evasive turn at midnight, but just as this began a nervous merchant captain fired a 'Snowflake' illuminant:

> Every ship in the convoy immediately followed suit with its own snow-flake; the sea was illuminated for miles around, and all benefit of the evasive turn completely lost.[8]

Not only that, but one merchantman, having fired her Snowflake directly over the corvette *Arvida*, followed this up with a shell which whistled past the officers on the bridge:

> the incident served to emphasize once again the strain under which merchant ships and escorts were carrying on.

447

The retribution was not long delayed. At 0235 *U 94* made a second attack and promptly sank two ships, bringing *Oberleutnant* Ites's score to three. Despite deteriorating weather, the *Hecht* Group maintained contact with ONS 92 all through the 13th, but the convoy succeeded by luck rather than by judgment in slipping through a gap in the U-boat patrol line on 14 May. The *Hecht* boats then refuelled from a 'milch cow' to await further opportunities.

Dönitz was not dissatisfied with the sinking of seven ships without loss to the U-boats. Nor, apparently, was Commander Heffernan unduly disappointed by the virtually complete failure of his Escort Group. In his report he wrote:

> The COs of all the escorts are entitled to credit for a highly satisfactory performance.[9]

This was not at all the view taken at Western Approaches Command, where the whole performance of A3 and ONS 92 recalled only too vividly the bad days of 1940–41. In particular, the Commodore's statement that '*Gleaves* was never there when ONS 92 was attacked' called to mind the lesson of the unhappy Commander Dickinson and SC 7 in October, 1940 (see p. 266). Representations were made to the Americans, 'and Heffernan was quietly moved to another command'. But all was not well with the Canadians, either. Commander C. D. H. Howard-Johnston, Western Approaches Staff Officer, Anti-Submarine, found it impossible to understand why senior officers of the RCN (Murray for one) actually *commended* the captain of *Arvida* for picking up survivors when a rescue ship was present. Furthermore, both Murray and his Captain (D) at St John's, Captain E. R. Mainguy, exonerated the captian of *Bittersweet* from blame for failing to attack a U-boat which her radar had detected, but which materialized only as a shape racing past the corvette's port side and disappearing into the night. 'This is awful,' said Howard-Johnston. Doubts and qualms about the Atlantic allies not unnaturally arose in Derby House and other quarters of Western Approaches.

The truth is that the whole Royal Navy in 1942 was suffering from a heavy dose of undigested new experience. Not only was it forced to admit that ships alone could no longer hold command of the sea, but for the first time in a major war during its long history it was encountering the pains of coalition. This was a condition that the Army was well acquainted with; in World War I a profound difference between the two Services lay in the fact that on the main front the Army fought always as a junior partner to the French, while the Navy was senior everywhere. In 1939–40 the Army had again been the junior, but the Navy by no means so. Now, in 1942, things were different. The RCN may still have been raw and often unhandy, but it was 46% of the Atlantic battle and very conscious of being *Canadian*, not just a contingent in another navy. The USN's Atlantic rôle was much reduced, and it showed alarming (if understandable) tendencies to preoccupation with the Pacific; but it was a mighty and growing force in the war and absolutely indisposed towards acceptance of junior status anywhere. So there were inevitable differences which were sometimes difficult to paper over.

When these reared up in the field of anti-submarine warfare, it was apparent that *doctrine* was at the centre of them – a visible difference of doctrine at both the strategic and tactical levels between the Royal Navy and the two transatlantic associates. At the strategic level – determining 'the object of the exercise' – there was a difference of view between the British approach to convoy operations and the American/Canadian attitude which lip-service could not hide, as the cases of ON 67 and ONS 92 revealed. The British doctrine was enshrined in the WACIS formula (see p. 288): the *primary* object of a convoy was and remained 'safe and timely arrival . . . at its destination'. And the strategic doctrine determined the tactical methods; prolonged absence from the convoy by escorts chasing U-boats was a bad tactic, even if the chase was successful, if it left the convoy unprotected. Indeed, *anything* that left the convoy unprotected was bad tactics. The Canadian and American view was different; both displayed

a tendency to concentrate on the offensive tasks of convoy escort – pursuit of nearby U-boats and hunting them to destruction.[10]

Both Canadians and Americans showed themselves

prepared to accept a certain scale of losses from convoys in 1942, provided that the escort displayed an aggressive spirit in the face of enemy attack. . . . For the British, the main Atlantic convoys were the lifeline of the nation, a perspective which gave a very different tone to their assessments of convoy battles.

449

This was, potentially, a dangerous divergence so close to the 'heart-beat of the war'. Partly, obviously, it was a matter of geography; it makes a difference, being a continent not an island, especially if the seat of war is in another continent altogether. Also, of course, it was to do with experience; as Milner says,

> although the RCN was primarily an anti-submarine navy by 1942 . . . it had not yet begun to think like one.

In the higher reaches of Canada's Naval Service Headquarters there were still dreams of the 'Big Battle' which would be fought by 'Big Ships' (see p. 331). And as the Pacific war gained momentum, the USN found no occasion to be other than a 'Big Ship navy', with aircraft-carriers displacing battleships as the real capital ships, protected by flocks of destroyers and covering a swelling amphibious campaign in which the chief small-vessel requirement would be swarms of vari-gated landing-craft. It is easy now to see, with such powerful tugs in different directions, how necessary a Supreme Commander, Atlantic, was – but also, unfortunately, how impossible to appoint by the very same token.

* * * * *

In that worst of all months, June, 1942, the various sections of the North Atlantic theatre – the Gulf, the Caribbean, the East Coast, a new intrusion into the St Lawrence estuary, and the convoy routes – contributed no less than 623,545 tons of shipping sunk (124 ships) out of the dreadful full total of 834,196 tons (173 ships). What makes the Atlantic U-boat achievement especially remarkable is the weather in the northern latitudes – heavy gales and dense fogs in mid-summer, maliciously bridging the brief time-gap between one bad winter and the next. On 1 June it was such a gale that ruined an intended attack on ONS 96. By contrast, further south, on 14 June an *ad hoc* U-boat group was able to sink five ships in a homeward-bound convoy from Gibraltar, HG 84. But the highlights of this grim month were the battles of ONS 100 and ONS 102, conducted by Group *Hecht*.

Refuelled and refreshed, this group re-entered the fray towards the end of May, only to be thwarted by the weather. On 8 June, however, it was able to make firm contact with ONS 100, escorted by Escort Group C1. 'C' stood for Canadian, but in fact the only Canadain ship

450

in the group on this occasion was the Senior Officer's River Class destroyer *Assiniboine*; with her were two RN and two Free French corvettes. All these ships had radar; unfortunately *Assiniboine's* was the obsolete Type 286, but all the corvettes had 271M, though the Free French *Mimosa's* set was out of order. She was accordingly placed astern of the centre column, where the lack of radar might be expected to matter rather less than in the other escort positions. Shortly after 0200 on 9 June, with the convoy making 7 knots, two unexplained explosions were heard on the starboard quarter, and soon afterwards an Admiralty signal was received to the effect that U-boats were pursuing the convoy, as the Senior Officer, Lieutenant-Commander J. H. Stubbs, had guessed. With no reports either from the other escorts or from merchantmen to enlighten him, he came to the conclusion that the explosions must have been torpedoes at the end of their runs.

With the dawn, however, he was able to see that *Mimosa* was missing, and at the same time received a message from the other Free French corvette, *Aconit*, saying that she had picked up a radar contact at 0215. Why she had not reported this before remained one of those random mysteries which could afflict every Senior Officer. *Assiniboine* raced back to make a search and soon found four survivors in the water who told Stubbs that *Mimosa* had been sunk by two torpedoes. It transpired later that these had been fired by the indefatigable Mohr's *U124*. With his reduced escort, Lieutenant-Commander Stubbs then conducted a courageous and intelligent defence of ONS 100, helped by fog. He could not, however, prevent Ites in *U94* slipping in and sinking two ships. On the 11th *U94* shared another sinking with *U569*, but on that day also Captain Prentice arrived with two ships of his roving training group, *Chambly* and *Orillia*, and took command. On 12 June *U124* returned to sink a fourth ship, but the next day bad weather and the proximity of land forced Group *Hecht* to break off the action. Considering the weakness of the very mixed escort group and the lack of HF/DF and air support, it could be said that a loss of no more than four merchantmen made honours roughly even, but the loss of the corvette tilted the advantage in favour of the Germans.

The story of ONS 102 is soon told. *U94* sighted the convoy on 16 June, and her signal brought in four more *Hecht* boats. Once again the Escort Group was A3 – but a very much stronger A3 than the unit that *Hecht* had met in May in the attack on ONS 92. Now commanded by an able US Coast Guard officer, Captain P. Heineman, it contained two destroyers, USS *Leary* and HMCS *Restigouche*, two Coastguard cutters and four RCN corvettes, with Prentice's Training Group (four corvettes) in support. In three days Group *Hecht* succeeded in sinking only one of the forty-eight merchantmen in the convoy – a final thrust by Mohr in *U 124*. And this time two U-boats suffered damage: *U 94* and *U 590*.[12]

This action marked the close of the *Hecht* group's operations. In the course of them twelve U-boats (at one time or another) had sunk twelve merchant ships and one corvette. A very good start, in other words, had sadly tailed away. And there was food for thought in the fact that only three U-boats were actually involved in the sinkings. *Korvettenkapitän* Mohr (*U 124*), a tough and experienced captain who had already marked up a considerable score on the American East Coast, was responsible for six of the merchant ships as well as the corvette *Mimosa*; *Oberleutnant* Ites's *U 94* claimed five and a half merchantmen, and *U 569* took a half share; the rest were nowhere. Nothing could more clearly illustrate the dilution of quality that comes with rapid expansion, as was now happening in the U-boat arm despite its rigorous training programme.

The June battles were a warning that full-scale convoy warfare was about to return to the North Atlantic, and it was heeded (with some apprehension) by the Allied navies. There were speculations in the USN that the U-boats might be using a new tactic – employing one or two boats as decoys to draw off the escorts, leaving the convoy exposed to the rest of the pack. ONS 92 seemed to offer a perfect example of this, and for a period on 16 June four out of eight escorts of ONS 102 were pursuing sighted U-boats, one of them 43 miles from the convoy. The supposition of a deliberate tactic, however, would seem to be a *post facto* deduction. The Dönitz system (see pp. 228–9) did not permit the degree of local control that would be required for such a ploy. The phenomenon of the packs delivering attacks in 'waves' separated by considerable time-lags was not the fruit of tactical agreement, which could only be arrived at by signalling, which was forbidden. It was due simply to the spread of the U-boat patrol line and the time inevitably taken by the more distant boats to reach the convoy. It was also due to tactical errors by the escorts themselves.

To British eyes the ONS 102 action was very satisfactory; to lose no more than one merchantman in three days, and damage two U-boats in the process, was good news. The Americans saw it differently, and their heart-searchings are reflected in their Official History. To the USN the salient fact was that 'all the attacking submarines escaped'.[13] Dr Morison lists various reasons for this: first, a tendency to drop depth charges too early, 'mostly due to over-eagerness'; secondly, and somewhat in contradiction, there was 'a tendency to economize on depth charges and not throw a large enough pattern'; thirdly, there was inadequate reporting by ASDIC operators; fourthly, the American escorts with their higher speed and greater turning circle were often baffled by the tight turns of the U-boats;[14] fifthly, 'although a ship has only one chance out of fifteen to catch a submarine after it has dived, the mathematically determined search course which would give her that one chance in fifteen of regaining contact was not always followed'; and, finally, 'the old jinx of communications continued to hamper anti-submarine warfare'. The catalogue was quite familiar to Royal Navy officers who remembered the early days.

Yet, says Morison, at the root of everything there was one underlying fault: 'the want of a definite anti-submarine doctrine for escort vessels'. It is not surprising that this should be so, since at this juncture each of the four USN destroyer training centres of the Atlantic Fleet – Key West, Miami, Staten Island and Boston – was issuing different attack instructions. Worse still, some smaller escorts were receiving no instruction at all. This thoroughly unsatisfactory state of affairs began to be corrected early in July when COMINCH brought out an anti-submarine information bulletin which became a manual for all ships, aircraft, shore installations and schools. Morison comments:

> Looking backward, this uniform doctrine, and the training and analysis systems set up, together with plain, hard experience, seem to be the most important contributions during that woeful year 1942 toward controlling the U-boat menace ... in the last analysis, the problem was human. All [the] devices and methods and gadgets would have been so much junk without proper knowledge of how to use them; and that is what doctrine, training and experience accomplished.

* * * * *

To those who were aware of it, the most ominous matter of all, as the storm-clouds of a new U-boat offensive gathered, was the continuing blackout of the *Enigma* decrypts. Do what it might, Bletchley Park could not overcome the obstacle of the fourth rotor. During all this period, as regards precise locations of individual boats and the gathering of packs,

> the radio location picture, derived from D/F-locating the U-boats sending messages, was the most important source to the Submarine Tracking Room in preparing the daily U-boat report.[15]

On the other side of the coin, the Germans were (unknown to the Admiralty) enjoying a windfall. The Merchant Navy Code, which the *xB-Dienst* had penetrated as far back as 1940 (see p. 257) was replaced in April, 1942, by a new Merchant Ships Code; but four weeks before the Code was introduced a copy of the book was captured from a merchant ship in northern waters. This, with the penetration of Naval Cipher No 3, meant a treble advantage to *B-Dienst* and the U-boat Command.

Responsibility for convoy and anti-submarine warfare in these circumstances lay heavily upon the senior officers – the Assistant Chief of Naval Staff (Trade), Vice-Admiral E. L. S. King, the C-in-C, Western Approaches, Admiral Noble, the Director of Operations, Captain Edwards, and the Director of Anti-Submarine Warfare, Captain Creasy, together with the AOC-in-C, Coastal Command, Air Chief Marshal Joubert. But the burden of preparing a daily Intelligence assessment to guide the decisions of these potentates fell upon Commander Rodger Winn. Was it, he had to ask himself, feasible to draw up such a document in existing circumstances? Would it have any value? Might it not be positively dangerous? It is indicative of Winn's robust personality and his faith in the general Intelligence system that had now been built up, that he concluded that an attempt must continue to be made, and that on balance the product was likely to be valuable rather than otherwise. It is indicative also of the confidence that he had been able to instil in his superiors (and of their enlightened attitudes, too) that he was able to persuade them to accept what he himself called a 'Working Fiction'. It was no trifling decison to agree

> that the Tracking Room's estimates, its best and most considered guesses, should be treated as facts and acted on accordingly until such time as they were proved wrong.[16]

Patrick Beesly affords us an inside glimpse of the kind of daily questioning that went on in the Submarine Tracking Room in order to produce Winn's 'Working Fiction'; while a U-boat remained within the Home Waters where HYDRA was still in use, there was little that Bletchley Park did not find out about it – but then:

Should this short position report, D/F'd on the hundred-fathom line in the Bay of Biscay, be associated with the U-boat that had recently sailed from St Nazaire or with that other one which had left about the same time from Lorient? A brief sighting by a Coastal Command patrol some days later might, if associated with one boat, indicate a Great Circle course for the Caribbean, while an attack on an independently routed ship south-west of Ireland might suggest a movement into the North-Western Approaches. Every U-boat was given a pin with two letters, AA, BB etc., representing its true identity. When a boat sailed, its pin was taken from the appropriate port board, placed on the end of the swept channel and plotted on every twenty-four hours with due allowance for weather conditions or the presence of strong air patrols, which might necessitate a slower than average speed of advance. Thereafter each and every incident, sighting, attack or D/F fix had to be related to a particular U-boat. . . . It was, of course, very much a hit-or-miss process and adjustments were continually having to be made, but Winn insisted on complete honesty and, no matter how involved and painstaking the process of re-estimating, fresh pins could not be added to the plot to account for awkward events, or old ones removed just because there had been no recent evidence to support that particular U-boat's presence where we were showing it. Despite all its errors and imperfections the plot did bear some relation to reality, with approximately the right number of U-boats on patrol or on outward or homeward passage.

That this could be so was due to the experience, the compendious knowledge, the imagination and the flair, above all of Rodger Winn, but also of the team that he had trained.

Since 1940 Rear-Admiral Godfrey (DNI) had worked to the best of his ability for the greatest cooperation between British and American Intelligence consonant with the fact that one country was at war and the other was not. Pearl Harbor erased that difficulty and in early 1942 it became apparent that what was needed as soon as possible was the creation of an American OIC for the anti-submarine war. There was, it must be understood, no question of 'letting America into the Ultra Secret'. America had possessed a German *Enigma* machine since

1927 when the Signal Corps had bought a commercial model for $144. In 1931 the Assistant Military Attaché in Berlin (a Signal Corps officer), having attended the German Army manoeuvres, reported that 'the German Signal Corps were using a typewriter type of enciphering device in the field'. So there was no lack of awareness of the German signal system in America; nor was there any serious doubt about how to attack it. The American position was simply that, for two decades, the whole thrust of cryptanalytical work had been directed against Japan – with remarkable results. The Japanese also had their enciphering machine, known to the Americans as the Purple; it was a complex affair and 'the mechanical processes involved were inherently different from those of *Enigma*'.[17] By August, 1940, a powerful and sustained American cryptanalytical effort (which cannot be even mentioned without reference, no matter how brief, to William F. Friedman, Director of the Signal Intelligence Service) had broken the Purple cipher:

> The interception, decryption and translation on a current basis of secret Japanese worldwide diplomatic messages then began.[18]

The fruits of this process were thereafter called, very reasonably, MAGIC, and very wonderful indeed were some of the treasures thus revealed. (The Japanese Ambassador in Berlin was a most helpful source of information on many subjects, not least the U-boat war).

There was, then, no question of 'junior partnership' in regard to American Sigint; it was just that the effort required to be re-directed and up-dated. There was, however, a status problem to be overcome within the US Navy. It has, for over forty years, been a matter of wonder and debate how it came about that, with this unceasing flow of invaluable information, the USN was taken utterly by surprise by the attack on Pearl Harbor.[19] This is not the time or place to examine that very large subject; a Congressional Inquiry was held, whose proceedings have been examined and re-examined, and the Defense Department in 1977 produced an eight-volume study of the rôle of MAGIC in the Pearl Harbor disaster. All that we need be concerned with here is the consequence, that senior operational officers of the USN in the immediate aftermath of Pearl Harbor viewed Intelligence with a considerable degree of disenchantment.[20] And it was against that background that the Royal Navy, in the early part of 1942, made the overtures intended to woo the American admirals into an OIC-style relationship. The man selected for the duty of wooing was Rodger Winn.

It is fair to say, from the sundry accounts of Winn's visit to America in May, 1942, that he had a rough ride, which was what he expected. Nothing would be achieved without Admiral King's blessing, and King's reputation as what a famous humourist would call 'a twenty-minute egg' was already well established. Rear-Admiral R. E. Edwards, the Assistant Chief of Staff, was another well-crusted personality, and so was the forthright Texan, Vice-Admiral Andrews, commanding the Eastern Sea Frontier. Winn soon found out that making allies in US Intelligence would be no help whatever in dealing with these intimidating shellbacks. However, he himself did not intimidate easily.

Winn's first 'admiral-encounter' was with Edwards, who told him bluntly that he did not believe it was possible to predict a U-boat's movements, and that it was therefore useless to try to re-route convoys to avoid it. According to Patrick Beesly, he also told Winn that the Americans were determined to learn their own lessons their own way, even if it did cost them ships, of which they had plenty in any case:

> Winn felt that Edwards, like so many Americans, would react well to plain speaking, so, taking his courage in both hands, he retorted with calculated heat, 'The trouble is, Admiral, it's not only your bloody ships you're losing: a lot of them are ours!' Edwards was taken aback for a moment but then gave a laugh. 'Well, maybe you've got a point there. Perhaps there's something in what you say. You had better see Admiral King.' He must have been more impressed than he appeared because, when Winn did see King, the ground seemed to have been well prepared. The Commander-in-Chief gave Winn a friendly hearing.[21]

Donald McLachlan tells us that when Winn explained the function and methods of the Submarine Tracking Room 'to an American admiral who was responsible for such activities', the admiral's immediate response was:

> I'm not buying all that boloney.[22]

We are not told who the admiral was; it may have been Edwards – it seems to chime with Beesly's account – or it may have been Andrews.

457

But what we have to remember is what it was that Winn was 'selling', to provoke this apparently 'shellback' reaction. He was selling the 'Working Fiction'. And if it was a bold and imaginative decision by the British admirals who knew Winn and his work to accept the inspired guesswork that was the foundation of it, it must be admitted that for the Americans who had only just met him also to 'buy' the 'boloney' was even bolder and not 'shellback' at all. For the outcome of Winn's meeting with King, says Beesly, was that the C-in-C

> instructed Edwards to set about the creation of a tracking room forthwith.
>
> Once convinced, the Americans moved with a speed and efficiency that was surprising to anyone accustomed to the ways of the Admiralty. Before Winn left Washington ... the necessary accommodation had been found and the additional staff required were being selected.[23]

The saving grace of the new organization, from the point of view of COMINCH, was that it stood quite apart from the despised Office of Naval Intelligence, and was part of Admiral King's own operational staff with the designation Op 20 (later F.21). The officer appointed to head the new 'Atlantic Section, Operational Intelligence' was Commander K. A. Knowles, a USN regular brought back from retirement; he turned out to be

> the perfect counterpart to Winn. ... The cooperation between Op 20 and OIC that grew up during the next two and three-quarter years was probably closer than between any other British and American organization in any Service and in any theatre.

The British Intelligence history tells us that:

> From then on communication between the two rooms, which were later joined by Ottawa,[24] was so good that they operated virtually as a single organization without any need to exchange or integrate their staffs.[25]

To Beesly, who saw the system working, the outstanding feature of this cooperation

> was the establishment, with the full approval of the 'High-Ups' on both sides, of a direct signal link between the two Tracking Rooms on the

458

understanding, scrupulously observed, that the messages exchanged were seen by no one other than Winn, Knowles and their two deputies. These messages ensured a completely free and unfettered exchange of ideas and information between the two organizations in which, if necessary, disagreement could be frankly expressed without offence being taken. This might not have been the case had the signals appeared, for example, on the desk of the irascible Admiral King or our own Andrew Cunningham[26]

In a period brimming over with sorrows, it is agreeable to be able to tell a story with such a swift and conclusive happy ending; among Rodger Winn's many services to his country in World War II, the establishment of this accord with the Americans must rank high.

Meanwhile, however, the blackout of *Enigma* and *B-Dienst*'s supremacy continued, with several desperate months to run.

* * * * *

Admiral Dönitz was now, at last, almost a happy man. By July, 1942, he was receiving thirty new operational U-boats a month, which by comparison with previous deliveries, and also by comparison with a loss of no more than twenty-six boats in the six months, January to June, was manna from heaven indeed. At last he had some real strength in his right arm; at last he could take hopeful stock of his strategic options. Dönitz never faltered in his assessment of the North Atlantic convoys as the veritable 'heartbeat of the war', and once again the most cost-effective area for U-boat operations. But not the *only* area; he could now contemplate both attacking the convoys and going further afield 'to deliver surprise attacks as opportunities occurred'.[27] The Caribbean, especially around Trinidad, was still a profitable place; West Africa – the Freetown route – might well yield fresh results to unexpected attack. Cape Town held out all the promise of a 'virgin field', especially suitable for the Type IXs;[28] and there was Brazil, which had announced in May that its aircraft were attacking U-boats and would continue to do so. He now had full permission to respond against Brazilian shipping. It was the Dönitz style to play every permutation that offered. One of his distinguished opponents called it 'always chopping and changing',[29] but the idea behind it never faltered – to sink ships wherever they could most conveniently be found. As he himself expressed it:

Taken as a whole, the Atlantic offered a great series of opportunities

459

and promise of very considerable success, and this I proposed to exploit as and when our operations against the North Atlantic convoys permitted.[30]

It is difficult to fault this strategy.

Tactically, too, Dönitz's ideas were mobile – to the extent of bringing him once more into dispute with the Naval Operations Staff. He proposed to make the fullest use of his newly-gained strength by forming the new boats into packs on the eastern side of the Atlantic which would then comb westward astride the convoy routes until they found a westbound convoy. This they would then pursue across the full breadth of the ocean, and when they had done with it they would refuel from the U-tankers, form a new patrol line facing eastwards and try to catch an eastbound convoy in the same way. It sounds a fairly straightforward, not to say obvious, notion, but here lay the dispute:

> Dönitz certainly did not agree with the views of Raeder and the German Naval Operations Staff that only the eastward-bound, loaded convoys were worth attacking, because if this view were adopted only one convoy operation per voyage would be possible, and thus the effectiveness of each individual U-boat would decline considerably.[31]

As ever, a ship sunk, no matter where, was a victory: 'and that's that'. But he knew it would not be easy:

> These operations, which would last four, six and even eight days, with only short pauses from time to time, imposed a great strain on both commanders and their crews, and demanded a high standard of training and determination; and many of them were, of course, newcomers to the game.

Thus, despite the advantages that had accrued to him, Dönitz remained only almost happy. He was still sadly conscious of lost time; he knew that many of his boats would now be in the hands of raw crews and untried captains, and more and more he was aware of increasing Allied air power.

It came about, for these reasons, that when the offensive began the U-boats did not have it all their own way. As it turned out, it was on the Sierra Leone route, against the outward-bound convoy OS 33, attacked on 12 July, that the U-boats scored their first noteworthy success: five merchantmen sunk for the loss of one U-boat, *U 136* (Zimmermann). A few days later *U 202* (Lindner), homeward bound from American waters, signalled a sighting of OS 34 which enabled the same pack to close in again; this time, however, only two merchant ships were lost, and Dönitz was disturbed to hear of four-engined aircraft (actually Coastal Command Liberators) 'equipped with locating device',[32] operating 800 miles out from their nearest base.

In the North Atlantic the packs made a slow start. The *Wolf* pack was one of those formed of new boats on passage westward: nine U-boats, all with inexperienced captains. On 13 July, 600 miles west of Ireland, the northern flank of this group found a convoy, but soon lost it again;

For the next three days the U-boats saw nothing but empty seas.[33]

B-Dienst, however, came to the rescue with information of a westbound convoy on 22 July, and this was duly intercepted by *U 552* on 24 July. It was ON 113, thirty-three ships escorted by Group C2, consisting of two Town Class destroyers (the 'four-stackers'), HMS *Burnham* and HMCS *St Croix*, with three RCN corvettes and one RN (*Polyanthus*). The SOE was Acting Captain T. Taylor RN, Commanding Officer of *Burnham*. It says much for Rodger Winn's 'Working Fiction' (and no doubt for the D/F plotting that informed it) that Taylor received an Admiralty warning of U-boats presence on the same day that the convoy was intercepted – in all probability from *U 552*'s sighting signal. The two destroyers immediately took up screening positions ten miles ahead of the convoy and very shortly *St Croix* (Lieut.-Commander A. H. Dobson RCNR) observed two U-boats on the surface. The Canadian destroyer pursued one of these, which dived some 6,000 yards ahead, well outside ASDIC range, giving the U-boat an excellent chance of escape. Lieut.-Commander Dobson, however, knew his business; he guessed the U-boat's movements correctly, found her and held her in ASDIC contact. Three depth-charge attacks produced oil and wreckage, but Dobson was not satisfied; he knew that it was normal for hard-pressed U-boats to discharge suitable débris through their torpedo tubes to mislead their pursuers. This hunter was not to be fooled in that manner; he ran in again over the point of last contact and dropped another pattern of charges, with results that could not be mistaken:

Over the place of the explosion, gathering slowly from the depths beneath, was a nasty, oily litter of timber, clothing, pocket books, cigarettes, food packages and bits of human flesh which immediately attracted the attention of the wheeling gulls. *St Croix* triumphantly gathered her grisly remnants, which were later found to include a once-filmy brassière labelled 'Triumph, Paris'.[34]

The U-boat was *U 90*; she was the RCN's second kill of the war.

The pack, however, remained with the convoy. During the night, obedient to instructions from the (American) shore authorities, ON 113 performed the unusual manoeuvre of a complete circle, but this did not save her from the loss of three ships. Lacking both HF/DF and 271M radar, there was not a great deal the escorts could do about it. Fog and generally deteriorating weather finally caused the U-boats to break off their attacks; one more ship was lost from ON 113, but this was not attributable to the *Wolf* Group – it was the work of an independent U-boat operating in Canadian waters, which attacked after the change of escort. C2 could claim honours even, the Germans attributing their lack of important success to the weather, to the strength of the escort (!), to the convoy's 'movements', and to the inexperience of the new captains. This last reason is by far the most convincing. On the Allied side, the order which caused the convoy to circle in mid-Atlantic understandably gave rise to further questions about the anomalies of the Atlantic command system.[35]

U-boat packs formed, fought, dissolved and disappeared into history; the ON 113 battle was not, however, the last fling of the *Wolf* Group. ON 115 was still in Irish waters and under the Coastal Command 'umbrella' on 26 July. Its escort was C3, consisting of two destroyers, *Saguenay* (Acting Commander D. C. Wallace RCNR, who was also SOE) and *Skeena*, with five RCN corvettes – among them *Wetaskiwin*, still under her regular RCN CO, Lieut.-Commander Guy Windeyer (see p. 350). C3 has been called 'the most stable and most successful of the C groups during 1942';[36] the two destroyers with *Wetaskiwin*, *Galt* and *Sackville* had been together for three months (which rated as a long time at that stage of the war), and these three corvettes were all Prentice-trained as a unit. Once again, there was no HF/DF and no 271M radar – lacks which would be severely felt. What C3 did have was medium-frequency (MF)/DF, using the commercial wavelength, monitored by a 'guard ship' – in this case the Commodore's vessel. It was from this source that Wallace on the 26th, having already ordered a 90° turn to starboard, received a U-boat bearing astern which took him off on a 30-mile search behind the convoy; it came to nothing, but marked the beginning of a nine-day ordeal for ON 115.

The following days were punctuated by MF/DF interceptions which led to a great deal of fruitless search activity, but on 31 July it was rewarded, thanks to admirable cooperation between two professionals, Lieut.-Commander K. L. Dyer RCN, of *Skeena*, and Windeyer. It was symptomatic of the professionalism that Windeyer, although the senior of the two, deferred to Dyer in the better-equipped destroyer as director of the U-boat hunt that began in the early hours of that morning. The signal exchange between *Skeena* and *Westaskiwin* is characteristic; as not infrequently happened at that time, it started with Bible references:

Skeena to *Wetaskiwin*: Acts xvi 9.[37]

This supplied the text:

And a vision appeared to Paul in the night; there stood a man of Macedonia and prayed him saying, come over into Macedonia and help us.

Windeyer replied:

Revelations xiii verse 1.

The meaning of that was:

And I stood upon the sand of the sea and saw a beast rise up out of the sea having seven heads and ten horns, and upon his horns ten crowns, and upon his heads the name of blasphemy.

It was an exaggeration, of course, in the cause of good entertainment; the 'beast' had not yet risen, but when it did the tone of the signals became very different:

Wetaskiwin:	You direct hunt. Give me my station and course.
Skeena:	Take station on my port beam; one mile, course 228°.
Skeena:	Turn 180° to port together.

Skeena:	Course 070°.
Skeena:	I am over my last contact. Now start square search from here.
Wetaskiwin:	Contact bearing 260°, 1,900 yards.
Wetaskiwin:	Contact is firm.
Wetaskiwin:	Contact bearing 280°, 600 yards.
Skeena:	Contact bearing 040°, 800 yards.
Skeena:	Contact bearing 070°, 1,400 yards.
Skeena:	Non sub.

[*Skeena* had been led astray by a false echo.]

Wetaskiwin:	Contact bearing 200°, 1,300 yards.
Wetaskiwin:	Attacking.

[*Wetaskiwin* dropped a pattern of depth charges.]

Wetaskiwin:	Lost contact at 600 yards.
Wetaskiwin:	By my plot you are over sub.
Wetaskiwin:	Contact bearing 210°, 1,900 yards.
Skeena:	Contact bearing 345°, 1,600 yards.
Skeena:	Attacking. Please keep to port.

[*Skeena* dropped a pattern of depth charges.]

Wetaskiwin:	Confirmed right spot.
Wetaskiwin:	Contact bearing 300°, 1,000 yards.
Wetaskiwin:	Attacking.

[*Wetaskiwin* dropped a pattern of depth charges.]

Wetaskiwin:	Lost echo.
Skeena:	Echo bearing 120°, 700 yards.
Wetaskiwin:	O.K. Let me do an attack now.
Skeena:	Unable to gain contact.
Wetaskiwin:	I will try to help you by directing.

[*Skeena* dropped a pattern of depth charges with settings changed from 350 feet to 550 feet.]

Wetaskiwin:	Excellent.
Skeena:	Did you hear that underwater explosion?
Wetaskiwin:	Yes. Definitely.
Skeena:	Your turn.
Wetaskiwin:	Plenty of wreckage over this way.
Skeena:	I am lowering a whaler to pick up the guts.
Skeena:	(General Signal): U-boat considered sunk by HMCS *Wetaskiwin* and HMCS *Skeena*. Floating wreckage and human remains recovered.

Such, highly compressed and intermittently accompanied by the thunder of depth charges exploding, was the audible record of a hunt which, in this case, lasted for five hours and led to the destruction of *U558*.

Thereafter, however, things did not go so well with ON 115. The following day both destroyers and *Wetaskiwin* were forced to leave the convoy and return to Newfoundland through lack of fuel – exhausted in their long chases. The half-dozen U-boats which had been shadowing them were now formed into a group (*Pirat*) across the course of ON 115. Before it could achieve anything, a Royal Navy and an RCN destroyer with an RCN corvette joined as replacements, but the cohesion of C3 was lost. On 3 August the corvette *Sackville* had a series of excitements and frustrations. A well-placed depth charge pattern brought *U 43* to the surface,

> breaching like a great whale, with a third of her hull pointing skywards at an angle of forty-five degrees. As the submarine hung momentarily, suspended by her momentum, a depth charge exploded under her keel and she then plunged into the sea, surrounded by a huge column of water.[38]

This looked like indubitable destruction – but *U 43* survived and returned to base. *Sackville* encountered two more U-boats within a few hours, hitting the second at the base of the conning tower with a 4-inch shell just as she dived – yet this boat, too, survived. Meanwhile the *Wolf* pack had arrived from further south, and *U 552* had sunk a merchantman, shortly followed by two more sunk by *U 553*. Further loss was only avoided by the onset of heavy fog on the Grand Banks. Thus the score stood at three merchant ships lost at a cost of one U-boat sunk and two more damaged: not at all a bad result. However, the ON 115 story did not please the hard taskmasters at Western Approaches. Commander Howard-Johnston's report said:

> This is an example of reckless expenditure of fuel and disregard of the object which must always include 'timely arrival'. The timely arrival was ignored to an exceptional degree [eventually] reducing the protection given by the escorts. The success achieved against the enemy in destroying a U-boat should not be allowed to cover up this basic failure. . . . I find in this story the ignorance of inexperienced officers who think that they are being offensive by acting in a reckless manner and without real consideration of their obligation to protect the convoy throughout the period it is entrusted to them.[39]

This judgment sounds harsh in the light of C3's anti-U-boat perform-ance, but clearly the RCN/USN preoccupation with offensive sweeps was now not at all acceptable to Western Approaches. More sympa-thetic was the recognition of the serious equipment deficiencies in the Canadian ships, HF/DF and modern radar; the Radar Officer at Derby House observed that

> *Sackville*'s two [sic] U-boats would have been a gift if she had been fitted with RDF type 271.

Thus began the final U-boat campaign to win mastery of the North Atlantic trade routes. Effectively it would last for eleven months and it is salutary to be reminded that, during that time, despite the *Enigma* blackout, out of 174 scheduled North Atlantic convoys, 105 (60.3%) were successfully re-routed and were never even sighted by the U-boats.

> Of the 69 ... which were partly located by the waiting U-boats ac-cording to plan and partly sighted by chance, 23 escaped without loss, 40 sustained minor losses, sometimes only stragglers. *Only 16 of the convoys lost more than four ships.*[40]

This startling calculation tells us how narrow the margin was between survival and disaster; if serious damage to only sixteen convoys could produce the acute crisis which later ensued, one can only speculate with dread about the likely effect of similar results in, say, only another sixteen. One sees again the force of Dönitz's haunting recollection of lost time in 1941, and the 300 ships that got away.

*   *   *   *   *

'The men who fought the Battle of the Atlantic,' says Cajus Bekker, 'asked little quarter and gave none.'[41] This is not entirely true; the Allied navies did not leave German submariners to drown except in very rare circumstances (like imminent risk of attack by another U-boat). But the search for pieces of human beings floating in the sea after a kill, 'picking up the guts', in order to satisfy the de-briefing officer, was a coarsening procedure, excused by the savage satisfac-tion of the kill itself after seeing too often what the effect of a U-boat attack could be.

Schrecklichkeit (see pp. 44–5) was never absent from U-boat and anti-

U-boat warfare by the very nature of the beast. One writes easily of a 'kill'; to form a real idea of the event that produced the lumps of flesh in the sea defeats imagination. There are no words to describe the violence of those underwater convulsions – words are mere palliatives. Indeed, all the conditions of the final moments of submarines, whether their crews die by the 'ordinary' processes of suffocation, by gas poisoning, or by lungs imploding under the pressure of the deeps, are unimaginable. A quick death was all that one could hope for – but we shall never know what the chances were of that when ruin reached the boat, nor how many times the agonies of destruction were long-drawn-out.

The fate of merchant seamen and escort crews under the harsh rule of *Schrecklichkeit* was visible and audible, but still at the very edge of understanding. On 3 January Hitler had discussed the war situation with the Japanese Ambassador, Baron Oshima; he spoke of the Atlantic battle and the task of the U-boats, and referred to American shipbuilding capacity. However many ships they built, he said, they would have a problem in finding crews:

> For that reason, merchant shipping will be sunk without warning with the intention of killing as many of the crew as possible. Once it gets around that most of the seamen are lost in the sinkings, the Americans will have great difficulty in enlisting new people. The training of sea-going personnel takes a long time. We are fighting for our existence and cannot therefore take a humanitarian viewpoint. For this reason I must give the order that since foreign seamen cannot be taken prisoner, and in most cases this is not possible on the open sea, the U-boats are to surface after torpedoing and shoot up the lifeboats.[42]

Dönitz did not demur; as we have seen (p. 218), already by November, 1939 he was telling his crews, 'We must be hard in this war.' He did not change his mind; never did he suppose that this form of warfare could be anything but 'unrestricted', and that word he took to mean exactly what it said. Certainly he agreed with Hitler's prescription for attack on merchant crews (as distinct from merchant ships); in May, 1942, referring to the need for a non-contact torpedo pistol, he remarked that this device 'will above all accelerate the sinking of torpedoed ships', with

> the great advantage that in consequence of the very rapid sinking of the

467

torpedoed ship the crew will no longer be able to be rescued. This greater loss of ships' crews will doubtless aggravate the manning difficulties for the great American building programme.[43]

There was a clear difference here but it was a small one: Hitler had spoken of shooting up the lifeboats, and Dönitz did not. This is not a matter that need long detain or puzzle us. Direct orders to commit atrocities are not frequently to be found; even the Nazis tended to clothe their outrages in emollient phrases – 'Final Solution', for example, meaning the Jewish holocaust – and even on the atrocious Eastern Front the responsibility for appalling deeds is usually screened by smooth or confusing words. To avoid brutalities in submarine warfare, very clear and firm orders are required, and also a consensus founded upon long tradition. None of these guidelines existed for the U-boats; in both wars, the decisions thus rested with the young captains, generally acting under stress, and now imbued with National Socialism, and the outcome would depend on their personal characters. Thus, in their 'massacre of shipping' on the American coast, says Dr Morison,

> Although they invariably attacked without warning, they commonly gave the crew a chance to get away before opening gunfire, and refrained from machine-gunning survivors in lifeboats, as had been done freely in the early part of the war.

Yet he adds in a footnote: 'There were many exceptions to this rule, however.'[44]

As regards the convoys, while shooting up of boats or rafts or men swimming in the water did occur, printing itself indelibly on the memories of those who had endured it, this was not the 'normal' hazard, and the truth about death in a convoy battle was that the 'normal' hazards were fully bad enough. What gave these losses their particular poignancy was the horrifying circumstances with which they were usually attended. An ore-ship, or a freighter laden with steel, could at one moment be sailing in station through the night, and the next there would be a terrifying explosion, the ship's back would be broken and she would sink instantly, taking her whole company with her; the horror lay in the suddenness and completeness of such a disaster – yet such swift deaths were merciful. They were preferable, certainly, to

468

being roasted alive in the blazing oil of a torpedoed tanker, or the alternatives of freezing to death or starving in open boats in mid-Atlantic. The quick numbing and swift death of a man alone in the icy waters of the Arctic was undoubtedly a mercy by such comparisons.

Robert Harling, a representative of the more reflective type of RNVR officer often to be found in corvettes, recalling a bad night in the London 'Blitz' and the somewhat nauseous 'shibboleths of the "purification through suffering" school of thought', remarked:

We never saw signs of spiritual grandeur upon the brows of broken seamen we helped from petrol-blazing seas. . . . German citizens suffered bombings as firmly as British; presumably they, too, by these same tokens, gained in spiritual grandeur, but I never heard this theory given credence.[45]

Nicholas Monsarrat noted the hardening that came with experience, with a second year of war in the Atlantic:

Yes, it's all the same now; the job is standardized; survivors are even wounded in the same way, and all corpses are alike.[46]

Yet this was not true, as he admits. The day came when his ship was detailed to search for survivors of a destroyer that had been torpedoed the night before. In all their minds was the thought

that not very far away, but out of effective reach, a virtual duplicate of our own ship's company, with the same trustworthy hands and humourists and rogues, was perishing man by man.[47]

It made a difference. In due course they found the raft they were looking for, 'an unforgettable picture':

Upright on it sat a handful of black-faced, oil-soaked men, surrounded by prone figures, sprawling in the lazy attitudes of the dead. One man, who raised a feeble arm in greeting as we came alongside, had a shipmate's head pillowed in his lap, his hand resting on the staring face with a cherishing touch which told the night's story in a single gesture. Another, whose filthy face split into a grin as we reached down for him, must have been in agony from his shattered leg. Of the others, some stared up at the ship as at a miracle: one might have been singing but,

469

heard close to, was in fact groaning softly: all were in an extremity of cold.

We set to work as carefully as we could, putting into our handling of them the overflow of compassion which the past night and the present sight of them called forth.

And then they brought the dead on board:

We had to rig a tackle for the dead men; their bodies dangled like hung criminals as they were hoisted up, their heads fell forwards and sideways and forwards again in a cycle of supreme ugliness. The hands detailed for the job had faces of stone as they worked the tackle. These men were themselves.

No, all corpses were *not* alike.

Robert Harling had a point; his reference to German civilians under bombing was taking on a new significance in 1942, which did not go unnoticed by the U-boat captains and their crews. Until this year, despite all its eagerness, its faith in the air offensive and the determination with which it pursued that task, Bomber Command had achieved little more than pin-pricks against the German war economy. Under the vigorous driving hand of Air Chief Marshal Harris, 1942 saw a significant change. This was the year of the 'thousand-bomber raids', the first of them, code-named MILLENIUM, delivered by 1,046 aircraft against Cologne on 30/31 May, followed by the attack on Essen by 956 aircraft two nights later, and a third, against Bremen, by 1,003 aircraft on 25/26 June. These were only the highlights of a campaign against German cities which included such shocks as the destructive fire attacks on Lübeck (March) and Rostock (April); it was a swelling theme. Neither the lasting damage done nor the casualties inflicted matched Bomber Command's claims, but U-boat men on leave could see with their own eyes that the Fatherland was being hurt: city centres (especially the older ones with historic associations) demolished, whole streets gone, houses – perhaps their own parents' homes – reduced to rubble. The next convoy at the end of their torpedo tubes would feel the force of their anger. And talk of 'morality' would have a strange ring.

It will be conveneint to take this account of the beastliness of U-boat warfare, and *Schrecklichkeit*, a little further into the year, and look briefly at an occurrence which held much ironic curiosity, and became a *cause célèbre* with loud reverberations at the War Crimes Trial at Nuremberg in 1945–46. In the second half of August, 1942, pursuant to his strategy of surprise diversions, Dönitz sent a group of four large Type IXC U-boats with a 'milch cow' towards Cape Town. As far as latitude 5°S, they were permitted to attack whatever they pleased (barring only due economy of torpedoes); beyond that line they were to refrain from attacking shipping, in order to preserve surprise when they reached the 'virgin' Cape Town area. On 12 September, at about 2000 hours, just south of the Equator, *U 156* (Hartenstein) torpedoed the 19,659-ton troopship *Laconia*, an armed White Star liner, homeward-bound.

It turned out that the *Laconia* was carrying, besides a crew of 436, 268 British Service personnel (including eighty women and children), 160 Polish ex-prisoners-of-war, and 1,800 captured Italians. Hartenstein became aware of this fact when he heard cries for help in Italian coming from the water. He reported what had happened, and requested instructions. Dönitz, in a passage that smacks of defence pleading in the Nuremberg court-room, says in his Memoirs:

> On receipt of this signal I decided to contravene one of the principles of maritime warfare accepted by all nations. This lays down that the exigencies of action take precedence over all rescue operations. Rescue work is undertaken only provided that it does not interfere with a warship's task. I know of no case in which the British or the American Navy have acted otherwise than in accordance with this principle.[48]

Hartenstein, to his credit, had already started the rescue work, and later that night he told Dönitz that he had 193 people on board, twenty-one of them British. Such a number could not fail to make operational difficulties for the U-boat, contrary to Dönitz's instructions. At 0400 Hartenstein broadcast a message in English, saying that providing he was not attacked he would not interfere with any ship that came to join in the rescue work. The *Laconia* herself had twice signalled her torpedoing just before she went down; it appears that no British ship or station received these messages, but Hartenstein's was received in Freetown, where it was regarded as a trap to lure other ships into a U-boat ambush. Dönitz, meanwhile, had ordered two more U-boats, *U 506* and *U 507*, to take part in the rescue, as well as an Italian submarine (*Cappellini*), and had requested the Vichy French at Dakar to send ships to lend further help.

All through the 13th and 14th Hartenstein continued with rescue work as best he could, collecting survivors on to rafts and lifeboats; on 15 September *U506* and *U507* joined, and the next day the Italian also arrived. *U156* was able to effect a redistribution of the rescued which left her with fifty-five Italians and fifty-five British (including five women). Some of these, on 16 September, were below, many were on the U-boat's deck, others in lifeboats which she had in tow. At 0925, a four-engined aircraft with American markings appeared, and Hartenstein at once displayed a large Red Cross flag, draped over the forward gun. He also tried to communicate by signal lamp with the aircraft, but without result. He recognized it as a B-24, correctly; it was, in fact, a patrolling B-24D of the 343rd Bombardment Squadron from the newly-opened and highly secret American air base called Wideawake Field on Ascension Island,[49] piloted by Lieutenant James D. Harden.

Harden and his crew took in all the details of the scene below, which was clearly quite out of the ordinary, and difficult to resolve. The pilot therefore turned away, flew off southward, and called up Wideawake for fresh instructions. The senior Air officer at Wideawake was Colonel James A. Ronin USAAF, and the operational air commander was Captain Robert C. Richardson. Harden's question, what to do next, put them both in the 'hot seat':

It could be answered in only one of two ways: return to base or attack . . . Richardson carefully weighed the alternatives. . . . If he ordered Harden to come in, he not only would jeopardize the safety of British ships but would leave the submarine free to continue its destruction of Allied shipping. Further, such an order would mean abandoning an important and legitimate military mission that had a chance of successful accomplishment. On the other hand, an order to attack would place in jeopardy the lives of some of the survivors. Harden had to have an answer soon. He could not remain in the area much longer and still have enough fuel to get back to Ascension. After conferring with Ronin, Richardson issued the order: 'Sink sub'.[50]

When Harden returned to *U156*, it appeared to him that 'lifeboats had moved away from the sub'. In his first pass he dropped three depth charges, claiming that one of these was only ten feet from the U-boat; in three more passes, the bombs [sic] failed to fall; finally, he reported:

Two bombs were dropped one on either side, not more than 15 to 20 feet away. The sub rolled over and was last seen bottom up. Crew had abandoned sub and taken to surrounding boats.

It is to be noted that Harden and his entire crew were flying their first combat mission, which goes far to account for the amazing errors of his report. Hartenstein's log, composed at the receiving end, tells a very different tale; his only important mistake was in believing that it was a second aircraft that was attacking him:

Dropped two bombs about three seconds apart. While four lifeboats in tow were being cast off, the aircraft dropped one bomb in their midst. One boat capsized. Aircraft cruised around for a short time and then dropped a fourth bomb 2,–3,000 metres away. Realized that his bomb-racks were empty. Another run. Two bombs. One exploded, with a few seconds delayed action, directly under the control room. Conning tower vanished in a tower of black water. Control room and bow compartment reported taking water. All hands ordered to don life jackets. Ordered all British off the boat. Batteries began giving off gas. Italians also ordered off (had no escape gear to give them).

Survivors confirmed that a lifeboat had been destroyed by a depth charge, drowning all aboard her (Italian prisoners); they also confirmed that damage had been done to the U-boat. This was perfectly true, but Harden was credited with a kill, which was not true. He and his inexperienced crew had obviously mistaken the capsized lifeboat for a 'bottom up' U-boat. The next day Harden was out on patrol again and at 1030 his crew sighted a U-boat which the B-24 at once attacked; on the first pass, with the submarine's decks already awash, the bombs (or depth charges) again failed to release; a second pass, only 45 seconds later, succeeded in placing two bombs and two charges very close, and an oil slick appeared. The Americans were all convinced that they had sunk another U-boat and congratulated themselves accordingly. But they were wrong; this was *U507*, with over 100 survivors aboard. At 1903 that night she informed Dönitz that she had met the Vichy sloop *Annamite* and transferred the rescued people to her; she also reported the whereabouts of two groups of lifeboats, which she had already notified to the French cruiser *Gloire*. Altogether, well over a thousand people, British, Poles and Italians, were rescued from the sinking of the *Laconia*, largely due to the prompt efforts of *Korvettenkapitän*

473

Werner Hartenstein. No doubt his action had been prompted entirely by hearing the voices of his Italian allies in the sea, but his work was no less well done for that.

By the 17th Dönitz, thoroughly alarmed by what had happened to *U156*, was becoming very unenthusiastic about the whole operation. At 0151 he signalled to *U506* and *U507*:

> Boats will at all times be kept in instant readiness to dive and must retain at all times full powers of under-water action. You will therefore transfer to the lifeboats any survivors you have aboard. Only Italians may be retained aboard your boats. . . . Beware of enemy counter measures, both from the air and by submarines.[51]

And later that day he followed this up with:

> Do not hoist Red Cross flag, since (i) that is not a recognized international procedure; (ii) it will not in any case, and most certainly not as far as the British are concerned, afford any protection.

But his most important signal of 17 September, which was flung back at him at Nuremberg, was at 2100, addressed to all Commanding Officers; as recorded in the War Diary it said:

> All attempts to rescue members of ships sunk, therefore also fishing out swimmers and putting them into lifeboats, righting capsized lifeboats, handing out provisions and water, have to cease. *Rescue contradicts the most fundamental demands of war for the annihilation of enemy ships and crews.*
> 2: Orders for bringing back Captains and Chief Engineers (issued previously) remain in force.
> 3. Only save shipwrecked survivors if [their] statements are of importance for the boat.
> 4. Be hard. Think of the fact that the enemy in his bombing attacks on German towns has no regard for women and children.[52]

The italics are mine; that sentence is the core of what became notorious as the '*Laconia* Order', and contributed to the imposition of the sentence that took Dönitz to prison for ten years. It might have done him even greater harm, but for the fact that at Nuremberg

Fleet Admiral Chester W. Nimitz testified that in the war with Japan the US Navy had followed the same general policy as was set forth in the German admiral's directive.[53]

The *Laconia* story is blurred at every edge; if there is any moral at all to be extracted from it, it would seem to be only a repetition, once again, of Admiral Fisher's perception in 1913 (already quoted more than once) to the effect that submarine warfare

is acknowledged to be an altogether barbarous method ... (but) the essence of war is violence, and moderation in war is imbecility.

Sometimes, however, it is impossible to withhold admiration from imbecility; in a rough and angry time, the name of Hartenstein must evoke respect. There would be very little more of the behaviour that distinguished him during this difficult incident. Cruelties, brutalities, *Schrecklichkeit* in some degree or other, would continue to be running themes of the U-boat war, too commonplace to mention.

* * * * *

On 21 July Churchill composed one of his periodical reviews of the war; his particular concern in this memorandum was seaborne tonnage, and he drew attention to the fact that nearly three-quarters of British-controlled shipping was at that stage 'primarily employed on the war effort, and only one-quarter is exclusively engaged in feeding and supplying this Island'.[54] From this he drew the conclusion:

It might be true to say that the issue of the war depends on whether Hitler's U-boat attack on Allied tonnage or the increase and application of Allied air-power reach their full fruition first.

Dönitz, from the opposite standpoint, would not have disagreed with him. When Churchill spoke of 'the application of Allied air-power', what he chiefly meant was the air offensive against Germany; what Dönitz was thinking about was the intervention of air power against the U-boats, a factor which preyed increasingly on his mind. On the day before Churchill drafted his paper, Dönitz was apprehensively noting in his War Diary the extending range of Allied land-based aircraft which, he said, has made the operation of boats very much more difficult, in some cases no longer worthwhile. This worsening of the operational situation must, if continued, lead to insupportable losses, to a decline in successes and so to a decline in the prospects of success of the U-boat war as a whole.[55]

This was a sobering thought, reinforced by the experience of August. The *Steinbrink* Group fought a hard battle between the 5–10th of that month in the seasonal fog that shrouded the Grand Banks. Its target was SC 94, thirty-six ships escorted by Group C1 (mixed RN/RCN) consisting of the Canadian destroyer *Assiniboine* and six corvettes. The Canadian ships were, as usual, badly hampered by lack of HF/DF and 271M radar; three of the corvettes, however, being RN, did possess the latter. Fog dominated the first phase of the battle; it prevented air escort, despite the proximity of airfields, and multiplied the confusions which normally characterized convoy actions. Thus, an alteration of course in the night of 5 August had to be signalled by siren, which was not heard on the port side of the convoy, with the result that six ships and two escorts became detached. Not until the following afternoon was this noticed, and while the missing ships were being rounded up the U-boats struck their first blow; *U 593*, the boat which had sighted the convoy, attacked at once and was rewarded with a sinking.

It was on the 6th, however, that HMCS *Assiniboine* chalked up another success for the RCN, after a running fight in and out of the fog against *U 210*. The unusual feature of this was that it was a gun-fight, the U-boat remaining surfaced to engage the destroyer, which stayed too close for it to hold a steady diving course. This was not the way that U-boats were intended to engage warships, but *U 210* made a good showing; her 40-mm cannon ignited some petrol drums stored outside the destroyer's wheelhouse, causing a dangerous fire on the starboard side. Inside the wheelhouse was *Assiniboine*'s coxswain, Chief Petty Officer Max L. Bernays, who promptly ordered his helmsman and telegraphman outside to help put out the blaze:

Then locking himself in the wheelhouse, with the full knowledge that he would never get out alive if the fire was not subdued, and with incendiary shells spattering the bulkheads about him and throwing splinters in his face, he proceeded to carry out faultlessly the 141 helm and engine room orders which were necessary during the wild chase.[56]

476

In the event, having killed the U-boat's captain (Lemcke) with a 4.7-in. direct hit on the conning tower, and rammed her twice, *Assiniboine* finally sent her to the bottom with another shell. The price to be paid, however, was the damage done to the destroyer by the ramming, which buckled her bows, and the fire. *Assiniboine* had to turn immediately for home, leaving the convoy escort without a destroyer.

By good luck, good handling and the use of 271M radar, the corvettes kept *Steinbrink* Group at bay throughout the next day. At 1325 on 8 August, however, the pack attacked using a new tactic: two boats, *U 176* and *U 379*, came in together, submerged and in broad daylight, and very quickly sank five ships. In the ensuing alarm and confusion, the crews of three more merchantmen abandoned ship, under the impression that they too, had been torpedoed. Two crews were persuaded to return to their ships, but the crew of the third, SS *Radchurch*, flatly refused to do so; although unharmed, she had to be abandoned by the convoy, and was duly sunk by *U 176*.[57] The U-boat successes on the 8th were not to pass unblemished; as daylight was fading, the RN corvette *Dianthus*, Lieutenant-Commander C. E. Bridgeman RNR, observed two U-boats at a range of six miles. She opened fire, forcing the U-boats to dive, and *Dianthus* began an ASDIC search which produced no result, but after dark a keen-eyed signalman with night glasses observed a dark object on the surface which proved to be *U 379* (Kettner). She dived again at once, but an accurate depth charge attack brought her to the surface once more. Four times *Dianthus* rammed the U-boat, and soon after midnight *U 379* finally went down, leaving some of her crew swimming in the dark water. *Dianthus* herself was now badly damaged, down by the bow with fore compartments flooded. As Dönitz said, 'the exigencies of action take precedence over all rescue operations'. *Dianthus* was only able to take five of the U-boat men aboard, but she launched a Carley raft for the rest before rejoining the convoy, where she took position among the merchantmen, being no longer capable of battle.

Two fresh destroyers joined SC 94 on that night and the next day, and on the 9th

At midday there came the heartening sight of the first of the Liberator aircraft which were thereafter intermittently to accompany and escort the convoy.[58]

On the morning of the 10th, however, there were no aircraft present, due to the variable weather conditions, and Group *Steinbrink* launched another simultaneous submerged daylight attack at 1022 hours. *U 348* and *U 660* succeeded in sinking a further four ships – but these were parting shots. In the afternoon the Liberators reappeared, and from then onwards air escort was virtually continuous, and surface escort also reinforced. So the final score stood at eleven ships lost, while out of some eighteen U-boats assembled to attack the convoy, two had been sunk and at least two more damaged, but to what degree is uncertain. SC 94 had suffered a loss of over 30%, yet there was no criticism of C1 this time. Indeed, taking into account the weakness of the escort group (the lack of a second destroyer was noticeable) and its want of modern equipment, it is difficult to see what there was to criticize. Milner remarks:

> The only stern comments to arise from the battle actually came from naval engineers in Britain and Canada who despaired that, with all their modern weaponry, escorts were still reduced to bludgeoning the enemy to death with their bows.[59]

From the U-boat point of view, there was food for thought in the fact that only five out of eighteen boats had actually done any damage to the convoy, one of these being lost in the process. Dilution was taking its toll.

For Dönitz the chief food for thought in this period was the ever-increasing presence of aircraft. He noted with apprehension the appearance of what he called 'especially long-range types'[60] as convoy escorts; the frustration of the *Vorwärts* Group, after a promising start on 31 August against SC 97, sinking two ships in a submerged attack, when USN Catalinas arrived next day from Iceland, drew him to the gloomiest conclusions. He wrote on 3 September:

> By systematically forcing the boats under water [air cover] made them lose contact at evening twilight, thus spoiling the best prospects for attack of all boats in the first four moonless hours of the night. . . . The convoy operation had to be broken off in the morning of 2.9 as it no longer seemed possible for boats to haul ahead in face of the expected heavy enemy air activity . . . by increasing the range of their aircraft the English have succeeded in gaining air control over a great part of the

North Atlantic with land-based planes and narrowing the area in which U-boats can operate without threat from the air.[61]

The perceptible steady closing of the 'Atlantic Gap' (see p. 345) was only one of Dönitz's preoccupations; he wrote on 21 August:

> the numerical strengthening of enemy flights, the appearance of a wide variety of aircraft types equipped with an excellent location device against U-boats have made U-boat operations in the eastern Atlantic more difficult.... The enemy daily reconnaissance extends almost as far as 20°W and has forced a movement of U-boat dispositions far into the middle of the Atlantic since a discovery of the dispositions would lead to convoys being re-routed around them.[62]

Dönitz's 'biggest headache', says Rohwer, 'was the system of radar location now being increasingly used by air patrols.'[63] This was, of course, ASV II, now being used, as we have seen, in conjunction with the Leigh Light. In the Bay of Biscay he had hoped to counter this in daylight by improved long-range air cover for the U-boats by Ju 88Cs, but Coastal Command was now meeting these with Beaufighters, which were very much superior for combat purposes.[64] Far more effective against the Leigh Light/ASV II combination was a device which made its appearance in mid-September, following the fortunate capture of an ASV II set in a Hudson which crashed in Tunisia in April. The new equipment was known as *Metox*, so named after one of the French firms which produced it. It was, quite simply, a receiver capable of picking up radar transmissions on any frequency in the band 113–500 megacycles, which amply covered ASV II. *Metox* was able to receive the radar signals at a distance of 30 miles, which was twice the effective range of the radar itself, thus giving the U-boat plenty of time to dive. Because of its cross-shaped wooden frame, the *Metox* aerial was known as the *Biscayakreuz* ('Biscay Cross'), and by the beginning of October every U-boat carried it. The result was a very marked falling-off of night sightings in the Bay. Such was the eternal pattern of the technological war, with advantages swinging rhythmically from side to side.

Two further possibilities of combating the growth of allied air power were explored. The first was to increase the anti-aircraft armament of the U-boats to the point where it would no longer be cost-effective to attack them. In retrospect, this expedient looks very far-fetched; a

U-boat, by comparison with even a four-engined aircraft, was a large, complicated object, full of sophisticated machinery and weaponry, and carrying crews of forty-four officers and ratings (Type VII) or forty-eight (Type IX). If we take the crew as a yardstick, an 'economic' exchange rate would require the shooting down of at least three and a half Sunderlands or five Liberators or seven Wellingtons or ten Hudsons per U-boat lost; this was asking a lot. Yet now Dönitz was ordering the installation of a second platform behind the conning tower to carry twin 20-mm AA guns (whose rate of fire was 150 rounds a minute and effective range one mile), and in some cases up to four 7.9-mm machine guns as well; the pressure hulls were strengthened, and bridges armour-plated against the coming battle. To one problem there was no solution, as Dönitz knew:

> when the boat submerged the guns remained where they were, and while she remained submerged were exposed to the danger of corrosion by sea water.[65]

It was, nevertheless, no joke to engage these heavily armed U-boats, even if the dice were, ultimately, loaded against them – as a Wellington of No. 311 (Czech) Squadron discovered on 7 September; her report stated:

> Attacked a U-boat which was fully surfaced. Our aircraft dived to attack from a height of 1,200 feet. U-boat opened fire with cannon and machine gun and our aircraft was hit in the fuselage. Most members of crew injured. The captain, however, pressed the attack home, and the six depth charges, dropped from seventy feet, straddled the conning tower. Our crew were unable to determine number each side of conning tower owing to their injuries. Rear-gunner observed the U-boat lift bodily in depth-charge explosions. Rear-gunner fired approximately 400 rounds, and observed tracers hit the conning tower. U-boat dived slowly, and submerged one minute after depth-charge attack. Owing to injuries to the crew the captain left the scene of the attack at once, climbed to 500 feet and set course for base. Crash-landed at St Eval, owing to failure of hydraulics. Navigator seriously injured in both legs, front-gunner small finger of left hand shot away, wireless operator splinter wounds in right arm, second pilot splinter wounds in leg.[66]

Such encounters were to continue, against steadily increasing AA armament on the U-boats, for many months; Dönitz and his men did not give in easily.

The second means of disputing Allied air superiority was obvious enough – if it was practicable: to meet the Allied VLR aircraft with German equivalents, and fight it out at long range. Once more Dönitz made a plea for He 177s, and for a short time it looked as though he might actually get them, but the promise was never fulfilled. He also urged, in a memorandum to Raeder on 3 September, the need 'for the development of a powerfully armed aircraft with a great radius of action, to help us in the Battle of the Atlantic in the more distant areas beyond the reach of the He 177'.[67] Raeder forwarded this request to *Luftwaffe* Headquarters, and was told:

> Desirable as the possession of such an aircraft undoubtedly is, we have not, at present, the necessary technical data from which it could be developed.

It was one more example of the uselessness of Göring as an economic overlord. Dönitz commented:

> The fact was that deficiencies in developments which should have been initiated in peace time, had our strategic thinking been logical, could not be made good in the midst of war.

By contrast, the outstanding Allied aircraft that Dönitz was hoping to outfight was the Liberator (B-24), so much prized by Coastal Command. This admirable machine was designed to a USAAF specification for a heavy bomber in 1939, and the prototype made its maiden flight on 29 December of that year. For maritime purposes it required considerable modification, and in 1942 it was always in short supply. But at least it was *there* – and it is wonderful what a very small number could achieve.

Now deeply concerned about the air threat, Dönitz constantly explored all possibilities of strengthening the U-boats with new weapons. On 9 September he composed a paper on this subject in which he even touched upon a possible adaptation of the rockets being developed at the Research and Experimental station at Peenemünde (birthplace of the V-weapons) for U-boat use. He took the opportunity of restating his war philosophy in the current context:

The U-boat arm today completes the third year of uninterrupted battle missions. It has remained in all the changes of the war always the chief weapon in the sea war, in the first line on grounds of its battle characteristics which allow it, not only to hit the enemy successfully, but also to exist in the face of a superiority in numbers and strength. If all forces are not used in the *first line* in order to keep the battle strength of the U-boats in the highest possible condition, the danger is clear that one day the U-boat will be crushed and eliminated by the defence forces.

The German sea war direction will thereby have the only weapon which it can set effectively against the great sea powers struck from its hand.[68]

The reader will not miss the remarkable prophetic quality of this assessment in September, 1942; making all allowance for a somewhat opaque translation, and for the need to pitch his argument in strong terms, to recognize so clearly the prospect of the U-boats being 'crushed and eliminated' is realism of a very high degree. Convoy Commodores and Senior Officers of the escort groups would not have dared to use such language or think such thoughts at that stage of the war; no one, on either side, would have believed how swiftly Dönitz's prediction would be fulfilled.

*   *   *   *   *

The remorseless see-saw of advantage in battle was reflected in the U-boat quotients for the third quarter of the year:

July	181 tons
August	204 tons
September	149 tons.

By comparison with the dreadful first half-year, this quarter saw some easing of the convoy and trade war, though the totals of sinkings were still high:

	Tonnage Total	By Submarines
July	618,133	476,065
August	661,133	544,410
September	567,327	485,413
	1,846,593	1,505,888

Out of the total sunk by Axis submarines, the U-boats claimed 1,298,000 tons at a cost of thirty-two boats. Taking the short term view, Dönitz was not displeased:

> Our successes had been won thanks to the efficiency and the fighting spirit of our submarines, while fortune had frequently smiled, too, on the U-boat Command in its direction of operations.[69]

It was the long-term view that was disturbing; quite apart from the air menace, other factors were coming into play which Dönitz did not view with favour. On 16–17 August *U 507* (Schacht) sank five Brazilian ships just outside territorial waters, and five days later Brazil declared war on Germany and Italy. The act did not come as any kind of surprise, and he laid no blame on the U-boat captain, but Dönitz did not welcome this development:

> Although this altered nothing in our existing relationship with Brazil, which had already taken part in hostile acts against us, it was undoubtedly a mistake to have driven Brazil to an official declaration; politically we should have been well advised to avoid doing so.[70]

Driving Brazil out of neutrality (no matter how unfriendly) was, says Roskill,

> an outstanding example not only of the Germans' political ineptitude, but of their lack of strategic insight. It was of course true that, measured in terms of ships, aircraft and fighting men, Brazil's assistance to the Allied cause was comparatively small; but the enormous length of her coastline and the fact that it juts right out in the South Atlantic were of inestimably greater advantage to us than her material aid. The Allied shipping control organisation could now be extended almost to the great focal area off the River Plate, defence of which was always one of Britain's major anxieties. But an even greater advantage was the stronger strategic control of the whole South Atlantic gained from the use of Brazilian bases.[71]

The end of August saw another important Atlantic development north of the Equator. The American 'Interlocking System' of convoys, 'by which ships were run almost like trains'[72] through the whole coastal and open water zone from Trinidad to New York, was now completed.

483

It was a masterpiece of organization, founded upon two central ideas: first, that all northbound convoys must be timed to arrive at New York just before a transatlantic convoy was due to sail, and secondly that the two 'master' convoys feeding the transatlantic line were Key West to New York and return (KN–NK) and Guantanamo to New York and return (GN–NG):

> These two may be likened to express trains; the rest to local trains, feeding freight into two big southern termini, Key West and Guantanamo, on schedules so carefully worked out that lost shipping days were kept to a minimum. For, if a coastal convoy arrived a day late, ships destined for an express convoy would lie idle until the next one came through. The local convoys, run on ten-day intervals, usually met every other express convoy, since they were run on intervals of four or five days.

The first NG convoy sailed on 27 August, and the first NK on 28 August; the first KN convoy arrived at New York on 9 September, and the first GN on 12 September. At the same time, the termini of the transatlantic convoys were shifted from Halifax and Sydney to New York, which thus became the focal point of the whole North Atlantic convoy system. However, even so great a port as New York could not, as it turned out, cope with such a mass of shipping as this, and the slow SC–ONS convoy terminal returned to Halifax in March, 1943.

Despite the 'Working Fiction', the U-boats in August and September located twenty-one out of sixty-three convoys that sailed, and mounted strong attacks on seven of them, sinking forty-three ships. Fortunes (always much at the mercy of the Atlantic weather) varied: the *Lohs* Group of nine boats, attacking ONS 122 at the end of August, could only sink four merchant ships and had two U-boats damaged in doing so. The escort, B6, contained four Norwegian corvettes for whom this was their first battle; they won golden opinions:

> The Norwegian navy was small and very professional throughout the war. Its reservists were deep-sea sailors in their own right, well trained for war even in peacetime, and all on active duty since 1939.[73]

The Senior Officer of B6, Lieutenant-Commander J. V. Waterhouse, reported that 'it was a pleasure to see (and hear) the Norwegians going into action'. His own ship, the destroyer *Viscount*, was well equipped, with 271M radar, HF/DF and a Hedgehog; there is no indication of this weapon being effective in the action or even noticed by the U-boats. That, however, is not surprising: any U-boat that noticed Hedgehog was lost anyway.

With greater numbers of boats available, Dönitz was able to form his packs into double patrol lines, making evasion that much more difficult. It was such a line that enabled the *Vorwärts* Group to fall upon ON 127 on 10 September, with impressive results. The escort was C4, under Acting Lieutenant-Commander A. H. Dobson in the destroyer *St Croix*, whom we last met as the killer of *U90* on 24 July. He had with him another destroyer, HMCS *Ottawa*, and four corvettes, three of which had been together in the group since June. It would seem that C4 was expecting daylight submerged attacks in the manner now too familiar, but was nevertheless taken by surprise when *U96* penetrated the screen at 1430 hours on 10 September and torpedoed three ships, two of which were sunk. This was just the beginning of a bad business for ON 127. Despite all the escort's vigorous activity, *Vorwärts* finally succeeded in sinking seven merchant ships, and as a parting shot on 14 September *U91* sank *Ottawa* with a loss of five officers (including the Commanding Officer) and 109 ratings. No U-boat was lost in this engagement, though one was severely damaged. This was not a good augury for the final months of the year, and

In addition, ON 127 gained the dubious distinction of being the only convoy during 1942–3 against which all the U-boats engaged were able to fire torpedoes.[74]

In October Dönitz had 196 U-boats operational and the OIC assessed the number at sea in the Atlantic as over 100. From this time onwards, he says,

there were always two U-boat groups permanently available in the North Atlantic for operations against convoys.[75]

The consequence, as may be supposed, was some very heavy fighting. Already, however, the steep Atlantick was laying down its own laws in familiar fashion: Dönitz tells us:

The weather in the Atlantic during October 1942 was exceptionally stormy, and the U-boats found that they were hard put to it merely to remain at sea.[76]

This was just the beginning of what would prove to be the most dreadful of a succession of dreadful Atlantic winters, taking its toll of U-boats, escorts and merchantmen with only this advantage to the U-boats, that they could from time to time dive under the worst of the sea's motion and obtain a little relief from the endless pitching and rolling of their boats. In the early part of the month, however, their operations on the convoy routes were entirely frustrated.

Elsewhere they did well, justifying Dönitz's decision to cast his net wide. October saw the conclusion of one successful campaign in the north and the opening of another, some 7,000 miles away in the south – an indication of how wide the net could be. On 5 October *U517* emerged from the Cabot Strait to make her way back to Lorient and a heroes' welcome after a three-month cruise in the Strait of Belle Isle and the Gulf of St Lawrence which saw the sinking of 31,101 tons of Allied shipping. Her commander, *Korvettenkapitän* Paul Hartwig,

was an extremely competent submarine officer and a hard drinker, apparently admired by his crew in both capacities.[77]

He was also an officer 'of great nerve and skill'; operating for so long in narrow waters, he needed to be. He calculated, at the end of his cruise, that as many as twenty-seven bombs and 118 depth charges had come close enough to cause danger to *U517* and discomfort to her crew. Among the devices he had used effectively to evade the attentions of escort vessels was the *Pillenwerfer*, or Submarine Bubble Target (SBT), now coming into general use. This was a perforated metal cylinder, about the size of a standard container of tinned fruit or vegetables, released by the submerged U-boat through a special vent. It contained a chemical which produced a cloud of bubbles; to any but the most experienced operator, this caused the ASDIC to pick up an echo practically indistinguishable from that of a submarine, to decoy the attacking escort away from a U-boat. Hartwig made good use of this equipment – and his natural cunning; his triumphant return (enhanced by the usual over-estimate of results) was marked by a well-earned Knight's Cross.

At the other end of the Atlantic, Dönitz's strategy of surprise attacks also produced striking successes. Against an opponent like Rodger Winn, who seemed to have a sixth sense of what U-boats might be doing or intending even without *Enigma* decrypts to guide him, surprise was not easy. As we have seen, Dönitz had been attracted by the 'virgin field' of Cape Town since June, and in August he formed the *Eisbär* (Polar Bear) Group of four Type IXCs and despatched it to the South Atlantic. We have already observed one of its more significant proceedings on the way, and it is interesting to see how Winn reacted to this at the time. In his weekly Submarine Report on 21 September he wrote:

> W/T evidence of half a dozen U-boats 200 miles NE of Ascension where the *Laconia* was sunk on the 12th is probably connected with the collection of the surviving passengers and the Italian prisoners of war.[78]

This was correct, of course – but it was not the whole truth, and Winn clearly had more than an inkling of that; on the same day he warned the C-in-C, South Atlantic, that 'a southward movement of U-boats seems imminent'.

It was indeed – not only the *Eisbär* Group, but *U 179* (*Fregattenkapitän* Sobe), the first of the Type IXD2s, whose superior speed (and the *Laconia* delay) had enabled her to catch up with the IXCs. Agents had informed *B-Dienst* that there were always up to fifty ships lying at anchor in the Cape Town roadstead; Dönitz and his captains looked forward to rich pickings. For Winn this was a frustrating period (one of many), but his instinct remained true. He wrote on 5 October:

> There have been no further reports from the South Atlantic and no real clue to the whereabouts of the ten U-boats estimated south of the Equator towards the end of September. A German broadcast has mentioned the arrival of U-boats in 'Far Eastern waters'. There is as yet no evidence to support this statement, but the appearance of up to six German U-boats in the Mozambique Channel by mid-October is theoretically possible.

There was not a lot that could be done about this threat; the total escort strength of South Atlantic Command in August, 1942, was seven destroyers, three sloops, twenty corvettes, seven armed merchant cruisers and sixteen anti-submarine trawlers.[79] Some re-routing and diversion was done, and inshore escorts were provided for ships actually calling at Cape Town. The result was that when the U-boats arrived three days later they found the roadstead empty. Not only that, but *U 179*, having sunk a merchantman on 8 October, was promptly sunk herself by the destroyer HMS *Active* on the same day. Thereafter, however, the fortunes of the *Eisbär* Group improved; finding nothing in the roadstead, they moved back to the shipping lanes, and were promptly rewarded by 9 October by the sinking of the liner/troopship *Oronsay* (20,043 tons) and on the following day her sister ship *Orcades* (23,456 tons). On that day also another of the Type IXD2s, on her way south, sank another troopship, the *Duchess of Atholl* (20,119 tons). Roskill remarks:

> These were grievous losses, for such fine ships could never be replaced during the war.[80]

Dönitz relates with understandable pleasure that thirteen ships were sunk in the Cape Town area in the space of three days:

> We had good reason to feel satisfied.[81]

And when, as Winn had predicted, the IXD2s entered the Indian Ocean to sink a further twenty ships by the end of the year, his satisfaction was even greater. As Roskill says,

> During these months U-boat Command's method of constantly seeking out the 'soft spots' in our defences, even when this involved sending the U-boats thousands of miles, reaped its rich harvest.

Patrick Beesly, however, remarks that in a bad time and a depressing scene, the South Atlantic foray

> shows the almost uncanny way in which (Winn) seemed to read Dönitz's mind, his ability to piece together an accurate picture from fragmentary and nebulous evidence, and perhaps above all his courage in maintaining for nearly two months and in the face of some scepticism a theory for which confirmatory evidence was for so long lacking.[82]

* * * * *

By mid-October the North Atlantic weather, while still awful, at least permitted active operations. Dönitz acknowledges the help he now received from the cryptographers of *xB-Dienst*, but sighting reports, accidental or otherwise, continued to be a main source of convoy information, and he frankly admits also

> how uncertain were the indications on which U-boat operations were based and how very considerable a part was played by chance in the vast areas over which the war at sea was being waged.[83]

Out of six attempts to bring convoys to battle in October, two failed completely, one produced no more than two sinkings of merchant vessels – but in the remaining three actions the U-boats succeeded in sinking no fewer than thirty merchantmen, which was a sign of very bad times indeed.

It was a chance sighting by *U258* on 11 October that drew the *Wotan* Group to SC 104, but the residual vigour of the storms that had been raging created such atmospheric disturbance that U-Boat Command did not receive an intelligible sighting signal until the next day. Then, as the U-boat pack closed in, the balance of disadvantage shifted; steep seas with tall waves gave wild motions to the ships of the escort (B6), reducing the effectiveness of both radar and ASDIC. *Korvettenkapitän* Trojer in *U221* took full advantage of this on the 13th; slipping through a screen which was weakened by the absence of three corvettes, drawn away in pursuit of HF/DF signals, he sank three ships in the space of just over 40 minutes. We may judge the quality of the 'improved' weather by the fact that in the howling south-west wind, and amidst the crash of the heavy seas, B6 was unaware of the first loss until Trojer had inflicted the next two.

This was another of those battles in which one U-boat performed most of the effective action. That night *U221* struck again, sinking two more ships; *U607* added another, and in the early hours of 14 October *U661* and *U618* each contributed one more. After that, with the weather now less wild, B6 did better; on the night of the 14th/15th the destroyer *Viscount* followed a radar detection and rammed *U619*. In the words of Commander S. Heathcote, the Senior Officer, the four Norwegian corvettes of the escort group, *Acanthus, Eglantine, Montbretia* and *Potentilla*, 'pounced like terriers' on every indication of a U-boat. On the 15th Liberators of No 120 Squadron made their welcome appearance, and the next day air cover continued in relays. Commander Heathcote's ship, the destroyer *Fame*, blew *U 353* to the surface by a well-judged depth charge attack, and then rammed her; the crew abandoned ship and the U-boat made her last plunge. It may be noted, incidentally, that both destroyers suffered such damage from their rammings that they could take no further part in the action. Command then devolved on Lieutenant-Commander C. A. Monsen, RNorN, in *Potentilla*; on the last night of the action, 16/17 October, she made a radar contact with *U571* and damaged her by gunfire. On the 17th the *Wotan* Group abandoned the attack. Dönitz was somewhat disappointed with this result, and indeed, after Trojer's excellent start it did have a poor look (eight merchant ships at a cost of two U-boats), especially in view of the numerical weakness of B6 – only six escorts for a convoy of forty-four ships.

The period of frustration then followed, when a succession of U-boat packs failed to obtain any results at all against ON 137 and ON 138, and succeeded only in sinking two ships in ON 139. Then, on 26 October *U 436*, a middle boat in the patrol line of Group *Puma*, signalled an eastbound convoy which proved to be HX 212. The escort was Group A3 (Senior Officer, Commander T. L. Lewis USCG in the 'Treasury' class cutter *Campbell*[84]), a USN destroyer, the RN corvette *Dianthus* and five Canadian corvettes – a reasonably strong escort, but again lacking the equipment which case after case had shown to be essential. Only one ship, HMCS *Summerside*, carried 271M radar; this was evidently quite inadequate, but rendered more so by the heavy seas, which also made it hard for the human eye to offer any useful substitute. And for two critical days this weather also robbed the convoy of air cover. The result was a loss of seven merchant ships, three of them to *U 436* (Seibicke), on the first day of attack, 27 October. The Liberators of No 120 Squadron in Iceland stopped the U-boats' run of success on the 29th, and the battle ended on that day without loss to *Puma* Group.

It was on that day, 29 October, however, that a large pack operation began, which turned into an Allied disaster. *B-Dienst* intercepted a signal giving the course of SC 107 and Dönitz was able to place the thirteen boats of the *Veilchen* (Violet)[85] Group, plus three Type IXs on passage to Canadian waters, across its path. *U 522* sighted the convoy on the 29th, forty-two merchantmen escorted by C4. This was a group not without experience; the Senior Officer was Lieutenant-

Commander D. W. Piers RCN, of the destroyer *Restigouche*, 'a very young man and a very junior officer',[86] but even so, he had performed the duties of SOE seven times already, and so far had never lost a ship. He had with him four regular C4 corvettes, and received the support of two others during the action. There was the usual lack of 271M radar; *Restigouche* had it, and so did the corvette *Celandine*, but unfortunately hers was out of action. *Restigouche* and the rescue ship *Stockport* had HF/DF, and this became 'a vital element in C4's valiant attempt to defend SC 107'.

It was not, however, the RCN which struck the first blows in this defence, but the RCAF. On 30 October two Hudsons of No 145 Squadron (I Group, Eastern Air Command), almost at the end of their endurance some 290 miles northeast of the airfield at Torbay in eastern Newfoundland, had the exceptional good fortune to see a conning tower breaking the surface only about two miles ahead; the leading Hudson at once ran in to attack from 2,000 feet:

> It was one of those rare occasions when everything clicked into place: 'at the time the depth charges were released the U-boat was almost fully surfaced. Four 250-lbs Mark VIII depth charges with Mark XIII pistol set to 25 feet at an angle of 30 (degrees) across the U-boat from port astern to starboard bow. All the charges functioned correctly and explosions were noted bracketing the U-boat, the center two charges on opposite sides of the hull and very close to it. The explosion raised the U-boat in the water and 60 feet of its stern raised on an angle of 40° to the horizontal. The U-boat then settled and a large oil slick and air bubbles merging with the rough sea appeared immediately.'[87]

This was no false promise. *U 658* had been destroyed. Eight hours later (2002) on the same day, a Douglas Digby[88] of No 10 Squadron sighted a surfaced U-boat 115 miles due east of St John's. This was *U 520*, surprised and straddled by four 450-lb Mark VII (Amatol-filled) depth charges which destroyed her also. It was a good day's work for the RCAF.

Nevertheless, it did not save SC 107 from misfortune. Passing through the gap in the *Veilchen* line caused by the loss of *U 658*, the convoy continued steadily on its course; whether it could have saved some loss by diversions we cannot tell – the fact remains that there were none, and on the night of 1/2 November *U 402* and *U 522* closed in for the first attack. On that first night the two U-boats sank six merchantmen, von Forstner's *U 402* taking four, and each boat also torpedoed one more ship which other *Veilchen* boats sank later. Deteriorating weather on the 2nd put the U-boat group out of contact with the single exception of *U 522*, which also succeeded in sinking another ship, bringing the tally to nine. And after a quiet night (apart from the weather) it was nine U-boats that regained contact on 3 November. That night five more ships were sunk; four U-boats were damaged in the process, but none lost. C4 received strong reinforcement on the 4th, but *U 89* was able none the less to claim one more victim, making fifteen in all. On the 5th the 120 Squadron Liberators appeared and the U-boats were kept down; *U 132* was sunk on this day, and it was believed in Britain for a long time that she had been the prey of one of the prowling Liberators. U-Boat Command, however, attributed the loss to damage sustained in the blowing-up of a munitions ship which she had torpedoed. The Naval Historical Branch now accepts that the cause of loss was an explosion of some kind, rather than aircraft attack.

The fifteen ships lost (87,818 tons) in the SC 107 battle constituted a disaster in themselves, and the total of thirty ships lost from three convoys (plus two from ON 139) made October an ominous month on the convoy routes. One hundred and one ships (637,833 tons) were sunk during the month, ninety-four of them by submarines (619,417 tons), and of these sixty-two (399,715 tons) in the North Atlantic. This month also saw, for reasons which we shall discuss below, the highest loss of shipping in the South Atlantic during the whole war: twenty ships (148,142 tons, of which 63,618 are accounted for by the three big liners on 9 and 10 October). The U-boat 'effective quotient' for October 1942 was 172 tons; the cost of the achievement was sixteen U-boats, one destroyed by a mine, one by causes unknown and, significantly, ten and a half by aircraft.

A footnote must be added to the October story. Virtually simultaneously with SC 107's bad time in the north, SL 125, homeward-bound from Freetown, had the bad luck to run into the arms of the *Xanthippe* Group. In a protracted running battle between 26 October and 5 November, thirteen merchantmen (85,686 tons) were sunk with no loss to the U-boat pack. This might be looked upon as another disaster, but for a quite unintended silver lining:

The first military convoys for North Africa were passing through adjacent waters at a time when the U-boats were occupied in attacking SL 125. Had the enemy not been thus engaged he might well have detected the great movements of troops and supply ships, have attacked them or guessed their destination, and so deprived our landing forces of the important element of surprise.[89]

* * * * *

The great decision taken at the ARCADIA conference, to concentrate Allied strength on the defeat of 'Germany first', evolved during the course of the year into a set of broad 'plans' which were actually no more than statements of intention, under the code-names ROUNDUP, BOLERO and SLEDGEHAMMER. The centrepiece of these was ROUNDUP, the direct assault on Hitler's 'Fortress Europe':

> This was first envisaged as taking place in 1943. . . . It would be proceded by a massive buildup of US forces in the United Kingdom, code-name BOLERO. But if, as then seemed more than likely, the Soviet Union should show signs of crumbling under the heavy blows that rained upon her, it was thought that it might be necessary to mount a desperate diversionary cross-Channel attack in 1942, SLEDGEHAMMER. One by one all these propositions were ruled out.[90]

The arguments which arose out of this fact caused much ill-feeling (some of it ineradicable) between British and American planners and leaders, and contentions which continue to inspire the historiography of the period to this day. And the fact itself, of course, profoundly affected the further course of the war; it meant that the great operation envisaged in the concept of ROUNDUP, ultimately called OVERLORD, would not take place until 1944. The military, political and social consequences of that are inexpressible except as a virtually inexhaustible series of speculations, a massive array of 'ifs' which compel some consideration in appropriate places (of which this is not one) but do not often reward it with greater enlightenment. The second fact, arising directly out of the first, is that instead of any SLEDGEHAMMER in 1942, and regardless of the likely effect upon ROUND-UP, the Allies embarked upon a landing in French North Africa under the codename of GYMNAST (or SUPER-GYMNAST), later changed to TORCH.

It is well established now that this change of strategy was more

493

welcome in Britain than, with one enormous exception, in America. Churchill and the British Chiefs of Staff had from the beginning grave trepidations about an opposed landing in north-western Europe (with all its evil connotations, for Churchill, of the Gallipoli landings in 1915) and a continental campaign against the still very powerful German Army. And as the year wore on, with what seemed an inexorable sequence of disasters in all theatres – loss of all Burma, bringing the Japanese threat to the borders of India in the north, and their landing on Guadalcanal in the south, threatening Australia; heavy losses to the Mediterranean Fleet in attempting to resupply Malta in August; the fall of Tobruk and Rommel's advance into Egypt; the PQ17 catastrophe and the renewal of the campaign on the Atlantic trade routes – the British leaders increasingly viewed a major operation across the Channel as an invitation to ruin. Yet the desirability of engaging the Germans as hard as possible somewhere was obvious – the more so when their 1942 offensive in Russia carried them right into the Caucasus, seemingly threatening the whole Middle East as far as Persia (Iran). The result was what Americans have always been inclined to dismiss as 'peripheral strategy' – with the one single exception of President Roosevelt who, from the first, took the view that the main thing was to get American ground and air forces into battle with the Germans at the earliest possible date. North-west Europe would clearly have been the best place, but North Africa was definitely better than nowhere at all. Furthermore, Roosevelt, like many other Americans, was sure that Vichy France was far less hostile to the USA than to Britain, and there was a tempting prospect of bringing a substantial French element back to the Allied cause by the 'liberation' of Morocco, Algeria and Tunisia. For these and other less important reasons he was prepared to take

one of the few strategic decisions of the war in which the President overrode the counsel of his military advisers.[91]

There is no doubt that all this was important background to the piecemeal abandonment of the strategy first intended at ARCADIA. But increasingly the foreground was occupied by more urgent matters. As we have seen, from the very beginning of any serious detailed planning of any project, the Allied staffs had discovered that 'shortage of shipping imposed an absolute ban'. That was before the 'roll of drums' and the massacre of American shipping along the coastal lanes. By mid-year the position had become calamitous; a sinking rate of 4,147,406 tons in six months obviously threatened to cancel out any possible increment from American productivity. The shipping shortage loomed over all TORCH planning, and the further drain imposed by that operation proved to be a serious matter indeed, especially when the campaign in North Africa unexpectedly dragged on well into May, 1943. The British planners were perhaps most at fault (if only because Britain was most concerned); they had estimated that an average of sixty-six ships per month would be required to support TORCH, but the reality turned out to be 106 ships per month – a very large increase. The result was a sharp fall in imports into Britain, with industry cutting into its reserves of raw materials and even the threat of unemployment. Living standards, already painfully lowered, faced the probability of further cuts. Indeed, it was this haunting shortage of shipping that gave TORCH its chief appeal to some British leaders; the CIGS, General Brooke, was a firm believer in the pressing necessity of clearing the Mediterranean which, he urged, would save a million tons of shipping – and 'to clear the Mediterranean, North Africa must first be cleared.'[92] According to his biographer, Sir David Fraser, this absorption with the shipping problem made 'the free passage of the Mediterranean the keystone of Alanbrooke's strategic philosophy'.[93] Such were the contradictory impulses evoked by the campaign in North Africa which opened on the night of 7/8 November.

Nor was shipping the only example of contradictory impulses. In January, 1942, before the 'roll of drums' began to sound, flushed with offensive enthusiasm, the Americans agreed to begin the mass-production of landing craft for their own as well as for British use. This involved an act of conversion in the USN, which had previously been sceptical about the need for such vessels; the missionary agents were the Japanese, now thrusting into the Pacific, and who would one day have to be dislodged by amphibious operations even more powerful than their own. So priorities for labour, steel and engines in America were allocated to landing craft in early 1942, and this, says Roskill,

> certainly contributed greatly to the continuing weakness of our Atlantic escorts, and to the heavy shipping losses we suffered at this time.[94]

It contributed also, of course, to the USN's great difficulties in creating

495

an effective convoy system in home waters, and to the increasing un-reality of an offensive in north-west Europe in 1942. When Dönitz's 'drums' beat out the measure of the truth, the priorities were altered; it was then recognized that the crying need was escort vessels and according to Robert E. Sherwood landing craft dropped to tenth place in the Navy's Ship-building Precedence List. Then, when the decision to carry out TORCH was taken in July, the pendulum swung back again:

> By October, just before the North African landings, [landing craft] had gone up to second place, preceded only by aircraft carriers, but the next month they dropped to twelfth place.[95]

So once more we see how much Allied offensive strategy was at the mercy of the U-boats, whose depredations, unless stopped, could cut at its very roots.

For the first TORCH landings over 350 ships were required, 102 of them sailing direct from America for the Casablanca area to land an all-American force under General George S. Patton. An Anglo-American landing at Oran and an all-British landing at Algiers required a further armada of over 250 ships sailing from British ports. Admiral Cunningham, C-in-C Mediterranean, who was responsible for the safe arrival of these huge numbers, later wrote:

> The defence for the 'Torch' convoys was marshalled in strength. But no imaginable defence could altogether have warded off the concentrated attacks of thirty to forty U-boats. The procession of large convoys con-verging on the Straits of Gibraltar passed close enough to submarine concentrations; but it is the almost incredible fact that they were not attacked and sunstained no casualties.[96]

This was, indeed, an 'almost incredible fact', explicable only by one sentence in Dönitz's memoirs:

> The Allied landing in North Africa was quite unexpected by the Axis Powers.[97]

It was not until 0630 on 8 November that a telephone call from the Naval High Command informed Dönitz that the Americans had landed on the coast of Morocco, and without waiting for further instructions

he ordered all the U-boats between the Bay of Biscay and the Cape
Verde Islands to move in on Morocco. After a further exchange with
the High Command, he ordered operations in the North Atlantic to be
broken off and the boats concerned to go to Gibraltar – an area which,
as we have seen, he disliked very much indeed. He wrote in the War
Diary on the 8th:

> The landings on the Algerian and Moroccan coasts are obviously part
> of a large-scale invasion to sustain which the enemy will require a broad
> and continuous stream of supplies and reinforcements. The U-boats
> will arrive too late to interfere with the initial landings, since the first of
> them cannot arrive before November 9–11 at the earliest. They should,
> however, be able to work effectively against the subsequent follow-up
> landings and against the supply line. *Prospects of success, however, must
> not be over-rated.* Every attack in these shallow waters will demand
> great determination. But the importance of dislocating the enemy's
> supply lines calls for the boldest possible intervention by the U-boats.[98]

The U-boat captains were rarely anything less than bold, and in
theory the targets awaiting them should have been ideal: shipping of
all sizes and denominations crowded in fixed localities, awaiting the
capture and clearance of harbours. In fact, however, matters transpired
as Dönitz had anticipated; surface and air defences were 'continuous
and strong', and the shallowness of the water 'a severe handicap'. The
first U-boat to arrive, off Fedala, was *U 173* (Schweichel), and her
success was limited to damaging a troopship, a tanker and a destroyer
on 11 November. *Fregattenkapitän* Kals in *U 130* reached Fedala on
the same day, but was located by radar and kept away from the roadstead by escort vessels. He then tried a new approach, deliberately using
the shallows to deceive the defence; his log recounted:

> November 12. 1321. 20 miles north of Fedala. My intention is to go
> inshore till I reach the 15 fathom line and then to proceed along the
> coast to the Fedala roadstead and attack. The patrols will hardly expect
> a U-boat to approach so close inshore.
> 1440. Grazed bottom. Depth 70 feet . . .
> 1600. Some twenty vessels observed lying in the roadstead, among them
> an aircraft carrier at the extreme southern end, a cruiser with tripod
> mast close inshore and two tankers. A few escort vessels to the west and
> in the vicinity of the warships. Proceeded with great caution on account

of completely unruffled surface. Periscope used only for brief glances. Decided to go for the ships nearest to me . . .

1828 to 1833. Fired four single torpedoes from bow tubes, then turned about and fired stern tube VI. Tube V out of action. Hits observed on three large modern freighters. Heavy explosions and clouds of thick smoke over whole formation . . . As I thought the enemy would certainly expect me to head north-west and make for deep water, I clung to the 10-fathom line and proceeded north-east along the coast without any difficulty.

Kals had, in fact, sunk three American transports, *Ewart Ruthledge*, *Hugh L. Scott* and *Tasker H. Bliss*. His attack was well conceived and displayed all the boldness that Dönitz could desire. It was, however, a flash in the pan; thereafter the U-boats conspicuously failed to interfere with the maintenance of the TORCH offensive. Only nine British merchant ships worthy of mention by the Official History were lost in the months November and December; they included two large liner/troopships, *Warwick Castle* (20,107 tons) sunk by *U 413* (Poel) on 14 November and the modern P & O *Strathallan* (23,772 tons) on 22 December. During the same period seven Italian and seven German submarines were lost in the central and western Mediterranean,[99] justifying Dönitz's worst fears. As early as 18 November, with six boats already missing, he addressed the High Command in familiar terms:

> U-boat Command is of the opinion that the relatively great success achieved initially, under particular circumstances and while the enemy was still in process of launching his offensive, cannot be taken as a yardstick which justifies a continuation of U-boat operations against his African reinforcement convoys; such a course offers a minimum prospect of success at probably a very high cost and can have no decisive bearing on the subsequent course of enemy operations.
>
> To employ the U-boats as suggested, however, would have disastrous effects on the war against shipping in the Atlantic, which U-boat Command has always regarded, and still regards, as the primary task of the U-boat arm. Indeed, its war on enemy shipping is perhaps the one great contribution that the U-boat arm can make towards winning the war.

The great wonder is that it was still necessary for him to spell out these fundamentals after three years of war; and a further wonder is that they still fell upon half-deaf ears. The High Command would only agree to a reduction of the numbers of U-boats to be used against TORCH, not the complete withdrawal that Dönitz wanted. The hard facts of profit and loss in war are difficult to ignore, however, and one senses the relief with which he records that on 23 December the Naval Command

> cancelled their previous orders to attack the enemy's Mediterranean traffic and U-boat activities against the Allied operations in North Africa came to an end.

Dönitz clearly considered this major defeat of the U-boats as a more or less self-inflicted wound; it was a major defeat, nevertheless. With 196 boats operational in October, the U-boat arm had absolutely failed to interfere with an operation which, theoretically, should have presented itself to the German submarines like a flock of sitting ducks to a fowler. The omens for the future required little reading, and when seen in conjunction with the great growth of Allied air power were discouraging to any German not blind to reality. Yet within this defeat there was an achievement that is not to be missed, and cannot have failed to be deceptive at the time.

November was the third 'black month' for shipping in 1942, when sinkings amounted to over 800,000 tons (to be precise, 134 ships, 807,754 tons). It was also the month that saw the highest-ever total of sinkings by submarines: 119 ships (729,160 tons), of which eighty-three (508,707 tons) were sunk in the North Atlantic. The reason for this is that the mounting of Operation TORCH was, in a sense, also a self-inflicted wound for the Allies. To protect the TORCH convoys the Royal Navy alone had to find 125 light craft, most of which could only come from trade convoy escorts; the hard-pressed RCN contributed seventeen of these, its best-equipped corvettes. To obtain the rest, the Arctic convoys to the Soviet Union were suspended (see pp. 584–5), and also the OG/HG (Gibraltar) and the OS/SL (Freetown) convoys. The ill-fated SL 125, which left Freetown on 16 October, was the last on that route for four months – SL 126 did not sail until 12 March, 1943. Most of the shipping involved was now routed across the Atlantic independently. Outward-bound ships for Gibraltar, West Africa and the Cape were given protection in the special 'KX TORCH' convoys, or merged with ON convoys on the southerly route as far as the Azores where they broke off to sail independently for South Africa or South

America. Homeward-bound ships, including those from South American ports, sailed independently across the South Atlantic to Trinidad to join the American Interlocking System, or through the Magellan Straits up the west coast of South America to pass through the Panama Canal and enter the Interlocking System in the Gulf of Mexico. It was these movements that accounted for seventy of the 119 ships sunk by U-boats, all 'independents', and many sunk in the Trinidad area or near the Cape of Good Hope. Indeed, never since that first gleeful onslaught in 1940–41 had such a mass of unprotected shipping been exposed to the periscopes and torpedo tubes; it was a situation made for a third 'happy time', and it is understandable that Dönitz was intensely anxious to exploit it to the full. And while it lasted, emphasizing its perils, was the fact that

the main North Atlantic convoys became . . . the only link between Britain and the rest of the free world.[100]

* * * * *

At last, in the closing months of 1942, Allied public opinion had a banquet of good news to feed upon. After sensational advances, the great German offensive on the southern front in Russia had come to an evident halt at Stalingrad, and in early November the Russians passed over to the counter-offensive. At Guadalcanal in the Solomon Islands the Japanese in that same month met their first serious defeat, which would shortly lead to their first retirement. British opinion, needless to say, was largely preoccupied by the counter-offensive against General Rommel in Egypt. The Second Battle of El Alamein opened on 23 October, and on 4 November General Sir Harold Alexander, C-in-C Middle East, was able to report to Churchill:

Such portions of the enemy's forces as can get away are in full retreat.[101]

This was electrifying news, bringing enormous relief after two years of hope deferred and bitter disappointment. Four days later came the TORCH landings and the first successes of the new campaign. All this helped to mask the hard truth of what was happening at sea, with its double threat to British survival and future Allied offensive capability. Well might Churchill say that the U-boat peril was 'the only thing that ever really frightened me' (see p. 264).

Back in August, on the suggestion of the Representative of the Australian Government, the Right Hon S. M. Bruce, it had been agreed to set up a small committee 'composed of those best equipped with knowledge and experience, those responsible for policy and those capable of rapidly translating policy into action'[102] to establish and ordain the priorities of the Battle of the Atlantic. It would be called the Cabinet Anti-U-boat Warfare Committee; it would consist of the appropriate Ministers and Service chiefs with scientific advisers, representatives of the United States Government and the USN, and it would meet weekly. Roskill observes:

> The fact that the Committee had Cabinet status enabled decisions to be quickly reached, and priorities firmly decided and enforced.

With the U-boats rampaging on the shipping lanes, it was high time for such a body to start work, and the first meeting took place on 4 November. The First Lord of the Admiralty (Right Hon A. V. Alexander) dwelt upon the increase in U-boat production, and gave the considered opinion that

> we were not destroying more than one-third of the monthly output of new U-boats. The first need was to fill the 'air gap' in mid-Atlantic, for which we required about forty long-range radar-fitted aircraft; the other need was for more and longer-range air patrols in the Bay of Biscay. The outstanding issues were thus at once placed in the foreground of the Committee's deliberations.

A fortnight after this inaugural meeting, a further important change took place in the organization of anti-submarine warfare; Admiral Sir Percy Noble left Western Approaches Command to head the British Naval Mission in Washington and represent the First Sea Lord there.[103] His successor was Admiral Sir Max Horton, a man of very different temperament. He unquestionably inherited from Sir Percy Noble a thoroughly 'going concern'; the staff at Command HQ in Derby House now numbered over 1,000 officers and ratings (of whom a large number were WRNS); liaison with No 15 Group, RAF, was intimate and continuous; liaison with the OIC and the Submarine Tracking Room was equally so; in its various sectors, at the turn of the year, Western Approaches disposed of over 170 escort vessels, which was still nothing like enough, but thanks to Nòble's emphasis on training and development of training facilities, a high degree of expertise had been produced.

To all this Horton brought new energy, a drive which was very soon felt throughout the Command. Vice-Admiral Gretton, who served under him as a (very distinguished) Escort Group commander, says that Horton was 'ruthless in weeding out the weak and replacing them by high-calibre officers'.[104] His grasp of the essentials was immediate; on his very first day in office he picked up where Noble left off in emphasizing the urgent need for 'Support Groups' to back up the close escort groups, and – yet again – for VLR aircraft. These were running refrains; regarding Support Groups, his biographer tells

> He wrote almost daily to the Admiralty stressing the need for such a force. Escort Groups and Support Groups could not be interchangeable.[105]

As always, it was a matter of simple availability. And the same, unless the Air Staff and the American Navy and Army Air chiefs could be brought to a change of heart, was true of the VLR aircraft which alone were the answer to the 'Gap'. What Horton could do, however, was gain strength by renewing the emphasis that Noble had given to training and even push it a stage further. His most fruitful innovation (in early February, 1943) was the setting up of a 'school of battle' at Larne with the object of 'exercising escort vessels in the art of sinking U-boats'.[106] The centrepiece of the 'school' was HMS *Philante*, a converted luxury yacht, with one or two RN submarines in attendance; the direction was in the hands, first, of Captain A. J. Baker-Cresswell, and later of Captain L. F. Durnford-Slater. Admiral Chalmers tells us:

> It was arranged that each Escort Group, before joining its convoy, should spend at least two days at sea with the *Philante* acting as a ship of a convoy. Exercises would than take place, in cooperation with Coastal Command aircraft, against submarines representing U-boats.
>
> The Commander-in-Chief took a keen interest in this 'school of battle' and would to go sea himself in the *Philante* for important tactical experiments.

The whole thing, says Gretton, was 'a thoroughly practical affair and of great value'. Horton was a training fanatic, especially for anti-submarine warfare; he was always adamant that experienced Group Commanders should not be removed from their groups even on promotion, and that all groups should be highly trained as teams. There were dangers, however, as an escort commander told Chalmers:

> He drove and drove and drove at training, shore training at their bases, sea training with *Philante*, and sea and air training all the time, even when with the convoys. His personal interest in training was so intense that he almost defeated his own – absolutely correct – object. Those responsible for training became so frightened of his insatiable enquiries that they were more interested in sending in satisfactory returns than in preparing ships to fight the enemy. However, when this was pointed out to him, he was – after an extremely tense period – a big enough man to recognize the situation and put it right.[107]

There is no doubt that Horton was a 'big man'. He came to Western Approaches from the post of Flag Officer, Submarines, after 35 years of specializing in submarine warfare, of which he had, in fact, been an important pioneer in 1914 and after. With this background, it was not difficult to see him as almost a personal adversary of Dönitz, whose own past career had been so similar. One naval writer commented:

> With due deference to 'Sir Max', one is tempted to think that the appointment was made in response to the old advice to 'set a thief to catch a thief'.[108]

And Roskill throws his weight behind this supposition:

> With his knowledge and insight, his ruthless determination and driving energy, he was without doubt the right man to pit against Dönitz.[109]

Gretton, on the other hand, having believed the same thing for a long time, concluded on studying the documents relating to *Enigma* and Winn's general contribution to the work of the Submarine Tracking Room and OIC,

> that in fact the two chief protagonists were Dönitz and Rodger Winn.[110]

This, says Beesly, may be going a little too far; certainly there is always a large gulf between the man holding executive operational responsibility, and the man who, valuable though his work may be, does not. The truth would seem to lie in the irrelevance of this kind of personalization to modern war. It does not lend itself to such simplifications – 'Churchill versus Hitler', 'Montgomery versus Rommel', 'Dowding versus Göring, etc., etc. The stature of Horton – like the stature of Air Chief Marshal Sir Hugh Dowding – lay in the ability to adapt to and make the fullest use of the whole apparatus that was to hand. The appreciation of the rôle of scientists as operational advisers and contributors is one aspect of this; appreciation of Intelligence is another. As Admiral Chalmers says, Horton and Winn were 'both gifted with prescience to a remarkable degree'[111]; their relations were entirely cordial, and one anecdote will serve to illustrate the bigness of Horton and the authority of Winn.

There was an occasion, says Patrick Beesly, when

> Horton was dissatisfied with appreciations given him by the Tracking Room which had led to an unsuccessful convoy battle, and attacked Winn at one of the fortnightly U-boat Warfare meetings presided over by the Assistant Chief of Staff (U-boats and Trade). Winn accepted the criticism in good part (indeed he had no option), but suggested that if he could be given half an hour, he would lay out all the intelligence available to the Tracking Room at the time the appreciation was made. The Admiral could then examine it himself and decide what different conclusions he would have come to. When Horton arrived in the Tracking Room he was confronted with a mass of Special Intelligence signals, D/F fixes, sighting reports and the last confirmed positions of the U-boats concerned. 'It's all yours, sir,' said Winn, 'and your Chief of Staff in Liverpool is in a devil of a hurry for the answer.' Horton settled down, but after a period of intense study turned to Winn and ... 'confessed that most of it was outside his province. With the old familiar smile, which some called 'cat-like', and others 'benign', he held out his hand and said, 'Goodbye, Rodger – I leave it to you.' And thereafter he did.[112]

It was, then, under a new C-in-C, experienced in all the ways of submarines, immensely energetic and dedicated to efficiency, and with the extra 'muscle' of a Cabinet Committee to speed the endeavour, that the battle against the U-boats entered its last phase. And as it did so, 1942, already the bringer of so many alarums, fired its parting shots.

* * * * *

The noticeable feature of the North Atlantic in the second half of November was the absence of U-boats, as they sped towards the TORCH landing areas. Only those that were becoming short of fuel remained near the convoy routes, reinforced by a few from northern waters. These boats, nine in all, were formed into the *Kreuzotter* (Adder) Group, and on 15 November the small convoy ONS 144 crossed their patrol line. The escort was once again B6, but seriously weakened by the lack of any destroyer; *Viscount* and *Fame* were under repair after their ramming exploits with SC 104 and the group's third destroyer (HMS *Ramsey*, 'Town' Class) had developed serious defects. That left only the Norwegian group of four corvettes, reinforced by another, HMS *Vervain*. The rescue ship in ONS 144, *Perth*, carried HF/DF and all the corvettes had 271M radar; what followed, under the skilful direction of Lieutenant-Commander Monsen, was a brilliant display of how these equipments should be used. Monsen was a believer in preserving a continuous radar barrier between a convoy and its attackers, and this he did to such effect that in a five-day battle he only lost five ships of the convoy and the corvette *Montbretia*. His own *Potentilla* took revenge on 20 November by sinking *U 184*. When the action was over, the U-boats were desperately short of fuel and had expended all their torpedoes. Dönitz reassuringly directed them to *rendezvous* with a 'milch cow', *U 460*, and nine boats duly gathered round her. To his dismay, a violent storm then came up, making refuelling impossible, dispersing the group, and putting the virtually helpless U-boats in extreme danger. This lasted for several days, and when it cleared the supply operation was successfully resumed:

> A great load was lifted from my mind. But I had once again learned that the endurance of even U-boats had limits, and that it was as well to bear that fact in mind.[113]

December was even-handed with its favours, beginning with another triumph for B6, now once more under its rightful Senior Officer, Commander S. Heathcote in his repaired destroyer, *Fame*. The group was now escorting Convoy HX 217, twenty-five ships which left New York on 28 November. U-boat Command was well aware that R/T intercommunication was now a regular feature of escort work and was experimenting with placing *B-Dienst* personnel in U-boats to intercept this VHF traffic. One such operator was aboard *U 524*, and on 4 December he heard speech on the appropriate wavelength emanating, he estimated, from some ten participants. They were, in fact, B6 and ships of HX 217, and their overheard chatter brought upon them no fewer than twenty-two U-boats belonging to the *Draufganger* and *Panzer* Groups.[114] They caught up with the convoy on 6 December as it was entering the dreaded 'Gap'.

Five U-boats were in contact on 7 December, but what the day provided was an object-lesson in the meaning and value of VLR air power. As it was beginning to get light, Liberator H of 120 Squadron, piloted by Squadron-Leader T. Bulloch, arrived over the convoy from Iceland, over 800 miles away, and began patrolling in poor light. This notwithstanding, during the next $5\frac{1}{4}$ hours Bulloch made eight U-boat sightings, seven of which he converted into attacks with depth charges, 20-mm cannon or machine guns. He spent $7\frac{1}{4}$ hours with the convoy, and finally returned to Reykjavik after a flight lasting 16 hours 25 minutes. H/120 was relieved by another Liberator of the same squadron piloted by Squadron-Leader D. Isted, who sighted five U-boats and attacked four. Thus the two aircraft had made sightings of U-boats thirteen times and carried out eleven attacks between them. It would be pleasant to round off this story with a report of a kill, but there was none on 7 December; on the other hand, there was no successful attack on HX 217 either, at the time of the convoy's maximum vulnerability. From the point of view of 'safe and timely arrival' one could scarcely ask more.

During the night a tanker with aviation spirit was sunk, but numerous attacks were driven off by B6 with the aid of radar and ASDIC. The Liberators returned at dawn on 8 December, and claimed during the day to have sunk *U 254*, but it was not so. *Korvettenkapitän* Gilardone's *U 254* was lost in an accident which, in the fourth year of war, seems only to have been miraculously delayed. Dönitz relates:

> Now and again during convoy battles U-boats had narrowly missed colliding, but in each case the alertness of the lookout and the swift reaction of the captain had succeeded in averting disaster. This time, however, fate had decreed otherwise.[115]

It was Trojer's *U 221* that, on a dark night amid squalls of rain, just failed to turn away sharply enough to avoid giving $U254$ what he called a

sharp blow on after pressure hull. Collision hardly noticeable to us.

$U254$ was less lucky; she soon began to settle in the water, and the crew abandoned her in a heavy sea. Trojer did his best, constantly using his searchlight for two hours, but was only able to pick up one petty officer and three ratings; all the rest were lost. It was, says Dönitz, 'a bitter blow'; when he received $U221$'s report on 28 December, he wrote in the War Diary:

> For the first time during our operations against convoys a collision has occurred between two U-boats and a boat has been lost. As far as we here know, the accident occurred on a dark night and in heavy seas, and no blame, presumably, can be attributed to the ramming boat. With the large number of U-boats engaged in these operations against convoys it was inevitable that something like this would occur some time or other. A study of this question of numbers had led to the conclusion that, in general, it is inadvisable to have more than thirteen or fifteen boats operating simultaneously against a convoy. But any tactical restrictions – regarding the number of boats attacking, the timing of the attack, the attacking formation adopted and so on – designed to minimize the dangers of a collison cannot be tolerated, for it would be a mistake to impose any restrictions on U-boats engaged in operations of so intricate a nature as an attack on a convoy.

This was not the end of the HX217 story; a second (and final) merchantman was sunk on the night of 8/9 December. The weather on the 9th deteriorated and prevented air support, while heavy seas interfered with radar and ASDIC; but the U-boats were more concerned with working ahead of the convoy than attacking on that day. The attacks came all through the night of the 9th, 'but B6 intercepted every attempt to penetrate the screen'.[116] It is worth pausing a moment to reflect upon what those nine words mean, to make the attempt to conjure up the non-stop activity, the mounting weariness but never-failing performance of the radar and ASDIC operators, and of the gun and depth-charge teams, and the constant pressure of decision-taking on the captains and the Senior Officer, that they tersely imply. But dawn on the tenth brought 'massive air support' which included

Hudsons of No 269 Squadron, Fortresses of 220 Squadron and USN Catalinas. On the 11th a B-24 of USN Squadron VP-84, operating from Londonderry, sank *U611* some 500 miles out from the Irish coast. Late that night Dönitz called off this entirely unsatisfactory pack operation; HX 217, says Milner, had provided

> perhaps the best example of *defence* of a convoy in the entire war.

If ONS 144 and HX 217 seemed once more to prove that a properly managed and well-escorted convoy could handle a U-boat attack, there remained the grim toll of independents. It looked at times as though the only thing that could halt this was the 'wild Atlantic winter' with its 'steady succession of cyclones sweeping across the convoy routes, whipping up monstrous seas'.[117] It was this, and according to Dönitz this alone, that brought operations to a stop in mid-December, and accounts for the steep fall in December sinkings: a total of seventy-three ships (compared with November's 134), 348,902 tons, of which, nevertheless, sixty ships (330,816 tons) were sunk by submarines, and of those forty-six in the North Atlantic (262,135 tons). There was not much doubt where the *schwerpunkt* of the war at sea still lay; the OIC certainly had no doubts, and on 22 November anxiety had reached such a pitch that Clayton (see p. 319) informed the GC & CS that the U-boat campaign was

> the one campaign which Bletchley Park are not at present influencing to any marked extent – and it is the only one in which the war can be lost unless BP *do* help. I do not think that this is any exaggeration.[118]

For nearly ten months Bletchley Park had been struggling to penetrate the 4-wheel *Enigma* with 3-wheel Bombes, a problem which may be partly comprehended by the fact that it took a 3-wheel Bombe

> 26 times longer to test the text of a four-wheel signal than to test that of a three-wheel signal.[119]

What was needed, once more, was a capture, as in 1941, when GC & CS obtained a copy of the code-book of the German short weather signals which had enabled it to break into the naval *Enigma*. In early 1942, however, the Germans had changed the book, and no amount of

508

effort at Bletchley Park could reconstitute the new one. Then, on 30 October, manna fell once more from heaven: *U 559* was sunk by the destroyer HMS *Petard* off Port Said, and the weather code-book was retrieved by a boarding-party before the U-boat went down. Mediterranean U-boats had their own *Enigma* settings (*MEDUSA*), and it took some time before this valuable prize could be made effective against *TRITON*. It may be imagined with what emotions the Submarine Tracking Room, the OIC, the Directorate of Anti-Submarine Warfare, the Board of Admiralty and the new Anti-U-boat Warfare Committee learned on 13 December that Bletchley Park had finally broken the 4-wheel *TRITON* key, and with what relief the First Sea Lord imparted this information to the US Chief of Naval Operations.

December, as stated, was even-handed with its favours. Patrick Beesly recounts how the Tracking Room received this long-awaited news on Winn's weekly rest day:

> Overjoyed, he [Beesly] at once telephoned his chief to explain in suitably guarded terms that the 'Oracle' could once more be consulted, expecting that Winn would say that he would be round at the Admiralty within half an hour, ready to work throughout the night on the tricky confusing situation that would certainly be revealed once Special Intelligence started to pour in.[120]

Instead, he was told that Winn had collapsed:

> His doctor advised him that he was suffering from total mental and physical exhaustion, that his blood pressure was dangerously low, that unless he took a complete and prolonged rest he would never again be fit enough to undertake serious work of any sort, and that in no circumstances could a return to the Admiralty be permitted.

This was dreadful news indeed; no one is absolutely irreplaceable, but as Beesly, his deputy, knew better than anyone, Winn 'was certainly irreplaceable in the short term, and time was indeed short.' He adds a footnote that could not be known in December, 1942:

> In the end the gods relented. Winn, being the man he was, defied his doctor and was back on duty in four weeks, but it had been a very close shave.[121]

The *TRITON* decrypts, says Beesly, began to flow in 'within an hour', but the backlog was enormous, and their immediate impact was not striking. It was, in fact, not until the battle was effectively over, that Bletchley Park regained complete current mastery of *TRITON* (see p. 627). The breakthrough in December, 1943, was certainly not in time to be of any help to ONS 154, which set out on a doomed passage on the 19th. This convoy's forty-five ships were escorted by Group C1, now commanded by Lieutenant-Commander Windeyer in the destroyer *St Laurent* with five Canadian corvettes in company. We have met Windeyer more than once already, and seen him to be a very competent professional officer; this was his first experience of command of a group, which is, of course, a different matter from command of a ship. From what was about to happen it seems likely that he was by now a very tired man – a condition not uncommon in the RCN. It was a weakness in C1 that two of the corvettes were new to it, and that there had been changes of Commanding Officers. It was a weakness, too, and a serious one, that there was no second destroyer. It was bad that a pre-sailing battle exercise for the group was prevented by foul weather and the breakdown of the submarine. It was worse that Windeyer made no attempt to redeem this by calling his captains together for a tactical conference. Worst of all, in the event, was a Tracking Room error (a failure of the 'Working Fiction' which still held sway) which set ONS 154 on what proved to be a fatal route.

There was nothing special to be said about the actual course of events. ONS 154 had the misfortune to be one of the bad convoy battles from the Allied point of view, indeed, in Milner's words, 'a disaster of the first order', weighing particularly heavily on the RCN. The Tracking Room's mistake was in sending the convoy on a south-westerly course towards the Azores, in the hope of enabling it to avoid the brutal weather of the North Atlantic (which could add days to the length of a voyage). What this routing actually did was to bring ONS 154 into the area of two U-boat packs – *Spitz* and *Umgestum* – totalling twenty boats. It was *U154*, by an unamusing coincidence, that sighted ONS 154 on Boxing Day, and Dönitz at once ordered a combined attack.

The first phase took place that very night, when *U356*, in poor visibility due to drizzle and high spray, made two runs through the convoy in which four ships were either immediately sunk or damaged so seriously as to sink later. Windeyer, however, took his revenge when *St Laurent* destroyed *U356* with accurate depth-charge attacks. That was his only success; on the 27th *U225* hit the tanker *Scottish Heather* while she was refuelling a corvette at sea. This was always a testing operation; in heavy seas and the immediate presence of U-boats it could only be hair-raising. On the 28th thirteen U-boats closed the convoy, and Windeyer's nightmare really began; at one stage four confident U-boats in line abreast about a mile apart were seen coming in. They were forced to submerge and split up, but very soon 'it seemed that the whole U-boat fleet was loose within the convoy'.[122] Actually only five of the boats were responsible for the damage that ensued: *U591*, *U225*, *U260*, *U406* and (later) *U435*. On the night of 28 December the best performer was *U225*, with hits on four ships including the Commodore's *Empire Shackleton*. 'Within two hours nine ships were plucked from ONS 154, producing a scene of chaos.'

Strangely, the next day brought no more activity against the convoy itself, the U-boats contenting themselves with sinking the wrecks (two of them burning) which littered the ocean. Two RN destroyers, ordered up by Horton, joined C1, but did not remain long, being short of fuel; with two of Windeyer's corvettes they parted company on the 30th, leaving only four vessels in the escort. That afternoon the U-boats claimed their last victim, the Special Service (converted merchant 'Q' ship) HMS *Fidelity*, making a total of fourteen ships sunk at a cost of one U-boat. Windeyer was by now in such a state of anxiety that he told the captains of two fast ships with civilian passengers aboard to use their own judgment as to whether or not to remain in convoy. They chose to remain. On 31 December the destroyer HMS *Fame* from B6 arrived with Heathcote who now relieved Windeyer as Senior Officer:

Windeyer, exhausted by the ordeal and now seeing torpedoes at every turn, was put to bed. The battle had cost the Allies fourteen ships and 486 lives. In exchange one U-boat was thought to have been damaged.

Dönitz remarked:

This was a good note on which to end the Battle of the Atlantic for the year.[123]

In each of the Twentieth Century's world wars there was one conspicuously awful year. In the First World War it was 1917 – the year of the Russian revolutions, of widespread mutiny in the French Army, of 'Passchendaele' the 'greatest martyrdom', of Caporetto, the year when air bombardment of cities became a distinct feature of war, the year when the U-boats exacted a toll of 6,235,878 tons of shipping. In World War II it was 1942, when the roll-call included the flood tide of Japanese victory, further calamitous losses and retreats on the Eastern Front, severe defeat in the Desert, a series of heavy blows to Allied sea power, and 7,790,697 tons of shipping (1,664 ships) lost. In this unprecedented and unequalled figure the Axis submarines – but above all the U-boats – were responsible for 6,266,215 tons (1,160 ships) and the North Atlantic accounted for 5,471,222 tons (1,006 ships). The cost to the U-boat Service was eighty-six boats, sixty-five of them between July and December. This brought their total loss in the war to date to 153 U-boats, as against a total of 393 in service and 212 operational as the year ended. It was in the light of these considerations, says Roskill, that

> To the British Admiralty it was plain that the Battle of the Convoy Routes was still to be decided, that the enemy had greater strength than ever before, and that the crisis in the long-drawn struggle was near.[124]

In December as in January,

> The Atlantic convoy was still the heartbeat of the war.

7

We Had Lost the Battle

'We had lost the Battle of the Atlantic.'
Dönitz, MEMOIRS

THE WATCHWORD OF the ARCADIA Conference in January, 1942, was 'Germany first', the slogan that spelt the ultimate defeat of Germany. The watchword of SYMBOL, the Casablanca Conference in January, 1943, was 'Unconditional Surrender', the slogan that ensured that Germany's defeat would be long delayed. We do not need to go into that matter in depth; it is worth noting, however, that the frame of mind that prompted the resurrection of that famous phrase,[1] and the warm approval of the great majority of the British and American people when they heard it, did stem in no small degree from the experience of unrestricted submarine warfare. Dönitz, as one might expect, has strong words to say about 'Unconditional Surrender' in his memoirs; for any German senior commander, he says, it was 'wholly unacceptable'. This is no doubt perfectly true, but the fact remains that Dönitz himself and his U-boats were considerably responsible for reviving this echo of another hard war in 1862.

Certainly all those present at Casablanca who had any inner knowledge of the U-boat war were deeply conscious of the threat it presented as the new year, 1943, came in. They saw

the stage set for Germany to fling into the Atlantic struggle the greatest possible strength, directed by the man who had from the beginning of

513

the war controlled the U-boats. . . . It was plain to both sides that the U-boats and the convoy escorts would shortly be locked in a deadly, ruthless series of fights, in which no mercy would be expected and little shown.[2]

The Submarine Tracking Room, in its January Anti-Submarine Report, warned that the evasive routing, on which the Admiralty had relied (supported by the 'Working Fiction') during much of 1942, might no longer work:

> it should be appreciated that with the growth of the operational U-boat force and the consequently greater areas covered by their patrols – which sometimes appear to approach ubiquity – the use of this method is limited and may soon be outworn . . . The potentially annihilating superiority which the enemy, given a favourable strategic situation, might bring to bear on a convoy unlucky enough to be caught early on a homeward journey and far away from effective air cover cannot be appreciated by reference to any past experiences . . . the critical phase of the U-boat war in the Atlantic cannot be long postponed.[3]

Among the many preoccupations of the British leaders as they prepared themselves for the Casablanca Conference was the awareness of an oil-fuel crisis which had been building up steadily since the first large-scale U-boat incursions in the Gulf of Mexico in 1942. By mid-December of that year commercial stocks were down to 300,000 tons, as against a monthly consumption of 130,000 tons – in other words, a reserve of less than $2\frac{1}{2}$ months' supply. Admittedly, the Admiralty held another million tons for emergency, but it would require a very dire emergency indeed to justify tapping this, since it could mean that the fleet would be immobilized, which would mean in turn that the foundation of all British strategies would disintegrate. The acuteness of this threat was brought home to the Americans also by a disaster on the very eve of the Conference.

On 3 January *U514* sighted an all-tanker convoy on a northerly course from Trinidad; she succeeded in sinking one ship but then lost contact. Dönitz, however, was able to draw the correct conclusions from this encounter, and bring to the scene a U-boat group (*Delphin*) which he had formed for the purpose of harassing the American supply and reinforcement convoys for TORCH. What *U514* had seen was, in fact, TM 1, a special convoy of nine tankers making its way from Trinidad towards Gibraltar with fuel for the American forces in North Africa. At the time of sighting, the *Delphin* Group was about a thousand miles away from the convoy, which it now proceeded to close, as Dönitz says, 'at the speed of a cyclist'.[4] Naturally, this took some time, during which alternative temptations seemed to be offered, but Dönitz steadfastly 'played his hunch' despite the doubts of his staff, and on 8 January TM 1 steamed right into the *Delphin* patrol line. For a convoy of such importance, it was very weakly protected; the escort consisted only of one destroyer and three corvettes, badly hampered by the simultaneous failure of their radar sets. Seven tankers were lost out of nine. General von Arnim, commanding the German forces in Tunisia, sent a grateful telegram to Dönitz, and the Allied staffs and statesmen at Casablanca on the 14th gathered with something more to think about. It is small wonder that when the Combined Chiefs of Staff presented their report to the final plenary meeting of the Conference on 23 January their first sentence read:

The defeat of the U-boat must remain a first charge on the resources of the United Nations.[5]

The word 'remain' invites a question mark. As we have constantly seen, the matter of VLR aircraft priorities was still unresolved and was not advanced at Casablanca. The dispute over first use of the airborne version of centimetric radar, whether by Coastal Command in the form of ASV III, or by Bomber Command in the form of H2S (carrying with it the certainty that this great technological forward leap would be revealed to the Germans in a crashed bomber, probably fairly soon),[6] ended in defeat for Coastal Command in December, 1942, when Churchill ruled in favour of H2S. In both these areas, when it came to implementing the 'first charge' on resources, there continued to be more lip-service than sincerity in responsible quarters. Indeed, as regards the VLR aircraft (which effectively meant American Liberators),

The whole story . . . is one of misunderstanding, argument, procrastination and delay, bedevilled throughout by inter-Service controversies in Washington and [Admiral] King's determination, *pace* Casablanca, to give priority to the Pacific. . . . King's obsession with the Pacific and the Battle of Washington cost us dear in the Battle of the Atlantic.[7]

It was now, to Air Marshal Harris's obvious dismay, that Bomber Command was called upon for its biggest direct contribution to the Battle of the Atlantic; on the day the Casablanca Conference opened he received a new Directive:

> to subject the following [U-boat] bases to a maximum scale of attack by your Command at night with the object of effectively devastating the whole area in which are located the submarines, their maintenance facilities and the services, power, water, light, communications, etc. and other resources upon which their operations depend. The order of priority of the bases is as follows:
>
> Lorient
> St Nazaire
> Brest
> La Pallice.[8]

Yet in the same Directive – one may say, in the same breath, such was the dedication of the Air Staff to the strategic offensive against Germany – Harris was also told:

> The operations are not to prejudice:
> (i) Any attack which you may be planning to undertake against Berlin.
> (ii) Any concentrated attack which suitable weather may enable you to direct against important objectives in Germany and Italy.

In obedience to the new Directive (with all its ambiguity) Bomber Command went to Lorient that very night, 14/15 January, and the next, and again on the 23rd/24th and 26th/27th, delivering 1,000 tons of bombs in these four nights. It was back again on the 29th/30th, then on four nights in February (1,000 tons dropped in the first three) and two nights in April. St Nazaire was attacked five times (two raids in March involving the dropping of 1,500 tons), and Brest once. In all, between 14 January and 6 April, when Bomber Command was released from this task, 3,170 sorties were flown against the Biscay bases. Two of these (Lorient, 13/14 February, and St Nazaire, 28/29 February) were by over 400 aircraft. Thirty-eight bombers failed to return and nine more were lost in accidents. And for reasons that we have already noted (see pp. 354–5) it was a futile exercise. Harris himself says:

> The U-boat shelters ... were covered with many feet of reinforced

concrete and were without question proof against any bomb we had at that time; when the bombs exploded on the roofs of these shelters they made no more than a slight indentation in the surface. . . . I protested repeatedly against this hopeless misuse of air power on an operation which could not possibly achieve the object that was intended.[9]

Against the Biscay towns themselves, Bomber Command's attacks were devastating, as the photographic records show; the bombers 'destroyed almost everything except the [U-boat] pens'.[10] *Enigma* decrypts, Photographic Reconnaissance and Secret Service reports ensured that this depressing fact was well known to the responsible authorities at the time. A far smaller number of long-range aircraft transferred in good time to Coastal Command would have been infinitely more useful – but the mere thought of such a thing would put Harris at risk of apoplexy.

The great Anglo-American conferences, and their later tripartite enlargements – Washington, Casablanca, Quebec, Cairo, Teheran, Yalta, Potsdam – were an essential feature of the Allied war-making machinery. They were the 'summits' at which strategy was evolved, approved and authorized; equally, they provided opportunities to paper over cracks, divergencies of opinion or interpretation between allies, between staffs and commanders. The official photographs of the Casablanca assembly tend to display the outward signs of perfect accord and an implausible degree of light-heartedness. In fact, the conference marked the opening of a year of strategic wrangling between the Western allies and, on the American side, mounting distrust of British intentions, and among commanders interpreting the conference 'decisions' – men like King and Harris – a bland indifference well summed up in Harris's words:

the new instructions therefore made no difference.[11]

In matters concerning the Battle of the Atlantic, it was still the U-boats themselves, rather than conference agreements, that provided the true Directive.

* * * * *

On 30 January, 1943, *Admiral* Karl Dönitz succeeded Raeder as Commander-in-Chief of the German Navy,[12] with the rank of *Grossadmiral*. This was the pinnacle of his naval career. It did not separate him from the arm of the Service to which he had dedicated his life; he remained *Befehlshaber-der-U-boote*, as he had been since October, 1939, on the simple ground that

> there was no senior officer in the Navy who possessed the same knowledge and had the same experience of submarine warfare as I.[13]

To make this situation workable, the U-boat Staff was incorporated in the Naval High Command under the designation 'Section II', and moved to Berlin, lodged in the Hotel am Steinplatz in Charlottenberg. The day-to-day conduct of the U-boat war was directed by *Konteradmiral* Godt as *FdU*, 'to whom I was linked by many years of close collaboration'. Godt's chief staff officer was Günther Hessler, Dönitz's son-in-law, who now enjoyed the reputation of a U-boat 'ace' in his own right.

As Commander-in-Chief, Dönitz now moved in the corridors of supreme power; until this date, he tells us, he had only had nine personal interviews with Hitler since 1934. Now they would be frequent, and as it turned out they would begin with a disagreement which caused Dönitz to wonder whether his days as C-in-C might not be numbered before they had properly begun. With Raeder's rank and title, he had also inherited the issue which had led to Raeder's resignation. For some time Hitler's discontent with the remains of the 'Z Plan' surface fleet had been mounting. The complete failure of a force consisting of the pocket battleship *Lützow*, the heavy cruiser *Hipper* and six large German destroyers against the escort of JW 51B, a small convoy making for Murmansk, occurred in the Barents Sea on 31 December. Against a British loss of one old (1929) destroyer and a minesweeper, the Germans had a destroyer sunk and substantial damage done to *Hipper*. Worse still, the pocket battleship had been completely ineffective and the convoy had sustained no loss at all. In a towering rage, Hitler announced his 'unalterable resolve' to scrap the big ships of the fleet and mount their guns on land for coastal defence. When Raeder jibbed at this, it became Dönitz's first task, and his immediate disposition, having himself argued against the priorities accorded to the surface fleet, was to agree. But closer inspection showed him that while savings in manpower and matériel by laying up the big ships would be negligible, and scrapping them would in fact make fresh demands on labour and dock services, the implementation of the project could not but react politically and militarily to our disadvantage.[14]

More succinctly, Hitler's naval *aide*, *Vizeadmiral* Krancke, had already told him that the scrapping policy 'would be the cheapest victory Britain could possibly win'.[15] This had merely provoked another explosion, and now it was Dönitz's turn to say it again; on 26 February he told Hitler that he no longer agreed with the directive, and asked the Führer to cancel it:

> He was disagreeably surprised, since he had not expected that I, as the former Flag Officer, Submarines, and the man who had always pressed for the expansion of the U-boat war, would adopt this attitude. He was at first extremely immoderate but in the end grudgingly agreed, and I was ungraciously dismissed.

Dönitz naturally saw himself following in Raeder's footsteps fairly soon, but to his surprise it turned out quite otherwise:

> From then onwards [Hitler] treated me with exceptional civility, and he continued to do so until the end of April, 1945. He never failed to address me with punctilious correctness and by my rank, and in my presence he never once lost his temper or was other than courteous and civil.

So, properly speaking, began the relationship which would end with Hitler nominating Dönitz as his successor on 29 April, 1945. It is one of the curiosities of history. As we have seen (p. 172) Dönitz was no half-Nazi; he was emphatically at one with those 17,265,283 Germans who cast their votes for Hitler in the election of March, 1933.[16] Returning to Germany from the Far East in 1935,

> Like the mass of the German people, I too, naturally regarded with pride and joy the increase in German prestige that had occurred since Hitler had come to power.[17]

He was in particular struck with the transformation of the status of officers:

> In the nineteen-twenties, for example, walking through a dockyard or

factory in uniform had by no means always been a pleasant experience. Then the working men had been hostile and unapproachable. Now things were very different.

For the ex-Imperial officer, what Hitler had given was a true homecoming at last, to a country in which unemployment appeared to have been abolished, the class war no longer tore the nation apart, and the shame of defeat in 1918 was being expunged:

> On the memorials of the first world war the words: 'Lord God, set us free!' are frequently to be found. We had become free. After the triumph of the Saar plebiscite, the declaration of our sovereign independence, the reoccupation of the Rhineland and the union with Austria and the Sudetenland had followed each other, a sequence of successes in the field of foreign policy. What patriotic citizen, what fighting man, would not have welcomed such a resurgence of his country after years of degradation and poverty? A united Greater Germany, the dream of our forbears, had become a reality.

When war came, Dönitz's officer ethos became even more firmly wedded to his Nazi faith:

> the die was cast, I was quite clear in my own mind that for me, as a member of the Armed Forces, there was only one possible course – to fight against our external enemies.

The same simple proposition held good now:

> When I was appointed Commander-in-Chief in January, 1943, I fully realized the heavy responsibility that I was accepting, but my belief that as a member of the Armed Forces in time of war my sole duty was to fight with all my strength against our external enemies was not affected in any way.

Hitler recognized this pure flame of patriotic determination and professional loyalty, and as the Third Reich disintegrated he found in this cool, unswerving naval officer a rock of reliability where once he would least have expected it. Dönitz, for his part, never forgot what he considered that he and his like owed to Hitler, even when the ruin the latter had wrought was engulfing them all. Thus it was, as Padfield says, 'from both their points of view an ideal relationship'.[18] Dönitz, and other specialist professionals (Speer comes at once to mind) were to a large extent insulated against what he calls 'the obverse side of the national socialist medal'. Locked in the exacting routines of their daily duty, facing always 'outwards' as it were, towards the sea and their powerful British foe, the naval commanders turned their backs as firmly upon the atrocities of the Third Reich as Nelson's telescope to his blind eye at Copenhagen:

> To expect a commander to accept the heavy responsibilities which de-volve upon him in war and at the same time to bother his head about internal conditions, let alone to enter upon a struggle against the political leadership of his own country, is asking altogether too much of him.

He and his naval colleagues, he tells us, 'most firmly disassociated ourselves from the excesses perpetrated against the Jews' – but these, he goes on to say, 'reached their culmination in the "crystal night"'.[19] They did not. The culmination was what the Nazis smoothly called the 'Final Solution' of the Jewish 'problem', which has gone down in history as 'The Holocaust'. On this he has nothing direct to say. He makes it clear that he could never have joined in the ill-fated 'July Plot' against Hitler's life in 1944, although he concedes that the con-spirators had sound 'moral motives', being aware of 'the mass murders that had been committed by the Hitler régime', and he continues:

> I cannot help asking myself how I myself would have acted, had I known of the crimes perpetrated by the National Socialist system.
>
> I feel sure that there were things which, on principle, I would never have tolerated and which I would have opposed to the best of my ability.
>
> But what I, as a responsible member of the armed forces of a country at war, would, in fact, have done, I cannot say.[20]

This is, at least, honest, and conforms to his generally uncringing post-war posture, from Nuremberg onwards. He *was* a Nazi, and it was with palpable pain that he submitted to massive evidence of the nature of the régime and accepted the unpalatable truth. Yet he stands always apart from the band of coarse-grained, ignorant, scheming, brutal bigots who made up most of the mephitic circle of the Nazi leadership.

His loyalty was that of a soldier; his patriotism was a burning fire; like many others, his ignorance of the evils was at least partly wilful. His Order of the Day, on taking up his new office on 30 January, reflects the working of his mind:

> As of today I take over the post of Commander-in-Chief of the Navy, by order of the Führer. I thank the submarine arm, which I have been permitted to command hitherto, for its death-defying readiness to fight, which it has shown at all times, and for its loyalty. I shall continue to retain command of the U-boats. I will command the Navy with the same hard, soldierly spirit. I expect from each one unconditional obedience, the highest courage, and devotion to the last. In that lies our honour. Gathered round our Führer, we shall not lay down our arms until victory and peace have been achieved.

One thing is clear: whatever questions such men as this may have asked themselves at different times, they would receive no help in answering them from the Casablanca formula of 'Unconditional Surrender'.

* * * * *

On the opposite side – and in an opposite manner – another Command change was also taking place. I wrote in *The Right Of The Line*:

> Air Chief Marshal Sir Philip Joubert de la Ferté, KCB, CMG, DSO, belongs to a familiar category of unfortunates: those officers, in different Services and in different wars, who preside over bad times, weather the worst storms, but do not remain in command when the change of fortune comes and the reward of strain and effort can be collected.[21]

Joubert, despite the evidently valuable work that he had done for Coastal Command since his return to it in June, 1941, did not collect universally golden opinions (see p. 367). On 5 February, 1943, he was replaced by Air Marshal Sir John Slessor, who had been Assistant Chief of the Air Staff (Policy) for nearly a year. He came to Coastal Command with a high reputation, much of it gained at the centre of RAF affairs, the Air Ministry. He had also enjoyed a spell as AOC of a Bomber Command Group (the redoubtable No 5). His heart was in the bombing campaign, and it is this author's belief that he never really understood the significance of Coastal Command's rôle. He saw it as a defensive weapon, an essential part of what could later be called

Britain's 'survival kit'. He did not perceive the *offensive* character, in so greatly helping to make OVERLORD possible, which gave the Command a true centrality. Yet in his 11-month period of office, he brought new energy and drive (as Horton had done at Western Approaches), a fierce aggressiveness which communicated itself to his crews and may be summed up in the indefinable but always recognizable quality, leadership. This Slessor undoubtedly possessed, to a degree that the more intellectual Joubert did not; and it was felt not only in the Command, but by his naval colleagues, by the Air Ministry – and by the U-boats.

Slessor inherited, as Horton had done, a definitely 'going concern', which is more than can be said for either of his two predecessors. He tells us:

> The sixty squadrons of Coastal Command in February, 1943, had a strength of some 850 aircraft and included units manned by Canadians, Australians, New Zealanders, Norwegians, Poles, Czechs and Dutchmen, as well as the three United States squadrons under our operational control. The anti-submarine squadrons made up the bulk of the force and amounted to thirty-four squadrons with a strength of some 430 aircraft. Of these, twelve squadrons were of flying boats, eight equipped with Sunderlands and the other four – including 84 Squadron USN based on Iceland – with the Catalina.[22]

The *prima donnas* of the Command were the Liberators, of which there were still only two squadrons, though 'these aircraft were to revolutionize the whole defence of convoys'.[23] Indeed, they had already gone some distance towards doing so, as we have seen, despite a daily availability of only about fourteen. As with Joubert, this matter would be one of Slessor's most urgent preoccupations.

* * * * *

It was in 1942 that the expanded U-boat building programme that Dönitz had repeatedly demanded at last took effect. In the last quarter of that year no fewer than sixty-nine new boats were commissioned. In January, 1943, the total stood at 393, of which 212 were operational. With the increase came, inevitably, dilution, and in any case, no increase could have offset the fierce strength of the 'steep Atlantick stream' which now presented a bravura performance. 'The elements,' wrote Dönitz, 'seemed to rage in uncontrolled fury.'[24] Herbert Werner, Executive Officer of *U 230*, recalled winds 'of up to 150 mph'; on watch, he said, the wind punished us with driving snow, sleet, hail and frozen spray. It beat against our rubber diver's suits, cut our faces like a razor, and threatened to tear away our eye masks; only the steel belts around our waists secured us to boat and life. Below, inside the bobbing steel cockle-shell, the boat's violent up-and-down motions drove us to the floor-plates and hurled us straight up and threw us around like puppets.

Werner speaks of waves 70 metres high breaking over the U-boat, 'forcing us on the bridge to ride for long seconds far below the surface'.[25] Between October, 1942, and February, 1943, there were more than 100 days when winds in the North Atlantic reached Force 7 on the Beaufort Scale or higher – that is to say, approaching gale strength:

During January alone, four merchant ships went aground, eight foundered, and forty were heavily damaged by weather. One rescue ship simply turned over and sank with the weight of ice which formed on her decks and superstructure. . . . Their escorts were in as bad or worse case. Of the 196 Canadian and 35 British ships now under Canadian operational command, less than seventy per cent could be kept operational at any time.[26]

In such conditions, frustrating both sides impartially, it is scarcely surprising that convoy battles were few, scrappy and inconclusive. Out of seventeen ON, ONS, HX and SC convoys operating during January, only three were involved in action against the U-boats, and only five merchant ships were lost from these convoys. The *Jaguar* Group sank one ship from HX 222 in the middle of the month, and a straggler from SC 117 towards the end of it, but in neither case was the group able to mount a concerted attack. In the wild storms that were prevalent, says Dönitz, 'systematic search for shipping became impossible';[27] and the U-boats found inter-communication difficult because of radio interference. At the very end of January *U 456* (Teichert) sighted HX 224; Teichert trailed the convoy for three days, attacked and sank two ships. On 3 February *U 632* found a straggler, making the total loss three. Five other boats, although alerted, failed to reach the convoy.

Making all allowances for the vile weather, the January performance was disappointing. The total loss of Allied shipping was 261,359 tons (fifty ships), of which 56,733 tons (sixteen ships) occurred in the

Mediterranean and the Pacific. U-boats accounted for 203,128 tons (thirty-seven ships) and the North Atlantic saw the loss of 172,691 tons (twenty-seven ships). It was a very severe fall from the high promise of November, and the U-boat Command was not satisfied that the weather accounted for all of it:

> In this month we had the impression that the hitherto very conservative manner in which the British conducted their convoy routing had undergone some modification. They now seemed to be diverting convoys to a far greater extent and to be dispersing them over far wider areas of the Atlantic. The whole system had obviously become more flexible.[27]

U-boat Command had its own equivalent of Winn's 'Working Fiction'. Every day a 'U-boat Disposition Chart' was drawn up, intended to match any such chart in the Admiralty (Dönitz did not know of the Submarine Tracking Room, but assumed that something of that kind must exist) and showing how it must have looked on the strength of sightings, other reports and radio interceptions (by which Dönitz meant D/F fixes). The U-boat staff then debated 'in the enemy's place, how would we react to these dispositions?' It was, says Dönitz, a 'game of chess', and at the beginning of 1943 it had suddenly become more complicated. Why?

So it came about that high among the pressing matters calling for attention by the new *Kriegsmarine* C-in-C at the end of January was yet another enquiry into security in the U-boat Service. Once more the Chief of the Navy Signals Department, *Vizeadmiral* Erhard Märtens, flatly pronounced that the *Enigma* ciphers were unbreakable, and once more this verdict was accepted by Dönitz and the U-boat staff. Ronald Lewin comments:

> The truth is that in spite of a professional instinct that told them something was wrong, the men in power at the head of the German armed services suffered from a limitation once defined by that shrewd sociologist Thorsten Veblen as 'trained incapacity'. Their minds had been dragooned and regimented into the belief that Enigma was totally secure: therefore they were incapable of assessing objectively any indications that it had become insecure. The error is repetitive.[28]

It must be said, however, in defence of the U-boat staff, that they did have plausible reasons for looking in other directions than *Enigma*. Acutely conscious, by now, of the growing power of Allied technology, they were quite ready to blame that for their disappointments: the real villain, they concluded, was airborne radar. But here they were in the realm of prophecy. ASV III had yet to make its impressive mark. Furthermore, there was something else altogether to persuade them that a big change had come over the 'game of chess':

> We now know that this was really so. In the middle of November 1942 Admiral Sir Max Horton had assumed command of the Western Approaches. . . As an outstanding submarine captain of the First World War and Flag Officer, Submarines, in the Second, Admiral Horton was better qualified than anyone else to read the mind of German U-boat Command and . . . render more difficult the prosecution of our U-boat campaign[29]

As we have seen, it was not so; it was not Horton who was really playing this chess game.

It was a difficult thing – indeed, impossible – for Dönitz and the Signals Staff to grasp that what had happened was that the *BdU* had now become the prisoner of his own system. With the coming of 'pack' warfare, the long-range tactical control which Dönitz had seen as a practical possibility in 1939 (see pp. 228–9) had become a routine reality – a reality involving a dense volume of radio signals:

> To carry the enormous burden of wireless traffic generated by this system the U-boat Command developed a signals network which, for complexity, flexibility and efficiency, was probably unequalled in the history of military communications. By the same token, however, it could not prevent the interception of the traffic or conceal its signals routines from the attention of Allied Traffic Analysis and, from the time when GC & CS broke the Shark [*TRITON*] key, it presented the Allies with an unprecedently rich flow of operational intelligence.[30]

This was what had gone wrong with the chess game: re-routing made more certain by the re-entry into *Enigma* in December, 1942, and the end of the black-out, reinforced by the return of Winn. So complete now was the Tracking Room's authority that the Assistant Chief of Naval Staff (U-boat Warfare and Trade), Rear-Admiral J. H. Edelsten, gave orders that no convoy or independent ship was to be routed against the advice of the Tracking Room without his express and personal permission (thus) setting the official seal of approval on a procedure which Hall and his assistants had long followed.[31]

And this, plus the Atlantic, was what stood between the U-boats and their prey in January and February, 1943.

Yet there were, in this Intelligence battle, always imponderables; so level was the exchange of pieces in the 'chess game' that no sooner had Bletchley Park effected its still partial entry into *TRITON*[32] than *xB-Dienst* obtained a compensating advantage. It still retained its own entry into the British Naval Cipher No 3, and now succeeded in decrypting both the Allied routing and re-routing signals and the daily U-boat situation reports that the Admiralty supplied to convoys. The significance of this needs no emphasis. Worse was to follow on 10 March, when U-Boat Command introduced a new code book for the short-signal weather reports which gave BP its most valuable entry-point into *TRITON*. This caused great alarm in the OIC and Admiral Edelsten felt obliged to inform the First Sea Lord that the Tracking Room might well face another black-out, possibly lasting for months. In the event it only lasted for nine days; from 20 March, subject to certain delays, *TRITON* was again read regularly. This was a brilliant performance by the GC & CS, partly due to an increase in the number of its 3-wheel Bombes from forty-nine at the end of 1942 to sixty in March, 1943, and also to the barely believable fact that the U-boats, for short signals and weather reports, used the *Enigma* as a 3-wheel machine. But chiefly it was the reward of that wise 'operation of the Bletchley establishment as a whole' to which we have referred above (p. 327).

The temptation to see Sigint as the very centrepiece of the final period of the Battle of the Atlantic is considerable; certainly the Admiralty was inclined towards this view in the dark days at the end of 1942. The British Official History seems to sway somewhat over this matter; thus we read:

Between February and June 1943 the battle of the Atlantic hinged to no small extent on the changing fortunes of a continuing trial of cryptographic and cryptanalytic resourcefulness between the *B-Dienst* and the Allies.[33]

527

However, as the same source tells us, complete mastery of TRITON did not come until after the battle, and until then, as a somewhat more reflective passage on another page also tells us,

> the value of the *Enigma* to evasive routing must be judged not by its failure to eliminate disasters to convoys, but by the extent to which it reduced the frequency and the scale of the disasters.

And elsewhere reflection produces a tempered verdict with which it is difficult to disagree:

> the battle which was fought in the Atlantic between December 1942 and May 1943 was the most prolonged and complex battle in the history of naval warfare, and when its outcome clearly hinged on many factors it is not easy to establish the extent to which it was influenced by the Allied decryption of the signals of the U-boat Command.[34]

* * * * *

On 5 February, 1943, Dönitz addressed a Directive to his staffs which well illustrates the 'hard, soldierly spirit' referred to in his first Order of the Day. He told them, with terse precision:

1. The question for us is winning the war. Considerations of how the Navy should appear after the war have no value.
2. The sea war is the U-boat war.
3. All has to be subordinated to this main goal.[35]

There is no hint here of any weakening of aggressive resolve, yet, being the realistic tactician that he was, always sensitive to the tides and currents of the war, Dönitz knew that a change, ominous for Germany, had come over it. 'We were already on the defensive,' he says, and cites the Eastern Front, where *Feldmarschall* von Paulus's Sixth Army had surrendered at Stalingrad on 2 February, and the Mediterranean, where combined Allied pressure was being brought to bear on the Axis forces in Tunisia. These factors could not fail to influence the war at sea:

> It was incumbent on the Navy to support these defensive campaigns. . . . There was yet another factor. Even if the enemy strengthened his forces in the Battle of the Atlantic to such an extent that we could no longer hope to inflict serious losses upon him, we should still have to continue

our efforts against the Allied sea lines of communication, in order to maintain our threat against them and so to tie down enemy forces.[36]

'To tie down enemy forces': this was a new emphasis, masked for general consumption by repetitions of the old objective, 'winning the war'. Yet these staff officers whom he was addressing were competent and reasonably well-informed; it is in a Staff appreciation of the tonnage war that we find these revealing words:

If the menace constituted by our attacks on tonnage were removed, a war potential of quite unpredictable strength would be released for action elsewhere.

This was the paradox: larger numbers of U-boats at sea in the central and North Atlantic than ever before – 100 boats – but at the same time a narrowing horizon of strategic possibility. The only hope of improvement lay in concentrating the new strength in the area of the 'Atlantic Gap' where air power did not yet reach, to do all the damage possible in the short remaining time before the Allies closed it, and while their resources were at full stretch because of TORCH.

By the time Dönitz's Directive reached its recipients, the final battle had begun. It started, in fact, as a sequel, a turning of the tables, of HX 224. It was a *B-Dienst* decrypt of a routing signal that alerted U-boat Command to the importance of SC 118, carrying quantities of war material destined both for Britain and for the USSR. *Konteradmiral* Godt accordingly collected all the available U-boats – twenty in all – into a new pack, *Pfeil* (Arrow) – across the anticipated course of the convoy. Then, on 3 February, the HX 224 straggler, the tanker *Cordelia*, was torpedoed by *U 632*, one of the boats which had failed to catch up with Teichert in his attack on that convoy. *Oberleutnant* Hans Karpf made a search for survivors, and the solitary one whom he found let fall the information that a large slow convoy was following two days behind the fast one on the same route. Karpf quickly reported this to U-boat HQ and *Pfeil* Group was thus fully informed of its intended prey's movements. Roskill comments:

The informant must have sacrificed many of his comrades' lives.[37]

However, this grim war of alternating advantages had not yet done with this story. At noon on 4 February *Oberleutnant* Ralph Münninch

($U\,187$) made a sighting report of SC 118. As was normal practice, the message was coded and brief, taking no more than 15–20 seconds for transmission. It was enough to constitute a death warrant for $U\,187$. The 61-ship convoy was numerically strongly escorted by Escort Group B2, normally commanded by Captain Donald Macintyre; however, his famous destroyer *Hesperus*[38] was undergoing a refit and the Senior Officer this time was Commander F. B. Proudfoot in *Vanessa*. This ship had HF/DF, but neither of the other two destroyers in B2 had that equipment. However, the rescue ship *Toward*, which we have met in this rôle with ON 67 a year earlier, was present with HF/DF equipment, which was also in the US Coast Guard cutter *Bibb*. Informed by them, Proudfoot sent off the destroyers *Vimy* and *Beverley* at full speed down the transmission beam of $U\,187$, and they duly sank her on that same day. It had been her first operation.

After that things went less well for the convoy and B2, though this proved to be, in Dönitz's words, 'perhaps the hardest convoy battle of the whole war'.[39] During the first night all the U-boat attacks on the convoy were driven off, and their only successes were the sinkings of two stragglers. The next day B2 was reinforced by two USN destroyers and a second cutter. $U\,465$ was located by HF/DF and severely damaged by a Fortress from Iceland. Air cover kept the pack down during 6 February, and when it closed in after dark the first three attacks were repelled by the very active escort, but in the early hours of the 7th *Oberleutnant Freiherr* von Forstner in $U\,402$ gave one of the best individual U-boat performances against a defended convoy of the whole war by sinking six ships (including SS *Toward*) in the space of four hours. With daylight, air cover once more kept the U-boats down and a Fortress of 220 Squadron sank $U\,624$. The Free French corvette *Lobelia* also sank $U\,609$. But that night Forstner returned to claim a seventh victim, and when the battle was finally broken off on the 9th the score stood at thirteen merchant ships lost from SC 118, with three U-boats sunk and four more severely damaged.[40] Effectively, this spelt a 20.6% casualty rate in the convoy, and a 35% rate in the *Pfeil* Group, a hard fight indeed.

The disturbing feature of the SC 118 battle, for Horton and all concerned, was that the heavy loss of merchantmen had taken place despite an unusually strong escort (with no fewer than five destroyers and two Coast Guard cutters after the second day). But once again it was shown that mere numbers are not everything; what these ships lacked was training as an integrated group – an old lesson which every month in the Atlantic seemed to find occasion to rub in. It was also clear that, in general, but during the long winter nights in particular, the aircraft operating at long ranges should be fitted with Leigh Lights, just as much as those hunting U-boats in the Bay of Biscay. And, says Roskill,

A further lesson was that in such a prolonged and severe battle expenditure of depth charges was enormous; replenishments for the escorts must therefore be carried in the merchantmen. And still more weight was added to the arguments in favour of support groups being used to reinforce threatened convoys. They were, in Admiral Horton's words, 'vital to secure reasonable safety'.[41]

It may be noted, too, that throughout this action seaborne HF/DF displayed itself as a major weapon in convoy defence, with an offensive potential which was also obvious. And, indeed, this is to be reckoned high among the 'many factors' on which, as Professor Hinsley says, the outcome of the Atlantic battle hinged.

After SC 118, as was normal, there was a lull in the heavy fighting, but this was Bletchley Park's bad time, and it was quite clear that the lull would not last. It is, incidentally, worth noting that the SC 118 battle was the first U-boat success of any significance since the end of December. Seven more convoys crossed the North Atlantic in February; three of them, SC 119, HX 225 and ON 164, had uneventful passages; one, HX 226, was diverted on the strength of a decrypt just before this source dried up; the remainder had different stories to tell. Between 17–20 February two U-boats of the *Haudegen* Group attacked ONS 165 in conditions of storm, fog and atmospheric radio interference which prevented the assembly of the pack. The result was a loss of two merchantmen, matched by the sinking of two U-boats. This was Escort Group B6 in action again; those two veteran (in every sense) destroyers, *Viscount* and *Fame*, were now repaired after the damage their victories had done to them in the SC 104 battle back in October. Working by HF/DF pointers, they pounced upon the U-boats; *Viscount* promptly sank *U 69*, and *Fame* sank *U 201*. It was a fine return for two 'old 'uns' – *Viscount* was launched in 1917 and commissioned in 1918, and *Fame* (modern by comparison) was part of the 1932 programme, launched in 1934. Dönitz did not like the arithmetic of this battle; 'for us,' he says, this engagement, which had resulted in the sinking of two enemy ships and the loss of two of our boats, was depressing.[42]

On 21 February *U664* (Graef), belonging to an improvised U-boat group, made a chance sighting of ONS 167, and succeeded in sinking two ships, but the group itself never came into action. What we can now see very clearly, though neither Senior Officers of Escorts, nor Commodores, nor Western Approaches Command could know this at the time, was that:

> The effectiveness of the U-boat assaults was far higher when they were delivered from positions taken up on the basis of advanced intelligence than when they had to be improvised in response to chance sightings of convoys that had not been expected or had been turned away.[43]

This is, after all, unsurprising.

Between these two U-boat setbacks, however, there was another cheering major victory. Escort Group A3, the last of the American groups operating in the North Atlantic (and only 'American' by courtesy) met sixty-three ships of Convoy ON 166 at EASTOMP in the North-West Approaches on 12 February. A3 was an experienced group, under an experienced Senior Officer, Captain Heineman, USN, whom we have already seen in action. At first it suffered from the drawback of having no destroyer at all; the two cutters, *Spencer* and *Campbell*, were fine, useful ships and well handled as they would shortly show, but they did not have a destroyer's speed, so valuable for swift response to a HF/DF fix. The arrival of the Polish destroyer *Burza*[44] on 22 February was therefore very welcome. The remainder of the escort was made up of four Canadian corvettes and one RN (*Dianthus*), of which all but one were regular members of this group. A3 was well supplied both with HF/DF and with 271M radar; none of these factors, however, availed to prevent serious losses of merchant ships.

It was not, on this occasion, an *xB-Dienst* intercept that gave U-boat Command the information it needed; this time it was the *Luftwaffe*'s Listening Service Regiment located in Paris which took in a signal from an escort aircraft identifying the convoy on 18 February. Godt assembled two packs, *Knappen* and *Ritter*, for the attack, which took the form of a running fight over 1,100 miles in a westerly direction which lasted from February 21 to February 25 and was conducted by both sides with great determination.[45]

During these five days twenty-one U-boats took part in the attack, keeping the escort at full stretch, but undaunted; indeed, it was Heineman in *Spencer* who opened the ball with the sinking of *U 225* on 21 February (although he did not have the satisfaction of certainty at the time). The next day *Campbell* and *Burza* shared the destruction of *U 606*, *Campbell* being badly damaged in an attempt to ram the U-boat. The whole action took place in dreadful weather conditions which, as usual, critically interfered with the essential equipment, radar and ASDIC. Thus six out of seven successful U-boat attacks came in undetected; the rescue ship was an early casualty, throwing an extra burden on the escorts, and the final result was fourteen ships sunk – 22.2%, a very grave loss.[46] We recall Professor Hinsley's words:

> the severe mauling of a convoy was the equivalent of a lost battle on land.[47]

There had now been two such in February, 1943. The crisis of the Atlantic battle had arrived.

A feature of the ON 166 operation that should be noted is the refuelling of escorts from tankers in the convoy while under way. This had been introduced as far back as June, 1942, but only slowly spread through the convoys owing to the continuing – indeed, increasing – shortage of tankers, and also to the great difficulty of the operation. Admiral Gretton describes it:

> The tanker first veered astern a light 'grass' steadying line which floated on the water. This was picked up right forward in the bows of the escort and was used to assist station-keeping and to steady the ship being fuelled. It was not used as a towing line. As soon as the grass rope had been secured, the tanker let out a rubber hose which was also buoyant. The escort picked this up with a grappling iron and hauled it inboard through a fair-lead. The end was joined to the connection piece on the forecastle. This was a comparatively simple matter in good weather, but if the sea was rough it might take a long time, station-keeping was difficult and there was danger of parting both the steadying line and the hose. Much depended on smart drill and skilled ship handling

533

and training was important. In bad weather, the men working in the bows of the escort got very wet and were in considerable danger.[48]

In the worst weather of the war it was Gretton's last sentence that chiefly applied. According to Dr Morison, there were three tankers on ON 166, and escorts were refuelled from these on nine days out of fourteen in the voyage, 'even during a 50-knot wind'. Even so, on 23 February, when HMS *Dianthus* found herself running badly short of fuel, the sea was too rough for this method, and she parted company. She reached St John's 'with every tank bone dry', having, according to her Commanding Officer,

> emptied 120 gallons of Admiralty Compound into Number 6 tank, also all gunnery oil, painting mixing oil, and two drums of special mineral oil. This increased fuel remaining by approximately half a ton, and eventually enabled me to get in.

'Apparently,' says Morison, 'only the castor oil in the sick bay was over-looked.'[49]

The U-boats also had fuel problems; it was two invaluable 'milch cows', *U 460* and *U 462*, that made possible the successive attacks on ONS 165, ON 166 and ONS 167:

> They lay between 400 and 600 miles to the north of the Azores and replenished no less than twenty-seven operational U-boats between the 21st of February and 5th of March.[50]

U 460 and *U 462* were 'broad beam' Type XIVs, with considerably greater cargo capacity than converted Type IXDs, and they fully demonstrated the superiority of boats specifically designed for definite rôles over improvisations.

The sharpening tempo of the battle was reflected in the February total of shipping losses: seventy-three ships (403,062 tons), of which sixty-three ships (359,328 tons) were sunk by submarines, forty-six of them (288,625 tons) in the North Atlantic. This was certainly a better performance than January's, but it had to be paid for. Only six U-boats had been sunk in January; in February the figure was nineteen, nine of them (eight and two halves) by aircraft. Taking the two months together, and given the current rate of new commissioning, this was a

534

containable figure; nevertheless, nineteen was the highest monthly figure of the war so far, a fact which cannot have escaped Dönitz's notice. At the same time, the Operations Staff at Naval High Command was estimating that merely to keep pace with Allied ship-building it would be necessary to sink a monthly average of 900,000 tons. With the substantially increasing number of U-boats now operating, says Rohwer,

> it was not unreasonable to suppose that it would still be possible to wage the tonnage war successfully in the future.[51]

Yet the average for the first two months of the year was only 332,210 tons. These were grave omens.

* * * * *

It was time to confer again. There were loose ends in the Allied conduct of the battle that needed to be tidied; an Atlantic Convoy Conference was accordingly convened in Washington under Admiral King on 1 March. The novelty of this event was that it was fully and formally tripartite for the first time. In this it differed very sharply from a previous meeting, also held in Washington, at the end of December, 1942, at which the Canadian naval delegation had felt itself to be invidiously 'junior' in status to the delegates of the big navies, the USN and RN, despite the 48% burden of escort work in the Atlantic that it was carrying. It was the Canadians who requested the March Conference in the first place, so a brief examination of their special position is required.

Only in November, 1942, did the Canadian Naval Service Headquarters (equivalent of the Admiralty) admit that it was fully engaged in its 'Big Battle', that the North Atlantic had undoubtedly become 'an anti-U-boat war zone of great strategic importance'. Milner comments:

> After three long years of hostilities the war had finally washed up on the shores of Canada, and the RCN was engaged on all fronts.[52]

With this realization came others that were displeasing; chief among them was mounting discontent with the now quite out-dated 1941 agreement that had given control of the North Atlantic as far as the 26°W CHOP (Change of Operational Control) line to the USN. With a major campaign on her doorstep, Canada was now in a mood to question severely an arrangement which, for example, made the dissemination of intelligence in the Western Atlantic a USN CTF-24 responsibility, so that even intelligence from the Canadian shore-based DF network could not be transmitted directly to RCN ships 'operating virtually within sight of Canada'.[53] It was time, Canadians felt, that their contribution to the war, and the proximity of one of its major theatres to their own country, should be recognized by the creation of a true Canadian command. It is easy to make retrospective lofty judgments on such sentiments – easy but foolish. No nation was exempt from them, and we shall shortly see British and American national pride vigorously at work in the same sense.

The difficulty of the RCN position at the end of 1942 was, quite simply, a very grave doubt, shared by both American and Royal Navies, about the efficiency of the 'C' escort groups. More perceptive officers in Western Approaches Command acknowledged that the Canadians were at a disadvantage in respect of essential equipment (radar and HF/DF above all). The stresses of expansion from practically nothing at the beginning of the war were also accepted. What was perhaps not sufficiently taken into account was the intense pressure of operational demands, which had time after time reduced schemes for improving training to pipe dreams. The net result, however, was what stuck in the throats of the British and American onlookers – such episodes as C4's two disasters in September (ON 127) and October (SC 107). And so it came about, in late December, that the Canadian Chief of Naval Staff, Vice-Admiral P. W. Nelles, learned with shock and disbelief that the British, with American support, were proposing to remove the Canadian groups from MOEF and send them to Western Approaches for intensive training. The Canadians would remain in the Eastern Atlantic as escorts for the TORCH convoys, benefiting from the powerful array of Allied air strength based on Gibraltar and North Africa, while eight 'B' groups handled the U-boat war.

Nelles's resentment was understandable. Although the RCN had responded unreservedly to every demand . . . Canadian interest remained focused on the mid-Atlantic: on convoy battles and U-boat packs. The RCN had been part of mid-ocean A/S escort since its inception. Now after stretching and scrimping for the common cause the Canadians were being asked to remove their escorts from the decisive theatre of the Battle of the Atlantic because the British believed they were inefficient. ... This was not in the spirit of load sharing that NSHQ had come to expect.[54]

To Nelles the efficiency question had the look of a camouflage – it had, in fact,

> quickly become a question of RCN operational control over its own ships and thereby of service independence.[55]

Such were the delicate nuances of international relations inside the Commonwealth. We have touched on this before (pp. 388–9). The fine shades of independent status were studied and cherished in the great Dominions, irrespective of their actual very great dependence on Britain and America for the sinews of war (at this very moment the RCN was asking Britain for fourteen reasonably modern destroyers to replace old ones damaged by the Atlantic storms and give the escort groups the thrust they needed). The British were painfully slow learners; as the Christmas Day conference convened in Washington, where disposition of Canada's Navy would be a large topic, the offer came from Western Approaches to send on the head of the British delegation, Horton's Chief of Staff, Commodore J. M. Mansfield, to Ottawa *after* the conference. No doubt no insult was intended; no doubt, too, that the Admiralty would have been genuinely surprised to hear that if Commonwealth ties were to be as real as the blood spilt on their behalf, it should have been axiomatic that Mansfield should come to an understanding in Ottawa first, and not turn up later, apparently as an afterthought. Fortunately, as so often happened, the 'man on the spot' was able to redeem some of the damage done by his masters. Mansfield overcame by his own tact and cheerfulness a great deal of the anger in the RCN. But, as so frequently occurred, it was not argument but the war itself that settled this matter; it was an inescapable fact, now established by Operational Research, that, as the Admiralty's Director of Anti-Submarine Warfare reported:

> 80% of all ships torpedoed in Trans-Atlantic convoys in the last two months were hit while being escorted by Canadian groups.

The dismal story of ONS 154 drove the lesson home; the Canadians had no option but to agree with the Anglo-American proposals. Three

RCN escort groups (1, 2 and 4) were thus absent from the North Atlantic during the final crisis.

To say that the Canadians liked this situation would be absurd. After the ONS 154 fiasco they could no longer argue the training issue – the pill was, in any case, sugared by the information that they were merely the first recipients of a general stepping up of training (Horton's fetish) throughout Western Approaches. What they could and did exert pressure upon was the Atlantic command position, and this was a main item on the agenda of the March Convoy Conference.[57] To the not inconsiderable surprise of both the British and the Canadians, the Americans quickly made it clear that they would be glad to be rid of the burden of North Atlantic convoy escort and the CTF-24 responsibility with it. Admiral King preferred to concentrate USN units in support of the North African campaign and confine Atlantic activity to the newly-formed Moroccan Sea Frontier,[58] an anomalous enclave within the British Strategic Zone, and to support for the US forces stationed in Iceland and Greenland. Roskill offers as one explanation of King's new proposal that he 'disliked escorts of mixed nationality'.[59] The larger truth would seem to be that he disliked wars of mixed nationality; Admiral King, like certain other high commanders – Field-Marshal Montgomery and General George Patton spring readily to mind – did not thrive in a coalition scene. However, 'it is an ill wind . . .'; the American withdrawal cleared the way for the fulfilment of the Canadian desire to see the end of CTF-24, and the British desire to extend the authority of Western Approaches Command right across the Atlantic. It was agreed that a Canadian North-West Atlantic Command would be created, under the Commanding Officer, Atlantic Coast (COAC, Rear-Admiral L. W. Murray in Halifax) with full authority westward of the new CHOP-line at 47°W, while Horton in Liverpool ruled over everything to the east of that. Thus

The Atlantic Convoy Conference was a watershed in Canadian and RCN history. . . . For the RCN the Canadian Northwest Atlantic was a dream come true and the only distinctly Canadian theatre of war.[60]

It is pleasant to record this 'happy ending'; but the conference, of course, had other work to do besides this. To enable the British and Canadians to shoulder their now unaided burden, it was agreed that some of the Canadian corvettes allocated to TORCH should be returned, and King also consented to the USN taking over the vital tanker convoys which ran between the Dutch West Indies and Britain. He went further: he even allocated an American Support Group, consisting of an escort carrier and five destroyers[61] to operate under British control in the North Atlantic, a splendidly cooperative gesture which may, perhaps, owe something to the conciliatory skills and charm of Sir Percy Noble. Other matters on the agenda were the speeding up of convoy cycles, the size of convoys and escorts (on which Western Approaches now had firm views based on Professor Blackett's Operational Research) and the all-important procedures of routing and diversion. In this field cooperation shortly produced one of its most striking examples of full partnership:

> The Naval Operational Intelligence Centres in London, Washington and Ottawa spoke with one voice so far as the Battle of the Atlantic was concerned.[62]

Admiral King was not a man to waste his shot on small birds, he saved it for big game; and if on matters of detail he could sometimes prove surprisingly generous, on big issues he was often obdurate. There were two big issues before the Atlantic Conference. One of them was the hardy perennial, VLR aircraft, the Liberators. The B-24, says one aviation historian of repute, was

> by far the most complicated and expensive combat aircraft the world had seen – though in this it merely showed the way things were going to be in the future.... In terms of industrial effort it transcended anything seen previously in any sphere of endeavour.[63]

The same source informs us:

> Yet it was built in bigger numbers than any other American aircraft in history, in more versions for more purposes than any other aircraft in history, and served on every front in World War II and with every Allied nation ... total production of all versions was a staggering 19,203.

Yet in 1943, whether under their American designations or by their RAF name, these essential instruments of long-range air war were still being doled out in tens and twenties. By the end of 1942 the US Navy possessed fifty-two of them; by February, 1943, Coastal Command had precisely eighteen available for the convoy routes, nine in Iceland (No 120 Squadron) and nine more in No 15 Group. The Atlantic Conference itself did nothing to improve this situation; once again it was the war that settled the arguments. As the grim events of March unfolded, Admiral King and the Navy Department were forced to revise their views of priority; at the end of that month,

> the Americans agreed that 255 Liberators (seventy-five from the US Army Air Force, sixty from the US Navy and 120 from British allocations) should be provided for the North Atlantic. This could not, of course, take effect at once.[64]

Indeed it could not. According to Slessor,

> That number was never reached, and a fair comment on the value of this sort of theoretical numerical assessment of 'requirements' is the fact that the U-boat campaign against the North Atlantic convoys was defeated by mid-summer with less than fifty VLR aircraft, in conjunction with the surface escorts and a couple of light carriers.[65]

In a footnote he adds that the less than fifty in question were

> All Coastal Command except six in 10 Squadron RCAF in Newfoundland.

The second big issue, also balked at this Washington conference, was that of a Supreme Allied Commander for the Atlantic theatre, a lack that we have touched upon above (p. 405). In fact there were two issues here: a Supreme Commander, sea and air and including such land forces as might be required, eg. for anti-aircraft defence of ports and bases and ship-borne gunners of the Maritime Regiment of Royal Artillery, and a 'Super Air Officer Commander-in-Chief' to pull together the all too separate threads of air activity, currently divided between Coastal Command, the USAAF, the US Navy and the RCAF. Indeed, it could in general be said that the whole top command situation constituted a real 'dog's breakfast', in the jargon of the day. This was well appreciated in Government and some Service circles, both in

Britain and in America. However, in both countries there was opposition to the creation of a Supremo from the Navies concerned. Admiral King, as he repeatedly showed, had an aversion to any kind of 'Supreme' authority that could impose itself on the United States Navy. Even the weight and majesty of the Combined Chiefs of Staff (of whom he himself was one) was liable to be set at nought if he considered that USN interests were being in any serious degree prejudiced. King liked to steer his own ship – he did not want a pilot on his bridge. Sir Dudley Pound and the British Naval Staff had trepidations (understandably) about the confusion and operational difficulties that might well arise from the sudden imposition of such an authority on an already complicated structure. They were also apprehensive on another score: it seemed that there was an idea among some influential Americans that the Supreme Commander, Atlantic, would be an American (King, perhaps?):

> To Britain victory in the Atlantic was a matter of life and death; to America it was only one part of a world-wide struggle. How could the British Admiralty delegate its responsibility to a national of another country? And what, asked the Naval Staff, would be the reaction of the House of Commons, the Press and the British people to such an idea?[66]

These were very serious questions. The idea was dropped.

The same fate befell the post of 'Super Air Officer'. This had been a favourite idea of Joubert's, endorsed by Slessor, and Slessor himself was regarded as a very likely candidate. Yet as he examined the practicalities, he shied away from the proposal; one practicality in particular seemed to him to be insuperable, and the name of it was 'King':

> I did not see King agreeing, for instance, to my coming to the conclusion on operational statistics that a US Naval squadron was not pulling its weight in the Caribbean and should be moved to Iceland. I think that's where it would break down.[67]

Slessor was certainly right. King was the stumbling-block. Churchill, at the beginning of April, took the trouble to write at length to a Conservative MP who had queried the apparent abandonment of the Supreme Commander principle. Churchill assured him:

that both His Majesty's Government and those fighting the day to day battle fully realize the general advantages of unified command.[68]

He acknowledged that continuous efforts had been made to achieve 'this ideal in the North Atlantic' and that the Washington Conference had been 'concerned largely with this question', and then he went on:

> There comes a point, however, in the development of all large commands where one must consider whether the general advantages of unity will outweigh the practical difficulties of administration as the size of the command and the complexity of the arrangements increase. In the North Atlantic there are very real practical limits which no paper arguments can possibly overcome.

It turned out that these unassailable 'practical limits' boiled down to

> different sets of escorts operating from bases on different sides of the Atlantic. It would be extremely difficult for a single command to control adequately escorts operating from bases thousands of miles away on the other side of the ocean.

This would surely have come as strange news to Admiral Nimitz, the Supreme Commander in the 7,000-mile wide Central Pacific, or General MacArthur, Supreme Commander in the South-West Pacific, and proved no deterrent, later in the year, to the setting up of a very far-flung South-East Asia Command under Admiral Lord Mountbatten. Yet in the aftermath of the Washington Conference, said Churchill,

> it is clear that the best practical arrangement is to have separate commands, working in close co-operation and unison, on either side of the Atlantic.

It all sounds very thin – a mask for failure. Yet Churchill did put a finger on the central matter: 'close co-operation'. Supreme commands necessarily depend upon goodwill – without it they are mere formalities and irritations. The simple truth was that separate commands would have King's goodwill, and a Supreme Commander would not.

There was a faint hope, nevertheless, that unity of practice, if not of protocol, might be achieved by the setting up of two joint bodies by this Conference: the Combined Procedure Board and the Allied Anti-

Submarine Survey Board. The object of the first was to set up a single system 'of operational intelligence and signals procedure for use by all Allied anti-submarine (air) squadrons in the Atlantic'; the advantages of this require no elaboration — indeed, the only wonder is that the thing had not been done before. The Combined Procedure Board set to work and drafted an acceptable scheme and was working on an agreement recommending its adoption,

> when the American Navy Department stepped in and brought the labours of the Board to an abrupt end.[69]

And it was the same with the Allied Anti-Submarine Survey Board; this consisted of two British and two American officers, representing equally naval and air interests.

They toured the Anti-Submarine commands and bases of the whole area, and produced a number of recommendations (including the abolition of the Moroccan Sea Frontier); none of these were acted upon and the Board was disbanded in September. This was all very discouraging. As Hilary Saunders says,

> A study of the orders issued and the plans propounded makes it difficult to escape the conclusion that Admiral King and his staff did not view the Battle of the Atlantic in the same light as General Marshall viewed the invasion of Europe in 1944.

Certainly, this was not what the Casablanca Conference had intended.

In defence of Admiral King it has to be recognized that he did have another war to fight as well. Allocating priorities among theatres of war is a conference-table exercise which the theatres themselves may reduce to mockery; campaigns gather their own momentum, whether defensive or offensive, calling inexorably for reinforcement, for equipment and supply. The war against Japan was now displaying both of these conditions: in New Guinea the Allies liquidated the last pockets of Japanese occupation on the coast, around Buna, in January, and in February the Japanese evacuated Guadalcanal — two important Allied successes which cried aloud to be followed up. In Burma, however, a British attempt to take the counter-offensive suffered heavy defeat which equally cried aloud to be avenged. Either way, irrespective of 'priorities', there would be demands on Allied resources of shipping, manpower, aircraft and landing craft that would be impossible to resist *in toto*. And meanwhile the stubborn Axis resistance in Tunisia was making the further strategy in Europe more and more difficult to plan, and ROUNDUP in 1943 was taking on a less and less likely look. The failures of the Washington Conference and Admiral King's intransigence have to be seen against this background, and it has to be admitted that the Americans did not have the monopoly of that quality. The proposals for unified command, says Roskill,

> seem . . . to have foundered on the unwillingness of Britain and the United States to surrender any measures of sovereignty within their own strategic zones.[70]

Jürgen Rohwer calls it a

> hard-to-understand mistake on the Allied side, that national and service rivalries combined with ignorance and preoccupation prevented a timely concentration of available forces at the decisive spot.[71]

These are the hazards of coalition war; by and large, the Anglo-American coalition in World War II was wonderfully successful, surviving strains which would have smashed a weaker structure. *How* successful it was is perhaps best measured by the occasions, such as the Atlantic Conference of March, 1943, when the coalition was *not* working well. And all examples proved, without fail, that coalitions live or die by goodwill or the lack of it.

* * * *

The decisions taken at the Atlantic Conference did not become effective until 1 April; before they could do so, the supreme crisis of the Battle of the Atlantic had come and gone. March, 1943, was the month when Allied 'fortunes in the mid-ocean reached rock-bottom'.[72] Macintyre called it 'the dark hour before the dawn'.[73] It is important to be clear about the precise meanings of these strong words. Macintyre also says that this month was

> one of the most disastrous of the war in terms of merchant shipping lost.

'One of': March, 1943, was definitely not *the* most disastrous – its total of 693,389 tons of shipping lost takes fifth place in a table of such losses, eclipsed four times in 1942, and almost matched (687,901 tons, 195 ships) in April, 1941. As regards losses caused by Axis submarines, its total of 627,377 tons (108 ships) is the third highest, and its total of 476,349 tons (eighty-two ships) in the North Atlantic is the seventh highest, being nearly 150,000 tons less than the highest of all – June, 1942. And in fact close inspection shows that out of seventeen convoys running on the North Atlantic routes during the month, only three suffered losses of five ships or more. Evidently the true nature of the crisis which undoubtedly ensued calls for some careful consideration.

As we have seen, this was the period of mounting numerical U-boat force, or, as Jürgen Rohwer puts it, when

> the German U-boat arm approximately reached the strength which the Commander, U-boats, had called for in his memorandum of 1939.[74]

There were, he says, on 1 March, a total of 400 U-boats in service, of which 222 were 'front-line boats':

> Of these front-line boats 18 were in the Arctic, 19 in the Mediterranean and three in the Black Sea. 182 were available for the Atlantic operations. Of the Atlantic front-line boats on March 1, 1943, 114 (62.6%) were at sea and 68 (37.4%) were in French harbours. Of the boats at sea 44 were on the way out or on the way back (24.2% of the front-line boats). The remaining 70 (38.4%) were in the operational areas: 45 in the North Atlantic, 13 in the Central Atlantic, 5 in the Western Atlantic and 7 in the South Atlantic.

While we trade in percentages, it is worth noting one more that Rohwer does not mention. It is salutary to observe that even a total of 400 U-boats in service reduces to a mere 11.25% of them in the North Atlantic, the prime operational area. Yet forty-five U-boats is a lot of U-boats, and the sheer quantity is an important contributory factor to the crisis that followed.

During this month, Rohwer tells us, all the HX (fast) and almost all the SC (slow) North Atlantic eastbound convoys were attacked; that amounts to eight convoys, five HX and three SC. In these attacks on convoys, forty-two ships were sunk – just over 51% of the North Atlantic total, which is a reversal of normal form by which independents suffered the chief loss, and also constitutes an important factor in the crisis. Furthermore, these losses fell largely on three convoys, SC 121, SC 122 and HX 229, which between them lost no fewer than thirty-five ships. That concentration of loss is another factor. But what it means is that a large number of convoys were still travelling without any, or with insignificant losses – for example, all nine of the ON and ONS outward-bound convoys moving at the same time.

There can be little doubt that a fair proportion of this immunity was due to the steep Atlantick, never steeper than during this long winter. March, says Rohwer, brought a succession of 'great storms sweeping across the Atlantic from west to east'.[75] The effect of these was, as usual, to interfere with U-boat communications and hamper their attacks. On the other hand, they made life exceedingly difficult for the convoys and escorts also. These gales, says Admiral Chalmers,

> played havoc with the existing escort forces, and the maintenance bases were working at full pressure to get the damaged ships back into service. On 3rd March, Horton wrote:
> 'The whole war situation depends upon the number of escorts available to protect convoys . . . I urge most strongly that the highest priority be given to refitting and no departure be made from this policy.'[76]

It is illuminating to follow the course of just one of the outward-bound convoys which did not encounter U-boats, but instead met the gales head-on. ONS 169 left Liverpool on 26 February with thirty-seven merchant ships under Commodore J. Powell, escorted by B4 Group with Commander E. C. L. Day as Senior Officer. B4 consisted of three destroyers, Day's *Highlander*, *Vimy* and *Beverley*, and four corvettes, *Pennywort*, *Anemone* and *Abelia* with the Canadian *Sherbrooke* attached. Immediately on 27 February, the convoy ran into a severe south-west storm which forced it to reduce speed. The next day the wind veered sharply to north-west, a shift which left several ships in trouble and damaged the ASDIC dome in *Highlander*. After that the weather abated for a couple of days, and three corvettes were able to refuel from tankers in the convoy, but the wind returned at storm force (10) on the night of 3/4 March and ONS 169 was at its mercy for the next six days. On 6 March the convoy was off the southern tip of Greenland; it was ordered to make an evasive turn to the west, but *Beverley*, not having been able to refuel, now had to make straight for St John's in order to do so. Five ships straggled from the convoy in the gale, and its speed was reduced to 3.4 knots. On 7 March the wind reached Force 11; the corvettes *Pennywort* and *Sherbrooke* also had to make for St John's for fuel. On 9 March the convoy's speed was down to 2 knots (virtually hove to); two destroyers, HMS *Montgomery* and HMS *Salisbury*, ordered from the Western Support Force[77] by Admiral Murray (then Flag Officer, Newfoundland Force), arrived that morning, and Commander Day was able to take the damaged *Highlander* on to St John's for urgent repair. Another ship straggled from ONS 169; the convoy struggled on with four escorts, and that night distant U-boat signals were picked up by the HF/DF in the rescue ship, *Gothland*. The next day, fortunately, the weather improved and a USN Catalina provided air cover. Icebergs and drifting ice-floes accompanied the convoy and *Salisbury*'s ASDIC was damaged and put out of action by this ice. By 11 March the whole of the B4 escort was back in St John's, *Highlander* and *Sherbrooke* in dock for repair. The Group had been scheduled to take over HX 229 on 13 March; this schedule clearly had to be abandoned. The storm-battered remains of ONS 169 finally reached Cape Cod on 19 March, after twenty-two days at sea, and there dispersed. This was what was sometimes called a 'peaceful passage'.

Such, too, were the accompaniments of 'unpeaceful' passages. The ordeal of SC 121 was concurrent with the worst times of ONS 169, though far more destructive, and played out against the same scenery of Force 10 winds and mountainous seas. This convoy consisted of fifty-nine merchantmen, escorted by A3, still under Captain Heineman, in the cutter *Spencer*. This time A3 contained a destroyer, USS *Greer*, whose place in history we have already noticed (see pp. 390–1), but with only four corvettes in company the group was weak for the task set; SC 121 was formed in fourteen columns presenting a front seven miles wide, a difficult span to protect with so few ships. Worse still was the effect of constant sea-going in this abominable winter weather; half the group's radar sets were out of action, three ships had defective ASDIC, and *Spencer*'s communication system broke down in the course of one attack. Among the merchantmen, straggling – if that is the word – was inevitable in such conditions; some of it may have been correctly named, but much of it was involuntary, a simple failure to keep station in towering seas with swirling snow and, to top it all, fog to follow.

Alerted by *B-Dienst*, two U-boat packs, *Burggraf* and *Wildfang*,

547

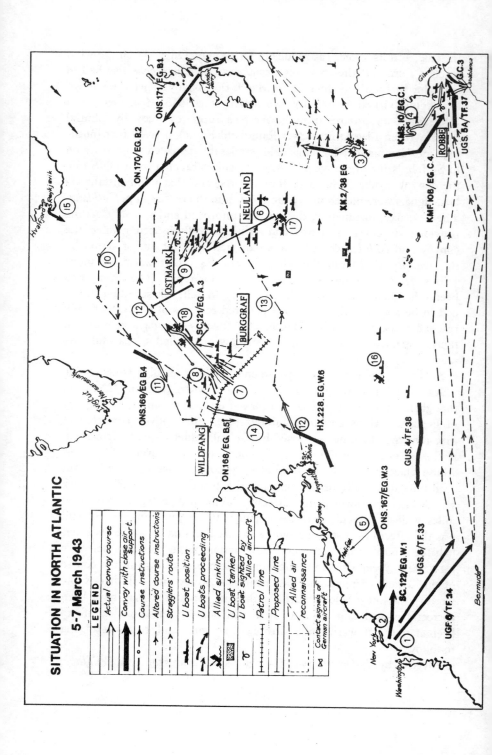

SITUATION IN NORTH ATLANTIC

5-7 March 1943

LEGEND

→ Actual convoy course
➡ Convoy with close air support.
―○― Course instructions
――― Altered course instructions
――― Stragglers route
⚓ U boat position
⚓ U boats proceeding
⚓ Allied sinking
▰ U boat tanker
⚓ U boat sighted by Allied aircraft
├┼┼┤ Patrol line
├──┤ Proposed line
⤻ Allied air reconnaissance
⋈ Contact signals of German aircraft

The situation in the North Atlantic: March 5 (1200 hrs GMT) to March 7 (1200 hrs GMT), 1943

No.	Date/time	Event
1	Mar 5 midday	Port Director New York sends by radio course instructions for UGF 6 and UGS 6 with stragglers' routes.
2	Mar 5 1330 hrs	SC.122 sets out from New York. It encounters a severe storm in the night Mar 6–7. 11 stragglers, of which 2 return, 6 make for Halifax, 2 rejoin convoy and 1 missing.
3	Mar 5 1645 hrs	U 130 attacks XK 2. 4 ships sunk in one approach. On Mar 6 and 7 19 Group, RAF Coastal Command, flies protective sweeps.
4	Mar 5 1730 hrs	German air reconnaissance again reports KMS 10, but opposite course steered temporarily on orders of CINCWA causes confusion. At 0830 hrs on Mar 6 U 107 reports the convoy, but is driven off. At 1420 hrs U 410 attacks: 2 ships hit and one of them sunk.
5	Mar 5 1900 hrs	ONS 167 passes HOMP.
6	Mar 5 evening	Neuland patrol line ordered for Mar 7 to operate against convoys on Southern route.
7	Mar 5 2200 hrs	SC 121 has passed the Burggraf group unobserved in the storm. The Cdr U-boats orders Burggraf and Wildfang to proceed to NE in the night, so as not to fall behind the convoy.
8	Mar 6 0956 hrs	U 405, one of the U-boats stationed in waiting positions in the rear of Burggraf and Wildfang, reports SC 122. The Cdr U-boats deploys the 17 favourably positioned boats of these groups as the Westmark group and
9	Mar 6	orders the 10 Northern Neuland boats to form a new patrol line for March 7 on the suspected convoy route.
10	Mar 6 afternoon	On the basis of U-boat signals picked up by D/F in the area of SC 121, CINCWA orders ON 170 to take new evasive action further to the North; at the same time
11	Mar 6	COMINCH orders ONS 169, which has been delayed by the storm, to take evasive action further to the West and
12	Mar 6	HX 228 to deviate sharply to the Southern route instead of maintaining Northern course ordered in the earlier course instructions.
13	Mar 6	ON 168, which has been delayed by the storm, does not arrive at WOMP at scheduled time.
14	Mar 6	2 escorts set out from Reykjavik as reinforcements for SC 121's screen.
15	Mar 6	
16	Mar 6 2207 hrs	U 172 reports the sinking of the independent Thorstrand.
17	Mar 7 morning	U 221 reports the sinking of the independent Jamaica.
18	Mar 7 morning	The U-boats deployed against SC 121 secure first successes against stragglers in the heavy storms.

totalling twenty-four boats, lay in a dog's-leg across the path of SC 121, with seven more forming a second line. Yet in such weather the patrol lines were ragged, visibility almost nil and communication chancy, with the result that even the great sprawl of SC 121 was able to pass clean through unobserved on 5 March. *Konteradmiral* Godt doggedly redeployed his boats, forming a new group, *Westmark*, to shadow the convoy, and another, *Ostmark*, to intercept it. *U 566* and *U 230* of *Westmark* made contact on the night of 6/7 March, and SC 121's tribulations began with the sinking of one merchantman that night. The next day came in with wind Force 10, and contact was understandably broken, but regained on the 8th. For the next three days, despite the strengthening of A3 with two more cutters and another destroyer, the U-boats (twenty-seven in the two groups) clung to SC 121 and sank twelve more ships, including the commodore's, with heavy loss of life since rescue was mostly impossible. A number of these casualties were 'stragglers', but when the wind blew Force 10 once more on 10 March even stragglers managed to escape. Well satisfied with what his boats had done, Godt broke off the action on 11 March; thirteen merchant ships had been sunk and no U-boat had been lost in this action. As Dönitz said, 'luck was on our side'.[78]

These North Atlantic convoy actions against the now vastly enlarged U-boat fleet took on the continuity of the convoy cycle itself, and simultaneous battles flared up in well-separated parts of the ocean. Hot on the heels of SC 121 on 6 March, HX 228 suddenly received orders from Admiral King's Convoy and Routing Section[79] to make a sharp evasive turn to the south. This was the result of HF/DF fixes picked up by Op 20 as the U-boat groups closed SC 121, showing the same groups right in the current path of HX 228. However, the new route instructions were intercepted by *B-Dienst* and decrypted by 9 March, and Godt at once ordered the *Neuland* Group to move in. At 1235 hours on the next day, 10 March, the southernmost boat of the Group, *U 336*, sighted and reported the convoy, and that night a fast and furious fight ensued which provided, in Roskill's words,

> a good example of the relentless giving and taking of lethal blows which was such a marked feature of the struggle.[80]

HX 228 was composed of sixty merchant ships, unusually strongly escorted by B3 (Commander A. A. Tait RN), an Anglo-French-Polish group which was 'a particular favourite of Horton's'.[81] B3 contained no fewer than four destroyers: Tait's *Harvester* and *Escapade*, both RN, with the Polish *Garland* and *Burza* (whose reputation we have noted); in addition there were two RN corvettes, *Narcissus* and *Orchis*, and three Free French, *Aconit*, *Roselys* and *Renoncule*. And this was not all: as well as B3, there was the promised American Carrier Support Group TU 24.4.1 (known as the 6th Escort Group to the Royal Navy) with USS *Bogue* and two of her escorting destroyers, *Belknap* and *Osmond-Ingram*. To carry out air operations, like *Audacity* before her, *Bogue* would move away from the convoy with her own escort, and return into it to a 'safe' station between the two centre columns when no longer operating her aircraft. With Force 10 winds occurring, flying on and off a carrier was not a feasible proposition, nor was night action a carrier *forte*. *Bogue*'s début was undistinguished, but she would soon make up for that.

U336 was quickly located by HF/DF and driven off, but *U444* (Langfeld) then arrived to keep up the rôle of contact-boat. *U221* (Trojer) came up in the evening of 10 March and sank two ships; she hit a third with a torpedo which failed to explode. Soon *U336*, *U86*, *U406* and *U757* were also present, and two more ships went down, one of them, *Brant County*, being a munitions ship which blew up with an enormous explosion which severely damaged her attacker, *U757*. The most dramatic action of the night, however, prompting Roskill's statement quoted above, concerned the escorts rather than the convoy. HMS *Harvester* was one of the six excellent destroyers which were building in British yards for the Brazilian Navy at the outbreak of war and were at once taken over by the Royal Navy (see p. 251). During the night of the 10th/11th, running down a radar contact, Commander Tait sighted *U444* on the surface; the U-boat submerged, but Tait brought her to the surface with depth charges and rammed her:

This usually most effective and certain way of destroying a submarine had its dangers, however. As the *Harvester* drove through and over, the submarine scraped and bumped its way along the destroyer's keel and became wedged under her propellers. The two vessels lay locked in this way for a time, and, by the time the U-boat finally broke free, *Harvester*'s propellers and shafts had suffered so much damage that she was reduced to a slow crawl on one engine.[82]

At this point the French corvette *Aconit*, which certainly deserves the accolade of 'fightin'est ship' of the group on this night, arrived and, finding *U 444* by some miracle still afloat, rammed her and sank her once and for all. Tait then ordered *Aconit* away to rejoin the convoy and limped along as best he could on one engine, picking up fifty merchant ship survivors as he went. During the morning of the 11th, however, *Harvester*'s second shaft broke and she came to a standstill. In this helpless condition she was found by *U 432* (Eckhardt) towards midday, and sunk by two torpedoes. Tait and most of his crew, together with the unfortunate merchant seamen, went down with her. *Lieutenant de Vaisseau* Lavasseur, the captain of *Aconit*, observed the distant column of smoke which announced this event and raced back to the spot. He soon obtained an ASDIC contact, and his depth charges brought *U 432* to the surface, where *Aconit* engaged her with gunfire and sank her by ramming once again. So the final tally for HX 288 was four merchantmen and one destroyer sunk, and two U-boats sunk with two more (*U 757*) and (*U 221*) badly damaged. On the 12th the weather eased sufficiently for *Bogue*'s aircraft to fly patrols, and No 15 Group of Coastal Command also provided air cover, making life very difficult for the U-boats; on the 13th Godt called them off.

HX 228 witnessed two significant innovations in this battle of unceasing technical advance and counter-advance. USS *Bogue* was one of them; the Royal Navy's escort carriers would shortly appear. They were still few in number – five to be precise – all converted merchant ships built and adapted in US yards. One, HMS *Avenger*, had already performed escort duty with PQ 18 on the Arctic route; the others were due to arrive in the Atlantic towards the end of 1942, but instead were diverted to protection of the TORCH convoys, work from which they were now released. They would become a permanent feature of escort operations, a new dimension of the battle whose value was seen above all in the dreaded 'Gap' where land-based aircraft could not reach.[83]

The second innovation was *FAT* torpedoes. We have mentioned a torpedo failure which robbed *U 221* of a victim on the night of 10 March. Dönitz complains of a much worse performance on 8 March, when *U 150* (Neitzel) attacked a Trinidad-bound convoy off Cayenne in French Guiana. In a two-day engagement, Neitzel sank three ships and his torpedoes damaged five more. Dönitz comments:

The fact that these five did not sink shows very clearly how greatly the

U-boats were handicapped through the lack of a really reliable magnetic pistol, which alone could ensure that one torpedo hit would suffice to sink a ship by breaking her back.[84]

Evidently the U-boat Service was passing through another period of difficulty with torpedoes, though nothing like the crisis which had afflicted it in 1940 (see pp. 231–40). The pistol problem had in fact been solved; deliveries had already begun in December of a new magnetic pistol which would also detonate on contact, a great step forward – but clearly *U 150* and *U 221* had not yet received the new equipment. 'At the same time,' says Dönitz,

a torpedo became available which, after having gone a specified distance, began to run in a circle. This, of course, greatly enhanced its chances – in an attack, for example, on a convoy – of scoring a hit.[85]

This was the *FAT*:[86]

These pattern-running torpedoes had a pre-set steering. The U-boat could fire the torpedoes at any desired angle up to 90°. The torpedoes ran a course, fixed by the distance from the convoy, at a speed of 30 knots. They could then make short or large loops at right angles to the course and in this way cut across the convoy's route several times.[87]

*FAT*s marked another stage in the see-saw of lethal technology; as it turned out, they proved to be more frightening than formidable, and would soon be overtaken by the next technical advance.

* * * * *

The cycle was inexorable; no sooner had a convoy passed, some on their way into history but the majority unnoticed, than another followed. After SC 121 came SC 122; after HX 228, HX 229; and with 100 U-boats at sea, these east-bound ships, laden with war-material and essential supplies, could depend on a reception committee. SC 122 and HX 229 were destined to provide the whole Atlantic battle with what has gone down as its ultimate climax, and is commonly regarded as a high peak of U-boat warfare never before or afterwards matched. As we have said, this projection is one that requires to be carefully examined.

Like their predecessors, these two convoys moved into their historic ordeal to the accompaniment of great storms and heavy following seas, with the additional spices of snow, ice and fog. No convoy actions are better documented than those which raged around these two numbers between 16–19 March. Two admirable books have been almost entirely devoted to them: *Convoy: The Battle for Convoys SC 122 and HX 229* by Martin Middlebrook (Allen Lane, 1976) and *The Critical Convoy Battles of March 1943* by Jürgen Rohwer (Ian Allan 1977). It is difficult to think of any aspect of these bitter engagements that is not dealt with in one or other of these valuable and thoughtful narratives[88] – or in both. Here it is impossible to pursue the story in anything like such detail, and we shall be concerned only with some highlights and reflections.

The first of these, prompted rather more by Middlebrook than by Rohwer, is that it is not really correct to view the event as one concerning only two convoys. There were, in fact, *three* east-bound convoys simultaneously at sea in mid-Atlantic during the period under review, and the full picture of the operation only emerges if all three are taken into account. As they finally formed up to join their ocean escorts at the Western Ocean Meeting Point (WOMP: about 49°W) they were:

		Commodore
SC 122	48 merchant ships, 2 LSTs, 1 rescue ship	Capt. S. N. White RNR
HX 229	38 merchant ships	Cdre M. J. D. Mayall RNR
HX 229A	37 merchant ships	Cdre D. A. Casey RNR

HX 229A requires explanation. At this stage Western Approaches and the USN authorities who still ruled the Western Atlantic were experimenting with the larger convoys recommended by Professor Blackett.[89] However, owing to a combination of circumstances, the USN Port Director at New York found himself with a superfluity of ships awaiting attachment to a fast HX convoy – eighty in all. As Middlebrook says,

> The Royal Navy was not yet prepared to escort such a large convoy across the Atlantic.[90]

This is understandable when one considers the width of front that such a convoy would have entailed, and the strain upon the escorts of providing all-round protection for that large mass of ships – to say nothing of the great difficulty of keeping station in the prevailing gale-force winds and mountainous seas. So the unusual decision was taken to split the fast sailers between two convoys. Middlebrook draws attention to the composition of the two parts of HX 229; 229A contained thirteen fast tankers, eight large refrigerated ships and four cargo liners:

> HX 229A would cross the Atlantic, therefore, with the fastest, largest and most valuable ships of the three convoys.[91]

An escort for this extra convoy inserted into the cycle was provided by sending over the long-range 40th Escort Group, normally employed on the Sierra Leone route, now in suspension due to Operation TORCH. EG 40's composition was decidedly different from the normal North Atlantic destroyer/corvette combination: four sloops and two of the new frigates that were now at last beginning to arrive in numbers.[92] The escort groups, as they arrived at the WOMP to collect their convoys, were:

SC 122	(12 March) B5	Commander R. C. Boyle RN (HMS *Havelock*)	2 destroyers (1 USN) 1 frigate 5 corvettes 1 anti-submarine trawler
HX 229	(14 March) B4	Lt.-Commander G. J. Luther RN (HMS *Volunteer*)	4 destroyers 1 corvette
HX 229A	(15 March) EG40	Commander J. S. Dalison RN (HMS *Aberdeen*)	4 sloops 2 frigates.

As we have seen, B4 had only arrived in St John's on 11 March, after its bruising passage with ONS 169. Commander Day's *Highlander* and three corvettes were still not ready to sail, and his proposal that HX 229 should be delayed 48 hours to give the group time to reform was turned down. The force that met the convoy on 14 March was thus a scratch collection (the thing most to be avoided). Lieutenant-Commander Luther and his *Volunteer* were transferred from B5, and two other destroyers, HMS *Witherington* and HMS *Mansfield*, were temporarily attached from the Western Support Force, both with limited fuel capacity. B4 was really a group only in name, and also weak in numbers. HMS *Volunteer* herself was a Modified 'W' Class ship of First World War vintage (though launched in 1919); to give these old vessels the necessary range for Atlantic escort work, their forward boilers were removed to make room for extra fuel bunkerage. She had only recently been recommissioned after a long refit, and though she was now equipped with HF/DF the operators were still unfamiliar with it and liable to the most elementary of errors – a bearing incorrect by 180°. It could be said that the dice were loaded against Lieutenant-Commander Luther.

Our second observation on the events that followed is that now we see the *B-Dienst* on the very peak of its form, and Bletchley Park once more in the shadow. The whole action took place during the period of the second Sigint blackout referred to above: 10–20 March. By contrast,

> Up to the first day of the attack, U-boat Headquarters had been able to read sixteen signals giving advance information of the movements of both convoys. Notable among them were the messages at 22.10 on 4 March giving ocean routes and stragglers' orders for HX 229, and a signal from Halifax at 19.32 on 13 March giving diversion orders for both convoys based on the Admiralty OIC's estimate of U-boat whereabouts.[93]

The *B-Dienst*, of course, knew nothing of the division of the fast ships, and continued to confuse HX 229A first with HX 229, then with SC 122, until 19 March. It is difficult to see that this had any noticeable effect on U-boat operations, but there may be a very small gleam of a silver lining for the convoys in this part of the cloud. In general, however, the Intelligence advantage lay heavily with the Germans through the whole of the coming battle, and this is an important factor in the assessment of it.[94]

Guided by a flow of sound information from the *B-Dienst*, U-Boat Command assembled its forces for attack. There was growing awareness of a rich prize in the offing, and it may be safely assumed that Godt and Dönitz were in close consultation during the early stages. Yet this major battle would become increasingly Godt's affair, and as it reached its climax on 17 March Dönitz was actually in Italy, conferring with the Italian Naval Command and with Mussolini on the mounting difficulties of the Axis in reinforcing and even maintaining its forces in the Tunisian bridgehead.

Three new Atlantic U-boat groups were formed for the occasion, the first to come into existence being *Raubgraf* on 6 March, with the intention of inflicting the same sort of damage on HX 228 as was being endured by SC 121. HX 228 was saved by a timely diversion, thanks once more to D/F fixes, but *Raubgraf* remained in being, well placed to intercept SC 122, whose approach was being watched by *B-Dienst*. Five days later the operations of the *Ostmark* and *Westmark* Groups against SC 121 concluded, and they were dissolved; in their place, across the anticipated course of the next convoys, the *Stürmer* Group was formed, and two days after that (13 March) the *Dränger* Group.[95] This was the cast. The precise number of boats in each attacking group varied from day to day according to proximity, preparedness, the need to refuel from one or other of the two U-tankers (*U 119* and *U 463*) currently present in mid-Atlantic, or in some cases to make the long haul back to base. Another factor, not often referred to, but real and of increasing importance in this rapidly expanded fleet, was the mood of the captain.[96] A total of forty-two U-boats was involved in the coming onslaught, but never all at once, and the first assembly was slow; on 16 March, when the main action began, it was thirty-eight of them that 'hurled themselves like wolves' (in Dönitz's words) upon the convoys.

The true beginning of the battle, however, was 12 March, when the U-boat War Diary informs us:

> On the basis of decoded messages received from the *B-Dienst*, the Command decided to commence operations against HX 229 which had been located.

Thus we see immediately the motive force of *B-Dienst* which would continue throughout, but with the irony that what it had discovered was not HX 229, but HX 229A. This was not important for what followed – certainly nothing like so important as an unfortunate (but understandable) decision by the USN Convoy and Routing Section, on the strength of D/F fixes, to divert SC 122 northwards, directly towards the *Raubgraf* group, which was forming for the attack on HX 229.

It was on this day, 12 March, that SC 122 met its ocean escort, B5; it may also be that it was on this day that it suffered its first casualty. The convoy had left New York on 5 March, accompanied by four Canadian corvettes of the Western Escort Force. The next day convoy and escort ran into a storm so violent that by dawn on 7 March SC 122 was thoroughly scattered and eleven ships were missing. Ten of these were accounted for: none were sunk though some were so badly damaged that they had to return to port, and two were even able to catch up with the convoy two days later. One ship, the 5,754-ton British freighter *Clarissa Radcliffe*, loaded with iron ore, could not be found. She was sighted by the escort leader, HMCS *The Pas*, on 9 March, only an hour's steaming from the convoy, and was given a course to follow. After that she was never seen again by Allied eyes, or heard of. After the war the Admiralty and Lloyds accepted that she had been abandoned by her crew, torpedoed by *U621* and had sunk in sight of the U-boat on 12 March. If so, she was the first SC 122 casualty. Middlebrook, however, disputes this supposition on strong grounds, and suggests that she was actually a victim of *U663* on 18 March. In any case, there were no survivors of her crew of fifty-five, and the *Clarissa Radcliffe* is reckoned in the tally of SC 122's losses. She remains one of the mysteries of the sea.

The first few days out were uneventful for SC 122. HX 229 duly met its ocean escort, B4, on the 14th, and by the 15th was only half a day's sailing behind SC 122. On that day, however, both convoys (and their enemies) were caught by another great storm coming up from the west. By 1300 hours (Central European time) this was hitting HX 229 with winds of Force 9–10 ('strong gale' and 'storm') and sea states of 7–8 ('very high' and 'precipitous'). Coming from behind the convoy, the storm certainly had the useful effect of pushing it along at a speed calculated by the SOE at $10\frac{1}{2}$ knots, but on the other hand the great seas were pounding up astern of the ships with the effect of 'pooping', which is something that sailors prefer not to experience: waves breaking on the ship's stern with tons of water tearing along the decks. The even-handedness of fate was once more demonstrated: the corvette *Pennywort*, delayed by engine trouble, caught up with HX 229, but no sooner had she done so than the Western Support destroyer *Witherington* was forced to heave to with damage to her deck plates, and her shortage of fuel made it impossible to rejoin the convoy afterwards. So Lieutenant-Commander Luther's weak group remained as weak as before.

In SC 122 even worse things were happening. This convoy's weather was not quite as bad as HX 229's, but sufficiently so to cause two small ships to fall out; one was the Icelandic freighter *Selfoss*, 755 tons with a cargo of timber, which never rejoined but completed her voyage to Reykjavik independently. The other was HMS *Campobello*. This

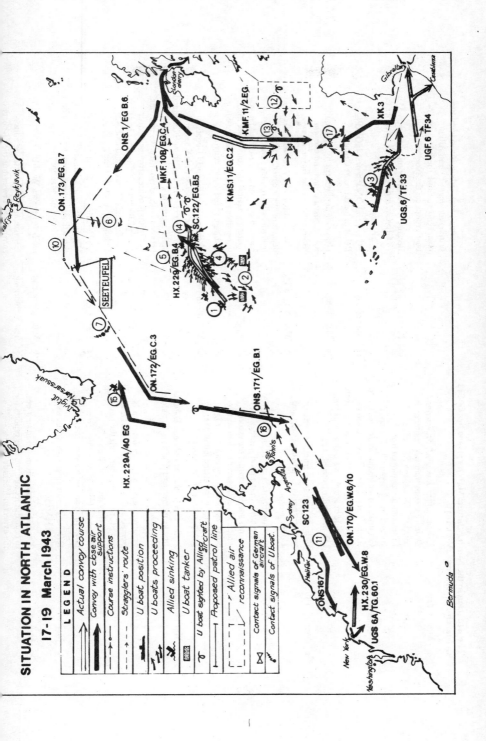

SITUATION IN NORTH ATLANTIC
17-19 March 1943

LEGEND

→	Actual convoy course
➤	Convoy with close air support
–○–	Course instructions
–·–	Stragglers' route
–·–>	U boat position
⟍	U boats proceeding
⤚	Allied sinking
▦	U boat tanker
⊤	U boat sighted by Allied aircraft
⊢	Proposed patrol line
⌐ ¬	Allied air reconnaissance
⋈	Contact signals of German aircraft
⌇	Contact signals of U boat.

HX.229A/40 EG

ON.173/EG.B.7

ONS.1/EG.B.6.

MKF.10B/EG.C.4

SC.122/EG.B5

HX 229/EG.B.4

ON.172/EG.C.3

ONS.171/EG.B.1

ON.170/EG.W.6/10

SC 123

HX.230/EG.W.8

ONS 167

UGS 6A/TG.60.1

KMS.11/EG.C.2

KMF.11/2EG.

XK.3

UGF.6 TF34

UGS.6/TF 33

SEETEUFEL

Bermuda

Reykjavik

Ivigtut

Narsarssuak

New York

Washington

Halifax

Sydney

St. John's

Gibraltar

Casablanca

The situation in the North Atlantic: March 17 (1200 hrs GMT) to March 19 (1200 hrs GMT), 1943

1	Mar 17 day	U-boats of the *Raubgraf*, *Stürmer* and *Dränger* groups maintain contact with convoys HX 229 and SC 122. 4 Liberators are deployed from N. Ireland by 15 Group, RAF Coastal Command over maximum ranges for air cover. They drive off many U-boats but during a pause at midday 3 U-boats are able to attack and sink 2 ships from HX 229 and 1 from SC 122.
2	Mar 17–18	U-boats turn away from the convoys and proceed to U-tankers *U 463* and *U 119*.
3	Mar 17–18	U-boats maintain contact with convoy UGS 6 but in the good weather they cannot succeed against the escorts which are equipped with long-range radar, especially since air cover is available on the afternoon of Mar 17. 1 ship is sunk in the evening.
4	Mar 18 night	In the case of SC 122 only one U-boat attacks in the night Mar 17–18. 2 ships are sunk.
5	Mar 18 day	15 Group sends 3 Liberators from N. Ireland and 4 from Iceland to HX 229 and SC 122. Together with the naval escort they drive off all attacks. However, *U 221* sinks 2 ships from HX 229 in an underwater attack.
6	Mar 18	Iceland aircraft sight U-boats as they fly to HX 229.
7	Mar 18	The radio signals from *U 229* sent out to transmit ice and weather reports for the expected blockade-runner meeting point with *U 161* to hand over search receiver = T) lead Allies mistakenly to think there are new U-boat groups on the Northern route.
10	Mar 18	Because of the situation picture on Mar 18 CINCWA diverts ONS 1 further to North.
11	Mar 18 day	SC 123 and ON 170 pass HOMP. Relief of local Escort Groups.
12	Mar 18 day	Heavy air deployment by 19 Group, RAF Coastal Command over the western part of the Bay of Biscay.
13	Mar 18 2000 hrs	*U 621* sights KMF 11 shortly after departure of air cover. Further operations by this boat and other outward and homeward-bound boats operating against the convoy are made impossible on Mar 19 by the air cover and high speed of the convoy.
14	Mar 18–19	In the night individual U-boats maintain contact with HX 229 and SC 122. 1 ship is sunk from SC 122 and in the morning a 'romper' of HX 229 between both convoys. In the morning 15 Group provides strong air cover with 5 Liberators, 2 Catalinas and 6 Sunderlands from Iceland and N. Ireland. U-boats fall back.
15	Mar 19 early	The whaling ship *Svend Foyn* with HX 229A is badly damaged in passing through an iceberg area and has to be abandoned on Mar 20.
16	Mar 19 morning	ONS 171 passes WOMP.
17	Mar 19 morning	German air reconnaissance finds convoy XK 3 twice but the U-boats

was a new Canadian-built Isles Class anti-submarine trawler intended for Home duties. Twice already this small (545-ton) vessel had been trapped in ice, which is the most probable reason for the fatal leak which she now developed under the coal in her bunkers. After a brave but unavailing fight to find and stop the leak, she had to be abandoned; her entire crew was rescued by the Belgian corvette *Godetia*, which then sank the slowly-foundering trawler with a depth charge. *B-Dienst* faithfully recorded a signal to *Godetia* giving SC 122's position, course and speed to help her to rejoin. It was a night when the phrase 'those in peril on the sea' required no explanation, or which, according to one corvette officer, 'brought home to me a sense of the power of Almighty God'; but there was one consolation – so far there were no U-boats.

The storm subsided about midnight, leaving a heavy swell; the night was very dark. Just as, in the bleakest periods of the Western Front of World War I, the drenching rain and the engulfing mud afflicted Germans and Allies alike, so it was in the Atlantic. A February storm had swept the watch officer and four lookouts of the *Raubgraf* boat *U 653* out of the conning tower to their deaths; now she had engine trouble and was low on fuel. *Kapitänleutnant* Gerhard Feiler was taking her to a tanker to refuel for her return to base in the early hours of 16 March when he was called to the bridge; he saw ships all around him at distances of 500 metres to half a sea mile. He dived at once, and a convoy passed over the U-boat; when the last ship had gone by and time had elapsed for all the escort to be gone also, *U 653* surfaced and Feiler made his sighting report. The convoy was HX 229, but U-boat Command believed it to be SG 122, leading the procession eastward. The eight remaining *Raubgraf* boats, plus two which had now refuelled, and eleven boats from the southern end of the *Stürmer* line were at once ordered to concentrate against the supposed SC 122, with the remaining six of *Stürmer* as a rear echelon, and *Dränger* with ten boats awaiting the supposed HX 229. As they closed, the spirits of their crews underwent a transformation. *Kapitänleutnant* Kurt Baberg of *U 618* (*Stürmer*) told Martin Middlebrook:

On receipt of that first message the mood in the boat changed completely. Everybody was waiting tensely for the next signal giving a further course of the convoy. We went flat out so as to reach the convoy before dark regardless of the state of the sea and waves often broke over the conning tower. All the tiredness and disappointments of preceding days vanished when you at last had the chance to see the target with your own eyes and you strained to spot the first spikes of the masts.[97]

U653 continued to shadow HX 229, making further signals at roughly two-hour intervals. Luther's *Volunteer* was the only escort equipped with HF/DF, and it appears that these early shadowing signals from *U653* were not picked up. During the afternoon of the 16th, however, more boats of *Raubgraf* Group came up and made their contact signals. Many of these were located by *Volunteer* and others by shore stations; there was no doubt that a serious attack was impending, but there was nothing to be done about it. B4 worked hard to keep the U-boats down, not without success, and the shore Commands did what they could to reinforce the convoys. Commander Day in HMS *Highlander*, with two more B4 corvettes, was on his way from St John's. B4's other destroyer, *Vimy*, was ordered to join from Reykjavik, but two more days would elapse before she could leave harbour; the US destroyer *Babbitt* and the large Coast Guard cutter *Ingham* were also ordered out from Iceland, but none of these ships would reach the convoys until 18 March. Meanwhile, on the 16th, another change of course by HX 229 had had the unfortunate result of taking it nearer to the U-boat packs rather than evading them. With only HF/DF to go on, and most of the D/F coming from shore station fixes, one can see at once how grave was the lack of instant *Enigma* decrypts; for both Commands the enemy picture was to some extent blurred, but thanks to *B-Dienst* the cloud of uncertainty was far less dense for the Germans. It should be noted, too, that with seas still high and often turbulent, the Type 271M radar was not giving its usual excellent service; there were few detections and even fewer attacks:

> The failure of the radar equipment was partly due to the fact that with visibility between 5 and 9 miles the U-boats could clearly recognize the escorts before they themselves could be located by radar in a state 3–4 sea. Visual observation from the conning tower of a surfaced U-boat proved, in the prevailing weather conditions, to be superior to radar location and the visual observation from the higher lookouts of the escorts and merchant ships.[98]

In some cases (HMS *Mansfield*, for example) the radar equipment was not working at all due to storm damage, and this was also sometimes the case with the ASDIC, for the same reason.

At 2000 hours HX 229 passed the CHOP line, thus leaving the jurisdiction of COMINCH in Washington and henceforth coming under Western Approaches; such arrangements, as we have seen, were shortly due to end. It would be difficult indeed to point to any particular advantage or otherwise accruing to either of the two convoys under consideration. On balance, to be wholly under the direction of the most experienced anti-U-boat organization could only be encouraging, but the greatest encouragement would come when the convoys had gone far enough into the Western Approaches area to benefit from the full array of its establishments and equipment, above all No 15 Group of Coastal Command. For the time being they were in the 'Gap', the U-boats were very close and High Command very far away. By the time it was past the CHOP line, SC 122 had had no U-boat contact, but no one had any illusion that this happy state would continue. HX 229A, having contributed its mite to the uncertainties at U-boat HQ, was also U-boat-free, but now its northward diversion brought it to a different enemy – the combination of blizzard, fog and ice that makes the latitudes between Canada and Greenland one of the most dangerous navigational areas in the world in the early months of the year. In March, 1943, the icebergs and floes were far further south than usual, and it would not be long before two escorts (*Waveney* and *Aberdeen*) had suffered serious damage – in the latter case it was to the ship's bottom and included the shattering of the ASDIC dome. To anticipate, five of HX 229A's merchantmen had to return to St John's with ice damage, and one, the 14,795 tanker (ex-whaling-factory ship) *Svend Foyn*, ran straight into an iceberg. She remained afloat for two days, but when a gale sprang up to add to the misery she sank suddenly with a loss of forty-three lives. To anticipate still further, *Svend Foyn* was the sole casualty in HX 229A, a victim not of U-boats but of that ancient foe of sailors, drifting ice.

The battle of HX 229 was joined at 2200 hours on 16 March. It was now a well-established understanding that in these convoy battles the first attacks were usually the most successful; as the fight wore on, partly because of expenditure of torpedoes, or of fuel (or both), and partly through strain, the U-boats would be less pressing with their attacks, and the escorts, no longer surprised, would often develop a curious 'second wind' and an anticipation of their enemies' movements. The story of HX 229 and SC 122 is no exception; two thirds of HX 229's losses were sustained on this night. *U 603 (Oberleutnant*

Bertelsmann) was the first to attack, with a salvo of three *FAT* torpedoes and one G7e (see p. 234); some five minutes later (suggesting the longer course of a *FAT*) one of these hit the 5,214-ton Norwegian freighter *Elin K.*; she sank within four minutes. In the hours that followed, *U758* (*Kapitänleutnant* Manseck), *U435* (*Kapitänleutnant* Strelow), *U91* (*Kapitänleutnant* Walkerling) and *U600* (*Kapitänleutnant* Zurmühlen) had all attacked the convoy; seven more ships had been hit and two had gone down. The most successful attack was the last, by *U600* at 456; she was one of Dönitz's favourite Type VIICs, with four bow tubes and one stern, from which Zurmühlen now fired a forward salvo of four *FAT*s and then turned to deliver a final normal torpedo from the stern tube. Four of these found targets: one hit the 8,714-ton British refrigerated ship *Nariva*, two hit the 6,125-ton American freighter *Irénée du Pont* and the fourth hit the 12,156-ton British tanker (ex-whaling-factory ship) *Southern Princess*. All three were brought to a halt, falling out of the convoy, and with two others already in similar condition adding to a difficult problem of rescue.

There was no rescue ship in HX 229; the last ship in each column was expected to give what help she could to casualties in that column, but this was not a rule that could be enforced and many ships ignored it. The only ones left for rescue work were the escorts, and we have seen how, from the very earliest days of convoy warfare, the necessity to free them from this duty had been recognized. An escort hove-to, perhaps with boats out, or hauling in drowning men and pitching rafts, probably silhouetted against the glare of a raging tanker fire, was an escort both extremely vulnerable herself and also lost to the convoy's protective screen until the work was done (which might be a matter of hours). Lieutenant-Commander Luther was an anti-submarine specialist, fully familiar with the current doctrines of the art, and well aware that the diversion of escorts to rescue work was frowned upon. Nevertheless we find not only the corvettes but the destroyers of B4 hard at work collecting survivors during this night, not least HMS *Volunteer* herself. It is important to understand what it was – apart from sheer compassion, which should not, in theory, overrule professional judgment – that caused him to do this, and fortunately we have the answer from his Number One, Lieutenant G. C. Leslie, who told Middlebrook:

The Captain and I had discussed the possibility on several occasions and our conclusion was that rescue was very important at a time when the worst disaster in the Atlantic battle would be a failure of morale in the merchant ships. In the absence of a rescue ship and with the failure of the last ship in the column to stop and pick up survivors, the Escort Group Commander had an almost impossible decison to make.[99]

It is to be remembered that no mantle of immunity covered the escorts: at 0418 HMS *Volunteer* was attacked by *U 616* (*Oberleutnant* Koitschka), which fired her full forward salvo at the destroyer, but missed. About an hour and a half later, *U 228* (*Oberleutnant* Christopherson) fired a salvo of three at HMS *Mansfield*, and he, too, missed, the destroyer not even being aware of the attack. And whenever possible the hyper-active B4 seized any opportunity that offered to counter-attack the U-boats. If it is not invidious to single out any particular member of the group, we may mention the corvette HMS *Anemone* (Lieutenant-Commander P. G. A. King RNR), which seemed to possess the secret of perpetual motion. To round out the picture fully, we must add that as well as radar failures and damage to radio equipment, the escorts had to contend with weapon shortcomings, non-functions of depth charge throwers and hedgehogs due to the storms.[100]

HX 229 went on its way on the 17th, leaving five wrecks behind; by the afternoon all had been sunk, four of them despatched by *U 91*. By that time SC 122 had also been attacked and had suffered casualties. The early hours of the day were illuminated by a bright, high moon which gave visibility up to twelve miles; at 0200 the lookout of the *Stürmer* boat *U 338* (*Kapitänleutnant* Manfred Kinzel), searching for HX 229, observed shadowy ships a long way off. Kinzel soon recognized the broad front of a convoy coming straight towards him – SC 122; he immediately made a sighting report which enabled the U-boat Command at last to sort out the two convoys and identify them. Orders went out to those *Stürmer* and *Dränger* boats that were nearest to close SC 122, and this they did to such effect that from 0900 until 2300 there was uninterrupted contact. But by then the main damage was done. *Kapitänleutnant* Kinzel had wasted no time; within minutes two merchantmen were sunk and another on fire, and by a quarter past two yet another had been wrecked (both of these were subsequently sunk). Early in the afternoon Kinzel attacked again, and sank a fifth ship – but that was the sum total of damage done to SC 122 in daylight on 17 March.

The reason for this – and for the loss of only two more ships from HX 229 during this day – was a transformation of the battle and of the whole Atlantic struggle that had taken place. The long-awaited, deeply desired VLR aircraft had arrived. Coastal Command now had two squadrons of B-24Ds – Liberator IIIs, the outstanding VLR aircraft. The normal squadron establishment was twelve aircraft, with four in initial reserve – a total of thirty-two; only thirteen were operational in mid-March. It was conversion of the B-24D from its intended rôle as a high-altitude bomber for the USAAF that caused the delays even when a thin flow of machines was reaching Coastal Command:

> extensive de-modification was necessary to prepare the Liberators for the very long-range, low altitude, anti-submarine rôle: the self-sealing liners to the fuel tanks and most of the pieces of protective armour plating were removed, as were the turbo-superchargers for the engines, and the underneath power-operated gun turret. This weight pruning made it possible for the aircraft to take off carrying more than two thousand gallons of high octane fuel, in addition to its load of eight 250 pound depth charges.[101]

The performances of the Liberators on 17 March justified their VLR description. M/86, captained by Flying Officer Cyril Burcher, an Australian, left its base at Aldergrove in Northern Ireland at midnight, and after a flight of 8 hours and 50 minutes the Liberator arrived over SC 122. On the way it had attacked *U 439* (*Oberleutnant* von Tippelskirch) and shaken her so severely that she remained submerged for most of the rest of the day. On arrival, M/86 came under the orders of Commander Boyle and carried out a protective sweep in the course of which she attacked Kinzel's *U 338*, but again only succeeded in putting the U-boat down. She then continued patrolling until 1115 hours, when fuel supply was becoming critical and she had to return to base. As it turned out, M/86 did not have enough fuel left to reach Aldergrove and landed instead at the Fleet Air Arm base at Eglinton near Londonderry. The aircraft had been airborne for 18 hours and 20 minutes. A second Liberator from Aldergrove failed to find SC 122 (but had brief contact with HX 229 in the late afternoon); its return flight was hampered by bad weather and it, too, had to land at Eglinton, having been in the air for 20 hours and thirty minutes. G/120 arrived over SC 122 at 1320 hours and remained with the convoy until 1705, returning to Reykjavik after a total flight time of 17 hours. J/120 was the only aircraft to reach HX 229 (two others being prevented from taking off by Force 7 winds across the runway); its patrol was action-packed with attacks, first on *Oberleutnant* Hans Trojer's *U 221*, which was badly shaken and had a man injured, then on *Kapitänleutnant* Struckmeier's *U 608*, which was also severely shaken, and finally with machine-gun fire (all depth charges having gone) on a third U-boat. J/120 was in the air for 18 hours. Maritime air warfare had entered a new dimension.

HX 229 lost two merchantmen on the 17th (in the interval between the departure of M/86 and the arrival of G/120) bringing its total to ten. During the night of the 17/18th SC 122 also lost two ships, making its total eight (including the *Clarissa Radcliffe*). Thereafter only three more ships in convoy were lost, two from HX 229 on the 18th, and one from SC 122 in the early hours of the 19th. By the morning of the 18th another full gale was blowing from NNWest, yet the U-boats were reporting 'very strong air escort' with the convoys; twelve of them had already broken off the action. On the afternoon of that day HMS *Highlander* caught up with HX 229; Commander Day was not able to inform himself of the full position immediately for the simple reason that a cipher clerk bringing a new code book to the cipher officer on the upper deck was knocked over by a strong wave and to save himself let go of the code books, which were washed overboard. However, at 1900 Commander Day resumed his responsibility as SOE with B4, for which relief Lieutenant-Commander Luther no doubt breathed a fer-vent 'much thanks'.[102] Bearing in mind the dictum that a major convoy battle was the equivalent of a major land battle, he takes his place high among the ranks of junior naval officers who were called upon to do the work of admirals (see p. 288). By the time he handed over to Day the weather was moderating, but there was little consolation in that fact since the U-boats could be expected also to benefit from it. The impression of the last two days' events on those who experienced them may be judged by a strange (and sad) performance aboard the 5,848-ton American freighter *Mathew Luckenbach*. The captain called a meet-ing of all crew who were off watch:

Then he gave his opinion of our situation. He explained that the *Mathew Luckenbach* was a 15-knot ship placed in a 9-knot convoy. Eighteen ships had been sunk so far. The escorts were ineffective against the subs. It was more than likely the submarine pack would sink most of the remaining ships. The *Mathew Luckenbach* had run alone on other trips without mishap and he was confident he could do it again, providing we lost the submarine pack. He said he could do this under cover of darkness by slipping out of the convoy and steaming ahead, leaving the submarine pack to go after the convoy.

He asked for a show of hands by those in favour of it. We all raised our hands. He also had a statement written out to this effect, which he asked us all to sign. We all signed.[103]

So the *Mathew Luckenbach* became a 'romper'. Commander Day saw her leaving the convoy and tried to persuade her captain to change his mind, but in vain; he preferred to rely on his 15 knots. By morning on 19 March the *Mathew Luckenbach* was some forty miles ahead of HX 229, but so far from taking her out of the U-boat packs, this only brought her to the area of the *Stürmer* attack on SC 122. It was not long before she was discovered, by *Kapitänleutnant* Uhlig's *U 527*, and very promptly torpedoed. The entire crew took to the boats, and had the good fortune to be picked up very quickly by the US Coast Guard cutter *Ingham*. The *Mathew Luckenbach* obstinately remained afloat (her crew flatly refused to go back aboard her) but at approximately 1910 hours she was hit again by a torpedo from *U 523* (*Kapitänleutnant* Pietzsch) and sunk very soon. She was the last casualty in the great battle of the convoys, and it is interesting to note that like the first (*Clarissa Radcliffe*) she was not lost while in convoy.

Until the morning of 19 March, despite vigorous action by all the surface escorts and many aircraft, no U-boat had been lost. By then, however, the two convoys were well into Western Approaches waters where they were met by what Milner calls 'the overwhelming power of Coastal Command'.[104] Fortresses and Sunderlands were now able to join in the work of protecting the two convoys. The two Fortress squadrons, No 206 and No 220, were stationed on Benbecula Island in the Outer Hebrides. It was aircraft B of 206 Squadron, flown by Pilot Officer L. G. Clark as cover for HX 229, that came upon *U 384* (*Oberleutnant* von Rosenberg-Gruszczynski) on the surface in a squall astern of the convoy. Clark made a perfect attack before the U-boat had time to dive, and it was never seen or heard of again. *U 384* thus became the solitary U-boat casualty of the battle, though Dönitz tells us:

568

Nearly all the other boats suffered from depth charges or bombs, and two were severely damaged.[105]

He adds: 'the success achieved was impressive', and this was certainly the feeling on both sides at the time. The U-boat War Diary entry on 20 March, 1943, claims:

A total of 32 ships of 186,000 tons and a destroyer were sunk; in addition, another nine hits were obtained on ships. This is the biggest success so far in a convoy battle. It is all the more gratifying because nearly 50% of the boats participated in the success.[106]

The claim, of course, is very wide of the mark and Dönitz did not repeat it in his Memoirs: the only naval vessel lost was the *Campobello*, and that had nothing to do with U-boats; the number of merchant ships lost was not thirty-two but twenty-two, and the tonnage sunk was 141,000 – which is still a very large amount.

It was large enough, certainly, to make blood run cold in the Admiralty. Reviewing the year at the end of 1943, the Admiralty recorded that

the Germans never came so near to disrupting communication between the New World and the Old as in the first twenty days of March, 1943.[107]

There would seem to have been an unusual degree of 'alarm and despondency' (the wartime phrase) in the Admiralty at that time, faithfully reflected in Roskill's commentary thirteen years later when he wrote that one could not

yet look back on that month without feeling something approaching horror over the losses we suffered. In the first ten days, in all waters, we lost forty-one ships; in the second ten days fifty-six. More than half a million tons of shipping was sunk in those twenty days; and what made the losses so much more serious than the bare figures can indicate was that *nearly two-thirds of the ships sunk during the month were sunk in convoy*. 'It appeared possible,' wrote the Naval Staff after the crisis had passed, 'that we should not be able to continue [to regard] convoy as an effective system of defence.' It had, during three-and-a-half years of war, slowly become the lynch pin of our maritime strategy. Where could the Admiralty turn if the convoy system had lost its effectiveness? They did not know; but they must have felt, though no one admitted it, that defeat stared them in the face.

'No one admitted it', says Roskill; but to Captain Donald Macintyre, whose credentials at the 'sharp end' are impeccable, even to think of abandoning the convoy system was

tantamount to an admission of defeat. For there was no possible alternative, as a glance at the record of ships sailed independently made abundantly clear. Disastrous as were the stories of a few of the trans-Atlantic convoys at this time, many others were being brought or fought through relatively unscathed, so that the total losses represented no more than 2.5 per cent of the ships sailed in convoy. Even considering the convoys which were attacked, the losses were only 11 per cent. . . . In fact a set-back on one part of the battlefield was being unreasonably looked upon as a herald of general defeat.[108]

The echoes are loud and clear; the Naval Staff collectively, in the spring of 1943, was in very much the frame of mind of Admiral Jellicoe when he had his famous conversation with Admiral Sims in April, 1917:

'It looks as though the Germans were winning the war,' I remarked.
'They will win, unless we can stop these losses – and stop them soon,' the Admiral replied.
'Is there no solution for the problem?' I asked.
'Absolutely none that we can see now,' Jellicoe announced.[109]

The parallel is very striking and suggests its own reason: Jellicoe in 1917 was a very tired man whose habitual realism had temporarily declined, as it not infrequently does, into pure pessimism, and he had tired men around him. Sir Dudley Pound and many of his staff officers were tired men in 1943; Pound had been First Sea Lord from the beginning of the war, and its burden had been very heavy upon him. The PQ 17 disaster, in which he felt deeply personally involved, had been a severe blow. He now had, in fact, only six more months to live – he died on Trafalgar Day, 1943. Looking back, one is nevertheless forced to say that Jellicoe's gloom, facing a totally unprecedented problem, for which there were no blueprints or guidelines, and all of whose technical solutions lay in an uncertain future, is the more understandable.

One thing is certain: there was nothing in the actual performance of the SC 122/HX 229 battle by itself to warrant such a degree of pessimism. SC 122, in fact, may be said to have got off lightly, in the face of the largest U-boat concentration ever, with a loss of only eight ships in convoy out of fifty-one – 15.7%, or nine with the straggler *Clarissa Radcliffe* – 17.6%. HX 229 fared far worse: twelve ships lost in convoy out of thirty-eight – 31.6%, or, if we include the *Mathew Luckenbach*, thirteen ships – 34.2%. If we take the joint total – and we may note that the U-boat Command increasingly viewed the whole operation as one single battle – we have to deduct the twenty-two ships sunk by U-boats from a full count of eighty-nine – 24.7%. To establish a perspective for all these percentages, we may recall a few of the loss rates in convoys that we have examined:

Convoy	Date	Ships	Losses	Percentage	Page
SC 42	September 1941	67	16	23.8	381
HG 73	September 1941	25	9	36	385
OG 74	September 1941	22	7	27	386
SC 94	August 1942	36	11	30.5	478
SC 107	October 1942	42	15	35.7	492
ONS 154	December 1942	45	14	31.1	511
SC 121	March 1943	59	13	22	480

It is immediately clear that neither the losses of SC 122 alone, nor of the two convoys combined, gave any special cause for alarm. It all really stemmed from HX 229, which takes its sad place as third in the list of high losses in the North Atlantic; yet there would seem to be nothing new, nothing calling for searching reassessments, in this fact. It was a very simple case of an unusually weak escort group facing an unusually large pack of U-boats. Lieutenant-Commander Luther handled his group with great courage and determination, but the odds against him were too high. On 17 March, to give just one example of a recurring situation, he was trying to protect HX 229 with only two destroyers – his own *Volunteer* and *Beverley* – all the other ships being away from the convoy for their own good reasons ('all', it may be noted, meaning one destroyer and two corvettes). Luther's only fault – if such it was – was his preoccupation with rescue, to which we have already referred and to which we shall return. But even if one takes a critical view of this, it is hard to see how HX 229 could have avoided heavy losses in such circumstances.

We have, furthermore, also to take into account the point made on p. 554, that this battle involved not two, but *three* convoys, all drawn from the same agglomeration of shipping. HX 229A lost no ship to U-boat attack. Deducted from the three-convoy total of 126 vessels, the loss then amounts to 17.5%.[110] These are all comparisons that fall within the purview of Operational Research, but of course that requires time to collect and sift its data; Professor Blackett's team should have had enough to work on by the end of the year, nevertheless. It looks as though nobody asked it the right questions.

How, then, do we finally account for this wave of gloom in the Admiralty, this 'unreasonable' fear (Macintyre's word; 'irrational' is perhaps better) that the convoy system itself had been found wanting and might have to be scrapped? We have mentioned fatigue, and this must certainly come high in any list of causes. It embraces the strain of three and a half years of ceaseless war, ceaseless danger of kinds and degrees that the ordinary citizen did not even guess at; tempers and nerves are bound to become overwrought in such conditions. And there is also the matter of sheer continuity to be taken into account: four consecutive North Atlantic convoys had been in virtually unbroken battle with U-boat packs for the first half of March:

Convoy	Action begins	Action ends	Losses
SC 121	March 6/7	March 11	13
HX 228	March 10/11	March 13	4
HX 229	March 16	March 19	13
SC 122	March 17	March 18/19	9

By the end of this time, from four consecutive convoys, thirty-nine ships had gone down; others (from HX 229a) had been forced to turn back by ice; some were scattered, and their fate unknown for a while. Nor was this all; Jürgen Rohwer's chart (No 2 in his admirable and informative series; see p. 549) shows the situation on 5 March as the U-boats gathered for their attack on SC 121; altogether sixteen convoys are featured on this chart, of which only three are in the list above. Some fall within or are destined for the Moroccan Sea Frontier for which the USN was responsible, but all the northern convoys were sooner or later Admiralty responsibilities. We may note unpleasantness taking place in the area of XK 2, a Gibraltar-UK TORCH convoy, which was attacked by *U 130* on 5 March and lost four ships. We see further unpleasantness with KMS 10, another military (UK – North Africa) convoy which had two ships torpedoed by *U 410* on 6 March, of which one sank. And this was just the North Atlantic; the war was in every ocean; the strain was unremitting. In March, 1943, it had rather got on top.

And there was another matter. One hundred and twenty British, Allied and neutral merchant ships were sunk in March, 1943, eighty-two of them in the North Atlantic. It was a figure that had been surpassed many times (eight times in 1942 alone); but Jürgen Rohwer comments:

> Losses on the scale of that of the last convoy battles in which convoy after convoy lost four, six, eight or even twelve ships, could not be sustained much longer. The morale and determination of the seamen was being undermined.[111]

March, 1943, was the 43rd month of the war, and the merchant seamen, like the Royal Navy, had been in the front line from the first. By the end of that month, no fewer than 4,486 merchant ships had been sunk, 2,385 of them by submarines; both figures are appalling. The SC 122/HX 229 battle itself had cost the lives of 292 officers, cadets and seamen in the ships that made up the two convoys. In the Admiralty, in Western Approaches and in the escort groups, these matters were not known as the precise statistics that post-war analysts were able to compile, but there was broad understanding of the gist of them – as Lieutenant-Commander Luther's conversation with his Number One, quoted above, well illustrates.

In the two convoys, as one may suppose with a heterogeneous collection of eighty-nine ships, there were variable performances displaying different states of morale. When the *Elin K.* went down, the corvette *Pennywort* came upon two of her lifeboats and at once stopped to take the survivors aboard. A sub-Lieutenant recalled:

> I was most impressed by the calmness and efficiency of the Norwegians. A lifeboat full was brought alongside by their captain, under great difficulty due to the shocking weather conditions. He saluted us, oars were tossed and laid down the centre of the boat. He ordered the crew aboard our ship, stepped aboard himself and the lifeboat was cut adrift. Their seamanship and general conduct was much to be admired.[112]

Norwegians are children of the sea; so were the Dutch of that time. When the refrigerated ship *Zaanland* was sunk on the night of 16 March, Middlebrook says that

> Once again, a well-trained crew of mainly pre-war sailors had been able to abandon their ship in good order.

With others, however, it is possible, he says, 'to read between the lines' of their reports 'and find an unhappy tale of panic'. It would be remarkable indeed if this were not so. The raw crews, hastily recruited for the now enormously expanding American merchant fleet, unsurprisingly gave patchy performances. In some ships the crews refused to sleep below deck; survivors sometimes astonished their rescuers by coming aboard with ready-packed suitcases.[113] The *Mathew Luckenbach's* behaviour speaks for itself.

The great majority of the ships in the convoys were always British, reflecting the predominance of the British Merchant Marine; the great majority of the seamen were British, too, and it would be hard to find a better summary of their achievement than Martin Middlebrook's:

> The Merchant Navy contained its fair share of heroes – 6,000 awards were made for gallantry – and also of slackers and cowards. Occasionally ships could not sail because crew members who had signed articles failed to appear and the law forbade ships to sail undermanned; statistically, firemen were the worst offenders. But, although there was the National Union of Seamen, there was never any strike action or even threat of such action, at a time when it would have been easy to press

574

for more money and at a time when many unions did call strikes among equally important groups of workers. Nor was there, so far as this writer is aware, any instance of mutiny among British seamen or of crews refusing to sail, however dangerous the conditions.

Although Britain had not treated him particularly well during peace-time, the merchant seaman served his country well in the years of war.[114]

It was chiefly to do with the kind of men they were. On the bridge of his corvette, Nicholas Monsarrat was very close to them day by day, and yet a planet apart by virtue of the different disciplines of the Royal and Merchant Services. Mustering a new convoy, he reflected upon these men who, from the beginning, had always been 'in the centre of the picture', and had perhaps become over-familiar:

> I had seen hundreds of convoys in this war; and if they did not always impress me with the same pride and the same admiration as at the beginning, that was simply because of the human inability to hold an impression, however strong or vivid, indefinitely. . . . There were ships that had seen scores of long-drawn out actions, and still came back cheer-fully for more; there were men – British and Allied sailors – who dared all, not as a job for money but simply as a chosen habit, who returned to the same task and the same run after two or even three hideous ordeals as survivors, who stuck to oil-tankers as other people stick to one brand of bottled beer. Even apart from action with the enemy, the men in these ships – some of them, old friends, were waving as I passed them now – had seen their job transformed by war into something a hundred times more difficult and hazardous: they had accepted loyally the irksome compulsion of convoys, of never moving except in crowded company – a discipline quite alien to sailors, whose foremost instinct is to beat it in the opposite direction when another ship comes over the horizon: they had accepted the necessity of wallowing along for hundreds of miles at the speed of the slowest, and of keeping close station in weather like a dirty blanket hanging all around them. . . . One could only feel proud to share a job with such men. Nominally we were in charge of them, on all their undertakings: but it was really a more complex relationship, in which admiration had its full share and a broth-erly regard seasoned all the discipline we had to enforce.[115]

Every veteran army, every *corps d'élite*, can be pushed too hard for too long; the day comes when any of them may falter. By March, 1943, the war was getting long in the tooth, the eternal cruelty of the sea was unabated. There is no immediately visible sign or proof that the Merchant Navy and its allies had reached a breaking-point – but there is plenty to justify the fear that they might be approaching one if the attrition of the battle continued. Only that priceless view of 'the other side of the hill' that all commanders yearn for could dismiss this fear, and Fate decreed that this was now to be restored.

* * * * *

That there was a crisis in the sea war in March, 1943, is not to be disputed. The only demur is as to its degree and justification: the question is, how great a crisis it was, how much of it was in the mind and how much in the facts of battle. That the mental and psychological factor in the Admiralty was of great – indeed, too great – importance has already been argued; it has, however, to be remembered that when one speaks of high commands in war a crisis in the mind may rate equally with a heavy defeat in the field. But there were material considerations at work as well as psychological, intimately bound up, as usual, with the state of the war itself. As Churchill said:

> The Battle of the Atlantic was the dominating factor all through the war. Never for one moment could we forget that everything happening elsewhere, on land, at sea, or in the air, depended ultimately on its outcome, and amid all other cares we viewed its changing fortunes day by day with hope or apprehension.[116]

If March did nothing else, its shocks underlined the rightness of the Casablanca decision to give top priority to the U-boat war; what now remained was to give effect to that decision. In other respects, in retrospect, the Casablanca Conference takes on the look of a distinctly unfortunate meeting. We have noted the baleful results of the 'Unconditional Surrender' pronouncement; we have touched on the vulnerability of conference directives in the face of strong personalities like Admiral King or Air Chief Marshal Harris; and there was another Casablanca decision which slipped quietly through – *dangerously* quietly for a matter of such vast importance: the burial of ROUNDUP.

All through 1942 the intention to carry out an Allied cross-Channel operation in 1943 had been the proclaimed centrepiece of Anglo-American strategy, with July in mind as the probable launching date. This was ROUNDUP, and steadily, as they considered its practicalities, the

British Chiefs of Staff had been cooling towards the concept; the experience of Dieppe, and of TORCH also,[117] gave a sharper edge to their doubts. Their spokesman, General Sir Alan Brooke, was quite firm on this matter. As his biographer says,

He simply knew that it would not work.[118]

The Americans, for their part, were already uneasily aware that the very acceptance of TORCH itself had already gravely compromised ROUNDUP in 1943.[119] When, on 19 January at Casablanca, the Allies so calmly agreed that TORCH should be followed by an invasion of Sicily, and that this should take place in July, ROUNDUP was buried without obsequies. The attack on Sicily (HUSKY) was a British concept, chiefly stemming from the desire to open up the Mediterranean sea lanes and effect that great saving of shipping which was, as we have seen, 'the keystone of Alanbrooke's strategic philosophy' at this time. The decision itself, however, was an entirely joint agreement; the American Chiefs of Staff did not put up any kind of last-ditch battle against it – largely because they had no alternative to offer. Nevertheless, as the year unfolded, and it became clear that, whether thus intended or not, the advance into Sicily was only the first stage of what became known as the 'Mediterranean strategy', American resentment steadily mounted. The US Chiefs had a sense of having been ambushed at Casablanca, dialectically outgunned by their better-prepared British opposite numbers (one almost says 'opponents') who came fortified by a strong expert secretariat. So the seeds were planted of serious misunderstandings and disputations which lasted well into 1944. What is quite clear, however, is that when one speaks of the U-boat threat to Allied offensive plans, after January, 1943, it is not the defunct ROUNDUP that we mean, but the buildup for OVERLORD in 1944. And that is a material consideration indeed in estimating the March crisis.

Not every senior officer was affected by the gloom that fell upon the Admiralty at the end of that month. On the 23rd, the day the two battered convoys reached their destinations, Admiral Horton was writing to an old friend in Submarines (Rear-Admiral R. B. Darke) in a distinctly un-gloomy vein:

This job has been pretty sombre up to date, because one hadn't the means to do those very simple things for which numbers are essential,

577

and which could quash the menace definitely in a reasonable time; but in the last few days things are much brighter and we are being reinforced, and I really have hopes now that we can turn to another and better role – killing them.

The real trouble has been basic – too few ships, all too hard worked with no time for training and all that that entails. The Air, of course, is a tremendous factor, and it is only recently that the many promises that have been made show signs of fulfilment, so far as shore-based stuff is concerned, after $3\frac{1}{2}$ years of war. The Air carried afloat is now turning up to an extent which may be almost embarrassing in the next few months, if they are to be properly protected. . . . All these things are coming to a head just now, and although the last week has been one of the blackest on the sea, so far as this job is concerned, I am really hopeful.[120]

We have already seen the VLR aircraft at work; there is no need to dwell further upon them, beyond noting Roskill's considered comment on their importance and that of the event in which they featured:

For what it is worth this writer's view is that in the early spring of 1943 we had a very narrow escape from defeat in the Atlantic; and that, had we suffered such a defeat, history would have judged that the main cause had been the lack of two more squadrons of very long range aircraft for convoy escort duties.[121]

Dönitz quotes this passage verbatim in his Memoirs, evidently with completely agreement. Others, however, were even now not persuaded; Air Chief Marshal Harris grudged every one of the VLR aircraft not allocated to the strategic offensive, and was backed up in this by the commanders of the now fast-growing US 8th Army Air Force, stationed in Britain precisely for the purpose of bombing Germany. In a paper addressed to the Anti-U-Boat Committee on 29 March, Harris said:

In the present case it is inevitable that at no distant date the Admiralty will recognize that U-boats can effectively be dealt with only by attacking the sources of their manufacture . . .

It cannot be pointed out too strongly that in the Bomber Offensive lies the only hope of giving really substantial help to Russia this year or in the foreseeable future . . . and that if it is reduced to lesser proportions by further diversions of large numbers of bomber aircraft for seagoing defensive duties, it will fail in its object and the failure may well extend to the whole of the Russian campaign. This in my opinion would be a far greater disaster than the sinking of a few extra merchant ships each week.[122]

This is one of Harris's wilder flights of fancy, all the more remarkable in the light of the fact that the surrender of the German Sixth Army at Stalingrad was now practically two months old,[123] marking a turning-point in the war on the Eastern Front as definite as the First Battle of Alamein on the smaller screen of the Desert War. The full implications of Stalingrad had yet to unfold, but it is amazing that Harris could continue to write about the Russian campaign in this way.

No less amazing was the barbed shaft that he could not resist planting in Coastal Command (see p. 432: 'merely an obstacle to victory'):

> I feel ... that too much emphasis is being given to the possibility of locating U-boats by means of ASV and too little to the difficulty of attacking them successfully when they are located. Our experience, which is considerable, is that *even expert crews* find it no easy matter to attack with accuracy even a city by means of H2S. I am therefore rather sceptical of the prospects of *inexperienced crews* with ASV. Indeed, I feel that the provision of aircraft equipped with this apparatus will mark the beginning rather than the end of the difficulties involved in sinking U-boats.[124]

Bomber Command's redoubtable AOC-in-C was on safer ground in rejecting yet another Admiralty appeal for bombing of the U-boat bases on the Biscay coast; as we have seen, this was an entirely unprofitable exercise, and known to be so. The appeal is, in fact, only further evidence of the Admiralty's shaken nerves. In other respects, however, one can only agree with Admiral Gretton's verdict:

> everything else which Harris said in these paragraphs proved to be wrong, and usually exactly the opposite was the case.

Harris was not by any means the only officer to cherish delusions at this time. Less than a fortnight after his paper to the Anti-U-boat Committee, his American colleague, Brigadier-General Ira C. Eaker, commanding the 8th USAAF, put forward what was known as the 'Eaker Plan', later rechristened Operation POINTBLANK, which laid down the lines of Allied air strategy for the year. The 'Eaker Plan' (officially known as the Combined Bomber Offensive) argued that

579

Allied bombing would be most usefully directed against a small group of selected industrial targets or target systems, and designated six whose destruction, said Eaker, would ' "fatally weaken" the capacity of the German people for armed resistance'. The six were:

submarine construction yards and bases,
the aircraft industry,
the ball-bearing industry,
oil production,
synthetic rubber production,
military transport vehicle production.

General Eaker looked forward to the expansion of his force for this purpose to 1,746 aircraft by 1 January, 1944, and 2,702 aircraft by 1 April of that year. Given these increases, and the cooperation of Bomber Command's night attacks,

the plan confidently asserted that submarine construction could be reduced by eighty-nine per cent, that forty-three per cent of the German fighter and sixty-five per cent of the bomber production capacity could be destroyed, that seventy-six per cent of ball-bearing production could be eliminated, etc. etc.[125]

For the American force, in daylight, to achieve results such as these would evidently depend on also achieving that magical condition, air superiority, which, in turn, would depend on defeating the German fighter force; and this was, indeed, done in 1944, but not before both the Americans and Bomber Command sustained heavy and unexpected defeats.[126] It was as well that the Anti-U-boat Committee had not taken Harris's protestations too seriously, though no one could know that this would be the last manifestation of the almost theological dispute between the bombing doctrinaires who believed that the best way to defeat U-boats was by attacking land targets, and the maritime school who thought it might be quicker and more effective to sink the U-boats at sea (see p. 429). That debate was now about to be decided.

Air Chief Marshal Sir Arthur Harris was a highly offensive-minded officer, who hated the thought that the air weapon should be in any way relegated to a 'defensive' rôle. Air Marshal Slessor was a chip off the same block. In giving effect to his offensive urge he was only following in his predecessor's footsteps, but with a considerably better-equipped Command than Joubert had ever disposed of. Slessor's target was the U-boats on passage through the Bay of Biscay to the Atlantic ('the trunk of the U-boat menace') and his instrument of attack was Air Vice-Marshal G. R. Bromet's No 19 Group. The 1943 Bay operations are collectively referred to as the 'Second Offensive', but each one had its own code-name, often reflecting intentions rather than realities. The first, already in progress as Slessor took command, was GONDOLA (a suitably neutral name) lasting from 4–16 February; this had the advantage of employing two USAAF B-24 squadrons on loan, both using SCR 517 (ASV III). A total of 300 sorties in the course of GONDOLA produced nineteen sightings and eight attacks, only one of which succeeded; unsurprisingly, it was one of the USAAF Liberators (No 2 Squadron) which achieved the solitary kill, *U519*. The American squadrons were then transferred to the Morocco Sea Frontier to deal with a U-boat alarm in that area, against protests by the British Chiefs of Staff.

The next round went to the Germans. We have seen how Harris had won his battle to have first use of centimetric radar in the form of H2S; the inevitable consequence was not long delayed. Bomber Command Pathfinder [127] aircraft with H2S began to operate over German-occupied territory at the end of January, and on 2 February, 1943, a Stirling carrying H2S was duly shot down near Rotterdam. The radar equipment was badly damaged, but not enough to conceal its character from the astonished eyes of the German electronics experts. All their prognostications and working hypotheses had been far wide of the mark, so much so that Göring, when he read the report, exclaimed:

> I expected the British and Americans to be advanced, but frankly I never thought that they would get so far ahead. I did hope that even if we were behind, we could at least be in the same race. [128]

Coming from Germany's ex-economic overlord, [129] this remark may stand as an epitaph of scientific progress in the National-Socialist state. It also meant, more immediately for the Royal Air Force Commands concerned, that the Germans would be slow to find an antidote for centimetric radar in either of its operational forms. At the same time it was evident that their scientists would be attacking the problem with all their powers.

The extension of the new device to anti-submarine warfare was soon revealed. Two squadrons of No 19 Group, No 172 and the RCAF No 407, were fitted with ASV III to supplement their Leigh Lights, which enabled a 172 Squadron Wellington to find *U 333* moving out across the Bay in the dark early hours of 5 March. As the U-boat commander, *Oberleutnant* Schwaff, reported:

> I was attacked by an enemy aircraft at night, but without receiving any previous warning.

And then he added:

> Little damage was done. Enemy aircraft shot down in flames.'

So one more victory was chalked up for German AA; and the U-boat Command was alerted quickly to its danger. Dönitz (or Godt) wrote in the War Diary on that same day:

> The enemy is making use of radar on frequencies outside the coverage of the present search receiver [i.e. *Metox*]. Until now the only confirmation of this is from an enemy aircraft shot down over Holland, which apparently carried a device with a wavelength of 9.7 centimetres.

No 172 Squadron soon took its revenge. Bromet's next operation over the bay was named ENCLOSE, and took place between 20–28 March: forty-one U-boats passed through the Bay during this period, with twenty-six sightings and fifteen attacks. Once more only one U-boat was sunk, *U 665*, but it was a Wellington of 172 Squadron that had the satisfaction of claiming it. Then came ENCLOSE II (6–13 April), during which twenty-five U-boats crossed the Bay; there were eleven sightings, four attacks and one sinking; 172 Squadron had taken blood-wite again – *U 376*. After ENCLOSE II came DERANGE, for which Bromet was able to deploy as many as seventy ASV III Wellingtons, Liberators and Halifaxes. The only U-boat casualty in the Bay by the end of April, however, was *U 526*, sunk by a mine. It must be stated that sinkings are not everything in judging the effectiveness of the Biscay offensives; many U-boats had hair-raising experiences in transit, especially nerve-racking for crews returning from hard actions in mid-Atlantic, perhaps with damage or injured men aboard. This pressure on morale at times when it would normally be expected to ease is a factor in the battle that is not to be ignored. Once again Coastal Command was interpreting 1917 experience with advantages – the 'Spider Web' patrol system described on p. 74; applied by a veteran squadron like 172, this could produce an average of one sighting in every four sorties. Yet the truth is, as Roskill points out, that up to 30 April, 1943, the broad results of the Bay Offensives could only be described as disappointing, despite the perseverance, the courage and the losses of the aircrews concerned. His table tells the story:

| Period | Flying hours | Aircraft lost | U-boats | | | Percentage kills to U/Bs on passage | Aircraft lost to U/Bs sunk |
			Sunk	Damaged	On passage		
1 Jan.–31 Dec., 1941	9,658	16	1	2	451	0.22%	16
1 Jan.–31 May, 1942	5,041	6	—	2	265	—	—
1 June, 1942– 30 Apr., 1943	65,744	148	9	20	959	1%	16
Total	80,443	170	10	24	1,675	0.6%	17 [130]

It could not possibly be said that a total of ten U-boats sunk, at a cost of 80,443 flying hours and seventeen aircraft for each one, in twenty-eight months of war, represented a satisfactory return or reward for the offensive spirit. Thus the Royal Air Force re-learned at much expense of time, effort and aircrew, what the Royal Navy had sorrow-fully learned in 1917–18 (see p. 33). As with other aspects of the U-boat war, a marked (but brief) alteration in this condition was about to take place; the condition itself, however, was at all times the norm.

March went out as it had come in – with a hurricane. *Kapitänleutnant* Purkhold of *U 260* described conditions on the night of the 28th:

Wind force 11. Sea force 9, SW hurricane. . . . While trying to run before the storm at full speed, the boat dived twice. By blowing tanks, putting my helm hard over and reducing speed I managed to hold her reasonably well on the surface. To remain on the bridge was impossible. Within half an hour the captain and the watch were half-drowned. Five tons of water poured into the boat in no time through the conning tower hatch, the voice pipe and the Diesel ventilating shaft. [131]

In the convoy that Purkhold was trying unsuccessfully to attack, HX 230, the commodore's ship capsized and was lost with all hands. The storm saved the convoy from the U-boats, but it is nevertheless odd that Roskill should call this 'a fortunate passage'.[132] Yet, compared with what had gone before, the last part of March was fortunate indeed; a total of some thirty U-boats was unable, in the prevailing conditions, to inflict more than one loss (a straggler) on the three convoys, ONS 1, SC 123 and HX 230. During the same period two U-boats were sunk in the North Atlantic, U 469 and U 169, both by Fortresses of 206 Squadron. The month's total was fifteen, bringing that for the first quarter to forty, a figure which requires to be set against the total for the whole of the rest of the war up to 1 January, 1943: 153. Clearly, if the Admiralty was in a state of deep dismay, there was food for sombre thought at U-boat Command also: this war was getting harder all the time.

It was at the end of March that Admiral Horton's chief hope came to fulfilment; his long-urged reinforcement appeared and at last Western Approaches could 'turn to another and better rôle – killing [the U-boats]'. As the virtually perpetual darkness of the Arctic winter began to give way again to daylight, the air and sea threat to the Murmansk convoys returned. The drain of these, in waters where the *Luftwaffe* could operate almost unhampered, where the remains of the German surface fleet (which still included the great battleship *Tirpitz*) continued to be a constant menace, and U-boats always added their contribution, was extraordinarily heavy – out of all comparison, in fact, with the Atlantic convoys which brought in much of the material that was then carried to the USSR. By way of illustration of this, Roskill tabulates the forces required to escort PQ 18 in September, 1942; the convoy itself comprised thirty-nine merchant ships, together with a rescue ship and an oiler, with three minesweepers for Russian waters and two fleet oilers. The naval strength allocated to the protection of these vessels by the Home Fleet consisted of:

1. *Close Escort:* 2 destroyers, 2 AA ships, 4 corvettes, 3 minesweepers, 4 trawlers, 2 submarines.
2. *Carrier Force:* HMS *Avenger* and 2 destroyers.
3. *'Fighting Destroyer Escort':* 1 cruiser, 16 destroyers.
4. *Spitzbergen Fuelling Force:* 2 fleet oilers, 4 destroyers.
5. *Cruiser Covering Force:* 3 cruisers.

6. *Reinforcements for Spitzbergen:* 2 cruisers, 1 destroyer.
7. *Distant Covering Force:* 2 battleships, 1 cruiser, 5 short-endurance destroyers.
8. *Submarine Patrols:* 7 submarines.

It will be observed that the deployment of such a force as this was equivalent to a major naval campaign; the effect of a regular diversion on this scale upon the Home Fleet was even more disastrous than the effect produced by U-boats on Beatty's Grand Fleet in 1917–18 (see pp. 117–8). The requirement of no fewer than thirty destroyers will also be noted. The decision had to be taken, whether it would not, in view of Atlantic happenings, be better to suspend this heavy commitment for a time. The Soviet Union was now, after all, rejoicing in a major victory and could certainly not plead the pressing necessity which had inspired the sacrificial endeavours of the Arctic Convoys in 1942. The Soviet Government was also, as it happened, for ineluctable secret reasons engaged in one of the periodic pin-prick performances against the Allied naval and air shore establishments in North Russia – though this would not affect high policy unless carried to improbable extremes. At all events, it was decided to risk Soviet displeasure and suspend the Murmansk convoys for an unspecified time. So at last there were some destroyers available for Horton's Support Groups.

Five such groups were formed at the end of March; they were misleadingly designated 'Escort Groups', but escort was not their purpose. This was, says Churchill,

> to act like cavalry divisions, apart from all escort duties. This I had long desired to see.[133]

It is not immediately clear to this author which cavalry division, belonging to what army in what war, Churchill means – unless it is the long-range raiding activity of General J. E. B. Stuart which robbed the Army of Northern Virginia of its mobile arm to no useful purpose on more than one occasion during the American Civil War. It is generally better not to risk dubious inter-Service analogies when referring to very different styles of war. What the Support Groups really implied was the recognition, at long last, that if serious U-boat killing was to be done, the place for it was not in the concrete Biscay bases, or the Baltic shipyards, or the transit 'trunk' of the Bay, but where the U-boats gathered for their pack attacks – across the convoy routes or all around them. And what was needed, as Captain Walker and others had demonstrated often enough, was a two-tier system: a close escort screen to defend the convoy and ensure 'safe and timely arrival', and another group to pursue located U-boats to the death, no matter how long this might take or how far they might travel (see p. 437). This was the Support Group rôle. In addition, there were the Carrier Groups, whose task was to close the 'Atlantic Gap' and bring air power to every part of that ocean. As we have seen, one such was already in action (the '*Bogue* Group'), now to be known as the 6th Escort Group; the other Support Groups were:

1st E.G.: Commander G. N. Brewer RN: sloop *Pelican*, ex–USCG cutter *Sennen*, frigates *Rother*, *Spey*, *Wear*, *Jed*;

2nd E.G.: Captain F. J. Walker RN: sloops *Starling*, *Cygnet*, *Wren*, *Kite*, *Whimbrel*, *Wild Goose*, *Woodpecker*;

3rd E.G.: Captain J. A. McCoy RN: Home Fleet destroyers *Offa*, *Obedient*, *Oribi*, *Orwell*, *Onslaught*;

4th E.G.: Captain A. K. Scott-Moncrieff RN: Home Fleet destroyers *Inglefield* (leader), *Eclipse*, *Fury*, *Icarus*, *Impulsive*, *Matchless*, *Milne*;

5th E.G.: Captain E. M. C. Abel Smith RN: carrier *Biter*, destroyers *Obdurate*, *Opportune*, *Pathfinder*.[134]

Thus fifteen destroyers (including one Flotilla Leader) came to join Western Approaches Command during April, the first to enter the battle being the incomplete 4th E.G., operating with HX 231 and B7 between 6–8 April. Roskill refers to the Home Fleet destroyers as 'these splendidly trained and led ships',[135] which they undoubtedly were. Admiral Gretton (then commanding B7) is somewhat less rhapsodical, remarking that

These destroyers were more familiar with escorting battleships and aircraft carriers with the Home Fleet and were not very experienced with Atlantic trade convoys.[136]

This is as we might expect, and so is his next statement:

They would be very welcome, however,

which is undoubtedly true, a fact undiminished by the record of actual U-boat sinkings by the new Escort Groups during the crucial months, April and May:

April 25	U 203	5th E.G.; aircraft from *Biter* (811 Squadron) and *Pathfinder*
May 6	*U 531*	3rd E.G.; Oribi
	U 438	1st E.G.; *Pelican*
May 12	*U 89*	5th E.G.; aircraft from *Biter* + destroyer *Broadway* and frigate *Lagan* (C2)
May 19	*U̇ 209*	1st E.G.; *Sennen, Jed*
May 22	*U 569*	6th E.G.; aircraft from *Bogue*
May 23	*U 752*	4th E.G.; aircraft from *Archer* (819 squadron).

It is to be noted for perspective that in this decisive period during which no fewer than fifty-six U-boats were sunk, only three and a half are attributable to the surface vessels of the Support Groups, compared with eight and a half to those of the now very experienced close Ocean Escort Groups.[137] It was, in fact, *after* the great battle had been decided that the Support Groups came into their own (Captain Walker's 2nd E.G., in particular, winning great renown as a U-boat killer as we shall see). What cannot be calculated, of course, is the extent to which the very presence of the Support Groups helped the close escorts to make their kills in April and May – yet this must have been a factor.[138] A very precise and apposite alternative statistic is provided by the losses of merchant ships in the North Atlantic during the same two months: seventy-three vessels (398,985 tons), compared with eighty-two vessels (476,349 tons) in March. 'Safe and timely arrival' was clearly in better health.

* * * * *

Dönitz was well pleased with the month of March:

> After three and a half years of war we had brought British maritime power to the brink of defeat in the Battle of the Atlantic – and that with only half the number of U-boats which we had always demanded.[139]

His satisfaction was fairly short-lived, for he continues:

> In the big convoy battles in March most of the U-boats engaged had

exhausted their supplies of both fuel and torpedoes and were forced to return to base. As a result, at the beginning of April there was a U-boat vacuum in the North Atlantic, and it was not until the middle of the month that there was once again a group – '*Meise*' – deployed northeast of Cape Race, Newfoundland.[140]

This is exaggerated; Jürgen Rohwer more moderately says that 'in the first ten days of April the number of U-boats operating in the Atlantic was considerably reduced'[141] because only one U-tanker was available at that stage. He points out that the *Löwenherz* pack of fourteen boats (actually fifteen) was in position southeast of Cape Farewell at the beginning of the month. This pack at once became involved in one of the last two convoy battles to cause a loss of more than five ships in a convoy – the attack on HX 231, for which purpose it was reinforced by another seven boats. A twenty-two boat pack is scarcely a 'vacuum', but Dönitz's account of the final passage of the Atlantic battle is in general vague and scrappy, reflecting his greater distance from the event as Commander-in-Chief of the Navy, and his understandable distress at developments after the HX 229/SC 122 action which he acknowledges to have been 'the last decisive success won by the Germans in the battle of the convoys'.[142]

The *Grossadmiral* is also being disingenuous. He was well aware that his beloved U-boat arm was not what it once had been; ninety-eight new boats appeared in the Atlantic during April,[143] which inevitably meant a great many inexperienced captains and junior officers and crews with a high proportion of young raw sailors. Despite their lengthy and admirable training, performances, in the face of the now highly developed anti-submarine techniques and equipment of the Allies, were distinctly variable, and in fact

it was from the last days of March that, both in the course of convoy operations and from the decrypts of the comments made on the operations by the U-boat Command, the Allies obtained the first substantial evidence of a decline in U-boat morale.[144]

Bletchley Park was now right back in the fray, and the Submarine Tracking Room benefited accordingly. Rodger Winn and his men had never shared the prevailing despondency, preferring to interpret the heavy and costly March battles as a gambler's last throw.[145] The Tracking Room, says Beesly, was alive to every sign, the slightest nuance, not only of the faltering morale which began to manifest itself among the growing proportion of U-boat COs and crews thrown straight into the heat of the conflict on their first war cruise, but also of the anxiety and lack of confidence displayed by Dönitz himself in his exhortations and admonitions to his U-boats at sea.[146]

As far back as February Winn's reports were drawing attention to such symptoms as (referring to HX 175):

> failure on the part of three U-boats, all new, to make a successful attack ... the large number of torpedoes fired without success ... fear of air attack, both by U-boats and *BdU*.

It was in that month also that Winn had predicted a possible change of basic U-boat strategy, as had occurred in mid-1942, saying

> if the switch comes it will be sudden and practically complete.

His sharp eyes were watching for every tell-tale sign of this, and as April wore on there was no shortage of these.

The reinforced *Löwenherz* Group made its attack on HX 231 between 4–7 April. This convoy of sixty-one merchant ships was fortunate enough to be escorted

> by one of the 'First Division' teams, led by Commander Peter Gretton.[147]

This was B7, with Gretton in the frigate *Tay* as Senior Officer, the 1918 destroyer *Vidette* and four corvettes. Vice-Admiral Gretton has given us an admirable stage-by-stage account of the HX 231 action in his book *Crisis Convoy* (1974) which authoritatively conveys the apprehensions, tensions, guesswork, doubt and the ultimate glow of satisfaction at work well done which are all contained in the bald summaries of history. Since only a bald summary is here required, it may as well come from one of Gretton's fellow Escort Group commanders, Macintyre:

> The reception awaiting any wolf-pack which accepted combat with a well-escorted convoy was demonstrated. Though handicapped by having

only one destroyer, only one ship fitted with HF/DF and by the absence of a rescue ship, Gretton's team, helped by good cooperation by Liberator aircraft from Iceland, beat off a concentrated attack, losing only three ships at a cost to the enemy of two of his submarines and others severely damaged, a rate of exchange the Germans could by no means afford.

As a matter of strict reckoning, one has to add three stragglers which, as Macintyre says, 'paid the inevitable penalty'. It is worth adding that this was another action fought in very bad weather conditions, with a strong north-west wind whipping up a rough sea and at night the phenomenon of the Aurora Borealis making the convoy feel 'particularly "naked"'. Rohwer informs us that most of the U-boats were on their first mission; out of eight which closed in on the convoy on the first night, only two were able to get into firing positions. Thereafter, only one or two U-boats were able to keep contact, a very poor performance which obviously owes much to Gretton's handling of his group. HMS *Tay* sank *U 635* on an HF/DF bearing; an 86 Squadron Liberator sank *U 632* and, according to Rohwer, four other U-boats were so badly damaged that they had to return to base. Four Home Fleet destroyers, all later to form part of the 4th Escort Group, joined on 6 April under Commander A. G. West, captain of *Inglefield*, who was considerably senior to Gretton. Yet the authorized procedure, for sound reasons, was that the close escort commander should direct the movements of the Support Groups as well as the aircraft working with his group. Gretton wrote in his report on the ensuing action:

I had been looking forward with some alarm to the prospect of directing the activities of a senior officer in the support group. In the event the situation was easy to control due to the ready co-operation of E. G. 4 and his ships. There is no doubt in my own mind that it is essential for the senior officer of the close screen to be in general charge.[148]

Surveying this action in which he had played such a distinguished part some thirty years later, Admiral Gretton added:

Of the convoys which came later, HX 232 lost three ships, HX 233 lost one ship and HX 234 had one ship torpedoed which did not sink. Perhaps the easiest way to sum up the passage of convoy HX 231 is to say that it represented 'the beginning of the end'.[149]

It would be difficult to dispute this contention. Nowhere is it better illustrated than in the signals which BP was now intercepting with great promptitude. The U-boat Command preferred not to dwell upon the performance of the escort groups with HX 231, and both its War Diary and other contemporary reports emphasize the inexperience of the U-boat commanders and the air rôle, even to the extent, in one case, of inventing non-existent carrier-borne aircraft.[150] But a signal decrypted at Bletchley after the action contained a reprimand for excessive use of W/T, which may be a sign of inexperience, but could also be a sign of nerves.

No sooner had the HX 231 action ended than another pack (*Adler*) attacked ON 176 on 8 April. This time the escort was Commander Day's B4, and against this battle-hardened unit the U-boats could achieve no more than the sinking of two merchantmen. Three days later the *Lerche* Group attacked HX 232, and the U-boat Command felt it necessary to call on the boats to display 'the healthy warrior and hunter instincts' (a phrase which would recur); once again the result was disappointing – three merchant ships. The attack on HX 233 was made by five passage U-boats on 17 April; not only did it fail to sink more than one ship, but the Senior Officer of the Escort (A3), Captain Heineman in the USCG cutter *Spencer*, sank *U 175*. This was one of the rare occasions when a U-boat (admittedly already damaged by depth charges) was despatched by gun fire, so effective that the crew abandoned ship, giving an opportunity for a well-trained American boarding party to make a thorough search. It is also worth mentioning that, in calm weather for once, the escorts were able to refuel seventeen times at the speed of the convoy. The U-boat War Diary recorded 'meagre success at the cost of heavy losses' in such conditions. The next day (19 April) Winn reported:

> It appears that a rumour has spread to the effect that our escorts sometimes leave depth charges suspended from buoys with a time release causing them to explode after the escorts have moved away. This device, [U-boat Command] said, was 'pure bluff, and it should be realized that bangs do not mean danger. The man who allows his healthy warrior and fighting instincts to be humbugged ceases to have any powers of resistance to present day enemy defences'.[151]

Winn called this a 'remarkable signal', as indeed it is; the repetition of

591

such a phrase as 'warrior and hunter (or 'fighting') instinct' is striking and indicative of grave misgivings at U-boat Command. Ronald Lewin speaks of

> a new tone in Dönitz's signals – a barely concealed desperation ... visible in the Ultra messages.[152]

This may be going a little too far for April, but the note of anxiety is unmistakable and the reiterated explanation of it was significant; it was in the same Tracking Room report on 19 April that Winn remarked:

> such manifestations of concern for the vulnerability of U-boats to air attack are suggestive of an incipient decline in morale amongst at any rate some U-boat crews.

This would now be a running refrain, and it is one more of the war's many ironies that at the very time that fear of a morale failure in the merchant crews was causing alarm in the Admiralty, it was in fact their opponents who were showing signs of a real moral collapse.

April went out on a note of anticlimax for the U-boats in the North Atlantic: attacks on three convoys, HX 234, ONS 3 and ONS 4,[153] carried out by the *Meise* and *Specht* packs, succeeded in sinking no more than four merchant ships (one straggler) for a loss of three U-boats. This was a wretched 'rate of exchange', and once more attributable substantially to aircraft: on 23 April a Liberator of 120 Squadron sank *U 189*; Macintyre in HMS *Hesperus* sank *U 191* on the same day; and two days later a Swordfish from HMS *Biter* shared the sinking of *U 203* with the destroyer *Pathfinder*. On the previous day *U 404* (von Bülow) had sighted *Biter* and tried a long shot with a salvo; four detonations were heard and spurts of flame observed, but von Bülow very properly made only a cautious report, clearly stating that a sinking could not be regarded as certain. This did not deter Dr Goebbels's propaganda machine from claiming the sinking of an aircraft carrier, but the truth was that all von Bülow's torpedoes had exploded short of their target, and HMS *Biter* was untouched.

The Tracking Room report on 26 April referred to a 'lack of boldness' spreading amongst the U-boat commanders; in the War Diary on 1 May, however, summarizing these operations, the Command asserted that they had failed 'only because of bad weather not because of the enemy's defences'. This was just whistling for a wind; yet even in 1956 Dönitz continued to blame the weather for the fact that 'no very great success could be scored'.[154] It was not a question of 'no very great success', it was a matter of no success at all – a far cry from the triumphs of March.

Yet Dönitz and Godt had some consolation:

> During April 1943 solid successes were achieved off Freetown. Five ships, sailing independently, were sunk in the immediate vicinity of the port. In addition, *U515* (*Kapitänleutnant* Henke) scored what must be regarded as a unique success against a convoy bound for Freetown. . . . After meticulous consideration he reported having sunk eight ships with a total tonnage of 50,000 tons. We now know, from official figures, that he had, in fact, sunk eight ships with a total tonnage of 49,196 tons . . . we are an honest firm!

The convoy was TS 37, on the Takoradi–Sierra Leone route, eighteen ships escorted by only one corvette and three trawlers. Roskill takes up the story:

> The Senior Officer of the escort had picked up U-boat transmissions, but did not break wireless silence to tell the shore authorities. Instead a message was sent through a patrolling Hudson. The aircraft merely included the message in its normal report, with the result that it did not reach the Headquarters of the Flag Officer, West Africa, until after the convoy was attacked that evening. Three destroyers were at once sent out to reinforce the escort, but they did not arrive until after a second attack had taken place early on the 1st of May.[155]

Churchill called the outcome 'deplorable', and a sinking rate of 44.4% makes it difficult to argue with that verdict. Yet with all his experience he must have been well aware that such accumulations of errors and mischances are all part of the familiar friction of war. *Kapitänleutnant* Henke was lucky; and for the U-boat Command his success, coming when it did, was highly suggestive.

U-boat losses remained constant: fifteen in March, fifteen again in April. It was not these that were causing concern at U-boat Command; it was morale, and the moment of crisis had arrived.

* * * * *

Convoy ONS 5, forty-two merchant ships including two refuelling tankers (one of which proved to be useless, having canvas instead of rubber hosepipes) under Captain J. Brooks RNR as commodore, sailed from Liverpool on 21 April. The escort was Gretton's B7, returning across the Atlantic only twelve days after bringing in HX 231. Gretton himself was now in the destroyer *Duncan* (actually a 1,400-ton flotilla leader, launched in 1932). The presence of a second destroyer was welcome, but perhaps even more so was that of two rescue trawlers in B7. ONS 5 was destined to be the last of the tragic convoys in the North Atlantic; to what extent foreknowledge of this might or might not have given consolation to the ship's companies of the merchantmen and escorts for what they were about to receive can only be a matter of speculation. What is beyond question is that for this last dramatic spectacle the full range of stage effects was produced, with the 'steep Atlantick' at its steepest and cruellest.

The misery began on the very second day of sailing, with a gale coming up and steadily worsening, causing two ships to collide, one having to be sent to Iceland for repair. A U-boat scare on the 24th turned out to be a false alarm, which was a relief, but there was no mistaking the mood of the sea: an attempt to refuel *Duncan* had to be abandoned when a hose parted in the vile weather. A Fortress of 206 Squadron was nevertheless able to draw first blood by sinking *U 710* in the convoy's path on that day, but thereafter the air escorts were grounded by conditions at base. A slight improvement in the weather enabled both destroyers to refuel on the 27th, but the next day U-boat signals were picked up dead ahead; battle was evidently about to begin.

As April drew to its end, 'the number of U-boats operating against the North Atlantic convoy routes was to reach its highest point of the whole war';[156] there were, says Rohwer, 193 boats now in the West:

	VIIB/C	VIID*	IXB/C	IXD†	XIV‡	Total
At sea	81	2	32	10	5	130
On North Atlantic routes	79	2	17	—	3	101

* = minelayers; † = transports; ‡ = tankers

These were formed into four packs: *Star*, south-west of Iceland, *Specht*, north-east of Newfoundland, *Amsel*, forming from new arrivals to the south of *Specht*, *Drossel*,[157] also made up of new arrivals, on the Gibraltar route. The three northern groups, totalling some forty-five boats with three tankers, were looking in particular for three homeward-bound convoys which the *B-Dienst* was carefully monitoring, HX 235, SC 127 and SC 128. But what *U 650*, at the northern end of *Star*, had found on 28 April was ONS 5. Fourteen more boats were ordered to home in on *U 650*'s showing reports, and the first attack came that night. Strong wind, heavy seas and skilful handling of a well-trained escort defeated it completely: no loss to the convoy, two U-boats damaged.

What Roskill calls 'the watchers on shore' – Bletchley Park, the Tracking Room and Western Approaches Command – were following all this activity as closely as the *B-Dienst*. The decrypts enabled all the home-bound convoys to evade the U-boat patrols, and also revealed the mounting threat to ONS 5. On 29 April Horton ordered the 3rd E.G. out from St John's to support the convoy with five of the ex-Home Fleet destroyers led by HMS *Offa* under Captain McCoy, and the first of them, *Oribi*, arrived on the night of the 30th. The remainder of the group had some difficulty in finding the convoy, which was now practically hove-to in weather which was reaching its worst. A full gale was blowing, visibility was low, pack ice and icebergs were present, ONS 5 was becoming very scattered and refuelling was impossible. On the other hand, so bad were the conditions that most of the U-boats dived and lost touch with the convoy; their sole success by 2 May was a single ship sunk by *U 258* in a bold attack in the early hours of 29 April. On 3 May, however, to his deep chagrin, Gretton found that his ship had only enough fuel to reach St John's at economical speed:

After much heart-searching I decided that the *Duncan* had to go. The weather would not allow boat work, nor transfer by jackstay, so I had to go with her. Command was therefore handed over to Lieutenant-Commander R. E. Sherwood RNR in the *Tay*, and we left at the best speed the weather would allow. After two days the wind shifted in our favour, we met an unexpected favourable current, and we managed to make St John's with 4 per cent fuel remaining. We were most depressed because we felt we left the group in the lurch and were thoroughly ashamed of ourselves, though there was really no one to blame except the staff who decided in the 1920s the endurance of such destroyers.[158]

As we know, Atlantic escort work was not what the Admiralty had in mind when it called for destroyer designs in the 1920s – nor, indeed, in the 1940s, for the next day two, and later a third, of the 1941–2 'O' Class ships of the 3rd E.G. had to follow Gretton for the same reason. He himself never ceased to regret that he had not decided to risk all and stay with the convoy:

> This decision has haunted me ever since . . . I had missed the 'golden moment' which comes but once in a lifetime.

Meanwhile, though neither Gretton nor Sherwood nor anyone else except, possibly, Rodger Winn, with his beady eyes fixed upon the Bletchley decrypts, could be aware of it, a real desperation was setting in at U-boat Command. Dönitz and Godt knew how many U-boats they had in play, they knew from *B-Dienst* how many convoys were in the area of operations, they could perceive the opportunities that were offering – yet nothing seemed to happen. Did it mean that the U-boats were not pressing their attacks? On 2 May the Command (and this must have been Dönitz himself) made a signal calculated to raise a cheer in the Tracking Room:

> With 31 boats something can and must be accomplished![159]

The next day, still hoping to catch SC 128, and under the impression that ONS 5 had been lost, U-boat Command reorganized its forces: the *Star* and *Specht* groups were amalgamated to form a new pack of thirty boats, *Fink*, in a tight patrol line into which to the surprise of all concerned ONS 5 duly sailed on 4 May. The U-boats closed in on both sides, and ahead the eleven boats of *Amsel* also lay in wait. As Dönitz says,

> our boats found themselves placed in a very favourable tactical position.[160]

The attack came on the night of the 4th, now with the familiar accompaniment of U-boats pressing right into the convoy; six ships were sunk that night, and the rescue trawlers 'proved their weight in gold'. The only U-boat loss was *U630*, sunk by 'a Canso of No 5 Squadron RCAF from Newfoundland, over 650 miles away.

Daylight brought a much-needed improvement in the weather, enabling some of the escorts to refuel, but during the course of the 5th four more ships were sunk in the convoy, and another from a group which had become detached in the storm. The B7 corvette HMS *Pink* exacted a price for this, however: *U192*, depth-charged to destruction. This was only the beginning of a splendid counter-attack by B7 under Sherwood and the two remaining destroyers of E.G. 3. Twenty-four times that night the U-boats tried to penetrate the escort screen, and each time they were repelled; the cost to the attackers was four U-boats. It was a second B7 corvette, *Loosestrife*, that caught *U638* on the surface and destroyed her with depth charges as she dived. The destroyer *Vidette* got *U125* with a Hedgehog. *Oribi* of E.G. 3 rammed and sank *U531* in the fog that now descended. And a reinforcement ordered up by Horton on the 4th, the sloop HMS *Pelican* leading E.G. 1, pursued a radar echo to destroy *U438*. At 0915 on 6 May the U-boat Command broke off the action and withdrew Group *Fink*.

The final tally of ONS 5 was twelve merchant ships lost, seven U-boats destroyed with two more (*U659* and *U439*) lost in collision on 3 May – a total of nine – and another five badly damaged. No escort was lost or heavily damaged. Thus a situation in which, in the words of Captain McCoy of E.G. 3, 'the convoy faced annihilation', had been transformed to the point where Dönitz would write:

> Such high losses could not be borne. . . . I regarded this convoy battle as a defeat.

For this defeat Dönitz blamed the sudden fog on the morning of 6 May 'which became thicker and which ruined . . . a golden opportunity', and the radar which, he said, placed his boats 'in an inferior and, indeed, hopeless position', and he added:

> While the U-boats continued to lack a receiver capable of picking up signals on these new wavebands, any further attacks on convoys in bad visibility would remain impossible.

He never did grasp the part that HF/DF played in the defence of convoys at this time. Yet, important though these technical advantages undoubtedly were, they do not fully explain a defeat in which

> in the end there were forty-one U-boats operating against ONS 5 – actually more boats than the convoy had ships.[161]

It is clear that the new boats with their raw crews did not have the battle skills and the rugged disposition of their peace-trained predecessors.

It is also clear that the Royal Navy had reached a high pitch of excellence. The loss of twelve merchant ships was a tragedy indeed – what else can one call it? But it was a tragedy within a triumph, and if one man is to be singled out as responsible for that triumph it must be Lieutenant-Commander R. E. Sherwood RNR in his smart frigate *Tay*. Sherwood comes across to us after nearly fifty years, through all the tightlipped traditions of the Silent Service, as an embodiment of the virtues of the Royal Naval Reserve. Mature, as Reserve officers are expected to be, wise in the ways of the sea and experienced in convoy battle, unflappable, this two-and-a-half-ringed officer won a battle that an admiral or a general could be well pleased with. Characteristically of the Service his report gave the credit to the men under him:

> All ships showed dash and initiative. No ship required to be told what to do and signals were distinguished both by their brevity and wit.

'Brevity and wit', in the face of forty-one U-boats, are matters to ponder; but Macintyre comments:

> These were the marks of the well-trained escort group.[162]

And Gretton sums up:

> Sherwood and his ships should be very proud of what they had done.[163]

It had been, indeed, truly a Royal Navy victory; for once there were no Allied ships engaged, and after 206 Squadron's success in sinking *U710* on 24 April Coastal Command was prevented by weather from playing any further part, though the RCAF brought the Air back into the picture on 4 May. Western Approaches now disposed of an escort fleet of reasonable size[164] and great efficiency; equipment and weapons were working well. Once the high winds and mountainous seas abated, the 271M radar came into its own: night or fog were the conditions in which it excelled.[165] HF/DF needs no further mention; seaborne or land-based, in combination with ASDIC in skilled hands, it was a war-winner. The teething troubles of Hedgehog were being cured, as the satisfying explosions after *Vidette*'s discharge indicated; a much needed forward-firing weapon had come into the armoury. But it was now well-established that the primary armament of an escort was the depth charge, and long and hard were the drills that made the best teams proficient.[166] Guns had few opportunities in anti-submarine warfare, and when these did occur it was usually at the acute disadvantage of engaging a fleeting target at very short range in darkness. Constant drill was essential, but all too often rewarded only by anti-climax. Gretton, after the HX 231 action, devised a special exercise which he, too, called 'Pointblank' (unconnected in any way with General Eaker's) for snap shooting at very short ranges. Tracer ammunition in the AA guns (Oerlikons) at maximum depression was found useful on such occasions. Normal torpedoes were of no use at all for this kind of fighting, but the tubes acquired new value with the introduction of the Mark X depth charge. This was a ten-foot cylinder containing 2,000 lb of explosive, fired out of a torpedo tube by a cordite charge. Accurately placed, this fearsome device 'had a devastating effect, particularly at great depths'.[167] The Navy was at last becoming convinced that the U-boats were diving very deep (see p. 437); depth charge technology was accordingly developing a new 600-lb streamlined Torpex-filled quick-sinking charge, but this was not yet available. There was still a great deal of luck as well as judgment in depth-charge attacks, whether by ships or aircraft:

> No method of accurately determining the depth of a submarine was ever found, and the most perfect attack failed if the depth-charge setting was too high or too low.[168]

* * * * *

One hundred per cent certainty is rarely vouchsafed in war, but in these late convoy battles the crews of the escorts have the air of men who know exactly what they are doing and have confidence in the instruments with which they have to work.

If, as Gretton claims, the battle of HX 231 marked 'the beginning of the end' of the big Battle of the Atlantic, ONS 5 was certainly its first milestone. It set the new pattern of heavy U-boat losses in exchange for small numbers of merchantmen. Before ONS 5 even approached port, *U 465* was sunk by a Liberator of 86 Squadron, while the convoy it was attacking, HX 236, suffered no loss at all. The litany continues in similar vein:

HX 237	12–13 May	3 stragglers lost, 3 U-boats sunk
SC 129	12–14 May	2 ships lost, 2 U-boats sunk
HX 238	mid-May	no loss on either side
ON 184	19–22 May	no merchant ship lost, 1 U-boat sunk
SC 130	19–20 May	no merchant ship lost, 5 U-boats sunk
HX 239	21–23 May	no merchant ship lost, 1 U-boat sunk

We do not need to follow the details of these actions which separately and collectively only display how the pendulum had swung, and how the ascendancy had unmistakably passed from the U-boats to the escorts, sea and air. It is worth, however, as a valediction, looking briefly at this change of fortune through the eyes and periscope of a tough and hardened First Officer, *Leutnant* Herbert Werner of *U 230*, soon to command a boat of his own with some distinction. On 11 May *U 230*, commanded by *Oberleutnant* Siegmann, another hard-bitten submariner, was ordered to attack a convoy which proved to be HX 237. At 0615 on 12 May Werner was on the bridge and sighted the distant smoke of the convoy, which *U 230* at once proceeded to close, preparing to attack. A change of course by the convoy delayed this, and Siegmann called Werner over to take a look through the periscope:

> I saw an amazing panorama. The entire horizon, as far and wide as I could see, was covered with vessels, their funnels and masts as thick as a forest. At least a dozen fast destroyers cut the choppy green sea with elegance. As many as two dozen corvettes flitted around the edges of the convoy. I said in awe, 'Quite a display of power, sir. It's probably the largest convoy ever'.[169]

It is said that distance lends enchantment to a view; clearly, angle of vision lends confusion. HX 237 was not an exceptionally large convoy – only forty-six merchantmen. Its close escort was C2,[170] under

Lieutenant-Commander E. H. Chavasse RN in the destroyer *Broadway*, with the RN frigate *Lagan* and corvette *Primrose* and three RCN corvettes. A support group, E.G. 5, was with the convoy, including HMS *Biter* with her three Home Fleet destroyers. It is likely that memory played tricks on Werner when he wrote his book in the late 1960s; for an experienced U-boat officer to multiply four destroyers and a frigate into 'at least a dozen destroyers', and four corvettes into 'two dozen', would require imaginative inclinations indeed. Yet even with such distortions it is salutary to see how the odds often looked from the other end of the torpedo tube.

At 0915 *U 230* surfaced and made her contact signal:

Convoy [grid position] BD 92. Course Northeast. Eleven knots. Strong defence. Remain surfaced for attack.

What follows is (perforce) a highly condensed version of Werner's narrative of *U 230*'s day from that time onwards, but even with severe cuts it throws searching light on the transformation of the U-boat war. Werner remained on the bridge after the contact signal had gone out:

0955: A startled cry at my back, '*Flugzeug!*'
I saw a twin-engined plane dropping out of the sun. The moment of surprise was total.
'Alarrrrmmm!' We plunged head over heels into the conning tower. The boat reacted at once and shot below surface . . .
Four short, ferocious explosions shattered the water above and around us. The boat trembled and fell at a 60-degree angle. Water splashed, steel shrieked, ribs moaned, valves blew, deck-plates jumped, and the boat was thrown into darkness. As the lights flickered on, I saw astonishment in the round eyes of the men. They had every right to be astounded . . .
Where had the small plane come from? . . . The conclusion was inescapable that the convoy launched its own airplanes . . . The idea of a convoy with its own air defence smashed our basic concept of U-boat warfare.

U 230 surfaced cautiously at 1035:

I glanced only occasionally at the dense picket fence along the horizon and concentrated on the sky . . .
1110: I detected a glint of metal between the clouds. It was a small aircraft, and it was diving into the attack.

'Alarrrmmm!'
Fifty seconds later, four explosions nearby taught us that the pilot was a well-trained bombardier.

U 230 dived to over 580 feet and surfaced again at 1125:

Instinct forced us ahead, kept us moving despite the constant threat from above . . .
1142: 'Aircraft – alarrrmmm!'
U 230 plunged into the depths. Four booms twisted the hull, but the boat survived the savage blows . . .
1204: We surfaced in an increasingly choppy sea and surged ahead . . .
1208: A call from below reached us on the bridge: 'Message for Captain, signal just received: '*Attacked by aircraft. Sinking. U 89.*' . . .
1217: 'Aircraft dead astern, alarrrmmm!'
U 230 dived once more and descended rapidly . . . At 45 seconds, four booms whipped the boat with violent force . . .
1230: We surfaced again . . .
1315: A twin-engined plane [171] dropped suddenly out of a low cloud only 800 metres astern. It was too late to dive. After freezing for a horrifying instant, Siegmann yelled 'Right full rudder!' I jumped to the rear of the bridge to shoot while the mate manned the second gun. The small aircraft grew enormous fast. It dived upon us, machine-gunning the open rear of the bridge as the boat turned to starboard. Neither the mate nor I was able to fire a single bullet; our guns were jammed. The aircraft dropped four bombs . . . then roared over the bridge so close I could feel its engines' hot exhaust brush my face . . . Four high fountains collapsed over the two of us at the guns. *U 230* was still afloat, still racing through the rising green sea . . .
1325: Our radio mate delivered an urgent message to the captain: '*Attacked by aircraft. Unable to dive. Sinking. 45 North 25 West. Help. U 456.*' . . .
1350: . . . my glasses picked up the bow of *U 456* poking out of the rough sea. The men clung to the slippery deck and to the steel cable strung from bow to bridge. Most of them stood in the water up to their chests. The aircraft kept circling above the sinking boat, making it foolhardy for us to approach . . . astern, a corvette crept over the horizon . . . We turned away . . .
1422: 'Aircraft astern!'
Again it was too late to dive. The single-engined plane came in low in a straight line exactly over our wake. I fingered the trigger of my gun. Again the gun was jammed. I kicked its magazine, clearing the jam.

Then I emptied the gun at the menace. The mate's automatic bellowed. Our boat veered to starboard, spoiling the plane's bomb run. The pilot revved up his engine, circled, then roared toward us from dead ahead. As the plane dived very low, its engine sputtered, then stopped. Wing first, the plane crashed into the surging ocean, smashing its other wing on our superstructure as we raced by. The pilot, thrown out of his cockpit, lifted his arm and waved for help, but then I saw him disintegrate in the explosion of the four bombs which were meant to destroy us. Four violent shocks kicked into our starboard side astern, but we left the horrible scene unharmed . . .

Running at highest speed, *U 230* gained bearing ahead of the convoy . . .

1545: A report from the radio room put our small victory into proper perspective: '*Depth charges by three destroyers. Sinking. U 186.*' This new loss was the 11th we had heard of since our patrol began. A naval disaster seemed to be in the making . . .

1600: *U 230* cut into the projected path of the convoy . . .

1603: 'Aircraft, bearing three-two-oh!'

We plummeted into depth. Four detonations, sounding like one, drove the boat deeper . . . Siegmann ordered his boat to periscope depth. He raised the scope but downed it instantly, cursing angrily, '*Verdammt! The fellow has dropped a smoke bomb and has dyed the water yellow.*'

Despite the dye marking the spot of our submergence, the captain ordered an attack on the convoy . . .

1638: Up periscope. Then: 'Tubes one to five stand ready.'

'Tubes one to five are ready,' I answered quickly, then held my breath.

Siegmann swivelled to check the opposite side. Suddenly he cried, 'Down with the boat, Chief, take her down for God's sake, destroyer in ramming position! Down to two hundred metres!' . . .

As the boat swiftly descended, the harrowing sound of the destroyer's engines and propellers hit the steel of our hull . . .

An ear-shattering boom ruptured the sea. A spread of six depth charges lifted the boat, tossed her out of the water, and left her on the surface at the mercy of four British destroyers . . . For seconds there was silence . . . After a whole eternity, our bow dipped and the boat sank – and sank. A new series of exploding charges lifted our stern with a mighty force. Our boat, entirely out of control, was catapulted toward the bottom five miles below. Tilted at an angle of 60 degrees, *U 230* tumbled to 250 metres before [Chief Engineer] Friedrich was able to reverse her fall.

250 metres is 817.5 feet; *U 230* finally levelled off at 230 metres, 752.1 feet. This was considered to be out of effective depth–charge range:

1657: Distinct splashes on surface heralded the next spread. A series of 24 charges detonated in quick succession. The bellowing roar slammed against our boat. The explosions again pushed her into a sharp tilt while the echo of the detonations rolled endlessly through depths . . .

1740: The uproar was at its peak. A sudden splash told us that we had 10 or 15 seconds to brace against another barrage. The charges went off just beyond lethal range . . . Perhaps we should risk going deeper. I did not know where our limit was, where the hull would finally crack. No one knew. Those who had found out took their knowledge into the depths. For hours we suffered the punishment and sank gradually deeper. In a constant pattern, spreads of 24 charges battered our boat every 20 minutes.

It would seem that this vigorous and persistent attack was the work of the close escort, which did not give up the hunt for nearly two hours. Then the attackers went away and *U 230*'s crew thought their ordeal was over, but very soon what Werner calls 'the killer group' arrived:

2000: The new group launched its first attack, then another, and another. We sat helpless 265 metres below [866.5 feet]. Our nerves trembled. Our bodies were stiff from cold, stress and fear. The mind-searing agony of waiting made us lose any sense of time and any desire for food. The bilges were flooded with water, oil and urine. Our washrooms were under lock and key; to use them could have meant instant death, for the tremendous outside pressure would have acted in reverse of the expected flow. Cans were circulated for the men to use to relieve themselves. Added to the stench of waste, sweat and oil was the stink of the battery gases. The increasing humidity condensed on the cold steel, dropped into the bilges, dripped from pipes and soaked our clothes. By midnight, the captain realized that the British would not let up in their bombardment, and he ordered the distribution of potash cartridges to supplement breathing. Soon every man was equipped with a large metal box attached to his chest, a rubber hose leading to his mouth and a clamp on his nose. And still we waited.

May 13. Over 200 canisters had detonated above and around us by 0100 . . .

0400: The boat had fallen to 275 metres [899.25 feet]. We had been under assault for 12 hours and there was no sign of relief. This day was my birthday and I wondered whether it would be my last. How many chances could one ask for?

The escorts – whichever they were – kept up their attacks. By midnight *U 230* had sunk to 280 metres; that is 915.6 feet – an incredible depth at a time when a 500-foot setting for a depth charge was considered to be the most that would be needed. At last, shortly after 0310 on 14 May, the attackers withdrew, and at 0430 Siegmann decided to risk taking his boat to the surface – if it could get there. Metre by metre it rose, using the last of the compressed air and battery power, and then

> *U 230* broke through to air and life ... Around us spread the infinite beauty of night, sky and ocean. Stars glittered brilliantly and the sea breathed gently. The moment of rebirth was overwhelming.

They had been under fierce attack in the deeps for thirty-five hours; the wonder is that no one had gone stark mad.

Werner's narrative must be the swan song of the North Atlantic U-boats in this account. For him, and many of those with him in *U 230*, this was only the first of a succession of such experiences now that all the 'happy times' were only memories and the tide of war had set against them. Whatever imprecisions his story may contain, the impression of the experience is exact, and prompts certain reflections yet again. The first is, as always, wonder at the extraordinary resilience of these young men – the birthday that Werner greeted with such painful conjecture over 900 feet below the surface of the Atlantic was his 23rd. One might suppose, despite the well-documented recuperative powers of youth, that seventy hours of incessant strain without sleep [172] would call imperatively for an intermission, however brief; instead, *U 230* passed straight into a succession of similar experiences in the equally unsuccessful action against SC 129 which lasted until the end of 15 May. Then came the long haul home, and the passage of the Bay under the merciless vigilance of Coastal Command. 'Home' was Brest, on 28 May, with no bands playing and the Commanding Officer of the 9th Flotilla (*Korvettenkapitän* Lehmann-Willenbrock) and his staff showing 'signs of shock'. Well they might – by then thirty-seven U-boats had already been lost in the month of May.

Yet again, also, one wonders at the resilience of the Type VIIC U-boat itself. Even without benefit of the deluge of high explosive that had been poured upon her, *U 230* must have been at the limit of her resistance to the pressures to which she was exposed at the depths that Werner mentions. Herr Schuerer's admirable hull design, adapted from the 1916 models, was doing everything that could be asked from it. Indeed, in the conditions of the rough-and-tumble fighting that had now developed, the Type VII's superiority was so marked that on 14 May Dönitz ordered all the Type IXs in the North Atlantic to transfer their fuel to Type VIIs and return to base.[173] Padfield calls this 'the first sign of retreat'; it is perhaps safer to say that it was a frank acknowledgement of a superior design (see pp. 196–7).

Our final reflection can only be on the awesome effectiveness of Allied anti-submarine warfare techniques by mid-1943 as perceived from the receiving end. Operational Intelligence was evidently central to this; when it was not available, or incomplete, responsible commanders felt crippled. When it was fully at work its most significant contribution was a silent one, to be found not in the battles that did take place, but in that huge number which did not – thanks to the evasive routing that frustrated so many promising U-boat combinations. Aircraft had long ago asserted their contribution – pushing the U-boats further and further out into the Atlantic towards the perilous 'Gap', and now, with the carrier groups, operating actually inside the 'Gap' itself. Werner leaves us in no doubt about what that felt like, but Dönitz, also reflecting on HX 237, sombrely remarks that

> it was once more perfectly obvious that the surface escorts alone would have been more than capable of locating the U-boats in ample time to prevent them from launching their attack.[174]

The impression of these May days on U-boat Command was dire. The HX 237 battle was particularly bad news because, in the words of the Admiralty report,

> no U-boat group operation . . . was so evidently guided by continuing intelligence of the convoy movements.[175]

Thus enlightened by the *B-Dienst*, the Command had assembled no fewer than thirty-six U-boats (the *Rhein* Group) to attack this convoy, but all they could achieve was the sinking of three stragglers. The convoy screen was never penetrated, and the price of this meagre success was three U-boats: *U 89*, *U 456* and *U 753* (all by joint air/sea action). When it was all over the Command tartly signalled:

We can see no explanation for this failure.

The disposition at U-boat Headquarters was still to lay the blame for these events on radar alone, and another of those tell-tale repetitive phrases had crept into the signals, to the deep satisfaction of Winn and his colleagues:

> In his efforts to *rob U-boats of their most valuable characteristic, invisibility*, the enemy is some lengths ahead of us with his radar location.
>
> I am fully aware of the difficult position in which this puts you in the fight with enemy escorts. Be assured that I have done and shall continue to do everything in my power as C-in-C to take all possible steps to change this situation as soon as possible.
>
> Research and development departments within and without the Navy are working to improve your weapons and apparatus.
>
> I expect you to continue your determined struggle with the enemy, and by pitting your ingenuity, ability and hard will against his ruses and technical developments yet to finish him off . . .
>
> Dönitz

This was on 14 May – a vain attempt to brace an obviously fast failing morale in the crews. The total fiasco of the attack on SC 130 on 19–20 May, when thirty-three U-boats failed to sink a single ship and lost five of their number,[176] showed that matters had gone beyond the powers of exhortation to cure. On 21 May, to the joy of the Tracking Room, the U-Boat Command turned from promises to rebuke:

> If there is anyone who thinks that fighting convoys is no longer possible, he is a weakling and no real U-boat commander. The Battle of the Atlantic gets harder but it is the decisive campaign of the war. Be aware of your high responsibility and be clear you must answer for your actions.[177]

It was to no avail; once more the *B-Dienst* supplied exact information of an approaching convoy (HX 239) and a pack of twenty-one boats (*Mosel*) was formed to intercept it. Dönitz resorted once more to exhortation:

> Do your best with this convoy. We must destroy it. If the conditions for this appear favourable, do not dive for aircraft but fight them off. Disengage from destroyers if possible on the surface. Be hard, draw ahead and attack. I believe in you.
>
> C-in-C

As it closed HX 239, the pack sighted ON 184; but attacks on the two convoys produced only the loss of two more U-boats, U_569 and U_752,[178] and not one merchant ship was sunk. It was as though suddenly the art of sinking ships had been totally lost. Roskill offers these impressive statistics for the period 6 April–19 May:

Ships sailed in convoy	Ships sunk in convoy	Stragglers sunk	U-boats sunk by escorts
912	17	6	27[179]

At last the message sank in:

> The overwhelming superiority achieved by the enemy defence was finally proved beyond dispute in the operations against . . . SC 130 and HX 239 . . . It was only bit by bit that I received definite details of the losses we had suffered in the action against these two convoys and among the boats on passage, particularly in the Bay of Biscay, off Iceland and the focal areas in the North Atlantic. Losses had suddenly soared. By May 22 we had already lost thirty-one U-boats since the first of the month, which came as a hard and unexpected blow.[180]

By the end of the month the total was forty-one U-boats lost, a figure as shocking to the Command as it was unprecedented. But Dönitz did not wait so long before taking his great decision:

> In the submarine war there had been plenty of setbacks and crises. Such things are unavoidable in any form of warfare. But we had always overcome them because the fighting efficiency of the U-boat arm had remained steady. Now, however, the situation had changed. Radar, and particularly radar location by aircraft, had to all practical purposes robbed the U-boats of their power to fight on the surface. Wolf-pack operations against convoys in the North Atlantic, the main theatre of operations and at the same time the theatre in which air cover was strongest, were no longer possible . . . and I accordingly withdrew the boats from the North Atlantic. On May 24 I ordered them to proceed, using the utmost caution, to the area south-west of the Azores.
>
> We had lost the Battle of the Atlantic.

So the fundamental change in German strategy prophesied by Winn in February had come to pass, but as Beesly says, 'even more suddenly and completely than Winn had predicted'.[181]

* * * * *

What is a 'decisive victory'? Admiral Dönitz, when he wrote his memoirs in the 1950s, still firmly believed that in the Second World War 'our main opponents were the two greatest sea powers in the world'.[182] He thus had little doubt about the significance of what had happened in the North Atlantic in May, 1943. Many in Germany would, of course, have disagreed with him totally, and would continue to do so; and it is unlikely that any Soviet citizen or Soviet historian or any Japanese, asked to name a turning point of the war, would think of that month as being a moment of decision. We need to recall that, as regards the European war, Germany's prime instrument, from first to last, was the Army, the main body of which was always, from June, 1941, deployed on the Eastern Front. From the Japanese point of view this was a profoundly important consideration as long as United States grand strategy adhered to the slogan 'Germany First'. We have to consider, then, what was the condition of Germany's prime instrument of war:

> The early spring of 1943 saw the German Army facing a supreme crisis which threatened its continued existence. Defeats on the Eastern Front and in North Africa had inflicted shattering losses on the field force of more than half a million men. The destruction of divisions between January and May had been severe: twenty were lost in Stalingrad, and six (of which two were *Luftwaffe*) outside, and another six in Tunisia – a total of thirty Army formations, roughly one eighth of . . . the German order of battle.[183]

In addition to this destruction of manpower, equipment sufficient for forty-five divisions had also been lost in this period, a damage increasingly difficult to repair. Soon (July) the German Army would attempt its last offensive throw, at Kursk, and when this failed (as it quickly did) the initiative passed to the Soviet forces. By May, 1944, they had advanced into Eastern Europe and the Third *Reich* was visibly crumbling.

There cannot, then, be any real doubt about the '*schwerpunkt*' of the war, the area of decision, in May, 1943. Not in the Atlantic; but the Anglo-American war – that was a different matter. And for Anglo-American planners this was also a time of distressing recognition that among its other errors (listed above) the Casablanca Conference had also, strategically, bitten off more than it could chew. The final Axis surrenders in North Africa did not take place until 13 May; already the decision for HUSKY had been taken and preparations begun; the British were pressing for an amphibious advance in Burma (ANAKIM); and there was BOLERO, the American build-up for the assault on Fortress Europe. BOLERO was languishing, and to General Brooke among others it looked as though American Pacific preoccupations had undermined the principle of 'Germany First'. And then, as the perception of Dönitz's change of strategy sank in, there came a change. BOLERO came to life again:

> the reason was not a change of heart or priority in Washington in 1943. It lay in victory in the Atlantic, which transformed the shipping situation. Meanwhile, in the first months of 1943, it became clear to all that the commitments undertaken at Casablanca were beyond the resources of the Allies. That BOLERO suffered was virtually inevitable. It did not suffer alone.[184]

So it emerges that the undoubted victory at sea did not decide the issue of the war – that had been decided already; indeed, it could be said that it had been decided from the first moments of *BARBAROSSA*. The nickname of a redoubtable Hohenstaufen emperor of the 12th century rings like a tolling bell for a later generation of Germans. What the Atlantic victory decided was whether the Western Allies would or would not be able to implement a strategy of their own at all. And this was no small matter.

Once again, then, we find our guiding light in the forbidding tables which reveal the statistics of the tonnage war (see facing page). Their meaning is unmistakable.

On no occasion after July, 1943, did sinkings in the North Atlantic exceed five figures. This was the first meaning of the Atlantic victory: 'safe and timely arrival' now became the norm.

The second and supreme meaning lies in the answer to the question, 'safe and timely arrival for what purpose?' Participants and historians alike have been strangely and sharply divided on this matter, and, as we have seen, the touchstone was always OVERLORD. Those whose

1943: January–May (incl.):			
Total losses		*Losses in North Atlantic*	
Tons	*Ships*	*Tons*	*Ships*
2,001,918	365	1,336,650	228

In June a drastic change was perceptible:

123,825	28	18,379	4

In July an upsurge of sinkings in the South Atlantic, Mediterranean and Indian Ocean swelled the total:

365,398	61	123,327	18

The final figures for June–December were:

1,218,219	232	322,951	57

After July, 1943, the total of monthly sinkings only exceeded 150,000 tons on three occasions:

September, 1943

156,419	29

December, 1943

168,524	31

March, 1944

157,960	25

hearts were not in OVERLORD never understood the Atlantic. One such was Slessor; in his end-of-year message in *Coastal Command Review* in December, 1943, he told his Command:

> For us this has been primarily a defensive victory. The main object of the operations against the U-boat was to prevent us losing the war.[185]

There is no doubt that Slessor spoke for many; OVERLORD was still in a questionable future; Britain's shortages, of food and raw materials of all kinds, were a daily reality. Thus even Roskill, writing in 1956, does not see beyond the defensive aspect of the May victory; it marked, he says

> one of the decisive stages of the war; for the enemy then made his greatest effort against our Atlantic life-line – and he failed.[186]

The RAF historian, Hilary St. G. Saunders, is thinking on the same lines when he says:

Coastal Command was essentially a defensive organization.[187]

Others have taken a different view; the German historians, certainly, have made no attempt to minimize the Atlantic defeat. Attributing it to 'close cooperation between (Allied) military and political leaders, their science and their technology', Jürgen Rohwer says:

> they won the Battle of the Atlantic, and their victory represented one of the most important turning points in the Second World War.[188]

Macintyre, a historian who could not have been closer to it, explains:

> The great assault on the Normandy beaches in 1944 could not have been attempted had the enemy not been first decisively beaten in the Atlantic.[189]

Beesly, who was also close enough, in 'another part of the field', confirms:

> The invasion of Normandy in 1944 would have been unthinkable if the second Battle of the Atlantic had not been won in 1943.[190]

Ronald Lewin goes even nearer to the centre of the matter:

> By the autumn of 1943 the Battle of the Atlantic had been reduced to an acceptable running skirmish. There were no more disasters. Certainly the path had been cleared for those immense movements of men and supplies without which the next year's return to Europe would have been impossible.[191]

Too often OVERLORD is seen simply as the assault landing on the Normandy beaches (and this was what frightened off many of the sceptics, with haunting and bloody memories of Cape Helles in 1915 and Dieppe in 1942). But OVERLORD was also the Battle of Normandy and the advance into Germany; it was a campaign lasting eleven months, during which the Allied forces under General Eisenhower deployed, from first to last, nearly 5,500,000 men. This figure may be compared with the 5,399,563 total of the British Expeditionary Force in France and Flanders in the fifty-one months between August, 1914, and November, 1918 (see p. 150). And in addition, in 1944-45, there were 970,000 vehicles and over 18,000,000 tons of supplies.[192] There can be no conceivable notion of building up and maintaining such a force as this with undefeated U-boats at its back.

The magnitude of the Allied enterprise is indisputable, and still breathtaking. The fact that, even so, it did not engage the main body of the enemy – that this was in process of being ground to dust on the opposite side of the Continent – is one of History's bitter ironies. It means that the ultimate victory turned out not to have been what it might have been, what 'fairness' requires it to have been. But war is rarely 'fair' and a victory is a victory nevertheless. Nobody can pretend that OVERLORD was anything else – certainly not a defeat – and few would now care to contemplate the absence of a Western presence in the West during those crucial years. In any case, OVERLORD was what the Allies had decided to do, what they had promised to do, and what they triumphantly did, thanks to the *offensive* victory in the Atlantic in 1943.

8

Unconditional Surrender

'I realized . . . that the darkest moment in any fighting man's life, the moment when he must surrender unconditionally, was at hand.'

Dönitz, Memoirs

IN MAY, 1943, the U-boats lost the Battle of the Atlantic; they had been soundly defeated in what had always been their main theatre of war, the transit area of the great Atlantic convoys. Yet two years would elapse before Germany, by then under the rule of Dönitz himself in succession to Hitler, arrived at the point of accepting the 'Unconditional Surrender' which the Allies had demanded at Casablanca. What was the rôle of the U-boats to be during that time? Dönitz tells us:

> In June 1943 I was faced with the most difficult decision of the whole war. I had to make up my mind whether to withdraw the boats from all areas and call off the U-boat war, or to let them continue operations in some suitably modified form, regardless of the enemy's superiority.[1]

Hindsight can be a dangerous blessing; its lofty overview can too easily suggest a steady and obvious progress from the U-boat defeat in May, 1943, to the débâcle in May, 1945, which culminated for the Western Allies at Lüneburg Heath and Reims. In June, 1943, all that was hidden; the Western Allies were not yet in Europe – the first of their great amphibious assaults only landed on Sicily in July. And it was in that month, also, that the last major German offensive was launched on the Eastern Front, at Kursk. Both of these operations turned out to be bitter pills for Germany: the attack on Sicily soon led to the Italian surrender, while in the East the Russians promptly counter-attacked and seized an initiative which they never lost. Meanwhile in the sky over Germany Bomber Command was fighting what is somewhat misleadingly called the 'Battle of the Ruhr'. In fact, its attacks fell

> on areas as widely separated from the Ruhr as Berlin, Stettin and Pilsen in the east, Munich, Stuttgart and Nuremberg in the south-east, Turin and Spezia in the south, and Lorient and St Nazaire in the west.[2]

Bomber losses were high, and the precise damage done is impossible to calculate; but Dönitz describes the mounting air offensive as 'increasingly severe', and Speer says of this period:

> In the burning and devastated cities we daily experienced the direct impact of the war.[3]

Dönitz explains his dilemma:

> Under these conditions what effect would the abandonment of the U-boat campaign have on our war situation as a whole? Could we afford to abandon it? Were we justified, in view of our inferiority, in calling upon our submarines to continue the unequal struggle?

He had no difficulty in enumerating the costs of the anti-submarine war to the Allies – the high tonnage requirements of the convoy system, the large numbers of escorts, the strain on bases, air stations, dockyards, labour and production:

> Were the U-boat campaign abandoned all this would become available for use against us elsewhere.

It would mean, he considered, among other things, the intensification of the air offensive, greater sufferings and higher casualties for the civilian population:

> Could the submariner stand aside as a spectator, saying there was nothing he could or would do and telling the women and children that they must put up with it?

On the other hand there was really no doubt that, if we carried on, U-boat losses would rise to an appalling height, in spite of anything we could do to accelerate improvements in their defensive equipment and afford them effective protection. A continuation of the U-boat campaign would involve certain and deliberate self-sacrifice.

I finally came to the bitter conclusion that we had no option but to fight on.

The question then arose, how would the U-boat-men themselves respond to continuing a battle which they could not win? Already the demands of U-boat warfare on the captains and crews were almost unbelievably high; would they be able to face even greater ones without the hope of great success to sustain them? There was only one way to find out: Dönitz called a conference at the headquarters of the Senior Officer, Submarines (West), *Kapitän zur See* Hans-Rudolf Rösing, to which all the Biscay flotilla leaders were summoned. He put the grim question to them directly:

they were unanimous both in their conviction that the campaign must be continued and in their confidence that the great majority of the crews would be in agreement with the decision. The U-boat arm proved that their confidence was fully justified, and to the end of the war it fought with undiminished determination.

It is not in any way to disparage the high courage and self-sacrifice of the U-boat crews during the next two years to remark that their spirit was yet another product of the Casablanca slogan. What alternative did they have, after all, in the face of Unconditional Surrender?

* * * * *

What makes the plight of the German submariners so peculiarly poignant is that by June, 1943, many of them were well aware of something that Dönitz had known for a year already: that despite their sterling qualities (to which he paid heartfelt tribute), in the face of new Allied technology and tactics the Type VIIs and Type IXs were now obsolete. For this he continued to blame airborne radar above all else; this, he was sure, was what had robbed the U-boat of its cloak of invisibility; this was what now gravely threatened 'our whole method of conducting submarine warfare, which was based on mobility and operations on the surface'.[4] Indeed, it threatened also the imminent fulfilment of his own prophecy in September, 1942, that one day the U-boat will be crushed and eliminated by the defence forces.[5]

The only solution, as Dönitz saw it, was one which he had urged as far back as 1936: a U-boat with high under-water speed. A design for such a boat, using hydrogen-peroxide propulsion, was put forward by the brilliant engineer and scientist, Professor Helmuth Walter in that year, and Dönitz (then commanding the 'Weddigen Flotilla') and his Chief Engineer, *Fregattenkapitän* Thedsen (see p. 189), had begged the Naval Command to back the invention. However,

> The immediate need for increasing conventional warship construction and the complexities involved in creating such a radical propulsion system discouraged its rapid development.[6]

Despite continuing pressure, both from Walter and from Dönitz, little progress was made with the Walter U-boat, in part at least because the Naval Command remained sceptical of its value. On 24 June, 1942, indeed, Dönitz was so apprehensive of the likely fate of the existing boats that he returned to the charge. The Walter U-boat, he told Raeder,

> would instantly render all but wholly ineffective the enemy's defensive measures, which are designed to defeat the current type of submarine. He would find himself suddenly faced with a completely new type of boat of quite astonishing performance, against which his defences, as they stand, would be of no avail, and which therefore would hold every prospect of achieving a decisive success.
>
> The immediate development, testing and most rapid construction of the Walter U-boat is, in my opinion, an essential measure and one which may well decide the issue of the war.[7]

This at last produced a result, and the Naval Staff had ordered 180 ocean-going Walter boats in June; persistent problems with the propulsion system[8] had led to a cancellation of this order in November. Experimental work, however, continued.

In June, 1943, in the crisis of U-boat warfare, Dönitz received a fresh draught of hope: blueprints of a new type of submarine, capable of very high under-water speeds (18 knots for $1\frac{1}{2}$ hours, 12–14 knots for 10 hours) and with the potential of remaining submerged for long periods, were shown to him. This was at last approaching what he called the 'one-hundred-per-cent under-water boat' – a true submarine, as opposed to a submersible. The Walter boat, if it could be perfected, still promised even higher under-water speeds, up to 25 knots, but the new boats, later known as the Type XXIs and smaller Type XXIIIs, might be ready sooner. Dönitz decided to press forward on both fronts – but here came the snag: the Construction Branch produced a schedule by which the first two Type XXIs would be completed by the end of 1944, mass production would not begin until 1945, and the type would not become operational until the end of 1946. How Dönitz dealt with this wholly unacceptable proposition we shall shortly see. In the meantime, he was left in the disagreeable situation of facing

a hiatus, between the end of the operational usefulness of the boats then in service, and the operational introduction of high under-water perform-ance boats[9]

During this ominous interval, his sole recourse would be the never-ending battle of technology.

* * * * *

In the summer of 1943 the advantages in the battle of technology lay firmly with the Allies. Those that they already possessed enabled them to win the decisive fights in May, and even as they did so more novel-ties of impressive promise made their appearance. It was in the course of the HX 237 action, on 13 May (while Werner and his ship-mates were tasting the pleasures of 280-metre depth), that a Liberator of No 86 Squadron made the first kill with a new weapon, the 'Mark 24 Mine'. This American invention (sometimes known as 'Fido' and sometimes as 'Wandering Annie') was a homing torpedo ingeniously devised for service against submerged U-boats. It was activated by cavitation: the sound made by popping bubbles as a ship's propeller rotates under water. The difficulty was that the torpedo's own propel-lers might drown the target sounds, which made it a definitely low-speed weapon (and a shallow-depth one, because cavitation decreased as the submarine went deeper, thus enabling it to go faster). 'Mark 24 Mine' was, of course, a cover name for security, and for the same reason there were strict rules about its use: *never* near enemy shores, in case it should be washed up, and *never* while in sight of the target or any other enemy vessel. On 13 May all the conditions were right, and *U 266* (Jessen) dived to her doom without ever knowing what had hit

618

her. The next day a Catalina of the USN Patrol Squadron 84 performed the same office for *U 657* (Göllnitz).[10] They were curious weapons to use, these homing torpedoes: there was always an anxious time-lag before any sign of a result, sometimes as long as 13 minutes. When it came, it might well consist of nothing more than a brief disturbance of the sea's surface, capable of being made by the occasional freak wave. It was not much to go by, and certainty of a kill would have to wait until the *Enigma* decrypts revealed it or until German records could be inspected – after the war. But 'Wandering Annie' entered the anti-submarine armoury and won increasing favour.

Only a week after the début of the homing airborne torpedo, a British development in turn made its mark. On 23 May, the day before Dönitz acknowledged his defeat in the Atlantic, HMS *Archer* was helping to escort Convoy HX 239; she sent out a Swordfish of No 819 Squadron and a Wildcat to investigate an HF/DF bearing, and shortly they sighted a U-boat about ten miles ahead. The Swordfish at once went into cloud for concealment, emerging to find *U 752* a mile away on the port side. The pilot, Sub-Lieutenant H. Horrocks, attacked at once with his new armament of eight rocket projectiles,[11] which he fired in pairs. The fourth pair struck the U-boat directly on her stern, but the serious damage had already been done, by a rocket of the third pair which went right through the pressure hull. The U-boat surfaced and attempted to engage the Swordfish with AA fire, but the Wildcat came in to pour .5-inch machine-gun fire into the conning tower, killing the captain and forcing the crew to scuttle and abandon ship. Rockets thereafter became standard equipment in the Fleet Air Arm and in the strike squadrons of Coastal Command. Early in 1944 Mark VI de Havilland Mosquitoes joined the Command, their eight 60-lb rockets, says Thetford,

> when fired as a complete salvo being equivalent to the broadside of a 10,000-ton cruiser.[12]

In the last month of the war, rocket-firing Typhoons of the Tactical Air Force did fearful execution among U-boats trapped on the surface in enclosed waters in the Baltic – unfortunately it has to be recorded that minesweepers of the Royal Navy had already discovered the meaning of 'fearful execution' as meted out by rocket Typhoons. The moral effect of this weapon, especially against young and inexperienced

U-boat crews, was as great as its destructive effect, as the German Navy Orders admitted; their only suggested remedy was an old-fashioned one:

It must be overcome by rigorous discipline.

Yet another addition to the airborne anti-submarine armament appeared early in 1944: the infantry's 6-pounder anti-tank gun (57-mm) mounted in Mark XVIII Mosquitoes. An automatic loader enabled the gun to fire forty rounds per miute; the armour-piercing shot travelled at a velocity of 2,800 feet per second and the gun was effective at ranges greater than those of the most heavily armed U-boats. It was a useful adjunct in the continuing fight against those boats that tried conclusions with their AA armament on the surface, and made its first kill in the Bay of Biscay on 25 March (*U 976*, returning to St Nazaire from an Atlantic cruise). The Mark XVIII ('Tse-Tse') Mosquitoes were really modifications of the Mark VI, which also had capabilities as a night fighter and as a low-level attack plane in the 2nd Tactical Air Force. Production priorities therefore went to the Mark VI and only twenty-seven Mark XVIIIs were produced; it was seldom that more than two were available at any given moment.

During this phase the Royal Navy also added to its now formidable armoury. The Hedgehog, after a slow start due to 'teething troubles' (chiefly a deplorable tendency of the bombs not to leave the spigots), was becoming a dependable and accurate weapon, preferred by some anti-submarine commanders to depth charges because it gave no warning of its arrival. It was still liable to accident – what lethal device is not? – and in September, 1943, a premature explosion of Hedgehog bombs in the destroyer *Escapade* caused many casualties and put the ship out of action.

Such occurrences tended to make Hedgehog unpopular with crews, but its improving efficiency guaranteed its retention; the US Official Historian, however, claims that it was in the Pacific rather than the Atlantic that Hedgehog found its chief usefulness. Meanwhile it was being supplemented by another version, 'Squid', a much heavier affair, consisting of three tubes each throwing a charge weighing 350 lbs to a distance of over 700 yards. The Squid was too heavy altogether for Flower Class corvettes, which confined it to destroyers, sloops and frigates, and it was a combination of the two latter classes that produced its first kill ($U\,333$) on 31 July, 1944. Thereafter its popularity steadily increased among anti-submarine warriors.

Other novelties would be added to these, as we shall see, but to the end of the war the main anti-U-boat weapon would continue to be the 300-lb depth charge. The outstanding practitioner with this was Captain Walker, whose 2nd Escort Group accounted for fourteen U-boats while under his command. Walker's high peak of achievement was his 27-day cruise in the Western Approaches between 31 January and 26 February, 1944. In the course of this the 2nd Escort Group sank no fewer than six U-boats; the full total of U-boats sunk during this strenuous four-week period was eleven, while twelve large Atlantic convoys passed safe and unmolested to their destinations. In these operations Walker made extensive use of what was known as his 'creeping attack' method, which he himself called 'Operation Plaster'. This was essentially a group tactic, already perfected by the end of 1943. It was designed not merely to overcome but to exploit the ASDIC characteristic generally regarded as a weakness (see pp. 439–40) – the loss of contact when the attacking ship's ASDIC beam passed right over the submarine. From the U-boat captain's point of view, although the constant ping of ASDIC on the hull of his boat could be somewhat unnerving, it was also useful for placing the attacker; when the pinging stopped, attack was imminent, and the U-boat would take all possible evasive measures. Walker's method was to make his attack while the U-boat was still in ASDIC contact, and pending the perfection of the ahead-throwing weapons, he saw that this could be done very satisfactorily by close cooperation in his Group.

Walker's method had all the merit of simplicity: its cardinal requirements were a superbly trained group, endless patience, stamina and a large supply of depth charges. In a typical 'creeping attack' on a U-boat that had dived deep, one ship (more often than not Walker's own sloop, *Starling* – he was, after all, known in the Group as 'the Boss') would take the rôle of directing ship. She would station herself some 1–1,500 yards from a located U-boat which she then stalked by ASDIC contact at a speed matching the U-boat's, which might be as low as 2 knots. If the U-boat captain was a skilful evader, or if the contact was made on a dark night with the risk of losing the quarry once depth charges broke the ASDIC link, the stalking might take a long time,[13] but while it continued it would be rare for a U-boat to shake off the skilled ASDIC operators of the 2nd E.G. So the U-boat captain (and his crew) would know from the steady ping that he was being pursued, but he would also know that the hunter was half to three-quarters of a mile away. And thus the manoeuvre would proceed until the moment came when the director called the attacking ship to pass him and take station ahead on the same course. She would then close the U-boat very slowly, probably at no more than 5 knots, so as not to be detected on the hydrophones, and also to avoid German acoustic torpedoes. The directing ship would range on her as she advanced, and at the moment when her range exceeded the ASDIC range of the U-boat by the distance this would travel while the depth charges were descending, the director would make the signal to fire. Operation 'Plaster' would now begin, perhaps with a salvo of as many as twenty-six charges, dropped in pairs and set to explode at 500–740 feet along the course of the unsuspecting U-boat. If the latter showed a disposition towards evasive action, Walker would have three attackers in line abreast, so that whichever way the U-boat turned, it would be caught. There were no reports on this tactic to U-boat Command, because once held in the vice of the 2nd EG's ASDIC, no U-boat survived. Walker hunted to the death.

On 31 January, 1944, the attacking ship was *Wild Goose* (Lieutenant-Commander D. E. G. Wemyss), the U-boat was *U592*, and the action was all over very quickly. Creeping attacks were elaborate affairs, and not always necessary. On 8 February it was the turn of HMS *Woodpecker*, attacking *U762*; her first salvo of twenty-two charges was so well placed that no more was needed and Walker made the famous signal to Commander H. L. Pryse,

Come over here and look at the mess you have made.

The next day was a big one for the 2nd EG: two U-boats were destroyed, both by creeping attacks. In the early morning (0615) *Wild Goose* once more obtained a contact some 10 miles from the homeward-bound convoy SL 147; she called up *Starling* and the two sloops began a creeping attack which lasted 3 hours and 25 minutes, ending in the destruction of *U734*. At almost the same time as *Wild Goose's* contact, HMS *Kite*, following an HF/DF bearing, sighted *U238* some 800 yards off, coming out of the mist. The U-boat dived at once, and *Kite*, later joined by *Magpie*, began a long vigil. *U238* was well-handled and elusive; the hours went by, *Kite's* depth charges were almost all expended, when *Starling* and *Wild Goose* arrived from their earlier victory, and Walker directed *Magpie* in a creeping attack which began with a Hedgehog salvo, continued with depth charges and destroyed the U-boat. It had taken 8 hours and 266 depth charges to perform the deed. The Group's fifth sinking came on 11 February, and once again it was *Wild Goose* that made the contact,[14] and in company with *Woodpecker* carried out the destruction of *U 424* after three attacks. The final (sixth) success had to wait just over a week – until February 19; once more *Woodpecker* was in the fray, obtaining a contact which, after seven hours, enabled her and *Starling* to force *U 264* to the surface. Her crew abandoned ship and the U-boat went down for the last time; the men were all picked up by the 2nd EG. They were the lucky ones.[15]

In this astonishing action (or series of actions), all, it should be noted, in the vicinity of convoys (hence the abundance of U-boat contacts), Walker's group had fired off no fewer than 634 depth charges (one wonders that any fish were left alive in the sea). The presence of convoys had a double value in the light of that figure; obviously, some means of replenishment was essential if these tactics were to continue, and sure enough, we find *Kite*, on 9 February, obtaining a fresh supply of depth charges from a merchantman in HX 277. So we perceive that the tried and trusted anti-submarine weapon remained the essential ingredient in a triumph which, amongst much else, underlined once more the obsolescence of the tried and trusted U-boats of 1939–42. These battles, says Roskill,

> marked the climax not only of Captain Walker's achievements but of the whole long-drawn, bitter offensive by the convoy escorts against their cunning and ruthless enemies.[16]

There was a price to pay, part of it only sad, part irremediable. On the day of her last success, HMS *Woodpecker* was hit by an acoustic torpedo and her stern blown off. Despite seven days of valiant effort to bring her home, she capsized on 27 February in a storm which finished off the U-boat's work; by great good fortune, her entire ship's company was saved. *Woodpecker* was the 2nd Escort Group's sole casualty in this whole climactic action; but it had taken a toll which exacted a further most grievous loss not long after. Walker, in these engagements, was like Nelson; every nerve vibrated in him, the battle burnt him like a flame. He hardly ever left the bridge; nourished by corned beef sandwiches and hot cocoa, clad in an old grey pullover and stained leather waistcoat, his senses were alert to every nuance of the action, he breathed his ardour into every phase of it. And Nature claimed its price: on 9 July, 1944, Captain F. J. Walker, CB, DSO and three bars, DSC and two bars, died of a stroke brought on by the cumulative strain of three years' high intensity war. He was buried at sea – fittingly, for as Admiral Horton said at his funeral service in Liverpool Cathedral,

> Not dust nor the light weight of a stone, but all the sea of the Western Approaches shall be his tomb.

And later, with an equally fitting allusion, Horton identified the ultimate secret of Walker's success:

> He trained and welded his own group into a splendidly efficient Band of Brothers.

The only consolation for such a loss was that the battle was now won.

There was less than a year of war against the German U-boats left to go when Walker died, but it was in that period that the battle of technology threatened to make a serious swing towards a fresh German advantage. In the meantime, they had not been standing still. As we have seen, Dönitz constantly named radar as the 'villain' of his story; he called it 'the modern battle weapon', the sinister device which 'has torn our sole offensive weapon against the Anglo-Saxons from our hands'. The discovery that the Allies were using centimetric radar greatly disconcerted the Germans; to the U-boat Command a first effect of this development was the nullification of *Metox* (see p. 478), assisted by a quick-witted RAF prisoner-of-war who told his interrogators that Allied aircraft were homing in on radiations from the U-boats' *Metox* receivers. It thus became a German priority to produce a non-radiating search receiver, and a whole generation of these soon appeared. The first to be developed was *Naxos*, which simply gave warning of the proximity of aircraft using centimetric radar; this was clearly on the right lines, though somewhat rudimentary, and had, moreover, a double value – in the air defence of Germany against Allied bombing as well as for the protection of U-boats. The maritime version was called *Naxos-U*, and by June, 1943, it was already at the trial stage. Then came a sudden change of course: naval trials during July and August revealed that there was indeed substance in the RAF prisoner's story – a sensitive receiver detected radiations from *Metox* at distances up to 30 miles. This discovery at once produced what has been called 'the great radiation scare'. Priorities in the German electronics industry switched from countering the present problems of ASV III/H2S to eliminating radiations which were not, in fact, a threat at all. The result was that *Naxos-U* did not begin to reach the U-boats until October, and the night-fighter version was delayed even longer, until January, 1944.

For the time being *Metox* was replaced by *Hagenuk*, also known as *Wanze*. *Hagenuk* was, in fact, the name of the manufacturer; *Wanze* (also written '*W-Anz-g2*') is an abbreviation of *Wellenanzeiger* (frequency indicator). *Hagenuk's* attraction was that it was non-radiating, and if that had mattered it would have been a success; but in the circumstances it was only a journey down a blind alley – in good company. In December, 1943, came *Hohentwiel*, a radar set used by the *Luftwaffe* as ASV; it was capable of detecting a 6,000-ton ship at 15 kilometres and a submarine at five and a half. The German submarines themselves used it to detect aircraft, and it gave useful service when conditions permitted. In 1944 the faults of *Naxos* were eradicated in its successor, *Fliege*; and when the Americans introduced their new and highly sensitive 3-cm radar (British ASV X) *Fliege* was replaced by *Mücke*. There was also a radar decoy device, *Thetis*, and an anti-radar decoy, *Aphrodite*; this last was a balloon, three feet in diameter, with 13-foot strips of aluminum foil attached to its cable, which was anchored on a float. It worked on the same principle as Bomber Command's WINDOW – producing blips on enemy radar sets exactly like those made by aircraft or, in this case, U-boats. The snag was that whereas the airborne version was perfectly easy to handle – the crew simply emptied the foil strips out by the boxful – the marine version in anything approaching bad weather, or on a dark night, was liable to beome entangled with the boat, a danger rather than a help. With all thése ingenious contributions it may be said that sometimes they worked, and sometimes they did not; they offered no magical solution to Dönitz's problems.

Yet there *were* scientific wonders which seemed to the U-boat Command to offer a touch of magic. As often happened, parallel developments had been taking place on both sides, in the field of offensive weapons: the Germans, too were about to produce acoustic homing torpedoes. The difference was that whereas the Allies' Mark 24 Mine was, and long remained, a secret from the Germans, the Allies themselves were fairly prepared for the German weapon. The story is a study in suspicion: as far back as 1941 the Germans suspected that the British had introduced acoustic torpedoes. Of course, they had done no such thing, but the Germans were sufficiently alarmed to begin their own development. In October of that year a prisoner reported that they were already carrying out trials; Naval Intelligence henceforth kept a close watch for all evidence of progress. In January, 1943, the *Engima* decrypts contained reference to the *FAT* torpedo which shortly made its appearance; an error in interpretation (Note 86 to the last chapter shows that this was not the only one) made this out to mean *Fernakustischtorpedo*, a long-range acoustic weapon, for which counter-measures were at once put in hand. The result was, as we shall see, that when the Germans produced the real thing, the *Zaunkönig* (Wren), known to the Allies as the GNAT (*G*erman *N*aval *A*coustic *T*orpedo), the counter was ready and operational only sixteen days after the first appearance. Suspicion thus had its reward, even if mistakenly founded.

The second wonder, more of technology than of science, was, as wonders frequently are, not exactly new; it was, in fact, an invention of a Dutch naval officer in 1927, and when the remains of the Dutch Navy came to Britain in 1940, four of its newest submarines contained this device: the *Schnorchel*. There was no great sophistication about this 16-year-old brainwave: it was simply an air pipe which could be extended above the submarine and retracted at will, with a ballcock valve like those in lavatory cisterns to prevent flooding in high seas. But the effect of it was that a submarine using it could remain submerged almost indefinitely, travelling on diesels, so that there was no need to surface to recharge batteries – indeed, there was little need to use up their current at all. Yet this simple affair constituted a large step into the future. As Richard Hough says, it

> brought the submarine half way towards being a true submarine craft
> rather than a submersible.[17]

Neither the Royal Navy, nor the Germans (who captured two *Schnorchel*-fitted submarines when they entered Holland) had any use for *Schnorchels* at that time. There was no present threat to the invisibility of the U-boats, and *Schnorchels* had serious disadvantages: they reduced mobility to a maximum of 7-8 knots (at higher speeds they would snap); they very greatly reduced vision, being only a few feet above the sea; on the other hand, the diesel exhaust fumes were highly visible to passing aircraft in daylight; not only were the watchkeepers virtually blinded, but they were also robbed of hearing by the steady throb of the diesels which blotted out sound from the hydrophones; the crews hated them because of the discomfort they brought, above all the unspeakable agony whenever a wave operated the cut-off valve; this shut off the air supply, the diesels would then suck in whatever air there was inside the boat and the men would begin to suffocate; when the air intake returned the sudden change in pressure would burst their eardrums. And in addition to all that it was believed that their very existence would make the captains defensive-minded. But centimetric radar worked wonders; if only the *Schnorchel* could restore invisibility, then *Schnorchel*-boats there must be. Conversion was put in hand in July, 1943, and by the following June there were thirty *Schnorchel*-boats in operation. The first of them to become operational, however, was not among those present; she was *U 264*, Walker's sixth victim on 19 February. Her consorts, however, gave the old Type VIIs and Type IXs a new lease of life and new possibilities of action, pending the arrival of the eagerly awaited new types.

The *Schnorchel*-boats did not take the Admiralty by surprise; their existence was confirmed by February, 1944, and *Enigma* decrypts were able to report progress with Baltic trials even as far back as December, 1943. Decryption was an area where the advantage so fortunately regained at the end of March remained firmly with the Allies. This is not to say that mastery of *Triton* was effortlessly complete from that time onwards.[18] On 1 July, 1943, the U-boat Command added an alternative fourth wheel to the *Enigma* machine, which had inevitable disruptive effects. Decrypts for the first three weeks of July and the first ten days of August were greatly delayed, and in September there was a 1–2 week delay early in the month, which was a very bad time for such a thing to happen, as we shall see. However, the arrival of the American 4-wheel high-speed Bombes in August made it possible to overcome these obstacles with far less trouble than ever before, and *Enigma* remained a first-class Intelligence source for the rest of the war.[19]

Bletchley Park had, in fact, won a double battle. Re-entry into the *Enigma* soon made certain what some had long suspected: that the British Naval Cipher No 3, known to *B-Dienst* and the U-boat Command as the 'convoy cipher', was insecure. At long last the Admiralty was persuaded, and in June, 1943, both No 3 and No 4 were replaced by No 5 and a secure ciphering system was introduced for both the Royal Navy and the RCN. The USN was fully integrated into this system by 1 January, 1944, by which time all three Navies were in process of adopting the Combined Cipher Machine (CCM) for all their Atlantic communications, and this was never penetrated by the *xB-Dienst*. And so, in his moment of greatest need, Dönitz was robbed of what he called 'the only reconnaissance service on which I can rely',[20] and reduced once more to the 'lack of eyes' which had been his bane in 1941 and much of 1942.[21]

* * * * *

When Dönitz wrote the despairing words, 'we had lost the Battle of the Atlantic', he was speaking with after-knowledge. At the time that he took the decision to keep the U-boat war alive, it was his fixed intention to return to the convoy routes as soon as new weapons or new boats allowed. There was therefore plenty of action on, under and above the Atlantic in the second part of 1943. But no part of it was more significant than the victory won in that area concerned with what Churchill feelingly called the

measureless peril expressed in charts, curves and statistics'.[22]

It was, said Roskill, in July, 1943,

that the rising curve of Allied merchant ship construction overtook and crossed the . . . curve of sinking by the enemy; and never again did the former fall below the latter.[23]

This was the statistic that capped the U-boat losses; this was the ripe fruit of 'safe and timely arrival'; this was what the battle had been about.

It would not be even decent not to refer here to the irreplaceable contribution of American shipbuilding to the rising curve on this chart. As Churchill said, in 1943

the foundation of all our hopes was the immense shipbuilding programme of the United States.[24]

The hopes – not without difficulties and discontents – were fulfilled,
and in a story full of minor miracles it is right to single out one firm
and one man as symbols of a great production triumph, just as the
famous ships they produced also bore a symbolic name: the 'Liberty
Ships'. The man was Henry J. Kaiser, one with no previous reputation
or experience in the arcane arts of shipbuilding; he was, like all such
people, viewed with considerable suspicion by naval and shipping authorities. Yet he succeeded in persuading the US Maritime Commission
to try his proposed new construction method: welding prefabricated
parts, instead of the time-consuming process of riveting. So the first of
the Liberty Ships, SS *Patrick Henry*, was launched at the Bethlehem-
Fairfield Yards, Baltimore,[25] on 27 September, 1941; she was the
leader of a line which totalled no fewer than 2,710 vessels, of which
more than 200 were sunk in the course of the war. The Liberty Ships
themselves were American adaptations of an original British design by
J. L. Thompson & Sons of Sunderland; they displaced 7,176 gross
tons (10,500 deadweight), and their 2,500-hp reciprocating engines gave
an average speed of 11 knots when loaded. They were far from handsome
– President Roosevelt, stirred by the sensitivity of a former Naval
Person, called them 'dreadful looking objects' – but they served well for
mass production (at an average rate of 42 days per ship) by Mr Kaiser's
methods, and masses were what the Allies needed to offset the depredations of the U-boats in their prime.

This style of production – and it is not to be supposed that Liberty
Ships were the only types that America produced – was something
that the British shipbuilding industry could not emulate. The British
tradition, never really overcome, was very different indeed:

> The ships themselves were built and fitted out much as had been medi-
> eval cathedrals – by swarms of craftsmen of many skills, and by masses
> of unskilled or semi-skilled deployed in working gangs; construction by
> hand pushed to the ultimate.[26]

Upon this antiquated means of production fell the main stress of the
first years of war; at the end of June, 1942, when the U-boats were
coming to the end of their 'massacre of shipping' along the American

east coast, British-controlled dry cargo ocean shipping comprised some 62% of world tonnage, but in the second half of that year 72% of shipping losses were British. Such a rate of loss – plus repairs, and naval construction in addition – was far beyond Britain's over-stretched resources,

And so the British merchant fleet steadily shrank.[27]

The shrinkage has never ceased.[28] In 1945 the omens of the distant future might be read in the grim statistic that, despite the huge American contribution, 54% of world shipping losses were British, as against America's 16%. But in 1943 the omens of the more immediate future were to be found in the steady scaling down of shipping losses, particularly in the North Atlantic, where 1942's dreadful 5,471,222 tons (1006 ships) fell away to a mere 175,013 tons (thirty-one ships) in the whole of 1944.

When the U-boats withdrew from the North Atlantic at the end of May, the Bay of Biscay became a busy place, and Air Marshal Slessor's strategy of 'cutting through the trunk' of the U-boats' transit routes at last held promise of success. In the first week of June the *Enigma* decrypts confirmed that there had been a major change in German strategy, and Coastal Command was freed to switch much of its strength into the Bay. There it found U-boats obeying not merely a new strategy, but also new tactical instructions: their orders now were to make the passage in groups, submerged at night, but on the surface in daylight to bring combined fire-power into action against Coastal Command's patrols. To improve their chances, their armament was strengthened, and the experiment was even tried of a submarine 'aircraft-trap'; the boat selected was the Type VII *U 441* (*Kapitänleutnant* Götz von Hartmann). Her 88-mm naval gun was removed and replaced by 'bandstands', one forward and one aft of the conning tower, containing two quadruple-barrelled 20-mm guns and one single-barrelled 37-mm gun, firing a 1.25 kg (2¾ lb) shot at a practical rate of 140 rounds per minute – a formidable weapon. *U 441's* task, says Dönitz,

was 'not to drive aircraft off, but to shoot them down'. We hoped that once they had been severely handled a few times by this type of AA submarine, British aircraft would lose their zest for attacking U-boats on the surface, or would at least have been made to feel that it had become a much more risky business.'[29]

For her new rôle, *U 441*'s crew was increased to sixty-seven, sixteen more than her regular establishment, mostly AA gunners but also including scientists (investigating Allied detection methods) and, significantly, a doctor. The effect of it all was disappointing; Coastal Command was not unfamiliar with *flak* – the strike squadrons operating against German shipping in the North Sea could write books on the subject. Slessor's instruction to the anti-submarine squadrons was very simple: if U-boats showed an inclination to fight on the surface, the aircraft were to go straight at them 'irrespective of the accuracy of the gunfire':

> A scientist asked him one day what would happen when the U-boats' anti-aircraft weapons forced our aircraft up, and reminded him how in 1940 we had made the *Luftwaffe* abandon low attacks on our convoys by using far less lethal weapons than those now being fitted in the U-boats. Slessor replied 'the one thing we want to see is the U-boat on the surface. We shall not be forced up'.[30]

It was no idle boast. Coastal Command's anti-submarine squadrons, whose war had been mainly exhausting until now – long, tedious hours of vigilance, quartering an empty sea in all the weathers the Atlantic could throw at them – entered a phase of hard fighting and heavy loss. It was not only the U-boats, fiercely wielding their new, heavier armament; there were also the Ju 88s to contend with. Yet by 17 June the aircrews had forced Dönitz to make another change of tactics: the U-boats were once again ordered to make their daylight passage of the Bay submerged. The consequence was a brief period during which the Command had no victories, and then another change in the texture of the battle:

> The period between the 1st of July and the 2nd August marks the climax of the air operations by the Bay of Biscay patrols, and was the period of their greatest success. We now know that eighty-six U-boats crossed the Bay during those weeks. Fifty-five of them were sighted, sixteen were sunk by aircraft and one by a surface ship, while six others were forced to turn back . . . Losses to our anti-submarine aircraft were, however, heavy. Fourteen did not return.[31]

631

This was the period when, in Herbert Werner's striking phrase,

the British ruled the sky and the Bay of Biscay trembled under their constant bombardments.[32]

Once again, the stark statistics say it all, and these that follow should be compared with those already quoted on page 583:

Period	Flying Hours	Aircraft Lost	U-boats			Percentage kills to U/Bs on passage	Aircraft lost to U/Bs sunk
			Sunk	Damaged	On Passage		
May 1–Aug 2 1943	32,343	57	28	22	270	10.37%	2.03
Aug 3 1943– May 31 1944	114,290	123	12	10	480	2.5%	10

As Roskill says,

never again did our patrols accomplish such good results as they had achieved in July.

August, however, saw another change; there were bitter pills for the U-boat Command to swallow – some of their own making. Two damaging cruises saw the end of *U 441*'s experiment; in the second, on 12 July, she encountered three Beaufighters of No 248 Squadron, disposing, between them, of a fire-power amounting to twelve 20-mm cannon and eighteen machine guns. The Beaufighters made skilful use of their speed and numbers, coming in at the U-boat from all sides; one well-aimed burst played havoc in her gun positions, killing ten of her crew and wounding another thirteen, including all the officers. The surgeon, Dr Pfaffinger, took charge, calmly directing the bringing-in of the wounded, then ordering a dive and commanding the boat all the way home to Brest. Dönitz remarks:

As far as U-boat Command was concerned . . . this action showed clearly that a U-boat was a poor weapon with which to fight aircraft, and all further modifications of U-boats as 'aircraft traps' were abandoned.[33]

The wonder is that such an experienced submariner, with an acute awareness of the value of the U-boat's invisibility, should ever have considered throwing that away and trying to operate them as surface warships.

The quietus of Dönitz's current tactics came at the end of July, when an entire group of three U-boats, including two of the milch cows on which all his hopes now rested, was sunk in the Bay by Coastal Command and the 2nd EG, followed by four more on 1 and 2 August, all by aircraft, including a USAAF Liberator. Dönitz then cancelled all group sailings and ordered returning boats to enter the Bay via Cape Finisterre, keeping close to the Spanish coast.[34] This seriously reduced the ability of Coastal Command to interfere with their movements, and at the same time the *Luftwaffe* became exceedingly active; seventeen anti-submarine aircraft and six fighters were lost in Bay operations in August for a loss of only one more U-boat in that area. It was also in August that the Royal Navy suffered a check in these operations: on the 25th a support group patrolling off the north-west corner of Spain was attacked by Ju 88s and Do 217 bombers. The latter were the E-5 variety, belonging to *II/KG 100*, and they carried yet another new weapon: the Hs 293A radio-controlled jet-propelled glider bomb with an explosive head of 1,000 lbs and a speed of 400 mph. Their *début* was disappointing; on 25 August, though distinctly disconcerting, they scored no hits. But they returned two days later to sink the sloop *Egret* and severely damage the Canadian Tribal Class destroyer *Athabaskan* – which would have been a prize indeed if she had sunk, but good seamanship and hard work got her back to Plymouth for repair. Jürgen Rohwer says 'the British support groups had to retire to the west',[35] which is true enough, but there was ample reason for a redeployment at the end of August quite apart from the nasty apparition of the Hs 293A.[36] Roskill's summary is safer:

> Dönitz had at least regained a large measure of safety on the Biscay transit routes, and never again did our patrols accomplish such good results as they had achieved in July.[37]

It is clear from the records that the undoubted success of Slessor's 'strategy of relentless and increasing pressure' in June and July was in fact a flash in the pan, due more than anything else to Dönitz's own faulty tactics.

His strategy was quite clear – dictated by circumstance and implicit in his decision to fight on: if he could no longer (or, as he preferred to think, for the time being) attack the great convoy routes, then he must attack elsewhere, he must transfer his offensive to more distant waters. One last attempt to operate a U-boat pack, against the flow of convoys carrying the American buildup in the Mediterranean, from the waters south-west of the Azores, failed dismally. When the sixteen boats of the *Trutz* Group attacked the westbound convoy GUS 7A on 4 June, well outside what they took to be the range of Allied air cover, the U-boats were dismayed to find themselves faced by the Avengers and Wildcats of USS *Bogue*. They were completely prevented from attacking the convoy, and the following day an Avenger sank *U 217*. A few days later *Bogue*'s aircraft sank *U 118*, and that concluded the operations of *Trutz* and, for a time, of packs against convoys. It marked also the beginning of a most fruitful campaign by the USN escort carriers, assisted by the renewed flow of *Enigma* decrypts.

U 118 was a Type XB, a supply-boat, and at the beginning of June, 1943, there were nine such in service.[38] Operations in distant waters were impossible without them: between May, 1942 and May, 1943 these boats had refuelled 170 U-boats on their way to the Caribbean, the South Atlantic or the Indian Ocean, in addition to 220 boats operating against convoys. The loss of *U 118* was bad news for U-boat Command, and soon the *Enigma* decrypts were revealing its effects: boats were recalled from their operational areas, others delayed in reaching them, and two were sunk after refuelling (no doubt as a result of HF/DF fixes on their reporting signals). Soon the decrypts revealed that the Type XIV *U 488* was also at work (she refuelled twenty-two U-boats in June) and the US Navy[39] decided that the time had come to eliminate this menace. Four escort carrier groups formed the spearhead of the attack: they were those centred around USS *Bogue*, the first and longest in Atlantic service, USS *Santee*, which came to the Atlantic on 13 June, USS *Core*, 27 June, and USS *Card*, 30 July. With pointers (rather than precise guidance) from the decrypts, the US carrier groups helped themselves to a feast: in the three months, June, July and August, they sank three supply-boats, *U 118*, another Type XB, *U 117* (USS *Card*) and a Type XIV, *U 487* (USS *Core*). Because refuelling operations drew U-boats together on the surface for lengthy periods, they presented great dangers which the American naval aircraft fully exploited. In addition to the three supply-boats, they sank eleven ordinary U-boats during this period, one of which was, in fact, acting as an emergency refueller, the Type IXD2 *U 847*. Herbert Werner gives us a graphic account of these operations from the submariner's point of view. *U230* had missed three meetings with U-tankers:

> By August 13, *U230* was floating along with only two tons of diesel oil. Our position: about 300 miles east of Barbados. That afternoon, we received a fourth date to meet a newly appointed supply boat, *U117* ... The rendezvous was set for August 17. ...
>
> *U117* never arrived. ... [*U230* was ordered to obtain some fuel from *U634*, which was in company, and both were to refuel more substantially from *U847* on August 27.]
>
> During the night of August 27, we entered the square of our new rendezvous and began scanning the surface for familiar silhouettes. But it was morning before we spotted three conning towers in the quiet sea. As we converged, the superstructure of the huge supply boat, *U847*, emerged from the ocean, increasing our number to five. ...
>
> Any assemblage of five U-boats was extremely dangerous ... Knowing that we were helpless while taking the heavy oil into our tanks, our boys manned the guns and stood ready to cut the hoses instantly. Not so the crew of the supply boat; they simply stood around the large superstructure like street-corner idlers. In disgust, I yelled to the Exec of *U847* through the megaphone, 'What's the matter with you people? Don't you have any respect for aircraft?'
>
> 'We haven't seen any since we passed Greenland,' he shouted back.
>
> 'You better change your attitude. Tell me, where do you fellows sail from here?'
>
> 'To Japan,' he replied nonchalantly. 'But after giving away 50 tons of fuel, I guess we'll only make it to Surabaja.'
>
> Sceptically I wished him luck. Soon afterward, our hoses were disconnected and *U230* withdrew from the uneasy meeting. ... Two hours after our departure, the supply boat broke radio silence and reported that she had completed the refueling of all four boats. By sending that message, *U847* not only jeopardized the four boats she had supplied but also sealed her own fate. Within minutes, the British direction-finding service had pinpointed her position. Three hours later she was attacked by US aircraft and sent to the bottom, a large iron coffin for every man aboard. That afternoon I heard the reverberations of many bombs some 60 miles astern, and I knew that *U847* had died a needless death.[40]

While the US carrier groups were gathering in their harvest, Coastal Command's Biscay patrols and EG 2 were disposing of four more supply boats, including three Type XIVs, *U 459*, *U 461* and *U 462*. So the 'milch cows' became a wasting asset, and the campaigns in distant waters faded with them. Operation *MONSUN* supplies a perfect illustration; at the end of June, eleven Type IX U-boats set out for the Indian Ocean, accompanied by *U 462*. They carried equipment for the construction of a U-boat base at Penang with a view to operating between Bombay and the Persian Gulf. Only five of the original twelve even reached the Indian Ocean – and as shown, the 'milch cow' *U 462* was not one of them. At the end of August there were only forty operational U-boats at sea (compared with seventy-one in July); their losses during the three months had been:

June	17
July	37
August	25
	79

In the same period eighty-two ships were lost to submarines in all theatres. Dönitz thus faced defeat on all fronts – but he did not despair; he had a new card up his sleeve, and now he was ready to play it.

* * * * *

As August wore on, the *Enigma* decrypts made it clear that movement was afoot among the Biscay U-boats once again; they were moving outwards, some (but by no means all) of them by the 'Piening Way' along the Spanish coast. The movement continued into September; but where were they going? On 6 September the Tracking Room reported that:

> apart from an indication that another group operation is planned in some area, there is as yet no information about the destinations or intentions of any of the fifteen or sixteen now estimated to be outward bound.[41]

By 13 September the number of U-boats at large had swollen to about twenty, but they were preserving very strict wireless silence; were they making for the Mediterranean, or were renewed operations planned in the area of the Azores? On 20 September the picture began at last to clear – and it was high time. A signal from U-boat Command told the waiting U-boats that operations were to be resumed in 'the main battle area', which spelt out 'North Atlantic' as clearly as the name itself. Furthermore, these operations would be 'the decisive struggle for the German race'; they would be conducted with 'new weapons and installations', and the tactic would be to 'decimate the escort for moral effect and to denude the convoy'. All in all, this signal offered plenty to think about, but there was no time left, for already the U-boats were in contact with their quarry.

This was Dönitz's long-meditated return to the convoy routes; for the purpose, he had formed his twenty-one available boats into the *Leuthen* group on a 350-mile patrol line. Nine of these U-boats were equipped with the *Hagenuk* search receiver and the *Zaunkönig* (*T5*) acoustic torpedo, the GNAT, which Dönitz referred to as the 'anti-destroyer torpedo' – hence the injunction to 'decimate the escort'. The *Enigma* decrypts had given no specific warning of this weapon, but fortunately the Tracking Room's general uneasiness had communicated itself to the Operations Division, which had already brought back the 9th Escort Group from the Bay of Biscay to help meet the threat in the North Atlantic if and when it materialized. So the stage was set for the last Atlantic convoy battle to give the U-boats any significant success.

Expectations were high at U-boat Command: a fair-sized pack in action once more, a deadly new surprise weapon, German electronic technology contributing handsomely – and a splendid target comprising two convoys. ONS 18 consisted of twenty-seven merchantmen including a Merchant Aircraft Carrier,[42] escorted by the eight ships of B3 under Commander M. J. Evans. Close behind came a fast convoy, ON 202, which left Liverpool 42-strong, escorted by six ships of C2 under Commander P. W. Burnett. The 9th EG was coming up astern as the two convoys left Iceland behind to the north-east on 19 September; first blood was drawn on both sides that day. It was a VLR Liberator of No 10 Squadron RCAF, returning from Iceland to Gander, that sank *U 341* at the northern end of the patrol line at 0855. And it was towards the end of the day that HMS *Escapade's* Hedgehog had the accident referred to above which forced her to return to base. The U-boat attacks began at 0300 on the 20th against ON 202, and scored early successes by sinking two merchant ships; then an acoustic torpedo struck the frigate *Lagan* causing such damage that she had to be taken in tow and also go home.

By now the two convoys were so close to each other that Horton ordered them to join up, which produced for a time the astonishing result that, in the words of Commander Evans, the two convoys gyrated majestically about the ocean, never appearing to get much closer, and watched appreciatively by a growing swarm of U-boats.[43]

However, plentiful air cover provided by the redoubtable 120 Squadron in Iceland[44] and skilful protection by the combined escorts saved the convoys from further loss on the 20th. Night brought a different story: at about 2000 the Canadian destroyer *St Croix* was hit by an acoustic torpedo, and about an hour later she was sunk by another torpedo. The corvette *Polyanthus* was also sunk by a GNAT at about this time. Survivors of both ships were rescued by the frigate *Itchen*.

September 21 and most of September 22 found the whole agglomeration of ships, escorts and U-boats wrapped in dense fog; when it lifted the RCAF's No 10 Squadron filled the air with Liberators whose attacks badly damaged *U 270*, forcing her to return to base, and wounding the commander of *U 377*, which was also forced to withdraw. Commander Evans's ship, the destroyer *Keppel*, following a D/F bearing, rammed and sank *U 229*. The night of the 22nd was full of action: four merchantmen were sunk, and by tragic chance *Itchen*, with the *St Croix* and *Polyanthus* survivors still aboard, was hit by a GNAT and went down, only three men surviving from all three ships' companies. This bad night marked the effective conclusion of the battle, ended, says Dönitz, by the fog.

At first Dönitz and his staff were very well pleased with the result of the return to the North Atlantic. The U-boats, he says,

> reported the destruction of twelve destroyers with the new torpedo and the sinking, in addition, of nine merchantmen by normal torpedo. Two U-boats were lost.
> We regarded this as a very satisfactory success.[45]

Hitler, not unnaturally, was equally pleased when Dönitz reported to him on the 24th; he called the U-boat war 'the only light in an otherwise dark situation' and pronounced that it 'must be stepped up with all available means'.[46] Both he and the Grand Admiral were badly mistaken; even by U-boat standards, the claims were wildly high. The actual losses inflicted were six merchantmen (36,422 tons) and three escorts sunk, and two escorts damaged, which was bad enough, but a very different story from what Dönitz believed at the time. Years later, when compiling his *Memoirs*, he attributed the large discrepancy to the fact that the U-boats, firing at short range, had to dive deep at once to avoid having the GNATS homing in on their own propellers:

> At short range, therefore, the detonation of a torpedo could not be observed, but only heard in the boat, and the explosion of depth charges could easily be mistaken for that of the torpedo.[47]

The assertion that only two U-boats were lost is readily accounted for by the fact that *U 341* was sunk some 160 miles away from the convoys before the main action had begun.

On the British side, there was no disposition towards rejoicing or even relief. The loss of six merchantmen was grimly reminiscent of the early months of the year and 1942, when such losses were normal, while for the naval forces this was a unique experience in the anti-submarine war. To have a destroyer, a frigate and a corvette sunk, with another destroyer and another frigate seriously damaged, all in the space of a four-day action, was ominous indeed. As Chalmers graphically puts it,

> Normally an efficient escort vessel should be able to hold her own against torpedo attack, but here they were falling down like ninepins before they could grapple with the enemy.[48]

Horton himself was disturbed, and having identified the nature of the beast he warned his commanding officers that acoustic torpedoes were being used against them. Thanks to the erroneous early warning to which we have referred, he was also able to assure them that counter-measures were already in the pipeline and would quickly be available (actually in just over a fortnight), and in the interval recommended 'certain tactical precautions'. The counter-measure was a device called FOXER, a noise-making machine which was to be towed astern of a ship in dangerous waters to attract and detonate the torpedo at a safe distance. It was a snag that FOXER could not be used at speeds above 15 knots, which left fast-moving destroyers still vulnerable. Furthermore, when working properly, FOXER interfered with the ASDIC. Improved models were devised in due course, and the Canadians produced a version known as the CAT which made a sustained screeching noise like a circular saw and had a distinct psychological effect on U-boat crews. But, as Joseph Schull says,

No one ever came to love foxers or the 'cat gear' and other refinements which were introduced later. Yet they proved effective; and the acoustic torpedo remained merely an added nuisance to the end of the war.[49]

This is a fair summary; the GNAT possessed a lethal sting, as further alarming occurrences revealed, but it could be contained. The 'tactical precautions' suggested by Western Approaches Command included the use of depth charges as counter-mines, and this was often effective. The echoing explosions of the torpedo 'prematures' as the depth charge reverberations died away were very reassuring. Slow speed, although it was unnerving – some would say, an invitation to sudden death – was also effective. In Walker's group it was considered the best form of defence against the acoustic attack, and, of course, it well suited Walker's own attack method. It was, in fact, a combination of treatments that overcame the GNAT menace, rather than any single one. It has been said that

No ship towing Foxer was ever hit by an acoustic torpedo.[50]

Jurgen Rohwer disputes this:

Of 464 *Zaunkönig*-shots we could analyze in detail, 77 were hits, but 8 of them were against ships which had their 'Foxers' or 'Cats' streamed.[51]

Eight out of seventy-seven is 10.4% – a factor not to be dismissed.

One thing soon emerged: the *Zaunkönig* was not going to achieve the reversal of the decision in the Atlantic that Dönitz fondly hoped. U-boat losses steeply declined in September, to only nine boats, but Allied shipping losses were no more than 156,419 tons, to which the North Atlantic contributed a mere 43,775. October saw a succession of fiascos as new groups of U-boats (*Rossbach* and *Schlieffen*) sought vainly for convoy after convoy, and gave up in frustration with only sunk and damaged boats to show for all their effort. For this Bletchley Park was considerably responsible, and the proficiency of the quickly redistributed escort and support groups and air patrols did the rest. The net result of the two months, September–October, was a loss of just nine ships out of 2,468 which sailed in sixty-four North Atlantic convoys. During October U-boat losses increased again, to twenty-six, of which six were claimed by the indefatigable USN carrier groups whose activities reduced the total of 'milch cows' to two and doomed the operations in distant waters.

By November the writing was on the wall, and 'the perplexity of the U-boat Command was beginning to reach neurotic proportions'.[52] The morale of the crews was strained almost to breaking point. *U 230* regained the bomb-proof pens in Brest after a nightmare crossing of the Bay of Biscay, which they called 'Death Valley'. Herbert Werner stepped ashore;

> Only then, with seven metres of reinforced concrete over our heads, were we safe. ... I took a deep breath, heaved a great sigh of relief. That was all I could do about our sinking fortunes in the U-boat war. Nowadays nothing went right for us. ... Two years before, our battle line had been far out at sea. Last spring, it had moved east to the Continental shelf. Now the front had settled at the very coast of France. ...
>
> The difference between then and now was dramatically evident in Brest. I noticed many empty berths in the bunker. ... The smell of death was everywhere.[53]

Dönitz did not give up hope; at last, towards the end of the fifth year of war, he overcame Nazi anti-intellectual prejudice to the point of setting up a Naval Scientific Operations Staff headed by the physicist Professor Küpfmüller. Science, after all this time, was given a voice at operational conferences which, says *Korvettenkapitän* Peter Cremer, created

> a direct dialogue with the fighting men, which had a positive effect.[54]

Indeed, this was better late than never, but it was very late indeed, and by the nature of his qualification Professor Küpfmüller's undoubtedly valuable contribution was largely in the engrossing field of radar, which was not the be-all and end-all of submarine warfare, despite its obvious importance. But neither Küpfmüller, nor Dönitz, nor even Speer could overcome the mounting crisis of the Nazi economy in the face of military defeat.

Defeat in the Atlantic, for the second time, became a fact on 16 November, when Dönitz, with a heavy heart, withdrew the U-boats from the great convoy routes. There was, he says, no repetition of the relatively successful first *Zaunkönig* operation. Indeed, the coming months were to show that even the improved weapons had not sufficed to restore adequate fighting powers to the U-boats. The era of success had ended. All we could now hope to do was to fight a delaying action and, with as economic a use of our forces as possible, continue to tie down the forces of our enemy.[55]

It was not a glittering rôle – but then there was little glitter left in Germany's situation. The Kursk offensive had collapsed in July amid unsurpassed scenes of slaughter and destruction, and the Soviet counter-offensive at Orel had set the pendulum of war swinging visibly in the opposite direction. The abler German generals were in no doubt that this had been a decisive defeat and that the initiative lost at Orel was unlikely ever to be regained.[56] Succeeding months made the position plain: between July and October the German Army lost about a million men,[57] while the Russians seemed to gain strength with each battle. In August they were back in Kharkov, in September they retook Smolensk, in November it was Kiev. This was the background of the successive defeats at sea: twice in the Atlantic, and once on the transit routes. U-boat losses in November were nineteen, and in December, when their activity markedly died away, it was eight, bringing the year's total to no fewer than 237. Their defeat, says Roskill,

> was most marked during the last two months of the year, and in the North Atlantic. In that period seventy-two ocean convoys totalling 2,218 ships reached their destinations without suffering any losses at all.[58]

The shadows of Unconditional Surrender were beginning to grow.

* * * * *

If 1943 had been a bad year for Dönitz and the U-boats, 1944 was even worse; it was a year not merely of defeat, but of sheer fiasco. As it opened, all Germany lay under three darkening clouds: the Russian advance, the swarming bombers, and the menace of the Second Front. There was nothing the U-boat arm could do about the first two of these, but it had already exerted considerable influence in delaying the third and would now be expected to make an even larger and perhaps decisive contribution to the defence of 'Fortress Europe'. Always westward-oriented, Dönitz saw the impending Allied attack as

of decisive importance to the subsequent course of the war.

The U-boat was the sole instrument which, with a few men aboard, could make a wholly disproportionate contribution to success in war by sinking, for instance, just *one* ship laden with munitions, tanks or other war material, even if it was itself lost in the process. How many soldiers would have to be sacrificed, how great an endeavour made, to destroy on land so great a mass of enemy war material?[59]

He had, he says, 'wrestled hard and long' with the problem of what to do; the answer, not merely with hindsight, stared him in the face:

I had come to the conclusion that, if invasion came, the U-boats must be there.

There were, on 1 January, 1944, 436 U-boats in commission, 168 of which were operational. Winn, with the Intelligence Officer's horror of anything resembling unjustifiable euphoria, tended to exaggerate the numbers in his reports; on 8 February he stated that 175 boats were operational, of which 130 were in the Biscay bases. He accepted that forty of these were of the larger types (IXs and XIVs) which were not suitable for Channel operations, but his summary warned that

a total of 175 to 200 U-boats will be used to prevent or impair landings and to reduce the forces conveyed and their stores and armour and to attack the Atlantic convoys necessary to maintain the build-up and renewal of men.[60]

As the weeks went by, the Tracking Room concentrated its attention on the Type VIIs, seeing them as the inevitable spearhead of the anti-invasion forces, and steadily becoming more realistic in assessing their numbers: on 1 May an estimate of forty-four, and towards the end of the month thirty-seven to forty, which was remarkably accurate. Winn added:

All boats of this group will sail on or before D Day or at least D + 1.

This was an intelligent surmise, but does not precisely express what took place.

Numbers, as Dönitz was now well aware, were not the main issue. Impatiently, he awaited the new types of U-boat, and the perfection and installation of the *Schnorchel* device with which he hoped to bridge the gap between the obsolete boats and the boats of the future. Ideally, an interval, a reduction of warlike activity all round, would have been desirable – but war does not submit to considerations of desirability. It was as March drew to an end that Dönitz received orders to build up a group of some forty U-boats to attack the invasion forces, which he at once proceeded to do, calling it the *Landwirt* Group and telling the captains that their one goal must be:

Angriff – ran – versenken! (Attack – close in – sink!)

This was on 27 March, and a fortnight later (11 April) he followed up with a further exhortation to what has been called 'Reckless Attack'. This would seem to be a matter of translation, for in the English text of his Memoirs, translated by R. H. Stevens in collaboration with the highly reputable naval historian David Woodward, it reads as follows:

> Every vessel taking part in the landing, even if it has but a handful of men or a solitary tank aboard, is a target of the utmost importance which must be attacked *regardless of risk.**
> Every effort will be made to close the enemy invasion fleet regardless of danger from shallow water, possible minefields or anything else.
> Every man and weapon destroyed *before* reaching the beaches lessens the enemy's chances of ultimate success.
> Every boat that inflicts losses on the enemy while he is landing has fulfilled its primary function *even though it perishes in so doing.***[61]

Padfield remarks that, in view of the opposition likely to be met,

> this was a suicide order; in the event it was not enforced, so it should perhaps be regarded . . . as exhortation to fanaticism rather than as a literal instruction.[62]

Certainly it would not have aroused any particular attention in the German Army, least of all that large part of it on the Eastern Front which was constantly trying to defend hopeless positions in obedience to Hitler's insensate strategy of 'no withdrawals'. In an altogether different category was something to which, said Herbert Werner in 1969, he had yet to see any published reference:

> a shocking order issued by U-Boat Headquarters just before the Allied

invasion of Normandy. It ordered the commanders of 15 U-boats to attack the vast invasion fleet and, after their torpedoes were spent, to destroy a ship by ramming – i.e. by committing suicide.[63]

In such matters as these, where a normally magniloquent vocabulary becomes overblown with fanatical declamation, we move for much of the time on the margins of mythology. But there is nothing of mythology, only stark realism, in the U-boat War Diary entry of 6 June as the boats cleared the Bay of Biscay and made for their battle stations:

For those boats without *Schnorchel* this means the last operation.

In the event, taken by surprise as all the German forces were, the U-boat Command (West) was only able to send out thirty-five boats on 6 June, late in the day, and of these only nine had *Schnorchels*. They had no idea of what they were about to face – indeed, the whole German High Command from Hitler downwards and including Dönitz were quite ignorant of the scale of the Allied D-Day effort. The naval forces allocated to Operation NEPTUNE (the naval aspect of OVERLORD) amounted to just under 7,000 vessels, 79% of them British and Canadian:

Naval Combatant Vessels	1,213
Landing Ships and Craft	4,126
Ancillary Ships and Craft	736
Merchant Ships	864
	6,939

Included in this array were five Support Groups with escort carriers and over 200 other escort vessels from Western Approaches Command, a contribution which emphasizes once again the significance of the Atlantic victory, since only the complete absence of the U-boats from that area could make this possible.

Coastal Command contributed on a matching scale. Air Chief Marshal Sir William Sholto Douglas saw his Command's rôle as 'putting the cork in the bottle' – the 'bottle' being the south-west approaches to the English Channel, where the U-boat threat was likely to develop.

The 'cork' consisted of twenty-nine squadrons of No 19 Group (Liberators, Wellingtons, Sunderlands, Beaufighters, Halifaxes and Mosquitoes with Swordfish and Avengers of the Fleet Air Arm and USN Liberators attached). To the north, watching for incursions of U-boats from Norway into the Atlantic, were further squadrons from the now very attenuated Nos 15 and 18 Groups and three strike squadrons of No 16 Group in Kent.[64] To the approximately 350 assorted aircraft of No 19 Group (Air Vice-Marshal B. E. Baker) fell the task of patrolling the 20,000-square-mile stretch of water lying across the Channel entrance between southern Ireland and Brest, and up the Channel to a line between Portland Bill and Cherbourg. The whole area was divided into twelve unequal rectangular blocks, their size and location suited to the type of aircraft on patrol; the aircraft flew along the (invisible) outlines of these blocks, sweeping the sea's surface with their radar. In this way 19 Group ensured that

> a U-boat on the surface anywhere in that area would be seen on radar at least once every thirty minutes.[65]

Not for nothing were such tactics as these known by the code-name SWAMP.

The makings of a real U-boat fiasco were evident from the start. It was, indeed, comprehensive: the fact is that while the huge mass of shipping which comprised the invasion armada was making its crossing, the Biscay U-boats (*Landwirt*) and the twenty-one boats in Norway (*Mitte*) designated for anti-invasion duties were still in harbour. *Landwirt* sailed belatedly in two groups: nine *Schnorchel*-fitted boats heading for the Isle of Wight, while seven without *Schnorchels* made for positions between the Scilly Islands and Start Point in Devon; all the remainder (eighteen boats) formed a line in the Bay of Biscay. Of the attacking group, fifteen boats came from Brest, and their fate is revealing. Of the seven without *Schnorchels* four were sunk and three so damaged that they had to return by 10 June. Two of these, *U 629* and *U 373*, were attributable to a fine performance by one of the approximately one thousand Canadian aircrew serving in Coastal Command:[66] Flying Officer Kenneth Moore of No 224 Squadron. In the early hours of 8 June his Liberator attacked and sank *U 629* and then, only 22 minutes later, *U 373* – a performance for which Moore won both the DSO and the US Silver Star. The non-*Schnorchel* boats achieved precisely nothing for all their heavy losses, and on 12 June the Admiral Commanding Naval Forces, West (*Marinegruppenkommando West*), *Admiral* Theodor Krancke, ordered their recall. He wrote in his War Diary:

> All submarines operating without the *Schnorchel* in the Bay of Biscay have been ordered to return to their bases, as the enemy air attacks are causing too many losses and too much damage. Only if an enemy landing seems imminent on the Biscay coast are the boats to operate. They will remain under shelter in a state of readiness.

It would be difficult to find a more abject confession of powerlessness, a more total revelation of the decline of a once devastating weapon.

The U-boats with *Schnorchels* did better; by 12 June six of the Biscay contingent were still in action, and they were soon joined by others of the *Mitte* Group coming down from Norway. It was one of these, *U 767*, that sank the frigate *Mourne* off Land's End on 15 June, and on the same day the Biscay boat *U 764* sank another frigate, HMS *Blackwood*, off Cap de la Hague. Three days later (18 June) the Royal Navy had its revenge: the destroyers *Fame* (a renowned U-boat killer), *Inconstant* and *Havelock* sank *U 767*, and on that day also a Wellington of 304 (Polish) Squadron made an end of the one-time 'aircraft-trap', *U 441*. So it went on: in all twenty-five U-boats were sunk in June, twelve of them in the Channel or the Bay, and of these seven and two half-shares were attributable to aircraft. The only appreciable success obtained against merchant shipping during this month was by *U 984* on the 29th, when she torpedoed four Liberty ships in quick succession off Selsey Bill. But this was untypical and *U 984* herself had less than two months to live: she was sunk by Canadian destroyers on 20 August.

Such was the fiasco of the U-boats against the assault on 'Fortress Europe' and the immediate follow-up. June, 1944, was, in fact, a month of utter disaster for Germany. Not only had her Western forces completely failed to repel the Allied invasion or destroy the bridgehead once it had been obtained, but in the East they had suffered a calamity roughly twice as great as that at Stalingrad. This was what the Russians called 'Operation BAGRATION' named after General Prince Peter Ivanovich Bagration, a hero of the 1812 campaign against Napoleon; it has gone down in history as the Battle of Byelorussia, or 'the destruction of Army Group Centre'. As that name implies, its effect was to smash clean through the vitals of the German line in the East on a front of some 250 miles. Twenty-eight divisions were destroyed and 350,000 men lost in a matter of about a fortnight (though the Russians continued to press their advantage for another three weeks). This 'apocalyptic' battle, as significant as Kursk-Orel a year earlier, marked another long stride towards the Unconditional Surrender which was now only ten months off.

July in the West was also a bad time, as the Allies tightened their grip in Normandy, and at the end of the month their long-awaited break-out began. The U-boats did not give up easily, but their successes were meagre; twenty-three of them were lost during the month, nine in the Channel and the Bay. But far more serious than the loss of twenty-three boats out of the 188 that were still operational was the threat that now developed to the Biscay bases themselves. On 30 July the US 4th Armoured Division entered the town of Avranches at the base of the Cherbourg Peninsula, and the next day the American armour seized the bridge over the little River Sélune at Pontaubault which opened the way into Brittany. The whole strategic position which had been the foundation of the U-boat war since June, 1940, was undermined.

The message was clear to read. After the taking of Avranches, the main thrust of General Patton's Third Army was eastward, the beginning of the great sweep through France that would carry the American armies to the Rhine. The US VIII Corps, however, turned westward and south-westward into Brittany, advancing on Brest, Lorient and St Nazaire; the Americans were actually in the outskirts of Lorient by the morning of 7 August. To the south, the French Resistance (*FFI: Forces Françaises de l'Intérieur*) closed in on La Pallice and Bordeaux. Each one of the bases, under the weight of Allied air bombardment during the last three years, had become a concrete fortress, virtually impermeable to artillery or bombing. Allied expectations of quick triumphs were due for disappointment. Churchill told Mr Harry Hopkins on 6 August:

St Nazaire and Nantes, one of your major disembarkation ports in the last war, may be in our hands at any time. Quiberon Bay, Lorient and Brest will also soon fall into our hands. It is my belief that the German troops on the Atlantic shore south of the Cherbourg peninsula are in a state of weakness and disorder and that Bordeaux could be obtained easily, cheaply and swiftly.[67]

Things did not turn out like that; if the Germans were in a state of 'weakness and disorder' they disguised the fact well. The *FFI* entered Bordeaux on the morning of 26 August, but all they found was the wreck of the scuttled Italian submarine *UIT 21*. All the other boats had gone, and the German garrison had withdrawn to two strong points on either side of the mouth of the Gironde, depriving the Allies of all use of Bordeaux port.[68] Brest held out against the US VIII Corps. until 18 September; it required a hard 3½-week battle by some 80,000 American troops and nearly 10,000 casualties (to say nothing of enormous consumption of precious ammunition) to eliminate the German garrison of 38,000. Once more the Allies were cheated of their reward:

> When Brest fell, the customary methodical German demolition had yet to be cleared, and so by the time Brest was safe and operating the war had left it too far behind to make much of a contribution to Allied logistics. . . . Lorient and St Nazaire remained in German hands until the end of the war.[69]

While the land forces advanced upon the U-boat bases from the rear, air and naval forces were delivering the last Allied offensive in the Bay. The U-boats began their evacuation of the bases in early August, together with the substantial light surface forces of the German Navy. The result was a massacre; out of thirty-six U-boats lost in August, twelve were sunk in the Bay and two more in the Channel. Three U-boats were scuttled in Bordeaux, one in La Pallice and two in Lorient. The surface units were hacked to pieces: two destroyers and fifty-three smaller craft sunk. Dönitz, unsurprisingly, writes distinctly equivocally about these transactions:

> In the end I myself could no longer match the moral fortitude displayed by the U-boat crews. The uncertainty regarding the fate of boats on operations and my fear that the enemy would progressively bring such strong defensive forces to bear that to continue U-boat operations would be an irresponsible act caused me on August 24 and 26 to recall all boats still operating in the invasion area.[70]

What he does not say is that 'recall' meant recall to Norway; the only faint gleam of satisfaction for the U-boat Command in this whole dismal débâcle was the successful passage of no fewer than thirty-one Biscay boats to the Norwegian bases at Bergen and Trondheim.

Equally equivocal is Dönitz's summary of the entire campaign during the OVERLORD period. Between 6 June and the end of August, he says, the U-boat achievement was:

Sunk	Damaged
5 escort vessels	1 escort vessel
12 merchantmen (56,845 tons)	5 merchantmen (36,800 tons)
4 landing craft	1 landing ship

The cost, he says, was twenty U-boats, 'nearly 1,000 men, of whom 238 had been rescued'. He wrote in the War Diary:

> This marked the end of the U-boat campaign in the Channel, in which the old spirit of the arm was once again magnificently displayed. An overall review of the operations shows that, contrary to all our previous misgivings and all the doubts which from time to time beset us, the decision to put in the U-boats had been a right one. After due consideration is given to the exceptional difficulties involved, the success achieved was satisfactory, and had been achieved at the expense of losses which were admittedly severe but were not intolerable.

What makes this judgment extraordinary is that the U-boat losses were over twice as large as he admits to: forty-two boats sunk in the Channel, the Bay and the bases (by scuttling) out of a grand total of eighty-two during the period; 51.2%. A price of two U-boats for each Allied vessel sunk does not seem to match the definition of a 'satisfactory success'. And in addition there was the loss of the inestimably valuable Biscay bases themselves, wrecking U-boat strategy and opening up for the first time in the war the possibility of bringing in large ocean convoys by the South-Western Approaches.[71] The inescapable truth is that once more the U-boats had suffered a grave defeat, part and parcel of the mounting defeat of Nazi Germany.

And this defeat was not the only one. The U-boat presence in the Mediterranean had existed for almost exactly three years during which what had begun as a simple but serious strategic error (see pp. 359–61) had not been without profit. Ninety-five Allied merchantmen, totalling 449,206 tons, had been sunk during that time, and twenty-four major

British warships as well, including the battleship *Barham* and the aircraft carriers *Ark Royal* and *Eagle*. The cost to the U-boats had been sixty-eight of their number, which was high, but not disproportionately so, for as Roskill says,

> by their mere presence they imposed on us the need to maintain strong sea and air anti-submarine forces, covering the whole theatre. Though the transfers to the Mediterranean, whose initial purpose had been to support a tottering Italy, did bring us an easement in the vital Atlantic theatre, on balance it seems that the price paid by the enemy was not excessive.[72]

On 15 August the Allied forces landed in the south of France between Cap Bénat and Cannes. To secure this operation (DRAGOON) against underwater attack, heavy air raids had been mounted by the USAAF on the U-boat base at Toulon in July and on 6 August, sinking four of the eight boats there and leaving only one (*U 230*) operational; she sailed on 17 August but ran aground, and was blown up by her crew on 21 August. This was the last U-boat at sea in the western Mediterranean; on 19 September the last one at sea in the eastern Mediterranean, *U 407*, was sunk to the north of Crete.[73] Five days later the last two were destroyed by the USAAF in the harbour of Salamis. Defeat in the Mediterranean was absolute.

Within this catalogue of woe there was a gleam of light, not yet fully perceptible to U-boat Command. After the brilliant successes of June, there had been a marked fall in the number of sightings and sinkings of U-boats by aircraft. This ominous change in the texture of the battle was due to the virtual invisibility conferred by the *Schnorchel*, and it was something whose implications could hardly be exaggerated, as Roskill points out:

> The dangerous significance of this development, which threatened to restore to the enemy the initiative which he had been forced to surrender in the early spring of 1943, was not lost upon the British authorities. Four years of continuous struggle had taught us that by far the most effective counter-measure to the U-boats was to employ radar- and Leigh Light-fitted aircraft in conjunction with radar- and asdic-fitted surface escorts – the aircraft to carry out side-spread searches, and the ships to hold contact and attack until the enemy was destroyed. By reducing the effectiveness of our air-borne radar, the 'Schnorkel' [*sic*] struck

a heavy blow at Allied anti-U-boat tactics. Taken with the construction of high-speed submarines, on which we knew the Germans to be actively engaged, it was plain that unless victory could be gained before the two developments had come into general use, we might find ourselves struggling against an enemy who was once again possessed of the inestimable benefit of the initiative.[74]

The great battles of 1944 had gone well for the Allies, which was a matter for deep relief. The U-boats had been soundly defeated time and again. Yet it was in no cap-over-mill mood that the Admiralty faced the sixth New Year of the war. And Dönitz, badly buffeted by its fortunes, did not despair; even now there were still strong cards in his hand and he could be depended on to play them.

* * * * *

When Dönitz became Commander-in-Chief of the Navy he quickly set in hand a new naval construction programme which, in sharp contrast with Raeder's misguided 'Z Plan', laid all its emphasis on light craft, in particular U-boats and E-boats. He quickly perceived a fundamental obstacle to expansion which had haunted all his predecessor's projects. The Navy was never able to obtain the amount of steel it needed, and Dönitz, unlike Raeder, could both see why and possessed the cool realism and determination to tackle the problem at its roots. All German armament production except the Navy's was in the hands of Albert Speer's Ministry of Arms and Munitions. This independence had been jealously preserved, but on investigation Dönitz concluded that the system actually worked against the Navy's own interests; it lacked elasticity to cope with breakdowns of production at any point, whereas with the other Services a shortfall in one sector could often be compensated in another. The Navy had no representative on the Central (Munitions) Planning Commission, no voice to champion its cause in the eternal battle of priorities; in effect, Speer and Göring fought these out between them and 'it was the Navy that went short'. Dönitz had vision enough to perceive that the only real solution was (with Hitler's consent) to put naval production under Speer, who in turn agreed to raise U-boat completions to forty per month, and build seventy-two E-boats a year. It all sounds very straight-forward at this distance in time, but amid the conspiratorial rivalries and jealousies of the Third Reich this was a very exceptional beam of light and sanity.

It served Dönitz well when the matter of the new types of U-boat arose, and he was faced with the wholly unacceptable building schedule proposed by the Construction Branch which we have noted on p. 618. Speer took up the cause of the new types with enthusiasm, and selected a fellow Swabian to organize their production; his name was Otto Merker, and he was a bold choice for naval work because his previous claim to fame lay in making fire engines:

> Here was a challenge to all marine engineers. On 5 July, 1943, Merker presented his new construction system to the heads of the Navy. As was being done in the production of Liberty ships in the United States, the submarines were to be built in inland factories, where the machinery and electrical equipment would also be installed. They were then to be transported in sections to the coast and quickly assembled there. We would thus avoid the problem of the shipyards, whose limited facilities had so far stood in the way of any expansion of our shipbuilding programmes. Dönitz sounded almost emotional when he declared, at the end of our conference: 'This means we are beginning a new life'.[75]

Dönitz might well be emotional. Merker's system promised to reduce building time for the 1,600-ton Type XXI to 260–300,000 man-hours per boat, compared with 460,000 man-hours for a boat of similar size by existing methods. The first Type XXI was to be ready by the spring of 1944 and considerable numbers – enough to conduct a proper campaign – by the autumn of that year. By that time some 140 of the 230-ton Type XXIIIs (suitable for coastal operations) would also be ready. All this was to be done by a crash programme, dispensing with prototypes and firmly rejecting all modifications. No further conventional U-boats were laid down after July, 1943, so that the full forty per month promised by Speer would consist of the new types of boats. It was a heady prospect; but there was a flaw.

An important part of Air Chief Marshal Harris's mounting offensive in 1943 was the Battle of Hamburg, the ten-day offensive between 25 July and 3 August in which Bomber Command attacked the great port on four nights (over 3,000 sorties) and the US Eighth Air Force attacked twice in daylight (626 sorties). The climax of this battle was the horrific fire-storm created on the night of 27/28 July; in all, some 50,000 people are believed to have died, many in indescribable agonies. This narrative is not concerned with those matters;[76] what concerns us here is the lesson of Hamburg for Speer, Dönitz and the U-boats. Speer was appalled:

Hamburg had put the fear of God in me. . . . \I informed Hitler that armaments production was collapsing and threw in the further warning that a series of attacks of this sort, extended to six more major cities, would bring Germany's armaments production to a total halt.[77]

A particularly significant casualty in the Hamburg holocaust was the Blohm & Voss submarine construction yard, where the damage was estimated as costing four to six weeks' production, besides three U-boats currently building. Merker took note. He at once ordered the building of a vast submarine assembly factory near Bremen: Code-named '*Valentin*', it takes its place among the many wonders of World War II:

> The Germans were artists in ferro-concrete without peer, and they were now able to take the factory in their stride: a structure with walls 10 to 15 feet thick, measuring 1,350 feet long and 320 feet wide, covering an area about twice that of the Houses of Parliament in London, with an inside headroom of 60 feet, the whole covered by a roof of reinforced concrete 22 feet thick; to enable the XXI boats to test their schnorkel equipment while *inside* the bunker, the water level at the outer end was to be dredged to 60 feet.[78]

Needless to say, such a structure, like the city of Rome, could not be completed in a day. As Dönitz ruefully says, the implementation of the Speer/Merker programme

> had to be achieved under the hail of bombs which, from the autumn of 1943, came pouring down on the German armament industry in ever-increasing volume. A long-term implementation according to plan was no longer possible.[79]

It is ironical – but satisfactory – to see how, at the very time that Coastal Command was meeting the discouragement of fewer sightings and sinkings, Bomber Command stepped into the breach with a highly effective series of attacks after many frustrations. By late 1944, thanks to the defeat of the German fighter force by the P-51Bs of the Eighth US Air Force, the Allied bombers could operate as easily by day as by night, but it is another of the war's ironies that this no longer mattered. Thanks in turn to the new bombing aids (especially OBOE, H2S and G–H) and the efficiency of Bomber Command's crews, 'precision and concentration could be achieved as well by night, or through ten-tenths cloud, as on a clear day'.[80] No clearer evidence of this is required than the attacks on the German canal system, above all the Dortmund-Ems and Mittelland which linked central Germany with the Ruhr and the North Sea ports. For Merker's work, which involved moving massive prefabricated U-boat sections, some of them about 27 feet long and 25 feet high ('the size of a two-storey suburban house') and weighing 150 tons, the canals were essential. No part of the Royal Air Force was better able to make a successful attack on such targets than 617 Squadron (the famous 'Dam-busters' of 1943). On the night of 23 September 617 Squadron attacked the Dortmund-Ems Canal aqueduct near Münster, wrecking it so severely that a six-mile stretch was drained, stranding the boats and barges on it and bringing all traffic to a standstill. The Germans made their usual tremendous effort of repair and succeeded in bringing the canal back into use by early November – whereupon Bomber Command returned and wrecked it again. In November and again in 1945 it turned its attention to the Mittelland, whose banks

were completely obliterated at Gravenhorst by night attacks on January 1st/2nd and February 21st/22nd, 1945. Both canals were kept out of action for the remainder of the war.[81]

Roskill remarks, somewhat tartly:

It therefore seems true to say that the heavy bombers' attacks on land targets first made an important direct contribution to the struggle against the U-boats in the autumn months of 1944.[82]

Merker would have agreed; he told Speer on 10 January:

The transport situation in general is catastrophically bad. . . . Ship-building has . . . been especially hard hit by the various stoppages of canal navigation, and must change over to rail transportation.

It was a counsel of despair; the bombs were falling on the railways too, and all forms of transportation had become, in Speer's words, 'the greatest bottleneck in our war economy'.[83]

The development of the new U-boat types had been carefully

watched by Bletchley Park from the beginning of 1944. Before it ended, the Admiralty was in possession of Intelligence which, for recency and precision, has rarely been matched. The GC & CS had for a long time been decrypting the Japanese diplomatic ciphers used by the Ambassador in Berlin to report on many matters of extreme interest. On 30 May he related a visit paid to Dönitz six days earlier by the Head of the Japanese Naval Mission, Vice-Admiral Abe, at which Dönitz disclosed the basic details of both the Type XXIs and Type XXIIIs.[84] On 29 August Admiral Abe, accompanied by the Naval Attaché and German technical experts, visited the Schichau yard at Danzig and made a thorough inspection of a Type XXI. They were given a full account of production methods, schedules and performance details. Cautiously the Japanese officers told the Ambassador that they had only seen one boat at its moorings and received only a word-of-mouth description of performance; they could not, therefore, reach definite conclusions, but, said the Attaché,

> it would seem at first glance that the Type XXI is an epoch-making U-boat.

This was a conclusion from which Winn, the OIC and the Board of Admiralty did not demur. Some comfort came on 12 December, when another Japanese signal stated that owing to delays caused by Allied bombing, the new boats would not be operational until March, 1945. We now know that ninety Type XXIs and thirty-one Type XXIIIs had been launched by the end of 1944, of which sixty of the former and twenty-three of the latter were in service, but none yet operational. It was not a pleasing prospect.

For the U-boats what it meant was that it was the old faithfuls, the Type VIIs, that would have to keep the war alive. Now, however, they had *Schnorchels*, and this did make a difference. It meant, for example, that they would generally submerge as soon as they left their bases in Norway and only surface when they returned, possibly eight weeks later. And continuous submergence meant, in turn, that there would be virtually no W/T communication from the U-boats, which meant no decrypts from Bletchley Park and no HF/DF; instead, for the Submarine Tracking Room, it would be back to a worse blackout than ever before and another 'Working Fiction'. It also meant 'an immense amount of unrewarding flying' for Coastal Command,[85] with very few real sightings but a spate of false excitements due to 'willywaws' – small moving water-spouts, well-known to seamen – and even spouting whales. Sinkings of U-boats decreased alarmingly: by all causes only 7 in November, and of the fourteen in December three were due to accidents and three to air raids on the bases.

As early as September the U-boats had begun to adopt a new strategy: while still trying to maintain an effort in distant waters, their main thrust switched from the Atlantic to British Home Waters where they had achieved great successes between 1939 – June 1941 (see Appendix F). In November, 1944, they returned in strength, and December saw a dramatic rise in the shipping losses in Home Waters: eighteen merchantmen (85,639 tons) compared with only three the previous month (8,880 tons). Only about half of this loss was directly due to U-boat attack – eight ships, but this was as many as the full total for the previous three months; and some more should be added to it, sunk by mines laid by the U-boats. The area in which this inshore campaign operated stretched round the north of Scotland from the Moray Firth to Cape Wrath, through the Minches and down to the Irish coast, with offshoots in the Bristol Channel and off Southern Ireland. The anti-submarine forces found themselves faced with serious and unexpected difficulties; in these waters ASDIC became confused by rocks and ledges, by the numerous wrecks and by tidal swirls.[86] The First Sea Lord (Admiral of the Fleet Sir Andrew Cunningham since October, 1943) was driven to say at the turn of the year:

> We are having a difficult time with the U-boats. . . . the air are about 90 per cent out of business. The asdic is failing us.[87]

Air, radar, ASDIC – to say nothing of cryptography and D/F – the inshore waters offensive played dangerous havoc with the anti-submarine armoury. A glimpse of what might be in store was provided by the exploits of *U 486* which sank four merchantmen[88] and a frigate in the Channel at the end of December. This, fortunately, was exceptional: the full total of losses in Home Waters in the two months was eleven merchantmen and two frigates, at a cost of five U-boats, of which only one was attributable to Coastal Command (a Leigh-Light Wellington of No 407 Squadron RCAF). But it was not the immediate losses of either ships or U-boats that mattered – it was what might all too clearly happen when the new types came into operation, if they pursued the same strategy. So 1944 went out, after all the NEPTUNE triumph, with a sense of the unappealing landscape of Square One having come back into view.

* * * * * *

In the event, the prophets of woe were confounded; the end was nearer than anyone dared to hope. By the end of 1944 Romania and Bulgaria had changed sides; the Red Army was encircling Budapest. In the West the Ardennes offensive marked the last flicker of German strength, and its collapse in January opened the way for the final advances of the Allied armies. In that month also the Red Army entered Germany; its next objective was Berlin. The *Luftwaffe*, by now, was almost powerless, and in a state of galloping disintegration. The pounding from the air continued, the bomb-deluge during the four effective months of 1945 reaching the proportions of fantasy:

	January	February	March	April
Bomber Command	32,800 tons	45,750 tons	67,500 tons	34,850 tons
8th USAAF	39,100 tons	51,500 tons	73,500 tons	46,631 tons

Unbelievably, through it all, U-boat production continued and actually increased, as the monthly averages show:

	U-boats	Tons
1940	4.1	2,656
1941	16.3	13,142
1942	19.9	16,380
1943	23.6	19,055
1944	19.5	18,374
January – March 1945	26	28,632

On 1 January the total was 425 boats, 144 of them operational; on 1 April the total was 429, with 166 operational.

As Germany shrank and crumbled in the vice that gripped her, the stark realities became starker and plainer:

The war could no longer be won by force of arms. To make peace was not possible since the enemy would have none of it until Germany had been destroyed.

658

For the fighting men there was nothing for it but to fight on.[89]

Dönitz threw every available weapon into the last phase of the U-boat war, and this included what the Germans called the 'small battle units' – a range of 'midget submarines' and manned torpedoes similar to those which the Italians had used with such frightening effect in Alexandria harbour in December, 1941 (see p. 404). These 'small units' had made their *début* in the Mediterranean in September, 1944, against DRAGOON, and it had not been encouraging: a story of exceedingly heavy losses for no result. It was practically a repeat of this performance when they were tried against the OVERLORD shipping; their only important success was the sinking of one 4,700-ton ship in December – at a cost of no fewer than 167 of Types *Linse* and *Biber*.[90] At this point the Admiral commanding Naval Forces, North Sea, proposed to suspend their operations until the new, improved *Seehund* type was ready, but he was overruled. Dönitz, possibly inspired by the Japanese Air Force's *Kamikaze* attacks on Allied warships in the Pacific, ordered that the 'small units' should continue with *Opferkampfer* – 'sacrifice' (i.e. suicide) missions. Suicide was, indeed, their main achievement, yet Roskill notes that, however high their losses,

there was never any lack of volunteers from the German Navy for this type of work.[91]

The *Seehund* two-man submarines, which appeared in January, 1945, were undoubtedly the most effective of these weapons; they sank nine ships and damaged three more (a total of 36,835 tons) at a cost of thirty-five of their own number. But the final verdict on the whole range of 'small battle units' is that they did not justify the very considerable productive effort that was spent on them at a time when all German production was under unremitting strain. They illustrate the somewhat hysterical German tendency in the final stages of the war to waste time and resources on 'wonder-weapons', rather than make good the deficiencies in the standard equipment with which they had to wage the war.

Considerably more effective in the last four months were mines, laid by aircraft, U-boats or surface vessels; twenty-four ships (79,241 tons) were sunk by this means. By the same token, minelaying by Bomber Command which, in 1944, had caused great inconvenience if no great loss to the Germans (perhaps above all in delaying the working-up of U-boats), now began to take a heavy toll of ships (eighty-three sunk between January and April) and also sank four U-boats outright and caused significant damage to three more. But far more serious for the U-boat arm than the loss, permanent or temporary, of seven boats was being forced to abandon the training area in the Gulf of Danzig. The U-boats, which had carried war to the doorsteps of their enemies, were now being harried on their own. The point was made with special emphasis when the USAAF sank three U-boats on one day (17 January) in Hamburg – *U 2515*, *U 2523* and *U 2530*[92] – and four days later (21 January) the Soviet Air Force sank another, *U 763*, in Königsberg.

The battle in the inshore waters was going harder for the U-boats; lacking now the great technological advantage that they had possessed in 1943–44, the anti-submarine forces nevertheless had one important advantage left: numbers. In 1945 there were no fewer than 426 escort vessels of all types operational; Western Approaches Command contained thirty-seven groups, of which fourteen were RCN. Even such numbers as these could not wipe out the inshore U-boats, but they could make life exceedingly difficult for them, and take a severe toll whenever a U-boat revealed its position by attacking. As Roskill succinctly says,

> once they knew where to seek for their adversary his prospects of survival were not good.[93]

Herbert Werner confirms this:

> The seas around England had become a sort of private pool in which the British eagerly played their game of killing off a helpless U-boat now and then; and if the hundreds of aircraft and surface vessels failed to sink our boats, then the hundreds of square miles of minefields did.[94]

This is an exaggeration, but it conveys the 'feel' of this phase of the war from the point of view of the men still trying to wage it in Type VIIs. In January they only succeeded in sinking seven ships (30,426 tons), and for that modest count six of them were destroyed.

The full tally of U-boats sunk in January was fourteen – and Coastal

Command could claim not one. What made this a particularly bitter consideration was that it was just at this time – in February – that the Command reached its peak strength: fifty-four squadrons (793 aircraft) of which thirty-eight and a half squadrons (528 aircraft) were allocated to anti-submarine duties. Furthermore, it was now in possession of a new low-altitude bomb sight which could have made possible swift attacks on a radar bearing without the need for the Leigh Light – if there had been anything for the radar to reveal. But even for the high-definition 3-cm radar, looking for a *Schnorchel* head in a choppy sea dancing with 'white horses' was, as has been well said, a problem like

that of a golfer looking for a ball in a limitless field of daisies'.[95]

The 3-cm radar was only one of a number of American inventions that came to life in the second half of the war. Once roused, American warlike inventiveness quickly hit a fertile streak, and American production methods soon translated this into weaponry in lavish quantities. It was now just a year since the first operational success of one ingenious invention, the Magnetic Airborne Detector (MAD). This was a development of the magnetometers used in mineral exploration to plot distortions in the earth's magnetic field. Adaptation to enable an aircraft by this method to locate so small an object as a submerged U-boat from an attacking height required some finesse, but the MAD was in service by 1943 – only to find that its targets had vanished. It was essentially a shallow water weapon, and not surprisingly its first successes were achieved in the Straits of Gibraltar, where the US Navy's Patrol Squadron VP-63's Catalinas (soon given the stage-musical name, 'Madcats') found and sank three U-boats between February and May, 1944. One invention calls forth another: since MAD only operated directly above its target, it was also necessary to devise a back-propelled bomb which would then fall vertically; this quickly came into existence – the 'retro-bomb'. Even such degrees of ingenuity, however, have their limits; applied to the different conditions of British Home Waters (the Irish Sea, for example) 'Madcats' were less successful and there is only one recorded kill by this method – *U1055* off Ushant on 30 April, 1945. An interesting multi-marriage of technologies had already borne fruit on 20 March, when 3-cm radar and a further American invention, the sonobuoy (a moored hydrophone with a transmitter enabling aircraft to hear and track a moving U-boat) joined with the Mark 24 Mine, judiciously used by a Liberator of No 86 Squadron, to put an end to *U905*. It was a sonobuoy once more, with the acoustic torpedo, that brought about the destruction of *U296* only two days later by another Liberator, of No 120 Squadron – blessed comforts for Coastal Command in a lean time.[96]

So we observe that the war of technology, at sea as in the air, continued to the very end. We must also acknowledge that, despite the sundry encouragements for the Allies listed above, it was now once more the Germans who held the ace. The first of the Type XXIIIs to become operational, *U2324* (*Oberleutnant* Hass), put to sea in January; a second followed in February. It was a serious weakness of this type that the boats carried only two torpedoes. Hass used up both of his in sinking a merchantman in the North Sea in February, and then returned to Bergen. It was not much to boast about, but it was a portent, and on the 28th of the month Dönitz was assuring Hitler that against the revolutionary qualities of the new types

the mighty sea power of the Anglo-Saxons is essentially powerless.[97]

With one all-important proviso, this was substantially true. Five more Type XXIIIs arrived in British Home Waters, and between them all they finally sank seven ships, two of them victims of *U2326* on the very last night of the war. Making good use of their submerged speed of 12½ knots, all of them escaped detection and destruction. If the little 230-tonners could perform like this, what might the Type XXIs not do, if and when they arrived? And this was the all-important proviso: 'if and when'. By the end of April, twelve Type XXIs had completed their working-up and ninety-nine more were doing their acceptance trials; on the 30th *U2511* (*Korvettenkapitän* Schnee) became the first and only Type XXI U-boat to become operational at sea, the harbinger of a threat more real and more disturbing than that of April, 1917, or of March, 1943. But it was too late. On 4 May Dönitz ordered the U-boats to cease hostilities.

And what of the Type VIIs, making their last forlorn endeavours in British Home Waters? Dönitz threw them into the scale with a spendthrift abandon; no fewer than fifty-one were present by the end of February – enough in theory to produce a fairly sensational result. Yet all they could achieve in the inshore campaign was the sinking of eleven ships (28,920 tons) at a cost of twelve to themselves. The full month's total, lost in all waters, was twenty-two, including three by mines, one by accident and one by cause unknown. In March there were fifty-three U-boats in Home Waters; their tonnage score was considerably higher than February's – 44,728 tons – but less by one ship, and fifteen of them were sunk. The total losses for the month were thirty-two, and this figure includes the beginning of the transformation of the last five weeks of war from a battle into a massacre: on 30 March the USAAF sank thirteen U-boats in massive attacks on Wilhelmshaven, Bremen and Hamburg. By now the Western Allies were over the Rhine and pressing into Germany; their aircraft roamed at will in the German skies. The Red Army entered Vienna on 13 April, and on 16 April the final battle began: the Battle of Berlin. Nevertheless, in that month forty-four U-boats (including *U 2511*) came out from their Norway bases to do battle, providing, says Roskill,

> convincing evidence of the way in which, almost to the end, the Germans managed to complete and commission new boats, and to train their crews.[98]

It was indeed an amazing performance. But it was hopeless: in fact, the operational U-boats on their stations were now safer than those in their bases and their own home waters. In distant seas they were reduced by the end to two in the Western Atlantic, one off Portugal and seven on passage; the last two sinkings were *U 548* on 30 April and *U 853* on 6 May, both off the American east coast.[99] In the British inshore waters during the last five weeks, the U-boats sank ten merchant vessels and two small warships for which they paid a price of twenty-three boats. Thus the campaign of the Type VIIs in 1945 cost a total of fifty-six U-boats for the meagre reward of thirty-eight merchant ships sunk (156,199 tons) and eight warships (two corvettes, three minesweepers and three smaller craft).

In the Baltic the Allied aircraft treated the U-boats to a 'happy time' in reverse. The last five weeks saw the destruction of eighty-three boats, fifty of them in the Baltic itself or in neighbouring waters, the Kattegat and the Skagerrak. The Allied heavy bombers continued the work well begun on 30 March, making the German bases themselves untenable. The US 8th Air Force sank six boats in Kiel on 3 and 4 April; Bomber Command took three more on 8 April; and between 9–25 April the RAF and USAAF between them destroyed another nine. This produced a flow of U-boats out of the Baltic, heading for the bases in Norway through the shallow, narrow, well-mined waters of the Belts and close to the Swedish shore. Coastal Command exultantly pounced on the U-boats travelling on the surface (for fear of mines) in this area: rocket-firing Mosquitoes of No 18 Group and Beaufighters of No 16 Group swept in, joined in May by more rocket-firing aircraft, the Typhoons of the Second Tactical Air Force now flying from fields well inside Germany. It was, appropriately enough, Coastal Command that made the final attack and the last kill: a Catalina of 210 Squadron commanded by Flight Lieutenant K. Murray inflicted so much damage upon *U 320* on 7 May that she foundered two days later with all hands.

It was against this background of ruin that on 1 May, 1945, Dönitz reached simultaneously the pinnacle and the nadir of his career. Hitler committed suicide on 30 April and on that day Dönitz received a radio message from Martin Bormann, the second-rate Nazi fanatic who ruled over the Party apparatus:

Grossadmiral Dönitz:
    In place of the former *Reichsmarschall* Göring the Führer has designated you as his successor. Written authorization on the way. Immediately take all measures required by the present situation.

                                            Bormann

The relatively obscure Flag Officer of Submarines of 1939 had become Head of the German State: this was the pinnacle. The nadir lay in the meaning of the words 'all measures' that he was required to take; there were few now who could have any doubt about what these must be. The Russians were deep into Berlin and conducting a battle of staggering ferocity even by Eastern Front standards.[100] In his Order of the Day to the *Wehrmacht* on 1 May Dönitz informed the Services of the death of Hitler, 'one of the greatest heroes of German history', and said:

I take over command of all arms of the Services with the intention of continuing the battle against the Bolshevists until the fighting forces and the hundreds of thousands of families of the German East are saved from slavery or destruction. Against the British and the Americans I must continue to fight as long as they persist in hindering the accomplishment of my primary object.

The position demands from you, who have already performed such great historical deeds, and who presently long for the end of the war, further unconditional commitment. I demand discipline and obedience. Only by the execution of my orders without reservation will chaos and collapse be avoided. Who now avoids his duty and thereby brings death or enslavement to German women and children is a coward and a traitor.

The oath of loyalty which you gave to the Führer is now due from each one of you to me as the Führer's appointed successor.[101]

No doubt this forbidding proclamation has to be interpreted to a considerable extent in terms of the internal power struggle against Heinrich Himmler who had the backing of the large and still potent SS organization, and had his own ideas about how the end of the *Reich* should be managed.[102] Yet it can have brought to those who heard it no such encouragement as Churchill's promise of 'blood, toil, tears and sweat' to the British in 1940. Indeed, it was only from the U-boats, despite what they were enduring, that Dönitz could rely on the discipline, obedience and loyalty that he demanded.

Any dream of exploiting inter-Allied differences quickly faded; on 4 May Dönitz ordered the U-boats to cease hostilities; and on that day he recognized that in Germany's desperate situation he must agree to the British demand that German warships should be surrendered, not scuttled, 'contrary to the traditions of our Navy'. Twice now in his lifetime he had witnessed the humiliation of German sea power, of the Service that he loved, and the nation which he had unfalteringly served with all his might, however misdirected. 4 May was also the day on which the German forces in the north surrendered to Field-Marshal Montgomery at Lüneburg Heath. Three days later the German delegates made the Reich's final submission to the Supreme Allied Commander, General Dwight D. Eisenhower, at Reims:

We the undersigned, acting by authority of the German High Command, hereby surrender unconditionally to the Supreme Commander, Allied Expeditionary Force and simultaneously to the Supreme High Command of the Red Army all forces on land, at sea, and in the air who are at this date under German control.

The German High Command will at once issue orders to all German military, naval and air authorities and to all forces under German control to cease active operations at 2301 hours Central European time on 8th May, 1945.

665

So it had come to that: Unconditional Surrender, after all. The first U-boats to obey this detested order came in on 9 May – the first of a total of 156; 221 were scuttled by their crews, whatever Dönitz might say. Two could not bring themselves to do either of these things: *U530*, coming from the American east coast, entered the River Plate in July, and *U977* from Kiel followed her in August; both were promptly interned by the Argentine Government.

On 23 May Dönitz was arrested on Eisenhower's orders to await trial as a war criminal (see p. 213 Note 4). At the famous – or notorious – Nuremberg trial he was sentenced to ten years' imprisonment. He died on Christmas Eve, 1980; at his funeral in January, 1981, a long line of old U-boat men, many wearing the ribbons of their war awards, or Iron Crosses, and some with Oak Leaves also, attended his burial and filed past his coffin to pay their last respects, bearing testimony to Lothar-Günther Buchheim's words:

> Hardly any units of the German armed forces can have had more blind faith in their commander than the submarine units had in Dönitz.

* * * * *

Evidently, the First and Second U-boat Wars had resemblances and contrasts; we have to remind ourselves that they were separated by only twenty-one years. This meant that they both fall within the same bracket of technology; until the advent of the new types in 1944, all U-boats were submersibles, rather than true submarines, and this was the operational truth for both wars. The campaign which effectively started in 1916 can thus be seen as a prologue to what followed in 1939, and there is no real cause for surprise at the fact that basic tactics were identical. The prime drawback of the submersible was its lack of underwater mobility, which meant that any operation requiring speed had to be conducted on the surface. By 1918 the U-boats well knew that this was fraught with danger if there were aircraft in the vicinity – hence the tactic of night approach and night attack on the surface. It was, of course, in World War II that this claimed its chief rewards, and if the final inshore campaign did nothing else, it proved this point. Roskill says,

> As destroyers of merchant shipping the surfaced U-boats of the 1941 'wolf packs' were immeasurably superior to the submerged 'Schnorkel-lers' of 1944, creeping unseen around our coasts; and, even if the latter

caused us much irritation and wasted effort, they never came near to becoming a serious threat to our Atlantic life-line – as the former certainly did.[103]

The strategic possibilities of the U-boats had also been clearly signalled in 1916–18. They did not yet have the performance for protracted and effective campaigns at great distances – this would have to wait for the Type IXs and the 'milch cows'; but their brief foray in American waters in August, 1918, was a clear portent which the United States Governments and their advisers neglected to their very grave cost. Nor was the 'happy time' on the American coast in 1942 the only exploitation of that unsuspected range revealed by the earlier boats: at different times between 1940–45, when things were not going well in the North Atlantic, Dönitz was able to take good pickings in the distant South Atlantic and in the Indian Ocean. It was not a novelty; it was a simple technological progression.

The conditions of U-boat warfare in the two wars were also very similar. Life in a U-boat on a long cruise meant much the same thing in both, as the comparison of the 1918-class boats with the Type VIIB on p. 197 indicates. Discomfort began as one stepped aboard, and continued until one crossed the gangplank to the shore. Cramped conditions, eternal damp and deteriorating food were the invariable concomitants of a long cruise, and for the duration of a long dive all those aboard were, in Werner's words, 'the captives of our own smells'[104] – which take little imagining. He records his amazement when he first inspected a Type XXI in 1945; he found the torpedoes in their own store, where all servicing and reloading took place, all hydraulically operated:

the crew, which on old boats slept crowded together among the steel fish, lived in a roomy compartment of their own. Officers' and petty officers' quarters were like first-class state-rooms on a passenger liner.

It is the authentic cry of the under-privileged, the man with the old-fashioned weapon when he first meets the man with the new one.[105]

As regards the submarine's own weapons, World War I had conclusively shown that, while guns had their uses from time to time, the primary armament of a U-boat was the torpedo. In this field, also, there were technological progressions, the culmination of them being

667

the 1944 *Dackel*, a pattern-running torpedo with a range of 57,000 metres. We have no record of achievement by this remarkable weapon, but we have ample evidence of the great effectiveness of the standard 21-inch variety delivered at the closest possible range. As we have seen, however, even these had grave defects in 1939, and Dönitz has bluntly told us that, until these were overcome in 1942,

> the effectiveness of our torpedoes was no greater than it had been in the First World War.[106]

It scarcely need be added that, as presaged in 1918, the prime anti-submarine weapon throughout the war was the depth charge, and it was a bad day for the U-boats when these began to be delivered effectively by aircraft as well as by surface ships.

Human stress is not a constant; it is liable to vary according to time and place – hence the fluctuation that we see in fleets and armies from one war to another. The World War I U-boat crews (like all other submariners) felt the excitement of pioneers, but also their apprehension at the unknown. There was still much novelty about submarines in 1939, and it is difficult to detect any significant difference in the responses and attitudes of the U-boat men in the two wars to their grim and testing trade. There is no one to report the hideous scenes of underwater destruction, so there is no way of making comparisons. All that we can securely go by is the posture of the survivors when it was all over. In 1918, when mutiny ran like a plague through the Imperial German Navy,

> Contrary to the generally-accepted opinion, the discipline of the German submarine crews was never broken. ... The submarine complements remained steadfast to the last. ... The nervous tension and physical discomforts; the terrible experiences of crews which had escaped death by a hair's breadth; the ever-increasing losses; the uncertainty as to the fate of those who never returned – all such were factors which might be expected to sap endurance and self-confidence in the bravest. Companionship in danger, active service, adventure – all these things preserved and upheld discipline. No instance has yet come to light of a submarine's crew refusing *en masse* to put to sea, no matter how dangerous an enterprise might be before them.[107]

When the war ended in November, the U-boat arm was still a going concern, an effective instrument of war. And so it was in May, 1945; *Korvettenkapitän* Schnee, for instance, in *U 2511*, had enough professional spirit left, even after receiving the order to surrender, to carry out a (highly successful) dummy attack on a British escort group on his way back to Bergen. On 14 May a token group of eight U-boats came into Lough Foyle to make their surrender to Admiral Horton in Londonderry. The crews were mostly very young; 'some were sullen and many were arrogant'; an officer of Horton's staff gave his opinion that the morale of the commanders was unbroken. The British officer supervising the surrenders said:

> I think the officers could be divided into three types – the young ex-Hitler [Youth] super-Nazi type, aged 22–23, who were perfectly bloody; the slightly older, and presumably pre-war *Kriegsmarine*, who were very 'correct' and not very forthcoming; and the ex-reservist type, perhaps from the Merchant Navy, who had knocked about the world a bit. These latter were quite pleasant.
>
> To sum up, I don't think that the U-boat morale had been crushed, and they certainly did not feel that they had been defeated. I think that these men, manning the new U-boats . . . would have given us the most awful headaches had the war continued.[108]

So much for resemblances; the contrasts are just as striking. First, there is the matter of numbers: between 1914–18, 390 U-boats were built; the 1939–45 figure was nearly three times as great – according to Bekker, 1,170 boats, according to Roskill 1,162. Curiously, the number of ships sunk by them was substantially larger in World War I: 4,837, as compared with 2,828 in World War II. The tonnage lost to submarines, chiefly to the Germans, was, however, as one might expect, much greater in the second war: 14,687,231 tons, compared with 11,135,460 in World War I. Each of these totals, it will be observed, constitutes a major factor in the waging of the war. In addition, the World War II U-boats sank 158 British Commonwealth warships[109] and twenty-nine American. The losses suffered by the U-boats themselves were also vastly different; 178 in World War I, 784 (including surrenders but not scuttles) in World War II. The human loss in the second war was nearly six times that of the first: the 5,409 officers and men of the first war grew to 27,491 dead of 1939–45, whose names are recorded on the U-boat Memorial near Kiel, plus another 5,000 who became prisoners of war – a total of over 32,000; a casualty rate of 85%.

The second profoundly important difference between the two wars is that in the first the U-boats did not seriously attack convoys, whereas in the second the major contests which decided the Battle of the Atlantic were the great convoy actions. These, alas, by their nature lack the names of the great naval battles of history – Salamis, Lepanto, The Nile, Trafalgar, Jutland, Leyte Gulf etc. – and have only the uninspiring convoy numbers to identify them, far out in the ocean where place-names do not abound. But this was the arena of a battle whose decisive character requires no further emphasis. The U-boats fought most of it in 'wolf packs', a tactic which had also been essayed in World War I, but only tentatively and briefly, for the simple reason that the control mechanism for it did not exist. This was entirely a product of the great advances in wireless telegraphy between the wars. It was these that made the long-range direct control of operations from U-boat Headquarters in Lorient or Paris (and finally Berlin) possible – a contrast indeed. And within the discipline of the same technology there was the contribution of the *B-Dienst* to the all-important matter of actually finding the convoys. Thus World War I emerges as the war of individual U-boats doing the best they could, often with most impressive results, and World War II as the war of pack attacks on convoys under tight radio control and guided by radio intelligence.

The third deep difference in the U-boat wars may be expressed in one word: Dönitz. He was an unique phenomenon, one of a very small number of men – less than a dozen all told – who left the unmistakable imprint of their personality on the war. In World War I the U-boats were commanded by officers whose names have little distinction, and who never rose above the rank of *Flotillenadmiral* (Commodore). This was not a very lofty position from which to guide the destinies and uphold the cause of the new, untested arm, to argue its priorities against the prestigious surface fleet of the Imperial Navy. Dönitz, by contrast, was already a *Konteradmiral* by October, 1939, and thereafter moved rapidly to the top of the naval profession and beyond. Yet it was the professionalism that he already brought with him in 1935, firmly founded on his practical First World War experience as a sea-going U-boat officer, that chiefly counted. This was something that, by the nature of things, his 1914–18 predecessors could not and did not have. Steeped in U-boat theory and well grounded in U-boat practice, he started the war with reputation and prestige, and despite all setbacks he never lost either. Always – and this was cardinal – he had the admiration and the ear of Hitler, who steadily became more disenchanted with the big surface ships and warmer towards the U-boats. Thus in the Second World War the U-boat arm always had a doughty champion; as he said himself, he was a submariner 'body and soul'.

Anti-submarine warfare has a somewhat different story of development, featuring no individual. When the lookouts on the battleship HMS *Monarch* saw the track of a torpedo approaching from an invisible source on 7 August, 1914, submarine warfare was born. When *U 24* torpedoed the French steamer *Amiral Ganteaume* without warning on 24 October, its 'unrestricted' nature stood revealed; it was, as Admiral Jameson says, 'a new and exceedingly unpleasant happening in the war at sea'.[110]

No apparatus for anti-submarine warfare existed in 1914; it was unknown. As late as 1916 there was considerable doubt in the Admiralty as to whether such an apparatus could even be created; as 'unrestricted warfare' began to make its impact, the Admiralty told Jellicoe:

> No conclusive answer has yet been found to this form of warfare; perhaps no conclusive answer ever will be found.[111]

As related on p. 24, one of Jellicoe's first measures when he became First Sea Lord in that year was to set up an Anti-Submarine Division of the War Staff. This, too, was a significant moment in history; two years later the 'conclusive answer' to the submarine threat of the day had been found. In World War I it was, above all, the introduction of convoy that produced it. Closely linked to this by 1918 was the valuable information provided by Room 40 and the ever-increasing rôle of aircraft, particularly in the protection of convoys. Technology, needless to say, ran through the whole business of anti-submarine warfare like a binding thread – or should one rather say, a range of technologies weaving the tapestry together: electronics, aeronautics, ballistics, explosives, underwater aural aids (hydrophones) etc., etc.? Certainly, in the brief period up to November, 1918, a sound and comprehensive foundation of anti-submarine practice and theory had been evolved.

As with so much else, a great deal of this was sadly lost between the wars. Yet it is worth noting that when war came again in 1939 certain valuable elements were ready waiting. It is difficult to exaggerate the importance of the OIC and above all (for our purposes) of the Submarine Tracking Room; equally difficult to over-rate is the existence of the GC & CS, after sundry trials and alarums, and the embryo at least of the astonishing organization that was to grow up at Bletchley Park. All these were truly new dimensions of processes which had made their first faint stirrings over twenty years before, but now came triumphantly into their own. There was also Coastal Command, weak and under-equipped, uncertain at first of its rôle, but a definite, specific commitment of air power to a maritime war which took little time to declare itself as mainly anti-submarine war. And, of course, once more there was convoy, a world-wide organization of shipping evolved from World War I instruction, only awaiting the starting-gun. And there was radar. If all of these had had to start from scratch in 1939, it is difficult to see how the victory could have been obtained. And on these foundations World War II proceeded, with all technologies in full flight towards an unrecognizable future.

The U-boat wars fully shared one attribute: the emotion they aroused. Writing of 1939–45, Roskill says of the British seamen who fought in the Battle of the Atlantic:

> there is no doubt that the German U-boats did finally arouse feelings of the strongest loathing in their minds.[112]

This is also true of the nation as a whole, and of both wars. The only quibble is with the word 'finally': the sinking of SS *Athenia* on 3 September, 1939, reawakened instantly the feelings which inspired Arthur Balfour to say, after the sinking of the mail boat *Leinster* on 10 October, 1918,

> Brutes they were, and brutes they remain.[113]

For World War I, this was a very understandable attitude; as I have said above (pp. 146–7), 'the contemplation of great vessels suddenly smitten, perhaps in the dead of night, by shattering explosions caused by unseen enemies and rapidly disappearing under the waves with passengers and crews drowned, blown up, or left exposed in open boats, came as a deeply shocking novelty'. Heavily dosed with propaganda, often of the crudest variety, as yet unaware of the vastly more savage capabilities of the industrial society in which it lived, and possessing in general only a highly selective and superficial sense of history, the British public at that time may be forgiven for an unreasoning reaction of outrage to a new and obviously cruel instrument. Even the introduction of poison gas did not have such a powerful emotive effect – poison gas was a battlefield weapon, but the U-boat struck at unarmed civilians and merchant seamen. It also threatened the public at large with starvation. Forgetting the unrefined activities of the heroes of the Elizabethan age in the Spanish Main, forgetting also the robust acceptance by their ancestors of the *guerre de course* of the French privateers, and almost totally unaware of Lord Fisher's pre-war prophecies, the British public response to the U-boats was mainly to howl with rage.

In World War II the same almost superstitious dread of the invisible enemies persisted. Better informed about the sufferings and often ghastly deaths of the ships' crews – the Merchant Navy's 35,000 dead[114] – and at least partially aware of the detestable qualities of Nazism, this generation hated as fiercely as its fathers. There were a great many convinced and loyal Nazis in the U-boat Service, and their arrogant demeanour as prisoners when they were brought ashore did not endear them to the British. Once more, too, the blockade peril made this quarrel personal for all sections of the population. There was no disposition at all to make any equation between the U-boat attack on merchant shipping and Bomber Command's attack on German cities. Today the affinities are more obvious. The two forms of war, both aimed primarily at civilian rather than military targets, and both liable to be targets of much odium themselves on that account, are not to be illuminated by moralization. Secure enough in evaluating the motivations and causes of war, moralization is far less so in judging its conduct. When nations are fighting for their lives, the only moral imperative likely to be accepted is sheer survival. That is the essence of total war.

Great modern wars, based on wide-ranging technology and intensive production techniques, and waged by mass populations, do not lend themselves to decision by single war-winning wonder-weapons. But if such a thing ever did exist, it would seem to have been firmly identified for both the World Wars by Ambassador Page in July, 1917:

> The submarine is the most formidable thing the war has produced – by far – and it gives the German the only earthly chance he has to win.

For as long as the people of the British Isles, and their friends and allies, depend for sustenance on the men who go down to the sea in ships to do business in great waters, the story of how the U-boats were twice defeated will deserve to be retold.

Notes

PART I: THE FIRST ROUND

I/1 *Free from All Scruple (pp. 3–16)*

1   Vol. xi p. 41, noted in the British Official History, *Military Operations, France and Belgium 1916* vol. ii pp. xiv–xv.
2   *My War Memories 1914–1918* vol. i p. 304; Hutchinson, 1919.
3   In the Imperial German Army, the *Kaiser* was designated as Commander-in-Chief, although he had no executive function; the Chief of Staff carried out the duties normally associated with a C-in-C.
4   Quoted in *The Most Formidable Thing* by Sir William Jameson pp. 112–13; Hart-Davis 1965.
5   Peter J. Parish, *The American Civil War* p. 421; Eyre Methuen, 1975.
6   Sir J. E. Edmonds (the Official Historian), *A Short History of World War I* p. 80; OUP 1951.
7   Lord Hankey, *The Supreme Command 1914–18* vol. i pp. 97–8; Allen & Unwin, 1961.
8   Peter Padfield, *Dönitz: The Last Führer* p. 73; Gollancz, 1984.
9   Jameson, op. cit. p. 137.
10 On that date the Admiralty had informed ship-owners that the hoisting of a neutral flag was a recognized *ruse de guerre*, often adopted in past wars, and not contrary to any 'international law', providing no hostile act was carried out under cover of the flag.
11 Jameson, op. cit. p. 154; cf. Dönitz, Order No. 154, December, 1940: 'Care only for your own boat ... We must be hard in this war' (see p. 218).
12 Admiral of the Fleet Lord Jellicoe, *The Crisis of the Naval War* p. 38; Cassell, 1920.

13 Patrick Beesly, *Room 40: British Naval Intelligence 1914–18* pp. 113–14; Hamish Hamilton, 1982.

14 Jameson, op. cit. p. 164.

15 The available statistics of ships sunk and tonnages lost vary considerably; I have chosen to use throughout the total supplied in the semi-official *Seaborne Trade* by C. E. Fayle (vol. iii p. 465; John Murray, 1924), which is also followed by Lord Hankey and Professor Arthur Marder in his majestic *From the Dreadnought to Scapa Flow* (vol. v p. 111).

16 *Thoughts and Adventures* p. 88; Odhams, 1947 (first published, 1932).

17 This quotation and those following relating to the Pless conference are from the official *Naval Operations* (Sir Henry Newbolt) vol. iv pp. 239 et seq.; Longmans, Green, 1928.

18 Sir John Wheeler-Bennett, in *Hindenburg: The Wooden Titan* (Macmillan Papermac, 1967, p. 89), says: '"I am not interested in a contest between armed mobs," replied the great Moltke when asked in 1864 his opinion of the operations of Grant and Lee before Richmond, and the opinion of the German General Staff had changed little in fifty years.'

19 Royal United Service Institution Journal, August, 1968: 'The High Seas Fleet 1917–18' by David Woodward.

20 Newbolt, op. cit. p. 241.

21 Ibid. p. 243, and next quotation.

22 Roger Parkinson, *Tormented Warrior: Ludendorff and the Supreme Command* p. 116; Hodder & Stoughton, 1978.

23 Ministry of Defence, Air Historical Branch: AHB/II/117/3(A): *The Royal Air Force in the Maritime War* i p. 24.

24 Newbolt, op. cit. pp. 345–6.

25 Ibid. p. 270.

I/2 *The Most Formidable Thing (pp. 17–39)*

1 As the war continued, five flotillas of submarines were formed to serve under the High Sea Fleet: No 1, Brunsbüttelkoog, No 2, Wilhelmshaven, Nos 3 and 4, Emden, and finally (September, 1917) No 5, Bremerhaven.

2 All U-boat statistics from R. H. Gibson & Maurice Prendergast, *The German Submarine War*, Constable 1931, Appendix III; 'Aces', ibid. p. 189.

3 *U 42* was built in Italy and never delivered to the German Navy.

4   Gibson & Prendergast, op. cit.

5   Colonel Repington, *The First World War* i p. 19; Constable 1920.

6   Padfield, op. cit. p. 67; the quotation is from K. Neureuther & C. Bergen (eds.), *U-Boat Stories*, Constable 1931.

7   Jameson, op. cit. p. 223.

8   AHB/II/117/3(A) p. 26.

9   Repington, op. cit. i p. 440; Jan. 24, 1917.

10 Hindenburg, *Out of my Life* p. 254; Cassell, 1920.

11 AHB/II/117/3 (A) op. cit.

12 e.g. the Battle of Amiens, 8 August, 1918, in which the Allied air component consisted of 800 aircraft of the R.A.F. and 1,104 French, a total of 1,904.

13 Except by perceptive individuals, the true nature of submarine warfare was not foreseen either in Britain or in Germany. The Admiralty, up to the outbreak of war, regarded the submarine primarily as a defensive weapon, an adjunct to coast defence; its scouting ability in the North Sea, and its offensive capacity in the Baltic and the Sea of Marmora came as surprises. As we have seen, the German Navy had no plan to use submarines against trade in 1914; the rôle which became characteristic of the U-boat in two wars was an improvisation.

14 This lack of small craft was in large part due to Admiral Fisher's sweeping programme of scrapping obsolete ships between 1904 and 1906. Small, slow ships were anathema to Fisher, who branded them as too weak to fight and too slow to run away. Critics of his measures suggested that these vessels might nevertheless have value for trade protection, but Fisher brushed this aside with the assertion that any attack on commerce would be made by powerful cruiser squadrons. It was not until the eve of war, when he was no longer First Sea Lord, that Fisher proclaimed the submarine danger (p. 5) – and very few were prepared to listen to him.

15 Jellicoe, op. cit. p. 185; a large part of the Auxiliary Patrol was permanently employed on minesweeping.

16 Richard Hough, *A History of Fighting Ships*, p. 114; Octopus Books 1975.

17 Churchill, *The World Crisis* i p. 109; Odhams Ed. 1938.

18 All destroyer statistics from F. J. Dittmar & J. J. Colledge, *British Warships 1914–1919* pp. 52–77; Ian Allen 1972. Churchill (op. cit. p. 106) is scathing on the subject of speed: 'Building slow destroyers! One might as well breed slow racehorses.'

19 It should be noted that in all navies destroyers carried only one torpedo per tube (Marder, op. cit. ii p. 440).

20 Jellicoe, op. cit. p. 59; the Admiralty Technical History (TH 7 pp. 18–19) says, 'Until the middle of June, 1917, the usual depth-charge armament for any vessel was two Type "D" *or* (my italics) "D*".' Jameson (op. cit. p. 213) adds that 'old destroyers on the East Coast carried only *one* depth charge apiece'.

21 R. M. Grant, *U-Boats Destroyed* p. 144; Putnam 1964.

22 Jellicoe, op. cit. pp. 56–7; the total includes, as well as the 7.5-inch howitzers, Stick Bomb Throwers 'on the lines of trench mortars' of 3.5-inch calibre throwing a 200-lb bomb with a 98-lb burster to a range of 1,200 yards or a 350-lb bomb with a 200-lb burster to a range of 650 yards (Admiralty TH 7 pp. 10–11).

23 Ibid p. 61; the reader will note the vivid contrast between the close-quarters fighting of the submarine war and the ranges of up to 20,000 yards at which the great ships of the surface fleets usually engaged.

24 Ibid p. 62.

25 Admiralty TH 7 p. 32.

26 Beesly, op. cit. p. 7.

27 Ibid, p. 30.

28 Gibson & Prendergast, op. cit. p. 88.

29 Beesly, op. cit. pp. 254–5.

30 *Naval Operations* iv. p. 380.

31 op. cit. p. 50.

32 Ibid p. 91.

33 Correlli Barnett, *The Swordbearers* pp. 187, 193; Eyre & Spottiswoode 1963. It may be noted that unsatisfactory torpedoes are a depressingly recurring factor in British defence. On 13 September, 1985, the Naval Correpondent of *The Daily Telegraph* related 'the dismal story of the Navy's post-war torpedo programme'. It had taken, he said, 20 years and £1 billion to get the Navy's only useful torpedo into service, due to reliance on pre-war machinery and technology.

34 These were: *Acacias* (1915): 24 vessels, 1,200 tons, overall length 262½ feet, 16½ knots, 2 12-pounder guns, 2 3-pdr. AA guns; *Azaleas* (1915): 12 vessels, characteristics as the *Acacias*, but armed with 2 4.7-inch or 4-inch guns; *Arabis* (1915–16): 36 vessels, 1,250 tons, oa length 268 feet, 16 knots, 2 4.7-inch (4-inch in 6 vessels), 2 3-pdr. AA guns; *Aubretias* (1916–17: 12 vessels, 1,250 tons, oa length 255 feet, 17½ knots, 2 4-inch, 1 3-pdr. AA guns; *Anchusas* (1917–18): 28 vessels, 1,290 tons, oa length 262½ feet, 16½ knots, 2 4-inch, 2 12-pdr. guns. Dittmar & College, op. cit.

35 Walter Raleigh, *The War in the Air* (Official History) i p. 389; OUP 1922 etc.

36 Ibid, p. 401. The Avro 504 was powered by one 80 hp Gnome engine, giving a maximum speed of 82 mph at sea level. One bomb failed to release.

37 Owen Thetford, *British Naval Aircraft 1912–1958*, p. 248; Putnam 1958.

38 Ibid, p. 72.

I/3 *Engage the Enemy More Closely!* (*pp. 40–56*)

1 British losses: February, 313,486 gross tons, March, 353,478.

2 C. R. M. F. Cruttwell, *A History of the Great War 1914–1918* p. 383 f.n.; OUP 1934.

3 See Terraine, *The Road to Passchendaele* p. 38; Leo Cooper, 1977.

4 Repington, op. cit. i p. 467.

5 Hankey, op. cit. ii p. 468.

6 Fayle, op. cit. iii p. 91.

7 Ibid.

8 *The Times History of the War* xiii pp. 57–8.

9 H. W. Wilson in *The Great War: The Standard History of the All-Europe Conflict* ix p. 255; ed. H. W. Wilson & J. A. Hammerton, Amalgamated Press.

10 See Terraine, *The Smoke and the Fire* pp. 22–33; Sidgwick & Jackson, 1980.

11 Jameson, op. cit. p. 182.

12 Ibid p. 221. It is to be noted that in the case of the first sinking of a merchantman by a submarine, the small British steamer *Glitra* by *U 17* (*Korvettenkapitän* Feldkirchner) on 20 October, 1914, fourteen miles off the Norwegian coast, the worst that could be charged against the behaviour of the Germans was 'a puerile exhibition of rudeness' in tearing up the British flag and trampling on the pieces. *U 17* stopped the *Glitra*, sent a boarding party to her, and, having given the captain ten minutes to abandon ship, proceeded to scuttle her by opening the seacocks. The U-boat then towed the boats some miles towards the coast until they could be picked up by a Norwegian torpedo-boat. It was noted with surprise and also, no doubt, relief, that 'More humanity has survived in modern naval warfare of the most scientific order than had been expected.' (David Hannay in *The Great World War*, ed. F. A. Mumby, i pp. 251–2; Gresham Publishing Co., 1915).

13 Op. cit. i p. 454.

14 *Journals and Letters of Reginald, Viscount Esher*, iv p. 115; Nicholson & Watson 1938.

15   The *Journal* of the Royal United Services Institute in December, 1977, carried a most interesting article by Captain R. A. Bowling (USN, Retd) entitled '*The Negative Influence of Mahan on Anti-Submarine Warfare*'. It well repays study.

16   See *The Smoke and the Fire*, op. cit., Table C, p. 46.

17   For number of ships see Admiralty T. H. 7 pp. 7–8; for tonnage see Fayle as above. The remaining 4% of losses were due to mines.

18   Fayle, op. cit. p. 91.

19   Ibid.

20   Newbolt, op. cit. p. 379.

21   Op. cit. ii p. 1233.

22   *The Road to Passchendaele* op. cit. p. 72.

23   Rear-Admiral W. S. Sims & B. J. Hendrick, *The Victory at Sea*, pp. 6–7; John Murray 1927.

24   Op. cit. p. 380.

25   Ibid.

26   Ibid p. 382.

27   Donald Macintyre, *The Battle of the Atlantic* p. 13; Pan Books 1983.

28   Ibid p. 14.

29   The advent of steam, which had the effect of making Britain's large reserve of sailing warships obsolete for all but minor purposes, caused considerable alarm. There was a serious scare of French invasion in the early 1850s, but it had little foundation in naval fact, and shortly afterwards (1854–55) Britain and France were allies in war.

30   Op. cit. pp. 15–16.

31   Fayle, op. cit. iii p. 469.

32   Captain A. T. Mahan, *The Life of Nelson* p. 611; Sampson Low, Marston, 1899. The cry dates from the period 1803–05 when Nelson was Commander-in-Chief, Mediterranean, a sea made perilous not only by French privateers but also by the Barbary corsairs of evil fame.

33   Ibid. p. 28; uttered by Nelson in 1781.

34   Admiralty War Staff, Operations Division; C. B. 0259, Jan, 1917 (Naval Historical Branch).

35   Op. cit. i pp. 69–70.

36   Later Admiral Sir Reginald, Third Sea Lord and Controller of the Navy 1934–39.

37   See Note 5.

38   Op. cit. ii pp. 1234–5.

39 *War Memoirs* i p. 688 (Odhams ed.); first published by Nicholson & Watson, 1933–6.

I/4 *Convoy Acted Like a Spell (pp. 57–84)*

1 *The Smoke and the Fire* p. 173; a good example of 'Military Mind' mythology will be found on pp. 130–41 of that work.

2 Sir Maurice Dean, *The Royal Air Force and Two World Wars* p. 6; Cassell, 1979.

3 The small number of British ships still trading with Holland had been organized in a loose convoy system on a roughly weekly basis in July, 1916, protected by the light forces under Commodore Tyrwhitt at Harwich.

4 Lord Beaverbrook, *Men and Power* pp. 155–6; Hutchinson, 1956.

5 Op. cit. ii p. 650.

6 Stephen Roskill, *Hankey: Man of Secrets* i p. 382; Collins, 1970.

7 Op. cit. v p. 44.

8 Rear-Admiral Sir Kenelm Creighton, *Convoy Commodore* pp. 55–6; Futura, 1976.

9 Cyril Falls, *The First World War* p. 273; Longmans, 1960.

10 Quoted in Beaverbrook, op. cit. p. 158.

11 The Convoy Committee consisted of: Captain H. W. Longden, RN, Fleet Paymaster H. W. E. Manisty, RN, Commander J. S. Wilde, RN, Lieutenant G. E. Burton, RN, Mr N. A. Leslie (later Sir Norman), Ministry of Shipping; it will be noted that this extremely important committee was not burdened with flag officers. It presented its report on 6 June.

12 Op cit. p. 60.

13 Naval Historical Branch: *The Defeat of the Enemy Attack on Shipping 1939–1945* by Lt-Cdrs F. W. Barley & D. Waters, 1b Table 4.

14 Admiralty Technical History, TH 14 p. 28; the same source informs us that the largest Atlantic convoy in World War I was HN 73, leaving New York on 18 June, 1918, with 47 ships and arriving without loss.

15 Barley & Waters, op. cit. 1b Table 5.

16 Op. cit. p. 227. The even greater trepidations of the US Navy should be noted. When asked in May to form a convoy of 16–20 Allied merchantmen, to accompany a division of 6 destroyers which was about to make the crossing, the Navy Department answered that this was too many, and that merchant vessels should only sail in groups of four. As a result, the destroyers crossed by themselves, and the merchantmen followed singly, without escort. (Newbolt, op. cit. pp. 44–5.)

17   Op. cit. p. 51; my italics.

18   Padfield, op. cit. p. 74.

19   Op. cit.

20   Quoted in Gibson & Prendergast, op. cit. p. 355. Jameson (op. cit. p. 225) says the U-boat fleet numbered 150, 50 at sea in British home waters.

21   F. S. Oliver, *The Anvil of War* p. 198; Macmillan, 1936.

22   CAB 27/6; War Policy Committee No 5, 18 June.

23   Op. cit. p. 17.

24   Ibid. p. 9.

25   Beesly, op. cit. p. 62 f.n.

26   *The World Crisis* i p. 362.

27   *Sir Douglas Haig's Despatches*, ed. Lt.-Col. J. H. Boraston p. 77; Dent, 1919.

28   Op. cit. i p. 579.

29   Op. cit. ii p. 1233.

30   Op. cit. v pp. 54–5; Jameson (p. 225) says that 31 destroyers and 10 submarines were involved.

31   *The Road to Passchendaele* p. 17.

32   Ibid. pp. 157–8, quoting CAB 27/6, War Policy Committee No 9, 20 June.

33   Ibid. p. 158.

34   *War Memoirs* i p. 699; Odham's ed.; 1936. Haig's private opinion of Jellicoe was less flattering; their last meeting had been in Paris, and Haig wrote to his wife on 7 May: 'I am afraid he does not impress me – indeed, he strikes me as being an old woman!' (Author's papers).

35   *The Supreme Command* ii p. 635.

36   Op. cit. i p. 700.

37   B. B. Schofield, *British Sea Power* p. 62; Batsford, 1967.

38   Op. cit. p. 15.

39   Air Historical Branch, Air Publication 125, *A Short History of the Royal Air Force* (1936) p. 254.

40   Ibid. p. 255.

41   R. M. Grant, *U-Boat Intelligence* p. 185; Putnam 1969.

42   Air Publication 125 p. 257.

43   Newbolt, op. cit. v p. 36.

44   CAB 27/6, op. cit.

45   H. A. Jones *The War in the Air* (Official History) iv p. 63; op. cit.

46　Air Publication 125 pp. 266–7.

47　Op. cit. p. 172.

48　Newbolt, op. cit. v pp. 61–2.

49　Gordon A. Craig, *Germany 1866–1945* p. 383; O.U.P. 1978.

50　Erzberger argued that world tonnage in 1914 had been 49,089,552 gross tons (a somewhat larger figure than the Lloyds Register; see p. 47). Since then 8,561,285 tons would have been built and launched, making a total of 57,650,837. On a very sanguine estimate, 19,450,000 tons would have been destroyed by all causes. This would reduce the available total to 38,200,837 tons – just under 78% of the 1914 total. The Entente Powers would thus have a tonnage far above their minimum requirements available. He asked the Naval Staff whether this was or was not the case, but received only a perfunctory reply

51　Hoch, Erzberger and other participants in the debate are quoted in *The First World War* ed. Richard Thoumin pp. 414–15; Secker & Warburg 1963.

52　Wheeler-Bennett, op. cit. p. 109.

53　Ibid. p. 122.

54　Op. cit. v p. 73

I/5　*Slack Water (pp. 85–104)*

1　Elizabeth Longford, *Wellington: The Years of the Sword* p. 475; Weidenfeld & Nicolson, 1969; Richard Aldington, *Wellington* p. 226; Heinemann, 1946.

2　Op. cit. v p. 136.

3　Op cit. iii p. 158.

4　Ibid.

5　R. M. Grant's list of U-boats sunk (*U-Boat Intelligence* p. 186) allocates *UC 21*, which sailed on 25 September for operations in the Shetlands area, to 'Sept.–Oct.'; the cause and exact location of her sinking are uncertain.

6　Four of the losses (*U 66*, *U 88*, *UC 42* and *UC 6*) are definitely attributed to mines; *UC 21* is a probable mine casualty; *U 28* is attributed to 'explosion'; two (*U 49* and *UC 33*) were rammed; *U 45* was torpedoed by Submarine *D 7*; *UB 32* was sunk by aircraft attack (see p. 77); *UC 55* was a loss by accident.

7　Beesly, op. cit. p. 262.

8　Op. cit. v p. 103.

9　Op. cit. v pp. 137–8; the next three quotations are from the same source.

10 Sir Henry Newbolt, with becoming tact, calls the existing anti-submarine system 'a scheme which has not yet succeeded'.

11 These figures are extracted from Newbolt, op. cit. v p. 139 and Appendix B I(a).

12 Naval Historical Branch: Barley & Waters, op. cit. 1B, Table 1.

13 Newbolt, op. cit. v p. 141; my italics.

14 AHB/II/117/3(A) pp. 29–30.

15 In 1916 the Germans had introduced large (1,510/1,870 tons) unarmed commercial submarine freighters. The first of these, *Deutschland*, left Kiel on 23 June and arrived at Baltimore on 9 July with a cargo of dyes and precious stones. She returned to Germany in August, loaded with zinc, silver, copper and nickel, all in short supply due to the blockade. Her sister ship, *Bremen*, should have arrived in America in September, but she mysteriously vanished. With America's entry into the war, the blockade-breaking rôle disappeared; *Deutschland* was converted into a warship (*U 155*) and a new class (*U 151–157*) was constructed on similar lines. They were slower than their contemporaries (12.4 knots on the surface, 5.3 submerged); their endurance, however, was remarkable: 13,130 miles. Their principal armament was two 150-mm guns. The menacing feature of these vessels was their ability to maintain a damaging cruise at distances where U-boats had previously paid only flying visits. They proved, however, to be considerably less dangerous than was at first feared.

16 Present in everyone's mind was the disappointing opening of the Flanders offensive. The first day, 31 July, had been a half-success: good progress at first, but gains later largely lost to German counter-attacks. Worst of all was the onset of drenching rain, which then proceeded to choke all the August operations in a sea of mud. It was not until late in September – long after the Naval Conference – that the offensive regained impetus. Meanwhile, hopes of capturing Ostend and Zeebrugge receded, and attempts to put those ports out of action by naval bombardment proved ineffective.

17 Newbolt, op. cit. v p. 157.

18 Op. cit. p. 173.

19 'Barrage' was a word correctly used by the Navy, being the French for 'barrier'. The Army had also used it correctly at first, meaning a barrier of artillery fire to prevent an enemy advance. By 1917, however, it had been corrupted to mean the curtain of shells in front of one's own attack – an altogether different matter.

20 Newbolt, op. cit. v p. 133; following quotations from the same source.

21 Ibid. p. 147; next quotation likewise.

22 Lt.-Commander Brooke was severely wounded almost immediately, but continued to command. Only when satisfied that all confidential papers and code books had been destroyed did he give orders to abandon ship, expecting to stay with her, but surviving crew members carried him to a Carley raft and took him off. Lt.-Commander Fox, having also given orders to abandon ship, was last seen swimming in the icy water.

23 Op. cit. v p. 157.

24 It is to be noted that *Partridge*, just before the action on 12 December, was able to transmit a signal to the C.-in-C. which was intercepted by the flagship of the covering force, which immediately hastened towards the scene. A second signal was picked up shortly afterwards, and though the call-sign was obliterated by German jamming, the message came clearly through.

25 Beesly, referring to the October attack on the convoys, remarks that Room 40 was working on the important decodes at high speed, placing the results with the Operations Division within a maximum of 50 minutes from the time of interception. He comments (p. 278): 'Whether it was the man or the faulty system, which he had devised and apparently refused to modify in the light of all experience, the *Mary Rose* disaster was yet one more example of Oliver's many inexplicable failures to make proper use of the priceless intelligence at his disposal.'

26 Newbolt's account (v pp. 189–90) makes sad but stirring reading.

27 Op. cit. v p. 194.

28 This and the next figure are from Newbolt v Appendix C.

29 Five U-boats were also sunk in the Black Sea – Bosporus – Sea of Marmora area between August and December, 1916.

30 Grant, op. cit. p. 186; *UC 62*, believed at the time to have been torpedoed by HM Submarine *E 45*, was almost certainly lost in a deep minefield off Portland.

31 Newbolt, op. cit. v pp. 195–6.

32 Op. cit. p. 231.

33 Op. cit. iii pp. 251–2.

34 Ibid.

35 AHB/II/117/3(A) p. 40 f.n.

36 Op. cit. v pp. 194–5.

37 Op. cit. i p. 711.

38 Captain S. W. Roskill, *The Dismissal of Sir John Jellicoe*; Journal of Contemporary History vol. 1 Number 4, October, 1966 p. 73; following quotation, ibid.; George V's letter, ibid. p. 77.

39 Op. cit. v pp. 4–5.

40 Beesly, op. cit. p. 272.

I/6 *Foiled Rather Than Defeated* (*pp. 105–128*)

1 See Terraine *To Win a War* pp. 140–41; Sidgwick & Jackson 1978.

2 See Terraine, *The Road to Passchendaele* p. 205.

3 In his very useful article, *The U-Boat Campaign and Third Ypres* (*RUSI Journal*, Nov. 1959), Captain Roskill shows that the danger from the Flanders flotillas was seriously over-rated; whereas they were responsible for one-third of ships sunk, the High Sea Fleet flotillas were responsible for two-thirds. On the other hand, General von Kuhl, Chief of Staff to Crown Prince Rupprecht of Bavaria's Group of Armies in the Flanders area, posing the question whether, after their heavy losses in the Battle of Messines in June, the Germans should have learned a lesson and withdrawn altogether in the Flanders sector, states among the reasons for not doing so: 'In Flanders a halt had to be called against further withdrawals so that the U-boat bases could be protected' (von Kuhl, *Der Weltkreig 1914–1918*; translated by Col. R. Macleod).

4 Op. cit. iii p. 255.

5 The Second Flanders Flotilla was formed in October, 1917.

6 Grant, op. cit. pp. 66–7.

7 Op. cit. p. 63; Grant lists *UC 1*, 18/19 July; *UB 20*, 28 July; *UC 6*, 27 Sept.; *UC 21*, Sept./Oct.; *UC 14*, 3 Oct.; *UC 16*, 14 Oct. (?). The very severe losses of the UC-boats at this time will be noted. Out of 63 U-boats lost in 1917, 32 were UC-boats.

8 Jellicoe (op. cit. p. 186) informs us that an average of 80–100 merchant vessels passed Dover every day in 1917.

9 Churchill (*World Crisis* ii p. 1239) states: 'The Dover passage saved a small Flanders U-boat nearly eight days on its fourteen days' cruise, and a larger boat from the Bight six days out of twenty-five.'

10 Vice-Admiral Bacon had retired from the Navy before war broke out, and was general manager of the Coventry Ordnance Works, a firm which, according to Churchill, represented 'one-third of our heavy-gun-producing power'. The 15-inch howitzer was at first manned by Royal Marine Artillery; eleven more were constructed, and Admiral Bacon managed to get himself appointed a Colonel, Royal Marines, to command them in action. In 1916 they were made over to the Army; they did not find great favour with the Royal Artillery, on account of their short range (10,795 yards maximum).

11 Haig Diary, 18 September, 1916; see Robert Blake, *The Private Papers of Douglas Haig* p. 167; Eyre & Spottiswoode 1952.

12 Haig Diary, 16 July, 1917; author's papers.

13 *Thoughts and Adventures*, op. cit. p. 102.

14 Op. cit. v p. 181.

15 *World Crisis* ii p. 1239.

16 Losses in the Dover Patrol and area were, according to Newbolt, 1 destroyer, 7 drifters and 1 (empty) transport sunk, 1 destroyer and 2 drifters badly damaged; Jellicoe says 1 destroyer and 6 drifters.

17 *Thoughts and Adventures* p. 105; Churchill is here describing the scene on 14 Feb. (see below).

18 *World Crisis* ii p. 1242.

19 Op. cit. v pp. 39–40.

20 Ibid.

21 *Thoughts and Adventures* p. 105.

22 Op. cit. p. 95.

23 Grant, op. cit. p. 88.

24 Jameson, op. cit. p. 239; the last U-boat to attempt the Dover Barrage was *UB 103* (Hundius), sunk at 5052/0127E on 16 September.

25 Cruttwell, op. cit. p. 388 f.n.

26 Op. cit. p. 109.

27 Barley & Waters, op. cit. pp. 11–12.

28 Ibid. (my italics).

29 January: 306,658 gross tons (179,973 British); February: 318,957 gross tons (226,896 British); March: 342,597 gross tons (199,458 British).

30 Cruttwell, op. cit. p. 338.

31 Op. cit. v p. 205.

32 Ibid. p. 206.

33 Jameson, op. cit. p. 254.

34 This and following statistics are from Gibson & Prendergast, op. cit. Appendix D; all figures are as of the 10th of each month. According to this table, the highest number of U-boats ever in commission was 140 in October, 1917, with 55 (39.2%) actually at sea. The highest number at sea was 61 in June, 1917, out of 132 (46.2%). In December of that year there were 60 at sea out of 134 (44.7%). Increasingly, as in World War II, it was not the numbers, either in total or at sea, that mattered, but what they were able to achieve.

35 Op. cit. ii p. 290.

36 Field-Marshal Sir Douglas Haig issued his famous 'Backs to the Wall' Order at the height of the Battle of the Lys on 11 April, 1918 ('With our backs to the wall, and believing in the justice of our cause, each one of us must fight on to the end.') See Terraine, *Douglas Haig: The Educated Soldier* pp. 432–3; Hutchinson 1963.

37 Jürgen Rohwer, *The Critical Convoy Battles of March 1943* p. 11; Ian Allan, 1977.

38 Op. cit. v pp. 278–82 including all following quotations on pp. 111–12.

39 Op. cit. p. 241.

40 L. Doughty Jnr. in *US Naval Institute Proceedings 61* (1935) p. 356, quoted in Grant, op. cit. p. 50.

41 Grant, op. cit. p. 178.

42 Op. cit. v p. 338.

43 AHB/II/117/3(A) pp. 41–3.

44 A.H.B.: Air Publication No. 125, *A Short History of the Royal Air Force* p. 333; revised edition, July, 1936. Three Anti-Submarine Groups were formed: No 9 (Plymouth), No 10 (Portsmouth) and No 18 (East Coast).

45 Edward Wright, *The Wonders of Wireless in the War*, in H. W. Wilson & J. A. Hammerton, *The Great War* vol. xiii; Amalgamated Press, 1919.

46 Barley & Waters, op. cit. p. 10.

47 I.e. 'offensive' action.

48 AHB/II/117/3(A) p. 43.

49 *The World Crisis* ii p. 1248.

50 Op. cit. p. 143, including all following quotations.

I/7 *Small Advantages* (*pp. 130–140*)

1 Gibson & Prendergast, op. cit. Appendix III D. The strength of the Flanders flotillas in 1918 was:

Month	Total	At sea	Month	Total	At sea
January	30	7	June	23	11
February	30	7	July	24	8
March	29	8	August	22	10
April	26	8	September	18	7
May	25	8	October	13	8

2   Op. cit. ii p. 1243.

3   Grant, *U-Boats Destroyed* p. 90. Not all UB- and UC-boats were in the Flanders flotillas, but the breakdown of U-boat losses by types is interesting; U-boats, 62; UB-boats, 64; UC-boats, 52.

4   Newbolt, op. cit. v pp. 298–9.

5   Scheer, qu. Jameson, op. cit. p. 244.

6   Ibid. p. 245.

7   Ibid. *U 117–21* were large boats displacing 1,510 tons submerged; *U 139–41* displaced 2,480 tons, the largest type built. *U 151–7* were 'U-cruisers', 1,870 tons, initially conversions of the *Deutschland* class cargo carriers.

8   Op. cit. v p. 348; Newbolt's figures for shipping sunk differ from Jameson's: 'From the time of their first arrival to the middle of August, when their activity was in its meridian, the U-boat commanders on the American coast had sunk thirty-six sailing vessels – some of which were mere coastal craft of between 20 and 50 tons – and twenty-nine steamships of all sizes.'

9   Ibid. pp. 336–7; the shipping losses of the last three months of the war are indicative:

Month	World	British
September	187,881 gt	136,859 gt
October	118,559 gt	59,229 gt
November	17,682 gt	10,195 gt

10 See Terraine, *To Win a War* p. 121.

11 Jameson, op. cit. pp. 247–8.

12 The progress of these negotiations is discussed in some detail in *To Win a War*, Chaps. VIII and IX.

13 Ibid. pp. 198–9.

14 Op. cit. ii p. 1962.

15 Harold Nicolson, *Peacemaking 1919* p. 24; University Paperbacks (Methuen) 1964.

16 Op. cit. ii p. 756.

17 *Sir Douglas Haig's Despatches*, p. 298, Dent, 1919.

18 See pp. 222–4.

19 Beesly, op. cit. p. 294.

20 Ibid. p. 295.

21 Ibid. p. 298.

22 Jameson, op. cit. p. 250.

23 Op. cit. v pp. 359–60.

24 Churchill, *The World Crisis* ii p. 1248; the phrase 'purchased so dearly' refers to the alienation of opinion which swung America towards the Allied cause.

I/8 *The Battle Done* (*pp. 141–150*)

1 Op. cit. p. 251; Gibson & Prendergast (Appendix III A) say that 7 U-boats were 'lost on the way to surrender'; Jameson is very reticent about his sources, but he was writing 34 years later, with access to more information.

2 *U-Boat Intelligence* pp. 182–90.

3 Jameson, op. cit. p. 249; Gibson & Prendergast say that 14 U-boats were scuttled.

4 Gibson & Prendergast, op. cit. Appendix III A.

5 U-Boats Destroyed pp. 143–4.

6 Op. cit. Appendix II.

7 *White Heat* p. 103.

8 *U-Boat Intelligence* p. 169.

9 Op. cit. p. 309 for this and following quotation.

10 *Ultra Goes to War* p. 71; Hutchinson, 1978. It may be noted that British GHQ Intelligence in 1918 was able to keep track of the German build-up for the great offensive which began on 21 March with startling speed and accuracy; but it takes a lot more than accurate Intelligence to withstand the onslaught of 50 battleworthy German divisions on the first day of battle alone.

11 Op. cit. p. 263.

12 *U-Boats Destroyed* p. 160.

13 Tirpitz, September 1917, quoted by Jameson, op. cit. p. 233.

14 The work of Robert Fulton (1765–1815) in pioneering submarines with his *Nautilus* (launched at Rouen in 1800) is succinctly described by Jameson, op. cit. pp. 28–35.

15 Quoted in Marder, *The Anatomy of British Sea Power* p. 355; Frank Cass, 1940.

16 See Alfred Price, *Aircraft versus Submarine* p. 23; William Kimber, 1973.

17 AHB/II/117/3(A) p. 44. Barley and Waters, op. cit. p. 8, make an interesting comparison: 'During the last six months of the First World

War the anti-submarine aircraft in Home Waters (excluding those with the Fleet, and kite-balloons) amounted to a daily average strength of 189 aeroplanes, 300 seaplanes and flying-boats, and 75 airships. Of this total of 564 aircraft an average of 310 were daily ready for service. Coastal Command in February 1943 – during the most critical period of the U-boat war in the Atlantic – had a strength of 118 flying-boats and 293 anti-U-boat aircraft based upon the United Kingdom and Northern Ireland, Iceland and Gibraltar. Of this total of 411 aircraft 210 were available for operations.' •

18 AHB/II/117/3(A) Appendix VIII p. 4.

19 Ibid. text, op. cit.

20 Marder, *From the Dreadnought to Scapa Flow*, 5, p. 103.

21 Totals vary from source to source; this (including fishermen) is from Edmonds, *Short History of World War I*, p. 426.

PART II: INTERVAL

The Insidious Submarine (pp. 153–207)

1 Schofield op. cit. p. 72.

2 Correlli Barnett, *The Collapse of British Power* pp. 248–9; Eyre Methuen, 1972.

3 Austen Chamberlain became Chancellor of the Exchequer on 10 January, 1919, following the Coalition victory, led by Mr Lloyd George, in the 'Coupon' or 'Khaki' Election of 14 December, 1918. The First Lord of the Admiralty in this administration was the Rt Hon Walter H. Long, and the First Sea Lord remained Admiral Sir Rosslyn Wemyss.

4 The overwhelmingly larger part of this debt (some £855 million) was to the United States. Britain herself was owed £1,825 million, but £483 million of this was by the USSR – in other words, a write-off – £90 million by Belgium, subsequently taken over by bankrupt Germany, and £446 million by France, who showed great unwillingness to pay anything until she had received 'reparations' from Germany. War Debts and Reparations proved to be the two intractable economic issues of the post-war years, and the Polonius-posture adopted by Britain was helpful to no one. The figures quoted here are from David Thomson, *England in the Twentieth Century* and Stephen King-Hall, *Our Own Times*; Nicholson & Watson, 1938.

5 The infant Royal Air Force, in its struggle for survival at this period, made great play with its comparative cheapness. The Government was much struck by the (well-advertised) rôle of an RAF squadron in suppressing the revolt of the 'Mad Mullah', a fanatic who had troubled the British forces in Somaliland for a decade. In the words of Mr Leopold Amery, then Under-Secretary at the Colonial Office, after the RAF's bombing attacks, 'All was over in less than three weeks. The total cost . . . worked out at £77,000, the cheapest war in history. For the next twenty years . . . Somaliland enjoyed the blessings of an undisturbed peace.' A somewhat similar performance in Iraq between 1921–23 helped to clinch the survival question. For better or for worse, between 1921–34 the Air Estimates were continuously held below £20 million.

6 This belief was widely shared; even so well-known a pacifist as Mr Ramsay MacDonald was heard to say, 'Our Navy is us'.

7 Roskill, *Naval Policy between the Wars* i pp. 106–7; Collins, 1968.

8 Stephen King-Hall, op. cit. p. 223.

9 Uneasiness about Japan was present in a number of minds; Colonel Repington, Military Correspondent of *The Morning Post*, was lunching with Mr Edwin Montagu on 3 July, 1918, and told him: 'It was only if Japan and Germany coalesced that we should have trouble, but I thought that Japan, though very ambitious, would not kick over the traces and risk her destinies.' (*The First World War* ii p. 325; Constable, 1920.)

10 Roskill, op. cit. pp. 278–83.

11 Barnett, op. cit. p. 272.

12 King-Hall, op. cit. p. 224; the Five-Power Treaty for Limitation of Naval Armaments was signed by Britain, the United States, Japan, France and Italy, who agreed that their respective naval strengths should be in the ratio of $5:5:3:1.7:1.7$. The Four Power Treaty was signed by Britain, the United States, France and Japan.

13 The High Sea Fleet made another sortie on 18–19 August, 1916, but the intention was purely to lure the Grand Fleet into a U-boat ambush. Eight Zeppelins scouted for the Germans with little success; 24 U-boats deployed in five lines succeeded only in torpedoing two light cruisers (a British submarine countered by torpedoing the battleship *Westfalen*). However, the episode gave Jellicoe great concern, and helped to restrict the movements of the Grand Fleet in the North Sea thereafter.

14 *Seaplane* carriers had been in regular use from the beinning of the war (see pp. 36–7).

15 HMS *Furious* (whose sister ships were *Courageous* and *Glorious*)

was originally designed as a fast battle cruiser with a speed of 32.5 knots and mounting two 18-inch guns. All three ships were launched in 1916, but almost at once the decision was taken to convert them. The forward 18-inch gun of *Furious* was replaced by a 228-foot flying deck. It was on this that Sqdn-Cdr Dunning made his landing. However, the difficulties of flying on were so great, and the remaining 18-inch gun so obviously useless, that a major reconstruction soon took place. The gun was removed, and replaced by a 284-foot flying-on deck. In 1919 she was laid up for a third reconstruction, giving her a flush deck, which was completed in 1925. She then carried 33 aircraft and served through World War II. Her sisters carried 48 aircraft, but were lost in 1939 and 1940. HMS *Eagle* was converted from a requisitioned Chilean battleship; launched in 1922, she was the first to have an offset superstructure. HMS *Hermes* (1923) was the first aircraft carrier to be built as such.

16 Roskill, *The War at Sea, 1939–45* i p. 50; HMSO, 1954. The same source informs us that the Navies of the British Empire contained 101 escort destroyers and sloops.

17 Jameson, op. cit. p. 250.

18 Padfield, op. cit. p. 93. I must here acknowledge my debt to Peter Padfield, the latest biographer of Grand Admiral Dönitz, for much of the information concerning him in the following pages.

19 Ibid. p. 35.

20 Ibid. p. 56.

21 This and the next quotation, ibid. pp. 60 and 61.

22 Ibid. p. 78.

23 *Memoirs: Ten Years and Twenty Days* by Admiral Dönitz, translated by R. H. Stevens in collaboration with David Woodward; Weidenfeld & Nicolson, 1958; p. 3 (next quotation, ibid.).

24 Jonathan Steinberg (*Yesterday's Deterrent* p. 40 fn 29; Macdonald, 1965) notes that in 1914, whereas just over 50% of the officers of the Army's Great General Staff belonged to the nobility, out of 57 admirals and senior officers who served as heads of departments in the Admiralty Staff between 1899–1918, only 7 belonged to the nobility and only 3 to the higher, titled nobility.

25 Steinberg, op. cit. p. 28.

26 Padfield, op. cit. p. 22. He describes Dönitz as belonging to 'the aspiring middle class' which, while imitating 'the bearing and the outlook and the manners of the Prussian nobility of the sword who stood behind the Kaiser at the head of the empire', were generally

better educated. Dönitz's father was an optical engineer in the famous firm of Karl Zeiss.

27   William L. Langer, *The Diplomacy of Imperialism 1890–1902* p. 656; New York, 1951.

28   Steinberg, op. cit.

29   This and the next quotation from Dönitz, op. cit. p. 5.

30   The naval mutinies were in July–August, 1917 (see pp. 83–4), November, 1918, and during the right-wing Kapp *Putsch* of March, 1920, with its concomitant communist counter-action.

31   Padfield, op. cit. p. 102; following quotations from same source.

32   Ibid. p. 111.

33   Roskill, op. cit. p. 441.

34   Quoted by Padfield, op. cit. p. 119; next quotation, ibid. p. 120.

35   Ibid. p. 125, quoting *40 Fragen an Karl Dönitz*, Munich, 1980.

36   Ibid.

37   Padfield, op. cit. p. 125. Canaris's report is dated 1 November 1931.

38   Ibid. p. 126.

39   Ibid. p. 129.

40   C. H. Müller-Graaft, quoted in *German History – Some New German Views*, ed. Hans Kohn, 1954.

41   Craig, op. cit. p. 338.

42   Padfield, op. cit. p. 130.

43   Ibid. p. 137.

44   Barton Whaley, *Covert German Rearmament 1919–1939* p. 28; University Publications of America, 1984.

45   Dönitz, *Memoirs* p. 7.

46   The first Japanese aggression in China took place between September, 1931, and February, 1933.

47   Barnett, op. cit. p. 407.

48   Schofield, op. cit. p. 130.

49   Cajus Bekker, *Hitler's Naval War* p. 27; Macdonald & Jane's, 1974.

50   Padfield, op. cit. p. 150.

51   Sir Maurice (later Lord) Hankey was Secretary to the Cabinet and the Committee of Imperial Defence and a number of other bodies of influence in the sphere of defence and rearmament.

52   Roskill, *Hankey: Man of Secrets* iii p. 61.

53   Roskill, *Naval Policy between the Wars* ii p. 227: Chatfield to Churchill, 28 May, 1936.

54   Ibid.

55 Ibid. p. 251.

56 Ibid. p. 228.

57 Ibid. p. 226.

58 Ibid. p. 228.

59 Ibid. p. 57 fn.

60 Ibid. i p. 536.

61 Roskill, *The War at Sea* i p. 34.

62 Roskill, *Naval Policy between the Wars* ii p. 383.

63 Later Admiral Sir Norman Denning, KBE, CB, the last Director of Naval Intelligence in the original line, 1959–64, and under the new Defence organization the first Deputy Chief of Defence Staff (Intelligence) 1964–65.

64 Beesly, *Very Special Intelligence* p. 21; Ballantine Books (NY) 1981, (Hamish Hamilton, 1977).

65 Roskill, op. cit. pp. 335–6.

66 The 'legend' of a warship class 'comprised the constructional, engineering and armament specifications (e.g. length, beam and draught, horsepower of main engines, and calibre of all guns).' (Roskill, op. cit. p. 223 fn 4).

67 After 1937, of course, the full cost of the Fleet Air Arm was borne in the Naval Estimates – a matter which the Treasury appeared to have difficulty in grasping.

68 Roskill, op. cit. p. 451.

69 Ibid. p. 283.

70 Correlli Barnett, *The Audit of War* pp. 88–9; Macmillan, 1986.

71 Ibid. p. 91.

72 See Terraine, *The Right of the Line: The Royal Air Force in the European War 1939–1945* pp. 40–3 (Hodder & Stoughton, 1985) for Typex development.

73 Ibid. pp. 223–5.

74 Denis Richards, *Royal Air Force 1939–45* i p. 19.

75 Terraine, op. cit. pp. 82–4.

76 Terraine, *The Smoke and the Fire*, op. cit. p. 179. It was a tragic irony that by 1915 it was possible to hear a voice speaking 4,000 miles away, but impossible to speak across a few hundred yards in land battle. The result was that generals 'became quite impotent at the very moment when they would expect and be expected to display their greatest proficiency'. Similarly, direct speech between ships and aircraft had to await a new advance in technology; air-to-ground speech (just intelligible) in fact made its début in 1918.

77 Sir David Fraser, *And We Shall Shock Them: The British Army in the Second World War* p. 91; Hodder & Stoughton, 1983.

78 Aileen Clayton, *The Enemy is Listening: The Story of the Y Service* p. 27; Hutchinson, 1980.

79 Terraine, *The Right of the Line* pp. 21–3.

80 Derek Wood and Derek Dempster, *The Narrow Margin* p. 15; Arrow Books, 1969.

81 Price, op. cit. p. 37.

82 Padfield, op. cit. p. 150.

83 King-Hall, op. cit. p. 695. *Deutschland* was renamed *Lützow* in November, 1939.

84 The 11-inch (280-mm) calibre was much favoured by the Germans in both wars, and in both it justified their confidence. As far back as 1909, Jellicoe as Controller of the Navy had pointed out that the German 11-inch gun had better ballistics and penetration equal to that of the British 12-inch. This was mainly due to defects of British steel production, compared with Germany's, even before the First World War. Schofield (op. cit. p. 139) draws attention to the difficulties faced by naval rearmament in the late '30s due to scrapping of plant and dispersal of the labour force resulting from the Washington Treaties: 'before they could even begin work on guns and armour for new battleships, the firms had to receive financial aid from the Government with which to re-equip themselves'.

85 Padfield, op. cit. p. 152.

86 King-Hall, op. cit. p. 725.

87 2 May, 1935; this went beyond and superseded the somewhat tentative Franco-Soviet Non-Aggression Pact signed on 29 November, 1932. The 1935 pact formed part of a pattern of Soviet diplomatic responses to the mounting Nazi threat.

88 Dönitz, op. cit. p. 25.

89 The time-scale was dictated by the Nazi Four-Year Plan (launched in October, 1936) and its successors under the aegis of Herman Göring (see Richard Overy, *Goering: The 'Iron' Man* pp. 86–7; Routledge & Kegan Paul, 1984). Overy says: 'The main structure of the heavy industrial expansion was only started in 1938 and the large military plans for the navy and air force were only worked out in detail in the winter of 1938–39. By the middle of 1939 the projects were all in the early stages of construction.... Germany needed five more years before her military forces and economic system would be ready.'

90 Dönitz, op. cit. pp. 13–14 for this and following three quotations.

91 Table compiled from various sources: Dönitz, *Memoirs* p. 29, Bekker, op. cit. Appendix I; Jürgen Rohwer in *Decisive Battles of World War II* (ed. H. A. Jacobsen and J. Rohwer) p. 260; André Deutsch, 1965.

92 Weddigen's most famous exploit was in *U9*; on 22 September, 1914, in the space of just over an hour, she sank three elderly British cruisers, *Aboukir*, *Hogue* and *Cressy*, with a loss of nearly 1,400 officers and men. Weddigen himself was killed with the entire crew of *U29* on 18 March, 1915, when she was rammed and sunk by the battleship HMS *Dreadnought*.

93 Dönitz, op. cit. pp. 16–17; unfortunately the commander in question is not named.

94 Ibid. p. 15 (my italics); following quotation from p. 16.

95 Ibid. pp. 15–16.

96 Ibid. pp. 19–22 for this and following three quotations.

97 Dönitz, p. 18; he is substantially correct, but see p. 120 for Commodore Bauer's 1917 proposal for a 'pack' attack under radio control (which Dönitz acknowledges) and Commodore Michelsen's unsuccessful experiment in 1918 (which he does not mention).

98 Dönitz, op. cit. pp. 30–1 for this and following quotation.

99 Ibid. p. 31 for this and following; Rohwer (op. cit.) gives a table of U-boats *laid down* as follows:

1935	26
1936	10
1937	19
1938	8
1939	9

100 Ibid. pp. 27–9 for this and following three quotations.

101 This table is compiled from Dönitz, Gibson & Prendergast, op. cit. and Price, op. cit.

102 Anthony J. Watts, *World War II Fact Files: Axis Submarines* p. 5; Arco Publishing Co. New York, 1977.

103 Lothar-Günther Buchheim, *U-Boat War*, Chapter 6; Bantam Books (New York), 1979, for this and following. Pages are not numbered in this edition.

104 Herbert A. Werner, *Iron Coffins* p. 15 which is also the source of the following information.

105 Buchheim, op. cit. for this and following quotation.

106 Werner, op. cit. pp. 35 and 27–8.

107 Terraine, op. cit. p. 521.

108 C. F. Rawnsley & Robert Wright, *Night Fighter* p. 20; Corgi Books 1959.

109   Buchheim, op. cit.

110   Bekker, op. cit. p. 29 for this and two following quotations.

111   Padfield, op. cit. p. 167.

112   Bekker, op. cit. p. 32.

113   Z = *Ziel* = target.

114   Overy, op. cit. p. 85.

115   Bekker, op. cit. p. 34.

116   Dönitz, op. cit. pp. 32–3 for this and three following quotations.

117   Ibid. p. 41.

118   Ibid. p. 42.

119   Captain D. V. Peyton-Ward RN, senior naval staff officer at Coastal Command HQ; see Terraine, op. cit. pp. 229–30 and 402.

120   Bekker, op. cit. p. 21.

121   Dönitz, op. cit. pp. 46–7.

PART III: THE SECOND ROUND

III/1   *Dearth of U-Boats* (*pp. 213–241*)

1   Dönitz, op. cit. p. 84.

2   Padfield, op. cit. p. 184.

3   Dönitz, op. cit. p. 120.

4   When Dönitz succeeded Hitler as *Reich Führer* on 1 May, 1945, he selected von Friedeburg (now Admiral Commanding Submarines) to head the German delegation to Field-Marshal Montgomery on 3 May to effect the surrender of all the German forces on the northern front, and it was von Friedeburg whose signature stood beside the Field-Marshal's on the instrument signed at Lüneburg Heath on 4 May. When Dönitz was arrested on 23 May, von Friedeburg was arrested with him; by this time he was in a state of acute depression. It is supposed that he was convinced that history (*German* history, at least) would attach to him the same stigma as that branded by nationalist elements on the signatories of the 1918 Armistice. As he was about to be taken to prison, he committed suicide by poison.

5   Wilhelmshaven was a port which had grown up with the High Sea Fleet. It was a naval base without frills and distinctly lacking in amenities. Seaman Stumpf, who served from 1914–18 in the battle-ship *Helgoland*, wrote: 'The sight of that horrible, inhospitable town

was not cheering. What a contrast with Kiel or Cuxhaven!' (*The Private War of Seaman Stumpf* p. 74; Leslie Frewin, 1969).

6   Dönitz, op. cit. pp. 38–9.

7   Bekker, op. cit. p. 26.

8   *Kapitän zur See* Viktor Oehrn to Padfield, 1982 (op. cit. p. 188). Oehrn was on Operations staff at U-boat HQ in 1939; in the course of the war, says Dönitz (op. cit. p. 367) he 'distinguished himself equally as a U-boat captain and a Staff Officer'.

9   Bekker, op. cit. pp. 19–20.

10   Padfield, op. cit. p. 191.

11   Dönitz, op. cit. pp. 54–5; my italics. The 'Agreement' referred to is the London Protocol on Submarine Warfare signed by Britain, the United States, Japan, France and Italy on 15 March, 1936; Germany acceded to this protocol on 23 November of that year.

12   Padfield, op. cit. p. 194.

13   Bekker, op. cit.

14   Padfield, op. cit.

15   Ibid. pp. 197–8 for this and following quotation.

16   Ibid. p. 206.

17   Ibid. p. 195.

18   Dönitz, op. cit. pp. 48–9 for this and following.

19   Two Polish submarines, *Orzel* and *Wilk*, and three destroyers escaped to join the Royal Navy. *Orzel* (*Eagle*) arrived in Britain on 14 October; on 9 April, 1940, she sank a heavily laden German troop transport in Norwegian waters, and shortly after that a trawler. On 23 May she set out on another patrol from which she did not return.

20   Dönitz, op. cit. pp. 123–5 for this and two following.

21   One reason for Göring's unhelpfulness was the prior claim of the *Luftwaffe*, of which he was also *Oberbefehlshaber* (C-in-C). As Richard Overy says, 'for most of his period in office the work with which he was associated was of a highly technical and complex nature. This was the case with both the air force and the economy. . . . Schacht's view that he had 'a complete lack of understanding of economics' is well known. . . . Göring himself was openly in agreement with this judgment . . . (his) political and administrative life . . . reflected both his personality and his intellectual make-up.'

22   Padfield, op. cit. p. 199.

23   Ibid. p. 207; the Order was 'presumably issued some time in November'.

24   *The Gathering Storm* p. 387.

25   Bekker, op. cit. p. 21.

26 Dönitz, op. cit. p. 67.

27 Geoffrey Cousins, *The Story of Scapa Flow* pp. 28–31; Frederick Muller, 1965.

28 Dönitz, op. cit. p. 69.

29 Quoted in *The War 1939–1945*, ed. Desmond Flower & James Reeves pp. 28–9; Cassell, 1960.

30 Dönitz, op. cit. p. 175.

31 William L. Shirer, *Berlin Diary* p. 190; Hamish Hamilton, 1941.

32 Dönitz recorded his thinking about the route for *U 47* in the War Diary on 15 October (the day after the sinking of *Royal Oak*, but three days before he had any contact with Prien):

> Holm Sound is completely blocked by two merchant ships, apparently sunk, which lie diagonally across the Channel of Kirk Sound, and a third vessel to the north of the other two. To the south thereof and running as far as Lamb Holm is a narrow channel about 50 feet wide, in which the depth is $3\frac{1}{2}$ fathoms and on either side of which are shallows. To the north of the merchant ships is a further small channel. The shore on both sides is practically uninhabited. Here, I think, it would certainly be possible to penetrate – by night, on the surface at slack water. The main difficulties will be navigational.

These were, in fact, the routes that Prien took to enter and leave Scapa Flow.

33 Cousins, op. cit. pp. 147–8.

34 U-Boat War Diary, 1 October; Dönitz op. cit. p. 61.

35 Price, op. cit. p. 45.

36 This, however, was the heyday of the German magnetic mine (in use by the Royal Navy in 1917; see p. 108). In November, 1939, mines claimed 27 Allied ships (120,985 tons) and in December 32 ships (82,557 tons). It was not until March, 1940, that this menace could be said to be contained.

37 Jacobsen & Rohwer, op. cit. pp. 261–2 for this and following.

38 Overy, op. cit. p. 86.

39 Donald McLachlan, *Room 39: Naval Intelligence in Action 1939–45* p. 82: '(*B-Dienst*) knew the closely guarded secret of the use of Loch Ewe as Home Fleet base.'

40 Shirer, op. cit. pp. 214–15.

41 Dönitz, op. cit. p. 62.

42 A conspicuous practitioner of this mode of command, who attracted

much admiration by it, was Field-Marshal Rommel. What tended to escape notice was that his German force in the Western Desert never amounted to more than 4 weak divisions – a corps, in other words. It is arguable whether Rommel's methods were actually effective or not – his famous 'dash to the wire' in November, 1941, has not gone down as a strategic masterpiece. In any case, a style appropriate to a corps commander (in certain circumstances) is not necessarily right for Army, Army Group and Supreme commanders.

43 See Terraine *The Right of the Line* p. 466: 'In Bomber Command, except on rare daylight occasions, each crew was on its own.' In 1943, beginning with the famous 'Dams Raid' in May, experiments were made with the technique of the 'Master Bomber' – a tactical director operating over the target. A notable example was the attack on Peenemünde on the night of 17/18 August. Improvements in the technology of bombing aids subsequently reduced the need for this function, just as improvements in the technology of communications made it possible for the U-boats to dispense with local control.

44 Dönitz, op. cit. p. 63 for this and two following.

45 Jacobsen & Rohwer, op. cit. p. 273.

46 Dönitz, op. cit. pp. 118–19 for this and following.

47 Bekker, op. cit. for this and following three.

48 Various versions of Beatty's cool remark have been published; this, from Roskill's *Admiral of the Fleet Earl Beatty: The Last Naval Hero*, p. 160 (Atheneum [NY] 1981), is authenticated by Captain A. B. Sainsbury's discovery of a manuscript note by Lord Chatfield, to whom the remark was addressed, dated 1937 and supplied by the latter for use in the *Oxford Dictionary of Quotations*. The second edition of that work omits 'There seems to be' and substitutes 'There's'.

49 Bekker, op. cit. pp. 132–3 for this and following.

50 It has been well remarked (Buchheim, op. cit.) that 'In fact, the torpedo is not a projectile at all. It is not expelled from the tube by the force of an explosion but by a blast of compressed air. Equipped with an engine, propellers, and a rudder of its own, the torpedo is itself a highly developed unmanned submarine streaking along just below the surface. Its cargo is the explosive charge.' The advantage of the magnetic torpedo, exploding some distance beneath the target, was that the violent blast of gas and water so produced would do considerably more damage than a contact explosion.

51 Dönitz, op. cit. p. 95.

52 Jacobsen & Rohwer, op. cit. p. 262.

53 Dönitz, op. cit. pp. 84–9 for this and following three.

54 In *The Right of the Line* (p. 237 Note 7), referring to the German torpedo failures, I said: 'These ... were rectified by June, 1940.' In fact, only the striker failure was corrected by that date.

55 Dönitz, op. cit. p. 94. As we have seen, the effectiveness of German torpedoes in World War I was not inconsiderable.

56 Ibid. p. 90.

57 Ibid. p. 96.

58 Bekker, op. cit. for this and following four.

III/2 *Nothing of Major Importance* (*pp. 242–254*)

1 See *The Right of the Line* pp. 118 & 144.

2 *Naval Policy Between the Wars* ii pp. 427–8 for this and following quotation.

3 Ibid. p. 420.

4 The 'cycle' is the number of days between convoys from the same port.

5 Op. cit. p. 428.

6 Roskill, *The War at Sea* i p. 134.

7 AHB/II/117/3(A) p. 221.

8 *Naval Policy between the Wars* ii p. 429.

9 *The War at Sea* i p. 135.

10 Churchill, *The Gathering Storm* p. 669; Churchill to Pound, 20 November, 1939.

11 AHB/II/117/3(A) Appendix V.

12 Thetford, op. cit. p. 442.

13 Op. cit. p. 71.

14 This was Exercise XKD, 15–21 August [AHB/II/117/3(A) pp. 252–4], and see p. 207.

15 Temporary Air Chief Marshal from 1 November, 1939.

16 Op. cit. p. 158.

17 AHB/II/117/3(B) p. 1.

18 On 5 September two RN submarines were attacked by mistake by Coastal Command Ansons; 'both escaped with nothing more than a slight shaking'. By a similar mistake on 3 December, 'the *Snapper* received a 100-pound anti-submarine bomb directly at the base of her conning tower. The only damage to her pressure hull occurred in

the control room, where four electric light bulbs were broken (Richards, op. cit. p. 61).

19 AHB/II/117/3(B) p. 48; a footnote adds: 'Of the 85 attacks on U-boats carried out by Coastal Command aircraft between September, 1939 and May, 1940, one resulted in the sinking of *U 55* in conjunction with HM ships, four attacks (two shared with HM ships) were assessed as probably compelling the U-boat to return to harbour immediately, and eight were considered to have possibly caused slight damage to the U-boat.'

20 Ibid.; this section, concerning anti-submarine bombs, is based upon the AHB Narrative, Roskill, *The War at Sea*, and Richards, *Royal Air Force 1939–45*.

21 U-Boats took the northern passage because once again, as in 1917–18, the Dover Straits had been closed by a barrage. Leaning on 1918 experience once more, this time the barrage was effective from the first; there was no repetition of the 1916–17 failure. Only one U-boat successfully passed through the Straits, on the night of 11–12 September, before the barrage was completed. By the end of October three (*U 12, U 40* and *U 16*) had been lost in the minefields and no further attempt was made.

22 Roskill, op. cit. pp. 104–5.

23 In *The Right of the Line* I referred to this as 'the numbers game'. It was perhaps seen at its most spectacularly misleading height in the Battle of Britain, but remained a conspicuous feature of the air war (on both sides) reflecting the difficulty of accurately estimating enemy losses in air combat. However, as I also pointed out, it recurred in other elements, and in both wars the men concerned – sailors and airmen – often found it hard to believe that U-boats had survived the punishment meted out and witnessed by impressive disturbance of the sea, large oil slicks and often even débris. Yet such was the case.

24 Roskill, op. cit. p. 90.

25 Barnett, *Audit of War* pp. 112–13 for this and following quotation. The author's title for this chapter of his book (No 6) is ' "The Fossilisation of Inefficiency" ' – taken from a memorandum by the First Lord of the Admiralty in March 1944 (Rt. Hon. A. V. Alexander) in which he says 'it is proving extremely difficult to get the industry itself to take the necessary steps to keep its plant up to date' and that it was necessary 'to keep a sharp look out for any tendency towards what I may term the fossilisation of inefficiency.'

26 Later Admiral of the Fleet Lord Fraser of North Cape.

27 Churchill, op. cit. p. 680.

28 H. T. Lenton and J. J. Colledge, *Warships of World War II* p. 172 fn; Ian Allan, 1980.

29 Vice-Admiral Sir Peter Gretton, *Crisis Convoy: The Story of HX 231*, caption to Fig. 3(a); Purnell Book Services, 1974.

30 Op. cit. p. 135.

31 Nicholas Monsarrat, *Three Corvettes*, Cassell, 1945, Granada Publishing, 1972, p. 26.

32 Joseph Schull, *The Far Distant Ships* pp. 58–9; Ministry of National Defence, Ottawa, 1961.

33 James B. Lamb, *The Corvette Navy* p. 12; Macmillan of Canada, 1978.

34 AHB/II/117/3(B) p. 51 for this and following.

35 In the course of the Norwegian campaign the Royal Navy lost:

Aircraft carriers	1
Cruisers	2
Destroyers	7
Submarines	4
Sloops	1

In addition, 6 cruisers, 8 destroyers and 2 sloops were damaged. The Allied Navies lost 1 destroyer (Polish) and 2 submarines (1 Polish, 1 Dutch).

36 Op. cit. p. 163.

37 B. H. Liddell Hart, *History of the Second World War* pp. 141–2, Cassell, 1970, for this and following.

III/3/i *The Steep Atlantick (pp. 255–274)*

1 Dönitz, op. cit. p. 110.

2 Ibid. p. 111.

3 AHB/II/117/3(B) pp. 120–1.

4 Op. cit. p. 102.

5 Ibid. p. 112.

6 This work was completed in September; in the meantime, U-boat HQ was lodged in Paris.

7 In the U-boat War Diary of 7 September, 1939, Dönitz was already hoping to 'score one great success, e.g. the destruction of a whole convoy.'

8 Official History: *British Intelligence in the Second World War* ii p. 639; F. H. Hinsley et al., HMSO, 1981.

9 *The Operational Use of 'Ultra' in the Battle of the Atlantic*; paper

presented at the Medlicott Symposium, University of Exeter, 1 November, 1985.

10 Official History: *Design and Development of Weapons* p. 390; D. Hay, M. M. Postan and J. D. Scott, HMSO, 1964.

11 Overy, op. cit. p. 173.

12 William Green, *Warplanes of the Third Reich* pp. 336 and 340 for this and following quotation; Macdonald & Jane's, 1970.

13 *The Rise and Fall of the German Air Force 1939–1945*, originally an Air Historical Branch Monograph by Wing Commander Cyril Marsh, was published by Arms and Armour Press in 1983. Page 38 informs us: 'The basic flying unit was the *Gruppe*, which consisted of about 30 aircraft.' Each *Gruppe* would normally contain *3 Staffeln*, roughly equivalent to Royal Air Force squadrons. Three *Gruppen* formed a *Geschwader* (equivalent to RAF Group). The working designation of the 'Condor' formation was I/KG 40 (*Kampfgeschwader* = Bomber Group).

14 Bekker, op. cit. p. 197.

15 Eric Brown (ed. William Green), *Wings of the Luftwaffe* pp. 7 and 18; Pilot Press, 1977.

16 Green, op. cit. p. 227.

17 Alfred Price, *Battle of Britain: The Hardest Day* p. 34; Granada, 1980.

18 Mines accounted for 22 ships (86,076 tons), surface vessels (warships, merchant raiders and 'E'-boats) accounted for 9 more (61,587 tons), and 29 (48,527 tons) were lost by causes unknown.

19 'The U-Boat War against the Allied Supply Lines' in *Decisive Battles of World War II* p. 263.

20 'tonnage king': Werner, op. cit. p. 21; 'exploits stood alone': Dönitz, op. cit. p. 174.

21 Dönitz, op. cit. p. 107.

22 See Roskill, *The War at Sea* i p. 348: 'The months of July to October 1940 were later called by the German U-boat commanders "the happy time".'

23 As Dönitz said, 'timely deciphering (of the signals) was largely a matter of luck' (op. cit. pp. 104–5).

24 Op. cit. p. 189.

25 AHB/II/117/3(B) pp. 270–1.

26 Op. cit. p. 106.

27 *Their Finest Hour* p. 529.

28 Hinsley, op. cit. vol. i pp. 188–9. His Official History contains no

reference to the decrypt on 17 September. It is treated at length in F. W. Winterbotham's *The Ultra Secret* pp. 58–9 (Weidenfeld & Nicolson, 1974), including an eyewitness account of it being presented to Churchill and the Chiefs of Staff. Ronald Lewin (*Ultra Goes to War* pp. 93 and 95) follows Winterbotham.

29   Patrick Beesly, in a paper on 'British Naval Intelligence in Two World Wars' presented at the Symposium at Exeter referred to in Note 9, says this: 'Information derived from decrypts is now erroneously if conveniently referred to as Ultra. The correct designation is Special Intelligence. Ultra was merely a security classification and followed a practice introduced by Hall in November, 1917. Godfrey [DNI in January, 1939] had reinstituted this method . . . in anticipation that Bletchley [GC & CS] would, sooner or later, again provide decrypts of enemy signals. On 13 May, 1940, Godfrey signalled the C-in-C Home Fleet and others that the previous security classification Hydro was to be replaced by the word Ultra, the first use of this term that I have been able to trace. The Royal Navy was well ahead of the other two Services in making provision for the prompt and effective dissemination of Special Intelligence.' The decrypts themselves are also referred to as Sigint. The word Ultra defined their source-nature. But Ultra also means a system of presentation, so that raw intelligence which might mean little to its Service recipients, could be given a context to indicate its value. Thus, on 17 September, a simple instruction to a German unit commander to dismantle some equipment only comes to life as part of what Lewin called 'a meaningful mosaic' when the unit and its function are also identified. Winterbotham was one of the special category of liaison officers who carried out this essential task.

30   Hinsley, op. cit. p. 189.

31   Dr Karl Klee (*Decisive Battles of World War II* p. 75), in his essay on the Battle of Britain, says:

> 'On May 23rd, 1939, Hitler communicated certain ideas to his military leaders, and these ideas later became the basis for still further plans. The main concept was that in view of her absolute dependence on imports, Britain could be forced to surrender by cutting off her supplies.'

32   Op. cit. p. 54.

33   Dönitz, op. cit. p. 102.

34   Macintyre, op. cit. p. 41; my italics.

35   There were no destroyers with *SC 7*; U-boat commanders habitually referred to all classes of escort vessels as 'destroyers'. It was widely believed in the U-boat Service that Kretschmer, in the course of his

career, sank three Royal Navy destroyers (Dönitz credits him with one); in fact, apart from three auxiliary cruisers (see p. 272), Kretschmer sank no naval vessel.

36   Op. cit. p. 50.

37   Ibid. p. 53.

38   Hinsley, op. cit. ii p. 555.

39   Kenneth Poolman, *Focke-Wulf Condor: Scourge of the Atlantic* p. 26; Macdonald & Jane's, 1978.

40   Op. cit. p. 102.

41   Ibid. p. 148.

42   Ibid. p. 131.

43   Richards, op. cit. p. 221.

44   Op. cit. p. 197.

45   Admiralty Anti-Submarine Report, November, 1940.

46   Dönitz, op. cit. p. 146.

47   Ibid. pp. 149–50.

48   Ibid. p. 130.

III/3/ii   *The Very Nadir of British Fortunes (pp. 275–310)*

1   See p. 269. The Royal Navy in Home waters in September, 1939, consisted of the Home Fleet, based at Scapa Flow, under Admiral Sir Charles Forbes, and four shore Commands: Portsmouth: Admiral Sir William James; The Nore: Admiral Sir H. Brownrigg; Rosyth: Vice-Admiral C. G. Ramsey. Western Approaches: (Plymouth): Admiral Sir M. Dunbar-Nasmith VC.

2   Shipping for East Coast ports passed north of Scotland via the Pentland Firth and the Fair Isle Channel.

3   Roskill, op. cit. i p. 359.

4   Charles B. MacDonald, *The Mighty Endeavour* p. 7; OUP 1969.

5   *Their Finest Hour* p. 23. 'This time next year we shall have plenty' was over-optimistic; 'plenty' was an inapplicable word until at least 1943.

6   Ibid. p. 117.

7   Ibid. p. 356.

8   A few were launched in 1919 and a very small number in 1920.

9   Op. cit. p. 368.

10   He used this phrase in an address to junior Naval Officers at an East Coast base entitled 'The First Sailor' in 1918. It may be found in the

collection, *Humourous Tales from Rudyard Kipling* (Macmillan 1931) and is highly recommended to students of naval history.

11 Schull, op. cit. pp. 56–7.

12 Martin Middlebrook, *Convoy* p. 32; Allen Lane 1976.

13 Schull, op. cit.

14 Churchill to First Lord and First Sea Lord, 18. XI. 40; op. cit. p. 612.

15 Ibid. pp. 553–4.

16 Schull, op. cit.

17 Op. cit. p. 65.

18 Quoted in Middlebrook, op. cit.

19 The Prime Minister presided over this powerful body, which worked in two panels: Operations and Supply. The Operations panel consisted of Churchill, the Chiefs of Staff Committee and the Vice Chiefs of Staff Committee, and under them the Joint Planning Staff and the Joint Intelligence Sub-Committee; there would be in addition Liaison Officers from the Ministry of War Transport, the Ministry of Economic Warfare, the Political Warfare Executive, the Ministry of Home Security and other Departments when necessary.

20 Op. cit. p. 532.

21 Eamonn De Valera, Eireann Prime Minister, 1932–48. In 1916 he took part in the Easter Rising, was captured and sentenced to death. The sentence was not carried out because he had American family connections. In 1922–3 he fought in the Irish Republican Army against the forces of the newly created Free State. His position in World War II was one of anti-British neutrality. He became President of Eire in 1959.

22 AHB/II/117/3(B) p. 272. The contrast with the Soviet Union's treatment of Finland in November 1939, when the USSR was still at peace, will not escape the reader.

23 Price, op. cit. p. 55

24 Ibid. p. 57. This equipment comprised two sets of aerials: the normal forwards-looking apparatus, and an elaborate sideways-looking set along the fuselage which gave detection across a 24-mile wide stretch of sea. Once contact was made, the aircraft made a 90° turn and homed in by use of the forward-looking aerials.

25 Op. cit. pp. 168–73 for this and following quotation.

26 E-boats = 'Enemy boats' – a useless definition opposed by Naval Intelligence, which would have preferred to call the very efficient German motor gun- and torpedo boats by their proper name: *Schnell* (fast)-boats, thus S-boats. Dönitz, as Naval Commander-in-Chief,

formed great admiration for the work of these vessels, and in 1943 tripled the production programme. Their theatre of action was the North Sea and the Channel, the 'quick-trigger corners of the war'.

27 Extracted from the Official History, *Merchant Shipping and the Demands of War* by Miss C. B. A. Behrens, Appendix VII; HMSO 1955.

28 Roskill, op. cit. p. 264. See p. 83 for 1917 comparison, p. 117 for 1918.

29 Creighton, op. cit. p. 124 for this and MN casualties below. Statistics in the Appendices of the Official History (Behrens) give a total of 37,651 deaths as a direct result of enemy action, including 5,743 Lascars. ('Lascar' is not a racial definition; it embraced natives of East Africa as well as Asia; normally some 75% of Lascars were Indians, most of the rest being Chinese.)

30 Marc Milner, *North Atlantic Run: The Royal Canadian Navy and the Battle of the Convoys* p. 150; University of Toronto Press, 1985. The SC cycle began in August, 1940.

31 The Assistant Chiefs of the Naval Staff (Trade) were: Rear-Admiral H. M. Burrough, 10.1.39; Rear-Admiral H. R. Moore, 25.VII.40; Vice-Admiral E. L. S. King, 21.X.41; Rear-Admiral J. H. Edelsten, 7.XII.42. The title was changed in February 1943 from 'Trade' to 'U-boat Warfare and Trade' – a indication of where the real threat was seen to lie.

32 Creighton, op. cit. p. 22.

33 Ibid. p. 49; Admiral Creighton here pays a heart-felt tribute to the NCSO at Halifax, Commander Richard Oland RCN.

34 Gretton, op. cit. p. 44.

35 Op. cit. p. 39.

36 Op. cit. p. 53.

37 Admiral Gretton (op. cit. p. 53) also tells us: 'The U-boats were fitted with excellent hydrophones which "listened" for propeller noises and could give accurate bearings of the target. When dived to about 100 feet, the hydrophones gave remarkable results, detecting convoys and large warships at up to fifty miles when the weather and water conditions were suitable.' The hydrophones were, of course, equally useful by night and by day, so noise rather than smoke was probably the main give-away of a convoy's position and course.

38 These were the 'runners' of Nelson's day (see p. 50).

39 Creighton, op. cit. p. 77 for this and following quotation.

40 Monsarrat, op. cit. p. 74.

41 Bekker, op. cit. p. 201 for this and following quotation; ibid. p. 210 for next two.

42 Bekker (p. 205) says that *Scheer* opened fire at 1640 hours, and that *Jervis Bay* went down 'soon after 1700 hours'.

43 Bekker, op. cit. p. 207.

44 Bekker (Appendix 7) lists 9 German merchant cruisers operating between 1940–3, of which 6 were sunk in combat and one by fire and explosion in dock.

45 Op. cit. p. 164.

46 Op. cit. pp. 213–5 for this and following.

47 Behrens, op. cit. p. 126.

48 Official History, *British War Economy* by W. K. Hancock and M. M. Gowing p. 252; HMSO 1949.

49 Op. cit. p. 56.

50 Behrens, op. cit. p. 143. M. M. Postan (*British War Production* p. 62; HMSO 1952) says that the tonnage under repair 'reached a peak of 2.5 million gross tons at the end of February 1941'. Churchill (*The Grand Alliance* p. 100) says: 'At the beginning of March over 2,600,000 tons of damaged shipping had accumulated, of which about 930,000 tons were ships undergoing repair while loading cargoes, and nearly 1,700,000 tons were immobilized by the need of repairs.' Table 115 in Sir Keith Hancock's *Statistical Digest Of The War* gives the numbers of ships under repair at various dates (HMSO 1951). The total from all causes never fell below 1,506, in March, 1944, though the lowest number totally immobilized was 576 in July, 1943. The worst period was February – May, 1941:

February	2,593
March	2,306
April	2,025
May	2,070

February, 1941 saw not only the highest total, but also the largest number totally immobilized – 1,585.

51 Hancock & Gowing, op. cit. pp. 256–7.

52 Hancock & Gowing (op. cit. pp. 257–8) inform us that 'in 1941, the total output of United States shipyards was only one million deadweight tons.'

53 *The Grand Alliance* pp. 100–1.

54 Behrens, op. cit. pp. 130–3 for this and four following.

55 Hancock & Gowing, op. cit. p. 261.

56 Behrens, op. cit. p. 142; my italics.

57 Op. cit. p. 103.

58 Commander Kenneth Edwards, *Men of Action* p. 142; Collins 1943.

59 Rear-Admiral W. S. Chalmers, *Max Horton and the Western Approaches* pp. 152–3; Hodder & Stoughton, 1954; Middlebrook (op.

cit. p. 204) says that somewhat later a WAAF attending to the Coastal Command plot fell off her ladder and was killed, after which all these girls were given harness.

60   Edwards, op. cit. p. 131.

61   Op. cit. p. 71.

62   Roskill, op. cit. ii p. 217 for this and following.

63   Edwards, op. cit. p. 132.

64   Ibid. p. 143.

65   Op. cit. for this and following.

66   Chalmers, op. cit. p. 170.

67   AHB/II/117/3(B) p. 300 for this and following.

68   *The Grand Alliance* p. 106 for this and two following.

69   Ibid. pp. 107–9.

III/3/iii *As Though the Defence had Won (pp. 311–352)*

1   Bekker, op. cit. p. 196.

2   Werner, op. cit. p. 13.

3   Op. cit. p. 137 for this and following quotation.

4   *KG 40* was commanded by *Oberstleutnant* Martin Harlinghausen, a former naval officer who was, says Dönitz, 'a man of exceptional energy and boldness, and under his leadership the Squadron did its admirable best'. (op. cit.)

5   Ibid. p. 141 for this and following. See p. 297 for *Hipper* reference.

6   According to Cajus Bekker (op. cit. p. 198) Captain Rowland's first indication of the presence of *U 47* was when 'his nostrils were assailed by the smell of engine exhaust gas'. This bears out an important passage in the lapidary work by Rudyard Kipling quoted on p. 279 (and Note 10):

> [he describes the Stone Age mariner's approach to battle in a dug-out log with unpredictable habits on a pitch-black night in the Thames Estuary with a crew of one – his very young son; the mariner's name appears to have been Clarke:] 'When they had collided with their fifth floating oak, Nobby calls forward to ask his son whether he was enjoying pleasant dreams, or what else.
> "But I can't *see* 'em," says the child, wiping his nose with the back of his hand.
> "See 'em," says Nobby. "Who the Hell expects you to see 'em on a night like this? You got to *smell* 'em, my son."

Thus early, gentlemen, was the prehistoric and perishing Watch Officer inducted into the mysteries of his unpleasing trade.'

Of course, in Captain Rowland's case it is just possible that radar may have had something todo with the business as well. See note 10.

7   Bekker, op. xcit. p. 199.

8   Macintyre, *U-Boat Killer* pp. 101–5; Weidenfeld & Nicolson, 1956.

9   Werner, op. cit. p. 21.

10 Op. cit. p. 175; it may be noted that according to Captain Peyton-Ward, in the case of each of the three aces, 'the improved RDF being mounted in escort vessels played a decisive part' (AHB/II/117/3(B) p. 102).

11 Bekker, op. cit. p. 200.

12 Today the ugliness of the thing is largely hidden by ivy, no doubt to the dismay of the contemporary 'brutalist' school of architecture.

13 The Admiralty's War Registry dated from 1914, and was responsible for the distribution of all incoming and outgoing signal traffic – a most important rôle which was at a discount for much of the inter-war period but never abolished. War brought a swift expansion of staff which mounted to some 500 when the Registry moved into the Citadel. Though part of the Admiralty, it was a civilian department mounting a continuous 24-hour watch with great efficiency throughout the war.

14 Roskill, op. cit. ii p. 461.

15 Beesly, *Very Special Intelligence* p. 18. It is in no critical spirit that I make the comment that I have always understood that nothing but the best was 'what was good enough for Nelson'.

16 McLachlan, op. cit. pp. 2–4 for this and following.

17 Beesly ('British Naval Intelligence in Two World Wars' pp. 6–13) lists three important similarities of NID in the two wars:
    (1) an enormous expansion, largely from civil life,
    (2) 'two exceptionally able and talented Directors' (Hall and Godfrey),
    (3) 'the absolutely vital part played by cryptanalysis and Sigint in general'.

18 Godfrey had the curious experience, in September, 1942, of being promoted to Vice-Admiral on the Active List, and on the same day being summarily dismissed from his post of DNI by the First Sea Lord, Sir Dudley Pound, on the grounds that cooperation with the other two Services was 'not possible so long as you were a member' of the Joint Intelligence Committee.

19 McLachlan, op. cit. p. 389; my italics.

20 'Station X' was the Security reference to the Government Code and Cipher School (GC & CS) which in 1919 replaced the Admiralty's 'Room 40' as the practitioner of cryptanalysis. At first it continued to be under the Admiralty for administrative purposes, but in 1922 it was transferred to the Foreign Office along with the Special Intelligence Service (SIS; commonly known as the 'Secret Service'). In 1923 the GC & CS was brought directly under the authority of the Head of the SIS, known as 'C'. This post continued to be a naval preserve until November, 1939, when the death of Admiral Hugh Sinclair brought in Colonel Stewart Menzies (ex-Life Guards) as 'C'. The Head of the GC & CS was Commander Alastair Denniston, an old 'Room 40' hand, as were a number of his staff.

21 McLachlan, op. cit. p. 57. He omits one further type of Intelligence material which was always highly valued: information gathered from interrogation of prisoners of war. The 'one man' to whom he refers was, of course, Admiral Hall.

22 Ibid. pp. 103–4 for this and preceding quotation.

23 Rodger Winn was later promoted to Captain, RNVR, a rare occurrence; he was also awarded an OBE and a CB, and the American Legion of Merit. After the war he returned to the Bar and became a Lord Justice of Appeal until his death in 1972.

24 McLachlan, op. cit. p. 105.

25 In the OIC, says Patrick Beesly, 'There were four principal sections, the Italian and Japanese Section under (Lieut.-Commander) Barrow-Green; the D/F plotters under Kemp; the Submarine Tracking Room under Thring; and the German surface ship section under Denning' (*Very Special Intelligence* pp. 22–3). At first Kemp's plotters were located away from the Tracking Room because their work seemed more directly useful to Denning. When the threat from the German surface fleet died away, Denning concentrated on the tracking of their armed merchant cruisers.

26 *The War at Sea* i p. 18.

27 Op. cit. p. 60.

28 See p. 194. *HYDRA* was the German name for the cipher called DOL-PHIN by the GC & CS cryptanalysts at Bletchley Park. This was the cipher used by all surface ships in the Baltic and the North Sea, then also by ships operating out of occupied territories, and at first also by all U-boats.

29 Hinsley op. cit. i p. 334.

30 Ibid. i p. 20 for this and following.

31 As Ronald Lewin (*Ultra Goes to War* p. 56) says: 'Just as the City of London and Balliol College Oxford (manipulators of two of the most

efficient Old Boy Nets in the country) became mainstays of SOE (Special Operations Executive), so Cambridge fed Bletchley. . . . The mathematical strength of Cambridge made the university an obvious hunting-ground.'

32 Gordon Welchman, *The Hut Six Story: Breaking the Enigma Codes* p. 14; Allen Lane 1982.

33 Andrew Hodges, *Alan Turing: The Enigma of Intelligence* p. 175; Unwin Paperback 1985. The name '*Bomba*', says Hodges, derived from the fact that when working the Polish machines produced a loud ticking sound.

34 Lewin op. cit. p. 119. Hinsley (op. cit. p. 489) calls the Bombe 'a machine devised for "finding" *Enigma* keys by automatic testing of several tens of thousands of possible combinations'. Gordon Welchman (op. cit. pp. 15–16) says: 'Rejewski's six-*Enigma* '*Bomba*' must have been the origin of the machine on which Alan Turing was working in the fall of 1939.' The Poles and Turing alike were working on the principle that 'what was done by a machine might all the more easily be undone by a machine' (Hodges, op. cit. p. 167). It was, he says, 'a brute force method'.

35 F. W. Winterbotham, op. cit.

36 Hodges op. cit. p. 191.

37 Hinsley op. cit. i p. 109 for this and following.

38 Lewin op. cit. pp. 120–1.

39 An excellent account of the boarding of *U 110* and retrieval of the *Enigma* machine and codebooks is to be found in Lewin, op. cit. pp. 204–7. It was Julius Lemp in *U 30* who had opened the U-boat account by sinking the *Athenia* on 3 September, 1939. Lewin says he 'had a fine record in the U-boat war', and Padfield (citing the British interrogation of the captured crews) says 'he was much respected and liked', but then adds that '*U 110* did not conform to Dönitz's ideal'. The interrogation indicated that the first lieutenant was a Nazi bully, the second officer incompetent, and the crew raw and ill-trained, 'drafted into U-boats without option' (conscription was, of course, the normal method of recruitment). The report concluded by saying: 'It would seem there is a real difficulty in manning U-boats'; May, 1941, was early days for such a supposition, which has all the sound of that classic Intelligence bane – wishful thinking. Lewin (p. 205) tells us: 'It is thought that when he realized what had happened Lemp committed suicide by allowing himself to drown.'

40 The GC & CS had established by May, 1941, that all German naval units were relying on the *Enigma* machine, and that they used two keys – Home and Foreign. The 'Home Waters' cipher was *HYDRA*

(see Note 28). The 'Foreign' key was used only for operations in distant waters; the pocket battleships and the armed merchant cruisers were the chief users, and this key was never broken.

41 Hinsley op. cit. ii p. 163. There is some discrepancy in the *Official History* of this phase of the 'battle of the decrypts'; the delay of 'only a few hours' of p. 163 becomes 'within an hour of its transmission' on p. 171. The difference could be operationally very significant.

42 Ibid i p. 339.

43 Hodges op. cit. p. 217.

44 Lewin op. cit. p. 207 for this and preceding.

45 Milner op. cit. p. 29.

46 Sir Charles Lucas, *The Empire at War* i pp. 215–7; OUP 1921, for this and the following.

47 Roger Sarty, *Hard Luck Flotilla: The RCN's Atlantic Coast Patrol 1914–1918*; paper presented by the Directorate of History, National Defence Headquarters, Ottawa 1985.

48 Milner op. cit. p. 6.

49 The destroyers *Saguenay* and *Skeena* were 'the first warships built specifically for the RCN' (Milner p. 6). They were ordered in 1929, built by Thornycroft's, launched in 1930 and commissioned in 1931. They belonged to the Royal Navy's 'A' Class: 1,540 tons, 32,000 hp, 35 knots, armament 5 4.7-in., 2 2-pdr AA guns, 8 21-in. torpedo tubes, complement 138.

In 1937 Canada purchased two 'C' Class destroyers, *Fraser* (ex-*Crescent*) and *St Laurent* (ex-*Cygnet*), built by Vickers Armstrong at Barrow and launched in 1931: 1,375 tons, 36,000 hp, 35½ knots, armament 4 4.7-in., 2 2-pdr, 8 .5 AA, 8 21-in torpedo tubes, complement 145. Two more of the same class were purchased in 1938: *Restigouche* (ex-*Comet*) and *Ottawa* (ex-*Crusader*). A flotilla leader, *Assiniboine* (ex-*Kempenfelt*), followed in 1939: 1,390 tons, machinery, speed and armament similar, complement 175. Milner (p. 7) says: 'These River-class destroyers formed the backbone of the RCN until well into 1943'.

50 *The Gathering Storm* p. 417.

51 Lamb, *The Corvette Navy* p. 8 for this and following.

52 Ibid. p. 9.

53 Between 1939–45 over one million Canadians served in the Armed Forces, distributed as follows:

Army	700,000
RCAF	222,501
RCN	99,407

So much for 'Never Again'! As Marc Milner says, 'The slow expansion of the navy could not keep up with the national desire to take up where the Canadian Corps had left off in 1918. . . . The great irony of unpreparedness in peace was that it severely limited what could be done in war, and it has always been easier and faster to raise battalions than to build ships' (op. cit. p. 21).

54 Milner (p. 35) refers to the original Canadian corvettes' 'inshore and jack-of-all-trades rôle'. A striking illustration of the failure to foresee an ocean-going anti-submarine function was the addition of a full mine-sweeping equipment which 'had an adverse effect on the operations of the anti-submarine gear'.

55 Milner, op. cit. p. 37.

56 Ibid. p. 26.

57 Schull, op. cit. p. 68.

58 Lamb op. cit. p. 21.

59 Ibid. pp. 23–4.

60 *Three Corvettes* p. 27.

61 Op. cit. p. 50.

62 The United States Official History (*The Battle of the Atlantic*, i, p. 95; see note 68) says that the area between Newfoundland, Greenland and Iceland 'is the roughest part of the Western Ocean. Winds of gale force, mountainous seas, biting cold, body-piercing fog and blinding snow squalls were the rule rather than the exception; U-boats could escape this by submerging, but the escorts had to face it.' The Meeting Points were where escorts handed over.

63 See Terraine, *The Right of the Line* p. 115.

64 *RUSI Journal* December 1975 pp. 45–7, *A Final Reappraisal of the British Occupation of Iceland*, 1940–42 by Donald F. Bittner USMCR.

65 Schull op. cit. p. 89.

66 Richards op. cit. p. 223. It was not until April, 1941, says Roskill (i, p. 451) 'when the fuelling bases in Iceland were ready, that any further extension of the escort vessels' protecting shield became possible. Once this had been accomplished, anti-submarine escort became possible to a greatly increased distance from our shores – as far as 35° West, which is more than half way across the North Atlantic.' On 30 June the Royal Navy's Iceland Command was created.

67 Op. cit. p. 41 for this and following.

68 Samuel E. Morison, *The Battle of the Atlantic* (US OH), i, p. 78; Little, Brown & Co. 1947. Bittner (see Note 64) says that 'In contrast to the British, the Americans in Iceland soon showed a disposition

for violence, both among themselves and in just enough cases against the Icelanders for the comparison to become even more obvious'. The Icelanders, he says, not unnaturally showed 'their dislike of the violent nature of parts of the American garrison' (op. cit. p. 49).

69 At a Press Conference on 30 May, explaining the American rearmament programme, Roosevelt said: '. . . there is no one of us can guess definitely as to what will be the decision on the part of Germany and Italy if they completely control all of Europe, including the British Isles. We don't know. That's the reason for this program. It is because we don't know. That is the primary reason. A good many other victors and conquerors in the world have said, "I only want so much", and when they got that they said, "I want only so much more", and when they got that they said, "I want all the whole known world"' (quoted in Joseph P. Lash, *Roosevelt and Churchill 1939–41* p. 147 [André Deutsch, 1977]; Lash comments: 'This was the viewpoint of most Americans.')

70 Morison, op. cit. p. 64.

71 Keith Sainsbury, in his informative book *The North African Landings 1942* (p. 43; Davis Poynter 1976) explains American attitudes to the South Atlantic: 'From Washington, Axis control of West Africa was seen as a major threat to US lines of communication with the UK and Latin America. From the French West African naval base at Dakar, only 1,600 miles from the nearest point on the Brazilian coast, German submarines, surface raiders and aircraft could harass Allied convoys far out into the Atlantic. Theoretically it was even possible for Axis troops to be airlifted from there to Latin America. German use of Dakar had been described by Secretary (of the Navy) Knox in April 1941 as "a disaster to US hemisphere safety and a threat to the Monroe Doctrine".'

72 Quoted in Lash, op. cit. p. 64.

73 Morison, op. cit. p. 45; this was known as the 'ABC-1 Agreement'.

74 Ibid. pp. 49–50. George B. MacDonald (op. cit. p. 30) says the ABC-1 talks 'actually marked the start of American participation in World War II'. (ABC = American-British Conversations.)

75 March 1941 saw the opening of US air bases on the east coast of Greenland and a naval and air base at Bermuda.

76 The American Coastguard cutters became 'Banff' Class sloops in the Royal Navy. Their displacement was 1,546 tons, their turbo-electric motors (shaft horse power 3,200) gave them a speed of 16 knots and they carried, in addition to one 5-in. gun, a very heavy anti-aircraft armament: 2 3-in., 4 20-mm., 10 .5-in., 4 .303 AA guns. Their considerable endurance made them very suitable for providing continu-

ous escort on the Sierra Leone convoy route. Six survived to be returned to the US Coastguard Service in 1946.

77 Roskill op. cit. i p. 455.

78 Morison op. cit. p. 57; the correction appears on p. 73.

79 Lash op. cit. p. 229.

80 *The Grand Alliance* p. 122.

81 Op. cit. p. 188.

82 Marshal of the Royal Air Force Lord Tedder, *With Prejudice* p. 105; Cassell 1966.

83 Morison op. cit. p. 64.

84 Lash op. cit. p. 325.

85 Robert Harling *The Steep Atlantick Stream* p. 162; Chatto & Windus, 1946. He also relates (pp. 170–1) a 'languid' dialogue overheard under the sweltering Freetown sun:
    "'When I was under training in Plymouth last summer, rig o' the day was piped as number threes, negative jumpers.'"
    "Muster bin 'ot."
    "Cos it was 'ot. And I seen a destroyer comin' in at 'Arwich, seven o'clock in the evenin', and all in 'alf whites."
    "Muster bin 'ot."
    "Cos it was 'ot, stoopid."
    "Not as 'ot as now, eh?"
    "No, nor so many daft bleedin' matelots about as now."
    "Muster bin nice.'"

86 Dönitz op. cit. p. 176. The seven boats comprised:
    | Type VIIC: | *U 69* |
    | Type IXA: | *U 38* |
    | Type IXB: | *U 103, U 105, U 106, U 107, U 124* |

87 Op. cit. p. 120. The first east-bound convoy to have complete trans-Atlantic surface escort was *HX 129* at the end of May, and the first west-bound was *OB 331* (June 2).

88 *Flak = Fliegerabwehrkanonen*, German AA. Flying Officer Kenneth Campbell of No. 22 Squadron won a posthumous VC on 6 April in a Beaufort torpedo-bomber which flew unhesitatingly into the *Flak* to attack *Gneisenau*. Campbell's torpedo hit the battleship's stern below the waterline, causing damage which took eight months to repair. The Beaufort was shot out of the sky, the whole crew of four being killed.

89 Harris, *Bomber Offensive* p. 68; Collins 1947. *Prinz Eugen* sustained such heavy damage from one bomb on 1/2 July (First Officer and 60 men killed) that she was out of action until the end of the year.

Scharnhorst, in La Pallice, was hit by 5 bombs on 24/25 July, which kept her, also, out of action for many months. Weighing up the pros and cons of the Channel dash in January, 1942, Hitler expressed the dilemma in these words:

'If the ships remain in Brest, they will be put out of action by the enemy air force. They are like a cancer patient: without an operation the patient is certainly doomed; with an operation he *may* be saved. So we shall operate' (Bekker op. cit. p. 232).

90   Dönitz op. cit. p. 167 for this and following.

91   Op. cit. p. 234.

92   op. cit. pp. 141–2; Macintyre (op. cit. p. 82) says: 'There followed several weeks of inactivity in the area off Newfoundland.'

93   Schull op. cit. pp. 77–8 for this and following.

94   It may be remarked that disobeying Admiral Fisher's orders was a course of action rarely to be recommended.

95   Op. cit. p. 189 for this and following. No frigates appeared in the battle until April, 1942.

96   *Decisive Battles of World War II* p. 268.

97   Memorandum to Grand Admiral Raeder; op. cit. p. 153 for this and following.

98   Ibid. pp. 176–7.

99   Op. cit. p. 267.

III/4: *By the Narrowest of Margins* (*pp. 353–402*)

1   By mid-July the German forces on the central front were two-thirds of the way to Moscow, having advanced an average of 20 miles a day. In the north they had cut Leningrad off, and in the south they were menacing Kiev. By mid-September, when Kiev fell, the Germans had captured nearly 1,500,000 Russian soldiers, over 7,000 tanks and some 9,000 guns.

2   Hinsley, op. cit. ii, pp. 168–9.

3   Roskill, op. cit. i, p. 467.

4   Fritz Todt first won fame as the creator of the *Autobahn* system, much admired by Hitler. In 1938 he was made responsible for the regulation of construction within the Four Year Plan. As such he was much concerned with all building work for defence. His career reached its height in 1940 when he added the post of Reich Minister for Armaments and Munitions to his other duties. He was killed in an air crash in February, 1942. The Todt Organization supplied the labour for defence constructions, increasingly from slave sources.

5   On 15 April, 1941, the AOC-in-C of Bomber Command, Air Marshal

Sir Richard Peirse, told the Chief of Air Staff that since 10 January, for the 'benefit' of *Hipper*, *Scharnhorst* and *Gneisenau* he had been 'compelled to throw about 750 tons of high explosive into Brest harbour'. The quantity was later corrected to 829 tons. Denis Richards (op. cit. p. 236) informs us that in 1,161 sorties in 8 weeks against Brest, only 4 bombs found their mark. Sir Richard Peirse said frankly to Portal: 'We are not designed for this purpose and we are not particularly effective in execution.'

6   AHB/II/117/3(C) pp. 30–31 f.n. The attitude of irritated condescension which the Air Staff and Air Ministry displayed towards the Battle of the Atlantic throughout the year is well expressed in a letter from Portal to Peirse on 1 March when he said: 'A very high proportion of bomber effort will inevitably be required to pull the Admiralty out of the mess they have got into.' The Air Staff was at that stage pinning its faith to a renewed attack on German oil targets – always very difficult to find and hit. The Official Historians comment: 'Whether Sir Charles Portal really believed that this directive would get the Admiralty out of the 'mess' or not, it was in effect the Admiralty which had got the Air Ministry out of the "mess", for if Bomber Command had . . . been left free to carry out the oil plan it would probably have done a great deal more damage to its prestige than to its targets.' (*The Strategic Air Offensive against Germany 1939–45* ii, p. 165).

7   *The Right of the Line* p. 278.

8   Richards, op. cit. p. 349.

9   Op. cit. p. 409.

10   Ibid. pp. 142–3 for this and following quotations.

11   Lewin, *Ultra Goes to War* p. 211.

12   Op. cit. p. 143.

13   As we shall see, 'continuous protection' was a manner of speaking. SL 81, for example, set out from Freetown on 15 July with 18 merchant ships under the protection of seven escort vessels, but when five of these returned to Freetown the sole defence of the convoy for the next 6 days was two Armed Merchant Cruisers. On 3 August, however, it was joined by the 7th Escort Group, which included the Fighter Catapult Ship *Maplin* with a Sea-Hurricane aboard (piloted by Lieutenant R. W. H. Everett RNVR) which succeeded in shooting down a FW 200, the first victory for a catapult ship, for which Everett was rewarded by a DSO.

14   Op. cit. i, p. 470.

15   In addition to the U-boats, Hitler also sent a force of 'E-boats' (see p. 285 Note 26) and R-boats (motor minesweepers).

16 In the last three months of 1941 9 U-boats were lost in the Gibraltar area and the Mediterranean, and one more in the Bay of Biscay on passage to those waters.

17 Edward P. von der Porten, *The German Navy in World War II* p. 132; Pan, 1972.

18 Macintyre, op. cit. p. 99.

19 Dönitz, op. cit. pp. 159–61 for this and following quotations. Dönitz adds that he was entirely sceptical of any British plan to reinforce the Middle East via Gibraltar and the full length of the Mediterranean when, as he knew, they could continue to use the far safer (though longer) Cape route.

20 *OKW = Oberkommando der Wehrmacht*, the central Command of the German Armed Forces, headed by *Generalfeldmarschall* Keitel with *Generaloberst* Alfred Jodl as his Chief of Staff and Head of Operations. *OKH, Oberkommando des Heeres*, was the High Command of the Army, headed until December, 1941, by *Generalfeldmarschall* von Brauchitsch. All these impressive designations were illusory; steadily Hitler concentrated military power in his own hands, holding the powers of Minister of War, Supreme Commander of the Armed Forces (to whom every soldier, sailor and airman was personally bound by oath) and Army C-in-C.

21 Padfield, op. cit. p. 229.

22 According to the diary of *Generaloberst* Franz Halder, the Army Chief of Staff, the original planning of *BARBAROSSA* was founded on the following very intelligible propositions:
'The quicker Russia is smashed the better. The operation only makes sense if we shatter the Russian state at a single blow. To gain tracts of territory is not enough. To stand still in winter is dangerous.'
The conclusion was that the whole operation should be completed in five months (Official History, *Grand Strategy* iii, Part I p. 52 by J. M. A. Gwyer, HMSO 1964). In other words, even granted the late start (22 June), the USSR should by now (November) have been defeated. Instead, its resistance was, if anything, hardening, and the Russian winter was fast approaching.

23 See Lewin, *The Life and Death of the Afrika Korps* p. 14 (Batsford 1977); *General* von Thoma told Sir Basil Liddell Hart that he had found 'that the Führer was noticeably indifferent to the idea of ejecting the British from Egypt – a fact not so surprising when one recalls Hitler's ambivalence about the invasion of the British Isles'.

24 See *The Right of the Line* pp. 365–9.

25 Padfield, op. cit.

26 Chlorine was the gas encountered by the Allies at Ypres on 22 April,

1915. Its effects are graphically described in the Official History (*Military Operations, France and Belgium 1915* i, p. 177 f.n. 3), which adds: 'prolonged inhalation or exposure to a high concentration of the gas will cause death by asphyxia, or, if not fatal, produce cardiac dilatation and cyanosis (blueness of the skin) as a result of the injury to the lungs.' (See p. 112: *UB 55*, 1918).

27 Richards, op. cit. p. 227.

28 The full list of Coastal Command aircraft in June, 1941 is: Avro Anson, Bristol, Beaufighter, Beaufort, Blenheim (Fighter & General Reconnaissance), Consolidated Catalina, Empire Flying Boat, Lockheed Hudson, Hawker Hurricane, Consolidated Liberator, Northrop sea-plane, Supermarine Spitfire, Short Sunderland, Fairey Swordfish, Vickers-Armstrong Wellington, Armstrong Whitworth Whitley.

29 See *The Right of the Line* p. 111.

30 AHB/II/117/3(B) p. 310.

31 The Catalina prototype, XPBY-1, first flew in 1935. In the RCAF the flying boat was called 'Canso' and the amphibian version 'Canso A'.

32 Quoted by Richards, op. cit. p. 223.

33 Ibid. p. 227.

34 Op. cit. p. 158.

35 Op. cit. for this and following quotation.

36 Ibid. p. 347. It took Dönitz a long time to believe that this could ever happen. In an interview with a Swedish journalist in August, 1942, he stated flatly: 'The aeroplane can no more eliminate the submarine than the crow can fight a mole.' It was a poor analogy; he should have been thinking about gulls and fish.

37 As with many innovations, there were early difficulties with R/T; Macintyre (op. cit. p. 75) says: 'Not until after the entry of the United States into the war, when the excellent VHF radio-telephone called TBS (Talk Between Ships) became a standard fitting in all escorts, was there the free, reliable and rapid inter-communication so essential to coordinated team-work.'

38 Op. cit. p. 156 for this and following quotation.

39 AHB/II/117/3(C) p. 43.

40 The problem was that 'The maximum height for release (of depth charges) was 300 feet – above this the depth charge would break up on hitting the water. But with the very inaccurate altimeters of the period, this meant that to carry out a depth charge attack by night meant a very real risk of flying into the sea' (*The Right of the Line* p.

233). The answer was to replace the barometric altimeters by radio versions which could be depended on; this was done – in due course. In June, 1941, they were a long way off.

41 AHB/II/117/3(C) p. 42; my italics.

42 The minimum diving time for a Type VIIB U-boat was 20 seconds (see p. 197).

43 AHB/II/117/3(B) pp. 305–6.

44 AHB/II/117/3(C) p. 40.

45 Marshal of the Royal Air Force Sir John Slessor, *The Central Blue* p. 512 (Cassell 1956) for this and following quotation.

46 AHB/II/117/3(C) p. 50. The reduced sightings were probably due to reduced numbers of U-boats.

47 Price, op. cit. p. 75.

48 Dönitz, op. cit. pp. 177–8.

49 The exact extent of these delays is not easy to state with confidence. The Official History (*British Intelligence in the Second World War*), vol. i, p. 338, tells us that from August, 1941, to the end of the war the *HYDRA* traffic 'was read within 36 hours'; on p. 163 of vol. ii, we see that 'maximum delay was 72 hours and the normal delay . . . often only a few hours'; on p. 171 this becomes 'within an hour of . . . transmission'; on p. 174 we learn that the average delay in August was 50 hours, in September 41 hours and in October 26 hours.

50 Roskill, op. cit. i, p. 468, says that SC 42 'originally comprised sixty-four ships'; Macintyre, op. cit. p. 89, says 65 ships from Sydney with 5 more from St John's; the Convoy Summary in the Admiralty Naval Historical Branch says firmly that the figures were 62 + 5, naming each ship.

51 *Decisive Battles of World War II* p. 267.

52 Op. cit. p. 67.

53 Hinsley, op. cit. ii, p. 174.

54 Weather description from Milner and Macintyre; the Admiralty Monthly Anti-Submarine Report for September says that the weather on 9/10 September was 'Wind ESE, light airs; moderate swell' and on 10/11 September 'Wind SSE, force 3–4; heavy swell'. Neither of these descriptions would account for the convoy having to heave-to, and being 72 hours late at its meeting-point, though the latter fact is also recorded in the Report.

55 Macintyre, op. cit. p. 92.

56 *Baron Pentland* did not sink either; she was found derelict by *U 372* on 19 September and duly sunk on that date.

57 Harling, op. cit. p. 111.

58 Two hundred and fifty merchant ships were selected for fitting with catapults. These were designated Catapult Aircraft Merchant (CAM) ships; they sailed under the Red Duster, and their aircraft were flown by pilots drawn from Fighter Command and forming the RAF's Merchant Ship Fighter Unit. They are not to be confused with the Fighter Catapult Ships, also converted merchant vessels, which were RN Auxiliaries, referred to as HMS and flying the White Ensign. Besides HMS *Maplin* (see Note 13) there were only 4 more of these, HMS *Pegasus* (a World War I seaplane carrier), HMS *Springbank*, HMS *Ariguani* and HMS *Patia*.

59 Schull, op. cit. p. 83.

60 Milner, op. cit. p. 46.

61 Schull, op. cit. p. 85 for this and following quotation.

62 Op. cit. p. 97.

63 Milner, op. cit. p. 57. One recalls the signal made by Admiral Sir Andrew Cunningham in 1941, when pressed by the Admiralty to report on the progress in gunnery in the Mediterranean Fleet:
'There has been NO progress in gunnery in the Mediterranean in the years 1940 and 1941, but certain old lessons well known to Noah and the Armada have been re-learned at much trouble and expense. The most notable lesson is that the right range for any ship of the Mediterranean Fleet, from a battleship to a submarine, to engage an enemy ship with gunfire is Point Blank (nowadays 2,000 yards or less) AT WHICH RANGE EVEN A GUNNERY OFFICER CANNOT MISS' (S. W. C. Pack, *The Battle of Matapan* p. 36; Batsford 1961).

64 Milner, op. cit. p. 61.

65 Between mid-August and the end of the year U-boats sank, in the Atlantic, the following RN and Allied warships:

Escort Carrier	*Audacity*	Dec. 21	*U 751*
Fighter Catapult Ship	*Springbank*	Sept. 27	*U 201*
Destroyers	*Bath* (RNorN)	Aug. 19	*U 201*
	Broadwater	Oct. 18	*U 101*
	Cossack	Oct. 23	*U 563* (?)
	Stanley	Dec. 19	*U 574*
Corvettes	*Zinnia*	Aug. 23	*U 564* (?)
	Levis (RCN)	Sept. 18	*U 74*
	Fleur de Lys	Oct. 14	*U 206*
	Gladiolus	Oct. 16	*U 568* (?)

66 Macintyre, op. cit. p. 101.

67 HMS *Springbank* was originally built by Bank Line, then converted to Auxiliary Anti-Aircraft Cruiser which endowed her with a heavy AA armament which she retained when she was re-converted to a

Fighter Catapult Ship. She was commissioned on 17 March and completed her trials on 8 August.

68 Creighton, op. cit. pp. 130–31 for this and following quotations.

69 Martlet was the British designation of the Grumman F4F-3, which made its first flight in December, 1937, and was ordered by the US Navy in 1940. In October of that year it also entered service in the Fleet Air Arm. The Mark II could attain a maximum speed of 315 mph (390–400 mph in a dive), but perhaps its outstanding feature for the FAA was its 4 (Mark II, 6) .50 calibre guns in the wings.

70 Op. cit. p. 103.

71 The operational figures were:

July	60	October	75
August	60	November	81
September	74	December	86

72 Lash, op. cit. p. 402, citing the Roosevelt papers and CAB 65 in the Public Record Office; my italics.

73 Ibid. p. 416.

74 *The Grand Alliance* p. 389.

75 The first QP convoy, bound for Britain, sailed on 28 September, and the first Russia-bound convoy PQ 1, taking the route north of Iceland, left Hvalfjord the following day.

76 Milner, op. cit. p. 59.

77 Morison, op. cit. p. 85.

78 Milner, op. cit. p. 155 for this and following quotation.

79 Lash, op. cit. p. 417.

80 Morison, op. cit. p. 80.

81 Lord Halifax, British Ambassador in Washington, to Churchill following an interview with Roosevelt on 10 October (see Lash p. 422).

82 Ibid. p. 421.

83 Morison, op. cit. p. 86; when the convoy and the US escort parted on 25 September the following exchange took place:
Commodore to SOE: 'Please accept my best congratulations on the brand of work and efficiencies of all your ships in looking after us so very well, and my very grateful thanks for all your kindly advice and help. Wish you all success with best of luck and good hunting. If you come across Admiral Nimitz, give him my love. We were great friends some years ago out in China.'
SOE to Commodore: 'This being our first escort job your message is doubly appreciated. As in the last war I know our people afloat will see eye to eye. You have my admiration for handling such a varied assortment so effectively. Will give your message to Admiral Nimitz.

I was in China later and knew Admiral Little and many of your people. I hope we shall meet again. Good luck.' Evidently the Americans were learning fast. Not all signal interchanges in the Royal Navy and its associates were couched with such courtesy, as witness; *SOE to corvette*: 'Why have you taken so long to rejoin convoy?' *Corvette to SOE*: 'It was uphill all the way.'

84 Roskill, op. cit. i, p. 472.

85 'We have fed our sea for a thousand years
  And she calls us, still unfed,
Though there's never a wave of all her waves
  But marks our English dead:
We have strawed our best to the weed's unrest,
  To the shark and the sheering gull.
If blood be the price of admiralty,
  Lord God, we ha' paid in full!'
Rudyard Kipling's Verse: Definitive Edition p. 173; Hodder & Stoughton, 1940.

86 As Morison (op. cit. p. 93) remarks: 'Fundamental lessons in escort duty were expensively learned from the battle of Convoy SC 48.'

87 Lash, op. cit. p. 456.

88 Milner, op. cit. p. 83. Volume II of the *Official History of the RCAF, the Creation of a National Air Force* by W. A. B. Douglas (University of Toronto Press 1986) pp. 483–4 also discusses SC 52, with an excellent map, which nevertheless contains two curiosities: the sighting of the convoy is credited to *U 375*, although the sinking of the merchantman is attributed to *U 374* (as Milner), and the tally of sinkings from SC 52 by the *Raubritter* pack comes to 5, not 4, merchant ships. The order to the convoy to return illustrates the peculiarities of the command system. Admiral Bristol and the USN were now responsible for the Western Atlantic where the action took place; but routing instructions could only come from the Submarine Tracking Room in the Admiralty.

89 Milner, op. cit. p. 89 for this and following quotation.

90 *Stork* was launched as a Survey Ship in 1937 and converted for escort duties in 1939. Her displacement was 1,190 tons; she carried a crew of 125, and had a maximum speed of $18\frac{3}{4}$ knots. Her armament was 4 4.7-inch guns, 6 4-inch AA guns and 4 .50 AA guns.

91 RAF Gibraltar Command was set up in November, 1941, under Air Commodore S. P. Simpson, directly responsible to Coastal Command HQ.

92 Dönitz, op. cit. p. 181.

93 For this account I am indebted to Kenneth Poolman, *Focke-Wulf*

Condor: Scourge of the Atlantic, Terence Robertson, *Walker R. N.* (Evans Bros. 1956), Roskill and Dönitz.

94 Hinsley, op. cit. ii, p. 176.

95 Paper, *The Operational Use of Ultra in the Battle of the Atlantic* p. 19 (see Note 8 to p. 226).

96 Hinsley, op. cit. ii, p. 169.

97 Op. cit.

98 *The Grand Alliance* p. 539.

III/5: *A Roll of Drums (pp. 403–443)*

1 Accompanying Churchill to Washington were Lord Beaverbrook, Minister of Supply, (a conspicuous absentee was the Foreign Secretary, Anthony Eden, who was in Moscow holding important talks with Stalin; Beaverbrook was thus the only other member of the Government with Churchill); the First Sea Lord, Admiral of the Fleet Sir Dudley Pound; the CIGS, General Sir John Dill (until 25 December, when he was succeeded by Brooke and promoted to Field-Marshal; Dill remained in Washington as Churchill's personal representative and his close relationship with General Marshall became an important and fruitful element in the Grand Alliance until his death in November, 1944; [a long-overdue study, *Very Special Relationship: Field-Marshal Sir John Dill and the Anglo-American Alliance 1941–44* by Alex Danchev, has been published by Brassey's Defence Publishers in 1986]); and Air Chief Marshal Sir Charles Portal, the Chief of the Air Staff.

2 By great good fortune a prime target, the American aircraft-carrier squadron, was absent from Hawaii when the Japanese attacked.

3 *Queen Elizabeth*, *Valiant* and *Barham* all belonged to the 'Fast Squadron' of battleships which began to come into service in 1915 and were the first British capital ships to be oil-fired.

4 Admiral of the Fleet Viscount Cunningham of Hyndhope, *A Sailor's Odyssey* p. 435; Hutchinson 1951.

5 *The Hinge of Fate* pp. 14, 15 for this and preceding Churchill quotations.

6 Louis Morton in *Command Decisions* p. 35 (and following quotation), compiled by the Office of the Chief of Military History, Department of the Army (USA), Methuen 1960.

7 Sainsbury, op. cit. p. 72; the United States did not suddenly leap at 'Germany first' in 1941; the first step towards this strategy had been

taken in June, 1939, with the development of the RAINBOW Plans, of which No. 5 proposed 'a strategic defensive to be maintained in the Pacific until success against the European Axis Powers permitted transfer of major forces to the Pacific for an offensive against Japan.' This was followed in November, 1940, by Admiral Stark's 'Plan Dog' –paragraph 'D' of an examination of four strategic possibilities which he phrased as questions: 'Shall we direct our efforts toward an eventual strong offensive in the Atlantic as an ally of the British, and a defensive in the Pacific?' These are well discussed in *Command Decisions* pp. 14–38.

8 Sainsbury, op. cit. p. 65–6.

9 See *The Grand Alliance* pp. 582–4 for text of this paper, entitled 'The Campaign of 1943' and dated 18 December, 1941. Churchill understandably remarks that this paper deserves close study whenever his attitude towards a campaign in north-west Europe is under discussion.

10 Gwyer, op. cit. p. 363.

11 *The Right of the Line* pp. 364 & 400.

12 Op. cit. p. 196.

13 At a conference on 22 January, Hitler announced that Norway was 'the decisive theatre of war'. He ordered 'all available U-boats' to proceed there at once. The next day, having learned the initial results obtained by such a small number of U-boats off the American coast, he rescinded this order. Nevertheless, on the day after (24 Jan.) the Naval High Command ordered Dönitz to send 8 boats to the area Iceland-Faroes-Scotland for the protection of Norway. On 6 February he was ordered to increase the numbers actually in Norwegian waters from 4 to 6, with 2 more in a state of instant readiness either at Narvik or Tromsø, 2 more at Trondheim and 2 at Bergen. This concentration of 20 boats in the Norwegian area was to be completed by 15 February; 'this put an end for the time being to any reinforcement of the Atlantic theatre'. Dönitz comments that clearly Hitler and OKW 'had no precise knowledge of the number of boats available nor of the total number that would be required to maintain operations off the American coast'. One cannot help recalling the complete failure of Napoleon and his advisers to grasp the fundamentals of naval strategy in 1805 (see Terraine, *Trafalgar* pp. 61–3; Sidgwick & Jackson 1976 [USA: Mason-Charter]). For Hitler's vacillations in 1942 see Dönitz, op. cit. pp. 206–10.

14 Dönitz, op. cit. p. 197 for this and following quotation.

15 Morison, op. cit. p. 126. *Admiral* Tirpitz was not, of course, responsible.

16 Op. cit. p. 202.

727

17   Op. cit. pp. 129–30; my italics. No country has a monopoly of un-
     thinking selfishness. In both wars front-line soldiers were infuriated
     by the spectacle of war profiteers ostentatiously doing themselves
     well. In World War II British sailors were also liable to fury, as
     Nicholas Monsarrat tells us (op. cit. p. 67):
     'When I am ashore, and hear (as I have done) one man telling another
     that he can get as much petrol as he wants, by licensing all four of
     his cars and only using one of them: when I see photographs of
     thousands of cars at a race-meeting for which a special fast train-
     service is run: when I read a letter to a newspaper complaining that
     the writer has had difficulty in obtaining extra petrol for the grouse-
     shooting season: when I hear of *any* instance of more than the bare
     essential minimum of petrol being used, this is what I think of:
        A torpedoed tanker ablaze at sea, with all its accompanying horrors.
        That's your extra ten gallons of petrol, sir and madam: that's last
     week's little wangle with the garage on the corner. You might re-
     member what you're burning, now and then: its *real* basic coupon is
     a corpse-strewn Atlantic.'

18   Morison op. cit. pp. 200–201.

19   Dönitz op. cit. pp. 204–5 for this and following quotation.

20   The Type IXs were specifically designed as long-range 'cruisers' (see
     p. 195); IXC characteristics were:

Displacement: surface	1,120 tons
submerged	1,232 tons
Maximum speed: surface	18.3 knots
submerged	7.3 knots (for 1 hour)
Endurance: surface	16,300 miles at 10 knots
	11,000 miles at 12 knots
	5,000 miles at 18.3 knots
submerged	128 miles at 2 knots
	63 miles at 4 knots
Diving depth	330 feet (could be greatly exceeded in emergency)
Torpedo tubes	4 bow, 2 stern; 19 torpedoes (maximum 22)
Guns	1 37-mm AA; 2 20-mm AA
Crew	48

21   *Decisive Battles of World War II* p. 272.

22   Churchill told the Lord Privy Seal (Clement Attlee, also Deputy
     Prime Minister) on 4 January: 'It was decided to raise United States
     output of merchant shipping in 1942 to 8,000,000 tons deadweight
     and in 1943 to 10,000,000 tons deadweight.' He adds: 'the new ton-
     nage built in the USA was as follows:

1942   5,339,000 tons

1943   12,384,000 tons.'

23 *The Hinge of Fate* p. 107.

24 Morison op. cit. p. 254; Vice-Admiral Adolphus Andrews, Commander Eastern Sea Frontier, coined this unhappy phrase.

25 Roskill, *The War at Sea* ii, p. 98 for this and following quotations. The first three lessons, of course, were all established in 1917–18.

26 When not desperately perilous, convoy work could indeed be humdrum. Monsarrat recalls telling his Number One that they were due for another convoy escort the next morning: '"It's like going to the office every morning," said the First Lieutenant, after a pause. "Backwards and forwards. One of these days I'm going to put in for a bowler hat and a season ticket."'

27 King to Gen. Marshall, 21 June, 1942.

28 Op. cit. p. 255.

29 See Note 22. The American historian Charles B. MacDonald, however, says (op. cit. p. 23) that 'Mr Roosevelt had waited dangerously long before taking steps to regulate the nation's resources for war. . . . Only with the creation of the Office of Production Management – just eleven months to the day before war came – and, within it, of the War Production Board, was any real regulation applied to the nation's material and industrial resources.' Only then, he argues, were 'priorities' established (the Florida Chamber of Commerce advertised, 'There are no priorities on sunshine'). Even so, 'the late start meant that gaping holes in the armaments of both Army and Navy would long despoil the entire fabric of defense preparations.'

30 Morison, op. cit. p. 229.

31 Ibid. p. 268.

32 By comparison with Coastal Command, this seems to have been a fairly brisk start. The USN did, of course, have the benefit of Coastal Command's long experience; it went to war, for example, fully cognizant of the value of depth charges, without which, as the RAF had mournfully discovered, an aircraft does not have a lethal anti-submarine weapon. Squadron VP-82 may also have enjoyed a degree of beginner's luck, which no one would begrudge it.

33 Op. cit. p. 157.

34 From January to April the Eastern Sea Frontier headed the table of sinkings by U-boats:

January	14
February	17
March	28
April	23

When the Caribbean/Gulf offensive opened in May, losses in the Eastern Sea Frontier dropped to 5, rising again to 13 in June, dropping back to 3 in July and thereafter zero for the remainder of 1942.

35 Op. cit. p. 219 for this and following quotation.

36 Ibid. p. 286.

37 Op. cit. p. 145.

38 All these figures are stated by Dr Rohwer in *Decisive Battles of World War II* p. 272.

39 Official History: *Oil: A Study of War-Time Policy and Administration* by D. J. Payton-Smith p. 284; HMSO 1971; following quotation on p. 298.

40 The Battle of Midway on 4 June, in which the Japanese Navy lost 4 carriers (the USN lost 1), was Japan's first serious check in the war; with the hindsight of later knowledge Sir Basil Liddell Hart wrote: 'it can reasonably be said that Midway was the turning point that spelt the ultimate doom of Japan.' That comforting appreciation was not, of course, immediately available in June, 1942.

41 Admiral King became Commander in Chief United States Fleet (COMINCH) on 20 December, 1941, and absorbed into that post the function of Chief of Naval Operations on 26 March, 1942.

42 Morison, op. cit. pp. 308–10 for this and following quotations.

43 Op. cit. p. 130.

44 Dönitz was promoted to full Admiral in March, 1942, a sign of Hitler's favour and, no doubt, gratitude for successful exploits to sugar the pill of the winter set-back to *BARBAROSSA*. The promotion, says Padfield (op. cit. p. 238), was 'one of the quickest sprints through the flag ranks ever achieved in the German service'.

45 Dönitz, op. cit. pp. 221–2.

46 *The Hinge of Fate* p. 96.

47 Ibid. p. 110.

48 *Very Special Intelligence* p. 65 f.n.

49 Op. cit. p. 223 for this and following quotation.

50 Beesly, op. cit. p. 117.

51 Rohwer, Medlicott Symposium Paper, 1985.

52 Dönitz, op. cit. p. 242.

53 The Gospel according to St Matthew, xxv 29.

54 Roskill, op. cit. p. 92.

55 Ibid. p. 78.

56 AHB/II/117/3(C) p. 7 f.n. 4.

57 The meaning of this expression is explained by Captain Peyton-

Ward: 'When formed in June, 1941 No. 120 Squadron were allocated 20 Mark I Liberators. These were to form the squadron's initial establishment of 9 aircraft and to provide for wastage. Loans and allotment of these Liberators during August and October to Ferry Command and BOAC had by 9 October, 1941, reduced the squadron to a total of 10 aircraft with no reserves for wastage except the possibility of two aircraft which were being used for experimental trials.'

58   AHB/II/117/3(C) pp. 10–7 for this and following quotation.

59   Op. cit.

60   AHB/II/117/3(C) p. 12 for this and following quotation.

61   Op. cit. p. 232 for this and following quotations.

62   See Terraine, *The Right of the Line* pp. 404–6 for greater detail; Alfred Price's *Aircraft versus Submarine* contains an excellent description of the attack on the *Luigi Torelli* and that submarine's subsequent career.

63   Op. cit. p. 234 for this and following quotation.

64   Webster & Frankland, op. cit. i, p. 341; Harris to Churchill, June 17.

65   These figures differ slightly from those that I presented in *The Right of the Line* (p. 428); the correction follows the latest very careful research by the Naval Historical Branch, for which I am grateful.

66   The AHB Monograph, *Armament* vol. i, informs us that true shallow detonation was achieved by a design in which the tail broke away on impact and the nose was completely reshaped on unusual lines: 'The principle of redesign was the control of underwater travel by means of a "spoiler nose" the effect of which was to make the depth charge unstable, and to cause it to travel broadside on. Tank trials at the Admiralty Research Laboratory at Teddington with models gave promising results, and a Mark XI charge was accordingly designed which had a concave nose, to give the desired instability on impact. By the middle of 1942, production of depth charges was concentrated on the Mark XI which in combination with a modified pistol had proved to be the most satisfactory anti-submarine weapon.'

67   'Born again' in 1942 had another connotation, as a Coastal Command officer discovered when, quite by chance, he came upon an Admiralty publication of April, 1918 entitled 'Notes on Aids to Submarine Hunting'. The author was Major J. G. Struthers, DSC, RAF, and the publication summarized the conclusions of nearly four years of anti-submarine warfare waged by the Airship Department. The finder was amazed to discover how up-to-date and applicable to 1942 procedures the publication was, and in an article for *Coastal Command Review* (the 'house journal' of the Command)* he stated that if the book and its author had been consulted in the early days of the war:

much experimentation would have been avoided, and the present stage of anti-submarine efficiency would have been reached earlier and would have been by now surpassed. *Coastal Command Review* No. 5, Sept., 1942.

68 *The Grand Alliance* p. 539.

69 Macintyre, op. cit. p. 138.

70 Rear-Admiral A. L. Bristol died suddenly of a heart attack on 30 April, and was replaced by Vice-Admiral R. M. Brainard.

71 Schull, op. cit. p. 101.

72 Macintyre (op. cit. p. 156) refers to another valuable discovery by Operational Research, namely that 'whereas the number of ships lost in a convoy battle depended, as might be expected, upon the number of U-boats attacking and the size of the escort, it was quite independent of the size of the convoy. Thus by increasing the size of convoys from an average of 32 ships to 54, which reduced the *numbers* of convoys open to attack at any one time, losses could be lessened by 56 per cent.'

73 Quoted in *Design and Development of Weapons* by M. M. Postan, D. Hay & J. D. Scott pp. 392–3.

74 Op. cit. p. 324.

75 Rohwer, *The Critical Convoy Battles of March 1943* p. 21 (op. cit.)

76 Morison, op. cit. p. 122.

77 Ibid. p. 211.

78 Op. cit. pp. 173–4.

79 Op. cit. p. 182 for this and following quotation.

80 Robertson *Walker, R.N.* pp. 53–4.

81 Op. cit. p. 155 for this and following quotation.

82 Milner, op. cit. p. 97.

83 AHB/II/117/3(C) p. 15; all italics are mine.

84 AHB/II/117/3(C) op. cit. for this and following quotation.

III/6 *The Heartbeat of the War* (*pp. 444–512*)

1 U-boat War Diary, 15 April (Dönitz *Memoirs* p. 228 for this and following quotation). It should be noted that U-boat HQ was now back in Paris. The British Commando raid on St Nazaire on 27–28 March was not directed against the U-boats, but intended to destroy the only dry dock on the Atlantic coast capable of holding the *Tirpitz*. However the success of the raid revealed the vulnerability of Dönitz's HQ by the sea at Kernével; it was accordingly moved to an apartment block in the Avenue Maréchal Maunoury.

2   Ibid. pp. 226–7 for this and following quotations.

3   see p. 423.

4   Roskill, op. cit. ii p. 614.

5   Dönitz, op. cit. p. 227.

6   Ibid. p. 222 for this and following.

7   Milner, op. cit. p. 113 for this and following.

8   Schull, op. cit. p. 112.

9   Quoted in Milner, op. cit. p. 115, as also following two quotations.

10 Ibid. p. 103 for this and following quotations.

11 On 27 June the ill-fated Arctic convoy PQ 17 set sail for Archangel; out of 36 merchant ships and 3 rescue ships, 23 merchantmen and 1 rescue ship were sunk by air and U-boat action, with a loss of 99,316 tons of cargo. It was the worst convoy disaster of the war.

12 HMCS *Restigouche* alone carried FH3 HF/DF which enabled her to locate 5 U-boats as they made their sighting reports. In December, 1941, this 'C' Class destroyer was very nearly sunk by damage caused in a tremendous gale. While she was being repaired in Britain, her enterprising captain, by undefined means, succeeded in 'acquiring' the FH3, which made her the pioneer of HF/DF in the RCN.

13 Morison, op. cit. pp. 306–8 for this and following quotations.

14 A wrong appreciation of the likely developments of anti-submarine warfare had led the USN to place too much emphasis on speed in its new specialized craft.

15 Rohwer, *Critical Convoy Battles of March 1943* p. 36.

16 Beesly, op. cit. pp. 117–8 for this and following quotation.

17 Lewin, *The Other Ultra* p. 43; Hutchinson 1982.

18 US Defense Department, *The 'Magic' Background of Pearl Harbor*, quoted in Lewin op. cit. p. 44.

19 A theory was evolved by some of President Roosevelt's numerous enemies that he 'was personally responsible for ensuring that available evidence about an imminent Japanese attack . . . somehow got manipulated and withheld from those who "needed to know".' Ronald Lewin comments: 'The conspiracy theory is moonshine' (op. cit. p. 50).

20 This is a recurring phenomenon; Telford Taylor told Ronald Lewin that 'the status of the intelligence officer in the pre-Pearl Harbor American armed forces was low' (*Ultra Goes to War* p. 251), and we have seen (pp. 177–8) that Intelligence was a backwater in the inter-war Royal Navy. The pre-1914 French Army also undervalued

its Intelligence Service (2eme Bureau), following the humiliations of the Dreyfus Case. In May, 1916, Admiral Jellicoe, commanding the Grand Fleet in the Battle of Jutland, lost faith in information from the Admiralty based on Room 40's decrypts of German signals. First, he suffered the shock of encountering the German Fleet in the middle of the North Sea only three hours after being told that it was still in the Jade River. This was not a fault of Room 40, but of the Admiralty's system of consulting its priceless source. Somewhat later, Jellicoe had another shock when the Admiralty's signals placed a German light cruiser in practically the identical position of Jellicoe's own flagship. This proved to be a fault of the German navigator, who caused a wrong signal to be sent – but Jellicoe was not to know that, and henceforth he disregarded Admiralty Intelligence. As a result, his efforts to intercept the retreating High Sea Fleet came to nothing and his enemies escaped at the end of the battle.

21   Op. cit. pp. 113–4.

22   *RUSI Journal*, August, 1967 p. 223, 'Naval Intelligence in the Second World War.'

23   Op. cit. p. 114 for this and following.

24   A footnote explains: 'In May, 1943, as well as receiving the intelligence summaries issued by Whitehall to the naval commands at home and overseas, the Tracking Room in Ottawa began to receive a full service of Enigma decrypts and from that time it carried on a completely free exchange of ideas and information by direct signal link with the Tracking Room in the OIC.'

25   Hinsley, op. cit. ii p. 48.

26   Op. cit. p. 175. Rodger Winn's deputy was, of course, Patrick Beesly.

27   Dönitz, op. cit. p. 238.

28   In particular Dönitz was looking forward to receiving in October some Type IXD2 boats, 1,365 tons with an endurance of 31,500 miles, which would enable him to attack shipping off the East African ports in the Indian Ocean.

29   Slessor, op. cit. p. 521.

30   Op. cit. p. 240.

31   Rohwer, *Decisive Battles of World War II* p. 274 for this and following.

32   This report came from *Fregattenkapitän* Suhren (*U 564*); the 'locating device' was the American centimetric radar, equivalent to ASV III, known as SCR 517, with which a number of Liberators were fitted before delivery.

33 Milner, op. cit. p. 125.

34 Schull, op. cit. p. 131.

35 It should be noted that *Korvettenkapitän* Topp (*U 552*) told Dönitz in a signal exchange to establish whether there was any point in pressing home further attacks, in answer to the question 'Did anything ... make the attack more difficult?' 'Attack further complicated by sudden advent of bad weather which enemy used skilfully to change course through 360°. As a result many boats lost contact.'

36 Milner, op. cit. p. 130.

37 Schull, op. cit. pp. 131–3 for this and following quotations. Among other noteworthy Biblical signals was one from a corvette towing a damaged merchantman to the C-in-C, Plymouth:
    '*Roman Emperor* in tow, badly damaged, please send tugs.'
    The C-in-C replied: 'Revelations Chapter 3 verse 11', which translates as: 'Behold, I come quickly; hold that fast which thou hast, that no man take thy crown.'
    Perhaps best of all was the response to congratulations to a corvette Commanding Officer on being promoted to Lieutenant-Commander:
    'VMT. Psalm 140, 2nd half of verse 5', which comes out as: 'Very many thanks. They have set gins for me.' There is nothing like a good grounding in religion.

38 Milner, op. cit. p. 137; Schull (op. cit. p. 134) adds that 'An uprush of oil flooded to the surface, followed by a heavy underwater explosion.' These misleading signs were common.

39 Milner, op. cit. pp. 139–40 for this and following.

40 Rohwer, *Critical Convoy Battles* p. 36 (my italics). In *Ultra Goes to War* (p. 196) Ronald Lewin refers to this as a time 'when the great Atlantic convoys began their death ride'. It is a striking phrase, but it has to be tempered by reference to Jürgen Rohwer's equally striking revelation that only 16 out of 174 convoys lost more than 4 ships.

41 Op. cit. p. 310.

42 Evidence and Documents of the International Military Tribunal (Nuremberg) quoted in Padfield (op. cit. p. 244).

43 Ibid. p. 245. Padfield also (p. 256) quotes Dönitz's Order of 7 October, in which he refers to the sinking of rescue ships and says: 'In view of the desired annihilation of ships' crews their sinking is of great value.'

44 Op. cit. p. 130. Dönitz (op. cit. p. 263) refers to *Fregattenkapitän* Eck of *U 852* who, on 13 March, 1944, opened fire on survivors of a sunken ship clinging to wreckage in the water. Eck was condemned

to death by a British court martial and shot on 30 November, 1945. His was, says Dönitz, 'the only one case in which a U-boat captain attacked survivors' – a statement which would be disputed by a number of the said survivors.

45   Op. cit. p. 18.

46   Op. cit. p. 57.

47   Ibid. pp. 116–17 for this and following quotations.

48   Op. cit. p. 256.

49   Mystery surrounded the *Laconia* incident for many years, and the appearance of the English translation of Dönitz's *Memoirs* brought speculation to a head. There was considerable doubt about whether the B-24 in question was American or one supplied to Coastal Command; there was also much doubt about who had given the order to attack *U156*. The whole tone of Dönitz's account seemed to suggest that the British were responsible, and the US Navy Department showed no enthusiasm for re-examining the matter. However, when two reputable writers approached the US Air Force they received a more helpful response. They were Dr Maurer Maurer and Mr Lawrence J. Paszek; they wrote a very detailed article entitled 'Origin of the Laconia Order' for the *US Air University Review*, and this was reprinted in the *RUSI Journal* in November, 1964. My narrative is almost entirely based upon it. Captain Roskill added an informative and lengthy note to the *RUSI*'s publication. Among minor but interesting matters mentioned by the authors is the origin of the name, Wideawake Field; this derived from the large numbers of 'wideawakes' (sooty terns) on Ascension Island.

50   This and following quotations from the above article, *RUSI* pp. 341–2.

51   Dönitz, op. cit. p. 260 for this and following quotations.

52   Quoted in Padfield, op. cit. p. 255. The version presented by Dönitz (op. cit. p. 263) differs significantly in tone and omits the last injunction (para. 4); it reads:

> 'All attempts to rescue the crews of sunken ships will cease forthwith. This prohibition applies equally to the picking up of men in the water and putting them aboard a lifeboat, to the righting of capsized lifeboats and to the supply of food and water. Such activities are a contradiction of the primary object of war, namely, destruction of enemy ships and their crews.'

53   *RUSI*, op. cit. p. 343.

54   *The Hinge of Fate* p. 783 for this and following qu.

55   U-boat War Diary, 20 July, qu. Padfield op. cit. p. 248.

56 Schull, op. cit. p. 136.

57 Macintyre (op. cit. p. 143) tells us that this was a coloured crew, the Lascars referred to in Note 29 to p. 251.

58 Macintyre, op. cit. p. 144.

59 Op. cit. p. 146. It is worth noting that following *U 593*'s attack on 5 August *Assiniboine* carried out a sweep which took her 30 miles from the convoy – at which distance she could verify that its smoke was clearly visible. Only destroyers could carry out such manoeuvres and hope to return in reasonable time, and for them this was nothing unusual.

60 Op. cit. (Note 55).

61 Ibid. pp. 249–50.

62 Ibid. p. 248.

63 *Decisive Battles of World War II* p. 283.

64 See Terraine *The Right of the Line* p. 431 for a narrative of a typical encounter.

65 *Memoirs* p. 268. Plate XXX shows how this armament expanded in 1943.

66 Richards & Saunders, op. cit. p. 112.

67 Dönitz, op. cit. pp. 269–70 for this and following quotations.

68 Qu. Padfield, op. cit. p. 251.

69 *Memoirs* p. 253.

70 Ibid. pp. 252–3.

71 Roskill, op. cit. ii, p. 203.

72 Morison, op. cit. pp. 260–2 for this and following. The GAT-TAG (Guantanamo-Aruba-Trinidad) convoys carried the bulk of the trade with South America. They were extended southward in October by TS (Trinidad South) convoys plying to Paramaribo (Surinam) and Rio de Janeiro.

73 Milner, op. cit. pp. 148 and 150 for this and following.

74 Ibid. p. 163.

75 Op. cit. p. 272.

76 Ibid. p. 274.

77 Schull, op. cit. p. 115.

78 Qu. Beesly, op. cit. pp. 149–50 for this and following quotations.

79 This number may be compared with the 70 destroyers, 18 sloops, 67 corvettes and 10 ex-US Coastguard cutters in Western Approaches at the beginning of the year.

80 Op. cit. pp. 269–70 for this and following Roskill quotations.

81   Op. cit. p. 294.

82   Op. cit. p. 150.

83   Op. cit. p. 274.

84   The 'Treasury' Class cutters began to appear at the end of June, 1942. They were large vessels, 327 feet long, displacing 2,750 tons (more than contemporary US destroyers), carrying a crew of 243 and with a maximum speed of 12 knots.

85   Dönitz (op. cit. p. 274) informs us that the naming of U-boat groups was done by his staff, who showed 'a predilection for the names of beasts of prey'. On special occasions they departed from this, and now, in deference to the wild Atlantic storms, they took another tack: 'The physical strain resulting from the boat's endless pitching and rolling must have filled the crew's hearts with a longing for some peaceful and sunny haven of retreat. To show his sympathy with such longings the operations officer of my staff chose for one group, which at the end of October was disposed in the wintry area to the north-east of Newfoundland and south of Greenland, the code name of "Violet". Little jokes like that did a great deal towards fostering mutual understanding between the staff at home and the crews in the far-flung ocean.' He may be right.

86   Milner, op. cit. p. 178 for this and following.

87   Douglas, op. cit. p. 527, quoting the RCAF attack report.

88   Four U-boats were destroyed on this day: one in the Eastern Mediterranean by the joint efforts of the Royal Navy and the RAF, one in the Atlantic by causes unknown, and two by the RCAF. Sadly, the latest researches compel the subtraction of 3 kills from the proud record of No. 120 Squadron to which I have paid tribute in *The Right of the Line*: *U661* on 15 October is now attributed to HMS *Viscount*; *U132* on 5 November to an explosion (see text) and *U254* on 8 December to collision (see text).

      The Douglas Digby (US designation B-18) was a twin-engined bomber-reconnaissance aircraft which made its first flight in 1935. It had a maximum speed of 215 mph, a service ceiling of 23,900 feet, and carried a bomb-load of 4,000 lb. Twenty were supplied to the RCAF in June, 1940, despite the Neutrality Act, by the simple expedient of running them up to the frontier and allowing them to roll down a slope into Canada. Their ability to make sustained patrols at a range of over 300 miles gave them an obvious maritime value in No. 10 Squadron, but they were already obsolescent and those that survived were phased out in 1943. *U520* was their only kill.

89   Roskill, op. cit. ii pp. 212–13.

90 Terraine, op. cit. p. 400.

91 Leo J. Meyer in *Command Decisions* op. cit. p. 129.

92 Fraser, *Alanbrooke* p. 247; Hodder & Stoughton 1982.

93 Ibid. p. 530.

94 Op. cit. ii pp. 92–3.

95 Sherwood *The White House Papers of Harry L. Hopkins* ii p. 558; Eyre & Spottiswoode 1949.

96 Op. cit. pp. 482–3.

97 Op. cit. p. 276; this complete surprise is itself the more surprising in view of the German High Command's unjustified sensitivity about French North Africa a year earlier (see pp. 359–61).

Derek Tangye, wartime Press Officer of MI5, says that when he joined that organization at the beginning of the war, 'the Germans as an intelligence force had the rating of a Fourth Division football team' (Anthony Masters *The Man Who Was M* p. 187; Blackwell, 1984). This is a strong statement, but in some respects not far from the truth; a conspicuous example of poor German Intelligence is the notorious Schmid Report to Göring in July, 1940, on the comparative striking power of the RAF and the *Luftwaffe* which, among many extraordinary errors, made no mention of radar though some British Chain Home stations were visible across the Channel with the naked eye. On the other hand, of course, the work of the Navy's *B-Dienst* was never less than excellent and competent judges have pronounced the German Listening Service (*Horchdienst*) as more efficient than the British 'Y' – which is saying a good deal.

98 Ibid. pp. 279–85 for this and following; my italics.

99 The U-boats in question were *U660*, *U605*, *U595*, *U411*, *U259*, *U331*, and *U98*. Aircraft, land- and carrier-based, were responsible for four of the sinkings. The corvette *Lotus* shared two sinkings, the second being *U605*, destroyed by a Hedgehog salvo. *Lotus*'s captain, in his Report of Proceedings, displayed once more the erudition of RNVR officers of that period, using the unusual word πομφολυγοπαφλάσμασιν from *The Frogs* by Aristophanes to give an onomatopoeic rendering of the underwater noises of the stricken U-boat. The Naval Staff were so struck with the appropriateness of this that they reproduced it themselves with suitable attribution, explanation and translation: 'loud and long bubble-bursting accompaniment'.

100 Milner, op. cit. p. 186.

101 Churchill, op. cit. p. 537. The First Battle of El Alamein was General Auchinleck's defensive victory between 1–22 July when he 're-peated his record as the first British general to defeat a German

general in the Second World War'. Thereafter Rommel was always on the defensive, so that 'First Alamein' was in fact 'the turning-point of the Desert campaigns' (see *The Right of the Line* p. 375).

102 Roskill, op. cit. ii pp. 88–9 for this and following quotations.

103 It was a fortunate circumstance for the Allied cause that the Army and the Navy should be represented in Washington by men of such stature and possessing such diplomatic flair as Field-Marshal Sir John Dill and Admiral Sir Percy Noble.

104 Gretton, op. cit. p. 169.

105 Chalmers, op. cit. p. 161.

106 Ibid. pp. 172–3 for this and following.

107 Ibid. p. 183.

108 Edwards, op. cit. p. 98.

109 Op. cit. ii p. 217.

110 Qu. Beesly, Medlicott Symposium 1985.

111 Op. cit. p. 180.

112 *Very Special Intelligence* pp. 162–3, quoting Chalmers p. 181 for closing lines.

113 Dönitz, op. cit. p. 286.

114 Rohwer (*The Critical Convoy Battles of March, 1943* p. 34), referring to the interception of R/T traffic by U-boats, comments: 'Since, with the existing equipment, the traffic could only be heard up to about 30 miles and could not be located by D/F, this method seemed to offer only limited possibilities.'

115 Op. cit. pp. 288–9 for this and following quotations.

116 Milner, op. cit. p. 194 for this and following quotations.

117 Macintyre, op. cit. p. 152.

118 Hinsley, op. cit. ii p. 548.

119 Ibid. p. 749.

120 Op. cit. pp. 157–8 for this and following quotations.

121 Rodger Winn died in 1972, aged 68. It is to be supposed that his original affliction (polio) plus the heavy strain of the Tracking Room may well have shortened his life to some extent, but it is pleasant to record that he had 30 useful years to go before his doctor's grim prognostication in December, 1942 took effect.

122 Milner, op. cit. pp. 205–10 for the ONS 154 narrative.

123 Op. cit. p. 289.

124 Op. cit. ii p. 218.

III/7 *We Had Lost the Battle* (*pp. 513–613*)

1   For the provenance of the slogan, 'Unconditional Surrender', at
Casablanca, see Major-General J. F. C. Fuller, *The Decisive Battles
of the Western World and their Influence on History* iii pp. 506–9;
Eyre & Spottiswoode, 1956. The phrase itself is embedded in American history by the reply sent to the Confederate commander of Fort
Donelson in Tennessee when he proposed an armistice in which to
discuss surrender terms, by the Union commander, General Ulysses
S. Grant, on February 16 1862:
'Sir,
    Yours of this date, proposing armistice and appointment of com-
missioners to settle terms of capitulation, is just received. No terms
except unconditional and immediate surrender can be accepted. I
propose to move immediately upon your works.
                    I am, sir, very respectfully,
                    Your obedient servant . . .'
United States opinion was much struck with Grant's brisk wording,
at a time when the Union was enduring mixed fortunes in the war;
but what may be an entirely appropriate procedure for procuring the
quick surrender of a small garrison is not necessarily so acceptable in
the case of great nations of over 100 million people. See Fuller, *The
Generalship of Ulysses S. Grant* p. 91; John Murray, 1929.

2   Roskill, op. cit. ii p. 355.

3   Admiralty Anti-Submarine Reports, Jan. 1943 vii p. 5.

4   Op. cit. p. 318.

5   Churchill, *The Hinge of Fate* p. 619.

6   See *The Right of the Line* pp. 436–8.

7   Slessor, op. cit. p. 499.

8   Webster & Frankland, op. cit. iv pp. 152–3 for this and following.

9   Op. cit. p. 137.

10 Hinsley op. cit. ii p. 754.

11 Op. cit. p. 144. The most implausible Casablanca photographs of
all, without any hint of lightheartedness in them, are those showing
Generals de Gaulle and Giraud enduring paroxyms of spurious cordiality.

12 Raeder's actual resignation, following a characteristically splenetic
outburst from Hitler attacking the Navy *in toto*, was on 6 January.
The lapse of time was partly attributable to him having to choose
between Dönitz and *Admiral* Rolf Carls, commanding Navy Group
North, and partly to mask disagreement following a defeat.

13   Dönitz, op. cit. p. 321 for this and following.

14   Ibid. p. 311 for this and following quotations.

15   Bekker, op. cit. pp. 292–3.

16   The statistics of the March 1933 Reichstag Election were:

Nazis	17,265,283 (288 seats)
Nationalists	3,132,595 (52 seats)
Social Democrats	7,176,505 (120 seats)
Communists	4,845,379 (1 seat)
Centre Party	4,423,161 (73 seats)
Bavarian People's Party	1,072,893 (19 seats)
German People's Party	432,105 (2 seats)

No other party obtained as many as 400,000 votes.

17   Op. cit. pp. 304–6 for this and following quotations.

18   Op. cit. p. 268.

19   On 7 November, 1938, a young Jew named Herschel Grynszpan shot Counsellor Ernst vom Rath in the German Embassy in Paris. Vom Rath died on 9 November, and immediately the Nazis carried out a ferocious anti-Jewish pogrom, looting shops, destroying homes and burning synagogues. According to the official statement, 36 Jews were killed, and 36 more injured, but the true figures were probably very much higher.

20   Op. cit. p. 404.

21   p. 401.

22   Op. cit. pp. 465–6. The aircraft types operational in Coastal Command were: Albemarle, Anson, Beaufighter, Catalina, Flying Fortress, Gladiator, Halifax, Hampden, Hudson, Liberator, Mosquito, Northrop (seaplane), Spitfire, Sunderland, Swordfish, Ventura, Wellington, Whitley.

23   Gretton, op. cit. p. 45.

24   Op. cit. p. 326.

25   Op. cit. pp. 90 and 93. The measurement and description of seas and winds are not an easy matter. To give, for example, a Force 8 wind (Gale Force: maximum 34–40 knots) an average is taken of the wind speeds during gusts and lulls. A lull (described by Adlard Coles in *Heavy Weather Sailing*, p. 23 as 'a transitory and sudden lack of wind speed') may last only a second; a 40-knot gust of the same duration will deliver 16 times the punch of a 10-knot wind in a lull. It is the gusts that do the damage and leave lasting impressions on those who endure them. In the hurricane of October, 1987, gusts of 94 mph were recorded in London, 110 mph on the south coast, and 145 mph in Brittany; Werner's 150 mph gusts in the North Atlantic are therefore quite probable.

His 70-metre waves are a different matter. It is likely that an error has crept into the translation here. Coles (p. 25) says that waves 35–40 *feet* high 'may be encountered in a West Indian hurricane'. He adds that: 'there are occasional abnormal waves which attain a height far in excess of the normal run of the seas. Such waves can attain heights as much as 100 ft. in violent ocean storms'. Francis Chichester (*Along the Clipper Way*, 1966) says that an American ship once encountered a 112-foot wave in the South Pacific, and a whaler claimed to have met one 120 feet high in the Southern Ocean. 120 feet = 36.6 metres.

26 Schull op. cit. pp. 163–4.

27 Op. cit. pp. 316–17 for this and following quotations.

28 *Ultra Goes to War* pp. 213–14.

29 Dönitz, op. cit. p. 217.

30 Hinsley, op. cit. ii p. 551.

31 This quotation is an amalgam of a sentence in *Very Special Intelligence* (pp. 171–2) and a similar sentence in his paper 'British Naval Intelligence in Two World Wars' (op. cit.).

32 I use the word 'partial' because Hinsley (op. cit. ii pp. 551–2) informs us that: 'By 17 February . . . the settings had not been broken for ten days in January, and no traffic had been read since 10 February. And between 10 March and the end of June the settings for a further 22 days were either not broken at all or broken only after a long delay.'

33 Hinsley, op. cit. ii pp. 554–5 for this and following quotations.

34 Ibid. p. 549.

35 Quoted in Padfield, op. cit. pp. 266–7.

36 Dönitz, op. cit. pp. 243–4 for this and following quotations.

37 Op. cit. ii p. 356.

38 In 1942 HMS *Hesperus* sank *U 93* (15 January) and shared *U 357* with the destroyer *Vanessa* on 26 December; in 1943 *Hesperus* sank *U 191* on 23 April and *U 186* on 12 May – all in the North Atlantic.

39 Op. cit. p. 322.

40 Bekker, op. cit. p. 320, says 4 U-boats were 'severely damaged by depth charges'; Roskill, op. cit. p. 356, tells us that three-quarters of the U-boats engaged suffered depth charge attacks, but only 2 were 'seriously damaged'.

41 Op. cit. ii pp. 356–7.

42 Op. cit. p. 323.

43 Hinsley, op. cit. ii p. 561.

44 *Burza* had escaped to Britain in 1939, together with two other Polish destroyers, *Blyskawica* and *Grom*; *Grom* was sunk by German aircraft off Narvik in May, 1940. According to Morison (op. cit. p. 340) the crew of USCGC *Campbell* called *Burza* 'the fighting'est ship they'd ever seen'.

45 Dönitz, op. cit. pp. 323–4.

46 Morison, op. cit. p. 341, says that ON 166 'lost seven merchant ships'. This reflects different methods of computation. He also tells us that by 22 February the 63 ships of the original convoy had been reduced to 42 in the prevailing foul weather. Clearly, he does not count losses among these stragglers as loss in convoy – yet it was to ON 166 that they belonged.

47 See p. 269.

48 Op. cit. p. 48.

49 Op. cit. p. 341.

50 Roskill, op. cit. ii p. 357; the Type XIVs all belonged to No. 12 *Flottille*, stationed at Bordeaux.

51 *Decisive Battles of World War II* p. 282.

52 Op. cit. p. 183.

53 Ibid. p. 189.

54 Ibid. p. 198.

55 Ibid. p. 205.

56 Ibid. p. 213.

57 The USN delegation at the Conference was headed by Admiral King, and consisted of 35 officers; the RN delegation was headed by Admiral Sir Percy Noble, with Vice-Admiral Sir Henry Moore, Vice-Chief of Naval Staff and Rear-Admiral J. M. Mansfield, Chief of Staff at Western Approaches, in support; at the head of the RCN delegation was Rear-Admiral V. G. Brodeur supported by Captain H. G. DeWolf and Captain H. N. Lay. It is always the misfortune of a smaller contingent that it is likely to be heavily outranked on such occasions.

58 Hilary St George Saunders (*Royal Air Force 1939–45* iii p. 39) instances one drawback of the Moroccan Sea Frontier:

'The American Officer Commanding the Moroccan Sea Frontier was in a position of complete independence. He had his own intelligence staff, which frequently provided him with information on the movements of U-boats differing markedly from that which the Air Officer Commanding at Gibraltar received from British sources. The American commander persistently used the long-range aircraft at his disposal for the escort of convoys classified by Admiralty intelligence as unthreatened, and for anti-submarine sweeps where, if that intelligence was correct, and it was, no U-boats were operating.'

59   Op. cit. ii p. 358.

60   Milner, op. cit. pp. 234 and 233.

61   Both the Royal Navy and the US Navy had taken to heart the lesson of HMS *Audacity* (see pp. 385–6 etc.) and had instituted programmes of escort carrier building. The first of these to see North Atlantic service was USS *Bogue* and the group built around her was the pioneer USN Support Group. USS *Bogue* had a flight deck 492 feet long, her displacement was 14,200 tons (large for an escort carrier) her maximum speed was 18 knots, she carried a heavy AA armament and on this cruise 9 Grumman Wildcat fighters (F4F-4) and 12 Grumman Avenger anti-submarine strike aircraft (TBF-1). In the course of six cruises to May, 1945, her aircraft accounted for 6 German U-boats and one Japanese blockade runner and shared in the destruction of two more U-boats. She became an important element in holding the Atlantic victory when it was won.

62   Beesly, Medlicott Symposium paper, 'British Naval Intelligence in Two World Wars'.

63   Bill Gunston, *Encyclopedia of the World's Combat Aircraft* p. 42; Salamander 1976, for this and following.

64   Roskill, op. cit. ii p. 364.

65   Op. cit. p. 499 for this and following.

66   Roskill, op. cit. ii p. 361.

67   Slessor, op. cit. p. 490.

68   The full text of Churchill's letter appears in Appendix P of Roskill's vol. ii, from which this and following quotations are taken.

69   Saunders, op. cit. pp. 37–8 for this and following.

70   Op. cit. ii p. 362.

71   Medlicott Symposium paper, op. cit.

72   Milner, op. cit. p. 234.

73   Op. cit. p. 159 for this and following quotation.

74   Rohwer, *The Critical Convoy Battles of 1943* p. 47 for this and following quotation.

75   *Decisive Battles of World War II* p. 289.

76   Op. cit. p. 186.

77   The Western Support Force was formed in November at the Admiralty's suggestion by removing all destroyers from the Western Local Escort Force. The experiment was not a success. Milner informs

us: 'The heavy weather of December and January, which kept U-boat activity low, also reduced WSF's ageing destroyers to hulks. By Christmas Day only four of the twelve destroyers assigned to WSF were operational, and this figure was no better two months later.'

78 Op. cit. p. 326.

79 The Convoy and Routing Section of the Office of the Chief of Naval Operations, which controlled merchant shipping in the US Strategic Zone, came into existence on 17 June, 1941. It was modelled upon the British Naval Control Service (see p. 288).

80 Op. cit. ii p. 365.

81 Chalmers, op. cit. p. 219.

82 Macintyre, op. cit. p. 162.

83 As stated in Note 61, the Royal Navy had been duly impressed by the performance of HMS *Audacity*, and had placed orders for 6 converted merchant-ship-aircraft-carriers for escort duty in American yards. Four of these belonged to the *Archer* Class: *Archer*, *Avenger*, *Biter* and *Dasher*. All had a displacement of 8,200 tons except HMS *Archer* (9,000); their overall length was $492\frac{1}{4}$ feet, maximum speed was $16\frac{1}{2}$ knots (*Archer*, 17); their armament was entirely AA: 3 4-in. and 15 20 mm guns; they carried 15 aircraft. The next two belonged to the more numerous *Attacker* Class: *Attacker* and *Battler*. Their displacement was 11,420 tons, overall length 492 feet, speed 17 knots, armament 2 4-in., 8 40-mm, 15 20-mm AA guns and they carried 18 aircraft. They were the forerunners of 41 White Ensign escort carriers, 38 of them built in the USA.

Delivery of these vessels began in the late summer of 1942 but before they could reach the Atlantic they were diverted to more pressing duties. HMS *Avenger* was sunk off Gibraltar by *U151* on 15 November. By March, 1943, the prospect of bringing the escort carriers to the Atlantic was brightening, but on the 27th of that month HMS *Dasher* was destroyed by a petrol explosion (see Roskill, *The War at Sea* ii p. 367 f.n. 2 for a discussion of this). That left *Archer*, *Biter*, *Attacker* and *Battler*; *Biter* was the first to arrive, in April, in the 5th Escort Group, one of Admiral Horton's long-desired Support Groups. She survived the war to be transferred to the French Navy in 1945.

84 Op. cit. p. 335.

85 Ibid. p. 95.

86 Two translations of this abbreviation are on offer: the official German manual of the weapon calls it *Federapparattorpedo* which is not particularly descriptive. Jürgen Rohwer translates it as *Fläch-*

enabsuchender, which can be readily rendered as 'surface-searching', and that is indeed what it did.

87 Rohwer, *Critical Convoy Battles* p. 119. A somewhat later refinement of the *FAT* was the *LUT* (*langen unabhangiger Torpedo*) which is described vividly in Herbert Werner's *Iron Coffins* (p. 161).

'It had become increasingly difficult to approach targets as closely as we had in previous years, and the new *LUT* torpedo was designed to overcome our inability to shoot at close range. It could be released at a great distance from a convoy and directed to pursue the target along its mean track, describing a number of predetermined loops, of any chosen size, at any chosen depth. A few of these torpedoes, released in a screening pattern, could form an effective barrier ahead of a convoy without forcing us to penetrate its tight defence:'

88 It is very sad that Jürgen Rohwer's publishers permitted a book so full of information of great reference value to be printed with so inadequate an index.

89 See p. 382, note 72. In January, 1942, Professor Blackett left Coastal Command and transferred his activities to the Admiralty.

90 Op. cit. p. 93.

91 Ibid. p. 94.

92 Ninety-nine frigates were ordered from American yards by the Admiralty. Four were delivered in 1942 ('Captain' Class, 1,085 tons, diesel-electric 20 knots, complement 200); 28 of the same class followed in 1943. In addition there were 46 of an improved 'Captain' Class (1,300 tons, turbo-electric 26 knots) and 21 of the 'Colony' Class, corresponding to the British-built 'River' class (1,318 tons, reciprocating 18 knots). The Americans called these vessels 'Destroyer Escorts'.

93 McLachlan, op. cit. p. 86.

94 Hinsley (op. cit. ii p. 561) says: 'It is . . . important to note that the battle on the intelligence front turned significantly against the Allies from the beginning of March. The *B-Dienst* continued to supply good convoy intelligence to the U-boat Command. But the Shark settings were read with greater than average delay for all but three of the first ten days of the month, and *between 10 and 19 March the decryption of the traffic suffered the longest interruption that GC & CS had experienced since the beginning of the year*.' (my italics).

95 '*Sturm und Drang*' is a familiar phrase in German literature, especially where military matters are concerned. Literally, it means 'storm and stress', and is often used to convey the heat of battle; an English equivalent might be 'sound and fury'.

96 Middlebrook (pp. 228–9) cites the interesting case of *Kapitän-*

leutnant Kurt Lange of *U 350*, 'a pre-war merchant officer who was now thirty-nine years old and was believed by his crew to be the second oldest captain in the U-boat fleet. He had never served in an operational U-boat before but during training had often told his crew that he intended to bring them back safely from every patrol, even though this might mean not always pressing home his attacks in dangerous conditions.' Despite very fierce and accurate attacks by HMS *Beverley* on 17 March, he succeeded in fulfilling this promise; his boat and crew were still intact when he went to a shore posting in January, 1945.

97 Op. cit. p. 159.

98 Rohwer, op. cit. pp. 189–90.

99 Op. cit. p. 182.

100 The Hedgehog mortars were still in the stage of 'teething troubles', made worse by the weather and sea damage. Rohwer cites two occasions when HMS *Anemone*'s hedgehog only loosed off 4 out of its pattern of 24 bombs.

101 Price, op. cit. pp. 123–6.

102 'For this relief much thanks; 'tis bitter cold
And I am sick at heart.' (Hamlet I.i.8)
    Lieutenant-Commander Luther could have echoed every part of this speech, especially 'sick at heart'. Middlebrook says, 'If his reputation is to be that of a man who erred on the side of compassion, he would not have regretted this. It is a fact that Luther died firmly convinced that he had failed to do enough for the crews of those merchant ships' (op. cit. p. 306). For every naval officer who had to face it, the decision was an appalling one: to go on, leaving men to drown, or to stop, risking more casualties to other ships while the rescue continued. Vice-Admiral Gretton describes one such moment as 'my most painful memory of the war'.

103 Middlebrook, op. cit. p. 255.

104 'Overwhelming power' is a manner of speaking; Rohwer (p. 141) tells us that out of 27 Fortresses in 3 squadrons of No. 15 Group, only 10 were operational, and out of 48 Sunderlands 22 were operational. But it shows how far the 'Cinderella Command' had come in four years of war that such a phrase should even occur.

105 Op. cit. p. 329 for this and following.

106 The full Diary entry appears as Appendix 9 in Rohwer (op. cit. 228).

107 Roskill, op. cit. ii p. 367 for this and following.

108 Op. cit. p. 165.

109   See p. 48.

110   We may further note that 101 merchant ships of the outward-bound convoys ON 170, ONS 171 and ON 172 arrived without loss during the period of the SC 122/HX 229 battle.

111   Op. cit. p. 187.

112   Middlebrook, op. cit. p. 173; pp. 176 and 188 for following quotations.

113   A land-warfare parallel could be the practice of sewing names and addresses of next-of-kin into the collars of uniforms in the Army of the Potomac during the Wilderness campaign of 1864, when life expectation appeared to be very much reduced.

114   Op. cit. p. 25.

115   Op. cit. pp. 190–1.

116   *Closing the Ring* p. 6.

117   The Official History (*Grand Strategy* vol. IV p. 269) refers to 'the near disasters of "Torch"', and informs us that 'On the American beaches 34% of the assault craft had been lost, chiefly through mishandling'.

118   Fraser, op. cit. p. 352.

119   It was, in fact, in July 1942, following a meeting in London at which an operation in French North Africa (then code-named GYMNAST) was agreed, that the US Joint Chiefs of Staff recognized that ROUND-UP in 1943 would be impossible. Contrary to general belief, the man who fought hardest against this recognition was Churchill, who continued to argue for a landing in north-west Europe even if it had to be delayed until October. As the Official History remarks, 'The latent misunderstandings remained unsolved; but an agreed military operation was at last under way' (*Grand Strategy* IV p. xxv).

120   Chalmers, op. cit. p. 188.

121   Op. cit. ii p. 371.

122   Gretton, op. cit. p. 22.

123   The German surrender took place on 2 February.

124   Gretton op. cit.; my italics. The reader will not miss the patronizing reference to Coastal Command's 'inexperienced crews', compared with Bomber Command's 'experts'.

125   Webster & Frankland, op. cit. ii pp. 16–17.

126   See Terraine *The Right of the Line* pp. 557–8.

127   Bomber Command's Pathfinder Force was created in August, 1942; it constituted a recognition that by no means all the Command was

'expert' at finding even very large targets in Germany and hitting them (see *The Right of the Line* pp. 498–503).

128 Price, op. cit. pp. 116–17 for this and following quotations.

129 Göring was relieved of responsibility for armament production in February, 1942.

130 Op. cit. iii Part I p. 263.

131 Dönitz, op. cit. pp. 330–1.

132 Op. cit. ii p. 366.

133 Op. cit. p. 8 (see p. 245).

134 Compiled from Roskill (ii p. 367) and Chalmers (p. 188); it is to be understood that every group would have ships under repair or refit at any given moment.

135 Op. cit. ii p. 401.

136 Op. cit. p. 94 for this and following.

137 These figures are extracted from Roskill op. cit. ii Appendix J.

138 See p. 600 for the impression made by these reinforcements on one U-boat officer.

139 Op. cit. p. 333.

140 Ibid. p. 335. In the battle of SC 122 and HX 229 97 torpedoes were fired (35 hits) according to Rohwer (*Critical Convoy Battles* p. 198).

141 *Decisive Battles of World War II* p. 296.

142 Op. cit. p. 330.

143 See Macintyre op. cit. p. 169.

144 Hinsley, op. cit. ii p. 567.

145 This recalls the GHQ Intelligence appreciation on 7 January, 1918 (two months before the great German offensive in March of that year): 'The German accession of morale is not of a permanent character . . . If Germany attacks and fails she will be ruined' – which proved to be totally correct.

146 Op. cit. pp. 180–2 for this and following quotations.

147 Macintyre, op. cit. p. 168 for this and following.

148 Op. cit. p. 145. A highly important feature of escort training was the post-convoy conference of all concerned 'where the lessons could be discussed, the mistakes analysed and new exercises designed to put things right' (ibid. p. 120). Command procedures would undoubtedly be a conference subject; Gretton remarks: 'We were never satisfied.'

149 Ibid. p. 147.

150 Even such an authority as Rohwer has been somehow misled into the belief that it was the 5th E.G. with the carrier HMS *Biter* that joined Gretton's B7 (*Decisive Battles* p. 296).

151 Beesly, op. cit. p. 186.

152 *Ultra Goes to War* p. 219.

153 The ONS series restarted at No. 1 on 15 March with the first convoy sailing once more to Halifax instead of to New York.

154 Op. cit. pp. 336–7 for this and following.

155 Op. cit. ii pp. 371–2.

156 Op. cit. p. 297; the accompanying table is on p. 297 of that work.

157 The U-boat staff had selected birds as their current code-name species: *Star* = Starling; *Specht* = Woodpecker; *Fink* = Finch; *Amsel* = Blackbird; *Drossel* = Thrush.

158 Gretton, *Convoy Escort Commander* (Cassell 1964) for this and following.

159 Hinsley, op. cit. ii p. 570.

160 Op. cit. pp. 338–9 for this and following quotations.

161 Bekker, op. cit. p. 333.

162 Op. cit. p. 175. It is evidence of the smooth running due to careful training of Western Approaches Command that Lieutenant-Commander Sherwood was able to carry out his task without 'let or hindrance' in the presence of two full RN captains.

163 *Crisis Convoy* p. 153.

164 The Command comprised 173 ships on 1 January, 1943.

165 An alternative version exists for the sinking of *U531* in the fog of the Newfoundland Banks on 5 May. The U-boat, he says, suffered 'crippling damage' but did not sink after being rammed by *Oribi*; her commander, *Leutnant* Ulrich Folkers, then made the mistake of signalling for help. Four U-boats were ordered to assist *U531*, but an HF/DF fix brought the corvette *Snowflake* to her first, to sink her by gunfire.

166 An example of high proficiency was HMS *Starling*, the leader of Captain Walker's 2nd Escort Group, whose 'guns could fire salvoes of six rounds in thirty seconds and the depth charge crews could fire a pattern of ten charges in fifteen seconds' (Robertson op. cit. p. 93).

167 Rohwer, *Critical Convoy Battles* p. 197. For aircraft, Slessor insists that 'the decisive weapon of the anti-submarine squadrons was the Mark XI torpex-filled depth charge, dropped in "sticks" of four to eight from point-blank altitude, fifty to a hundred and fifty feet' (*The Central Blue* p. 466).

168 See p. 439, note 77.

169 Werner, op. cit. pp. 119–29 for this and following quotations relating to *U230*.

170 With the exception of C3 which never left the convoy routes, the RCN groups began to reappear in mid-March.

171 Werner's references to 'twin-engined' aircraft must be another example of memory playing tricks. The standard aircraft equipment of escort carriers was Martlets, Seafires, Swordfish, Avengers, Corsairs, Wildcats and Hellcats. All these were single-engined. At this early stage the chief strike aircraft was that 'grand old warrior', the Fairey Swordfish; it was Swordfish that so plagued *U 230*, and a Swordfish that she shot down that day.

172 In the foul, toxic air of the submarine at great depths, it was one of Werner's tasks to force men to stay awake: 'Whoever fell asleep might never be awakened.'

173 Michael Hadley, in a conference paper delivered at Halifax in October, 1985, says that the Type VIIC 'is considered by many to have been the best integrated maritime combat system of the day'.

174 Op. cit. p. 340.

175 Hinsley, op. cit. ii p. 570 for this and following (17 May).

176 Among those lost was *U 954*, sunk by a Coastal Command Liberator; she went down with all hands, including Dönitz's 21-year-old son Peter, on his first cruise. In keeping with the officer traditions of the German Services, 'Dönitz showed no emotion when he learned of his son's death' (Padfield, op. cit. p. 299).

177 Hinsley, op. cit. ii p. 571 for this and following.

178 Both were sunk by escort carrier aircraft: *U 569* by one from USS *Bogue*, and *U 752* by one from HMS *Archer*.

179 Op. cit. ii p. 381.

180 Dönitz, op. cit. pp. 340–1 for this and following.

181 Op. cit. p. 190.

182 Op. cit. p. 333.

183 Matthew Cooper *The German Army 1939–1945* p. 451; Macdonald & Jane's 1978.

184 Fraser, op. cit. p. 338.

185 Even more amazingly, in May, the month of victory itself, Slessor wrote in the *Coastal Command Review*:
  'Many of us in Coastal no doubt sometimes envy our friends in Bomber and Mediterranean Commands their share in the shattering offensive which has been such a heartening feature of the last month's news. But if we can keep up this rate of killing against the U-boats, or anything near it, we are doing as much as anyone to hasten the collapse of the Axis. If we could really kill the U-boat menace once and for all many of us could be spared to take part in the

more direct offensive against objectives on German and Italian soil.'

For a Command which had just succeeded in destroying 41% of the very large number of U-boats lost in May, it is fairly poor praise to be told that soon it may be lucky enough to take part in the real work of the war!

186 Op. cit. ii p. 377.

187 *Royal Air Force 1939–45* iii p. 62.

188 *Decisive Battles* p. 308.

189 Op. cit. p. 12.

190 *Room 40* p. 308; by 'second' Beesly means the World War II campaign, as opposed to 1914–18.

191 Op. cit. p. 220.

192 See Macdonald op. cit. p. 513.

III/8 *Unconditional Surrender (pp. 614–673)*

1 Op. cit. p. 406 for this and following quotations.

2 Webster & Frankland, op. cit. ii pp. 108–9.

3 *Inside the Third Reich*, p. 278; Weidenfeld & Nicolson, 1970.

4 Dönitz, op. cit. p. 234.

5 See p. 482.

6 Von der Porten, op. cit. p. 31.

7 Dönitz, op. cit. pp. 236–7.

8 A prime feature of the Walter boats was his closed-cycle diesel and turbine engine and a grave disadvantage was discovered when experiment revealed the very high fuel consumption at high speeds of the Walter turbine.

9 Price, op. cit. p. 180.

10 In actual fact the first U-boat to be hit by a Mark 24 Mine was *U 456* (Teichert) the previous day (12 May), attacked by a Liberator of No. 86 Squadron. Badly damaged, the U-boat surfaced and fought back; being close to his endurance limit the pilot left the obviously crippled *U 456* to her fate, which was not long delayed. She was destroyed by surface escorts of convoy HX 237 on 13 May. The essential thing was that neither Teichert nor U-boat Command had any inkling of what had done the fatal damage; Dönitz believed it was 'an aerial bomb'.

11 The first test of rocket projectiles for Fleet Air Arm work was carried out by a Swordfish on 12 October, 1942; the attack on *U 752* was their first operational success.

12 See Thetford, op. cit. p. 170; but we should note that HMS *Belfast* (10,000 tons, launched 1938) had a main armament of 12 6-inch guns whose shells weigh 100 lb each, giving the full broadside a weight more than twice that of 8 rockets.

13 Long hunts were a commonplace of Support Group work; Walker's destruction of *U 202* on 1 June, 1943, took 14 hours, but the longest hunt of the war was that carried out by EG 1 at the beginning of March, 1944, which destroyed *U 358*: 38 continuous hours. Very shortly afterwards the mixed RN/RCN group C2 carried out a 30-hour hunt to destroy *U 744* (see p. 30 for hydrophone comparison).

14 Commander D. E. G. Wemyss pays well-deserved tribute to the assured and competent operation of *Wild Goose's* ASDIC by Leading Seaman Wilkinson in this action.

15 See p. 627 for further reference to *U 264*.

16 Roskill, op. cit. iii Part I p. 254.

17 Op. cit. p. 122.

18 Hinsley (op. cit. ii pp. 551–2) says that mastery of SHARK/ *TRITON* 'was to be total by August, 1943, from which time till the end of the war all the traffic for each day was read as a matter of course with little or no delay'; he later modifies this statement, as we see.

19 This remained true even after the introduction of a totally new form of signal traffic by the Germans in 1943. This was based on a machine known as *Geheimschreiber*, using the Baudot-Murray teleprinter code instead of Morse. It produced a stream of radio traffic (known at Bletchley Park as 'Fish') as secure as landline teleprinter messages – or so it seemed. The Germans used the *Geheimschreiber* for the highest-level (and therefore most important) communications and BP responded with a top-level counter-attack which included Alan Turing and Professor M. H. A. Newman FRS of St John's College, Cambridge, who presided over the evolution of a mechanical answer to the fresh mechanical problem: BP's famous 'Colossus', which has been (inaccurately) called the father of modern computers. At the end of 1943 BP was handling a flow of some 250 'Fish' decrypts per month, compared with 84,000 per month of *Enigma*. This figure remained roughly constant for the rest of the war.

20 Dönitz to *Kapitän zur See* Heinz Bonatz, spring 1943; see Bekker op. cit. p. 314.

21 In addition to FW 200s and Blohm & Voss BV 222 six-engined flying boats, HE 177s and the newly-converted transport Ju 290B-2 with a maximum range of 4,970 miles, were promised in the autumn

of 1943. However, in mid-November the U-boat Diary confessed: 'The enemy has all the trumps in his hand . . . On our side, as yet no air reconnaissance; the U-boat its own scout, with a minimum of scouting range.' (see p. 258).

22 See p. 301.

23 Op. cit. ii p. 379 (and see Appendix D).

24 *Closing the Ring* p. 4.

25 A subsidiary of the great Bethlehem Steel Corporation, a good friend to Britain in both wars. It is interesting, and possibly revealing, that Mr Kaiser earns no mention for this invaluable work in either the American or British Official Histories (though Morison gives him a paragraph for his contribution to production of CVEs – the escort carriers). Ruffled authority has a long arm.

26 Barnett, op. cit. p. 107 (and see p. 250).

27 Hancock & Gowing, op. cit. p. 416.

28 *The Daily Telegraph*, on 16 December, 1987, informed its readers that 'The Merchant Navy has lost its place among the major fleets of the world for the first time, according to *Lloyds' Register*. It had dropped from 8th to 11th place, having been overtaken by the fleets of Cyprus, the Bahamas and the Philippines'.

29 Op. cit. p. 410.

30 Roskill, op. cit. iii Part I pp. 25–6.

31 Ibid. pp. 29–30 for this and following Roskill quotation.

32 Op. cit. p. 155.

33 Op. cit. p. 412.

34 This was known as the 'Piening Way', after the commander of *U 155* who, says Rohwer, 'successfully confused the radars of the British planes with the echoes of the hills at the coast behind' (Halifax RCN conference paper, October, 1985).

35 Ibid.

36 The Germans also produced a heavier version of this, the FX 1400 (*Fritz*), weighing 3,000 lb, first used at Salerno with considerable effect on 11 September, 1943; 'if released at 18,000 feet, this bomb was travelling at 800 feet per second at the end of its trajectory and it could neither be shot down by gunfire nor avoided by manoeuvring, especially the congested waters of the assembly areas' (G. A. Shepperd, *The Italian Campaign 1943–45* p. 125; Arthur Barker 1968). The Dornier 217 was specially modified to carry these weapons: the Do 217K-2.

37 Op. cit. p. 30; ibid. p. 25 for following.

38 The supply-boat types were IXD2s, XBs and XIVs. The most successful were the 'Broad Beam' Type XIVs.

39 American anti-submarine operations were centralized on 1 May, 1943, when Admiral King announced: 'It is arranged to set up immediately in the Navy Department an anti-submarine command to be known as the Tenth Fleet.' This was a necessary and overdue administrative arrangement, completed on 20 May when Admiral King himself took direct command of the Tenth Fleet.

40 Op. cit. pp. 153–5.

41 Hinsley, op. cit. iii pp. 221–2 for this and following.

42 These were merchant ships, either 8,000-ton grain carriers or 11,000-ton tankers, carrying normal cargoes but fitted with 400–460 feet flight decks, and equipped with three or four Swordfish each. They entered Atlantic operations in May, 1943, when the decision of the battle had already been declared. The MAC with ONS 18 was SS *Empire MacAlpine*.

43 Schull, op. cit. p. 178.

44 A Liberator of 120 Squadron piloted by Flying Officer J. Moffat found *U 338* on the surface and at once attacked. *Kapitänleutnant* Kinzel, an able and combative commander who had distinguished himself in the SC 122/HX 229 battle in March, gave the Liberator a warm reception. Moffat was in no hurry; he circled the U-boat, waiting for her to dive. As soon as she did so, he came down on the swirl and dropped a Mark 24 Mine which quickly found *U 338*. Alfred Price remarks: 'So it was that Manfred Kinzel met his end, because he did not allow for the fact that his enemy might be carrying weapons as advanced as those in his own torpedo tubes.'

45 Op. cit. p. 419.

46 Padfield, op. cit. pp. 327–8.

47 Op. cit. It is also likely that some U-boat commanders were misled by hearing the detonations of *Zaunkönig* torpedoes at the end of their runs.

48 Op. cit. pp. 208–9.

49 Op. cit. p. 181.

50 Hinsley, op. cit. iii p. 223.

51 Halifax RCN Conference, October 1985.

52 Hinsley, op. cit. p. 225.

53 Op. cit. p. 172.

54 Peter Kremer, *U 333: The Story of a U-boat Ace* p. 167; Bodley Head 1984.

55 Op. cit. p. 420.

56 This includes two of the ablest of them: *Feldmarschall* von Manstein, who said that after Kursk 'the initiative in the Eastern theatre of

war finally passed to the Russians', and *Generaloberst* Guderian who said that this defeat was decisive because 'it damaged the German Army to an irreparable degree and the loss of the war dates from this defeat even more than from that of Stalingrad'.

57　See Albert Seaton, *The German Army 1939–45* p. 206; Weidenfeld & Nicolson 1982.

58　Op. cit. iii Part I pp. 55–6.

59　Op. cit. pp. 421–2 for this and following.

60　Beesly, op. cit. p. 248 for this and following.

61　Op. cit. p. 422; the italics marked by asterisks are mine.

62　Op. cit. p. 358.

63　Op. cit. p. xv.

64　Sholto Douglas had succeeded Slessor as AOC-in-C on 20 January. See Humphrey Wynn and Susan Young, *Prelude to Overlord* pp. 45–6; Airlife 1983, for strength of Coastal Command.

65　Price, op. cit. p. 202.

66　Douglas, op. cit. p. 587.

67　*Triumph and Tragedy* p. 59.

68　See *After the Battle* No. 55, February, 1987: *U-Boat Bases* p. 40.

69　Russell F. Weigley, *Eisenhower's Lieutenants* pp. 283–6 (a clear short narrative of the battle for Brest); Sidgwick & Jackson, 1981.

70　Op. cit. pp. 422–3 for this and following quotations.

71　The first large ocean convoy to come in via the South-Western Approaches was the combined SL 167/MKS 58 from Sierra Leone and Gibraltar on August 27.

72　Op. cit. iii Part II p. 108.

73　*U 407* was betrayed by a wisp of smoke which proved to be a *Schnorchel* funnel, sighted at a distance of 8 miles by the Polish-manned destroyer *Garland* – a remarkable piece of alert observation.

74　Op. cit. iii Part II p. 68.

75　Op. cit. p. 273.

76　For fuller discussion of the Battle of Hamburg see the author's *The Right of the Line* pp. 545–9.

77　Op. cit. p. 284.

78　Price, op. cit. p. 184.

79　Op. cit. 356–7.

80　*The Right of the Line* p. 679.

81　Air Marshal Sir Robert Saundby, *Air Bombardment: The Story of its Development* p. 208; Chatto & Windus 1961.

82 Op. cit. iii Part II 182.

83 Op. cit. p. 224.

84 *Type XXI* (123 built)
Displacement: Surfaced 1,621 tons, Submerged 1,819 tons; Maximum speeds (laden): Surface 15½ knots, Submerged (1 hour) 17 knots; Endurance: Surfaced at 10 knots 15,500 miles, at 12 knots 11,150 miles; Maximum sustained at 15½ knots 5,100 miles; Submerged on electric motor: at 5 knots 365 miles, at 6 knots 285 miles, at 8 knots 170 miles, at 10 knots 110 miles; Diving depth: 376 feet; Armament: Torpedo tubes 6 bow; Torpedoes (maximum) 20; Guns 4 × 30-mm AA; Crew 57.
Type XXIII (59 built)
Displacement: Surfaced 232 tons, Submerged 256 tons; Maximum speeds (laden): Surfaced 9¾ knots, Submerged (1 hour) 12½ knots; Endurance: Surfaced at 6 knots 4,300 miles, Surfaced at 8 knots 2,800 miles; Maximum sustained at 9¾ knots 1,350 miles; Submerged on electric motor at 4 knots 175 miles, at 6 knots 113 miles, at 8 knots 70 miles, at 10 knots 43 miles; Diving depth: 330 feet; Armament: Torpedo tubes 2 bow; Torpedoes (maximum) 2; Guns None; Crew 14.

85 Roskill, op. cit. p. 287.

86 The Germans also launched, in late 1944, an inshore offensive in Canadian waters with Type IXs. The selected areas were the Gulf of St Lawrence (where *U517* had operated so successfully in 1942: see p. 486) and the waters round Nova Scotia. ASDIC conditions here were notoriously bad for most of the year; wrecks were plentiful; rock outcrops gave false echoes and reverberations in rough seas up to about 25 miles offshore; and temperature variations in the water layers trapped, bent or refracted sound waves at different depths. Fortunately, the Woods Hole Oceanographic Institute in Massachusetts had realized the problem of temperature variation before the war, and an instrument had been devised for measuring it: the bathythermograph. So a new science entered the armoury of war: Bathythermography (BT). By 1942 the Americans were already issuing ASDIC charts for the North Atlantic. Even so, the Canadians had a bad time; their best anti-submarine units were on the other side of the Atlantic, and though the U-boats in 1944–5 showed far less enterprise than *Korvettenkapitän* Hartwig in 1942, to their sorrow the Canadians were never able to destroy even one of them.

87 Roskill, op. cit. p. 285.

88 Among them was the 11,500-ton Belgian steamer *Leopoldville*, under charter to the Admiralty. She was carrying 2,235 soldiers of the US 66th division, reinforcements for the Ardennes battle. 802 of these

men were killed or missing. It was amazingly rare for troopships to be sunk by U-boats; this case offers a clear indication of what might have happened off Normandy if the U-boats had not been so soundly beaten by the Royal Navy and Coastal Command.

89   Dönitz, op. cit. p. 397.

90   The 'Small Battle Units' comprised:

Marder (Marten): a one-man electrically propelled carrier for one torpedo; maximum speed 2.5 knots, range 35 miles;

Molch (Salamander): a one-man midget submarine; displacement, 10.5 tons; endurance 43 miles at 5 knots; 2 torpedoes;

Biber (Beaver): a one-man midget submarine; displacement 6 tons; surface endurance 13 hours at 7 knots, submerged 1.5 hours at 6 knots; 2 torpedoes or 2 mines;

Hecht (Pike): a two-man midget submarine (U-boat Type XXVII); displacement 12 tons; range 60 miles at 4 knots or 42 miles at 6 knots (maximum); originally intended to carry limpet mines, later adapted for torpedoes;

Seehund (Seal): a two-man midget submarine (U-boat Type XXVIIB); displacement 12.3 tons surfaced, 15 tons submerged; maximum surface speed 8 knots for 15 hours, submerged 5 knots for 4 hours; 2 torpedoes; 'by far the most successful of the many types' (Roskill);

Linse (Lentil): a radio-controlled motor boat unit comprising two manned explosive boats with 300-kg charges and a control boat; maximum speed 31 knots for 2 hours; the explosive boats were steered by their pilots to striking distance; the pilots then jumped overboard and were picked up by the control boat which guided the explosive boat in to the target;

Dackel (Dachshund): a long-range pattern-running torpedo with a range of 57,000 metres, beginning with a straight run of 27,000 metres; speed 9 knots.

91   Roskill, op. cit. p. 153.

92   The reader will note these high numbers; they should not be taken too seriously. The German Submarine Service's highest numbering was the class, *U6301–U6351*, but this order was cancelled and none were ever built. This was the fate of most boats once the *U 1000* mark was passed.

93   Op. cit. iii Part II p. 292.

94   Op. cit. p. 289.

95   Price, op. cit. p. 212.

96   The homing torpedo which killed *U 905* took 6 minutes to make its run; no doubt the Liberator crew became exceedingly anxious during that time, but *U 296*'s killer took even longer: 13 minutes,

by which time the aircrew must have given up hope.

97 Padfield, op. cit. p. 382.

98 Op. cit. iii p. 298.

99 In April Dönitz despatched 7 *Schnorchel* Type IXs to the West Atlantic as a spoiling operation. Well warned by the *Enigma*, the US Navy prepared a 'Barrier Force' to meet them in mid-Atlantic and a second to greet them closer to the American coast. The U-boats (*Seewolf* Group) achieved a few sinkings, but nothing of consequence, and 5 of the 7 were sunk by USN forces.

100 For the Battle of Berlin (16 April–8 May) the Red Army assembled some 2½ million men, nearly 17,000 guns, some 6,500 tanks and self-propelled guns and 7,500 aircraft. Its total casualties in the three weeks were 304,887 men and over 2,000 tanks.

101 This is an amalgam of Dönitz p. 446 and Padfield p. 412.

102 It is characteristic of the leadership of the Third Reich that at his last interview with Himmler on 30 April Dönitz had a pistol with the safety-catch off hidden under papers on his desk: 'I had never done anything of this sort in my life before, but I did not know what the outcome of this meeting might be' (op. cit. p. 443).

103 Op. cit. iii Part II p. 179.

104 Op. cit. p. 251; following quotation ibid. p. 283.

105 Examples of this abound; the southern African tribesman must have had similar feelings when, armed with his old-fashioned and uncertain throwing assegai, he encountered the Zulus armed with the *iKlwa*, the heavy, broad-bladed, nicely balanced stabbing assegai which was to the Zulu *impi* what the short stabbing sword was to the Roman legion.

106 Op. cit. p. 94; see p. 237.

107 Gibson & Prendergast, op. cit. p. 182.

108 Chalmers, op. cit. pp. 276–7.

109 They consisted of: 2 battleships; 3 aircraft carriers; 2 auxiliary or escort carriers; 1 catapult aircraft merchantman; 5 cruisers; 33 destroyers; 3 submarines; 6 sloops; 10 frigates; 21 corvettes; 6 minesweepers; 1 minelayer; 10 armed merchant cruisers; 2 depot ships.

110 Op. cit. p. 133.

111 Newbolt, op. cit. p. 324.

112 Op. cit. iii Part II p. 306.

113 See p. 137.

114 In addition to 'a large proportion' of the Royal Navy's 73,642 casualties (50,758 killed, 820 missing); Roskill, op. cit. p. 305.

APPENDIX A

BRITISH, AMERICAN AND GERMAN NAVAL RANKS

RN/RCN	USN	*Kriegsmarine*
Admiral of the Fleet	Fleet Admiral	*Grossadmiral*
Admiral	Admiral	*Admiral*
Vice-Admiral	Vice Admiral	*Vizeadmiral*
Rear-Admiral	Rear Admiral	*Konteradmiral*
Commodore	—	*Flotillenadmiral*
Captain	Captain	*Kapitän zur See*
Commander	Commander	*Fregattenkapitän*
Lieutenant-Commander	Lieutenant-Commander	*Korvettenkapitän*
		Kapitänleutnant
Lieutenant	Lieutenant	*Oberleutnant zur See*
Sub-Lieutenant	Lieutenant Junior Grade	*Leutnant zur See*
Midshipman ·	Ensign	*Fähnrich zur See*
	Senior Chief Petty Officer	*Hauptbootsmann*
Chief Petty Officer	Chief Petty Officer	*Oberbootsmann*
—	Petty Officer First Class	*Bootsmann*
—	Petty Officer Second Class	*Obermaat*
Petty Officer	Petty Officer Third Class	*Maat*
—	—	*Hauptgefreiter*
Leading Seaman	Seaman	*Obergefreiter*
Able Seaman	Seaman Apprentice	*Gefreiter*

APPENDIX B

THE GERMAN U-BOATS OF WORLD WAR I

(See notes on p. 765)

U-boat Nos	Ordered	Completed	Displacement[a] Surface	Displacement[a] Submerged	Torpedoes Tubes	No.[c]	Cal. (cm)	Guns No. × cm	Endurance[d] Surface	At[e]	Submerged	At	Speed[f] Surface	Submerged	Diving Times[g]	Engines[h] Surface	Submerged	Officers	Ratings
3–4	VIII.07	V.09	420	510	2B,2S[b]	6	45	1 × 5	3,000	9	55	4.5	11.5	9.5	60	2 × 200	2 × 505	3	19
5–12	IV.08	VII.10–VIII.11	500	620	2B,2S	6	45	1 × 5	3,400	8.6	80	5	14.2	8.1	65	4 × 225	2 × 580	4	24
13–16	XII.09	XII.11–IV.12	540	635	2B,2S	6	45	1 × 5	1,920	14.8	90	5	15	10.7	40	2 × 250 / 2 × 350	2 × 550	4	24
17–18	V.10	XI.12	560	690	2B,2S	6	45	1 × 5	1,210	13.5	75	5	15	9.5	70	4 × 350	2 × 550	4	24
19–22*	XI.10	VII.13–XI.13	650	840	2B,2S	9	50	1 × 5 or 1 × 10.5	5,200	8	80	5	15.5	9.6	75	2 × 850	2 × 550	4	35
23–26	III.11	IX.13–V.14	670	860	2B,2S	9	50	2 × 8.8	5,020	8	85	5	16.8	10.3	84	2 × 900	2 × 550	4	35
27–30	II.12	V.14–VIII.14	680	870	2B,2S	10	50	2 × 8.8	5,520	8	85	5	16.7	9.9	45	2 × 1,000	2 × 550	4	35
31–41†	VI.12	IX.14–II.15	680	870	2B,2S	6	50	1 × 10.5	4,440	8	80	5	16.5	9.5	50	2 × 925	2 × 550	4	35
42		Not Delivered																	
43–50	VII.13–VIII.14	IV.15–VII.16	720	940	4B,2S	6	50	1 × 10.5	4,840	8	51	5	15.2	9.3	?	2 × 1,000	2 × 550	4	35
51–56	VIII.14	II.16–VI.16	720	902	2B,2S	8	50	1 × 10.5 or 8.8	5,260	8	55	5	17	9.2	?	2 × 1,100	2 × 550	4	35
57–62	X.14	VII–XII.16	780	950	2B,2S	7	50	1 × 10.5 or 8.8	5,800	8	50	5	16.5	8.5	?	2 × 1,100	2 × 550	4	35
63–65	III.15	III–V.16	810	930	2B,2S	8	50	1 × 10.5	6,020	8	60	5	16.6	9.1	?	2 × 1,100	2 × 550	4	35

| | | | Displacement[a] | | Torpedoes | | | Guns | Endurance[d] | | | | Speed[f] | | Diving | Engines[h] | | | |
U-boat Nos	Ordered	Completed	Sur-face	Sub-merged	Tubes	No.[c]	Cal. (cm)	No. × cm	Sur-face	At[e]	Sub-merged	At	Sur-face	Sub-merged	Times[g]	Sur-face	Sub-merged	Offi-cers	Rat-ings
66–70‡	?	VII–IX.15	810	930	4B,1S	12	45	1 × 10.5	3,980	8	115	5	16	10.6	?	2 × 1,150	2 × 620	4	35
71–80‡§	1.15	X.15–VI.16	750	830	1B,1S§	4	50	1 × 10.5	4,610	7	83	4	10.6	8	40	2 × 450	2 × 450	4	35
81–86	VI.15	VIII–XII.16	810	950	2B,2S	10	50	1 × 10.5 or 8.8	7,630	8	56	5	16.8	9.1	?	2 × 1,200	2 × 550	4	35
87–92	VI.15	II–X.17	760	1,000	4B,2S	12	50	2 × 10.5	7,660	8	56	5	15.6	8.6	45	2 × 1,200	2 × 550	4	35
93–98	IX.15	II–V.17	850	1,000	4B,2S	16	60	1 × 10.5 or 8.8	3,800	8	50	5	16.8	8.6	45	2 × 1,200	2 × 550	4	35
9–104	IX.15	III–VIII.17	750	950	2B,2S	12	50	1 × 10.5 or 8.8	4,080	8	45	5	16.5	8.2	45	2 × 1,200	2 × 550	4	35
105–114	V.16	VII.17–VI.18	800	1,000	4B,2S	16	50	1 × 10.5 or 8.8	3,900	8	50	5	16.4	8.5	45	2 × 1,200	2 × 550	4	35
115–116		Unfinished																	
117–121	V.16	III–VIII.18	1,160	1,510	4B	24	50	1 × 10.5	5,860	8	35	4.5	14.7	7.1	30	2 × 1,200	2 × 600	4	36
122–126	V.16	V–X.18	1,160	1,470	4B	12–22	50	1 × 15	6,080	8	60	4.5	14.7	7.1	30	2 × 1,200	2 × 600	4	36
127–134		Unfinished																	
135–138	V.16	VI	1,180	1,530	4B	14	50	1 × 15	2,780	8	50	4.5	18	8.5	30	2 × 1,700	2 × 890	4	42
139–141	VII.16	III–VIII.18	1,930	2,480	4B	19	50	2 × 15	4,000	8	53	4.5	17.7	8.1	30	2 × 1,700	2 × 890	6	56
142–150		Unfinished																	
151–157	II.17	V.17–II.18	1,510	1,870	2B	18	50	2 × 15 or 8.8	13,130	5.5	65	3	12.4	5.3	?	2 × 400	2 × 400	6	50
158–159		Unfinished																	
160–172	II.17	V–X.18	820	1,000	4B,2S	19	50	1 or 2 × 15	2,900	8	62	4.5	16.2	8.2	45	2 × 1,200	2 × 550	4	35
173–276		VI.17–VI.18 Never came into service																	

| U-boat Nos | Ordered | Completed | Displacement[a] | | Torpedoes | | | Guns | Endurance[d] | | | | Speed[f] | | Diving Times[g] | Engines[h] | | Officers | Ratings |
			Surface	Submerged	Tubes	No.[c]	Cal. (cm)	No. × cm	Surface	At[e]	Submerged	At	Surface	Submerged		Surface	Submerged		
UB-boats																			
1–17	XI.14	I–V.15	127	142	2B	2	45	1 MG	1,650	5	45	4	6.7	6	22	1 × 60	1 × 120	1	13
12	XI.14	III.15	147	161		minelayer		1 MG	1,650	5	45	4	6.7	6	22	1 × 60	1 × 120	1	13
18–47	IV.15–VII.15	XI.15–VIII.16	260	290	2B	4	50	1 × 5 or 8.8	5,700	6	45	4	9.2	5.8	32	2 × 140	2 × 140	2	21
48–71	V.16	VI–XI.17	510	650	4B,1S	10	50	1 × 8.8 or 10.5	4,200	6	55	4	13.4	7.8	30	2 × 550	2 × 380	3	31
72–87	IX.16	IX.17–XII.17	520	650	4B,1S	10	50	1 × 8.8 or 10.5	4,000	6	50	4	13.4	7.7	30	2 × 550	2 × 380	3	31
88–132	II.17	12.17–VII.18	510	640	4B,1S	10	50	1 × 8.8 or 10.5	3,500	6	50	4	13.5	7.5	30	2 × 550	2 × 380	3	31
133–249	VI.17–VI.18	Never came into service; no significant variations																	
UC-boats																			
1–15	XI.14	IV.15–VII.15	168	183		12 mines		1 MG	850	5	50	4	8.4	5.5	23	1 × 90	1 × 175	1	13
16–33	VIII.15	VI.16–IX.16	410	490	2B,1S	18 mines		1 × 8.8	6,910	7	55	4	11.5	6.9	40	2 × 250	2 × 230	3	23
34–48	XI.15	IX.16–XI.16	420	500	2B,1S	18 mines		1 × 8.8	7,100	7	55	4	11.7	6.9	40	2 × 250	2 × 230	3	23
49–79	I.16	XI.16–VI.17	420	500	2B,1S	18 mines		1 × 8.8	8,000	7	59	4	12	7.2	33	2 × 300	2 × 310	3	29
80–118	VI.17	VII.18–X.18	480	560	2B,1S	14 mines		1 × 10.5	8,200	7	40	4.5	11.5	6.6	15	2 × 300	2 × 310	3	29
119–192		Unfinished																	

Notes to Appendix B:

a   gross registered tons
b   B = bow, S = stern
c   number of torpedoes
d   in miles (nautical)
e   knots
f   knots
g   seconds
h   horse power

*   the first diesel, and first ocean-going boats
†   the 'Thirties' class
‡   built for Austria-Hungary
§   minelayers, carrying 36 mines
¶   both tubes above water
‖   minelayers, carrying 42–48 mines
**   plus a prize crew for boarding: 1 officer, 19 ratings
††   only 6 boats completed

U-boat characteristics are discussed on pp. 19–21. These tables, however, make certain points of their own. They clearly show the experimental phase of the submarine arm at this stage of development. One is nevertheless struck by the early achievement of effective speed: the 14.2 (surface) knots of the *U5–12* class, ordered in 1908, in relation to the maximum speeds of most merchant ships, is impressive. The 16.8 knots of the 1911 *U23* class may be compared with the 16 knots of a 1940 corvette; the 18 knots of the 1916 *U135* class was greater than the maximum speeds of all World War II U-boats except the Type IXs.

The *U151* class, laid down in 1917, is also remarkable for its great surface endurance (13,130 miles at $15\frac{1}{2}$ knots), and for the extraordinary phenomenon of the 'prize crew' – contrary to the very nature of sub-marine warfare.

Certain 'firsts' may be noted: the 1911 *U27* class, the first to have 1,000-hp engines and the first to carry ten torpedoes; the 1916 *U117* class, the first to to have both surface and submerged displacements of over 1,000 tons; and the *U139–141* class (1916) with the massive dis-placements of 1,930 tons (surface) and 2,480 tons (submerged).

GROSS TONNAGE OF MERCHANT SHIPPING LOST THROUGH ENEMY ACTION, TO 11TH NOVEMBER, 1918

N.B.: These figures exclude Commissioned Auxiliaries. The British figures include merchant vessels only; the world total includes British and foreign fishing vessels. The figures include steam and sailing vessels of all sizes.

	British	World Total		British	World Total
1914			**1917**		
August	40,254	62,767	January	153,666	368,521
September	88,219	98,378	February	313,486	540,006
October	77,805	87,917	March	353,478	593,841
November	8,888	19,413	April	545,282	881,027
December	26,035	44,197	May	352,289	596,629
			June	417,925	687,507
Total	241,201	312,672	July	364,858	557,988
			August	329,810	511,730
			September	196,212	351,748
1915			October	276,132	458,558
January	32,054	47,981	November	173,560	289,212
February	36,372	59,921	December	253,087	399,111
March	71,479	80,775			
April	22,453	55,725	Total	3,729,785	6,235,878
May	84,025	120,058			
June	83,198	131,428			
July	52,847	109,640			
August	148,464	185,866			
September	101,690	151,884			
October	54,156	88,534	**1918**		
November	94,493	153,043			
December	74,490	123,141	January	179,973	306,658
			February	226,896	318,957
Total	855,721	1,307,996	March	199,458	342,597
			April	215,543	278,719
			May	192,436	295,520
1916			June	162,990	255,587
January	62,288	81,259	July	165,449	260,967
February	75,860	117,547	August	145,721	283,815
March	99,089	167,097	September	136,859	187,881
April	141,193	191,667	October	59,229	118,559
May	64,521	129,175	November	10,195	17,682
June	36,976	108,855			
July	82,432	118,215	Total	1,694,749	2,666,942
August	43,354	162,744			
September	104,572	230,460	Grand total	7,759,090	12,850,814
October	176,248	353,660			
November	168,809	311,508			
December	182,292	355,139			
Total	1,237,634	2,327,326			

C. E. Fayle: Seaborne Trade, iii, p. 465, Table I(a); John Murray, 1924.

APPENDIX D

SHIPPING AND U-BOAT LOSSES 1939–45, YEARLY AND MONTHLY*

	TOTAL		NORTH ATLANTIC		
	Tons	Ships	Tons	Ships	U-boats
1939					
September	194,845	53	104,829	19	2
October	196,355	46	110,619	18	5
November	174,269	50	17,895	6	1
December	189,768	72	15,852	4	1
Total	755,237	221	249,195	47	9
1940					
January	214,506	73	35,970	9	2
February	226,920	63	74,759	17	4
March	107,009	45	11,215	2	3
April	158,218	58	24,570	4	5
May	288,461	101	49,087	9	1
June	585,496	140	296,529	53	—
July	386,913	105	141,474	28	2
August	397,229	92	190,048	39	3
September	448,621	100	254,553	52	—
October	442,985	103	286,644	56	1
November	385,715	97	201,341	38	2
December	349,568	82	293,304	42	—
Total	3,991,641	1,059	1,805,494	349	23
1941					
January	320,240	76	214,382	42	—
February	403,393	102	317,378	69	—
March	529,706	139	364,689	63	5
April	687,901	195	260,451	45	2
May	511,042	139	324,550	58	1
June	432,025	109	318,740	68	4
July	120,975	43	97,813	23	1
August	130,699	41	83,661	25	3
September	285,942	84	184,546	51	2
October	218,289	51	154,593	32	2
November	104,640	35	50,215	10	5
December	583,706	285 †	50,682	10	10
Total	4,328,558	1,299	2,421,700	496	35

	TOTAL		NORTH ATLANTIC		
	Tons	Ships	Tons	Ships	U-boats
1942					
January	419,907	106	276,795	48	3
February	679,632	154	429,891	73	2
March	834,164	273	534,064	95	6
April	674,457	132	391,044	66	3
May	705,050	151	576,350	120	4
June	834,196	173	623,545	124	3
July	618,113	128	486,965	98	11
August	661,133	123	508,426	96	10
September	567,327	114	473,585	95	10
October	637,833	101	399,715	62	16
November	807,754	134	508,707	83	13
December	348,902	73	262,135	46	5
Total	7,790,697	1,662	5,471,222	1,006	86
1943					
January	261,359	50	172,691	27	6
February	403,062	73	288,625	46	19
March	693,389	120	476,349	82	15
April	344,680	64	235,478	39	15
May	299,428	58	163,507	34	41
June	123,825	28	18,379	4	17
July	365,398	61	123,327	18	37
August	119,801	25	10,186	2	25
September	156,419	29	43,775	8	9
October	139,861	29	56,422	12	26
November	144,391	29	23,077	6	19
December	168,524	31	47,785	7	8
Total	3,220,137	597	1,659,601	285	237
1944					
January	130,635	26	36,065	5	15
February	116,855	23	12,577	2	20
March	157,960	25	36,867	7	25
April	82,372	13	34,224	5	21
May	27,297	5	—	—	22
June	104,084	26	4,294	2	25
July	78,756	17	15,480	2	23
August	118,304	23	5,685	1	36
September	44,805	8	16,535	3	21
October	11,668	4	—	—	13
November	37,980	9	7,828	3	7
December	134,913	26	5,458	1	14
Total	1,045,629	205	175,013	31	242

| | TOTAL | | NORTH ATLANTIC | | |
	Tons	Ships	Tons	Ships	U-Boats
1945					
January	82,897	18	29,168	5	14
February	95,316	26	32,453	5	22
March	111,204	27	23,684	3	32
April	104,512	22	32,071	5	55
May (1–7)	17,198 ‡	4	5,353	1	28
	411,127	97	122,729	19	151

* *Note:* annual totals include 2,229 tons (2 ships) undated in 1942.

† 431,673 tons (241 ships) in the Pacific.

‡ 7,176 tons (1 ship) in the Pacific.

APPENDIX E

U-Boat Deployment in the Biscay Bases (July 1943)
Senior Officer, U-boats (West): *Kapitan zur See* Hans Rudolf Rösing*

Base	Flotilla	Commander
Lorient	Flotille No. 2 ('Saltzwedel' †)	*Korvettenkapitän* Ernst Kals
	Flotille No. 10	*Korvettenkapitän* Günter Kuhnke
Brest	Flotille No. 1 ('Weddigen' †)	*Korvettenkapitän* Werner Winter
	Flotille No. 9	*Korvettenkapitän* Heinrich Lehmann-Willenbrock
La Pallice	Flotille No. 3 ('Lohs' †)	*Korvettenkapitän* Richard Zapp
Saint-Nazaire	Flotille No. 6 ('Hundius' †)	*Korvettenkapitän* Wilhelm Schultz
	Flotille No. 7 ('Wegener' †)	*Korvettenkapitän* Herbert Sohler
Bordeaux ‡	Flotille No. 12	*Korvettenkapitän* Klaus Scholtz

---

* This was a purely administrative post; the Senior Officer, U-boats had no operational responsibility beyond planning the boats' transit across the Bay of Biscay. At 12°W they came under direct control of U-boat HQ.

† Rheinhold Saltzwedel, World War I U-boat commander.
Otto Weddigen, World War I U-boat commander.
Johannes Lohs, World War I U-boat commander.
Admiral Wolfgang Wegener
Paul Hundius, World War War I U-boat commander.

‡ Home of most of the supply U-boats and the Italian flotilla.

Shipping Losses in British Home Waters, 1939–45
(by all causes including submarines, surface vessels and aircraft)

Month	1939			1940			1941			1942			1943			1944			1945		
	Tons	Ships	Tonnage % of total	Tons	Ships	Tonnage % of total	Tons	Ships	Tonnage % of total	Tons	Ships	Tonnage % of total	Tons	Ships	Tonnage % of total	Tons	Ships	Tonnage % of total	Tons	Ships	Tonnage % of total
January				178,536	64	83.2	36,975	15	11.5	19,341	14	4.6	15,849	4	6.0	6,944	8	5.3	46,553	12	56.1
February				152,161	46	67.0	51,381	26	12.7	11,098	5	1.6	4,925	2	1.2	4,051	3	3.5	48,551	19	50.9
March				95,794	43	89.5	152,862	73	28.8	15,147	8	1.8	884	2	0.1	—	—	—	83,864	23	75.4
April				133,638	54	85.5	99,031	40	14.4	54,589	14	8.0	9,926	5	2.9	468	1	0.6	49,619	14	47.5
May				230,607	90	79.3		99	19.7	59,396	14	8.4	1,568	1	0.5	—	—	—	4,669	2	27.1
June				208,924	77	35.7	86,381	34	19.9	2,655	5	0.3	149	1	0.1	75,166*	19	72.2			
July				192,331	67	49.7	15,265	18	12.6	22,557	9	3.6	72	1	0.01	19,038	8	24.1			
August				162,956	45	41.0	19,791	11	15.1	—	—	—	19	1	0.01	54,834	12	46.3			
September	84,965	33	43.6	131,150	39	29.2	54,779	13	19.1	1,892	1	0.3	—	—	—	21,163	3	47.2			
October	63,368	24	32.3	131,620	43	29.7	35,996	12	16.5	12,733	6	1.9	—	—	—	1,722	2	14.7			
November	155,668	43	89.3	92,713	48	24.0	30,332	20	28.9	6,363	5	0.8	13,036	7	9.0	8,880	3	23.3			
December	152,952	65	80.6	83,308	34	23.8	56,845	19	9.7	9,114	10	2.6	6,086	1	3.6	85,639†	18	63.4			
	455,953	165	60.4		650	44.9	740,293	350	17.1	214,885	91	2.7	52,484	25	1.6	277,905	77	26.6	233,256	70	51.4

* This was the month of D-Day; submarines (world-wide) accounted for 57,875 tons (55.6%; 11 ships out of 26).
† This month marked the onset of the *Schnorchel* boats in inshore waters; submarines (world-wide) accounted for 58,518 tons (43.4%; 9 ships out of 26).
Annual sinkings by E-boats were: 1939: —; 1940: 47,985 tons (23 ships); 1941: 58,584 tons (29 ships); 1942: 71,156 tons (23 ships); 1943: 15,138 tons (6 ships); 1944: 26,321 tons (13 ships); 1945: 10,222 tons (5 ships).

APPENDIX G

Analysis of U-boat Losses 1914–1945

(i) 1914–1918*
    Sinkings by:
    Surface Vessels:

Naval patrols, hunting groups, random encounter	38	
Convoy escorts	17	
'Q'-ships	11	66
Merchant ships		6
Submarines		18
Aircraft		1
Mines		48
Accidents		19
Unidentified explosion		1
Unknown		19
		178

Methods of sinking:

Torpedoes	18
Ramming	19
Gunfire	20
Depth charges	31

* Between 1914–16 forty-six U-boats were sunk (fourteen by accidents or unknown causes), all the remainder being sunk in 1917 and 1918.

(ii) 1939–1945
    Sinkings by:
    Surface Vessels:

British & Allies	206	
US	37	
Shared	3	246
Shore-based Aircraft		
British & Allies	195	
US	48	
Shared	2	245

Ship-borne Aircraft
British & Allies	14	
US	29	
British, shared between ship- and shore-based aircraft	2	45

Shared by ships and shore-based Aircraft
British and British	21	
US and US	5	
British ships and US aircraft	5	
US ships and British aircraft	2	33

Shared by ships and ship-borne Aircraft
British and British	9	
US and US	6	15

Submarines
British	19	
US	2	21

Mines
laid by ships and submarines (British)	9	
laid by aircraft (British)	16	25

Bombing
British	22	
US	40	62

Soviet action	7

Accidents
Collision	27
Other	4

Marine causes	9
Scuttling or scrapping (pre-surrender)	17
Unknown	29
	———
	785

Bibliography

Unpublished Material:

Air Historical Branch: Air Publication 125, *A Short History of the Royal Air Force* (1936); Narrative, *The RAF in the Maritime War* (AHB/II/117), 8 vols; Monograph: *The Rise and Fall of the German Air Force* (published by Arms & Armour Press, 1983) (AHB/II/116/19); Monograph: *Armament* (AHB/II/116/4), 2 vols; *Coastal Command Review* (1942–5).

Naval Historical Branch: Admiralty Technical History (1914–1918); Lieutenant-Commanders F. W. Barley and D. Waters, *The Defeat of the Enemy Attack on Shipping 1939–45*; *Convoy Summaries*; *Monthly Anti-Submarine Reports*.

Conference Papers: Patrick Beesly: *British Naval Intelligence in Two World Wars*: Some Similarities and Differences, Medlicott Symposium, 'Intelligence and International Relations', Exeter University, 1985; Michael Hadley: *Inshore Anti-Submarine Warfare in the Second World War: The U-Boat Experience*, Halifax, 1985; Marc Milner: *Inshore ASW: The Canadian Experience*, ibid.; Jürgen Rohwer: *The Final Convoy Battles in the North Atlantic in Autumn 1943*, ibid.; *The operational use of 'Ultra' in the Battle of the Atlantic*, Medlicott Symposium, 1985; Roger Sarty: *Hard Luck Flotilla (1914–1918)*, Halifax, 1985.

Journals, Magazines etc.: *After the Battle* [No. 55: U-Boat Bases (February, 1987)]; *Military History*, February, 1983: 'The Eagle is Free' by Barry Gregory (escape of Polish submarine *Orzel* in 1939); Ibid., April, 1983: 'Torpedoes' by Edwyn Gray; Ibid., July, 1983: 'The Four-Stackers' by Kenneth Poolman; Ibid., December, 1983: 'Convoy HX 84) by Peter Chatt; *Royal United Services Institute for Defence Studies Journal* November, 1959: 'The U-boat Campaign and Third Ypres' by Stephen Roskill; November, 1964: 'Origin of the *Laconia* Order' by Dr Maurer Maurer and Lawrence J. Paszek; August, 1967: 'Naval Intelligence in the Second World War' by Donald McLachlan; August, 1968:

'The High Seas Fleet' by David Woodward; December, 1975: 'A Final Appraisal of the British Occupation of Iceland 1940–42' by Donald F. Bittner; December, 1977: 'The Negative Influence of Mahan on Anti-Submarine Warfare' by Captain R. A. Bowling (USN, rtd.); *Journal of Contemporary History* vol. i No. 4, October 1966; 'The Dismissal of Sir John Jellicoe' by Captain S. W. Roskill.

Official Histories: World War I:

Naval Operations, vols iv and v by Sir Henry Newbolt; Longmans 1928.

Military Operations, France and Belgium 1916 vol. ii by Sir James Edmonds, Macmillan 1938; 1915 vol. i, Macmillan 1927.

The War in the Air vol. i by Walter Raleigh, Clarendon Press 1922; vol. vi by H. A. Jones, Clarendon Press 1937.

(Semi-official) *Seaborne Trade* (3 vols) by C. E. Fayle, John Murray 1922–4.

Official Histories: World War II:

The War at Sea (4 vols) by Captain S. W. Roskill, HMSO 1954–61.

British Intelligence in the Second World War (3 vols) by F. H. Hinsley et al.; HMSO 1981–4.

Merchant Shipping and the Demands of War by Miss C. B. A. Behrens; HMSO 1955.

British War Economy by W. K. Hancock and M. M. Gowing; HMSO 1949.

British War Production by M. M. Postan; HMSO 1952.

Oil: A Study of War-Time Policy and Administration by D. J. Payton-Smith; HMSO 1971.

Statistical Digest of the War by W. K. Hancock; HMSO 1951.

Design and Development of Weapons by D. Hay, M. M. Postan, J. D. Scott; HMSO 1964.

Grand Strategy iii Part I by J. M. A. Gwyer; HMSO 1964; Ibid. iv by M. Howard; HMSO 1972

Royal Air Force 1939–1945 (3 vols) by Denis Richards and Hilary St George Saunders, HMSO 1974.

The Strategic Air Offensive Against Germany by Sir Charles Webster and Noble Frankland vol. ii; HMSO 1961.

The Far Distant Ships by Joseph Schull; Ministry of National Defence, Ottawa 1961.

The Creation of a National Air Force vol. ii by W. A. B. Douglas; University of Toronto Press 1986.

History of United States Naval Operations in World War II vol. i: *The Battle of the Atlantic* September 1939–May 1943; vol. x: *The Atlantic Battle Won* May 1943–May 1945 by Samuel Eliot Morison; Little, Brown and Company 1947.

Command Decisions, Office of Chief of Military History, Army Department; Methuen 1960.

Other Published Works:

Aldington, Richard, *Wellington*; Heinemann 1946.

Barnett, Correlli, *The Swordbearers*; Eyre & Spottiswoode 1963; *The Collapse of British Power*; Eyre Methuen 1972; *The Audit of War*; Macmillan 1986.

Beaverbrook, Lord, *Men and Power*; Hutchinson 1956.

Beesly, Patrick, *Room 40: British Naval Intelligence 1914–18*; Hamish Hamilton 1982; *Very Special Intelligence: The Story of the Admiralty's Operational Intelligence Centre 1939–1945*; Hamish Hamilton 1977.

Bekker, Cajus, *Hitler's Naval War*; Macdonald and Jane's 1974.

Brown, Eric (ed. William Green), *Wings of the Luftwaffe*; Pilot Press 1977.

Buchheim, Lothar-Günther, *U-Boat War*; Bantam Books (N.Y.) 1979.

Chalmers, Rear-Admiral W. S., *Max Horton and the Western Approaches*; Hodder & Stoughton 1954.

Chichester, Francis, *Along the Clipper Way*; Hodder & Stoughton 1966.

Churchill, Winston S., *The World Crisis* (2 vols); Odhams 1938; *Thoughts and Adventures*; Odhams 1947 (first published 1932); *The Second World War*: (i) The Gathering Storm; (ii) Their Finest Hour; (iii) The Grand Alliance; (iv) The Hinge Of Fate; (v) Closing The Ring; (vi) Triumph And Tragedy.

Clayton, Aileen, *The Enemy is Listening: The Story of the Y Service*; Hutchinson 1980.

Coles, Adlard, *Heavy Weather Sailing*; Adlard Coles 1967.

Cooper, Matthew, *The German Army 1933–1945*; Macdonald and Jane's 1978.

Cousins, Geoffrey, *The Story of Scapa Flow*; Frederick Muller 1965.

Craig, Gordon A., *Germany 1866–1945*; OUP 1978.

Creighton, Rear-Admiral Sir Kenelm, *Convoy Commodore*; Futura 1976.

Cremer, Peter, *U 333: The Story of a U-Boat Ace*; Bodley Head 1984.

Cruttwell, C. R. M. F., *A History of the Great War 1914–1918*; OUP 1934.

Cunningham, Admiral of the Fleet Viscount, *A Sailor's Odyssey*; Hutchinson 1951.

Danchev, Alex, *Very Special Relationship: Field-Marshal Sir John Dill and the Anglo-American Alliance 1941–44*; Brassey's 1986.

Dean, Sir Maurice, *The Royal Air Force and Two World Wars*; Cassell, 1979.

Dittmar, F. J. and Colledge, J. J., *British Warships 1914–1919*; Ian Allan 1972.

Dönitz, Admiral, *Memoirs: Ten Years and Twenty Days* (trans. R. H. Stevens in collaboration with David Woodward); Weidenfeld & Nicolson, 1958.

Edmonds, Sir J. E., *A Short History of World War I*; OUP 1951.

Edwards, Commander Kenneth, *Men of Action*; Collins 1943.

Esher, Reginald, Viscount, *Journals and Letters*; Nicholson and Watson 1938.

Falls, Cyril, *The First World War*; Longmans 1960.

Flower, Desmond and Reeves, James, *The War 1939–1945*; Cassell 1960.

Fraser, Sir David, *Alanbrooke*; Hodder & Stoughton 1982; *And We Shall Shock Them*; Hodder & Stoughton 1983.

Fuller, Major-General J. F. C., *The Decisive Battles of the Western World and their Influence on History* vol. ii; Eyre & Spottiswoode 1956; *The Generalship of Ulysses S. Grant*; John Murray 1929.

Gibson, R. H. and Prendergast, M., *The German Submarine War*; Constable 1931.

Grant, R. M., *U-Boats Destroyed*; Putnam 1964; *U-Boat Intelligence*; Putnam 1969.

Green, William, *Warplanes of the Third Reich*; Macdonald and Jane's 1970.

Gretton, Vice-Admiral Sir Peter, *Crisis Convoy: The Story of HX 231*; Purnell Book Services 1974; *Convoy Escort Commander*; Cassell 1964.

Gunston, Bill, *Encyclopedia of the World's Combat Aircraft*; Salamander 1976.

Haig, *Sir Douglas Haig's Despatches* (ed. Lt.-Col. J. H. Boraston); Dent 1919.

Hankey, Lord, *The Supreme Command 1914–1919* vol. i; Allen & Unwin 1961.

Harling, Robert, *The Steep Atlantick Stream*; Chatto & Windus 1946.

Harris, Sir Arthur, *Bomber Offensive*; Collins 1947.

Hindenburg, Field-Marshal von, *Out Of My Life*; Cassell 1920.

Hodges, Andrew, *Alan Turing: The Enigma of Intelligence*; Unwin Paperback 1985.

Hough, Richard, *A History of Fighting Ships*; Octopus 1975.

Jacobsen, Dr Hans-Adolf and Rohwer, Dr Jürgen (ed.), *Decisive Battles of World War II: The German View*; André Deutsch 1965.

Jameson, Sir William, *The Most Formidable Thing*; Hart-Davis 1965.

Jarman, T. L., *The Rise and Fall of Nazi Germany*; Signet Book (New American Library) 1956.

Jellicoe, Admiral of the Fleet Lord, *The Crisis of the Naval War*; Cassell 1920.

King-Hall, Stephen, *Our Own Times*; Nicholson & Watson 1938.

Kipling, Rudyard, *Humorous Tales*; Macmillan 1931; *Verse: Definitive Edition*; Hodder & Stoughton 1940.

Lamb, James B., *The Corvette Navy*; Macmillan of Canada 1978.

Langer, William L., *The Diplomacy of Imperialism*; New York 1951.

Lash, Joseph P., *Roosevelt and Churchill*; André Deutsch 1977.

Lenton, H. T., *World War II Fact Files: British Escort Ships*; Macdonald and Jane's 1974; *American Gunboats and Minesweepers*; Arco Publishing Co., New York 1974.

Lenton, H. T. and Colledge, J. J., *Warships of World War II*; Ian Allan 1980.

Lewin, Ronald, *Ultra Goes to War*; Hutchinson 1978; *The Other Ultra*; Hutchinson 1982; *The Life and Death of the Afrika Korps*; Batsford 1977.

Liddell Hart, B. H., *History of the Second World War*; Cassell 1970.

Lloyd George, David, *War Memoirs* (2 vols) Odhams 1936.

Longford, Elizabeth, *Wellington: The Years of the Sword*; Weidenfeld & Nicolson 1969.

Lucas, Sir Charles, *The Empire at War*; OUP 1921.

Ludendorff, General, *My War Memories 1914–1918* i (2 vols); Hutchinson 1919.

MacDonald, Charles B., *The Mighty Endeavour*; OUP 1969.

Macintyre, Donald, *The Battle of the Atlantic*; Pan Books 1983 (first published Batsford 1961); *U-Boat Killer*; Weidenfeld & Nicolson 1956.

Mahan, Captain A. T., *The Life of Nelson: The Embodiment of the Sea Power of Great Britain*; Sampson Low, Marston 1897.

McLachlan, Donald, *Room 39: Naval Intelligence in Action 1939–45*; Weidenfeld & Nicolson 1968.

Macleod, Colonel R., translation of extracts from *Der Weltkrieg 1914–1918* by General von Kuhl and the German Official Account, *Der Weltkrieg 1914 bis 1918: Die militarishen Operationen zu Lande*, Mittler 1939.

Marder, A. J., *From the Dreadnought to Scapa Flow* (5 vols); OUP 1961–70; *The Anatomy of British Sea Power*; Frank Cass 1940.

Masters, Anthony, *The Man Who Was M*; Blackwell 1984.

Medlicott, W. N., *British Foreign Policy Since Versailles*; Methuen, revised edition 1968.

Middlebrook, Martin, *Convoy*; Allen Lane 1976.

Milner, Marc, *North Atlantic Run: The Royal Canadian Navy and the Battle of the Convoys*; University of Toronto Press, 1985.

Monsarrat, Nicholas, *Three Corvettes*; Cassell 1945.

Mumby, F. A. (ed.), *The Great World War* (9 vols); Gresham Publishing Co. 1915–20.

Nicolson, Harold, *Peacemaking 1919*; Constable 1933.

Oliver, F. S., *The Anvil of War*: Letters between F. S. Oliver and his Brother 1914–1918; Macmillan 1936.

Overy, Richard, *Goering: The 'Iron' Man*; Routledge & Kegan Paul 1984.

Pack, S. W. C. *The Battle of Matapan*; Batsford 1961.

Padfield, Peter, *Dönitz: The Last Führer*; Gollancz 1984.

Parish, Peter J., *The American Civil War*; Eyre Methuen 1975.

Parkinson, Roger, *Tormented Warrior: Ludendorff and the Supreme Command*; Hodder & Stoughton 1978.

Poolman, Kenneth, *Focke-Wolf Condor: Scourge of the Atlantic*; Macdonald & Jane's 1978.

Porten, Edward P. von der, *The German Navy in World War II*; Pan 1972.

Price, Alfred, *Aircraft Versus Submarine*; William Kimber 1973; *Battle of Britain: The Hardest Day*, Macdonald & Jane's 1979.

Rawnsley, C. F. and Wright, Robert, *Night Fighter*; Collins 1957.

Repington, Lieutenant-Colonel C. à Court, *The First World War* i (2 vols); Constable 1920.

Robertson, Terence, *Walker RN*; Evans Bros. 1956.

Rohwer, Jürgen, *The Critical Convoy Battles of March 1943*; Ian Allan 1977.

Roskill, Captain S. W., *Admiral of the Fleet Earl Beatty: The Last Naval Hero*; Antheneum (N.Y.) 1981; *Naval Policy between the Wars* (2 vols); Collins 1968; *Hankey: Man of Secrets*; Collins 1970–74.

Sainsbury, Keith, *The North African Landings 1942*; Davis Poynter 1976.

Saundby, Air Marshal Sir Robert, *Air Bombardment: The Story of its Development*; Chatto & Windus 1961.

Schofield, B. B., *British Sea Power*; Batsford 1967.

Seaton, Albert, *The German Army 1939–45*; Weidenfeld & Nicolson 1982.

Shepperd, G. A., *The Italian Campaign 1943–45*; Arthur Barker, 1968.

Sherwood, Robert E., *The White House Papers of Harry L. Hopkins* (2 vols); Eyre & Spottiswoode 1949.

Shirer, William L., *Berlin Diary*; Hamish Hamilton 1941.

Sims, Rear Admiral W. S. and Hendrick, B. J., *The Victory at Sea*; John Murray 1927.

Slessor, Marshal of the Royal Air Force Sir John, *The Central Blue*; Cassell 1956.

Speer, Albert, *Inside the Third Reich*; Weidenfeld & Nicolson, 1970.

Steinberg, Jonathan, *Yesterday's Deterrent*; Macdonald 1965.

Stumpf, Richard, *The Private War of Seaman Stumpf* (ed. and trans. Daniel Horn); Leslie Frewin 1969.

Tedder, Marshal of the Royal Air Force Lord, *With Prejudice*; Cassell 1966.

Terraine, John, *Trafalgar*; Sidgwick & Jackson 1976; *The Road to Passchendaele*; Leo Cooper 1977; *The Smoke and the Fire: Myths and Anti-Myths of War 1861–1945*; Sidgwick & Jackson 1980; *To Win a War: 1918 The Year of Victory*; Sidgwick & Jackson 1978; *Douglas Haig: The Educated Soldier*; Hutchinson, 1963; *The Right of the Line: The Royal Air Force in the European War 1939–1945*; Hodder & Stoughton 1985; *White Heat: The New Warfare 1914–18*; Sidgwick & Jackson 1982.

Thetford, Owen, *British Naval Aircraft 1912–1958*; Putnam 1958.

Thomson, David, *England in the Twentieth Century*; Pelican History of England vol. ix 1965.

Thoumin, Richard (ed.), *The First World War*; Secker & Warburg 1963.

The Times History of the War (22 vols).

Watts, Anthony J., *World War II Fact Files: Axis Submarines*; Arco Publishing Co., New York 1977.

Weigley, Russell F., *Eisenhower's Lieutenants*; Sidgwick & Jackson 1981.

Welchman, Gordon, *The Hut Six Story: Breaking the Enigma Codes*; Allen Lane 1982.

Werner, Herbert A., *Iron Coffins*; Arthur Barker 1969.

Whaley, Barton, *Covert German Rearmament 1919–1939*; University Publications of America 1984.

Wheeler-Bennett, Sir John, *Hindenburg: The Wooden Titan*; Macmillan Papermac 1967.

Wilson, H. W. and Hammerton, J. A., *The Great War: The Standard History of the All-Europe Conflict* (13 vols); Amalgamated Press.

Winterbotham, F. W., *The Ultra Secret*; Weidenfeld & Nicolson 1974.

Winton, John (ed.), *Freedom's Battle: The War at Sea 1939–45*; Hutchinson 1967.

Wood, Derek and Dempster, Derek, *The Narrow Margin*; Arrow Books 1969.

Wynn, Humphrey and Young, Susan, *Prelude to Overlord*; Airlife 1983.

General Index

A

ABC-1 (Anglo-US talks, Jan. 1941): 340 & Notes 73, 74; 388; 405

Abe, Adml.: Japanese Naval Mission, Berlin, on new U/Bs, 656

Abel-Smith, Capt. E. M. C. (RN): SO 5th EG, 586

Abwehr: 170–1

Abyssinia: Italy attacks, 1935, 173–5; 257

Achilles, *Kapitänleutnant* A.: in Caribbean, 1942, 421

Admiralty, The:

1914–18:

see Royal Navy, Room 40, Hall, ASW: Convoys, Northern Barrage; 1916 changes at, A/S Division formed, 24, 671; 1917 'apathy and incompetence', 45; divided opinions in, 49–56; Lloyd George's visit, 58–9; favours large escorts, 63–4; 'dragged into 20th Century', 65–9; 'not a good office', 66; Jellicoe on unique rôle, 66; function of CNS, 66–7; younger officers at, 69; see Oliver, Carson, Geddes, Wemyss; Plans, Statistics Division, 68, 73–4; Mercantile Movements Division, 80; disappointment at, Dec. 1917, 99; dispute with Bacon, 110; control of maritime air, 124; addiction to hunting groups, 126–7; improved Intelligence system, 138–9, 143

1918–39:

neglect of ASW, 154; and Japan, 156–7; and economic crisis, 160; and Anglo-German Naval Agreement, 1935, 174–5; ASW delusions, 176–9; and hunting groups, 180; and 'capital ships', 182; and German rearmament, 185

1939–45:

see Convoys 1939–45, ASW, ASDIC, RAF: Coastal Command, Western Approaches, Churchill, Pound, Alexander, A. V., Cunningham; Trade Division assumes control of Merchant Shipping, Aug. 1939, 244; abandons SW Approaches, 275; Naval Control Service (NCS), officers (NCSO), 287–8; 295; 'the Citadel', 317; War Registry, 317 & Note 13; see OIC, Godfrey, Submarine Tracking Room, Thring, Winn; requests RCN escorts, 333; and Iceland, 337, 246; and German ships in Brest, 348; D/F chain, 356; 1941 A/S system, 363; 381; 382; 384; 411; and Far East, 1942, 428; 'Battle of the Air', 429–30; 'command of the sea', 1942, 442; 1943 prospects, 512; and 'Working Fiction', 514; and RCN sensitivity, 537; 541; 558; 'alarm and despondency', March 1943, 569–73; doubts efficacy of convoy, 569–71; 'unreasonable' fear, strain, 572–3; and bombing of U/B bases, 579; 584; and *Schnorchel*, 627; 1945 New Year mood, 652; and new U/Bs, 656; 'Square One', 658

Admiralty Research Laboratory (Teddington): 433 Note 66

Adriatic Sea: 32; U/B bases, 1915–18, 115–16; 126; see Otranto Barrage

Africa (East): Japanese threat, 427

Africa (North): Allied landing, 360–2; 493–9; oil for, 514–15; 536; 609–10

Africa (West): USA and, 339 Note 71; 459; U/B success off, April 1943, 593; see Freetown

Afrika Korps: 342
Air Ministry: 150; and Coastal Command, 1939, 247; see Portal; and bombing of U/B bases, 354–5 & Notes 5, 6; 366; 'Battle of the Air', 429–30: and maritime air force, 443; 522; 523
Air power:
1914–18:
see RFC, RNAS, Airships; in ASW, 1917, 36–8; deterrent value, 77; air escort, 90; 1918 advances, 124–5; RN/Air ASW cooperation, 125–6; aircraft types and uses, 126; and convoys, 148–9; expansion of maritime, 148 & Note 17, 158–60; bombardment of cities, 512
1918–39:
1920s fear of, 160; inter-war strides, 182–3; see German Air Force, RAF, FAA
1939–45:
see German Air Force, RAF, FAA, USAAF, USN, VLR; sanction of sea power, 343; dispute on use of, 1942, 429–30; increasing effectiveness in Atlantic, 432–3 & Note 65; Admlty demand for maritime use, 443; Dönitz's fear of, 1942, 475–6; in N. Atlantic, 478–9; 529; U/B dread of, 1943, 591; in Bay of Biscay, 601–5; 606; and Atlantic victory, 608; RAF rules sky, 632; effect of *Schnorchel*, 657; 1945 bombing of Germany, 658; commitment to ASW, 672
Aircraft: see separate Index
Aircraft Carriers: British, 159; cost of, 160; need for as escorts, 385; see RN Ships, *Audacity*; see Escort Carriers; US construction, 1942, 496; USN and 'milch cows', 1943, 634–5
Airships: see Zeppelins; British, 1915–18, 37–8; as escorts, 78–9; 126
Alamein, El: Battles of, 1942, 500 & Note 101; 579
Alanbrooke, F-M Lord: CIGS, at ARCADIA Conference, 403 Note 1; and shipping, 495; and ROUNDUP; 'Mediterranean strategy', 577; 610
Alcock, John: crosses Atlantic, 1919, 159
Aldegrove, RAF station: 566
Alexander, Rt. Hon. A. V.: 1st Lord of Admlty, 250 Note 25; on 1942 crisis, 428; on need for VLR aircraft, 501
Alexander, F-M Lord: 500

Alexandria: Italian 'human torpedoes' in, 404; 659
Algeria: 494; 497
Algiers: British landing, 1942; 496
Amatol (explosive): replaced by Torpex, 434
Amery, Leopold: 155 Note 5
Amiens, Battle of, 1918: air forces in, 23 Note 12; 'black day of German Army', 135
Amsterdam: 7
ANAKIM, Operation: 610
Andrews, V/Adml A. (USN): on convoys, 413 Note 24; and Eastern Sea Frontier, 418; bans coast lights, 419; 457
Anti-aircraft (AA): British lack of, 1939, 181; U/B training, 191; shortage for M/Vs, 1939; Oerlikons, 243; RCN lack, 333; Brest *Flak*, 346 & Note 8; in U/Bs, 432, 582; increasing U/B armament, 479–81; Maritime Regiment, RA, 540; use in ASW, 599; rockets 57-mm guns versus, 619–20; U/B equipment, 1943, 630–1
Anti-Submarine Warfare (A/S; ASW):
1914–18:
RN A/S Division formed, 1916, 24; lack of weapons, 24; see Western Approaches, Hydrophones, Depth Charges, Weapons, Wireless Telegraphy, Destroyers, Direction Finding, Auxiliary Patrol, Sloops, Jellicoe; offensive patrolling, 35; pre-1917 failure, 38; geography and, 41–2; lack of analysis, 53; no previous experience of, 58; see Convoys; 'young man's job', 66; R/Adml Duff, 67; June 1917 A/S offensive, 69 & Note 30; balloons in, 78; see Airships; air contribution, 79; sinking U/Bs a bonus, 87 (see Marder); Allied Naval Conference, Sept. 1917, 90–3; and 'real' war, 93; U/B 'ambush', Oct. 1917, 93–6; unidentified explosions, 95, 113; strategic effect of, 98; failure to destroy U/Bs, 99; resistance to convoy, 100; Lloyd George on 1917 triumph, 101; see Dover Straits, Northern Barrage, Otranto Barrage, Mediterranean Sea; first-line forces engaged, 117; turning-point, 119; failure of U/B packs, 120–3; improvements in, 124; professionalism, 125; Admlty belief in 'hunting groups', 126–7; victory of 'small advantages', 134–5; safe convoys more important than U/Bs sunk, 144–5; 'two-tier victory; Tirpitz on, 145; 1914–18

784

summary, 147–50; air escort doctrine, 1918, 149; ignored, 434 Note 67

1918–39:
ASW backwater, 160, 193; 1930s delusions, 176–7; 'whalers' in 1939 Estimates, 180; see OIC, S/M Tracking Room

1939–45
persisting RN belief in 'hunting groups', 244–6; Churchill on 'cavalry division', 245, 585; bombs v depth charges, 248–9; growth of A/S forces, 1939–40, 251–3; see Corvettes, Frigates, Sloops; RN taken by surprise, 1940; lack of escorts, 265–8; ASW shortages, 271; see Depth Charges; see Western Approaches; SW Approaches abandoned, 275; A/S Schools, 275–6; see Training, Noble (CinCWA), Derby House; WACIS, 288, 429; WA Tactical Unit, 307–8; 1941 Atlantic Directive, 309–10; era of U/B 'aces' over, 313–16; Creasy Director, ASW, 319; Operational Intelligence and, 326; USN training begins, 340; elaborate machinery of, 1941, 357–8; higher direction (cf. Germany), 363; Coastal Command Operational Research, 368–70; see Escorts, Escort Carriers; USA unprepared for, 410–18; Air contribution, 1942, 432–3; see HF/DF, Radar; equipment and technique, 441; no unified A/S doctrine in USN, 453; 'Working Fiction', 454–9; ramming, 478; Cabinet Anti-U-boat Warfare Cttee, 501, 578–9; TRITON breakthrough, 509; VLR new dimension, 566–7; sea/air 'theological dispute', 580; gunnery, 599; U/B deep diving, 599; 'awesome effectiveness', May 1943, 606; Dönitz accepts Atlantic defeat, 608; cost of ASW, 615; new weapons, 1943–, 618–20; 'Mark 24 Mine', see Torpedoes; 'Operation Plaster', 621–3; long ASDIC hunts, 621 Note 13; 'FOXER' (CAT), 639–40; effect of *Schnorchel*, 656–8; 'Square One', 658; strength of ASW forces, 1945, 660; 1914–45 summary, 671–3; commitment of air power to, 672

Antilles Is.: 414

Antwerp: 36

America: see United States of (USA)

Aphrodite: German anti-radar decoy, 625

ARCADIA Conference, Dec. 1941–Jan. 1942:

403–8 & Note 1, 412, 493–4; watchword, 513

Arctic Ocean: 286; 351–2; 413; 469; 545; winter darkness, 584

Ardennes Offensive, 1944–45: 657 Note 88; 658

Argentia, Newfoundland: US base, 336; 340; 418; 434

Argentina: U/Bs interned in, 666

Aristophanes, playwright: quotation from 'The Frogs', 498 Note 99

Armada, Spanish, 1588: 383 Note 63

Arms Race (1930s): 185–6

Arnauld, *Korvettenkapitän* von, de la Perière: 1914–18 'ace of aces', 19–20; final cruise, 135–6; return to Kiel, 1918, 160–1

Arnim, *Gen.* von: and TM 1, 515

Arras, Battle of, 1917: 46; 70

Aruba Is.: 414; *U 156* at, 420; GAT/TAG convoys, 483 Note 72

Ascension Is.: Wideawake Field; bombing of *Laconia* survivors, 472 & Note 49; 487

ASDIC: 1917–18 development, 30; 147; 1930s Admlty faith in, 177–8; 184; Dönitz sceptical of, 188; 191; exaggerated RN belief in, 1939, 245, 250; nullified by U/B surface attacks, 1940, 264; 278; 280; and *U 99*, *U 100*, 315; RCN lack, 333; 341; and HX 133, 349; complement to radar, 357–8; and SC 42, 377–80; and *U 127*, 396; and *U 434*, 397; damage to, 398; and *U 567*, 399; 437; faults of, 439–40; poor use by A3, 453; 461; 477; and SBT, 486; weather and, Oct. 1942, 489; and HX 217, 506–7; and ON 166, 533; damage with ONS 169, 546–7; defective in A3, 547; 562; damage with HX 229A, 563; ONS 5 and, 599; and 'Operation Plaster', 621–3 & Note 14; long U/B hunts, 621 Note 13; 'FOXER' and, 639; inshore difficulties, 657 & Note 86

Asia, SE: Japanese advance in, 403–4; SEAC, 542

Asquith, Rt. Hon. H. H. (Prime Minister 1908–16): and Flanders U/Bs, 69

Athens: Germans enter, 1941: 342

Atlantic, Battle of the, 1940–5: 186; Germany's unfavourable position, 214; begins, 1940, 256; *Luftwaffe* and, 259–60; 261; nadir of British fortunes, 269; westward shift, 171; public slow to understand, 275;

785

285; 'measureless peril in charts, curves, statistics', 301; British fear defeat, 1941, 303–4; Churchill proclaims, 308; 1941 Directive, 309–10; RCN and, 1941, 331; British optimism, 1941, 352; see Atlantic 'Gap'; Air Ministry and, 354–5 & Note 6; fundamental change in U/B strategy, 359–61 & Note 16; see North Atlantic, South Atlantic; USN participation, 1941, 392; 1941 true moment of decision, 400–1; 'never doubt about outcome', 401; no SAC for, 405; and Allied landing in Europe, 405–6; USN unprepared for, 1942, 410–11; 'terrible event in very bad time', 424; 426; air power and, 433; SAC necessary but impossible, 450; 'no quarter', 466; priorities for, 501; at end 1942, 511–12; Adml King and, 515; Bomber Command and, 516–17; Sigint and, 527–8; final battle begins, 529; crisis arrives, 533; Convoy Conference, March 1943, 535–44; NW Command created (RCN), 538; question of SAC, Super Air Officer, 540–4; Combined Procedure Board, Allied A/S Survey Board, 542–3; 'dark hour before dawn', 544 ff.; climax, 553–76; transformed by VLR aircraft, 566; 'dominating factor all through war', 576; 'last decisive German success', 588; 'beginning of end', 590; ONS 5 'tragedy within triumph', 594–600; U/B defeat, 597; 607; Dönitz accepts defeat, 608; meaning of 'victory', 609–13; 614; 619; 628; second U/B defeat, 641–2; U/Bs and, 670, 672

Atlantic Charter: 387

Atlantic City, NJ: waterfront lights, 1942, 410

Atlantic Cttee, 1941: 308–9

Atlantic Fleet: see USN

Atlantic 'Gap': see VLR aircraft; 345; 366; steady closing, 1942, 479; A. V. Alexander on, 501; increasing significance, 529; escort carriers and, 552; HX 229/SC 122 in, 563; Carrier Groups and, 586; aircraft operating in, 606

Atlantic Ocean: 19; 31; U/Bs in, 1917, 41; 61; 64 Note 14; 69; shipping dispersal points, 88; 91; 99; U/B across, 1918, 142; W/T and, 143; non-stop air crossing, 1919, 159; 193; U/B passage to, 1939, 249–50 & Note 21; see 'steep Atlantic stream', Weather; Italians unfamiliar

with, 273–4; 278; 'Town' Class unsuited to, 280; German surface ships in, 295–7; winter 'frozen malice', 300; German weather-ships, 326; worst part of, 334, 336 & Note 62; 338; US Security Zone, 341–2; *Bismarck* in, 343; 381; USN and, 388; tanker losses in, 421; 424; St Nazaire dry dock, 444 Note 1, 552; 663

Atlantic (North): D/F stations, 356; 371; U/B offensive Sept. 1941, 372–82; M/V losses, Oct.–Dec. 1941, 387; last 1941 actions, 394–9; 400; U/Bs return, 1942, 423; USN withdrawal, 434; U/Bs in, 446; June M/V losses, 450; Dönitz and, 459; 461; final U/B campaign begins, 466 & Note 40; air power and, 478–9; Oct. M/V losses, 492; 494; U/B operations suspended, Nov., 497, 505; *schwerpunkt* of sea war, 508; 510; 532; 'Big Battle' of RCN, 535–8; US Support Group for, 539; March 1943 M/V losses, 545; continuity of convoys, 550; comparative convoy losses, 571; continuous action, 572–3; April–May M/V losses, 587; U/B 'vacuum', April, 588; ONS 5 'last of tragic convoys', 594–600; 608; meaning of victory, 609–13; declining M/V losses, 630; U/B return, Sept., 636–40; U/B second defeat, 642; BT and, 657 Note 86

Atlantic (South): 41; 62; convoy dispersal points in, 1917, 88, 296; US view of, 339 & Note 71; Brazil and, 483; U/Bs move into, 487–8; Oct. 1942 M/V losses, 492; convoys in, 500; 545; 634

Atlantic Plot: in Derby House and Admlty, 304 & Note 59

'Atlantick stream, steep': 255; 258; 274; 280; 290; 308; 395; 437; Oct. 1942, 485–6; 'bravura performance', 1943, 523–4; 546; 'steepest and cruellest', 594–5

Attlee, Rt. Hon. C. R. (Deputy Prime Minister): 412 Note 22

Auchinleck, F-M Sir C.: and First Battle of El Alamein, 500 Note 101

Aurora Borealis: 590

Australia: 62; 156–7, and pre-1914 naval Defence, 328; 389; RAN, 396; Japanese threat, 1942, 494; 500

Austria: *Anschluss*, 1938, 201

Austro-Hungarian Empire: 4; effect of Allied blockade, 1917, 80–1

Auxiliary Patrol (RN 1914–18): 25; 95; losses in Dover Straits, 1917, 1918, 110 Note 16, 111; 416; see Index of Merchant Ships 1914–18

Avranches: US Army captures, 648

Axis, Rome-Berlin 1936: forces advancing, 1941, 342; Dec. defeat, 401; 419; surprised by TORCH, 496 & Note 97; pressure on, 1943, 528; resistance in Tunisia, 544, 556, 610; 611 Note 185; Italian surrender, 615

Azores, Is.: Italian S/Ms off, 273; 342; 352; 499; ONS 154 directed towards, 510; 534; 634; 636

B

Baberg, *Kapitänleutnant* K.: and SC 122, 561

Bacon, V/Adml. Sir R. (RN): Dover Command, 108–10 & Note 110; and tank landing-craft, 1917, 109; replaced by Keyes, 110

BAGRATION, Operation (Battle of Byelorussia): destruction of Army Group Centre, June 1944, 647–8

Bahama Is.: 414

Baker, AVM B. E. (No. 19 Group): SWAMP operations, June 1944, 646

Baker-Cresswell, Capt. A. J. (RN): Larne Battle School, *Philante*, 502–3

Balfour, Rt. Hon. A. J.: on U-boats, 1918, 137, 672

Baltic Sea: 6, 24 Note 13; Jellicoe proposes blocking ports, 91; 139; 187; U/B exercises in, 1937, 193; Germany's 'front door', 214; frozen, 1939–40, 234; 326; 351; 358–9; *TETIS* cipher used in, 425; 545; 585; 627; massacre of U/Bs in, 1945, 663–4

Baltimore, Md.: 91 Note 15; 414; 629

Bangor, Maine: 418

Banks, Cdr. W. E. (RN): SOE SC 42, 381

Bapaume, Battle of, 1918: 135

BARBAROSSA, Operation, June 1941–: 351–2; 353 & Note 1, 359; 362 & Note 22; 'great folly', 401; German 1942 offensive, 494, 500; 610; see Stalingrad, Kursk, Operation BAGRATION, Eastern Front

Barbary Coast: 52 Note 32, 146

Barents Sea: 518

Barnett, Correlli: on British technology, 34, 180–81, 284–5

Bathythermography (BT): 667 Note 86

Battenberg, A-F Prince Louis of: 5

Bauer, *Flotillenadmiral* H.: U/B *Führer*, 1914–17, 9; on unrestricted warfare, 22; replaced, 65; proposes 'pack' tactics, 1917, 120, 122; and 'milch cows', 142; 194 Note 97

Bauer, *Oberst* M. H.: 81

Bawdsey Research Station: 184

Bayly, V/Adml. Sir L. (RN): 74

B-Dienst: see *xB-Dienst*, Intelligence (German); 32; 215; and Loch Ewe, 227 & Note 39; Norwegian Campaign success, 257; and MN Code, 257–8; 262; 356; and new MN Code, 454; 459; 461; and SC 107, 490; excellence, 496 Note 97; personnel in U/Bs, 505; 527; 529; 547; 550; on peak of form, 556–7 & Note 94, 561–2; and ONS 5, 595–6; 606; 607–8; 628; 670

Beatty, A-F Lord: 1917 misgivings, 24; on ASW, 49; and Scandinavian convoys, 97–8; and Northern Barrage, 115; and fundamental change of RN strategy, 117; see Grand Fleet; 156; and aircraft carriers, 159; and Anglo-German Naval Agreement, 1935, 174; 175; 'something wrong with our bloody ships', 233 & Note 48; 296; 585

Beaufort Scale: 524 & Note 25

Beaumont Hamel: capture of, 1916, 3

Beaverbrook, Lord: 58–9; 403 Note 1

Beesly, Patrick: deputy to Winn, 321

Beharrel, Lt.-Col. J. G.: at Admlty Statistics Division, 1917, 73

Belgium: coast occupied, 1914, 17; German atrocities in, 44; amphibious operations, 1917, King of, 135; corvette *Godetia* and SC 122, 561

Belgrade: 342

Belle Isle Straits: 394; *U 517* in, 1942, 486

Belts, Danish: 214; U-boat massacre in, 664

Benbecula Is.: RAF station, 568

Bengal, Bay of: Japanese in, 427

Bentley Priory: Fighter Command HQ, 304

Bergen, Norway: 96; 97; 98; 113; 115; 257; U/Bs ordered to, 1942, 409 Note 13; U/Bs withdraw to, 1944, 650; 662

Berlin: *Marineleitung* in, 167; 219; 221; 224; 298; 327; Japanese Ambassador at, 456; U/B HQ, 1943, 518, 670; Japanese Embassy reports, 656; Allies advance on, 658; final battle, 663–4 & Note 100

Bermuda Is.: US base in, 279, 340 Note 75, 341–2; D/F station, 419; 420

Bernays, CPO M. L. (RCN): courageous action, 476–7

Bertelsman, *Oberleutnant*: and HX 229, 563

Bestelmeyer, Dr A.: torpedo designer, 234

Bethlehem-Fairfield Yards, Baltimore: 629 & Note 25

Bethmann Hollweg, T. von: Imperial Chancellor (1909–17), 4; opposes U/B blockade of Britain, 8; *Lusitania* &, 10; at Pless Conference, 1916, 12–13; accepts unrestricted U/B warfare, 15; resigns, 82

Bevin, Rt. Hon. E. (Minister of Labour): and Regional Port Directors, 302

Bigalk, *Oberleutnant*: sinks *Audacity*, 399

Binney, V/Adml T. H. (RN): on ASW, 1939, 245

Biscay, Bay of: U/Bs in, 1917, 88; Germans reach, 1940, 255; 260; 275; 'trunk of U/B menace'; 1st RAF Offensive in, 371–2; 425; early 1942 operations, 430; *Luigi Torelli* attacked with Leigh Light, 431; 479; 497; 531; 2nd RAF Offensive, 1943, 581; effect of air offensives, 582–3; 585; 605; 608; 620; 3rd RAF Offensive; 630–3, climax of, 631–2; 'Death Valley', 641; U/B operations, June 1944, 645–7

Biscay, U/B bases: 19; establishment, 1940, 255–6; Italians join, 273; 326; 344; and German surface ships, 347–8; Hitler and shelters ('pens'), 354–5; 'milch cows' and, 420; Casablanca Conference orders bombing, 516–17; Harris on, 579; 585; 616; 636–7; elimination of, 648–50

Bismarck, Prince Otto von: Imperial Chancellor, 1871–90, 172

Black Sea: 14, 99 Note 29; Dönitz in, 162

Blackett, Prof. P.: Scientific Adviser to Coastal Command, 368–70; at WA, 539; at Admlty, 554 & Note 89; 'nobody asked right questions', 572

Blackman, Mr A. H.: on *Alnwick Castle* survivors, 1917, 42–3

Blériot, M. Louis: cross-Channel flight, 1909, 158

Bletchley Park (BP): 31; see GC & CS; 265 Note 29; 'central to conduct of war', 322; Huts, 322–3; Index, 325; and *Heimische Gewässer* traffic, 326 & Note 41; attack-

ing German communications as whole, 327; 348; and HX 133, 349–50; 353; recruiting for, 357; 363; 371; and U/B grid disguise, 1941, 373 & Note 49; 394; and *TRITON*, 425; 1942 crisis, 426–7; 438; and *Enigma* blackout; 'Working Fiction', 454–5; 4-wheel *Enigma* & 3-wheel Bombes, 508; *TRITON* breakthrough, 509–10; fears second blackout, March 1943, 527; bad time at, 531, 556; monitors U/B morale, 588–92; and ONS 5, 595–6; *Geheimschreiber* ('Fish') and 'Colossus', 627 Note 19; double victory, June 1943, 628; 640; monitors new U/Bs, 655–6; 672

Blockade: meaning of, 5–6; of Germany, 1914, 8; of Britain, 8–9; Hitler declares, 1940, 262

Blohm & Voss: S/M building yard damaged, 654

'Bloody Foreland': 268

Blum, *Korvettenkapitän*: on numbers required for U/B blockade (pre-1914), 9, 17

Bohm, *Adml*. H.: backs U/Bs, 1938, 203

BOLERO, Operation: US buildup in UK, 493; 610

Bolsheviks: take Russia out of war, 105–6

Bomba: Poles develop, 323

Bombe: Turing develops, 323–4; 325; 327; permutations, 424; 'brutal assault', 425; 508; increasing number, 1943, 527; US 4-wheel, 627

Bomber Command: see Royal Air Force

Bombs: A/S. 1918, 148; A/S 1939, 248; new sight needed, 1941, 366; German radio-controlled glider-, 633 Note 36

Bonatz, *Fregattenkapitän* H.: and *B-Dienst*, 257

Bone (Algeria): *Breslau* at, 161

Boot, Dr H: and centimetric radar, 285

Bordeaux: 255; Condors at Bordeaux-Mérignac, 259–60, 383; Italian S/Ms at, 273–4; U/B shelters at, 354; Allies advance on, 648–9

Bormann, Martin: 664

Borneo: Japanese in, 404

Bosporus: 99 Note 29

Boston, Mass.: 414; USN destroyer training centre, 453

Boswell, Lieut. H. G. (RNAS): attack on U/B, 76

Bowen, Dr E.: and ASV radar, 184; 283
Bowhill, A/M Sir F.: AOC Coastal Command; and depth charges, 247–9 & Note 15; 271; 365–8
Boyle, Cdr. R. C. (RN): SOE SC122, 555, 566
Brainard, V/Adml R. M. (USN): CTF24, 434 Note 70
Brauchitsch, F-M von: C-in-C German Army (1938–41), 361 Note 20
Brazil: destroyers for, 51, 551; strategic significance, 339 & Note 71; aircraft attack U/Bs, 459; declares war on Germany, 483
Bremen: 214; Bomber Command attack, 1942, 470; 'Valentin' U/B factory, 654; 663
Bridgeman, Lt.-Cdr. C. E. (RNR): CO Dianthus, sinks U379, 477
Brest: 255; operational U/B base, 262; Hipper at, 297; He 111s at, 308; German ships in; Flak, 346; U/B shelters, 354 & Note 5; Bomber Command attack, 1943, 516; U230 returns to, 1943, 605; empty berths in U/B pens, 641; losses of U/Bs from, June 1944, 646; Americans capture, 648–9 & Note 69
Brewer, Cdr. G. N. (RN): SO 1 EG, 586
Bristol: 41–2; Channel, 221, 299, 657; 1940 air raid, 300; Regional Port Director, 302–3; 1941 air raid, 308
Bristol, R/Adml. A. LeR Jnr (USN): CTF24, 1941, 388–9; 394 Note 88; death, 434 & Note 70
Britain: decline of technology, 34; public discontent with RN, 1917, 45; unawareness of U/B peril, 48; see Convoys; change of Govt., 70; see Home Waters; reaction to unrestricted S/M warfare, 1916–18, 146–7; dependence on sea-borne supplies, 153; tradition of post-war retrenchment; National Debt, 1918, 154–5; 'Coupon Election', 153 Note 3; faith in RN, 155 & Note 6; Ten Year Rule, 155–6; naval supremacy no longer cornerstone of policy, 1919, 156; economic crisis, 160; Anglo-German Naval Agreement, 1935, 174–5; obsolescence of steel industry, 180–1; declares war, 1939, 214; 1920–1940 madness, 242; munitions shortage, 243; run-down economy, 250–1 & Note 25; 'no compromise equivalent to slow suicide',

254; enemies on all sides except West, 256; see Battle of; unawareness of naval peril, 1940, 275; 'Blitz' on cities, 283, 299–300; weakness of radio and electrical industries, 284–5; merchant shipping pre-dominance, 285; war direction, 362; procedures more modern than German, 363; failure to understand Dominions, 389, 537; selfish civilian behaviour, 410 Note 17; doubts about ROUNDUP, 494; and Battle of Atlantic, 541; 1943 shortages, 611; shipping decline, 629–30 & Note 28; and U/B wars, 672–3
British Army: in Battle of Arras, 1917, 46; convoys for BEF, 50; 'Backs to Wall', 1918, 119 & Note 36; in final Allied Offensive, 135; strength on Western Front, 150, 612; 1919–23 Estimates, 156; 180; 'walkie-talkies' and, 183; and training, 190; 1939 BEF safely convoyed, 242; Dunkirk evacuation, 254; flung out of Europe, 1941, 342; Commandos, 44 Note 1; see Desert War, CRUSADER, TORCH, HUSKY, OVERLORD, Auchinleck, Brooke, Montgomery; junior partner in both wars, 449; Maritime Regiment, RA, 540
British Broadcasting Company: 183
British Empire: forces on Western Front, 1914–18, 49, 150, 612; shipping tonnage, 1917, 52; 153; 363; US difficulty in understanding, 388–9; Dominions dependent on Britain and USA, 537
British Guiana: US base in, 279
British Overseas Airways Corporation (BOAC): 429 Note 57
Brittany: 1940 evacuation, 261; see Brest, Cherbourg; Allies enter, 1944, 648
Brodeur, V/Adml. V. G. (RCN): at Atlantic Convoy Conference, 1943, 538 & Note 57
Bromet, AVM G. R.: AOC 19 Group and 2nd Bay Offensive, 581–2
Brooke, F-M Sir A.: see Alanbrooke
Brooke, Lt.-Cdr. E. (RN): CO Mary Rose, 1917, 96 & Note 22
Brown, A. W.: crosses Atlantic, 1919, 159
Brown, Capt. E., RN test pilot: on Condors, 260; shoots down Condor, 396, 398
Brown, Stoker W. (RCN): 379
Brownrigg, Adml. Sir H. (RN): C-in-C Nore, 1940, 275 Note 1

Bruce, Rt. Hon. S. M. (Australia): and Cabinet Anti-U-boat Warfare Cttee, 500–1
Bruges, Belgium: 1915 U/B base, 17–9; 106–7; Allied offensive towards, 1918, 135; 354
Brunsbüttel: Kiel Canal terminal, 214
Brusilov, Gen. A.: and Russian 1916 offensive, 3–4
Bucharest: fall of, 1916, 14
Budapest: Red Army at, 1944, 658
Bulgaria: changes sides, 1944, 658
Bulloch, S/L T.: and HX 217, 506
Bulow, *Kapitän zur See* von: 13
Burcher, F/O C.: and SC 122, March 1943, 566
Burma: Japanese occupy, 424, 494; British defeat, 1943, 543; 610
Burnett, Cdr. P. W. (RN): SOE ON 202, 637–8
Butcher, Flight Lieut. O. A. (RNAS): sights U/B from balloon, 1917, 78
Byron, Lord, poet: 255

C

Cabinet (British): 1916 War Policy Ctee, 66; note on Belgian ports, 69–70; June 1917 meetings, 70; Economic Policy Cttee, 1940, 301; Port Clearance Ctee, 301–4; 387; Anti-U-boat Warfare Cttee, 1942, 501, 504, and *TRITION* breakthrough, 509
Cabot Strait: 486
Cairo Conferences: 517
Calcutta: Japanese threat to, 427–8
Callaghan, Adml. Sir G. (RN): demands depth charges, 1914, 27
Cambridge University: and GC & CS, 322–3 & Note 31, 627 Note 19
Campbell, F/O K.: VC at Brest, 1941, 346 Note 88
Campbeltown: A/S School at, 276
Canada: 42; convoys from 1917, 62; corvettes built in, 253; 279; and Naval Defence, 328–9; 'Never Again', Mackenzie King, 329; seeking VLR aircraft, 366; not consulted in Anglo-US 1941 agreement, 388–9; Can. Coastal Zone (US Sea Frontier) 414; and Tripartite Convoy Conference, March 1943, 535–8; watershed in history (NW Atlantic Command), 538;

weather, 563; Canadians in Coastal Command, 646; inshore U/B campaign, 1944, 657 Note 86
Canadian Air Force (RCAF): 329; competes with RCN for skills, 332; total recruitment, 332 Note 53; 389; 394; 418; 145 Sqdn sinks *U658*, 10 Sqdn sinks *U520*, Oct. 30 1942, 491; Liberators in 10 Sqdn, 540; ASV III in 407 Sqdn, 582; 5 Sqdn sinks *U630*, 597; 10 Sqdn sinks *U341*, 637, and ONS 18/ON 202, 638; 407 Sqdn sinks inshore U/B (British Home Waters), 657
Canadian Army: Can. Corps at Vimy, 1917, 46; and US War of Independence, 328; 1914–18 recruiting, 329; total 1939–45 recruiting, 332 Note 53; 389
Canadian Navy (RCN): 'Town' Class destroyers join, 281; 1941 expansion, 264; 1914–18 weakness; 1933 nadir, 329; desire for fleet destroyers, 330–1 & Note 49; 'corvette navy', 330–3; 1939–45 expansion, 331, 332 Note 53; expansion problems, 332–3; see AA, ASDIC; ASW corvette rôle unforeseen, 333 Note 54; request to perform escort duty, 333; see NEF; and continuous Atlantic escort, 345; deficiencies, 349; 378; 381; and Anglo-US 1941 agreement, 388–9; 46% of Atlantic burden, 434; MOEF ('Newfy-Derry run'), 435; 439; training, 442; and ONS 92, 447–9; RN criticism, 448–9; 'Big Battle' dreams, 450; and ONS 102, 452; and ON 115, 462–6; lack of HF/DF and 271 radar, 466, 476; and TORCH, 449; ONS 154 disaster, 510–1; and ON 166, 532; 48% of Atlantic burden, 'Big Battle', 535; escorts withdrawn for training, 538; NW Atlantic Command created, March 1943; 'watershed', 538; corvettes in WLEF, 557, 600–1 Note 170; and CCM, 628; 'CAT' (FOXER), 639–40; NEPTUNE contribution, 645; sinks *U984*, 647; escort groups, Jan. 1945, 660
Canaris, *Adml.*: 1931 report on Dönitz, 170–1
Cannes: 651
Cap Bénat: 651
Cape Cod: 547
Cape Farewell: 345; 588

Cape Finisterre: 633
Cape Gallinas: 414
Cape of Good Hope: 62; 359; 500
Cape Gris Nez: 107
Cape Hatteras: 416
Cape Helles: 612
Cape Henry: 416
Cape Lookout: 418
Cape Race: 394; 588
Cape St. Vincent: 313
Cape Town: first convoy to, Sept. 1939, 244; 'virgin field', 1942, 459; U/Bs sent to, 471, 487–8
Cape Trafalgar: 140
Cape Verde Is.: 497
Cape Wrath: 657
Capelle, *Adml* von: 4; at Pless conference, 11–12
Caporetto, Battle of, 1917: 511
Caribbean Sea: 42; 62; 286; 371; 408; 419; returning U/Bs attacked, 432; 444; 634
Caribbean Sea Frontier (USA): 414; U/Bs in, 1942, 420–3; shipping losses, 421; July–Aug. losses in, 423; 450; 459
Carls, *Adml* R.: 518 Note 12
Carson, Sir E.: First Lord of Admlty, 1916–17, 24; and Plans Division, 68; replaced, 72
Casablanca: US landings, 1942, 496; 1943 Conference (SYMBOL), 513–17; and U/B war, 513–15; Air Directive, 516–17; see Unconditional Surrender; photographs of, 517 & Note 11; 522; 543; 'unfortunate meeting', 576–7; US Chiefs of Staff 'ambushed', 577; 610; 614; 616
Caston, 1st Air Mechanic W.P. (RNAS): in attack on U/B, 76
Castries Harbour (St. Lucia): *U 161* in, 1942, 421
Catapult Aircraft Merchant (CAM) ships: and SC 42, 377 & Note 58; 385
Cattaro: German U/B base, 115; U/Bs defeated, 131–2; U/Bs withdrawn, 138; U/Bs scuttled, 141
Caucasus: Germans reach, 424; 1942 offensive, 494
Cavendish, Lt.-Cdr. J. R. C. (RN): 1917 destroyer action, 98
Ceylon: 428

Chamberlain, Rt. Hon. Austen: Chancellor of Exchequer, 1919, 154 & Note 3
Chamberlain, Rt. Hon. Neville: Prime Minister, 1937, 176; 177; and Iceland, 337
Charleston, SC: 414
Chatfield, A-F Lord (RN): on S/Ms, 1936, 175; pre-eminence, 180
Chavasse, Lt. E. H. (RN): SOE, HX 237, 60
Cherbourg: 646; 648
Chesapeke Bay: 414
Chiefs of Staff Cttee.: 362; Combined (British/US), 405; British doubts about ROUNDUP, 494–5, 576–7; 581
Chlorine gas: UB 55 and, 1918, 112; 364 & Note 26
CHOP (Change of Operational Control) Line: at 26°W, 434; moved to 47°W, 535–8; HX 229 passes, 563
Christopherson, *Oberleutnant*: and HX 229, 565
Churchill, Rt. Hon. Winston S.:
1914–39:
First Lord of Admlty, 1914, 4–5; on first U/B campaign, 10; on destroyers, 26 & Note 18; on 'cemetery of British shipping', 47; and Naval War Staff, 53, 65; on convoys, 55; on Oliver, 67; 69; on Jellicoe, 71; 108; and Keyes, 110–11; and Ten Year Rule, 1919, 155–6; says S/M 'mastered', 1939, 177; on Munich Agreement, 179
1939–45:
accused of *Athenia* sinking, 217; 224; wants ASW 'cavalry division', 245, 585; and 'whalers', 252; Prime Minister, 254; 'only thing that ever frightened me', 264; 270; suggests Clyde Command, 276, 304; correspondence with Roosevelt, 277, 339; and US destroyers, 277–81 & Note 5; and Defence Cttee., 281–3 & Note 19; tends to downgrade ASW, 282; 'perils expressed in charts, curves, statistics,' 301, 628; Atlantic Cttee and Directive, 308–10; 321; on size of destroyers, 330; 337; 341–2; 343; and continuous escort, 345; and ASW organization, 363; at Placentia Bay, 387–8; and radio, 390; 394; on meaning of Pearl Harbor, 402; and ARCADIA Conference, 403–8 & Note 1; and landing in

Europe, 407 & Note 9; on U/B campaign in US waters, 1942, 423–4; war depends on U/Bs v air power, 475; doubts about landing in NW Europe, 494; and U/B peril, 500; 'versus Hitler', 504; orders H2S priority, 515; on SAC, Atlantic, 541–2 & Note 68; Atlantic 'dominating factor', 576; on TS 37 disaster, 593; on capture of U/B bases, 648–9; 665

Clarke, P/O L. G.: and HX 229, sinks *U 384*, 568

Clayton, R/Adml J. (RN): head of OIC, 319; and *Enigma* blackout, 508

Clyde, River: 42; firth mined, 1940, 227; Churchill suggests Command in, 276, 299, 304; Regional Port Director, 302–3; 1941 air raids, 308

Cole, E. K. Ltd.: ASV II ordered from, 1940, 283–4

Collett, Flight Lieut. (RNAS): attacks Düsseldorff Zeppelin shed, 1914, 36

Cologne: RNAS attack, 1914, 36

Colombo: Japanese threat, 1942, 427

'Colossus': see BP

Combined Bomber Offensive, 1943 (CBO): 579–80

Combined Chiefs of Staff: Cttee formed, 405; Adml King and, 541

Combined Cipher Machine (CCM): 628

COMINCH: see Adml. King; ASW bulletin, 453; Op 20 (F 21) directly under, 458; 563

Commodores (Convoy): Mackinnon, SC 7, 266; killed, 287; 288–90; 292–3; HX 126 decision, 345; Mackenzie, SC 42, 373–7; Creighton, HG 73, 383–5; Fitzmaurice, HG 76, 396; ONS 154, 511; Powell, ONS 169, 546–7; SC 121, ship sunk, 550; White, SC 122, Mayall, HX 229, Casey, HX 229A, 554; HX 230, ship capsizes, 584; Brooks, ONS 5, 594

Commons, House of: 5; 45; 540

Communism: in Germany, 1930s, 172–3

Condors: see Aircraft Index (*Luftwaffe*)

Confederate States of America: 1861 blockade of, 6

Constantinople: *Goeben*, *Breslau* at, 1914, 162

Contraband: 1914 definition, 6

Convoys, Arctic (PQ/QP, JW/RA), Sept.

1941–May 1943, Nov. 1943–May 1945: PQ 17, 229; 352; beginning, 1941, 388 & Note 75; 428; PQ 17 disaster, 450 Note 11, 494; Pound and, 570; JW 51 13, Barents Sea, 518; PQ 18, 532; strength of escort, 584–5; suspended, 585

Convoys, General:

1917–18:

BEF convoys, 1917, 50–6; in 18th Century, 'runners' etc., 50–2; Compulsory Convoy Act, 1798, 50–1; arguments against, 51–3; effect of steam-power, 51; coal, to France, 54–5; Churchill on, 55; adoption of, 58–60; first, May 10–18, 60–1; not 'a spell', 61–2; Scandinavian, 62; Convoy Cttee, 62 & Note 11; speed problem, 63; escorts, 63–4 & Note 14; invisibility, 64; 1917 success statistics 90; Sims on, 92–3; surface attacks on Scandinavian, Oct., 96–8; in Mediterranean, 99; effect of U/Bs coming inshore; night attacks, 101; difference between World Wars, 120–1; pack attacks on HS 38, HG 75, HL 33, HJL 2, 122–3; OLX 39, 132–3; 134; rôle in defeat of U/Bs, 144–5; air escort doctrine, 148–9; Dönitz on, 192

1918–39:

Admiralty confusion on, 176–7; no exercise in protection, 1919–39, 177; Adml. James on, 1937, 179; Trade Division organizes, Aug. 1939, NCS, 244

1939–45

cycles, designations, success, 1939, 244; 1940 air escort out of date, 263; Oct. catastrophes, 265–8; 'mauling equivalent to lost battle on land', 269, 533, 567; 90% convoys not attacked, 272; Dönitz on nature of convoy battles, 274; SW Approaches abandoned, escorts dispersed, 275–6; 1917–18 lesson relearned, majority 'drab, monotonous, unending', 286; Commodores, fast, slow convoys, 287; Trade Division and, 287–8; SOE, WACIS, 288; impression of Commodores, vice-, rear-, signalling, 289–90; size of convoys, 290; formation, escorts, 290–1; slow notoriously unruly, smoke, straggling, etc., 290–2 & Note 37; HX cycle interrupted, Nov. 1940, 296; 307; no attacks, June–Sept. 1941, 354; to Malta, 359; Sept. 1941 losses, 382; USN increasingly responsible for, 388; MOMP, 392; re-routing, 1941, 400–1; USN and, 413–4 & Note 25; Marshall/King correspondence on, 422–3; losses not related to size, 436 & Note 72; 438; U/Bs resume attacks, 1942, 446; RN/RCN/USN differences on doctrine, 449–50; Dönitz and, 459; 1942 re-routing, 'death ride', 466 & Note 40; hazards, 468–9; 'Interlocking System', 417, established, Aug. 1942, 483–4; 500; Aug.–Sept. U/B attacks, 484; Oct. 1942 battles, 489–91; OG/HG, OS/SL suspended, Nov. 1942, 499; 'heartbeat of the war', 512; evasive routing, 1943, 514; effect of Jan. weather, 524; SC 118 'hardest battle of war', 530; HF/DF and, 531; Atlantic Conference, March 1943, 535–44; 80% of losses while under RCN escort, 539; Operational Research and, 539; March 1943 losses, 545–6; N. Atlantic continuity, 550, 553; HX 229, HX 229A, SC 122, major battle, 553–76; large convoys, 554–5; main action begins, 557; VLR aircraft transform battle, 566; tonnage sunk, 569; Admlty doubts efficacy, 569–70; loss rates, various, 571–2; continuity and strain, 572–3 & Note 110; need for 'two-tier' escorts, 586; 'last decisive German success', 588; HX 231 'beginning of end', 590; ONS 5 'last of tragic convoys', 594; rescue trawlers, 594, 597; U/B defeat, 597; analysis of April–May losses, 608; and Atlantic victory, 1943, 610–12; U/Bs renew attack, Sept. 1943, 636–40; Sept.–Oct. losses, 640; second U/B defeat, 640–1; SW Approaches reopened, 650; ASW rôle, 672

Convoys, individual: see Index of Main Trade Convoys

Copenhagen: 7; Battle of, 1801, 521

Cornelius, Prof.: torpedo expert, 234

Corsairs: Barbary, 52 Note 32; Barbary and St. Malo, 146

Corvettes: in 1939 Estimates, 180; 'Flower' Class, 251–3; 'way of life', 253; early problems, 268; 327; RCN 'Flower' Class, 332–3 & Note 54; in bad weather, 335–6; in NEF, 336; and HX 133, 349–50; radar in, 357; SOCC and, 378; 1941 production, 381; USN and, 417; in WA, 1942, 427;

distribution, 435–6; Norwegian, 484–5; 490; 510; Squid and, 620

Creasy, A-F Sir G. (RN): Director of ASW, 319, 320; 454, 537

Creighton, R/Adml Sir K. (RN): and HG 73, 385–6

Cremer, *Korvettenkapitän* P.: 641

Crete: 1941 evacuation, 342; RN losses, 343; 442; 651

CRUSADER, Operation, 1942: 360

Cryptography: see Room 40, GC & CS, BP, Sigint, *XB-Dienst*

Cuba: 414; 418

Cunningham, A-F Lord (RN): on gunnery, 382 Note 63; on 'Human torpedoes', 404; 459; on TORCH convoys, 496; 657

Curaçao: 414

Cuxhaven: RNAS attacks Zeppelin sheds, 1914, 36–7; 214 & Note 5

Cyrenaica: German 1941 offensive, 342

Czechoslovakia: 1938 crisis, 179; RN orders armour plate from, 1938, 151; 201–2; Germans enter, 206

Czernin, Count: Austrian Foreign Minister, on need for peace, 1917, 80

D

Dakar: 62; strategic significance, 1941, 339 Note 71; Vichy French base, 471

Dalison, Cdr. J. S. (RN): SOE HX 229A, 555

Danzig: 1937 elections, 201; 656; U/Bs abandon Gulf, 660

Dare, V/Adml P. C. H. (RN): on A/S patrols, 1917, 99–100

Day, Cdr. E. C. L. (RN): SOE ONS 169, 546–7; 555; 562; and HX 229, 567–8; and ON 176, 591

De Gaulle, Gen. C.: 360; 517 Note 11

De Valera, E.: Irish Prime Minister, 282 & Note 21

Defence Cttee., 1940: 281–3 & Note 19

Defence Policy and Requirement Cttee, 1934: 180

Deloraine, Prof.: and HF/DF, 438

Denmark: 7; 12–13; 23; Belts and Sounds, 214, 664; *KG 40* in, 259

Denning, Adml. Sir N. (RN): father of OIC, 178 & Note 63; and Operational Intelligence, 318–19; 321 Note 25; 357

Depth Charges: 1917 development, 27–8 & Note 20; 74; 123; weapon of future, 142; 147; airborne, 148; bombs and, 248–9; 271; 314–15; 364; Mark XI, shallow setting, 366, 397; USN and, 418 Note 32; 419; Torpex, new pistols, 433–4 & Note 66; different requirements for RN and RAF, 437; 491; enormous expenditure, 531; primary escort armament, 531; Mark X, 599, Mark XI, Note 167; 621; 'Operation Plaster' expenditure, 621–3; use against GNAT, 640; 668

DERANGE, Operation, April 1943: 582

Derby, Lord, Sec. of State for War, 1917: 'Navy at wits' end', 40; 'we have lost command of sea', 47; 145

Derby House (Liverpool): WA HQ, 305–7; 448; 466; WA staff in, 501

Desert War (1940–42): see Rommel, CRUSADER, El Alamein; 512; 579

Destroyers: in ASW, 1917, building time, 25–7; Churchill on speed, 26 Note 18; armament, 27 Note 19; as escorts, 1917, 63; German in N. Sea, 97–8; 107; RN 1918 total, 153; 1918–39 decrease, 160; 'Hunt' Class, 180, 251; 'Brazilian', 251, 551; Dunkirk losses, 254; 'Town' Class (ex-US), 277–81, 331, 336; in Mediterranean, 1940, 278; RCN wants 'Tribals', 330–1 & Note 49; 381; in WA, 1942, 427; 1942 losses, 435; US training centres, 453; 'W' and 'V' boilers removed, 555; Home Fleet, for Support Groups, 586; 'O' Class not designed for Atlantic escort, 596

Devonport: 60

Dickinson, Cdr. N. V. (RN): SOE SC 7, errors, 266; 288; 448

Dieppe: 1942 Raid, 577; 612

Dietrich, Dr: and Prien Press Conference, 224

Dill, F-M Sir J.: in Washington, 403 Note 1, 501 Note 103

Direction Finding (D/F): 1915 achievement, 31; French, 33, 356; use in Spider Web, 74; 80; 183; Lt.-Cdr. Kemp in charge, 321 & Note 25; and Sigint, 322; 'Short Signals' and, 326; N. Atlantic stations, 356, 419; see HF/DF; 1942 effectiveness, 425; MF/DF, 462–3; and SC 122, 557; 562; effect of Schnorchel, 656–7

Disarmament, 1930s: 156–7; 160; 234

Dobson, Lt.-Cdr. A. H. (RCNR): 461–2

Don, River: Germans reach, 1942, 424

Donegal Bay: 269

Dönitz, Grossadmiral K. (1891–1980): Order No. 154 (Dec. 1940), 9 Note 11, 218; 144; prisoner of war, 161; and S/Ms, 162–4; first command, 163; UB 68, 163–4; return to Germany, 1919, 164–6; middle-class background, 165; anti-British feeling, 165–6; rejoins Navy, 166–7; on U/B mystique, 166; at Marineleitung, 167–8; and torpedo boats, 1928, 169–70; Canaris reports on, 1931, 170–1; and Nazism, 172; Far East tour, 1934, return to U/Bs, 1935, 173; 183; 185; 'body and soul a submariner', 187; and ASDIC, 188; 'Weddigen Flotilla', 188–92; and tactical control, 190–4; Führer der U-boote (FdU), 192; on nature of S/M, 194, 196; preference for small U/Bs, 196–8; 202; not consulted on naval plans, 203; wants 300 operational U/Bs, 1939, 205; 206; 207; HQ at Wilhelmshaven, 213–4; and outbreak of war, 215; and Athenia, 216–8; and paucity of U/Bs, 218–9, 270–1, 311–12; 220; and 'surrender to deeps', 221; and Scapa Flow, 222 & Note 32; Befehlshaber der U-boote (BdU), 225; on slow U/B repairs, 226; 227; evolution of command method, 228–30; bond with U/B crews, 230; and 1939–40 torpedo crisis, 231–41; and Biscay bases, 255–7; attempt to obtain air support, 258–61; doubts about SEALION, 260; on 'grey wolves', 261–2; and first pack actions, 262–4; HQ at Kernével, 265; 269; and U/B 'quotient', 270–1; 272; on Italian S/Ms, 273–4; on convoy battles, 274; 275; 285 & Note 26; 286; 295; on rôle of big ships, 297; and training, 311–12; quarrel with Göring, 312–13; 317; 326; on US Security Zone, 342; and G. Hessler, 344; and surface ships, 345–8; and BARBAROSSA, 351–2; 353; and bombing of U/B pens, 354–5; and Enigma security, 356–7; tactical flexibility, 358; and Mediterranean 'mousetrap', 359–62 & Note 19; and U/B staff, 363; and N. Atlantic, 1941, 372–81; defeat, 386; 394; 396; 399; and 'roll of drums', 408–10; and Caribbean, 419–20; second Enigma security enquiry, 4th rotor, 424; 427; and RAF at tacks,

430–2; philosophy of war, 444–5; renewed attack on convoys, 1942, 446–8; 452; 'almost a happy man', 459; 'chopping and changing', 459–60; 461; sense of lost time, 466; and M/V crews, 467–8 & Note 43; and *Laconia*, 471–5 & Note 52; Nuremberg sentence, 474–5, 466; and Allied air power, 475–6, 478–9; and U/B AA, 479–81; on need for new weapons, 481; fears U/Bs 'will be crushed & eliminated', 482; 483; 485; strategy, 486–8; 489; 490; surprised by TORCH, 496–9; and Horton, Winn, 503–4; and 'milch cows', 505; on collisions, 506–7; 508; on 'Unconditional Surrender', 513; 515; *Grossadmiral*, Navy CinC, 517–19; and Hitler, Nazism, 518–22; Jan. 30 1943 Order of Day, 522; and 1943 security enquiry, 525–7; Feb. Directive, 528–9; 530; 531–2; 534; 550; on 1943 tor- pedo defects, 552–3; in Italy, 556; and HX 229/SC 122, 568–9, 587–8; 582, on excessive use of W/T, 591; 'barely concealed desperation', 592; 583; 596–7; 606; fears U/Bs losing invisibility, 607; exhortations to captains, 607–8; accepts Atlantic defeat, 608–9; 'most difficult decision', 614–16; need for new U/Bs, 617–18; and radar, 624–5; 628; 'fighting back', 630–3; 634; 636; and return to N. Atlantic, 637– 40; second Atlantic defeat, 641–2; OVER-LORD preparations, 642–3; D-Day instruc- tions, 643–5; and withdrawal to Norway, 649; 650; and Speer, 652–3; and Battle of Hamburg, 653–4; and 'small unit' suicide missions, 659; on new U/Bs, 662; *Reich President*, 664–5 & Note 102; orders end of hostilities, 665; arrest, imprisonment, death, 666; 667; 668; unique pheno- menon, 670–1
Dönitz, Peter: killed, 1943, 607 Note 176
Dortmund-Ems Canal: 655
Douglas, MRAF Lord: AOC Coastal Command, 645 & Note 64
Dover Straits and Barrage: 91; 107–8 & Notes 8, 9; Adml. Bacon and, 108–9; German attacks, 1916, 1917, 110 & Notes 16, 17; *UB 56* destroyed in, Dec. 1917, 110; U/Bs destroyed in, 1918, 111–3; *UB 55* in, 112; 113; 142; 1939 U/B losses in, 249 Note 21
Dowding, ACM Lord: 'versus Goring', 504
DRAGOON, Operation: 651; 659

Drake, Adml. Sir F.: 33
Duff, R/Adml. A. L. (RN): and A/S Division, 24; on ASW, April 1917, 49; and adoption of convoy, 58; Assistant CNS, 67; 74
Duguay-Trouin, Adml.: corsair activity, 146
Dunbar-Nasmith, Adml. Sir M. VC (RN): CinCWA, 271; 275
Dunkirk: 1917 seaplane base, 77; BEF evacuation, RN losses, 1940, 254; 342
Dunning, Sqdn. Cdr. E. H. (RNAS): lands on *Furious*, 159; 160 Note 15
Dunoon: A/S School moves to, 276
Durnford-Slater, Capt. L. F. (RN): and Larne Battle School (*Philante*), 502–3
Düsseldorff: RNAS attack, 1914, 36
Dutch East Indies: Japanese attack, 404
Dutch West Indies: 539
Dutch Wars (17th Century): 24
Dyer, Lt.-Cdr. K. L. (RCN): CO *Skeena*, and ON 115, 463

E

Eaker, Brig.-Gen. I. C. (USAAF): commands 8th AAF, POINTBLANK Plan, 579– 80
Eastern Front (1941–45): 362; 1942 Soviet defeats, 512; Germans on defensive, 1943, 528; 579; 609; last German offensive, 614–15; Soviet initiative, 615; 642 Note 56; 644; 647; 664; see Stalingrad, Kursk, BAGRATION
Eastern Sea Frontier (USA): 414; 1942 air defence, 418; perceptible change in, 419 & Note 34; U/Bs disappear from, 423
EASTOMP: 532
E-boats: 261 Note 18; 285 & Note 26; 299–300; in Mediterranean, 359 Note 15
Eck, *Fregattenkapitän*: executed as war criminal, 468 Note 44
Edelsten, R/Adml. J. H. (RN): ACNS, and S/M Tracking Room, 526–7
E-Dienst: 32
Eden, Rt. Hon. A.: 402 Note 1
Edmonds, Flight Cdr. C. H. K. (RNAS): first airborne torpedo sinking, 37
Edwards, Capt. (RN): Director of Operations Division, and Winn: 319–20, 454
Edwards, R/Adml. R. E. (USN): Assistant Chief of Staff, 457–8

795

Eglinton: FAA station, 566
Egypt: Axis advance on, 342; Hitler indifferent to, 362 Note 23; Rommel advances to, 424, 494; 500
Eire: Defence Cttee and, 1940, 282–3 & Note 22
Eisenhower, Gen. of the Army D. D. (USA): forces in NW Europe, 612; German surrender to, 665
Eliot, T. S., poet: 'April cruellest month', 46
Ely, Eugene: 158–9
ENCLOSE, Operations I & II: March–April 1943, 582
Endrass, *Kapitänleutnant* E.: 'grey wolf', 261; and SC 7, 267; death, 399
Enigma: 1930s development, 194; BP progress against, 264; *HYDRA* cipher, 321, penetrated, 1940–41, 322–5; captures, *U 110* etc., 325–6 & Note 39; 327; 346; 348; 1941 security enquiry, 356–7; 365; 1942 security enquiry, 4th rotor added, 424; *TRITON* (SHARK) replaces *HYDRA*, 425; insecurity masked, 427; continuing BP blackout, 454; US acquires machine (1927), 456; 459; 487; 503; 508; Mediterranean setting, 509, 517; 1943 security enquiry, 'trained incapacity', 525–7; end of BP blackout, 526; 527; 528; new blackout threat, March 1943, 562; and declining U/B morale, see BP, 619; and *FAT*s, 626; and *Schnorchel*, 627; alternative 4th rotor, 627–8; volume of monthly traffic (BP), 627 Note 19; and 'milch cows', 634; 636; and U/B return to N. Atlantic, 637; effect of *Schnorchel*, 656–8; 663 Note 99
English Channel, 1914–18:
17; coal convoys, 1917, 54; 62; vulnerable patrols, 71; seaplane bases, 77; air cover, 79; 88; U/Bs in, 107–8; 1917 Barrage Cttee, 109–10; 113; 126; W/T across, 143; corsairs in, 146; 150; Blériot crosses, 158
1939–45:
244; 1940 RN concentration in, 261; E-boats in, 285 & Note 26; German ships pass through, 1942, 348; Allies plan to cross, 493–4; 643; Coastal Command and OVERLORD, 645–7; see NEPTUNE; 1944 U/B losses in, 648–50; sinkings in, 657
Equator, The: 471; 483; 487

Erzberger, Matthias: opposes U/B campaign, 1917, 81–2 & Note 50; 86
Escorts (RN & Allied): see Corvettes, Destroyers, Frigates, Sloops; question of, 1917, 63–4; RNAS and, 148–9; 1939–40 shortage, 265; lack of doctrine, 266; lack of training and experience, 268; see Training; formation with convoy, 290–1; improved performance, 1941, 314–6; USCG utters as, 340 & Note 76; continuous across Atlantic, 345; U/Bs ordered to attack, 359; R/T (TBS) in, 368; VHF, 505–6; see RCN, NEF, MOEF, 383; USN 1942 lack, 411; US types, 416–17 & Note 29; US building programme, 417; Naval Cipher No. 3 and, 426; RN and USN requirements, 1942, 428; 437; defects of US, 453 & Note 14; in WA, 1942, 501; 'Support Groups', see Noble, Horton; *Philante* Battle School and, 502–3; 530–1; refuelling from tankers, 633–4; RCN deficiencies, 537–8; US Support Group for N. Atlantic, 539 & Note 61; March 1943 weather and, 546; 'second wind', 563; Arctic convoy requirements, 584–5; Support Groups, 585–7; 'two-tier' system, 586; 587; SOE of close escort directs Support Group, 590; 'O' Class destroyers unsuitable, 596; 'brevity and wit', 598; WA strength, 1943, 599; weapons, 599; RCN return to convoy routes, 600 Note 170; in NEPTUNE, 645; see Walker, Home Waters; 1945 numbers operational, 660
Escort Carriers (CVEs): RN, 552 & Note 83; Carrier Groups, 586; aircraft equipment, 602 Note 171; in 'Gap', 606; A. J. Kaiser and, 629 Note 25; USN and 'milch cows', 634–5
Escort Groups:
Close escort:
A3: and ONS 92, 447–8; and ONS 102, 452; and HX 212, 490; and ON 166, 532–3; and SC 121, 547–50; and HX 233, 591
B2: and SC 118, 530–1
B3: and HX 228, 550–2; and ONS 18, 637–8
B4: and ONS 169, 546–7; and HX 229, 555–76; and ON 176, 591
B5: and SC 122, 555–76

B6: and ONS 122, 484–5; and SC 104, 489–90; and ONS 144, 505; and HX 217, 505–8; 511; and ONS 165, 531–2

B7: and HX 231, 586, 589–91 & Note 150; and ONS 5, 584–9

C1: and ONS 100, 451; and SC 94, 476; and ONS 154, 510–1

C2: and ON 113, 461–2; and *U 89*, 587; and HX 237, 600–1 & Note 170; and *U 744*, 621 Note 13

C3: and ON 115, 462–6; 600 Note 170

C4: and ON 127, 485; and SC 107, 490–2

Support Groups

EG 1: 586; sinks *U 438*, *U 209*, 587; longest hunt sinks *U 358*, 621 Note 13

EG 2: 586–7; 'Operation Plaster', 1944, 621–3; sinks *U 202*, 621 Note 13; 633; 635–6

EG 3: 586; sinks *U 531*, 587; and ONS 5, 595–7

EG 4: 586; sinks *U 752*, 587

EG 5: 586; sinks *U 203*, *U 89*, 587, 591 Note 150; and HX 237, 601

EG 6: (TU 24.4.1): and HX 228, 551–2; 586; sinks *U 569*, 587

EG 9: and ONS 18/ON 202, 637

EG 24: and SC 42, 373–81

EG 36: and HG 76, 396–9

EG 40: and HX 229A, 555–76

Esher, Lord: on Admlty, 1917, (ref Mahan), 45 & Note 15; on Geddes as First Lord, 68

Essen: Bomber Command attack, 1942, 470

Europe: 342; 'Fortress', 642, 647

Evans, Cdr. M. J. (RN): SOE ONS 18, 637–8

Everett, Lt. R. W. H. (RNVR): shoots down Condor, 358 Note 13

F

Falkland Is.: 1982 Campaign, 229

Falls, Capt. C.: on convoys, 61

Falmouth: convoys from, 1917, 62

Far East: Dönitz in, 1934–35, 173; equipment requirements, 1942, 428

Faroes Is.: 409 Note 13

Fastnet Rock: 42; 88

Fedala (Morocco): U/Bs operating off, 1942, 497

Fegen, Capt. E. S. F. (RN): killed in *Jervis Bay*, 295–6

Feiler, *Kapitänleutnant* G.: and HX 229, 661

Feldkirchner, *Korvettenkapitän*: humane behaviour in *U 17*, Oct. 1914, 44 Note 12

Felixstowe: Flying Boat, 37; 74

'Final Solution' (Jewish Holocaust): 468; Dönitz and, 521 & Note 19

Finland: builds U/B, 1930, 169; S/M types, 188; USSR attacks, 282 Note 22

Firth of Forth: 97; 138; 223; mined, 1939, 227

'Fish' signals: 627 Note 19

Fisher, A-F Lord: on S/Ms, 1913, 4–5, 7; orders 'whalers', 1915, 25; scrapping programme, 25 Note 14; on speed, 26; opposed to Naval Staff, 65; on Oliver, 67; 146; 218; 'any fool can obey orders', 350 & Note 94; 475; 673

Flak: see AA

Flamborough Head: *UB 41* sunk off, 96

Flanders Offensive, 1917,: U/B connection with, 69–70; 91 Note 16; 105

Flanders U/B Flotillas, 1915–18: 10; 11; UB-, UC-boats, 17–21; 50; and Ypres Offensive, 69; danger over-rated, 105 Note 3; 2nd Flotilla formed, 1917, 106; 108; 1918 losses, 118; bombed, 126; decline, 130 & Note 3; end of, 135; U/Bs scuttled, 141

Fleet Air Arm (FAA): RN acquires, 159; cost, 179 Note 67; 181; 241; in Mediterranean, 359; 428; 646

FAA Squadrons:

802: in *Audacity*, and OG 74, 385–6; and OG 76, HG 76, 395–9

804: 383

811: 587

819: 587; rocket-firing Swordfish in, 619 & Note 11

Flensburg-Mürwik: U/B School, 162

Fletcher, Sub.-Lt. G. (FAA): death, 396–7

Fliege: 625

Florida: fears for 1942 tourist season, 410; 414; 416 Note 29

Foch, Marshal: 130

Folkestone: 107; 115

Forbes, Adml. Sir C. (RN): 275 Note 1

Forster, *Korvettenkapitän* H.: 379–80

Forstmann, *Kapitänleutnant* W.: 20; report on Dönitz, 163

Forstner, *Oberleutnant* Freiherr von: and SC 107, 491–2; and SC 118, 530
Fort Donelson (Tennessee): 'Unconditional Surrender', 1862, 513 Note 1
Fox, Lt.-Cdr. C. L. (RN): death, 1917, 96 & Note 22
FOXER (CAT): 639–40
France: D/F system, 1914–18, 33, 356; coal convoys to, 1917, 54–5; Franco-Soviet Pact, 1935, 186 & Note 87
1939–45:
Hitler determined to attack, 220; fall of, 1940, 254, 275, 337; Battle of, 255–6, 261; and *Enigma*, 323; Vichy, 473; and USA, 494; Allied advance through, 1944, 648; Resistance (*FFI*), 648–9; see De Gaulle
France: Army: 83; 1917 mutiny, 105, 511; undervalues Intelligence, pre-1914, 456 Note 20
France: Navy: opposed to convoys, 1917; 55; in Mediterranean, 99; Intelligence, 143; corsairs, 146, 673; and 1930s naval race, 185; in Mediterranean, 1940, 278; see Index of Warships, RN
Franz, *Kapitänleutnant*: 281
Fraser, A-F Lord: 252
Frauenheim, *Korvettenkapitän*: 227; 261; and SC 7, 267
Freetown: convoys, 244; 344 & Note 85; continuous protection to, 358 & Note 13, 382; 459; 471; convoys suspended, 1942, 499; U/B successes, 1943, 593
Fremantle, Adml. Sir S. R. (RN): 138
Friedeburg, *Adml.* H. von: and U/B training, 214 & Note 4
Friedman, W. F.: and 'Purple' cipher, 456
Friedrichshafen: Zeppelin sheds attacked, 1914, 36
Frigates: naming, 251; 351 Note 95; first arrivals, qualities, 436; in EG 40, March 1943, 555 & Note 92; see Index of Warships, RN
Fulton, Robert: 145 & Note 14
Funakoshi, Adml. (Imp. Japanese Navy, 1917): 91

G

Gallipoli: 1915 landings, 494; see Cape Helles

Gander (Newfoundland): 637
Geddes, Sir E.: Controller of Navy, 1917, 67–8; First Lord of Admlty., 72–3; deteriorating relations with Jellicoe, 101–3
Geheimschreiber ('Fish') signals: 627 Note 19
George V, King: and Adml. Wemyss, 103
Georgetown, SC: F/F station, 419
German Air Force (*Luftwaffe*; GAF): reborn, 1935, 186; training, 190; triumph in Poland, 219–20; Goring C-in-C, 220 Note 21; 222; lack of maritime aircraft; KG 40, 249–60 & Note 13; M/V sinkings, May, June 1940, 261; 263; defeated, 1940, 264–5; 285; 293; begins 'Blitz', 299; attacks on British ports, 308; Dönitz and, 312–13 & Note 4; see Goring; ciphers attacked, 322–5; and *Scharnhorst*, *Gneisenau*, 347, 362; Intelligence, 1940, 496 Note 97; Listening Service Regiment, 532, 584; field divisions, 609; 625; 628 Note 21; and Bay operations, June 1943, 631–3; almost powerless, 658
German Army: 1916 losses, 3; change in High Command, 4; fundamental change in strategy, 1916, 13–5; and U/Bs, 81; High Command supreme in Germany, 1917, 82; 1918 offensives, 119; wrecking of, 130; 'Black Day', 135; helpless condition, 137; overshadows Navy, 164; 187; training, 190; prepares attack on Poland, 206; triumph in Poland, 1939, 219–20; offensive in West, 253–6; ciphers attacked, 322–3; see Desert War, Rommel; attack on Greece, 342; Command structure, Hitler and, 361 Note 20; see BARBAROSSA, Eastern Front, Stalingrad, Kursk, BAGRATION; 1943 condition, 609; 1943 losses, 642 & Note 56; 644; see Berlin
German Navy:
1914–1918:
and S/Ms, 1914, 5; see High Sea Fleet, U-boats; main rôle transferred to, 15; see Jutland, Intelligence (German); 1917 mutiny, 83–4; gunnery, 98; torpedo boats, 107; end of, 1918, 140; destruction of German sea-power, 153; social composition, 164–5 & Note 24; over-shadowed by Army and RN, 164; like Teutonic Knights, 165; 1918, 1920 mutinies, 167 &

798

Note 30; outstanding failure of World War I, 185

1918–1939:
awaits *Der Tag*, 166; resumes U/B warfare studies, 167; see U-boats; *Marineleitung* and rearmament, 167–8; 1932 expansion, 169; and Nazis, 172; Anglo-German Naval Agreement, 1935, 174–5, 195, 203, 206; 'big-ship' policy, 185–7 & Note 84; training, 190; Staff opposes U/B pack tactics, 194; belief in U-cruisers, 194–5; 1938 building programme, 202–3; see 'Z' Plan; ships enter Atlantic, Aug. 1939, 206; unready for war, 207; and air cooperation, 258; see Dönitz, Raeder

1939–45:
Naval Group West, 213, 647; see U-boats, E-boats, Torpedoes, *B-Dienst*; Norwegian Campaign, 235–7; continued belief in big ships, 293–5; zenith of surface fleet, 295–8; see *HYDRA*; 'Short Signals', 'Home Waters' cipher, 326 & Note 40; and *Bismarck*, 343; ships in Brest, 346–8 & Note 89; see R-boats; High Command says Mediterranean 'main theatre', 360–1; and US shipbuilding, 445; surprised by TORCH, 496–7 & Note 97, 498–9; Dönitz C-in-C, 517; Hitler and surface fleet, 518–19; 1943 security enquiry, 525–7; Feb. 1943 Directive, 528–9; and Allied ship-building, 535; and need for new U/Bs, 617–18; and rocket-firing aircraft, 620; Scientific Operations Staff, 641; losses in Bay of Biscay, 1944, 649; steel, Dönitz/Speer agreement, 652–3; 'small battle units', 659 & Note 90; surrender 665; see *TRITON*, Godt, Index of Warships (German)

Germaniawerft: 168

Germany:
Imperial:
blockade of, 6; declares 'War Zone' round Britian, 9; and *Lusitania*, 10; ends first U/B campaign, 11; Pless Conferences, 1916–17, and 'unrestricted S/M warfare', 11–16; Reichstag Peace Resolution, 1917, 81–3; military dictatorship, 82; peace negotiations, 1918, 136

1918–33:
clandestine rearmament, 167–8; last days of Republic, 171; and Disarmament, 234;

and March 1933 Election, 519 & Note 16

1933–45:
see Hitler; Anglo-German Naval Agreement, 1935, 174, 193; Rome-Berlin Axis (1936), Anti-Comintern Pact (1936), Nazi-Soviet Pact (1939), 186; Rearmament, 187; Four-Year Plan, 187 Note 89; see Göring; Dönitz on Nazi achievement, 519–20; Hitler and war with France and Britain, 206; production bottlenecks, 239; Press exultation over *Empress of Britain*, 269–70; and Iceland, 337; *BARBAROSSA* and, 351, 610; amateurishness of war effort, 361–2; Nazi system, 391; war with USA, 401; see 'Final Solution'; civilians under bombing, 469–70; see 'Unconditional Surrender'; July Plot, 1944, 171, 521; on defensive, 1943, 528; epitaph for science, 581; Third *Reich* crumbling, 609; effect of air offensive, 615; 'under three clouds', 1944, 642; June 1944 disasters, 647; mounting defeat, 650; rivalries and jealousies in, 652; transportation system attacked, 655; Allied advances, bombing, 658; surrender, 665

Gibraltar: first convoy from, 1917, 58, 60, 62–4; 140; first convoy from, 1939, 244; 313; continuous protection to, 358; U/Bs gather, 1941, 360–1; currents in Straits, 361; 371; 384; 385; and OG 76, HG 76, 395–6; RAF Command, 396 & Note 91, 409; 496; U/B 1942 concentration, 497; convoys suspended, 499; 515; 536; 573; 'Madcats' at, 661

Gilardone, *Korvettenkapitän: U 254*, sunk in collision, 506–7

Giraud, Gen.: 517 Note 11

Gironde, River: Germans block, 1944, 649

Glattes, *Kapitänleutnant:* 231

GNAT: see *Zaunkönig*

Godfrey, R/Adml. J. (RN; DNI): 178; 265 Note 29; qualities, 317–20 & Note 18; supports Winn, 320; promotes Anglo-US cooperation, 455

Godt, *Konteradmiral* E.: U/B Chief of Staff, 213; 215; *FdU*, 1943, 518; and SC 118, 529; and ON 166, 552; and SC 121, HX 228, 550–2; and HX 229/SC 122, 556; 582; 593; 596

Goebbels, Dr J.: 390; 592

GONDOLA, Operation: Bay Offensive, Feb. 1943, 581
Goodwin Sands: 106
Göring, *Reichsmarschall* H.: and 4-Year Plan, 187 Note 89; 195; economic overlord, 220–1; 226; and U/Bs, 258–60; promises to defeat RAF, 259; and *SEELÖWE*, 260; 311; and Dönitz, 312–13; 'disruptive disaster', 362; 481; and *Luftwaffe* Intelligence, 496 Note 97; and centimetric radar, 581 & Note 129; 652
Gotting, *Vizeadmiral*: dismissed for torpedo failures, 240
Government Code & Cipher School (GC & CS; 'Station X'): see Bletchley Park (BP), Sigint; progress against *Enigma*, 1940, 264; Bletchley, 265 Note 29, 321 Note 28; attack on *Enigma*, 322–5; US counterpart, 394; and 1941 re-routing, 400–1; and *TRITON*, 424–6; and *Enigma* blackout, 508; brilliant performance, March 1943, 527; decrypt interruption, 1943, 556 Note 94; and new U/Bs, 656; 672
Grand Banks (Newfoundland): 334; 465; fog, 476; 599 Note 165
Grand Fleet (1914–18): 6; ammunition defects, 1917, 24, 34; and convoy protection, 58; 68; 93; 96; 98; 103; 115; USN battleships join, 116; change of fundamental strategy, 117–18; and final HSF sortie, 118; HSF attack on planned, Oct. 1918, 138; see Beatty, Oliver, Room 40; 156; see Jutland; obsolescence, 160; 585
Grant, Gen. U.S. (USA): and 'Unconditional Surrender', 1862, 513 Note 1
Gray, Lieut. G. T. S. (RN): and *U 574*, 398
Greece: 1939 shipping, 285; ships in convoy, 292; German conquest, 1941, 342
Greenland: US base in, 340 Note 75; 342; 344; 352; D/F station, 356; 372; 490 Note 85; USN and, 538; 546; weather, 563
Gregory, Lieut. R. (RNAS): lands on moving ship, 1912, 158–9
Greswell, S/L J.: first Leigh Light attack, 431
Gretton, V/Adml. Sir P.: on corvettes, 252; on Horton, 502; on fuelling at sea, 533–4; on Harris, 579; on Home Fleet destroyers, 586; and HX 231, 589–91; and ONS 5, misses 'golden moment', 594–6

Guadalcanal Is.: 494; Japanese defeat, 500; Japanese evacuate, 543
Guam Is.: Japanese capture, 404
Guantanamo (Cuba): 417; GAT/TAG convoys, 483 Note 72; GN/NG convoys, 484
Guderian, *Generaloberst* H.: 642 Note 56
Guiana, French: 552
Gulf Sea Frontier (USA): 414; U/Bs in, 420–1; U/Bs disappear from, 423
Guse, *Vizeadmiral* G.: 202–3
GYMNAST, Operation: SUPER-GYMNAST, 493; 577 Note 119

H

Habekost, *Leutnant*: 221; 227
Hagenuk (Wanze): receiver, 625; 637
Hague Conferences, 1899, 1907: 5
Haig, F-M Lord: 40; 45; 47; tribute to Geddes, 68; 69; on Jellicoe, 71–2 & Note 34; urges Geddes as First Lord, 72; and Bacon, 109; and 1918 offensive, 135; 145
Halder, *Generaloberst* F.: on *BARBAROSSA*, 362 Note 22
Halifax (NS): convoys from, 244; 268; US destroyers arrive at, 1940, 279; fast convoys from, 287; RCN corvettes at, 1941, 333; 378; 417; 446; no longer HX terminal, 484
Hall, R/Adml. Sir R.: at Trade Plot, relations with Winn, 320–1
Hall, R/Adml. Sir W. R.: DNI, 1914–18, 31; 74; 79; 138; 178; 250; 265 Note 29; and Godfrey, 317–18 & Notes 17, 21
Hamburg: 214; Battle of, 1943, 653–4; 660; 663
Hampton Roads: 62, 64
Hanbury-Brown, Mr: designs airborne radar scanner, 284 & Note 24
Hankey, Lord: fears defeat at sea, 1917, 41; supports convoys, 54; at Admlty with Lloyd George, April 1917, 59; considered as First Sea Lord, 1918, 72; 1932 view of S/Ms, 175 & Note 51
Harden, Lieut. J. D. (USAAF): and *U 156*, *Laconia* survivors, 472–3
Harlinghausen, *Oberstleutnant* M.: and *KG 40*, 313 Note 4
Harris, M/RAF Sir A.: on German ships in Brest, 346; on U/Bs and air offensive, 366; at Bomber Command, 429–30; Coastal

Command 'obstacle to victory', 432; 1942 offensive, 470; Casablanca directive to, 516; 'bland indifference', 517; 576; on VLR aircraft, Eastern Front, ASV etc., 578–81; and Battle of Hamburg, 653–4

Hartenstein, *Korvettenkapitän* W.: and *Laconia* survivors, 471–5

Hartland Point (Devon): D/F station, 419

Hartmann, *Fregattenkapitän*, 225

Hartmann, *Kapitänleutnant* G. von: and *U 441*, 630–2

Hartwig, *Korvettenkapitän* P.: in Gulf of St Lawrence, 1942, 486; 657 Note 86

Harwich Force (RN 1914–18): 58 Note 3; 96; 116; 141

Hass, *Oberleutnant*: and first operational Type XXIII, 662

Hawkcraig Experimental Station (1917): 29

Heathcote, Cdr. S. (RN): SOE SC 104, 489–90; SOE HX 217, 505–8; SOE ONS 154, 511

Hedgehog: 23; description, 440–1; 485; *U 125* sunk with, 597, 599; improving efficiency, 620–1; explosion in *Escapade*, 620, 637; 623

Heffernan, Cdr. J. B. (USN): and ONS 92, 447–8

Heineman, Capt. P. (USCG): and A3, 452; SOE ON 166, 532–3; SOE ON 166, 532–3; SOE HX 233, 591

Helfferich, Karl: at 1916 Pless Conference, 12

Heligoland: Bight, 91; U/Bs seek base in, 1918, 139

Henderson, Adml. R.: and convoys, 1917, 54–5

Henke, *Kapitänleutnant*: and TS 37, 593

Hessler, *Korvettenkapitän* G.: Knight's Cross, 344; at U/B HQ, 1943, 518

Heye, *Kapitän zur See* H.: and 1938 naval plan, 202–3

HF/DF (High Frequency Direction Finding): 438–9; and ON 67, 439; and ONS 92, 447; and ONS 100, 451; 462; 476; 485; and SC 104, 489; 491; and ONS 144, 505; and convoy defence, 530–1; and ON 166, 532; RCN and, 536; and HX 228, 550–1; in *Volunteer*, March 1943, 556; 562; and HX 231, 590; and ONS 5, 597–9; 619; 634; effect of *Schnorchel*, 656–7

Hibbard, Cdr. J. C. (RCN): SOE SC 42, 373–81

High Sea Fleet (HSF): 8; U/B flotillas, 1914, 17–20 & Note 1, 24; 32; 50; 1917 mutiny, 83–4, 106 Note 3; 108; 117; final sortie, 118; effect of inaction, 130; 131; 135; 1918 mutiny, 137–9; 143; 144; scuttled, 154; 156; and Jutland, 158 & Note 13, 456 Note 20

Himmler, H.: interview with Dönitz, April 1945, 665 & Note 102

Hindenburg, *Feldmarschall* P. Von: 4; and U/Bs, 13–14; and Battle of Somme, 24; 'Hindenburg Line', 105, 135; President, 168

Hipper, *Adml.* von: commands HSF, 138–9

Hitler, A.: rising star, 171–2; oath of obedience to, 1934, 172; orders U/B building, 173; denounces Versailles Treaty, 1935, 174; 185; and Saar Plebiscite, 186; announces rearmament, 186; 195; warlike policies, 201–2; approves 'Z' Plan, 204–5; repudiates Anglo-German Agreement, 206; and U/B procedure, 1939, 216; visit to U/Bs, 219–20, 221; and Norway, 234; 259; declares blockade of Britian, 262; prepares attack on USSR, 265 & Note 31, 311; and KG 40, 312; and *Scharnhorst*, *Gneisenau*, 346 Note 89; and *BARBAROSSA*, 350–1; and U/B shelters, 354; orders U/Bs to Mediterranean, 359–62 & Notes 15, 20; 'intuition', 362 & Note 23; 387; use of radio, 390; 391; strategic blunder, 400–1; says Norway 'decisive theatre', 408–9 & Note 13; 1942 advance in USSR, 424; on merchant crews, 467; 475; and surface fleet, 1943, 517–19; and Dönitz, 519–20; 'July Plot' against, 1944, 521; 614; 638; 'insensate strategy', 644; 645; 652; 654; 662; death, 664; admiration for Dönitz, 670–1

Hoch, Gustav: and Reichstag Peace Resolution, 1917, 81

Hohenborn, *Gen.* von: 4

Hohentwiel: ASV radar, 625

Holland: 7, 12–13; 23; convoys to, 1917, 58 Note 3, 62; mines laid off coast, 96; and VLR aircraft, 1941, 366; high morale of seamen, 574; and *Schnorchel*, 626

Holtzendorff, *Adml.* von: Chief of Naval Staff, 1916, 4; at Pless, 11–13; Dec. 1916

Memorandum, 15; 'victory before harvest', 41, 84

Home Fleet (1939–45): driven out of Scapa Flow, 1939, 222–4; in Loch Ewe, 227; and U/B menace, 231; 265 Note 29; 275 Note 1; 296; sinks *Bismarck*, 343; and Arctic convoys, 584–5; destroyers, 586, 596, 601

Home Waters (British): disappointing A/S performance in, 1917, 99–100; 131; maritime RAF in, 1918, 148; 1944 U/B campaign in, 657–8; Type XXIIIs and, 662; Type VIIs and, 662–3

Hong Kong: 403; surrender of, 404

Horchdienst: German 'Y' Service, 215; 496 Note 97

Horrocks, Sub.-Lieut. H: (FAA): sinks *U 752* with rockets, 619 & Note 11

Horton, Admiral Sir M. (RN): CinCWA, 501–4; and Support Groups, 502; as adversary of Dönitz, 503–4; and Winn, 504; 511; 523; Dönitz on, 526; and SC 118, 530–1; 537; 538; and B3, 551; 1943 optimism, 577–8; obtains Support Groups, 584–5; and ONS 5, 595; and Walker's funeral, 624; and ONS 18/ON 202, 637, 639; 669

Howard-Johnson, Cdr. C. D. H. (RN): criticism of RCN, 448; and On 115, 465–6

Howell, P/O W.: Leigh Light attack, 432

Huns: depredations of, 154

HUSKY, Operation: agreed, 577; 610

Hutchinson, Sub.-Lieut. (FAA): shoots down Condor, 395–6

Hvalfjordhur: 'dreary and unforgiving', 338; 344; first PQ convoy at, 358 Note 75

HYDRA (DOLPHIN) cipher: 321 & Note 28; 323; settings captured, 1941, 326–7; effect of breaking, 353; replaced by *TRITON*, 425; Home Waters continue use, 455

Hydrophones: 1917–18, 29–30; long hunts with, 30; failures, 99; on Channel bed, 108; in aircraft, 126–7; 147; 269; German, 292 Note 37; in U/Bs, 622

I

Iceland: 315; 326; NEF terminal, 336; Allied occupations of, 1940, 1941, 337–9, 344; enables continuous escort, 345; D/F station, 356; 358; 364; 365; 120 Sqdn in,

366; 373; 375; 381; USN and, 1941, 388; 393; 394; 409 Note 13; 435; 478; 490 & Note 85; 506; 530, 537; Liberators in, 540; 562; 608; 637–8

India: 156; Japanese threat to, 429, 494

Indian Ocean: 296; tankers for, 422; Japanese in, 427; aircraft requirement, 1942, 428; U/Bs in, 442, 488; 634; Operation *MONSUN* fiasco, 636

Indicator Loops (S/M detectors): 108

Indies, East: 18th Century convoys from, 51; Japanese threat to, 404

Indies, West: 18th Century convoys from, 51; US bases in, 1941, 279; D/F stations, 356

Industrial Revolution: see Technology; 5; inventions, 30; 51; 'unrestricted industrial technology', 146

Ingenieursburo fur Wirtschaft und Technik (*Igewit*): 169

Ingenieurskantoor voor Scheepsbouw (*IvS*): 168–9

Ingenohl, *Adml.* von: 8

Intelligence (British):

1914–18:

see Hall, Room 40; W/T, D/F; 23; 1914 victory, 31; Admiralty misuse, 79; 97 Note 25; and U/B pack operations, 1918, 121–3; 133; 138; rôle in U/B defeat, 143–4 & Note 10

1918–39:

RN backwater and revival, 178; RN and RAF failure, August 1939, 207

1939–45:

see W/T, D/F, HF/DF, 'Y' Service, *Enigma*, BP, GC & CS, Sigint; NID scepticism, 250 & Note 23; strength of NID, 1942, Operational Intelligence, 318; Sigint superior to espionage, 322; 1941 success equivalent to major victory, 326–7; mobilization, 357; 1942 crisis, Sigint and PR, 425–6; and U/B diving ability, 437; and Biscay bases, 527; March 1943 disadvantage, 556 & Note 94; and *FAT*s, 620; attack on 'Fish', 627 Note 19

Intelligence (German):

1914–18:

1914 defeat, 31; E-*Dienst*, 32; U/B lack of, 142–5

1939–45:
see *B-Dienst*, *xB-Dienst*, *Horchdienst*, *Abwehr*; U/B sources, 228–9; penetration of British naval codes, 1935–40, 257–8; quality of, 496 Note 97; advantage with, March 1943, 556 & Note 94; defeated by CCM, 628

Intelligence (US):

1941–45:
see MAGIC, see Purple, downgraded after Pearl Harbor, 456; Op. 20 (F.21) set up, 458–9; and HX 228, 550

Iran: 494

Iraq: 1922 campaign in, 155 Note 5

Ireland: see Eire; 47; Irish Sea, 126, 137; 260; lack of RN bases, 1940, 274; 334; US base in north, 340; D/F stations, 356; 358; 364; MOEF terminal, 435; 461–2; 507; 566; 646; 657

Isonzo, River: Battles of, 1915–18, 14

Isted, S/L D.: and HX 217, 506

Italian Navy: 1918, 99; 154; S/M *Iride* attacks RN, 1937, 177; 178; S/Ms at Bordeaux, 1940, 273–4; 'human torpedoes', 404, 659; S/Ms in Caribbean, 1942, 421; Leigh Light attack on S/M, 431; and *Laconia* survivors, 471–2; S/M losses, 1942, 498; 556; S/M in Bordeaux, 1944, 649

Italy: 1916 offensives, 14; naval power, 99; attack on Abyssinia, 1935, 173–5; threat to Malta, 176; enters war, 1940, 254, 278; and Mediterranean, 360; war with USA, 401; surrender, 1943, 615

Ites, *Oberleutnant*: and ONS 92, 447–8; and ONS 100, 451; 452

J

Jackson, Adml. Sir H. (RN): First Sea Lord, 1916, 31; 69

Jacksonville, Fla.: 414; 418

Jade, River: 214; 456 Note 20

Jagow, G. von (German Foreign Minister, 1916): 4; and Unrestricted S/M Warfare, 12

James, Adml. Sir W. (RN): and Naval Intelligence, 178; on convoys, 1937, 179; 275 Note 1

Japan: threat of war with, 1919, 156–7; Anglo-Japanese Alliance, 157; and Washington Treaties, 1922, 157–8; aggression

in China, 1935, 173 & Note 46; 174; military party in power, 1941, 394; 417; see MAGIC, PURPLE; unchecked advance, 1942, 422 & Note 40, 442, 494, 495; first defeat, 500; 1942 victories, 512; campaign against, 1943, 543; 'decisive victory' and, 609; *Kamikaze* operations, 659

Japanese Navy: destroyers in Mediterranean, 1917, 68, 99, 157; 91; 154; 1919 battleships, 158; 159; 160; see Pearl Harbor, Midway, Battle of

Jellicoe, A-F Lord (RN): First Sea Lord, 1916, 24, 671; 25; 28; on hydrophones, 29; on mines, 34; on Western Approaches, 41–2; and Adml. Sims, 48, 570; A/S proposals, 48–9; 52; 55; and convoy, 58–9; on rôle of Admlty, 66; CNS, 66–7; agreements with Lloyd George, 67–8; and War Policy Cttee, June 20 1917, 70–2; no longer an asset, 71; see Geddes, Wemyss; 74; on seaplanes, 77; 91; opposed to convoy at heart, 100; dismissal, 101–3; 1919 Far East tour, 156–7; 296; 304; see Jutland, Battle of

Jenisch, *Oberleutnant*: 'grey wolf', 261; sinks *Empress of Britain*, 269; captured, 270

Jeschen, *Leutnant*: Dönitz and death of, 1918, 164

Jews: see 'Final Solution'

Johnson, Leading Seaman (RCN): and *U 501*, 379–80

Joubert de la Ferté, A/M Sir P.: AOC-in-C, Coastal Comnand, 1941, 365–72; making aircraft a U/B killer, 367; 'Sunday Soviets', 372; 1942 problems, 428–30; 454; replaced, 1943, 522–3; 581

'July Plot', 1944: see Hitler

Jutland, Battle of, 1916: 24; 85; 158; 159; 175; 181; Beatty at, 233; Room 40, Jellicoe and, 456 Note 20; 670

K

Kaiser, Henry J.: and 'Liberty Ships', 629 & Note 25

Kals, *Fregattenkapitän* E.: attacks TORCH shipping, 497–8; see Appendix E

Karl, Emperor of Austria-Hungary: 80

Karpf, *Oberleutnant*: and HX 224 survivor, 529

Kattegat, The: 115; 663
Keitel, *Feldmarschall*: OKW Chief of Staff, 361 Note 20
Kemp, Cdr. P. (RN): heads D/F Section in OIC, 321 & Note 25
Kendrew, Sir J. (FRS): and Coastal Command Operational Research Unit, 368
Kernével: 256; U/B HQ at, 265; U/B HQ leaves, 444 Note 1
Key West, Fla.: 414; 417; destroyer training centre, 453; KN/NK convoys, 484
Keyes, A-F Lord: and Plans Division, 1917, 73; and Channel Barrage Cttee, 109–10; and Dover Command, 110; see Zeebrugge
KG 40: see Focke-Wulf FW 200 (Index of Aircraft, German)
Kharkov: Red Army recaptures, 642
Kiel: 91 Note 15; mutiny at, 1918, 139; in 1918, 160–1; Dönitz in, 163; 167; 168; 193; 206; Canal, 214 & Note 5; 227; 232; 239; 296; 663; U/B Memorial, 669
Kiev: Red Army recaptures, 642
King, Fleet Adml. E. J. (USN): and Atlantic Fleet, 1941, 340; 342; 414; Marshall correspondence, 1942, 422–3; COMINCH, 422 Note 41; and Winn, 457–9; '20-minute egg', 457; informed of TRITON breakthrough, 509; obsession with Pacific, 515; 517; convenes Convoy Conference, 1943, 535; 'disliked wars of mixed nationality', 538; and VLR aircraft, 539–40; 550; 576; and Tenth Fleet, 634 Note 39
King, V/Adml E. L. S. (RN): ACNS (Trade), 454
King, Lt.-Cdr. P. G. A. (RNR): and HX 229 (*Anemone*), 565
Kingston, Jamaica: D/F station, 419
Kinzel, *Kapitänleutnant*: *U 338* and SC 122, 565; death, 638 Note 44
Kipling, R., 'packet of assorted miseries', 279 & Note 10; 'smell 'em, my son', 314 Note 6; 'Price of Admiralty', 392 & Note 85
Kitchener, F-M Lord: 357
Kitty Hawk: first flight at, 158
Knowles, Cdr. K. A. (USN): heads Op. 20 (F.21), and Winn, 458–9
Knox, F.: (US Navy Secretary): 339 Note 71

Koitschka, *Oberleutnant*: and HX 229, 565
Königsberg: 214; 660
Konoye, Prince: fall from power, 394
Krancke, *Vizeadmiral*: 519; recalls U/Bs, 1944, 647
Kretschmer, *Fregattenkapitän* O.: 'tonnage king', 261; and SC 2, 263; and SC 7, 267–8 & Note 35; Oakleaves, 272; and OB 290, 293; captured, 313–16
Kuhl, *Gen.* von: on Flanders U/Bs, 1917, 105 Note 3
Kuhnke, *Korvettenkapitän* G.: and SC 2, 263; and SC7, 267; see Appendix E
Kummetz, *Konteradmiral*: Torpedo Inspector, 1940, 234
Küpfmuller, Prof.: 641
Kursk, Battle of, 1943: 609; 615; German defeat, 641 & Note 56; 648

L

Laborde, Cdr. (French Navy, 1917): 77
Labrador: fog, 290; Current, 334
Lagos: U/B success off, 1941, 344
Lamlash: convoys from, 1917, 62
Landing craft: for tanks, 1917, 109; US mass-production, 495–6
Land's End: D/F station, 356; 647
Lange, *Kapitänleutnant* K.: *U 350*, intention to bring crew safe home, 557 Note 96
Langsdorff, *Kapitän zur See* H.: 165
La Pallice: U/B base, 1940–, 262; shelters built, 354; Bomber Command and, 1943, 516; Allies advance on, 648–9
Lascars: 287 Note 29
Lavasseur, *Lt. de Vaisseau* (*Aconit*): and HX 228, sinks *U 444*, *U 432*, 552
'Law of the Sea': 5, 218
League of Nations: 'collective security', 156–7; Japan joins, 157; Abyssinia appeals to, 174; sanctions against Italy, 175, powerless against Hitler, 202
Lehmann-Willenbrock, *Korvettenkapitän* H.: 9th Flotilla, 605; see Appendix E
Leigh Light: introduction of, 431–2; '*verdammte Licht*', 433; 474; need in LR aircraft, 531; 657
Lemp, *Leutnant* J.: sinks *Athenia*, 215–17; in *U 110*, 315; death, 326 & Note 39
Lend-Lease Agreement: 279; 336; 340

Lenin, V. I.: 46
Lepanto, Battle of, 1571: 670
Lerwick: convoys from, 1917, 58; 96; disuse, 97
Leslie, Lt. G. C. (RN): on picking up survivors, 564–5
Leslie, Sir Norman: 54; 62 Note 11
Letch, Sir R.: and Clyde shipping, 1941, 302–3
Lewis, Butt of: 231
Lewis, Cdr. T. L. (USCG): and HX 212, 490
Leyte Gulf, Battle of, 1944: 670
'Liberty Ships': 629; *U 984* sinks 4, 647
Liddell Hart, Sir B.: 362 Note 23; on Midway, 422 Note 40
Liebe, *Korvettenkapitän*: and SC 7, 257
Lisbon: 342
Lithuania: 206
Liver House: 307
Liverpool: 41–2; 215; 244; 1940 air attacks on, 300; May 1941 air attacks, 303–4; Western Approaches Command at, 304–8; 395; 446; 546; 624; 637
Lloyd George, Rt. Hon. D.: Prime Minister, 1916, 24; on Admlty., 45; 54; on convoys, 55; on 'Military Mind', 57; visit to Admlty., 58–9; and Jellicoe, 67–8, 72; on 1917 defeat of U/Bs, 101; 137; and 'Coupon Election', 154 Note 3; 304
Lloyds (of London): 558
Loch Ewe: Home Fleet in, 1939, 223; mined, 227 & Note 39
Lockyer, Capt. H. C. (RN): first convoy Commodore, 60
Lofoten Is.: Commando raid on, 1941, 325
London: Gotha attacks on, 1917, 48; imports through Port, bombing, 1940, 299; 302; 352; 'Blitz' on, 469
London, Declaration of, 1909: 5–7
London Naval Conference, 1918: 116–17
London Protocol on S/M Warfare, 1936: 216 & Note 11
Londonderry: 344; 'Newfy-Derry' run, 435; 507; 566; 667
Long, Rt. Hon. W.: First Lord of Admlty., 1918, 154 Note 3
Lorient: U/B HQ at, 256–7, 670; 262; shelters built, 354–5; 486; Bomber Command attacks, 1943, 516, 615; Allies advance on, 648–9

Lough Foyle: U/B surrender in, 1945, 669
Lough Swilly: escort base, 1917, 63
Lübeck: Bomber Command attack, 1942, 470
Ludendorff, *Gen.* E.: 4; and unrestricted S/M warfare, 13–14; change of strategy, 14; loses faith in U/Bs, 81; on 'black of German Army', 135; on end of unrestricted U/B warfare, 137
Luftwaffe: see German Air Force
Lüneburg Heath: 214 Note 4; 614; German surrender, 665
Luther, Lt.-Cdr. G. J. (RN): temporary SOE, HX 229, 555–6; 558; and rescue of survivors, 564–5; relieved, 567 & Note 102; appreciation, 571–2; 573
Lütjens, *Vizeadmiral* G.: and *Jervis Bay*, 295

M

MacArthur, Gen. D. (USA): SAC, SW Pacific, 542
McCoy, Capt. J. A. (RN): OC 3rd EG, 586; and ONS 5, 595, 597
MacDonald, Rt. Hon. Ramsay: belief in RN, 155 Note 6
MacIntyre, Capt. D. (RN): SOE HX 112, and capture of *U 99*, 314–16; 530; on B7, 589–90
Mackendrick, Cdr. D. W. (RN): commanding *Audacity*, and OG 74, 385–6; and HG 76, death, 398–9
Mackenzie King, Rt. Hon. W. (Canadian Premier): attitude to Forces, 329
Maclay, Sir J. (Shipping Controller, 1916): 24; says Admlty. 'not good office', 66
MAD, 'Madcats': 661–2
Madras: Japanese threat to, 427
Magellan Straits: 500
MAGIC: US Japanese decrypts, 394; Friedman and, 456
Magor, Flight Sub.-Lt. N. (RNAS): sinks *UB 32*, 77
Mahan, Adml. A. T. (USN): '*Influence of Sea Power upon French Revolution and Empire*', 45–6 & Note 15; on Nelson, 52
Mainguy, Capt. (D) E. R. (RCN): 448
Malaya: Japanese in, 403–4

Malta: 163; untenable, 1935, 176; convoys, 359; key to Mediterranean, 362; 1942, 494
Manila: Japanese capture, 404
Manisty, Fleet Paymaster H. W. E. (RN): on 1917 Convoy Cttee., 62 Note 11; heads Convoy Section, 80; and Naval Control Service, 243
Manseck, *Kapitänleutnant*: and HX 229, 564
Mansfield, Cdre. J. M. (RN): WA Chief of Staff, in Ottawa, 537
Marconi, Signor: 143
Marder, Prof. A. J.: 'sinking S/Ms is a bonus', 87, 288, 400
Marineleitung: se German Navy 1918–45
Marix, Flight Lt. (RNAS): attacks Düsseldorff Zeppelins, 36
Marmora, Sea of: 24 Note 13; 99 Note 29
Marne, Second Battle of, 1918: 130
Marshall, Gen. G. C. (USA): at ARCADIA Conference, 1942, 403 Note 1; strategy, 407; and U/B crisis, correspondence with King, 422–3
Martens, *Vizeadmiral* E.: Chief of Signals, 525
Matz, *Korvettenkapitän*: captured, 1941, 314, 316
Max, Prince, of Baden: Imperial Chancellor, 136
Mediterranean Sea: 19; 41; Valentiner in, 44; 45; corsairs, 52 Note 32; Japanese destroyers in, 1917, 68; 86; shipping graveyard, 90; U/B feast in, 1917, 98–9; divided Allied command, 99; 100; see Otranto Barrage, Cattaro, Pola, Malta; convoys introduced, 116; 124; U/B 1918 defeat, 130–2; 138; 140; 156; Italian threat, 1935, 175–6; 187; 257; 273; 1941 shipping losses, 342–3; U/Bs in, 1941, 359–62 & Note 16; 'mouse-trap', 361; 371; 387; 394; RN losses, 1941, 404; 409; 413; 424; RN position precarious, 1942, 442; Alanbrooke and, 495; see TORCH, Casablanca Conference; 499; MEDUSA cipher, 509; 528; 545; 'Mediterranean strategy', 577; see HUSKY; 634; 636; 659
MEDUSA: Mediterranean *Enigma* setting, 509
Memel: Germany seizes, 1939, 206

Mentor Bilanz: 168–9
Merchant Aircraft Carriers (MAC ships): 637 & Note 42
Merchant Navy (MN; Merchant Marine):
1914–18
53; opposed to convoy, 55; and first convoy, 60; and RN, 60–61; surprise at efficiency of convoy, 64; 1914–18 casualties, 149, 669
1918–39:
179; training for war, 243
1939–45:
Germans capture Code, 1940, 257–8; total dead, 1939–45, 287 & Note 29, 673; Noble and, 306–7; 325; and 'Newfyjohn', 334; new Code captured, 1942, 454; convoy 'death ride', 466 Note 40; Hitler, Dönitz on killing M/V crews, 467–8; survivors, 469; fear for morale, 565; HX 229/SC 122 losses, 573; 1943 morale, 574–6; relations with RN, 575; no sign of breaking-point, 576; 592; shrinkage, 629–30 & Note 28
Merchant Shipping (M/Vs): see Index of Merchant Vessels
1914–18:
arming of M/Vs, 7–8; 1915 losses, 10; 1916 losses, 11; Aug.–Oct. 1916 losses, 15; Dec. 1916–Jan. 1917 losses, 22–3; Shipping Ministry, see Maclay; Feb.–March 1917 beginning of massacre, 40; *Alnwick Castle* sinking, 41–4; April 1917 losses, 46–8; 'cemetery of British shipping', 47; see Convoys; 'runners', 50; 1914 World and British tonnage, 52; Henderson analyses port clearances, 54–5; May 1917 losses, 61; 63; June 1917 losses, 65; Geddes and, 67; summer 1917, 80; Sept.–Oct. 1917 losses, damage, 86; losses of independents, 90; first year of unrestricted U/B warfare, 106; Jan.–March 1918 losses, 116; turning-point, 119; and US forces, 120; June–Aug. 1918 losses, 131; 1914–18 total losses, 149, 669
1918–39:
no inter-war exercise in trade protection, 177; Shipping Defence Advisory Cttee, 179, 243; Insurance, arming, 243; Admlty assumes control, Aug. 1939, 244
1939–45
Sept. 1939 losses, 221; Oct.–Dec. 1939

losses, 225–6; losses to May 31 1940, 241; shipbuilding blight, 250–1; average monthly losses to May 1940, 253; May, June losses, 261 & Note 18; *Empress of Britain* sunk, 1940, 269–70; Nov. 1940 losses, 272; British predominance, 285–6; air raids and, 300 & Note 50; acquisition of foreign, 300–1; dependence on US building, 301 & Note 52; Churchill on, 301; Port organization, 1941, 301–4; Feb. 1941 losses, 308; April–May losses, 342; June–Aug. losses, 352; 1941 half-yearly losses, 353; see CAM ships; Oct.–Dec. 1941 losses, 386–7; 'shortage imposed absolute ban', 407; US coast massacre, 412–13; US coast losses, 419; losses in Caribbean & Gulf, 421; tanker losses, 421–2; Jan.–June 1942 losses, 424; June 1942 losses, 450; July–Sept. losses, 482–3; losses in Gulf of St Lawrence, 486; Oct. 1942 total, 492; influence on strategy, 494–5; Nov. 1942 losses, effect of TORCH, 499–500; Dec. 1942 losses, 508; 1917/1942 comparison, 512; Jan. 1943 weather and, 524; Jan. losses, 524–5; Feb. losses, 534; occasions of disastrous loss, 544–5; HX 229/SC 122 losses, 569, 571–2; March 1943 losses, 573; April–May 1943 losses, 587; Atlantic victory and, 610; Jan.–May 1943 losses, 610–11; 'safe and timely arrival', 610; production exceeds sinkings, 1943, 628; US triumph, British decline, 629–30; June–Aug. 1943 losses, 636; see MAC ships; Sept. 1943 losses, 640; see 'Liberty Ships'; Mediterranean losses, 650–1; Home Waters losses, 1944, 657 & Note 88; losses by Type XXIIIs, 662; losses by Type VIIs, 662–3; total losses, World War I and II, 669

Merker, Otto: and U/B construction, 653–5

Mersey, River: 299; Regional Port Director, 302; 303; 1941 air raids, 308

Messina: 162

Messines, Battle of, 1917: 105 Note 3

Methil: convoys to Bergen, 1918, 97–8

Metox: and ASV II, 479; 582; and ASV III, 624

Metzler, *Korvettenkapitän*: success off West Africa, 344

Mexico, Gulf of: 62; 334; 414; see Gulf Sea

Frontier, 444; June 1942 losses, 450; 500; 514

Miami: waterfront lights indimmed, 1942, 410; Subchaser School, 416; Destroyer Training Centre, 453

Michaelis, Georg: Imperial Chancellor, 1917, 62

Michelsen, *Flotillenadmiral* A.: U/B *Führer*, 65; and 1918 mutiny, 139–40; 194 Note 97

Middlebrook, Martin: '*The Battle for Convoys SC 122 and HX 229*', 554

Middlesborough: Smith's Dock, 251

Mid-Ocean Escort Force: see MOEF

Midway Is.: 403; Battle of, 1942, 422 Note 40; 442

Milford Haven: convoys from, 1917, 62; 101

MILLENIUM, Operation: RAF attack on Cologne, 1942, 470

Milton, John: 255

Minches, The: 657

Mines:

1914–18:

1917 British defects, 33–4; in barrages, 91–2; U/Bs sunk by, Aug.–Oct. 1917, 95–6; continuing poor quality, 106–7; magnetic and acoustic, 108; in Northern Barrage, 113–15; chief U/B killer, 1914–18, 142; 147

1939–45:

magnetic, 1939, 225 & Note 36; effect, to May 1940, 241; 299; use off W. Africa, 344; 'Mark 24', see Torpedoes; German, 1945, 659; RAF use in E. Baltic, 660

Ministry of Labour: 1935 Shipbuilding Report, 250–1

Ministry of Munitions: Geddes at, 1915, 68

Mittelland Canal: 655

MOEF (Mid-Ocean Escort Force): 435; 536

Moffat, F/O J.: sinks *U 338* with Mark 24 Mine, 638 Note 44

Möhle, *Korvettenkapitän*: and SC 7, 267

Mohr, *Fregattenkapitän*: and ONS 92, 447; and ONS 100, 451; and ONS 102, 452

Moltke, *Feldmarschall* von: and American Civil War, 13 Note 18

MOMP (Mid-Ocean Meeting Point): 336; 338; 345; SC 42 and, 375; at 22°W, 392

807

Mongols: depredations of, 154

Monsen, Lt.-Cdr. C. A. (RNorN): SO B6, 490; and ONS 144, 505

Montgomery, F-M Lord: 214 Note 4; 'versus Rommel', 504: and coalition warfare, 538; German surrender to, 665

Montreal: 215

Moore, V/Adml Sir H.: Director, Trade Division, 1940, 287; VCNS, 538 & Note 57

Moore, F/O K.: sinks U 629, U 373, 1944, 646

Moray Firth: 657

Morocco: 494; US landings, 1942, 496–7; U/Bs and, 497–9; Moroccan Sea Frontier, 538 & Note 58, 543, 573, 581

Morrish, Flight Sub.-Lt. C. R. (RNAS): attack on U/B, 1917, 74–6

Moscow: German defeat at, 401

Mountbatten, A-F Lord: and Typex, 181; SACSEA, 542

Mozambique Channel: 487

Mücke: radar receiver, 625

Muller, *Korvettenkapitän* K.: 165

Munich Agreement, 1938: 179; 186

Munninch, *Oberleutnant* R.: and SC 118, 529–30

Murdaugh, Cdr. A. C. (USN): 439

Murmansk: 518, 584–5

Murray, F/L K.: last U/B kill, May 1945, 664

Murray, R/Adml L. W. (RCN): and NEF, 336; 350; 378; and USN control, 389; 448; COAC, 538; 547

Mussolini, B.: and 'Pact of Steel', 206; 'fate sealed', 402; 556

N

Napoleon I, Emperor (1769–1821): 50; 156; Hitler and, 408 & Note 13; 1812 campaign, 647

Narvik: U/Bs ordered to, 1942, 409 Note 13

National Physical Laboratory: 184

Naval Agreements: Declaration of London, 1909, 5, 7; see Washington Treaties, 1921–22; Anglo-German, 1935, 174–5; 193, 195, repudiation, 206–7; London Protocol, 216 & Note 11

Naval Control Service: 243: Officers (NCSOs), 244; 287–8; see Manisty

Naval Vessels: see Index of Warships

Naxos, Naxos-U: radar receiver, 624–5

Nazi-Soviet Pact, 1939: 186

Nelles, V/Adml P. W. (RCN): and RCN status, 536–7

Nelson, V/Adml Lord (RN): 33; 45; 50; and convoys, 52 & Note 32; 85; 156; and Trafalgar, 158; 292; 317 & Note 15; 'only numbers can annihilate', 435; and frigates, 436; 521; and Walker, 623–4

NEPTUNE, Operation, 1944: D-Day scale of, 645; 658

New Guinea: Allied victory, 543

New York: 1917 assembly port, 62; 342; 414; 417; 'Interlocking System' terminal, 483–4; trans-Atlantic terminal, 484; 505; too many ships at, March 1943, 554; SC 122 leaves, 557

New Zealand: 156; 389

Newfoundland: US base in, 279; Crown Colony, 1939; geography, 334; D/F station, 356; USA and, 389; 394; 418; 435; 465

Newfoundland Escort Force (NEF): 336; 338; 345; first convoy battle, 248–50; and SC 42, 373–81; first kill, 380; expansion, 381; and training, 382 & Note 63; USN control, 1941, 388–9; abolished, 1942, 435

Newman, Prof. M. H. A.: and 'Fish', 627 Note 19

Nile, Battle of the, 1798: 670

Nimitz, Adml. C. W. (USN): at Nuremberg, 475; SAC Central Pacific, 542

Nivelle, Gen. R.: 23; 1917 offensive, 46–7; failure of, 70; 83; 105

Noble, Adml Sir P.: CinCWA, 305–8; and HX 133/OB 336, 349–50; and need for numbers, 435; 441; 442; 454; at Washington, 501 & Note 103; 502; 538 & Note 57; 539

Norfolk, Va.: 414; 418

Normandy: 1940 evacuation, 261; 1944 assault on, 612–13; 645; 648; 657 Note 88

North Cape: 252 Note 26; 256

North Sea: see High Sea Fleet, Dover Straits, Northern Barrage, Holland, Flanders U/B Flotillas, Harwich Force, Scandinavian Convoys; U/Bs withdrawn, 1916, 11; 17; U/B tracked across, 1915,

31; 35; airships, 38; 'Spider Web' in, 74–7; 88; German ports, 91; ambush for U/Bs, 1917, 93–6; 108; U/B losses, 1918, 115; strategic change in, 116; 126; U/B defeat, 1918, 130–1; 141; 156; 174; 175; U/Bs in, 1939, 207; 214; 235; 249; E-boats in, 285 & Note 26; 299; 326; 456 Note 20; 655; 662

North-West Atlantic Command (RCN): created, 1943, 528

Northern Barrage, 1918: Admlty faith in, 91–2 & Note 19; operations, mysterious explosions in, 113–15

Northern Virginia, Army of, 1861–65: 585

Northwood: Coastal Command HQ, 368

Norway: 7; 44 Note 12; convoys to, 1917, 58; 91; 98; 113; whalers for, 251; 255; evacuation, 261; 295; 308; RAF Sqdn, 338; 358–9; Hitler and, 1942, 409 & Note 13; 425; 'children of the sea', 574; 646–7; U/Bs withdraw to, 1944, 649–50; 656; 663–4

Norwegian Campaign, 1940: U/B failure in, 235–41; RN losses, 253 & Note 35; B-Dienst success, 257; 337

(Royal) Norwegian Navy: corvettes, (B6), 484–5; 505

Nova Scotia: 122; D/F station, 356; 414; 657 Note 86

Numbers: importance in 2 world wars, 23, 147

'Numbers game': 250 Note 23

Nuremberg War Crimes Trial, 1946: 471; sentence on Dönitz, 474, 666; Adml Nimitz at, 475; 521

O

Oerlikon AA guns: Britain obtains manufacturing rights, 243; use in ASW, 599

Oehrn, Kapitän zur See V.: 215 Note 8; 'grey wolf', 261; and HG 53, 313

Oil: Caribbean refineries, 414; 1942 tanker losses, British crisis, 421–2; Oil Executive, 422; 1942–43 crisis, 514

OKH (Oberkommando des Herres): 361 Note 20, 362

OKW (Oberkommando der Wehrmacht): 361 Note 20; 362; 363; ignorance about U/Bs, 1942, 409 Note 13

Oliver, A-F Sir Henry: Chief of War Staff, 1915–17, 31; Deputy CNS, Fisher and Churchill on, 67; old age, 68; opposes Statistics Division, 73; misuse of Room 40, 79; and Mary Rose disaster, 1917, 97 Note 25; leaves Admlty, 103

Onomatopoeia: see Aristophanes

Operational Intelligence Centre (OIC): 149; 178; in 'Citadel', 1941, 317–21; daily input, 318 & Note 21; see Submarine Tracking Room; and Trade Division, 320; sub-divisions of, 321 Note 25; 357; 363; and U/B strategy, 399; need for US ASW equivalent, 455–9; and Op 20. 458–9; and WA HQ, 501; 503; and Enigma blackout, 508; and TRITON breakthrough, 509; March 1943 alarm, 527; Ottawa and, 539; central to ASW, 606; and new U/Bs, 656; 'Square One', 658; 671

Oran: Allied landings, 1942: 496

Orel, Battle of, 1943: 642; 648

Orkney Is.: 24; 42; 113; 115; 222; Prien's visit, 224; 231

Oshima, Baron (Japanese ambassador in Berlin): 467; reports on new U/Bs, 656

Ostend: U/B exit port, 1915–18, 17–19; 69; 91 Note 16; amphibious attack planned, 1917, 105, 109; exit mined, 106; Allied advance towards, 1918, 135

Ottawa: S/M Tracking Room, 456 & Note 20; WA delegation in, Dec. 1942, 537; OIC, 539

Otranto Barrage: hunting operation in, 1918, 115–16; 163

OVERLORD Operation, 1944: Atlantic victory and, 405–6, 610–13; 493; Coastal Command and, 523; U/B threat, 577; U/B fiasco, 643–7; 659

P

Pacific Ocean: 156; Japanese advances in, 1942–43, 403–4, 495; US aircraft requirement, 417; SACs, 542; 610

Padfield, Peter: acknowledgement to, 161 Note 18

Page, Ambassador Walter (USA): calls U/Bs 'most formidable thing', 38, 673; 'each side losing where it thought itself strongest', 62

Panama: 62; Declaration of, 1939, 339; Sea Frontier, 414; Canal, 500
Paramaribo (Surinam): 483 Note 72
Paria, Gulf of: 421
Paris: Declaration of, 1856, 5; Germans in sight of, 1918, 119; 265; U/B HQ at, 444 Note 1, 670; GAF Listening Service in, 532
'Passchendaele', Battle of, 1917: 511
Patton, Gen. G. S. (USA): 496; and coalition warfare, 538; 1944 advance, 648
Paulus, *Feldmarschall* von: Stalingrad surrender, 528
Pearl Harbor: Japanese attack, 401; 403; 434; 455–6 & Note 19
Peenemunde: 228 Note 43; Research and Experimental Station, 481
Peirse, A/M Sir R.: 354 Notes 5, 6
Penang: 636
Pentland Firth; 69; 115; sea states in, 222
Persian Gulf: 636
Peyton-Ward, Capt. D. V. (RN): 207 & Note 119; 247–9; and Operational Research, 368–9
Pfaffinger, Dr: brings *U 441* home, 632
Philippeville: bombarded by *Goeben*, 161
Philippine Is.: Japanese attack, 403; conquest of, 424
Phillips, Adml Sir T.: on ASW, 1939, 245; 281; supports Winn, 320
Photographic Reconnaissance: see Intelligence (British)
'Piening Way': 633 Note 34; 636
Pietzsch, *Kapitänleutnant*: sinks *Mathew Luckenbach*, March 1943, 568
Pillenwerfer (SBT): see Weapons
Pitt, Rt. Hon. William (1759–1806): and R. Fulton, 145
Placentia Bay (Newfoundland): 336; 339; Churchill, Roosevelt meet, 387–8; 434
'Plaster', Operation: ASW group tactic, 621–3
Plate, River: Battle of the, 1939: 249; 483; U/Bs enter, 666
Pless (Silesia): Imperial HQ, 4; 1916 conference at, 11–13; 1917 conference agrees Unrestricted S/M Warfare, 15–16
Plymouth: convoys from, 1917, 62; escort base, 63; WA HQ, 1939–41, 275 & Note 1

Pocket battleships: see German Navy 1918–45 (*Deutschland* [*Lützow*], *Admiral Graf Spee*, *Admiral Scheer*)
Pohl, *Admiral* von: proposes S/M blockade of Britain, 1916, 8
Pola: Austro-Hungarian naval base, 115; 163
Poland: 201; Hitler prepares attack, 1939, 206–7; 213; fall of, 219 & Note 19; 255; and *Enigma*, 323
Port Arthur, siege of, 1904: 91
Port of Spain: *U 161* in, 1942, 421
Portal, M/RAF Lord: 354 & Notes 5, 6; CAS, at ARCADIA Conference, 1942, 403 Note 1; 422
Porte, Wing Cdr. J. C. (RNAS): 37; 76
Portland, escort base, 1917, 63; deep minefield off, 99 Note 30; A/S School, 275; Bill, 646
Portsmouth: air raid on, 1940, 308
Portugal; 663
Potsdam; 1945 Conference, 517
Pound, A-F Sir D. (RN): plans Division, 1917, 73; and PQ 17, 229; favours 'hunting groups), 1939, 245; 298; supports Winn, 320; at ARCADIA Conference, 1942, 403 Note 1; and 'Battle of the Air', 429; and *TRITON* breakthrough, 509; 527; 541; tired man, 1943, death, 570
Prentice, Cdr. J. D. (RCN): SOCC, 78; and SC 42, 378–80; and ONS 100, 451; and ONS 102, 452; 462
Prien, *Kapitänleutnant* G.: sinks *Royal Oak*, 223–4; and torpedo failures, 235–7; 'grey wolf', 261; and SC 2, 263; and OB 290, 293, death, 313–16
Proudfoot, Cdr. F. B. (RN): SOE SC 118, 530
Purkhold, *Kapitänleutnant*: and March 1943 hurricane, 583
Purple: Japanese enciphering machine, 456
Puttkamer, *Fregattenkapitän* von: 221
Pye Radio Ltd.: ASV II ordered, 1940, 283–4

Q

Q-ships: 8; *Fidelity*, sunk Dec. 1942, 511
Quebec: 269; conferences, 517
Queenstown (Eire): convoys from, 1917, 62;

escort base, 63; US destroyers at, 74; convoys abandoned, 101

R

Radar: 'Chain Home', ASV, 183–5; German, 184; 271; ASV I, II, AI, centimetric, 283–4; Type 271, 314–15 & Notes 6, 10; ASV III and 271M, 357–8; ASV II in Coastal Command, 1941, 365; in *Audacity*, 397; ASV II and Leigh Light, 1942, 431; advances in 1942, 433; increasing RN dependence on, 437–8; and ONS 92, 447; Type 286, 451; US Type SCR 571, 461 Note 32; and ON 113, July 1942, 462; in C1, Aug., 476–7; ASV II and *Metox*, 479; 485; weather and, Oct. 1942, 489; 490; and HX 212, 491; German Air Intelligence unaware of British, 496 Note 97; 505; and HX 217, 506; contest for ASV-III/H2S, 515, 579, 581; German fear of, 526; and ON 116, 532–3; RCN lack, 536; weather damage, 1943, 547, 562; SCR 517 and GONDOLA, 581; ASV III début, 581–2; and ONS 5, 599; and Atlantic victory, 608; makes Type VII, IX U/Bs obsolete, 616; German developments, 1943–44, 624–5; 3-cm (ASV X), 625, 661–2; effect of *Schnorchel* on, 656–7; and ASW, 672

Radio: see W/T; altimeters, 434; controlled glider-bombs, 633 & Note 36

Radio-Telephony (R/T): 126; 271; RCN lack, 349; in escorts, TBS, 368 & Note 37, 505–6 & Note 114

Raeder, *Grossadmiral* E.: first impression of Dönitz, 167–9; and big ships, 185–6; 195; 202; deceived by Hitler, 1939, 204–6; and *Athenia*, 217; 219; and U/B production, 1940, 220–1; and torpedo crisis, 240; 1941 naval initiative, 298; 344; 345; 359; and U/Bs for Mediterranean, 362–3; and Hitler's intuitions, 409; 460; replaced, 1943, 517–19 & Note 12, 617; 652

Rahmlow, *Korvettenkapitän* H.: and capture of *U 570*, 364–5

RAINBOW: US contingency plans, 1939, 406 Note 7

Ramsey, V/Adml C. G. (RN): Rosyth Command, 1940, 275 Note 1

Randall, Prof. J. T.: and centimetric radar, 284

Ransome, Lt.-Cdr. R. H. (RN): in *Partridge*, Dec. 1917, 98

R-Boats: 359 Note 15

Red Sea: Japanese threat to, 427

Regional Port Directors: 301–4

Reichstag: 13; 1917 Peace Resolution, 81–3; fire, 1933, 173

Reims: German surrender, 1945, 614, 665

Rejewski, M.: develops *Bomba*, 323

Repington, Col.: 'could armies win war before navies lost it?', 1916, 23; 40–1; discusses Admlty with Lloyd George, 45; on Naval Plans Division, 68; on Flanders Flotillas, 118

Reykjavik: 337–8; 376; 506; 558; 562; 567

Rhine, River: 648; Allies across, 663

Richardson, Capt. R. C. (USAAF): and *Laconia* survivors, 472 & Note 49

Rio de Janeiro: 483 Note 72

Ritchie, R/Adml (RN): Flag Officer, Liverpool, 307

Robb, AV/M J. M.: AOC No. 15 Group, 305

Robertson, Prof. J. M. (FRS): and Operational Research, 368

Robertson, F-M Sir W. R.: on submariner's life, 1917, 21; 69

Rockets: possible U/B use, 481; and ASW, 619–20

Rohwer, Prof. J.: on 1941 Atlantic decision, 400–1; inevitability of, 401; charts of HX 229/SC 122 battle, 548–9, 559–60; '*The Critical Convoy Battles of March 1943*', 554 & Note 88; 573

Rollman, *Leutnant*: and SC 42, 377–80

Romania: 4; Germans fear threat, 1916, 13–14; 23; changes sides, 1944, 658

Rommel, *Feldmarschall* E.: command method, 228 Note 42; 1941 offensive, 342; OKW and, 362; advance to Egypt, 1942, 424; 494; and El Alamein, 500 & Note 101

Ronin, Col. J. A. (USAAF): and *Laconia* survivors, 472

Room 40: 31–2; 46; tracking S/Ms, 79–80; W/T intercepts, 93, 96; Dec. 1917 failure, 97 & Note 25; and A/S strategy, 107; and Dover passage, 109; and U/B packs, 1918,

121–3; and HSF mutiny, 138–9; and U/B defeat, 143–4; disbanded, 1920s, 178; and Jutland, 456 Note 20, 671

Roosevelt, Pres. F. D. (1882–1945): 'all aid short of war', 277; and Lend-Lease, 278–9; and US war policy, 339–44 & Note 69; and Stimson, 341; 'Unlimited National Emergency', May 1941, 343–4; and Placentia Bay meeting, 387–8; final moves towards war, 390–4; and ARCADIA Conference, 403–8; 411; and production priorities, 416 Note 29; Pearl Harbor 'conspiracy theory', 456 Note 19; and N. Africa, 494; and 'Liberty Ships', 629

Rosenberg-Gruszczynski, *Oberleutnant* von: and *U 384*, 568

Rösing, *Kapitän zur See* H-R.: 'grey wolf', 261; and SC 7, 266; U/B Senior Officer (West), 616; see Appendix E

Rostock: Bomber Command attack, 1942, 470

Rosyth: RN base, 1915, 116; 138; RN Command, 1939, 275 Note 1

Rotterdam: 7; 581

ROUNDUP, Operation: 1943 plan, 493; British doubts, 494–5; 544; burial of, 576–7 & Note 119

Rowland, Capt. J. M. (RN): sinks *U 47* (Prien), March 1941, 314 & Note 6

Royal Air Force: birth, April 1918, 124; and ASW, 125–6; effect of expansion, 144–5; maritime strength, 1918, 148; no lethal A/S weapon in 1939, 149; 1920s struggle for survival, 155 Note 5; 1919–23 Estimates, 156; and control of maritime air, 159; 180; 1930s transformation, 182–3; Fighter Command W/T control, 183; see Bomber Command, Coastal Command; 190; unaware of German entry to N. Atlantic, 207; 229; 241; Bowhill joins, 247; Fighter Command limitation, 1940, 276–7; competition for ASV, 283–4; competition for VLR aircraft, 345; and German ships in Brest, 345–8; and Mediterranean, 359; Merchant Ship Fighter Unit, 377 Note 58; Gibraltar Command, 396 & Note 91; and US aircraft, 418; Far East requirement, 1942, 428; Ferry Command, 429 Note 57; Air Staff and Strategic Offensive, 516; Mediterranean Command,

611 Note 185; 2nd TAF in Baltic, 1945, 619–20, 664; prisoner misleads Germans on ASV III/H2S, 624–5

RAF Bomber Command:
and German radar, 1939, 184; 'Master Bomber' technique, 228 Note 43; 1940 weakness, 276–7; and H2S, 284; and VLR aircraft, 345, 366; and *Scharnhorst, Gneisenau*, 346–7 & Note 89; and Biscay U/B bases, 354–5 & Notes 5, 6, 1942 1,000-bomber attacks, 470; first use of H2S, 515, 581; Casablanca Directive to, 516–17; and Combined Bomber Offensive, 578–80, 611 Note 185; and Battle of Ruhr, 1943, 615; and WINDOW, 625; and Battle of Hamburg, 1943, 653–4; bombing aids, attacks on canals, 654–5; 1945 attacks on Germany, 658; final U/B sinkings, 663; equation between U/Bs and bomber offensive, 673

RAF Coastal Command:
see Bowhill, Joubert, Slessor, Peyton-Ward, 124; 'Cinderella', 182; 1939 Intelligence failure, 207; condition and rôle, 246–9; Northwood HQ, 247; bombs v depth charges, 248–9; 'becoming U/B-minded', 249 & Note 19; Dönitz wants similar support, 258; 262; outdated escort system, 1940, 263; equipment needs, 271; reinforcement ASV, 283–4; No. 15 Group in WA, 304–5, 501, 563; and Iceland, 338; see Atlantic 'Gap'; attacks on Brest, 346 & Note 88; and U/B shelters, 354; 363; and *U 570*, 364–5; 1941 expansion and improvement, 365–72 & Note 28; 'Scarecrow' phase, 367–70; Operational Research Unit, 368–70; Tactical Instruction for attacking U/Bs, 369 & Notes 40, 42; 'White Crows', 370; first Bay offensive, 371; first kill, Nov. 1941, 371–2; 'Sunday Soviets', 372; Gibraltar station, 396; and USN, 418 Note 32; 427; 1942 demands upon, 428–9; Bay operations, 430; Leigh Light, 431–2; 'obstacle to victory', 432; turning-point in performance, 433; 'born again', 434 & Note 67; 437; 462; Beaufighters in, 479; and *Philante* school, 502–3; and HX 217, 507; loses ASV III fight, 515; 517; 1943 order of battle, 523 & Note 22; Liberators in, 1943, 540; VLR

sqdns in, 566; 'overwhelming power', 568
& Note 104; Harris and, 579 & Note 124;
second Bay offensive, 1943, 581–3; 598;
'merciless vigilance', 605; and Atlantic victory, 611–12 & Note 185; and rockets,
619; third Bay offensive, 630–3; and
'milch cows', 635–6; 'cork and bottle',
June 1944, 645–7; No. 19 Group SWAMP
tactic, 646; Canadians in, 646; 654; effect
of *Schnorchel*, 656–7; peak strength, lean
time, 660–1; final U/B sinkings, 664; and
ASW, 672

RAF Squadrons:

Nos. 22 (Beaufort): attack on Brest,
March 1941, 346 Note 88

24 (Hudson): first RAF air victory,
246

86 (Liberator): and HX 229/SC
122, March 1943, 566–7; sinks
U 632, 590; sinks *U 465*, 600;
and Mark 24 Mine, 618 Note 10;
sinks *U 905*, 662

98 (Battle): in Iceland, 1940, 338

120 (Liberator): 429 Note 57; and
SC 104, 489–90; and HX 212,
490; correction to record, 491
Note 88; and SC 107, 492; and
HX 217, Dec. 1942, 506; 540;
and HX 229/SC 122, 566–7;
sinks *U 189*; and ONS 18, ON
202, sinks *U 338*, 638 & Note
44; sinks *U 296*, 662

172 (Wellington): and Leigh Light,
431–2; ASV III in, 582

206 (Fortress): sinks *U 384*, 568;
sinks *U 169*, *U 469*, 584; sinks
U 710, 594, 598

209 (Catalina): 364

210 (Catalina): last U/B kill, 664

220 (Fortress): and HX 217, 507;
sinks *U 624*, 530

224 (Liberator): sinks *U 629*, *U 373*,
June 1944, 646

248 (Beaufighter): and *U 441*, 632

269 (Hudson): and *U 570*, 246,
364–5, and HX 217, 507

304 (Wellington; Polish): sinks
U 441, 647

311 (Wellington; Czech): fight with
U/B, 1942, 480

330 (Northrop seaplane; Norwegian): in Iceland, 338

502 (Whitley): sinks *U 206*, 371–2

617 (Lancaster): attacks on canals,
655

Royal Aircraft Establishment (Farnborough): 260

Royal Canadian Air Force, Royal Canadian
Navy: see Canada

Royal Flying Corps: 'Bloody April', 1917,
46, 233; 124; 125

Royal Indian Air Force: 428

Royal Naval Air Service (RNAS): 1914 attacks on Zeppelin sheds, 36–7; increasing
ASW effectiveness, 74–9; only U/B sinking, 77; expansion, 79; 367; see Royal Air
Force

Royal Naval Reserve (RNR): virtues of, 598

Royal Navy: War Staff created, 1912, 53;
and Imperial Defence, 328; see Fisher,
Index of Warships

1914–18:

see Admiralty, Beatty, Churchill, Geddes,
Grand Fleet, Hall, Jellicoe, Jutland,
Keyes, Oliver, Wemyss; distant blockade,
6–7; Q-ships, 8; small craft, 25; see Destroyers, Sloops; offensive tradition, 33;
public discontent with, 1917, 45–6; desire
to 'engage enemy more closely', 56; dominated by technology, 58; see Weapons,
Convoys; surprise at efficacy of convoy,
64, 69; 'main campaign', 71; new A/S
craft, 74; U/B ambush failure, 93–6; and
German cruiser sortie, self-sacrifice, 96–
7; and German destroyer sortie, 'minor
epic', 97–8; failure to destroy U/Bs, 99;
blamed for Dover disaster, Feb. 1918,
111; see Dover Straits and Barrage, Northern Barrage, Otranto Barrage; S/M
ambush in Skagerrak, 115; U/Bs cause
fundamental change of strategy, 117–18;
see Mediterranean; better understanding
of air power, 125–6; attitude to U/Bs,
146–7; approach to Submarine Tracking
Room and OIC, 149

1918–39:

See Ten Year Rule, Naval Agreements,
Operational Intelligence Centre; apogee of
British supremacy, 153; costs, Estimates,
1919 proposals, 155; naval supremacy

no longer cornerstone of policy, 156; dual control of air, 159; ASW backwater, 160; and German Navy, 164; 1935 bad year, 173–4; Spithead Review, 175; Mediterranean Fleet weakness, 175–6; rearmament begins, 1934, 176; Estimates, 1933–39, 179; 180; defects, 181–2; training, 190; 193; 1939 Intelligence failure, 207, 247; Mediterranean Fleet signal insecurity, 1935–6, 257

1939–45:
See Corvettes, Cunningham, Destroyers, Escorts, Fleet Air Arm, Frigates, Home Fleet, Horton, Intelligence (British), Noble, Pound, Sloops, Walker, Winn; *Courageous* sunk, 221–2; *Royal Oak* sunk, 222–4; and Trade Protection, see Convoys, Naval Control Service; vulnerability to air attack, 243; continued addiction to 'hunting groups', 244–5, 454; Northern Patrol, 247; 1939 euphoria, 249; NID scepticism, 250 & Note 23; 1939 U/B sinkings, 250; Norway losses, 1940, 253 & Note 35; Dunkirk losses, 254; ciphers penetrated, 257–8; pressure on, 261; and U/B tactics, 263; Portsmouth, Nore, Rosyth Commands, 275 Note 1; SW Approaches abandoned, 275; and Trade protection, 285; total 1939–45 casualties, 287, 673 Note 114; junior officers' responsibility, 288; tradition of self-sacrifice, 295; WA Command in Liverpool, 305–7; see Atlantic, Battle of the, GC & CS; capture of German weather-ships, 326; surface-ship fixation, 331; criticism of RCN, 333; and Newfoundland, 334; and NEF, 336; Iceland base and Command, 338 & Note 66; and ABC-1, 1941, 340 & Note 74; repairs in US yards, 340–1; Crete losses, 343; and air power, 343; Atlantic fuelling problem, 344; and *Bismarck*, 344; 356; AMCs as escorts, 358 Note 13; Mediterranean losses, 359–60; Fighter Catapult Ships, 377 Note 58, 385; gunnery, 382 Note 63; 1941/1942 disasters, 404 & Note 3; and US aircraft, 418; 50% of Atlantic burden, 434; value of training, 441–12; and command of sea, 442; senior partner in two wars, 449; rescuing survivors, 469–70; S. Atlantic Command, 487–8 &

Note 79; Mediterranean Fleet losses, 1942, 494; and TORCH, 499; and ONS 154, 511; and large convoys, 554; 'high pitch of excellence', 590; and Typhoons, 619; ciphers secured, CCM, 628; and glider bombs, 633 & Note 36; NEPTUNE contribution 645; losses by U/Bs, 699 Note 109

Royal Navy, Signals (various): 'uphill all the way', 392 Note 83; Biblical, 463–4 & Note 37; see Aristophanes; 'brevity and wit', 598

Royal Society: see Science and Scientists; Coastal Command Operational Research Unit, 368

Rozycki, J.: and *Enigma*, 323

Ruhr, Battle of the, 1943: 615; 655

Rupprecht, *Feldmarschall*, Crown Prince of Bavaria: commands Flanders Army Group, 1917, 105 Note 3

Russia, Imperial: 1916 offensive, 3–4; Lenin returns to, 46; Revolution, 79, 83; second Revolution, 105, 511

Ryan, Capt. C. P. (RN): and hydrophones, 29

S

Saar: 1935 Plebiscite, 186

Salamis: 651; Battle of, 480 BC, 670

Salerno: glider bombs at, 633 Note 36

Scandinavian convoys: 62; 1917 attacks on, 96–8; 118

Scapa Flow: Grand Fleet base, 24; 98; 116; *U 116* at, 1918, 132 & Note 18; 142; Prien in, 1939, 222–4 & Note 32; 261

Scheer, *Admiral*: Chief of Naval Staff, 1918, 132; 133; ends Unrestricted U/B Warfare, 137; 143

Schepke, *Kapitänleutnant* J.: 'grey wolf', 261; and SC 7, 267; death, 315–16

Schichau (Danzig S/M yard): new U/Bs under construction, 1944, 656

Schleicher, *Gen.* von: approves U/B building, 1932, 169

Schlieffen, *Generaloberst* Graf von: 220

Schnee, *Korvettenkapitän*: and operational Type XXI U/B, 622; 669

Schnorchel: U/Bs fitted with, 626–8; 643; U/B suicide without, 645; June 1944 and, 646–7; 651 Note 73; implications of, 651–2; operations with, 656

Scholtz: *Korvettenkapitän* K.: see Appendix E

Schrecklichkeit: 44–5 & Note 12; 146; 466–8

Schrott, *Korvettenkapitän*: 316

Schuerer, *Herr*: U/B designer, 605

Schultz: *Korvettenkapitän* W.: see Appendix E

Schultze, *Korvettenkapitän* O.: 167

Schultze, *Kapitänleutnant*: reports torpedo failure, 1939, 232

Schutze, *Kapitänleutnant*: reports torpedo failure, 1939, 232

Schwaff, *Oberleutnant*: and Leigh Light/ ASV III attack, 582

Science and Scientists: and ASW, 357; and Atlantic victory, 612; see Bathythermography, Bawdsey Research Station, Blackett, Bletchley Park, Boot, Bowen; and Cabinet Anti-U/B Warfare Cttee, 501; French HF/DF progress, 438; FRS and Operational Research, 368; see GC & CS; Horton and, 504; see Joubert (N.B. 'Sunday Soviets'), Kendrew, National Physical Laboratory, Newman, Poland (N.B. attack on *Enigma*), Randall, Robertson, Sigint, Telecommunications Research Establishment, Tizard, Turing, ULTRA; US inventiveness, 661–2; see Watson-Watt, Welchman

German: Nazi state and, 581; 1944 advances, 624–6; *Geheimschreiber* ('Fish'), 627 Note 19; *Marineleitung* Scientific Operations Staff, 1944, 641; see Küpfmuller, Walter

Scilly Is.: 41; 60; 79; 88; 646

Scotland: A/S operations north of, 1917, 69; US base preparations, 340; D/F stations, 356; 365; 409 Note 13; 657

Scott-Moncrieff, Capt. A. K. (RN): SO 4th EG, 586

Seaplanes: see RNAS, RAF; first use of word, 1913, 158; Jutland failure, 159

SEELÖWE (SEALION), Operation: 259–60; abandoned, 264–5 & Notes 28, 29; 311; 401

Shaw, Petty Officer (FAA): 384

Sherwood, Lt.-Cdr. R. E. (RNR): and ONS 5, 595–8, achievement, 598 & Note 162

Shetland Is.: 78, 91

Shipping, Ships: see Index of Merchant Vessels

Shipping Defence Advisory Cttee, 1937: 179

Shirer, W.: and Prien, 224; Christmas visit to U/Bs, 1939, 227

Shorter, Leading Mechanic (RNAS): in attack on U/B, 1917, 76

Sicily: invasion of (HUSKY), 577; 614–15

Siegmann, *Oberleutnant*: and *U 230* return to Brest, May 1943, 600–5

Sierra Leone: 344; 395–8

Sigint: 265 & Note 29; 'superior to espionage', 322; 1941 'embarrassment of riches', 325–6; 1942 blackout, 425–7; in USA, 456; Traffic Analysis, 526; end of blackout, 526–7; and Battle of Atlantic, 527–8; 1943 blackout, 536; and 'Fish', 627 Note 19; effect of *Schnorchel* on, 656–7

Sims, R/Adml W. S. (USN): and Jellicoe, 1917, 48, 570; percipience of, 92–3; wisdom ignored, 1942, 413; opinion on convoy accepted, 423

Simmons, Lt. (RCN): 379

Singapore: 158; RN base, 160, 173; 'main fleet to', 174; 403; fall of, 424

Skagerrak, The: 115; 214; 663

SLEDGEHAMMER, Operation: 1942 plan, 493

Sleigh, Sub.-Lt. (FAA): attacks Condor, 398

Slessor, M/RAF Sir J.: and 'Battle of Washington', 515; replaces Joubert, 522–3; and VLR aircraft, 540; and 'Super Air Officer', 541; and 2nd Bay Offensive, 580–1; on depth charges, 599 Note 167; and Atlantic victory, 611–13 & Note 185; and U/B AA, 630–1; 633; replaced by Douglas, 645 Note 64

Sloops: 1917 types, and P-boats, 35 & Note 34; available for escort, 1917, 63; 147; 1939 paucity, 160 Note 16; in 1933–36 Estimates, 179; *Black Swan* Class, 1939, 251; 252; *Banff* Class (USCG cutters), 340 & Note 76, 383; in WA, 1942, 427; see EG 2

Smolensk: Red Army recaptures, 642

Snowflake illuminant: misuse by ONS 92, 447

Sobe, *Fregattenkapitän*: U 179, 487–8

Sohler, *Kapitänleutnant* H.: reports torpedo failure, 1939, 232; see Appendix E

Somaliland: 1920 campaign 155 Note 5

Somme, Battle of the, 1916: 3; 14; 23; 105
Sonobuoy: 661–2
South Africa: 343; Air Force, 428; 499
South America: see Brazil; 483 Note 72;
    499–500
Southampton: 41; 269; 1940 air raids, 300
Spain: 42; 138; U/B built in, 1928, 169; Civil
    War, 177–8, 195; torpedo reports from,
    240–1; Germans at frontier, 256; 278;
    Spanish Armada, 1588, 382 Note 63; U/Bs
    hug coast, 619 & Note 34, 636; Spanish
    Main, 673
Speer, Albert: on 1943 bombing, 615; 641;
    and naval construction, 652–3; and Strat-
    egic Air Offensive, 653–5
'Spider Web': 1917, 74; UB 32 sunk in, 77;
    revived, 1944, 583
Spiess, Kapitänleutnant: 139–40
Squid: 441; description, 620–1
St Abb's Head: 126
St Germain: Treaty of with Austria, 1919,
    201
St John's (Newfoundland): 'Newfyjohn',
    333–4; 344; 373; 378; NEF Corvettes at,
    381; 382; 394; 448; 534; 546–7; 555; 562;
    M/Vs with ice damage in, 563; 595;
    escorts forced back to, 595–6
St Lawrence, River: spring freshettes, 1941,
    327; 331; Gulf of, 409; losses in, June
    1942, 450; U 517 in, 1942, 486, 657 Note
    86
St Malo: corsairs, 146
St Nazaire: 1942 Raid, 281, 444 Note 1; U/B
    shelters built, 354–5; Bomber Command
    attacks, 1943, 516, 615; 620; Allies ad-
    vance on, 648–9
St Vincent, Adml. Lord (RN): on S/Ms,
    145
Stalin, J.: 219; 403 Note 1
Stalingrad: German offensive halted, 1942,
    500; German surrender, 1943, 528; 579 &
    Note, 123; German losses, 609; 642 Note
    56; 647
Stanley, Lord: on convoys, 1935, 176; 179
Stark, Adml. H. R. (USN): 278; and Greer,
    391; 'Plan Dog', 406 Note 7; and Sea
    Frontiers, 414
Staten Island: USN destroyer training
    centre, 453
Stavanger: KG 40 detachment at, 260

Stephenson, V/Adml Sir G. (RN): and
    Tobermory A/S School, 276; 307; 382
Stimson, Henry L. (US Secretary for War):
    and Roosevelt discuss support for Britain,
    1941, 341; 1942 strategy, 407
Stockhausen, Leutnant von: 215; and SC 2,
    262
Strelow, Kapitänleutnant: and HX 229, 564
Struckmeier, Kapitänleutnant: and SC 122,
    567
Struthers, Major S. G. (RAF): 'Notes on
    Aids to Submarine Hunting', 1918, 434
    Note 67
Stuart, Gen. J. E. B. (CSA): 585
Stubbs, Lt.-Cdr. J. H. (RCN): SOE, ONS
    100, 451
Stumpf, Seaman: on Wilhelmshaven, 214
    Note 5
Submarine Warfare: see 'Law of the Sea',
    Shrecklichkeit, ASW, Convoys, Unre-
    stricted S/M Warfare; Fisher on, 4–5;
    no German plans for, 1914, 5; nature not
    foreseen, 24 Note 13; close range action,
    28 Note 23; 1918 abandonment, 137;
    permanent truths of, 142; lineaments
    defined, 147; Dönitz in control, etc.,
    190–4; pressures of, 274; comparison in
    two wars, 666–7; birth of true S/M war,
    671
Submarines (S/Ms): Fisher on, 5, 7; Blum
    on numbers for blockade of Britain, 9;
    1915 instructions to, 9; paucity in first
    campaign 10–11; second campaign, 15–
    16; diving time, 27; strength of hulls, 28;
    'most formidable thing', 38, 673; Anglo-
    German Naval Agreement, 1935, and,
    174–5; Hankey and Chatfield on, 1932,
    1934, 175; Dönitz on nature of, 194; not
    meant to fight own kind, best size, 196;
    'fear of flying', 'fear of deeps', 200–1;
    'surrender to deeps', 221; reconnaissance
    disadvantage, 258; 1914–44 types really
    submersibles, 264, 666; diving to escape
    storms, 336 Note 62; approach to true
    S/M, 617–18; Schnorchel and, 626; Type
    XXI and XXIII operations, 1945, 662
Submarine Tracking Room (NID 8[S]): 80;
    149; 178; 'centre of A/S war', 319; Winn
    and, 319–21 & Note 23; 24-hour routine,
    321; familiarity with U/Bs, 326–7; 357;

369; and SC 42, 375; 394 & Note 88; and 1941 re-routing, 400–1; and 1942 Sigint crisis, 425; 'Working Fiction', 454–9, 484; and WA HQ, 501; 503; Horton and, 504; and *TRITON* breakthrough, 509; and ONS 154, 510; Jan. 1943 warning, 514; authority of, 526–7; March alarm, 527; and U/B morale, 588–9 & Note 145, 592; and ONS 5, 595–6; and U/B return to Atlantic, Sept., 637; and D-day, 643; prospect of worst blackout, 656; 'Square One', 658; 671

Suhren, *Fregattenkapitän*: reports SCR 517 radar, 461 Note 32

Supreme Allied Commander (SAC): system instituted, 405; need for Atlantic SAC, 450; Adml King and, 540–4

Surcouf, Capt. Robert: St Malo corsair, 146

Sweden: 7, 664

Sydney, NS: HS from, 1918, 122; 262; 268; slow (SC) convoys from, 287; 373; 378; 381; 484

Sylt, Is.: U/Bs seek refuge, 1918, 140

T

Tait, Cdr. A. A. (RN): SOE, HX 228, 550–2

Takoradi: U/B success off, 1941, 344; 593

Taylor, Capt. T. (RN) SOE, ON 113, 461–2

Technology: see Air Power, Airships, ASDIC, ASW, Bathythermography, Bombe, CCM, Depth Charges, D/F, HF/DF, Hydrophones, Industrial Revolution, Mines, Radar, *Schnorchel*, Sigint, Torpedoes, Weapons, W/T; early U/B development, 19–21; destroyers, 25–7; 'Military Mind' and, 57; RN and, 58; constant 1914–18 progress, 108; decline of British, 180–1, 284–5; 1914–18 takeoff and development, 182–5; U/B 'miracles', 198; ASW, 1941, 358; power of Allied, 526; 'seesaw', 552–3; 612; never-ending battle, 618; 1943 Allied progress, 618–21; German progress, 624–8, 637; new U/Bs, 656 & Note 84, 662; MAD, retrobomb, 661; sonobuoy, 661–2; and two wars, 666–7; 'binding thread' of ASW, 1914–45, 671–2

Tedder, M/RAF Lord: on Sea and Air Power, 343; 442

Tehran Conference: 517

Telecommunications Research Establishment (Swanage): ASV development, 284; 'Sunday Soviets' at, 372

Ten Year Rule: 155–6

TETIS cipher: used by Baltic U/Bs, 425

Thailand, Japanese in, 403

Thames, River: 138; 244; imports through, 1939, 299

Thedsen, *Fregattenkapitän*: 188–90; and Type VII range, 197; 617

Thetis, radar decoy: 625

Thirty Years' War (1618–1648): 154

Thompson, S/L J.H.: and *U 570*, 364; 366

Thring, Fleet Paymaster E. W. C. (RN): and S/M tracking, 1917, 80; heads Tracking Room, 1939, 178; retirement, 319; 357

Tiarks, Mr F.: heads Admlty D/F Section, 1917, 80

Tippelskirsch, *Oberleutnant* von: and SC 122, 566

Tirpitz, *Admiral* von: on change in U/B war, 1917, 145, 409 & Note 15

Tizard Cttee, 1935: and radar defence, 184

Tobermory: A/S Sea Training School, 276; 307; 382

Tobruk: 424; 494

Todt Organization: and U/B shelters, 354 & Note 4

TORCH, Operation, 1942–43: 362; 493–5; landings, 496–9; shipping requirement, convoys, 499–500; TM 1 and, 514–15; 519; 536; 538; 552; 555; 573; British COS and, 577 & Note 117

Torpedoes:

1914–39:
in 1917 destroyers, 27 & Note 191 defects of British, 34 & Note 31; first sinking by airborne, 37; and U/Bs, 44; 74; significance in U/B war, 146–7; S/M ideal carrier, 194

1939–1945:
German 1939–40 crisis, 231–41; 1915–39 development, 234; characteristics, 234 Note 50; Norway failures, 235–7; nature of faults, 237–8; German Torpedo Organization, 239–40, 249; 1943 defects, FATs,

817

552–3 & Note 86; LUTs, 553 Note 87; FATs and HX 229, 564; expenditure against HX 229/SC 122, 588 Note 140: 'Mark 24 Mine', 618–19 & Note 10, 626, and *U 338*, 638 Note 44; FATs, 622–3, 626; see *Zaunkönig*; in two wars, 667–8; 759 Note 90

Torpex (explosive): in Depth Charges, 434; 437; in Mark X Charges, 599 & Note 167

Toulon: U/B base, 1944, 651

Trafalgar, Battle of, 1805: RN Signal No. 16, 33; crisis of, 85; 117; 158; 1943 for U/Bs, 400; Pound dies on Day, 1943, 570; 670

Training (RN): 190; inter-war lack of A/S, 266–8; A/S Schools, 275–6; see Tobermory; importance of tactical coherence, 276; WA 'Game', 307–8, 441; USN and ASW, 340; RCN lack, 381–2; see Prentice; vital importance of, 441; USN and doctrine, 453; WA, 501; *Philante* battle school, 502–3; Horton fanatical on, 503; 530–1; RCN escorts withdrawn for, 1943, 536–8; post-convoy conferences, 590 Note 148; 598 Note 162

Training (U/B): duration of, 190; *Adml* von Friedeburg and, 214 & Note 4; value of peacetime, 261; Werner on, 312

Transport and General Workers' Union: 302

Trinidad: 414; 421; 459; 'Interlocking System' terminal, 483; TS convoys, 483 Note 72; 500; TM 1 and, 514–15; 552

TRITON (SHARK) cipher: replaces *HYDRA*, Nov. 1941, 425; broken, Dec. 1942, 509–10; 526; BP and, 527–8 & Note 32; 556 Note 94; mastery of, 627 & Note 18

Trojer, *Korvettenkapitän*: *U 221*, 489–90; and *U 254* collision, 506–7; 551; 567

Tromsø: U/Bs ordered to, 1941, 409 Note 13

Trondheim: 347; U/Bs ordered to, 1941, 409 Note 13; U/Bs withdrawn to, 1944, 650

Troup, R/Adml J. A. J. (RN): DNI, 1937, 179

Tunisia: 479; 494; Allied advance in, 1943, 528; Axis resistance, 544, 556; 609

Turing, Alan (GC & CS): and *HYDRA*, develops Bombe, 323–4; 424–5; and 'Fish', 627 Note 19

Turkey: enters war, 1914, 162; buys U/B, 169

Typex Ciphering Machine: 181

Tyrwhitt, R/Adml Sir R. (RN): 58 Note 3

U

U-Boats (U/Bs): see Submarines, Torpedoes, ASW, Convoys

1914–18:
see HSF, Flanders Flotillas; numbers and categories, 17; types and characteristics, 19–21; conditions aboard, 22; increase in, 23; commanders' behaviour, 24, see *Schrecklichkeit*, 44 & Note 12, war criminals and 'aces', 45; diving time, 27; strength of hull, 28; 'unduly garrulous', 1917, 32; 'most formidable thing', 38; 1917 operations mainly off-shore, 41; numbers operational, April, May, 61; surprise at effect of convoy, 64; losses, new commissions, numbers, June, 65; 71; and aircraft, 77; losses and new commissions, Sept.–Dec., 86–7 & Notes 5, 6; sinkings a bonus, not necessity, 87; first sign of defeat, 87–90; change of tactics, 88; U-cruisers, 90–1 & Note 15; triumph in Mediterranean, 98–9; Sept.–Dec. losses, 99; move inshore, 100; 106; robust construction, 107; 1917 UC-losses, 107 Note 20; losses in Dover Straits, 1915–17, 108; 1918, 111; and Northern Barrage, 113–15; effect on RN strategy, 117–18; no dreadnought sunk by, 117; 1918 numbers, building programmes, losses, 118 & Note 34; turning-point of campaign, 119; and US buildup, 120; first 'pack' operation, May 1918, declining activity, 124; morale, losses, 127–8 & Note 51, 130; new orders, June 1918, 132; dying kicks, 132–3; attack on US East coast, 133–4, 195; resolute commanders, 135; final blows, 136–7; plan to attack Grand Fleet, Oct. 1918, 138; commanders undefeated and defiant, 140, 668; surrender, 141 & Note 1; total losses and casualties (causes of), 141–2; basic truths about, 142–3; effect of losses, 144–5; Tirpitz on, 145; performance in two wars, 146, 263; night surface attacks, 147; British attitude to, 1918, 161; Weddigen, 189 & Note 92; U/Bs 'fought alone', 192; 1917 sinkings by, 512; 1918 morale, 668–9

1918–39:
Versailles Treaty forbids, 154; no sense of defeat, 166; 1921 war studies, 167; revival, 168–9; Hitler orders building, 173; 1935 programme, Type VII, 175, 188; and air power, 183; 1930s neglect of, 186–7; Dönitz's faith in, 187–8; see Dönitz; 'Weddigen Flotilla', 1935–36 morale, 189–92; tactical control, Dönitz on, 190–4; types built, 1936–39, 195–8 & Note 99; Type IX, 196–7; Type VII compared with 1918, 197–8; officers, crew, conditions, 199–200; Dönitz demands 300, 1939, 205; entry into Atlantic, August, 206–7

1939–45:
see Training (U/B), Dönitz, Atlantic, Battle of the; Wilhelmshaven HQ, 213–15; unrestricted warfare returns, 217–18; paucity of, 218–19; slow production, 220–1; Sept. 1939 sinkings by, 221; and *Courageous*, 221–2; *U 47* in Scapa Flow, 222–4 & Note 32; Oct.–Dec. sinkings and losses, 225–6; long repair time, 226; high morale, Christmas 1939, 227; control problems, 228–9; Intelligence sources, 229; bond with Dönitz, 230; torpedo crisis, 231–41; Norwegian campaign, 235–7; losses to May 1940, and 1939 BEF deployment, 242; and northern passage, 250; 253; Biscay bases, 255–7; continuing dearth, 256; 'lack of eyes', 257; see *B-Dienst, xB-Dienst*; 'grey wolves', 'happy time', 261–2; first 'pack' actions, 262–4; revival of 1918 tactics, 263–4, Kernével HQ, 265; 'grey wolves' ' zenith, 265–8; U/B 'quotient', 270; numbering, 271; Nov. 1940 sinkings; losses to March 1941, morale, 272; 283; 293; 299; 300; continued dearth, training, 311–12; loss of 'grey wolves', 313–16; and W/T 321; capture of *U 110*; 344; April, May 1941 sinkings, 344; West Africa operations, 344 & Note 86; 345; and dock labour, 346–7; 1942 production, 348; Jan.–June 1941 losses, 350; attack on USS *Texas*, 350–1; and *BARBAROSSA*, 351–2; U/B war stagnating, 353; shelters, 354–5; and D/F 356–7; diversions, order to attack escorts, 358–9; Mediterranean, fundamental change of strategy,

359–62 & Note 16; inadequacy of HQ Staff, 363, 372; and SC 42, 373–81; sinkings of Allied warships, 1941, 382 Note 65; numbers operational, July–Dec. 1941, 387 Note 71; and SL 91 and HG 76, 395–9; 1941 failure, 399–401; Type IXC, 408–10 & Note 20; distribution, Jan. 1942, 409; second 'Happy Time', 410; US coast offensive, 412–13, 419; first quarter losses, 413; 417; Caribbean offensive, 420–3; Type XIV 'milch cows', 420; M/V sinkings in Caribbean and Gulf, 1942, 421; return to N. Atlantic, 423; effect of US campaign, 423–4; 4th rotor added to *Enigma*, 424; AA in, 1942, 432; losses from air action, 1942, 432–3; 435; diving ability, 437; 439; value of training, 441–2; height of powers, 442; HQ moves to Paris, 444 Note 1; 1942 quotients, 445; return to convoy routes, numbers, 446; June 1942 sinkings, 450; decoy tactics, 452; 453; S/M Tracking Room and, 455; strategic and tactical permutations, 459–60; Type IXD, 459 and Note 28; 462; final N. Atlantic campaign begins, 466 & Note 40; *Schrecklichkeit*, 466–75; National-Socialism and, 468; and bomber offensive, 470; *Laconia* incident, 471–5; air power and, 475; dilution, 1943, 478; *Metox* installed, 479; fighting on surface, 479–80, *U 441*, 630–3; Dönitz fears U/B 'will be crushed', Sept. 1942, 482; quotients, July–Sept., 482–3; Aug.–Sept. convoy operations, 484; numbers operational, Oct. 1942, 485; in S. Atlantic, 497–8; in N. Atlantic, 489–92; and Allied strategy, 496; withdraw from N. Atlantic, 1942, 497; Morocco operations, 497–9; Mediterranean losses, Nov.–Dec. 1942, 498 & Note 99; major defeat, 499; 504; Atlantic refuelling, 505; collision, 506–7; and ONS 154, 510–1; 1942 M/V sinkings, U/B losses, 512; bombing of Biscay bases, 1943, 516–17; Dönitz C-in-C Navy, 517–18; numbers operational, 523; 1943 security enquiry, 'trained incapacity', 525–7; short-signal weather code, 527; new strategic emphasis, 528–9; and SC 118, 530 & Note 40; and Intelligence, 532; 'milch cows', Feb.–March 1943, 534; numbers,

March 1943, 545; 550; 1943 torpedo defects, FATs, LUTs, 552–3 & Notes 86, 87; high peak, 553–76; and HX 229/SC 122 556–76; offensive morale, 561–2; threat to OVERLORD, 577; effect of Bay offensives, 582–3; and HX 230, 584; March 1943 losses, 584; 'vacuum' in N. Atlantic, expansion, 588; declining morale, 588–9; Dönitz demands 'healthy warrior instincts', 591–3; Freetown successes, April, 593; March–April losses, 593; April numbers (table), 594; and ONS 5, 595–8; collision, 597; return of *U 230*, May 1943, 600–5; deep diving, 602, 603, 604, 605; diving conditions, 604–5 & Note 172; Type VIIC 'best integrated maritime combat system', 605–6 & Note 173; May losses, 605, 608; losing 'most valuable characteristic', 607; Dönitz's exhortations, 607–8; Atlantic defeat, 608–13; rôle after defeat, 614–16; 1943 flotilla deployment, Appendix E; Types VII and IX obsolete, 616–17; Walter boats, Types XXI, XXIII, production schedule, 617–18, Speer and, 652–3; and 'Mark 24 Mine', 619 Note 10; and rocket-firing aircraft, 619–20; and Operation 'Plaster', 1944, 621–3; *Zaunkönig, Schnorchel*, 626–8; lack of 'eyes', 628 & Note 21; USN carriers and 'milch cows', 634 & Note 38; Operation MONSUN, 636; June–Aug. 1943 losses, 636; return to N. Atlantic, Sept., 636–40; and ONS 18/ON 202, 638–9; Sept.–Oct. losses, 640–1; Command becoming neurotic, 1943, 641; second Atlantic defeat, 641–2; 1943 losses, 642; OVERLORD fiasco, 642–7; numbers, Jan. 1944, 643; Dönitz's D-day Orders, 643–5; suicide attacks, 645; Brest Flotilla losses, 646; elimination of Biscay bases, 648–9; August massacre, 649; withdrawal to Norway, 649–50; losses against OVERLORD, 650; Mediterranean operations, 650–1; Japanese report on new U/Bs, 656 & Note 84; *Schnorchel* and Type VII inshore campaign, 656–8 & Note 86; 1945 production, 658; losses by bombing, 659– 60 & Note 92; Jan. 1945 sinkings and losses, 660–1; Type XXIII and XXI operations, 662; Type VII operations, 622–3; 1945 massacre, 663–4; and

US coast, 633 Note 99; surrender, 665–6; loyalty to Dönitz, 666; comparison of two wars, 666–7; effectiveness of packs, 666–7; weapons, 667–8; 1945 morale, 669; numbers built, sinkings, losses, casualties, 669 & Note 109; and Battle of Atlantic, 670; Dönitz and, 670–1; British attitude, 672–3; see Index of U-Boats

U-Boat Groups:

Adler: and ON 176, 591
Amsel: and ONS 5, 595 & Note 157, 596
Burggraf: and SC 121, 547
Delphin: and TM 1, 514–15
Dränger: and HX 229/SC 122, 556 ff & Note 95
Draufganger: and HX 217, 506
Drossel: and ONS 5, 595 & Note 157
Eisbär: 487–8
Fink: and ONS 5, 596–7
Haudegen: and ONS 165, 531–2
Hecht: and ONS 92, 446–8; and ONS 100, 102, 450–2
Jaguar: 524
Knappen: and ON 166, 532–3
Kreuzotter: and ONS 144, 505
Landwirt: and D-Day, 644, 646
Lerche: and HX 232, 519
Leuthen: and ONS 18/ON 202, 637–8
Lohs: and ONS 122, 484–5
Löwenherz: 588; and HX 231, 589–91
Meise: 588; 592
Mitte: 646–7
Mordbrenner: and SC 52, 394
Mosel: and HX 239, 607–8
Neuland: and HX 228, 550–52
Norden: and SC 42, 373–81
Ostmark: and SC 121, 550; 537
Panzer: and HX 217, 506
Pfeil: and SC 118, 529–30
Pirat: and ON 115, 465
Puma: and HX 212, 490
Raubgraf: and HX 228, HX 229/SC 122, 556 ff
Raubritter: and SC 52, 394–5 & Note 88
Reisswolf: and SC 52, 394
Rhein: and HX 237, 606
Ritter: and ON 166, 532–3
Rossbach (1943): 640
Schlagetod (1941): 394
Schlieffen (1943): 640

Seewolf (1945: 633 Note 99
Specht: 592; and ONS 5, 595–6 & Note 157
Spitz: and ONS 154, 510
Star: and ONS 5, 595 & Note 157
Steinbrink: and SC 94, 476–8
Stoerbrecker: 395
Stürmer: and HX 229/SC 122, 556 ff & Note 95
Trutz (1944): 634
Umgestum: and ONS 154, 510
Veilchen: and SC 107, 490–2 & Note 85
Vorwärts: and SC 97, 478; and ON 127, 485
Westmark: and SC 121, 550; 557
Wildfang: and SC 121, 547
Wolf: and ON 113, 461–2; and ON 115, 462–5
Wotan: and SC 104, 489–90
Xanthippe: and SL 125, 492–3
Uhlig, *Kapitänleutnant:* and *Mathew Luckenbach*, 568
ULTRA: see 'Y' Service, W/T, Bletchley Park, GC & CS, Sigint, *Enigma*; 139; 144; 265 Note 29; and 1941 U/B defeat, 400–1; USA and, 455–6; and evasive routing, 528
'Unconditional Surrender': see Casablanca Conference; origin, Feb. 1862, 513 Note 1; and anti-Nazi Germans, 522; 576; 614; 616; 642; 648; 666
Union of Soviet Socialist Republics (USSR): Soviets, 139; German trade missions, 1926, 168; Nazi–Soviet Pact, 1939, 186; 187 & Note 87; Hitler plans to attack, 219–20; and Finland, 282 Note 22; Germany attacks, June 1941, 351; first convoys to, 388 & Note 75; Moscow counteroffensive, 1941, 401; convoys suspended, Nov. 1942, 499; 1942 counter-offensive, 500; see Stalin, Stalingrad; 529; 584; convoys suspended, 1943, 585; and 'decisive victory', advance into E. Europe, 609; gaining strength in 1943, 642 & Note 56; 1944–45 Red Army advances, 658; Battle of Berlin, 664 & Note 100
United Nations: 387
United States of America (USA): Wars of Independence and of 1812; Civil War, 1861–65, 6, 8, 585; see 'Unconditional Surrender, Grant, Stuart

1914–18:
and *Lusitania*, 10; ultimatum to Germany, 11; Germany and war with, 12–13; declares war, 16; U/Bs off coast, 41; 42; 46; 70; shipbuilding, 1918, 86; and Northern Barrage, 92; U/B Coast offensive, 1918; 142, 195
1919–45:
and Peace Treaty, 156; and Japan, 157; see Naval Agreements; Neutrality Act, 277, 393; Lend-Lease Agreement, 279, 336; 'Security Zone', 336, 339, moves east, 341–2; and Iceland, 338–9 & Note 68; war policy, 339–44 & Note 69; 'Neutrality Zone', 339 & Note 71; see ABC-1; first ship sunk, 343; and *Bismarck*, 343; 345; 362; 371; and Canada, 388–9; *Greer* episode, Sept. 1941; 'reluctant rattlesnake', 390–2; public opinion, 391; declares war on Germany and Italy, Dec., 401; and ARCADIA Conference, 403–8 & Note 1; 'Germany First', 405–6 & Note 7, 609–10; E. Coast unpreparedness, 1942, 408–10 & Note 17; see USN; 1942–43 shipbuilding, 412 & Note 22; two-ocean war, 414; 418; and tanker shortage, 422; and French HF/DF, 438; 'hub' of Allied supply, 444–5; and Military Intelligence, 456 Note 20; and 'peripheral strategy', 494; and Anti-U-boat Warfare Cttee, 501; and VLR aircraft, 502; inter-Service rivalries, 515; and Mediterranean, 577; and 'Mark 24 Mine', 618–19; 4-wheel Bombes, 627; Liberty Ships, 629; warlike inventiveness, 661–2; 1945 U/B threat, 665 Note 99, 666; See Intelligence (US)
United States Army: see Marshall; slow 1917 deployment, 106; 1918 buildup, 120; on Western Front, 150; 1944 advances, 648; capture of Brest, 649 & Note 69; troopship sunk, 1944, 657 Note 88
United States Army Air Force (USAAF): demarcation with USN, 417–18; airfields, 418; 422; and *Laconia* survivors, 472–3; 540; 8th AAF, 578; Eaker Plan, 579–80; B-24 sqdns in GONDOLA, 581; 633; 651; and Battle of Hamburg, 653; 1945 attacks on Germany, 658; and massacre of U/Bs, 663–4

United States Coast Guard (USCG): Cutters, see Index of Warships (USN), Sloops (Banff Class); 1941 transfer to RN opposed, 340 & Note 76, 417; A/S successes, 1942, 418; in WA, 427, 488 Note 79; and SC 118, 530

United States Navy (USN): see Index of Warships, Index of Aircraft, King; blockade of Confederacy, 1861, 6

1917–18:
and convoys, 1917, 55; and escorts, 64 Note 16; destroyers at Queenstown, 74; in Mediterranean, 99; and Northern Barrage, 113–15; battleship sqdn with Grand Fleet, 116, 153, 159

1939–45:
see RAINBOW, ABC-1; Senate Naval Affairs Cttee., 278; see Atlantic Fleet; Atlantic activity, April 1941, 342; and *Bismarck*, 343; 344; and control of W. Atlantic, 388; *Greer* episode, 390–2; *Kearney* torpedoed, Oct. 1941, *Reuben James* sunk, Oct., 393; 'not enough navy to go round', 394; and SC 52, 394 Note 88; Pearl Harbor damage, 404 & Note 25; 1942 unpreparedness, 410–1; and RN ASW lesson, 413–14 & Note 25; Sea Frontiers, length of shipping lanes, 414; 'Bucket Brigades', 414–17; 'Donald Duck Navy', first successes, 418–19; Marshall/King correspondence, 422–3; escort shortage, 427–8; CTF-24 and W. Atlantic, 434; withdrawal from N. Atlantic, two-ocean war, 434–5; and ON 67, 439; 'Mousetrap', 441; and training, 441–2; Pacific preoccupation, 440–50; ASW failings, 453 & Note 14; need for OIC equivalent, 455–9; Winn and, 457–9; Op 20 (F. 21) created, 458–9; 'Interlocking' convoy system established, 483–4; see Landing Craft; and Convoy Conference, March 1943, 535–44; CTF-24 and A/S Intelligence, RCN resentment, 536–8; sheds N. Atlantic responsibility, 538; Moroccan Sea Frontier, 538 & Note 58; *Bogue* characteristics, 539 Note 61; and B-24s, 1943, 540; Convoy and Routing Section, 550 & Note 79; diverts SC 122, 557; 573; and *U 657*, 619; and CCM, 628; Tenth Fleet formed, 634 & Note 39; carriers and

milch cows, 634–5; 'MADCATS' at Gibraltar, 661; 'Barrier Force', 1945, 663 Note 99; sinkings by U/Bs, 699 Note 109

USN Air Squadrons:
VP-74: sinks *U 158*, 419
VP-82: sinks *U 656*, 418
VP-84: inks *U 611*, 507

Unrestricted Submarine Warfare: start of, 1916, 8–9; decision to declare, 15–17; formal declaration, Feb. 1 1917, 22; reasons for timing, 23–4; immediate success, 40; passes peak, 46; 'crunch', 47–8; 70; no 'victory before harvest', 80; first year of, 106; failure, 119; and pack actions, 120–3; ends, 137; assessment, 145–7; 'unrestricted industrial technology' and, 146; return, 1939, 217 ff *passim*; nature revealed, 671

V

'Valentin': bomb-proof U/B factory, 1944, 654
Valentiner, *Korvettenkapitän* Max: cruel reputation, 44; warns of torpedo defects, 1937, 239–40
Verdun, Battle of, 1916: 3; 14
Versailles, Treaty of, 1919: 150; naval terms, 154; 156; German Navy and, 166; 167; opposition to, 168; 172; Hitler denounces, 1935, 174, 186; 185
Vienna: Red Army enters, 1945, 663
Vimy Ridge: storming of, 1917, 46
VLR (Very Long Range) aircraft: maritime need for, 271; and Atlantic 'Gap', 345; 365–6; and 'Battle of the Air', 429; 434; A. V. Alexander on, 501; Horton and, 502; flight durations, 506; priority unresolved, 515; King and, 539–40; and HX 229/SC 122, 566; and maritime warfare, 567; Harris and, 578; 637
Volga, River: Germans reach, 424
V-Weapons: 481

W

WACIS: 228; 429
Waddington, Prof. C. H. (FRS): and Operational Research, 368
Wake Is.; Japanese at, 404

Walker, Capt. F. J. (RN): and HG 76, 396–9; 437; and *U 252*, 441; and 'two-tier' escorts, 586–7; and Operation 'Plaster', 621–3; death, 623–4; and GNAT, 640

Walkerling, *Kapitänleutnant*: and HX 229, 564

Wallace, Cdr. D. C. (RCNR): SOE, ON 115, 462–3

Walter, Prof. H.: and new U/B, 617–18 & Note 8

Wanze: see *Hagenuk*

War Office: difference from Admlty, 66; 68

Washington, DC: 339 Note 71; RCN attaché in, 389; ARCADIA Conference, 403–8 & Note 1; 'Battle of', 515; conferences, 517; Convoy Conference, March 1943, 535–44; OIC, 539; 563; 610

Washington Treaties (1921–22): 157–8 & Note 12; Japan repudiates, 1934, 173; 185 Note 84

Waterloo, Battle of, 1815: 85

Watson-Watt, Sir R.: and radar, 184; and HF/DF, 438

Weapons: see ASDIC, Barrages, Bofors guns, Bombs, Depth Charges, FOXER, Hedgehog, Hydrophones, Indicator Loops, Oerlikon Guns, *Pillenwerfer*, Radar, *Schnorchel*, Squid, Torpedoes, *Zaunkönig*; howitzer, 1917, 28 & Note 22, 147; 1916–18 development, 145; Browning guns, 181; Mousetrap, 441; rockets, 619–20; 57-mm gun, 620; HS 293A, FX 1400 glider bombs, 633 & Note 36; bombing aids, 654–5; MAD, retrobombs, sonobuoy, 661–2

Weather: N. Sea, 1917, 93–5; Baltic frozen, 1939–40, 234; see Atlantic Ocean, 'Steep Atlantick'; wind Force 8, 262; gale, 266; 1940–41 storms, 274; 287; fog, 293; 'frozen malice', 1940–41, 300; spring, 1941, 327; St. John's winter, 334–5; Oct. 1941, 393; 'macabre & desolate winter', 395; June 1942 gales, 450; and ON 113, 462; fog and SC 94, 476; winter, 1942–43, 486, 508; Oct. 1942, 489; Nov. 1942 storm, 505; Dec., 507; 510; Atlantic winds and waves, Jan. 1943, 523–4 & Note 25; and ONS 165, 531; and ON 166, 533; March 1943, 546; wind Force 11, 547, Force 10, 530; and HX 229/SC 122, 554–76; sea states, 'pooping', 558–61; and *U 653*, 561;

ice comes south, 1943, 563; March hurricane, 583; and HX 231, 590; and ONS 5, 'full range of effects', 594–9

Weddigen, *Leutnant* O.: 189–90 & Note 92

Weedon: birthplace of British radar, 183–4

Wehr, *Konteradmiral*: at Torpedo Test Institute, 239–40

Welchman, G.: and GC & CS, 322–3; 357

Wemyss, Adml. Sir R. (RN): Deputy First Sea Lord, 73–4; First Sea Lord, and George V, 103; 138; 154 Note 3

Werner, *Korvettenkapitän* H.: on U/B conditions, 200; on training, 312; and loss of 'aces', 316; on Atlantic weather, 1943, 523–4; and *U 230*'s return to Brest, May 1943, 600–5; and sinking of *U 847*, 635; 'smell of death everywhere', 641; on Dönitz's 'suicide order', 645

West, Cdr. A.G. (RN): and HX 231, 590

Western Approaches (WA):

1914–18:

'cones of approach', 41–2; 'cemetery of British shipping', 47; 61; 64; 69; US destroyers in, 74; U/Bs abandon, 1917, 100–1; Dover route to, 108; pack operations in, May 1918, 121–3

1939–45:

see Dunbar-Nasmith, Noble, Horton, Stephenson, Liverpool, Derby House; 271; SW Approaches abandoned, 1940; HQ at Plymouth, 275 & Note 1, 278; destroyers available for, Nov. 1940, 280; 282–3; Convoy Instructions (WACIS), 1941, 288, 449, 610; 'the Game', 307–8; and Iceland, 337; 344; and HX 133/OB 336, 349–50; 363; and NEF, 1941, 388; 1942 strength, 427; and Atlantic control, 435; criticism of RCN, 448–9, 465–6; staff, WRNS, escorts, 1942, 501; *Philante* battle school, 502–3; 523; 532; and RCN difficulties, 536–7; Operational Research, 539; and HX 229/SC 122, 1943, 563; 573; and Support Groups, 584–7; and ONS 5, 595; training, 598 Note 162; strength, Jan. 1943, 599 & Note 164; death of Walker, 623–4; and NEPTUNE, 645; SW Approaches reopened, 650 & Note 71; strength, Jan. 1945, 660; U/Bs surrender, 669

Western Front 1914–18: 3; '*Materialschlacht*', 14; German defeat, 1914–16,

15–6; British forces, 49; Americans on, 106; German 1918 offensives, 119; German defeat, 1918, 130; U/Bs powerless to affect, 150; 561
Western Local Support Force (WLEF) 547 Note 77; 557
Western Support Force, 1942: 547 & Note 77; 555; 558
Western Ocean Meeting Point (WOMP): 336; 554–5
Wight, Isle of: 646
Wilamowitz-Möllendorf, *Korvettenkapitän*: U 459, 420
Wilhelm II, *Kaiser*: C-in-C, 4 Note 3; and S/M blockade, 1914, 9; changes mind, 15; and *Reichstag*, 82; 185
Wilhelmshaven: July 1917 mutiny, 83; 138–9; Dönitz at, 1930, 170; 206; U/B HQ in, 213–14 & Note 5; Hitler visits, 1939, 219–21; 232; 663
Wilkinson, Leading Seaman (RN): ASDIC proficiency, 624 Note 14
Williams, Prof. E. J. (FRS): and Operational Research, 368
Wilmington, NC: 414
Wilson, Pres. W.: and U/B sinkings, 11; and 1917 election, 14–15; 61; Oct. 1918 protest at U/B sinkings, 136–7
Windeyer, Lt.-Cdr. G. (RCN): and 'hot seat', 350; and ON 115, 463; and ONS 154, 510–1
Winn, Capt. R. (RNVR): and S/M Tracking Room, 319–21 & Note 23; and BP, 327; see 'Working Fiction'; in USA, 1942, 457–9; 461; 'sixth sense', 487–8; and Dönitz, 503–4; and Horton, 504; collapse, Dec. 1942, 509 & Note 21; return, 526; and U/B morale, 588–9 & Note 145, 591–2; 596; and Atlantic victory, 608; and D-Day U/B plans, 643; and new U/Bs, 656
Winter, *Korvettenkapitän* W.: see Appendix E
Wintour, Lt.-Cdr. (FAA): death, 395–6
Wireless Telegraphy (W/T):
1914–18:
   30–3; decryption and D/F, 31; *E-Dienst*, 32; 1917 German transmitter range, 'garrulous' U/Bs, 32; intercepts, 93; value of silence, 97; jamming, 97 Note 24; *U 70*

signals, 106–7; and U/B packs, 1918, 120–3; see R/T; still unreliable, 143
1918–45:
   'wireless war', 183 & Note 76; U/B dependence on 192; see D/F, HF/DF, *Enigma*, Sigint, BP, HYDRA, TRITON, MEDUSA, TETIS; and U/B command system, 228–30; British codes penetrated, pre-war, 256–7; 1940 rôle, 258; British radio industry, 284–5; and convoys, 289–90; 321; German 'Short Signals', 'Home Waters' cipher, 326 & Note 40; and propaganda, 390; N. Atlantic reception, 394, 524; *BdU* prisoner of, GC & CS and, 526; excessive use by U/Bs, April 1943, 591; effect of silence, 656
Witzell, Adml. K.: 203
Women's Royal Naval Service (WRNS): and Atlantic Plot, 305 & Note 59; at Derby House, 501
Woods Hole Oceanographic Institute, Mass.: and BT, 657 Note 86
Woodward, D.: 644
'Working Fiction': 454–9; 484; 510; 525
World War I: turning-point, 3; 33; and World War II, 41; 50; High Commands in, 57; innovations in, 57–8; technology and, 108; highest monthly U/B loss (cf 1943), 123; Armistice, 140–1; ASW reasoning clarified, 148; main front, 150; War Debts and Reparations, 154 & Note 4; 'no voice control', 183; 187; 193; command in, 228; ASW lesson, 245–6; Sigint and, 322; 361; 367; U/B diving ability, 437; rescue ships, 439; 'command of sea' echo, 1942, 442; difference between Services, 449; 1917 worst year, 511; 561; relearning lessons of, 583; GHQ predicts German collapse, 588 Note 145; strength of BEF, 612; comparison of two wars, 666–73
World War II: Sigint, 32; 55; 62; balloons in, 78; 80; 93; and barrages, 116; 1941 U/B tactics, 120; highest monthly U/B loss (cf 1918), 123; and hunting groups, 127; US taken by surprise, 1942, 134; 150; hindsight, 154; and W/T tactical control, 183; outbreak, 214; command in, 228; and Sigint, 322; turning-point, 351, 433; 439; generals, 500 Note 101; personalizations irrelevant, 504; 1942 worst year, 512; coali-

tion, 544; 'getting harder all the time', 584; 'schwerpunkt', 1943, 609; NW Europe Allied total, 612; comparison of two wars, 666–73
Wright Brothers: 58; 158

X

xB-Dienst: 215; and RN ciphers, 257; 264; and Naval Cipher No. 3, 426–7; and convoy routes, 446; 454; 489, and re-routing signals, sitreps, 1943, 527; 532; defeated by CCM, 628

Y

'Y' (Listening) Service: origins, 31; intercepts, 93, 96; 107; 1091 and Northern Barrage, 113–15; and U/B packs, 1918, 120–3; and HSF mutiny, 138–9; and Sigint, 322, 496 Note 97
Yalta Conference, 1945: 517
Ypres, Third Battle of, 1917: 69

Yucatan Channel: 414
Yugoslavia: German conquest, 342

Z

'Z' Fleet: plan, 204–6; abandoned, 220; 295; Hitler and, 1943, 518, Dönitz and, 518–19; 652
Zahn, Kapitänleutnant: reports torpedo failure, 1939, 232
Zapp, Korvettenkapitän R.: see Appendix E
Zaunkönig (T5; GNAT) acoustic torpedo: 626; and ONS 18/ON 202, 637–40 & Note 47; and FOXER, 639–40; 641
Zeebrugge: U/B exit port, 1915–18, 17–19; 69–71; 91 Note 16; U 70 returns to, 106–7; Raid on, 1918, 111–12
Zeppelins: L 59 over Khartoum, 1917, 32; RNAS attacks on, 1914, 36–7; L 54, L 60 destroyed, 159
Zulu assegai: and Type XXI U/B, 667 Note 105
Zurmuhlen, Kapitänleutnant: and HX 229, 564
Zygalsky, H.: and Enigma, 323

Index of Aircraft

Luftwaffe

1914–18:

Gothaer Wagonfabrik G IV, G V bomber: attacks on London, 1917, 48

1939–45:

Blohm & Voss BV 222 flying-boat: 628 Note 21

Dornier Do 18 flying-boat: 246

Do 217E-5 bomber: and HS 293A glider bomb, 633; 217K-2 and FX 1400 (*Fritz*) glider bomb, 633 Note 36

Focke-Wulf 200C-1 recce bomber ('**Condor**'): 259–60; Achilles' Heel, 260; and *Empress of Britain*, 269–70; 293; 299; 308; *KG 40* under Dönitz, 312–3; and HG 53, 313; 358 Note 13; 366; 383; and HG 73, 384; and OG 74, 386; and SL 91, 395–8; 628 Note 21

Heinkel He 111 bomber: 308

Heinkel He 177V heavy bomber: 259; Dönitz demands, 1942, 481; 628 Note 21

Junkers Ju 88C6 bomber etc.: as L/R fighter in Bay, 432; 479; 631; 633

Ju 290B transport: 628 Note 21

see Zeppelins

Royal Flying Corps (RFC), Royal Naval Air Service (RNAS), Royal Air Force (RAF)

1914–18:

Admiralty Type 135 seaplane: Cuxhaven raid, 1914, 35–7

Avro 504: attack on Friedrichshafen, 1914, 36 & Note 36

Blackburn Kangaroo 125

Curtiss H-12 ('Large America') flying-boat: in RNAS, 1917, 37; in 'Spider Web', 74

sinks *UB 32*, 77; convoy escort, 79; see Porte

De Havilland DH 6 trainer, A/S patrol: 125

Felixstowe F 2A flying-boat, 1917, 37

'Folder' seaplane: Cuxhaven raid, 1914, 36–7

Short Type 74 seaplane: Cuxhaven raid, 36–7

Type 184 seaplane: 'mainstay of A/S patrol', 37

Sopwith Tabloid: attacks Dusseldorff Zeppelin sheds, 36

1½ Strutters, Pups, Triplanes, 78

Camels, 78; attack Tondern, 1918, 159

Cuckoo torpedo bomber, 1917, 159

Vickers Vimy bomber: Atlantic crossing, 1919, 159

see Airships

RAF, FAA 1939–45:

Armstrong-Whitworth Whitley bomber: 276; for Coastal Command, 283, 429; patrol endurance, 365–6 & Note 28; and *U 206*, 371–2

Avro Anson GR etc.: 125; characteristics, 246; 365 Note 28

Lancaster L/R bomber: 429

Boeing Flying Fortress (B-17) L/R bomber: 429; and HX 217, 507; 530; 568 Note 104; 584; 594

Bristol Beaufighters: 365 & Note 28; in Coastal Command, 479; and *U 441*, 632; 646; 664

Beaufort torpedo bomber: 346 Note 88, 365 & Note 28

Blenheim bomber, fighter, GR: 365 Note 28

Consolidated Catalina (RCN 'Canso'; PBY-5) L/R flying boat: see USN; and *U 570*, 364; 365; patrol endurance, 366 & Note 31; 428; 597; 664

Liberator (B-24) bomber: see VLR aircraft, USAAF, USN; 365 & Note 28; 120 Sqdn and, 1942, 429 & Note 57; with SCR 571 radar, 461 Note 32; and SC 94, Aug. 1942, 477–8; 480; contrast with He 177, 481; and SC 104, 489–90; and HX 217, 506; '*prima donna*', 523; transforms HX 229/SC 122 battle, March 1943; modifications for VLR rôle, 566; performances, 566–7; 582; 590; 592; 600; 618 & Note 10; 637; 638 & Note 44; 646; with 'Mark 24 Mine'/ sonobuoy combination, 662

De Havilland Mosquito bomber, fighter, PR etc.: Mark VI rocket-firing, 619 & Note 12; Mark XVIII, 57-mm gun, 620; 646; 664

Douglas Digby (B-18) bomber, maritime patrol (RCAF): 491 & Note 88

Empire Flying Boat: 365 Note 28

Fairey Battle bomber: in Coastal Command, 283; in Iceland, 338

Fulmar carrier-borne fighter (FAA): 383–4

Swordfish torpedo bomber, GR etc.: 37; 365 Note 28; and *U 230*, 602 & Note 171; rockets in, 619 & Note 11

Grumman Avenger torpedo bomber & A/S strike aircraft (FAA; TBF-1): 646

Martlet carrier-borne fighter (FAA; F4F-3): and OG 74, 385–6 & Note 69; and OG 76/HG 76, 395–9

Wildcat carrier-borne fighter (FAA; F4F-4): and *U 752*, 619

Handley Page Halifax L/R bomber: 366; 582; 646

Hampden bomber: 276

Hawker Hurricane fighter: 365 & Note 28; Sea-, 384

Typhoon rocket-firing fighter-bomber: in Baltic, 1945, 619; 664

Lockheed Hudson bomber and GR (PBO-1, A-29): in Coastal Command, 246; and ASV, 283; in Iceland, 338; captures *U 570*, 364–6; 479; 480; RCAF sinks *U 658*, 491; and HX 217, 507; 593

Northrop N3P-B seaplane: in Iceland, 338; 365 Note 28

Saro London flying-boat: 246

Short Sunderland L/R flying-boat: characteristics, 246; 262; and U/Bs, 263; and SC 7, 266; 271; 283; in Iceland, 338; 120 Sqdn, 366; 429; 480; 568 Note 104; 646

Supermarine Seafire carrier-borne fighter: 602 Note 171

Spitfire Mark IV (PR): 365 & Note 28

Stranraer flying-boat: 246

Vickers Vildebeest torpedo bomber: 246

Vickers Wellington bomber: 276; 365 & Note 28; patrol endurance, 366; 429; and Leigh Light, 431–2; fight with AA U/B, 1942, 480; 172 Sqdn sinks *U 665*, *U 376*, 582; 646; 657

USAAF, USN

1914–18:

Curtiss H-12 'Large America' flying-boat: see RNAS

1939–45:

Boeing B-17 L/R bomber: see RAF, Flying Fortress

Consolidated PBY-5 L/R flying-boat: see RAF, Catalina; 417–18; and SC 97, 478; 507; 547; and 'Mark 24 Mine', 619; 'Madcats', 661

B-24 (PB4Y-1) VLR bomber: see RAF, Liberator, 417; and *Laconia* survivors, 472–3 & Note 49; 481; 507; Pacific and, 515; production of, 539–40; USAAF in GONDOLA, 581; 633; 646

Douglas B-18 bomber: see RAF, Digby

Grumman TBF-1 torpedo bomber and A/S strike: see FAA, Avenger; in *Bogue*, 539 Note 61, 602 Note 171; 634

F4F-4 carrier-borne fighter: see FAA Wildcat; in *Bogue*, 539 Note 61, 602 Note 171; 634

F6F-1 carrier-borne fighter (Hellcat): 602 Note 171

Lockheed PBO-1, A-29 bomber and GR: see RAF, Hudson; first USN A/S successes, 418

Martin PBM flying-boat (Mariner): 418; sinks *U 158*, 419

Vought V-166B carrier-borne fighter-bomber (Corsair): 602 Note 171

Index of Main Trade Convoys

HG (Gibraltar–UK, 1939–42)
HG 53, Feb. 1941: Condors and, 313
HG 73, Sept. 1941: 382–5; 571
HG 76, Dec. 1941: U/B defeat, 396–9; 437
HG 84, June 1942: 450
HX (Halifax–UK, 1939–42, New York–UK, 1942–45)
HX 72, Sept. 1940: 263
HX 79, Oct. 1940, 268
HX 79A, Oct. 1940, 268
HX 84, Nov. 1940: *Jervis Bay* and, 295–6
HX 89, Nov. 1940: 296
HX 90, Dec. 1940: 272
HX 106, Feb. 1941: 297
HX 112, March 1941: 314–16
HX 126, April 1941: heavy losses, 345; 348
HX 133, June 1941: 348–50; 354
HX 150, Sept. 1941: USN escort, 392 & Note 83
HX 156, Oct. 1941: and USS *Reuben James*, 393
HX 175, Feb. 1942: 389
HX 212, Oct. 1942: 490
HX 217, Dec. 1942: 505–8
HX 222, Jan. 1943: 524
HX 224, Feb. 1943: 524, 529
HX 225, Feb. 1943: 531
HX 226, Feb. 1943: 531
HX 228, March 1943: 550–2; 553
HX 229, March 1943: 546; 553–76; 588; 638 Note 44
HX 229A, March 1943: 554–76
HX 230, March 1943: 584
HX 231, April 1943: 584
HX 231, April 1943: 586; 588; 589–91; 600

HX 232, April 1943: 590–1
HX 233, April 1943: 590–1
HX 234, April 1943: 590; 592
HX 235, April 1943: 595
HX 236, May 1943: 600
HX 237, May 1943: 600–1
HX 238, May 1943: 600
HX 239, May 1943: 600; 607–8; 619
HX 277, Feb. 1944: EG 2 and, 623
HXF 1, Sept. 1939: fast, 244
OA (Thames outward, 1939–40)
OA 1, Sept. 1939: 244
OB (Liverpool outward, 1939–41, then ON)
OB 288, Feb. 1941: 313
OB 290, Feb. 1941: losses by Condors, 313
OB 293, March 1941: 313–14
OB 336, June 1941: 348–50
OG (UK–Gibraltar, 1939–43)
OG 74, Sept. 1941: *Audacity* and, 385–6; 571
OG 76, Nov. 1941: U/B defeat, 395–6
OG 82, April 1942: 441
ON (UK–N. America, 1941–)
ON 26, Oct. 1941: 394
ON 67, Feb. 1942: rescue ship with HF/DF, 439; 441; 449; 530
ON 113, July 1942: 461–2 & Note 35
ON 115, July 1942: 462–5
ON 127, Sept. 1942: 485; 536
ON 137, Oct. 1942: 490
ON 138, Oct. 1942: 490
ON 139, Oct. 1942: 490; 492
ON 164, Feb. 1943: 531
ON 166, Feb. 1943: 532–4 & Note 46

ON 176, April 1943: 591
ON 184, May 1943: 600; 608
ON 202, Sept. 1943: 637–8
ONS (UK–Halifax, slow, 1941–)
ONS 92, May 1942: 447–9; 452
ONS 96, May–June 1942: 450
ONS 100, June 1942: 450–1
ONS 102, June 1942: 450–2; differing RN,
   USN views, 453
ONS 122, Aug.–Sept. 1942: 484–5
ONS 144, Nov. 1942: 505; 508
ONS 154, Dec. 1942: 510–11; 537–8; 571
ONS 165, Feb. 1943: 531–2; 534
ONS 167, Feb. 1943: 532; 534
ONS 169, Feb.–March 1943: 'peaceful pas-
   sage', 546–7; 553
[renumbering of ONS series, March 15]
ONS 1, March 1943: 584
ONS 3, April 1943: 592
ONS 4, April 1943: 592
ONS 5, April–May, 1943: 'triumph within
   tragedy', 594–9; 600
ONS 18, Sept. 1943: 637–8
OS (UK–West Africa)
OS 33, July 1942: 460–1
OS 44, July 1942: 461
SC (Sydney, NS–UK, 1940–)
SC 2, Sept. 1940: 262–3
SC 7, Oct. 1940: 265–8; 288; 448
SC 26, April 1941: 344
SC 42, Sept. 1941: 372–82 & Notes 50, 54;
   571
SC 44, Sept. 1941: 382
SC 48, Oct. 1941: 393 & Note 86; 394
SC 52, Nov. 1941: only convoy driven back,
   394–5 & Note 88
SC 94, Aug. 1942: 476–8
SC 97, Aug. 1942: 478; 571
SC 104, Oct. 1942: 489–90; 505; 531
SC 107, Oct.–Nov. 1942: 490–2; 571
SC 117, Jan. 1943: 524
SC 118, Feb. 1943: 529–31
SC 119, Feb. 1943: 531
SC 121, March 1943: 546; 547–50; 553; 556;
   571

SC 122, March 1943: 546; 553–76; 588; 638
   Note 44
SC 123, March 1943: 584
SC 127, April 1943: 595
SC 128, April 1943: 595
SC 129, May 1943: 600
SC 130, May 1943: 600; 607
SL (Sierra Leone–UK, Sept. 1939–)
SL 81, July 1941: 358 Note 13
SL 87, Sept. 1941: 382–3
SL 91, Nov. 1941: 395–6
SL 125, Oct.–Nov. 1942: and TORCH con-
   voys: 492–3; 499
SL 126, March 1943: 499
SL 147, Jan.–Feb. 1944: 622
SL 167/MKS 58, Aug. 1944: return to SW
   Approaches, 650 Note 71

Miscellaneous:
GAT/TAG   (Guantanamo–Trinidad,
   Trinidad–Guantanamo), Aug. 1942–: 483
   Note 72
GN/NG (Guantanamo–New York, New
   York–Guantanamo), Aug. 1942–: 484
GU (S & F; military, North Africa–USA),
   Nov. 1942: GUS 7A, 634
KMF (military, UK–North Africa), Oct.
   1942: KMF 11, 560
KMS (N. Africa–UK), Oct. 1943: KMS 10,
   549; 573
KN/NK (Key West–New York, New
   York–Key West), May 1942: 484
KX (TORCH, UK–N. Africa), Oct. 1942: 499
TM (tanker, Trinidad–Gibraltar), Jan.
   1943: TM 1, 514–15
TS (Takoradi–Sierra Leone), Aug. 1942–:
   TS 37, April–May 1943, 593
UGF (USA–N. Africa, fast), Oct. 1942–:
   UGF 6, March 1943, 549
UGS (USA–N. Africa, slow), Oct. 1942–:
   UGS 6, March 1943, 549
WS (military, UK–Middle East), June
   1940–: WS 5A, Dec. 1940, 297
XK (TORCH special, Gibraltar–UK), Oct.
   1942–: XK 2, 549, 573; XK 3, 560

Index of Merchant Vessels (M/Vs)

1914–18:

Alnwick Castle, liner: sunk March 1917, 41–4

Amiral Ganteaume, packet: sunk Oct. 1914, 671

Chieftain, trawler (Auxiliary Patrol): 95

Denbigh Hall, freighter: sunk May 1918, 122

Glitra, freighter: sunk Oct. 1914, 44 Note 12

Hiramo Maru, freighter: sunk Oct. 1918, 136–7

Hurunui, freighter: sunk May 1918, 122

Justicia, liner: sunk July 1918, 132–3

Leinster, mail boat: sunk Oct. 1918, 136–7; 672

Lusitania, liner: sunk May 1915, 10–11; 216

Olympic, troopship: 121

Oyama, trawler (Auxiliary Patrol): 95

San Andrew, freighter: sunk May 1918, 121

Scholar, freighter: sunk May 1918, 122

Sir John French, trawler (Auxiliary Patrol): 95

Sussex, Channel packet: sunk March 1916, 11

Swallow, trawler (Auxiliary Patrol), 95

William Tennant, trawler (Auxiliary Patrol): 95

1939–45:

Athenia, liner: sunk Sept. 1939, 215–17; 315; 326 Note 39; 672

Avoceta, freighter: Commodore's ship, HG 73, sunk Sept. 1941, 383–4

Baron Pentland, freighter: and SC 42, sunk Sept. 1941, 376 & Note 56

Berury, freighter: and SC 42, sunk Sept. 1941, 380

Brant County, freighter: and HX 228, sunk March 1943, 551

Bulysse, freighter: and SC 42, sunk Sept. 1941, 379

Bury, freighter: ONS 92 rescue ship with HF/DF, 447

City of Waterford, collier: and OG 74, sunk by collision, 386

Clarissa Radcliffe, freighter: and SC 122, disappearance March 1943, 558; 567–8; 571

Cordelia, tanker: survivor betrays SC 118, Feb. 1943, 529

Duchess of Atholl, liner (troopship): sunk Oct. 1942, 488

Elin K., freighter: and HX 229, sunk March 1943, 564, 574

Empire Crossbill, freighter: and SC 42, sunk Sept. 1941, 380

Empire Hudson, CAM ship: and SC 42, sunk Sept. 1941, 377

Empire Shackleton, freighter: Commodore's ship, ONS 154, sunk Dec. 1942, 511

Empire Springbuck, freighter: and SC 42, sunk Sept. 1941, 376

Empress of Britain, liner (troopship): sunk Oct. 1940, 269–70

Ewart Ruthledge, transport: sunk Nov. 1942, 498

Garm, freighter: and SC 42, sunk Sept. 1941, 380

Gothland, freighter: ONS 169 rescue ship, 547

831

Gypsum Queen, freighter: and SC 42, sunk Sept. 1941, 379
Hugh L. Scott, transport: sunk Nov. 1942, 498
Irénée du Pont, freighter: and HX 229, sunk March 1943, 564
Jamaica, freighter: 549
Laconia, liner (troopship): sunk Sept. 1942, 471–5; 487
Leopoldville, troopship: sunk Dec. 1944, 657 Note 88
Mathew Luckenbach, freighter: romps from HX 229, sunk March 1943, 567–8; 571; 574 & Note 113
Muneric, freighter: and SC 42, sunk Sept. 1941, 375
Nariva, refrigerated ship: and HX 229, sunk March 1943, 564
Orcades, liner (troopship): sunk Oct. 1942, 488
Oronsay, liner (troopship): sunk Oct. 1942, 488
Patrick Henry: first 'Liberty Ship', 629
Perth, freighter: ONS 144 rescue ship with HF/DF, 505
Radchurch, freighter: and SC 94, sunk Aug. 1942, 477 & Note 57
Regin, freighter: and SC 42, 377
Robin Moor, freighter: sunk May 1941 (first US casualty), 343
Sally Maersk, freighter: and SC 42, sunk Sept. 1941, 377
Scania, freighter: and SC 42, sunk Sept. 1941, 380

Scottish Heather, tanker: and ONS 154, 510
Selfoss, freighter: and SC 122, 558
Southern Princess, tanker: and HX 229, sunk March 1943, 564
Stargaard, freighter: and SC 42, sunk Sept. 1941, 377
Stockport, freighter: SC 107 rescue ship with HF/DF, 491
Stonepool, freighter: and SC 42, sunk Sept. 1941, 380
Strathallan, liner/troopship: sunk Dec. 1942, 498
Svend Foyn, whaler: and HX 229A, sunk by ice, March 1943, 563
Tahchee, tanker: and SC 42, Sept. 1941, 376
Tasker H. Bliss, transport: sunk Nov. 1942, 498
Thistleglen, freighter: Vice-Commodore's ship, SC 42, sunk Sept. 1941, 378
Throrstrand, freighter: 549
Toward, freighter: ON 67 rescue ship with HF/DF, Feb. 1942, 439; sunk Feb. 1943, 530
Walmer Castle, liner: and OG 74, sunk by Condor, Sept. 1941, 386
Warwick Castle, liner/troopship: sunk Nov. 1942, 498
Winterswijk, freighter: and SC 42, sunk Sept. 1941, 377
Zaanland, refrigerated ship: and HX 229, sunk March 1943, 574

Index of U-Boats

1914–18:
U 1: (1907) 19
U 8: 108
U 9: (Weddigen) 189 Note 92
U 17: first M/V sinking, 44 Note 12
U 23 class: 19
U 24 and unrestricted warfare, 67 1
U 27 class: 19
U 28: 86 Note 6
U 29: 189 Note 92
U 31 class: 19; 20
U 32: 56 Note 6
U 35: 19
U 37: 108
U 38: 44; 239
U 39: 20; Dönitz in, 163
U 42: 20 Note 3
U 43 class: 20; 121
U 45: 86 Note 6
U 46: 121
U 49: 86 Note 6
U 50: 95
U 55: 44; 121–2
U 60: 113
U 66: 86 Note 6; 95–6
U 69: 78
U 70: 106–7; 121–2; 124
U 78: 139
U 81 class: 20
U 82: 135
U 86: 113–15; 121
U 88: 86 Note 6
U 92: 121
U 93: 20
U 94: 121–2

U 99: 20
U 103: 121
U 105: 197–8
U 106: 95–6
U 117: 133
U 135: 139
U 139: 135–6; 160
U 140: 133
U 151 class: 91 Note 15; 120
U 156: 133
Bremen: 91 Note 15
Deutschland: 91 Note 15
UB 1 class: 20
UB 18 class: 20
UB 20: 76; 107 Note 7
UB 29: 108
UB 32: sunk by aircraft, 77; 86 Note 6
UB 41: 96; 99
UB 48 class: 21
UB 50: 140
UB 55: 112
UB 56: 108; 110
UB 57: 135
UB 64: 132–3
UB 68: Dönitz and, 161; 163–4
UB 72 class: 21; 121; 123
UB 87: 135
UB 88 class: 21
UB 116: 138–9; 142
UB 124: 133
UC 1: 76; 107 Note 7
UC 6: 86 Note 6; 107 Note 7
UC 14: 107 Note 7
UC 16 class: 21; 107 Note 7
UC 21: 86 Notes 5, 6; 107 Note 7

UC 25: Dönitz commands, 163
UC 33: 86 Note 6
UC 34 class: 21
UC 36: 76; 108
UC 42: 86 Note 6
UC 49 class: 21
UC 55: 86 Note 6
UC 62: 99 Note 30
UC 80 class: 21

1939–45:
UA: 169; 314
U 1: 235; 241
U 2: 235
U 3: 235
U 4: 235
U 6: 235
U 7: 235
U 9: 235
U 10: 235
U 12: 249 Note 21
U 13: 235
U 14: 235
U 16: 249 Note 21
U 19: 235
U 21: 227
U 22: 241
U 25: 232, 235–6
U 27: 231
U 28: 263; 267–8
U 29: 221–2; 231
U 30: and *Athenia*, 215–17; 235; 256
U 31: 221; 227
U 32: 261; 269; 270; 272
U 33: 325
U 36: 227; 250
U 37: 261; 313
U 38: 235; 267–8; 345 Note 21
U 39: 231
U 40: 249 Note 21
U 43: 235; 465 & Note 38
U 46: 232; 235; 261; 267–8
U 47 (**Prien**): 223–4 & Note 32; 235–6; 261; 263; 313–14
U 48: 232; 235–6; 261; 268
U 49: 235; 241
U 51: 235–6
U 52: 235
U 55: 248 Note 19
U 56: 232–3; 235

U 57: 235
U 58: 235
U 59: 235
U 60: 235
U 62: 235
U 62: 235; 241
U 65: 235; 262
U 69: 343; 344 & Note 86; 531
U 70: 314
U 74: 382 & Note 65
U 81: 360; 377
U 82: 377–80
U 85: 418
U 86: 551
U 89: 492; 587; 602; 606
U 90: 485
U 91: 485; 564–5
U 93: 530 Note 38
U 94: 447–8; 451; 451–2
U 96: 485
U 98: 498 Note 99
U 99 (**Kretschmer**): 261; 267–8; 315–16
U 100 (**Schepke**): 261; 267–8; 315
U 101: 261; 267–8; 382 note 65
U 103: 345 Note 86
U 105: 345 Note 86
U 106: 345 Note 86
U 107: 344; 345 Note 86
U 108: 420
U 110: 315; captured, 326
U 116: 420
U 117: 634
U 118: U-tanker, 634
U 119: U-tanker, 537
U 123: 267–8
U 124: 345 Note 86; 384–5; 386; 447; 451–2
U 125: 597
U 127: 396
U 130: 573
U 131: 397
U 132: 491 Note 88; 492
U 136: 461
U 150: 497–8; 552–3
U 151: 532 Note 83
U 154: 510
U 155: 633 Note 34
U 156: 420; and *Laconia*, 471–5
U 157: 418
U 158: 418
U 159: 432

U 161: 421
U 169: 584
U 173: 497
U 175: 591
U 176: 477
U 179: 487–8
U 184: 505
U 186: 530 Note 38; 603
U 187: 530
U 189: 592
U 191: 530 Note 38; 592
U 192: 597
U 201: 382 Note 65; 385; 531
U 202: 394; 461; 621 Note 13
U 203: 350–1; 384; 394; 587; 592
U 206: **first Coastal Command kill,** 371–2, 382 Note 65
U 207: 380–1
U 209: 587
U 210: 476–7
U 217: 636
U 221: 489; 506–7; 551–2; 552–3; 567
U 225: 510–11; 533
U 228: 565
U 229: 638
U 230: 523; 550; **600–5**; 635; 651
U 238: 622
U 254: 491 Note 88; 506–7
U 258: 489; 595
U 259: 498 Note 99
U 260: 511; 583
U 264: 623; 627
U 266: 618
U 270: 638
U 296: 662 & Note 96
U 320: **last kill of the war,** 664
U 331: 360; 498 Note 99
U 333: 582; 621
U 338: 565–6; 638 Note 44
U 341: 637–8
U 348: 478
U 350: 557 Note 96
U 352: 418
U 353: 490
U 346: 510
U 357: 530 Note 38
U 358: **sunk after 38-hour hunt,** 621 Note 13
U 373: 646
U 374: 394 & Note 88

U 375: 394 & Note 88
U 376: 582
U 377: 638
U 379: 477
U 384: 568
U 402: 491–2; 530
U 404: 592
U 406: 511; 551
U 407: 651 & Note 73
U 410: 573
U 411: 495 Note 99
U 413: 498
U 424: 623
U 432: 375–7; 552
U 435: 511, 564
U 436: 490
U 438: 597
U 439: 566; **sunk in collision,** 597
U 441: **'aircraft trap',** 630–2; 647
U 444: 551–2
U 456: 524; 602; 606; 618 Note 10
U 459: **Type XIV tanker,** 420; 636
U 460: tanker, 420; 505; 534
U 461: tanker, 636
U 462: tanker, 534; 636
U 463: tanker, 557
U 465: 600
U 469: 584
U 486: 657
U 487: 634
U 488: tanker, 634
U 501: 379–80
U 502: 432
U 503: 418
U 506: 471–4
U 507: 471–4; 483
U 514: 514
U 515: 593
U 517: 486
U 519: 581
U 520: 491 & Note 88
U 522: 490–2
U 523: 568
U 524: 505–6
U 526: 582
U 527: 568
U 530: **interned,** 666
U 531: 587; 597; 599 Note 165
U 548: 663
U 551: 316

U552: 461 & Note 35; 465
U553: 465
U556: 350
U557: 360
U558: 252; 463–5
U559: 508–9
U562: **sinks USS** *Reuben James*, **Oct.
1941**, 393
U563: 382 Note 65
U564: 382 Note 65; 461 Note 32
U566: 550
U567: 399
U568: 382 Note 65
U569: 394; 447; 451–2; 587; 608 & Note
178
U570: **captured by RAF**, 364–5; 366; 370
U571: 490
U574: 382 Note 65; 397–8
U591: 511
U592: 622
U593: 476
U595: 488 Note 99
U600: 564
U603: 564
U605: 498 Note 99
U606: 533
U607: 489
U608: 567
U609: 530
U611: 507
U616: 565
U618: 489; 561
U619: 490
U621: 558
U624: 530
U629: 646
U630: 597
U632: 524; 529; 590
U635: 590
U638: 597

U650: 595
U651: 350
U652: **and USS** *Greer*, 390
U653: 561–2
U656: 418
U657: 619
U658: 491
U659: **sunk in collision**, 597
U660: 478; 498 Note 99
U661: 489; 491 Note 88
U663: 558
U665: 582
U710: 594; 598
U734: 622
U744: 621 Note 13
U751: 382 Note 65; 399
U752: 587; 608 & Note 178; 619
U757: 551–2
U758: 564
U762: 622
U763: 660
U764: 647
U767: 647
U847: **tanker**, 634–5
U853: 663
U905: 662 & Note 96
U954: **P. Dönitz killed in**, 607 Note 176
U976: 620
U977: **interned**, 666
U984: 647
U1055: 661
U2324: **first operational Type XXIII**,
662
U2326: 662
U2511: **first operational Type XXI**,
662–3; 669
U2515: 660
U2523: 660
U2530: 660

Index of Warships

French:

Aconit, FF corvette: and ONS 100, 451; and HX 228, sinks *U 444*, *U 432*, 551–2

Annamite, Vichy sloop: and *Laconia* survivors, 473

Dunquerque, battleship: and 1930s naval race, 185

Gloire, Vichy cruiser: and *Laconia* survivors, 473

Lobelia, FF corvette: and SC 118, sinks *U 609*, 530

Mimosa, FF corvette: 380, sunk, 451–2

Renoncule, FF corvette: and HX 228, 551

Roselys, FF corvette: and HX 228, 551

Strasbourg, battleship: and 1930s naval race, 185

German:

1914–18:

Bremser, minelaying cruiser: and Scandinavian convoys, 96–7

Breslau, light cruiser: Dönitz in, 161–2

Brummer, minelaying cruiser: and Scandinavian convoys, 96–7

Emden, light cruiser: 165

Friedrich der Grosse, battleship: 1917 mutiny, 83

Helgoland, battleship: and 1918 mutiny, 139; 214 Note 5

Kaiserin, battleship: 1917 mutiny, 83

Pillau, light cruiser: mutiny, 1917, 83

Prinzregent Luitpold: 1917 mutiny, 83

Rheinland, battleship: 1917 mutiny, 83

Westfalen, battleship: 1917 mutiny, 83

1918–45:

Admiral Graf Spee, pocket battleship: 165; 185; enters Atlantic, 1939, 206; sunk, 249; 295

Admiral Hipper, cruiser: 186; 295; 296–7; 308; 313; 354 Note 5; 518

Admiral Scheer, pocket battleship: 185; and *Jervis Bay*, 295–6

Bismarck, battleship: 186; 295; 298; sunk, 1941, 343; 345

Deutschland, pocket battleship: 185; renamed *Lützow*, 1939, 185 Note 83; enters Atlantic, 207; 295; 518

Emden, light cruiser: Dönitz in, 173

Gneisenau, battleship (-cruiser): 185; 295; in Brest, 297; 308; Channel dash, 345–7 & Note 88, 354 Note 5

Krebs, armed trawler: *Enigma* rotors captured, 325

Lauenburg, weather-ship: captured, 326

München, weather-ship: captured, 326

Nymphe, cruiser: Dönitz in, 169

Prinz Eugen, cruiser: 346 & Note 89

Scharnhorst, battleship (-cruiser): 185; 295; in Brest, 297; 308; Channel dash, 345–7 & Note 88, 354 Note 5

Tirpitz, battleship: 186; 295; 298; 444 Note 1; 584

T 157, torpedo-boat: Dönitz commands, 167

VP 2623, patrol boat: captured, 325

Polish:

Burza, battleship: and ON 166, sinks *U 606*, 532–3 & Note 44; and HX 228, 551

Garland, destroyer: and HX 228, 551; and *U 407*, 651 Note 73

Orzel, S/M: 219 Note 19

Wilk, S/M: 219 Note 19

Royal Canadian Navy:

Alberni, corvette: and SC 42, 373–80

Arvida, corvette: and ONS 92, 448

Assiniboine, destroyer: 330 Note 49; and ONS 100, 451; and SC 94, sinks *U 410*, 476–7 & Note 59

Athabaskan, destroyer: damaged by glider-bomb, 633

Bittersweet, corvette: and ONS 92, 447–8

Chambly, corvette: and SC 42, 378–80; and ONS 100, 451

Fraser, destroyer: 330 Note 49

Galt, corvette: and ON 115, 462

Kenogami, corvette: and SC 42, 373–80

Levis, corvette: sunk, 1941, 382 & Note 65

Moose Jaw, corvette: and SC 42, 376–80

Orillia, corvette: and SC 42, 373–6; and ONS 100, 451

Ottawa, destroyer: 330 Note 49; and HX 133, 248–50; sunk, 485

Restigouche, destroyer: 330 Note 49; 1941 gale damage, 395; and ONS 102, 452 & Note 12; and SC 107, 491

Sackville, corvette: and ONS 115, 462; 465–6

Saguenay, destroyer: 330 Note 49; and ON 115, 462

Sherbrooke, corvette: and ONS 169, 546–7

Skeena, destroyer: 330 Note 49; and SC 42, 373–81; and ON 115, signals to *Wetaskiwin*, 462–4

St Croix, destroyer: and ON 113, sinks *U 90*, 461–2; and ON 127, 485; sunk, 1943, 658

St Laurent, destroyer: 330 Note 49; and ONS 154, 510

Summerside, corvette: 490

The Pas, corvette: 558

Wetaskiwin, corvette: and OB 336, 349–50; 380; and ON 115, signals to *Skeena*, 462–5

Windflower, corvette: sunk, 1941, 395

Royal Navy:
1914–18:

Aboukir, cruiser: sunk, 1914, 189 Note 92

Argus, aircraft carrier, 1917: 159

Britannia, battleship: sunk, 1918, 140

Cressy, cruiser: sunk, 1914, 189 Note 92

Dreadnought, battleship: sinks *U 29*, 1915, 189 Note 92

Furious, aircraft carrier: first landing on, 1917, 159; 160 & Note 15

Gaillardia, sloop: sunk, 1918, 113

Hogue, cruiser: sunk, 1914, 189, Note 92

Mary Rose, destroyer: sunk, 1917, 96–7 & Note 25

Monarch, battleship: 671

Pellew, destroyer: and Scandinavian convoy, 1917, 98

Partridge, destroyer: and Scandinavian convoy, sunk, 1917, 98

Patriot, destroyer: with balloon, sinks *U 69*, 1917, 78

Strongbow, destroyer: sunk, 1917, 96

Tancred, destroyer: 95

Viper, destroyer (1899): high speed, 25

1918–45:

Abelia, corvette: and ONS 169, 546

Aberdeen, sloop: and HX 229A, 563

Active, destroyer: sinks *U 179*, 488

Anemone, corvette: and ONS 169, 546; and HX 229, 'perpetual motion', 565

Arbutus, corvette: 314

Archer, escort carrier: 552 Note 83, 587; rocket-firing aircraft, 619–20 & Note 11

Ariguani, Fighter Catapult Ship: 377 Note 58

Ark Royal, aircraft carrier: 231; sunk, 1941, 404; 651

Attacker, escort carrier: 532 Note 83

Audacity, escort carrier: 382 Note 65; and OG 74, 385–6; and OG 76, 395–6; and HG 76, 396–9; sunk, 1941, 399; 539 Note 61, 551

Avenger, escort carrier: sunk, 1942, 552 Note 83; 584

Barham, battleship: sunk, 1941, 404 & Note 3; 651

Battler, escort carrier: 552 Note 83

Belfast, cruiser: mined, 1939, 227; weight of broadside, 619 Note 12

Beverley, destroyer: sinks *U 187*, 530; and ONS 169, 546; 572

Biter, escort carrier: 552 Note 83; 586; 591 Note 150; sinks *U 203*, 592; and HX 237, 601

Black Swan, sloop: 251

Blackwood, frigate: sunk, 1944, 647

Bluebell, corvette: and SC 7, 266

Broadwater, destroyer: sunk, 1941, 382 Note 65; 393

Broadway, destroyer: 587; 601

Bulldog, destroyer: captures *U 110*, 1941, 326 & Note 39

Burnham, destroyer: and ON 113, 461–2

Buttermere, trawler: 380

Camellia, corvette: 314

Campbeltown, destroyer: and St Nazaire Raid, 1942, 281

Campobello, A/S trawler: sunk by ice, 558–61

Celandine, corvette: and SC 107, 491

Cossack, destroyer: sunk, 1941, 382 Note 65

Courageous, aircraft carrier: 160 Note 15; sunk, 139, 221–2; 231; 249; 251

Cygnet, sloop: 586

Dasher, escort carrier: sunk by explosion, 552 Note 83

Deptford, sloop: 386; 396; sinks *U 567*, 399

Dianthus, corvette: and SC 94, rams *U 379*, 477; and HK 212, 490; and ON 166, 532, 534

Douglas, destroyer: 381

Duke of York, battleship: 403

Duncan, destroyer: and ONS 5, 594–6

Eagle, aircraft carrier: 160; 651

Eclipse, destroyer: 586

Egret, sloop: sunk by glider-bomb, 633

Enchantress, sloop: 251

Escapade, destroyer: and HX 228, 551; Hedgehog explosion in, 620, 637

Fame, destroyer: and SC 104, 490; and HX 217, 505; 511; sinks *U 201*, 531; shares *U 767*, 647

Fidelity, Q-ship: 511

Fleur de Lys, corvette: sunk, 1941, 382 Note 65

Forester, destroyer: shares *U 27*, 1939, 231

Forfar, Armed Merchant Cruiser: sunk, 1940, 272

Fortune, destroyer: shares *U 27*, 1939, 231

Fowey, sloop: and SC 7, 266

Foxhound, destroyer: sinks *U 39*, 1939, 231

Furious, aircraft carrier: see 1914–18

Fury, destroyer: 586

Gladiolus, corvette: career, 252; 380; sunk, 1941, 382 Note 65; 393

Glorious, aircraft carrier: 160 Note 15; sunk, 1940, 253

Harvester, destroyer: and HX 228, sunk, 551–2

Havelock, destroyer: shares *U 767*, 647

Havock, destroyer: attacked by Italian S/M, 1937, 177

Heartsease, corvette: and SC 7, 266

Hermes, aircraft carrier: first purpose-built, 160 & Note 15

Hesperus, destroyer: 530 & Note 38

Highlander, destroyer: and ONS 169, 546–7; damaged, 555; 562; 567

Hood, battleship: 181

Icarus, destroyer: 586

Impulsive, destroyer: 586

Inconstant, destroyer: 586

Inglefield, flotilla leader: 586

Itchen, frigate: sunk, 1943, 638

Jed, frigate: 586–7

Jervis Bay, Armed Merchant Cruiser: sunk, 1940, 295–6

Kite, sloop: 586; in EG 2, 1944, 622–3

Lagan, frigate: 487; 601; 637

Laurentic, Armed Merchant Cruiser: sunk, 1940, 272

Leamington, destroyer: and SC 42, 381

Leith, sloop: and SC 7, 266

Lobelia, corvette: 393

Loosestrife, corvette: sinks *U 638*, 597

Lotus, corvette: sinks *U 605*, 498 Note 99 (see Aristophanes)

Magpie, sloop: sinks *U 238*, 622–3

Mansfield, destroyer: 555; and HX 229/SC 122, 562; 565

Maplin, Fighter Catapult Ship: 358 Note 13, 377 Note 58

Matchless, destroyer: 586

Milne, destroyer: 586

Montgomery, destroyer: and ONS 169, 547

Mourne, frigate: sunk, 1944, 647

Narcissus, corvette: and HX 228, 551

Nelson, battleship: cost of, 1925, 155; mined, 1939, 227

Nestor, destroyer (RAN), sinks *U 127*, 396

Obdurate, destroyer: 586

Obedient, destroyer: 586

Offa, destroyer: 586; and ONS 5, 595

Onslaught, destroyer: 586

Opportune, destroyer: 586

839

Orchis, corvette: 437; and HX 228, 551

Oribi, destroyer: 586–7; and ONS 5, 595; sinks *U 531*, 597 & Note 165

Orwell, destroyer: 586

Pathfinder, destroyer: 586–7; sinks *U 203*, 592

Patia, Fighter Catapult Ship: 377 Note 58

Patroclus, Armed Merchant Cruiser: sunk, 1940, 272

Pegasus, Fighter Catapult Ship: 377 Note 58

Pelican, sloop: 586–7; sinks *U 438*, 597

Pennywort, corvette: and ONS 169, 546–7; 558; 574

Petard, destroyer: captures *U 559* code-book, 508–9

Philante, steam yacht: Larne Battle School, 502–3

Pink, corvette: sinks *U 192*, 597

Polyanthus, corvette: sunk, 1943, 638

Primrose, corvette: and HX 237, 601

Prince of Wales, battleship: sunk, 1941, 404; 442

Queen Elizabeth, battleship: damaged by 'human torpedo', 404 & Note 3

Ramillies, battleship: 297

Ramsey, destroyer: 505

Rawalpindi, Armed Merchant Cruiser: sunk, 1939, 249

Repulse, battlecruiser: sunk, 1941, 404; 442

Rother, frigate: 436; 586

Saladin, destroyer: 381

Salisbury, destroyer: and ONS 169, 547

Scarborough, sloop: and SC 7, 265–6

Sennen, sloop (ex-USCG): 586–7

Skate, destroyer: 381

Snowflake, corvette: sinks *U 531*, 597 Note 165

Spey, frigate: 436; 586

Springbank, Fighter Catapult Ship: 377 Note 58; 382 Note 65; 383–5 & Note 67

Stanley, destroyer: 382 Note 65; sinks *U 434*; sunk, 1941, 396–7

Starling, sloop: 586; proficiency of, 599 Note 166; 621; shares *U 734*, 622; shares *U 264*, 623

Stork, sloop: 396–9 & Note 90; sinks *U 574*, 397–8; sinks *U 252*, 441

Tay, frigate: and HX 231, sinks *U 635*, 589–90; and ONS 5, 595; 598

Valiant, battleship: and 'human torpedoes', 404 & Note 3

Vanessa, destroyer: and SC 118, 530 & Note 38

Vanoc, destroyer: sinks *U 100*, 315 & Note 10

Verity, destroyer: and *U 47*, 314

Vervain, destroyer: 505

Vetch, corvette: and *U 252*, 441

Veteran, destroyer: and SC 42, 381

Vidette, destroyer: and HX 231, 589; sinks *U 125*, 597

Vimy, destroyer: sinks, *U 187*, 530; and ONS 169, 546; and HX 229, 562

Viscount, destroyer: and ONS 122, 485; rams *U 619*, 489; 491 Note 88; 505; sinks *U 69*, 531

Visenda, trawler: sinks *U 551*, 316

Volunteer, destroyer: and HX 229, 555; 562; and rescue of survivors, 564–5; 572

Walker, destroyer: sinks *U 99*, 315–16 Note 10

Waveney, frigate: and HX 229A, 563

Wear, frigate: 586

Western Isles: A/S Sea Training School, 276

Whimbrel, sloop: 586

Wild Goose, sloop: 586; and ASDIC, 621 Note 14; sinks *U 592*, shares *U 734*, 622; shares *U 424*, 623

Witherington, destroyer: 555; 558

Wolverine, destroyer: sinks *U 47*, 314 & Notes 6, 10

Woodpecker, sloop: 586; sinks *U 762*, 622; shares *U 264*, sunk, 623

Wren, sloop: 586

Zinnia, corvette: sunk, 1941, 382 Note 65

RN Submarines:

1914–18:

total U/Bs sunk by, 34; 4 U/Bs sunk, May 1918, 124; and U/Bs, 147; and torpedoes, 233

D 4: sinks *UB 72*, 121; 123

D 7: 86 Note 6

E 45: 99 Note 30

E 51: minelaying, 1917, 96

G 2: sinks *U 78*, 139

1939–45: in Mediterranean, 359

Graph (*U 570*): 365

Orzel (Polish): 219 Note 19

Porpoise: sinks *U 1*, 1940, 241

Salmon: sinks *U 36*, 1939, 227; 250
Snapper: and RAF bomb, 248 Note 18
Trident: and *Prinz Eugen*, 346
Wilk (Polish): 219 Note 19

RNorN:

Acanthus, corvette: and SC 104, 489
Bath, destroyer: sunk, 1941, 382 Note 65
Eglantine, corvette: and SC 104, 489
Montbretia, corvette: and SC 104, 489; sunk, 1942, 505
Potentilla, corvette: and SC 104, 489–90; sinks *U 184*, 505

USN:

Babbitt, destroyer: and HX 229/SC 122, 562
Belknap, destroyer: and HX 228, 551
Bibb, USCG cutter: 530
Bogue, CVE: 539 Note 61; and HX 228, 551–2; 586–7; operations against milch cows, 634
Campbell, USCG cutter: 490 & Note 84; and ON 166, sinks *U 606*, 532–3
Card, CVE: operations against milch cows, 634
Core, CVE: operations against milch cows, 634

Gleaves, destroyer: and ONS 92, 447–8
Greer, destroyer: 'attacked', 1941, 390–92; and SC 121, 547
Icarus, USCG cutter: sinks *U 352*, 418
Ingham, USCG cutter: and HX 229/SC 122, 562; and *Mathew Luckenbach*, 568
Kearney, destroyer: torpedoed, 1941, 393
Leary, destroyer: and ONS 102, 452
Minnesota, battleship: damaged, 1918, 133
Nibleck, destroyer: 341
Osmond-Ingram, destroyer: and HX 228, 551
Pennsylvania, cruiser: aircraft landing on, 1911, 158
Reuben James, destroyer: sunk, Oct. 31 1941, 393
Roper, destroyer: sinks *U 85*, 418
San Diego, cruiser: sunk, 1918, 133
Santee, CVE: operations against milch cows, 634
Spencer, USCG cutter: and ONS 92, 447; and ON 166, sinks *U 225*, 532–3; and SC 121, 547; sinks *U 175*, 591
Texas, battleship: attacked by U/B, 1941, 350–51
Thetis, USCG cutter: sinks *U 157*, 418